History of the Office of the
CHIEF OF NAVAL OPERATIONS
1915–2015

History of the Office of the
CHIEF OF NAVAL OPERATIONS
1915–2015

THOMAS C. HONE
CURTIS A. UTZ

NAVAL HISTORY AND HERITAGE COMMAND,
Department of the Navy
Washington, DC
2023

Use of ISBN: This is an official U.S. Government edition of this publication and is herein identified to certify its authenticity. Use of ISBN 978-1-943604-02-9 is for this hardcover edition only.

Library of Congress Cataloging-in-Publication Data
Names: Hone, Thomas, author. | Utz, Curtis A., 1962– author.
Title: History of the Office of the Chief of Naval Operations 1915–2015 / Thomas C. Hone, Curtis A. Utz.
Description: Washington, D.C.: Naval History and Heritage Command, [2020]
Identifiers: LCCN 2018028545| ISBN 9781943604029 | ISBN 9781943604036 (.pdf)
Subjects: LCSH: United States. Office of the Chief of Naval Operations—History—20th century. | United States. Office of the Chief of Naval Operations—History—21st century.
Classification: LCC VA58 .H55 2018 | DDC 359.60973—dc23
LC record available at https://lccn.loc.gov/2018028545

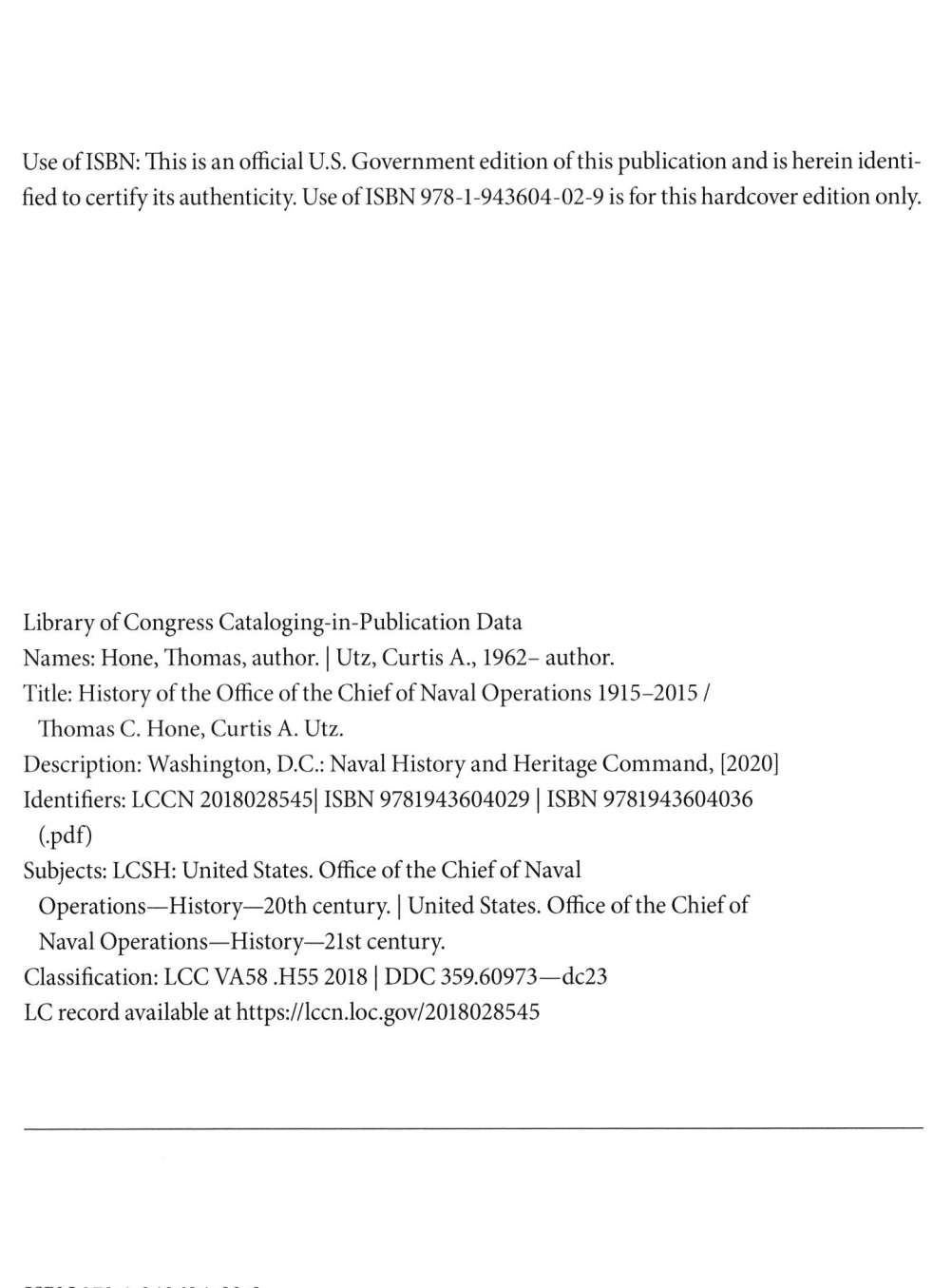

ISBN 978-1-943604-02-9

CONTENTS

Introduction xix
    Our Three Audiences xix
    General Themes xx
Acknowledgments xxiii

Chapter 1—The Office of the Chief of Naval Operations
    Introduction 1
    Navy Secretaries and "Modern" Navy Management 2
    The Traditional and Legal Domination of the Secretary 3
    Changes Under President Taft 9
    The Creation of the Office of the Chief of Naval Operations 12
    Enduring Issues 17

Chapter 2—World War I: The First Test of the Chief of Naval Operations and His Organization
    Introduction 25
    CNO Benson and the Navy's Bureaus 26
    Tightrope Walkers: CNO Benson and Secretary Daniels 29
    1916: A Key Year for both the Secretary and the CNO 32
    1917: War 36
    1918–1919: War and Its Aftermath 44
    Final Assessment: The CNO at War 47

Chapter 3—The Early Interwar Period: Reorganization, Arms Limitation, and Money
    Introduction 55
    The Role of the CNO 56
    Rear Admiral Sims vs. Secretary Daniels 57
    The Role of the General Board 59
    The Key to OPNAV's Influence: The Planning Process 61
    Policy Challenges: Budgets, Bombs, and Battleships 63
    An Excess of Economy 65
    Arms Limitation: The Washington Naval Treaty 67
    Consequences of the Treaty 69

    Coontz as Chief of Naval Operations 71
    Eberle Takes Over 73
    Making an Effective Treaty Fleet 73
    Debates About Naval Aviation 74
    The Fleet Problems 76
    Beyond the Washington Treaty 78
    Hughes Takes Over 80
    Planning for War 81
    Conclusion 83

Chapter 4—The Thirties: From the "Treaty System" to Mobilization
    Introduction 93
    CNO Pratt and the "Treaty System" 94
    Sustaining American Naval Power 97
    Pratt and Naval Administration 98
    Army-Navy Relations 101
    Pratt's Command Philosophy 102
    Franklin Roosevelt and the "Treaty System" 103
    Building the Navy to Treaty Strength 105
    Maturing the Interaction with Congress 109
    The End of the "Treaty System" 110
    Organizing the Fleet for War 111
    Shifting Away from Peace 112
    Admiral Leahy as CNO 114
    Preparing for War 118
    Conclusion 126

Chapter 5—Admiral Ernest J. King: CNO and Commander-in-Chief—at Last
    Introduction 137
    Preliminaries: King as COMINCH 138
    King as CNO-COMINCH 141
    Initial Challenges Facing CNO-COMINCH 145
    King and the Secretariat 149
    The Bureaus Continued to Matter 150
    Rounding Out the High Command 151
    OPNAV: Struggling Through 1942 152
    OPNAV Matures: 1943–1945 154
    End Game: After Japan Surrendered 167
    CNO-COMINCH King: An Assessment 170

Chapter 6—OPNAV Postwar: No End of Challenges

Introduction 187
A Late Start for Navy Planning for a Postwar World 188
Demobilization and Service Unification 189
The Critical Role Played by James V. Forrestal. 190
Congress and the Navy Postwar 193
The Challenges of Technology. 196
OPNAV Organization Postwar 197
Operating Under the National Security Act 199
The "Revolt of the Admirals". 201
After the "Revolt of the Admirals". 205
Conclusion 206

Chapter 7—The Eisenhower Years

Introduction 213
Office of the Chief of Naval Operations in 1953. 214
Eisenhower's 1953 Reforms 214
The Navy's Response to Reorganization Plan 6 216
Burke Becomes CNO 221
Conclusion 225

Chapter 8—Burke: Shielding the Navy

Introduction 229
The Campaign for Defense Reorganization Resurfaces 229
Burke's Response to Defense Reorganization 230
The Franke Board 232
The Fine Line Between Lobbying and Arguing 235
Burke's Tenure Reviewed 237
Conclusion 240

Chapter 9—The McNamara Revolution

Introduction 245
Robert McNamara: A Strong Defense Secretary 246
The Planning, Programming, and Budgeting System (PPBS) 246
The Response to McNamara: Secretariat and CNO. 248
The Response to McNamara: The Bureaus 254
McNamara's Changes: An Attack on Navy Values? 256
The Bureaus Go Away 259
The Benson Study: OPNAV's Response to McNamara 260
Following the Benson Study 265

    The McNamara Years: A Conclusion....266
    After McNamara: Melvin Laird....268

Chapter 10—Zumwalt: A Cultural Revolution
    Introduction....279
    Admiral Elmo Zumwalt....280
    Organizational Reform....281
    "Project Sixty"....282
    Zumwalt's Changes to OPNAV....282
    Zumwalt Compared to Arleigh Burke....284
    More Organizational Changes....285
    Corralling Admiral Rickover....286
    Still More Organization Changes....287
    Were the Organizational Changes Working? Could They?....290
    Investing in Personnel....292
    Conclusion....296

Chapter 11—From Project Sixty to the Maritime Strategy
    Introduction....303
    Background....304
    Holloway's Initial Actions....304
    The Issue of Fleet Modernization....305
    Managing Innovation....309
    Holloway and the Carter Administration's Defense Reform Effort....310
    Holloway and the Joint Chiefs of Staff....312
    Restructuring the Fleet....313
    Holloway as CNO....314
    CNO Hayward: The Roots of the Maritime Strategy....316
    Hayward's Primary Concerns....317
    Making Changes to OPNAV....317
    The Genesis of the Maritime Strategy....319
    Strategic Arms Limitation....321
    Readiness Challenges....321
    The Stage Was Set for Navy Secretary John F. Lehman Jr.....322

Chapter 12—Resurgence of the Navy Secretariat
    Introduction....329
    Background....330
    Lehman's Influence Over Navy Programs....331

    Lehman and Hayward 334
    Lehman and CNO James D. Watkins (I) 336
    The Maturing of the "Maritime Strategy" 337
    Lehman and CNO Watkins (II) 339
    Secretary Lehman and Goldwater-Nichols 344
    Admiral Watkins and the Strategic Defense Initiative 346
    Enduring Issues 347

Chapter 13—After Lehman's Regime
    Introduction 355
    Refashioning OPNAV: Lehman's Legacy 356
    Refashioning OPNAV Part 2: Trost's Changes 358
    Fiscal Stringency 361
    Dealing with Fiscal Stringency Through Analysis 361
    Implications of Goldwater-Nichols 365
    The Packard Commission, Goldwater-Nichols, and Defense Acquisition 369
    The Strategic Environment Trumps the 600-Ship Navy 372

Chapter 14—The Continuing Response to Goldwater-Nichols and the End of the Cold War
    Introduction 377
    The "Base Force" 378
    Changing Minds and Changing Processes 378
    Troubled Waters, Part I: Tailhook 385
    Troubled Waters, Part II: The A-12 387
    The Cold War's End and Partial Demobilization 394
    The Effects of the Reorganization of OPNAV 395

Chapter 15—Following Kelso: Consolidating Changes
    Introduction 403
    The Consequences of the Bottom-Up Review 404
    CNO Boorda and the Bottom-Up Review 405
    Boorda's Leadership of OPNAV and the Navy 407
    Problem-Solving and CNO Boorda's OPNAV 412
    Admiral Johnson Takes Over 415
    The Devil Is Always in the Details 422
    CNO Johnson's Initiatives 424
    Richard Danzig: Another "Activist" Secretary 426

Chapter 16—Admiral Vernon Clark: Readiness, Reorganization, and War

Introduction 437
Clark Takes Command 438
The Impact of Defense Secretary Rumsfeld 441
Operational Implications of the 11 September 2001 Attacks 444
Managerial Implications of the 11 September 2001 Attacks 445
CNO Clark's Initial Response 448
Further Implications of 9/11 for CNO Clark and OPNAV 451
A Renaissance of Strategy 456
Unresolved Issues 459
Conclusion: Two Reformers and War 460

Chapter 17—A Dramatic Two Years: Michael G. Mullen as CNO

A Running Start 471
The Genesis of the 1,000-Ship Navy 474
Reorganizing OPNAV 477
Navy and Marine Corps Acquisition Disappointments 482
Conclusion 489

Chapter 18—Admiral Gary Roughead: Déjà Vu All Over Again?

Introduction 499
Roughead's Concerns 500
The Management of Defense: From Rumsfeld to Gates 500
Planning According to Desired Joint Capabilities 502
The Concept of the "Chief Management Officer" 504
Gates Takes Over 505
The Great Recession 506
Shipbuilding Programs 507
The "Balisle Report" 514
Roughead and OPNAV 515
Information and the Cooperative Strategy 519
The Navy and the Marines 521
Conclusion 523

Chapter 19—Admiral Jonathan W. Greenert as the 30th CNO

Introduction 531
Reorganizing OPNAV—Again 532
The "End Game" 534
"Wholeness" 536

    Implementing the OPNAV Reorganization 537
    The Purpose of the Reorganization 537
    Partisan Politics Intervenes. 538
    Shipbuilding Problems Persist 541
    The Navy and the Marines 544
    OPNAV and the Navy Secretariat 545
    The Hidden But Always-Present Danger: Cybernetic Warfare. 550
    Sex and "Officer Detachment for Cause". 552
    "Managers" vs. "Executives" 554
    Conclusion: The Hurricane Years 555

Chapter 20—Conclusion
    Introduction 565
    Historical Background 566
    Does the CNO Matter? 567
    OPNAV: Responding to Change 567
    The Chiefs of Naval Operations 570
    Obstacles to a CNO's Leadership 573
    The CNO Compared with a President 576
    The CNO as Chief Programmer 579
    The Influence of Strategic Issues 580
    The Influence of Technology 582
    Personalities 585
    Bureaucracy 587
    The CNO as Actual and Symbolic Leader 589

Epilogue 593
Bibliography 597
Appendix 1— Secretaries of the Navy and Chiefs of Naval Operations, 1915–2015 619
Appendix 2—Abbreviations 623
Index 629

List of Illustrations

Chapter 1—The Office of the Chief of Naval Operations
Figure 1-1. Rear Admiral Bradley A. Fiske, 1912 13

Chapter 2—World War I: The First Test of the Chief of Naval Operations and His Organization
Figure 2-1. Navy Secretary Josephus Daniels and Admiral William S. Benson 36

Chapter 3—The Early Interwar Period: Reorganization, Arms Limitation, and Money
Figure 3-1. CNO Robert E. Coontz 69
Figure 3-2. CNO Edward W. Eberle 76
Figure 3-3. CNO Charles F. Hughes 82

Chapter 4—The Thirties: From the "Treaty System" to Mobilization
Figure 4-1. Admiral William V. Pratt and Rear Admiral Joseph M. Reeves Inspect Crew 101
Figure 4-2. Vice Admiral William H. Standley on *Chicago* (CA-29) 108
Figure 4-3. CNO William D. Leahy and President Franklin D. Roosevelt 113
Figure 4-4. Rear Admirals Harold R. Stark and Chester W. Nimitz Inspect Sailors 119

Chapter 5—Admiral Ernest J. King: CNO and Commander-in-Chief—at Last
Figure 5-1. Admirals Ernest J. King and Chester W. Nimitz 156
Figure 5-2. Fleet Admiral Ernest J. King 170

Chapter 6—OPNAV Postwar: No End of Challenges
Figure 6-1. CNO Chester W. Nimitz 191
Figure 6-2. Navy Secretary John Sullivan and CNO Louis E. Denfeld 202
Figure 6-3. CNO Forrest P. Sherman 205

Chapter 7—The Eisenhower Years
Figure 7-1. CNO William M. Fechteler 219
Figure 7-2. CNO Robert B. Carney 220

Chapter 8—Burke: Shielding the Navy
Figure 8-1. CNO Arleigh A. Burke on Ship's Bridge 231
Figure 8-2. CNO Arleigh A. Burke, 1959 235

Chapter 9—The McNamara Revolution
Figure 9-1. CNO George W. Anderson Jr. on *Enterprise* (CVAN-65) 249
Figure 9-2. CNO George W. Anderson Jr. and Vice Admiral David L. McDonald . . .253

Figure 9-3. CNO David L. McDonald 258
Figure 9-4. CNO Thomas H. Moorer. 264

Chapter 10—Zumwalt: A Cultural Revolution
Figure 10-1. CNO Elmo R. Zumwalt Jr.. 281
Figure 10-2. CNO Elmo R. Zumwalt Jr. confers with
VADM Robert S. Salzer, May 1971 284
Figure 10-3. CNO Zumwalt with Vice President Gerald R. Ford on 29 June 1974 295

Chapter 11—From Project Sixty to the Maritime Strategy
Figure 11-1. CNO James L. Holloway III during commissioning
of *Dwight D. Eisenhower* (CVN-69). 307
Figure 11-2. CNO Thomas B. Hayward 316

Chapter 12—Lehman—Resurgence of the Navy Secretariat
Figure 12-1. CNO James D. Watkins. 336
Figure 12-2. Secretary of the Navy John F. Lehman Jr.,
Virginia Senator John W. Warner, and CNO Carlisle A. H. Trost in 1986 348

Chapter 13—After Lehman's Regime
Figure 13-1. CNO Carlisle A. H. Trost. 365

Chapter 14—The Continuing Response to Goldwater-Nichols and the End of the Cold War
Figure 14-1. CNO Frank B. Kelso II at the commissioning of
George Washington (CVN-73). 388

Chapter 15—Following Kelso: Consolidating Changes
Figure 15-1. CNO Jeremy Michael Boorda. 405
Figure 15-2. CNO Jay L. Johnson 424

Chapter 16—Admiral Vernon Clark: Readiness, Reorganization, and War
Figure 16-1. CNO Vernon E. Clark 442
Figure 16-2. CNO Clark testifies before Congress 455

Chapter 17—A Dramatic Two Years: Michael G. Mullen as CNO
Figure 17-1. CNO Michael G. Mullen meets with sailors
from *John Stennis* (CVN-74) 490

Chapter 18—Admiral Gary Roughead: Déjà Vu All Over Again?
    Figure 18-1. CNO Gary Roughead at the Marinette Marine shipyard 508
    Figure 18-2. CNO Gary Roughead before the House Armed Services Committee. . . .520

Chapter 19— Admiral Jonathan W. Greenert as the 30th CNO
    Figure 19-1. CNO Jonathan W. Greenert and Navy Secretary Ray Mabus 546

Chapter 20—Conclusion
    Figure 20-1. CNO Frank B. Kelso with Former CNOs 19 October 1990. 572

List of OPNAV Charts

Chapter 2—World War I: The First Test of the Chief of Naval Operations and His Organization
    Chart 1. Select Elements of OPNAV Organization as of January 1916 32

Chapter 3—The Early Interwar Period: Reorganization, Arms Limitation, and Money
    Chart 2. Select Elements of OPNAV Organization as of June 1920. 63
    Chart 3. Select Elements of OPNAV Organization as of January 1923 72

Chapter 4—The Thirties: From the "Treaty System" to Mobilization
    Chart 4. Select Elements of OPNAV Organization as of January 1931 100
    Chart 5. Select Elements of OPNAV Organization as of January 1939 117

Chapter 5—Admiral Ernest J. King: CNO and Commander-in-Chief—at Last
    Chart 6. Select Elements of OPNAV Organization as of June 1942. 144
    Chart 7. Select Elements of OPNAV Organization as of June 1944. 162

Chapter 6—OPNAV Postwar: No End of Challenges
    Chart 8. Select Elements of OPNAV Organization as of December 1947 198

Chapter 8—Burke: Shielding the Navy
    Chart 9. Select Elements of OPNAV Organization as of 1958. 234

Chapter 9—The McNamara Revolution
    Chart 10. Select Elements of OPNAV Organization as of 1966. 261

Chapter 10—Zumwalt: A Cultural Revolution
    Chart 11. Select Elements of OPNAV Organization as of 1971. 287

Chapter 12—Lehman—Resurgence of the Navy Secretariat
    Chart 12. Select Elements of OPNAV Organization as of 1986. 344

Chapter 13—After Lehman's Regime
    Chart 13. Select Elements of OPNAV Organization as of 1987. 358

Chapter 14—The Continuing Response to Goldwater-Nichols and the End of the Cold War
    Chart 14. Select Elements of OPNAV Organization as of August 1992. 384

Chapter 16—Admiral Vernon Clark: Readiness, Reorganization, and War
    Chart 15. Select Elements of OPNAV Organization as of November 2000. 439
    Chart 16. Select Elements of OPNAV Organization as of December 2002 453

Chapter 17—A Dramatic Two Years: Michael G. Mullen as CNO
    Chart 17. Select Elements of OPNAV Organization as of August 2007. 479

Chapter 18—Admiral Gary Roughead: Déjà Vu All Over Again?
    Chart 18. Select Elements of OPNAV Organization as of January 2010 518

Chapter 19—Admiral Jonathan W. Greenert as the 30th CNO
    Chart 19. Select Elements of OPNAV Organization as of December 2012 534

ABOUT THE AUTHORS

Thomas C. Hone received a PhD in political science from the University of Wisconsin (Madison) in 1973. He served as Principal Deputy Director for the Office of the Secretary of Defense Office of Program Analysis and Evaluation in 2001–2002, and was Special Assistant to the Commander, Naval Air Systems Command, in 1992–1994. Mr. Hone is the author of *Power and Change: The Administrative History of the Office of the Chief of Naval Operations, 1946–1986*, and the co-author of *American & British Aircraft Carrier Development, 1919–1941*; *Battle Line: The United States Navy, 1919–1939*; *Innovation in Carrier Aviation*; and *Vol. 1, Part 2 of the Gulf War Air Power Survey*. He has taught at the Naval War College (in the departments of Military Operations and Defense Economics and Decision-Making), the National Defense University, and the George C. Marshall Center for European Security Studies in Germany. In 2003–2006, he was Assistant Director for Risk Management, Office of Force Transformation, Office of the Secretary of Defense.

Curtis A. Utz earned an MA in U.S. history from the University of Maryland (College Park) in 1989. He has held several positions in the Naval History and Heritage Command and its predecessor, the Naval Historical Center (NHC), including leading the Naval Aviation History and Archives Branches from 2003–2014. Mr. Utz authored *Cordon of Steel: The U.S. Navy and the Cuban Missile Crisis* and *Assault from the Sea: The Amphibious Landing at Inchon* while with the NHC. He was a historian and analyst with the Defense Intelligence Agency 1994–2003. He has lectured in history at the University of Maryland, the Joint Military Intelligence College, and the Joint Military Intelligence Training Center.

INTRODUCTION

This is a centennial history of the Office of the Chief of Naval Operations (OPNAV). It is organized by the individuals who had the greatest impact on OPNAV. Most of those individuals have been admirals, especially the Chiefs of Naval Operations. At times, however, a Secretary of the Navy, a Secretary of Defense, or a President has taken center stage, forcing the Navy's senior officers to react. In addition, the Navy obviously does not operate in a vacuum. What affects the country certainly influences the Navy. Yet the story of the interaction between the Navy and the nation is too great to be covered in depth here. To cover OPNAV's first century in a reasonable number of pages meant that the authors had to pick and choose among a number of potential topics that were relevant to OPNAV in each segment of its history. Readers, including active and retired officers with experience in OPNAV, may disagree with our choices of topics and our treatments of them. But our choices were shaped by the audiences that we were writing for.

Our Three Audiences

The first of our audiences is composed of younger officers committed to a career in the Navy. To them we say, "Here is our 'biography' of OPNAV and our study of the officers who have led it. Read this to learn where OPNAV came from, what it was, how it has changed, and why it has survived. This is a story about your Navy. It's designed to help you understand it."

The second of our audiences is composed of senior active duty officers searching for ways to make OPNAV work better. One theme that is constant across OPNAV's history is the desire of the Chiefs of Naval Operations to leave the Navy stronger and better managed than they found it. How have they done that—or attempted to do that? What has worked? What has not? How can a Chief of Naval Operations (CNO) lead OPNAV effectively? What is the relationship between leading OPNAV and leading the Navy? What are a CNO's "measures" of effectiveness and/or success? Though this study was not intended to be a manual of leadership at the highest levels, in a sense it is that, though readers should be aware that the leadership required of a CNO changes as the environment—both in Washington and in the world—changes.

The third audience we have written for is composed of interested citizens. "Just what do those people do in the Pentagon?" This book will give a citizen some idea of what's done in the Navy's portion of the five-sided building and why it's done. We think the story of OPNAV and the CNOs is a fascinating one—bureaucratic "battles" instead of actual combat—and we hope that readers will agree with us. If not fascinating, the stories in this book may at least be useful in helping readers understand what usually does not make the around-the-clock news cycle.

Our work has been shaped by our desire to inform these three audiences and by one major constraint—the need to keep the study unclassified. The farther back we go in OPNAV's history, the less concern there is for classification and the more we can rely on the work of other investigators—historians, especially. That is why you will see secondary sources used extensively in the chapters that deal with the early years of OPNAV and the changes in OPNAV during World War II. Some very good historians have covered those periods. Where we needed to, however, we relied on primary sources, especially the documents preserved in the National Archives.

The closer we got to the present, the more we had to rely on material in open sources such as the *Proceedings* of the U.S. Naval institute and the institute's oral histories, and "trade press" publications such as *Inside the Navy*. As far as governments go, that of the United States is surprisingly open. A careful reader, with an understanding of what to search for, can glean a great deal from unclassified reports and publications.[1] The Navy wanted this history to be open and available. We have written it accordingly. Does this mean that we have not included some interesting facts because they remain classified? Yes. But we believe that what we have written will stand up well once more recent files have been declassified and opened to researchers.

General Themes

There are some general themes that we can describe here and return to in our conclusion. The most important is the way that Chiefs of Naval Operations have, over time and through deliberate acts of the Congress, lost command of actual military operations. The CNO is no longer a "chief of naval operations." Does this mean that a Chief of Naval Operations is not important? No. Every CNO has both formal powers and access to a variety of audiences, ranging from the public to the President. Effective CNOs know how to use their formal authority (over appointments, for example) and they also know how to address the very different audiences who watch and comment on what they do. CNOs necessarily represent the Navy to members of Congress, deal directly with the other military service chiefs and with officials in the Office of the Secretary of Defense, and communicate with the public and with the men and women, uniformed and civilian, in the Navy and the Marine Corps.

In a sense, the CNO is like the President of the United States. Like the President, the CNO must persuade others to take up his causes and act to put them into effect. The CNO, like any President, must have a "program," and must know how to help his supporters and disarm his opponents. Like Presidents, CNOs must persuade. They must also know how to bargain, appealing if necessary to public opinion. True, CNOs today find layers of decision makers between themselves and their Presidents. There can hardly be a repeat of the later 1930s, when President Franklin D. Roosevelt could pick up the phone and call CNO William D. Leahy directly when Claude Swanson, then the Navy secretary, was ill and absent from the Main Navy building on Constitution Avenue. But despite the existence of the Office of the Secretary of Defense, a persuasive and knowledgeable CNO can influence the other members of the Joint Chiefs of

Introduction

Staff, members of the Congress, and even a President—as CNO Admiral James Watkins did in shaping President Ronald Reagan's ideas about ballistic missile defenses in the 1980s. Politics in Washington is not just about formal authority and informal influence. It is also about access, and the CNO's official role gives him (or her) access—directly and indirectly—to many important people.

Since 1898, the Navy has been a tool of American power. At the same time, advocates of a large, strong Navy have had to contend with political opponents critical of the cost of such a navy, especially if it is deployed around the world in force. CNOs are right in the middle of the back-and-forth between proponents of a "big Navy" and their opposites. That means CNOs have to walk a kind of tightrope. If they are not careful, they will generate political opposition to a large and powerful Navy, especially when budgets are tight. But they must also be aggressive enough to represent the modern, forward-deployed Navy in such a way as to satisfy the legitimate concerns of members of Congress.

Put another way, any CNO must be a "politician" in the highest sense of that term—as a leader with great public responsibilities and (as with a President) limited authority to fulfill those responsibilities. No CNO is a dictator. A CNO may be a hard-driving executive, but no CNO can ignore the leadership qualities that have brought him (or her) to the Navy's highest uniformed position. The CNO must never forget the fact that every officer holding that office must work in tandem with the Secretary of the Navy (SECNAV) and subordinate to the Secretary of Defense (SecDef).

If there is one theme that flows through writings by naval officers in the last century, it is distaste for partisan politics. Military officers are sworn to protect and obey the Constitution. They support Presidents and respond to members of Congress because Presidents and members of Congress have constitutional standing and authority. In that sense, CNOs are "political." They are—and must be—public officials participating in debates about how the public's resources and authority should be used.

At the same time, CNOs must heed their sincere doubts about engaging in partisan politics. To venture there openly is to endanger the authority of the office they hold and the standing of the Navy in the eyes of the public. And so, with rare exceptions, they don't. Yet they must still "organize, train, and equip" the Navy. To do this effectively, they must interact with the political partisans in Congress and with the President's men and women serving as appointees in the executive branch. Under the overall leadership of the Secretary of the Navy, the CNO must work with the Commandant of the Marine Corps to field maritime forces that are equal or superior to any found elsewhere in the world. OPNAV exists to aid a CNO to do that. OPNAV is the CNO's immediate tool for influencing the Navy.

But no CNO can take OPNAV (or the Navy's systems command) for granted. OPNAV must be led. Leading it requires a deft hand. Tommy Lasorda, former successful manager of the Los Angeles Dodgers, was once asked what it was like to "manage" aggressive and energetic young baseball stars. He said it was like holding a bird in your hand. Hold too tight and you crush the bird. Hold too loose and the bird flies away. This is an appropriate model for any CNO. But how should OPNAV be structured to enable a CNO to lead the Navy? How can a CNO delegate authority without losing it? If the manager of a professional baseball team has to have a knack for leadership in order to foster winning teams, then what must a CNO have to lead the much larger and far more diverse OPNAV?

Our history may provide some answers to these questions—and to others. As an earlier study of OPNAV put it in 1989, "The Office of the Chief of Naval Operations is not the way it is by accident. . . . In plain terms, [OPNAV] must be understood as an organization assigned certain crucial tasks. How it carried out those tasks and how the nature of the tasks themselves changed over time are [the] central topics of this study."[2]

Notes

[1] For an excellent example of this sort of study and analysis, see Thomas C. Lassman, *Sources of Weapon Systems Innovation in the Department of Defense, The Role of In-House Research and Development, 1945–2000* (Washington, DC: Center of Military History, 2008).

[2] Thomas C. Hone, *Power and Change, The Administrative History of the Office of the Chief of Naval Operations, 1946–1986* (Washington, DC: Naval Historical Center, 1989), xii.

ACKNOWLEDGMENTS

This study could not have been completed without the assistance of a number of individuals and organizations. First are the professionals who provided the bulk of the source material:

- Ms. Dara Baker, Archivist, Naval War College, Newport, RI.
- Ms. Robin Lima, Senior Librarian, and her colleagues at the Naval War College Library.
- Mr. Michael Vansickle, DNS-33 (Director, Navy Staff Organization and Management Branch).
- Mr. Glenn Helm, Director, Navy Department Library, and his staff.

These four individuals and their colleagues were extraordinarily helpful. Because this history had to be unclassified, and because various files in the archives of the Naval History and Heritage Command were not available, the historical materials from DNS-33, the National Archives, the Naval War College, and the Navy Department Library, augmented by interviews, were the foundation of this study.

Next in line to be acknowledged are the readers of the draft chapters:

- Prof. Donald Chisholm, Joint Military Operations Department, Naval War College.
- Dr. Jeffrey Barlow, retired historian, Naval History and Heritage Command.
- Mr. Paul Stillwell, formerly with the U.S. Naval Institute and a superb interviewer.

These three were very patient, thorough, and—therefore—quite helpful. If any errors survive in the final manuscript, they are the fault of the authors alone and not of the panel of readers.

Because various files in the archives of the Naval History and Heritage Command were not available due to security considerations, the assistance provided by Dale J. "Joe" Gordon, John Hodges, John Greco, and Dan Jones of the reference staff of the NHHC Archives was especially helpful. The reference staff provided updates regarding collections transferred from the command to the National Archives that allowed Mr. Curtis Utz to update the history's footnotes. Lisa Crunk, Dave Colamaria, and Jon Roscoe of the NHHC's photo archives section were very helpful with many of the images in the book. History Branch interns Jeffrey Beaver and Sarit Laschinsky also helped with the imagery effort.

Other members of the History Branch who provided assistance were Branch Head Dr. Kristina Giannotta and her former deputy, Scott Anderson, who took care of the administrative coordination of the project, and historians Dr. Gregory Bereiter, Dr. Frank A. Blazich Jr.,

Robert J. Cressman, Mark L. Evans, Christopher B. Havern Sr., Chris Martin, Dr. Ryan Peeks, and Dr. John D. Sherwood. Dr. Michael J. Crawford, the NHHC Senior Historian, and Dr. Sarandis "Randy" Papadopoulos, the Navy Secretariat historian, also provided advice and guidance.

Thanks to the Communication and Outreach Division's Publishing and Website Management Branch members that edited the work, Wilma Haines and Jim Caiella, especially the latter's work with our charts and the interactions with GPO.

Significant encouragement was provided by the following individuals:

- Captain Peter M. Swartz, USN (Ret.), who has produced a series of briefings that describe the evolution of the Navy's deployments, its force structures, and OPNAV's various organization charts. His briefings are encyclopedic in scope and comprehensiveness. He generously shared information and ideas with Thomas C. Hone.
- Dr. Norman Friedman. The modern U.S. Navy is a "technology-heavy" organization, and Dr. Friedman has explained the way that the Navy has acquired and used technology in a series of volumes that are required reading for anyone trying to understand the modern Navy.
- Captain Ronald R. Harris, USN (Ret.), who shared his experiences as a member of the OPNAV staff and also his thoughts on the nature of leadership in OPNAV and the Navy Secretariat.
- Captain John L. Byron, USN (Ret.), who supported the writing of *Power and Change* in the mid-1980s and typifies those Navy officers who are willing and able to go in harm's way and also to serve as intelligent and creative staff officers.
- Ms. Mary B. Hundley, a superb programmer—an expert on how Navy programs are put together in OPNAV and on the people who do that work.
- Mr. Frank Uhlig Jr., Editor Emeritus of the *Naval War College Review.*
- Captain Henry J. Hendrix, USN (Ret.), who was Director of the NHHC when the study began, Commander James Kuhn, USN (Ret.), the former Deputy Director, Gregory Martin, Asst. Director of the Histories and Archives Division, and Lieutenant Colonel Justin "Lance" Eldridge, U.S. Army (Ret.).
- Experienced and capable Navy civilians, including Dr. William E. Turcotte, Dr. John B. Hattendorf, Bruce Powers, Dr. Irving Blickstein, Dr. William Armstrong, Robert J. Murray, Kenneth E. Miller, and Dr. Allan R. Somoroff. Also Andrew Marshall, former director of the Office of Net Assessment, Office of the Secretary of Defense.
- The staff of the Defense Systems Management College (now the Defense Acquisition University), especially Commander E. P. Vollmer, USN (Ret.), Lieutenant Colonel Charles B. Cochrane, U.S. Army (Ret.), and Lieutenant Colonel Kurt Dieterle, USMC (Ret.).
- Trent Hone, who shared his insights into Navy innovation before and during World War II.
- Parts of *Power and Change, The Administrative History of the Office of the Chief of Naval Operations, 1946–1986,* have been incorporated into the present study. Those individuals and organizations acknowledged in *Power and Change* should also be remembered for their contributions, especially that superb archivist, the late Bernard F. Cavalcante.

Any errors of fact in the text are the fault of Thomas C. Hone and Curtis A. Utz.

CHAPTER 1

The Office of the Chief of Naval Operations

Introduction

Why is there an Office of the Chief of Naval Operations? Where did it come from? Who wanted it? What was it meant to do? In 1900, according to Captain Henry C. Taylor, a former President of the Naval War College, and soon to be chief of the Bureau of Navigation (BuNav), "The need for a General Staff in our Navy is not unnatural: All military organizations, afloat and ashore, experience the same necessity, as do all large business enterprises in civil life, though under other names than that of General Staff."[1] But Secretary of the Navy John D. Long, a contemporary of Taylor's, argued that, "Under the circumstances [proposed by Captain Taylor], the Secretary [of the Navy] could hardly fail to lapse into a figurehead in the administration of the Navy."[2] What was going on? Why were these individuals in conflict? Why were there such strong and different opinions about how the U.S. Navy should be directed? To answer these questions, it's necessary to go back 15 or so years before the creation of the position of the Chief of Naval Operations.

Along a portion of the Pentagon's "E" ring is a collection of portraits of secretaries of the Navy from the late 19th and early 20th centuries. Just looking at these gentlemen brings to mind a now-very-distant past, and that past seems settled, tradition-bound, and not especially exciting. But the portraits are deceiving. For the Navy and the U.S. Army, the period from the end of the war with Spain in 1898 to the beginning of American participation in World War I in 1917 was a time of great change and great uncertainty. The government of the United States was committed to building a world-class navy and a modern army, but getting that navy and army would require a dramatic transformation in how the two military services were managed, directed, and financed.

Put another way, political and military leaders in the United States proposed to create a modern navy and a modern army without knowing quite how to do it. There were European models of army and navy command staffs, but those models were often judged by American political leaders as being incompatible with the American constitutional tradition of civilian leadership. This history focuses on the efforts by Secretaries of the Navy and senior Navy officers to find a particularly "American" solution to this problem, but readers need to keep in mind that the problem was also one for the civilian and uniformed leaders of the Army.[3]

These efforts at change and reform took place in the context of increasing professionalism in American life. Often through regulations imposed by states or the federal government, citizens required education and specialized training of practitioners in a number of fields, including medicine, education, and engineering, and in many industries, such as railroading, manufacturing, mining, and food processing.[4] The demand for professionalism in the Navy by a group of dedicated officers was a part of this general movement, reflecting what was happening in fields like medicine and also building on the general pressure to make people in specialized areas of endeavor both more skilled and more accountable. Being "modern" meant being educated and trained. It also meant that a practitioner was judged on the basis of performance—on what he could do instead of his political connections or his seniority. This is the "deep background" to the history that follows.

Navy Secretaries and "Modern" Navy Management

During this period, successive Navy secretaries created three different combinations of organizations to shape and direct the Navy. The first was established in March 1900, when SECNAV Long created the General Board, a small organization of senior line and staff officers who advised the secretary directly.[5] With the General Board in place, the Navy's work was directed by it and by (a) the Navy secretary, (b) the Naval War College, (c) the Board on Construction, and (d) the Navy's bureaus. These five organizations decided Navy policy and planned the Navy's future. George von Lengerke Meyer, Secretary of the Navy from 6 March 1909 to 4 March 1913, changed this confederation of organizations. He eliminated the Board on Construction and used a staff of senior uniformed "aids" (later called "aides") to assist him in setting policy and developing building programs and strategic plans. In 1915, SECNAV Josephus Daniels eliminated the system of "aides," and Congress provided for a "chief of operations," a senior military officer serving under the Navy secretary, but responsible for fleet operations and readiness. This chapter will explain why those organizational changes were made and show how members of Congress and senior officials in the Navy Department gradually came to accept a uniformed chief of operations.

The Traditional and Legal Domination of the Secretary

By law and by tradition, the Secretary of the Navy—a civilian—was in charge of the Navy—in charge of both operations and shore-based support of the fleet. For example, it was SECNAV Long who sent Commodore George Dewey, in command of the American squadron in Hong Kong, his orders after the United States government declared war on Spain. "War has commenced between the United States and Spain," cabled Long. "Proceed at once to Philippine Islands. Commence operations at once, particularly against the Spanish fleet. You must capture vessels or destroy. Use utmost endeavors." But the war with Spain made it clear to Long and others that the SECNAV needed help. Long created the advisory Naval War Board during the war, but it was only a temporary organization.[6] Already in existence in 1898 were (a) the Board on Construction, formed in 1889 and composed of the Navy's bureau chiefs; (b) the Naval War College, founded in 1884; (c) the Office of Naval Intelligence, created in 1882; and (d) the Navy's bureaus, most of which dated back to 1842.[7]

The bureaus were semi-independent organizations that had their own budgets and were led by rear admirals or their equivalents. The bureau heads sat on the Board on Construction; their task was to provide the Navy with ships, weapons, equipment, trained sailors, and facilities. By contrast, the Naval War College existed (in the words of its first president, Rear Admiral Stephen B. Luce) to "*raise naval warfare from the empirical stage to the dignity of a science*" (emphasis in the original).[8] To do that, a small number of officers studied and taught at the college, developed war plans, and refined the art of war gaming. But Long wanted—and needed—more assistance, especially in Washington. Captain Taylor had therefore suggested to the SECNAV that Long persuade Congress to create a naval general staff. Strong opposition to this proposal from Senator Eugene Hale (R-ME), Senate Naval Affairs Committee chairman, led Long to instead create the General Board, composed of Admiral of the Navy George Dewey; Taylor, the Navy's senior intelligence officer and his principal assistant; the president of the Naval War College and his principal assistant; the chief of the Bureau of Navigation; and three other senior line officers.[9]

Admiral Dewey, in a 29 June 1901, letter to Secretary Long, explained that the War College was "an essential part of a General Staff—a place for the consideration of war plans, the working out of schemes of campaigns, for the study, in a word, of the art of war in its broadest and highest sense." The college and the Office of Naval Intelligence were "two indispensable adjuncts of the General Board—the three together constituting a General Staff. The whole bears a close analogy to the German General Staff system . . ."[10] This comparison with Germany's naval command did not please Secretary Long or his successors. The civilian secretaries were very suspicious of the German General Staff model and they made sure that the senior officers of the Navy knew it.[11] At the same time, they were often frustrated by the fragmented nature of naval administration. In April 1904, for example, Navy secretary William H. Moody told the members of the Naval Affairs Committee of the House of Representatives that the Secretary of the Navy needed a senior uniformed advisor. But before the same committee, Assistant Secretary of the Navy

Charles H. Darling argued that the recently created General Board had "already invaded the province of civil administration and planted there the standard of conquest."[12]

So why did Navy officers continue to argue for a general staff? Because they wanted a *modern* navy—one capable of deterring or fighting other modern navies, navies equipped with the latest naval technology and directed by formally trained officers. The key to such a navy was professionalism. Navy veteran and author Frank Uhlig Jr., put it this way:

> The war with Spain . . ., the strategic views expressed by Captain Mahan (one of the most important of which was "do not divide the fleet"), the growing concentration of foreign navies into coherent battle fleets, and the sense that at some time in the future the United States might have to fight one or another of those fleets, meant that the U.S. Navy must also form its ships into a tactically coherent fleet.
>
> Such fleets require that . . . the ships of which they are comprised be as much alike as possible, that those ships sail together and exercise together, and that the formerly independent captains become used to following the tactical commands of the flag officers placed over them.[13]

This shift from a navy where individual ships or small squadrons of ships protected commerce and showed the flag to a navy of powerful fleets required innovations. One was measuring the skill of enlisted and officer personnel through regular and fair peacetime competitions, such as gunnery and engineering performance contests. A second was promotion by ability instead of seniority or favoritism. A third was creating vigorous training and education programs. A fourth was weaning the Navy's "shore establishment," especially its dockyards, from being primarily a source of largess for the constituents of members of Congress.[14]

Secretary Long contributed to this process by giving the Navy's Bureau of Construction and Repair (BuC&R) control over ship design and construction in July 1899.[15] The Navy relied on private firms for the detailed designs of its ships, but Long wanted to begin a process that would give uniformed officers the skills to make systematic trade-offs among the critical characteristics (speed, firepower, and protection, for example) of warships *before* the Navy sought bids from commercial ship builders. He also wanted to focus responsibility on one bureau for construction, maintenance, and modernization. The Navy already relied on institutions like the Massachusetts Institute of Technology (MIT) to train the brightest graduates of the Naval Academy in the fields of naval architecture and marine engineering. Long wanted to give these officers authority commensurate with their technical skills.

Secretary Moody picked up where his predecessor—Long—left off. In December 1902, for example, Moody had most of the Navy's new ships participate in a "war game" in the Caribbean to test the ability of the new fleet to quickly assemble and then move *as a fleet* a great distance in order to confront an enemy force. Admiral Dewey was in overall command of this "game" and Henry C. Taylor, now a rear admiral, was his chief of staff. The exercise showed the need for effective scouting; scouting—reconnaissance—was the necessary prerequisite to fighting, and the Navy needed both ships to do the scouting and a doctrine to link scouting with a fleet engagement.[16] Navy ships staged another major scouting exercise in the Caribbean in 1903—again, to learn how best to maneuver and control a fleet.

At the urging of Rear Admiral Taylor, the Secretaries of the Navy and of the War Department created in July 1903 a joint board to coordinate Navy and Army strategy and planning. This board proved its worth later, when the government of the United States supported the separation of Panama from Colombia in late 1903 and early 1904.[17] Secretary Moody also asked the General Board in September 1903 to put together a long-range building program. The General Board, under the leadership of Admiral of the Navy George Dewey, produced a confidential report the next month; it recommended that the Navy construct 48 powerful battleships by 1920—32 of the warships for the Atlantic Fleet and 16 for the Pacific Fleet.[18] But the battleships were just the core of an enlarged force. "Every two battleships [would] be supported by one armored cruiser, seven protected and scout cruisers, three destroyers, and two colliers, and each division of four battleships [would] be supported by five auxiliaries, supply, repair, and hospital ships, and two transports."[19]

Why so many battleships? First, because it was estimated that such ships would have an effective life of only ten years; after that, they would need to be replaced. The first group, once built and sent to sea, would be wearing out as others were being designed and built to replace them. Second, because other navies—especially Britain's Royal Navy—were building numbers of battleships, and the U.S. Navy had to keep up the pace. Third, because a planned program of construction would support an industrial base; firms would deal with the Navy if they were certain of a long-term relationship with the service. Fourth, because technology was advancing rapidly; as a consequence, ships were becoming obsolete at a rate much faster than before, and more modern ships would polish off obsolescent opponents the way that Admiral Dewey's ships had overwhelmed obsolete Spanish ships at Manila Bay in 1898.

Secretary Moody was pleased with the work of the General Board. He wanted to strengthen its authority and make one of its members the official military advisor to the Navy secretary.[20] He favored the creation of a naval general staff.[21] He also sanctioned and supported meetings among the members of the General Board, the faculty of the Naval War College, and officers from the fleets every summer at the Naval War College in Newport, Rhode Island.[22] Supporting and shaping Moody's initiatives was President Theodore Roosevelt. Roosevelt made no secret of his desire for a large and modern U.S. Navy. He was quite capable of acting as his own Secretary of the Navy, as well as the commander-in-chief of the nation's military forces. In October 1903, for example, Roosevelt broke a "three-year bureaucratic logjam surrounding the selection of a new gun sight for the fleet's large-caliber weapons."[23] Roosevelt also supported the work of Lieutenant Commander William S. Sims, whom Rear Admiral Taylor had appointed the Navy's Inspector of Target Practice in November 1902.

Sims was one of a group of officers—including Bradley A. Fiske, Albert L. Key, and Reginald R. Belknap—pressing for reforms in the Navy. In 1901, Sims had written to President Roosevelt directly, expressing his concerns about naval gunnery. Roosevelt answered and encouraged him.[24] In 1902, Sims challenged the leaders of the Bureau of Ordnance (BuOrd) by writing "The Crushing Superiority of British Naval Marksmanship over Ours, as Shown by Comparisons of Recent Record Practice."[25] He wondered if it might get him disciplined. Instead, under Rear Admiral Taylor's mentorship, it gave him a chance to prove that his proposals for improving Navy gunnery were sound. They needed to be. If the Navy was to operate as one or more fleets (there was no Panama Canal at this time), its gunnery needed to be first-rate; so did its engineering and seamanship. In urging Congress to support the creation of a world-class fleet, Roosevelt needed not only modern ships but also professionally minded officers and trained sailors. Though outspoken and at times confrontational, Sims was aggressively professional. As he noted in 1902, "I loathe indirection and shiftiness, and where it occurs in high places, and is used to save a face at the expense of the vital interests of our great service . . ., I want that man's blood and I will have it, no matter what it costs me personally."[26] In effect, the behavior of a reforming officer like Sims was an inevitable consequence of Roosevelt's desire for a world-class navy. The President understood this; when he and Sims finally met face-to-face in January 1904, they began a "long and fruitful personal relationship."[27]

Navy officers around the world perked up when Russia and Japan went to war in February 1904. What would the war at sea tell them about the performance of modern ships and about the ability of naval officers to use them effectively? Theodore Roosevelt followed the fighting closely. "He depended on [the Office of Naval Intelligence] to provide him with reports to justify his naval building plans," and he was instrumental in getting the Russian and Japanese governments to a resolution of the conflict.[28] In June 1904, Secretary Moody resigned to become Attorney General. Roosevelt appointed Paul Morton to take Moody's place, but Morton—unlike Moody—was not interested in administrative reforms. However, Lieutenant Commander Sims and his officer allies were. In a series of trials, Sims's ideas about continuous aim firing were shown to be correct, and by 1905 it was clear that his "system of gunnery" had become the standard.[29] The major naval engagements between the Russian and Japanese fleets, especially the battles of the Yellow Sea in August 1904 and Tsushima in May 1905, prompted a debate about the value of the all-big-gun battleship, but Roosevelt sided with Sims's argument that the all-big-gun ship was superior.[30]

Roosevelt's next Navy secretary was Charles J. Bonaparte. Bonaparte, distantly related to Napoleon Bonaparte of France, was a political reformer from Baltimore. From 1901 to 1905, he had served as chairman of the Council of the National Civil Service Reform League.[31] However, Roosevelt had not selected him for the post of Navy secretary to make major changes. Accordingly, in his 1905 annual report to the President and the Congress, Bonaparte approached the issue of reforming the Navy's leadership cautiously. On the one hand, he argued that "The system of autonomous bureaus seems to me open, in theory, to very serious objection, and it is in practice attended with some measure of friction, circumlocution, and delay."[32] On the other hand, he was convinced that the Navy Department's "work is done, on the whole, with great fidelity and marked efficiency," though he considered "these results the fruits not of the system but of the high character, both with respect to integrity and with respect to competency, of the officers employed."[33]

Bonaparte did not favor the sort of change that Rear Admiral Taylor had proposed. As the secretary noted, "before deciding upon any changes in an organization which fulfills its purposes we should feel a reasonable certainty that these changes will prove improvements. I do not advise, therefore, any immediate changes in the organization of the Department . . ."[34] At the same time, however, Bonaparte's own report cited just the sorts of problems that Rear Admiral Taylor and other officers had said needed to be dealt with, including (a) the debate within the department over the proper speed, size, and gun power of new battleships, (b) the inability of BuOrd to deal effectively with its increasing workload, (c) the frustration of the chief of BuC&R with repair work done "at private shipyards on the Asiatic Station," and (d) the slow progress of amalgamating the line and engineering officer groups.[35]

Indeed, Rear Admiral George A. Converse, Taylor's successor as the chief of BuNav, went against Secretary Bonaparte in his own report, first asking "Is our departmental organization the best we can have for efficiently providing, organizing, preparing, and directing the fleet?" and then answering by saying, "In the opinion of the Bureau it is not. . . .[C]ommon sense dictates that the highest naval efficiency, demanded as never before for national success in war, must come from knowledge born of study, training, and experience—a knowledge that is essential to intelligent organization and preparation." The problem, according to Converse, was "the lack of military initiative and directive force—military administration under the Secretary."[36]

One cause of the problem identified by Rear Admiral Converse was rapid technological change. In a series of detailed studies, Norman Friedman has traced the progress in naval technology during Theodore Roosevelt's presidency.[37] In 1905, for example, studies at the Naval War College suggested that long-range torpedoes could well drive battleships from the seas. Soon thereafter, however, the ability of battleship guns to shoot accurately beyond effective torpedo range kept the battleship in play. And battleships were not the only ships changing dramatically. What had been small torpedo boats (like *Cushing*, Torpedo Boat No. 1), at 105 tons in 1890, had become larger—like *Blakely* (Torpedo Boat No. 27) of 196 tons in 1901. Soon the torpedo boats were superseded by torpedo boat destroyers such as the 408-ton *Hopkins* (Destroyer No. 6) of 1903 and—eventually—torpedo boat destroyers of 700 tons, such as *Flusser* (Destroyer No. 20) and *Reid* (Destroyer No. 21) of 1909. Other actual or potential technological additions to the Navy included submarines (or, as they were known, "submarine torpedo boats"), aircraft, and radio.

These rapid and dramatic changes strongly influenced Secretary Bonaparte. In his 1906 report (published in 1907), he therefore returned to the issue of Navy Department organization, arguing that "a very radical and thoroughgoing change should be made in the organization of the Department."[38] Rear Admiral Converse was even more emphatic than Bonaparte:

> [W]ith each year that passes the need is painfully apparent for a military administrative authority under the Secretary, whose purpose would be to initiate and direct the

steps necessary to carry out the Department's policy, and to coordinate the work of the bureaus and direct their energies toward the effective preparation of the fleet for war.[39]

The bureaus had been created in the first place to pursue special fields of technology—ordnance, for example, navigation, and steam engineering. They continued to do that, and their efforts had produced better torpedoes, improved engines, guns of greater hitting power and longer range, and electric motors and control systems on ships. But how were all these innovations to be combined in one or more fleets? And how was any fleet to be used?

Use is what Theodore Roosevelt cared about. Navy "reformers" such as Lieutenant Commander Albert L. Key, Roosevelt's naval aid from 1905 to 1907, and Commander William S. Sims, Key's successor from 1907 to 1909, knew this. They had watched Roosevelt in action. In 1902, ships of the German, British, and Italian navies had blockaded Venezuelan ports, demanding payment of Venezuelan government debts. Admiral Dewey and President Roosevelt could not stop the blockade, but they determined to field a Navy that could force foreign navies to forego such action in the future. By the end of 1905, the rapid build-up of the U.S. Navy had produced such a force, and Roosevelt did not hesitate to threaten to use it.[40] This was real drama—the United States government asserting what became known as the "Roosevelt Corollary" to the Monroe Doctrine. The United States, said Roosevelt, would decide whether and when European navies would act against the nations around the Caribbean. The next step was to use the Navy to influence world—and not just regional—events, as Roosevelt did when he acted to help settle the 1904–1905 Russo-Japanese War.

But if the Navy was to serve as Roosevelt's "big stick," then the Navy had to be *modern*—professional, and properly managed. This was the argument that Bonaparte and officers like Sims made. Roosevelt listened. The President dispatched the "Great White Fleet" on its around-the-world cruise in December 1907 in order to show other naval powers that the U.S. fleet had a long reach. But while the fleet was away, Roosevelt returned to the issue of how best to make it a truly world-class force. In January 1908, Henry Reuterdahl, the American editor of *Jane's Fighting Ships*, had published an article entitled "The Needs of Our Navy" that was critical of Navy Department administration. The article triggered hearings conducted by the Senate Naval Affairs Committee in February and March of that year.[41] Commander Sims then persuaded the President to hold a major conference on battleship design at the Naval War College. The now-famous conference may have begun by focusing on the design of new battleships such as *North Dakota* (Battleship No. 29), but it quickly enlarged its scope to cover the way the Navy Department was organized and led. Sims, however, did not get what he and the other "reformers" wanted, which was an organization for *operations*, headed by a senior officer. President Roosevelt's time in office was running down by the fall of 1908, and Sims and his allies had no strong champions in Congress. But the Newport conference did recommend that all future warship designs be reviewed by a board of "seagoing" officers. This board would be a modified General Board, and it would do what President Roosevelt wanted—"to lead other nations" in the development of modern warships.

Yet Sims was not done. He kept after Roosevelt, telling the President at the end of 1908

> that the great improvement we have made in the last few years was really due to the fact that your powerful influence has largely suspended the evils of the bureau system; but that if you should leave us with an unsound organization, unrestrained by your influence, not only must we relapse into our former condition, but our failure in this respect would be remembered long after our minor improvements were forgotten.[42]

Supporting Sims was the famous Alfred Thayer Mahan, who told Roosevelt that "The only means by which such consecutive knowledge can be maintained is by a corporate body continuous in existence and gradual in change. That we call a General Staff." Moreover, the head of this staff needed to be "solely responsible for information and advice given the Secretary."[43]

In early 1909, Roosevelt convened a special board, composed of three ex-secretaries of the Navy and five accomplished admirals, to review and evaluate all the different reorganization proposals. After a month, the board came down on the side of change. No administrative system, the board informed the President and Congress,

> can possibly be effective which does not recognize that the requirement of war is the true standard of efficiency in an administrative military system; that success in war and victory in battle can be assured only by that constant preparedness and that superior fighting efficiency which logically result from placing the control and responsibility in time of peace upon the same individuals and the same agencies that must control in time of war. There should be no shock or change of method in expanding from a state of peace to a state of war. This is not militarism; it is a simple business principle based upon the fact that success in war is the only return the people and the nation can get from the investment of many millions in the building and maintenance of a great navy.[44]

Congress, however, was not then moved to act.

Changes Under President Taft

Roosevelt's successor, William H. Taft, took action. On Roosevelt's suggestion, he appointed George von Lengerke Meyer as Secretary of the Navy. Meyer understood what Roosevelt's board had suggested. But he also knew that there was strong opposition to those suggestions within the Congress and even within the Navy. Senator Hale, still chairman of the Senate Naval Affairs Committee, disliked Sims, distrusted Secretary Meyer, and blocked every effort to have Congress review the recommendations of Roosevelt's special board. Hale was supported by Rear Admiral Washington L. Capps, the Chief Constructor of the Navy and the Chief BuC&R, and by Rear Admiral Caspar F. Goodrich, who had commanded the Navy's Pacific Squadron.

Meyer was committed to "reforming" the Navy, and, to keep both the opponents and the supporters of change occupied, he set up a special board in July 1909, headed by Rear

Admiral William Swift, a former Commandant of the Boston Navy Yard, to consider existing reorganization proposals.[45] While the Swift Board was considering the different views, he took actions that were clearly within his responsibility as Navy secretary but not a direct threat to those officers and members of Congress set against creating a Navy "general staff." In the early spring of 1909, Meyer toured the navy yards at Norfolk, Boston, Philadelphia, and New York. In May, he met with the navy yard commandants and explained to them that he planned to restructure the ways that they performed their work. He then "prohibited the sending of ships to yards merely because the [yards] needed work" and "assigned to yards only officers knowledgeable of the needs of operating ships . . ."[46] After gaining President Taft's permission to experiment with new methods of managing the navy yards, Meyer hired an accounting firm to overhaul the method used in the Boston yard for cost accounting. After seeing it work, Meyer "gradually extended" the method to the remaining navy yards.[47]

In June 1909, Meyer began removing retired officers from "temporary" active duty and replacing them with younger men. He also openly criticized the officer promotion process, which he said produced admirals who were too old. Unfortunately, his efforts were sometimes blocked by Congress. As former Naval Academy historian Paolo Coletta observed,

> On providing the rank of admiral and vice admiral, Congress did nothing. Meyer sought authority to bring capable young officers to early promotion . . . Congress did nothing. He wished to amalgamate the Pay Corps and Construction Corps with the line. Congress did nothing. He recommended the abolishment of the restriction . . . on the employment by the department of retired officers in a civilian capacity. Congress did nothing.[48]

But Meyer persisted. He worked with Congress when he had to, but he also adroitly used what powers he had as navy secretary. As he informed his mentor, Theodore Roosevelt, in July 1909, "we must have our navy yards and our fleets in actual readiness for any emergency, and . . . this is as important as it is for a fire-engine to be prepared to quell a fire at a moment's notice."[49]

The Swift Board issued its report to Meyer on 11 October 1909.[50] As historian Henry Beers noted, "Secretary Meyer, familiar with the temper of Congress, acted before [the legislature] came into session" and chose to implement those of its recommendations that did not require congressional action. On 18 November 1909, Meyer promulgated changes in Navy regulations that created a set of "aids"—four senior officers in the fields of personnel, material, inspections, and operations.[51] As Meyer put it in his 1912 annual report, these officers "are without executive authority, but have a supervisory function and serve in an advisory capacity." Through them, "the Secretary of the Navy receives expert responsible advice and is kept informed daily of what is going on in the department. They also serve in coordinating the work of the various bureaus of the department."[52]

The Aid for Personnel was "instrumental in coordinating the work of the Bureau of Navigation, the Bureau of Medicine and Surgery, the Marine Corps, the Offices of Naval Militia,

Naval Reserve, Aviation, Radio Telegraphy, and of the Judge Advocate General . . ." The Aid for Material was a member of the General Board and "has labored to coordinate the work of that board and the work of the technical bureaus . . ." The Aid for Inspections was "specially charged with the supervision of the work of the two permanent departmental inspection boards, the one for ships and the other for shore stations."[53]

But it was the aid for operations who mattered the most. Secretary Meyer noted that this aid devoted

> his entire attention and study to the operations of the fleet. He works in conjunction with the War College and the General Board on war plans and strategic matters. . . . In any emergency the aid for operations is prepared to advise promptly as to the movements of ships and to submit such orders as are necessary to carry into effect campaign plans recommended by the General Board and approved by the Secretary.[54]

This position was very close to what reform-minded officers like Sims wanted. As historian Beers recognized, "The creation of [the operations] division initiated the decline of the Bureau of Navigation as the most powerful organization in the department." A clear sign of the change was the fact that the aid for operations "took the place of the Chief of the Bureau of Navigation on the General Board."[55]

Meyer described how the aids supported him: ". . . the aids meet in full council daily and take up questions of departmental policy, general orders and changes in regulations, and submit recommendations on those that require action by the department." The SECNAV met with his "Council of Aids . . . at least once a week," whereas Meyer met with the bureau chiefs *and the aids* once each month. Meyer acknowledged that the bureau chiefs could "confer freely" with him "whenever any matter arises that affects their particular bureaus," but it was clear that it was the aids who were closer to the secretary and that Meyer wanted it that way.[56]

Using his system of "aides," Meyer made further changes. In January 1910, the House Naval Affairs Committee agreed with Meyer's decision to eliminate the Bureau of Equipment and also agreed to give the Navy secretary time to test his plans to reorganize the navy yards. This was a sticky point. If Meyer could improve the efficiency of the yards, and if he could consolidate yard functions, then it was obvious that he would try to eliminate yards that he considered unnecessary. That was a direct attack on the desire of many in Congress to use the yards as sources of largess for their constituents. Meyer understood this and therefore moved carefully. But he also proposed to the naval affairs committees in both houses of Congress a way to set the officer and enlisted levels for the Navy—a way that depended on the Navy's overall ship tonnage. It's important to recall the detail with which Congress then managed the Navy. The Congress set pay scales, decided how many officers and enlisted personnel the Navy could have, decided what ships to authorize, and even told the Navy what sorts of food could be served to sailors aboard ships. In pressing for modern forms of management, Meyer ran up against tradition—a tradition that had not been based on modern notions of business efficiency and military effectiveness. In his campaign against the past, Meyer usually had the support of the General Board.[57]

Meyer continued to use his authority to make changes. In 1910, he approved the organization of torpedo and submarine flotillas in the three Navy fleets (Atlantic, Pacific, and Asiatic). On the advice of the Aide for Operations Rear Admiral Richard Wainwright, Meyer also reorganized the Atlantic and Pacific fleets to make each a force better suited to its mission.[58] You see in these changes further efforts to figure out how best to use the technology that was coming from the Navy's bureaus. How could destroyers be combined with the battleships? What was the mission of the submarine—coast defense, or work with the fleet? Meyer did not stop. He persuaded President Taft to create two Navy "oil reserves" in 1910. The fleet was switching from coal to oil, and Meyer understood the need to have sources of oil that were under the Navy's direct control. He even tried to modernize the weapons and infrastructure of the Marine Corps.[59]

But Meyer's greater contribution was to prepare the Navy for a major campaign. He directed "all the first line and reserve ships of the Atlantic fleet to mobilize on 30 October 1911 and the Pacific fleet to mobilize at San Diego on 1 November."[60] In 1912, the Atlantic fleet mobilized again—123 ships of all classes, including 31 active and "reserve" battleships. The "reserve" was another product of Meyer's diligence. He wanted a force of older ships kept in readiness for an emergency. On his own authority, he could create a reserve fleet, but he needed the support of Congress to man it, and so he proposed enlarging the Navy Reserve and training members of the state naval militias at sea on active ships. He didn't get the funding for more reserve personnel, but he used the authority of his office to improve the training of the state naval militias.[61] And on 12 May 1912, Rear Admiral Austin M. Knight, author of a classic book on seamanship, took command of the Atlantic Reserve Fleet.[62]

President Taft was impressed. After watching the 1912 fleet review, he complemented Meyer and the Navy's officers for their efforts. As he said, Meyer had worked to "bring about a system of control in the Navy Department which shall be military rather than civil, and directed to fighting rather than merely to manufacture and industrial work."[63] But Meyer wasn't done in 1912. On 10 February 1913, with just three weeks remaining to the Taft presidency, Meyer appointed Rear Admiral Bradley A. Fiske his Aide for Operations, and he "made the Aide for Operations his liaison man with all the offices and bureaus of the department."[64] This elevation of the operations aide to the role of *de facto* naval military chief was a dramatic move—a fitting end to a busy and productive term as Navy secretary.[65] As Meyer told then-Commander Yates Stirling Jr., before he left office, "Congress was violently against" creating a Navy general staff, but Congress would approve reforms "peacemeal" [*sic*].[66]

The Creation of the Office of the Chief of Naval Operations

Meyer's successor as secretary was Josephus Daniels, and Daniels came with an agenda. First on that list, as he said in his first annual report, was his plan to "make the Navy a great university,

The Office of the Chief of Naval Operations

Figure 1-1. Rear Admiral Bradley A. Fiske, 1912. Admiral Fiske was an articulate and persistent advocate of what would become the Office of the Chief of Naval Operations (OPNAV). In 1915, he went around Secretary of the Navy Josephus Daniels and worked directly with congressional allies to get the necessary legislation passed. He knew Daniels would then keep him from becoming the first CNO.
(NHHC Archives NH 49555)

with college extensions afloat and ashore. Every ship should be a school, and every enlisted man, and petty and warrant officer should be given the opportunity to improve his mind, better his position and fit himself for promotion."[67] Daniels had other ideas, too. He's still remembered as the secretary who shut down the officer's wine mess and in doing so made coffee ("cup a'joe") the Navy's staple beverage. Daniels did much more than that, however. He was an odd combination of reformer—successfully advocating "the Navy, school of the nation"—and at the same time a supporter of racial segregation. If you were a white enlisted sailor, Daniels was for you. If you were black, he wanted no part of you, except as a steward. In that, he was very much like his political ally and mentor, President Woodrow Wilson.

Daniels inherited Admiral Fiske as his Aide for Operations. As Fiske noted in his published memoir, "the upper officers of the navy realized that while the navy was in good condition for times of peace, it was not organized for war," and it was thinking about possible war with either Germany or Japan that troubled him deeply. As he recalled, he and his closest colleagues

> did not like the German idea of war or the German belief that might makes right . . . But we realized that the German naval machine was immeasurably better than ours . . . and the only man in the United States Navy who could remotely pretend to occupy the position of a naval strategist was myself![68]

And *that* was the problem. Like Sims, Fiske had a strong personality, and for that reason debates over the proper direction of the Navy took on a personal cast, with people taking sides based on their like or dislike for Fiske or Daniels.

The two men—so different in temperament, yet so alike in intelligence—locked horns almost immediately. What held them together for two years may be guessed from Fiske's assessment of his boss: "a man of refinement, sympathy, and good nature, whose serenity was rarely ruffled and whose politeness was unfailing." Fiske liked Daniels personally, but he also felt that Daniels "did not see the Navy as a whole, but only certain parts of it; with the natural result that the parts upon which he fixed his attention seemed to him larger than they really were." Fiske set out to show Daniels that "the navy was really a vast and highly specialized machine, and not an aggregation of separate parts."[69] The Navy as a *fighting machine*. In 1916, Fiske published a book with that title. It was a powerful image, but not one that Daniels was comfortable with.

As Fiske recalled, by the fall of 1914 "I had done all I possibly could to impress the Secretary with the fact that our navy was not prepared for war with any navy like the German navy, and that there was an actual danger of our being drawn into [World War I]; but I could make no impression on him."[70] Frustrated, Fiske chose to do an end-run around Daniels and testify to the Committee on Naval Affairs of the House of Representatives. He persuaded Representative Richmond P. Hobson (D-AL), a retired Navy hero in the war with Spain, to sponsor him. Fiske's December 1914 testimony made the papers, made him popular among Navy officers, and was the first step in a deliberate campaign to maneuver Secretary Daniels into asking Congress for a naval general staff.

Step one in this campaign was to win the support of Representative Hobson. Step two was to develop the basis of legislation that would create what would be called the "chief of naval operations." It was the stuff of a matinee drama. As Fiske's diary for January 3, 1915, put it,

> I asked Capts. H[enry] S. Knapp, [John] Hood & [James H.] Oliver, & Lt. Comdrs. [William P.] Cronan, [Zachariah H.] Madison & [Dudley W.] Knox to be at Hobson's at 8:30 p.m. We all met there in Hobson's study, & sat till after 11 p.m. when we adjourned. We agreed on program whereby Chief of Naval Operations is to be legislated for & to have 15 assts!![71]

Fiske had the six other officers keep the meeting secret "because they were engaged on an exceedingly dangerous mission."[72] On January 4, Fiske met again with the six officers who had worked with him the night before, and they wrote a draft of the proposed addition to the naval appropriations act.

Step three was for Representative Hobson to persuade his subcommittee to accept the idea for a chief of naval operations. Hobson first picked up the draft proposal that morning (January 4) from Fiske. Then, according to Fiske, Hobson approached Daniels and "took up the matter" with the secretary. Daniels was completely opposed, but he apparently did not know that Fiske and the others had actually drafted the proposal and given it to Hobson. By 2:20 that afternoon, Hobson informed Fiske personally that his subcommittee had "passed the proposition unanimously!"[73]

Step four was to persuade the House Naval Affairs Committee to accept the recommendation of Hobson's subcommittee. To do that, Fiske worked with Madison, Cronan, and Knox to draw up a brief, which Knox delivered to Hobson the next morning. As Fiske noted in his diary, "Hobson telephoned me at 1 p.m. [on January 6] that full House Naval Committee agreed unanimously on incorporating in naval appropriation bill the provisions for a 'Chief of Naval Operations'!!"[74]

Step five was to get around the objection that the provision creating the office of the Chief of Naval Operations was not germane to an appropriations bill. Hobson expected that and persuaded his counterparts in the Senate to put the provision back in the legislation. Before that could happen, however, Secretary Daniels had to be given the opportunity to suggest changes, which he did. The version of the bill prepared by Fiske and his colleagues read as follows:

> There shall be a Chief of Naval Operations, who shall be an officer on the active list of the Navy not below the grade of Rear Admiral, appointed for a term of four years by the President, by and with the advice of the Senate, who, under the Secretary of the Navy, shall be responsible for the readiness of the Navy for war and be charged with its general direction.[75]

Daniels's version—the one finally passed in March 1915—read differently:

> There shall be a Chief of Naval Operations, who shall be an officer on the active list of the Navy appointed by the President, by and with the advice and consent of the Senate, from the officers of the line of the Navy not below the grade of Captain for a period of four years, who shall, under the direction of the Secretary, be charged with the operations of the fleet, and with the preparation and readiness of plans for its use in war.[76]

Note the differences. Fiske's younger supporters thought he was the obvious choice to be the new Chief of Naval Operations, but Fiske knew otherwise. He would receive no reward for going behind Daniels's back. Accordingly, Fiske compared himself to "the well-known gentleman who sawed off the branch of a tree at a point between himself and the branch, except that that man did not realize what he was doing, and I did."[77] Secretary Daniels could—and did—reach down into the ranks of the Navy's captains for the first Chief of Naval Operations. Daniels also denied the office of the chief the "general direction" of the fleet, and he made sure that the law put the new Chief under "the direction" of the civilian secretary. Fiske nevertheless thought the whole struggle had been worth it. As he put it in his memoir, "Most officers said that it was as great a boon to the navy as the act of Congress, in 1880, which had authorized the 'new navy' in the shape of the steel ships *Chicago*, *Atlanta*, *Boston*, and *Dolphin*."[78]

But Fiske was not done. Step six was to give the new Chief of Naval Operations the rank of admiral, the pay commensurate with that high rank, and a staff of "no less than fifteen officers of and above the rank of lieutenant commander of the Navy or major of the Marine Corps." Congress took that step in August 1916, and also changed the wording of the law to "All orders issued by the Chief of Naval Operations in performing the duties assigned him shall be performed under the authority of the Secretary of the Navy, and his orders shall be considered as emanating from the Secretary, and shall have full force and effect as such."[79]

Secretary Daniels tolerated the change. As he put it in his annual report for 1915, the

> reorganization and realignment of the machinery of the Navy Department was finally rounded out and completed by the creation of the Secretary's Advisory Council, composed of the Assistant Secretary of the Navy, the Chief of Naval Operations, the Chiefs of the Bureaus of Navigation, Ordnance, Steam Engineering, Construction

and Repair, Yards and Docks, Supplies and Accounts, and Medicine and Surgery, the Major General Commandant of the Marine Corps, and the Judge Advocate General.[80]

Daniels added that "The result of this reorganization has been the using to better purpose all existing departmental machinery while securing the maximum of cooperation between its constituent units."[81]

And there, in just a few words, was the view opposed to Fiske's. Fiske wanted a senior officer *from the* fleet to direct Navy operations, supervise war planning, and coordinate among the bureaus to make sure that what they did in fact supported war planning. Daniels, by contrast, wanted all this done *under the authority* of the secretary. But how could the SECNAV best exercise that authority? The answer was through an advisory council, where there would be no officer between the secretary and the bureau chiefs. Like his predecessors, Daniels did not want to be insulated from the bureau chiefs by a serving officer.

Daniels also got the last word:

The present plan of organization accords with the genius of American institutions. The militaristic idea does not. And, if ever our country seriously desires to reverse its traditional policy of civilian authority in the Navy Department it ought to do so with eyes wide open and with full knowledge of all that such a radical departure from Americanism means. . .[82]

But why did Secretary Daniels, a confidante of President Wilson, accept the establishment of the post of Chief of Naval Operations if he was basically opposed to it? Charles Oscar Paullin suggested the reason in his 1914 essay on Navy administration:

It is scarcely too much to say that the Secretary of the Navy, the chiefs of naval bureaus, the members of the General Board, the President of the United States, the Speaker of the House and the leading members of the two naval committees, constitute a grand committee on naval legislation, whose members . . . resolve differences, compromise conflicting interests, bring the legislature and executive to an understanding and reach an approximate agreement upon naval legislation.[83]

Over a period of about 15 years, a majority of the most influential members of that "grand committee" had participated directly or indirectly in changing the administration of the Navy—from the creation of the General Board by Secretary Long to the creation of the system of "aides" by Secretary Meyer. Gradually but steadily, the executive and legislative branches had made these changes and then assessed their value. Put another way, by 1915 there was a coalition favoring a chief of operations, and Josephus Daniels knew it, and so he compromised.

But what was the new office of the chief of operations like? What did it consist of? The most important elements of the new office were those that had reported to Rear Admiral Fiske: the Office of Naval Intelligence, the Naval War College, the Office of Target Practice and Engineering Competitions, the Naval Radio Service, and the Office of Naval Aeronautics.[84] But Secretary

Daniels also gave the new Chief of Operations—William S. Benson—the duties that had been performed by the Aide for Material. Rear Admiral Benson then appointed Captain Josiah S. McKean, "an expert in logistics and a graduate and former member of the faculty of the Naval War College," his deputy for material.[85] The bureau chiefs approved. Though small, the new office of operations had the basics for effectiveness: legitimacy and authority.

Enduring Issues

Could the very different views of Admiral Fiske and Secretary Daniels be made compatible? If so, then reconciling them would not be easy. Historian Elting E. Morison got to the heart of the problem in a book published in 1942: "Any successful system of administration . . . must bring into combination the three elements which can claim an interest in the Navy—that is, the professional who fights the ships, the civilian who superintends the maintenance of the establishment, and the politician who represents the people for whom the Navy exists."[86] Balancing these elements is the job of the Congress, which writes the laws empowering Navy officials, and of the senior civilian and uniformed leaders of the Navy. As Morison put it in his biography of Admiral Sims, all three "elements" must be present in the administration of the Navy Department, "the influence of each must be permitted to operate, and the predominance of any one avoided"—without at the same time stripping the gears of effective leadership and efficient management.[87]

But Rear Admiral Taylor had put his finger on a problem: How to coordinate the various parts of the Navy Department without at the same time weakening civilian control of the Navy. Taylor knew what he was talking about. For example, when he became chief of BuNav in 1902, he directed "the widely scattered individual units of the Fleet to come together for yearly manoeuvers" in order to give ship and squadron commanders experience they would need in the event of war.[88] Some senior officers objected to this and resisted Taylor's order. They could not see the need for the Fleet to concentrate. After all, it had not done that during the war with Spain, and their separate squadrons had been victorious. But Taylor knew that the new, modern Navy the nation was creating—a navy able to challenge the naval forces of Germany or Japan—needed to be built and run on a level of professionalism significantly greater than that of the past.

Rear Admiral Taylor died suddenly in 1904, but the issue he had raised—the proper administration of the Navy in Washington—did not go away. By law, the Secretary of the Navy was responsible for the operations and management of the Navy Department. By law, the chiefs of the seven Navy bureaus (Yards and Docks, Construction and Repair, Steam Engineering, Ordnance, Supplies and Accounts, Medicine and Surgery, and Navigation) were the senior advisors of the secretary and managers of their own organizations, with their own congressionally approved budgets. The fleet's commander and his subordinates were responsible to the SECNAV. But Navy officers wanted one of their own to direct operations and, if possible, coordinate the work of the Navy's bureaus. As already noted, Secretary Long was opposed to this idea. However, he did create a General Board of the Navy on his own authority in Washington in 1900.

This board, composed mostly of Navy line officers, was responsible for developing war plans and for helping the secretary see to it that what the bureaus produced did in fact support those plans. The creation of the General Board, an organization intended to assist the Secretary of the Navy, was actually a step toward the creation of the position of the Chief of Naval Operations. The reason it became that was because the General Board gradually grew to be a place where critical trade-offs were made by line officers who held hearings—often adversarial—where bureau representatives and fleet officers offered their opinions and presented supporting evidence. If the Navy was to become truly modern, then its leaders would have to be able to make decisions about force structure and strategy based on the systematic analysis of evidence. You can see this in the debate in 1906 between Sims and Rear Admiral Mahan over the meaning of the major engagements of the Russo-Japanese War. Who had better interpreted the evidence? Theodore Roosevelt (no mean thinker himself) sided with Sims. The General Board was a place where the sort of analysis done by Sims was becoming routine. This analysis was the basis—as Sims and many other officers recognized—of modern command.

This changed the nature of the debate over whether a Navy officer should share power with the civilian secretary. For example, the basis for the authority of Navy secretaries such as Meyer and Daniels was the Constitution. Sims and Fiske wanted to root the authority of officers in their proven abilities to lead and to think. In effect, the "reformers" who wanted a chief of naval operations saw the chief's authority based on his competence—on his professionalism, and his professionalism would be based on his intellectual integrity, or, putting it another way, on his willingness and ability to analyze evidence objectively. Both Daniels and Fiske were concerned about accountability. Daniels feared that a senior naval officer would not be as faithful to the Constitution as he was. Fiske feared the damage a secretary could do if he were not as faithful to the "new Navy's" commitment to intellectual integrity as Fiske was. In short, what you had was an argument about the source of integrity—not a confrontation between integrity and the lack of it. This argument is still with us.

Notes

[1] RADM Henry C. Taylor, quoted in *Naval Administration: Selected Documents on Navy Department Organization, 1915–1940*, ed. by LT Elting Morison, USNR (Washington, DC: Dept. of the Navy, 1945), Navy Dept. Library, I-2.

[2] Ibid., I-3.

[3] This approach, which portrays the civilian and military leaders of the Navy as "problem-solvers," is presented and critiqued in detail by Donald Chisholm in his *Waiting for Dead Men's Shoes: Origins and Development of the U.S. Navy's Officer Personnel System, 1793–1941* (Stanford, CA: Stanford Univ. Press, 2001), 779–881 and 795. See also, *Establishment and Evolution of the Office of the Deputy Chief of Staff for Operations and Plans, 1903–1983*, by Terrence J. Gough (Washington, DC: Dept. of the Army, 1983).

[4] The literature on this topic is very large. One award-winning example is *The Social Transformation of American Medicine*, by Paul Starr (New York: Basic Books, 1984). See also, *The Engineer in America: A Historical Anthology from Technology and Culture*, ed. by Terry S. Reynolds (Chicago: Univ. of Chicago Press, 1991).

[5] Ltr, ADM George Dewey, Chairman of the General Board to Secretary of the Navy John D. Long, 30 March 1900, (GB No. 2), in General Board Letters, vol. I, Box 3, General Records of the Department of the Navy, 1798–1947, Record Group 80, National Archives (hereafter RG 80, NARA).

[6] Charles Oscar Paullin, "A Half Century of Naval Administration," U.S. Naval Institute *Proceedings*, vol. 40, no. 1 (January/February 1914), 116–17.

[7] Henry P. Beers, "The Development of the Office of the Chief of Naval Operations, Part I," *Military Affairs*, vol. 10, no. 1 (Spring 1946), 40–68.

[8] Ltr, RADM Stephen B. Luce to RADM Alfred T. Mahan, 15 July 1907, in Naval War College Records, 1884–1914, Folder 2 ("Correspondence"), Manuscript Collection, Library of Congress.

[9] Secretary Long's 13 March 1900 directive stated that the Admiral of the Navy (George Dewey) was the new board's president. The General Board's membership was changed in April 1901 and again in 1905. Paullin, "A Half Century of Naval Administration," 118–119; https://www.history.navy.mil/research/library/online-reading-room/title-list-alphabetically/g/general-orders/general-order-no-544-1900-establishment-general-board.html.

[10] Ltr, General Board to Secretary of the Navy John D. Long, 29 June 1901, (GB No. 197), in General Board Letters, Vol. I, Box 3, RG 80, NARA. In 1900, as part of his work while attending the Naval War College, CAPT Asa Walker prepared for Navy Secretary Long a "Memorandum on a Naval General Staff" in which he argued that "the American Navy has *for some years* (italics added) felt instinctively that [a general staff], or something like this, was needed for future efficiency." Walker had been promoted as a result of his command of gunboat *Concord* in the Battle of Manila Bay. He served briefly on the General Board in 1904 and retired as a rear admiral in 1906. Walker's memo is in the Collection 8, Box 70, Folder 1, Naval War College Archives (Hereafter cited as NWC Archives).

[11] Paullin, "A Half Century of Naval Administration," 120–21.

[12] Ibid., 121. When Darling gave his testimony, William H. Moody was Secretary of the Navy. Long had relinquished the secretary's position in 1902.

[13] Ltr, Frank Uhlig Jr. to: Thomas C. Hone, "The Nature of a Modern Navy," no date. This was also the view of RADM Henry C. Taylor, Chief of the Bureau of Navigation in 1902. See Elting E. Morison, *Admiral Sims and the Modern American Navy* (Boston, MA: Houghton Mifflin, 1942), 70.

[14] See CDR (later RADM) Yates Stirling, "Organization for Navy Department Administration," U.S. Naval Institute *Proceedings*, vol. 39, no. 2 (June 1913), 435–99, and "Discussion," 501–502.

[15] Paolo E. Coletta, "John Davis Long," in *American Secretaries of the Navy, Vol. I*, ed. by Paolo E. Coletta (Annapolis, MD: Naval Institute Press, 1980), 452.

[16] Norman Friedman, *U.S. Cruisers, An Illustrated Design History* (Annapolis, MD: Naval Institute Press, 1984), 67.

[17] Henry J. Hendrix, *Theodore Roosevelt's Naval Diplomacy: The U.S. Navy and the Birth of the American Century* (Annapolis, MD: Naval Institute Press, 2009), 76.

[18] Paul T. Heffron, "William H. Moody," in Coletta, *American Secretaries of the Navy, Vol. I*, 463.

[19] Robert W. Love Jr., *History of the U.S. Navy, 1775–1941* (Harrisburg, PA: Stackpole Books, 1992), 420.

[20] Heffron, "William H. Moody," in Coletta, *American Secretaries of the Navy, Vol. I*, 465.

[21] Ibid., 464.

[22] Norman Friedman, *U.S. Battleships, An Illustrated Design History* (Annapolis, MD: Naval Institute Press, 1985), 17.

[23] Hendrix, *Theodore Roosevelt's Naval Diplomacy*, 140.

[24] Morison, *Admiral Sims and the Modern American Navy*, 101–102.

[25] Ibid., 116–18.

[26] Ibid., 130.

[27] Ibid., 137.

[28] Hendrix, *Theodore Roosevelt's Naval Diplomacy*, 114.

[29] Morison, *Admiral Sims and the Modern American Navy*, 147.

[30] Ibid., 170. See also Hendrix, *Theodore Roosevelt's Naval Diplomacy*, 142.

[31] Paul T. Heffron, "Charles J. Bonaparte," in Coletta, *American Secretaries of the Navy, Vol. I*, 475.

[32] Charles J. Bonaparte, Secretary of the Navy, *Annual Reports of the Navy Department for the Year 1905* (Washington, DC: GPO, 1906), 3.

[33] Ibid.

[34] Ibid., 4.

[35] Ibid., Report of the Chief of the Bureau of Construction and Repair, 543.

[36] Ibid., Report of the Chief of the Bureau of Navigation, 369.

[37] Norman Friedman, *U.S. Destroyers: An Illustrated Design History*, rev. ed. (Annapolis, MD: Naval Institute Press, 2004); and *U.S. Submarines Through 1945: An Illustrated Design History* (Annapolis, MD: Naval Institute Press, 1995); also his *U.S. Cruiser's; U.S. Battleships*.

[38] Charles J. Bonaparte, Secretary of the Navy, *Annual Reports of the Navy Department for the Year 1906* (Washington, DC: GPO, 1907), 5.

[39] Ibid., report of RADM George A. Converse, Chief of the Bureau of Navigation, 402.

[40] Hendrix, *Theodore Roosevelt's Naval Diplomacy*, 25.

[41] Beers, "The Development of the Office of the Chief of Naval Operations, Part I, 59.

[42] Morison, *Admiral Sims and the Modern American Navy*, 222.

[43] Ibid., 223.

[44] Ibid., 227–28.

[45] As a captain, Swift was court martialed after his command, battleship *Connecticut* (Battleship No. 18), ran aground in 1907. Denied any further command at sea, Swift accepted command of the Charlestown (Boston), Massachusetts, Navy Yard, and was promoted to rear admiral on 30 January 1908. He retired from the Navy in mid-March 1908, but served as an advisor to Navy secretaries Victor H. Metcalf and Truman H. Newberry. Secretary Meyer selected Swift to head a board "to consider the question of the organization of the Navy Department" on 13 July 1909. Secretary Meyer's letter establishing the board is in Collection 8, Box 42, Folder 6, NWC Archives.

[46] Paolo E. Coletta, "George von Lengerke Meyer," in Coletta, *American Secretaries of the Navy, Vol. I*, 500.

[47] Ibid.

[48] Ibid., 506.

[49] Mark A. DeWolfe Howe, *George von Lengerke Meyer, His Life and Public Services* (New York: Dodd, Mead & Co., 1920), 438.

[50] The so-called "Swift Board" report is in Collection 8, Box 42, Folder 6, NWC Archives. On the first page, its authors noted that they had found "many defects in existing organization both of the Navy Department and of Navy Yards; and these defects have become emphasized with the growth of a modern navy, the expenditures of large appropriations, the advent of new industrial and business method [sic], the increased importance of strictly military features involved in the assemblage of fleets, the tactical and strategic questions arising in connection therewith, and the imperative necessity of methodical preparation for war." The report went on to recommend the creation of the posts of the four "aids"—for operations, personnel, material, and inspections.

[51] Beers, "The Development of the Office of the Chief of Naval Operations," Part I, 63–64.

[52] George von Lengerke Meyer, Secretary of the Navy, *Annual Reports of the Navy Department for the Fiscal Year 1912* (Washington, DC: GPO, 1913), 5.

[53] Ibid., 7.

[54] Ibid., 6.

[55] Beers, "The Development of the Office of the Chief of Naval Operations," Part I, 66.

[56] Meyer, *Annual Reports of the Navy Department for the Fiscal Year 1912*, 8.

[57] Ltr, General Board to the Secretary of the Navy, 15 June 1909, GB No. 446, General Board letters, Vol. VI, Box 5, RG 80, NARA. In this letter, the members of the General Board noted that

there was not, "... under the present practice of the Navy department, anything that insures reference of the details of military features as they are developed in the elaboration of the designs and in the building of the [*Wyoming* and *Arkansas*] to seagoing officers for their comment and recommendation." The board would soon make this task its own.

[58] Coletta, "George von Lengerke Meyer," in Coletta, *American Secretaries of the Navy, Vol. I*, 512.

[59] Ibid., 511.

[60] Ibid., 513.

[61] Ibid., 510–11.

[62] Benjamin Franklin Cooling, *U.S.S. Olympia, Herald of Empire* (Annapolis, MD: Naval Institute Press, 2000), 173. Knight's book is *Modern Seamanship* (New York: Van Nostrand, 1918).

[63] Coletta, "George von Lengerke Meyer," in Coletta, *American Secretaries of the Navy, Vol. I*, 514.

[64] Ibid., 499.

[65] In a paper completed in August 1913 for a conference at the Naval War College, CDR (later RADM) Reginald R. Belknap noted that "opposition to a single Aid, the Aid for War," was "certain." But he argued that "no effort should be spared to win the single Aid system; for until we get it there can be neither unity of effort, nor military spirit, in our naval administration." As a captain, Belknap was in charge of the laying of the North Sea Mine Barrage—more than 56,000 mines put into the water between June and the end of October 1918. He was head of the strategy department at the Naval War College from 1921 to 1923. His paper is in Collection 8, Box 77, Folder 1, NWC Archives.

[66] CDR Yates Stirling Jr., "Memoranda from Memory of Remarks Made by the Secretary of the Navy, Mr. Von Meyer, Upon Navy Department Organization," 2 and 3, 1913, Collection 8, Box 42, Folder 6, NWC Archives. In his memoirs, Stirling argued that "Organization is lifeless. It is merely a skeleton. . . . A faulty organization may achieve successful results because of a great leader who controls it. It is far wiser not to place too great faith in genius but to perfect the organization in order to give effective results." *Sea Duty: The Memoirs of a Fighting Admiral* (New York: G. P. Putnam's Sons, 1939), 138.

[67] Josephus Daniels, Secretary of the Navy, *Annual Reports of the Navy Department for the Fiscal Year 1913* (Washington, DC: GPO, 1914), 6.

[68] RADM Bradley A. Fiske, USN, *From Midshipman to Rear-Admiral* (New York: The Century Co., 1919), 526–27 and 530.

[69] Ibid., 532.

[70] Ibid., 554.

[71] Ibid., 567.

[72] Ibid.

[73] Ibid., 569

[74] Ibid.

[75] Josephus Daniels, Secretary of the Navy, *Annual Reports of the Navy Department for the Fiscal Year 1920* (Washington, DC: GPO, 1921), 359. Digital version at https://babel.hathitrust.org/cgi/pt?id=mdp.39015025950646;view=1up;seq=369.

[76] *Naval Investigation: Hearings before the Subcommittee of the Senate Committee on Naval Affairs*, 66th Cong., 2nd sess., Vol. I, 720 (Hereafter Naval Investigation).

[77] Ibid., 568.

[78] Ibid., 570.

[79] RADM Julius Augustus Furer, USN (Ret.), *Administration of the Navy Department in World War II* (Washington, DC: Divison of Naval History, Dept. of the Navy and GPO, 1959), 110.

[80] Josephus Daniels, Secretary of the Navy, *Annual Report of the Secretary of the Navy for the Fiscal Year 1915* (Washington, DC: GPO, 1915), 11.

[81] Ibid.

[82] Secretary of the Navy Josephus Daniels, quoted in Morison, *Naval Administration: Selected Documents on Navy Department Organization, 1915–1940*, I-6.

[83] Paullin, "A Half Century of Naval Administration," 124.

[84] Henry P. Beers, "The Development of the Office of the Chief of Naval Operations, Part II," *Military Affairs*, vol. 10, no. 3 (Fall 1946), 13.

[85] Ibid., 14.

[86] Morison, *Admiral Sims and the Modern American Navy*, 70.

[87] Ibid.

[88] Ibid., 127.

CHAPTER 2

World War I: The First Test of the Chief of Naval Operations and His Organization

Introduction

> There shall be a Chief of Naval Operations, who shall be an officer on the active list of the Navy, appointed by the President, by and with the advice and consent of the Senate, from among the officers of the line of the Navy not below the grade of Captain, for a period of four years, who shall, under the direction of the Secretary of the Navy, be charged with the operations of the fleet, and with the preparation and readiness of plans for its use in war.[1]

The legislation creating the post of Chief of Naval Operations was passed on 3 March 1915. Captain William S. Benson was confirmed as the first CNO eight days later and promoted in his new position to rear admiral. Benson had three subordinates (one captain and two lieutenants), no clerical staff, and primitive office space.[2] Rear Admiral Benson could not issue orders except through Secretary of the Navy Josephus Daniels; the CNO's authority consequently depended on his relationship with the secretary and on his standing in the minds of his fellow Navy officers. Though it was the policy of President Woodrow Wilson and the Congress to remain neutral, many Navy officers suspected that the United States would enter the war. To prepare for war—without at the same time violating the nation's official neutrality—the new Chief of Naval Operations would not have much time—just about two years.

Benson therefore had two tasks. The first was to turn his legal authority into actual authority within the Navy Department. The second was to hedge against the possibility of war by preparing the Navy for it. To understand Benson's position in March 1915, put yourself in his place. By law, the Navy secretary was in charge of the Navy Department. By law, the Navy's "shore establishment" was managed by its bureaus, and the leaders of the bureaus reported directly to the secretary. By law, the Secretary of the Navy was accountable to the President and to Congress, especially the naval affairs committees of the Senate and the House of Representatives. Finally, the CNO was not the fleet commander. Instead, the CNO's job was to develop operations plans and prepare the fleet for war.

To become a successful CNO, therefore, Benson had to first show Secretary of the Navy Daniels that his office posed no threat to the secretary's proper authority. While he was doing that, Benson had to demonstrate his personal loyalty to the secretary. Officers like Bradley Fiske, who had campaigned—some would say "plotted"—for the creation of the CNO's position, wanted an aggressive, even assertive, CNO, but that was asking for too much. If Benson had confronted Daniels, the secretary would have cut him off from the business of the Navy Department and would probably have asked President Wilson to remove Benson from his post.

CNO Benson and the Navy's Bureaus

But Benson had much more to do than establish a good working relationship with Secretary Daniels. He also had to determine how best to fulfill his legal responsibilities. Benson's permanent rank was captain; he was a rear admiral because—and just as long as—he was the CNO. He had to deal with the Navy's major bureaus (like BuOrd), all of whose chiefs were rear admirals. Benson also had to deal with the General Board of the Navy, an organization of senior line officers who advised the secretary on ship designs, naval strategy, and any major policy issue that the secretary chose to hand to them. Fortunately, Secretary Daniels made the new CNO an ex officio member of the General Board, and Benson "on the very day of his installation as CNO attended a meeting of its executive committee and continued to do so regularly."[3]

Influencing the bureaus was a separate challenge for Benson. He was not a part of their routine activities. But he did inherit some sources of information and analysis, including the Office of Naval Intelligence (ONI), the Naval War College, the Office of Target Practice and Engineering Competitions, and the Board of Inspection and Survey. The latter had to approve new ships built for the Navy before they could be accepted and paid for. The Board of Inspection and Survey also examined and counted merchant ships registered in the United States, giving the CNO a window on the size and strength of the U.S. Merchant Marine. The Office of Target Practice and Engineering Competitions would eventually turn out to be a major tool used by Benson to gather information about and improve fleet readiness.

The only plans for the Navy's deployment in 1915 were those already developed by the General Board. Though useful, these plans were not adequate for Benson's use. He and his subordinates needed to see the plans developed within the Navy's bureaus. Accordingly, Benson "drafted an order for Secretary Daniels's signature implementing the shelved 'General Plan'" that Benson's predecessor, Rear Admiral Fiske, the former Aid for Operations, had left for Secretary

Daniels on 13 March 1915. Daniels quickly signed the order and sent it to the bureau chiefs. The order directed the bureau chiefs to send their reports to the secretary and *through* the CNO to the General Board. This order was essential if Benson and his small staff were to serve as developers of plans and coordinators of the planning that was already being done in the bureaus.[4]

Daniels later explained why he had directed the bureaus to funnel information through Benson's staff. As he informed members of Congress,

> My theory of the Chief of Naval Operations is—and I think it is a very important position—that he shall be the thinking man about plans, about tactics, about strategy . . . he has no direction or control over anything in the Navy except the thinking, the planning, the operating. . . . whenever you make the Chief of Naval Operations . . . responsible for the direction of the Navy, you will then make him an administrative officer and not a thinking and operating officer.[5]

This "theory" of Daniels required him to support the position of Benson that the CNO's staff needed information direct from the bureaus—not in order to manage them but instead to monitor their major activities, including their own planning.

And the leaders of the bureaus *were* planning. For example, Rear Admiral Samuel McGowan, the youngest paymaster general in the Navy's history, was convinced as early as the fall of 1914 "that the Navy's 1914 peacetime supply and logistical plans should be no different from those necessary" in time of war. McGowan believed that the United States would become involved in the European war, and he acted to prepare the Bureau of Supplies and Accounts (BuSandA) for that possibility.[6] His was not the only bureau that was preparing for war. Since 1904, the Bureau of Yards and Docks (BuDocks) had possessed the authority by statute to design and supervise the construction of navy yard power plants. In 1911, Congress expanded the BuDocks authority to cover the development of all "the public works and public utilities of the Navy, wherever located, and irrespective of the bureau or office of the Navy" that used them.[7] This policy gave the civil engineers in BuDocks valuable experience in planning and management, experience that would allow them to greatly expand the Navy's shipyards and bases during the war.

The Bureaus of Construction and Repair, Steam Engineering, and Ordnance had already gained valuable experience developing the "new" Navy of the 20th century. You can see the progress these technical bureaus had made if you compare a battleship authorized in 1890 (*Indiana*, Battleship No. 1) with one authorized in 1902 (*Connecticut*, Battleship No. 18). *Indiana* mounted four 13-inch and eight 8-inch guns, displaced 10,225 tons on her sea trials, and was propelled by triple-expansion reciprocating engines that were rated at 9,498 indicated horsepower (ihp). *Connecticut* mounted four improved 12-inch and eight 8-inch guns, displaced approximately 16,000 tons, and her triple-expansion reciprocating engines had an ihp rating of 16,500. *Indiana* was described as a "coast defense battleship," while *Connecticut* was clearly ocean-going. But the real change came with battleship *Michigan* (Battleship No. 27, authorized in 1905), which was an "all-big-gun" design, with eight 12-inch guns and no "secondary" 8-inch guns—all on about the same displacement as *Connecticut*.⁸ Unlike *Connecticut*, *Michigan* was designed for truly long-range gunfire; she would fight beyond the effective range of the 8-inch guns carried by earlier battleships.

In addition to Rear Admiral McGowan, there was another impressive bureau chief: Rear Admiral David W. Taylor, chief of BuC&R. Taylor, appointed to head BuC&R in December 1914, had built the Navy's first towing tank for model testing in 1898 and had supervised the design of the Navy's first wind tunnel in 1914. By the time he was appointed bureau chief, he was an acknowledged world expert in the relationship between hull design and engine power. His 1910 *The Speed and Power of Ships* was a classic analysis and stayed in print for a generation, and by 1914 he was deeply involved in aeronautics as well as ship design.

In 1913, when Daniels became Secretary of the Navy, he dealt directly with the bureau chiefs and, like his predecessors, set up temporary boards to review major issues. In July 1914, for example, Daniels created a "Board on Increased Efficiency of the Personnel of the Navy." Its senior member was Assistant Secretary of the Navy Franklin D. Roosevelt, and Roosevelt was assisted by Rear Admiral Taylor and Rear Admiral Victor Blue, chief of BuNav. Secretary Daniels directed the three members of the Board to consider drafting a bill

> to increase the efficiency of the Navy, applicable to the Line, and the Medical, Pay, Construction, and Civil Engineer Corps, by causing a healthy flow of promotions through the various grades at an age when they are capable of rendering the most efficient service in those grades and with experience commensurate with the duties and responsibilities thereof.[9]

Another example of an influential temporary board was the Naval Consulting Board, created by Secretary Daniels in the fall of 1915 in an effort to draw on the work of American scientists and inventors just in case the United States entered World War I.[10] A third example was the May 1915 board on gunnery control and calculations ("fire control"), also headed by Assistant Secretary Roosevelt.[11]

In a letter written later to a congressional committee, Captain William V. Pratt, Benson's Assistant CNO, argued that such ad hoc boards were a mistake, especially if and when the Navy secretary was not a master of the issue involved. As Pratt put it,

> The Secretary, no matter how wise a man he may be in his own particular affairs, must accept the advice of his naval counselors; but if somebody is not charged with the responsibility for the advice [a counselor] gives and the head man does not know the details, the result is an indifferent state of affairs. . .[12]

Pratt's point was that the Office of the Chief of Naval Operations was created to deal with this problem—not to challenge the SECNAV's authority, but instead to make decision making in the Navy Department more accountable. The term used today is "transparency." Though temporary boards established by the SECNAV could be an effective tool, the secretary's effectiveness was actually undermined if and when it was not clear just how the recommendations of such boards were implemented.[13]

Tightrope Walkers: CNO Benson and Secretary Daniels

CNO Benson was walking a tightrope. He had to steer a course between seeming to bow to Secretary Daniels's wishes—and thereby alienating officers such as Captain William S. Sims—and creating friction between himself and the SECNAV. But Secretary Daniels was also walking a tightrope all his own. Daniels knew from the beginning of his time in office that he needed the support of the Navy's officers if he wished to make "every battleship a school" and change the way that officers were selected for higher rank.[14] He knew in 1913 that a "considerable number of the officers spent much of their time criticizing" him, and that many were not by any means his loyal supporters.[15] He apparently realized that some Navy officers thought of him and President Wilson as "pacifists."[16] Wilson would quickly show them he was not.

After President Wilson took office in 1913, he made his hostility to Victoriano Huerta, the virtual dictator of Mexico, very clear. Starting in October 1913, Wilson ordered the Navy to place ships near Mexico's Caribbean coast in order to protect or evacuate U.S. citizens. In early April 1914, Mexican authorities in Tampico took unarmed U.S. sailors into custody temporarily, and the Navy admiral in charge of the U.S. force demanded that they be returned and that a formal apology be given. The sailors were returned to their ship, but Rear Admiral Henry T. Mayo, the senior U.S. officer, required the Mexican authorities to hoist and salute the U.S. flag. President Wilson backed him up.

That stand-off was made even more dangerous by the effort of a German merchant ship, the *Ypiranga*, to deliver a cargo of arms to the Heurta regime through the port of Veracruz. On 20 April 1914, Secretary Daniels directed Rear Admiral Frank F. Fletcher, commanding U.S. warships at Veracruz, to keep the *Ypiranga* from unloading. Fletcher sent Marines and sailors into Veracruz on 21 April to gain control of the customs house, but their presence was contested by Mexican forces. In fighting in the streets of the city, 17 American military personnel and at least 126 Mexicans were killed. The sailors and Marines were replaced by U.S. Army forces at the end of April, and Huerta resigned as Mexico's "provisional president" on 15 July. Wilson's decision to intervene militarily in Mexican affairs set a pattern. The so-called "pacifist" was anything but that when it came to Mexico and the Caribbean.[17]

Secretary Daniels and the Navy also had to back up the neutrality policy that President Wilson adopted after the outbreak of World War I in August 1914. That policy led to a series of serious diplomatic disputes between the government of the United States and the government of Great Britain. In a lengthy and revealing study, Nicholas Lambert has demonstrated why Great Britain was the pivot point of international trade in 1914. Three developments had put the British in this position. The first was the security of worldwide shipping lanes—guaranteed by the Royal Navy—that made the movement of commodities and finished products reliable and predictable. The second was the London credit market, which facilitated orderly and secure payments between buyers and sellers in international markets. The third was the network of submarine cables that tied together vendors, purchasers and banks.[18] The British Admiralty realized before World War I that the second factor—the London credit market—could be closed to an enemy; that is, firms in one country using that credit market in order to buy or sell to firms in a different country could be excluded from it. This meant that industrialized nations such as Germany could be "blockaded" both by driving the German merchant marine from the sea and also by making it impossible for German buyers and sellers to use the London credit market.

As Lambert put it, "Economic warfare necessarily entailed large-scale state intervention in the workings of both the domestic *and international economy* (italics added), starkly challenging traditional ideas about the role of government. In so doing, moreover, it far exceeded established boundaries of what constituted grand strategy and indeed the very nature of war."[19] That is, any effort by Great Britain to shut down German trade with financial tools would also harm the economies of other nations by paralyzing the London-based credit markets and curtailing *all* international trade. President Wilson therefore opposed any move by the British government to implement measures that would deny U.S. firms and banks access to the London credit market. He did so because, in 1914, "the financial world viewed the United States as a debtor nation with a checkered financial past and its dollar as a second-class currency."[20] In fact, the war could not have come at a worse time for American agricultural exports, especially grain and cotton. To protect American producers' exports, Wilson warned the British not to disrupt the London credit market.

But that left the British with only the option of imposing a traditional naval blockade—interdicting merchant ships with "contraband" cargoes heading for German and neutral ports. In 1908, major trading nations had sent delegates to a formal conference in London to review international maritime law. One of the products of this conference was a 1909 declaration that merchant ships of belligerents could not legally switch flags in order to avoid a naval blockade. That is, merchant ships owned and operated by German firms could not, at the outbreak of war, seek refuge in a neutral port and then be sold by their owners to a firm in a neutral country—and resume shipping commodities to Germany *through* ports in neutral nations.[21] The British government was adamant about this.

As it happened, the Wilson administration in 1914 was "quietly shepherding a bill through Congress to repeal a law that prevented foreign-built merchantmen from being added to the U.S. merchant marine register."[22] Secretary Daniels warned President Wilson that a Joint State Department and Navy Neutrality Board had ruled that such legislation violated the London declaration of 1909. In pursuing such legislation, President Wilson and his congressional supporters were actually violating the notion of neutrality that Wilson had said was at the core of U.S. policy.[23] Wilson, however, was in a corner. Without ships, agricultural exporters in the United States could not get what they had for sale to those purchasers overseas who were willing and able to pay. But if the U.S. government bought German ships in U.S. ports or allowed private American buyers to purchase the ships, the U.S government would be guilty of trying to avoid the British blockade of Germany—in effect helping a belligerent. What would U.S. claims to neutrality mean then?

World War I: The First Test of the Chief of Naval Operations and His Organization

The important point is that an essential element of Britain's war policy was its blockade of German maritime shipping and shipments of war material from neutral nations to German ports. The British government considered imposing a financial blockade on Germany, but protests from governments like that of the United States forced the British to back away from that approach. Instead, the British government used the Royal Navy to intercept and inspect merchant ships suspected of heading for German ports or suspected of carrying contraband to a neutral port for eventual shipment to Germany. The question, of course, was what was contraband? When the British government put American agricultural exports on the list of contraband items, the U.S. government objected, and the result was a months-long back-and-forth between the two governments.

In fact, President Wilson was on the verge of a showdown with British Prime Minister Herbert Asquith when a German submarine sank, without warning, the British liner *Lusitania* on 7 May 1915, killing 1,201 passengers, including 124 U.S. citizens. Wilson almost broke off relations with Germany in retaliation, but he also authorized Colonel Edward House, his personal emissary, to discuss with British Foreign Secretary Sir Edward Grey the possibility that the British government would stop claiming grain and other foodstuffs were contraband if the German government would halt its U-boat attacks.[24] In 1914, Wilson had defended U.S. neutrality, asserting that the American position was essentially the same as it had been for a century. In 1915, he continued to do so, but he also began a process of trying to find some way to mediate the European conflict because it was clear that both British and German respect for neutral shipping was wearing thin.

Wilson's effort to stay out of World War I and also to find some way to end it formed the background to the official actions of Secretary Daniels. That background has to be considered in discussing the Daniels-Benson relationship. Daniels, for instance, had taken his position as secretary without wanting to oversee the construction of a larger Navy, yet if President Wilson wanted to protect American neutrality, he might find a larger, more powerful U.S. Navy a useful bargaining chip to have. Historians of the Benson-Daniels relationship have usually focused just on those two men. It is better to see both in the context of events such as the sinking of *Lusitania*, the struggle to sustain American neutrality, and even the perceived need to intervene in Haiti in July and August 1915. In all of this, Daniels needed help, and Benson acted to offer it.

In June 1915, Benson "convinced Daniels to create an advisory council" composed of the bureau chiefs, the CNO, and the SECNAV, and this group "worked out to the great satisfaction" of both Daniels and Benson. That same month, Benson also appointed Captain Josiah S. McKean his first assistant for materiel (or logistics, as we would say now), and he persuaded Secretary Daniels to assign more officers to the Board of Inspection and Survey and to reestablish the Joint Army and Navy Board (with Benson as its Navy member). Benson had ideas about how to improve the organization of the naval districts and the assignment of battleships to the Atlantic and Pacific coasts; Daniels eventually approved both. Daniels also accepted Benson's recommendations that

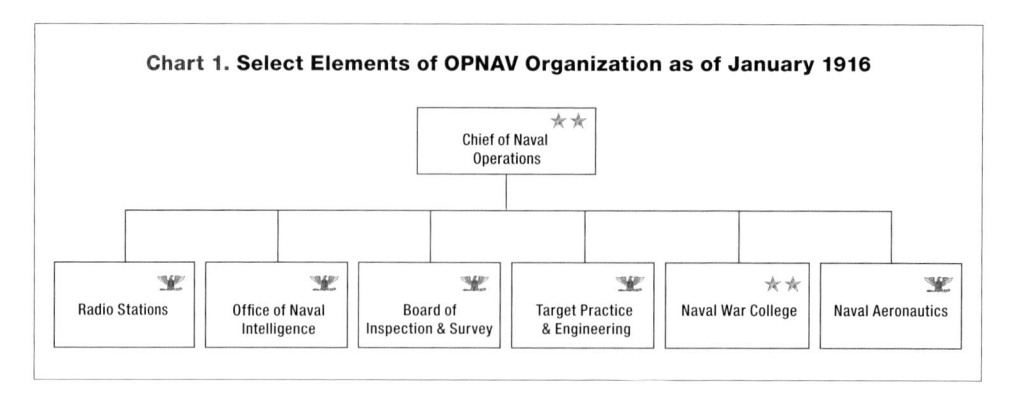

Chart 1. Select Elements of OPNAV Organization as of January 1916

- Chief of Naval Operations
  - Radio Stations
  - Office of Naval Intelligence
  - Board of Inspection & Survey
  - Target Practice & Engineering
  - Naval War College
  - Naval Aeronautics

the SECNAV create an Atlantic Submarine Flotilla and place naval aviation inside the Office of the CNO. In July 1915, Benson drafted the rules governing the new Naval Consulting Board chaired by Thomas Edison.[25] In all this, we see Benson aiding his chief and also filling out his new office—making sure that the CNO was involved in important decisions affecting the Navy.

One of Benson's more important tasks was to explain to Secretary Daniels what various ships were for and how newer ones differed from older models. The General Board, for example, wanted the Wilson administration to authorize construction of the world's most powerful navy. But what would that navy look like? How would it be structured? Where would it be based? On 7 October 1915, Secretary Daniels directed the General Board to draw up a five-year program for a Navy "as powerful and as well balanced as possible."[26] He could not have done that in an intelligent way without the assistance of both Benson and Rear Admiral Taylor, Chief of BuC&R. It surprised no one, then, when Benson was promoted to the permanent rank of rear admiral on 26 November 1915. It was also no surprise to see the following in the 1916 Naval Appropriations Bill: giving to the CNO the rank of full admiral; authorizing the CNO to issue orders to the fleet "in the name of the secretary of the Navy, designating a certain number of officers as assistants to the CNO, and stipulating the retirement of the CNO at his permanent lineal rank."[27]

1916: A Key Year for both the Secretary and the CNO

By early 1916, Benson divided his work into five basic categories: intelligence (using the information provided by ONI); officer education (primarily at the Naval Academy and the Naval War College), planning (in consultation with the General Board), monitoring inspections (to ascertain the readiness of ships and sailors); and exercising "operational responsibility" for approved policies and plans.[28] Benson described how his office worked in the following way:

> Certain conditions are known to exist, . . ., through information obtained from force commanders and detailed information obtained through Naval Intelligence. The information, with the objects to be attained, is sent to the Planning Division. The Planning Division makes a study of the subject and calls a meeting of a certain

plans committee. This committee deliberates on the information at hand and on the mission. It then prepares definite recommendations of what it proposes in order to insure the success of the mission. The matter is then taken up with the Chief of Naval Operations, and if approved by him (or the Secretary if required) is referred to [appropriate divisions]. These divisions proceed with the preparation of the material and personnel which may be necessary to make the approved plan effective.[29]

This ability to link plans with resources (human and otherwise) was the key to the success of Benson's office—called then the "Office of Operations," but soon referred to as OPNAV, the Office of the Chief of Naval Operations.

On 15 January 1916, Colonel House advised the President that British Minister of Munitions David Lloyd George believed that Wilson's influence in Europe would be increased if the United States Congress passed large military and naval programs.[30] On 3 February, Wilson, by now convinced that the United States had to prepare militarily in order to convince the Europeans that the nation would fight if necessary, told an audience in St. Louis that he wanted "incomparably the greatest navy in the world."[31] CNO Benson supported the President in testimony to the House Naval Affairs Committee on 16 and 17 March, and then and later defended the work of his own office, saying that it was operating as expected "in a purely American and businesslike manner."[32] The concern of Daniels and others that the CNO's office would function like a Prussian general staff was gone, replaced by a concern for whether the CNO and his staff could successfully implement the president's "preparedness" policy.

By June 1916, the Office of the Chief of Naval Operations was organized as follows: There were eight divisions—Operations, Plans, Naval Districts (transferred to OPNAV by Secretary Daniels in April 1916), Regulations, Ship Movements, Communications, Publicity, and Materiel. Operations served as a link between the fleet commanders and the General Board. Plans took the strategic concepts developed at the Naval War College and reviewed by the General Board and translated them into operational designs. The division of Naval Districts coordinated the efforts of the naval district commanders to provide for coast defense and to furnish support for the fleets. Ship Movements reviewed and coordinated movement orders and tracked the locations of ships while scheduling port visits and navy yard overhauls. Communications covered the Navy's rapidly developing radio network and produced signal and code books. Publicity provided stories, information, and photographs to newspapers. The Materiel Division coordinated the work of the bureaus.[33] For a year, Benson and his assistants had been "loaned" clerks and secretaries by BuNav and the secretary's office, but Congress authorized a permanent "clerical force" for OPNAV in May 1916.[34]

On 3 June 1916, Congress passed the National Defense Act, which dealt mostly with the organization of the Army and the National Guard. But the law also authorized the president to compel private firms to take on work for the government so long as what the government had ordered was an item that a given private firm was already producing or had the capacity to produce.[35] This provision would support the decisions on priorities and production issued by the War Industries Board once the United States entered World War I. But the immediate issue before the Congress was the writing of the appropriations acts for the Army and Navy.

Both bills became law on 29 August 1916. The Army's appropriation act authorized the Council of National Defense. Its members would be the secretaries of War, Navy, Interior, Agriculture, Commerce, and Labor. Though the Council's authority was limited to "advising" the president, creating the Council was the first step toward government direction of the economy. The Navy's appropriation act authorized an assistant to the chief of BuDocks, advanced funds to BuOrd that allowed the bureau to begin preparing for wartime expansion, and included the "Line Personnel Act of 1916," which Professor Donald Chisholm of the Naval War College has shown was more important than any other provision of the whole act because it required selection boards to promote Navy "officers based on their comparative fitness to perform the duties of the next higher grade."[36]

The Navy's appropriation act also mandated what Fiske, Sims, and others had argued for—giving the CNO the rank of admiral, second only to Admiral of the Fleet Dewey. That "placed the Chief of Naval Operations above the commanders-in-chief of the fleet."[37] The law also gave the CNO the 15 senior assistants that Fiske had attempted to persuade Secretary Daniels to approve. The law also provided that "All orders issued by the Chief of Naval Operations in performing the duties assigned to him shall be performed under the authority of the Secretary of the Navy, and his orders shall be considered as emanating from the Secretary, and shall have full force and effect as such." This was a significant change, and it was reflected in changes to Navy regulations, one of which gave the CNO the authority to "freely consult with and have the advice and assistance of the various bureaus, boards, and offices of the department, including the Marine Corps headquarters, in matters coming under their cognizance." Moreover, once a war plan had been approved, Navy regulations stipulated that "it shall be the duty of the Chief of Naval Operations to assign to the bureaus, boards, and offices such parts thereof as may be needed for the intelligent carrying out of their respective duties in regard to such plans." In plain language, the CNO was the SECNAV's chief deputy—not just his chief military advisor.[38]

But what mattered more to President Wilson was the Navy force structure authorized by the law: 157 ships in three groups. Ten battleships were authorized; four were appropriated for. Three of the remaining six would be appropriated for in March 1917, and Congress would appropriate funds for the last three of the ten in July 1918. Six large, swift, and powerful battle cruisers were authorized—funds for the first four were appropriated in the 1916 act, while one would be funded in 1917 and another in 1918. The law also authorized ten scout cruisers, 50 destroyers, nine "fleet" submarines, 58 "coast" (i.e., short-range) submarines, and 11 auxiliaries, including one hospital ship. Funding for these ships would also be spread across three fiscal years.[39] When this ship construction program was complete, the U.S. Navy would indeed be "second to none," and hopefully Wilson would have more bargaining power with the Europeans even as the ships were being built. Congress also gave the President the authority to increase the number of sailors in the event of an emergency, and the 1916 law "transformed the naval militia into the Naval Reserve Force."[40] President Wilson would get his ships *and* the men to drive and fight them.

The year running from the summer of 1915 through August 1916 was the transition year for the Navy—the shift from peacetime operations (which, remember, had included combat with Mexicans on Mexican territory in 1914) to preparation for war. As late as the spring of 1915, Wilson was adamant about sustaining American neutrality with regard to the war in Europe. But over the fall and winter of 1915–1916, his view changed, and he came to support "preparedness." The sinking of *Lusitania* shifted the views of numbers of Americans from stubborn neutrality toward hostility to Germany's U-boat campaign, and the wrangling over compensation for the families of the American victims of *Lusitania*'s sinking did not add to the reputation of Germany in the United States.[41] But despite the passage of the dramatic Naval Appropriation Act of 1916, the Navy was not prepared for war. It lacked adequate numbers of trained sailors and experienced officers, and its senior officers lacked an understanding of the true nature of Germany's submarine offensive against Britain and France.

The Army was even less prepared for war than the Navy. In June 1916, a conference on Army-Navy cooperation was held at the Naval War College. Rear Admiral Austin M. Knight, President of the Naval War College, had hoped that "a large number of officers of high rank in the Army and Navy" would attend, and that they would thrash out the details of Army-Navy cooperation in planning both modern coast defenses and joint overseas expeditions.[42] Unfortunately, "it proved impossible to assemble a completely representative group of officers of the two Services," and, as Knight wrote to Benson, "the conference took a much narrower range than had been anticipated."[43] That meant too little attention was paid to coordinating Army and Navy programs and doctrines for coast defense, and nothing was really done about planning for Army-Navy operations overseas. Knight informed Benson that "the Army knows nothing about the possibilities, the methods, or the limitations, of submarine operations." In addition, the two services had not even begun to develop plans for "joint scouting operations" with aircraft, and there was "no cipher code used by, or familiar to, both the Army and Navy."[44]

Knight argued to Benson that the existing Joint Army and Navy Board was not capable of doing the joint planning that was necessary because its members were "officers who have many other duties demanding their almost constant attention." The basic problem was that efforts to develop joint plans and doctrines would continue to fail to be effective "unless the co-operation is brought to its logical focus in the offices of the Secretary of the Navy and the Secretary of War, where the last word in co-operation must necessarily be said."[45] As Knight put it, "Two and a half years of experience as President of the War College, Member of the General Board, and Supervisor of the Second Naval District" had made clear to him "the danger of the existing conditions," and he was surprised that the obvious lack of Army-Navy coordination "should have been allowed to exist so long."[46]

However, there was some good news: Secretary Daniels and Rear Admiral (full Admiral after September 1916) Benson had learned to work together. Their ability to continue to do so would be put to a severe test soon enough.

1917: War

By January 1917, CNO Benson's office had a staff of 75. It was barely adequate. Fortunately, the Navy's bureaus had already started preparing for war. BuDocks began doing so in November 1916, and that same month the Navy Department's Logistics Committee, composed of the chiefs of the Bureaus of Supplies and Accounts, Steam Engineering, Ordnance, Yards and Docks, Construction and Repair, and Medicine and Surgery, called Admiral Benson's attention to measures that would have to be taken within their organizations if the United States went to war. It was not war mobilization, but it was as close as the Navy could get to mobilization short of war being declared.

In February, the German government began a campaign of "unrestricted submarine warfare" around Great Britain, off the Atlantic coast of France, and in parts of the Mediterranean. Though it was clear to senior German military leaders that attacking American-flagged ships could bring the United States into the war on the side of the British and French, they were willing to gamble that the U-boat campaign could knock Britain out of the war in less than six months, long before the United States could turn the tide of war on the Western Front. In response to the changed situation at sea, Benson advised Daniels that the United States could lawfully take steps short of war to protect seaborne commerce, including convoying and arming merchant ships.

In a long memorandum to Secretary Daniels, Benson put forward a general statement of U.S. naval policy. Acknowledging the traditional American commitment to "freedom of the seas," Benson stressed looking beyond the war to the postwar setting. In his view, there were no permanent alliances, but only temporary combinations. Nations pursued their interests, and those interests would change with time. One's ally today could be one's opponent tomorrow. For that reason, the government of the United States had to realize that the "possible combinations,

Figure 2-1. Secretary of the Navy Josephus Daniels (left) welcoming CNO William S. Benson back from France, where Benson had advised President Woodrow Wilson at the Versailles peace conference. Daniels chose Benson as the first CNO because Benson seemed to be the opposite of RADM Bradley Fiske, whom Daniels distrusted. But Benson's quiet personality masked a shrewd decision maker who was a match for the aggressive, well-connected, and talented Daniels. (NHHC Archives NH 5313)

of powers and circumstances, are too numerous and too pregnant with possibilities adverse to our interest to permit us to consider any plan other than one which will permit us to exercise eventually the full naval and military strength of the United States in the defense of our interests." As historian Mary Klachko put it, Benson was warning Daniels that the British and French might negotiate an end to their part in the war, perhaps leaving the United States to confront Germany alone.[47]

What, then, should be the general naval policy of the United States? For the immediate future, the U.S. Navy should support the British and the French. At the same time, the United States should develop its "full military and naval strength," which was another way of saying that the ship construction program adopted in 1916 should be completed. Benson argued that the United States should "build up our fighting power as an independent nation," looking ahead to what might happen after the war was over. Assuming Secretary Daniels and President Wilson accepted this general policy, it had certain implications for how the Navy would fight if war were declared. First, the President should retain control over U.S. naval forces and deploy them primarily in areas near the United States. There would be no combined naval command. Second, Benson realized that the Navy had to "make war on enemy submarines . . . and deflect sufficient commerce to the transatlantic trade to ensure the full support of the entente powers," but he insisted that "vessels should be built not only to meet present conditions but conditions that may come after the present phase of the world war." Third, the leaders of the United States should "expect the future to give us more potential enemies than potential friends so that our safety must lie in our own resources."[48]

While Admiral Benson and his staff focused on policy and plans, the bureaus continued to gear up for war. On 3 February 1917, for example, BuOrd

> received word that all diplomatic relations with Germany had been severed. A conference of the bureau's officers was at once called and instructions were issued for the procurement of machine guns [for the Marines] and certain types of ammunition, and the bureau directed that guns in reserve batteries be shipped to the fitting-out yards of the auxiliary vessels.[49]

To facilitate these actions, "60 shipment orders were placed at once in the hands of the Bureau of Supplies and Accounts, the necessary letters having previously been typed and placed in the allowance books of the merchant vessels concerned. Thus it was a small matter to sign, date, and mail instructions."[50] The other bureaus had also prepared for war, including BuNav, which had drawn up tables for the allocation of officers and enlisted personnel among existing and planned Navy ships.[51]

Secretary Daniels was also very busy. The Council of National Defense, created by the Army Appropriation Act of 29 August 1916, created a Munitions Standard Board on 28 February 1917 to set specifications for munitions used by the Army and the Navy. A month later, the Council created the General Munitions Board to coordinate Army and Navy munitions requirements. It was clear that the anticipated needs of the services far outstripped the capacity of existing production facilities, both public and private.[52] Military procurement officials were helped on 4 March 1917, when Congress passed a law authorizing cost-plus-percentage-of-cost contracts. Prior to this date, production contracts had been let on a fixed-price basis. That is, the government (Navy, in this case) would announce a procurement, publish the specifications of the item to be procured, solicit sealed bids from qualified vendors, and then select the winning vendor or vendors after all the eligible vendors had submitted their (as yet unopened) bids. This was the process that Secretary Daniels was comfortable with. It protected the government from cost escalation by placing the risk of artificially low bids on the vendor. Cost-plus-percentage-of-cost contracts, however, reversed that situation; they placed the risk of cost overruns squarely on the back of the government.[53] But what were Daniels and the other members of the Council of National Defense to do? In peacetime, cost was the most important factor in acquisition. In wartime, time would be the critical factor. That was why Rear Admiral McGowan, head of BuSandA, had insisted on stockpiling critical materials in 1915 and 1916, and why he had overseen the preparation of the Navy's Standard Stock Catalog in 1914 (so that commercial suppliers could learn how to supply the Navy with its essential wartime materials in peacetime).

On 23 March 1917, Walter H. Page, U.S. Ambassador to Great Britain, recommended that President Wilson send an American admiral to consult with the British Admiralty. Wilson agreed on 24 March, and on 28 March Secretary Daniels ordered Rear Admiral William S. Sims—then serving as President of the Naval War College—to London. Sims left the United States in secrecy on 31 March, disguised as a civilian, with only one young officer as an aide. After all, war had not yet been declared. But Congress declared war on 6 April, and so Sims became the U.S. Navy's official representative to the British naval authorities starting on 9 April 1917.

Two issues confronted Daniels, Benson, and Sims right away. The first was dramatic—the British were losing the U-boat campaign. The Germans might soon starve Britain into submission. The British government had hidden this disaster from the British public and the government of the United States, but Admiralty officials realized that they had to be candid with Sims, and the American admiral quickly alerted Daniels and Benson, recommending that the U.S. Navy provide immediate support to the Royal Navy. The General Board had already informed Benson that destroyers were the best existing naval weapons against submarines, so Sims's urgent pleas for destroyers were in line with the best naval thinking in Washington. But Benson hesitated to support Sims's case. As already noted, Benson had argued to Secretary Daniels that it was essential that the United States complete its 1916 ship construction program. He was not certain that British merchant ship losses in the campaign against the U-boats were so serious that the U.S. Navy had to forego its planned shipbuilding program in favor of destroyers for use in support of the Royal Navy. But Sims, supported by Ambassador Page, went to work to persuade the British that convoying merchant ships was essential. The corollary of this policy was that the U.S. Navy needed to provide ships (and later aircraft) quickly in great numbers to escort those convoys.[54] By the end of July 1917, Benson and Daniels were convinced that Sims was correct, and they began work to shift the U.S. Navy's building program to anti-submarine vessels.

The second issue confronting Daniels, Benson, and Sims was developing effective liaison with the British and French. Sims was in some ways ideal as the U.S. Navy's representative in London. He had good contacts with British naval officers and he spoke French well. But was he just a liaison officer, or would he command U.S. naval forces once they had made the journey across the Atlantic? Indeed, how would U.S. Navy commanders work with their British and French counterparts? Who would set strategy and policy? No effective foundation for cooperation had been laid. A start toward cooperation (and even integration, though it was not called that) was a meeting on 10 April 1917, at Hampton Roads, Virginia, of Admiral Benson and Admiral Henry T. Mayo, Commander of the Atlantic Fleet, with British Vice Admiral Montague E. Browning and French Rear Admiral Maurice F. A. de Grasser. The British and French admirals were the commanders of their nations' naval forces in the Caribbean. The next day, the admirals journeyed to Washington to confer with Secretary Daniels, Assistant Secretary Franklin Roosevelt, and the members of the Navy's General Board. While Rear Admiral Sims was meeting with Admiral Sir John R. Jellicoe, Britain's First Sea Lord, in London, Daniels and the others decided to order six destroyers to Great Britain to serve under British naval authorities.[55]

Thus was a precedent set. Command of U.S. naval forces would remain in the hands of Secretary Daniels through Admiral Benson. Sims's authority would have to be specified by Daniels—which it was, when Daniels appointed Sims Commander, U.S. Naval Forces, Europe in mid-April 1917.[56] In the short run, however, U.S. naval forces would fall under the control of the Royal Navy, which would also provide them with fuel, other supplies, and dockyard facilities. Back in Washington, Daniels and Benson would seriously consider altering the 1916 ship construction program to meet the needs of the campaign against the U-boats. On 22 April British Foreign Secretary Arthur Balfour reached Washington to begin folding the military potential of the United States into the Allied war effort. Balfour's naval representative, Rear Admiral Sir Dudley R. S. de Chair, accompanied by Admiral Benson, met with congressional leaders to encourage them to authorize a major change in the U.S. Navy's 1916 building program.[57]

Naval historians have made much of differences between Admirals Benson and Sims—partly because Sims also made much of it in his writings. Sims was desperate to provide support to the British and French in order to stave off the U-boat offensive. Benson and Daniels hesitated to come around to Sims's view because of the long-term implications of Sims's argument for the U.S. Navy. But the more basic issue—setting aside the particular question—was this: Just how much authority did a theater commander have? Sims was not called a theater commander, or an operational commander, but that's what he was, and it wasn't clear whether he could direct his superiors in Washington to do what he thought was necessary to deal with the German U-boat campaign.[58] One historian cites President Wilson's apparent invitation to Sims to "bypass Daniels and Benson on issues of policy and grand strategy and report instead to the White House" as a sign of the confusion in Washington regarding Sims's proper role.[59] That interpretation is correct. The

United States Navy had no useful experience with the role that Sims had to play. Confusion—even leading to open disputes between Sims and his superiors in Washington—was inevitable.

But in the meantime, there was a war to be won. In May, Congress authorized an increase in the number of enlisted and officer personnel for the Navy. The 4,376 officers and 69,680 sailors of the existing Navy would not be enough for the fight with Germany. Also in May, George Goethals, who headed the Emergency Fleet Corporation (a spinoff from the Council of National Defense), asked Secretary Daniels if the shipways being built for the battle cruisers authorized in 1916 could be used instead for merchant ship construction. Early in June, 1917, Captain Pratt, Benson's assistant, supported the idea and persuaded Benson to accept it.[60] To rationalize the Navy's efforts to build ships to combat German submarines, Secretary Daniels appointed Pratt to head a special anti-submarine warfare board. Pratt's board made its report on 6 July 1917. The report argued that the Navy should stop building its existing destroyer design and instead build a destroyer especially tailored for anti-submarine operations. However, Rear Admiral Taylor, Chief, BuC&R, and Rear Admiral Robert S. Griffin, chief of the Bureau of Steam Engineering, opposed this recommendation. They argued that it would be better to simply enlarge the existing destroyer construction program by bringing more builders into the project.[61]

There was clearly a high level of uncertainty in Washington about how best to deal with the U-boat threat. For example, by the end of June 1917, Benson and Daniels (as well as members of the General Board) agreed that more destroyers or destroyer-like ships needed to be built, but could they be built in time? They might appear only after the German submarine offensive had forced Britain out of the war. In the short term, the Navy's solution was to acquire almost anything that might help, including converted yachts and wooden-hull subchasers of about 80 tons that had to be towed to Europe. Captain Pratt, appointed Assistant CNO after the untimely death of Captain Volney Chase at the end of June 1917, was a protégé of Sims, and he kept in nearly constant communication with his former mentor. On 2 July 1917, he wrote again to Sims, saying "This office does not have to be scared into sending ships because we do not realize the seriousness of the situation. We do. Every man jack in the Plans Department has laid [sic] awake nights." But the British needed to inform Washington just what they planned to do about the U-boats. As Pratt noted, the Navy Department was "directing every effort, building, concerning shipping, to arrive at a successful conclusion of this war, even to the possible sacrifice of our own individual good later."[62]

To help Sims in the latter's dealings with the British, Pratt sent him "a general policy statement drafted by Captain Chase shortly before his death." The three critical elements of that statement of policy were, first, "most hearty cooperation with the allies to meet the present submarine situation in European waters." Second, that principle of "hearty cooperation" would extend to "any future situation during the present war." Third, the U.S. Navy would cooperate closely with allied navies so long as doing so did not seriously weaken U.S. postwar naval strength.[63] Sims could reveal that policy to the British and French so that they would know what the official U.S. naval position was. It seems that both Secretary Daniels and Admiral Benson expected the British to show their hand if the U.S. Navy did that first. President Wilson, however, had already judged British policy a failure. He told Daniels in early July 1917 that the British Admiralty "had done absolutely nothing constructive in the use of their navy and I think it is time we were making and insisting upon plans of our own . . ." In a letter to Sims dated early July, Wilson wrote, "From the beginning of the war I have been greatly surprised at the failure of the British Admiralty to use Great Britain's great naval superiority in an effective way. In the presence of the present submarine emergency they are helpless to the point of panic."[64]

As this incident shows, Sims, Benson, Daniels, and Wilson not only had to decide what authority Sims should have, they also had to agree on how the United States should deal with its allies, and they had to reach a consensus among themselves about this while the war was in a critical stage. Everything was happening at once. Daniels was legally responsible (with the Navy's bureau chiefs and the advice and assistance of the CNO) for providing the fleet with ships, sailors, and supplies. He was up to his ears in work. But he was also President Wilson's chief Naval deputy, and he had to respond to the President. Benson was trying to plan—to create both a force suited to the war as it was happening and to make sure that that same force did not rob the Navy of its postwar strength. He, too, was working long hours while trying to make sure that his Navy wasn't sacrificed to save the British Empire. For his part, President Wilson was frustrated with the British and they with him. In London, meanwhile, Sims was trying to command U.S. naval forces streaming into European waters while at the same time encouraging the British to explain their naval plans and operations to Daniels and Benson.

It should not come as any surprise that these dedicated and determined individuals sometimes grated on one another. It might, however, come as a surprise to know that one key to their working together (or at least not working at cross purposes) was Captain Pratt. Pratt, as Assistant CNO became close to both Benson and Daniels, and drove himself tirelessly in an effort to link his immediate chief (Benson) and his former mentor (Sims). After the war, Pratt remembered the problems facing Benson's staff this way:

> The reorganization and expansion of the Office of Operations and the bureaus had to be undertaken; the coordination of the bureaus with this office had to be developed; the methods of administration had to be divested of their prewar conservatism; the red tape abolished and more authority given to subordinates in matters of detail. Habits of quick and accurate thinking and quick decision under stress of war had to be formed.[65]

In addition, coordination had to be developed among the various government agencies and then between the U.S. government and its allies, especially the British.[66]

These problems were solved, partly by "voluntary and hearty cooperation of every distinct departmental organization, including the Secretary . . ." According to Pratt, the bureaus practically placed "themselves under the control of the Office of Operations," and planners in the United States actually depended heavily on Vice Admiral Sims's planning section for operations in Europe.[67] There was such a shortage of officers as the Navy expanded almost tenfold that "many of the officers then assigned to the General Board were detached and ordered to sea duty, [and] others were assigned to duty on various other boards such as the War Industries Board."[68] In short, the CNO's staff grew while that of the General Board—not large to begin with—shrank. The Naval War College also shut down so that its military faculty could go to sea or shore commands. As Pratt well understood, it did not make sense to send the best officers to sea and leave the training of the many new recruits in the hands of those less qualified.[69]

Pratt was also a particularly energetic officer. He had to be. As historian Gerald Wheeler recognized, Pratt

> occupied the unenviable position of being the man in the middle between a variety of powerful contending interests. . . . Sims was to badger him unmercifully; he had to fend off the attempts of Admiral Mayo to weaken CNO's control over the operating forces . . . At all times he was an interested party in the power struggle between CNO and the . . . chiefs of the various bureaus. Many of the battles . . . were really Benson's, but Pratt made them his own because so much of the CNO's detailed work had fallen on him.[70]

Wheeler was surprised that Pratt was able to retain the confidence of both Benson and Sims, both of whom evaluated his performance highly.[71] But Pratt was enterprising and creative, able to continually assess his own performance realistically. In his unpublished autobiography, he told a story that suggests he had not completely lost his sense of humor under the trying circumstances of managing OPNAV on Benson's behalf. While serving as assistant CNO, he often did not wear a tie or his uniform coat. One day, rushing to yet another meeting, he bumped hard into a typist. "I looked so disheveled . . . that turning to a companion she said 'If that carpenter bumps into me again I will tell him where he gets off.'" Humor aside, the job (and the war) took its toll. Pratt wrote that he "entered upon my work without a gray hair on my head or a nerve in my body," and he "left with both . . . and with a resolve never to enter that cursed hole again."[72]

By July 1917, though, there was agreement in Washington that Sims was correct—more destroyers were needed and needed fast. The War Industries Board began issuing priorities for production and for raw materials. The Navy had something of a free hand; but what should it produce? An ad hoc committee of staff officers (Pratt was a member) sided with Rear Admiral Taylor, rejected the earlier recommendation that the Navy develop and procure a special anti-submarine destroyer, and advised Secretary Daniels to maximize the construction of the standard destroyer. Daniels accepted the group's proposal the same day they made it.[73] On 20 August, Daniels met with American shipbuilding executives and asked them to help him find ways to build more destroyers.

Daniels met with the shipbuilders again on 5 September. It seemed that they could provide most of the destroyers that the Navy wanted, but Secretary Daniels had to obtain the funding for both the ships and construction of their building ways. He was able to gain support for this project in both the House and Senate Naval Affairs Committees, and on 6 October 1917, Congress passed the Urgent Deficiencies Act, giving the Navy the funds for the destroyer program and for advanced procurement (by BuOrd) of weapons for these ships.[74] By the end of September 1917, then, the Navy had acquired 35 new destroyers, but another 244 were being built or were on order.

World War I: The First Test of the Chief of Naval Operations and His Organization

At the beginning of November 1917, Admirals Sims and Benson met in London with First Lord of the Admiralty Sir Eric Geddes and Admiral Jellicoe, the First Sea Lord. Jellicoe and Sims had been friends since they first met, and Jellicoe had been corresponding with Benson for over a month, so the officers were not strangers to one another. Benson agreed to send four coal-burning battleships to reinforce the Royal Navy's Grand Fleet, and he persuaded the British to cooperate in creating "mine barrages" in the North Sea and the Strait of Dover in order to impede the movement of German submarines.[75] Admiral Benson "also arranged for Sims to take on the additional duty of naval attaché in London, and authorized a planning section in London that would work closely with the British Admiralty." He also helped draft "plans for the creation of the Allied Naval Council" on which Sims would serve as his representative.[76]

Captain Pratt said at the time that Benson had "all the threads in his hand, and was controlling them."[77] Rear Admiral McKean, Benson's materials deputy and successor to Pratt as Assistant CNO, expressed a similar view but in a somewhat different way:

> Had we listened only to Sims, and we did listen to him hardest, it would have been all destroyers. Had we listened only to [Rear Admiral Albert] Gleaves, it would have been cruisers and transports. Had we listened only to [Commander Hutchinson] Cone, the whole Navy and Navy Department would have been in the air. Had we listened to [Rear Admiral William] Fullam only, the navy yards and appropriations would have been devoted to his old armored cruisers. Had we listened to [Rear Admiral Albert] Grant only it would have been subs at one time and old battleships at another.[78]

This wry comment captured Benson's ability to avoid extremes in a time when uncertainty about just what to do—what to build, what to develop, what to send to Europe, and whom to place in command of the rapidly growing Navy—was very great.

After the war, Admiral Sims charged that the Navy had not been properly prepared for the conflict. He argued that the service lacked an effective plan for the war. But his accusation missed two points. First, official American policy was to *not* prepare for war. Wilson and Daniels had made that clear in 1914. Second, once war came, the changes that had to be made were daunting. As already mentioned, the shipbuilding program specified in 1916 had to be reexamined. That was a demanding and contentious task. But there were other urgent tasks for OPNAV, including specifying the wartime powers and responsibilities of the recently created naval districts, finding enough transports for the new divisions being raised by the Army, turning the new Naval Overseas Transportation Service into an effective organization, and coordinating convoy routing with the British. Doing the latter required Captain Pratt to meet with the convoy commanders to plan their routes across the Atlantic, supervise the preparation of the orders for their journeys, and then make sure that Sims's staff in London knew when to expect the ships. In March 1917, Congress had given the Navy the authority to "commandeer" ships, but that meant the Navy would have to establish a board to appraise the value of ships thus taken up; they could not be taken over arbitrarily. Qualified officers had to be found to staff that board. The fact that OPNAV was at the center of much of the naval mobilization effort gave the CNO and his staff great influence, but it also forced a punishing pace of work in OPNAV.[79]

It was said after World War I that, in time of war, the authority and prestige of the Office of the Chief of Naval Operations inevitably grew while that of the SECNAV and the Navy's bureaus declined—as though an increase in the CNO's influence came at the expense of the authority and influence of the secretariat and the bureaus. However, it would be more accurate to say that in 1917 the CNO enlarged his authority and influence so that the Secretary of the Navy and the bureaus could fulfill their legal responsibilities. The secretary and the bureaus were responsible for industrial mobilization and for day-to-day coordination with other government agencies. These Navy organizations carried on the often intense negotiations that were required by industrial and human mobilization. For much of 1917, by contrast, the CNO and his staff coordinated the activities of the Navy's organizations by leading or participating in the negotiations that took place *inside* the Navy Department. That is why Captain Pratt said that Admiral Benson had all the threads in his hand. In 1918 and 1919, however, Benson would be tapped to move into the highest circles, working eventually as an official advisor to Colonel House and President Wilson.

1918–1919: War and Its Aftermath

Industrial, agricultural, and human mobilization continued in the United States through 1918. Managing the Navy's activities in this mobilization effort and justifying it to Congress took a great deal of Secretary Daniels's time. For example, Daniels supervised the negotiations with the Ford Motor Company for the production of 100 "Eagle Boats" in January 1918. Henry Ford had responded to the Navy's urgent request for more ships to escort convoys by proposing to use assembly line techniques to manufacture a small destroyer-like ship, 200 feet in length and displacing about 500 tons. The Ford Motor Company had never built anything like it before 1918, but the need for escorts and anti-submarine vessels was so great that the Navy was willing to gamble that the small ships would be both useful and affordable.

At the same time, BuDocks, which had taken its final wartime form only in October 1917, was supervising a major program of building construction, some of the results of which you can still see in the Washington Navy Yard in Washington, D.C. BuDocks also oversaw the creation of several large drydocks in places such as the Philadelphia Navy Yard—bringing the Navy's shore infrastructure up to date (and also creating facilities that turned out to be very useful in World War II). BuOrd contracted for the construction of a huge ordnance complex along the Kanawha River near Charleston, West Virginia, that opened just as World War I ended, then closed almost immediately—but was useful for the next world war.

In May 1918, the Overman Act had given the President the authority to reorganize and streamline executive branch agencies in order to facilitate mobilization, and President Wilson used his new authority to reorganize the War Industries Board and give the Board the authority it needed to manage the nation's mobilization. The mobilization effort for World War II has received more attention from historians,[80] but what happened "on the home front" in World War I was equally impressive, if often somewhat chaotic. The point to remember, however, is that the leadership of the War Industries Board was civilian, though the Board's various committees were often staffed in part by military officers assigned to them by the secretaries of the War and Navy Departments. In 1914, Secretary Daniels had insisted on civilian control of the Navy. He feared that having a uniformed "chief" of naval operations might rob the Navy secretary of his rightful authority. The same basic issue came up during the war, and the War Industries Board, under the its chairman Bernard Baruch, was first created and then strengthened to both coordinate mobilization and preserve civilian control of the war program.

In effect, the responsibility of the Secretary of the Navy was enlarged during the war, and consequently his workload grew. The same sort of thing happened to the CNO, but in a different way: Admiral Benson became a close advisor to Colonel House, President Wilson's confidante, and through House to the President. That is, the CNO's responsibilities, which had been confined initially to issues *inside* the Navy, spread in 1918 to larger diplomatic and strategic concerns, and Admiral Benson found himself trying to direct his own office while supporting House and Wilson in Paris.[81] It all began when Benson accompanied Colonel House to Europe in October 1918. Benson remained in Europe after the Armistice as a member of the committee of allied naval leaders that drafted the naval elements of the peace treaty, and, as President Wilson's advisor, he insisted that the United States be equal in naval terms to Great Britain once the peace treaty was signed. Benson must have been perceived by President Wilson as useful because Wilson would not let him return to the United States until the Treaty of Versailles was signed in June 1919.

Under Admiral Benson, OPNAV (and the Navy) had mushroomed. The 75 officers, enlisted personnel, and civilians who staffed OPNAV in January 1917 had become 1,462 by war's end. Of that total, only 80 were regular Navy officers, and just 3 were Marine officers. 184 Navy officers and 912 of the 962 enlisted Navy personnel were reservists. 141 members of the staff were civil servants. OPNAV had ten "sections" (including the major ones for planning and material), some of which (such as aviation and anti-submarine operations) were new.[82] Other offices—Gunnery Exercises and the Office of Naval Intelligence—had existed under the "aide system" established by former Navy secretary Meyer in 1909. When the Armistice was signed in November 1918, the individuals manning OPNAV did not go home right away. The Navy had to decommission ships no longer needed, pull up the anti-submarine "mine barrages" it had sown in the North Sea and the Dover Straits, and fight a dangerous influenza epidemic. The Office of Naval Communications had to dismantle its powerful stations in Europe, the lessons of anti-submarine warfare had to be codified, and the organization and direction of the Navy's own submarines had to be assessed in light of war experience.[83] The secretary's office was especially busy, demobilizing the Naval Overseas Transportation Service, canceling contracts for a host of supplies and equipment, and compensating individuals and firms whose property was taken or damaged by the Navy during the war.[84]

Benson's term as CNO was supposed to end on 10 May 1919 (four years after his initial appointment), but Secretary Daniels asked President Wilson to extend Benson's appointment, and Wilson agreed to do so. Benson still had some work to do. At the end of June 1919, Benson's proposal that the Navy's forces at sea be divided into two fleets—one in the Atlantic and the other in the Pacific—was put into force by Daniels. Though the Panama Canal allowed ships to be moved back and forth from the Atlantic and the Pacific, Benson had argued that, with the defeat of Germany, it would be wise to shift the more modern fleet units to the Pacific, where his planners had said they would serve as a deterrent to the Japanese.[85]

Benson also reorganized OPNAV into two main divisions—Planning and Operating Forces.[86] The members of the Planning Division had no administrative responsibilities and instead "considered policy, strategy, tactics, education, submarines, aviation, logistics, and administrative plans."[87] The Division of Operating Forces oversaw the "movements of all naval craft" and aircraft not involved in training. "This arrangement," according to historian Klachko, "strengthened the role of the Office of Naval Operations as a centralized command post."[88] This development was one of the consequences of the war. Another was the decision by Secretary Daniels to require all Navy officers to be addressed by rank rather than by titles (such as "paymaster" and "doctor"). This was a significant symbolic victory for Rear Admiral McGowan, the BuSandA chief.[89] McGowan and his subordinates had taken the role of paymaster and transformed it into that of logistician, placing the methods of BuSandA at the forefront of modern material management.[90]

Benson's final organization for OPNAV was laid out in "Organization Orders of the Office of Naval Operations," August 1, 1919, a pamphlet that was sent to all the Navy's bureaus and also published by the Government Printing Office.[91] These orders described a top-down planning process still in use today: "National policy, naval policy, national strategy, naval strategy, logistics, naval tactics, form a descending series from the general to the concrete which may be used as a partial guide in . . . problem solving."[92] The orders also authorized OPNAV's Director of Plans "to consult directly with officers of the service" and to ask the CNO "to order such officers for temporary duty with the Planning Division."[93] Clearly, the idea was to keep the OPNAV staff from being isolated from the officers actually commanding, training, and supporting the fleet.

The 1919 "Organization Orders" stressed that "Nothing helps so much in an organization as large as this office as a wise dissemination of proper information, and this fact must be a guiding principle." To encourage that spread of information, the "Orders" informed officers in OPNAV that they were *"responsible for the dissemination of . . . information to others, whether they be in this office, in the bureaus, the* [naval] *districts, or the forces afloat."* [italics in original] To facilitate this sharing, the "Orders" also forbid formal correspondence among the divisions within OPNAV. "Matters in which two or more divisions are jointly concerned must be taken up informally in conference, or, if this is not necessary, by informal memorandum." Benson did not want OPNAV to become a collection of feuding offices, each representing its own constituency. As the "Orders" put it, "Officers must bear constantly in mind the fact that the Office of

Naval Operations is the coordinating center of all the various naval activities of the service. The function of the office is, therefore, largely one of rendering decisions upon which the various bureaus and offices concerned may base their administrative work."[94]

Benson's term as the first CNO was extraordinary. Not considered by some of his peers to be the right choice for the post, Benson nevertheless left after having established the CNO at the center of Navy operational and strategic planning, tactical training, and logistics. The latter was particularly important as the Navy planned for a trans-Pacific campaign against the Imperial Navy of Japan. The post of CNO was ill defined when Benson stepped into it, and he fleshed it out—even opening up the possibility that the CNO could serve as one of a President's closest strategic and diplomatic advisors.[95]

Final Assessment: The CNO at War

War is the ultimate test of the quality of the Navy's organization and of the individuals who lead that organization. War was—and is—a particularly difficult test of American military institutions because of the American constitutional requirement that civilian secretaries head the military services. When Benson was approved by the Senate as the first CNO, he found himself face to face with an energetic and talented SECNAV who had opposed the creation of his office. Only in 1927 did Benson finally give this assessment of his civilian superior:

> It was unfortunate that . . . we had as Secretary of the Navy a man who, while he was honest, earnest and sincere in his efforts to do the best with the situation, due to a very meager experience and lack of knowledge of international affairs, could not appreciate the fact that we could be drawn into the European struggle, and in addition to that, was more or less suspicious of military and naval men, believing their principal effort was to do things that would redound to their military glory [rather] than to the best interests of the country. He was honestly and firmly of the opinion that we could not be drawn into the war, consequently when requests were made upon him for increased appropriations, more officers or material, he often could not see his way clear to give full and wholehearted cooperation and sometimes even refused consent. He was at times suspicious of changes in organization and things of that sort.[96]

Of course he was. Secretary Daniels came from a background that was suspicious of what historian Peter Karsten called "the naval aristocracy"—the officers schooled at the Naval Academy to become "national darwinists," believers in a world of competitive nation states where only the strong survived.[97] Daniels came into his office disdainful of these beliefs. To show the Navy's officers who was boss, he shut down the officer's wine mess and made them implement his policy of "every battleship a school," and he was always alert to what he regarded as unacceptable arrogance on the part of Navy officers. Daniels selected Benson as the first CNO because Benson did not seem to regard himself as superior to the civilian secretary. After disagreeing with Admiral Fiske and being politically outmaneuvered by him, Daniels did not want to have to deal day-in and day-out with officers like Fiske or Sims. Benson grasped this; he could see Daniels's strengths and weaknesses, and he made up his mind to support the secretary instead of challenging or manipulating him.

Benson first won Daniels's confidence, partly by keeping a low public profile and partly by working hard. Benson demonstrated the qualities that a man like Daniels held in high regard—competence, stability, intelligence, integrity, and attention to detail. In relying on Benson, Daniels did not weaken his own position, and he repaid Benson's reliability and loyalty by giving the CNO more resources, more responsibility, and more authority. All this comes out in the records of hearings held by the Senate Naval Affairs Committee in 1920.[98] The hearings were an effort by Admiral Sims to show that the Navy had been unprepared for World War I because the office of the CNO lacked authority and because Benson himself was not the right man for the job. But Sims did not win his case. A careful reading of the record of the hearings suggests that Benson in fact enlarged the role of his office and also grew into the increased responsibilities given him.

Benson was not the dynamic personality that Sims was. The latter won hearts and minds in Europe. He was articulate, committed to an Allied victory, spoke excellent French, and got along very, very well with senior military officers and influential civilians in Britain and France. By comparison, Benson seemed provincial.[99] Yet it was Benson that Colonel House and President Wilson looked to for advice on naval matters in the run-up to the Versailles Treaty of 1919. Under Benson, OPNAV for the first time promulgated "Action Doctrine" for the whole fleet. In December 1917, for example, that doctrine stressed always taking a *"vigorous offensive,"* [italics in the original] and emphasized that "Time is everything, never waste it, keep ahead of it, deny it to the enemy."[100] Benson also worked effectively with the Navy's bureau chiefs. Just as important was Benson's ability to select and support capable subordinates. Historian William Braisted's words bear repeating: Benson "had the happy capacity to command effective work from brilliant subordinates with whom he disagreed."[101]

Notes

[1] *Naval Investigation*, Vol. I, 720.

[2] Mary Klachko, "William Shepherd Benson: Naval General Staff American Style," in James C. Bradford, ed., *Admirals of the New Steel Navy* (Annapolis, MD: Naval Institute Press, 1990), 304.

[3] Ibid., 305.

[4] Ibid., 306.

[5] Statement of Navy Secretary Josephus Daniels, in Morison, *Naval Administration: Selected Documents on Navy Department Organization, 1915–1940*, III-A-25.

[6] RADM Frank J. Allston, SC, USN (Ret.), *Ready for Sea, The Bicentennial History of the U.S. Navy Supply Corps* (Annapolis, MD: Naval Institute Press, 1995), 162, 191.

[7] Bureau of Yards and Docks, *Activities of the Bureau of Yards and Docks, World War, 1917–1918* (Washington, DC: GPO, 1921), 17. Electronic version at https://archive.org/details/activitiesofbure00unit.

[8] Data on ships from *Ships' Data, U.S. Naval Vessels*, 1 Jan. 1938 (Washington, DC: GPO, 1938) and from Friedman, *U.S. Battleships*.

[9] Chisholm, *Waiting for Dead Men's Shoes*, 558.

[10] "Daniels Names Naval Advisors. Announces Makeup of Board of Inventors Headed by Thomas A. Edison." *New York Times*, 13 Sept. 1915.

[11] Ltr, F. D. Roosevelt to CAPT Roy C. Smith, 1 May 1915, Box 8, Folder 120-1 (II), Fleet Training Division, General Correspondence, 1914–1941, Records of the Office of the Chief of Naval Operations, Record Group 38, National Archives (hereafter RG 38 NARA). See also the letter from Secretary Daniels to Smith's successor, CAPT Charles P. Plunkett, 28 Dec. 1915, in Box 7, Folder 120-1, RG 38, NARA.

[12] Morison, *Naval Administration: Selected Documents on Navy Department Organization, 1915–1940*, III-A-31.

[13] For an overview of the Navy in this time period, see "The U.S. Navy," by Trent Hone, in *To Crown the Waves: The Great Navies of the First World War*, ed. by Vincent P. O'Hara, W. David Dickson, and Richard Worth (Annapolis, MD: Naval Institute Press, 2013), 257–307.

[14] Josephus Daniels, *Our Navy at War* (New York: George H. Doran, 1922), 34.

[15] Interview, Frank Freidel with FADM William D. Leahy, 24 May 1948, in Thomas B. Buell papers, NWC Archives.

[16] Ibid.

[17] Jack Sweetman, "Take Veracruz at Once," *Naval History*, April 2014, 34–41. See also *The Landing at Veracruz: 1914*, by Jack Sweetman (Annapolis, MD: U.S. Naval Institute, 1968).

[18] Nicholas Lambert, *Planning Armageddon: British Economic Warfare and the First World War* (Cambridge, MA: Harvard Univ. Press, 2012).

[19] Ibid., 122.

[20] Ibid., 252. Lambert cites Eric Rauchway, *Blessed among Nations: How the World Made America* (New York: Hill and Wang, 2007).

[21] Ibid., 240.

[22] Ibid., 241.

[23] Ibid., 244.

[24] Ibid., 424.

[25] Klachko, "William Shepherd Benson: Naval General Staff American Style," Bradford, *Admirals of the New Steel Navy*, 306–308.

[26] William R. Braisted, *The United States Navy in the Pacific, 1909–1922* (Austin: Univ. of Texas Press, 1971), 192.

[27] Klachko, "William Shepherd Benson: Naval General Staff American Style," Bradford, *Admirals of the New Steel Navy*, 311.

[28] Mary Klachko, with David F. Trask, *Admiral William Shepherd Benson, First Chief of Naval Operations* (Annapolis, MD: Naval Institute Press, 1987), 39.

[29] *Naval Investigation*, Vol. I, 681.

[30] Braisted, *The United States Navy in the Pacific, 1909–1922*, 194.

[31] Klachko, *Admiral William Shepherd Benson, First Chief of Naval Operations*, 48.

[32] Ibid.

[33] Beers, "The Development of the Office of the Chief of Naval Operations, Part II," 17.

[34] Ibid., 18.

[35] Randall B. Kester, "The War Industries Board, 1917–1918: A Study in Industrial Mobilization," *American Political Science Review* (Aug. 1940), 676–77.

[36] Chisholm, *Waiting for Dead Men's Shoes*, 587.

[37] Beers, "The Development of the Office of the Chief of Naval Operations," Part II, 19.

[38] Ibid., 20–21.

[39] Memo, "C&R Statistics," 11 April 1921, in Secret and Confidential Correspondence of the Chief of Naval Operations and the Office of the Secretary of the Navy, 1919–1927," M 1140, Microfilm Roll 39, RG 80, NARA.

[40] Beers, "The Development of the Office of the Chief of Naval Operations, Part II," 19.

[41] There was also the "Zimmermann telegram," which promised German assistance to Mexico in the event of a war between Mexico and the United States. The British had intercepted this telegram, decoded it, and given it to the U.S. ambassador in London, and it was released to U.S. newspapers in late Feb. 1917. As historian Thomas Boghardt showed in his *The Zimmermann Telegram: Intelligence, Diplomacy, and America's Entry into World War I* (Annapolis, MD: Naval Institute Press, 2012), the link between British intelligence and the U.S. government went through the U.S. State Department and not the U.S. Navy.

[42] Ltr, President, Naval War College, to Navy Department (Operations), 6 July 1916, Box 55, Folder 7 (633-4, AMK-ma), NWC Archives, 1–2.

[43] Ibid., 2.

[44] Ibid., 6.

[45] Ibid., 6–7.

[46] Ibid., 7.

[47] Klachko, *Admiral William Shepherd Benson, First Chief of Naval Operations*, 59.

[48] Ibid., 60.

[49] Bureau of Ordnance, U.S. Navy, *Navy Ordnance Activities, World War, 1917–1918* (Washington, DC: GPO, 1920), 17. Electronic version available at https://archive.org/details/navyordnanceact00ordngoog.

[50] Ibid.

[51] ADM Harris Laning, USN, *An Admiral's Yarn*, ed. by Mark Russell Shulman (Newport, RI: Naval War College Press, 1999), 226.

[52] Kester, "The War Industries Board, 1917–1918," 657–58.

[53] Daniels, *Our Navy at War*, 352.

[54] Morison, *Admiral Sims and the Modern American Navy*, 355–59.

[55] Klachko, "William Shepherd Benson: Naval General Staff American Style," Bradford, *Admirals of the New Steel Navy*, 314.

[56] Love, *History of the U.S. Navy, Vol. One, 1775–1941*, 484.

[57] Klachko, "William Shepherd Benson: Naval General Staff American Style," Bradford, *Admirals of the New Steel Navy*, 315.

[58] Sims issued directives under his authority as Commander, U.S. Naval Forces Operating in European Waters. His first "force instruction" was issued on 22 Sept. 1917. The Naval War College Archives contain the amended instructions dated 16 Aug. 1918. See *Force Instructions No. 25* ("Doctrine and General Instructions"), Collection 8, Box 40, Folder 4, NWC Archives.

[59] Love, *History of the U.S. Navy, Vol. One, 1775–1941*, 484.

[60] William J. Williams, "Josephus Daniels and the U.S. Navy's Shipbuilding Program during World War I," *The Journal of Military History* 60 (Jan. 1996), 22–23.

[61] Ibid., 25–26.

[62] Klachko, *Admiral William Shepherd Benson, First Chief of Naval Operations*, 75.

[63] Ibid.

[64] Ibid., 76–77.

[65] Morison, ed., *Naval Administration: Selected Documents on Navy Department Organization, 1915–1940*, III-A-36.

[66] Ibid., III-A-31.

[67] Ibid., III-A-37.

[68] Ibid., III-B-32, "Statement of CDR W. S. Pye, USN, Concerning Desirability of Reorganization of the Navy Department," 3 June 1920.

[69] Gerald E. Wheeler, *Admiral William Veazie Pratt, U.S. Navy* (Washington, DC: GPO, 1974), 105.

[70] Ibid., 95.

[71] Ibid., 118.

[72] Craig L. Symonds, "William Veazie Pratt," in *The Chiefs of Naval Operations*, ed. by Robert W. Love Jr. (Annapolis, MD: Naval Institute Press, 1980), 75 and then 71. See also Wheeler, *Admiral William Veazie Pratt, U.S. Navy*, 123. Pratt collapsed from overwork in June 1918, and Benson made him take a month off.

[73] Williams, "Josephus Daniels and the U.S. Navy's Shipbuilding Program during World War I," 29.

[74] Ibid., 30.

[75] For information about the Northern Mine Barrage laid by the U.S. Navy, see *Fighting the Great War at Sea, Strategy, Tactics and Technology*, by Norman Friedman (South Yorkshire, England: Pen & Sword Books, 2014), 342–44. Friedman puts the mine barrage in the larger perspective of the U.S. and British campaign against German U-boats.

[76] Klachko, "William Shepherd Benson: Naval General Staff American Style," Bradford, *Admirals of the New Steel Navy*, 317–18.

[77] Klachko, *Admiral William Shepherd Benson, First Chief of Naval Operations*, 87.

[78] Ibid., 84.

[79] Beers, "The Development of the Office of the Chief of Naval Operations," Part II, 25–36.

[80] *A Call to Arms, Mobilizing America for World War II*, by Maury Klein (New York: Bloomsbury Press, 2013) is a recent example of a very impressive literature.

[81] Klachko, *Admiral William Shepherd Benson, First Chief of Naval Operations*, 154.

[82] Henry P. Beers, "The Development of the Office of the Chief of Naval Operations, Part III," *Military Affairs*, vol. XI, no. 2 (Summer 1947), 92.

[83] CAPT L. S. Howeth, *History of Communications-Electronics in the United States Navy* (Washington, DC: Bureau of Ships and the Office of Naval History, 1963), 289. Also, "Antisubmarine Information," 1 Dec. 1918, Office of Naval Intelligence, Fleet Training Div., General Correspondence, 1914–1941, Box 7, Folder 116, item 41, RG 38, NARA. U.S. Submarine policy is addressed in Circular Letter, "Administration and Operation of Submarines," Op-51-H, 2 Jan. 1919, Fleet Training Div., General Correspondence, 1914–1941, Box 12, Folder 304-1, RG 38, NARA.

[84] Daniels, *Our Navy at War*.

[85] See *War Plan Orange, The U.S. Strategy to Defeat Japan, 1897–1945*, by Edward S. Miller (Annapolis, MD: Naval Institute Press, 1991).

[86] This organization was explained in a public document: "Revised Organization Orders of the Office of Naval Operations," 1 Aug. 1919 (Washington, DC: GPO, 1919). This is an extraordinary document with relevance to today's OPNAV.

[87] Miller, *War Plan Orange*, 82. Also, "A discussion of the War Plans, U.S. Navy and the Cooperation and Coordination necessary for their preparation," 29 Dec. 1923, in Box 21, Folder 484-72, Fleet Training Division, General Correspondence, 1914–1941, RG 38, NARA.

[88] Klacho, "William Shepherd Benson: Naval General Staff American Style," Bradford, *Admirals of the New Steel Navy*, 323–24.

[89] Allston, *Ready for Sea, The Bicentennial History of the U.S. Navy Supply Corps*, 193.

[90] U.S. Navy, Bureau of Supplies and Accounts, "Historical Record of the Activities of the Bureau of Supplies and Accounts during the War with Germany," no date. Copy in Navy Department Library.

[91] "Revised Organization Orders of the Office of Naval Operations," 1 Aug. 1919.

[92] Ibid., 5. As the "Orders" noted, "the most general problems should be solved first, and subsequent problems should arise from the decisions of the more general problems."

[93] Ibid., 7.

[94] Ibid., 13–14.

[95] A useful summary of the Navy's post–World War I organization is *Information Concerning the U.S. Navy and Other Navies*, compiled by the Office of Naval Intelligence and published by the Government Printing Office in July 1919, especially 10–20. Electronic version at https://babel.hathitrust.org/cgi/pt?id=mdp.39015074170898;view=1up;seq=4.

[96] Klachko, *Admiral William Shepherd Benson, First Chief of Naval Operations*, 177–78.

[97] Peter Karsten, *The Naval Aristocracy: The Golden Age of Annapolis and the Emergence of Modern American Navalism* (New York: Free Press, 1972), esp. ch. 5, "The Naval Mind."

[98] Morison, *Admiral Sims and the Modern American Navy*, 445–60.

[99] See Tracy Barrett Kittredge, *Naval Lessons of the Great War* (Garden City, NY: Doubleday, Page & Co., 1921). Kittredge was a well-educated reserve lieutenant who served under Sims in London and greatly admired him. Kittredge's comments on Secretary Daniels are especially pointed. They reflect Sims's own very bitter views—views he voiced in private but tempered in public.

[100] "Doctrine," Navy Department, Washington, D.C., 1 Dec. 1917, 3. This pamphlet was signed by ADM Benson. Collection 8, Box 55, Folder 1, NWC Archives.

[101] Braisted, *The United States Navy in the Pacific, 1909–1922*, 183.

CHAPTER 3

The Early Interwar Period: Reorganization, Arms Limitation, and Money

"Suppress friction and a machine runs fine. Suppress friction, and a society runs down."

John D. MacDonald, *A Deadly Shade of Gold*

Introduction

At the beginning of 1919, the civilian and military leaders of the Navy faced a series of significant challenges. The first was the need to bring the Navy back to its "proper" peacetime size. How many ships, submarines, and planes were needed to fulfill the nation's strategic requirements? The second was to harvest the meaningful lessons of World War I. The third challenge was to assess the relationship between the Secretary of the Navy and the Chief of Naval Operations in light of wartime experience. The fourth was to comprehend rapidly evolving technologies such as aviation, submarines, and radio communications. The fifth was to deal with the numbers of officers who had been commissioned in the Navy during the war. What was their role in the postwar years? The sixth was to clearly define the role of the CNO as the Navy's chief planner. What did planning mean? How could the CNO lead the planning process? By the end of 1921, there were two additional challenges. One was to find a way to implement the Budget and Accounting Act of June 1921. The other was to cope with the consequences of the negotiations in Washington in 1921 that would lead in February 1922 to the signing of the Treaty for the Limitation of Armament, or what was usually referred to as the "Washington Treaty."

The magnitude of these challenges can be inferred from some figures. On 1 December 1918, there were 32,208 commissioned officers and 494,358 enlisted personnel manning and supporting 1,362 ships. By 1 January 1922, there were 6,163 officers, 100,000 enlisted sailors, and 900 ships.[1] In January 1914, the Navy's aviation contingent consisted of nine officers, 23 enlisted sailors, and seven planes. "By the end of World War I, U.S. Naval Aviation Forces had increased to approximately 7,000 officers, 33,000 enlisted men, and over 2,100 aircraft."[2] Six months later, the number of officers in aviation was 580 (370 were pilots), and there were 4,879 enlisted personnel.[3] The congressional naval authorization of 1916 had set a peacetime ceiling of 137,500 enlisted sailors "and an officer corps of four percent of the enlisted strength—5,500 line and staff officers."[4] Otherwise, the reductions in personnel might have been even greater.

At the same time, the end of World War I left the U.S. Navy with a large and still growing fleet. For example, the destroyer construction program, which put into service almost 160 vessels from 1918 to 1921, could not be immediately shut off with the signing of the Armistice in November 1918. In addition, the building plans started under the 1916 program were continuing or were about to be continued, and included—by war's end—ten battleships, six battle cruisers, ten light cruisers, and more than 60 submarines. However, many members of Congress asked to what end? The defeat of Germany removed what the General Board had said before the war was the major threat in the Atlantic, and, although Japan remained a potential threat in the Pacific, it was not obvious that the only way to deal with the Japanese was to compete with Japan in a naval arms race.

There was also the problem of returning to a peacetime economy. Economists and financiers accepted the idea that payments on the wartime debt drew down the funds available for private investment. Accordingly, they favored paying off the debt quickly. At the same time, they were also concerned about the inflation that had weakened the currency during and right after the war. The fact that the immediate postwar inflation was followed by a severe recession justified for many members of Congress a great reduction in naval expenditures.[5] The Army was like an accordion. It could be expanded quickly in an emergency through conscription and then deflated once a war or emergency had ended. Why, wondered some members of Congress, couldn't the Navy expand and contract in the same way?

When the administration of President Warren G. Harding took office in March 1921, the new President and his Secretary of State Charles Evans Hughes decided to deal with congressional calls for reduced naval expenditures by sponsoring an international conference on arms limitation. Their position was that the nation's interests would be secure if the three major naval powers—the United States, Great Britain, and Japan—agreed to keep their navies at a size that would not allow any one of them to quickly defeat one of the other two with an aggressive naval campaign. The result was what was termed "the Treaty system," which was an extended international program for constraining naval expenditures and technology that shaped the actions of Navy leaders right up until 1940.

The Role of the CNO

Rear Admiral Robert E. Coontz stepped right into this challenging world when he became CNO on 1 November 1919.[6] Coontz had temporarily spelled Captain Pratt as Assistant CNO when Pratt journeyed to Paris in December 1918. Coontz had also chaired a Navy "demobilization board" that same month. What he really wanted, however, was command at sea, directing a division of battleships, and he got it after Pratt returned to Washington in January 1919. Coontz was a solid, reliable officer who commanded the Bremerton Navy Yard before being detailed to OPNAV. He was noted for being a "trustworthy, anti-radical officer" because of the way that he dealt with organizational efforts of the radical Industrial Workers of the World and with suspected labor agitation by pro-Bolshevik agents.[7]

Coontz lacked the experience, reputation, and personality of Admiral William S. Sims, and some in the Navy thought Sims should be the next CNO. Admiral Coontz, however, was supported by officers such as Rear Admiral Eustace B. Rodgers, the West Coast Pay Inspector, who wrote to Senator (and former Secretary of the Navy) Truman H. Newberry (R-MI) that Coontz "has the very qualities needed in Washington: infinite tact, sound judgments, quiet decision, pleasant personality and a remarkable facility for getting things done rightly."[8] In other words, he was not Sims; Coontz's facility with people and his low-key approach had not created enemies who would oppose his selection.

Admiral Coontz became CNO somewhat unsure of his authority and responsibilities. Secretary Daniels clearly wanted to maintain civilian control, and he was comfortable working through the Navy's bureaus and the General Board for that purpose. Coontz apparently did not concur; he later asserted that he was "a firm believer in the authority of the Chief of Naval Operations over all the bureaus."[9] In the short term, however, he found that Secretary Daniels was "eminently successful" in dealing with Congress, and he also "found the weekly councils of the Chief of Operations, and also the conferences of the Secretary of the Navy, were real clearing houses" for resolving a variety of issues.[10] To make them even more effective, Coontz prepared memoranda which listed the exact duties of each bureau and circulated the memoranda among the bureau chiefs. He also presided over weekly meetings of a bureau chiefs council; these meetings took on the challenge of reducing the overall size of the Navy while still completing the ships authorized by the 1916 act. The meetings were necessary, according to Coontz, because "There is scarce a financial question arising in any bureau that is not, to some extent, dependent on one or more of the bureaus."[11] Daniels, although more in favor of working directly with the bureau chiefs, eventually came around to Coontz's approach.

Rear Admiral Sims vs. Secretary Daniels

Unfortunately for Coontz, he was CNO for just over two months when Rear Admiral Sims, President of the Naval War College,[12] sent an official letter to Secretary Daniels criticizing the performance of the Navy Department during World War I and demanding that "errors of policy, tactics, strategy, and administration" be investigated and eliminated.[13] Sims later argued that "our state of preparedness when we entered the war was dangerously inadequate," and "our administrative methods, especially during the early stages of our participation, were seriously at fault."[14] Publicity surrounding Sims's letter triggered an investigation by a subcommittee of the Senate Committee on Naval Affairs.

Once the hearings began in March, 1920, Sims argued to the subcommittee that "a civilian head of the military branch of a democratic government is essential." But Sims went on to charge that the Navy had not been prepared for war, that it was not in adequate material condition when the war began, and that the Navy lacked a clear plan for waging the conflict once the United States declared war on Germany.[15] He also claimed that "the apathy of the Navy delayed victory for four months and cost the Allied cause 2,500,000 tons of shipping, 500,000 lives, and $15,500,000!"[16] Daniels was not about to be intimidated, however. He told the subcommittee that

> if Congress believes that civilian control is a 'great evil,' that the policy which has prevailed from the foundation of our Government [sic] should be reversed and that the Navy should be removed from civilian control, let it follow Sim's [sic] lead—create a general staff on the German model, and name some Von Tripitz [sic] to rule the Navy.[17]

As historian Elting Morison noted in his commentary on the hearings 20 years later, what quickly came to center stage was the animosity between Sims and Daniels. As a result, the hearings "took the form of an ill-natured and destructive debate," and such intense "heat was generated, so clearly divided in loyalties were the opposing sides, so many feelings were deeply injured that the subject of change was buried away and not raised again in fundamental form for a generation."[18] Moreover, the acrimony among those testifying at the hearings cast a poor light on the Navy. Coontz and some other senior officers even demanded that Sims be court-martialed, especially for his comment that CNO Benson "lacked the will to win." The service, however, chose not to prosecute Sims; as Admiral Henry B. Wilson, Commander of the Atlantic Fleet, stated: "We want to make no martyrs. Admiral Sims has ruined himself. . ."[19]

Yet imbedded in the approximately 3,500 pages of testimony was evidence that the issue of civilian control was real and not just a matter of personalities. Captain Pratt, who would eventually become CNO, put it this way:

> To administer the duties of the chief executive of this department, there is called a civilian . . . who . . . is best able to coordinate the Navy's activities with Congress, and who in his person is the strongest connecting link between us and the people. He comes to the office as an individual . . . able, efficient, highly trained in some subject, but not technically trained in the activities of the Navy nor a student of the art of war. This system functions after a fashion in peace but does not function when preparation for war becomes necessary, nor does it function in war.[20]

Secretary Daniels was unmoved by Pratt's argument. His view of the CNO and OPNAV was clearly laid out in his final annual report. He stated that the CNO, in accordance with the act of 1915, was the ranking officer of the Navy, and that the law also guaranteed a "direct relationship" of the CNO with fleet commanders and other commanding officers. Daniels added that the CNO was provided with "a large staff of the best trained officers," to prepare war plans and make plans for the operation of the fleet, and he defined the position of the CNO as "one of thinking, of planning, of leadership, of cooperation, with all needed executive power that makes ... for the operation of the fleet in peace and in war." Daniels also stated that because of the CNO's interaction with the bureau chiefs and the secretary, his position on the General Board, his direction of naval intelligence, Navy communications and the War College, and the definition of his powers in legislation, the CNO "holds a position ... without the inherent executive weaknesses found in the position of any Chief of Staff." Most critically, to Daniels and many others, the complementary relationship between the secretary and the CNO "avoids the substitution of military for civilian control while insuring the cooperation of all naval agencies in perfect team work."[21]

After Daniels had left the Navy as its secretary, Coontz was free to comment candidly on Daniels's views of the relationship between the SECNAV and the CNO. Coontz felt that Daniels took up matters directly with Congress, asking advice from the bureau chiefs as needed; hence Coontz's belief that Daniels favored the staff (bureaus) over the line (fleet and operations) officers. Coontz considered Daniels's successor, Edward Denby, to prefer the line to the staff, and credited Denby's preference to his service as an enlisted man in both the Navy and the Marine Corps, and his service as a Marine officer in World War I.[22]

The Role of the General Board

In 1919, it was the General Board that took up the issue of what had been learned from the Navy's experience in World War I. By the time Coontz became CNO, for example, the board had already spent much of 1919 considering the future role of aviation in the Navy. Starting in January 1919, a number of officers testified at the board's secret hearings and provided the members of the board with information and insights regarding Navy aviation during World War I. For example, on 5 March 1919, Captain Noble E. Irwin, the Director of Naval Aviation in OPNAV, testified that

> The fleet is very enthusiastic about the use of heavier-than-air craft for spotting. I had a report yesterday from the commanding officer of the *Texas* (Battleship No.35), which stated in the recent target practice at the range of 20,000 yards they had one seaplane spotting and kite balloons and that the spotting of the seaplane was 200% better than the spotting by any other means.[23]

Irwin added that "the urgent thing is to go ahead with the development of the use of aircraft with the fleet proper, particularly now when the move is for a united air service, and we strengthen our hand every time we can show that we are using it with the fleet."[24]

Board hearings covered all aspects of using aircraft at sea, including training pilots and aircrew, training aircraft engine mechanics, aircraft tactics, progress in aircraft design, the roles played by aircraft in World War I, seaplanes versus aircraft flying from land bases and aircraft carriers, and the design of carriers that could take aviation to sea. How had aircraft performed in combat? What had been learned from the Royal Navy's use of the *Furious*, a battle cruiser converted in stages to a carrier? What did the U.S. Navy need *now*? Would existing aircraft and any aircraft carrier soon be obsolete? As pioneer aviator Commander John H. Towers told the board at the end of March 1919, "I don't think we can continue beyond . . . 1925 . . . in building aircraft carriers, because I think it will be quite possible that ships will all become more or less aircraft carriers and be so designed." He added that "the development of aviation is so startling that any one is foolish if he attempts to lay down a six year's aviation program."[25] But of course that is exactly what the board was trying to do.

The board also solicited testimony from the Army's aviators, including Brigadier General William "Billy" Mitchell, an ardent advocate of the British model for organizing military aviation as a separate service, from Marine Corps aviators, and from a representative of the Royal Navy. Though there were disagreements among the Navy's aviators about how the available funds should be spent, there was general agreement among them that the captain of battleship *Texas* was on the mark when he asserted that the Navy was "far behind in the development of our Fleet Aviation," and that "Quick and energetic steps must be taken to place it on an efficient basis."[26] On 23 June 1919, the board sent a memo to Secretary Daniels stating that "fleet aviation must be developed to the fullest extent. Aircraft have become an essential arm of the fleet. A Naval air service must be established, capable of accompanying and operating with the fleet in all waters of the globe." The memo also recommended that "airplane carriers for the fleet be provided in the proportion of one carrier to each squadron of capital ships."[27] Finally, in several of its hearings, the board also considered the possibility that Congress should create a new bureau for Navy aviation.[28]

The General Board did not work in isolation. Its regular members were senior officers with command experience at sea, and they worked "in closest cooperation with the Plans Division of Operations, and with the Bureaus."[29] The CNO, the Commandant of the Marine Corps, the Director of the Office of Naval Intelligence, and the President of the Naval War College were ex officio members, but the real work of the board was done by its regular members and younger officers "ordered to duty in connection with the Board."[30] On behalf of the Secretary of the Navy, the board had prepared drafts of the 1916 shipbuilding program, and in 1919 its members were committed to resuming battleship and battle cruiser construction with the goal of making the U.S. Navy "second to none." They were concerned about the possibility that Japan and Great Britain, allied by treaty, might combine their fleets to intimidate the United States.

In carrying out its responsibilities to the secretary, the board linked the technical expertise of the "hardware" bureaus (Ordnance, Construction and Repair, and Steam Engineering) with the strategic perspective of the planners in OPNAV.[31] As the members of the General Board understood, "to determine a building program and to decide upon the military characteristics of ships, it is really necessary to consider the whole subject of the material of a navy in its strategic and tactical aspects."[32] In contemporary terminology, the General Board played an "integrating role," and its secret hearings were a place where representatives of the CNO, the bureau chiefs, and the commander-in-chiefs of the fleets could discuss issues and then build a consensus to support the solutions to those issues that they had hammered out.

The Key to OPNAV's Influence: The Planning Process

However, before the CNO's staff could weigh in on issues, its members had to develop positions that were consistent with the overall strategic goals of the country. Once they did that, and after they had discussed thoroughly the implications of their positions with members of the General Board and representatives of the bureaus and the fleet, they had to make sure that the negotiated solutions were in fact implemented. How was this done?

The answer is that it was done through the planning process. OPNAV staff had not had time to develop an efficient and effective planning process before war began in April 1917. In August 1919, then-CNO Benson attempted to rationalize OPNAV's planning process by dividing it into two parts—war plans and administrative plans. This division was described in the official "Organization Orders of the Office of Naval Operations," and its intent was described in the previous chapter of this volume. But how, precisely, would it work? That was the question left for CNO Coontz.

Fortunately, Admiral Benson had made sure that the talent needed to find an answer was in OPNAV. In addition to Captain (later Rear Admiral) Noble E. Irwin, the following future flag officers were on the OPNAV staff in 1919: Captain Joseph M. Reeves, Captain Harry E. Yarnell, Captain Thomas C. Hart, Captain William D. Leahy, Commander Charles A. Blakely, Commander Chester W. Nimitz, Commander Walter B. Woodson, Commander William S. Pye, and Commander Robert L. Ghormley. This group of talented officers, along with many others, formed a team that, under CNO Coontz, shook the kinks out of OPNAV, creating a process that allowed the CNO to direct Navy war planning and coordinate the activities of the bureaus.

Coontz's successor, Admiral Edward W. Eberle, explained how the process worked in a December 1923 paper. As Eberle put it, the "Chief of Naval Operations should guide, as a whole and toward a common end, all activities of the Navy."[33] He would do this by issuing and updating the "Basic War Plans," which served as "the basis of all the Navy's activity in preparation for war and operation in war." The "various responsible agencies, afloat and ashore," would then write their Contributory War Plans "on matters under their cognizance."[34] For example, the Contributory Plan of the Commander-in-Chief of the Fleet would draw on the Basic War Plan developed under the supervision of the CNO. The CNO's Basic War Plan was the "Orange Plan," the trans-Pacific campaign plan against Japan.[35]

As the December 1923 paper made clear, each officer responsible for preparing a Contributory Plan had to make sure that the plan developed under his supervision supported the Basic War Plan. Each Contributory Plan also had to contain two sections—a readiness plan for peacetime and an operating plan for war. The planning process was deliberately decentralized: "The Contributory Plans will be prepared by the officers who will also execute them. They, therefore, are not the Chief of Naval Operations' plans, but the plans of the officers who will execute them." These plans "will be inspected by the Chief of Naval Operations only to see that they are sufficiently comprehensive to carry out the Basic Plans." Coordinating the various plans "will require a great deal of give and take, frequent conference, and mutual helpfulness." However, as the paper noted, "It is well to remember that we have for many years built ships with this system."[36]

This planning process was very much in the tradition of Navy command and control. As the December 1923 paper observed, "The Chief of Naval Operations does not wish to absorb functions that are, can be, and ought to be, better performed by those agencies especially organized, trained, and qualified for such functions. He desires to encourage and strengthen these agencies, interposing his authority only so far as to effect coordination of effort and unity of action."[37] In plain terms, the Basic War Plan was not a straitjacket. It projected a broad campaign and then left it to the fleet and the bureaus to demonstrate how they would support that campaign. As historian Edward Miller recognized, this was the approach that allowed OPNAV to take the overall strategic planning function away from the General Board.[38] It also kept the OPNAV staff from being buried under staff work that could best be done by others.

In July 1921, Coontz appointed the highly experienced and intelligent Rear Admiral Clarence S. Williams director of OPNAV's War Plans Division (WPD), and Williams began a process of using staff papers to develop and test ideas for a trans-Pacific campaign against the Imperial Navy of Japan. Historian Miller's view is that Williams was "the most astute campaign strategist of the pre–World War II era," with "the right temperament for a war planner: analytical, mature in judgment, unswayed by eloquence, yet a good listener who demanded facts and asked penetrating questions."[39] Miller credits Williams with integrating "the innovative ideas brewing among the [War College], marine, and logistical staffs into a rational island-hopping campaign plan."[40]

By the time CNO Eberle sent around his paper on planning, Coontz and Williams had already defined the roles of the key offices within the OPNAV staff. The WPD wrote the Basic War Plans. The Director of the Policy and Liaison Section planned the operations necessary to "further the Readiness Plan. That is he adjusts what should be done with what can be done. . . . Consequently there comes from his office current departmental plans, Operating Forces Plans, and current policy."[41] The Director of the Material Division was responsible to the CNO "for the general direction and coordination of all agencies engaged in meeting the material requirements of the Navy." There was one exception to his authority, and that was determining the "number, types, and military characteristics of ships." That authority rested with the Secretary of the Navy, who acted on the advice of the General Board and the CNO. But the General Board and the CNO were linked through the Basic War Plans, which were an "attempt to harmonize the Chief of Naval Operations' advice with the General Board's." Finally, the Director of the Ships' Movement Division monitored readiness and "the peace disposition of naval vessels."[42]

If there was one seriously harmful myth about the relationship between planners in OPNAV and officers commanding the ships of the fleet, it was that the relationship between the planners and the "operators" was one-way, from the planners to the "operators." The reality was that there was a two-way relationship between them. The planning process was fluid, even messy. OPNAV officers developed plans. Fleet officers developed plans. Bureau personnel developed plans. The General Board worked to develop a formal naval policy, reviewed plans for the SECNAV from the perspective of that policy, and fulfilled its responsibility of initiating and reviewing preliminary ship designs in light of the naval policy and war plans. It took several years for the OPNAV

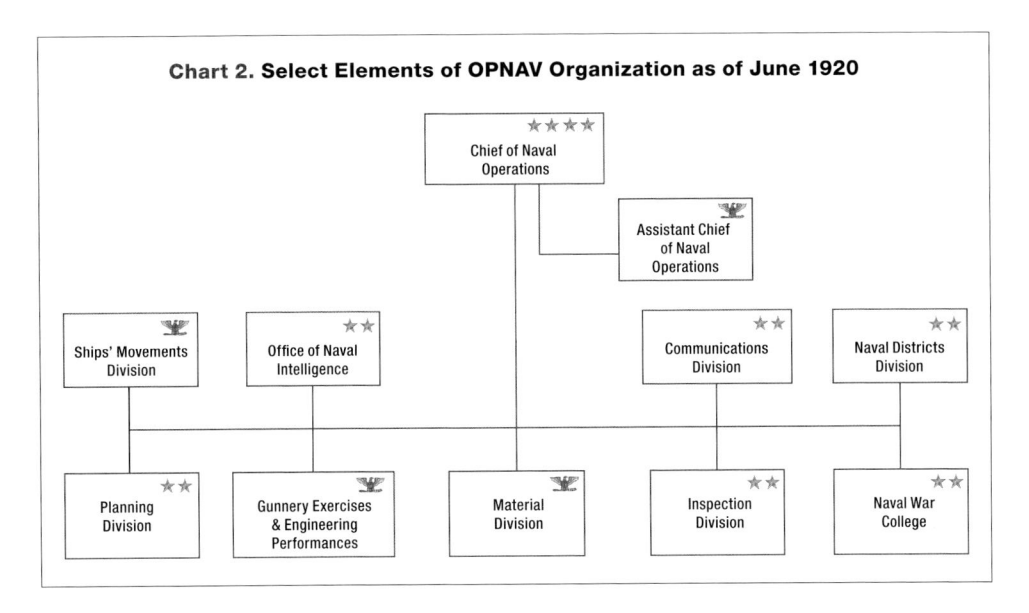

Chart 2. Select Elements of OPNAV Organization as of June 1920

- Chief of Naval Operations (★★★★)
  - Assistant Chief of Naval Operations
  - Ships' Movements Division
  - Office of Naval Intelligence (★★)
  - Communications Division (★★)
  - Naval Districts Division (★★)
  - Planning Division (★★)
  - Gunnery Exercises & Engineering Performances
  - Material Division
  - Inspection Division (★★)
  - Naval War College (★★)

staff, under CNO Coontz, to develop an effective planning process, and it was never meant to be tightly disciplined. Authority within the Navy Department was dispersed—divided among the secretariat, the bureaus, OPNAV, and the fleet. The activities of these different organizations had to be coordinated. Under CNO Coontz, a process for doing that came to be accepted. It was Coontz's gift to his successor, Admiral Eberle.

Policy Challenges: Budgets, Bombs, and Battleships

When Admiral Coontz became CNO, the Navy was already dealing with constraints on its spending and ahead lay a challenge from General Mitchell of the Army to subject a modern battleship to aerial bombardment. By the end of the summer of 1920, the congressional investigation of the issues in dispute between Secretary Daniels and Rear Admiral Sims was over. At that time, major decisions about Navy expenditures were not in the hands of the CNO. The bureau chiefs submitted their own budgets to Congress, and Secretary Daniels's submission covered the remaining expenditures. This would change with the passage of the Budget and Accounting Act of 1921 on 10 June 1921.

The year 1921 was busy for the Navy's leaders for two other reasons. The first was focus of the media on the bombing tests conducted by the Navy and Army against German warships ceded the United States under the Versailles Treaty of 1919. The bombing tests were carried out in June and July, 1921. The run-up to them was pure grist for the newspapers' mills. General Mitchell and his supporters had been claiming that bombing from the air made battleships—and by implication the fleet that Congress had authorized in 1916—obsolete. The Navy had detonated explosives against the hulls and superstructures of the obsolete battleships *Indiana* (BB-1), *Alabama* (BB-8), and *Massachusetts* (BB-2) in the fall and winter of 1920–1921, and it was planning to conduct similar tests on the German ships in the summer of 1921. At the beginning of February 1921,

Secretary Daniels offered the Army a role in the upcoming tests, the Army accepted, and the Joint Board of the Army and Navy approved the arrangement. The bombing tests provided lots of drama but did not demonstrate conclusively that the battleship was obsolete.[43]

Unfortunately, a good deal of bad blood between the Army and the Navy came out of the dispute over the implications of the bombing tests.[44] But what really mattered to CNO Coontz was that Congress had passed a bill creating a new Navy bureau for aviation on 12 July 1921, right in the middle of the bombing tests against the German ships. The legislation, which had been drafted by Rear Admiral David W. Taylor, Chief, BuC&R, gave Navy aviation a new and more politically secure bureaucratic "home."[45] Also in July, the General Board recommended to Edwin Denby, the new SECNAV, that he ask Congress to authorize the construction of three large built-for-the-purpose aircraft carriers.[46] In August, the Joint Board of the Army and Navy reviewed the reports of the bombing trials and, on that basis, rejected Mitchell's claim that the battleship was obsolete.[47]

The second reason why 1921 was such a busy year was because the administration of President Harding saw a reduction of Navy expenditures as a complement to the Budget and Accounting Act. However, the General Board remained wedded to the 1916 program; its members had recommended to Secretary Daniels in 1919 that the 1916 program be completed without delay, and they wanted to add more battle cruisers to it. The Philippines were America's outpost in the western Pacific. The Army had built strong defenses around Manila Bay that were designed to hold that harbor in the event of war with Japan. But if Britain and Japan combined against the United States, then the U.S. Navy would find itself fighting in two oceans simultaneously. Given this possibility, the General Board regarded the 1916 program as essential, plus the additional battle cruisers. Officers in OPNAV's Planning Division, by contrast, believed that the current building program allowed for enough capital ships; they recommended instead laying down four airplane carriers and 20 light cruisers, plus destroyer flotilla leaders and submarines.[48] Coontz supported this view and called for a more well-rounded fleet and bases in the western Pacific. It was there that the country confronted "the most serious and irreconcilable clashes." The planners also called for increases in personnel to restore naval efficiency.[49] Even after significantly reducing the number of ships in active commission, the Navy was still short of sailors.[50]

The restructuring of the Navy's operating forces in 1919 to have both an Atlantic and a Pacific Fleet, each with its own battleships, seemed to be one way to safely economize. However, as Coontz and his staff understood, the real challenge in operating against Japan would be logistics. It was about 2,300 miles from the Pacific Fleet's bases in San Diego and San Pedro, California, to Pearl Harbor. It was almost 4,800 miles from Pearl Harbor to Manila. In 1919, Pearl Harbor had not been dredged sufficiently to hold battleships. Even the U.S. bases on the West Coast, including San Francisco, were not sufficient to support the large number of ships, especially capital ships, which would be based there in the event of a war with Japan. The island of Oahu was well garrisoned by the Army, but Guam had neither Army defenses nor an adequate base for the fleet. The Philippines also lacked the infrastructure for a major naval base. If war came, Japanese forces would surely attack the Philippines. How could the Pacific Fleet rescue the garrison there?[51]

The Planning Division addressed these critical issues. There were different approaches to the move against Japan: a direct move from the West Coast, usually via Pearl Harbor to the Philippines (the "through ticket to Manila"), or a more cautionary approach seizing bases, including the former German Pacific Micronesian colonies, which the Japanese had received as mandates at Versailles. Strengthening and assessing these plans, known collectively as War Plan Orange, would be the primary focus of OPNAV planners during the interwar period.[52] They would also be tried out multiple times on the war game boards at the Naval War College.

These plans also assumed that the United States still considered defense of the western Pacific and the maintenance of the Open Door Policy in China critical to national security. In 1919 Captain Harry E. Yarnell of the OPNAV staff realized this was not a question for OPNAV or, even, the Navy Department but a question for the State Department and the President. Inquiries in 1921 regarding this policy elicited no response from Harding's Secretary of State Hughes. The Navy, including OPNAV, therefore proceeded as before. The importance of the Far East, however, was not settled policy for the U.S. government, and this mattered once the government of the United States convened the conference on the limitation of armaments in November 1921.[53]

An Excess of Economy

The push to reduce expenditures by the newly elected Republican majorities in both the Senate and the House in 1919 hindered the development of a sensible naval policy. Matters grew even worse after the inauguration of President Harding in March 1921. In 1920, CNO Coontz had found members of Congress eager to reduce Navy expenditures, but reluctant to close unneeded shore facilities that were located in their districts. Despite Coontz's well-known interpersonal skills, his relations with the members deteriorated over such issues.

The passage of the Budget and Accounting Act of 1921, which established the Bureau of the Budget, also required all major departments to have a budget officer.[54] Coontz thought this should fall within the CNO's responsibilities, and Secretary Denby appointed him as the Navy Budget Officer in the summer of 1921. This work brought him into close and frequent contact with the members of the Senate and House Navy Subcommittees of the Appropriations Committees. However, his relations with Congress were already often sour, and he was frustrated by the unwillingness of the Congress to properly fund the Navy, including already approved programs, and their continuing opposition to any proposed reductions or closures of Navy facilities within their states or districts.[55] Being Navy Budget Officer also added to the CNO's workload. Coontz did not have a staff to help him review budget submissions from the bureaus until the summer of 1922.[56]

The need for funding was real. In January and February 1921, the major units of the Atlantic and Pacific Fleets met on the Pacific side of the Isthmus of Panama for a cruise south of the equator. After conducting various exercises, the combined fleets separated, with Atlantic Fleet ships heading for Peru and the Pacific ships steaming for Chile. After their successful South American visits, the separate fleets combined once again before the ships based in Atlantic ports passed back through the Canal and returned to the United States. The 1921 deployment tested the readiness of almost 60 ships and their thousands of sailors. It also gave a number of ships experience in making their way through the Panama Canal. Finally, the deployment tested the capability of the Navy's seaplanes, a number of which flew in stages from their home bases in the United States to join the ships in the Caribbean and in the Pacific near Panama.[57]

Unfortunately—and despite the success of the Pacific cruise—the Navy lacked the funds to stage a similar exercise in 1922. Financial stringency in that year impeded operations and training. The CNO Annex to *Annual Reports to the Navy Department 1922* had one sentence for the section for the winter maneuvers for the year: "The winter maneuvers contemplated for the year were abandoned on account of the lack of fuel."[58] The Navy lacked funding to carry out necessary training; Coontz wrote: "An arbitrary sum was appropriated to be expended for fuel. This sum proved absolutely inadequate . . ." In previous years, the fuel estimate was made with the "understanding that deficiencies could be incurred" and paid from later years or supplements. This appropriation was the first where Congress "indicated that this practice would no longer continue." Coontz emphasized that "operations relied entirely on fuel," either coal or oil, not "an amount to be paid for fuel."[59]

In this constrained fiscal environment, it was going to be difficult to support naval aviation. CNO Coontz had supported the establishment of the new Bureau of Aeronautics (BuAer), which Congress authorized in the Navy Appropriation Act of 12 July 1921. The bureau stood up on 10 August 1921 with Rear Admiral William A. Moffett, whom Coontz considered "a strong and experienced man," as its first chief. However, Coontz also believed this bureau would be temporary until the technology was better integrated into the Navy, and then "this bureau should go back into its component parts, just as other bureaus have had to do in the past."[60]

Moffett, however, had no intention of allowing BuAer to exist only temporarily. He wrote Navy General Order Number 65 to give BuAer the authority to supervise the training of pilots and mechanics, and the order also gave BuAer the responsibility for assigning aviation personnel to their posts at sea and ashore. This authority over personnel put BuAer at loggerheads with the Bureau of Navigation (BuNav), which had the legal authority over Navy personnel policy and training. To fend off those critics who thought that BuAer had too much authority compared to the other bureaus, Moffett had carefully cultivated support for his ideas among members of the General Board, members of Congress, and bureau chiefs such as David W. Taylor, the highly respected chief of the Bureau of Construction and Repair (BuC&R). Moffett had also recruited some of the Navy's most accomplished younger officers as supporters of the new bureau, including Captain Henry C. Mustin, Commander John H. Towers, and Commander Emory S. Land, Construction Corps. These individuals and others formed a talented cadre of staff officers and aviation commanders who could defend naval aviation from its critics and simultaneously demonstrate what naval aviation could do with and for the fleet.[61]

Moffett also stayed in close touch with Rear Admiral Sims, President of the Naval War College. In February 1922, he informed Sims that the BuAer staff was "getting up a plan for Fleet aviation, which will cover the next five years, and this is to be submitted to the General Board for approval. We are trying above all else to get Aviation afloat."[62] Communicating regularly with Sims was a sound tactic in Moffett's drive to sustain and improve Navy aviation. As War College President, Sims was an *ex officio* member of the General Board. Sims and his colleagues at the War College had also developed a program of operational and tactical simulations, and the results of those exercises on the college's war game boards suggested that the potential of naval aviation was very great. Was the Navy still short of long-range scouts? Yes. Could aviation—whether aircraft or dirigibles—fill that gap? The simulations suggested that aviation could. Under Moffett and Sims, BuAer and the War College developed an important relationship, one where ideas and proposals went back and forth. The point to remember is that Moffett and Sims could communicate in this way without having to go through OPNAV. In supporting the creation of BuAer, Coontz had helped create a new and special kind of bureau, and Moffett took advantage of every resource that being chief of BuAer gave him.

Arms Limitation: The Washington Naval Treaty

President Harding and Secretary of State Hughes decided in the spring of 1921 to pursue arms reduction as a way of husbanding resources for domestic economic growth and of reducing the potential for future military conflicts. With the support of congressional leaders, Harding called for a conference in Washington in November 1921 to discuss naval arms reduction and other issues that were a source of tension in the Far East. Delegates attended from the major naval powers (the United States, Great Britain, and Japan), the naval powers in the Mediterranean (France and Italy), and nations with clear interests in the western Pacific (China and The Netherlands, for example).

In 1919, the Navy had shifted its strongest units to the Pacific on the assumption that the western Pacific was the main area of potential conflict with Japan. On becoming Secretary of State, Hughes had provided no definite direction regarding this assumption. So the Navy prepared and planned for conflict against Japan. CNO Coontz was very concerned about ratios of ships, especially battleships and battle cruisers. OPNAV planners thought that the United States should have a 10:5 ratio over Japan in such warships. This was based on the idea that for every thousand miles a fleet traveled from its base, it would lose 10 percent of its effectiveness. Advancing from Pearl Harbor to the western Pacific would reduce the effectiveness of the U.S. force by at least 40 percent, but a 10:5 ratio in heavy combatants left a marginal superiority at the point of conflict.[63]

Preparing for the conference strained relations between the President and the Navy. According to historian Gerald Wheeler, Secretary of State Hughes "insisted that the conference be an assemblage of diplomats and not naval ministers. Harding agreed that Hughes should lead the American delegation and passed [Navy secretary] Denby by." Hughes also did not select any Navy officers as delegates, drawing instead on the Assistant Secretary of the Navy, Theodore

Roosevelt Jr., for advice and staff support. CNO Coontz and Captain Pratt assisted Roosevelt. "In the background," according to Wheeler, "was a very fretful General Board."[64]

The General Board had reason to be fretful; Secretary Hughes did not accept the board's proposal that the 1916 building program be completed. But the President and the Secretary of State were not the only obstacles to the board's recommendations. As the General Board's push for more ships continued, it became clear that there was not congressional support even for the existing ships under construction. Within OPNAV, Rear Admiral Williams, Director of War Plans, repeated to Coontz the argument of his planners that any treaty must give the United States at least a 10:5 ratio of battleships and battle cruisers over Japan. However, Secretary of State Hughes, convinced that limiting naval armaments was essential to national security, took the drastic step of proposing to halt battleship and battle cruiser production for ten years. According to Wheeler, the "General Board objected strenuously, but Hughes won over his delegation and the President as well."[65] Then Hughes asked Assistant Secretary Roosevelt what would be required actions by the Japanese and the British if the United States stopped all new capital ship construction under the treaty. Roosevelt, Coontz, and Pratt weighed options and presented their final draft to the Secretary of State on 4 November 1921; the document was so sensitive that Pratt typed it. Hughes did not release it to the Government Printing Office until the first day of the conference. Hughes stunned the conferees with the proposal to halt all capital ship construction, reduce arms by scrapping older ships, build an arms limitation agreement based on the current strengths of the countries involved, and place a limit on capital ship tonnage.[66]

As historian Wheeler observed, "The most important treaty to come out of the conference was the Five Power Naval Treaty signed on 6 February 1922" by the United States, Japan, Great Britain, France, and Italy.[67] The treaty as accepted limited the number, tonnage, gun size, and total tonnage of battleships and battle cruisers, the tonnage and total tonnage for aircraft carriers, declared a 10-year "holiday" on new battleship construction and set a restriction on gun size for all other warships to no larger than 8 inches and a weight (ship displacement) limitation of 10,000 tons. The treaty also called for the non-fortification of U.S. possessions west of Hawaii as well as the Japanese Mandated Islands. In addition, the Four Power Treaty between the United States, France, Great Britain, and Japan was an agreement to consult with each other in the event of a crisis in East Asia; significantly, this treaty also ended the Anglo-Japanese Treaty of 1902.[68]

Many U.S. naval officers were displeased with the result, not only the loss of capital ships, but also with the failure to secure more controls on other combatants. Dudley Knox, a retired captain serving on active duty in the Historical Section of the Office of Naval Intelligence and a friend of Admiral Sims, criticized the treaty publicly in his widely read book *The Eclipse of American Sea Power*, published in 1922. The Navy, however, was never given the chance to present official comments on the Washington Treaty to the Congress, and Senator Henry Cabot Lodge (R-MA), a delegate to the conference, forced the treaties through the Senate without formal hearings. The Senate ratified the treaty on 29 March 1922.[69]

The Early Interwar Period: Reorganization, Arms Limitation, and Money

The treaty was not well-understood by many in the country. Coontz commented on the public misconceptions about the treaty in an appendix that was included in the Secretary of the Navy's Annual Report:

> There is throughout the country a prevailing opinion that the 5-5-3 ratio, which applies to capital ships only, applies to navies as a whole. This is far from correct, and the United States Navy is still far short of other powers in light cruisers, and will still be short after the completion of the present building program, and has no battle cruisers.[70]

Coontz apparently believed it to be a bad bargain in the long run; he later stated that he thought Secretary of State Hughes acted from the desire to get a treaty, even a poor one, because of the efforts expended and the priorities of the administration.[71] The assumption behind the treaty was that not allowing any one of the three major naval powers—the United States, Great Britain and Japan—to threaten war would add to the security of all three. That was never the view of the Navy's General Board.

However, some American naval leaders saw advantages to the treaties. The naval treaty codified "parity between the U.S. Navy and the Royal Navy" and established the "U.S. Navy's superiority in capital ships over the Imperial Japanese Navy." It was accepted by some naval leaders as a rational solution to ensuring further development if the forces were built to treaty strength. The fortification clause had shocked many in the Navy; others in the service thought that neither Guam nor Manila was suitable for a major naval base and those funds could be better spent elsewhere.[72] Most importantly for OPNAV planners, the treaty broke the official link between Japan and Great Britain. That meant the United States would probably not have to wage a naval campaign in two oceans simultaneously.

Figure 3-1. Admiral Robert E. Coontz, selected as the second CNO, was an experienced professional sailor and successful commander, and he usually worked well with members of Congress. After leaving the CNO's post in July 1923, he served as fleet commander, deploying the battleships to Australia in 1925 to test the idea that the fleet could steam directly to the Philippines in the event of war. (NHHC Archives NH 51699)

Consequences of the Treaty

The implementation of the treaties signed in Washington in 1922 forced CNO Coontz to reorganize the fleet. The major change was codified in Navy Department General Order No. 94 of 6 December 1922, "Organization of Naval Forces." The order eliminated the Pacific and Atlantic Fleets and established the U.S. Fleet built around four components: The Battle Fleet (to defeat the

69

main enemy force), the Scouting Fleet (to find the main enemy force), the Control Force (to protect the Navy's key bases) and the Fleet Base Force (to sustain the fleet as it steamed across the Pacific). The Battle Fleet, with the newer battleships, was based in the Pacific; the Scouting Fleet, based in the Atlantic, had the older battleships. Additional commands that were part of the Navy included the Asiatic Fleet, other regional forces, naval district forces, and separate submarine divisions for the Atlantic and the Pacific.[73] The treaty also allowed Coontz and Denby to scrap numbers of obsolete ships, thereby saving the money that would have been spent to maintain them.[74]

How many sailors would be needed to man this "treaty" Navy? After World War I, a number of reserve Navy officers had requested that they be given the chance to qualify for regular commissions. Given the building program authorized in 1916, it looked as though a percentage of these officers would be needed to augment the ranks of the officers commissioned from the graduating classes of the Naval Academy. In the Naval Appropriation Act of June 1920, Congress therefore had allowed the Navy to administer examinations to the non-Academy graduates in order to select those qualified for regular commissions.[75] Once the Washington Treaty was signed, however, the officers who had successfully passed the examinations and been commissioned became a "hump" or "bulge" in the officer corps. As they rose through the commissioned ranks of the "treaty" fleet, they would outnumber the billets available to officers of their experience.[76]

So began a long back-and-forth discussion between the Navy and the congressional naval affairs committees about how best to structure the officer corps. To trim the ranks of those newly commissioned officers and their peers who had graduated from the Naval Academy but who were not qualified for higher rank, Congress in December 1924 required the Navy to retire them once they reached certain years of service.[77] In March 1925, Congress eliminated the Naval Reserve Force it had created in 1916 and replaced it with the Naval Reserve Officer Training Corps (NROTC), which allowed college graduates to gain reserve commissions in exchange for a limited number of years of active service in the fleet and a correspondingly limited number of years in the Navy's reserves.[78]

The nature of the officer corps was not the only personnel issue facing Coontz. At the beginning of fiscal year (FY) 1922 the Navy had to reduce the number of enlisted personnel from 115,000 to 106,000. Given the political support for fiscal retrenchment, Coontz anticipated further reductions. However, the Navy hoped to maintain a force of 96,000 sailors. Later that year, during the budget process, the Republican leaders of the House Appropriation Committee recommended a reduction to 67,000 enlisted men, despite President Harding's support for a force of 86,000. CNO Coontz and his staff obtained a copy of the committee report before the vote and prepared a response supporting the minority view that such reduced manning would all but nullify the 5:5:3 provisions of the Washington Treaty. Fortunately for Coontz, Representative William S. Vare (R-PA) introduced an amendment to the appropriations bill that restored the 86,000 level. Although this effort saved almost 20,000 billets, the Navy faced additional manning challenges as the new scout (light) cruisers approved under the 1916 Act finally joined the fleet. Coontz's actions also caused lasting enmity with several Republican leaders in the House. Even so, Coontz considered the passage of Vare's Amendment one of his greatest achievements as CNO. A less visible but in the long run a very important achievement was the establishment of the Naval Research Laboratory in 1921.[79]

Coontz as Chief of Naval Operations

Admiral Coontz's tenure as CNO is not today generally regarded as significant. That is a mistake. Critics of Coontz as an officer pointed to his inability to block the Washington Naval Treaty or control the negotiations that led to its signing. The evidence, however, is that this was not a failing of Coontz personally. Instead, it reflected a larger development. If Navy officers were going to lead a navy "second to none," then they were going to have to accept more than the legal authority of a civilian secretary and the decisions of the Congress. They were going to have to be prepared to anticipate international events. They were going to have to think about strategy in a broad context, broader than force structure or plans to deal with a specific enemy of the United States. It is no accident that the General Board gradually but steadily lost its domination of the process by which the Navy's force structure was determined. Part of the reason for this loss was the death of its highly respected president, Admiral of the Fleet Dewey, in January 1917. But the deeper reason was the General Board's refusal to adopt a more far-reaching approach to strategy.

Coontz's tenure as CNO was also important because he and his OPNAV staff created the most important bureaucratic tool that a CNO could have—a rigorous but not suffocating planning process. By law and regulation, there were multiple centers of authority in the Navy—the secretary, the General Board, the bureaus, the fleet's commander, and the CNO. By the end of Admiral Coontz's time as CNO, these centers of authority had worked out sensible ways of dealing with one another that allowed decisions to be effectively made and efficiently implemented.

You can think of each center of authority as an inkblot. Coontz oversaw a process that allowed the ink blots to overlap and coordinate their separate authorities. For example, when the General Board held hearings on warship design, representatives of OPNAV, the fleet, and the bureaus would routinely testify, offering arguments and evidence to support their positions. When the fleet planned exercises, the planning was done through cooperation and communication between OPNAV's Ships' Movements Division and the staff of the commander of the fleet. When the War Plans Division of OPNAV developed tentative operational-level plans, the planners communicated regularly with planning officers in the bureaus.

This looks like a messy process, and it was. The only time the Navy could be a strictly hierarchical organization was in wartime, when the fleet's commander assumed extraordinary powers. In peacetime, the different centers of authority had to work together, and adherence to two principles made this possible. The first principle was delegation of authority down to the appropriate level. Rear Admiral Moffett based his leadership of the Bureau of Aeronautics on the general acceptance of this principle within the Navy. As a bureau chief, he was initially responsible for his bureau's budget, and he wrote the regulations defining his bureau's authority. He also recruited his own staff and reached out to other senior officers in the Navy who could help him guide the development of naval aviation and protect it from calls for a separate aviation department along the lines of the British Air Ministry.

But Moffett could not act without being accountable to the CNO. The second principle—the need for planning—constrained Moffett and the other bureau chiefs. The term "planning" may be misleading here, especially for readers not familiar with how a complex organization works. In any such organization, it's essential that those in its different parts tell the truth about what they are doing, what it costs, and whether what they are doing is working the way it's supposed to. The key to effective planning is information. When Coontz ceased being CNO and moved to the post of fleet commander-in-chief, he left behind two working planning processes. The first one, already described in this chapter, was based in OPNAV. It was the source of OPNAV's influence. The second one was the conceptual ship design process used by the General Board. Both these processes were essential to the Navy's preparation for war.

Was Coontz successful in all his endeavors as CNO? No. He was not a success as the Navy's first budget officer, for example. Near the end of his term as CNO, Secretary Denby appointed Rear Admiral Joseph Strauss, a former commander of the Asiatic Fleet, Budget Officer for the Navy and his position transferred from OPNAV to the Office of the Secretary. No other serving CNO would ever serve as budget officer, though three budget officers went on to become commanders of the U.S. Fleet.[80]

Coontz became CNO at a time when enough was happening that he could well have been overwhelmed. Yet he tackled the problems of demobilization, adopting aviation, the tension between Secretary Daniels and Rear Admiral Sims, fiscal constraints, and arms reductions while building an OPNAV planning process that would be the base of influence inside the

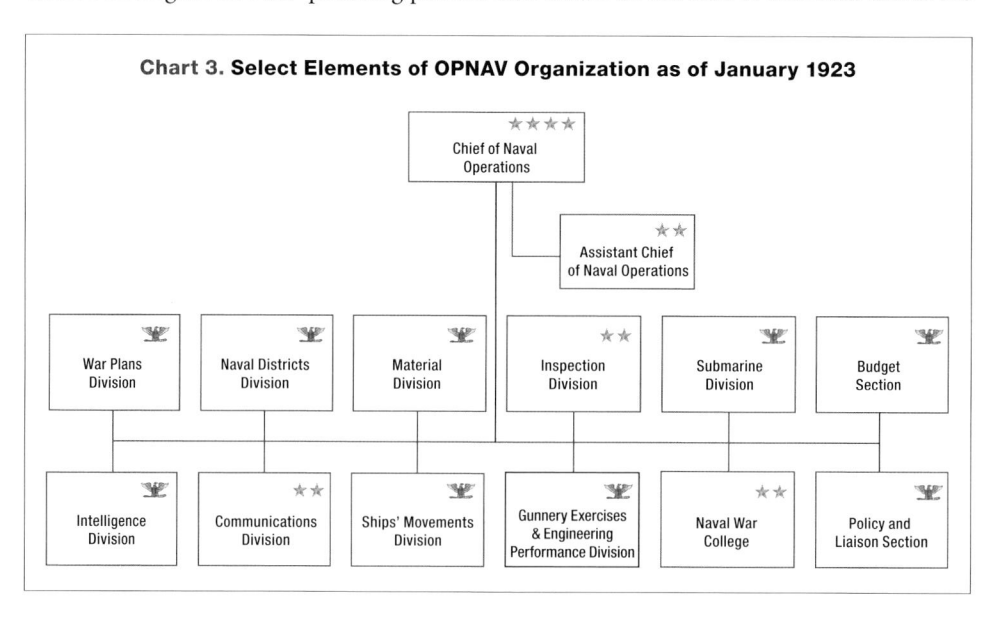

Chart 3. Select Elements of OPNAV Organization as of January 1923

- Chief of Naval Operations (★★★★)
  - Assistant Chief of Naval Operations (★★)
  - War Plans Division
  - Naval Districts Division
  - Material Division
  - Inspection Division (★★)
  - Submarine Division
  - Budget Section
  - Intelligence Division
  - Communications Division (★★)
  - Ships' Movements Division
  - Gunnery Exercises & Engineering Performance Division
  - Naval War College (★★)
  - Policy and Liaison Section

Navy for his successors. After Coontz, the Navy's overall agenda was set. How was the "treaty fleet" to remain modern and effective in times of fiscal stringency?

Eberle Takes Over

Admiral Edward W. Eberle became the CNO on 21 July 1923. Eberle was an expert on gunnery and wireless telegraphy, and, according to historian Richard Turk, "His interest in technology never waned."[81] At the time of his selection as CNO, Eberle was serving as Commander of the Pacific Fleet, which became the Battle Force. From retirement, Admiral Sims wrote that he was not impressed with Eberle as the choice; he thought that personal relationships rather than professional development had more do with the selection. He feared Eberle lacked an adequate understanding of strategy. Eberle, however, was no stranger to learning. He had completed the short course at the Naval War College, served there briefly as an instructor, and also served as the Superintendent of the Naval Academy during World War I.[82]

Eberle inherited the staff process brought to maturity under Coontz and confronted the same basic issues as Coontz—treaty restrictions and fiscal constraints. The battles over appropriations consumed much of the new CNO's energy; Eberle had been warned a year earlier by Admiral Hillary P. Jones, the Commander of the Atlantic Fleet, that the service "was laboring under economy run wild."[83] Eberle also had to deal with issues of developing technologies (especially aviation and submarines), renewed calls for greater naval arms limitation, and the challenges to Navy logistics inherent in War Plan Orange. The existence of the "treaty system" meant that his role as CNO would be strongly affected by political factors and leaders over whom he had no control. But the CNO and the Navy did have one very important tool after 1923—the so-called "fleet problems"—and those would turn out to be an essential part of preparing for war.

Making an Effective Treaty Fleet

In the aftermath of Washington, improvements to a fleet built around aging battleships were limited; there was only so much that could be done to bring the older capital ships (such as *Arkansas* [BB-33]) up to the performance levels of the newer ones (such as *Colorado* [BB-45]). However, senior officers wanted to at least replace the coal-fired steam plants in the older battleships with oil-fired boilers. They also wanted to improve the armor and underwater protection of all the surviving battleships. The Treaty allowed the addition of no more than 3,000 tons of alterations per battleship or battle cruiser, so there was the potential for some modernization, especially if newer equipment (like boilers) actually weighed less than the old. Another improvement was to increase the elevation of the main battery guns of the battleships, thereby increasing their range; whether this was allowed under the treaty was a matter of concern. In 1923, Captain Frank Schofield of the General Board wrote a memo included as Appendix C of the Navy Secretary's Annual Report that argued that the change in elevation did not violate the treaty.[84] However, the Royal Navy objected to the change. Unfortunately, most of the U.S. Navy's 12-inch and 14-inch battleship guns could not elevate beyond 15 degrees. Therefore, accepting the Royal Navy's objection effectively limited their combat range to 21,000 yards. The Commander-in-Chief of the U.S. Fleet (CINCUS) judged that a "grave defect."[85]

The treaty had also allowed the U.S. Navy to convert the incomplete battle cruisers *Lexington* (CC-1, later CV-2) and *Saratoga* (CC-3, later CV-3) to very large aircraft carriers displacing 33,000 tons each. Eberle stated in his 1 July 1925 annual report that they would likely be completed by the end of 1926. However, the limited funds provided by Congress slowed construction. As historian John Kuehn observed, this lack of action with *Lexington* and *Saratoga* not only saved money in the short term but also allowed the U.S. to be "a good example" to the other powers regarding restrained naval developments.[86]

The construction of cruisers by "other powers" became increasingly important. Allowed to do so by the Washington Treaty, both the British and the Japanese improved their cruiser forces, which were already substantially larger and more modern than the U.S. force. By 1924, the Japanese and British navies had ordered several 10,000 ton ships armed with 8-inch guns, the maximum ship displacement and armament allowed under the treaty, while the United States was still completing the last of the *Omaha*-class scout (light) cruisers (with 6-inch guns) authorized under the 1916 program. The need for the larger cruisers was understood within the Navy but by few others. Eberle, however, did convince Congress to authorize eight of the new 10,000 ton cruisers in late 1924, but the appropriations act only provided funds for two. Did the rush by the British and the Japanese to construct larger and more heavily armed cruisers mean that their governments were planning to build up their long-range naval striking forces in advance of any future naval arms negotiations? Was a new arms race in the offing?[87]

Even if there was no new arms race, manning was critical to sustaining the treaty fleet. The enlisted force remained authorized at 86,000 men, but the number was often lower than this. In his reports of 1926 and 1927, Eberle noted that the Navy operated with an average of about 82,000 men. The delay in the commissioning of *Lexington* and *Saratoga* eased the problem somewhat in 1926, but by 1927, the CNO included a specific section in his annual report about the problems caused by lack of sufficient numbers of enlisted men. In the same report he also pointed out the growing need for both officers and men to be assigned to aviation, including a projected shortfall of 12.5 percent by 1929. As already noted, the Navy appropriation act for fiscal 1926 included the formation of the NROTC; Eberle had supported the law as a means to help alleviate the manning situation.[88] As he and his fellow flag officers knew, the "treaty system" was based on the assumption that the three main navies—British, Japanese, and American—would keep their "treaty fleets" up to strength.

Debates About Naval Aviation

Aviation remained a controversial topic, even as the technology matured. Trying to understand the developing role and missions of aircraft was critical, especially as the Army Air Service pushed for greater funding and responsibilities; some Army aviation officers even advocated an independent air force. BuAer Chief Moffett had captured the dilemma facing the Navy and the nation in a memo he had sent to CNO Coontz and Secretary Denby in the summer of 1922. Moffett's argument was that:

> fleet aviation cannot successfully be expanded rapidly upon declaration of war; it is true that we can make a rapid increase in the production of aviation material, but experience has shown that a year of training and indoctrination is necessary for an aircraft squadron before it can operate in the fleet efficiently and safely...[89]

This fact had a powerful implication for planning. What BuAer needed, according to Moffett, was a planned program of aircraft construction and pilot training "that extends several years ahead of each year's aeronautic appropriation." Without this, Navy aviation would be prey to charges by the Army that its aviation was inadequate because the Navy had refused to support creation of a single, separate air force.[90]

In September 1924, Curtis D. Wilbur, Denby's successor as Secretary of the Navy, appointed Eberle to lead a board reviewing naval policy, especially naval aviation policy. The board contained no aviators, but Eberle, in the words of historian William Trimble, "was generally supportive of the need for expanding its role in the Navy."[91] Over several months of testimony, the board heard from a number of witnesses, including General Mitchell, the outspoken leader of the Army faction calling for an independent air force. The Eberle Board issued its final report in January 1925; it was relatively conservative. The battleship was still the main arbiter of sea power; the limitations in range and payload of aircraft consigned them to a complementary role in the Navy. The issue of manning, especially how best to train enough aviation officers, was not fully resolved. But the board also officially recognized the growing need for aviation, particularly in the Pacific, and it called for the rapid completion of *Lexington* and *Saratoga* and the building of additional carriers to bring the force up to treaty limits. The report also stated "the operation of aircraft in battle may be so important that among the first objectives of attack are the enemy's aircraft carriers."[92]

The public debates about whether or not to create a separate air force continued, however, and they came to a head in September 1925. That month, the large airship *Shenandoah* (ZR-1) had crashed in a violent thunderstorm over Ohio. An attempt by Navy aviators to fly the 2,200 miles from California to Hawaii had also failed. Colonel William Mitchell (Mitchell reverted to his permanent rank of colonel when his term as Assistant Chief of the Air Service ended in March 1925) claimed that the loss of men and material was due to "incompetency, criminal negligence and almost treasonable administration of the national defense by the war and navy departments."[93] Mitchell's aggressive public statements cost him his career, but it led President Calvin Coolidge Jr. to create a special board, headed by the experienced banker Dwight Morrow, to review the state of military aviation and suggest changes the members thought necessary.

The recommendations of the Morrow Board came down on Moffett's and the Navy's side of the debate.[94] The board said there was no need for an independent air force, that the Army and Navy did not have to purchase their airplanes from a common agency, and that Congress needed to authorize a five-year procurement plan that would add 1,000 aircraft to the nation's air forces.[95] In June 1926, Congress authorized the Navy to purchase 1,000 planes under the five-year program. This not only provided aircraft for the large carriers, it also allowed the construction of specialized types of aircraft instead of multipurpose aircraft that often turned out to be unsatisfactory compromises and less than useful militarily.[96]

In the wake of the Morrow Board's recommendations, CNO Eberle appointed Rear Admiral Montgomery M. Taylor, head of OPNAV's Fleet Training Division, to chair a panel to develop a five-year plan for naval aviation. The members of the panel rejected the argument that Navy carrier aircraft needed to be multipurpose. The panel's report also supported the development of long-range airships as fleet scouts and endorsed the idea of flying small planes from surfaced submarines and destroyers. It also suggested that the remaining aircraft carrier tonnage allowed by the Washington Treaty be allocated among smaller carriers.[97]

One reason why this board was so optimistic about naval aviation in general and carrier aviation in particular was because of the success that Captain Joseph M. Reeves was having with the experimental carrier *Langley* (CV-1) in exercises off the California coast. In November and December 1925, for example, *Langley*'s aviators and flight deck crew, under the direction of Reeves, dramatically reduced the amount of time it took to get *Langley*'s planes into the air. Based on his work as a student and instructor at the Naval War College, Reeves knew how important it was to get lots of planes into the air quickly. He also understood the need to land them rapidly so that they could be refueled and rearmed. By June 1926, *Langley* had a "deck park"—a safe way to protect planes that had already landed aboard from any aircraft that might miss the arresting gear wires. In August, Reeves recommended that *Langley*'s status be changed from experimental to operational.[98]

Figure 3-2. Admiral Edward W. Eberle was fleet commander when he was selected as the third CNO. In 1924, he headed a special board that recommended that the Navy take its aviation to sea in strength aboard numbers of carriers, and he supported the conversion of battle cruisers *Lexington* and *Saratoga* to carriers. (NHHC Archives NH 49797)

The Fleet Problems

Under CNO Eberle, OPNAV, the Naval War College, and the staff of the Commander-in-Chief, U. S. Fleet developed a process to plan and execute one or more "fleet problems" each year. These "problems" were major fleet exercises; they were called "problems" and not just "exercises" because they divided the ships and aircraft involved into two opposing forces. Each force had a mission that the opponent was instructed to block or defeat. The idea was to approximate wartime conditions as much as possible in order to highlight gaps in the Navy's ability to execute the sorts of missions it would have to undertake as part of War Plan Orange. The problems also helped prepare officers for the planning and command tasks that they would have to perform in wartime.

CNO Eberle set the pattern for his successors in the summer of 1923 when he appointed "a committee of three captains, five commanders, and a marine [sic] lieutenant-colonel" to develop candidate problems. Historian Albert Nofi found that Eberle also directed this committee to "include in their report 'how such problems shall be supervised and directed'" and how their efforts were to be coordinated with the staff of the fleet's commander.[99] Planners on the OPNAV and fleet commander's staff were free to draw on the reports of the war games conducted at the Naval War College, and they often did. In fact, the planning process for the fleet problems was open to all the fleet's senior commanders. Even though the CNO had to approve the products of this process because he was the officer who would provide the ships, aircraft, and personnel to execute them, Eberle and his successors did not want the problems to emerge from a "closed loop" of planners in OPNAV and the students and staff conducting war games at the Naval War College.[100]

The fleet problems put in place the last piece of the Navy's interwar planning system. OPNAV reviewed the basic war plan and the contributory plans from the fleet and the bureaus. The General Board applied Navy strategy, bureau expertise, and fleet experience to ship designs before making its recommendations to the Secretary of the Navy. The War College fed the results of its war games and studies to the fleet, OPNAV, and the bureaus, and the War College faculty received the reports of the fleet problems and any advances in naval technology from the bureaus. OPNAV staff made sure that the fleet problems were properly supported. The Secretary of the Navy oversaw the process and drew on it to explain Navy programs to members of Congress. This system was continuous; it ran every year until World War II. It can be thought of as a learning device or process.[101]

Strategy is both a process and a product. To focus OPNAV on supporting this process, CNO Eberle directed the WPD to write the annual "Estimate of the Situation," the classified basic document that was the touchstone for all Navy planning, including the Navy's budget. The "Estimate," based on a War College model of a campaign planning aid, discussed critical issues of force structure to assist planners. What were the Navy's missions? What forces did it need to perform those missions? How did the list of available forces stack up against what was required? The "Estimate" was an introduction to Navy force requirements—a useful summary of what the Navy had and a reminder of what OPNAV planners knew the Navy needed.

The WPD prepared the document by first looking at the broadest possible issues, including the various war plans. Then the focus narrowed to specific campaign plans, mainly the Orange Plan against Japan. Then it moved systematically to force structure. What forces were needed? Eberle chose Rear Admiral William R. Shoemaker to direct the WPD and Shoemaker persuaded Eberle to allow him to establish a structured planning process. Shoemaker also brought in additional staff, including Captains William H. Standley (a future CNO) and William S. Pye (a future vice admiral), and they stressed material preparations for war.[102] The "Estimate of the Situation" written in March 1924 as the foundation for the Navy's budget submission for fiscal year 1926, described the process:

> This system is so constructed that the whole field of naval endeavor is covered and there is a definite, sharp and compelling allocation of authority and responsibility. As the plans are built up, the needs of the Navy will become more clearly defined and the view of all responsible officers should become more pointedly set toward the common end in view. The adherence to this system will make for economy and should become the main stay for the budget.[103]

All elements of the Navy—every board, bureau, naval district, and fleet staff—contributed to the war plans. While this was burdensome to many, especially in a time when funds were scarce, it was necessary because it was the only way that OPNAV could identify gaps between what the plans required and what the Navy possessed and planned to acquire. Eberle recognized this, noting that complex war plans were not written ". . . on a few sheets of paper or in words of one syllable." Future heads of the WPD differed about the best way to conduct the campaign against Japan—whether as a direct "thrust" to Manila, or a "cautionary" campaign through the Mandates, but they stayed with the process that produced the estimates of the situation.[104]

Beyond the Washington Treaty

It is difficult now—in a time of great federal spending, a string of federal deficits, and a large national debt—to appreciate the personal intensity behind President Coolidge's effort to reduce federal expenditures. As Amity Shlaes has shown, Coolidge "believed higher taxes were wrong because they took away from men money that was their property; he believed lower rates were good precisely because they encouraged enterprise, but also because they brought less money. Low rates starved the government beast." Though he also believed in reducing federal taxes, Secretary of the Treasury Andrew Mellon had a different reason for thinking that lower taxes were advisable. He believed that reducing marginal tax rates would actually increase tax revenue as individuals invested what was not taken in taxation in productive enterprises or in housing and automobiles. As Shlaes put it, Mellon was sure that money "that flowed when he cut the taxes would enable him to pay off the federal debt faster."[105]

Unfortunately, for the Navy, it would take some time to see if Mellon's idea would prove effective. In the meantime, Eberle and his staff accordingly faced a continuing push for greater arms limitation from the Coolidge administration. The Navy wanted to build more cruisers, particularly cruisers up to the 10,000 ton and 8-inch gun limits allowed by the Washington Treaty. The President opposed this and called for a conference at Geneva to extend the tonnage ratios agreed to in Washington in 1922 to other classes of warships. This gambit appealed to the British, who were considering limits upon cruisers as well, particularly the number of larger cruisers; they had opted for more light cruisers of about 6,500 tons and armed with 6-inch guns to meet their requirements for Imperial defense and trade protection. To Coolidge's disappointment, his approach was not favored by the majority of Navy officers. War games and experience in the fleet problems had convinced many Navy officers that the newer 10,000 ton cruisers, armed with 8-inch guns, were vital for operations in the expanse of the Pacific. The British and American naval officers had very different strategic concerns. As a result, neither group could accept the mix of cruiser types acceptable to the other.[106]

At the conference in July 1927, the American delegates could not find enough common ground with the British and Japanese delegates. As a result, the Geneva Conference was a failure. CNO Eberle was pulled in two opposite ways simultaneously. Simulations at the Naval War College and the fleet problems showed the need to maintain at least the "treaty" Navy force structure, including bases in the Pacific, but the Coolidge administration was committed to extending the terms of the Washington Treaty that governed battleships to future cruisers. Eberle chose to stand by the commitment to the 1922 agreement that allowed the Navy to possess numbers of 8-inch gunned cruisers, and he directed the senior U.S. naval delegates at the Geneva Conference, Rear Admiral Hillary P. Jones of the General Board and the WPD's Director Rear Admiral Frank Schofield, to immediately reject the British proposals. Secretary of State Frank B. Kellogg later noted that the naval delegates had been told to not even discuss the status of American bases in the Pacific.[107]

Eberle and his peers regarded the Washington Treaty's force structure agreement as a floor below which the Navy was not going to be allowed to fall. President Coolidge looked at it very differently. He saw it as a ceiling that the government of the United States could not and would not break through. The next President, Herbert Hoover, took the same stance. This basic disagreement persisted across the terms of Eberle and his successor, Admiral Charles F. Hughes, who served as CNO from November 1927 to September 1930.

There was, however, one area of naval life that President Coolidge supported—aviation. In December 1926, Coolidge asked Congress for funds to "regulate the skies and promote aviation commerce."[108] Secretary Wilbur also supported aviation. He sent a cruiser to return aviator Charles Lindbergh from France in 1927, signaling the government's interest in and commitment to both civil and military aviation. Wilbur also reappointed Rear Admiral Moffett to a second term as chief of BuAer in 1925, and he supported Moffett's five-year program to acquire more than 1,600 aircraft—plus two very large airships—for the Navy by the end of fiscal year 1931.[109]

Eberle's time as CNO was stressful and in many ways frustrating. Congress and the administration stymied his efforts to increase ship construction, but aviation's role in the Navy improved during his term. There was clear evidence his health was suffering at the end of his tenure; correspondence indicates he had at least one surgery during his last year as CNO.[110] Eberle went on to serve on the General Board until mandatory retirement at 64 in 1928. Hospitalized again in early 1929, he died on 6 July.

Hughes Takes Over

Admiral Charles Frederick Hughes relieved Eberle on 14 November 1927 after having already held the major sea-going commands, the Battle Fleet and Commander-in-Chief of the U.S. Fleet. He also had held a vital post in OPNAV, the Director of Fleet Training, earlier in the decade. An imposing figure and an accomplished seaman, he had a reputation as a hard-working and independent-minded officer not given to self-promotion. When asked by his Annapolis classmate Secretary Wilbur to be CNO, Hughes did not think he was the man for the job. Some comments from other leaders in the fleet convinced him otherwise, including one that wrote: "He is the one man I know who can keep those stuffed-shirted Bureau chiefs in line." With such encouragement, Hughes agreed to accept the post.[111]

Hughes faced the same challenges as his predecessor. Hughes, however, took the responsibilities of CNO quite literally on many occasions; historian William Braisted noted that if a junior officer in the fleet received an order by direction, he could be assured that Hughes had actually sent it.[112] The CNO's extreme dedication to duty and hard work undermined his health and highlighted a negative consequence of not promoting talented officers rapidly enough. Hughes's advanced age was also a problem when it came to sustaining the "treaty system." It was obvious that the tension between President Coolidge and the Navy would continue into the administration of Herbert Hoover. That meant CNO Hughes would have to walk the same tightrope as his predecessor, trying to make sure that the Navy did not suffer severely from efforts to trim naval armaments. As it had been for Admiral Eberle, the position of CNO demanded tact and discretion when the opposite seemed called for.

For example, in the spring of 1929, the Hoover administration attempted to find a way around the dispute about numbers of cruisers that the Washington Treaty allowed the United States and Great Britain; that dispute had blocked any agreement at the Geneva Conference in 1927. American diplomat Hugh S. Gibson, representing the United States in disarmament talks at the League of Nations in Geneva, argued that there might be a "yardstick" that would allow the United States and Britain to come to an agreement where what mattered was the overall capability of a group of ships and not just their number. Hughes was alarmed; how could civilians lacking naval experience accurately gauge the combat potential of different types of warships? Hughes immediately convened the General Board and chaired all of its meetings that were concerned with the concept of a "yardstick." He also signed all of the board's papers that covered the topic.[113]

As historian Braisted revealed, "Relations between Hoover and the General Board reached a climax when Hughes and the board were called to the White House on the morning of 11 September 1929 to recommend a response" to a proposal from British Prime Minister Ramsay MacDonald. Hughes and his colleagues were not convinced that the British proposal had in fact followed the concept of a "yardstick," and, as Braisted noted, there was "some evidence that the meeting broke up after Hughes bluntly told the president that the General Board had completed its last study of the cruiser question."[114] From that time until the convening of the

London Conference in January 1930, Hughes and the General Board were without much influence with President Hoover. Instead, the President and Secretary of State Henry L. Stimson relied on Admiral Pratt, by that time the Commander-in-Chief of the U.S. Fleet.

Planning for War

The WPD remained focused on Japan as the most likely opponent in a war, but the failed negotiations at Geneva disturbed some officers, especially Rear Admiral Schofield. After the talks, Schofield stated in his next "Estimate" that the British had "no intention of surrendering supremacy of the sea," a fact that the United States was not "prepared to acknowledge." Schofield was also concerned by the Japanese and British reaching agreements that were not shared with the United States; he was convinced that Japan would never attack America without a European ally.[115]

Hughes accepted Schofield's estimate, and approved the completion of new Orange (Japan) and Red (Britain) war plans. Work also began on a Red-Orange Plan, the case of a two-ocean naval conflict. In Schofield's words, the United States needed to be prepared "for a strategic offensive in the Pacific and a strategic defensive in the Atlantic." While Schofield may have been overly wary of the British, he represented the view of those in the Navy who felt that Great Britain could still be an enemy.[116]

That was all the more reason to bring the "treaty fleet" to full strength. To Presidents Coolidge and Hoover, Hughes therefore argued for more ships and the sailors to man them to provide a balanced fleet. This was especially true in regard to cruisers, which had caused such trouble for the negotiators in 1927 at Geneva. Secretary Wilbur had already called for the completion of the cruisers authorized in 1924, and he asked the General Board to prepare a five year building program. The main element of the program was a batch of just over two dozen 10,000 ton 8-inch-gunned cruisers, plus new battleship construction in 1931, five small aircraft carriers, numerous destroyers and submarines, and a floating dry dock. The number of cruisers was impressive, but less than that called for by OPNAV's WPD and lower than Naval War College estimates that were based on its war games. President Coolidge approved much of the program, striking only new battleship construction, most of the destroyers, and the floating dry dock. Would Congress go along?[117]

Hughes went to the House Naval Affairs Committee in January 1928 and stated simply that he wanted ships for the Navy and that he relied on Congress to provide them. While some in Congress were impressed by his presentation, the committee only funded 15 cruisers to be laid down over three years, and one small (13,500 ton) carrier. The bill, which became known as "the Cruiser Bill," then stalled in the Senate. News of an Anglo-French agreement that any new naval limitation should be only on the 8-inch gun cruisers and long-range submarines, both of which the Navy wanted, spurred new activity. Even Secretary of State Frank B. Kellogg supported the passage of the bill as the best response to the British. The Senate passed the bill in early 1929; this was the zenith of Hughes's term as CNO.[118]

Figure 3-3. Admiral Charles F. Hughes commanded the U.S. Fleet when he was chosen as the fourth CNO. An intensely hard worker, Hughes nearly worked himself to death as CNO, suffering a stroke in February 1930 that led him to retire after 46 years of service to the Navy. (NHHC Archives NH 49933)

A solid battleship man, Hughes requested funds to complete the modernization of the commissioned battleships carrying 14-inch guns, but he also supported the completion of BuAer's 1,000 plane program. The Navy finally commissioned the large carriers *Lexington* and *Saratoga* in late 1927 and aviation went to sea on a large scale as the two carriers exercised with their air groups in 1928. Fleet Problem IX, in January 1929, demonstrated the capabilities of these large, fast carriers and their aircraft when *Saratoga* and a single escort avoided detection by opposition forces, including the Army Air Service, and successfully "attacked" the Panama Canal. Manning, however, remained a challenge, and as more ships and aircraft entered service, and personnel numbers remained stagnant, effectiveness suffered. In his 1929 report, Hughes's concerns about the lack of enlisted personnel was the first item discussed. A small increase (500 men) was authorized for fiscal 1930, despite the fact that 2,655 men were required for the new ships commissioning in the same fiscal year.[119]

Despite the concerns of CNO Hughes and the members of the General Board, the treaty negotiations in London produced an agreement. United States, British, and Japanese representatives signed the London Naval Treaty on 22 April 1930. The United States agreed to build fewer "treaty" cruisers and accepted building additional 6-inch gun cruisers. This was possible because very recent simulations at the Naval War College had suggested that 10,000-ton cruisers armed with 12 of a new-model 6-inch gun could actually defeat the older cruisers armed with 8-inch guns. The treaty also extended the battleship building holiday by five years, set a "treaty" ratio on the tonnage of cruisers and destroyers, continued the tonnage limits for carriers from the Washington Treaty, and limited the size of destroyers and submarines. Hughes' Senate testimony during the ratification process was restrained, but clearly showed his opposition to the treaty. Hughes' views were representative of most Navy officers, but it was of no avail. The Senate ratified the London Treaty in July 1930.[120]

The Navy was tasting the bitter consequences of the "treaty system." It was not just that successive presidents and Congresses had favored restrictions on the Navy's strength. It was that the "treaty system" put the power to set the Navy's planning agenda into the hands of political leaders who were more concerned about constraining the Navy's size and cost than about preserving it in sufficient strength to deter the Japanese. Setting the agenda is one way to control the actions of an organization. The "treaty system" derailed the ability of the Secretary of the Navy and the CNO to set the Navy's basic agenda.

Conclusion

Under CNOs Coontz and Eberle, the Navy had matured its planning process. The WPD in OPNAV wrote the Basic Plan. Every other organizational element in the Navy added contributory plans. The plans themselves were tested on the game boards of the Naval War College and in the fleet problems at sea. The conduct of the war games was the product of exchanges between OPNAV's WPD and the CINCUS staff. The war games and simulations conducted at the War College drew on information provided by the bureaus and were shaped by what had been learned in previous fleet exercises. In turn, the war games provided scenarios to the planners of the fleet problems, and the experiences of the fleet were provided to the General Board. In today's terms, this planning process had a "feedback loop" between the plans and the war games and fleet problems that tested them.

OPNAV's influence in the Navy was a consequence of its coordination and review of plans. Yet OPNAV staff and the CNO did not do everything. For example, the General Board shaped ship design, doing so with an eye toward the requirements generated by the fleet problems. The bureaus provided information about technological developments to the War College, to the Secretary of the Navy, to the General Board, and to OPNAV. Rear Admiral Moffett, BuAer's first chief, was an aggressive, audacious leader, claiming broad authority for his bureau and, with the aid of officers such as Rear Admiral Reeves, moving ahead steadily in the development of aviation at sea. The CNO's job was to keep this collection of organizations and professional officers in balance.

Unfortunately, the "treaty system" was not structured like the Navy planning process. It did indeed involve a great deal of negotiation within the U.S. government. But it was ultimately a process that had to respond to the direction of the President. To a great degree, the process of treaty negotiation distracted and perturbed the Navy's internal planning process. In addition, the CNO's influence in the "treaty system" depended on his willingness to influence the President, and the most obvious way to build a relationship to the President was by adopting the President's goals. Only then could a CNO use his "political" skill to try to shape the President's point of view. But if the CNO was perceived as "political" by his Navy peers on the General Board or in the fleets and forces at sea, then his influence within the uniformed Navy declined.

Is it any wonder that both Eberle and Hughes were ill at the end of their terms? From the times both officers became CNO, they fought rearguard actions against those members of Congress and two presidents who were committed to naval arms limitation (in the case of President Coolidge) and, in President Hoover's case, actual naval disarmament. The strife over the Geneva and London conferences distracted the attention of many senior officials from the what really mattered within the Navy—whether the Navy's personnel were learning what they needed to learn to keep the Navy trained, up-to-date technologically, and tactically proficient.

CNOs Coontz and Eberle had been creative in promoting the fleet problems. That's where so much of what mattered for the Navy took place. For example, the early problems had made clear the need for a mobile base that the fleet could take with it during any trans-Pacific campaign against the Imperial Japanese Navy. By 1926, the "Estimate of the Situation" for fiscal year 1928 noted that "the Naval Transportation Service will become a large command in war, second only in size to the U.S. Fleet. The success of an Orange War will largely rest on the early mobilization and efficient operation of such a service."[121] Thus did the inferences drawn from war games and the fleet problems lead senior officers to a detailed appreciation of the critical role that auxiliaries (such as submarine tenders) and merchant ships would play in war. Congress and President Hoover would not respond to this appreciation, but the evidence of the need was clear enough, and it would eventually stimulate a future President (and a future Congress) to act. Much of this understanding was confidential. In the case of naval aviation, to take another case, not everyone understood how it was rapidly improving. But arms control advocates were vociferously opposed to any development that they considered added to the Navy's offensive capability. They wanted a "defensive" Navy. What this meant was that CNOs Eberle and Hughes had to serve as buffers, shielding the Navy from what they considered harm while trying as best they could to participate in a political and diplomatic process where they did not set the agenda. As one historian put it, the CNOs and the OPNAV staff in this period had to fight extraordinary political and bureaucratic battles in order to protect the service from "the ravages of peace."[122]

Notes

[1] Gerald E. Wheeler, "Edwin Denby," in *American Secretaries of the Navy, Vol. II 1913–1972*, ed. by Paolo E. Coletta (Annapolis, MD: Naval Institute Press, 1980), 587.

[2] Thomas C. Hone, "Navy Air Leadership: Rear Admiral William A. Moffett as Chief of the Bureau of Aeronautics," in *Air Leadership*, ed. by Wayne Thompson (Washington, DC: GPO, 1986), 83.

[3] Ibid., 84.

[4] Wheeler, "Edwin Denby," in Coletta, *American Secretaries of the Navy, Vol. II*, 587.

[5] Adam Tooze, *The Deluge: The Great War, America and the Remaking of the Global Order, 1916-1931* (New York: Viking Press, 2014), 342–47. In the first nine months of 1919, the cost of living in the United States surged, wiping out the real value of wage increases gained by salaried workers during the war. The Federal Reserve responded by increasing interest rates. The intent was to dampen inflationary pressures by soaking up as much of the available money as possible. Unfortunately, as Tooze pointed out, "The abrupt tightening of credit tipped the American economy over a cliff." (345). The result was a severe recession.

[6] RADM Robert E. Coontz, USN (Ret.), *From the Mississippi to the Sea* (Philadelphia, PA: Dorrance and Co., 1930), 399. As Coontz pointed out in his memoir, he took the oath of office as CNO on 1 November 1919, but he was not awarded the permanent rank of rear admiral until

4 November 1919. His promotion, however, was backdated to 25 September 1919, and so he was formally a rear admiral when appointed CNO.

[7] Lawrence H. Douglas "Robert Edward Coontz," in Love, *The Chiefs of Naval Operations*, 27.

[8] Ibid., RADM Rodgers, the retired former Paymaster General of the Navy had been recalled to active duty; Newberry had served as the Assistant Secretary of the Navy, 1905–1908, and then Secretary of the Navy 1908–1909.

[9] Coontz, *From the Mississippi to the Sea*, 400.

[10] Ibid.

[11] Ibid.

[12] When Sims completed his tour in Europe and returned to the War College, his rank reverted to two stars; rank was based on the billet filled, so three- and four-star admirals often reverted to two stars prior to retirement.

[13] Morison, *Naval Administration, Selected Documents on Navy Department Organization, 1915–1940*, III-A-2.

[14] Ibid.

[15] Paolo E. Coletta, "Josephus Daniels," in Coletta, *American Secretaries of the Navy, Vol. II*, 566–67.

[16] Ibid., 567. The transcript of the testimony of the witnesses called by the subcommittee is in *Naval Investigation*.

[17] Morison, *Naval Administration, Selected Documents on Navy Department Organization, 1915–1940*, III-A-12.

[18] Ibid., III-A-3.

[19] Coletta "Josephus Daniels" in Coletta, *American Secretaries of the Navy, Vol. II*, 569.

[20] Morison, *Naval Administration, Selected Documents on Navy Department Organization, 1915–1940*, III-A-36.

[21] The final 10 pages of the Daniels report is an overview of the organization of the Navy, and he again emphasizes the importance of true civilian control, and specifically cites the Senate hearings from the winter and spring of 1921 as a thinly veiled attempt by certain naval officers to remove effective civilian control. Further, he includes extracts from his Senate testimony as an appendix to the report which is even more direct in criticizing those who would remove effective civilian control. *Annual Reports of the Navy Department 1920: Report of the Secretary of the Navy* (Washington, DC: Government Printing Office [hereafter, GPO], 1921), 198–210, 348–80. As to the size of the staff, in December 1920, OPNAV consisted of 151 officers (active, retired, reservists, and temporary), including the staff at the Naval War College and the attachés in ONI assigned overseas. The Planning Division included 21 officers. See *Navy Directory: Officers of the United States Navy and Marine Corps 1 Dec. 1920* (Washington, DC: GPO, 1920), 186–87.

[22] Coontz, *From the Mississippi to the Sea*, 400.

[23] *Hearings of the General Board of the Navy*, 5 Mar. 1919, "Development of Naval Aviation," 160, microfilm roll 4, RG 80, NARA.

[24] Ibid., 177.

[25] *Hearings of the General Board of the Navy*, 27 Mar. 1919, "Development of Naval Aviation Policy," 371, microfilm roll 4, RG 80, NARA.

[26] *Hearings of the General Board of the Navy*, 12 May 1919, "Naval Aviation Policy—Fleet Aviation," 930, microfilm roll 4, RG 80, NARA. The captain of *Texas* was Captain Nathan C. Twining, who in 1920 was a rear admiral and chief of staff to the commander of the Pacific Fleet.

[27] Memo, the General Board to the Secretary of the Navy, subj: "Future Policy Governing Development of Air Service for the United States Navy," paragraphs (a) and (g). General Board No. 449, Serial 887, 23 June 1919, RG 80.7.3, NARA.

[28] Thomas Hone and Mark Mandeles, "Interwar Innovation in Three Navies: USN, RN, IJN," *Naval War College Review*, vol. 40, no. 2 (Spring 1987), 63–83.

[29] CAPT Frank H. Schofield, USN, "The General Board and the Building Program," a lecture given to the students of the Navy's Postgraduate School at the U.S. Naval Academy, 14 Oct. 1922 (2711-23/X/22), 13, File UNC, 1922–171, NWC Archives.

[30] Ibid., 1.

[31] For details and examples, see *Agents of Innovation, The General Board and the Design of the Fleet that Defeated the Japanese Navy*, by John T. Kuehn (Annapolis, MD: Naval Institute Press, 2008).

[32] CAPT Frank H. Schofield, USN, "The General Board and the Building Program," 3.

[33] Memo, E. W. Eberle, Chief of Naval Operations, to Basic War Plans Distribution List, subj: War Plans, (SC 198-1:2/1), 29 December 1923, with accompanying paper, "A discussion of the War Plans, U.S. Navy and the Cooperation and Coordination necessary for their preparation," 3, Fleet Training Division, General Correspondence, 1914–1941, Box 21, Folder 484-72, RG 38, NARA.

[34] Ibid., 4.

[35] Ibid., 10.

[36] Ibid., 11–12.

[37] Ibid., 3.

[38] Miller, *War Plan Orange*, 82.

[39] Ibid., 114–15.

[40] Ibid., 83.

[41] "A discussion of the War Plans, U.S. Navy and the Cooperation and Coordination necessary for their preparation," 17.

[42] Ibid., 18.

[43] See Alfred F. Hurley, *Billy Mitchell: Crusader for Air Power* (Bloomington, IN: Indiana University Press, 2006, but the book was published originally in 1964), and Hone, "Navy Air Leadership: Rear Admiral William A. Moffett as Chief of the Bureau of Aeronautics," in Thompson, *Air Leadership*, 83–117.

[44] VADM Alfred W. Johnson, USN (Ret.), *The Naval Bombing Experiments Off the Virginia Capes, June and July 1921: Their Technological and Psychological Aspects* (Washington, DC: Naval Historical Foundation, 1959). Electronic copy at https://www.history.navy.mil/research/library/online-reading-room/title-list-alphabetically/n/the-naval-bombing-experiments.html.

[45] See Hone, "Navy Air Leadership: Rear Admiral William A. Moffett as Chief of the Bureau of Aeronautics," in Thompson, *Air Leadership*.

[46] Thomas C. Hone, Norman Friedman, and Mark D. Mandeles, *American & British Aircraft Carrier Development, 1919–1941* (Annapolis, MD: Naval Institute Press, 1999), 29.

[47] Ibid., 30.

[48] Soon after the war, mid-career officers with destroyer experience opened a "Destroyer Staff College" in the naval base at Charleston, SC to distill lessons of the war. Collection 8, Series 1, Box 55, Folder 1, UNT, Staff College, 1915–1920, Destroyer Force, Atlantic, NWC Archives.

[49] Braisted, *The United States Navy in the Pacific, 1909–1922*, 472–78.

[50] Ltr, Chief of Naval Operations to All Bureaus, Offices, and Stations concerned, subj: "Current Operating Force Plan and Replacement Plan," 24 Sept. 1921, World War II Command File, Naval Historical Center (NHC), Box 213, folder "Operating Force Plans, Fiscal Year 1922;" NHC transferred this collection to NARA, and is now in Record Group 38.2.4 "Records relating to U.S. Navy operations received from the Operational Archives Branch, Naval Historical Center."

[51] Braisted, *The United States Navy in the Pacific, 1909–1922*, 459–60.

[52] Orange was the color assigned to Japan. See Miller's *War Plan Orange* for the best discussion on this topic.

[53] Thomas C. Hone and Trent Hone, *Battle Line: The United States Navy 1919–1939*, (Annapolis, MD: Naval Institute Press, 2006), 177–178; George W. Baer, *One Hundred Years of Sea Power: The U.S. Navy, 1890–1990*, (Stanford, CA: Stanford University Press, 1994), 92.

[54] As Professor Donald Chisholm of the Naval War College noted in a comment to the authors, the Budget and Accounting Act of 1921 was "a huge innovation that radically altered budgetary processes" by forcing the heads of executive branch departments to submit their budget proposals to the President for review before those proposals went to the Appropriations

Committee of the House of Representatives. The law therefore made possible "the first genuine national annual budget."

[55] Douglas, "Robert Edward Coontz," in Love, *The Chiefs of Naval Operations*, 29. See also, Robert G. Albion, *Makers of Naval Policy, 1798–1947*, ed. by Rowena Reed (Annapolis, MD: Naval Institute Press, 1980), 175. Also, Coontz, *From the Mississippi to the Sea*, 410.

[56] Coontz appears to have worked budget issues without any specifically detailed staff until the summer of 1922 when a "Budget Section" (a captain and a commander) was created. See *Navy Directory*, 1 Sept. 1922. See also *Annual Reports of the Navy Department 1921*, "Appendix A, Office of the Chief of Naval Operations" (Washington, DC: GPO, 1921), 23.

[57] CAPT Richard C. Knott, USN, *The American Flying Boat: An Illustrated History* (Annapolis, MD: Naval Institute Press, 1979), 76.

[58] *Annual Reports of the Navy Department 1922: Appendix A: Office of the Chief of Naval Operations* (Washington, DC: GPO, 1923), 39.

[59] Ibid.

[60] Coontz, *From the Mississippi to the Sea*, 408–409, Henry P. Beers, "The Development of the Office of the Chief Of Naval Operations, Part IV," *Military Affairs*, vol. 11, no. 4 (Winter, 1947), 230–31; Roy Grossnick, *United States Naval Aviation, 1910–1995*, (Washington, DC: Naval Historical Center, 1996), 49–50.

[61] Hone, "Navy Air Leadership: Rear Admiral William A. Moffett as Chief of the Bureau of Aeronautics," in Thompson, *Air Leadership*, 92–94.

[62] Ltr, RADM W. A. Moffett to RADM W. S. Sims, 28 Feb. 1922, William Adger Moffett Collection, MS 234 Special Collections and Archives Department, Nimitz Library, U.S. Naval Academy.

[63] Baer, *One Hundred Years of Sea Power*, 95–96.

[64] Wheeler, "Edwin Denby," in Coletta, *American Secretaries of the Navy, Vol. II*, 585.

[65] Ibid.

[66] Braisted, *The United States Navy in the Pacific, 1909–1922*, 589–91.

[67] Wheeler, "Edwin Denby," in Coletta, *American Secretaries of the Navy, Vol. II*, 586.

[68] Kuehn, *Agents of Innovation*, 181–97; https://history.state.gov/milestones/1921-1936/naval-conference.

[69] Kuehn, *Agents of Innovation*, 28–29; Baer, *One Hundred Years of Sea Power*, 101–102.

[70] *Annual Reports of the Navy Department 1922: Appendix A: Office of the Chief of Naval Operations* (Washington, DC: GPO, 1923), 40.

[71] Coontz, *From the Mississippi to the Sea*, 413–14; Douglas, "Robert Edward Coontz", *The Chiefs of Naval Operations*, 30.

[72] See "A Treaty Between the United States of America, The British Empire, France, Italy, and Japan, Limiting Naval Armament," Conference on the Limitation of Armament, Senate,

67th Cong., 2nd sess., Document No. 126 (Washington, DC: GPO, 1922), 871–87; Kuehn, *Agents of Innovation*, 2–3; Coontz, *From the Mississippi to the Sea*, 413–14. Also see Miller's *War Plan Orange* and Braisted's *The United States Navy in the Pacific, 1909–1922*.

[73] Department of the Navy, General Order 94 "Organization of Naval Forces." 6 Dec. 1922, Navy Department Library.

[74] Hone and Hone, *Battle Line*, 6.

[75] "Report of the Chief of the Bureau of Navigation," Appendix B of the *Annual Reports of the Navy Department 1921* (Washington, DC: GPO, 1921), 24.

[76] Chisholm, *Waiting for Dead Men's Shoes*, 605–606.

[77] Ibid., 635. See also the "Report of the Chief of the Bureau of Navigation," in *Annual Reports of the Navy Department 1925* (Washington, DC: GPO, 1925), 8.

[78] Chisholm, *Waiting for Dead Men's Shoes*, 646.

[79] Douglas, "Coontz", in Love, *The Chiefs of Naval Operations*, 31, 35; Coontz, *From the Mississippi to the Sea*, 416–19.

[80] *Annual Reports of the Navy Department 1923: Report of the Chief of Naval Operations* 121; Beers, "The Development of the Office of the Chief Of Naval Operations," Part IV, 233. The three budget officers who became fleet commanders were Claude C. Bloch, James O. Richardson, and Husband E. Kimmel.

[81] Richard W. Turk, "Edward Walter Eberle," in Love, *The Chiefs of Naval Operations*, 38.

[82] Ibid., 39.

[83] Ibid., 40.

[84] *Annual Reports of the Navy Department 1923: Appendix C: The Gun-Elevation Question* (Washington, DC: GPO, 1924), 114–17.

[85] Trent Hone, "The Evolution of Fleet Tactical Doctrine in the U.S. Navy, 1922–1941," *Journal of Military History* 67 (Oct. 2003), 1117.

[86] Kuehn, *Agents of Innovation*, 98–99; *Annual Reports of the Navy Department 1925: Report of the Chief of Naval Operations* (Washington, DC: GPO, 1926), 85.

[87] Baer, *One Hundred Years of Sea Power*, 40–41; *Annual Reports of the Navy Department 1925: Report of the Chief of Naval Operations* (Washington, DC: GPO, 1926), 85. In these reports, the 10,000-ton ships are referred to as light cruisers, which caused some confusion because the cruisers with 6-inch guns were also called "light cruisers."

[88] Turk, "Eberle," in Love, *The Chiefs of Naval Operations*, 44; *Annual Reports of the Navy Department 1925: Report of the Chief of Naval Operations*, 92–93; *Annual Reports of the Navy Department 1926: Report of the Chief of Naval Operations* (Washington, DC: GPO, 1927), 63, 83; *Annual Reports of the Navy Department 1927: Report of the Chief of Naval Operations* (Washington, DC: GPO, 1928), 92–93.

[89] Hone, "Navy Air Leadership: Rear Admiral William A. Moffett as Chief of the Bureau of Aeronautics," in Thompson, *Air Leadership*, 97–98.

[90] Ibid.

[91] William F. Trimble, *Admiral William A. Moffett: Architect of Naval Aviation* (Washington, DC: Smithsonian Institution Press, 1994), 142–44.

[92] Turk, "Eberle," in Love, *The Chiefs of Naval Operations*, 40–41.

[93] Hone, "Navy Air Leadership: Rear Admiral William A. Moffett as Chief of the Bureau of Aeronautics," in Thompson, *Air Leadership*, 99.

[94] See Chisholm, *Waiting for Dead Men's Shoes*, ch. 25, for a detailed discussion of the Morrow Board's deliberations.

[95] Hone, "Navy Air Leadership: Rear Admiral William A. Moffett as Chief of the Bureau of Aeronautics," in Thompson, *Air Leadership*, 99.

[96] Hone, Friedman, and Mandeles, *American & British Aircraft Carrier Development*, 46–47. British carrier planes were usually multipurpose designs that had severe limitations when used as fighters.

[97] Hone, "Navy Air Leadership: Rear Admiral William A. Moffett as Chief of the Bureau of Aeronautics," in Thompson, *Air Leadership*, 101.

[98] Hone, Friedman, and Mandeles, *American & British Aircraft Carrier Development, 1919–1941*, 41–45.

[99] Albert A. Nofi, *To Train the Fleet for War, The U.S. Navy Fleet Problems, 1923–1940*, Naval War College Historical Monograph Series No. 18 (Washington, DC: GPO, 2010), 20.

[100] Ibid., 21. See also, "Report of United States Fleet Problem, Number One," February 1923, Collection 8, Series 1, Box 55, Folder 2, NWC Archives. That report noted that the actual statements of the problem given to the commanders of the opposing forces were written by CDR (later VADM) Adolphus Andrews, who worked with the Naval War College staff.

[101] There was also, at times, cooperation between the Naval War College and the Army War College in the making and running of war games. See the correspondence between RADM J. R. P. Pringle, Naval War College President, and MGEN W. D. Connor, Army War College Commandant, in File UNT, "1928–29, Naval War College," Collection 8, Series 1, Box 59, Folder 4, NWC Archives.

[102] Miller, *War Plan Orange*, 135.

[103] "Budget 1926, Estimate of the Situation and Base Development Program," Office of the Secretary of the Navy, Confidential Correspondence, 1927–1939, File L1-1, "Annual Estimates of the Chief of Naval Operations," RG 80, NARA, 28.

[104] Eberle as quoted by Miller in *War Plan Orange*, 135.

[105] Amity Shlaes, *Coolidge* (New York: HarperCollins, 2013), 265–66.

106 Baer, *One Hundred Years of Sea Power,* 109–10.

107 Turk, "Eberle," in Love, *The Chiefs of Naval Operations,* 44–45.

108 Shlaes, *Coolidge,* 349.

109 Roger K. Heller, "Curtis Dwight Wilbur," in Coletta, *American Secretaries of the Navy, Vol. II,* 616.

110 Turk, "Eberle," in Love, *The Chiefs of Naval Operations,* 46.

111 William R. Braisted," Charles Frederick Hughes," in Love, *The Chiefs of Naval Operations,* 49–50.

112 Ibid., 53.

113 Ibid., 62.

114 Ibid., 63.

115 Ibid., 54.

116 Ibid, 54–55; Baer, *One Hundred Years of Sea Power,* 111.

117 Braisted, "Hughes," in Love, *The Chiefs of Naval Operations,* 56.

118 Ibid., 58.

119 Ibid., 58–60; see also *Annual Reports of the Navy Department 1928: Report of the Chief of Naval Operations* (Washington, DC: GPO, 1929), 21–28; *Annual Reports of the Navy Department 1929: Report of the Chief of Naval Operations* (Washington, DC: GPO, 1929), 79. For Fleet Problem IX, see Nofi, *To Train the Fleet for War: The U.S. Navy Fleet Problems,* ch. X.

120 Hone and Hone, *Battle Line,* 9; https://history.state.gov/milestones/1921-1936/london-naval-conf.

121 "Budget 1928, Estimate of the Situation and Base Development Program," RG 80, Office of the Secretary of the Navy, Confidential Correspondence, 1927–1939, File L1-1, 30, NARA.

122 Braisted, "Hughes," in Love, *The Chiefs of Naval Operations,* 66.

CHAPTER 4

The Thirties: From the "Treaty System" to Mobilization

Introduction

The appointment of Admiral William V. Pratt as CNO on 17 September 1930 brought an advocate of arms control and of cooperation among the major navies to the Navy's most senior post. Admiral Pratt's career prior to his appointment had covered the key events in OPNAV's history, from the debates between Admiral Sims and Secretary Daniels over the proper form of civilian control of the Navy to the resistance of the General Board to the naval arms control treaties. Pratt's predecessors had created an effective staff process that was guided by the restrictions of the Washington Treaty, the requirements of War Plan Orange, and the inferences drawn from the fleet problems. By 1930, OPNAV had become a mature organization that linked the operations of the fleet with policies worked out by the President and the Congress.

The Navy was fortunate that OPNAV had matured because the decade of the 1930s would be full of challenges. The first was shaping the Navy for what was called "the treaty system." Was that "system" a way of limiting naval arms competition and thereby saving the resources of the nations with large navies while reducing tensions among them? Or was it the first step along a road to military disarmament? Or was it just an empty dream? The second challenge was dealing with continuous technological advances in fields such as naval aviation. Could the U.S. Navy exploit these advances with limited financial resources? The third challenge was whether the Navy could find ways to make the Orange Plan more than a concept on paper. Could the fleet actually defeat its Japanese counterpart in the waters around the Philippines in the event of war? Finally, could the Navy survive the economic consequences of the Great Depression?

The decade began with CNO Pratt; the "treaty system" was to some degree his creation. Under Pratt and his successor, Admiral William H. Standley, the "treaty system" would first be followed and then abandoned. Under CNO Standley's successors, Admirals William D. Leahy and Harold R. Stark, the Navy built to and then beyond the limits set by the Washington and London naval treaties. In addition, during Stark's tenure, the Navy also began mobilizing for war. Through this decade of challenges and change, the OPNAV staff supported the chiefs of naval operations and worked effectively with the other elements of the Navy that participated in making and implementing Navy policy, including the General Board and the Navy's bureaus.

CNO Pratt and the "Treaty System"

Historian Robert G. Albion described Admiral Pratt as "the most influential naval professional policymaker throughout the Hoover administration."[1] As well he might have been, given his prior service in OPNAV as Assistant Chief of Naval Operations under the first CNO, William S. Benson. A protégé of Rear Admiral Sims, Pratt wanted to accompany Sims to London in 1917. Instead, he was detailed to Washington. He "escaped" from OPNAV in January 1919 to command battleship *New York* (Battleship No. 34), left her to lead the Pacific Fleet's destroyer squadrons, played an important role in the naval limitation negotiations in Washington in 1921–1922, rejoined the fleet as an admiral and battleship division commander, then served as President of the Naval War College on the way to higher operational commands, culminating in his appointment as CINCUS in 1929. Along the way, his papers defending the efforts to limit naval arms competition through the use of negotiated treaties were published in various journals.[2] Pratt's views on arms control were no secret. Though an experienced and skilled naval professional, the admiral was also a diplomat, strategic thinker, and thoughtful essayist.

He was also courageous. In an essay he wrote as CNO, published in the *Proceedings* of the U.S. Naval Institute in July 1932, CNO Pratt argued that the key to an effective peacetime Navy was the development of a "clean-cut, definite naval policy."[3] As he observed, once the Washington naval treaty had been approved, "the General Board of the Navy set out to formulate a naval policy which would be adequate for our needs." Secretary of the Navy Denby had approved the board's draft on 1 December 1922. The policy statement was revised in 1928 and approved by then Secretary Wilbur. A third revision was approved by Secretary Charles F. Adams on 1 June 1931. Pratt succinctly condensed that policy as follows: "The Navy should be maintained in sufficient strength to support the national policies and commerce and to guard the continental and over-seas possessions of the United States."[4] To Pratt, that also meant adhering to the limits set by the Washington and London naval treaties. This was not the position of President Herbert C. Hoover, however, and Pratt was risking his own standing with the President by not agreeing with Hoover in public.

Pratt knew that, with a clear naval policy in place, it was possible to take the next step and determine the size and fighting strength of the Navy. As Pratt noted, a clear naval policy would allow the President and Congress to craft "a steady, orderly program stretching over a term of years and based on the laying down of new craft as the old reach the end of their lives of usefulness." A long-term program "should bring economy and efficiency."[5] These words should be read as Pratt meant them to be read—as a reminder to President Hoover that there was more to the "treaty system" than an effort to forestall a naval arms race. The "treaty system" was not just a means to implement a strategy of achieving international stability through widespread arms reductions. It was also a guide to a naval program. The treaties told the governments that signed them what to build and when, allowing, as Pratt put it, "the country, the Navy, and Congress [to] know what to expect."

By the time Pratt's essay was published in 1932, the admiral had already spent almost two years serving a President who did not accept the logic of his argument about a treaty-driven naval policy. In April 1929, Herbert M. Lord, whom former President Coolidge had appointed Director of the Bureau of the Budget, had warned recently inaugurated President Hoover that building the Navy to the levels permitted by the Washington treaty would be very costly. Over 12 years, the Navy would need to build new battleships, aircraft carriers, destroyers, and submarines, and it would obviously need to maintain these ships and provide for their crews. Lord summed up his assessment of these likely costs by saying that "it appears that the program sponsored by the Navy Department, commencing with the fiscal year 1932 and continuing for at least ten years, would, if approved, involve an annual expenditure of between $450,000,000 and $500,000,000."[6] This was significantly more than Hoover was willing to accept; he was thinking of a total annual cost of the Navy coming in under $350,000,000. As historian Gerald Wheeler documented, the President decided that "The Navy could not be allowed to carry out its plans" and proceeded to both reduce naval expenditures and arrange another naval arms limitation conference—in London this time, starting in January 1930.

Admiral Pratt, serving as the fleet's commander through 1929, went to London in January 1930 as a member of the American delegation to the conference. Pratt's actions in London, based on his confidence in the value of the "treaty system," embittered the CNO, Admiral Hughes. Hughes and the members of the General Board were effectively cut out of the negotiations in London, and Hughes did not give Pratt a warm welcome on the latter's return.[7] However, President Hoover and British Prime Minister MacDonald were satisfied with the treaty that was signed on 22 April 1930. Among other limits, the new agreement held off any new battleship construction until 1936, settled the dispute over cruiser size and armament that had torpedoed the conference in Geneva in 1927, and limited the displacements of new destroyers and submarines.[8] The delegations also agreed to meet in London again in 1935.

However, if Pratt thought that the London treaty would smooth his relations with President Hoover when he became CNO, Pratt was to be very disappointed. As we pointed out in the previous chapter, Hoover was more interested in disarmament than in arms reduction. The worsening economic contraction in 1930 made the President even more opposed to building the Navy to "treaty strength."[9] Yet if the United States did not build new ships to "treaty limits" and recruit and train sailors to man those ships, Japan and Great Britain would. Pratt was apparently unable to convince Hoover of the logic of the "treaty system," which required the three major navies to build to the levels set by the treaties. If one or two navies did not build to those levels, then the stability that was supposed to follow from the treaties would be threatened. Put another way, Hoover's insistence on restricting spending on the U.S. Navy actually endangered the "treaty system," undermining the stability that the "system" was intended to encourage.

Pratt tried another tack with the President, and he explained what that was in his July 1932 article in *Proceedings*. Pratt first acknowledged that, "To the average mind, the naval establishment is regarded as all overhead, and frequently as unnecessary overhead, particularly in hard times." He also admitted that it was "difficult to reduce the standing expenses [of the Navy] during the times of financial depression when available money is scarce, the country at large is on short rations, and when budgets are extremely hard to balance."[10] However, "If the total annual charge against the Navy is less than the minimum interest charge on the capital investment it takes to finance a war, and the Navy through the protection given, either keeps a country out of war or helps bring success if it is forced into war, then the yearly sum it takes to run a navy would seem to be a good investment in the matter of national insurance." Pratt then proceeded to show that such was indeed the case, using numbers from World War I.[11] Hoover was not moved, but two important members of Congress were—Republican Senator Frederick Hale of Maine and Democratic Representative Carl Vinson of Georgia, the Chairman of the House Naval Affairs Committee. Both introduced legislation in 1932 to authorize the construction of ships allowed the United States by the London treaty.[12]

Admiral Pratt and President Hoover respected one another. Though it was obvious that the two men disagreed about the implications of the "treaty system," Pratt was careful to respect the President's authority. He did not question civilian control of the Navy and maintained a good working relationship with Secretary of the Navy Adams. In his biography of Pratt, historian Wheeler compared Pratt favorably with Army Chief of Staff General Douglas MacArthur.[13] For example, MacArthur used the press and public relations to influence political leaders. Pratt did not. MacArthur was a national public figure and wanted to be. Pratt deliberately avoided that sort of notoriety. Wheeler put it this way: "By a consistent display of loyalty to the President's programs, and a demonstrated willingness to meet Congress's desires where reasonable, the admiral built up a reputation for honesty and common sense . . ." Unfortunately, Pratt's ability to work with Hoover and his regard for the President did not change Hoover's basic position. Pratt's "support and defense of the London Treaty was premised on the assumption that President Hoover and Congress would build the fleet to ratio strength," but Pratt's "acceptance of cuts in 1930 simply led to further reductions in 1931, 1932, and 1933."[14] As CNO, Pratt confronted a President who rejected the logic of the "treaty system." It would be up to the next President and the next CNO to adopt that logic and implement it.

Sustaining American Naval Power

As CNO, Pratt was responsible for assisting SECNAV Adams in drawing up and defending the Navy's annual budget. The budget estimates from Pratt's time as CNO were mostly not happy ones. For example, in December 1924 Congress had authorized the construction of eight "heavy" cruisers; five had been commissioned by the time Pratt became CNO.[15] In February 1929, Congress had authorized five more (in addition to the eight then built or building). However, President Hoover had suspended work on three of the five "pending the outcome" of the London conference.[16] This was an understandable move on the President's part. What if the conferees meeting in London decided to end the construction of "heavy" cruisers altogether? However, not having enough heavy cruisers—or even more modern "light" cruisers—was made worse by the shortage of modern submarines and destroyers. The battle fleet was supposed to be a whole and balanced force. If one part were lacking in strength or firepower, then the whole fleet could suffer. That was why OPNAV's War Plans Division judged the pending mass obsolescence of destroyers a "precarious" situation.[17]

Fortunately, Pratt inherited a relatively strong naval aviation program. Enough had already been learned through the annual fleet problems for the WPD to write that "In view of our existing inferiority in capital ship [i.e., battleship] tonnage, the reduced [gun] range of certain of our capital ships, and our lack of light cruisers, it should be our constant effort to maintain our present superiority in seaborne aviation, which, to a degree, can compensate . . ."[18] In addition, the five-year aircraft procurement program suggested by the Morrow Board in the fall of 1925 had been implemented by Congress in June 1926, and Pratt was advised by the war planners that "No recession should be made from the terms of the authorizing act which established this program, and every effort should be made to obtain the much needed expansion of it . . ."[19]

As CNO, Pratt worked to find ways to add to the fleet's strength while working within three major constraints—the limits on force structure set by the London treaty, President Hoover's policy regarding the Navy, and resistance to increasing the strength of the Navy among many members of Congress. As Norman Friedman noted in his detailed and thorough history of Navy cruiser designs, the CNO "presided over the development of four warship types intimately linked to the treaty provisions."[20] One type was a cruiser with a flight deck; it was a possible way of getting more aircraft into the fleet without using up scarce aircraft carrier tonnage. Another was a class of large 6-inch-gun cruisers. A third was a large gunboat armed with 6-inch guns that could fulfill some of the missions performed by regular cruisers without eating into the cruiser tonnage allowed by the London treaty. The fourth was a new type of large and fast "battle cruiser" that could escort fast aircraft carriers and hunt down Japanese cruisers raiding American "lines of communication" in the Pacific.

Only one of the proposed designs was a success. It was the large light cruiser. The hybrid cruiser-carrier turned out to be too small for the coming generations of larger, faster aircraft, but there was clearly a need for some way to augment the squadrons that flew from the existing carriers. Accordingly, BuAer, BuC&R, and the General Board studied the cruiser-carrier hybrid plus the potential of converting passenger liners and cargo ships into "ORANGE war" carriers. However, these studies did not lead to any ship production or conversions, and the escort carriers of World War II came about years later because of decisions made by Hoover's successor, Franklin D. Roosevelt.[21] The large gunboats were an effort on CNO Pratt's part to get numbers of smaller but heavily armed ships. So long as their displacement and the caliber of their guns were less than the limits set at the London conference, the United States government could build as many of them as it wished. Two of the large gunboats were indeed built, but they were not suited for service with the fleet.[22] Pratt's hope that numbers of them could compensate for the limited number of regular cruisers allowed the Navy by the London treaty was not realized.

The one successful design was a cruiser of 10,000 tons displacement armed with 6-inch guns. Pratt, like most of his colleagues, had initially favored the 10,000-ton cruiser armed with 8-inch guns. However, in the late 1920s BuOrd developed a new metric of protection for surface ships against gunfire. It was called the "immune zone." It was a range from an enemy ship within which a U.S. ship—whether destroyer, cruiser, or battleship—could survive the gunfire of a similarly armed opponent. The General Board adopted this new metric in 1929 as a way of comparing ship designs, and the Naval War College used it in its tactical simulations.[23] The War College simulations suggested that a large, well-protected cruiser with 12 to 15 6-inch guns could defeat an 8-inch-gun cruiser. For Pratt, that meant that the U.S. Navy could accept the limits on 8-inch-gun cruisers desired by the British navy and still provide the U.S. Fleet with enough cruisers for an "Orange" war.

Pratt's insight, which he and Secretary Adams carried to the London conference in January 1930, broke the deadlock with the British that had prevented an agreement about numbers and strengths of cruisers at Geneva in 1927. In his history of the "treaty system," British historian Stephen Roskill noted that "much of the credit" for the improvement in Anglo-American relations was due to Pratt, "whom members of the [Royal Navy's] Board of Admiralty soon began to like and to trust . . ."[24] But it was not just Pratt's confidence in the "treaty system" that smoothed his relations with his British counterparts. It was also his understanding of the implications of an analytic tool developed by the specialists in BuOrd and explained to Pratt and others through the mechanism of the confidential hearings before the General Board.

Pratt and Naval Administration

Soon after becoming CNO in September 1930, Pratt set up what was called a "Planning Section" to help him oversee OPNAV. According to an article in the *Army Navy Journal*, the section was "to handle routine and dispose of minor matters related to operations."[25] The article listed seven officers assigned to the section, including Rear Admiral Montgomery M. Taylor, the Director of the WPD and leader of the section; Captain Emory S. Land (Construction Corps), head of the Central Division in OPNAV; and Pratt's former flag lieutenant and flag secretary, both of whom had served with the admiral when he had held the post of fleet commander.[26] Rear Admiral John Halligan Jr., ordered to be Assistant CNO, met with the section once he reported. The article also mentioned a proposal to have each bureau detail an officer to this section. BuAer

The Thirties: From the "Treaty System" to Mobilization

had apparently already done so because aviator Lieutenant Commander Marc A. Mitscher, who had been working in BuAer's Plans Division, was one of the eight officers named.[27]

This ad hoc organization was, in the first months of Pratt's term as CNO, an "inner staff." It was an impressive group of officers. Rear Admiral Taylor had served in OPNAV in 1917, commanded the modern battleship *Florida* (Battleship No. 30) in 1918, served on the staff of the Naval War College from 1919 to 1921, headed the Fleet Training Division in OPNAV as a rear admiral from 1925 to 1927, commanded the Scouting Fleet with the rank of vice admiral, and headed the WPD of OPNAV from May 1929 to April 1931 as a rear admiral, when he left Washington to take command (as an admiral) of the Asiatic Fleet. Captain Land would be promoted to rear admiral and chief BuC&R in October 1932. Rear Admiral Halligan, who had commanded carrier *Saratoga* in 1928–1929, was a contemporary of Rear Admiral Moffett and had served as Commander Aircraft Squadrons, Scouting Fleet.[28] Lieutenant Commander Mitscher had been the executive officer of carrier *Langley* before joining the BuAer staff. Halligan, Land, and Mitscher were, like Pratt, advocates of naval aviation. Taylor was an advocate of better relations with Japan. Together, these officers and several others in this section could advise CNO Pratt on issues of policy and monitor the implementation of the London naval treaty.

Pratt also chose to change his relationship to the Navy's General Board. As CNO, Pratt was an *ex officio* member of the General Board. There were three other *ex officio* members: the Major General Commandant of the Marine Corps, the President of the Naval War College, and the Director of Naval Intelligence. Remember that the General Board worked for and reported directly to the Secretary of the Navy. Pratt believed that making the CNO "president" of the General Board was a mistake. In March 1932, the SECNAV approved a reorganization of the Board recommended by Pratt. All four *ex officio* members were formally removed, though they could and did appear before the General Board to offer their views. As *Navy Regulations* specified, the board would have "not less than five members who are line officers of the Navy, a majority of whom shall be of flag rank." A Marine general officer "may be designated as a member of the Board."[29] After his retirement, Pratt wrote in a letter to Representative Vinson that the Board was "the balance wheel of the Navy. It should be free to express an opinion, not tied." Pratt also argued that the CNO "likewise should be free. It cramps his style to be tied to the Board."[30]

Did Pratt give up an opportunity to influence the Navy by taking himself off the General Board? Not necessarily. Historian John Kuehn has argued that Pratt had it right when he referred to the General Board as the Navy's "balance wheel," a counter to the immediate concerns of both the CNO and the Secretary of the Navy.[31] Pratt did not believe in the value of centralized management of the Navy Department. He accepted the "ink blots" of separate and overlapping authority among OPNAV, the secretariat, the bureaus, the fleet, and the General Board. Pratt was confident that this was the correct way to operate and support the Navy. He was not afraid of disagreements among these sources of authority. As he said, the Navy secretary, the CNO, and the Chairman of the General Board "ought to be able to iron out any matters likely to come up either in peace or in war."[32]

However, Representative Vinson, who had introduced a bill to build up the Navy to treaty strength in January 1932 and was therefore a supporter of Pratt's force level policy, did not share Pratt's management philosophy. In June 1933, Vinson, still Chairman of the House Naval Affairs Committee, introduced a bill to reorganize OPNAV. "Vinson wanted to create, under the CNO, an Office of Naval Material to coordinate the activities of the . . . bureaus of Construction and Repair, Steam Engineering, Ordnance, and Aeronautics." Vinson also proposed to create in the Navy secretariat an office to "coordinate Navy strategic planning with the Army."[33] Vinson knew that CNO Pratt was about to be replaced by Admiral William H. Standley. Secretary Adams had also been replaced that March by Senator Claude A. Swanson (D-VA), an appointee of newly inaugurated President Franklin D. Roosevelt. Vinson apparently thought that the time was right to float a new reorganization proposal.

Vinson was also aware that in May 1933, Secretary Swanson had directed the new Assistant Secretary, Henry L. Roosevelt, to lead a study of the Navy Department's organization and the relationship between the Navy's line and staff officers. Would the study dovetail with Vinson's recommendations? It didn't. Instead, the study agreed with both CNO Pratt and the General Board that "no radical change in the existing organization of the Navy Department gives sufficient promise of improvement in the war efficiency of the Fleet or of economy in the expenditure of public funds to justify its adoption at the present time."[34] This conclusion agreed with the views that Pratt and the General Board had expressed privately to Secretary Adams and then to Secretary Swanson.[35] It also was in line with the opinions of both Swanson and the new President. Vinson, however, was not done with the matter. As we shall see, he returned to the issue of Navy Department reorganization later in the decade.

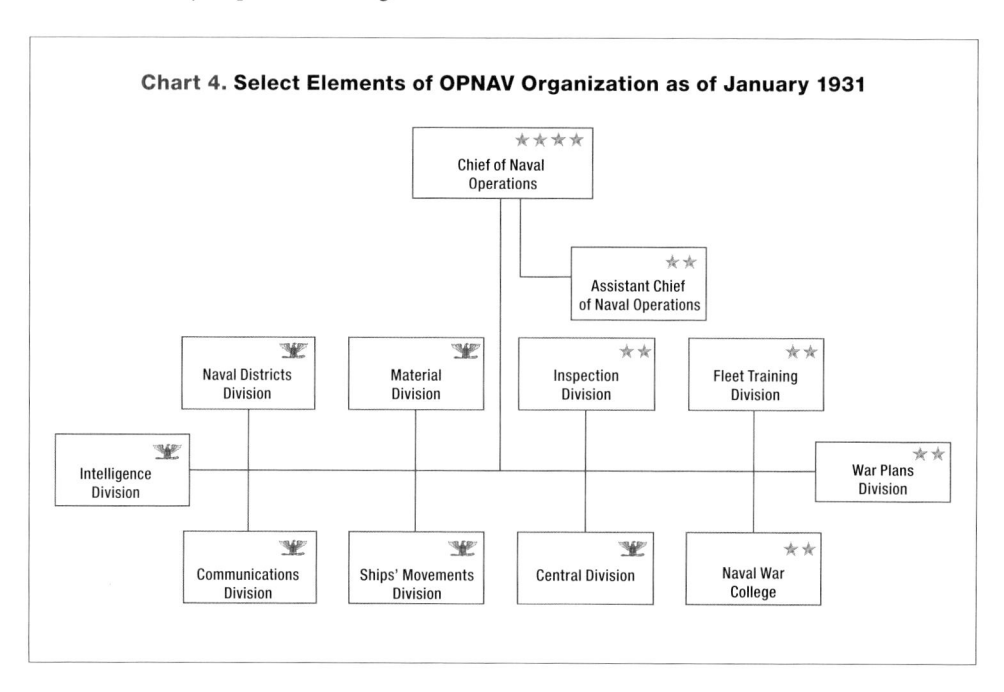

Chart 4. Select Elements of OPNAV Organization as of January 1931

Army-Navy Relations

After World War I, the Secretary of War had added a war plans division to the staff of the Chief of Staff of the U.S. Army. The head of that division and his counterpart on the OPNAV staff were members of the Joint Planning Committee of the Joint Army and Navy Board. Together, Army and Navy planners on the Committee had worked in the 1920s to develop and refine the Orange war plan. Beginning in 1924, they had also cooperated to design joint exercises, including the "Grand Joint Exercise" in Hawaii in 1925.[36] When he was President of the Naval War College, then–Rear Admiral Pratt had commissioned a major joint war game, held from March to May 1926 at the Naval War College. It was clear from that event that no Orange war could be fought successfully unless the Army and the Navy cooperated closely, and the Army and Navy war colleges therefore planned and staged an even more extensive joint war game in May 1929, sharing information and analysis between the staffs and students of the two schools.[37]

Pratt's appreciation of the need for Army-Navy cooperation facilitated his ability to reach several agreements with Army Chief of Staff MacArthur while the two officers were the uniformed chiefs of their services. In October 1931, they agreed on a plan to coordinate their services' radio communications networks, and the previous January they had signed a very important agreement on Army and Navy responsibilities for the defense of the coasts of the United States. The background to so-called "Pratt-MacArthur agreement" was Admiral Pratt's promulgation of a new naval air policy the previous November.

Figure 4-1. Admiral William V. Pratt (left) and Rear Admiral Joseph M. Reeves (right) inspect sailors on board *Saratoga* (CV-3) around 1930. This image was likely taken about the time Admiral Pratt became CNO. (NHHC Archives NH 75870)

The issue then was the control of naval aviation. Were planes based in a given naval district under the command of the district commander or the fleet commander? Pratt ruled in favor of the latter. Navy aviation forces, including air bases in "strategic naval operating areas," were assigned to the fleet. Coast defense from Navy land bases was no longer a primary mission. This change in policy, which made naval aviation an integral part of the fleet, also meant that the Navy would stress taking its aircraft with it, whether on aircraft carriers, as floatplanes mounted on battleships and cruisers, or as seaplanes based on mobile tenders. The agreement between Pratt and MacArthur was a logical consequence of the change in Navy policy and the increasing range and ordnance-carrying capability of land-based Army bombers. After 1931, responsibility for coast defense, including the defense of Hawaii and the Panama Canal, would be the Army's, especially Army aviation.[38] Pratt's biographer considered the agreement a victory for the Army's aviators on the grounds that it justified investment in long-range bombers. However, Pratt may have been hoping that one benefit of the agreement would be the Army's strong opposition in 1932 to any effort to create a department of national defense.[39]

Pratt's Command Philosophy

Pratt had revealed his approach to leading the Navy in a lecture he gave at the Army War College on 1 April 1927 while he was President of the Naval War College. In that presentation, the admiral distinguished between "high naval command and administration."[40] At the same time, he noted that he could not "conceive of an organization built for command which does not also comprehend within its scope the organization which must work for it," and he called this supporting organization's actions "the administration of affairs in peace." His argument to his audience was that "Command and administration must be so blended that the instant we go into war, administration disappears into a subordinate place and command stands out where it belongs, the *two working together as the fingers of your hand*"[41] [emphasis added].

How could this be done? Pratt's answer was that the Navy did it by organizing by type and in task forces. In peacetime, the structure by "types" of platforms—whether ships, submarines, or aircraft—facilitated training in tactics and the adoption of common communications and means of material support. However, peacetime training also included the shift from "type commands" to "task force" commands because in war the elements of the fleet would be organized into task forces composed of different classes of ships that had to work together smoothly.[42] How would those task forces be led? Through the application of a process taught at the Naval War College called the "Estimate of the Situation"—a process practiced and applied in peacetime *and* in war. As Pratt well knew, this meant that the Navy could never demobilize the way that the Army had after World War I. At the same time, the President and the Congress had to know at what level of strength to keep the Navy so that it could deter a conflict or defeat an enemy if conflict could not be avoided.

Keeping the Navy adequately sized and supported was Pratt's major concern as CNO. The Washington and London naval agreements had, in Pratt's view, solved the issue of the Navy's size. However, the friction between Pratt and President Hoover pointed to a potentially grave weakness in Navy-Presidential relations. The fact that the President ultimately reviewed the Navy's budget meant that the President could become the Navy's chief planner. Both Pratt and Secretary Adams wanted a long-range plan to construct and maintain a "treaty Navy." Unfortunately, neither could bring President Hoover around to that policy. Pratt had seen the conflict between political and military leaders before—between former Secretary Daniels and Admiral Sims, for example, and he knew that civilians possessed the authority to decide the Navy's force structure. As Pratt told his audience at the Army War College in 1927, conflict was therefore inevitable because of "the superimposition of untrained minds, men who have been working at something else all their lives, placed over the trained men who have spent their lives working with the object in view of conducting war," and he regarded it as "a grave danger."[43] There was only one good way of forestalling it, and that was to have "men of character" in the highest military and civilian positions. As Pratt discovered in his struggle with President Hoover, however, "men of character" might still disagree, even fundamentally.

Franklin Roosevelt and the "Treaty System"

When Franklin D. Roosevelt was inaugurated as President of the United States on 4 March 1933, the banking system of the country was on the verge of collapse and the rate of unemployment was almost 25 percent. There was a sense of desperation in Washington, and it was not lessened by the news from overseas. On 30 January 1933, Adolf Hitler had been appointed Chancellor of Germany, and Hitler and his Nazi party began a process of destroying the parliamentary democracy of the Weimar Republic and replacing it with a dictatorship. On 7 March 1933, Engelbert Dollfus, leader of the Austrian Christian Socialist Party, dissolved that nation's parliament and assumed power. On 9 March, followers of Hitler seized control of the government of Bavaria. It seemed that there was a growing tide of fascist movements. Even in Britain, where unemployed families had staged a "National Hunger March" in September and October 1932, there was an organized fascist party modeled after Benito Mussolini's in Italy. The sense that the American Republic was also in danger was very real.

The Roosevelt administration acted quickly to deal with the economic and social crisis. Starting on 9 March 1933, the President and his cabinet sent a wave of proposed laws and new regulations to Capitol Hill. However, the new administration showed no signs of supporting the Navy, and CNO Pratt was not influential with the new President. Indeed, the admiral felt that he had been taken advantage of.[44] As historian Wheeler noted, "There was no commitment [from Roosevelt] to building the Navy to treaty strength, nor of adopting a long-term construction program."[45] Pratt felt it was therefore necessary to put into practice his "rotating reserve" plan. Under this program, one-third of every ship class and one-third of every aircraft squadron would be placed temporarily in reserve, and "in reserve" meant having just 60 percent of the normal complement of personnel. After six months "in reserve," those ships and aircraft squadrons would resume "full" operations with "80 to 85 percent" of their nominal peacetime complements while another set of ships and aircraft squadrons went into reserve. It was like locking part of the Navy away in the attic.[46] Angry opposition to the idea, especially on the part of the chief of BuNav, led members of Congress and President Roosevelt to relent, and Pratt cancelled the "rotating reserve" program.

Admiral William H. Standley, Pratt's successor, was also not close to the President. Even worse, Standley's relationship with the new Assistant Secretary, Henry L. Roosevelt, was "poisonous."[47] Yet Standley knew his way around OPNAV; he had been Assistant CNO under Admiral Hughes. Moreover, there was some good news for Standley when he became CNO on 1 July 1933. First, Franklin Roosevelt took a keen interest in the Navy, a Navy he had seen a lot of in his eight years as assistant secretary under Josephus Daniels. Indeed, Roosevelt knew a number of senior Navy officers personally, and he never hesitated to deal directly with the Chief of Naval Operations when Secretary Swanson was ill—as he often was. Second, Roosevelt was a strategist in a way that his predecessor was not. In April 1933, Roosevelt had announced in a speech to the Pan-American Union in Washington that his administration would pursue a "Good Neighbor Policy" in Latin America. In plain terms, that meant that in 1933 the government of the United States would refuse to claim the right to interfere in the affairs of its Caribbean neighbors. The Marines would no longer be acting as a sort of "colonial infantry."

The importance of Roosevelt as a strategist was often overlooked, even by his peers. As historian Johnathan Utley noted, Roosevelt was "quite capable" of "thinking strategically," but he was also averse to "seeing that a strategic plan was drafted."[48] From today's perspective, Roosevelt can be seen as taking deliberate steps to protect the United States from the danger of another world war. First, he attempted to improve relations with the nations and regimes of the Western Hemisphere. Then, at the same time, he tackled the Great Depression and slowly built up the Navy's strength. As the 1930s went on, Roosevelt supported improved relations with Great Britain and the Soviet Union. It all looks like a gradual and deliberate strategy to prepare for the "Grand Alliance" that would defeat Germany and Japan in World War II.

But it was not that. Historian Waldo Heinrichs's characterization of Roosevelt was more accurate:

> The most characteristic feature of FDR's relationship with his subordinates was his unorthodox administrative style. Complaints abound in the records: those who came to ask and tell had to listen; important diplomatic conversations went unrecorded; he secreted information; he embellished and otherwise contorted the truth; he played officials against each other; he shifted position from one caller to the next; bureaucratic lines of authority were subverted; he generally sowed confusion. He seemed positively medieval in his methods, an enemy of modern, rational organization.[49]

In other words, he was quite the opposite of Herbert Hoover.

Building the Navy to Treaty Strength

A key element in the Roosevelt administration's emergency effort to counter the economic depression was the signing of the National Industrial Recovery Act on 16 June 1933. Title II, Section 202, paragraph (e) of the law noted that "if in the opinion of the President it seems desirable, the construction of naval vessels within the terms and/or limits established by the London Naval Treaty of 1930 and of aircraft required therefor" was authorized.[50] The legislation also authorized spending on "public works" such as dry docks and created the Public Works Administration to contract for such work. Because Navy ship construction was labor-intensive, Representative Vinson had been able to justify it as a form of "public works" covered by the intent of the law. In August, authorized by the President, the Navy contracted for the construction of two aircraft carriers (*Yorktown* [CV-5], and *Enterprise* [CV-6]), four 6-inch-gun cruisers (CL-40 through CL-43), four destroyer leaders, 16 destroyers, four submarines, and two sloops.[51] Fortunately, CNO Pratt had "prepared a study called 'The Navy's Needs'" in March 1933, and that study provided the basis for "the progressive laying down of new vessels required to bring the Navy to treaty strength."[52]

Unfortunately, building new ships would have a limited military effect if there were not enough sailors to man them properly. In January 1933, in testimony to the Subcommittee on Naval Appropriations of the House Appropriations Committee, Secretary Adams claimed that "The ratio between the average number of men allowed the vessels in the operating force plan and the number to man efficiently the same vessels in war has shown a steady and gradual decrease." The ratio was 87.5 in 1931; in 1932 it fell to 84.6; in 1933, it was 78.9 percent and still likely to fall below 75.0 in 1934.[53] Testifying alongside Adams, Pratt was just as emphatic. He told the members of the subcommittee that "to keep the *Arkansas* going and working in the Pacific, we have had to include a marine [sic] battalion on board, doing the work of the bluejackets." Pratt intended to obtain more Marines to man the new ships as soon as Marine units returned from Nicaragua.[54]

There were still not enough sailors to properly man the fleet when CNO Standley and Rear Admiral William D. Leahy, Chief of BuNav, testified before the same subcommittee in February 1935. As Leahy warned the representatives, with just 80 percent of its complement—all that was allowed in 1935—a battleship could man its main battery, but it would not be able to steam "at battle speeds for a long period," only one-half of the broadside battery of 5-inch guns could be manned, and the antiaircraft guns could only be "partially manned." Even with 85 percent of its complement, a battleship would be short of sailors to maintain the ammunition supply, fight fires, and conduct repairs in an emergency.[55] The only good news in Leahy's testimony was that "we are now being very careful in our choice of men for enlistment in the Navy. We have very many more times the number of applicants than we have vacancies and we have been able within the last few years to get a very superior type of recruit in the Navy."[56]

What disappointed Standley and Leahy, both of whom had lobbied hard and somewhat successfully in 1933 and 1934 to persuade Congress "to restore the 15 per cent pay cut that had been imposed on naval officers and enlisted men by the Hoover administration," was that

President Roosevelt had not strongly supported them.[57] Roosevelt also did not lobby Congress to build more auxiliary ships (submarine, seaplane and destroyer tenders, for instance) that the Navy would need in order to wage a naval campaign across the Pacific. The President avoided any naval policy that he thought could be construed as supporting a naval offensive against Japan. Building ships to "treaty levels" was portrayed by the President and his supporters in Congress as essentially defensive and therefore not provocative. Recruiting more sailors and building up the Navy's auxiliaries suggested preparing for a conflict, and public opinion seemed strongly opposed to such a move. Whether it was or not, Roosevelt acted with great caution.

Representative Vinson did not. In the fall of 1933, he worked with Standley, who was acting secretary in place of the ill Swanson, to craft a bill authorizing the Navy to build ships to the limits allowed by the Washington and London treaties. The bill became law on 27 March 1934; it was commonly referred to as the "Vinson-Trammell Act" after its sponsors in the House and Senate.[58] The law set the "composition" of the Navy "at the limit prescribed by" the Washington and London treaties. In so doing, it added the following to the ships authorized the previous summer: one aircraft carrier (*Wasp*, CV-7), 99,200 of destroyers, and 35,530 tons of submarines.[59] The law also authorized President Roosevelt to "procure the necessary naval aircraft for vessels and other naval purposes in numbers commensurate with a treaty navy."

As a means of holding down the costs of the new ships, the law specified that "the first and each succeeding alternate vessel of each category," except for the carrier, "shall be constructed or manufactured in the Government navy yards, naval stations, naval gun factories, naval ordnance plants, or arsenals of the United States." The government-built ships would serve as "yardsticks" against which the costs of privately built ships could be evaluated. In addition, ships built in private shipyards were held to a 10 percent profit level.[60] Another cost-saving move was to require the Navy to manufacture "not less than" 10 percent of the aircraft in government facilities.[61] If the Naval Aircraft Factory in Philadelphia could not assemble that many planes, then the President, "at his discretion," could expand that facility or solicit bids from private firms. The governments of the United States, Japan, and Great Britain had already agreed to send delegations to another naval arms limitation meeting in London in 1935. If a new naval treaty came out of that meeting, then the Vinson-Trammell Act authorized the President "to suspend" construction of the ships authorized by the law "as may be necessary to bring the naval armament of the United States within the limitation so agreed upon, *except that such suspension shall not apply to vessels actually under construction on the date of the passage of this act.*"[62] (emphasis added) This last clause protected private shipbuilders against the chance that their work would suddenly be cut off. It also guaranteed the Navy new classes of destroyers and submarines, no matter what happened in the next arms control conference.

Admiral Standley considered the drafting and passage of this law his most important achievement as CNO. In October 1933, under the sponsorship of the Navy League, a lobbying organization, he even went on the radio to appeal for its passage. His message was that the law would "have a great stabilizing effect upon the economic and industrial activities" of the nation.[63]

Once Vinson-Trammell was law, Standley wanted to make sure that he was directly involved in the development of the new ships. On 5 September 1934, he issued a memo to "All Bureaus and Offices" directing that "All plans of new ship construction will, before being submitted to the Secretary of the Navy for approval, be referred to the Chief of Naval Operations."[64] On 24 September, he sent to all the bureau chiefs a memo reminding them that by a SECNAV memorandum promulgated on 16 January 1923, the CNO had cognizance "of the progress of new construction." He went on to say that he "desired" the bureau chiefs to inform him when any "conflicting interests of [the] Bureaus cannot readily be reconciled."[65]

Standley had wanted more influence over bureaus such as Ordnance, Aeronautics, Engineering, and Construction and Repair. Secretary Swanson and President Roosevelt had chosen not to grant him (or any CNO) direct control over those four bureaus, but by inserting his office into the ship design process, the CNO gained influence that OPNAV otherwise would not have had.[66] For example, in March 1935 Standley "approved the characteristics for the 10,000-ton cruisers which the General Board had submitted on 7 January." At the same time, however, he also directed the Preliminary Design section of BuC&R to conduct studies of smaller cruisers.[67] Toward the end of 1935, the CNO commissioned "a general review of destroyer policy" that combined the views of the Bureau of Construction and Repair and the fleet. As Norman Friedman pointed out in his history of destroyer design, "At this time only the eight *Farragut*s, which had been designed in 1931, were in service; the succeeding large classes [made possible by Vinson-Trammell] had been designed almost without modern operational experience. This situation was unique among the major sea powers, the rest of which had started new construction programs in the mid-twenties."[68]

The notion that constructing a navy was something that the nation's political leaders could turn on and off hindered public understanding of what the Navy had to do once the Vinson-Trammell Act was passed. It was true that the Navy had in fact purchased ships in the 1920s, and it was true that for a number of reasons, including the passage of the Merchant Marine Act of 1928, major American shipbuilders "entered the depression with firm work commitments for at least three years."[69] However, much expertise in the field of military ship design and construction had been lost in the years when no battleships, aircraft carriers, and destroyers had been built.[70]

Making matters even worse was the need for the government and commercial shipyards to innovate if they were to avoid the mistakes that occurred in the rapid naval build-up in World War I. Rear Admiral Harold G. Bowen, Assistant Chief and then Chief of the Bureau of Engineering, understood that the traditional shipyard practice of building all elements of a warship that didn't directly relate to firing a gun or launching a torpedo was outmoded. As he said, "The industry did not appreciate the fact that the old ship-and-engine builder was gone and that shipyards must become assembly yards."[71] Accordingly, major shipbuilders resisted the Navy's pressure to become assembly yards, where they would combine "subsystems already fabricated outside their building ways or even outside their yards."[72]

Navy shipbuilding was becoming an important source of work for both government and private shipyards, and many of the latter, starved for work by 1934, were anxious to win Navy contracts. The government contracting process, though, tended to help the yards with more experience win the new contracts. The process of contracting began with the Navy circulating a package of ship specifications and requirements among the interested yards. Interested yards could then respond by submitting a "confidential bid along with proof of their ability to build what the navy wanted." Navy officials would then open the bids, compare them, and make an award to the lowest bidder. "Theoretically, this system would drive down costs by giving an advantage to efficient firms," which "would get better over time at estimating and controlling costs, thereby reducing both the government's outlay and the number of firms able to bid. . . . The hitch was that the navy did not want to reduce the number of yards able to build its vessels."[73] Given OPNAV's limited size and the limits on the authority of the CNO, Admiral Standley had to trust bureau leaders such as Rear Admiral Bowen to do two things at the same time. The first

Figure 4-2. Vice Admiral William H. Standley, Commander Cruisers, Scouting Force, transits the Panama Canal aboard his flagship *Chicago* (CA-29), circa 1932. Standley had extensive experience in OPNAV, having led the War Plans and Fleet Training Divisions and later serving as Assistant CNO. He also held critical staff and command billets at sea, culminating in command, albeit briefly, of the Battle Force in 1933. (NHHC Archives NH 50860)

was to build ships and aircraft to treaty limits. The second was to make sure that industry could respond with a surge of production if the "treaty system" broke.

Maturing the Interaction with Congress

It was difficult to coordinate the Navy's interactions with Congress because the Appropriations Committee of the House of Representatives was accustomed to receiving justifications of budget requests "directly from the subdivisions of the Department having immediate cognizance and detailed knowledge."[74] But it made sense for the Navy to have an officer to coordinate the Navy's communications with Congress if it already had an officer who coordinated the Navy's budget submissions that were sent to the Bureau of the Budget before the President sent them on to Congress. Rear Admiral Claude C. Bloch had served as the Navy's Budget Officer in 1933 and the first half of 1934. In June 1934, Secretary Swanson appointed him to the post of Judge Advocate General (JAG). Bloch then convinced Swanson that the JAG "should take a principal part in the framing of laws affecting the Navy." Accordingly, on 18 December 1934, Swanson directed that "all proposed legislation (except the Navy Appropriation Bill) be submitted to the Judge Advocate General in order that it may be cleared through the proper channels."[75] This gave the SECNAV two senior management deputies—the Budget Officer and the JAG—who could link the process of building the budget and then of shepherding it and other legislation through Congress.

Rear Admiral Bloch consolidated his authority within the Navy Department and then proceeded to attend "the Naval Affairs Committee hearings . . . Before long, Congress looked to him for advice on all sorts of naval matters. During his two years in office [1934–36], Bloch firmly established the new routine."[76] Eventually, one of the JAG's deputies was given the title of "Legislative Counsel," and as the 1930s progressed, the bureau chiefs appointed their own legislative liaison officers. As historian Robert Albion revealed, "all this activity was under the Secretary of the Navy, who remained the primary channel of contact between the Navy and Congress."[77]

The budget process itself was based on two plans—the Orange war plan and the operating force plan. Each year, OPNAV's War Plan Division drew up a classified "Estimate of the Situation and Base Development Program" for the fiscal year two years hence. That "Estimate" was based on the requirements for a trans-Pacific war against Japan. For example, the "Estimate" for fiscal year 1936, which began on 1 July 1935 and ended on 30 June 1936, was approved by the CNO in April of 1934. At about the same time the "Estimate" was approved, the CNO issued the "operating force plan" for fiscal year 1936 (FY-36). This plan was "a letter of instructions to the fleet, and to the bureaus and offices of the Navy Department and shore establishments."[78] It was sent out by the CNO after it was approved by the Secretary of the Navy. It listed which ships would be in commission in the fiscal year being budgeted for, and it usually also spelled out the manning of the shore bases that supported the fleet. As Rear Admiral Ernest J. King, then–chief of BuAer testified in December 1933, "Before we can prepare our [bureau] budget estimates we have to have the operating force plan [for FY 1935], showing the number of ships and the different types that will be in commission in the active Navy."[79]

With the operating force plan in their hands, the bureaus and other Navy offices prepared preliminary estimates and submitted them to the Navy's budget officer in early summer.[80] After a review by the budget officer, the SECNAV met with the assistant secretary and the CNO to consider any remaining issues. Under CNO Pratt and Secretary Adams, the bureau chiefs began meeting with the secretary and the CNO to find ways to deal with the severe budget cuts required by President Hoover. This practice continued under CNO Standley because, despite the Vinson-Trammell Act, Navy funding was still tightly constrained. Once the preliminary budget estimates were accepted by the Secretary of the Navy, they were sent to the Bureau of the Budget. Even before that happened, however, "investigators from the Bureau of the Budget" visited each Navy bureau and "discussed the character and amount of the preliminary estimates," and the investigators returned after the Navy's preliminary estimates were approved by the SECNAV and sent to the budget bureau.

After a review, the budget bureau would send the preliminary estimates back to the Navy Department, the Navy's budget officer would review them with the secretary, and they would go back out to the Navy's bureaus. The bureau budget staffs would then conduct their own reviews and either accept the estimates or submit supplemental estimates back to the Navy budget officer. The last step before sending the secretary's final budget to the Bureau of the Budget in mid-September of the year before the next fiscal year was a review by the secretary, the assistant secretary, and the CNO.

> Conferences are then sometimes held between the director of the Bureau of the Budget and the Secretary of the Navy, or between the director of the Bureau of the Budget and the navy budget officer, or between the director of the Bureau of the Budget and such other bureau chiefs as the Secretary of the Navy may designate . . .[81]

This back-and-forth process was and remains typical of budget negotiations. Yet what anchored the Navy's position in any negotiation with the Bureau of the Budget was the classified "Annual Estimate of the Situation." The operating force plan and the budget of any given fiscal year were supposed to support the goals set out in the "Annual Estimate." Even if spending was inadequate, the Orange war plans and the "Annual Estimates" that were based on those war plans remained firm.

The End of the "Treaty System"

After the London Naval Treaty had been signed in 1930, contacts continued between American disarmament negotiator Ambassador Norman H. Davis and the British government.[82] The election of Franklin Roosevelt in November 1932 had not dimmed hopes for further arms limitation talks, and Davis spent a great deal of time in London preparing for the next London conference, scheduled to begin in December 1935.[83] CNO Standley joined him there for a time in the fall of 1934. President Roosevelt wanted to know if the "treaty system" could survive, given the rising tension between the United States and Japan in the Far East and the unsettling developments in Europe. The prospect that the "treaty system" would continue to block any naval arms race depended on whether Japan, Britain, and the United States could agree on force limits in 1936.

The story of the London conference of 1935–1936 has been told in detail by other researchers.[84] What matters here is, first, that preparing for the conference and participating in it took a great deal of CNO Standley's time and the time of the General Board.[85] Second, the "treaty system" fell apart once the conference officially convened because the Japanese government refused to agree to extend the force limits set by the London Treaty of 1930 unless and until Japan was given parity in naval forces with the United States and Great Britain, and the U.S. government refused absolutely to accede to that demand. Third, the British, French and American delegates, supported by their respective governments, did negotiate a treaty that was signed on 25 March 1936. The more important clauses of that treaty restricted battleships to 35,000 tons standard displacement, limited the heavy guns of battleships to 14 inches, held aircraft carrier tonnage to 23,000 tons standard displacement, and limited new cruisers to a maximum of 8,000 tons and new submarines to 2,000 tons. If any of the governments that had signed the original Washington Treaty refused to abide by the limit of 14-inch guns for battleships, the other governments could equip their new battleships with 16-inch guns.[86] Finally—and importantly for the future—"British-American relations had been excellent on all levels, and . . . there was every reason to expect co-operation to continue and be extended."[87]

Organizing the Fleet for War

As CNO, Admiral Standley favored the appointment of Admiral Joseph M. Reeves as CINCUS because of Reeves's performance in a fleet problem. But once in that post, Reeves proved a disappointment for Standley, and the CNO regretted that he had recommended Reeves to President Roosevelt.[88] Why was there tension between the two officers? Some of the reason was due to their different personalities. But the essential cause of their disagreement lay in the different responsibilities of the fleet commander and the CNO.

After the London Naval Treaty of 1930, it was clear that the Navy wasn't going to get any new battleships for some time, and it was essential to write "a set of battle instructions designed with the capabilities and limitations" of the existing battleships "in mind."[89] Tentative battle plans were drafted in 1930 and tested over time in exercises and the fleet problems. These battle plans proved a major advance over existing battle doctrine. As Vice Admiral William C. Cole, Commander of the Scouting Fleet, put it in his comment on Fleet Problem XI in 1930, "We must have the tactical forms to admit of quick change, and the flexibility of mind to use them."[90]

But what was the best way to develop those forms and that flexibility of mind? Part of the answer was the fleet problems, which the Navy continued to plan and conduct even when Navy expenditures were at their lowest levels under Presidents Hoover and Roosevelt. The CNO could, if he wished, influence the design of the problems; Admiral Pratt certainly did. But conducting the problems and then altering battle plans and fleet tactical publications on the basis of what was learned in the problems was the responsibility of the fleet's commander. Under Pratt, the fleet was organized into the Battle Force (the battleships, light cruisers, destroyers, and aircraft carriers), the Scouting Force (the heavy cruisers, destroyers, and long-range patrol planes), the Submarine Force, and the Base Force (auxiliaries). This organization was judged the best for training purposes. The elements of the Battle Force, for example, trained together and developed a battle doctrine and battle maneuvers that were suited for a clash of battleships.

The Navy made a distinction between "type" commanders and "tactical" commanders. Type commanders and their staffs were the link between the bureaus and the fleet, informing the bureaus how equipment was working and making sure that the fleet's sailors were properly trained. In addition, in cooperation with offices in OPNAV, they oversaw training and maintenance for their "types" of ship, documented fleet battle doctrine, and managed the various competitions (gunnery, navigation, communications and engineering) among the crews of similar ships. Tactical commanders were responsible for leading some part of the fleet to war. In practice, flag officers commanding elements of the fleet were "double-hatted." That is, they served as both type and tactical commanders.

Admiral Reeves felt that the structure of the fleet into standing "forces" was unrealistic. In August 1934, he testified to the General Board that "In all Fleet Problems which simulate actual war conditions, the Battle Force and Scouting Force inevitably and naturally disappear...."[91] His point was that keeping the fleet organized more or less permanently as those forces hindered the ability of fleet commanders and their subordinates to shift to a task force structure if and when war broke out. However, both the members of the General Board and CNO Standley disagreed. Standley objected that disrupting the force structure as it existed in order to train senior officers for task force commands would hinder the training of the various ship types. Standley's point was that the fleet's "type" commanders could not simultaneously serve as tactical commanders until war was imminent or underway.

Reeves argued back that what mattered was the organization of the fleet for war—and that in war the fleet would likely fight as task forces. There weren't enough admirals to have adequate numbers of "type" commanders *and* tactical commanders, but training needed to focus more on tactical command. In 1936, Vice Admiral Clarence S. Kempff, Commander Battleships, Battle Force, observed that "In war the Force Commanders would be done away with and their supporting battle plans with them. The fleet would operate under *task forces evolved to meet practical situations* and any supporting battle plans would be produced by appropriate commanders to meet *existing conditions*." (emphasis in the original)[92] Reeves and Kempff were right; in wartime, "individual ships and small task units would have to be interchangeable."[93] However, Standley was responsible for preparing the fleet for war, and he did not agree with them because he feared that their ideas, if implemented, would actually reduce the fleet's readiness.

Shifting Away from Peace
The shift from the "treaty system" to a naval build-up was facilitated by the growing maturity of OPNAV, the value of the fleet problems, and the Navy's budget process. It was also facilitated

The Thirties: From the "Treaty System" to Mobilization

by Carl Vinson in the House of Representatives and Franklin Roosevelt in the White House. The shift was accelerated by events, especially Japan's invasion of China in July 1937 and the Japanese sinking of the U.S. gunboat *Panay* (PR-5) in the Yangtze River in December. Yet Roosevelt remained cautious. He denied, for example, that the second London conference had been a failure, even though Japan's abandonment of the "treaty system" had clearly killed hopes for further arms limitation. At the same time, however, his administration had been able to gain passage of the Merchant Marine Act of 1936, which provided subsidies to American shipbuilders if they would produce ships that the Navy could modify and turn into naval auxiliaries.[94]

Opposition to rearmament within the United States remained strong. The same month (January 1937) that Admiral William D. Leahy was appointed CNO, Congress passed a joint resolution making it illegal for Americans and American firms to sell or ship arms to Spain, then in the midst of a brutal civil war. In May 1937, Congress passed the Neutrality Act of 1937 to replace the Neutrality Acts of 1935 and 1936. The 1937 law prohibited American ships from carrying both passengers and cargo to countries at war or to nations divided by a civil war. However, it also

Figure 4-3. Together on heavy cruiser *Houston* (CA-30) in February 1939, President Franklin D. Roosevelt (left) and CNO William D. Leahy had known and liked one another since Roosevelt had served as Assistant Secretary of the Navy in World War I. In Roosevelt's second term as President, Secretary of the Navy Claude Swanson was often ill, and Leahy was the acting secretary, a situation that the President preferred. (NHHC Archives NH 49475)

allowed European nations to purchase material in the United States so long as their governments paid in cash and shipped the purchased material in ships that were not registered in the United States. The Chinese government could also obtain material and supplies in the United States, even though the military forces of Japan and China were fighting. President Roosevelt was able to avoid applying the Neutrality Act of 1937 to trade with China because Japan and China had not declared that their conflict was a war. Yet his "Quarantine Speech" of October 1937, where he proposed to isolate aggressive nations politically, economically, and diplomatically, had not been a success politically, and so the President backed away from that alternative.

Admiral Leahy as CNO

The new CNO had reached the pinnacle of a distinguished naval career. He had served as chief of both BuOrd and BuNav, and he was familiar with many members of Congress and at ease with press reporters (he was the first CNO to hold a formal press conference).[95] His operational credentials were firm: He had commanded the battleships of the Battle Force and then the Battle Force itself. Moreover, his personal and professional ties with President Roosevelt reached back to World War I. The President trusted Leahy, and Leahy was very careful about what he said to others about Roosevelt. In 1948, Robert Sherwood, a Pulitzer Prize–winning playwright and speech writer for Roosevelt, published his award-winning *Roosevelt and Hopkins, An Intimate History*.[96] The book is fascinating—until you go looking for an in-depth assessment of Leahy. You won't find it. The admiral was extraordinarily discreet. Though one of Roosevelt's confidantes, he's hardly mentioned at all.

His close relationship to the President shows in the story of the Navy's relationship with efforts by the government of the Soviet Union to purchase ships for its navy in the United States. The United States had recognized the USSR in November 1933. In the spring of 1936, the Soviet Union's two import-export firms in New York had attempted to purchase armor steel plate from Bethlehem Steel. "The Soviet government had also asked for drawings and specifications of an aircraft carrier and several battleships, and had expressed an interest in purchasing a submarine from the Electric Boat Company."[97] The American firms had informed the Soviet-sponsored firms that they would have to first speak with the Navy and State Departments. Secretary Swanson told their representatives that his department "did not have the staff to furnish the plans for the carrier and the battleships," and at the State Department they were told that they had to be cleared by the Navy in order to see any ship plans. So back the Soviet representatives went to the Navy's bureaus, where the chiefs of the bureaus of Engineering and Ordnance "told them that the Espionage Act of 1917 restricted what the Navy could offer in the way of technical help. This was not a lie."[98] To avoid violating the law, the export-import firms would have to obtain export licenses from the State Department.

Back at the State Department, the representatives of the import-export firms were informed that Navy Secretary Swanson had written to the Secretary of State saying that "any export of 16-inch guns would (a) threaten the desire of the United States government to hold the size of new battleship guns to 14-inches and (b) involve the Navy in the testing of the weapons, violating an established policy...." The Russians then went back to the Bethlehem Shipbuilding Company, but the firm said it could not get a "yes" or a "no" from the Navy. By this time it was 1937, and Bethlehem Steel accused the Navy of "stonewalling." After another visit to the State Department to renew their export license and another trip to Bethlehem Steel, the representatives of the Soviet-sponsored firms learned that CNO Leahy had told Bethlehem that the Navy would not assist in the proposed sale because "active and prolonged cooperation in the manufacture of battleships for a foreign power . . . would be definitely contrary to the policy of the Government."[99]

Though the State Department was willing to grant the Soviet-sponsored American firms export licenses for naval material, it claimed that "subordinate officers in the Navy Department have repeatedly told the ship builders and the representatives of the other interested American companies not to enter into contracts with representatives of the U.S.S.R."[100] The Navy could offer one good reason for backing away from supplying its approval for the potential sales, especially of destroyers and any battleship: If war broke out between the Soviet Union and another country, the Neutrality Act of 1937 would halt construction and trade with both belligerents. It wasn't as though the Navy was lying outright. So "The merry-go-round kept spinning through the fall of 1939," when war forced the President to apply the provisions of the 1937 Neutrality Act.[101] It was a classic case of a runaround. The Russians had to renew their export license each year, and it was possible for the Navy to drag out negotiations so that time ran out before any deal could be made. President Roosevelt got political credit for trying to aid the Soviet Union while at the same time making sure that there was no real aid, and as CNO after January 1937, Leahy went along with the charade.

Leahy was comfortable with Roosevelt's methods. Though they often frustrated members of his own administration, in the case of the Navy the President was a consistent if demanding supporter. Leahy described Roosevelt as having "little confidence in some of his executive departments," leading him to take "detailed action with his own hands," in the process becoming "completely familiar with the details of all his written orders and other official communications."[102] This was, it seems, somewhat similar to Leahy's own style.

However, Leahy's two-and-a-half years as CNO were almost too busy for him to emulate the whole range of Roosevelt's bureaucratic tactics. For starters, the signing of the second London agreement in March 1936 signaled the end of the "treaty system," and Leahy had to oversee a re-evaluation of the War Plan Orange, especially conferences with the Army about Pacific strategy. Leahy also had to work with Representative Vinson on three critical projects—strengthening the fleet with additional ship and aircraft authorizations, ironing out the complications of the officer selection process, and modifying the structure of the Navy Department.

In April 1937, Leahy and Assistant Secretary of the Navy Charles Edison tried unsuccessfully to persuade the Bureau of the Budget to grant the Navy Department funds to procure 48 auxiliaries of different kinds.[103] That experience convinced Leahy that Congress needed to add to the authorizations of the Vinson-Trammell Act of 1934. The State Department, concerned about Japanese aggression in China, urged the CNO to press for "an accelerated schedule of battleship replacement."[104] Leahy did so in a 15 December letter to the President. On 28 January 1938, President Roosevelt therefore asked Congress for a 20 percent increase in "authorized under-age combat tonnage." Leahy vigorously defended the President's proposal to Vinson's House Committee on Naval Affairs, and on 17 May 1938 the "second Vinson bill" became law.[105]

The act authorized an additional three battleships (105,000 tons), with the proviso that each of the three could displace 45,000 tons if there was evidence that "other nations" were no longer observing the 35,000-ton limit set by the Washington treaty and reaffirmed at London in 1930. Two 20,000-ton aircraft carriers were also authorized, along with 68,750 tons of cruisers, 38,000 tons of destroyers, 13,650 tons of submarines, "not less than three thousand" aircraft, and a total of 20 auxiliaries (15 tenders, one repair ship, and four modern tankers), one mine layer, three mine sweepers, and two fleet tugs.[106] Leahy made it clear in his congressional testimony that this added naval strength would not allow the Navy to do more than defend American territory and interests.

Proof of the government's peaceful intent was Section 9 of the law, which stated that "The United States would welcome and support an international conference for naval limitations." If that conference produced limits, the President was "authorized and empowered to suspend" the new ships authorized by the law unless they were already being built. However, Section 10 of the law authorized the SECNAV to appoint a board "to investigate and report upon the need, for purposes of national defense, for the establishment of additional submarine, destroyer, mine, and naval air bases on the coasts of the United States, its territories and possessions." To careful readers of the act, that meant the Navy was going to consider modernizing and enlarging its bases in the Pacific, including the very limited facilities on the island of Guam. Section 9 was a consolation to the congressional opponents of any naval alliance with Britain and any effort to "quarantine" Japan. Section 10 was a clear sign that the Roosevelt administration was planning for war, and the dispute over the study that the section authorized was long and bitter.[107] In effect, the Navy was implementing part of the preliminaries to the Orange Plan.[108]

CNO Leahy and Representative Vinson had two other matters to deal with once they had completed enlarging and strengthening the Navy. The first was selection of officers for promotion. This was a complex issue with a long and detailed history. Resolving the issue was going to affect how the Navy prepared for and then performed in wartime. In parallel with the bill to increase the size of the Navy, Vinson and his fellow committee members tried to find a way to balance the need of the Navy for qualified officers with the fair treatment of officers compelled to face a rigorous evaluation of their abilities at successive stages of their careers. Rear Admiral Adolphus Andrews, Chief, BuNav, testified to the House Naval Affairs Committee that "we must give the best fitted officers adequate sea duty on combatant ships." That could mean that officers rated by their superiors as "fitted" but not "best fitted" could never have an opportunity to serve in a significant position on a combat ship. Yet a "fitted" officer might turn out to be an excellent commanding officer. Andrews made the CNO's position clear: The "principle of giving preference for sea billets to best fitted officers should be followed, *even though it becomes necessary to employ fitted officers only on shore . . . if the Navy is to produce the best officers for high command, it must be able to give the best fitted officers ample sea duty in the fleet.*"[109] As the committee members knew, this policy tended to produce a kind of class structure within the Navy. It also tended to make junior officers hesitant to take risks for fear of being judged "only" fitted.

Yet a policy favoring the "best fitted" was what both the President and the CNO wanted, and the House and Senate Committees on Naval Affairs accepted that policy. The good news for CNO Leahy was that Congress agreed to increase the number of Navy line officers, allowed the Navy to subject all promotions above junior lieutenant to review by selection boards, permitted officers with long service who were not selected for promotion to retire with a pension, and "Defined the eligibility of officers for consideration for selection."[110] Unfortunately, the Navy was still short of officers after the passage of legislation in June 1938. However, the work of the naval affairs committees had made a positive difference over time. For example, in 1916, the average age of a commander was 55; in 1938 it was 42.5. The numbers for captains were 59 and 49.5, respectively, and the numbers for admirals were 61.5 and 55.[111] This was done despite the growth of naval aviation, which produced continuously a large block of young pilots—a bulge or "hump" in the officer corps that threatened to block advancement as its members rose through the ranks.

What about reorganizing the Navy Department? President Roosevelt was against it. Representative Vinson sent a draft of a reorganization proposal to the bureau chiefs and five senior fleet officers in June 1939, but it went nowhere.[112] As Rear Admiral James O. Richardson, Assistant CNO, explained in December 1937:

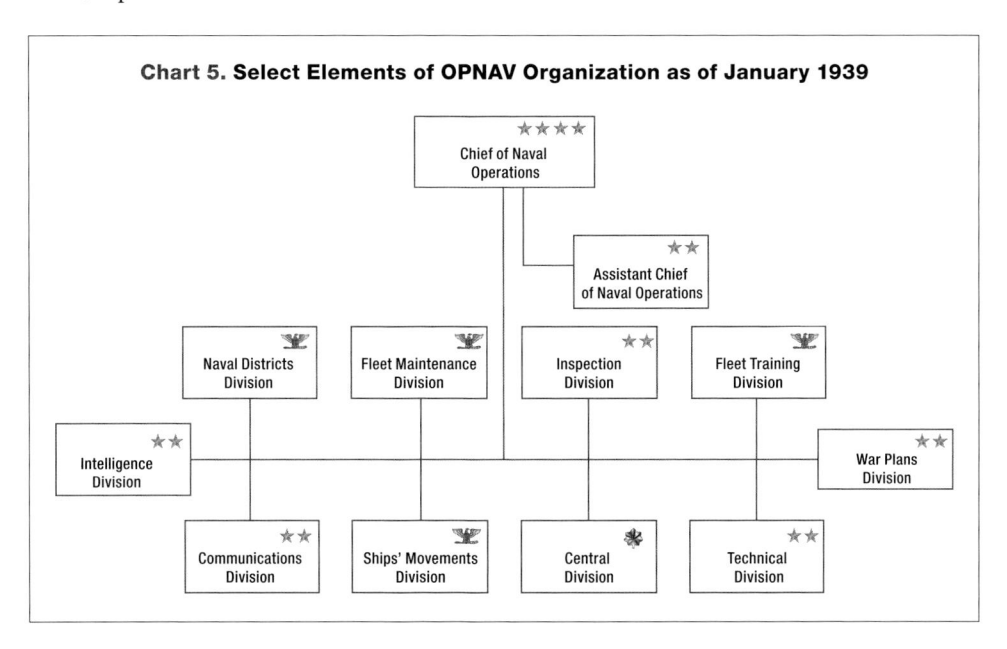

Chart 5. Select Elements of OPNAV Organization as of January 1939

> While the Chief of Naval Operations has no direct control over the personnel or the expenditures . . . for the Naval Establishment (all the money that is spent by the Navy is appropriated directly to the control of the bureaus), by the Annual Operating Force Plan, Aeronautical Organization and Shore Establishment Operating Plan flowing from the decisions in the Annual Estimate of the Situation he practically determines the personnel requirements; and by virtue of his responsibility for the readiness of the Fleet and his duty of coordinating all efforts to this end he largely influences the expenditures of appropriations without interfering with detailed duties of the Material Bureaus.[113]

Leahy knew how to make this process work; he saw no reason to change it.

Preparing for War

When Admiral Harold R. Stark became CNO on 1 August 1939, the Congress and the President had already begun creating organizations that would manage the war effort. On 3 April 1939, the Congress passed the Reorganization Act of 1939. The new law authorized the President to create the Executive Office of the President.[114] This was a very significant step. On 8 September 1939, using the authority granted him by this legislation, President Roosevelt signed Executive Order (EO) 8248, which pulled the following organizations into the new office: the Bureau of the Budget, the National Resources Planning Board, the Office of Government Reports, and the Liaison Office for [civilian] Personnel Management. They joined several other agencies installed there as a consequence of Military Order 2786, issued by the President acting as Commander-in-Chief on 1 July 1939: the Joint Board of the Army and Navy, the Aeronautical Board, the Joint Economy Board, and the Joint Army and Navy Munitions Board.[115] In August 1939, the Assistant Secretary of War, acting under authority given him by the President, had created the civilian-staffed War Resources Board to advise the Joint Army and Navy Munitions Board. The War Resources Board was the first of a series of economic mobilization committees, all created to coordinate the allocation of resources, manufacturing capacity, and human labor of the country among the military departments and civilian agencies such as the War Shipping Board.[116]

On 5 September, President Roosevelt issued a proclamation affirming American neutrality in the European war (which had started on 3 September). Three days later, he assumed additional executive powers as a means of protecting and enforcing that neutrality. In addition to signing EO 8248 on 8 September, he also signed EO 8244, which authorized an increase in Army personnel; 8245 did the same for the Navy and the Marine Corps. Both 8244 and 8245 were justified by Presidential Proclamation 2352 of 8 September 1939, which declared the existence of a national emergency and gave the President limited authority to deal with it. The proclamations of 5 and 8 September captured the two-sided nature of the U.S. government's response to the war. One side emphasized American neutrality. The other side stressed preparedness in case war came.

Over time, however, the emphasis shifted to preparedness and what preparedness implied— economic and military mobilization. For example, in his proclamation of 5 September 1939, President Roosevelt had declared an arms embargo against all the nations at war. That was in

The Thirties: From the "Treaty System" to Mobilization

line with the Neutrality Act of 1937. Later that month, however, Roosevelt asked Congress to modify the Neutrality Act, precipitating extensive debate. The President's position eventually prevailed, and Congress passed the Neutrality Act of 1939 in early November. The law lifted the arms embargo that was at the heart of the 1935 Neutrality Act, allowing the sale of arms to belligerents on a "cash and carry" basis only. The 1939 law also extended a 1936 amendment to the 1935 law prohibiting loans to warring nations, and it stipulated that arms purchased under "cash and carry" had to be transported on ships not registered in the United States.[117]

The debates and decisions in the fall of 1939 set a pattern for the next two years. The United States would be officially neutral, but its Navy would gradually shift in the Atlantic from an active "neutral" stance to one of overt confrontation with German U-boats. At the same time the federal government would move closer and closer to full-scale mobilization. In June 1939, Congress had passed the Strategic Materials Act, which allowed the Treasury Department to allocate funds for critical raw materials. But with the increase in orders for both raw materials and finished products such as aircraft, the British and French governments were actively competing with the Army and Navy. What was needed was a means to coordinate all orders for war material placed in the United States, whether those orders were placed by Britain and France or by the U.S. Army and Navy. Accordingly, President Roosevelt established a special liaison committee in the Executive Office in December 1939 to balance foreign and domestic orders for military equipment.[118] This was just another step in the move toward greatly expanded executive authority and the creation of a complex bureaucracy to implement executive policy.

Admiral Stark inherited the organizations and procedures developed by his predecessors, but were they adequate for the new national emergency? Stark was no "outsider." He had served as an executive aide to SECNAVs Adams and Swanson, and according to his biographer was also "intensely loyal to Roosevelt, with whom he shared a long and intimate friendship."[119] Stark had also served as chief of BuOrd from 1934 to 1937, commanded a cruiser division in the Battle Force and then became Commander, Cruisers, Battle Force. He possessed knowledge of Washington and had credibility within the fleet. However, the structure of government in Washington was steadily changing.

Figure 4-4. Rear Admirals Harold R. Stark (left) and Chester W. Nimitz inspect sailors in 1939 before Stark's promotion to CNO. In 1940, he was instrumental in persuading President Roosevelt to adopt a war strategy for the United States. He also helped persuade Congress to drastically increase the size and strength of the Navy. (NHHC Archives NH 62817)

Could the new CNO maintain a position of influence in the middle of all this change?

CNO Stark's position and role within the Navy Department was secure. Secretary Swanson had died on 7 July 1939. President Roosevelt did not replace him with Assistant Secretary Edison until 5 August, and even then Edison was only "Secretary of the Navy *ad interim*."[120] Given his friendship with the President, the new CNO had to some degree a "free hand." Yet the challenges facing Stark were many and serious, and some important decisions had been made even before he became CNO that constrained what he could do. For example, Navy force planning was based on its war plan, and its war plan had to further national strategy. In May 1939, Army and Navy planners had developed five "joint blueprints" for war. These were the Rainbow Plans. Each covered a different basic option such as hemispheric defense, a conflict in the Atlantic, or a conflict in the Pacific.[121] No one knew what the future held; no one knew what the role of the United States would, could, or should be. Nevertheless, as George Baer pointed out, "It was essential that President Roosevelt clarify the position of the United States. Fundamental executive decisions were needed to guide naval strategy." Instead, "Roosevelt waited."[122] This put great pressure on CNO Stark and Army Chief of Staff General George C. Marshall.

Stark, however, had a clear agenda for the Navy, no matter what war plan the President adopted: Get more ships, planes, submarines, and sailors for his service and prepare for war without announcing that preparing for war with Japan and Germany was in fact what the Navy was doing. In November 1939, Stark went to Vinson with a proposal: enlarge the Navy by another 25 percent over the next five years. Vinson said it was too much and reduced it to 11 percent. However, Vinson also left open the possibility of another 11 percent increase in two years and still another two years after that.[123] Stark had also decided that the rules governing submarine warfare, as published in *Instructions for the Navy of the United States Governing Maritime Warfare*, needed to be changed. He had the WPD, assisted by the JAG and advised by the State Department, prepare a new draft in April 1940.[124] Just a month later, after a fleet problem that had taken the fleet to Hawaii, President Roosevelt ordered Admiral James O. Richardson, the fleet's commander, to keep his ships there. "Stark told Roosevelt plainly what Richardson's problems would be if the fleet were not sent back to the West Coast," but the President would not change his mind.[125]

That same month, starting on 12 May, the German army rolled into France; on 14 June, German troops occupied Paris. That same day, President Roosevelt signed congressional legislation to increase the size of the Navy by the 11 percent Stark and Vinson had agreed upon. The legislation added 167,000 tons of warships to the Navy, including 79,500 tons of aircraft carriers, 66,500 tons of cruisers, and 21,000 tons for new submarines. The legislation also authorized an additional 75,000 tons of auxiliaries based on commercial ship designs. The law also gave the President permission to "acquire or construct" new airplanes to bring the Navy's number of useful aircraft up to 4,500, and it authorized additional sums for base construction, new shipbuilding ways, and the production of armor and armament. There was even a provision to modernize the obsolete battleships *New York* (BB-34), *Texas* (BB-35), and *Arkansas* (BB-33), and another to authorize the President to create a seven-member Naval Consulting Board that could help the Navy tap the research being done outside of the federal government.[126]

The shock of the defeat of the French and British armies galvanized Congress. On 22 June 1940, the House of Representatives again voted to increase the Navy's ship and aircraft strength. The Senate voted to do the same on 10 July. On 19 July, the President signed the bill to add 1,325,000 tons of warships to the Navy, including 385,000 tons for battleships, 200,000 tons for aircraft carriers, 420,000 tons for cruisers, 250,000 tons for destroyers, and 70,000 tons for submarines. The law also authorized the President to acquire 100,000 tons of auxiliaries. The number of "useful naval airplanes" was authorized to reach 15,000, and the SECNAV was allowed to procure more aircraft if he could gain the consent of the President.[127] This was no longer expansion; it was mobilization.

The President was being given more and more authority and enlarging his own office and the responsibilities of the federal departments. On 16 May 1940, Roosevelt had announced that the country needed to produce 50,000 military aircraft in 1941—an unrealistic figure given the lack of any clear American strategy, and his Army and Navy air chiefs knew it, but Roosevelt's initiative forced them to work with Representative Vinson to come up with a more realistic goal.[128] Roosevelt might be worrying his military chiefs by withholding approval of any strategy document, but he could boost aircraft production dramatically and still call it "defensive," especially in light of what was happening in Europe.

To achieve his grand production goals, Roosevelt needed to persuade Congress to alter the rules that governed Navy and Army procurement. The law requiring the use of sealed bids for items such as ships, submarines, and aircraft had to be modified to allow for negotiated contracts, and those negotiated contracts had to be written to allow for the flexibility in production that was needed in wartime, when what was needed and when it was needed might change quickly. Accordingly, on 28 June Congress overturned the rule—first established in the Vinson-Trammell Act of 1934—that limited a vendor's profits on Navy contracts over $10,000 to 10 percent. Congress also handed the SECNAV the authority to negotiate contracts for the repair and construction of ships and planes. The pre-war practice of soliciting sealed bids was over.[129]

On 25 May, to deal with the sometimes redundant contracts negotiated by the Army and Navy, Roosevelt had established an organization in the executive office of the president to coordinate existing and planned Army and Navy procurement contracts. On 27 May, the President had declared an "unlimited national emergency," and two days later he had set up the National Defense Advisory Commission to advise him on production priorities. On 20 June, Congress established the position of Under Secretary of the Navy and also merged BuC&R with the Bureau of Engineering to form the new Bureau of Ships (BuShips).[130] On 25 June, Congress authorized the Reconstruction Finance Corporation to stockpile strategic materials, and on the 28th, Congress gave the President the authority to give firms producing war material for the Army and Navy priority in the purchasing of raw material.

Things were moving fast and it was only June of 1940. In July, Chicago newspaper publisher and prominent Republican politician Frank Knox accepted President Roosevelt's invitation to become Secretary of the Navy, and he was sworn in on the 11th. Fortunately, Knox and Stark got along. However, the new secretary had his own ideas about how to support the country's efforts to prepare for war. In August, Knox developed what became the "destroyers for bases" deal between the United States and Great Britain.[131] The idea was that the British would receive 50 mothballed destroyers in exchange for granting long-term basing rights to British bases in the Western Hemisphere. When the exchange deal was revealed publicly on 3 September, Stark was faced with a dilemma. Congress had denied the SECNAV the authority to make such a ship transfer unless the CNO showed that the ships were not needed for the defense of the country. Stark had asked for funds to bring the destroyers out of mothballs; he'd based his request on his claim that they were needed by the U.S. Navy. Now the President was planning on exchanging them for leases for bases. Stark believed that complying with the President's directive "would compromise his reputation with Congress; he concluded that he could not change his position overnight and still serve as chief of naval operations."[132] After consulting with the President, Knox, and Attorney General Robert H. Jackson, Stark came up with a solution: trading the destroyers for "the bases would result in a net advantage to the United States."[133] Stark could stay on as CNO.

Adding to the general sense of urgency, the governments of Germany, Italy, and Japan signed the Tripartite Pact on 27 September 1940. The pact pledged those three governments to declare war on any nation that declared war on any of them. The lines of conflict were now drawn. The United States would find itself in a two-ocean conflict if it went to war with Japan or Germany. Admiral Stark and General Marshall wanted and needed a clear statement from the Commander-in-Chief describing the nation's strategy. That strategy would set priorities. It would tell the leaders of the Army and Navy what mattered most and why, and they needed that guidance to develop their war plans. Yet still Roosevelt hesitated. He was risking his political future by turning his back on a precedent set by George Washington and running for a third term as President. He was also determined to avoid as long as possible the criticisms of those who believed that the President was pushing the nation into the European war.

Once the President won re-election, Stark realized that he could finally force Roosevelt to make some choices that the President had been avoiding. The CNO "submitted to Knox and Roosevelt a memorandum" that presented and assessed four major strategic alternatives. As historian B. Mitchell Simpson noted, "It was a paper [Stark] had worked on for several weeks and which he drafted with consummate skill." Its argument that Germany posed the greatest danger to the United States led Stark to endorse the fourth alternative, "a defensive strategy in the Pacific and an offensive strategy in the Atlantic to defeat Germany first."[134] This was Plan D, or, by the military's alphabet, Plan Dog. It "expressed a consensus among military and naval planners which was tacitly accepted by the president."[135] It was the foundation of U.S. strategy in World War II. George Baer summed up the effect of Stark's memo succinctly: "Thus did Stark turn attention from aid to war, from assistance to participation, from the Pacific to the Atlantic, and from hemisphere defense to an overseas offensive war that would be taken onto the European continent."[136] Roosevelt's tacit acceptance of the plan also opened the door to confidential talks with the British, and Stark promptly invited Britain's first sea lord to dispatch Royal Navy officers to Washington. "Only after he had issued the invitation did Stark tell Roosevelt what he had done."[137]

Recall that CNO Stark had served on the London staff of Vice Admiral Sims in World War I. Stark made contacts there that he sustained in the years after the war. The standing of the U.S. Navy in the eyes of British political leaders and senior officers in the Royal Navy had been enhanced in the 1930s by the face-to-face relationships established and nurtured by former CNOs Pratt and Standley. If Plan D were to become the foundation of U.S. war strategy, Britain would be the base from which Germany would be assaulted, and Stark knew how important it therefore was to be on good terms with that nation's civilian and military leaders. As it turned out, once contact with Britain's government was acceptable, there were specific benefits to a "partnership" for the Navy, including the designs of an escort carrier and various landing craft. All this was still in the future in the fall of 1940, but Stark's initiative put down the foundation for it.

The President continued to edge toward war. He endorsed the "destroyers-for-bases" agreement with British Prime Minister Winston Churchill early in September 1940. On 16 September, the President signed the Selective Service Act in order to create a huge citizen Army. On 17 December, CNO Stark cancelled the Orange war plan. However, the essential element of the plan, which was a trans-Pacific offensive against Japan, had already left its mark on the Navy—the naval authorizations of June and July. On 29 December, Roosevelt proclaimed in a speech that the United States would be the "Arsenal of Democracy." The speech signaled two significant changes. The first was the end of the policy of "cash and carry." The second was the creation of a quasi-alliance and the end of neutrality. After all, if the United States was the arsenal, then how could the enemies of democracy not attack it? How could they stand by and allow it to sustain their enemies?[138]

While Washington was trying to develop a strategy that could deter war, Admiral James O. Richardson, Commander-in-Chief of the U.S. Fleet, was stewing in Hawaii. Stark had told Richardson that the presence of the fleet in Hawaii was meant to deter Japanese aggression in Southeast Asia, but the CNO also admitted that no one knew what Roosevelt would do if the Japanese navy and army attacked British or Dutch possessions there.[139] Richardson decided to fly to Washington to see the President. In a meeting with Roosevelt on 8 October, Richardson said that "The senior officers of the Navy do not have the trust and confidence in the civilian leadership of this country that is essential for a successful prosecution of a war in the Pacific."[140] Richardson followed up with a 22 October official letter to Stark, arguing that "successful operations in war can rest only on sound plans, careful specific preparation and vigorous prosecution," noting that without the sound planning, preparation would be confused or inadequate and defeat probable.[141] This was too much for Stark and Roosevelt, and Richardson was relieved on 1 February 1941 when Navy General Order 143 made the post of Commander-in-Chief of the U.S. Fleet an administrative command and established the Atlantic and Pacific Fleets, with their own commanders, as well as retaining the existing Asiatic Fleet.[142]

British and American staff negotiations, "conducted in great secrecy," began in January 1941 and ran to the end of March. The product was an agreement called ABC-1, which made defeating Germany the strategic objective in the event the United States entered the war and also committed the U.S. Navy to aiding the Royal Navy in the Atlantic. Approved by CNO Stark, Army Chief of Staff Marshall, and the secretaries of the Army and Navy, ABC-1 led to Rainbow Plan 5 (Navy War Plan (WPL) 46), which finally made it clear to their services that the Atlantic was the primary theater of any war with the parties to the Tripartite Pact. In parallel with this strategic planning, Congress passed the Lend-Lease Act on 11 March 1941. As economic historian Maury Klein noted, the President "could sell, exchange, transfer, lease, or loan any defense article to any other country without regard to existing laws . . . [and] To pay for such articles, he received what amounted to a blank-check authorization from any unappropriated funds in the treasury."[143] The immediate purpose of the legislation was to keep Britain in the war, but the Soviet Union was also aided under Lend-Lease once it was attacked by German forces on 22 June 1941.

Lend-Lease actually worsened a problem for the Navy, however, because it led to greater British demands for items, such as aircraft, that were also needed by U.S. naval forces. The Army and Navy had created a Joint Aircraft Committee in September 1940 to provide the National Defense Advisory Commission with suggested priorities for the allocation of aircraft to the Army, Navy, and the British Purchasing Commission.[144] What this meant was that, before British and American war planners began learning to work together, British and American procurement officers had already carried on a string of negotiations about which nation had first claim on critical war material.[145] Perhaps ironically, given the way that past CNOs had campaigned for more authority over the bureaus, CNO Stark got a lot of help at this time from the Navy's bureau chiefs, especially Rear Admirals John H. Towers at BuAer and Samuel M. Robinson at the newly created BuShips.[146]

War in the Atlantic was coming ever closer. On 21 May 1941, a German submarine sank the first American merchant ship to be lost in the Atlantic. On 27 May, President Roosevelt declared a state of "unlimited national emergency" and authorized the Navy to extend its "Atlantic Neutrality Patrol" farther out into the Atlantic Ocean. The President also revealed that three battleships, an aircraft carrier, and supporting cruisers and destroyers had been shifted from the Pacific to the Atlantic. On 12 June, the SECNAV recalled all naval reservists without selective service deferments to active duty. On 7 July, the Navy landed Marines in Iceland to begin relieving British occupation forces. On the 19th, Admiral Ernest J. King, Commander-in-Chief of the Atlantic Fleet, dispatched U.S. Navy ships to convoy supplies to U.S. forces in Iceland. Six days later, President Roosevelt froze Japanese assets in the United States and stopped the sale of U.S. oil to Japan. That same month, Stark wrote to a friend that "Policy seems something never fixed, always fluid and changing."[147]

Roosevelt and Prime Minister Churchill met secretly in Argentia, Newfoundland, at the beginning of August and produced the Atlantic Charter, which was a statement of war aims. At the beginning of September, a German submarine fired torpedoes at destroyer *Greer* (DD-145), and Roosevelt ordered U.S. ships escorting convoys to "shoot on sight" any submarine that they discovered. Two U.S. destroyers were torpedoed in October, and one, *Reuben James* (DD-245), was sunk. Light cruiser *Omaha* (CL-4) captured a German blockade runner on 6 November, and Congress authorized putting guns on American merchant ships on 17 November.[148] In effect, the Navy was at war with Germany in the Atlantic. The conflict created a constitutional crisis for the United States. Just how close to war could the President push the Navy before he would be usurping the war power given to Congress in Article I, Section 8 of the Constitution?

The answer to that question would come from the Pacific. On 27 November, after consulting with President Roosevelt, Secretary of State Cordell Hull, and General Marshall, Stark sent the following message to fleet commanders King and Husband E. Kimmel in Hawaii: "This dispatch is to be considered a war warning. . . . an aggressive move by Japan is expected within the next few days . . ." Kimmel was ordered to deploy his fleet defensively while he prepared to execute the Navy's war plan, WPL 46.[149] What happened next—the Japanese navy's attack on Pearl Harbor—has been covered in a great number of publications and the subsequent events are well known, but some points need to be made here.

First, the run-up to war illustrated both the strengths and weaknesses of the Navy's military command structure. If Stark had been both CNO and fleet commander-in-chief, there would have been no need to find just the right way to communicate the grave danger developing in the Pacific to Admiral Kimmel. It was no accident that Admiral King, Atlantic Fleet commander, spent as much time in Washington as he could. Based in Narragansett Bay, Rhode Island, he was relatively close and could consult personally with Stark. He needed to. His fleet moved gradually but inevitably from armed neutrality to combat, and he needed to understand the wishes of the President. Kimmel did not have that opportunity.

Second, the Navy needed a four-star officer in Washington to deal with the President, the Army, and Congress and to provide guidance to the Navy's bureaus. Proof of this was provided by Admiral King when he became both CNO and Commander-in-Chief of the U.S. Fleet in March 1942. King did not eliminate OPNAV. Instead, as former CNO Pratt had predicted, OPNAV became subordinate to the commander-in-chief, and King assumed that the officers he put into OPNAV could and would respond to his guidance. He would not have to direct OPNAV day-to-day. Stark had already begun this process by focusing much of his effort on dealing with offices and individuals outside of OPNAV, especially President Roosevelt. Stark could do that because he had talented deputies in OPNAV such as Rear Admirals Royal E. Ingersoll (the Assistant CNO), Richmond K. Turner (Director of WPD), and Captain Willis A. Lee Jr. (Director of Fleet Training).

Third, the actions of CNO Stark and SECNAV Frank Knox in the second half of 1940 and through 1941 showed how important personal relations were when it came to sustaining civilian authority without having civilians clash with military professionals. Both Stark and Knox admired Franklin Roosevelt. This was very important. To his credit, the media-savvy Knox held weekly press conferences, which took pressure off Stark (and would do the same later for Admiral King). In April 1941, Knox appointed Rear Admiral Arthur J. Hepburn as the Navy's Director of Public Relations, placing Hepburn and his staff in the secretary's own office.[150] Knox was also an outspoken advocate of Roosevelt's efforts to arm and work with the British. Just as important was Knox's ability as a manager. His 23 August 1940 memo outlining the duties of the Secretary, the new Under Secretary, and the Assistant Secretary is a model worth studying.[151]

Finally, President Roosevelt made the right move in sending Stark to London as the Navy's senior officer there after Admiral King was made both CNO and commander-in-chief in March 1942. By getting Stark out of Washington, he protected the former CNO from the furor of indignation and incrimination that erupted after the attack on Pearl Harbor—a furor that cost Admiral Kimmel his command and his career. By contrast, Admiral Stark continued to serve his country as a valued colleague of the British, as the next chapter will show. Decades later, Vice Admiral William R. Smedberg III, who served as CNO Stark's flag lieutenant, recalled that Stark was a contrast to President Roosevelt. Unlike Roosevelt, Stark was "not devious in any way," and, "because of his honesty," was trusted by members of Congress as well as by the President.[152] That seems just the sort of individual whom a president would want to send to work alongside the senior officials of an ally.

Conclusion

This chapter has been long because so much happened between the appointment of CNO William Pratt and the beginning of World War II. The nation's strategic policy went from disarmament, to arms limitation, to armed neutrality, and then to mobilization and war. First the Navy was deliberately starved, despite CNO Pratt's point that tightly constraining the Navy would actually undermine the "treaty system." Then the Navy was built (but not really manned) to treaty strength, despite the severest economic depression the nation had ever known. Then, after Europe had gone to war, the Navy was suddenly turned into the largest and most effective navy the world had ever seen. Making this roller-coaster ride even more hazardous—and the lives of the CNOs often nerve-racking—was the running, acrimonious debate in the country about the role of the United States in the world.

However, by the time Admiral Stark was appointed CNO on 1 August 1939, OPNAV had matured as an organization. Its members planned for war, coordinated schedules for fleet operations and maintenance, crafted budgets to finance new construction and ongoing operations, supported the annual fleet problems, coordinated with the Army and the State Department, and had effective liaison with Congress. OPNAV also had found the funds and the personnel to create OP-20G—the codebreakers. Listed as communicators, the staff of OP-20G would, with its intercept stations in places such as Hawaii and the Philippines, provide some of the most important intelligence the Navy was to have in both peace and war.

In his 1953 novel *The Deep Six*, author and World War II Navy veteran Martin Dibner had the father of his main character say, "Knew an ensign once . . . In the First World War. Came to no good, I understand. They made him an admiral."[153] In the 1930s, that droll anecdote was taken by many people, including numbers of sailors, as a sly and somewhat mischievous portrait of the Navy's senior officers. This chapter should alert readers of this misconception, at least as far as the Chiefs of Naval Operations were concerned.

Notes

[1] Albion, *Makers of Naval Policy, 1798–1947*, 239.

[2] See, for example, RADM William V. Pratt, "Naval Policy and the Naval Treaty," *North American Review*, vol. 215, no. 798 (May 1922), 590–99, and "Disarmament and the National Defense," U.S. Naval Institute *Proceedings*, vol. 55, no. 9 (Sept. 1929), 751–64.

[3] ADM W. V. Pratt, "Our Naval Policy," U.S. Naval Institute *Proceedings*, vol. 58, no. 7 (July 1932), 953.

[4] Ibid., 958.

[5] Ibid., 959.

[6] Wheeler, *Admiral William Veazie Pratt*, 285–86.

[7] Craig L. Symonds, "William Veazie Pratt," in Love, *The Chiefs of Naval Operations*, 74–75.

[8] Thomas C. Hone, "The Effectiveness of the 'Washington Treaty' Navy," *Naval War College Review*, vol. 32, no. 6 (Nov.–Dec. 1979), 38.

[9] Federal government tax and other income fell from $4.1 billion in fiscal 1930 to $3.1 in fiscal year 1931 and $2.0 billion in fiscal year 1932. As he watched this collapse, Hoover first attempted to reduce funding already appropriated for the fiscal years 1931 and 1932. Then he used his authority under the Budget Act of 1921 to force the Navy Department to accept a nearly 18 percent reduction of its fiscal year 1933 budget request. See Albion, *Makers of Naval Policy*, 245–46.

[10] Pratt, "Our Naval Policy," 965.

[11] Ibid., 965–67.

[12] Albion, *Makers of Naval Policy*, 239, 249.

[13] Wheeler, *Admiral William Veazie Pratt*, 371.

[14] Ibid.

[15] These cruisers carried 8-inch guns and did not displace more than 10,000 tons. At first they were referred to as just "cruisers" or even as "light cruisers." But soon the term "heavy cruisers" was accepted. "Light" cruisers were those carrying 6-inch guns, even if they displaced the same tonnage as a "heavy" cruiser.

[16] "Budget 1932. Estimate of the Situation and Base Development Program," in "Annual Estimates of the Chief of Naval Operations," Office of the Secretary of the Navy, Confidential Correspondence, 1927–1939, File L1-1, 23, RG 80, NARA.

[17] Ibid., 25.

[18] Ibid., 22.

[19] Ibid.

[20] Friedman, *U.S. Cruisers*, 163.

[21] Friedman, *U.S. Aircraft Carriers, An Illustrated Design History* (Annapolis, MD: Naval Institute Press, 1983), Chap. 6.

[22] Friedman, *U.S. Cruisers*, ch. 6. The two gunboats that were built were *Erie* (PG-50) and *Charleston* (PG-51). They were authorized in June 1933 and commissioned in July 1936. See *Ships' Data, U.S. Naval Vessels*, 1 Jan. 1938 (Washington, DC: Navy Department and GPO, 1938), 158–59.

[23] Friedman, *U.S. Cruisers*, 142.

[24] Stephen Roskill, *Naval Policy Between the Wars, Vol. II, The Period of Reluctant Rearmament, 1930–1939* (Annapolis, MD: Naval Institute Press, 1976), 25, 85.

[25] *Army Navy Journal*, 4 Oct. 1930, 101.

[26] CAPT Land would be appointed Chief, BuC&R, and promoted rear admiral in Oct. 1932 and serve in that post until Apr. 1937. In Feb. 1938, he was appointed head of the Maritime Commission. In Feb. 1942, he was made Administrator of the War Shipping Administration and served in that position and also as head of the Maritime Commission for the duration of World War II. Land was an early supporter of naval aviation, learning to fly while working for RADM Moffett in BuAer in the early 1920s.

[27] Another officer assigned to this section was CAPT John W. Greenslade, a member of the General Board. In World War II, Greenslade served as Commandant of the Twelfth Naval District and Commander, Western Sea Frontier, retiring from the Navy as a vice admiral.

[28] According to Gerald Wheeler, Pratt thought that Halligan would be chosen CNO, but Halligan declined to replace RADM Moffett on the latter's death in the crash of the airship *Akron* in March 1933, and that blocked Halligan from further promotion. See Wheeler, *William Veazie Pratt*, 316, 318.

[29] *United States Navy Regulations, 1920*, as reprinted in 1941 (Washington, DC: GPO, 1941), 137–39.

[30] Wheeler, *Admiral William Veazie Pratt*, 323–24.

[31] Kuehn, *Agents of Innovation* For more details on the role of the General Board, see "Managerial Style in the Interwar Navy: A Reappraisal," by Thomas C. Hone and Mark D. Mandeles, *Naval War College Review*, vol. 32, no. 5 (Sept.–Oct. 1980), 88–101, and Hone and Mandeles, "Interwar Innovation in Three Navies: USN, RN, IJN," 63–83.

[32] Wheeler, *Admiral William Veazie Pratt*, 324.

[33] Thomas C. Hone, *Power and Change, The Administrative History of the Office of the Chief of Naval Operations, 1956–1986* (Washington, DC: Naval Historical Center and the GPO, 1989),

6. See also, "Organization of the Navy Department," General Board Study No. 446 (1933–1939), 24 Jan. 1934, Record Group 80, NARA (Hereafter cited "Organization of the Navy Department," General Board Study No. 446).

[34] "Report of the Board to Consider and Recommend upon the Reorganization of the Navy Department and the Amalgamation of Certain or All Staff Corps and the Marine Corps with the Line of the Navy," 6 Dec. 1933, in "Organization of the Navy Department," General Board Study No. 446, 9, para. 9.

[35] On 17 Dec. 1932, in a letter to the Secretary of the Navy, CNO Pratt had opposed any major reorganization of the Navy Department. On 28 June 1933, the chairman of the General Board had taken the same position in a memo to Secretary Swanson. See "Organization of the Navy Department," General Board Study No. 446.

[36] MAJ George B. Eaton, USA, "General Walter Krueger and Joint War Planning, 1922–1938," *Naval War College Review*, vol. 48, no. 2 (Spring 1995), 94–95, 98.

[37] Ibid., 100–101. See also Wheeler, *Admiral William Veazie Pratt*, 245.

[38] Wheeler, *Admiral William Veazie Pratt*, 356–57.

[39] Ibid., 357–58.

[40] RADM William V. Pratt, "The Preparation of the United States Fleet for Battle and Its Conduct Therein. The Exercise of High Naval Command," lecture given at the Army War College, Washington Barracks, Washington, DC, 1 Apr. 1927, RG 38, Strategic Plans Division Reports, Box 9, 3, NWC Archives.

[41] Ibid.

[42] Ibid., 5.

[43] Ibid., 7.

[44] On 10 April 1933, Secretary Swanson sent a memo to "All Bureaus and Offices, Navy Department," detailing drastic reductions in Navy expenditures. Subj: "Reduction in Expenditures for Fiscal Year 1934," SONYD-C-Kr-4/8, (SC) L1-1 (1934) in "Organization of the Navy Department," General Board Study No. 446.

[45] Wheeler, *Admiral William Veazie Pratt*, 365.

[46] Ibid., 367.

[47] John C. Walter, "William Harrison Standley," in Love, *The Chiefs of Naval Operations*, 92.

[48] Jonathan G. Utley, "Franklin Roosevelt and Naval Strategy, 1933–1941," in *FDR and the U.S. Navy*, ed. by Edward J. Marolda (New York: St. Martin's Press, 1998), 51.

[49] Waldo Heinrichs, "FDR and the Admirals: Strategy and Statecraft," in Marolda, *FDR and the U.S. Navy*, 116.

[50] *An Act to encourage national industrial recovery, to foster fair competition, and to provide for the construction of certain useful public works, and for other purposes,* [National Industrial

Recovery Act] Public Law 67, 73rd Cong., 1st sess. (16 June 1933), Title II, Sec. 202, para "e."

[51] "Budget 1936. Annual Estimate of the Situation, including Shore Establishment Projects," in "Annual Estimates of the Chief of Naval Operations," Office of the Secretary of the Navy, Confidential Correspondence, 1927–1939, File L1-1, RG 80, NARA, 65. The two "sloops" were ADM Pratt's heavy gunboats.

[52] Ibid.

[53] House Committee on Appropriations, *Navy Department Appropriation Bill for 1934, Hearings Conducted by the Subcommittee of the Committee on Appropriation*, 72nd Cong., 2nd sess., 23 Jan. 1933, 24. Digital version at https://babel.hathitrust.org/cgi/pt?id=uc1.b3637072;view=1up;seq=1.

[54] Ibid., 25.

[55] House Committee on Appropriations, *Navy Department Appropriation Bill for 1936, Hearing before Subcommittee of the Committee on Appropriations*, 74th Cong., 1st sess., 25 Feb. 1935, 89. Digital version at https://babel.hathitrust.org/cgi/pt?id=uc1.b3637097;view=1up;seq=99.

[56] Ibid., 118.

[57] Walter, "William Harrison Standley," in Love, *The Chiefs of Naval Operations*, 92.

[58] Both sponsors were Democrats—Vinson from a district in Georgia and Park M. Trammell a senator from Florida.

[59] *An Act to establish the composition of the United States Navy with respect to the categories of vessels limited by the treaties signed at Washington, 6 Feb. 1922, and at London, 22 Apr. 1930, at the limits prescribed by those treaties; to authorize the construction of certain naval vessels; and for other purposes*, [Vinson-Trammell Act/First Vinson Act] Public Law 135, 73rd Cong. 2nd sess. (27 Mar. 1934), Sec. 2. (Hereafter, Vinson-Trannell Act). Digital version at http://legisworks.org/congress/73/publaw-135.pdf.

[60] Ibid., Sec. 3. In the 25 Feb. 1935 hearing on Navy Appropriation Bill for 1936 before the subcommittee of the House Appropriations Committee for the, RADM Christian J. Peoples, (SC), who headed BuSandA and also served in the air procurement division of the Treasury Department, provided an explanation of how the profits of private firms could be limited under the Vinson-Trammell Act. See 322–24.

[61] This meant the Naval Aircraft Factory. See *Wings for the Navy: A History of the Naval Aircraft Factory, 1917–1956*, by William F. Trimble (Annapolis, MD: Naval Institute Press, 1990).

[62] Vinson-Trammell Act, Sec. 4.

[63] Walter, "William Harrison Standley," in Love, *The Chiefs of Naval Operations*, 93.

[64] Memo, CNO to All Bureaus and Offices, subj: "Ship Development Board," Op-23-RSM, QB (94)/A3-1 (340905), 5 Sept. 1934, paragraph 5, in "Organization of the Navy Department," General Board Study No. 446. The Ship Development Board was responsible to the Director of

the Fleet Maintenance Division in OPNAV.

65 Memo, CNO to Bureau Chiefs, subj: "New Construction; Coordination of work of Bureaus in connection with, By Chief of Naval Operations," Op-23-RSM, FS/L8-3 (340921), 24 Sept. 1934, paragraphs 2 and 3, in "Organization of the Navy Department," General Board Study No. 446.

66 In a letter to Secretary Swanson dated 2 Mar. 1934, President Roosevelt argued that "it is of the utmost importance that the Secretary of the Navy himself shall know what is going on every day in all major matters affecting all bureaus and offices." Put another way, Swanson was to resist granting any more authority to the CNO. The letter is in General Board Study No. 446, "Organization of the Navy Department."

67 Friedman, *U.S. Cruisers*, 206.

68 Friedman, *U.S. Destroyers*, 92.

69 Thomas C. Hone, "Naval Reconstitution, Surge, and Mobilization: Once and Future," *Naval War College Review*, vol. 47, no. 3 (Summer 1994), 70.

70 Once the Washington treaty was signed in 1922, the industrial base for armor for battleships almost completely collapsed. See *U.S. Navy Bureau of Ordnance in World War II*, by Buford Rowland and William B. Boyd (Washington, DC: Bureau of Ordnance, Dept. of the Navy, and GPO, 1954), ch. 3.

71 Hone, "Naval Reconstitution, Surge, and Mobilization," 71.

72 Ibid.

73 Thomas C. Hone, "Fighting on Our Own Ground: The War of Production, 1920–1942," *Naval War College Review*, vol. 45, no. 2 (Spring 1992), 103.

74 Memo, from: The Chief of the Bureau of Navigation; to; The General Board; subj: "Bill for Reorganization of the Navy Department and for Amalgamation of certain Corps with the line as proposed by Congressman Vinson," Nav-HH, EN/93-1(4), 10 Jan. 1934, 4, in, "Organization of the Navy Department," General Board Study No. 446.

75 Albion, *Makers of Naval Policy*, 176.

76 Ibid.

77 Ibid., 177.

78 *Statement of Rear Admiral Ernest J. King, Chief, Bureau of Aeronautics*, Hearing before the Subcommittee of the House Committee on Appropriations, Navy Department Appropriation Bill for 1935, 6 Dec. 1933 (Washington, DC: GPO, 1934), 402.

79 Ibid.

80 CAPT David Potter (SC), "The Annual Naval Appropriation Bill: How It Becomes a Law," U.S. Naval Institute *Proceedings*, vol. 58, no. 358 (Dec. 1932), 1723. See also the comment on Potter's paper by BGEN George Richards, Marine Corps Paymaster, in the same issue of *Proceedings*, 1802–1809.

[81] Potter, "The Annual Naval Appropriation Bill: How It Becomes a Law," 1724.

[82] Roskill, *Naval Policy Between the Wars, Vol. II,* ch. X.

[83] Baer, *One Hundred Years of Sea Power*, 131.

[84] See Roskill, *Naval Policy Between the Wars, Vol. II*, and Harold and Margaret Sprout, *Toward a New Order of Sea Power* (Princeton, NJ: Princeton University Press, 1940).

[85] Walter, "William Harrison Standley," in Love, *The Chiefs of Naval Operations*, 95.

[86] *Ships' Data, U.S. Naval Vessels*, 1 Jan. 1938, ix. The definition of "standard displacement" is on page vii: "The standard displacement of a surface vessel is the displacement of the vessel, complete, fully manned, engined, and equipped ready for sea, including all armament and ammunition, equipment, outfit, provisions and fresh water for crew, miscellaneous stores and implements of every description that are intended to be carried in war, but without fuel or reserve feed water on board." The standard displacement for a submarine was based on the submarine's surface displacement without counting its fuel or ballast water.

[87] Roskill, *Naval Policy Between the Wars, Vol. II*, 299.

[88] Walter, "William Harrison Standley," in Love, *The Chiefs of Naval Operations*, 94.

[89] Trent Hone, "The Evolution of Fleet Tactical Doctrine in the U.S. Navy, 1922–1941," 1118–1119.

[90] Ibid., 1125.

[91] Hone and Hone, *Battle Line*, 131.

[92] Ibid., 132 (emphasis in the original).

[93] Trent Hone, "U.S. Navy Surface Battle Doctrine and Victory in the Pacific," *Naval War College Review*, vol. 62, no. 1 (Winter 2009), 69.

[94] The head of the newly created Maritime Commission was RADM Emory S. Land, (Ret.), who had been Chief, BuC&R. In effect, the Maritime Commission's subsidies were an indirect form of Navy spending. See VADM Emory S. Land, USN (Ret.), *Winning the War with Ships* (New York: Robert M. McBride, 1958).

[95] John Major, "William Daniel Leahy," in Love, *The Chiefs of Naval Operations*, 102.

[96] Robert E. Sherwood, *Roosevelt and Hopkins, An Intimate History* (New York: Harper & Brothers, 1948).

[97] Thomas C. Hone, "The Evolution of the U.S. Fleet, 1933–1941: How the President Mattered," in Marolda, *FDR and the U.S. Navy*, 87.

[98] Ibid.

[99] Ibid., 88.

[100] Ibid.

[101] Ibid., 89.

[102] Ibid., 90.

[103] Roskill, *Naval Policy Between the Wars, Vol. II*, 363.

[104] Major, "William Daniel Leahy," in Love, *The Chiefs of Naval Operations*, 106.

[105] Ibid., 106–107.

[106] *An Act to Establish the Composition of the United States Navy, to Authorize the Construction of Certain Naval Vessels, and for Other Purposes*, [Naval Expansion Act/Second Vinson Act] Public Law 528, 75th Cong., 3rd sess., (17 May 1938) Sections 1 through 4. Digital version at http://legisworks.org/congress/75/publaw-528.pdf.

[107] See "The Decline and Renaissance of the Navy, 1922–1944," prepared by David I. Walsh, Chairman of the Committee on Naval Affairs, U. S. Senate, 7 June 1944 (Washington, DC: GPO, 1944).

[108] In October 1937, before *Panay* was attacked and sunk on the Yangtze River, ADM Harry E. Yarnell, Commander-in-Chief of the Asiatic Fleet, sent CNO Leahy "an outline plan for a maritime war against Japan which would avoid deployment of huge land forces." Leahy sent this on to the president, though he knew that considering seriously such a plan would force a reassessment of the accepted Orange Plan. The opponents of war who did not trust Roosevelt had reason to be concerned. See Roskill, *Naval Policy Between the Wars, Vol II*, 365.

[109] Chisholm, *Waiting for Dead Men's Shoes*, 718, emphasis added by Chisholm.

[110] Ibid., 720–21.

[111] Ibid., Table 27.1, 749.

[112] See "Organization of the Navy Department," General Board Study No. 446, which cites a memo (Op-13/PS, (SC) A3-1, Serial No. 34) from CNO Stark dated 12 Aug. 1939.

[113] Hone and Hone, *Battle Line*, 128.

[114] The genesis of this piece of legislation was the *Report of the President's Committee*, The President's Committee on Administrative Management (Washington, DC: GPO, 1937).

[115] *United States Government Manual*, Feb. 1940, Office of Government Reports (Washington, DC: GPO, 1940), 98–99.

[116] On 4 Aug. 1939, President Roosevelt instructed the War Resources Board to study the Army and Navy Munitions Board's plan for industrial mobilization. See Furer, *Administration of the Navy Department in World War II*.

[117] "Neutrality Act" of 31 August 1935 (49 Stat. 1081; 22 U.S.C. 441 note), Joint Resolution. See also, Public Resolution 54, 76th Congress, 54 Stat. 4 (http://legislink.org/us/stat-54-4), 4 Nov. 1939. The consequences of the Neutrality Acts for the American aircraft industry are spelled out in *Buying Aircraft: Materiel Procurement for the Army Air Forces*, by Irving Brinton Holley Jr. (Washington, DC: Office of the Chief of Military History, Dept. of the Army, 1964), ch. IX.

[118] This was the "Interdepartmental Committee for Coordination of Foreign and Domestic

Military Purchases" under the Secretary of the Treasury.

[119] B. Mitchell Simpson III, "Harold Raynsford Stark," in Love, *The Chiefs of Naval Operations*, 131.

[120] Allison W. Saville, "Charles Edison," in Coletta, *American Secretaries of the Navy, Vol. II*, 670.

[121] Miller, *War Plan Orange*, 215.

[122] Baer, *One Hundred Years of Sea Power*, 148.

[123] Mitchell Simpson III, "Harold Raynsford Stark," in Love, *The Chiefs of Naval Operations*, 121–22.

[124] Joel Ira Holwitt, *Execute Against Japan, The U.S. Decision to Conduct Unrestricted Submarine Warfare* (College Station: Texas A&M University Press, 2009), 92.

[125] Mitchell Simpson III, "Harold Raynsford Stark," in Love, *The Chiefs of Naval Operations*, 124.

[126] *An Act to Establish the Composition of the United States Navy, to Authorize the Construction of Certain Naval Vessels, and for Other Purposes*, [Third Vinson Act] Public Law 629, 76th Cong., 3rd sess. (14 June 1940). Digital version at http://legisworks.org/congress/76/publaw-629.pdf.

[127] *An Act to Establish the Composition of the United States Navy, to Authorize the Construction of Certain Naval vessels, and for Other Purposes*, [Two-Ocean Navy Act] Public Law 757, 76th Cong., 3rd sess. (19 July 1940). Digital version at http://legisworks.org/congress/76/publaw-757.pdf.

[128] The almost constant negotiations within the executive branch and between executive branch officials and members of Congress is discussed in *Admiral John Towers: The Struggle for Naval Air Supremacy*, by Clark G. Reynolds (Annapolis, MD: Naval Institute Press, 1991), ch. 11.

[129] See *The Navy and the Industrial Mobilization in World War II*, by Robert H. Connery (Princeton, NJ: Princeton University Press, 1951). Connery was correct to highlight this authorized shift to negotiated contracts as one of the major keys to wartime mobilization.

[130] See Furer, *Administration of the Navy Department in World War II*, 219–21. In Aug. 1939, Secretary of the Navy Charles Edison first directed the two bureaus (C&R and Engineering) to consolidate their design divisions. Then he appointed RADM Samuel M. Robinson as chief of the Bureau of Engineering. Later, he made Robinson Coordinator of Shipbuilding, and soon thereafter (on 18 Sept. 1939) Edison appointed RADM Alexander H. Van Keuren, who was the chief of Construction and Repair, the Asst. Coordinator of Shipbuilding. That's as much consolidation as Secretary Edison could do under his existing authority.

[131] George H. Lobdell, "Frank Knox," in Coletta, *American Secretaries of the Navy, Vol. II*, 688–90.

[132] Mitchell Simpson III, "Harold Raynsford Stark," in Love, *The Chiefs of Naval Operations*, 123.

[133] Ibid.

[134] Ibid., 125.

[135] Ibid.

[136] Baer, *One Hundred Years of Sea Power*, 154.

[137] Ibid.

[138] "Cash and Carry" had been allowed under the 1937 Neutrality Act for everything except arms; that limitation was removed with the 1939 Neutrality Act. See https://history.state.gov/milestones/1921-1936/neutrality-acts . Mitchell Simpson III, "Harold Raynsford Stark," in Love, *The Chiefs of Naval Operations*, 124–26; Miller, *War Plan Orange*, 270. The full text of the "Arsenal of Democracy" speech can be found at http://www.presidency.ucsb.edu/ws/?pid=15917.

[139] Ibid., 149–50.

[140] Ibid., 151.

[141] Ibid., 150.

[142] Department of the Navy, Navy General Order 143, 3 Feb. 1941, Navy Department Library. The order also stated that the CINCUS would be "appointed from among" the fleet commanders, and ADM Husband Kimmel, in addition to commanding the Pacific Fleet, also was designated CINCUS. *Navy Directory*, 1 Apr. 1941, 323.

[143] Klein, *A Call to Arms, Mobilizing America for World War II*, 134.

[144] Reynolds, *Admiral John H. Towers*, 339.

[145] That required setting up a "Material Procurement Section" in OPNAV. See also, Reynolds, *Admiral John H. Towers*, 306, 347.

[146] Reynolds, *Admiral John H. Towers*, and the detailed warship design histories of Norman Friedman.

[147] Thomas B. Buell, *Master of Sea Power: A Biography of Fleet Admiral Ernest J. King* (Annapolis, MD: Naval Institute Press, 2012), 139.

[148] Robert J. Cressman, *The Official Chronology of the U.S. Navy in World War II* (Annapolis, MD: Naval Institute Press and Washington, DC: Naval Historical Center, 2000), 49–56.

[149] Mitchell Simpson III, "Harold Raynsford Stark," in Love, *The Chiefs of Naval Operations*, 129.

[150] Lobdell, "Frank Knox," in Coletta, *American Secretaries of the Navy*, Vol. II, 695–96.

[151] Ibid., 686. The secretary focused on the budget, legislation, and public relations. The undersecretary dealt with other government agencies concerned with procurement, with Navy contracting, and the Judge Advocate General's preparation of routine legislation for Congress. The assistant secretary focused on personnel, the shore stations and bases, civilian employees, labor relations, and the flow of paper.

[152] Paul Stillwell, ed., *Air Raid: Pearl Harbor! Recollections of a Day of Infamy* (Annapolis, MD: Naval Institute Press, 1981), 91.

[153] Martin Dibner, *The Deep Six* (New York: Doubleday & Co., 1953), 90.

CHAPTER 5

Admiral Ernest J. King: CNO and Commander-in-Chief—at Last

". . . life in the navy, although it seemed to move from one crisis to another, was really one continuous crisis, that even while dealing with one emergency it was necessary to be making plans to deal with the next."

C. S. Forester, *Mr. Midshipman Hornblower*

Introduction

When Admiral Ernest J. King, Commander-in-Chief of the United States Fleet (now known as COMINCH), relieved Admiral Harold R. Stark as Chief of Naval Operations on 26 March 1942, the hopes of the officers who had worked in 1915 to create the CNO's position and give it significant authority were realized. EO 9096 of 12 March 1942 specified that

> The duties of the Commander in Chief, United States Fleet, and the duties of the Chief of Naval Operations, may be combined and devolve upon one officer who shall have the title 'Commander in Chief, United States Fleet, and Chief of Naval Operations', and who shall be the principal naval adviser to the President on the conduct of the War, and the principal naval adviser and executive to the Secretary of the Navy on the conduct of the activities of the Naval Establishment.[1]

As far as command was concerned, EO 9096 gave it to King: ". . . the officer holding the combined offices as herein provided shall have supreme command of the operating forces comprising the several fleets, sea-going forces, and sea frontier forces of the United States Navy and shall be directly responsible, under the general direction of the Secretary of the Navy, to the President . . ."[2] But King was also

> charged, under the direction of the Secretary of the Navy, with the preparation, readiness, and logistic support of the operating forces comprising the several fleets, seagoing

forces and sea frontier forces of the United States Navy, and with the coordination and direction of effort to this end of the bureaus and offices of the Navy Department except such offices (other than bureaus) as the Secretary of the Navy may specifically exempt.[3]

Executive Order 9096 did not grant the new CNO-COMINCH more *legal* authority than the Secretary of the Navy and his civilian deputies, but it put Admiral King in the driver's seat, and he worked to stay there and even to increase his *actual* authority within the Navy Department.[4] However, this grant of authority to Admiral King raised two major questions. One was administrative: How could he carry out both jobs simultaneously and well? The second was constitutional: How could he work effectively without challenging the authority of the civilian leaders of the Navy Department? In short, how could King be both effective and responsible?

The Navy expanded tremendously during the war. In June of 1940, there were 189,000 men in the Navy and Marine Corps. In August 1945, that number (including the women who had volunteered to serve) had grown to 3,890,000. In 1940, the Navy had 510 ships; by August 1945, it had 8,149. In 1940, the Navy and Marines flew 1,741 aircraft; by 1945, they were flying more than 40,000.[5] How could one individual oversee this huge expansion, command the fleet, and serve as the President's principal naval adviser "on the conduct of the War"? Remember that CNO-COMINCH was the principal naval advisor on the conduct of the *whole* war and not just on the naval side to it. President Franklin Roosevelt regarded King as perhaps the military's most sound strategic thinker, which meant that King would be a pivotal member of what came to be called the Joint Chiefs of Staff (JCS). But because the war was a coalition war, King was also one of the key members of the Combined Chiefs of Staff (CCS). How could King do all these things without exhausting himself? EO 9096 had authorized the new CNO-COMINCH to have deputies and assistants, but King's challenge was to use his staffs and his authority to *direct* the Navy without immersing himself in the many details of *managing* the Navy. Similarly, King and the other members of the JCS had often impressive staff support, but advising the President on strategy was a demanding task, and one that could not be delegated.

King had spent his career aiming for the Navy's top job.[6] He well understood that the naval forces under his command were supposed to defeat those of Imperial Japan and Nazi Germany, despite the fact that prewar planning had not been based on a two-ocean war. When King became CNO-COMINCH, Rear Admiral Bradley A. Fiske, the instigator behind the creation of the CNO's position in 1915, was still alive. Would King fulfill Fiske's vision for the office?

Preliminaries: King as COMINCH

Then–Rear Admiral King had thought his career was at an end when he was ordered in the summer of 1939 to serve on the General Board in Washington. Being placed on the General Board was definitely not what King had aimed for. His career "track" had been an impressive one. He had qualified to command submarines, had learned to fly, and had served as an acquisition manager when he headed BuAer after Rear Admiral Moffett's death in April 1933. He had commanded at sea (carrier *Lexington* in 1930–1932), attended the Naval War College, and served as Commander, Aircraft, Battle Force, beginning in January 1938, where he held the temporary rank of vice admiral.

However, even before King had taken his place on the General Board, something very important was happening within the Navy that would take him out of the board and back into command at sea. On 12 February 1939, CINCUS sent a memo to the Chief of Naval Operations describing experiments with "radio controlled target airplanes." The targets, controlled from piloted airplanes, had made diving passes at ships, and the ships had found it extremely difficult to shoot them down.[7] As the memo noted, "the accepted procedures and technique are not uniformly capable of being extended successfully to firings on a maneuvering target."[8] In plain language, the antiaircraft gunners on the ships could not shoot the targets out of the sky. Or, to put it another way, antiaircraft defense of the fleet was incredibly poor. Something had to be done. Aircraft were flying faster, farther, and carrying heavier bombs. This was true of land-based aircraft *and* carrier planes, especially dive-bombers. The threat from the skies had suddenly increased dramatically. Experience in the European war soon confirmed that.

In response, Secretary of the Navy Edison asked King to review fleet antiaircraft defense. King reported to Edison and then to Frank Knox, Edison's successor, that the need for improved antiaircraft guns and fire control devices was "urgent and immediate."[9] As a result, Secretary Knox established the Antiaircraft Defense Board in early August 1940 to come up with a comprehensive solution to the problem. In the meantime, King's hard work, intelligence, and decisiveness had impressed Secretary Edison. In his last memo to President Roosevelt, dated 24 June 1940, Edison strongly recommended that King be appointed Navy commander-in-chief. King, said Edison, would shake "the service out of a peace-time psychology."[10] After spending time with King on an inspection trip to the Caribbean in October 1940, Frank Knox seemed to agree.[11] Both Navy secretaries saw at first hand that King had both operational and organizational skills. In so rigorously criticizing the Navy's antiaircraft weapons programs, for example, King had challenged BuOrd—and gotten away with it. That was the sort of officer that both Edison and Knox knew would be essential in wartime.[12]

King left Washington when he was appointed commander of the Navy's Patrol Force in the Atlantic on 17 December 1940. In January 1941, President Roosevelt and Secretary Knox decided to reorganize the U.S. fleet, and the new organization went into effect on 1 February 1941.[13] King was made Atlantic Fleet commander and promoted, first to vice admiral and then to four stars. Secretary Knox sent a warm letter of congratulations to the new vice admiral, saying, "I am still a great deal of a novice in this Navy business, and I am depending upon you [fleet commanders] to help me along in my education."[14] King's fleet increased in size in April 1941 when CNO Stark shifted three battleships, a carrier, four cruisers, and two destroyer squadrons from the Pacific Fleet to King's command. King did not apparently know how close the United States was to supporting British convoys against German submarines.[15] But what he was certain of was that he had to stay close to the decision making in Washington, and he maintained an office in "Main

Navy" on Constitution Avenue so he could consult with Admiral Stark and Secretary Knox. He also moored his flagship, heavy cruiser *Augusta* (CA-31), in Narragansett Bay near the Naval War College and the Newport Naval Station.[16] He wanted to stay in close touch with Washington.

King went to Washington the day after the attack on Pearl Harbor, but he did not stay. However, he returned on 16 December to be informed by Secretary Knox that he had been appointed overall fleet commander and that Rear Admiral Chester W. Nimitz had been selected to command the Pacific Fleet.[17] King quickly made some decisions about his new position. The first was that he would command from Washington. As he said, "Where the power is, that is where the headquarters have to be." The second was to determine just what his relationship with CNO Stark would be. Knox put two senior admirals to work on that issue. Then Knox, Admiral Stark, and King went to see President Roosevelt. To Roosevelt, King said that he wanted his official acronym changed from CINCUS to COMINCH. He also told the President that he wanted to avoid as much as possible press conferences and testifying to congressional committees. The new COMINCH also said that he wanted "command authority over the bureaus in the Navy Department." The President said that last wish would require a change to the law, one he wasn't ready to ask the Congress to make, but he also reassured King that "any bureau chief who did not cooperate with King" would be replaced.[18]

The next day, 17 December 1941, King approved what his biographer Thomas B. Buell called "one of the most remarkable documents of the Second World War." It was the draft executive order defining the duties of the CNO and the COMINCH.[19] The order, published on 18 December as EO 8984, declared that COMINCH "shall have supreme command of the operating forces comprising the several fleets of the United States Navy and the operating forces of the naval coastal frontier commands, and shall be directly responsible, under the general direction of the Secretary of the Navy, to the President of the United States therefor."[20] COMINCH was directed by EO 8984 to "keep the Chief of Naval Operations informed of the logistic and other needs of the operating forces." In turn, the CNO was directed to keep COMINCH "informed as to the extent to which the various needs can be met."[21] Then EO 8984 specified that, subject to the authority given COMINCH, "the duties and responsibilities of the Chief of Naval Operations under the Secretary of the Navy will remain unchanged." The CNO "shall continue to be responsible for the preparation of war plans from the long range point of view."[22] As historian Buell recognized, the distinction between the authority of COMINCH and that of the CNO was not clear. Even worse, "Left unsaid were such crucial matters as who would advise the President, and who would represent the Navy during conferences with the British."[23]

After gaining a strong grant of authority, the new COMINCH had to quickly create a staff that would enable him to exercise that authority effectively. He selected Rear Admiral Russell Willson, Naval Academy Superintendent, to be his chief of staff. Willson's deputy would be Rear Admiral Richard S. Edwards, commander of submarines in the Atlantic. Willson was a good choice; Edwards was an inspired one. As it turned out, King and Willson did not work well together, and Willson was moved out and Edwards up. King valued Edwards because the latter "never promoted his own interests" but always put those of King first. As Buell observed, "Edwards remained with King throughout the war, an exception to King's policy of frequent rotation between COMINCH staff and sea duty."[24]

King wanted as his chief planning officer Captain (later Vice Admiral) Charles M. Cooke Jr., known as "Savvy" because of his sagacity and calm. When Cooke's submarine had sunk bow-first "in 180 feet of water off the coast of New Jersey in September 1920," he and his crew survived by raising the stern "above the water, laboriously punching a small hole through the sub's pressure hull, and then attracting the attention of a passing merchant ship with a jury-rigged 'flag.'"[25] It was an extraordinary, breathtaking, achievement, and one King had not forgotten. Cooke, in command of fleet flagship *Pennsylvania* (BB-38) at Pearl Harbor, at first resisted King's summons to Washington, but eventually he gave in. To round off his team, King chose Captain John L. McCrea to serve as naval aide to President Roosevelt. McCrea would become a sort of two-way communicator—telling Roosevelt what King wanted the President to hear and also telling King what Roosevelt wanted King to know.[26]

King deliberately wanted a small staff with three divisions: plans, readiness, and operations. The personnel in these divisions would do strategic planning in both the Atlantic and Pacific, link COMINCH with anticipated joint and combined staffs, guide training and readiness across fleet boundaries, track and assess fleet operations, and provide OPNAV with the requirements that the OPNAV and secretariat staffs needed to construct and sustain the fleet. To avoid having his COMINCH staff cover the same ground as OPNAV, on 15 January 1942 King had requested that CNO Stark transfer elements of OPNAV's War Plans, Fleet Training, and Ship Movements Divisions to COMINCH. Stark told his OPNAV deputies that his one thought was "to have Admiral King free to do nothing but operate the Fleet," and he and King then engaged in a back-and-forth exchange about which elements of OPNAV should move immediately to COMINCH.[27]

King as CNO-COMINCH

But the relationship between the CNO and the new COMINCH could not be an easy one. There was too much overlap, as both Stark and King realized. King informed the President that "he was perfectly willing as COMINCH to be placed under CNO," and Roosevelt told him that the problem would be taken care of.[28] The President did so with EO 9096, moving Stark aside instead of King. A sign of the President's confidence in King was the letter Harry Hopkins, the President's confidante, sent the new CNO-COMINCH on 13 March 1942. "I can't tell you how pleased I was," said Hopkins, "when the President told me of the action he was going to take about you. I think it is perfectly grand and I have a feeling it is going to be one of the most important things the President has done during the war."[29] This was high praise, indeed, but it was based on the assumption—held by Roosevelt and Hopkins—that the Navy would halt the Japanese and deal with the German U-boats beginning to operate off the East Coast.[30]

Admiral Stark resigned as CNO and was appointed to the post that the late Admiral William S. Sims had held during World War I—Commander, U.S. Naval Forces, Europe. The former CNO reached London on 30 April 1942. The British were glad to see him. Stark had served on the staff of Vice Admiral Sims in London in 1918, and he was both known and respected in the United Kingdom. He immediately gained access to Admiral Sir Dudley Pound, First Sea Lord and Chief of the Naval Staff, and Pound selected one of his closest friends, retired Vice Admiral Sir Geoffrey Blake, to serve as Stark's "personal liaison officer."[31] With Blake's assistance, Stark and his staff gained the confidence of their British counterparts, which was essential if the Allied governments were to win the conflict in the Atlantic with German U-boats. By the time the struggle with the U-boats reached its climax in March 1943, Stark and American diplomat W. Averell Harriman were regular participants in the meetings of the British War Cabinet that dealt with anti-submarine warfare.[32]

When King became CNO-COMINCH in March, 1942, the basic administrative machinery of wartime mobilization management was in place. Moreover, the basic American strategy had also been agreed upon: Germany was the greater danger and would be the primary focus of U.S. military attention. However, the war against Germany was a coalition war, and of the two major U.S. Allies (the Soviet Union and Great Britain), the British were by far the closer, and King and his colleagues on the JCS would have to work closely with them. The war against Japan was also a coalition war, but by the end of March 1942, only the United States had enough forces in the Pacific to form a barrier against further Japanese expansion. King's Navy would have to fight the Pacific war basically alone, and it soon became clear that the new CNO-COMINCH preferred it that way.

King had served on the staff of Vice Admiral Henry T. Mayo in World War I. He had come away from that experience disappointed in the performance of most of the Navy's flag officers.[33] An arrogant, confident "egoist," he was determined to gain control of the Navy and not lose that control to any challenger.[34] Accordingly, the new CNO-COMINCH immediately began thinking about "providing COMINCH/CNO with effective control over all aspects of the department that he viewed as contributing directly to the Navy's prosecution of the war."[35] This goal of control was an audacious claim against the Navy secretariat. King acknowledged the authority of the Secretary of the Navy, but he was thinking about "streamlining" the Navy Department so that CNO-COMINCH would serve under the SECNAV and senior officers would serve under CNO-COMINCH.[36] He circulated his proposals "to the bureau chiefs and principal officers" on 22 May 1942.

When he read King's proposals, Under Secretary of the Navy James M. Forrestal, the Navy's procurement executive, sent a memo to Secretary Knox saying,

> There are three main divisions of the activities of the Navy: procurement, supply and operations—the only reason for the existence of the first two being the third. I believe the operational side of the Navy should control the material side to the extent of determining what kind of ships, ordnance, aircraft, etc., it wants to use. *The procurement of*

this program should then be left to the procurement side with a minimum of interference in the way it is done[37] (italics in the original).

Forrestal, who had been president of a Wall Street bond-trading firm before becoming a special assistant to President Roosevelt in the spring of 1940, had also served in the Navy as a pilot in World War I. He had even spent most of 1918 working in the Navy Department in Washington, so he knew his way around. In terms of experience, intelligence, and energy, Forrestal was suited to his position. Over time, and especially after Forrestal took Knox's place after the latter's death from a heart attack in April 1944, he and King would become wary competitors for the authority and power to manage the Navy.

But what killed King's May 1942 reorganization proposal was the adamant opposition of President Roosevelt. The President told Secretary Knox that King's ideas amounted to "a reorganization and not a streamlining" of the Navy Department.[38] When King persisted in his effort to enlarge the authority of OPNAV at the expense of the secretariat, Roosevelt lost his temper and directed Knox to cancel King's latest reorganization directives and provide the White House with all recent orders from King regarding Navy organization and procedures. To Knox, Roosevelt termed King's actions "outrageous," particularly in light of his earlier rejection of King's 22 May proposals. Knox responded by telling King that "I have just received from the President a specific directive directing me to order the cancellation of the order of the Chief of Naval Operations, dated 15 May, creating an Assistant Chief of Naval Operations (ACNO) for Air and the order of 28 May creating the ACNO for Personnel and Material..." King had no choice but to comply.[39]

King may have been balked in his efforts to alter the relationship between OPNAV and the secretariat, but he had the authority to modify the structure of OPNAV, and he did so. OPNAV's organization chart on 27 March 1942 showed King as CNO-COMINCH, with his Vice Chief of Naval Operations (VCNO), Vice Admiral Frederick J. Horne, responsible for liaison with the British, the Army, and the Navy's own bureaus. Under VCNO Horne was the commandant of the Coast Guard and OP-13, the Central Division, responsible for liaison with the State Department and for reviewing proposed legislation and preparing statements for congressional hearings. Also under the VCNO was OP-11, the office of the Sub Chief of Naval Operations, responsible for liaison with the Marine Corps. The following divisions were directly under the authority of OP-11: Plans (OP-12), Naval Communications (OP-20), the Board of Inspection and Survey (OP-21), and the Naval Districts Inspection Board (OP-31). Also under the sub chief were three assistant CNOs: for operations, information and security, and maintenance.[40]

By 15 July 1942, the basic structure of OPNAV had not changed dramatically, but the organization chart showed some significant differences. The VCNO was still responsible for liaison with the British and the Navy's bureau chiefs, but he was also chief liaison officer with the commandants of the Marine Corps and the Coast Guard. Under the VCNO was the Sub Chief of Naval Operations, directly responsible for the following divisions: Naval Intelligence, Naval Communications, Pan American (i.e., Central and South America), the Hydrographic Office,

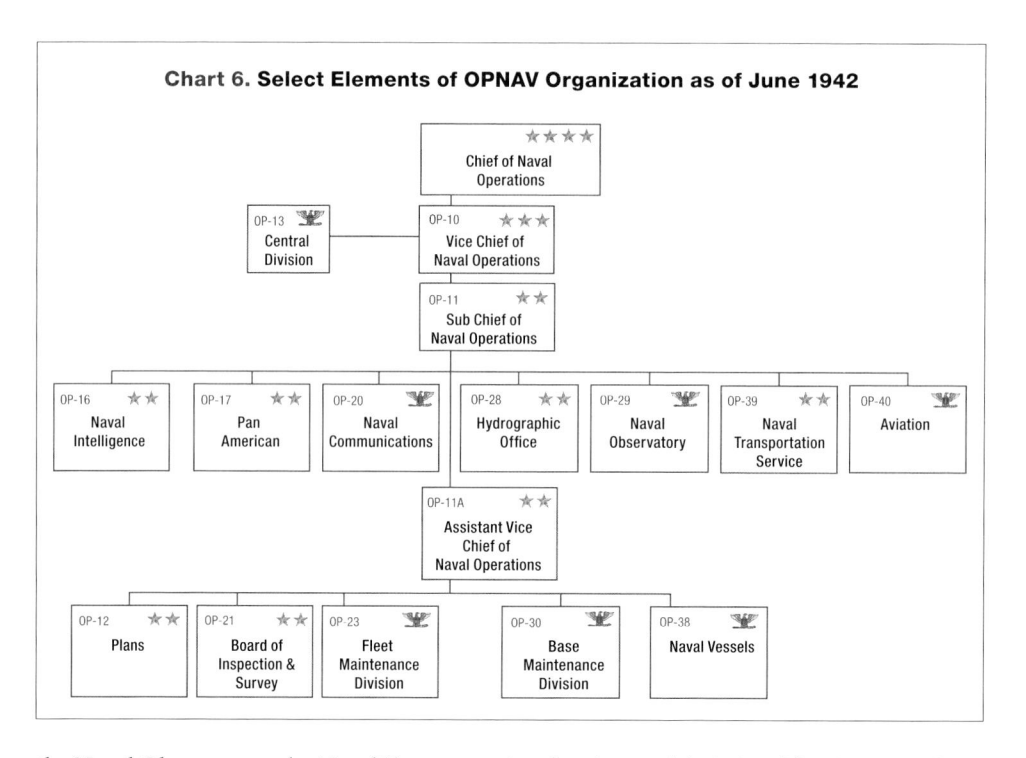

Chart 6. Select Elements of OPNAV Organization as of June 1942

- Chief of Naval Operations (★★★★)
  - OP-13 Central Division
  - OP-10 Vice Chief of Naval Operations (★★★)
    - OP-11 Sub Chief of Naval Operations (★★)
      - OP-16 Naval Intelligence (★★)
      - OP-17 Pan American (★★)
      - OP-20 Naval Communications
      - OP-28 Hydrographic Office (★★)
      - OP-29 Naval Observatory
      - OP-39 Naval Transportation Service (★★)
      - OP-40 Aviation
    - OP-11A Assistant Vice Chief of Naval Operations (★★)
      - OP-12 Plans (★★)
      - OP-21 Board of Inspection & Survey (★★)
      - OP-23 Fleet Maintenance Division
      - OP-30 Base Maintenance Division
      - OP-38 Naval Vessels

the Naval Observatory, the Naval Transportation Service, and Aviation. The Assistant CNO reported to the sub chief and supervised the following divisions: Plans, the Board of Inspection and Survey, Fleet Maintenance, Base Maintenance, and "Naval Vessels." There were more than 300 officers serving in OPNAV, compared to fewer than 90 in the COMINCH staff.[41]

Each bureau also had its headquarters staff in Washington: 98 officers in BuOrd's headquarters, for example, and 217 in BuShips' headquarters.[42] BuShips also had 129 officers serving away from Washington as "Inspectors of Naval Material," and 136 active and retired officers serving as "Supervisors of Shipbuilding" at various civilian shipyards. There were more officers serving as inspectors than there were in the offices of BuShips in Washington.[43] As a former bureau chief, King well knew that a major problem facing the Navy was to make sure that the bureaus—each a major organization in its own right—were responsive to the needs of the fleet. He believed that they would not be responsive if they held on to peacetime routines.

King had kept his COMINCH staff as small as possible so that he could communicate his energy and command philosophy all through it. It was his personal creation. But OPNAV and the bureaus were not his creations. Once President Roosevelt denied King the power to alter the relationship between OPNAV and the secretariat and gain control of the bureaus, the new CNO-COMINCH had to rely basically on the patterns of organization that already existed in the Navy. He could modify the structure and working patterns of OPNAV, and he could dominate the bureau chiefs with his aggressive personality and the tacit support of the President, but he had to take the existing organizations as he found them and then bend them to his purposes.

Initial Challenges Facing CNO-COMINCH

King inherited the "Washington Treaty" Navy that was already built and the Navy that was building—the force Congress had authorized and funded in the summer of 1940. But the forces on hand were not adequate for the initial demands of the war.[44] For example, the "Naval Coastal Frontier Forces," or "Sea Frontier Forces," as they were known after 6 February 1942, were inadequate as a deterrent to German submarine attacks along the East Coast and Japanese submarines prowling along the West Coast. As in 1917, there was an acute shortage of destroyers and smaller convoy escorts. The result was something of a disaster for the nation and an acute embarrassment for the Navy.[45] King—who regarded the situation as "desperate"—was unfortunately and inevitably at odds with retired Rear Admiral Emory S. Land, head of the War Shipping Administration.[46] King wanted more escort ships—combatants. Land wanted to increase the production of merchant ships. Which would it be—a policy of building merchant ships faster than German submarines could sink them, or a crash program of building more and better convoy escorts?[47]

There was no consensus on a solution, and so the War Shipping Administration kept producing merchant hulls and the Navy had to defer the production of what came to be called destroyer escorts (designated DE, they were ocean-going combatants tailor-made for anti-submarine warfare [ASW]) in favor of amphibious assault craft. In the first part of July 1942, President Roosevelt told King in a memo, "I still do not understand the long delay in making all ships sail under escort." In the President's view, it had taken "an unconscionable time to get things going . . ." Accordingly, "We must speed things up and we must use the available tools even though they are not just what we would like to have." King had to respond. As he explained, he agreed with the President's call for escorted convoys. "I have established convoy systems, beginning with the most dangerous areas, as acquisition of escort vessels permitted." King continued, "My goal—and I believe yours also—is to get every ship under escort. For this purpose . . . the United States and Great Britain . . . need a very large number—roughly 1000—of sea-going escort vessels of DE or corvette type. I am doing my best to get them quickly."[48] Doing that would take longer than King anticipated. There was only so much shipyard capacity in the United States, and since the beginning of April 1942 it had been increasingly taken up with the production of amphibious ships and landing craft.

There were also less dramatic moves that King had to take once he became CNO-COMINCH. One was to standardize the "type commands" in the Atlantic and Pacific fleets. Type commanders were responsible for prescribing "standards and methods of training for all of the seagoing forces and aircraft of the Navy."[49] Operational commanders were often also type commanders. When that was the case, they were referred to as "double-hatted." But double-hatted or not, the type commanders played an invaluable role. They reviewed and sometimes even wrote tactical publications, making sure that shipboard sailors knew the tactics and procedures for their types of ships, and also making sure that sailors were trained in new technologies such as radar fire control and underwater sound detection and ranging. On 10 April 1942, COMINCH directed the Pacific Fleet to adopt the same type command structure as the Atlantic Fleet.[50]

King's goal was the standardization of training and the creation of an organizational arrangement that would facilitate the rapid spread of changes in fighting doctrine, training methods, and official publications.

King was also concerned about the growth in the size of the Navy's bureaus. Accordingly, the new CNO-COMINCH set his sights on the Navy's "shore establishment." On 31 March 1942, for instance, he issued a memo to the bureau chiefs critical of the way the bureaus were growing in size. As King said, "We are . . . now operating a 'one-ocean Navy' and preparing for a 'two-ocean Navy' as to material, yet the 'overhead' in Washington has increased some 500% *estimated* [his emphasis]—perhaps more." He demanded that the bureau chiefs "reduce the mass of detail that is now dealt with in Washington."[51]

The President could also be a source of problems. In February 1942, for example, Roosevelt had approved the Navy's "Master Plan for Maximum Ship Construction," but he did not leave all the shipbuilding decisions to King once the latter became CNO as well as COMINCH. A case in point was the design of a new class of carriers, proposed by King in May. If built, these ships would be significantly larger than both the *Enterprise* then fighting in the Pacific and the new *Essex*-class carriers that would join the Pacific Fleet in 1943—45,000 tons for the new ships as against 27,000 tons for *Essex* (CV-9) and her sisters. The new carriers would also be much better protected against attack. Roosevelt, however, responded by pointing to the need to augment the existing carrier force quickly. He criticized the plan to build the very large carrier and even argued that the tonnage King wanted to devote to the *Essex* class should be reduced so that more small carriers, converted either from merchant ships or cruiser hulls, could be built.[52] King argued right back, defending the 45,000-ton carrier and the planned construction of more *Essex*-class ships. He disparaged anything smaller than *Essex* as not useful in the sort of trans-Pacific naval campaign that he intended to direct. On 17 May, however, King gave in completely on the carrier issue, recommending to Secretary Knox that the 1942 June Naval Expansion Act include 48 "escort" carriers and "100 escort vessels of the corvette type, of Navy design and characteristics, modified as found essential for mass production."[53] On 29 May, King agreed that "further consideration is to be given to conversion of 4 additional [light cruisers] or [heavy cruisers] to [carriers].[54]

President Roosevelt also wanted something done in the Pacific to take the bitter taste of Pearl Harbor out of the mouths of Americans. He wanted Japan bombed. But how? In January, Captains Francis S. Low and Donald B. Duncan of King's COMINCH staff came up with the idea of having Navy carriers transport Army B-25 medium bombers close enough to Japan to bomb Tokyo.[55] On 3 February, two of the bombers successfully flew from the deck of the new carrier *Hornet* (CV-8), proving that launching the B-25s from a carrier was feasible. The raid against Japan, staged successfully by a two-carrier task force commanded by Vice Admiral William F. Halsey, took place on 18 April. By that time, King's COMINCH staff was already considering occupying one of the Solomon Islands as a means of blocking further Japanese expansion.[56] King did not want to waste any time once the Pacific Fleet stopped the Japanese, as he was certain it would.

King also worked to develop a sound working relationship with Army Chief of Staff General Marshall. The first test of his ability to do that came in January 1942, when Marshall had proposed creating "a single head for the Army and the Navy, with a Joint Staff, responsible solely to the Commander in Chief."[57] Admirals Stark and King opposed this idea from the start, and, after he became CNO-COMINCH, King pointed out to Marshall that the two of them were the President's immediate subordinates and therefore had access to Roosevelt—access they would lose if some officer were put in place above them.[58] Marshall apparently accepted this idea and also realized that he could work with King. The product of their working together was a series of agreements and directives to subordinate commanders about areas of command responsibility in the Pacific theater of war. The governing directives (CCS 57/1) to General Douglas MacArthur and Admiral Nimitz, for example, guided the American military effort for the remainder of the war in the Pacific.[59]

But two developments in the late spring and summer of 1942 threatened to derail the Army-Navy cooperation necessary to direct a worldwide war effort. The first was the issue of amphibious shipping and landing craft. The second—closely related to the first—was the matter of the sizes of the Army and Navy. General Marshall, following the President's lead and his own strategic sense, wanted to come to grips as quickly as possible with the German army. He favored an invasion of France at the earliest possible date. The idea—dubbed Operation Sledgehammer—was rejected by the British, but Marshall had made a point. It made no sense to fight the campaign against the U-boats and send U.S. troops to England if those troops were not going to go into action soon. Indeed, the size of the Army was to a great degree dependent on the amount of available transports, the number and quality of amphibious ships and craft, and the success in the struggle against the U-boats. The British insisted that their forces should not bear the brunt of any amphibious assault against German defenses in France. What was the alternative? Roosevelt eventually chose North Africa—Operation Torch instead of Sledgehammer.

Yet that decision still did not eliminate a major divide between the Army and the Navy. Both services needed to know what forces to build even as they were in the process of building them. In July and August 1942, service and joint staff planners had to estimate their personnel and equipment requirements for the spring of 1944—18 months in the future. They had to do that without knowing for sure what the strategic situation would be in 1944, or even what operations the British and Americans would be staging in 1943. Not surprisingly, they projected "requirements" for great numbers of tanks, ships, aircraft, soldiers and sailors. As Joel Davidson has shown, President Roosevelt's demand on 24 August 1942 that Marshall and King tell him what forces they had to develop in order to win the war led to a crisis. Army planners came up with a total force figure of 8.5 million soldiers, 3.5 million of them overseas. Navy planners estimated 2.5 million. Army Air Force (AAF) planners argued that the nation could produce no more than 10 million fighting men while also serving as the "arsenal" for the Allies (including the Soviet Union). They said the Army and Navy would have to reduce their estimates because it was only the AAF that could, with the British Royal Air Force, reach Germany in 1943 and early 1944. As Davidson noted, the newly organized joint staff planners in September 1942 had to reconcile for the joint chiefs "no less than three versions of how the nation's armed forces should expand."[60]

Given the "Germany first" strategy, American military leaders and their British counterparts were acutely conscious of links between and among factors such as recruiting, training, housing and moving personnel, transporting fuel supplies, producing merchant ships and warships, the through-put of ports and anchorages, the production of equipment and munitions, and the construction of bases. In World War I, the Allies had controlled access to French ports. In this war, they would have to fight their way ashore, and in 1942 there was no combined American-British force that could conduct such operations successfully. In a way, Roosevelt's decision to invade North Africa instead of France forced a sort of reconciliation among the Army, Navy, and Army Air Force. Marshall and King warned the President that Operation Torch and the conquest of North Africa would set back the hoped-for invasion of France by a year, but the American campaign planners and logisticians needed time to master their related arts while building the forces needed for the invasion of the continent.

As King told an audience of officers at the National War College in 1947, "We all came to realize the meaning of the term logistics, particularly, I think, the Chiefs of Staff."[61] This was logistics at the strategic and operational levels of war, where concerns for war production combined with equally important concerns for shipping and personnel. Having senior officers—King, especially—simply demand that this sort of logistics happen was to be dangerously unrealistic. The Joint and Combined Chiefs of Staff could not make sensible strategic decisions without being constantly aware of the constraints put on them by factors such as the availability of shipping, numbers and quality of landing craft, and supplies of fuel and ammunition. The strategy planners and the logistics planners were like a pair of Siamese twins—inextricably joined, and each group dependent on the other.

There is a tendency to ignore this intimate and often frustrating connection. Given King's many responsibilities, it should surprise no one that Vice Admiral Horne, King's VCNO, "was CNO in every way except title alone." It was Horne who usually explained the Navy's material needs and defended its budgets in Congress. According to Buell, King and Horne "had an informal agreement that King would manage the war and Horne would manage the logistical matters."[62] But fighting the war could not be separated from logistics. In both the Atlantic and the Pacific, U.S. forces could not come to grips with their enemies without being carried across long distances, supported at and by distant bases, and then moved ashore in the face of enemy resistance. From the perspective of the war leaders of the United States, World War II was a huge and demanding amphibious campaign. American military strategy was essentially maritime, involving tremendous amounts of shipping, the protection of that shipping, and then the support of Army and Marine units that had to fight their ways ashore and overcome enemy forces in two different operational theaters. Admiral King and General Marshall could not avoid the details; logistics both constrained them and offered them opportunities.

King and the Secretariat

King understood this. It was why he wanted to be both COMINCH and CNO. As CNO, however, he had to contend with the bureaus and with an influential secretariat. The hand of the Navy secretary had been strengthened by Navy General Order Number 166, which had created the Office of Procurement and Material (OP&M) at the end of January 1942. The order gave the new office the authority to "coordinate all the material procurement activities of the Navy Department, supervise programs for the procurement of ships and materials of every character as approved by the Secretary of the Navy, and perform such other duties as the Secretary of the Navy may direct." At the same time, the order stipulated that the head of OP&M "shall be an officer on the active list of the Navy of the rank or grade of captain or above and shall have the rank, pay, and all allowances of a vice admiral while so serving."[63] Rear Admiral Samuel M. Robinson, a naval engineer officer who had been appointed the first chief of BuShips, became OP&M's new director. By making that post one for a vice admiral, Secretary Knox hoped to place the director beyond the reach of the CNO's influence over the promotion process for flag officers and at the same time give the director the status he would need to be effective.

Knox's decision to create in the secretariat the Office of Procurement and Material and give it—subject to Under Secretary Forrestal's leadership—responsibility for "the overall coordination of the Navy Department's material procurement activities"[64] was significant. Experienced officers in uniform from OP&M would represent the Navy before higher-level material management boards such as the newly created (on 16 January 1942) War Production Board. These officers included Rear Admiral Henry Williams, who was the Navy's representative on the War Production Board's requirements committee, Captain (later Rear Admiral) James M. Irish, who ran OP&M's statistics branch, and Captain (later Rear Admiral) Claud A. Jones, head of the production branch.[65] Creating OP&M also put the under secretary in the middle between national war production agencies and the Navy's bureaus.[66] The War Powers Act of 18 December 1941 had given the President the authority to set up or reorganize executive agencies, and he delegated that power selectively to the secretaries of War and the Navy.[67] Accordingly, Secretary Knox simply created OP&M as his own procurement coordinating organization inside the Navy secretariat.

The Secretary of the Navy had another source of influence in his office: the Navy's Budget Officer. Rear Admiral Ezra G. Allen, who had served with Vice Admiral Sims in London in 1918, held the budget officer's position from 1938 to 1946. Historian Robert Albion credited Allen with being on a first-name basis with almost all the members of Congress involved in the appropriations process. But Allen was not just an intermediary between the Navy and congressional committees. On behalf of the SECNAV, Allen's Estimates Division "received the budget estimates from the bureaus and offices, made analyses of the estimates, conducted hearings, recommended amounts to be allowed by the Secretary, and supervised hearings before the Budget Bureau and Congressional Committees."[68] The key phrase is "conducted hearings." Such hearings were, if Secretary Knox chose to use them as such, a source of information and a means of disciplining the otherwise independent bureaus.[69]

As Albion found, the "liaison between the Navy and Congress became constantly more complex as the war progressed. In addition to the Budget Officer, the Legislative Counsel, and the liaison officers attached to the Naval Affairs Committees," Vice Admiral Horne had his own liaison officer, and CNO-COMINCH King was on familiar terms with Carl Vinson, the Georgia representative who had served on the House Naval Affairs Committee since 1917.[70] In fact, Commander George L. Russell, King's flag secretary when King was in command in the Atlantic and, later, when King was CNO-COMINCH, had worked for Representative Vinson in 1939 and 1940. Russell told Thomas Buell that he had written some of Vinson's speeches and "many" of the House Naval Affairs Committee's reports before the war. As Russell recalled, "I was the number one assistant, messenger boy, and aide" to Vinson.[71] This obviously helped King later.

The Bureaus Continued to Matter

Just before and after King was appointed CNO-COMINCH, there developed a complex web of connections between the secretariat and the bureaus, the secretariat and the Congress, the bureaus and the Congress, the Congress and CNO-COMINCH, and the secretariat and CNO-COMINCH. The bureaus occupied an important place in this web because there were some critical issues that could only be solved by the specially trained officers who staffed the bureaus. One such issue was amphibious and assault shipping. Before the war, the Navy's Bureau of Construction and Repair had experimented with a number of different types of landing craft, including modified ship's boats and barges. These experiments, described by Norman Friedman in his detailed *U.S. Amphibious Ships and Craft*, were largely unsuccessful until two things happened.[72] First, the Navy opened up the design process to civilian builders, especially the flamboyant Andrew J. Higgins. Second, the creation of the Lend-Lease program in 1941 meant that U.S. boat and ship builders and the Navy's BuShips could interact openly with Royal Navy ship designers who had been working for almost two years on specialized amphibious ship and boat designs. Under Lend-Lease, the British could specify what they wanted, and so they shared their experience and designs.

Then-Captain Edward L. Cochrane, head of the preliminary design section in BuShips, was critical to the success of the amphibious ship and assault craft programs. It was Cochrane who recognized the superiority of the British amphibious ship designs and of the assault boats produced by Higgins. It was also Cochrane who understood that all amphibious craft would have to be produced in large numbers and that therefore they had to be built to standardized designs and produced quickly.[73] British Prime Minister Churchill pressured President Roosevelt to mass produce such ships during the Arcadia conference (22 December 1941 to 14 January 1942) in Washington, and by July 1942 both the U.S. Navy and the Royal Navy had agreed on a set of standardized designs for what became the Landing Ship, Tank (LST); the Landing Ship, Dock (LSD); the Landing Ship, Infantry (LSI); and the Landing Craft, Tank (LCT). The three landing ships and the LCT were absolutely essential to Allied success in World War II. So were the scads of assault boats carried by amphibious transports. King and his closest deputies, as well as Secretary Knox and his staff, had to rely on the bureaus for this sort of innovation and for the management of the production that followed from the agreement on standard designs. Put another way, the bureaus had to work; the officers leading them had to demonstrate that their demands for relative autonomy were justified. In the case of Captain (later Rear Admiral and chief of BuShips) Cochrane, there was the right sort of exchange—he had decision authority, used it successfully, and Admiral King got his amphibious ships and boats.

Given the talent resident in the bureaus and in the Navy secretariat, why did King continue to press for more control over Navy logistics? The answer is that logistics, broadly defined, was the key to King's concept for defeating Japan. When it was clear in Washington that the Battle of Midway had been a defeat for the Imperial Japanese Navy, King directed Admiral Nimitz to take the offensive against Japanese efforts to sever the line of communications between the United States and Australia. King knew that the key to an American victory in the Pacific war was the ability of the Navy, Marines, and Army to take the operational initiative from the Japanese and never give it up. It's true that General MacArthur's plan to mount an offensive from Australia competed with Admiral Nimitz's plan to "island hop" across the Central Pacific, but King realized that the logistical and manufacturing strength of the United States could support both offensives, *especially if one or both stole a march on the Japanese*. King wanted to make sure that no element of the Navy delayed the ability of the fighting forces to go on—and stay on—the offensive. This is why King put landing craft production at the top of the Navy's priority list in July 1942.

Rounding Out the High Command

That same month, President Roosevelt appointed former CNO and retired Admiral William D. Leahy as "chief of staff to the commander in chief." It was a wise choice for an unprecedented position. King was strongly—even vehemently—opposed to any officer standing between him and the President, and Leahy did not try to do that. Instead, Leahy defined his role as "the maintenance of daily liaison between the President and the Joint Chiefs of Staff." In this role, Leahy passed "on to the Joint Chiefs . . . the basic thinking of the President on all war plans and strategy." At the same time, Leahy, whose office was in the White House, "brought back from the Joint Chiefs a consensus of their thinking."[74] As historian Paul Miles has noted, "Leahy's terse description [failed] to convey the full scope and complexity of his responsibilities."[75] The point that matters here is that Leahy was aware that he would serve neither the President nor the Joint Chiefs of Staff by acting as a gate-keeper between Roosevelt and his military chiefs.[76] At the same time, he knew what the President needed, which was a senior military officer obligated to the President and yet not involved in the political disputes that were inevitable in wartime. Leahy was chosen to be the officer who could understand the connections between strategy and policy and move easily back and forth from one area to the other *on behalf of the President*.

OPNAV: Struggling Through 1942

In a note to historian Walter M. Whitehill, King recalled that he gave VCNO Horne two major responsibilities—to facilitate and coordinate the work of the material bureaus and to see to it that new naval forces were well trained and sent forward prepared to engage in combat. As King put it, "I believed that my top job was to manage the war especially as to fighting so I told Horne to go ahead as if he was [sic] C.N.O. in such matters . . . but to keep me informed of what he was doing and to tell me when he got 'stuck'."[77] Horne got "stuck" rather soon over the issue of operational planning vs. logistics planning.

The distinction between the two types of planning seemed clear enough after war was declared. When King was appointed COMINCH, for example, he and Admiral Stark agreed that most of the officers in the War Plans Division of OPNAV needed to join King's staff. Officers from Fleet Training and Ship's Movement Divisions also shifted from OPNAV to COMINCH. Given the traditional distinction in the Navy between operations and logistics, this transfer seemed logical. Accordingly, on 17 June 1942, Horne suggested that COMINCH do the strategic planning and coordination with the JCS while OPNAV coordinate the execution of COMINCH's plans by the Navy's bureaus. On 29 June, Horne went a step further and recommended that he be permitted to eliminate OPNAV's separate planning section and shift the responsibility for whatever execution planning was necessary to the Fleet Maintenance Division (OP-23).[78] OP-23 would coordinate the support of operational plans among the bureaus and see to it that those plans were executed.[79] But this seemingly logical distinction could not be maintained in practice. As Duncan Ballantine argued, there was no clear difference between "the planning of operations and the planning of their material support,"[80] and, as a result, Horne was "stuck" with a problem he could not resolve.

Several factors combined to make OPNAV's task of logistics planning even more difficult. The first was the level of secrecy of joint staff planning. The Navy's bureaus needed to know in 1942 what levels of support they would need to provide to the commanders fighting the war in 1944, but how could they know what those levels of weapons and trained manpower would be if they were not privy to the decisions of the JCS, decisions that were closely held? This dilemma was highlighted in an organizational study commissioned by Secretary Knox and performed by the firm of Booz, Fry, Allen & Hamilton in the late summer and early fall of 1942.[81] The firm's analysts also found a second basic problem—that the shift of planning authority and activity from OPNAV to COMINCH had "made it necessary for the project divisions in Naval Operations such as Base Maintenance to do individual project planning," thereby creating confusion within the "material and service bureaus."[82]

Horne's solution to this problem was to bolster the authority of OP-23. But making OP-23 his (and King's) agent for the coordination of naval logistics was not an obvious way to overcoming being "stuck." For example, Horne wanted to give OP-23 "cognizance" over the production and support of aircraft material, but Rear Admiral John Towers, chief of BuAer, was opposed. Rear Admiral Towers was also opposed to giving that authority to OP&M in the Navy secretariat. His reason was simple: only he and his colleagues in BuAer understood both the needs of the fleet and the capabilities of industry.

To back up his objections, Rear Admiral Towers pointed to the huge aircraft production quotas set by President Roosevelt; they were unrealistic—not based on any specific operational plans, and, if followed, threatened to unbalance the overall aircraft production program. Knowing that Roosevelt's demands were dangerously overoptimistic, Towers and his Army counterpart, Lieutenant General Henry H. Arnold, cooperated to develop their own targets in the early summer of 1942 and then actually hid those numbers from Roosevelt. When the President realized that the goals he set were not being implemented by the Navy and Army, he demanded—and got—explanations. King and Towers, along with other officials, argued their case to Roosevelt and Harry Hopkins, and Roosevelt accepted their lower and more realistic production targets.[83] This incident and others showed that senior civilian and military leaders could not dictate production goals without consulting the experts. In the Navy, the experts were most likely to be in the bureaus.

The second factor causing problems for Horne and OPNAV was the nature of the war itself. The war didn't wait for officials in Washington to work out solutions to administrative problems. For example, the commander of Service Forces Pacific, based in Hawaii and under the command of Admiral Nimitz, established a South Pacific Service Squadron in New Zealand in April 1942 and directed it to serve as the clearing house for all requests for supplies from base commanders in the area.[84] But some of the base commanders were Army officers, and so Horne's staff had to negotiate a joint logistics plan with Lieutenant General Brehon B. Somervell's Services of Supply detailing which items of supply and maintenance each service would be responsible for. In doing this, the Army and Navy staff officers created a joint purchasing board (to acquire provisions and services locally, in New Zealand) and also decided that control of shipping into the South Pacific would be under the control of the region's commander.[85] They thereby set a precedent for Army-Navy logistics coordination and cooperation.

The third factor was the difficulty in defining logistic "requirements." The imperatives of fighting a war clashed with the need for a deliberative process that reduced the chance of error. Before and during World War II, for example, the General Board set the general requirements (size, armament, endurance, etc.) for Navy ships. To do that, the board asked the preliminary design section of BuShips to prepare conceptual plans for a ship type (destroyer, aircraft carrier, etc.). Then the board held hearings, where bureau, OPNAV, and fleet or COMINCH officers could comment on the "balance" among a conceptual design's general characteristics. The members of the board would then select the optimal "balance" that they considered best fit the needs of the fleet. Before the war, when the board had made its recommendation regarding a design to the Secretary of the Navy and the secretary had approved it, the preliminary design was turned into a contract design by BuShips. During the war, BuShips continued to prepare the detailed designs of new ship types for review by the COMINCH staff. The latter then forwarded final permission to proceed to the contract specialists in OP&M (in the secretariat). The major difference with the prewar process was that OP-23 had to monitor this process closely in order to be certain that final designs could be supported in the field.[86]

These cases illustrate how and why VCNO Horne got "stuck" multiple times. On King's behalf, Horne had to have OPNAV monitor and support the fleet—even though it wasn't always clear where the fleet would be in 12 or 18 months' time. Horne's deputies also had to deal with OP&M in the secretariat and with the Navy's bureaus. OPNAV also had to participate in the larger war mobilization process, usually by sending officers from OP-23 to serve on joint and civilian-military committees. OP-23's staff had 38 specific duties to perform routinely, and the division provided members to 16 important coordinating and review boards.[87] One reason OP-23 performed as well as it did was its director, Rear Admiral William S. Farber. Farber had worked in OPNAV's Material Division from 1932 to 1935, served ably at sea, and studied industrial mobilization at the Army Industrial College. In June 1941, Captain Farber was Director of OP-23. He was promoted to rear admiral under Vice Admiral Horne and later vice admiral and the first Deputy CNO for Logistics. OP-23 gradually became responsible "for supervising and coordinating the execution of plans for building and improving the fleet."[88] There was no straightforward "fix" when Horne and his deputies were "stuck." Instead, they improvised, smoothing out inefficiencies as they went along.

1942 had been a difficult year for both the fighting forces and those dedicated to supporting them. At sea, the Navy had not yet won its campaign against the U-boats, though it was able to transport the Army to North Africa and sustain it there, and turn back the Japanese offenses in the Pacific. At home, the division of authority among COMINCH, OPNAV, the Navy secretariat (especially OP&M), and the bureaus had to be worked out. As Duncan Ballantine pointed out, in peacetime, "The entire continental shore establishment of the Navy was geared to the process of rendering support to a home-based fleet."[89] This had to change. Admiral King, acting as COMINCH, had directed Admiral Nimitz to take the offensive in the Pacific as soon as possible after the Navy's victory at Midway in June 1942. Indeed, King sent his chief war planner, Rear Admiral Richmond K. Turner, to the South Pacific to serve as the amphibious force commander in the campaign to wrest the Solomon Islands from the Japanese. But the Solomons were just the first step of a gigantic offensive that would take the Navy and the Army to the shores of Japan. As COMINCH, King wanted Admiral Nimitz to jump from one set of islands to another across the Pacific, keeping the Japanese on the defensive and denying them the chance to create an effective defense against U.S. forces. To do that, Nimitz had to have a Navy that could support a *forward-based fleet*, and King and Horne had to produce that Navy. In effect, King had to turn the peacetime Navy's support establishment on its head. Senior officers such as Horne and Farber were his lieutenants, charged with doing that.

OPNAV Matures: 1943–1945

As histories of naval logistics in World War II make clear, the task facing King and OPNAV was to link Washington with the deployed fleet via an incredibly long logistics pipeline. OPNAV got a break on 5 October 1942, when King "directed that an estimate should be prepared of Navy shipping requirements for all purposes during the period from December 1942, through June 1943. For the first time by this directive the disclosure to the bureaus of information on operational plans was authorized."[90] King's directive also had another benefit:

> By drawing a distinction between requirements for the establishment of bases (which would be furnished by the bureaus) and requirements for the maintenance of bases and forces afloat (which would be furnished by the Commander in Chief Pacific Fleet), Admiral Horne was able . . . to draw theater agencies into participation in the determination of requirements.[91]

If the devil is in the details, then who better to consult than the officers struggling with the details? In producing an authoritative estimate of shipping requirements for use in OPNAV, King allowed the OPNAV staff, the bureaus, and the fleet staffs to begin an honest discussion about how best to meet those requirements. Horne also took advantage of a Navy tradition of giving responsibility to commanders at sea and ashore.

But though the promulgation of an authoritative estimate was the first step toward solving one problem, it created another, which was the need for Army-Navy coordination and cooperation. The Navy didn't exist for itself. It fought other navies so that it could transport the Army and the Marines to places where they could take the war to the enemy and then support them while they defeated the enemy. It should therefore have come as no surprise to Vice Admiral Horne when Lieutenant General Somervell encouraged General Marshall to create a "standing supply committee" with himself and Horne as the members.[92] Nor should Horne have been surprised when Somervell on 13 December 1942 proposed that the Army and Navy "consolidate [their] two ocean transportation services."[93] As it happened, the Navy did not see value in consolidating its shipping or its logistics with those of the Army. As Rear Admiral Oscar C. Badger, head of OPNAV's Logistics Plans office, told his Army counterparts, it would be a mistake in the middle of the war to try to merge Army and Navy logistics. Coordination and cooperation would be better than "effecting drastic changes in the internal organizations of the War and Navy Departments."[94]

Badger and Horne received support for their position with the creation of the Joint Army–Navy–War Shipping Administration Ship Operations Committee in San Francisco in February 1943. The Navy representative was Vice Admiral John W. Greenslade, commandant of the Twelfth Naval District. Representing the Army was Major General Frederick Gilbreath, commander of the Army's port of embarkation; the War Shipping Administration's representative was a senior civilian. The committee's purpose was to "consider all matters pertaining to the handling of shipping or cargo and personnel . . . to the end that the maximum use will be made of ships and facilities available."[95] In effect, the committee was a model for use in other areas. It also showed that coordination and cooperation could work.

However, to avoid documented inefficiencies in logistics, Admiral King and General Marshall promulgated on 7 March 1943 a joint directive ("Basic Logistical Plan for Command Areas

Involving Joint Army and Navy Operations") directing subordinate joint commanders to create "suitable unified logistical supply staffs" or facilitate "joint staff planning and operations on the part of respective Army and Navy staffs."[96] The directive was obviously a compromise, "the result of three months of negotiations," and it placed the primary responsibility for coordination and cooperation on the theater commanders. The Army's historians judged it "a practical achievement of considerable import. It left a great deal to the discretion of theater commanders so that co-ordinating arrangements could go ahead at the pace they deemed practicable and desirable."[97] Admiral Halsey, joint commander in the South Pacific, promptly sent to Washington "a single consolidated [logistics] priority list . . . for both services for May shipments to the South Pacific, instead of following his former practice of sending separate priority lists for each service."[98] It was a smart move. "The War and Navy Departments instructed their port agencies on the west coast to honor Halsey's preference, and on 26 May [1943] followed up with a directive extending the principle to cover all Pacific theaters except the North and Southeast Pacific."[99]

As the Navy fended off the Army's desire for truly joint *service* logistics in 1943, Vice Admiral William L. Calhoun's Hawaii-based Service Force was learning to keep the Navy's carrier task forces supplied with fuel and ammunition so that they could stay at sea and keep the Imperial Japanese Navy off-balance.[100] This was not a concept of logistics familiar to the Army.

Figure 5-1. Commander-in-Chief, U.S. Fleet and CNO Ernest J. King (third from left) with Pacific Fleet commander Admiral Chester W. Nimitz (second from right) in 1943. King had observed the disputes and misunderstandings between Vice Admiral Sims in London and Admiral Benson in Washington in World War I. By meeting regularly with Admiral Nimitz, he made sure that similar problems did not hinder the war effort in the Pacific in World War II. (NHHC Archives NH 62957)

Consequently, it should surprise no one that when the JCS created a committee in June 1943 "to study the problem of overlapping and duplication in Army-Navy functions . . . differences in approach by the two services prevented any effective action."[101] Despite this, the two services improved their material cooperation, creating joint committees to coordinate ship repairs, transport personnel, and standardize vehicle parts and construction materials.[102]

In the Pacific, Admiral Nimitz drew on the authority granted him by Admiral King and General Somervell and placed two senior Army logisticians on Vice Admiral Calhoun's staff and then appointed an Army general to be his logistics deputy for his theater of operations.[103] If the Army and Navy officers on the Joint Staff's planning committee in Washington could not agree on combining Army and Navy logistics from production through deployment, the theater commanders had the authority to create what the Army's historians called "congeries of local arrangements, . . . providing at least an element of cohesiveness to the widely differing supply systems of the Army and Navy." This lack of what might be termed "systematization," because it was flexible and adaptable, suited the Navy and apparently satisfied the planners who worked for the Joint Chiefs.[104]

While all this was taking place, Admiral King put yet another Navy reorganization plan on the table, triggering something of a repeat of the controversy in March 1942. He first proposed in March 1943 to establish three new posts under Horne—

> a Chief of Procurement and Material, who would supervise the Bureaus of Ships, Ordnance, Docks, and Supplies & Accounts for the Under Secretary of the Navy; a Chief of Naval Aviation, who would oversee the activities of the Bureau of Aeronautics for the Assistant Secretary of the Navy for Air; and a Chief of Personnel, who would supervise the work of the Bureaus of Personnel and Medicine and Surgery for the Assistant Secretary of the Navy.[105]

After receiving comments from members of the General Board, King modified his basic proposal, proposing the creation of four new deputy chiefs of naval operations instead of three. However, the chiefs of BuOrd and BuDocks strongly opposed King's initiative, as did President Roosevelt. Roosevelt was willing to allow King to create the post of Deputy Chief of Naval Operations for Aviation (DCNO) [Air]), but he told Secretary Knox in mid-August 1943, "Tell Ernie *once more*: No reorganizing of the Navy Dept. set-up during the war. Let's win it first."[106]

The new post of DCNO (Air) was a mixed blessing for Horne and King. On the one hand, it pulled the aviation policy and planning staffs out of BuAer and put them under King and Horne. On the other hand, the new office was directly linked to the Assistant Secretary for Air and was therefore not so directly subordinate to King and Horne as the chiefs of fleet and base maintenance. As Duncan Ballantine noted, "In planning and executing logistic programs no real integration of air under the general divisions of the Office of Naval Operations was accomplished."[107]

King and Horne (and Secretary Knox, as well) also ran afoul of Roosevelt when they proposed to reorganize the structures of the naval districts. The commandants of the naval districts were under the authority of CNO-COMINCH, and the districts themselves had been created as defense organizations, intended to support the sea frontier commanders. But by the summer of 1943, most of the military activity in the naval districts was concerned with logistics—warehousing, moving and loading supplies and equipment, and housing and training Navy personnel. There was no overall supervision of the many logistic organizations and activities in the naval districts.

According to Ballantine, "In general the pattern of regional logistic activity was one of many separate autonomies over which district organization had almost ceased to exercise any influence."[108] This fragmentation of authority was impeding the smooth and constant flow of men and material that was essential to the Navy's trans-Pacific campaign. Horne therefore proposed—and King and Knox supported—the creation of vice commandants in each naval district where there was increasing logistic activity. These senior officers would report directly to OPNAV.[109] Once the President stated his opposition to such a reform, the best that Secretary Knox could do was to create assistant district commandants who *advised* their superiors regarding logistic matters—*except* in Hawaii (the 14th Naval District), where King, acting on his authority as COMINCH, was able to create a senior logistics officer with the power to cut across bureau lines of authority.[110]

For Roosevelt, civilian control mattered more than improved efficiency, and he always resisted King's efforts to—as Roosevelt perceived it—shift control from civilian to military hands. At the same time, the President pressed his war leaders for a more rational system of logistics. In a letter to the Joint Chiefs of Staff on 17 July 1943, Roosevelt argued that "Joint logistics planning should parallel joint strategic planning. . . . The supply program of each service should be carefully scrutinized as to its relationship to the programs of the other services to the end that there shall be one unified and balanced supply program consistent with up-to-date strategic concepts."[111] General Marshall told his colleagues on the JCS that Roosevelt's letter had likely been drafted by the director of the new Office of War Mobilization (OWM), former senator and Supreme Court Justice James F. Byrnes, an individual whom many in Washington would soon call "the assistant president."[112] But what precisely did the President want? Lieutenant General Somervell drafted a response to Roosevelt's letter suggesting that existing joint coordination was satisfactory, but the evidence suggests that it was not, and the President's letter compelled the JCS to modify the existing joint committee on administration and make it the Joint Logistics Committee—an equal with the already functioning committee of JCS planners.[113]

President Roosevelt had created OWM in May 1943 as an overarching committee directing both the War Production Board and the Office of Economic Stabilization.[114] Director Byrnes had earlier chaired the Navy Subcommittee of the Senate Appropriations Committee; he was knowledgeable, persistent, and very influential because of his skills and his link to Roosevelt. In the summer of 1943, Byrnes, evidently concerned that the Navy's ship construction program was not being adequately assessed by Secretary Knox, was able to force the Navy to create a Procurement Review Board. Byrnes was after information that would substantiate his suspicion that the shipbuilding program was not responsive to OWM direction.[115]

As it happened, King had Horne's staff present a summary of the Navy's ship construction program that refuted Byrnes's criticism, but it was clear that Byrnes was still suspicious of the Navy's plans. In September 1943, as King, Secretary Knox, Horne and the head of BuShips debated the number of destroyer escorts that should be produced, Byrnes claimed again that the Navy's huge ship construction program was robbing men and material from other areas that needed them more. He received support from Under Secretary of the Navy James Forrestal, who argued that "piecemeal cancellations like those in the destroyer escort program would ultimately prove wasteful and were the product of poor requirements planning."[116] President Roosevelt said that the issue should be turned over to the "newly created Joint Production Survey Committee," which "had been created through arrangements made at a meeting between the Joint Chiefs" and OWM head Byrnes.[117]

King believed that the creation of the Joint Production Survey Committee was a mistake because it gave Army staff officers the chance to examine and criticize Navy shipbuilding. As it happened, Army and Navy staff officers supporting the committee bickered over the Navy's ship construction program for months, and the Navy officers assigned to support the committee adamantly refused to allow their Army counterparts to gain any control over the program. The Navy officers had the clear support of Admiral King, who did not want to face any obstacle in his effort to build a fleet that would both subdue Japan and leave the Navy superior to any competing force once the war was over. King and General Marshall had carefully avoided criticizing one another's acquisition programs, but the creation of the Joint Production Survey Committee opened up that possibility, and King's reaction against it was strong. The President, however, wanted the committee to review the "entire national shipbuilding program" (i.e., both the Army and Navy efforts).[118]

It was time for King to build a coalition against Byrnes. To do its work, the Joint Production Survey Committee had to rely on Secretary Knox to produce the information it needed. Knox turned to King and Horne. King's response was to argue that the Committee's study was unnecessary; at the same time, he quietly worked to make sure that the information given Knox would support the Navy's (i.e., King's) position. To keep from being totally dependent on CNO-COMINCH for information and analysis, Knox asked the General Board in October 1943 to review the shipbuilding program. When the board sided with King, Knox told the Joint Production Survey Committee that he could not recommend further reductions in the Navy's shipbuilding effort. In consequence, the committee accepted the Navy's program, and on 18 November 1943, "Admiral Horne duly notified Justice Byrnes that the Joint Chiefs had concluded that continued prosecution of the full navy building program was necessary to the war effort."[119] King's campaign against OWM chief Byrnes had been a success. Later, when Byrnes served as Secretary of State under President Harry S. Truman and traveled with Truman to the Potsdam conference in July 1945, Admiral Edwards, King's deputy in COMINCH, quipped that "The State Department fiddles while Burns [sic] roams."[120] The comment is a clever indication of the standing of Byrnes in the eyes of King and King's senior deputies.

The Navy got its way with its building program. In March 1944, King, acting in his role as CNO, asked Under Secretary Forrestal to direct the General Board to review the Navy's shipbuilding program to see if there were planned vessels that could be cut. This may have been a deliberate move to repeat what had happened the previous October, when the board had supported the shipbuilding program in the face of claims that it was too large. King also wanted to begin planning the postwar Navy, and some of the ships in the program (such as the *Midway*-class carriers) were, he thought, essential to begin while the wartime expenditures were still high. Horne supported King, recommending that the Navy build to the congressionally authorized tonnage levels; the General Board also backed King.[121]

After the death of Secretary Knox at the end of April 1944, Roosevelt nominated Forrestal as his replacement. After being approved by the Senate on 19 May, Forrestal began again surveying the shipbuilding effort. In June 1944, Rear Admiral Donald B. Duncan told his colleagues on the Joint Staff Planning Committee that the Navy's shipbuilding program was "outside the sphere of the Joint Chiefs of Staff or any of the supporting joint agencies."[122] But the program was not outside the jurisdiction of the new SECNAV, and Forrestal set up a "Special Committee on Cutbacks" in June.

What prompted this move by Forrestal was a looming shortage of personnel. The Navy was in danger of building more ships than it could man. Or, if it could somehow man the ships it was building, it would siphon off manpower desperately needed by the Army.[123] That would bring the President into the decision process, and King apparently did not want that. Yet as Joel Davidson pointed out, "With pressure building to reduce ship production, the navy's senior officers were instead contemplating still further increases in fleet strength."[124] Though King clearly had cause to want to come out of the war with the strongest possible fleet, there was another reason why he opposed reducing ship construction in 1944—the need to prepare for the possible invasion of Japan in the fall of 1945. In the summer of 1944, no one knew how long or just how hard the Japanese would fight. In addition, just how they might resist was not certain. So King was hedging his bets. Forrestal, unfortunately, was not privy to the strategic discussions carried on by the JCS. He did not know what King knew. So on 25 September 1944, Forrestal asked King for "studies, documents and recommendations" prepared by the Joint Chiefs and the joint committees that supported them. Buell found evidence that King made an effort to give that information to Forrestal, but for some reason it seems it did not work to the satisfaction of either Forrestal or King.[125]

One very important reason it did not was probably the effort to break apart the positions of CNO and COMINCH. King suspected that Forrestal had favored placing all material matters under the secretariat since his appointment as under secretary in 1940. According to King, the more Forrestal

> learned about Horne's job the more he wanted to change Horne's job or rather to change my two jobs into one (Cominch) only and leave Horne as 'C.N.O.' But that couldn't work against the basic EO so he went to work on Mr. Knox . . . saying that I

had *too* much power and the best thing was to change . . . my double job so that I would carry on *only* as 'Cominch'.[126]

King said that nothing serious had happened until Secretary Knox informed him at the Quadrant conference in August 1943 that a change had to be made in King's position as CNO-COMINCH. King's response was "to educate [Knox] all over [again] on the basic 'set-up' of the office of 'C.N.O.' and how I got the so-called double job because only one man could manage the military part of the Navy."[127] But the proposal put to King by Knox soured the relationships between King and Horne and between King and Forrestal.[128]

The issue of the proper relationship between CNO and COMINCH, and between CNO-COMINCH and the SECNAV did not go away. Indeed, it intensified at the end of 1943, and Secretary Knox actually recommended breaking the link between CNO and COMINCH in order to improve the logistic support of the fleet. King argued against the proposal. He maintained that those wanting to split CNO from COMINCH were reluctant to accept the fact that the "enormous expansion of the Navy, particularly in small craft that can carry few supplies and no repair facilities, has created administrative problems of a scope never approached in pre-war days."[129] The argument that such problems could only be dealt with by "a corps of 'logisticians only'" was wrong because it "did not work when the Supply Corps had this exclusive function."[130] King did admit that the Supply Corps had a legitimate and important role to play, but he insisted that supply was "a function of operational command." As he noted, "the Army Services of Supply was under the Secretary of War at the commencement of hostilities, but later on it had to be shifted to the control of the Chief of Staff, in order to unify supply and operations under a single command."[131] This was a form of the argument that President Roosevelt himself had made in the summer of 1943—that operational planning could not be separated from logistics planning.

To wrap up his objections to any proposal to break the official link between CNO and COMINCH, King pointed to his own effort to establish the Logistic Organization Planning Unit. This idea had its roots in the mind of Captain Paul E. Pihl, who worked for Vice Admiral Horne in 1943. Just before the United States had entered the war, then-Commander Pihl, trained as an aeronautical engineer, had served as assistant naval attaché in Berlin. As a protégé of Rear Admiral John Towers, Pihl had headed BuAer's production section before moving over to OPNAV.[132] But Pihl had more going for him than successful experience in the fields of intelligence and acquisition. He and his wife were friends of Admiral King, and Pihl drew on their friendship in 1943 to gain access to King and press COMINCH to create a logistics study group within the COMINCH staff.[133]

King did so, and the group developed means to measure and depict the flow of logistics from the West Coast to and through the Pacific. In April 1943, members of Pihl's staff visited West Coast ports; they came back with bad news: ". . . the shore establishment . . . was clogging the pipeline to Nimitz." In response, King told Secretary Knox "that all construction in all shore establishments of the Navy" should be halted.[134] Material was piling up at the West Coast ports, according to King, because there were people who thought that storing it was their mission;

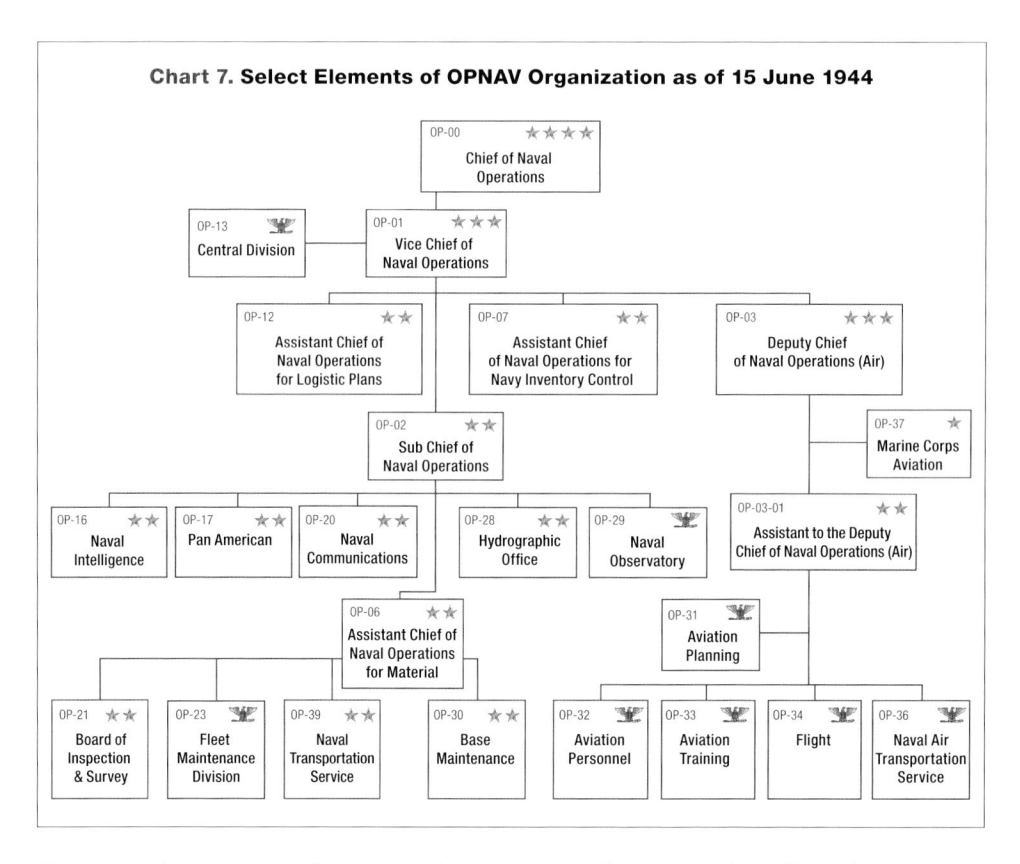

Chart 7. Select Elements of OPNAV Organization as of 15 June 1944

- OP-00 ★★★★ Chief of Naval Operations
  - OP-13 Central Division
  - OP-01 ★★★ Vice Chief of Naval Operations
    - OP-12 ★★ Assistant Chief of Naval Operations for Logistic Plans
    - OP-07 ★★ Assistant Chief of Naval Operations for Navy Inventory Control
    - OP-03 ★★★ Deputy Chief of Naval Operations (Air)
      - OP-37 ★ Marine Corps Aviation
      - OP-03-01 ★★ Assistant to the Deputy Chief of Naval Operations (Air)
        - OP-31 Aviation Planning
          - OP-32 Aviation Personnel
          - OP-33 Aviation Training
          - OP-34 Flight
          - OP-36 Naval Air Transportation Service
    - OP-02 ★★ Sub Chief of Naval Operations
      - OP-16 ★★ Naval Intelligence
      - OP-17 ★★ Pan American
      - OP-20 ★★ Naval Communications
      - OP-28 ★★ Hydrographic Office
      - OP-29 Naval Observatory
      - OP-06 ★★ Assistant Chief of Naval Operations for Material
        - OP-21 ★★ Board of Inspection & Survey
        - OP-23 Fleet Maintenance Division
        - OP-39 ★★ Naval Transportation Service
        - OP-30 ★★ Base Maintenance

there were also too many places to put it, suggesting to less innovative officers that storing it was acceptable. The key to victory, however, was to keep the material moving. But how? King attacked what he thought was a traditional problem: the tendency of shore-based organizations to grow faster than the fleet in wartime. But was that the real problem?

After studying West Coast logistics, Pihl's Logistic Organization Planning Unit wrote a report in April 1944 arguing that there was "no overall coordinated supervision of the operation of logistic activities on the Pacific Coast." Admiral Horne responded that "the present working organization, despite certain deficiencies of logistic organization and control, has supported the war in the Pacific effectively and, except for some minor delays imposed by shipping and production difficulties, the requirements of our forces have been adequately met."[135] But Pihl and his colleagues in the Logistic Organization Planning Unit believed that the final campaigns against the Japanese—campaigns fought in the near vicinity of the Japanese home islands—would require something different in kind than of degree. Doing more of the same would not work.

King agreed. His "solution" was to shift Vice Admiral Royal E. Ingersoll from command of naval forces in the Atlantic to the command of the Western Sea Frontier in November 1944. Ingersoll was also appointed deputy COMINCH and deputy CNO. Ingersoll had had extensive command experience at sea and multiple tours in OPNAV, where he had been serving as assistant CNO when King made him commander of the Atlantic Fleet. He had the experience, the reputation, and also the contacts that were necessary to facilitate the flow of material to the Pacific theater. Ingersoll was to pull all the threads on shoreside Navy logistics together and link the material flowing across them to Admiral Nimitz's joint logistics and shipping organization in Hawaii. As Ingersoll later put it, "If I couldn't accomplish what I wanted under one hat, I could accomplish it under another."[136] Command of the Western Sea Frontier was not the combat command that Ingersoll wanted (he had wanted the Pacific command [PACOM] held by Nimitz), but he took it, and Buell argued that "Things improved considerably" as a result.[137]

In 1944, King was trying to get OPNAV organized the way he wanted while at the same time he found a solution to the logistic problems that had to be overcome if the Navy was to blockade Japan (after defeating the Japanese fleet) and carry the Marines and Army to Japanese home waters. Appointing Admiral Ingersoll as the chief deputy commander for logistics was one of King's measures. Before moving Ingersoll, however, King elevated and promoted Admiral Edwards, making him Deputy CNO-COMINCH effective 1 October 1944. In a Navy Department press release on 4 October, King announced that he would henceforth have three senior deputies—"Vice Admiral Edwards as Deputy Commander in Chief-Deputy Chief of Naval Operations, Vice Admiral Horne as Vice Chief of Naval Operations, and Vice Admiral Cooke as Chief of Staff, U.S. Fleet." However, King also asserted that "the duties now assigned to Vice Admiral Edwards do *not* constitute a demotion of Vice Admiral Horne or of anyone else."[138] But Vice Admiral Horne had in reality been superseded by Edwards. Proof of that came on 23 October 1944, in a headquarters memorandum that gave Edwards "cognizance" over post-war planning (including demobilization), shipbuilding and aviation acquisition programs (and cutbacks), joint intelligence and communications, lend-lease, and major personnel "problems."[139]

King and his bureaucratic opponents—from Byrnes to Forrestal and the Navy's bureau chiefs—expended a lot of energy debating King's various reorganization proposals in 1943 and early 1944. Was the conflict worth it? Was OPNAV more effective because of the debates? Historians are not of one mind on this issue. Joel Davidson, for example, argued in *The Unsinkable Fleet, The Politics of U.S. Navy Expansion in World War II*, that the Navy kept cranking out ships that were not really needed. Rear Admiral Furer, in his lengthy and detailed *Administration of the Navy Department in World War II*, took a different view. As he put it,

> The lack of an Overall Logistic Plan was . . . not too serious because of the cordial and intelligent personal relations that existed between the hierarchy in CNO . . . and the hierarchy in the Bureaus. Such relationships made for a team of extraordinary effectiveness in keeping logistics in step with the ever changing strategic situation.[140]

Was Furer correct? Buell said yes as far as the Pacific was concerned, but Buell was critical of King's approach to Europe, where, according to Buell, "Shipping requirements were seen only dimly."[141] Ballantine had a more nuanced view. He appreciated that "operational planning in the Pacific in 1944 took on a highly flexible and opportunistic character" because "the war had now become a war of movement. Its duration depended directly upon the mobility of operating forces and hence upon the rapid projection forward of base facilities, staging areas and airfields."[142] As a result, "the logistic system was kept under constant pressure. Any slack offered by the build-up of surplus resources was immediately taken up by further acceleration in the operational schedule . . ."[143]

What happened to Vice Admiral Horne? Ballantine pointed to Horne's obvious strengths, including his excellent memory and intelligence, and especially his temperament: "Placed at the cross-roads of civilian-military pressures, he had a remarkable capacity for recognizing the many sides of the Navy's administrative problem and for reconciling its many contradictions in harmonious working relationships."[144] Horne himself acknowledged the importance of his role when he admitted that "The Bureau Chiefs were good men; they trusted me, and they did what I asked them."[145] In addition, Horne understood that "the bureaus . . . contained in themselves all the elements necessary to create, expand and maintain the working establishment of the Navy." Horne knew that—to use Ballantine's words—"Like water flowing beneath the frozen surface of a stream, the workings of the bureau system were hidden, but not essentially impeded by the overlay of authority" in OPNAV.[146] King could not accept this point of view. Accordingly, he assigned the Logistic Plans Division in OPNAV (OP-12) the task of developing an Overall Logistic Plan that would cover "the requirements for support for the entire naval establishment."[147] Issued at the end of September 1944, the "Top Secret" plan signaled the end of Vice Admiral's Horne's approach to Navy logistics. Unfortunately, the plan lacked enough detail to serve as definite guidance to the Navy's bureaus. It was also so secret that the only officials who could see it were the chiefs and assistant bureau chiefs and a few planners on their staffs.[148]

Thus it was ironic that King's effort to gain real control over the shore-side Navy seemed to fail even while the operational Navy in the Pacific was successfully executing, with the cooperation of the Marines and the Army, an extraordinary trans-Pacific campaign. But the culmination of that campaign might be the invasion of Japan, and the Navy's logistics process—which would have to dovetail with the Army's—was probably not prepared for it. It was one thing to move several divisions to assault positions and then support them with an air and sea bombardment, but the April–June 1945 campaign against Okinawa showed what determined Japanese defenders could do to an invasion force. This is why King wanted the Overall Logistics Plan. To get that plan, however, would require restructuring the relationship between the Navy's bureaus and OPNAV because the OPNAV planners lacked the data they needed to plan for an operation as extensive as the invasion of Japan.[149]

Did that mean that creating the Logistics Organization Planning Unit in April 1944 had been futile? No. There were three goals that King wanted the unit to achieve. The first was to create a method for charting the logistic requirements of any major operation and then mapping them against bureau programs. This would create a "picture" of what was needed and when it was needed. The second goal was to develop a logistics plan for the rest of the Pacific campaign that would project material and maintenance requirements and also be flexible enough to handle changes in the operational plans developed by Admiral Nimitz's staff. The third goal was to create an organizational structure that would allow the Navy's leaders to make major logistics decisions that they knew subordinates could implement. Not all these ambitious goals were achieved, but some significant progress was made.

For example, in the summer and fall of 1944, a study group headed by an executive from General Motors and another from United States Steel considered Navy logistics management.[150] The group recommended that Secretary Forrestal set up an Organization Control Board headed by the SECNAV "or his designated representative" to consider "all matters of policy which relate to organization planning, development, procedure and functional assignment."[151] To support the board, the study group suggested an "Organization Planning and Procedure Unit," headed by a rear admiral, to serve as the control board's executive agent and coordinator for "the work of various Organization and Planning and Procedure Units to be established in each bureau."[152] Secretary Forrestal established the senior board, calling it the "Organizational Policy Group." He also set up the planning and procedure unit, "headed by Admiral [Charles P.] Snyder, the Naval Inspector General." However, the "suggestion that subordinate units be established at lower levels was not adopted."[153] That should not have surprised anyone. The most that King wanted was advice on how best to perform his responsibilities under EO 9096 of 12 March 1942. He did not want a parallel chain of command from the Secretary of the Navy running down through the bureaus.[154]

But the Planning and Procedure Unit headed by Admiral Snyder did persuade Secretary Forrestal to set up the Requirements Review Board under Assistant Secretary of the Navy H. Struve Hensel on 9 February 1945. Hensel had served as General Counsel of the Navy Department from 10 July 1940 to 30 January 1945, and he was a close associate of Forrestal. Vice Admiral Horne, Vice Admiral Samuel M. Robinson, head of OP&M, and Rear Admiral Walter S. DeLany, Assistant Chief of Staff for Readiness in COMINCH, were his colleagues on the Requirements Review Board. Ballantine noted that "together they represented the sum of authority in the Navy Department which was exercised over the bureaus."[155] One of the most important steps taken by the Requirements Review Board was to organize the reporting of logistics. Every month, the Requirements Review Division of the board would publish the "Monthly Progress Report of the Navy Logistic Program." This was an extraordinary document, containing logistic requirements, delivery schedules, charts and graphs outlining Navy finances, Navy ship and aircraft deliveries, the production and procurement of special items, and descriptive statistics on personnel.[156] In effect, it provided the staffs of the senior executives in the Navy Department with data useful for planning and for controlling the production and distribution of material.[157]

Forrestal himself headed the "so-called 'Organization Top Policy Group' or 'Top Policy Board'." The secretary intended that this group should serve as the Navy's "board of directors." Admiral King had wanted to give that responsibility to the General Board because the board's role was already part of Navy regulations. But Forrestal already knew in late 1944 of

King's criticisms of the General Board, and so Forrestal did not turn to the General Board but instead put together his "Top Policy Group" without giving it formal authority. Robert G. Albion called it "experimental."[158] Composed of Forrestal, Under Secretary Artemus L. Gates, Assistant Secretary Hensel, King, Vice Admiral Edwards, Vice Admiral Robinson, Admiral Snyder, and Vice Admiral Horne, it first met on 13 November 1944. Though this "group" had no collective responsibility, it was apparently a success as an arena where major issues of procurement, finance, and personnel could be hashed out. Albion, who examined the notes of the group's meetings, believed that its members participated "freely."[159] After the death of Franklin Roosevelt in April 1945, Forrestal was able to use this group in a way he had not while the President—King's patron—was still alive. In at least one group meeting, for example, Forrestal challenged the Navy's shipbuilding targets, prompting a spirited back-and-forth between him and King.[160] The incident can only have increased King's dislike of Forrestal.[161]

Another change that followed from the creation of the Requirements Review Board was the establishment of the Ship Characteristics Board (SCB). Secretary Forrestal directed that it be set up on 15 March 1945 as a complementary organization to the General Board. Secretary Forrestal was concerned that the senior admirals on the General Board could not keep up with all the changes in warfare that had taken place during the war, and on that point Admiral King agreed with him.[162] As a result, the members of the SCB (the DCNO [Air]), the Director of the Electronics Division in BuShips, a representative of COMINCH, and representatives of the chiefs of the Bureaus of Personnel, Ordnance, and Ships) were inserted into the process of ship design after the members of the General Board had made their recommendation. OP-02, the Sub-Chief of Naval Operations, was "ex-officio the senior member" of the SCB, and the assistant director of the Fleet Maintenance Division in OPNAV provided the staff support for the board.[163] The mission of the SCB was "To insure that the characteristics of all naval vessels (projected, building, and on hand) not only meet, but anticipate wherever possible, the requirements of all phases of Naval Warfare."[164] To fulfill this mission, the SCB had the same authority as the General Board—to require the bureaus to provide information and recommendations. The new board was a success; it indeed did draw, through younger officers, on the learning that had become almost constant, especially within the Pacific Fleet, and it eventually replaced the General Board as the forum where basic ship design decisions were thrashed out.[165]

One more example of organizational change bears mentioning: the centralization of the Navy's aviation supply process. As Rear Admiral Edwin D. Foster of the Supply Corps noted in a lecture he presented at the Naval War College in October 1946, "determination of requirements for and procurement of aeronautical material were decentralized and almost uncoordinated functions" before World War II.[166] The "system" worked well enough in peacetime, but it was overwhelmed by the quantity of demands on it once the Navy began to seriously prepare for war. In effect, the cooperative and informal prewar process depended on personalities and the fact that demands for aviation material were limited. As he remarked, "Seven aircraft carriers were operating. Compare this . . . with the 35–40,000 aircraft of 152 models and 50 prototypes and over 100 aircraft carriers operating" on the day Japan surrendered.[167] To deal with the tremendous ramp-up in demands for material, the Secretary of the Navy on 1 October 1941 established the Aviation Supply Office "under the joint cognizance of the Bureau of Aeronautics and the Bureau of Supplies and Accounts."[168]

But "joint cognizance" didn't work well enough, especially as one important supplier to aviation was BuOrd. There was a crisis; in 1942, there were too many items in the hands of the Aviation Supply Office that were not "critical" and not enough that were critical. The reason was because there was no one organization with the authority to review requirements and set priorities among the different claimants for aviation supplies. To try to overcome this problem, the Bureaus of Ordnance, Supplies and Accounts, and Aeronautics recast the authority of the Aviation Supply Office on 8 September 1942. Then they did it again on 10 September 1943.[169] There were still problems, and so Vice Admiral Horne appointed a review board, headed by Rear Admiral Arthur W. Radford, on 12 April 1944 to go at the problem one more time. Radford and his colleagues wrote a report that persuaded Secretary Forrestal to assign to the Aviation Supply Office on 24 June 1944 "those authorities and responsibilities required for successful operation of the aviation, or any other, inventory control program."[170] The change worked. In effect, aviation logistics went through the same period of confusion as much of the rest of Navy logistics and then had to have its chain of authority straightened out and the quality of its information improved.

Both Forrestal and King could point to this case and say that they had been after the same basic rationalization of authority and information collection and flow since the spring of 1942, and both could point to the statutory authority of the bureaus as an obstacle to achieving this essential goal. However, as the "First Draft Narrative" of the history of the Logistics Plan Division in OPNAV pointed out, in 1942 "the constant necessity for action on problems of pressing importance inevitably left many questions of departmental organization to be worked out on lines of least resistance."[171] And one important line of least resistance was to put off decisions.

End Game: After Japan Surrendered

The relationship between CNO-COMINCH and Forrestal "had become unbearably strained" by the time Japan surrendered on 14 August 1945 (the formal surrender ceremony took place on 2 September).[172] Forrestal believed that the Navy secretary had the legal right and obligation to direct the activities and set the policies of the Navy Department. King believed that in time of war this would impede victory. This conflict between the two senior Navy officials might well have caused major problems if the United States had invaded Japan proper.

There is a tendency to see the end of World War II in the Pacific in August 1945 as inevitable. The JCS could not and did not see it that way. They and the joint staff planners, as well as planners on the Army and Navy Washington and Pacific staffs, had already begun preparing for an invasion. The "wheels" of planning and organizing forces had already been turning for some time when the Japanese regime capitulated. Had Japan been invaded, General MacArthur and

Admiral Nimitz would have been the operational-level commanders, but King and Forrestal would have been responsible for sustaining their attack. One must wonder how the friction between them could have been worked out. Under the late President Roosevelt, it was one thing. Under President Truman, it was something else.

Secretary Forrestal moved to protect the authority of the secretariat three days after the fighting in the Pacific ended. He first sent President Truman a draft of an executive order specifying the postwar organization of the Navy Department. That same day—18 August—Forrestal commissioned a "Board to make recommendations concerning the Executive Administration of the Naval Establishment."[173] Known as the "Gates Board" after its chairman, Under Secretary of the Navy Artemus L. Gates, the board's membership was revealing. Most of the members were naval officers—Admirals Snyder, Horne, Edwards, Robinson, and, for a month, Rear Admiral Radford. Gates and Assistant Secretary Hensel were the civilian members. All those on the board had been heavily involved in managing the Navy's wartime material logistics, though Radford had also served as an outstanding carrier task force commander. Moreover, the Navy officers could not be accused as being somehow the protégés of Secretary Forrestal. The SECNAV wanted the support of experienced officers, and placing them on the board was his means to obtain it.

While the Gates Board was still deliberating, President Truman issued EO No. 9635 on 29 September 1945. The order declared that "The Marine Corps is an integral part of the naval establishment," and the naval establishment was defined as "sea, air and ground forces . . . and the naval agencies necessary to support and maintain the naval forces and to administer the Navy as a whole . . ."[174] The order also specified that the Chief of Naval Operations "shall be the principal adviser to the President and to the Secretary of the Navy on the conduct of war, and principal naval advisor and military executive to the Secretary of the Navy on the conduct of the activities of the naval establishment." EO 9635 also gave the CNO "command of the operating forces," and made the CNO "responsible to the Secretary of the Navy for their use in war and for plans and preparations for their readiness in war." The CNO was also "charged, under the direction of the Secretary of the Navy, with the preparation, readiness and logistic support of the operating forces . . . and with the coordination and direction of effort to this end of the bureaus and offices of the Navy Department."[175] The order also allowed the CNO to have on his staff enough vice chiefs, deputy chiefs, and assistant chiefs "as may be considered by the Secretary of the Navy to be appropriate and necessary . . ."[176]

The order further stated that the Secretary of the Navy could create an office "to effectuate common policies of procurement, contracting and production of material throughout the naval establishment," as well as another office to direct and coordinate naval research.[177] Paragraph 9 of the order stated that "Nothing in this order is intended to modify the statutory authority, duties, or responsibilities of the Secretary of the Navy, nor shall it be so construed." That was clearly Forrestal's effort to return to the intent of the language used by Secretary Daniels in 1915: "under the direction of the Secretary," and *not* "under the general direction of the Secretary," as EO 9096 had phrased it in 1942. To hammer home the point, Paragraph 10 of EO 9635 revoked

"Executive Orders 8984 of December 18, 1941, and 9096 of March 12, 1942." The authority that King had exercised no longer existed.

The Gates Board put out its report on 7 November 1945, and elements of that report served as the basis for General Order 230 on 12 January 1946. The order set the Naval Establishment (the operating forces, the Navy Department, and the shore establishment) "four principal tasks." The first was described as "policy control," which meant the proper interpretation of national policy and the development of means for its effective application. The second task was "naval command" of the Naval Establishment. The third task was "logistics administration and control." The fourth task was "business administration," which meant economically efficient operation of all the elements of the Naval Establishment.[178] As far as the "executive administration of the Naval Establishment" was concerned, General Order 230 referred to EO 9635. The bureaus were not placed under the authority of the CNO but were responsible "to the Secretary, the Civilian Executive Assistants, and the Chief of Naval Operations."[179]

General Order 230 gave to the secretary "direct and complete 'policy control' of the Naval Establishment," but also asserted that the secretary would exercise that control "through his Civilian Executive, and his Naval Professional Assistants." The secretary was charged with recommending "to the President the appointment, removal, or reassignment of the incumbents of the legally constituted positions of the Naval Establishment," and he was given the authority to "control the selection and assignment of all other principal naval officials."[180] King had controlled the selection process for senior officers during the war, and he had tried, against Forrestal's wishes, to go back to the formal process of selection boards in the summer of 1945. This section of General Order 230 was Forrestal's response to King's position. General Order 230 also made the secretary responsible for the "business administration" of the "bureaus, boards, and offices of the Navy Department (except such boards and offices as are assigned to the Chief of Naval Operations)." In effect, the Secretary of the Navy was the chief executive officer of the Navy's business side, responsible for setting material procurement policies, organizing research and development (R&D), and defining personnel policies. The secretary was also directed to collaborate with the CNO "in reconciling difficulties encountered in meeting the requirements of the Operating Forces due to scarcity of funds, materials, products, facilities, or personnel."[181]

The CNO was given command of the operating forces, the responsibility for advising the President and the Secretary of the Navy "on the conduct of war," and executive powers on behalf of the secretary. The CNO was also responsible for that part of "logistics administration and control" which applied to planning for the needs of the operating forces, stating those needs as official requirements, reviewing the performance of the bureaus in meeting those requirements, and collaborating with the SECNAV's civilian assistants "in evaluating and strengthening the policies and procedures governing the determination of stock levels and replenishment requirements, and the administration of inventory control systems."[182] General Order 230 named the "Naval Technical Assistants" (the bureau chiefs, the Judge Advocate General, the Commandant of the Marine Corps, and the Commandant of the Coast Guard when the Coast Guard was placed under Navy control), and made them responsible for implementing the directives of the secretary, the "Civilian Executive Assistants," and the CNO.[183]

Besides helping to write what became Navy General Order 230, the Gates Board spread the idea that there were two sides to logistics—the "producer" side and the "consumer" side. "Producer logistics" referred to the development of ships, submarines, weapons, and aircraft, as well as the training of personnel to man, direct, and maintain all those items. "Consumer logistics" referred to the ways that those items were placed in commission, the ways they were fueled and maintained, and the process by which the "users" (elements of the fleet) could tell the "producers" what was needed in and by the operating forces. This distinction between "producers" and "consumers" would carry on for another generation as the conceptual foundation of Navy logistics.[184]

At Fleet Admiral King's insistence, the office of COMINCH was disestablished on 10 October 1945, and King resigned as CNO on 12 November (though he did not retire).[185] His war was over, his extraordinary command ended. Nothing like his position has existed since.

CNO-COMINCH King: An Assessment

Admiral King can be assessed at three levels—the personal, the organizational, and the institutional. What was he like as an officer? What personal characteristics made him effective or robbed him of influence and authority? What did he do with OPNAV? How did he shape OPNAV? Did he wield OPNAV and COMINCH as an effective team? Finally, how did King affect the Navy and the nation's institutions of national security? These are the questions to ask, and this concluding section will attempt to answer them.

What kind of officer was King? His biographer characterized King as personally arrogant, stubborn, ambitious, tenacious, intelligent, incredibly hard working, and demanding of himself and his subordinates—and possessed of a violent temper.[186] Buell described King as a "dispassionate professional warrior who held his own political system in contempt and spurned all civilian authority except that of his commander in chief."[187] However, at the same time as he built a reputation for severity, King

Figure 5-2. CNO-COMINCH Fleet Admiral Ernest J. King led the Navy to its great victories in two oceans in World War II. Brilliant, irascible, and incredibly determined, he was an excellent strategist. Despite the fact that his personality was in some ways the opposite of that of Army Chief of Staff General of the Army George C. Marshall, King worked well with Marshall, and both worked well with President Roosevelt. (National Archives 80-G-416886)

"could be extraordinarily kind to his junior officers." Uncomfortable testifying before Congress and making speeches in public, King nonetheless "worked well in private with [Representative Carl] Vinson" and worked effectively with General Marshall, whose personality was very different.[188] As Naval Academy historian Robert Love argued, "The hinge of the higher direction of the American war effort was the working relationship between Admiral King and General Marshall, two men quite different in tastes, personality, and background. The chief of staff was a man of great tact and breadth; the CNO was a man of blunt speech and agonizing precision." Love was impressed with the way that King, "the greater strategist, often gave way to Marshall, the greater man" as the war progressed. Love credited King's "willingness to engage in remorseless self-examination" as the cause of King's ability to thoughtfully defer to Marshall.[189]

King also possessed the ability to identify and then recruit talent. Buell discovered that King's COMINCH staff was composed of "the finest professional naval officers obtainable," and that King and Admiral Nimitz "were so well informed and had so much in common that their minds could shift easily from strategy to tactics, logistics to administration, or from people to weapons." As a consequence, "Policy decisions with momentous consequences were frequently made in moments" when the two senior officers met.[190] King was even closer intellectually to his chief COMINCH planner, then–Rear Admiral Cooke. Buell described Cooke as King's alter ego in all matters dealing with strategy.[191] King's most important personal relationship, however, was with President Roosevelt. Roosevelt blocked King's efforts to enlarge the powers of the CNO, and Buell notes that King considered Roosevelt "tricky," but it was clear that Roosevelt had confidence in King as a strategist and war leader, despite their personal differences. Indeed, in some ways they were very similar. Both could present very different faces to different audiences. Both could be cleverly manipulative. Both could identify real talent. But it was clear all through the war who was the chief, and King accepted that because he was dependent on Roosevelt's support, just as Roosevelt depended on King for strategic advice.[192]

The point is that King had the sort of personal characteristics and skills that helped him fulfill his three great responsibilities—commanding and directing the Navy, serving as an effective CNO, and working successfully with President Roosevelt and with his colleagues on the JCS.

King's COMINCH headquarters initially had three divisions, plans (F-1), operations (F-3), and readiness (F-4); King added a fourth division, combat intelligence (F-2), on the advice of Vice Admiral William S. Pye, who had briefly commanded the Pacific Fleet after Admiral Kimmel had been relieved of command after the Japanese attack of 7 December 1941. The plans division worked closely with the Logistics Plans Division (OP-12) in OPNAV and with the Joint Staff Planners. The staff of the readiness division also cooperated with the various offices in OPNAV, though a special responsibility of the readiness division was the improvement of tactics. The operations division coordinated "anything and everything that may be necessary to carry out fleet operations." Combat intelligence focused on the location and employment of U.S. and enemy forces. King created the Tenth Fleet, "in effect the Anti [sic] Submarine Division" on 20 May 1943 and took formal command of it himself.[193] Because the COMINCH staff was small and the personal creation of King, "No CominCh 'Staff Instructions' were published, nor were the specific duties of senior staff officers defined in writing."[194]

What about OPNAV and the Navy? When he became COMINCH, King had to create his staff from scratch; in his own words, "I had to start with nothing."[195] But with OPNAV, the situation was different. OPNAV was a large staff, and had been continually growing since the prewar build-up started in 1939. King did not have time to restructure it, nor could he risk disrupting OPNAV's established routines in that phase of the war. But he did choose Rear Admiral Horne to take Rear Admiral Ingersoll's post as assistant CNO while Ingersoll moved to take King's former command in the Atlantic. King had come to know and respect Horne when both served on the General Board. But could King infuse OPNAV with his intensity without at the same time undermining Horne's authority? As COMINCH, King selected his own staff, kept it small, and was able to recruit superb officers, such as his deputy, Rear Admiral Edwards. In OPNAV, King had to work through officers most of whom he had not selected, many of whom were not familiar to him, and some of whom were doing things that King was not familiar with. The potential for confusion and even chaos was great.

The confusion is apparent in the "first draft narratives" written by officers attached to the various OPNAV staff offices. "The History of the Naval Transportation Service," for example, noted that "the Naval Transportation Service lacked within the Navy Department the administrative status and prestige required for its task" in 1942.[196] Another example is the fate of OPNAV's Convoy and Routing Section. It became a section in the Ship Movements Division only on 18 November 1941; then it was transferred to COMINCH F-3 in mid-May 1942; then it was made a part of the Tenth Fleet in the late spring of 1943.[197] At least the task of its officers was given special consideration. Mine warfare was another matter. Because "No mining policy had been enunciated by the Joint Chiefs of Staff or CominCh," Rear Admiral Farber on Horne's staff apparently worked through COMINCH F-3 to gain Admiral King's attention. That led to a memo from King to Horne officially defining the duties of OPNAV's mine warfare division.[198]

When the war began, matters were just as confused in the field of fuel supplies as they were in transportation and convoying. Procuring and transporting fuel was an area where the Army and Navy had separate responsible offices and where they therefore had been competing with one another in securing adequate quantities of certain fuels. To overcome this problem, Vice Admiral Horne and Lieutenant General Somervell in July 1942 created the Army-Navy Petroleum Board to coordinate fuel purchases. In January 1943, the JCS designated the Petroleum Board as one of their joint agencies. Though this action helped set a sensible petroleum supply policy, it did not solve the problems of the operating forces. As the history of the Petroleum Board pointed out, "The volume of petroleum products required in the various theaters was so great and constantly increasing [that] it was necessary to establish" area petroleum offices that were responsible to the theater commanders.[199]

These cases are indicators of the many complex day-to-day problems that OPNAV staff officers had to face. How were they dealt with? The answers to that question are in the cases themselves. For example, if a problem was serious enough, it was dealt with by Horne or by Rear Admiral Farber. In the case of mine warfare, it turned out that "the Bureaus were willing and indeed anxious for direction."[200] Personnel in the relevant bureaus were eager to help and so could be left to work on solutions with OPNAV and COMINCH staff and across bureau organizational boundaries.[201] Convoying and routing problems had been anticipated in OPNAV's series of Orange War Plans, and port directors in San Francisco and New York had acted on their own as war neared to prepare for the assembly of convoys. After the fall of 1939, they were aided in this endeavor by a reactivated Joint Merchant Vessel Board.[202] Pre–World War II planning, and sometimes memories of successes and failures in World War I, helped Navy staffs to get through many of the problems they had to deal with. When this happened, it significantly reduced the management burden on Horne, which also helped King.

The staffs were also helped by the fact that, once war began, money was not an issue. Human resources were scarcer than financial ones. But the military services also drew on reservists and even on older individuals who had served in World War I. As a result, a lot of talent and experience flowed into Washington, and in many cases it was put to good use. Even King, the admiral who normally disdained the press, changed his ways and met regularly with a coterie of reporters starting in November 1942. The sessions with the reporters were off the record, but both King and the reporters found the informal meetings extremely useful. King usually avoided the press; he did not like to be questioned. At the off-the-record sessions, however, he was allowed to set the topic and talk at ease. He quickly won and kept the loyalty of the small group of assembled reporters, and they were careful not to quote him in their subsequent writing.[203]

King was adept at holding on to critical information and using it for his purposes. In 1942, he deliberately withheld news of Navy ship losses from both Secretary Knox and General Marshall. King thought that Knox would inadvertently reveal secrets, so "he did not tell Knox anything."[204] But King also knew that he had an advantage over Knox; the secretary lacked a sophisticated understanding of the Navy, and King knew it. Knox and King could nevertheless get along. After all, Knox was one of King's early supporters. Moreover, King was apparently quite willing to allow Knox to direct the Navy's shore establishment. As Buell observed, however, "On matters of serious policy their differences could become brutal."[205] In Secretary Forrestal, King encountered a more aggressive bureaucratic opponent. Forrestal turned the conflict over information around, eventually using the Requirements Review Board to produce some of the information that King had earlier been hesitant to reveal as a matter of routine.

King's reluctant deference to civilian authority and his efforts "to consolidate his power within the Navy Department" had several roots.[206] The first was his memory of World War I; he did not want that experience repeated—either the confusion over waging the anti-U-boat campaign of 1917–1918 or the recriminations that took place after the war was over. The second was his intense desire to take the offensive against the Japanese coupled with his understanding of how important it was to avoid playing to Japanese naval strategy. The Japanese military leaders wanted to gain territory in the Western Pacific and Southeast Asia and then go on the defensive, where they could fight for time and gamble that the United States would be willing to reach an armistice with them. King knew that an aggressive offensive campaign could deny the Japanese military leaders that option, and he pressed Admiral Nimitz to wage that campaign.

There are three questions that the leader of any complex organization has to answer. The first is, "Why do we exist? What's our purpose?" The second is, "How must we be organized in order to fulfill our purpose?" The third is, "What should be our future, and how do we act now to put down the foundation for that future?" AS CNO-COMINCH, King tried to make sure that the staffs under his command knew the answers. First, the Navy existed to defeat the navies of the enemies of the United States. Second, the Navy existed to take the Army and Marines to key points in Europe and the Pacific. Those might seem such obvious answers that the question prompting it didn't need to be asked in the first place. But King knew from experience that there were always other answers. The Navy was a career for some, a job for others, and a source of revenue for individuals and businesses. Those answers had to be constantly shoved aside enough so that they didn't get in the way of the task that mattered.

As far as answering the second question was concerned, King's position was clear. To win the war, it was essential to combine OPNAV and COMINCH. Indeed, King wanted the bureaus subordinated to the Chief of Naval Operations. But President Roosevelt (and then President Truman) would not allow him that option. Civilian control mattered so much that it was better to take the risk of impeding the war effort than to cripple effective civilian direction of the war production program. King accepted that response so long as his Navy could obtain the material and personnel that it needed. That is, the war effort was never so hampered that King's Navy could not achieve its objectives—at least until the summer of 1945. The campaign in Okinawa had shown that invading the Japanese home islands could be so costly that the Army and Navy would be pushed to the limits of their capabilities. King's view as a commander was that Japan could be blockaded and starved into submission, but as CNO-COMINCH he had to plan for an invasion. With Germany defeated, the United States had the human and material resources to invade Japan, but they had to be moved into position by sea, protected while at sea, and then shielded while being set ashore on bitterly hostile territory in the face of a suicidal defense. The projected losses in personnel and equipment were heavy.

The answer to the second question influenced the answer to the third. King was well aware that the Navy came out of World War I "unbalanced." There were too many war-built destroyers, not enough modern cruisers, and no aircraft carriers. The Navy emerged from World War I saddled with ships built for World War I and not designed for a possible future war. Soon after the war, the Washington Treaty limited the sizes of navies, and the desire of several Presidents and the Congress for financial savings cut the Navy's budget and consequently its readiness. In King's mind, he had two reasons to press for as many new ships, submarines, and aircraft as he could get. The first was to have enough material to replace the losses anticipated in the event Japan was invaded. The second was to stock the fleet with as many new types of ships, submarines, and aircraft as possible so that the U.S. Navy's superiority at sea would go unchallenged.

King had used his authority to leave the Navy both stronger and different than it had been in 1940. As Love observed, King "personally selected most of the new admirals who rose through the ranks during the conflict."[207] King had also accepted the suggestion that aviator admirals have unrestricted line officers as their deputies and vice versa. This policy would produce two CNOs in the 1950s—Admirals Robert B. Carney and Arleigh A. Burke. King had also emphasized through his leadership the importance of the habit of "getting the most out of what was available." This implied—as Love grasped—the need to take risks, especially in operations, but also in procurement.[208] This positive, aggressive, confident attitude would pay dividends during the Cold War.

This chapter has largely ignored King's role on the JCS. That part of his commanding career has been well covered by others, but it's important to remember that King wanted the Joint Chiefs given legal status[209] and that his ability to work with Generals Marshall and Arnold, and his good relationship with Admiral Leahy, created a positive attitude toward the notion of a standing joint chiefs' organization. President Roosevelt sought King's counsel. King was able to develop an effective working relationship with Marshall. Out of these relationships came agreements on overall strategy. The only time Roosevelt overruled his Joint Chiefs was in the fall of 1942, when the President insisted on the invasion of North Africa. This is an extraordinary record. Roosevelt was confident that he could leave much of the direction of the war in the hands of two extraordinary officers. They rarely disappointed him.

Of King's three roles—war leader as a member of the JCS, Navy supreme commander, and Chief of Naval Operations—the first and second have been paid most attention to by historians. In doing that, however, they may miss King's ability to see the larger strategic picture and simultaneously pay attention to the details that mattered. From 12 March 1942 until the end of the war, King balanced the three roles and used his leadership in each to make his service in the other two more valuable to the Navy and the nation. The effort wore him out physically and mentally, but he carried on and seemed never to give a damn if he was liked or not.

On 10 March 1942, former CNO Admiral William V. Pratt wrote to congratulate King on his soon-to-be-announced appointment as CNO-COMINCH. Pratt told King that for months he had been "sick at heart, unable to open my mouth—seeing the job and the office which I helped create in war—knowing how strong it can be if run with a firm hand—one that keeps its grip on the Bureaus, and at the same [time] holds the general directive of the Fleet—has deteriorated until its main purpose was to be a mouthpiece . . . has made me very sore." According to Pratt, "it is the CNO job [sic] in Washington to be the Fleets [sic] defender against the Bureaus—I have seen the job go straight to Hell with well meaning men leading it there," but at last the Navy would have a CNO "who knows the only way to win a war is to fight—and who also knows that this war in the East, at least in its preliminary phases is an air war."[210] Pratt was right—the Navy had found the admiral who knew how to fight to win.

Notes

[1] Appendix IV in Buell, *Master of Seapower*, 528–30.

[2] Ibid.

[3] Ibid.

[4] Executive Order 9096 specified that the CNO-COMINCH was next in line of succession *behind* the Navy secretary and the secretary's deputies. Ibid., 529.

[5] "The Naval Establishment: Its Growth and Necessity for Expansion, 1930–1950," Office of the Comptroller of the Navy, Executive Office of the Secretary of the Navy (NavExos-P-1038), July 1951, i.

[6] King said, "I had a proper ambition to get to the top, either Commander in Chief of the United States Fleet, or even to become Chief of Naval Operations." See Buell, *Master of Seapower*, title page to ch. I, "Before the War."

[7] Memo, Commander-in-Chief, United States Fleet to Chief of Naval Operations, subj: "Radio Controlled Target Airplanes—Exercises with during current quarter, advance partial report," 12 Feb. 1939, General Board File 436, Serial No. 3908, F41-10/0245, RG 80, NARA.

[8] Ibid.

[9] Rowland and Boyd, *U.S. Navy Bureau of Ordnance in World War II*, 220. For the pre–World War II and wartime evolution of antiaircraft guns, see *U.S. Naval Weapons*, by Norman Friedman (Annapolis, MD: Naval Institute Press, 1982), 62–67 and 74–81.

[10] Buell, *Master of Seapower*, 125.

[11] Ibid., 128.

[12] In addition, being a member of the General Board gave King access to the transcripts of earlier confidential hearings and proceedings of the board, and these were an invaluable source of information about many bureau activities, as Norman Friedman has shown in his series of studies of ship design.

[13] "Organization of the Naval Forces of the United States," General Order No. 143, 3 Feb. 1941, in Furer, *Administration of the Navy Department in World War II*, 178–80.

[14] Buell, *Master of Seapower*, 133.

[15] Ibid., 137.

[16] Ibid., 139.

[17] Ibid., 152.

[18] Ibid., 153.

[19] Ibid.

[20] See Appendix III of Buell, *Master of Seapower*, 526.

[21] Ibid.

[22] Ibid., 526–27.

[23] Ibid., 154.

[24] Buell, *Master of Seapower*, 178.

[25] Hone and Hone, *Battle Line*, 125.

[26] Buell, *Master of Seapower*, 240–41.

[27] Jeffrey G. Barlow, *From Hot War to Cold, The U.S. Navy and National Security Affairs, 1945–1955* (Stanford, CA: Stanford University Press, 2009), 15–16.

[28] Ibid., 17.

[29] Buell, *Master of Seapower*, 179.

[30] Hopkins was Roosevelt's emissary, responsible for sizing things up for the President. Hopkins correctly assessed the consequences of the 4 June Battle of Midway. As he said in a letter to Winston Churchill after receiving news of the battle, "The Japs simply cannot stand the attrition and I am sure we can beat them down gradually in the air and on the sea until finally they must collapse." See *Roosevelt and Hopkins*, by Robert Sherwood (New York: Harper & Brothers, 1948), 580.

[31] "FOLUS: British Liaison with COMNAVEU," in COMNAVEU Records, Series II, Item 54, "British Liaison With," 1940–1943," in MS Collection 37, NWC Archives, 3.

[32] See *Admiral Harold R. Stark, Architect of Victory, 1939–1945*, by B. Mitchell Simpson III (Columbia: University of South Carolina Press, 1989), 129, 131–32, and 136–40.

[33] Buell, *Master of Seapower*, 52.

[34] Ibid., 11.

[35] Ibid., 18.

[36] Barlow, *From Hot War to Cold*, 19.

[37] Ibid., 20.

[38] Ibid.

[39] Ibid., 21.

[40] The organization chart is in folder "OPNAV Organization, Feb. 42–May 48," in File "Historic OPNAV Org Manuals," N09B1, Office of the Chief of Naval Operations.

[41] The 15 July 1942, organization chart is from the same file as that for 27 Mar. 1942. The number of officers in OPNAV is from the 1 Apr. 1941, *Navy Directory* (Washington, DC: GPO, 1941), 366–70. The number of officers on King's staff is from the list for battleship *Texas* (BB-35), King's nominal Atlantic Fleet flagship.

[42] *Navy Directory*, 1 Apr. 1941, 366–70 for the OPNAV numbers, 373–74 for the Bureau of Ordnance, and 374–78 for the Bureau of Ships. The OPNAV phone book for 18 June 1941, however, lists only 120 active and retired officers. In the 1 April 1941 *Navy Directory*, 86 officers are listed in OPNAV's Communications Division. In the phone book for 18 June 1941, only 12

officers are listed. Part of the difference may be accounted for by the presence in the 1 Apr. 1941 *Navy Directory* of 56 naval reservists. The source for the phone book is "OPNAV Organization Manual, Nov. 1941," a folder in the "Historic OPNAV Organization Manuals" file in N09B1, Office of the Chief of Naval Operations.

[43] See *Navy Directory*, 1 Apr. 1941, 374–78. The Navy's officer corps was like an iceberg: most officers were stationed or assigned away from Washington, just as most of an iceberg's bulk is under water.

[44] Hone, "The Effectiveness of the Washington Treaty Navy, 35–59.

[45] Michael Gannon, *Operation Drumbeat: Germany's U-Boat Attacks Along the American Coast in World War II* (New York: Harper Collins, 1990).

[46] King's use of the term "desperate" is cited in Buell, *Master of Seapower*, 287.

[47] Buell, *Master of Seapower*, 285.

[48] Both Roosevelt's memo and King's reply are in Buell, *Master of Seapower*, 289.

[49] "Organization of the Naval Forces of the United States," General Order 143, quoted on 179 of Furer, *Administration of the Navy Department in World War II*.

[50] Furer, *Administration of the Navy Department in World War II*, 181.

[51] Memo, Chief of Naval Operations to Chiefs of Bureaus and Other Material Offices, subj: "Over-centralization of Material Control in the Navy Department," 31 Mar. 1942, KN3/A3-1, in MS Collection 37, NWC Archives.

[52] Buell, *Master of Seapower*, 309.

[53] Memo, CNO-COMINCH to Secretary of the Navy, subj: "Mass Production of XCV's and Corvettes," Confidential Correspondence of the Secretary of the Navy, 17 June 1942, Microfilm Roll No. 2, Scholarly Resources, Inc.

[54] Memo, King to Roosevelt, 29 May, 1942, COMINCH File, Official Papers of Fleet Adm. E. J. King, Series I (May 1942–Feb. 1943), Microfilm Roll No. 2, Scholarly Resources, Inc.

[55] CAPT Low was Operations Officer under RADM Richard S. Edwards, head of the Operational Division of COMINCH. CAPT Duncan was the Air Officer. See Appendix 14, "Commander in Chief, United States Fleet, Headquarters," First Draft Narrative, Historical Section, by CDR W. M. Whitehill, in the Navy Department Library, Washington Navy Yard, Washington, DC.

[56] Samuel Eliot Morison, *History of United States Naval Operations in World War II, Vol. 4, Coral Sea, Midway and Submarine Actions* (Edison, NJ: Castle Books, 2001), 245–47.

[57] Buell, *Master of Seapower*, 184.

[58] Ibid.

[59] See "Development of U.S. Joint and Amphibious Doctrine, 1898–1945," by Barry P. Messina, (Alexandria, VA: Center for Naval Analyses, 1994), especially Appendix B and Appendix C.

[60] Joel R. Davidson, *The Unsinkable Fleet, The Politics of U.S. Navy Expansion in World War II* (Annapolis, MD: Naval Institute Press, 1996), 49.

[61] FADM E. J. King, "Some Aspects of the High Command in World War II," presented at the National War College, Washington, D.C., 29 Apr. 1947, in MS Collection 37, NWC Archives, 16.

[62] Buell, *Master of Seapower*, 237–38.

[63] "Office of Procurement and Material," Gen. Order No. 166, Navy Department, 30 Jan. 1942, Appendix 8 of "The Logistics of Fleet Readiness: The Fleet Maintenance Division in World War II," First Draft Narrative, Historical Section, Office of the CNO, Navy Department Library.

[64] Furer, *Administration of the Navy Department in World War II*, 442, 839.

[65] "Organization and Functions," Office of Procurement and Material, 1 July 1944, Folder "Naval Material Command: 1941–1970," in File "Historic OPNAV Organization Manuals," N09B1, Office of the Chief of Naval Operations.

[66] Connery, *The Navy and the Industrial Mobilization in World War II*, 11.

[67] The Act of 8 December 1941 authorized the President "to make such redistribution of functions among executive agencies as he may deem necessary, including any functions, duties, and powers hitherto by law conferred upon any executive department." See *Makers of Naval Policy, 1798–1947*, 452.

[68] Albion, *Makers of Naval Policy, 1798–1947*, 478.

[69] Furer, in his *Administration of the Navy Department in World War II*, 68, called the Budget Officer one of "the tools available to Frank Knox for managing the Naval Establishment."

[70] Albion, *Makers of Naval Policy, 1798–1947*, 485–86, on legislative liaison officers who worked for the Judge Advocate General (who in turn worked for the Secretary). The quotation from Albion is from 456. Material on Carl Vinson is on 454–55, while that on Senator David I. Walsh, chair of the Senate Naval Affairs Committee, is on 454.

[71] Interview, Thomas Buell with George Russell, 11 Dec. 1974, in MS Collection 37, NWC Archives, 2.

[72] Norman Friedman, *U.S. Amphibious Ships and Craft* (Annapolis, MD: Naval Institute Press, 2002), especially ch. 4 and 5.

[73] Ibid., 98, 117.

[74] Paul L. Miles, "Roosevelt and Leahy: The Orchestration of Global Strategy," in Marolda, *FDR and the U.S. Navy*, 150.

[75] Ibid., 154.

[76] As Buell pointed out, ADM King visited President Roosevelt in the White House 32 times in 1942—and those were the official visits. There were unofficial visits as well. Marshall and King were not kept away from Roosevelt. At the same time, once Leahy accepted his new post as chief of staff to the commander-in-chief, he was much more than simply another member

of the Joint Chiefs. For example, Leahy and King were friends, but Leahy rarely visited King. Leahy kept his distance—both to show his link to Roosevelt and to avoid being seen as another "Navy man." See Buell, *Master of Seapower*, 242–43, and Robert W. Love, "Ernest Joseph King," in Love, *The Chiefs of Naval Operations*, 162.

[77] *Flight Log Book No. 3*, Year 1944, typed notes to CDR Whitehill from FADM King, Buell Papers, NWC Archives, 10–11.

[78] Duncan S. Ballantine, *U.S. Naval Logistics in the Second World War* (Princeton, NJ: Princeton University Press, 1949), 105.

[79] Ibid., 105–106.

[80] Ibid., 106.

[81] Ibid.

[82] Ibid., 107.

[83] Reynolds, *Admiral John H. Towers*, ch. 13, especially 400.

[84] Ballantine, *U.S. Naval Logistics in the Second World War*, 98–99.

[85] Ibid., 99–100.

[86] "The Logistics of Fleet Readiness: The Fleet Maintenance Division in World War II," 38.

[87] Ibid., 34, 38–39.

[88] Ibid., 12.

[89] Ballantine, *U.S. Naval Logistics in the Second World War*, 34.

[90] Ibid., 121.

[91] Ibid.

[92] Richard M. Leighton and Robert W. Coakley, *Global Logistics and Strategy, 1940–1943* (Washington, DC: Office of the Chief of Military History, U.S. Army, and GPO, 1995), 651.

[93] Ibid., 657.

[94] Ballantine, *U.S. Naval Logistics in the Second World War*, 126. Also Leighton and Coakley, *Global Logistics and Strategy, 1940–1943*, 658.

[95] Coakley and Leighton, *Global Logistics and Strategy, 1943–1945*, 429.

[96] Ibid., 427.

[97] Ibid., 428.

[98] Ibid., 431.

[99] Ibid.

[100] Thomas C. Hone, "Replacing Battleships with Aircraft Carriers in the Pacific in World War II," *Naval War College Review*, vol. 66, no. 1 (Winter 2013), 56–76. Also see Ballantine, *U.S. Naval Logistics in the Second World War*, 162, 176.

[101] Coakley and Leighton, *Global Logistics and Strategy, 1943–1945*, 425.

[102] Ibid., 246, 430, 432.

[103] Ibid., 446–47.

[104] Ibid., 453–54.

[105] Barlow, *From Hot War to Cold*, 22.

[106] Ibid., 24.

[107] Ballantine, *U.S. Naval Logistics in the Second World War*, 138.

[108] Ibid., 146.

[109] Ibid., 147–48.

[110] Ibid., 148.

[111] Coakley and Leighton, *Global Logistics and Strategy, 1943–1945*, 94.

[112] Ibid., for GEN Marshall's comment to his colleagues.

[113] Ibid., 94–95.

[114] Executive Order 9024, 16 Jan. 1942, established the War Production Board to replace the Supply Priorities and Allocation Board and the Office of Production Management. The War Production Board facilitated the conversion of civilian industry to war production, rationed scarce material, allocated critical materials such as copper, shut down unnecessary civilian production, and set production priorities. It continued to function through the end of the war, though both it and the Office of Economic Stabilization were placed under the Office of War Mobilization.

[115] Davidson, *The Unsinkable Fleet*, 99.

[116] Ibid., 102.

[117] Ibid.

[118] Ibid., 104.

[119] Ibid., 109.

[120] Ltr, to: CDR Thomas B. Buell, from: ADM Malcolm F. Schoeffel, USN (Ret.), 9 Sept. 1974, in MS Collection 37, NWC Archives, 4.

[121] Davidson, *The Unsinkable Fleet*, 143–44.

[122] Ibid., 114.

[123] Ibid., 119, 132–33.

[124] Ibid., 144.

[125] Buell, *Master of Seapower*, 452.

[126] ADM Ernest King, "Flight Log Book No. 3, Year 1944," in MS Collection 37, NWC Archives, 11.

[127] Ibid., 12.

[128] Ibid. See also Buell, *Master of Seapower*, 238.

[129] Memo, COMINCH to the Secretary of the Navy, subj: "Draft of Report to the President—Comments thereon," 30 Dec. 1944, MS Collection 37, NWC Archives, 1.

[130] Ibid., 3.

[131] Ibid.

[132] Reynolds, *Admiral John H. Towers*, 348.

[133] Buell, *Master of Seapower*, 406.

[134] Ibid., 407.

[135] Ibid., 408.

[136] Ibid., 409.

[137] Ibid.

[138] "Commander-in-Chief, U.S. Fleet, Headquarters," First Draft Narrative, Historical Section, Office of the Commander-in-Chief, U.S. Fleet, 1946, Navy Department Library, Washington, DC, 43.

[139] Ibid., 44.

[140] Furer, *Administration of the Navy Department in World War II*, 732.

[141] Buell, *Master of Seapower*, 409.

[142] Ballantine, U.S. Naval Logistics in the *Second World War*, 170.

[143] Ibid., 172.

[144] Ibid., 149.

[145] Ibid., 165.

[146] Ibid., 164.

[147] Ibid., 190.

[148] Ibid., 191–92.

[149] Ibid., 193.

[150] The executives were T. P. Archer, a vice president of General Motors, and George Wolf, head to U.S. Steel's export company. They were brought in at the request of Secretary Knox. Their work continued after Knox died and was succeeded by Under Secretary of the Navy James Forrestal. See Ballantine, 185. See also Connery, *The Navy and the Industrial Mobilization in World War II*, 419–20.

[151] Ballantine, *U.S. Naval Logistics in the Second World War*, 186.

[152] Ibid.

[153] Ibid., 187.

[154] ADM King had commissioned VADM Horne on 26 May 1944 to survey the functions of the Office of Procurement & Material in the Navy secretariat to learn if there were areas where

OPNAV and the secretariat had similar functions. King halted his study effort in order to wait for the recommendations of the study that Secretary Knox had initiated. See Connery, *The Navy and the Industrial Mobilization in World War II*, 421.

[155] Ibid., 274.

[156] The 25 July 1945 edition of the "Monthly Progress Report of the Navy Logistic Program" is especially revealing because it contains statistics on five years of Navy logistics. As the "Foreword" to the Report notes, "As requirements, delivery schedules and other yardsticks of performance have been omitted, this issue affords a quantitative report on Navy procurement and growing strength, essentially along bureau lines."

[157] According to Connery, the staff supporting the Requirements Review Committee (which supported the Requirements Review Board) kept "the major material and personnel procurement programs of the Navy under constant audit review." *The Navy and the Industrial Mobilization in World War II*, 425.

[158] Albion, *Makers of Naval Policy, 1798–1947*, 542.

[159] Ibid.

[160] Davidson, *The Unsinkable Fleet*, 180.

[161] Barlow, *From Hot War to Cold*, notes that King treated Forrestal as an enemy, 27.

[162] "The Logistics of Fleet Readiness: The Fleet Maintenance Division in World War II," 62.

[163] Furer, *Administration of the Navy Department in World War II*, 166.

[164] "The Logistics of Fleet Readiness: The Fleet Maintenance Division in World War II," 63.

[165] There was also an "Informal Advisory Board on Ships' Characteristics to DCNO (Air)," and the "head of the carrier type desk in Fleet Maintenance was a member of this new board." See "The Logistics of Fleet Readiness: The Fleet Maintenance Division in World War II," 66.

[166] RADM Edwin D. Foster, "Aviation Supply System," lecture, Naval War College, 14 Oct. 1944, NWC Archives, 1.

[167] Ibid., 2.

[168] Grossnick, *United States Naval Aviation, 1910–1995*, 108.

[169] Foster, "Aviation Supply System," 4.

[170] Ibid., 5. Clark Reynolds, in *Admiral John H. Towers*, 464, noted that VADM Towers in Hawaii did not want to see Radford sent to Washington when there was a real need for experienced carrier commanders.

[171] "Aspects of Logistics Planning," First Draft Narrative, Historical Section, Office of the CNO, 1946, in the Navy Department Library, Washington, DC, 37.

[172] Buell, *Master of Seapower*, 501.

[173] Furer, *Administration of the Navy Department in World War II*, 13.

[174] "Organization of the Navy Department and the Naval Establishment," Executive Order No. 9635, para. 3. This order was based on the authority given the President by Title I of the First War Powers Act (55 Stat. 838; 50 U.S. Code 601, Supp. IV).

[175] Ibid., para. 4.

[176] Ibid., para. 5.

[177] Ibid., para. 6.

[178] General Order No. 230 [Series of 1935], 12 Jan. 1946, "Policies and Principles Governing the Distribution of Authority and Responsibility for the Administration of the Naval Establishment," Section A, Part. 3. Copy in the Navy Department Library.

[179] Ibid., Section A, Part 4.

[180] Ibid., Section B, Part 6.

[181] Ibid., Section C, Part 7.

[182] Ibid., Section D, Part 8.

[183] Ibid., Section D, Part 9.

[184] In his *Administration of the Navy Department in World War II*, for example, RADM Furer wrote as though the distinction between consumer and producer logistics was both well established and had been for some time the basis of Navy logistics. That may have been the case in 1959, when Furer's history was published, but it was not the case in 1945.

[185] King had been promoted to the five star rank of fleet admiral in December 1944. Love, "Ernest Joseph King," in Love, *The Chiefs of Naval Operations*, 179.

[186] Buell, *Master of Seapower*, 11.

[187] Ibid., xxxiii.

[188] Ibid., 100.

[189] Love, "Ernest Joseph King," in Love, *The Chiefs of Naval Operations*, 162–63.

[190] Buell, *Master of Seapower*, 227, 357.

[191] Ibid., 267.

[192] The classic description of Roosevelt as political leader is in *Roosevelt: The Soldier of Freedom*, by James M. Burns (New York: Harcourt, Brace, Jovanovich, 1970), 347–50.

[193] "Commander-in-Chief, U.S. Fleet, Headquarters," First Draft Narrative, Historical Section, Commander in Chief [sic], U.S. Fleet, 1946, Navy Department Library, Washington, DC, 29–30.

[194] Ibid., 38.

[195] Buell, *Master of Seapower*, 154.

[196] "The History of the Naval Transportation Service," First Draft Narrative, Office of the Chief of Naval Operations, Navy Department Library, Washington, DC, 38.

[197] "History of Convoy and Routing, HQ COMINCH and Commander, Tenth Fleet, 1939–1945 (FX-37)," Historical Section, COMINCH, Navy Department Library, Washington, DC, 12-I through 14-I.

[198] "Mine Warfare in the Naval Establishment," History of Mine Warfare Section, Base Maintenance Division of OPNAV, Navy Department Library, Washington, DC, 96.

[199] "History of Army-Navy Petroleum Board and Petroleum and Tanker Division of the Office of the Chief of Naval Operations," Vol. II, Appendices 1–62, Director of Naval History, Navy Department Library, Washington, DC, 1, 7.

[200] "Mine Warfare in the Naval Establishment," 86.

[201] Robert C. Duncan, *America's Use of Sea Mines* (Silver Spring, MD: U.S. Naval Ordnance Laboratory, 1962).

[202] "History of Convoy and Routing," 10-I.

[203] Glen C. H. Perry, "Dear Bart," *Washington Views of World War II* (Westport, CT: Greenwood Press, 1982). Thomas Buell also describes these off-the-record meetings. See *Master of Seapower*, 259–263.

[204] Buell, *Master of Seapower*, 200. King feared that admitting the losses at Guadalcanal in August 1942 would weaken his standing in Washington, and to avoid giving the Japanese important intelligence information he kept the loss of carrier *Yorktown* (CV-5) at the Battle of Midway a secret until September 1942. *Master of Seapower*, 222.

[205] Buell, *Master of Seapower*, 234.

[206] Ibid.

[207] Love, "Ernest Joseph King," in Love, *The Chiefs of Naval Operations*, 178.

[208] Ibid.

[209] Buell, *Master of Seapower*, 181.

[210] Ltr, from retired ADM and CNO William V. Pratt, to King, 10 Mar. 1942, in Buell Papers, NWC Archives, Newport, RI.

CHAPTER 6

OPNAV Postwar: No End of Challenges

Introduction

When President Truman signed EO 9635 at the end of September 1945, Secretary Forrestal had achieved his goal of making clear the responsibilities and authority of the Chief of Naval Operations. However, there was much more to be done, especially in the area of Army-Navy relations. For many Army officers, as well as for many members of Congress, one major source of inefficiency and ineffectiveness during the war had been the Navy's independence. What if the Army and Navy were merged into one organization, with one experienced military officer serving as the deputy to a senior civilian department head? Would that eliminate the disputes that, in the eyes of many, had hampered the war effort? Admiral King and General Marshall had agreed during the war that such centralization would not be a good idea, but the idea came up again after the war, and debating it would consume much time and energy on the part of senior military officers and civilian political leaders in the post-war years.

In addition, World War II had ushered in a revolution in technology. Military aviation, for example, had grown tremendously in importance, and innovations developed during the war—such as jet aircraft engines and long-range heavy bombers—encouraged the leaders of the Army's air component to demand that it was time to create a separate military department for all military aviation. This claim was disputed by the Navy and the Marines, both of which regarded their air forces as integral and necessary elements of their fighting power. However, it was clear that the creation of the atomic bomb had significant implications for the military services. The nuclear weapon, which was the most spectacular result of wartime investment in advanced technology, promised to revolutionize warfare. What agency or department should control this new weapon, and how should it be used? Did it make the Navy's carrier task forces and its amphibious armada obsolete?

The end of World War II brought in its wake issues like those that had arisen after World War I—the role of aviation, how to manage the development of new technology, how to demobilize without at the same time dangerously weakening the Army and Navy, and how best to manage the American military at a time when military expenditures were declining dramatically. There was also something that the Navy's leaders had not had to consider after World War I: the fact that the Navy and its allies had eliminated any naval force able to challenge their domination of the oceans. Did the nation even need a powerful navy if its air forces controlled the skies and carried atomic bombs?

There was no rest for the armed services of the United States after World War II. On the one hand, they were demobilized rapidly, with all the confusion that entailed. On the other hand, they were given new missions, requiring new organizations such as the Sixth Fleet in the Mediterranean and the Strategic Air Command. Geopolitical events also presented a cluster of serious challenges to the United States and its military. China and Southeast Asia were in turmoil—the former from a civil war between Nationalists and Communists, and the latter from the desire of various nationalist groups for independence from colonial powers (the British in Burma, India and Malaya; the French in Indochina; and the Dutch in the Netherlands East Indies) that had been allies of the United States during World War II.[1] Europe needed to be rebuilt economically and socially. There was also the great danger that European regimes would "go communist" through elections or insurrections—both fomented by the Soviet Union. Finally, there was the challenge of technology, especially that posed by nuclear weapons. Though the United States was the strongest economic and military power on the globe in 1946, there could be no turning away from the rest of the world. In particular, how should the nation's military power be organized, directed, and used to attain the strategic goals of the nation's leaders?

A Late Start for Navy Planning for a Postwar World

As Navy historian Jeffrey G. Barlow noted, "[N]either COMINCH Headquarters nor the Office of the Chief of Naval Operations gave postwar planning serious attention until mid-1943."[2] This late start was unfortunate because the Army's General Staff, at the request of the Secretary of War, had already begun postwar planning. Accordingly, in July 1943, the Under Secretary of War, Robert P. Patterson, invited SECNAV Frank Knox to provide means "to enable the War and Navy Departments' postwar planners to collaborate with one another on matters of common interest."[3] VCNO Frederick J. Horne had not set up a committee in OPNAV to conduct postwar planning, and he told CNO King that in his view there was no need for one, though he said a senior officer should be selected to "give his entire thought as to what planning will be necessary and how it should be carried out . . ."[4]

As it happened, the General Board had already conducted a postwar strategy analysis for the Secretary of the Navy. Such an analysis was the first step in tailoring the Navy and Marine Corps to the postwar needs of the nation. In early August 1943, retired Admiral Harry E. Yarnell wrote on his own to a former colleague in the Office of Procurement and Material (OP&M) arguing for a high-level board, headed by a civilian, to plan for the shift from a mobilized to a civilian economy. Yarnell's letter caught VCNO Horne's attention, and in late August Admiral Yarnell found himself in charge of a special planning section in OPNAV responsible for charting demobilization.[5] Based on Yarnell's work, VCNO Horne produced "Navy Basic Demobilization Plan No. 1" and circulated it within the Navy Department in November.

The COMINCH staff responded in January 1944 with its own projection of the bases and forces required postwar. In the meantime, Yarnell wrote a second demobilization plan, and VCNO Horne suggested to CNO King that this revised version of the demobilization plan be shared with the other members of the JCS. King chose not to do that, but in October 1944, after he had appointed Vice Admiral Edwards Deputy CNO–Deputy COMINCH, King put Edwards in charge of all Navy postwar planning.[6] By May 1945, Captain Charles J. Moore, whom Edwards had selected to be his assistant for planning, had managed the publication of "Basic Post-War Plan No. 1," which historian Barlow judged "a far cry from the early analytical efforts in 1943 and 1944."[7]

Demobilization and Service Unification

The Army also planned for demobilization—and also for something far more dramatic: unification of the services within a single department of war. Army Chief of Staff General George C. Marshall changed his mind and embraced it as a means of improving cross-service cooperation, providing a separate service for the Army's aviation component, and creating unity of command at the highest level. Marshall promoted the idea to his colleagues on the Joint Chiefs of Staff in late 1943. Once he did so, "unification [became] the defining issue of the early postwar period" for the Army and Navy. "By 1944, the Army and the Army Air Forces, its increasingly vocal, largely autonomous component, strongly supported unification of the services, while the Navy and Marine Corps firmly opposed it."[8] Unfortunately, what began as a proposal to prevent demobilization from decimating the Army became over time a bitter controversy that scarred almost all the senior military and civilian officials caught up in it.

While Admiral King and General Marshall went back and forth in March 1944 about the value of a special committee to study postwar defense reorganization, the House of Representatives created a select committee to consider postwar military requirements.[9] The committee began its hearings on 24 April 1944, and the Army witnesses testified first. Their argument was simple. First, unification of the armed services would eliminate redundancies, especially in basic activities such as recruiting, training, and the procurement of basic supplies. Second, unification would give the JCS and the staffs that supported the Joint Chiefs permanent standing. But what rang alarm bells in the Navy was the testimony of Assistant Secretary of War for Air Robert A. Lovett. Lovett argued that a separate air force should control all land-based military aviation, develop and purchase all military aircraft, and conduct all flight training.[10] This proposal, described as an economy measure, was seen in the Navy as a means of destroying naval aviation. Appearing before the committee as Under Secretary of the Navy, James Forrestal set the tone for all the Navy witnesses by saying that unification required more study. In its report of 15 June 1944, the committee agreed.[11]

Before the committee finished its report, the JCS had agreed to create a temporary committee to consider defense organization. The members of the committee—two each from the Army and Navy, plus alternates—began their work by interviewing senior officers stationed in Washington. Then the committee went to Europe and the Pacific theater, interviewing still more commanders before returning to Washington in December 1944. In its April 1945 report to the Joint Chiefs, the committee recommended that there be one department of national defense headed by a civilian secretary. Under the secretary would be a senior military officer who was both commander of the armed forces and chief of staff to the President. There should also be a separate Air Force, a permanent chiefs of staff organization, and a civilian business manager for the whole department.[12] In a preview of debates to come, the head of the committee, retired Admiral James O. Richardson, a former commander of the U.S. Fleet, dissented from the final report, arguing that the concentration of authority in one secretary and one commander was too risky. What if they made unwise decisions? What process would subject those unwise decisions to scrutiny and lead the two top officials to correct their mistakes before too much damage was done?

The Critical Role Played by James V. Forrestal

Secretary Forrestal was concerned by the intensity with which the Army advocated service unification. He did not want the nation to rush into a sort of merger that was not based on a careful sifting of experience. For a more thoughtful assessment, Forrestal turned to Ferdinand A. Eberstadt, "an old friend and former business associate" who had chaired the Army and Navy Munitions Board and then served as the War Production Board's vice chairman. Eberstadt and his small staff handed in their 250-page report at the end of September 1945. It rejected the Army's concept of unification but advocated much improved coordination at the highest levels, especially between the Joint Chiefs of Staff and the State Department and between the Joint Chiefs and the organizations in charge of industrial mobilization. The report also supported independence for the Air Force. It came just in time. The Military Affairs Committee of the Senate began hearings on two military service unification bills on 17 October 1945, and Navy witnesses drew on the "Eberstadt Report" in their opposition to the Army's arguments in favor of service unification.

That same month, Forrestal—on the advice of aviator (and later Chairman of the JCS) Vice Admiral Arthur W. Radford—established what became known as the Secretary's Committee on Research on Reorganization (SCOROR). This committee was Forrestal's counsel in the legislative struggle over service unification.[13] Forrestal attained his goal of blocking—at least in 1945—unification legislation when the Senate committee declined to report out either of the two bills after two months of hearings, but President Truman dispatched a strong message in December in favor of unification to the House of Representatives. Truman did not intend to allow the debate over service unification to stop, but because the unification issue involved two sets of committees—two in both the Senate and the House—it was difficult to build majorities behind a unification bill.

On 15 November 1945, a special joint committee of Congress convened to begin a long series of hearings on the Pearl Harbor attack.[14] The hearings revealed a number of problems that had given the attacking Japanese task force the advantage of surprise, especially the lack of a standing joint command in the Pacific. To avoid future Pearl Harbors, the committee recommended peacetime "unity of command," especially in each primary theater of operations. The Pearl Harbor investigation also gave the Army's air leaders more justification to establish the Strategic Air Command (SAC) in March 1946. SAC's specially equipped B-29 bombers were the only operational aircraft that could carry nuclear weapons, and the argument of officers such as General Carl A. Spaatz, commander of the Army's air arm, was that war experience had demonstrated that only an organization like SAC could serve as the nation's primary long-range striking force.[15]

To Forrestal the unification debate was essentially political and not a matter of organizational streamlining. Unlike Admiral King, he feared that the very existence of the Navy as a separate force might be at stake. An active and media-conscious Secretary of the Navy, Forrestal responded to what he saw as the threat of unification by cultivating public opinion in favor of a strong, independent Navy. At the same time Forrestal began talking publicly about the Soviet Union as the likely enemy in the next war. He exhorted Navy officers to think about means of using naval forces to attack the Soviet Union and to face the task of bringing American naval power to bear in the Mediterranean and Atlantic as well as the Pacific.

As one part of his effort to reorient the thinking of Navy officers, Forrestal announced on 4 December 1945 that half of the important positions below the CNO level in OPNAV would go to aviators and that, for the first time, aviators would be as eligible for fleet commands as other line officers.[16] At Forrestal's request, President Truman asked Congress to lower the statutory retirement age for officers and to increase the authorized peacetime strength of the Navy while making room for a higher proportion of officers.[17] Congress did both, with the result that the proportion of aviators among all Navy officers and within the ranks of flag officers increased markedly, despite the effects of demobilization.[18]

Figure 6-1. CNO Fleet Admiral Chester W. Nimitz on the bridge of a destroyer in May 1946. Pacific Fleet commander in World War II, Nimitz led a huge fleet that fought its way to the shores of Japan. Vice Admiral Lloyd M. Mustin, who was a young subordinate of Nimitz on cruiser *Augusta* (CA-31) in the late 1930s, remembered Nimitz as the finest teacher he ever encountered in the Navy. (NHHC Archives NH 62967)

As Navy historian Barlow pointed out, Forrestal did not initially want Fleet Admiral Chester W. Nimitz as Fleet Admiral King's successor. When you consider Forrestal's efforts to change the Navy from within, you can understand why. To Forrestal, Nimitz represented the prewar Navy—the Navy Forrestal wanted left behind. But King favored Nimitz. As it turned out, Forrestal and Nimitz got along, perhaps surprising both individuals. But Forrestal dragged his feet on the appointment, and Nimitz did not succeed King until 15 December 1945, some weeks after King himself was ready to retire. To balance Nimitz, Forrestal selected as Vice Chief Admiral Dewitt C. Ramsey, a pioneering naval aviator, and former chief of BuAer.[19]

The official powers of the CNO were later codified in Public Law 432 of 5 March, 1948. The 1948 law repealed the law of 3 March 1915 that had created the position of Chief of Naval Operations in the first place.[20] It also repealed the 20 June 1940 law that had reorganized the Navy Department[21] and the 27 May 1930 law that had provided for an assistant to the Chief of Naval Operations.[22] P.L. 432 of 1948 specified that the CNO "shall take rank above all other officers of the naval service," and that the duty of the CNO was "to command the operating forces and be responsible to the Secretary of the Navy for their use, including, but not limited to, their training, readiness, and preparation for war, and plans therefore." The CNO was also the "principal naval adviser to the President and to the Secretary of the Navy on the conduct of war, and the principal naval adviser and naval executive to the Secretary of the Navy on the conduct of the activities of the Naval Establishment."[23] The law also allowed the CNO to have six deputy chiefs, each with the authority to issue orders "considered as emanating from the Chief of Naval Operations."

At the same time, P.L. 432 added to the powers of the Secretary of the Navy by authorizing the creation of "an Office of Naval Material which shall be headed by a Chief of Naval Material . . ." This chief material officer was charged, "under the direction of the Secretary of the Navy," to "effectuate policies of procurement, contracting, and production of material throughout the Naval Establishment, and plans therefor, and his orders shall be considered as emanating from the Secretary of the Navy and as having full force and effect as such." This was essentially the organization that Navy Secretary Forrestal had put into place at the end of the war.[24]

How would these two "chiefs"—of operations and material—coordinate their respective responsibilities? The framers of the law understood that coordination was essential, and they provided for it by directing the CNO, "under the direction of the Secretary of the Navy," to "determine the personnel and material requirements of the operating forces, . . ., and [to] coordinate and efforts of the bureaus and offices of the Navy Department as may be necessary to effectuate availability and distribution of the personnel and material required where and when they are needed."[25] The New Chief of Naval Material, also "under the direction of the Secretary of the Navy," was responsible for setting "procurement and production policies and methods . . . and shall coordinate and direct the efforts of the bureaus and offices of the Navy Department in this respect."[26]

Forrestal understood that there were three key components of OPNAV: its structure, the authority of the CNO, and the identities of the Navy's uniformed leaders. He left his stamp on all three. He did so for several reasons. One was to protect and preserve civilian authority. Another was to keep the Navy strong in the postwar world. A third reason was because Forrestal thought and planned and acted with a grasp of power and influence. He was very much a sophisticated bureaucratic actor. Yet Forrestal also left the Chief of Naval Operations in a strong position. As Barlow noted, OPNAV

> successfully incorporated COMINCH's control of the Navy's operating forces with CNO's responsibilities, under the direction of the Secretary of the Navy, for coordinating and directing the bureaus and offices of the Navy Department . . . Because of this new arrangement, the Chief of Naval Operations in December 1945 was far better equipped to handle the manifold responsibilities that would come his way in the challenging postwar years.[27]

Congress and the Navy Postwar

Congress was quick to take control over military spending after Japan formally surrendered on 2 September 1945. On 5 September, President Truman began the process of rapid demobilization by requesting that the Congress cancel approximately $50 billion in war spending. On 14 September, the President focused on Navy spending in particular, asking Congress to take back from the Navy Department the authority to spend or obligate almost $17 billion. By comparison, the Navy's expenditures from 1 July 1940 through 30 June 1945 totaled $90.5 billion.[28] Further cuts came in February and May 1946, and by that time the Budget Bureau had severely trimmed Navy funding for FY 1947.[29]

However, the members of Congress did more than change the levels of funding for the Army and the Navy. On 2 August 1946, President Truman signed the "Legislative Reorganization Act of 1946," making legal a major change to the structure of the committees where the members of Congress did the bulk of their work.[30] What most mattered in the law to the Navy was that the formerly separate naval and military authorizing committees were combined in both the House of Representatives and the Senate to form "armed services" committees.

This change was long overdue. The passage of the Budget and Accounting Act in 1921 had made executive branch agencies (including the Navy) more accountable to both the President and the Congress. That law had created the Budget Bureau to assist the president and compelled the Navy and other executive branch agencies to establish budget officers. After the law went into effect, the budget proposals of the executive departments went to the Budget Bureau for review after they had been subjected to reviews by the department budget officers. The Navy's first budget officer was CNO Admiral Robert E. Coontz. As we pointed out in an earlier chapter, Coontz did not appreciate the addition to his workload, and he did not apparently enjoy defending the Navy's budget proposal to the congressional naval affairs committees.

The CNOs after Coontz did not have to serve as budget officers, and, according to historian Robert Albion, the officers who did serve as budget officers "reported directly to the Secretary." Albion also found that the officers holding the post of budget officer after CNO Coontz "had distinguished careers before or after their service in this billet." As Albion observed, officers "of this caliber were needed to impose unwelcome cuts on bureau chiefs." Navy budget officers before World War II included Admirals Joseph Strauss, formerly head of BuOrd, Charles B. McVay Jr., another chief of BuOrd, and two officers who became CINCUS, Claude C. Bloch and James O. Richardson.[31]

Having a budget officer, however, did not eliminate the problem of placing each year's budget proposal within the context of all the legislative proposals considered each year by the Congress. As we showed in an earlier chapter, the Navy needed someone with both operational and administrative experience to perform this task. The first officer to do so was Rear Admiral Bloch, who was appointed JAG after having served for a year as the Navy's budget officer. Bloch, as described earlier, decided that the JAG should take a "principal part" in drawing up "laws affecting the Navy." Secretary Swanson agreed with him, and in 1934 handed Bloch—as JAG—the responsibility for reviewing all legislative proposals related to the Navy, except for the annual proposed Navy appropriations. Bloch soon became the man that Congress consulted on a variety of naval matters.[32] This prewar arrangement carried on through World War II, but with one critical difference: The budget officer's post was less of a "stepping stone" to higher command than it was a special staff post. The incumbent from 1938 to 1946 was Rear Admiral Ezra G. Allen, who "was on a first-name basis with almost everyone [in the authorizing committees]."[33]

What you can see from the evolution—over 20 years—of the budget officer's position and the eventual participation of the Navy's JAG in the legislative process is the gradual modernization of the Navy's internal management process along with its legislative liaison. The two processes had to go together and complement one another. Congress intended the innovation of the budget officer to improve the administration of the executive branch. To the degree that was done, the ability of Congress to perform its appropriating function would improve, as in fact it did. At the same time, the Navy Department also needed more effective liaison with the Congress on issues that were outside the budget process. Giving the JAG the responsibility for overseeing the Navy's "package" of legislative proposals outside the budget submission added to the authority of the SECNAV and at the same time also improved the efficiency of the legislative process.

The next logical step was to reform the authorizing process, which was far too complex. As it happened, this was done first on the Navy side of the executive-legislative divide, and it was performed at the instigation of then Under Secretary Forrestal. In January 1941, the Navy's budget office was changed to the office of the "Director of Budget and Reports." Forrestal persuaded Secretary Knox to make the change so that the secretariat would have the information necessary to plan for the growth of the Navy as the service gradually mobilized. By early 1942, the office of the "Director of Budget and Reports" had three divisions—Estimates (of Navy resource and manpower needs and the funding to meet those needs); Lend-Lease (what allies would need and how to pay for meeting those requirements); and Financial Reports. These divisions within the secretariat were essential to providing the Congress with information required by the naval affairs committees.[34]

As Congress began the hearings and studies that would lead to the Legislative Reorganization Act of 1946, it was evident that the Navy would have to modify its own processes for dealing with the reorganized Congress. The budgeting process had been gradually improved over more than 20 years. There was no pressure to change it in any major way. However, it needed to be reconciled with the streamlined authorization process that Congress intended to adopt. The initial step to do this was taken on 1 August 1946, when the office of the "Director of Budget and Reports" was made a part of the office of the Navy's Fiscal Director. The latter office had been created in December 1944 in order to improve the management of Navy expenditures. It was one thing to get the funds from Congress; it was another matter to track where those funds went and then decide whether they had gone to the right place at the right time. Both the authorizing and appropriating committees would want that information. In 1946, it was first thought by Forrestal and his deputies that combining supervision of fiscal "input" (appropriations) and "output" (expenditures) under one officer (the Fiscal Director) would improve the effectiveness of the Navy secretary.

However, after Secretary Forrestal was installed as the first Secretary of Defense (SecDef) on 19 September 1947, his successor, John L. Sullivan, pulled the Office of Budget and Reports out of the Office of the Fiscal Director and gave it the following responsibilities: "analyze budget requirements," "review and coordinate estimates," set "budget policies and procedures," "supervise the preparation and submission of reports to the Bureau of the Budget and the Treasury Department," and "administer" the personnel ceilings directed by Congress.[35] This was the Navy's approach. It was not developed in concert with the Army or the newly created (on 18 September 1947) United States Air Force.

However, by 1949 the Commission on the Organization of the Executive Branch of the Government (also known as the Hoover Commission because it was chaired by former President Herbert C. Hoover) was calling for the federal executive departments (including the military services under the SecDef) to use "performance budgeting," where the output of any agency program could be matched against the input of funds appropriated by the Congress. Congress responded to the Commission's report by providing for a comptroller in the Office of the Secretary of Defense and comptrollers in each of the military services. The goal was the make the budget proposals and fiscal accounts of the three services "comparable as to form and to follow a uniform pattern." To make this happen, the comptroller working for the SecDef was given the authority to "fix standards for budgeting, fiscal, accounting, progress, and statistical programs."[36]

Rear Admiral Herbert G. Hopwood, the head of the Office of Budget and Reports, informed the Navy's General Board in early April 1949 that he and his staff applauded the implementation of performance budgeting ("it embodies the same principles that the Navy tried to get through in 1948"). When asked how the appointment of a Navy comptroller would affect the work of his office, Hopwood answered, "Not at all." Hopwood also told the members of the board that he supported "the present Naval [sic] policy of having the budget and accounting features under the Secretary and not under the Chief of Naval Operations." Indeed, he supported "centralized control" of fiscal and budget "activities" in the secretariat. At the same time, he distinguished between authority and direct supervision. As he noted, if the Navy's bureaus used modern techniques of financial management effectively, they were more likely to get their budget submissions through the reviews conducted by his office.[37] That is, the Navy was already most of the way along toward using a comptroller. Again, what the record shows is an effort on the part of the Navy and the Congress to do two very important things. One was to provide for more efficient and effective management inside the Navy. The other was to facilitate the intelligent and informed direction of the Navy by the President and Congress.

The Challenges of Technology

"Building a new navy from scratch, . . . , is simplicity itself compared with the job of transforming a navy that already exists . . ." Capt. Wayne P. Hughes Jr., *Fleet Tactics, Theory and Practice*, 1st ed.

The new military technologies developed during the World War II posed particularly severe tactical and budgetary problems for the Navy. The prospect that the Soviet Navy would build on captured German technology to produce large numbers of submarines with high submerged speed and underwater endurance, for example, promised to make the Navy's antisubmarine equipment, ships, and tactics obsolete within five years. The development of nuclear weapons also threatened the Navy's strategic role. In August 1945, no operational Navy carrier attack plane could loft an atomic bomb. Only the Army Air Forces' B-29s could carry the bulky five-ton weapons, and then only after special modifications, which left the aircraft unable to carry conventional bombs, were made. If naval aircraft could not carry nuclear weapons, then what role did the Navy's carriers have in a future global war? Indeed, if future conflict with the Soviet Union were to be exclusively nuclear, then what was the purpose of the Navy? Showing that the Navy had a real strategic mission in an age of nuclear weapons was hard enough. It was an even more difficult task in the immediate postwar years, when conventional forces were rapidly demobilized because both President Truman and senior members of Congress feared a round of post–World War II inflation that would be as severe as the one that followed World War I.[38]

The Army Air Forces espoused the new nuclear technology, but its leaders also understood that they would need new bombers and a specially trained force to carry atomic weapons.[39] As historian and strategic analyst Norman Friedman noted, nuclear weapons "threatened to make existing forms of warfare obsolete," so the need to make more nuclear bombs, develop smaller and more effective bombs, and produce long-range bombers while demobilizing quickly led to a fiscal squeeze.[40] The Air Force's solution to this "squeeze" was to assert that only it had the systems and the expertise to develop a strategic nuclear force. But the Navy's decision to develop a new carrier that could launch bombers carrying nuclear weapons "put the Navy on a collision course with the Air Force over the question of which service had the right to employ atomic weapons."[41] The dispute over this carrier, and the related dispute over what American nuclear doctrine should be, came to dominate and even dictate the relations between the postwar Navy and the postwar Air Force.[42] The conflict between the Navy and the Army, and after 1947 between the Navy and the Air Force, over the nature of war in the nuclear age strongly colored the attitudes of Navy officers toward service unification and interservice cooperation. As historian Barlow noted, "By the spring of 1948, concerns about the proposed strategic air offensive were taken so seriously within OPNAV that they were raised in the meetings of the Joint Chiefs of Staff."[43]

The disputes about service unification and about service roles and missions were rooted in large measure in the uncertainties created by technological change. For example, early jet aircraft accelerated slowly, and the catapults on Navy carriers in service in 1945 were not strong enough to assist the early jet bombers to launch speed.[44] The situation worsened when planes carried nuclear weapons. Such aircraft needed special boost engines to lift off a carrier's deck. Indeed, one reason the Navy so strongly opposed service unification in 1946 was because it seemed that the Army Air Forces were correct in their claim that carrier aircraft had no future role in strategic warfare.

As Vice Admiral Robert B. Carney, DCNO for Logistics (OP-04), phrased it in an "Eyes Only" memo for CNO Nimitz in November 1946: "The entire role of aviation, as understood in 1945, may be due for an enforced change as a result of (a) aircraft improvement, and (b) the difficulties in adjusting carrier characteristics to further aircraft improvement." Carney was blunt: "Current trends in the weight, size, speed, and characteristics of aircraft may have a serious adverse effect on the utility of existing carriers and even on the overall importance of carrier aviation in the future."[45] In short, the Navy did in fact have reasonable doubts about the future of carrier aviation. The Air Force also had reason to doubt the ability of its B-36 intercontinental bomber to fulfill the nuclear mission in the way its proponents claimed.[46]

Given the climate of fiscal stringency, as well as the limited number of nuclear bombs, neither Navy nor Air Force senior officers wanted to admit that their services could not perform the nuclear bombing mission. Any such admission would be ammunition for the other side in what had become a "war" over unification and service roles and missions. This did not mean there were not any real issues dividing the services. The debates over how to use nuclear weapons against the Soviet Union if war broke out and the disputes over the value of conventional forces in a war fought with nuclear weapons were very serious and not simply smokescreens for professional and personal rivalries.[47]

OPNAV Organization Postwar

OPNAV emerged from the war with both functional and weapons directorates: deputy chiefs for Personnel (OP-01), Administration (OP-02), Operations (OP-03), Logistics (OP-04), Air (OP-05), and Special Weapons (OP-06, disestablished in 1946). In 1939 none of the five flag officers in OPNAV below the CNO and the assistant chief held rank greater than that of

CHART 8. Select Elements of OPNAV Organization as of December 1947

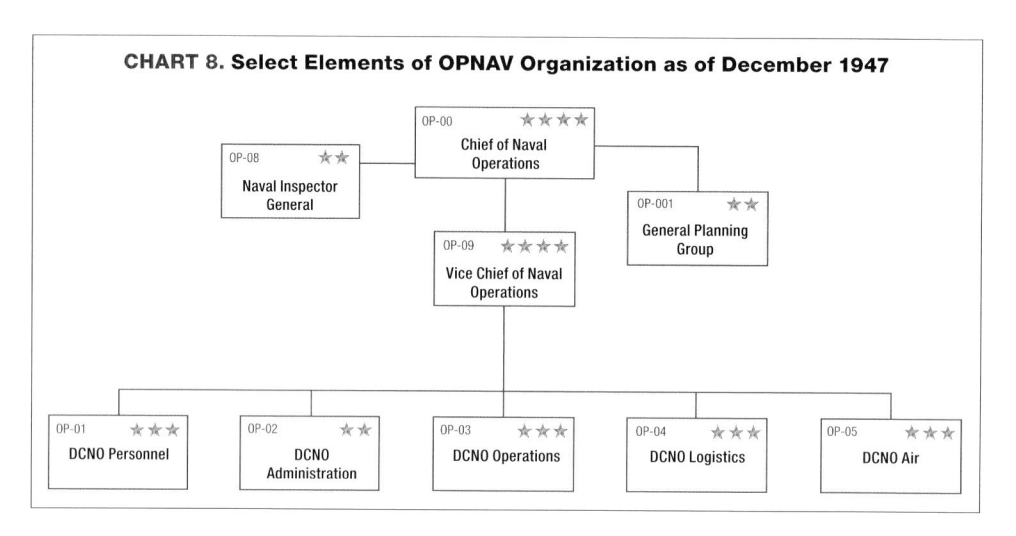

- OP-00 ★★★★ Chief of Naval Operations
  - OP-08 ★★ Naval Inspector General
  - OP-001 ★★ General Planning Group
  - OP-09 ★★★★ Vice Chief of Naval Operations
    - OP-01 ★★★ DCNO Personnel
    - OP-02 ★★ DCNO Administration
    - OP-03 ★★★ DCNO Operations
    - OP-04 ★★★ DCNO Logistics
    - OP-05 ★★★ DCNO Air

rear admiral (two-star). After the war, however, all the deputy chief positions were filled by vice admirals, and rear admirals served as their senior assistants. Flag officers also directed the OPNAV offices of naval intelligence and communications, and a full admiral served as Navy Inspector General (OP-08). This was a major change from OPNAV's prewar structure.

In this postwar organization, functional deputies (e.g., Personnel) worked alongside deputies for weapons (e.g., Air). Functional deputies administered areas that stretched across what are now referred to as the major warfare, or platform, communities—for aviation, submarines, and surface ships. The weapons deputies, especially the DCNO for Air, gave their communities a form of vested representation in the Navy's top policy making institution. The tension that developed between the functional and the platform community deputies became a major issue within OPNAV after the war and continued to be an issue over the next 25 years.

A sign of OPNAV's growing importance was the fact that many of the Navy's most respected young flag officers took OPNAV posts in 1946–1947: Arthur W. Radford (OP-05), Forrest P. Sherman (OP-03), Louis E. Denfeld (OP-01), Richard L. Conolly (OP-02), Robert B. Carney (OP-04), and William H. P. Blandy (OP-06).[48] Radford later became Chairman of the Joint Chiefs of Staff; Denfeld, Sherman, and Carney were eventually appointed Chiefs of Naval Operations; Conolly and Blandy were serious candidates for the CNO's post.

However, the issue of OPNAV's optimal structure was never finally resolved after the war. There were too many distractions. Congress wanted to institutionalize the lessons of the war; President Truman wanted to unify the services; and the Joint Chiefs and the services were concerned about the possible military threats from the Soviet Union. These and related issues dominated the agendas of CNO Nimitz and his deputies. In January 1947, for example, the Navy's part of joint war plan Pincher called for conventional attacks by carrier aircraft on Soviet submarines in their bases. The Russian threat appeared to be basically one of submarine attacks on ships linking the United States to Europe and Asia. That same December, however, the Assistant Chief of Naval Operations for Guided Missiles argued in a memo to the CNO that the Navy could and should compete head-to-head with the newly created Air Force for the mission of strategic nuclear bombing.[49] Just what were the proper Navy missions? With changes in technology, Navy roles and capabilities were a matter of debate, even within the Navy.

Operating under the National Security Act

The Secretaries of the Army and Navy agreed in May 1946 that there should be no single military chief of staff and that the Navy would keep the Marines and the aviation forces necessary for seagoing operations. Despite this agreement, in November 1946 Major General Lauris Norstad, Army Director of Plans and Operations, began working with Vice Admiral Sherman, DCNO for Operations, on the issue of service unification. Sherman convinced Norstad to accept the proposals first presented to Forrestal by the secretary's friend and advisor Ferdinand Eberstadt in September 1945, and those proposals were later incorporated into the National Security Act of 1947.

The act (Public Law 253), passed in July 1947, created a National Military Establishment of three executive departments (Army, Navy, and Air Force—the latter separate from the Army) under the general direction of a Secretary of Defense. The law also created the National Security Council (NSC) and the Central Intelligence Agency (CIA). The Joint Chiefs of Staff (JCS) were given statutory legitimacy and charged with developing strategic plans and providing for the "strategic direction of the military forces," as well as preparing "joint logistic plans," "policies for joint training," and "policies for coordinating the education of members of the military forces."[50] The law also gave the JCS a joint staff of no more than 100 officers to keep the JCS from engaging in operations (as opposed to strategic) planning. Finally, the National Security Act set forth the combat roles of the armed services, touching off a disagreement between the Navy and the Air Force that would lead to a national political crisis in October 1949.

As early as May 1946, it was clear to Marine Corps Commandant General Alexander A. Vandegrift that the Marine Corps might be drastically reduced in size as a consequence of statutory changes in the nation's military organization. That month, Vandegrift told the Senate Naval Affairs Committee that "the War Department's intentions with respect to the Marine Corps are well advanced and carefully integrated." Moreover, under the proposed reorganization, "the single Secretary for Common Defense and the all-powerful National Chief of Staff are entirely free, either to abolish the Marine Corps outright or to divest it of all its vital functions, leaving only a token organization in order that the name of the Corps may be preserved."[51] In April 1947, Vandegrift testified to the Senate Armed Services Committee that the proposed law, though it affirmed the survival of the Marine Corps, excluded the "Marine Corps from participation in the joint bodies and agencies which the bill would establish."[52]

Vandegrift's efforts, supported by congressional allies, saved the Marine Corps. The National Security Act of 1947 stipulated that the Marine Corps,

> within the Department of the Navy, shall include land combat and service forces and such aviation as may be organic therein. The Marine Corps shall be organized,

trained, and equipped to provide fleet marine forces of combined arms, together with supporting air components, for service with the fleet in the seizure or defense of advanced naval bases and for the conduct of such land operations as may be essential to the prosecution of a naval campaign.[53]

This was the minimum that General Vandegrift wanted, but he actually got more because the law gave the Marine Corps the authority to expand "to meet the needs of war."[54]

Even before Congress had passed the National Security Act, however, the President appointed an Air Policy Commission to develop an "integrated national aviation policy."[55] Congress established its own joint Aviation Policy Board that same month (July 1947), and the two groups considered the same set of problems. In January 1948, the President's commission issued its report, arguing that the nation's defense and its defense organization had to "be built around the air arm."[56] The congressional panel argued that the first objective of any future war would be "the industrial organization and the resources of the enemy."[57] President Truman considered the report of the Air Policy Commission so politically charged that he delayed making it public until the day after he submitted the Fiscal Year 1949 budget, the first with joint figures for the three services.[58]

Tension among the services, especially between the Air Force and the Navy, grew worse in 1948. Early that year, the Strategic Plans Division of OP-03 prepared a detailed critique of the Air Force's war strategy, especially the claim that a massive offensive air campaign against the Soviet Union would force an early end to any major war and therefore eliminate the need for the sorts of campaigns fought against Germany and Japan in World War II.[59] In March, Forrestal, who now held the new post of Secretary of Defense, called the service chiefs to Key West, Florida, to clear up the debate about service roles and missions—a debate that the National Security Act of 1947 had not ended. The resulting agreements, entitled "Functions of the Armed Forces and the Joint Chiefs of Staff," promulgated by Forrestal in April, spelled out in some detail the areas of responsibility of each service.[60] The service chiefs also used the meetings in Key West to press Truman to ask Congress for a restoration of conscription, which he did.

However, the Key West agreements did not end the conflict in the press and in the JCS between the Navy and the Air Force.[61] One unresolved issue was the question, "Which service (if any) would be the executive agent for the JCS in the area of strategic nuclear weapons?" The issue stemmed from the limited supply of weapons-grade nuclear material. Only one service would be assigned responsibility for the small number of weapons. The Air Force wanted sole responsibility for strategic nuclear weapons, but Forrestal had already approved Navy plans to construct a large carrier equipped with aircraft that could carry atomic bombs. Air Force plans to organize and control strategic air warfare seemed threatened by Navy claims that carrier-based bombers had a better chance of surviving Russian air defenses than the heavy land-based bombers of SAC.

In August 1948, Forrestal called the service chiefs together in Newport, Rhode Island, in an effort to resolve the dispute over which service would be the agent for the Joint Chiefs in controlling strategic nuclear air warfare. "After lengthy and sometimes heated debate," the service chiefs agreed that "although the Air Force would be designated the interim executive agent" for nuclear weapons, the Navy "would be allowed to participate in atomic bombing, both for tactical purposes and, in assisting in the overall air offensive, for strategic purposes."[62] To Secretary of Defense Forrestal's disappointment, this agreement did not put an end of friction between the Air Force and the Navy over this issue.[63] The two services continued their dispute through all of 1948 and 1949.[64]

This conflict between the Air Force and the Navy was an obstacle to Secretary Forrestal's concern for the mobilization potential of the United States. As SecDef, for example, Forrestal had supported what became the Selective Service Act of 1948, particularly because the law "empowered the President, through the head of any government agency, to use a mandatory order on any manufacturer or producer for supplies or services when necessary for defense."[65] It was, as Forrestal knew, one step toward rearming the nation for a possible confrontation with the Soviet Union. Forrestal was moving away from his previous opposition to a strong Defense secretary heading a unified department. That movement on Forrestal's part caused Navy officers to fear yet another attempt at unification. Their fears seemed substantiated by Forrestal's decision in May 1948 to unify Army and Navy aviation transport organizations in the Military Air Transport Service. Senior Navy officers who opposed the consolidation interpreted Forrestal's decision as the beginning of a process that would gradually strip the Navy of its less central components until it was forced to rely on support from the Air Force and the Army. As historian David Rosenberg noted, "Misunderstanding and conflict between the services was worse by the fall of 1948 than it had been before passage of the National Security Act a year before."[66]

The "Revolt of the Admirals"

To some senior Navy officers, SecDef Forrestal appeared to be behaving more like an enemy, and they felt compelled to develop their own response to the pressures from the Air Force and from the advocates of a centrally managed Defense Department. In 1946, CNO Nimitz had created a General Planning Group in the Office of the Vice Chief of Naval Operations to coordinate the actions of the Deputy Chiefs of Naval Operations.[67] However, this organization was not prepared for the interservice struggles that marked 1948 and 1949. Admiral Louis E. Denfeld, Nimitz's successor, turned to the General Board for long-range plans in 1947, and later, in December 1948, created in OPNAV the Organizational Research and Policy Division (OP-23), the successor to Forrestal's Committee on Research on Reorganization. The head of the new division, Captain Arleigh Burke, was charged with countering arguments favoring service unification, and he eventually became one of the most articulate spokesmen for the Navy's views on defense organization.

Admiral Denfeld, who had "served for most of World War II in senior positions in the Bureau of Naval Personnel," was on good terms with many members of Congress. As Barlow observed, however, Denfeld "was not seen as a strong CNO," and in dealing with the other members of the Joint Chiefs of Staff, the CNO sought "consensus with his colleagues," making

Figure 6-2. Secretary of the Navy John Sullivan (left) welcomes Admiral Louis E. Denfeld as the new CNO on 15 December 1947. Both men were caught up in the 1949 political struggle over the future of Navy aviation. Sullivan resigned in May 1949 to protest the policies of Secretary of Defense Louis A. Johnson. Sullivan's successor, Francis P. Matthews, relieved Denfeld in early November 1949 at the request of President Harry S. Truman. (National Archives 80-G-704743)

"him ill equipped for the vital role of defending [the Navy] in interservice battles over roles and missions."[68]

Captain Burke began his work just in time to land in the middle of major flap over defense policy and organization. In March 1949, President Truman forced Forrestal from office and appointed Louis A. Johnson, a "quarrelsome, efficient, and ambitious executive," and a former Assistant Secretary of War, as Secretary of Defense.[69] Johnson promptly cancelled construction of the Navy's supercarrier *United States* (CVA-58) on the grounds that the newly created North Atlantic Alliance gave the Strategic Air Command access to bases in England from which its bombers could reach targets within the Soviet Union. Publicly, Johnson claimed that the country could not afford such large ships and their accompanying air groups. With the cancellation, Secretary of the Navy John L. Sullivan resigned. Captain Burke warned CNO Denfeld that Johnson would eventually try to shift naval aviation to the Air Force and the Marines to the Army.[70]

Moreover, in March 1949, in a memo to CNO Denfeld, Burke argued that the advantage of the National Military Establishment, created by the National Security Act of 1947, was that it divided and balanced the powers of military leadership, thereby preventing rash action—a real possibility if military leadership were concentrated in one individual or organization. Burke's point was that a division of power among coequal services was essential to preserve civilian authority. He also refused to accept the contention that divided powers in the hands of multiple service chiefs led to significant waste and inefficiency.[71]

In an August memo to Vice Admiral Carney, Burke opposed any moves to increase the authority of the Navy Comptroller and the Management Engineer, both uniformed officers who advised the Secretary of the Navy. About the latter, Burke wrote: "The change of the Management Engineer from an advisory position to one where he exercises functional control over Bureaus and Offices in effect clothes him with responsibilities which have traditionally been reserved for command." He objected to giving the comptroller authority over Navy officers

> because unless the Comptroller were a line officer, a civilian or a staff corps officer would be exercising authority in the purely military sphere. On the other hand, if the

> Comptroller is a line officer, he will be functioning in a field which has heretofore been reserved as the province of the civilian executive assistants to the Secretary.[72]

Burke argued further that a strong comptroller's office might "provide a stronger impetus for the creation of a Departmental General Staff."[73]

In September, in a memo for the Chairman of the General Board on "the Applicability of the General Staff System to the Navy," Burke admitted:

> The merger controversy found the Navy with no firm objective of its own, and no firm ideas as to how to combat a concept which the Navy . . . found undesirable. This lack of naval objective was in part, at least, a result of there being incomplete naval recognition of the political function of a national service headquarters.[74]

In other words, OPNAV had two basic responsibilities: to plan and prepare for war, and to deal with political threats external to the Navy. Burke's ideas both built on and rejected the Navy's tradition of command. Burke endorsed the concept of civilian control, but only if and when that control respected the military chain of command. In this regard he was very traditional. At the same time, however, Burke placed the duty of understanding and manipulating the Navy's external environment on uniformed military officers in OPNAV. That was not traditional at all. Carney gave the reason for the break with tradition in another memo for the General Board:

> The Air Force labored under great difficulties as a part of the Army and was often forced into paths of circuitousness and rebellion to achieve its proper place in the sun. Many now in key positions in the Air Force are men who participated in their Revolution, and their general approach to their problems still reflects their personal experiences.[75]

Burke took the same view—that conspiratorial organizational tactics, coupled with adroit public relations techniques, were for the Air Force legitimate tools to get what it wanted. The Navy had to respond—with or without leadership from the civilian Secretary of the Navy and his assistants.

As far as Navy aviators were concerned, the future looked especially bleak. In September 1949, Vice Admiral Gerald F. Bogan, Commander of the First Task Fleet, sent a confidential memo "through the chain of command" to Navy secretary Francis P. Matthews. In his memo, Bogan told Matthews, "The morale of the Navy is lower today than at any time since I entered the commissioned ranks in 1916. . . . In my opinion this descent, almost to despondency, stems from complete confusion as to the future role of the Navy and its advantages or disadvantages as a permanent career."[76] CNO Denfeld agreed with Bogan, and the stage was set for a showdown between the Navy secretary and the CNO. In October, Denfeld testified before the House Armed Services Committee hearings on the unification controversy in opposition to the views of Secretary Matthews. Denfeld's testimony led to his dismissal.

In "Trends in Unification," a memo prepared on 16 October 1949 after Denfeld was pushed out, Burke expressed some of the bitterness felt within OPNAV toward the whole unification issue. Burke argued that there was a trend toward robbing the Navy of its ability to fulfill the functions assigned it by law.

> First, constant pressure is exerted toward the reassignment and redistribution of . . . the roles and missions of the armed forces. Second, continuing efforts are being made to reduce, either by budgetary action, executive order, or statutory proposals, the forces of the Navy. . . . Third, there is an obvious trend in the field of organization and management toward greater centralization of control over the three military departments.[77]

As Burke put it, the Navy supported "the principle of decentralized operation under authoritative policy direction," but the cumulative effect of postwar changes in law and administration was to undermine that principle.[78]

The story of the passage of the amendments to the National Security Act, approved by Congress on 10 August 1949, is told elsewhere, as is the struggle between the Navy and the Air Force over the B-36 bomber.[79] What is important is the way in which the Navy's leadership interpreted actions taken in the name of "efficiency," or in the name of improving cooperation among the services. Naval leaders regarded them as part of an overall strategy to destroy the Navy and its tradition of decentralized command. The OP-23 October memo expressed this view: "The many developments, of course, are being undertaken separately and without any outward acknowledgment of interrelationship. Yet viewed as a whole they bear striking resemblance to a pattern of military development described by General Heinz Guderian, Hitler's last Chief of Staff."[80] The issue was not one of budgets or resources or careers:

> The ultimate development . . . appears to be the establishment of a supreme general staff to coordinate all military functions with a subordinate "armed forces office" to manage such non-combat functions as procurement, medical service, personnel policy, recruiting, and research. The individual services, then, would be reduced virtually to technical branches of the military establishment.[81]

These memos portrayed the struggle over service unification and service roles more as one over ideas than over resources. Although they rarely admitted it, Burke and other officers involved in the controversy were debating constitutional principles. They were arguing about the proper role and organization of military leadership. For Burke, the chief duty of a CNO was political—to represent the Navy at the highest levels of the executive branch and in Congress, where the fundamental battles over authority and responsibility were fought. Burke believed that the Army and Air Force neither understood nor accepted the Navy's unique tradition of executive leadership. Indeed, the October memo suggested that the Navy's view on the distribution of authority was in fact the more proper one—the more constitutionally correct one. But the Air Force, clearly, did not see matters that way, which forced the Navy to wage a partisan struggle to preserve what it considered to be the proper, or constitutional, relationship between military and civilian powers.

Burke strongly opposed any efforts to consolidate service activities because he believed all such efforts were motivated by a kind of misguided ideology. In his view, terms like "efficiency" and "jointness" were used in congressional hearings to disguise attacks on the Navy. The Navy's task was to deflect and defeat both the ideologues and the well-intentioned, but misinformed, politicians. When Forrestal was Navy secretary, the Navy had a civilian champion for its cause. By October 1949, OP-23 was arguing that the uniformed service leadership had to do what the secretary's office would not. The CNO, then, was as much a political and constitutional warrior as an operational commander.

OP-23's arguments in 1949 formed the basis for the Navy's later positions toward the Joint Chiefs of Staff and the Defense Department. The Navy suspected that both institutions were following a long-term strategy to strip the Navy of its independence and to over centralize the military leadership of the country. OP-23 memos presented an argument familiar to readers of James Madison's Federalist Paper No. 10: competition among factions (in this case the services) was beneficial because it allowed civilians both to retain control of the military and to consider alternative national military strategies. Burke carried that view, to which many Navy officers subscribed, with him into office when he became CNO in 1955. It remained a widely held, if sometimes not well-argued, position among senior Navy officers.

Figure 6-3. CNO Admiral Forrest P. Sherman on the bridge of battleship *New Jersey* (BB-62) during the Korean War. A fine writer, wartime planner, and student of the Navy's history, Sherman was godfather to what became the Sixth Fleet. He also reestablished sound relations with the Air Force and Army after CNO Denfeld was relieved in November 1949.
(National Archives 80-G-431253)

After the "Revolt of the Admirals"

Admiral Forrest P. Sherman, Nimitz's Deputy Chief of Staff for Plans during the last two years of World War II, replaced Denfeld as CNO. Sherman, reputedly one of the best strategic minds in Washington, had represented the Navy in talks with the Army when the services developed the outlines for the National Security Act of 1947. Building on his reputation and on his contacts in the other services, he acted quickly to restore service morale and to gain friends and allies for the Navy. As Rosenberg noted, Sherman's positive "impact was felt almost immediately."[82]

Before SecDef Johnson cancelled construction of *United States* and fired Denfeld in October 1949, the Air Warfare Division (OP-55) in the Office of the DCNO for Air had produced (that August) a new study that justified large aircraft carriers. In 1947 Navy planners perceived the Soviet threat as one primarily of submarines at sea. They had accordingly advocated carrier air strikes as a means of striking Soviet submarines at their bases before they could slip into the Atlantic and Pacific and prowl the shipping lanes linking the United States and its European and Asian clients. In 1949, naval aviators, as reflected in the OPNAV study, decided that Soviet air forces posed the greater immediate threat, especially to U.S. naval forces deployed in the Mediterranean. To overcome such land-based air forces, Navy carrier groups needed large numbers of high-performance aircraft to attack Soviet air bases.[83] As Friedman noted, "sea control and power projection were associated, rather than opposed, naval missions."[84] The OP-55 study was important because it provided a justification for large aircraft carriers that was *not* based on plans for staging nuclear strikes against the Soviets. Consequently, it did not add fuel to the fire generated by the B-36 controversy.

Gradually, under Sherman, the tension between the Air Force and the Navy declined, and the Navy began conceptualizing the missions that matured in the late 1950s and early 1960s: using the mobility and striking potential of naval forces—especially carrier air groups able to deliver conventional bombs and tactical nuclear ordnance—to deter or respond to threats from Soviet or Soviet client forces in areas distant from the dividing line between North Atlantic Treaty Organization (NATO) and the Warsaw Pact.

Conclusion

At the close of World War II, some major strategic issues were solved, but others tested the mettle of American political and military leaders. Germany and Japan had been defeated, but parts of Europe were a wreck and the European colonial empires in Asia were being challenged. The leaders of the United States had to define the place of their nation in the world, and that task was made more difficult by the tension between the United States and the Soviet Union. For example, should the United States demobilize to a level similar to that of 1939, or would the nation have to gear up for a military conflict with the USSR? Would the United States help along the process of "decolonization," or would it shield the pre-war colonial empires in order to gain needed political support in Europe? Returning veterans may have been eager to get home and back to work, but the United States finished the war as the most economically powerful nation and its leaders needed to decide how best to wield that power.

Demobilization of the armed services created an obvious challenge to the military leaders of the country: What forces and bases to keep and what to abandon? However, while trying to answer that question, they also had to decide where they stood on the issues of the control and possible further use of nuclear weapons, service unification, military access to the civilian economy in peacetime, race relations, and civil-military relations. Where should U.S. forces be stationed, and what were their roles in the post-war world? There would be no rest for the post-war CNOs and the OPNAV staff.

Soviet actions and heavy-handedness in 1949 helped resolve some of these issues. By detonating an atomic weapon and trumpeting the defeat of Chiang Kai-shek and his Nationalist regime in China as the beginning of the end of the capitalist world, the Soviet Union spurred U.S. policymakers into reassessing their attitudes toward military spending. The result was

National Security Council Study 68, reviewed by President Truman in April 1950 and approved by him that September, while fighting raged in Korea. NSC-68 was the beginning of a program to increase military expenditures, especially on conventional forces.

The Korean War brought more money to the services, along with (in 1953) tactical nuclear weapons and the programs to produce thermonuclear explosives. It also tested the postwar military command structure. Perhaps most importantly, Korea helped Army general and former NATO commander Dwight D. Eisenhower win the presidency, and, as we shall show, Eisenhower was committed to resolving the issues of civil-military relations and service unification.

Notes

[1] Ronald H. Spector, *In the Ruins of Empire: The Japanese Surrender and the Battle for Postwar Asia* (New York: Random House, 2008).

[2] Barlow, *From Hot War to Cold*, 35.

[3] Ibid., 40.

[4] Ibid., 41.

[5] Ibid., 42.

[6] Ibid., 52.

[7] Ibid., 55–56. CAPT Moore had served on the staff of ADM Raymond A. Spruance in World War II, and he was therefore no stranger to planning.

[8] Ibid., 57.

[9] This was the "Woodrum Committee," named after its chairman, Rep. Clifton A. Woodrum (D-VA). The senior Republican on the committee was James W. Wadsworth of New York. Barlow credited Wadsworth with having "a long-standing allegiance to the Army." See Barlow, *From Hot War to Cold*, 69.

[10] Barlow, *From Hot War to Cold*, 72.

[11] See Vincent Davis, *Postwar Defense Policy and the U.S. Navy, 1943–1946* (Chapel Hill: Univ. of North Carolina Press, 1967), 54–65.

[12] Barlow, *From Hot War to Cold*, 83.

[13] Davis, *Postwar Defense Policy and the U.S. Navy, 1943–1946*, 238.

[14] Joint Committee on the Investigation of the Pearl Harbor Attack, *Investigation of the Pearl Harbor Attack: Report*, 79th Cong., 2nd sess., 1946, S. Doc. 244; see also *Investigation of the Pearl Harbor Attack: Hearings*, 39 vols., 79th Cong., 2nd sess., 1946; and Gordon Prange, *At Dawn We Slept* (New York: McGraw-Hill, 1981).

[15] For details of the long debate between the Air Force and the Navy over strategic firepower, see *Revolt of the Admirals: The Fight for Naval Aviation, 1945–1950*, by Jeffrey G. Barlow (Washington, DC: Naval Historical Center and GPO, 1994).

[16] Robert Greenhalgh Albion and Robert Howe Connery, *Forrestal and the Navy*, (New York: Columbia University Press, 1962), 204–205.

[17] Ibid., 203.

[18] Ibid., 126–27.

[19] Barlow, *From Hot War to Cold*, 30, 33.

[20] 38 Stat. 929.

[21] 54 Stat. 494.

[22] 46 Stat. 430.

[23] *An Act Making certain changes in the organization of the Navy Department,* Public Law 432, 80th Cong., 2nd sess., (5 Mar. 1948). Section 1 of the law defined the term "Naval Establishment" as "vessels of war, aircraft, auxiliary craft and auxiliary activities, and the personnel who man them—and the naval agencies necessary to support and maintain the naval forces and to administer the Navy as a whole; the Marine Corps . . ." Digitial version at http://legisworks.org/congress/80/publaw-432.pdf.

[24] Ibid., Section 7.

[25] Ibid., Section 9.

[26] Ibid.

[27] Barlow, *From Hot War to Cold*, 34.

[28] "Navy Logistic Program, Monthly Progress Report, Issued as of 25 July 1945," Requirements Review Board, Requirements Review Division (NAVEXOS, RR20), 2. Compare that figure with "Total appropriation expenditures 1940" of $885,769,793.59. See "Naval Expenditures 1940," Bureau of Supplies and Accounts, Navy Department (Washington, DC: GPO, 1941), 1.

[29] Albion, *Makers of Naval Policy, 1798–1947*, 464–67.

[30] Pub. Law 601, ch. 753. The number of committees in the House was reduced from 48 to 19; in the Senate, the reduction was from 33 committees to 15.

[31] Albion, *Makers of Naval Policy, 1798–1947*, 175.

[32] Ibid., 176.

[33] Ibid., 477.

[34] Ibid., 477–78.

[35] Ibid., 480.

[36] Connery, *The Navy and the Industrial Mobilization in World War II*, 459.

[37] RADM Herbert G. Hopwood, Chief, Office of Budget and Reports, *Hearings before the General Board of the Navy*, 8 Apr. 1949, 1, 12–14, National Archives Microfilm Publication M-1493, Roll 27.

[38] Norman Friedman, *The Postwar Naval Revolution* (Annapolis, MD, 1986), ch. 1.

[39] John T. Greenwood, "The Emergence of the Postwar Strategic Air Force, 1945–1953," in *Air Power and Warfare*, Proceedings of the 8th Military History Symposium, U.S. Air Force Academy, eds. Alfred F. Hurley and Robert C. Ehrhart (Washington, DC, 1979), 218–21.

[40] Friedman, *The Postwar Naval Revolution*, 9.

[41] Barlow, *From Hot War to Cold*, 175.

[42] Greenwood, "The Emergence of the Postwar Strategic Air Force, 1945–1953." In Hurley and Ehrhart, *Air Power and Warfare*. See also David A. Rosenberg, "American Postwar Air Doctrine and Organization: The Navy Experience," in Hurley and Ehrhart, *Air Power and Warfare*, 245–78.

[43] Barlow, *From Hot War to Cold*, 179.

[44] See *Innovation in Carrier Aviation*, Thomas C. Hone, Norman Friedman, and Mark D. Mandeles, Newport Paper 37 (Newport, RI: Naval War College Press and GPO, 2011), ch. 5.

[45] Memo, Carney to Nimitz, 25 Nov. 1946, subj: Merger Discussions, file 31 (Memos, CNO, Personal, 1942–47), box 2, Records of the Immediate Office of the CNO (hereafter 00 File), originally in the Operational Archives of the Naval History and Heritage Command (hereafter NHHC).

[46] See Barlow, *From Hot War to Cold*, 511n68.

[47] Ibid., 179.

[48] Michael A. Palmer, *Origins of the Maritime Strategy, American Naval Strategy in the First Postwar Decade* (Washington, DC: Naval Historical Center, Dept. of the Navy, 1988), ch. 3.

[49] Rosenberg, "American Postwar Air Doctrine and Organization," in Hurley and Ehrhart, *Air Power and Warfare*, 11.

[50] Historical Division, Joint Secretariat, Joint Chiefs of Staff, *A Concise History of the Organization of the Joint Chiefs of Staff, 1942–1978* (Washington, DC, 1979), 17.

[51] BGEN Albert E. Brewster, USMC (Ret.), "The Commandant of the Marine Corps and the JCS," *Marine Corps Gazette*, vol. 92, no. 3 (Mar. 2008), 59–60.

[52] Ibid., 60.

[53] Ibid.

[54] Ibid.

[55] Robert Frank Futrell, *Ideas, Concepts, Doctrine: A History of Basic Thinking in the United States Air Force, 1907–1964* (Maxwell AFB, AL, 1971), 115.

[56] Ibid., 117.

[57] Ibid., 116.

[58] Steven L. Rearden, *History of the Office of the Secretary of Defense, vol. 1, The Formative Years, 1947–1950* (Washington, DC 1984), 316.

[59] Barlow, *From Hot War to Cold*, 179.

[60] Ibid., 395–96; see also Futrell, *Ideas, Concepts, Doctrine*, 99–100.

[61] Paolo E. Coletta, "Louis Emil Denfeld," in Love, *The Chiefs of Naval Operations*, 196–97.

[62] Barlow, *From Hot War to Cold*, 190.

[63] Ibid., 199. Barlow put it this way: "From the outset of his appointment as Secretary of Defense, James Forrestal had expected to be a creative mediator between the competing interests of the President, who wanted military spending kept within strict limits despite America's increasing overseas commitments, and the military services, who sought increased funding to adequately handle the commitments mandated by the administration." This situation convinced the first Secretary of Defense that the 1947 law would have to be revised significantly.

[64] Ibid., 190.

[65] Connery, *The Navy and the Industrial Mobilization in World War II*, 440.

[66] Rosenberg, "American Postwar Air Doctrine and Organization," in Hurley and Ehrhart, *Air Power and Warfare*, 256.

[67] See Robert Greenhalgh Albion and Samuel H. P. Read Jr., *The Navy at Sea and Ashore* (Washington, DC, 1947).

[68] Barlow, *From Hot War to Cold*, 184.

[69] Coletta, "Louis Emil Denfeld," in Love, *The Chiefs of Naval Operations*, 197.

[70] Ibid., 198.

[71] Memo, Burke to Denfeld, 3 Mar. 1949, subj: Comments on "The National Security Organization" by the Commission on Organization of the Executive Branch of the Government, A20/4 National Security Organization folder, Records of the Organizational Research and Policy Division (hereafter OP-23 File), NHHC Archives.

[72] Memo, Burke to Carney, 5 Aug. 1949, subj: Comptroller of the Navy, A1/EM-3/4, OP-23 File, NHHC Archives.

[73] Ibid.

[74] Memo, Burke to Chairman, General Board of the Navy, 7 Sept. 1949, subj: Study of the Applicability of the General Staff System to the Navy, A1/EM-3/4, OP-23 File, NHHC Archives.

[75] Memo, Carney to Chairman, General Board of the Navy, 4 Aug. 1949, subj: Study of the General Staff System Applicability to the Navy, folder 70, box 5, Records of the Plans, Policy, and Command Organization Branch (unprocessed) (hereafter OP-602 File), NHHC Archives.

[76] Barlow, *Revolt of the Admirals*, 236–37.

[77] Memo, "Trends in Unification," 16 Oct. 1949, 1, A1/EM-3/4, OP-23 File, NHHC Archives.

[78] Ibid.

[79] U.S. Statutes, *National Security Act Amendments of 1949*, Public Law 216, vol. 63, pt. 1 (10 Aug. 1949), 578–90; see also Futrell, *Ideas, Concepts, Doctrine*, 129–34, 136.

[80] Memo, "Trends in Unification," 16 Oct. 1949, 13, A1/EM-3/4, OP-23 File NHHC Archives.

[81] Ibid., 14.

[82] Rosenberg, "American Postwar Air Doctrine and Organization," in Hurley and Ehrhart, *Air Power and Warfare*, 263.

[83] Ibid., 261–62.

[84] Friedman, *The Postwar Naval Revolution*, 9.

CHAPTER 7

The Eisenhower Years

Introduction

The Eisenhower years were a time of great change for the nation and the Navy. For the nation, the prosperity of the middle and late 1950s wiped out the fears of another Great Depression. At the same time, the fear that the "Cold War" might turn "hot" created what was later called "the military-industrial complex." Other changes were underway, too. The 1950s have often been thought of as a decade where "conventionality" ruled. In some ways, that was true, but the seeds of change—especially in race relations and in the relations between women and men—planted in World War II were beginning to sprout, and the 1960s would bring waves of social change, waves that would undermine old behaviors in the Navy.

When he took office in 1953, President Dwight D. Eisenhower was neither satisfied with the existing level of service cooperation (as demonstrated in the campaign in Korea) nor impressed with the ability of the Joint Chiefs of Staff to link the President with his theater military commanders. He wanted to strengthen the hand of civilian defense officials and to streamline the national military command system. And in 1953 he went to Congress with proposals to do just that. Eisenhower's initiative and his strong views on national strategy led to the creation of the doctrine called the "New Look," less accurately termed "massive retaliation." By the summer of 1953 the relative cost of making nuclear weapons had drastically declined, while their versatility had dramatically improved. The question was this: Could the United States use its superior nuclear weapons technology to support North Atlantic Treaty Organization

(NATO), deter the Communist Chinese in the Far East, and reduce the reliance on large and costly conventional forces?

The answer, reached through close consultation with the Joint Chiefs, was yes, and the services considered means to adapt their forces and skills to the requirements of strategic and tactical nuclear warfare. The Navy, for example, began developing the forces to deploy tactical nuclear weapons against submarines, supplementing its existing arsenal of weapons for use against submarine bases. The emphasis on nuclear warfare enhanced Eisenhower's already deep interest in altering the highest levels of national security administration. As the Soviet Union developed its own nuclear strategic forces, the U.S. government would have to be prepared to respond to any swift surprise attack. Accordingly, Eisenhower went back to Congress in 1958 to ask for more changes in the laws governing national security decision making.

Office of the Chief of Naval Operations in 1953

CNO Forrest P. Sherman had died suddenly on 22 July 1951 after less than two years as the Navy's senior officer. His successor was Admiral William M. Fechteler, then serving as Commander-in-Chief, Atlantic Command (CINCLANT). Rear Admiral Richard W. Bates, a member of the staff of the Naval War College, characterized Fechteler as "an outstanding officer of brilliant professional attainments." Fechteler had served as Deputy Chief of Naval Operations for Personnel, and so he was familiar with how things worked (or didn't) in Washington, and Bates believed that Fechteler was "ideally suited for the responsibility" of serving as the CNO.

But one of the other candidates to succeed CNO Sherman was Admiral Richard L. Conolly, formerly Commander, U.S. Naval Forces Eastern Atlantic and the Mediterranean and, in 1951, President of the Naval War College. Admiral Bates contrasted his two superiors by first noting that "there is more to the responsibility of the Chief of Naval Operations than simply . . . commanding the uniformed side of the service. There is, in addition, the responsibility of the Joint Chiefs of Staff. Here the destiny of our Nation and the World will be worked out, and here should be our finest brain." As Bates continued, "I think Admiral Conolly has this brain . . ."[1]

Eisenhower's 1953 Reforms

The new President had a mind like Conolly's. Eisenhower was comfortable with strategic issues and the complexities of world politics. He also had strong views about defense organization and had campaigned on a platform that called for changes in the structure of defense decision making. After his victory in the 1952 elections, he asked prominent Republican Nelson A. Rockefeller to chair a committee of experts who would suggest a list of reforms.[2] The Rockefeller Committee was guided by four objectives: to make the lines of "authority and responsibility" within the Defense Department "clear and unmistakable"; to give the Secretary of Defense (SecDef) the responsibility for clarifying "the roles and missions of the services"; to make planning effective by using "our modern scientific and industrial resources"; and "to effect maximum economies without injuring military strength and its necessary productive support."[3] In its April 1953 report, the committee recommended the following:

- "The direction, authority, and control of the Secretary over all agencies of the Department, including the three military departments, . . . should be confirmed by decisive administrative action, and if necessary by statutory amendment."
- "The Secretaries of the military departments, subject to the direction, authority, and control of the Secretary of Defense, should be the operating heads of their respective departments in all aspects, military and civilian alike."
- "The command function" should be removed "from the Joint Chiefs of Staff, in order to enable them to work more effectively as a unified planning agency."
- The SecDef, not the JCS, should decide which military department should serve as the executive agent for a unified command.
- The SecDef should be "free to adjust from time to time the assignment of staff functions within his own office in a flexible and expeditious manner." The assistant secretaries "should not be in the direct line of administrative authority between" the secretary "and the three military departments."
- The Joint Munitions Board and Research and Development Board created by the National Security Act of 1947 should be dissolved and their functions transferred to Assistant Secretaries of Defense.[4]

On the basis of these recommendations, Eisenhower submitted Reorganization Plan 6 to Congress at the end of April 1953. Former Navy Department officials were divided in their views about defense reorganization. Ferdinand Eberstadt, who had advised former Navy and Defense Secretary James Forrestal, recommended to the Rockefeller panel that its members avoid making the structure of defense leadership too hierarchical. However, H. Struve Hensel, who had served as Navy counsel under Forrestal, accepted the need to have a more structured decision-making process but wanted the flow of authority to run from the President to the secretaries of the three military departments and then to the unified and specified commands.[5]

What concerned serving senior Navy officers was that the Rockefeller Committee met in secret. The new President did not want the committee's deliberations made public until the committee's report was ready to be sent to Congress. Admiral Donald B. Duncan, the VCNO, was taken by surprise when he learned that Reorganization Plan 6 was going to be sent to Congress on 30 April without first being sent to the service secretaries and service chiefs for comment.[6]

Minor opposition in Congress to the President's proposals failed to block his suggested reforms. Consequently, the joint military boards were broken up and their functions were transferred to the Office of the Secretary of Defense (OSD). The Defense secretary was allowed to appoint an additional six assistant secretaries and a general counsel. The JCS and the service chiefs were removed from the operational chain of command, which ran from the President to the unified and specified commanders. The service secretaries were preserved as nominal heads

215

of the military services, but they were supported by their chiefs of staff, or, as in the Navy's case, by the CNO. The Chairman of the Joint Chiefs was authorized to review appointments to the Joint Staff and to manage the staff.[7]

Department of Defense Directive 5158.1 of 26 July 1954 implemented Eisenhower's reorganization proposals. Perhaps the most important part of the directive was the first statement under the "Implementation" section: "The Joint Staff work of each of the Chiefs of Staff shall take priority over all other duties."[8] Part 6 of that section read, "Development of strategic and logistic plans will be based on the broadest conceptions of over-all national interest rather than the special desires of a particular service."[9] The President, displeased with the way he believed the Joint Chiefs had functioned during the World War II, now directed the service chiefs to focus their time and energy on joint issues through an institution that had adequate staff support and that was tied closely to OSD.

What about the Marines? Congress had specified the minimum force structure of the Marine Corps in the summer of 1952 "to include not less than three combat divisions and three air wings, and such other land combat, aviation, and other services as may be organic therein." Congress capped the peacetime strength of the Corps at 400,000 (not including the Marine Corps Reserve), but Congress also amended the National Security Act of 1947 to give the Marines something they had wanted when that legislation was passed—a seat on the Joint Chiefs of Staff. The amended law specified that:

> Unless the Secretary of Defense, upon request from the Chairman of the Joint Chiefs of Staff . . ., determines that such matter does not concern the United States Marine Corps, the Commandant of the Marine Corps shall meet with the Joint Chiefs of Staff when such matters are under consideration by them and on such occasion and with respect to such matter the Commandant of the Marine Corps shall have co-equal status with the members of the Joint Chiefs of Staff.[10]

The Defense Cataloging and Standardization Act, passed by Congress in 1953, created a single, standard catalog for the Defense Supply Management Agency to use when it procured material for all three services. DOD Directive 5158.1 abolished the Defense Supply Management Agency, but did not shift the agency's functions back to the services. Instead, the authority to procure common articles was given to the Secretary of Defense, who was empowered to create "single manager" agencies in procurement areas such as clothing, medical supplies, petroleum products, and food. Nearly 20 years later, Navy logisticians would interpret this act as the beginning of a tug-of-war between the services and the Secretary of Defense that the latter would eventually win.

The Navy's Response to Reorganization Plan 6

Secretary of the Navy Robert B. Anderson responded to congressional acceptance of Reorganization Plan 6 by appointing Under Secretary of the Navy Thomas S. Gates Jr. to head a special study committee to consider the Navy's organization. The Gates Committee struggled with the problem of how to give the Secretary of the Navy administrative control over the department without diluting the CNO's authority on the Joint Chiefs of Staff. If the CNO, as a member of the JCS, had access to the Defense secretary and the President, then was he subordinate to the Navy secretary? And, if the Navy secretary were in fact the "manager" of the Navy Department, then did he need special access to OPNAV for information and reports necessary to monitor the department's performance? Moreover, if the SECNAV could authorize the CNO to act for him, then was the CNO still as powerful as he had been before Reorganization Plan 6? Finally, there was the problem of time. After Reorganization Plan 6, both the Secretary of the Navy and the CNO seemed to have additional duties that were not easily delegated. How could the OPNAV and secretariat staffs best support the managerial and decision-making responsibilities of their leaders?

To answer these questions, the Gates Committee went back to basics. First, it considered the three general orders from the Navy secretariat which distributed authority and responsibility within the department: Number 5, which covered the administration of the department; Number 9, which specified the organization of the Navy's operating forces; and Number 19, which covered the shore activities of the department. Then the committee reviewed the basic structure of the Naval Establishment—the Navy Department and its bureaus, the operating forces, and the shore support facilities—observing that it was a divided, decentralized organization. The bureaus, for example, reported to the Secretary of the Navy, but were supposed to satisfy the requirements set by OPNAV for weapons, training, and personnel, so there was a dual chain of command within the Navy Department itself. The CNO was subordinate to the SECNAV, but the secretary did not participate in the deliberations of the Joint Chiefs, and traditionally did not interfere in the CNO's organization and (at times) direction of the operating forces (a heritage of World War II). Through the OPNAV staff, the CNO linked the "consumer" side of the Navy so that the "producer" side—the bureaus—could develop programs to meet the present and future needs of the operating forces in areas such as weapons and weapons platforms.

What held the whole Naval Establishment together, according to the committee, was ongoing consultation among Navy leaders. As the committee observed in its report, "many working level committees and groups are dealing with specific technical and management areas."[11] But the committee also noted that only two such committees were "concerned with top level problems," so "more effective coordination of all aspects of operation and management of the department would result from the establishment of a group of internal advisory committees made up of key executives and designed to deal with specific categories of problems."[12] The Navy's two high-level coordinating committees were the Navy Management Council, chaired by the under secretary and consisting of senior military and civilian Navy officials, and a weekly conclave of the bureau chiefs, which met under the auspices of the assistant secretary. The Gates Committee recommended that the secretary create six senior-level groups for general department policy, material procurement, Navy facilities and base construction, personnel policy, reserve forces, and for research and development.

The Gates Committee also proposed that the Navy secretary act as congressional liaison, coordinate public relations and relations with the OSD, and supervise the "producer logistics segment" of the department through the under secretary. The committee recommended making the seven bureaus and other assistants to the secretary "accountable" to the undersecretary "for total performance." Gates and his colleagues also advocated giving the undersecretary an office of analysis and review, which would prepare "consolidated statistical and analytical performance appraisals of each important program." Other recommendations included:

- Designating an Assistant Secretary of the Navy for Financial Management—a comptroller;
- Making the Assistant Secretary of the Navy responsible for "policy, management and control of production, procurement, supply, distribution and maintenance of material";
- Coordinating the Navy's "producer logistics" by the Under Secretary of the Navy through the assistant secretaries (especially Assistant Secretary for Material) and the bureaus;
- Relieving the Assistant Secretary for Air of his personnel powers, but giving him responsibility "for policy, management and control of functions relating to aeronautical matters (except those aspects concerned with producer logistics under the cognizance of the other Assistant Secretaries), and for Research and Development"; and
- Designating a new Assistant Secretary for Personnel and Reserve Forces, with responsibility "for policy, management and control of functions relating to personnel . . . and matters relating to policy and administration of public housing and quarters."[13]

The Gates Committee deliberations attempted to balance the new duties of the SECNAV and the CNO with the Navy's traditional, decentralized form of management. The proposals to create committees, which would determine the policies of the Naval Establishment, avoided giving too much authority to individuals, but still created institutional settings where these same individuals could and would act jointly to set policy. The basic reform of Reorganization Plan 6, which placed the service secretaries directly in the chain of command, caused severe administrative problems because it gave both the Navy secretary and the CNO access to the Defense secretary and the President without clearly dividing their respective duties. The committee tried to avoid head-to-head conflicts and to encourage consensus by creating joint administrative boards.

In the meantime, CNO Fechteler was eased out by President Eisenhower and Secretary of Defense Charles E. Wilson. There is evidence that both Eisenhower and Wilson simply did not understand that Fechteler had only served two years of what was supposed to be a four-year term.[14] As Fechteler recalled, he was called into Navy secretary Anderson's office on 11 May 1953 and told that the President wanted to make changes in the nation's high command and that Admiral Robert B. Carney would be the new CNO. Commander Edward L. Beach, Eisenhower's naval aide, told the President that the change had embarrassed Admiral Fechteler; it looked as though he had been fired. The CNO offered to retire immediately. According to Barlow, "Beach urged the President to make a gesture in Fechteler's direction, suggesting that the admiral be encouraged to accept another position." There was then a scramble to find Admiral Fechteler a suitable post. Fechteler and his superiors were in a bind. Wilson offered

Figure 7-1. Admiral William M. Fechteler inspecting Marines on battleship *Iowa* (BB-61). Before being appointed CNO, Fechteler had commanded U.S. naval forces in the Atlantic. Though he did not receive a second two-year term as CNO, he went on to serve three years as the commander of U.S. naval forces in the Mediterranean and the commander of NATO forces in Southern Europe. (NHHC Archives NH 49544)

Fechteler the job that Admiral Radford—who had been nominated as JCS chairman—was about to vacate, but Fechteler pointed out that taking it would be a demotion, and that he would rather resign. Eventually Fechteler accepted the post of Commander-in-Chief, Allied Forces, Southern Europe, a NATO command.

VCNO Duncan told Admiral Radford that he "was profoundly distressed" by the relief of CNO Fechteler. In Duncan's view, Fechteler had been:

> the best Chief of Naval Operations we have had since the War. He has engendered in all quarters—Congress, the press and DOD, and in other directions, too—a great confidence in the Navy and what it can do. *The manner in which it was done seems to me to have very little of the human element in it.* [italics in the original] The only reason for it that I can think of is that it is the wish of the President.[15]

It was. Eisenhower wanted as senior military officers individuals whom he knew, such as Admiral Carney.

The changes suggested by the Gates Committee were not successfully implemented. While Secretary Anderson delegated authority to Admiral Carney, his successor, Charles S. Thomas, was more jealous of his prerogatives. Carney also irritated Secretary of Defense Charles Wilson when he communicated directly—as service chiefs were authorized to do—with the President.

It was not clear whether Carney or Thomas was the principal naval advisor to the President. Finally, the CNO had to deal with a very assertive and capable senior admiral, Arthur Radford, Chairman of the Joint Chiefs and a very powerful advocate of long-range strategic bombing. As historian Paul Schratz pointed out, Admiral Radford "retained tremendous influence within the Navy Department and he actively cultivated the support of Secretary of the Navy Thomas, who soon fell under his sway."[16] The connection between Thomas and Radford, and Carney's strong insistence on his command and presidential advisory prerogatives as CNO (codified in Public Law 432 of 5 March 1948), kept the Gates Committee's proposals for collegial leadership committees from ever getting off the ground.

Figure 7-2. CNO Admiral Robert B. Carney had served as chief of staff to Admiral William F. Halsey in World War II and as a deputy to General of the Army Dwight D. Eisenhower when Eisenhower was NATO Commander-in-Chief in Europe after the war. Carney and Fechteler traded places when Carney was chosen to replace Fechteler by President Eisenhower in May 1953. (NHHC Archives NH 83604)

Carney, however, did heed the committee's call for improved institutional planning and DOD Directive 5158.1's instruction that the services work closer with the Joint Chiefs and the Defense secretary. In April 1954 he set up an ad hoc group to consider future shipbuilding plans and programs. The following year, in February 1955, he established the Long Range Objectives Group (OP-93) to consider major Navy programs ten to 15 years into the future.[17] To enable the CNO to serve as an effective member of the Joint Chiefs, Carney placed the responsibility for JCS matters and strategic planning in a new office, the DCNO for Plans and Policy (OP-06). OP-06's predecessor in the area of joint military policy and planning was the DCNO for Operations (OP-03). The changes in defense organization initiated by President Eisenhower required Admiral Carney to change OPNAV's organization so that the Navy would not be outmaneuvered in competition at the JCS level. He said later:

> As CNO and a member of the JCS I was under pressure to defend Navy interests against Army/Air Force proposals to preempt the major theater and unified commands. My staff spent too much time in defensive effort. Curiously, my combat-proven deputy was reluctant to generate comparable power-grab proposals, typical of a widespread mentality that was basically conservative, honest—and, I thought, naive.[18]

The Gates Committee had responded to Reorganization Plan 6 by trying to strengthen the secretariat so that it could fulfill its new, mandated responsibilities. Admiral Carney responded to Plan 6 by becoming more aggressive in the Navy Department and in the JCS. He perceived that the plan left more authority in the hands of the service secretaries than the average civilian appointee could handle.

The CNO expressed his concerns in a letter to Eisenhower after SECNAV Thomas had refused to extend Carney's appointment because Thomas regarded Carney as having been insubordinate.[19] As Carney told the President,

> The increasingly close supervision and checking by the civilian Secretariat on virtually every operation of the Navy Department, including the office of the Chief of Naval Operations, is something which is slowly but surely sapping military initiative, slowing down business, and diluting the exercise of command and executive direction formerly carried out by senior officers experienced in the needs of the fleet and the military establishment ashore.[20]

But Eisenhower took a very different view. As he said, "Carney holds that there are certain matters within the direction and operation of the Naval chiefs, with which the Secretary has no possible concern or right to interfere." As the President knew, however, the secretary—legally and constitutionally responsible for the direction of the Navy Department—needed to be "constantly informed and to demand and have all the inspectional rights as to operations, reports, communications and so on, which are necessary to him in order to form his own judgment in these matters. Unless that is so, there could be no control over any CNO . . ."[21]

Carney also realized that the New Look, which Admiral Radford had helped to shape for the President, had major long-range implications. The same question was asked again: what mission would the Navy have if the nation's major war strategy were a nuclear one? The Navy needed strong representation in the JCS, and that representation required a staff capable of dealing with strategic issues. Carney acted to build OP-06 as a competent link to and a shield against the JCS. He also started a process of long-range planning to give the CNO some warning of future military and technological developments that would affect the Navy's strategic role.

Burke Becomes CNO

In mid-1955, after Navy secretary Thomas decided not to ask for Admiral Carney's reappointment, President Eisenhower appointed Rear Admiral Arleigh Burke the Chief of Naval Operations. If the President and Secretary of Defense Wilson ever thought that Burke was less likely to resist defense reorganization than Carney, they were in for a surprise. Indeed, Burke himself told the Senate before his confirmation that he had not abandoned the positions that he had presented so forcefully in 1949, when he was head of OP-23. As the President and the other services would learn, Burke meant what he said.

As CNO, Burke was an energetic administrator and a shrewd leader. He moved quickly to win the support of OPNAV and the Navy by retaining Carney's "entire immediate staff," by consulting with the Navy's senior commanders in the Atlantic and Pacific, and by personally writing a monthly newsletter for flag officers.[22] As he earned the support of officers senior to him in service, Burke began a process of giving the Navy a principal role in Eisenhower's New Look strategy. In October 1955 Burke pursued a joint project with the Army to put an intermediate-range ballistic missile to sea. When the solid-fueled Polaris missile was developed, the Navy pursued its program separately from the Army, eventually placing Polaris on nuclear-powered submarines. He also initiated a study of Navy organization, appointing Vice Admiral Ruthven E. Libby chairman of a special board of inquiry "to study and report upon the adequacy of the Bureau System of organization." Burke believed that the Navy's future was in jeopardy, and he wanted to make sure that his service was organized to stay at the cutting edge of military technology.

Burke convened the Libby Board because he and other senior officers were concerned about the lack of success of the Navy's antiair missile program—the three "Ts" (Terrier, Tartar, and Talos missiles). Shifting the surface Navy from guns to missiles took longer than planned, but it was an essential move because existing middle- and short-range antiaircraft guns were inadequate against modern jet aircraft. Moreover, the fact that those aircraft could carry nuclear weapons meant that they had to be engaged at the longest ranges practicable. The basic idea behind the three "T" program was to build a layered air defense around Navy formations, with missiles of different ranges engaging attacking aircraft as they flew closer to the center of the U.S. formation. The idea was sound, but getting the new weapons into the fleet took longer than anticipated. Burke wanted to know if the problem was an engineering or organizational one.[23]

In his letter of instruction to the board, Burke observed:

> Weapons and weapons systems are becoming more and more complicated, with more and more interdependent components. Interest in, and in some cases, cognizance of certain of these components, is common to the three so-called material bureaus, as a result of which constant interchange of information and constant coordination is required.[24]

The question was whether this constant exchange and coordination was being done properly. In March 1956 the Libby Board issued its report. Classified at the time, it first summarized the developmental process and then suggested changes. The key to the developmental process in the Navy was the generation of "operational requirements," or statements of "*what, when, and where* of desired specific systems or equipment."[25] As the report declared:

> Nowhere in the present system is there provision specifically for performing the function of conceiving, in general physical terms, new weapon systems and system complexes *which relate to the entire field of naval warfare*. . . . Such system development planning as is going on now is fragmentized among the several warfare desks [in OPNAV] . . . Thus the systems here developed tend to be entities within their own operational categories;

no one agency correlates the systems between or among categories; and no one agency is charged with coordinating all the systems with their essential logistic support.[26]

But the board was uncomfortable with the suggestion that the Bureaus of Ordnance, Aeronautics, and Ships be given certain areas of absolute technical dominance. Its report observed that "it has been impossible to arrive at a determination of Bureau cognizance" in missile design and development "because the development of almost any guided missile system requires the specialized skills and capabilities of more than one bureau."[27] Indeed, two successful missile designs—the Sidewinder air-to-air missile and the Regulus surface-to-surface cruise missile—emerged from bureaus (Ordnance and Aeronautics, respectively) whose primary duties did not cover those types of weapons. The board suggested that the CNO establish a conceptual weapons systems group in OPNAV. Board members wanted to preserve the bureau system and opposed using special "task forces" to develop new weapons, just as they voted against "arbitrary and rigid assignment of cognizance over an entire weapon system."[28]

At the same time, the Libby Board placed the initiative for new systems development in OPNAV rather than with the bureaus. Praising a study on long-range shipbuilding ordered by former CNO Carney, the board endorsed the establishment of the Long Range Objectives Group (OP-93). Board members also supported Admiral Burke's decision to form a special Naval Warfare Analyses Group (NAVWAG), composed of both civilian and military analysts, to support OP-93.[29] In so doing, they were admitting that the traditional system of training line officers as ordnance or aviation specialists and alternating them between the fleet and the bureaus was not working effectively.

Organizational differences between the Bureaus of Ordnance and Aeronautics and the Bureau of Ships had always existed. The latter was managed more by uniformed specialists (later called Engineering Duty Only officers) who followed career paths different from those of line officers. Ordnance and Aeronautics were dominated by line officers who, because of their abilities, received postgraduate training in ballistics, engineering, or chemistry and then shuttled back and forth from the operating forces to their bureaus. Burke had been trained as an ordnance officer, and many of the Naval Academy's most outstanding graduates were guided into postgraduate ordnance work before World War II. That tradition marked the origins of the prejudice toward the Navy's "Gun Club," or the ordnance-trained line officers, who before the war had been singled out by their superiors for outstanding careers. This system of giving qualified line officers special training leading to career advantages was defended on the grounds that it promoted communication between the operating forces, the bureaus, and the latest advances in applied science. The Libby Board's report was the first sign that this pattern of special training might not be adequate for the missile age.

The board also suggested that the CNO direct newer, complex systems development because the task of generating operational requirements was too important to be left to the various warfare desks in offices like OP-05. Burke used the force of the recommendation to justify his decision to ask the Secretary of the Navy to create a Special Projects Office (SPO) to develop the

Polaris missile and its platform, or platforms. Burke placed a special board, with senior civilian and Navy members, over the new organization and gave the SPO first priority in funding and staffing. It was the Navy's bootstrap effort to make a place for itself in the strategic missile forces and it worked. Rosenberg characterized Burke's strong, unswerving support for the SPO as "probably the single most significant action of his six years as chief of naval operations."[30] The significant point, however, was that Burke refused to accept the Air Force claim to primacy in the strategic field, and he took control of the planning processes in OPNAV in order to carry on that fight with the Air Force.

The Libby Board also recommended that the Secretary of the Navy establish an Inter-Bureau Technical Group and an Executive Council (with bureau representation) for Development and Production. It also endorsed the concept of the "lead bureau," whereby OPNAV would give coordinating authority to a bureau in a particular area of development, such as surface-to-air missiles. The Navy's shift from guns to missiles, and then from analog to digital technology, had caused the coordination problems among the major bureaus. So long as sensors, such as radar, were essentially "add-ons" to existing fire control and plotting systems and missiles had little influence on ship and aircraft designs, coordination problems were limited. Systems could be added to, or subtracted from, basic hull and powerplant designs with simple modifications. The difficulty arose when the missiles and their sensors and guidance systems began to dominate surface ship and aircraft design. Platform designers were on the edge of a revolution—integrated ship and aircraft systems design—and the bureaus had to rethink their accepted boundaries.

The process would not be easy. Navy leaders wanted the bureaus to be centers of applied expertise and the Navy's laboratories to be centers of research and innovation. But rapid advances in technology required a stronger technical education for line officers and constant retraining. As Rear Admiral Charles D. Wheelock of BuShips had informed the General Board as early as 1948, "[A] great deal of emphasis has to be placed on technical training . . . [and] technical training excellence has got to be emphasized much more than it has been."[31]

At the same time, however, bureau personnel wanted assurance that their chosen careers would last; they did not want to make a commitment to naval engineering and development and then lose their jobs when a new technology replaced the old. In the nuclear submarine program, for example, Vice Admiral Hyman G. Rickover had solved the problem of training and holding skilled personnel by fostering simultaneously military and civilian technology. The one nourished the other. The Navy supplied trained operators for the civilian nuclear power program, while the civilian manufacturers maintained development efforts to benefit the Navy. There were dangers in this close military/civilian relationship, however. On the one hand, the military risked losing control of the direction of technology. On the other, if the Navy retained control by freezing design development, it risked missing technological opportunities. These dangers were not apparent either to Burke or to the Libby Board in 1956, but were realized by the late 1970s.

Conclusion

The 1950s were full of challenges to CNOs Fechteler, Carney, and Burke. There were the operational challenges posed by the Korean War, the need to work out command relationships in the NATO, the numerous engineering and technological challenges stemming from the many advances in multiple areas of science and engineering, and the debate between the Air Force and Navy over how the nation's strategic nuclear forces would be directed in the event of war.[32] There was also the challenge put to his military chiefs by President Eisenhower: Find a way or ways to deter the Soviet Union without going to all-out nuclear war. After World War II, the military services demobilized; in the early 1950s, they had to re-arm without remobilizing. That was Eisenhower's decision. It had dramatic implications for the military services.

There would be no return for senior Navy officers to the concerns of their own service. In the 1950s, Navy officers had to become skilled and active diplomats. They had to think strategically and become articulate advocates of well-thought-out positions about American strategy. They had to be able to stand up to senior civilians—even the President—without challenging the concept of civilian control embedded in the Constitution. Burke was able to do all of this, and he was therefore a particularly effective CNO.

The Eisenhower administration made it final: The United States would not go "all out" to rearm and confront an aggressive Soviet Union. President Eisenhower wanted to deter a major war in order to avoid a nuclear conflict. At the same time, he wanted his military chiefs to help him field and develop forces that would be technologically sophisticated and yet not so expensive that creating and sustaining them would harm the American economy. Strategically, Eisenhower walked a tightrope during his two terms. In 2012, historian Evan Thomas called Eisenhower's approach a "bluff."[33] But the "bluff" would work only if there were signs that the leaders of the Soviet Union could see that would convince them that Eisenhower was not bluffing. Admiral Arleigh Burke's Navy provided some of the more important of those signs.

Notes

[1] Barlow, *From Hot War to Cold*, 321. For more on ADM Conolly, see "Enthusiasm—Richard Lansing Conolly (1892–1962)," by Jeffrey G. Barlow, *Nineteen-Gun Salute, Case Studies of Operational, Strategic, and Diplomatic Naval Leadership during the 20th and Early 21st Centuries*, ed. by John B. Hattendorf and Bruce A. Elleman (Washington, DC, and Newport, RI: GPO and Naval War College Press, 2010), 92–104.

[2] The Rockefeller Committee was chaired by Nelson Rockefeller; other members were GA Omar N. Bradley; Vannevar Bush, president of the Carnegie Institution; Milton Eisenhower, president of then-Pennsylvania State College; Arthur Flemming; Robert Lovett, former Secretary of Defense; and David Sarnoff, head of Radio Corporation of America (RCA).

[3] Senate Committee on Armed Services, *Department of Defense Organization: Report of the Rockefeller Committee*, 83rd Cong., 1st sess., 1953, 1.

[4] Ibid., 2–3, 5, 9, 11, 12.

[5] Barlow, *From Hot War to Cold*, 342–47.

[6] Ibid., 344.

[7] *Message from the President of the United States, Reorganization Plan No. 6 of 1953, Relating to the Department of Defense*, 83rd Cong., 1st sess., 1953, H. Doc. 136, 9–10.

[8] Historical Division, Joint Secretariat, Joint Chiefs of Staff, Chronology, *Functions and Composition of the Joint Chiefs of Staff* (Washington, DC, 1979), 209.

[9] Ibid., 210.

[10] Brewster, "The Commandant of the Marine Corps and the JCS," 62.

[11] Department of the Navy, *Report of the Committee on Organization of the Department of the Navy* (Thomas S. Gates Committee Report) (Washington, DC, 1954), 34.

[12] Ibid., 34–35.

[13] Ibid., 41–44.

[14] Barlow, *From Hot War to Cold*, 369–72.

[15] Ibid., 372.

[16] Paul R. Schratz, "Robert Bostwick Carney," in Love, *The Chiefs of Naval Operations*, 248.

[17] "Historical Perspectives in Long Range Planning in the Navy," draft, pt. 1: "The Planning Process in Overview, 1900–1978, for the Naval Research Advisory Committee," May 1979, vi–1, collection of Thomas C. Hone.

[18] Schratz, "Robert Bostwick Carney," in Love, *The Chiefs of Naval Operations*, 256.

[19] Barlow, *From Hot War to Cold*, 396–97.

[20] Ibid., 399.

[21] Ibid.

[22] Rosenberg, "Arleigh Albert Burke," in Love, *The Chiefs of Naval Operations*, 275.

[23] Friedman, *U.S. Naval Weapons*, 150–58.

[24] Department of the Navy, "Report of the Board Convened by the Chief of Naval Operations to Study and Report Upon the Adequacy of the Bureau System of Organization" (R. E. Libby Board Report), 14 Mar. 1956, Ref (A) LTR from CNO to VADM R. E. Libby, 6 Jan. 1956 Ser 115P02, iii, in Libby, R.E. VADM, Individual Personnel, Box 1795, Post 1946 Command File, NHHC Archives. The issues covered by the Libby Board were not new. They had been raised with the General Board in November 1948, when the Board reviewed the Fiscal Year 1951–1960 shipbuilding program. See *Hearings before the General Board of the Navy*, 2, 4, 8, and 10 Nov. 1948, NARA, Washington, DC, Microfilm M-1493, Roll 27.

[25] Ibid., III–9.

[26] Ibid., III–11.

[27] Ibid., III–32.

[28] Ibid., I–1, I–2.

[29] Ibid., III–9.

[30] Rosenberg, "Arleigh Albert Burke," in Love, *The Chiefs of Naval Operations*, 279.

[31] "Shipbuilding Program, Fiscal Year 1951–1960," *Hearings before the General Board of the Navy*, 4 Nov. 1948, 36. National Archives Microfilm M-1493, Roll 27.

[32] See *Nuclear Weapons and Aircraft Carriers*, by VADM Jerry (Gerald E.) Miller, USN (Ret.) (Washington, DC: Smithsonian Institution Press, 2001), ch. 9. VADM Miller was directly involved in the development of the SIOP, or "Single Integrated Operations Plan," and his explanation of how that planning came about is brief and to the point.

[33] Evan Thomas, *Ike's Bluff: President Eisenhower's Secret Battle to Save the World* (Boston: Little, Brown, 2012).

CHAPTER 8

Burke: Shielding the Navy

*"Most so-called social scientists seem to think
that organization is everything.
It is almost nothing—except when it is a straitjacket."*

Robert A. Heinlein, *Glory Road*

Introduction

After his first two years as Chief of Naval Operations, Burke clearly saw that President Eisenhower was not satisfied with service cooperation, joint planning, and the type of defense management allowed by existing laws. Neither was Congress. By 1957, for example, all three services were developing or producing both long-range cruise missiles and intermediate-range ballistic missiles. This appeared to be an expensive case of unnecessary duplication. To reduce such apparently wasted effort, Congress wanted to give the Secretary of Defense (SecDef) the power to cancel programs, not simply coordinate program development among the military services. Congress and the President also wanted some central, unified planning for nuclear war. Outside the government, the Rockefeller Foundation had funded a series of studies on national security. One such study, completed while Admiral Burke was CNO, had recommended that the service chiefs be removed from the chain of command and that the Joint Staff of the Joint Chiefs of Staff be both reorganized and strengthened.[1]

The Campaign for Defense Reorganization Resurfaces

As it became obvious to the services that the President would submit another proposal for Department of Defense reorganization to Congress, Burke prepared for a rerun of the unification debates. The chronology of Navy responses to the recommendations of the Rockefeller panel on defense reorganization shows how carefully Admiral Burke prepared and managed the Navy's position:

October 1957: The CNO formed a special committee in OPNAV to study the alternatives to the panel's likely recommendations. (That same month Eisenhower privately said that he favored eliminating separate military services.)

December 1957: The Deputy Chief of Naval Operations for Plans and Policy (OP-06) solicited comments within the Navy (not just within OPNAV) regarding possible changes to DOD and service organization.

January 1958: The Rockefeller reorganization report was released.

January 1958: The first DOD reorganization bill cleared the House of Representatives, and the President supported reorganization in his "State of the Union" address.

January 1958: The Office of the Secretary of Defense began a formal study of DOD organization.

February 1958: The OPNAV staff completed its study, begun in October 1957, on the consequences of JCS control over theater operations and joint commands.

April 1958: The administration's reorganization bill was introduced in the House.

May 1958: Largely at the request of the Navy Department, Carl Vinson, Chairman of the House Armed Services Committee, introduced his own reorganization bill.

June 1958: With Senate Armed Services Committee hearings on several reorganization bills underway, Admiral Burke created the Ad Hoc Committee to Review the Navy Department Organization to consider the effects of these bills should they become law.[2]

Burke opposed all proposals to merge the military departments, to create a single chief of staff of the armed forces, and to fashion the Joint Staff into an effective general staff. He began a time-consuming correspondence, arguing his case with influential retired flag officers. He ordered the DCNO for Plans and Policy to develop a special proposal to send to Congress for reorganizing OSD. He tried to dissuade President Eisenhower from submitting a bill that would strip the CNO of operational authority, and he welcomed the support of Carl Vinson and Vinson's colleague, Representative Paul Kilday (D-TX), the second ranking majority member of the House Armed Services Committee. To Burke's relief, Vinson and Kilday insisted that any reform legislation *not* authorize the SecDef to merge the services, or create a single chief of staff, or establish an "overall armed forces general staff.[3]

Burke's Response to Defense Reorganization

Despite Burke's opposition, however, the Department of Defense Reorganization Act of 1958 did eliminate the operational authority of the service chiefs. The new law removed the service secretaries from the chain of command; the revised chain of command ran from the President to the Secretary of Defense, through the Joint Chiefs of Staff, to the unified (such as Commander-in-Chief, Pacific [CINCPAC]) and specified (Strategic Air Command [SAC], for example) field commanders. The Joint Chiefs did not act as their organization's delegated representatives in the chain of command. However, the JCS advisory role was strengthened by giving the chairman a vote in their deliberations, by increasing the size of the Joint Staff, and by permitting the Joint Staff to organize along traditional staff lines and abandon the joint committee structure in use since 1947.

Figure 8-1. CNO Admiral Arleigh A. Burke on a ship's bridge. Though clearly an outstanding officer, Burke had not served as commander of a numbered fleet when he was selected as CNO Carney's replacement. He won the respect and confidence of President Eisenhower, initiated the ballistic missile submarine program in the Navy, and served three terms as CNO. (National Archives 80-G-1019527)

Before 1958 the Joint Staff consisted of several major staff committees: strategic plans, intelligence, logistics, military assistance, and advanced studies. After 1958, the Joint Staff was set up along Army lines with directorates: J-1 for personnel, J-2 for intelligence, J-3 for operations, J-4 for logistics, and so forth. CNO Burke had always regarded the JCS as less a military organization than a political one in which service chiefs had to struggle for resources and authority, and he drove his staff to keep one step ahead of the other services, especially the Air Force. But the reorganization of the Joint Staff along Army lines meant an organizational philosophy that felt alien to Navy officers, and the Navy developed a strong prejudice against sending its best officers for joint work.[4]

What concerned Burke, however, was the increased authority that the 1958 law gave the Secretary of Defense. Subject to a veto by either house of Congress, the Secretary of Defense could alter service functions. The SecDef could also reorganize the department's supply and service activities and assign new weapons systems development and use to one service. Finally, the SecDef could delegate his authority to assistants, giving them responsibility for functions that he himself created. Within eight months of the law's passage, the commander of SAC took advantage of its provisions by requesting that SAC be given operational "control" of the Navy's Polaris submarine force then under construction.[5] As historian David Rosenberg noted in his study of Burke's tenure as CNO, "Over the next fifteen months, Burke stubbornly fought the proposal, not only within the Joint Chiefs, but before Congress and in the press."[6] Burke won that contest but lost a later debate over whether there should be a Joint Strategic Target Planning Staff (JSTPS) with SAC's commander as its director.[7]

During the debate over defense organization in 1958, Burke asked Rear Admiral Allan L. Reed of OP-92 (Intelligence) to study OPNAV. Burke particularly wanted to know why the Navy appeared to be on the defensive in the debates over national security organization. Reed's answers, in a confidential report, were revealing:

> The habit of thinking of naval officers has always been more individualistic than that of officers in the other services. This makes for vigor in action and produces good ideas, but it . . . tends to inhibit the teamwork and support of officially stated

policies and doctrines necessary in the highest staffs.[8] Naval officers in general do not consider it an honor to be assigned to the Office of the Chief of Naval Operations. . . . The degree of identification with special interests such as naval aviation, the submarine service, or surface specialties tends to encourage the formation of cliques and to discourage viewpoints and thinking oriented toward the best interests of the Navy as a whole.[9]

The solution: "encourage the development within the line of the Navy of a group of officers of all ranks and branches, thoroughly trained in staff work, and qualified through experience to assist the highest commanders in the solution of problems and in formulating and implementing policy." But there was a catch, as he realized: "This is admittedly coming close to the concept of a 'General Staff Corps.'"[10]

To avoid that apostasy, Reed suggested breaking down the "distinct feeling of compartmentation" by making sure that all warfare specialties represented in OPNAV understood current Navy doctrine.[11] He argued that OPNAV organization hindered the development of a shared sense of mission because too many officers reported directly to the Chief and Vice Chief of Naval Operations instead of working together to iron out problems. Moreover, the lines of authority in OPNAV were uncertain, and Navy officers capable of exercising delegated authority were often not given it.[12] Reed advised Burke to increase the size of his immediate staff under the vice chief and create a "central point for the review, coordination and dissemination of policy and doctrine."[13] As part of the latter effort, Reed recommended reducing the sweeping responsibilities of the DCNO for Air (OP-05).[14]

Reed's study was important for several reasons. First, it revealed how influential the Navy's traditions and unwritten rules for success were as the Navy battled bureaucratic challenges from both the Air Force and the Office of the Secretary of Defense. Second, it uncovered a Navy dilemma that survives to the present day. Burke considered himself and the Navy under attack by "ideologues," officers and civilians who had strong beliefs about what national strategy would be successful and what defense organization would be best but little evidence to back up those strong beliefs. But the obvious means of opposing his attackers—using the same kind of tactics in return—would not make the Navy the kind of institution that Burke argued the nation needed to resist an over concentration of military command power. That was the dilemma. Burke did not trust military ideologues, no matter what uniform they wore. Yet he admitted that opposing them successfully sometimes demanded as much theater as rational argument. Finally, the Reed study prompted Burke to consider adding responsibilities to OP-06 (Plans and Policy), and to review his own style of leadership.

The Franke Board

The more immediate task for the Navy, however, was to respond to the Department of Defense Reorganization Act of 1958. Secretary of the Navy Thomas Gates appointed a board in August 1958 to address the impact of the new law on the Navy's organization. Chaired by

Under Secretary of the Navy William B. Franke, the board convened for six months before recommending the following:

- Retain the Navy's bilinear system of parallel civilian and military administration (the Secretary of the Navy and the CNO).
- Change General Orders Numbers 5 and 9 to reflect the 1958 law, which eliminated the operational command authority of the CNO.
- Reorganize the assistant secretaries of the Navy, appointing one each for finance, manpower, material, and research and development.
- Create a DCNO for research and development.
- Combine the bureaus of Ordnance and Aeronautics.[15]

To make room for the new Assistant Secretary of the Navy for Research and Development, Gates abolished the office of the Assistant Secretary for Air. He also ordered the CNO to shift aviation personnel matters from OP-05 to the Bureau of Naval Personnel (BuPers [later became BUPERS]), and authorized the merger of the bureaus of Ordnance and Aeronautics.[16]

Burke's special Ad Hoc Committee to Review the Navy Department Organization had reported in July, before the 1958 reforms became law. It recommended that OPNAV be reorganized along functional lines, with the DCNO for Air losing influence and the bureaus losing their independence. The original, uncorrected draft of the ad hoc committee's report argued that the "Chief of Naval Operations must exercise appropriate direction over Bureau operations and finances. To achieve this, the Department must bring the Bureaus and Comptroller under the Chief of Naval Operations."[17] That first draft was amended later, when the words "subject to the policy of the Secretary of the Navy" were appended to the first sentence. The Franke Board also considered subordinating the bureaus to the CNO, but it rejected the idea on the counsel of Navy line officers who worked in the bureaus.[18]

Burke's committee was taking an audacious stand in recommending that the CNO, not the secretary, control the bureaus. That issue had divided former Secretary of the Navy Forrestal and former CNO Ernest King. The issue surfaced again because Burke felt pressured from the SecDef and indirectly from the Navy secretary. The 1958 reforms not only eliminated the operational authority of the CNO but also made the service secretaries de facto line managers for the Secretary of Defense. In that capacity, a strong Navy secretary, who was also a loyal subordinate of the Secretary of Defense, could exploit the limits on the CNO's authority to control Navy research, development, and acquisition, thereby reducing the influence of the CNO.

When the Franke Board recommended merging the bureaus of Aeronautics and Ordnance, CNO Burke began considering directors for the new organization, named the Bureau of Naval Weapons (BuWeps). In June 1959, an OP-06 memo informed Burke that Vice Admiral Rickover, director of the Navy's nuclear propulsion program in the Bureau of Ships, had "a campaign going" to get the new position. The memo, apparently written for Burke by Captain Joseph W. Leverton, laid out a strategy for Burke to use in getting his own choice to head the new bureau.[19]

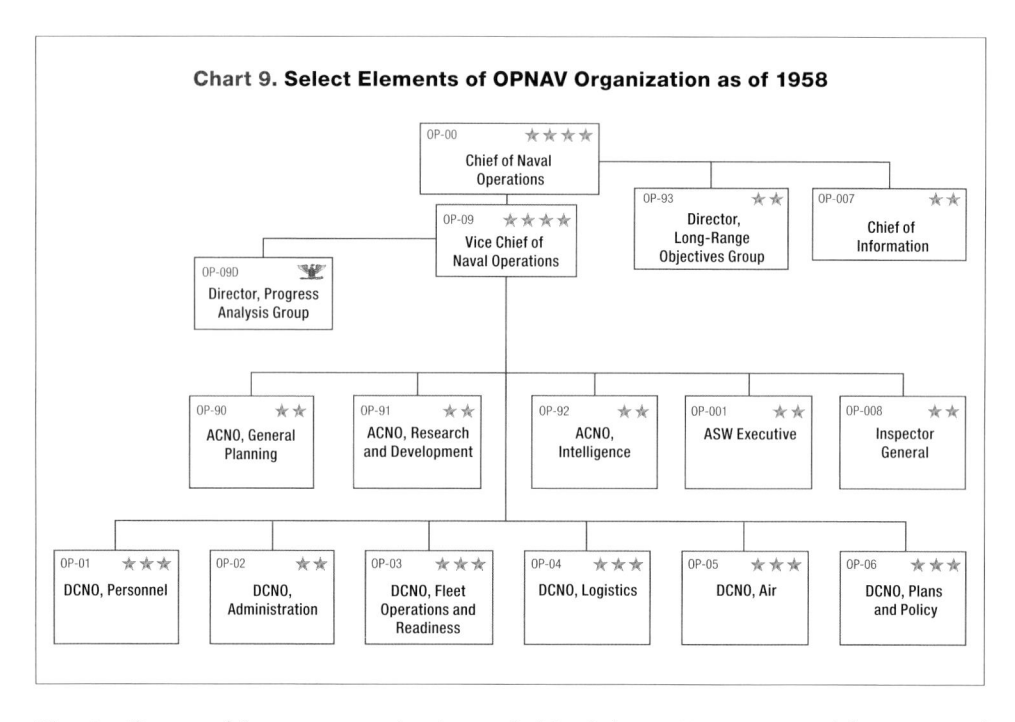

Chart 9. Select Elements of OPNAV Organization as of 1958

- OP-00 ★★★★ Chief of Naval Operations
  - OP-09 ★★★★ Vice Chief of Naval Operations
    - OP-09D Director, Progress Analysis Group
  - OP-93 ★★ Director, Long-Range Objectives Group
  - OP-007 ★★ Chief of Information
  - OP-90 ★★ ACNO, General Planning
  - OP-91 ★★ ACNO, Research and Development
  - OP-92 ★★ ACNO, Intelligence
  - OP-001 ★★ ASW Executive
  - OP-008 ★★ Inspector General
  - OP-01 ★★★ DCNO, Personnel
  - OP-02 ★★ DCNO, Administration
  - OP-03 ★★★ DCNO, Fleet Operations and Readiness
  - OP-04 ★★★ DCNO, Logistics
  - OP-05 ★★★ DCNO, Air
  - OP-06 ★★★ DCNO, Plans and Policy

The significance of the memo was that it revealed Burke's sensitivity to one of the sources of his organizational influence—his appointment authority. For example, when the 1958 DOD Reorganization Act was passed, the service chiefs legally lost their operational authority. Burke retained his command authority, however, by simply ignoring the 1958 law and acting as though his position was unchanged. To bolster his authority, he also relied on the need of naval component commanders in the unified commands, such as Commander-in-Chief, Pacific Fleet, in CINCPAC, to get the CNO's approval for reorganizations.[20] Burke understood that the CNO, through OPNAV, influenced the number and kind of billets under the component commanders. He used that influence to remind these commanders of his authority.[21]

Burke had learned to use all the resources at his disposal to shield the Navy from what he regarded as "misguided" outside pressure. Where he lacked resources, he relied on the strength of his personality. As the Franke Board prepared its report, for example, Burke had Captain Leverton informally solicit OPNAV personnel for impressions of Burke's managerial style. Leverton summarized his findings in two memos:

- Subordinates often did not know what the CNO expected of them.
- Burke's quick temper rubbed senior officers the wrong way.
- Subordinates felt that Burke lacked time for the really important matters because too many people with trivial issues were vying for the CNO's attention.
- Subordinates disliked Burke's habit of bypassing channels.
- Burke was seen as not delegating enough authority to his deputies.

- Despite Burke's energy and "no compromise" style, OPNAV operated like Congress: advocates of important change had to build a coalition behind their ideas through persuasion, bargaining, and compromise.
- Burke relied heavily on OP-06, ignoring other portions of OPNAV. OP-06 felt buried under work because it had to respond immediately to JCS issues.

Leverton closed by commenting that Burke's leadership style "has caused a lot of uncertainty within the staff—but it has kept them on their toes—it has been productive."[22]

At Burke's request, Leverton quietly monitored Congress to detect further efforts to "reform" the Defense Department and the services. Burke also continued his letter-writing campaign. That October (1959), he expressed his views on defense organization to retired Vice Admiral Walter G. Schindler, explaining his opposition to unifying the services:

> [O]ur present organization is . . . much better than a single Service for getting answers that are really thought through, for controlling the power contests among the many contending interests, for broadening and deepening the rigid Service concepts that would put us at the mercy of a flexible enemy. . . . A single Service would give effective control of the power of over $40 billion-plus a year into the hands of a single man, or a group of disciplined men all oriented in exactly the same direction, and this power would directly threaten the government of the country.[23]

It is important to note that Burke considered these points "basic and decisive," because what he did later appeared to violate the line dividing military and civilian authority.

The Fine Line Between Lobbying and Arguing

In June 1960, Burke set up the Technical Studies Group (OP-06D) "to study the organization of the Department of Defense and to prepare studies . . . which the Secretary of the Navy and the Chief of Naval Operations could use in the event their views were sought by Congress or the executive branch of government."[24] The group, headed by Rear Admiral Denys W. Knoll, was created because "five bills had been introduced in the eight-sixth Congress, 2nd session, which proposed substantial modification of the National Security Act of 1947 (Amended)."[25] Burke believed that the legislative furor was caused by

Figure 8-2. Admiral Arleigh A. Burke, 1959. In the six years Burke was CNO, the Navy began shifting from analog to digital technology, turned its larger aircraft carriers into nuclear strike platforms, developed nuclear-powered surface ships, and pioneered operational-level antisubmarine warfare.
(National Archives 428-KN 573)

an Air University study of defense organization and by an Air Force "Black Book" written for senior officers by the Air Staff. OP-06D thought that the Air Force intended to make one final push for service unification, but with proposals unlike those of 1947 or 1949. Instead, the Secretary of Defense would set the stage for unification with administrative changes, only asking for congressional approval after merger of the services was largely a fact.[26] It was one reason why Burke strongly opposed creating the Joint Strategic Target Planning Staff—he viewed it as part of a more sweeping package, the end result of which would be Air Force domination of the military services.

Burke ordered Knoll to send weekly papers and letters to journalists sympathetic to the Navy's cause and Navy-oriented material to major public relations groups, expressing forcefully "what the Navy stands for and what the Navy will do."[27] Knoll also corresponded with many reserve and retired Navy personnel throughout the nation, asking them to "follow closely the public utterances of political candidates for national office and leading citizens in your area, and forward (direct to OP-06D as expeditiously as possible) a brief on what they are saying." As Knoll put it, his correspondents could "provide us in Washington with timely information concerning what we might expect when the New Congress convenes in January."[28] Not all recipients of this plea agreed that it was the proper procedure for the Navy Department to follow. One letter, which Knoll preserved, came back sharp:

> Are we . . . to become Gallup Pollers [sic] to give strength of statistics to lobbying representatives of the Navy in the congressional corridors? This would seem to be a gross misuse of the men and funds appropriated to the Navy by that same Congress. I will not use the Navy mails to send this sort of information to you unless you reply with some justification I have not foreseen.[29]

Knoll did not have a good answer to this complaint. He could not. He was fighting fire with fire.

Burke and Knoll had reason to be concerned. The political party platforms of both presidential candidates in 1960 called for a more efficient defense organization, and the Democrats at their convention supported wholesale changes. In September 1960, John F. Kennedy, the Democratic nominee, chose Senator Stuart Symington (D-MO), the Air Force Secretary during the unification hearings in the late 1940s, to head a committee on defense reorganization. In response, Burke ordered the Navy's JAG to draft a response to what Burke thought the Symington Committee might produce. In October the JAG study, "Reorganization of the Department of Defense: Philosophy and Counter-Philosophy," was circulated in OPNAV. The JAG's position was that "any tendency to resist fundamental reorganization through attacks on the Air Force or response to the 'sinister conspiracy' theory not only misconstrues the basic issues, but may well bring about the very results which we seek to avoid."[30] The key issue was the relationship between "organizational problems" and "strategic problems. They cannot and must not be separated at any point."[31] Therefore, the Air Force favored unification, according to the JAG study, because of its approach to strategic warfare. Because the Navy considered that approach erroneous, the Navy opposed unification—not simply because the Air Force favored unification.

In an October 1960 conference at the Pentagon, CNO Burke evaluated the JAG study. He criticized it for taking too long to make its important points and for containing "too much Air Force Phraseology."[32] In short, it was not partisan enough. The JAG responded that his study group had concluded that the only alternative to unification was "increasingly effective civilian control vested in the Secretary of Defense." Those at the conference took up the issue of the Navy's optimal strategy. Was the JAG's conclusion correct? The alternatives were as follows: (1) to increase the powers of some collective body instead of just those of the Secretary of Defense; (2) to go on the offensive against the Air Force by suggesting that the Tactical Air Command be given to the Army; (3) to give the Secretary of Defense more influence, but reduce the size of his office staff; and (4) to advocate a single chief of staff to counterbalance the powers of the Secretary of Defense. The conference rejected these alternatives. As the legal counsel to the Secretary of the Navy pointed out, "The Navy's greatest concern right now is to prevent another major DOD reorganization, or at least postpone it, for the Navy's position is stronger now than it has been for years and getting stronger all the time."[33]

Burke was not happy with a delaying strategy; that was not his style. The Navy was let off the hook, however, when the Symington Committee reported to the President-elect that December. The committee recommended eliminating the military departments and service secretaries, replacing the Assistant Secretaries of Defense with two powerful undersecretaries, one each for weapons and administration, and substituting a single chief of staff for the JCS.[34] The report was seen as so extreme that it was largely ignored, and efforts in Congress to promote changes in defense administration fizzled. But CNO Burke well understood that the Secretary of Defense already had enough authority to reshape the Defense Department. The question was whether the next secretary would do it.

Burke's Tenure Reviewed

Burke's tenure as CNO lasted six years. When he was appointed CNO in 1955, OPNAV had just begun long-range force planning. Burke gave more influence to that planning process by linking it to Navy programming, the procedure by which operational requirements for new systems were translated into development goals for the Navy's bureaus. By linking programming to long-range planning and by giving OPNAV planning responsibility, Burke kept the leadership of Navy force development in OPNAV, which he dominated. The increased influence of planning should not have surprised anyone. The producer/consumer distinction was really a product of World War II, when the short-term and urgent production of men and machines was in fact the major job of the bureaus, led by the Under Secretary of the Navy, and OPNAV. After the war, however, the Navy's needs changed. Systematic long-range force planning became the only way the Navy could anticipate technological and strategic changes and respond effectively to such changes. The cost of weapons and sensors grew more expensive in the 1950s, and getting ships and planes from the design stage to actual delivery in the fleet took longer. The relative scarcity of funds, time, and even personnel made long-range planning essential.

One very real problem with long-range planning was that it was a potentially powerful process. Consequently, questions such as, "Who will the planners be?" or "Which OPNAV office will plan?" or "How will plans be converted into specific programs?" were contentious. For that reason CNOs Carney and Burke placed their long-range planners in OP-93 (Long Range Objectives Group) close to the CNO. The proximity to Burke meant that planners had greater visibility at the highest levels. Eventually, long-range force level planning rivaled, and then superseded, war planning as a place for younger flag officers to make names for themselves.[35]

It is also important to remember that long-range planning could not be done effectively in a vacuum, isolated from the operations-oriented parts of OPNAV. The deputy chiefs acted as the key links to the bureaus and to the fleet. No planner who thought in terms of programs could ignore them. Indeed, turning plans into programs was impossible without including them in the process. But including the deputy chiefs made the programming side of force planning a consultative, pluralistic, interactive process—more a matter of coordination than direction, more a political process than one of command. The necessary emphasis on long-range planning gave the CNO an opportunity to lead the programming process. Whether he did or not was his choice, dependent on his skills.

By the end of Burke's third term (summer 1961), the program planning process within OPNAV was fairly comprehensive. The Director of the Long Range Objectives Group was responsible for projecting Navy missions and force requirements for 10 to 15 years. Guidance for OP-93 emanated from the CNO Advisory Board, whose membership included the Vice Chief of Naval Operations (chair), the director of OP-93, the deputy chiefs, the Assistant Commandant of the Marine Corps, the head of the Office of Naval Material, the Assistant Chief of Naval Operations for General Planning (OP-90), and the Director of Naval Administration (an assistant CNO). As "the most influential body in the military requirements determinations and programming cycle," the advisory board evaluated "strategic concepts, research requirements and material and logistic readiness requirements."[36]

Directed by the CNO Advisory Board, OP-93 produced two plans: Long Range Requirements, for the next 10–15 years, and Long Range Objectives, reasonable goals for fulfilling the requirements. The next step in the process rested with the ACNO for General Planning. Working from the Long Range Objectives, his office drew up guidelines for the deputy chiefs to follow as they put together their program objectives for the next fiscal year and for the nine years thereafter. Another Burke creation, the Program Evaluation Center, tracked the progress of the deputy chiefs and conducted "analyses of approved naval objectives; analysis, measurement of progress and display of approved programs of the Department of the Navy and evaluations of the impact of decisions and alternatives on program requirements."[37]

In the next step of program planning, DCNO planning staffs developed operational requirements based on the guidelines prepared by OP-90. Planning directorates and sometimes operations analysis groups of OP-01 (Personnel), OP-03 (Fleet Operations), OP-04 (Logistics), OP-05 (Air), and OP-07 (Development) worked with the Program Evaluation Center in OP-90. The deputy chiefs proceeded collectively from general force requirements, projected by OP-93, and fiscally constrained objectives, developed by OP-93, to program objectives, with performance milestones attached, prepared by the staffs of the DCNOs. They forwarded their milestone requirements to the bureaus, where line managers entered detailed cost figures for each requirement. The link between the deputy chiefs and the bureaus was a group of officers called "program coordinators"—Navy captains and commanders who ensured that the detailed plans drawn up by the bureaus remained faithful to the program objectives worked out by the DCNOs.[38]

The Navy's civilian leadership participated in the program planning process in several ways. First, the Secretary of the Navy chaired a top-level policy council, whose members included the under secretary, the CNO, the VCNO, and the Marine Corps commandant. This group met at least every week to review Navy plans and policies. Second, the secretary used his Office of Analysis and Review to monitor Navy programs. Third, the comptroller reported Navy expenditures directly to the secretary, so the secretary could monitor the consequences of Navy program actions. Finally, the Program Evaluation Center in OP-90 reported simultaneously to the Navy secretary, the CNO, and the Marine Corps commandant.[39] The secretary's office was also the Navy's link to Congress. The assistant secretaries reported to Congress via the secretary in areas such as manpower, financial management, research and development, and procurement. Except through the CNO, however, the Secretary of the Navy did not participate in major Navy force structure decisions.

Burke developed the organization of program planning over time. The first Long Range Requirements document, for example, was not produced until April 1960. It took time because Burke had to reconcile his command philosophy, which emphasized decentralization, with a program planning system that was centralized. Burke described his approach to command as "management at the lowest possible competent level . . . [s]o that, in the ideal situation, with . . . competent people and experience up and down the line, the top of the organization makes policy decisions, only."[40] That philosophy was consistent with his experience as a line officer and a bureau (Ordnance) manager. But the need to do serious program planning, coupled with the need to do battle with the proponents of unification and those hostile to the Navy's strategic role, forced Burke to shape OPNAV more like a *personal* staff—in short, to do what Burke criticized the Army and Air Force for already having done. The centralization of the Army staff system insinuated itself upon OPNAV despite Burke's efforts to keep the programming activity open to ideas from officers fresh from the fleet. For example, he classified both the Long Range Requirements and the Long Range Objectives no higher than Secret, so that OPNAV's junior officers could see and comment on them.

Burke was able to make OPNAV a staff, yet keep it Navy, because of his own fierce dedication and hard work. Rosenberg quoted Burke's comments on fatigue: ". . . you get very tired. It takes a lot of stamina for that job. You work seven days a week and you're lucky if you can get seven hours sleep a night."[41] In OPNAV, Burke's energy and time were spent leading and pushing the program planning process that he had devised. As the Assistant Secretary of Defense (Comptroller) noted in November 1961, "the making of critical decisions in the

Navy (e.g., force structure) involves the collective participation of the entire CNO organization." The comptroller also observed that the CNO and the Secretary of the Navy more often *approved* than *decided:* "The real decision-making occurs during the collective process of staffing, review, approval, and agreement as the development of the planning document proceeds from stage to stage."[42] The danger of such a system was apparent to Burke: officers outside senior leadership positions could in fact influence major decisions without bearing a commensurate share of responsibility for those decisions. But that was a danger unavoidable in any complex organization. The benefit of such a system was that it tapped the multiple sources of expertise within the organization.

Conclusion

Arleigh A. Burke was an extraordinary Chief of Naval Operations. He held that office for six years, *despite* differing with the very experienced and accomplished President Eisenhower on the important issue of defense organization. The comedian Bob Hope is supposed to have quipped that "of course the President found golf very relaxing. That's understandable. Only someone who had been through World War II would find golf relaxing." There was something to this bit of humor. Both Eisenhower and Burke had spent time as senior officers under very great pressure. Both had come through their experiences as military leaders convinced that those experiences had offered them vital clues about how to lead large organizations in an emergency, and both Burke and Eisenhower saw the Cold War of the mid-1950s as a state of emergency.[43] At the same time, both leaders wanted subordinates who could work extremely hard and take the initiative. Burke could certainly do that. He and his Navy did not need careful tending, and Eisenhower, determined as he was to keep the Soviet Union contained while avoiding nuclear war, knew that and counted on it.[44]

Ideally, the Navy's military and civilian leaders should have taken time after World War II to sort through the lessons of leadership, management, and organization that war experience had highlighted. They could have said to one another, "Here's what we did under the pressure of war. What worked and what didn't, and what can we do about it?" The General Board did just that sort of thing in 1919, and the board tried to do it again after the end of World War II. But there was too much happening after the war to calmly review the wartime experiences of CNO King, the Navy's commanders at sea, and the OPNAV staff. Robert Connery put it very well in 1951:

> Few of the men who held posts of responsibility during the war years are still left in the Navy's organization, and in not so many years at best, there will be only a handful of them available for active duty. It is not to particular individuals, therefore, but primarily to a sound administrative structure, efficient administrative procedures, and good personnel practices that the Navy must look in the future.[45]

As it happened, however, it was "particular individuals," veterans of the war years, that had to take on the post–war world—Eisenhower, for example, and Carney and Burke, and SECNAV Thomas Gates. They did in fact try to create the structure, procedures, and practices that Connery described. They were sometimes aided by Congress and by various special committees such as the Hoover Commission, as well as by officers and civilians in and out of the Pentagon. Eventually, by the end of the 1950s, they had created a national security administration—most prominently the Office of the Secretary of Defense, the Central Intelligence Agency, and the National Security Council—designed to eliminate the worst sorts of command problems that had bedeviled President Franklin Roosevelt and his subordinates. Yet for the Navy, what mattered again and again in all of the activity that characterized the late 1940s and 1950s was the personality, energy, and resourcefulness of CNO Admiral Arleigh Burke.

Notes

[1] John R. Wadleigh, "Thomas Sovereign Gates Jr.," in Coletta, *American Secretaries of the Navy, vol. 2*, 883.

[2] Memo for the Record, subj: Chronology–Reorganization Act of 1958, 30 Aug. 1961, folder 33, 1958 Bills–DOD Reorganization, box 3, Chief of Naval Operations (CNO), Deputy Chief of Naval Operations (DCNO) (Plans, Policies and Operations) Strategy, Plans and Policy Division (hereafter OP-602 File, Archives of the Naval History and Heritage Command (NHHC). For Eisenhower's views, see Stephen E. Ambrose, *Eisenhower, vol. 2, The President* (New York, 1984), 428.

[3] Memo for the Record, 1 June 1961, subj: Appointment of Rep. Paul Kilday to Court of Military Appeals, folder 49, DOD Reorganization–1961, box 3, OP-602 File, NHHC Archives.

[4] Rosenberg, "Arleigh Albert Burke," in Love, *The Chiefs of Naval Operations*, 280–82.

[5] Ibid., 302.

[6] Ibid., 303.

[7] Ibid., 303–304. ADM Burke had to accept the concept of joint strategic targeting, but he did shield Polaris missile targeting from the Strategic Air Command by placing that function under the Commander-in-Chief Atlantic (CINCLANT) and then moving the commander of submarines in the Atlantic from New London, Connecticut, to Norfolk, Virginia, to support CINCLANT. He also made sure that Navy participants on the Joint Strategic Targeting Planning Staff were highly qualified officers. Email, Paul Stillwell to Thomas C. Hone, subj: "Burke Chapter," 28 Mar. 2016. Paul Stillwell has compiled the oral histories of many senior officers from the Burke years and after. His email was based on several of those oral histories.

[8] Department of the Navy, "Staff Study on Organization of the Office of the Chief of Naval Operations" (A. L. Reed Study), 5430 OPNAV/OP–00, 1–2, Aug. 43–Dec. 61 folder, OPNAV Historical Records, Organization and OPNAV Resource Management Division (OP-09B2), Pentagon (hereafter OP–09B2 Records). Note, the functions of OP-092B2 are in DNS-33 in 2017.

[9] Ibid., 2.

[10] Ibid.

[11] Ibid., 3.

[12] Ibid., 5.

[13] Ibid., 6.

[14] Ibid., 7.

[15] Department of the Navy, *Report of the Committee on Organization of the Department of the Navy* (Franke Board Report) (Washington, DC, 1959), 17–37, 56–58.

[16] Wadleigh, "Thomas Sovereign Gates Jr.," in Coletta, *American Secretaries of the Navy*, vol. 2, 888.

[17] Memo, OPNAV Ad Hoc Committee to Review the Navy Department Organization to Burke, 25 July 1958, subj: Preliminary Report, 3, folder 70, box 3, OP-602 File, NHHC Archives.

[18] Edwin B. Hooper, "Draft to Form the Basis of a Possible Study on Navy Department Reorganization," Navy Department Library, NHHC.

[19] Memo, Leverton to Burke, 19 June 1959, subj: Chief of Bureau of Weapons, folder 39, DOD Reorganization–1959, box 1, OP-602 File, NHHC Archives. The memo is unsigned, but it was apparently written on the same typewriter used for other memos prepared by CAPT Joseph W. Leverton, and is stored with other papers written and signed by Leverton.

[20] "ADM Hopwood's Three Fleet Concept for the Pacific," folder 12, CINCPACFLT–1948–DATE, box 3, OP-602 File, NHHC Archives.

[21] Memo, Burke to OP–06, DCNO (Plans and Policy), OP-00 Memo 511–59, 2 Oct. 1959, subj: Revised Joint Table of Distribution for CINCPAC Staff, folder C22, Command in the Pacific, vol. 1, OP-602 File, NHHC Archives.

[22] Memos, unsigned, but probably meant for CNO Burke, 9 Apr. 1959, subj: Dealing out of Channels; OPNAV Opinion, 6 Apr. 1959, folder 39, box 1, OP-602 File, NHHC Archives. Both memos appear to have been written on CAPT Leverton's typewriter.

[23] Ltr, Burke to Schindler, 5 Oct. 1959, subj: Organization of the Dept. of Defense, folder 39, box 1, OP-602 File, NHHC Archives.

[24] "The Need for a Look at DOD Organization," OP-06D, ser 109P06D, 15 May 1961, folder 49, DOD Reorganization–1961, box 1, Organizational files, OP-602 File, NHHC Archives.

[25] Ibid.

[26] "Symington Committee Report to Senator Kennedy on Defense Reorganization–Brief of Legislative Versus Administrative Changes," folder 50, Monograph: DOD Reorganization, box 3, OP-602 File, NHHC Archives.

[27] Knoll, Memo for the Record, "Meeting with Admiral Burke on 15 August," OP-06D, 16 Aug. 1960, folder 41, DOD Reorganization, 1 Jan.–30 Sept. 1960, box 2, OP-602 File, NHHC Archives.

[28] Ltr, Knoll to address list, 8 Aug. 1960, subj: Following the Presidential Campaign, folder 41, box 2, OP-602 File, NHHC Archives.

[29] Ltr, Andrew Hoyem, CO, USN&MCRTC, to Knoll, 19 Aug. 1960, subj: Response to Knoll's Letter of 8 Aug. folder 41, box 2, OP-602 File, NHHC Archives.

[30] "Reorganization of the Department of Defense: Philosophy and Counter–Philosophy," A–14, folder 45, JAG Studies on DOD Reorganization–1960, box 3, OP-602 File, NHHC Archives.

[31] Ibid., A–15.

[32] Memorandum to the File, 10 October 1960 meeting of CNO Burke and aides, 12 Oct. 1960, para. 4, folder 49, box 1, OP-602 File, NHHC Archives.

[33] Ibid., para. 15.

[34] Memo, Acting Deputy Chief of Legislative Affairs, Navy Department, to SECNAV, CNO, and Commandant of the Marine Corps, 7 Dec. 1960, subj: Report to Senator Kennedy from Committee on the Defense Establishment, Historical Evolution folder, box 1, OP-602 File, NHHC Archives.

[35] A number of future CNOs and VCNOs served as Long-Range Planning chiefs or heads of OP-96 (Systems Analysis), including ADMs Thomas H. Moorer, Elmo R. Zumwalt Jr., and Horacio Rivero.

[36] OASD (Comptroller), "Department of the Navy, Organization and Decision–Making Study," 3 Nov. 1961, Executive Summary, 12, Historical Evolution folder, box 1, OP–602 File, NHHC Archives.

[37] Ibid., 19.

[38] Ibid., 13.

[39] Ibid., 19.

[40] Arnold R. Shapack, ed., *Proceedings Naval History Symposium*, U.S. Naval Academy 27–28 Apr. 1973 (Annapolis, MD, 1973), 90.

[41] Rosenberg, "Arleigh Albert Burke," in Love, *The Chiefs of Naval Operations*, 297.

[42] OASD (Comptroller), "Department of the Navy, Organization and Decision-Making Study," Summary, 46–47.

[43] Stephen E. Ambrose, *Eisenhower, Vol. II: The President* (New York: Simon & Schuster, 2014).

[44] See 28–37 in Recollections of Admiral Arleigh A. Burke, USN (Ret.), Years 1955 to 1961, Naval Historical Center (now the Naval History and Heritage Command), in *Navy/Chiefs of Naval Operation/Commandants of the Marine Corps, 1951–1985*, compiled by Bernard F. Cavalcante, 2000, in the Navy Department Library. Early in his time as CNO, Burke won the confidence of President Eisenhower, and Eisenhower would sometimes invite Burke to the White House for a drink and a talk about some matter the President was dealing with. Burke didn't have to agree with the President. He only had to speak his mind. Eisenhower trusted him.

[45] Connery, *The Navy and the Industrial Mobilization in World War II*, 432.

CHAPTER 9

The McNamara Revolution

Introduction

President John F. Kennedy took office with an aggressive foreign-policy agenda. He made that very clear in his inaugural address, when he said, "Let every nation know, whether it wishes us well or ill, that we shall pay any price, bear any burden, meet any hardship, support any friend, oppose any foe to assure the survival and the success of liberty." At the same time, he characterized the United States and the Soviet Union as "overburdened by the cost of modern weapons, both rightly alarmed by the steady spread of the deadly atom, yet both racing to alter that uncertain balance of terror that stays the hand of mankind's final war." His rhetoric proposed a solution to this dilemma: Both nations should "begin anew the quest for peace, before the dark powers of destruction unleashed by science engulf all humanity in planned or accidental self-destruction."[1]

    This combination of toughness and apparent reasonableness was a hallmark of the Kennedy administration. It required a new approach to defense. Whereas the Eisenhower administration had relied on an implicit threat to use nuclear weapons to constrain the political and territorial ambitions of the Soviet Union, the Kennedy administration favored a more "flexible" approach, combining a limiting of the U.S. nuclear arsenal with bilateral nuclear arms control and a simultaneous investment in U.S. "conventional" forces. In the 1950s, the bulk of defense investment went to the Air Force and the Navy. Now defense spending would increase, and much of the increase would go to the Army, especially Army Special Forces. Yet the new administration was nevertheless committed publicly and privately to holding down the cost of national defense.

Robert McNamara: A Strong Defense Secretary

Consequently, when President Kennedy appointed Robert S. McNamara Secretary of Defense in 1961, he instructed him to increase the effectiveness of the nation's armed forces—especially the strategic nuclear forces—without spending significantly more funds. Representative George H. Mahon (D-TX), chairman of the Defense Appropriations Subcommittee of the House Appropriations Committee, had already encouraged the Defense Department to adopt a mission approach to defense programming and budgeting, and McNamara knew that Charles J. Hitch and Hitch's colleagues at the RAND Corporation were conducting research in the field.[2] At the same time, Congress was waiting to see how McNamara would use the authority granted his office by the 1958 Department of Defense Reorganization Act. McNamara was under pressure from both the President and the Congress to create a stronger, more effective military force and simultaneously economize on the defense budget. McNamara thought he could do both, and as part of his effort to achieve these goals, he instituted the Planning, Programming, and Budgeting System (PPBS).

Secretary McNamara believed that "the role of the public manager is very similar to the role of a private manager; in each case he has the option of following one of two major alternative courses of action. He can either act as a judge or a leader." If a judge, then "he sits and waits until subordinates bring him problems for solution, or alternatives for choice." If a leader, then "he immerses himself in the operations of the business or the governmental activity, examines the problems, the objectives, the alternative courses of action, chooses among them and leads the organization to their accomplishment."[3] McNamara intended to be a leader.[4]

But how could he do that in an organization as large and diverse as the DOD? The answer was by creating and then using a new financial management system—PPBS. McNamara appointed Charles Hitch as Defense comptroller in 1961, and Hitch proposed devoting "18 months developing and installing [PPBS], beginning in the first year with a limited number of trial programs, with a view to expanding the system to include all programs during 1962. The Secretary approved the proposed system but shortened my timetable from 18 months to 6."[5]

The Planning, Programming, and Budgeting System (PPBS)

What was PPBS? Hitch defined it as a "financial management system" that provided "the data needed by top Defense management to make the really crucial decisions, particularly on the major forces and weapon systems needed to carry out the principal missions of the Defense establishment."[6] When McNamara and Hitch moved into the Pentagon, they agreed that there was only a very weak link between the planning done by the military staffs in the services and the budget preparation done by the civilians working for the service secretaries and the SecDef. As Hitch put it, "Planning was performed in terms of missions, weapon systems, and military units or forces—the "outputs" of the Defense Department; budgeting . . . was done in terms of such "inputs" or intermediate products [such] as personnel, operation and maintenance, procurement, construction, etc.; and there was little or no machinery for translating one into the other." If the two functions (planning and budgeting) were not effectively tied together, then planning would remain unrealistic and budgeting would be the only tool for forcing the military staffs to recognize "fiscal realities."[7]

Moreover—and making matters worse and not better—the SecDef "each year found himself in a position where he had, at least implicitly, to make major decisions on forces and programs without adequate information and all within the few weeks allocated to his budget review."[8] The result was a rush to fit the service budgets under the president's budget ceiling for the coming fiscal year. The solution to this problem was a uniform programming process throughout the Defense Department. The SecDef and his staff would have to provide guidance to the military planners at the beginning of the process, the programmers would have to shape their short-term and long-term spending by the plans produced in conformity with the secretary's high-level guidance, and the budget officers would translate the programming numbers into the numbers used by Congress. If Secretary McNamara and Comptroller Hitch could define "program" in a meaningful way, then senior defense executives could look across separate service programs and apply cost-effectiveness analysis to improve the overall defense program.

As Hitch explained, McNamara "would have to know in order to optimize the allocation of resources, the cost of, for example, a B-52 wing—not only the cost of equipping the wing but also the cost of manning and operating it for its lifetime or at least for a reasonable period of years in the future. Only then would he be in a position to assess the cost and effectiveness of a B-52 wing as compared with other systems designed to perform the same or similar tasks."[9] The Five Year Force Structure and Financial Program, later called the Five Year Defense Program (FYDP), emerged from this effort to relate mission to cost.

But creating an analytical management process inside the Defense Department was only part of what McNamara and Hitch achieved. As Hitch testified before Congress, "the functional arrangement of the budget [i.e., the one used by Congress] . . . does not focus on forces and military programs in relation to missions, the key decision-making area of principal concern to top management in the Defense Department."[10] That meant the defense program had to be turned into a budget proposal that aligned with the congressional authorization and appropriations processes.

What linked data from program categories with that from the categories used in Congress was the concept of Total Obligational Authority, defined as "the full cost of an annual increment of a program regardless of the year in which the funds [were] authorized, appropriated, or expended."[11] By dividing each major program, such as strategic forces, into basic elements, such as the Polaris ballistic missile/nuclear-powered submarine combination, McNamara and Hitch could determine how much that element cost in terms of personnel, operations and maintenance, and procurement. They could also decide how much each element contributed to the overall program (strategic forces, or nuclear deterrence) over a five-year period. Under Burke, program planning in OPNAV had not been directly linked to the budgeting process because the budget categories did not coincide with program categories, which were stated in terms of force structure. McNamara and Hitch deliberately changed that, and Navy leaders had to accept PPBS despite the fact that it displaced their own methods of programming. But what really concerned military service chiefs was Secretary McNamara's use of cost-effectiveness studies, conducted by his own Directorate of Systems Analysis, in determining which service systems were approved by the SecDef and included in the overall defense budget sent to Congress.[12]

A classic example of programming in action was McNamara's recommendation to President Kennedy in November 1962 regarding fiscal year (FY) 1964 through FY 1968 strategic nuclear retaliatory forces. The Air Force and Navy wanted to increase the number of air-launched missiles and ballistic missiles with nuclear warheads from 1,074 in 1961 to 5,227 in 1968. That increase would push the megatons of explosive power in the U.S. strategic nuclear arsenal from 1,771 to 8,851. McNamara recommended to the President that the number of warheads be reduced from 5,227 to 3,568, thereby shrinking the projected megatons of explosive power from 8,851 to 6,577. McNamara's argument was that "the extra capability provided by the individual Service proposals runs up against strongly diminishing returns and yields very little in terms of extra target destruction. In my judgement, it is an increment not worth the cost of $12.5 billion over the five year period."[13] This sort of analysis was what some influential members of Congress had been asking for—a force structure based on an assessment of what was needed to perform a specific mission (in this case, to provide a secure nuclear retaliatory force).

PPBS was a major shock for the services, but not because it brought the concept of programming to military administration. The shock came from McNamara's claim that his office could and would define program categories across service boundaries, monitor the services in meeting program goals, and, if necessary, enforce service compliance with the secretary's policies.[14] The Office of the Secretary of Defense put into place standard operating procedures that gave OSD both the initiative and the power of review in the programming and budgeting process. In effect, this management system allowed McNamara and his deputies to shape the planning and programming of organizations like OPNAV. According to historian David Rosenberg, "Burke felt that he was never able to find out just what it was that McNamara believed in or wanted to accomplish as Secretary of Defense."[15] Was it any wonder? What Burke and his colleagues had already created in their separate service staffs McNamara would have to control if he were to act as the leader he intended to be.

The Response to McNamara: Secretariat and CNO

The memory of McNamara's management style is fading now, but his ideas, attitudes, and methods colored every aspect of defense decision making during the years he was SecDef. Indeed, McNamara was so convinced that his concepts and procedures of defense management were correct that he deliberately kept forceful personalities out of service chief and service secretary positions, and he moved ruthlessly against those military officers who criticized his authority. In the Navy's case, historian Paul Schratz observed: "McNamara also wished to prevent the naval leadership from undercutting his authority via a traditional end run to a sympathetic naval ear

The McNamara Revolution

in the White House. The naval secretary's chair, therefore, required ... the least enthusiastic Kennedy supporter in government."[16] That meant the man who had managed Senator Lyndon Johnson's campaign for the Democratic Party's presidential nomination in 1960, John B. Connally Jr.

Burke's successor as Chief of Naval Operations was Admiral George W. Anderson Jr., an aviator with extensive command and joint staff experience. He barely made it through one two-year term (1961–1963) as CNO because he angered the SecDef twice: first, privately, during the blockade of Cuba in October 1962; and then, publicly, in congressional testimony against McNamara's controversial proposal for a multiservice fighter plane, the TFX.[17] CNO Anderson regarded McNamara as an obstacle to sound decision-making by the President. As he said, "[T]he President needs good advice administratively, economically, politically, as well as military. I think when you have dominant people like McNamara playing, they throw the whole thing off balance."[18]

Despite public and private criticism, the SecDef kept the bureaucratic initiative. Once PPBS was in place, he avoided naming service secretaries who might challenge its suitability. "McNamara saw a strong, analytical type of service secretary" could become a "rallying point for service loyalties" and "hence a divisive threat to his own exercise of authority."[19] The secretary's actions were aimed at preventing the services from challenging his control. For example, McNamara chose not to release the original studies of Defense Department management, undertaken right after the Kennedy administration entered the White House.[20] Moreover, the continuous administrative changes emanating from McNamara's office kept the services off balance. As Assistant Secretary of Defense for Administration Sol Horwitz said in an interview: "Not only is the Defense structure highly dynamic, it is safe to say that it will continue to be highly dynamic.... A static condition would be a certain sign of management stagnation."[21] Although a faith in reorganization was a tenet of modern management; the process of redistributing responsibility and authority was (and remains) a tool for keeping the opposition from coalescing.

Secretary Connally's replacement (Connally had resigned to run for governor of Texas), Fred H. Korth, responded to the changes emanating

Figure 9-1. CNO George W. Anderson Jr., on the bridge of *Enterprise* (CVAN-65). Anderson was commander of the Sixth Fleet when President John F. Kennedy chose him as Admiral Burke's successor. Anderson thought he might be nominated to be the next Chairman of the Joint Chiefs of Staff after serving two years as CNO. However, he did not get along with Secretary of Defense Robert S. McNamara and was forced to retire after two years as CNO.
(National Archives 428-KN 13115)

from McNamara's office by appointing John S. Dillon, a career assistant to Navy secretaries since 1947, chairman of a board of inquiry. Composed of uniformed and civilian officials drawn from the Navy Department, the Dillon Board examined internal Navy management and policymaking and external influences that affected Navy decisions. In six months of study (June through November 1962), the Dillon Board reviewed the management of the Navy Department and specifically recommended changes that would foster a more effective organization for OPNAV and the Navy secretariat.

With regard to OSD, the Dillon Board's *External Environmental Influences Study* took a long-standing Navy position that the Secretary of Defense was encroaching on service prerogatives. However, the "consolidation of decision making is being accomplished not by the reorganization of existing components but by requiring the presentation of detailed information so that it can be evaluated and acted upon at top levels."[22] The Dillon Board viewed programming as "the primary tool of both financial management and military management."[23] Expressed another way, "the management information system must be designed to account not only for the traditional documents of obligation and expenditure, but must consider many other events that provide controls over the physical aspects of the projected military structure."[24] In short, McNamara was indeed taking over.

The Dillon Board concluded that the Navy would have to change its internal management to respond to McNamara's aggressive use of program budgeting and analysis. However, the services were not the only institutions that felt threatened by the new budget process. The armed services and appropriations committees of Congress also feared that PPBS was reducing their control over defense policy and expenditures. The appropriations committees believed that the traditional congressional budget categories (e.g., operations and maintenance, research and development), were no longer adequate to give Congress real control over military force structure. The armed services committees, by contrast, feared that their traditional control over force structure and composition was being transferred to the appropriations committees because of PPBS. Accordingly, the armed services committees required the services to get their permission annually to purchase aircraft, missiles, or ships. Concerned that McNamara had taken complete control over defense planning, Congress retaliated by ignoring McNamara and demanding information from the military services. As the Dillon Board recognized, the need to give both OSD *and* Congress the data they demanded placed a new burden on OPNAV.

According to a Dillon study, the Navy found it difficult to respond to OSD and congressional pressures because the Navy was not well enough organized internally. The board's *Planning, Programming, Budget, and Appraising Study* reported that "all bureaus have established their own internal programs, which in most cases do not coincide with programs identified in the OSD program system or the OPNAV system. Bureau programs are generally more closely associated to the appropriation structure than to the OSD program structure."[25] Put another way, the bureaus were still oriented toward Congress. Moreover, the Assistant Chief of Naval Operations for General Planning and Programming (OP-90) "does not have direction authority for the over-all programming process with respect to major Departmental components, or within the Office of the Chief of Naval Operations."[26] Yet OP-90 was responsible for submitting the Navy's programming data to the Office of the Secretary of Defense. If OSD held the Navy accountable to the program choices made by the SecDef, then the Navy's civilian and military leaders would have to create a programming office with more authority to meet OSD's demands. McNamara was forcing versions of his management institutions on the services.

Secretary Korth's initial response to this situation was to create, in July 1963, the Office of Program Appraisal (OPA) within the secretariat. Rear Admiral Draper L. Kauffman was appointed OPA's first director. Kauffman was not new to the Pentagon. He had held posts in both OPNAV and the Joint Staff, and he had spent two years as an aide to former SECNAV Gates. However, Kauffman quickly realized that the responsibilities—and powers—of the new OPA were very broad. His first impulse was to tell Secretary Korth that OPA belonged within OPNAV, but he knew that Korth wanted what he sometimes referred to as "the Navy's System Analysis Division" in his own office.[27] OPA's charter stated that the office existed to "assist" the Secretary of the Navy "in assuring that existing and proposed Navy and Marine Corps programs provide the optimum means of achieving the objectives of the Department of the Navy and that approved programs are executed in a timely, effective, and economic manner."

This was a very broad mandate, and it included doing the following:

- Analyzing Navy Department objectives "and the validity, adequacy, feasibility, and balance of proposed programs" so that the Secretary could "assess the overall direction and priority of efforts" in the Department.[28]
- "Conduct or provide the guidelines for and coordinate special studies as requested by the Secretary of the Navy and his civilian executive assistants, *including projects for the Secretary of Defense.*"[29] [emphasis added]
- ". . . obtain, analyze, and present timely and complete data on the status of approved" Navy programs, "so that performance against service requirements and objectives may be evaluated."[30]
- "Administer for the Secretary of the Navy the [Defense Department] program-change control system within the Department of the Navy."[31]
- "Review and evaluate the responsiveness of the Navy Programming system in meeting the needs of the Secretary and present recommendations as required."[32]
- "Ensure that the analytical capability and the necessary information are available to permit a knowledgeable view of the cost and effectiveness of both proposed and approved programs."[33]
- "Prepare such other analyses, statements and reports as the Secretary may direct."[34]

When Vice Admiral William R. Smedberg III, chief of the Bureau of Naval Personnel (BuPers), read the charter, he phoned Kauffman and said, "Draper, if you have a friend left in uniform two years from now, it will prove to me that you have done a lousy job."[35]

Secretary Korth was McNamara's agent. With the creation of OPA, Kauffman became Korth's. How could this work without generating intense friction between Kauffman and the senior officers in OPNAV? Kauffman knew he had to find a way. If he didn't, the actions of OPA would either be irrelevant or simply add to the frustration the CNO and his deputies felt over the implementation of PPBS. Thinking back on it 15 years later, Kauffman explained how he solved this dilemma. First, he deliberately kept OPA small so that it could not get into too many issues. As he noted, "A large staff would permit us to sin more frequently and to a greater extent than we could with a small staff."[36]

Second, the VCNO, Admiral Claude V. Ricketts, worked with Kauffman to set up OPA. As Kauffman recalled, Admiral Ricketts came up with "a modus operandi for [OPA] that really worked quite well." It was to make OPA a liaison office between the OPNAV staff and the secretariat staff, reducing friction between the two organizations. In addition, Ricketts made sure that senior officers in OPNAV did not see OPA as a threat to their own authorities.[37]

Third, Captains Elmo R. Zumwalt Jr., and Isaac C. Kidd Jr., respectively the executive assistants to Korth's successor Paul H. Nitze and CNO Admiral David L. McDonald, worked very well together, and Kauffman was a close friend of Zumwalt, which created informal and positive links between the secretariat and OPNAV.[38]

Fourth, Kauffman developed a very collegial relationship with Dr. Alain C. Enthoven, a Deputy Assistant Secretary of Defense and PhD in economics whom McNamara had recruited from the RAND Corporation. Unlike many others in the military services, Kauffman regarded Enthoven as "an exceptionally brilliant young man, very gifted." Before setting up OPA, Kauffman spent a week with Enthoven and his team of systems analysts, and later he sent Navy Lieutenant Commander Charles J. di Bona and Captain Stansfield M. Turner to work inside Enthoven's organization.[39]

The creation of OPA reads like something out of a novel. CNO Admiral George W. Anderson Jr., was not going to be given a second two-year term. He and Secretary McNamara did not get along. Not surprisingly, Navy secretary Korth and CNO Anderson "almost literally were not speaking to each other."[40] On 1 August 1963, Anderson was relieved by Admiral David L. McDonald and Korth approved the charter of OPA. Korth and McDonald got along, reducing the tension between the secretary's office and OPNAV. Criticized because of the way he used his influence to return favors to his former business associates, Korth resigned as secretary that November. The way was open for Kauffman and his staff in OPA to build links to the new SECNAV, Paul H. Nitze, McDonald's OPNAV staff, and Enthoven's cadre of systems analysts in McNamara's office. According to Kauffman, that's what happened.

Kauffman was linked informally to Nitze through Zumwalt. Kauffman was linked to McDonald in a similar way through Ricketts and Kidd. Kauffman was also linked to McNamara through Enthoven.[41] It helped a great deal that Enthoven respected Vice Admiral Horacio Rivero Jr., the head of OPNAV's new Program Planning Division (OP-090). CNO McDonald had decided that it would not be wise to leave "systems analysis" to OPA, and he

The McNamara Revolution

Figure 9-2. Vice Admiral David L. McDonald (left), then Sixth Fleet commander, with CNO Admiral George W. Anderson Jr., on McDonald's flagship, cruiser *Springfield* (CLG-7). McDonald was made CNO because he was diplomatic and because his temperament was such that he could avoid confronting Secretary of Defense Robert McNamara. (National Archives USN 711075)

and VCNO Ricketts created OP-090 in the spring of 1964 as OPNAV's central programming office, appointing Admiral Rivero its head.[42] As Kauffman remembered,

> Rivero was at the very least the intellectual equal of anyone in [OPNAV], his judgment was exceptionally sound, and, very important, he knew which battles to fight . . . And, of course, he had a personality that was such that Enthoven and other top people in Defense were delighted to work with him even when they disagreed with him completely.[43]

With Rivero as OP-090, Kauffman was satisfied to have OPA "operate very happily in the shadow of [Rivero] and his people insofar as paralleling Enthoven's office was concerned."[44]

However, as Kauffman admitted, the resulting "very weird procedures that we had to go through to satisfy the Secretary and the Chief of Naval Operations and [his] Staff were very laborious and highly inefficient."[45] Put another way, the relations between the Navy secretariat and OPNAV, influenced as they were by the actions of Secretary of Defense McNamara, were essentially unworkable so long as all the senior people stuck to their formal roles. Perceiving this, uniformed officers such as Kauffman, Ricketts, McDonald, and Rivero engaged in informal and ongoing talks and negotiations with Navy secretaries Korth and Nitze and their immediate uniformed aides (Zumwalt and Kidd). This informal contact was given formal sanction when McDonald and Ricketts created OP-090 and appointed Rivero as its head.

The importance of the many informal relations was emphasized in June 1964, when Navy Secretary Nitze moved CNO McDonald into the office of the Under Secretary of the Navy and moved Under Secretary Paul B. Fay Jr., out. The secretary and the under secretary had adjacent offices and had shared the same bathroom. By moving McDonald into Fay's office, Nitze was sending a signal: The CNO had become his de facto chief of staff. As Rear Admiral Kauffman put it, "No SecNav instruction could possibly increase the power of the CNO as much as a simple maneuver which results in SecNav and CNO using the same head."[46]

Formal organizational relations still mattered, however. In the summer of 1966, CNO McDonald created OP-96, the systems analysis division within OP-090, and made then–Rear Admiral Elmo Zumwalt its director. Under Zumwalt, OP-96 began to conduct a series of systematic studies to identify the factors that should shape the fleet that was going to take shape as the modernized World War II ships were gradually replaced. To aid this effort, Zumwalt recruited Lieutenant Commander di Bona and a team of younger officers, and one of their first projects was to "establish sound, basic characteristics for a large class of replacement destroyers."[47] Another was to assess the potential of surface-to-surface missiles at sea. A third was to study carefully Defense Secretary McNamara's proposal to develop a multipurpose fighter (the TFX, later F-111) that would be used by both the Air Force and the Navy. The story of the often bitter debate over the F-111 has been told in detail elsewhere.[48] The key point here is that OP-96 completed a triad of systems analysis offices—one in the Office of the Secretary of Defense, another (OPA) in the Navy secretariat, and a third (OP-96) in OPNAV.

The Response to McNamara: The Bureaus

Former Secretary of the Navy Forrestal once claimed that the Navy was administered by "mutual consent": "The bureaus have legal existence; they enjoy a mutual independence; they have . . . concrete, well-defined jobs to do. . . . They have also information and they have money. In other words they possess everything which gives purpose, logic, and meaning to action."[49] Burke had acted to reduce bureau independence; McNamara was reducing it further. But technology had already made the bureau system obsolete. As officials in BuShips reported, the relationship between a modern ship's hull and machinery, on the one hand, and its weapons and sensors, on the other, was becoming so intimate and complex that "there is in many cases . . . a complete intermesh of [bureau] responsibilities and in fact no clear responsibility or authority."[50] The Dillon Board understood the cost of maintaining bureau autonomy: "Of the nine DLG's under construction in a recent month, six were behind schedule an average of 6 months each. The estimated additional cost . . . is $200,000 per month per ship. A substantial portion of this added cost may be attributed to incompatibility of companion equipments developed by [the Bureau of Ships and the Bureau of Naval Weapons]."[51]

To deal with the administrative challenge posed by new technology, the Dillon Board proposed that OPNAV reorganize its program sponsorship. "For example, the Deputy Chief of Naval Operations (Air) is the appropriation sponsor for the Procurement of Aircraft and Missiles Appropriation, which includes among other things surface-to-air missiles. The latter are the *programming* responsibility of the Deputy Chief of Naval Operations (Fleet Operations and Readiness)."[52] In short, the board proposed that program sponsors serve also as appropriation sponsors, so that the same OPNAV office would defend its work in both Congress and OSD.

The long and detailed Dillon Report in fact contained inconsistencies. The report accepted the Navy's traditional approach to the distribution of authority within the department, recommending that the bureaus continue to function and that the Secretary of the Navy oversee logistics. At the same time the board argued that the "lead bureau" system of management, originally proposed by the Libby Board in 1956, was not giving the Navy the advanced systems it needed at a cost it could afford. The board also found some assignments of responsibility "ambiguous," particularly in the bureaus of Naval Material (created to coordinate the actions of the other bureaus) and Supplies and Accounts (nominally subordinate to the Chief of Naval Material). The responsibilities of these chiefs overlapped so much that "neither knows exactly when his responsibilities begin and end."[53] Faced with closer congressional scrutiny and a determined, able defense secretary, the board temporized, unwilling to recommend major changes.

To improve coordination among programs, the Dillon Board wanted the Secretary of the Navy to appoint a chief of naval support as the Navy's "producer executive." Although the board accepted the traditional distinction between producers and consumers, it believed that an office *above* the bureaus could pull together the different threads of Navy development and production. While the board accepted the distinction between OPNAV as consumer and the bureaus as producers, it reaffirmed the Navy secretary's control over "logistics administration." In a strongly worded dissent to the report, VCNO Ricketts asserted that the proposed chief of naval support would never be effective because the Dillon Board had refused to recommend giving the position the resources to function effectively as a new office.[54]

Ricketts was on the right track. The Dillon Report reaffirmed the Navy's traditional bilinear administration at the same time it cited examples of confusion caused by decentralized administration. One of the major points in the report, for example, criticized the fragmented responsibility for managing shore activities.[55] Yet the board did not recommend that one office in the Navy be given sole responsibility in that area. Similar criticism was leveled against "double-hatting" the jobs of Deputy Chief of Naval Operations for Personnel and Naval Reserve (OP-01) and Chief of Naval Personnel. The two positions had been combined so that the bureau director could better advise the CNO on staffing, recruiting, and training. But the combination was not working. As Admiral Charles K. Duncan, who later held both positions, observed, "I consider the position of Chief of Naval Personnel with its concurrent position of Deputy Chief of Naval Operations for Manpower and Reserve, to be such a complex one and such a demanding one that it is in a sense almost beyond the capabilities of any one person to do what I would term a perfect job."[56] The Dillon Report suggested separating the positions again, especially because the Secretary of Defense was demanding explicit justification of the Navy's billet structure. As the board admitted, the CNO had to "assume the full responsibility to determine both the qualitative and quantitative requirements for military manpower."[57] The dilemma remained: there was no obvious way to separate the positions and still work out their respective spheres of authority.

Yet some means had to be found to administer a personnel and training system capable of producing the skilled people required to operate all the new systems entering the fleet. Unlike the 1950s, younger officers now actually feared that postgraduate work in technical fields would "endanger their opportunities for promotion," especially if a system they trained in became obsolescent. The Dillon Report showed that "current personnel practices tend to substantiate that view. The truth is that the Navy has not yet worked out a logical career pattern of technical subspecialization."[58] The shortage of technically trained officers meant that OPNAV could not provide the essential requirements for new weapons systems. It also meant that bureaus would lack talented commanders.

Senior Navy officers, including former CNO Burke, had insisted that the structure of an organization counted for less than the quality of its people. In that sense, the Navy's officer corps was going downhill. As the board admitted: "The view that tours of duty in key technical positions in bureaus and shore activities adversely affect promotional opportunities to flag rank is widely held among officers. These problems are most serious."[59] The Dillon Board had avoided saying that the Navy, with its emphasis on operations and on decentralized authority and administration, had backed itself into a corner. The pressures from the Office of the Secretary of Defense only made more apparent the costs of preserving a very loose staff in OPNAV and semiautonomous bureaus. Given the new and growing influence of the Secretary of Defense and OSD, the Navy had to reform its own administration.

The Dillon Report provided a detailed snapshot of the Navy's administration in 1962. Although the study presented an excellent diagnosis of the Navy's administrative problems, it failed to dig deep enough. Was the bureau system outmoded? If so, what should replace it? Could an organization as splintered as OPNAV defend itself against the new Secretary of Defense? If so, how? Should OPNAV be organized along functional lines, such as personnel, operations, and logistics, or should the major deputies to the CNO represent the major Navy platform communities (submarines, surface ships, and planes)? These questions would surface later in another study.

McNamara's Changes: An Attack on Navy Values?
In early 1962, however, the bureaucratic aggressiveness of the new SecDef and his assistants was perceived by certain officers in OPNAV as far more of a threat to sensible naval administration than the unification proposals put forward right after World War II. To these officers, McNamara and his colleagues were cloaking a campaign to suffocate "the military profession

as an authoritative voice" in the guise of promoting efficiency.[60] An OP-06 (Plans and Policy) study put it this way: "There is every evidence that every function performed by the Military Department Secretaries, other than problems of military strategy, the management of military forces, and the related development of weapons systems, will come under the immediate policy control of some functionary or activity in the Office of the Secretary of Defense."[61] This development threatened the Navy's line officers who needed a leader "to stand up for the operating forces and the men who operated them in the everlasting battle to protect their (and the Nation's) interests against unduly restrictive administrative procedures in the name of economy and the democratic ethic."[62] This complaint sounded like the lament from a member of a threatened "aristocracy."

But this "aristocracy" was not based on privilege, nor in the modern Navy did it govern arbitrarily. The concept of command in the Navy in the early 1960s could best be expressed by two accepted maxims: (1) "No question should ever be decided without considering *primarily* its effect on the efficiency of the fleet for *war*," [sic] and (2) "Avoid hostile criticism of authority."[63] The emphasis was always on operations and the chain of command. Operations would succeed only if "proper" leadership were based on a clear understanding of the problem at hand, of the abilities of the men ordered to solve it, and of the risks involved.

The old Navy tradition was that sailors and Marines, properly led and organized, could do almost anything. But that tradition assumed that "good" leaders would focus on the real problem—what would bring victory in war. It also assumed that Navy officers governed, instead of ruled, the men entrusted to them. That is, officers established their legitimacy through their own performance—leading instead of coercing. The chain of command was in fact a chain of obligations; seniors felt bound to support subordinates and subordinates felt bound to accept the authority of seniors. The chain of command was not primarily an organizational structure, but was basically an ethical bond, linking warriors as commanders and commanded in settings where no other kind of link—especially that found in bureaucracies—would work.

Since the end of the World War II, OPNAV had had problems linking the concepts of management and leadership as understood by Navy line officers. That had been easy when the CNO was both manager and operational leader. Indeed, a CNO's influence often varied with his image as a strong operator. Through operations, a CNO like Burke, for example, could affirm and strengthen his authority within the Navy. When the CNO lost operational command authority, he and his office lost much of their legitimacy. When Secretary of Defense McNamara increased the authority of OSD at the expense of the service headquarters, he further undermined the stature and authority of the Chief of Naval Operations. In addition, he attacked the twin pillars of Navy command tradition—the chain of command and the emphasis on operations. If, as seemed true, the CNO was just a bureaucratic subordinate to a Navy secretary who, in turn, was a subordinate to a dominant SecDef, then the Navy's chain of command led ultimately to an official who was not necessarily experienced in command. And if systems analysts could make decisions that were once made by officers with years of operational command experience, then it would seem that operations were no longer considered a source of legitimacy for naval officers. But, of course, operations mattered because the legitimacy of officers in the fleet—the right to command—would crumble if they did not.

McNamara could not understand the intimate connection between legitimacy and operations. His concept of authority worked well in business areas but inadequately in military institutions. For example, in May 1965 the SecDef directed the services to apply the project manager concept to major development efforts.[64] The project manager held the power and the responsibility to push through a major project, like the Polaris ballistic missile–armed submarine, from design to delivery. So long as this manager and his subordinates met production and testing deadlines agreed upon with OSD, they were guaranteed support. The project manager concept undermined the programming authority of OPNAV and sent a signal to the bureaus that they were seen as obstacles to effective technological development. McNamara interpreted the management and coordination problems in OPNAV and between OPNAV and the bureaus, which were highlighted in the 1962 Dillon Report, as evidence of a poorly organized and managed Navy. Conversely, senior Navy officers viewed the problem of interbureau coordination as a price they had to pay for the Navy's bilinear, decentralized administration. These uniformed leaders failed to make McNamara understand that the Navy's shared, decentralized, and often confusing administration was something worth preserving and vital to the Navy's concept of command authority.

From one perspective, however, Secretary McNamara was correct. The Navy's bilinear organization made sense when the Secretary of the Navy was the senior civilian in the Navy Department, ensuring civilian control, and when the CNO held the operational authority. But after 1958, OSD replaced the service secretaries as the agency of civilian control, while the commanders in chief displaced the service chiefs in the chains of command.[65] Because the commanders in chief did not in fact command their component commanders the way the CNO had commanded the Navy before the 1958 law passed, the CNO had to contend with other senior officers, such as the Commander-in-Chief, U.S. Pacific Fleet, for the image of senior Navy commander. Moreover, the need for administratively separate bureaus reporting to the Secretary of the Navy no longer existed.

Figure 9-3. CNO Admiral David L. McDonald was the youngest four-star admiral in the Navy when he was selected as CNO. His oral history, in the collection of the U.S. Naval Institute, reveals how important McDonald's diplomatic skills were as he dealt—more or less successfully—with Secretary of Defense Robert S. McNamara. (National Archives USN 1143706)

Instead, the real need was for responsiveness to the Office of the Secretary of Defense. As CNO David L. McDonald discovered to his disappointment, the duty to OSD increased his "managerial and administrative responsibilities" while "the number of his command prerogatives shrank."[66]

The Bureaus Go Away

Supported by Secretary of the Navy Nitze (McNamara's former Assistant Secretary of Defense for International Security Affairs [ISA]), McNamara asked Congress in 1966 to eliminate the Navy's material bureaus and to allow the Secretary of the Navy to subordinate them to the CNO through the Chief of Naval Material.[67] Secretary Nitze shared McNamara's belief that the Navy needed reorganizing. As one of "McNamara's men," Nitze came to his post committed to bringing the Navy in line with what he and McNamara considered modern organizational practices.[68] In 1963, Secretary of the Navy Korth had responded to the Dillon Board recommendations by requiring the material bureaus (Weapons, Ships, and Yards and Docks) to report to him through the Chief of Naval Material. General Order Number 5 was altered in July 1963 to reflect the new relationships, and the Chief of Naval Material formally became the head of what was called the Naval Material Support Establishment. Two years later, however, Secretary Nitze expanded the order to clarify the role of the Chief of Naval Material. He asked Vice Admiral Ignatius J. Galantin, the new chief, to consider changes and additions to the Naval Material Support Establishment. By 1966, Nitze had a proposal for McNamara, which the latter submitted to the congressional armed services committees.

In a March 1966 letter to the Chairman of the House Armed Services Committee, McNamara noted, "The Secretary of the Navy believes that the organizations performing the Navy's material support functions should be so structured as to subject them to more effective command by the Chief of Naval Material under the Chief of Naval Operations."[69] In response, Congress abolished the statutory basis of the bureaus and gave the Secretary of the Navy the responsibility (once the prerogative of Congress) for assigning the bureau organizations their functions. Defense Secretary McNamara then described what the altered organization would look like: "the Naval Material Command [NAVMAT] will be divided along functional lines into six subcommands—namely, the Air Systems Command, the Ship Systems Command, the Ordnance Systems Command, the Electronic Systems Command, the Supply Systems Command, and the Facilities Engineering Command, each under a commander."[70] The bureaus of Medicine and Naval Personnel were also placed under the Chief of Naval Operations. The traditional consumer/producer distinction was dropped, and the CNO became responsible for all naval support elements that had once reported to the secretary through the Naval Material Support Establishment.

To make the transition from the bureaus to the newly formed systems commands a smoother one, Admiral Galantin and the Assistant Chief of Naval Operations for Program Planning (OP-090) analyzed the functions of the new commands and their relationships to OPNAV during April and May 1966.[71] The transition from bureaus to systems commands took over four months to implement and was complete by August 1966. It was achieved only through lengthy negotiations over the respective powers of OPNAV and the Naval Material Command because former bureau personnel, accustomed to a certain level of autonomy, had feared that their independence would dissipate in the systems commands.[72]

The Benson Study: OPNAV's Response to McNamara

An in-depth study of OPNAV, supervised by Rear Admiral Roy S. Benson, Assistant Vice Chief of Naval Operations, paralleled the transition to systems commands.[73] Prodded by McNamara's defense "reforms," OPNAV had changed by fits and starts under CNOs Anderson and McDonald. The Benson Task Force reviewed those changes and devised a reorganization plan to prepare the office for its new role of directing systems commands in a setting where OSD dominated service program planning. To hold down the size of OPNAV, the task force recommended that the Chief of Naval Operations create intelligence and communication commands separate from OPNAV. The ACNO positions for Communications (OP-94) and Intelligence (OP-92) could be "double-hatted," serving simultaneously as members of the CNO's staff and as directors of their own commands.[74] The task force was compelled to recommend this organizational gimmick because supervising the systems commands would impose new demands on OPNAV.

Benson and his colleagues formally completed their study of OPNAV organization at the end of 1966. They observed the following:

- OPNAV's organization and working procedures have not been reoriented to conform to the 1 May 1966 reorganization of the Navy Department.
- The basic organization of OPNAV is not responsive to some of the demands placed upon it and is unwieldy in operation.
- [T]he OP-090 [Program Planning] organization is a layer between the DCNO's [sic] and the VCNO, slowing down the processing of paperwork and preventing the DCNO's [sic] from exercising a level of authority which would relieve more senior officers of some of the burden placed upon them.
- OPNAV personnel are involved too deeply in the details of functions performed by subordinate commands.
- The span of control of the VCNO and certain other officials in OPNAV is excessive.
- A common complaint of certain DCNO's [sic] is that so many of their personnel are involved in studies that it detracts to a degree from their ability to carry out their primary duties.[75]
- [OPNAV program sponsors dealt directly with project managers in the systems commands without going through the new Naval Material Command.][76]

These findings suggest that the problems plaguing OPNAV in 1966 were much like those afflicting OSD at the same time. That is, as McNamara forced his management form and style on the service headquarters, the problems of over-centralization, overwork, and continual appraisal and review grew more serious in his own office.[77] The emphasis on programming as the key management tool caused most of the major problems. If programming were indeed the

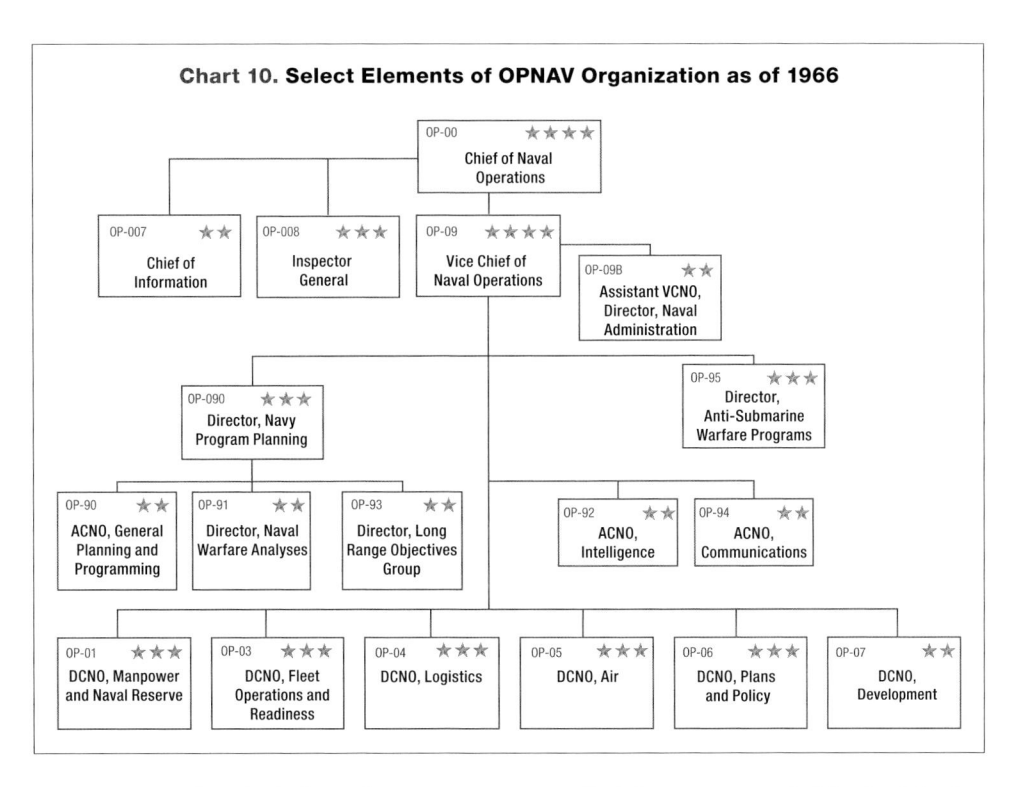

Chart 10. Select Elements of OPNAV Organization as of 1966

- OP-00 ★★★★ Chief of Naval Operations
  - OP-007 ★★ Chief of Information
  - OP-008 ★★★ Inspector General
  - OP-09 ★★★★ Vice Chief of Naval Operations
    - OP-09B ★★ Assistant VCNO, Director, Naval Administration
    - OP-95 ★★★ Director, Anti-Submarine Warfare Programs
    - OP-090 ★★★ Director, Navy Program Planning
      - OP-90 ★★ ACNO, General Planning and Programming
      - OP-91 ★★ Director, Naval Warfare Analyses
      - OP-93 ★★ Director, Long Range Objectives Group
      - OP-92 ★★ ACNO, Intelligence
      - OP-94 ★★ ACNO, Communications
    - OP-01 ★★★ DCNO, Manpower and Naval Reserve
    - OP-03 ★★★ DCNO, Fleet Operations and Readiness
    - OP-04 ★★★ DCNO, Logistics
    - OP-05 ★★★ DCNO, Air
    - OP-06 ★★★ DCNO, Plans and Policy
    - OP-07 ★★ DCNO, Development

primary means by which the Defense secretary controlled the services, and if the CNO had to apply the same technique to control the Navy, then the Navy's tradition of decentralization and delegation would collapse. Under the new system, a conflict between the ACNO for Program Planning and the deputy chiefs was inevitable because the latter were authorized deputies of the CNO and the former only a staff assistant to the CNO. Who was actually in charge—the authorized deputies or the staff analysts? Similarly, the military had criticized McNamara for placing too much power, through PPBS, in the hands of an OSD staff responsible only to the Secretary of Defense. The same critique applied to Program Planning and the newly created Systems Analysis Division. The Navy was developing what it was criticizing in OSD. (See Chart 10.)

Similarly, the CNO and the VCNO's workload had grown too great. Under the Planning, Programming, and Budgeting System, neither dared to allow authorized deputies to act independently. But the DCNO positions were originally created to shield the Chief and Vice Chief of Naval Operations from work that was better delegated. The villain was McNamara's concept of programming. For programming to be an effective tool of organizational control, top management must monitor the program proposals, which lower layers (divisions) of the organization periodically prepare. In a large organization like the Defense Department, however, top managers have neither the time nor the energy to monitor all the program documentation, which the service staffs prepare. As a result, they must use their own staff analysts to review proposals from the services, and influence over programming decisions devolves unavoidably to those analysts. To counter this influence, the service chiefs hire or train their own program analysts. The process repeats itself within each service as deputies of the service chief develop or hire their own analytical experts to shield their branches against the service chief's analysts.

This process of using analysis as the primary decision tool creates friction between staff analysts and line deputies. This friction was unavoidable, however, because the CNO's perspective was strongly influenced by the studies done in OP-96 (Systems Analysis), which tried to anticipate the analyses performed at the OSD level. As McNamara realized, reviewing program elements only gave his office veto power. To stay ahead of the services—to push defense policy instead of just regulating it—he needed to conduct analyses independently of the services. Although the Navy opposed this policy, the only way a CNO could deal with it was to create a staff analysis organization able to justify Navy programs in terms that OSD would accept.

McNamara's approach to PPBS had a domino effect. The concept of systems analysis cascaded down the levels of the Navy's organization. Studies, once a luxury, became essential. As the CNO's deputies acquired analytic support, either directly from the Center for Naval Analyses, or indirectly from outside contractors (the so-called Beltway Bandits), a "shadow" OPNAV staff grew.

The emphasis on programming also had other side-effects: the bypassing of the chain of command and the reduction in the influence of OP-06 (Plans and Policy) as the CNO's role in the JCS was overshadowed by his programming responsibilities. Deputies of program sponsors (the DCNOs) dealt directly with project managers in the systems commands, often ignoring the offices in the Naval Material Command with official cognizance over programs. Officers in NAVMAT and in the systems commands found that OPNAV program directors, responsible to program sponsors, would go around them and deal directly with the managers of key projects. As Rear Admiral Benson pointed out to the OPNAV staff, its proper function was review and approval, "not day to day detailed monitoring." But that statement missed the point.[78] Programming was a form of control, and control was now OPNAV's responsibility. The bilinear Navy was gone. The question was, what would take its place?

There was already one alternative in place, one structured around a weapons system. Vice Admiral Hyman Rickover had recreated in the Bureau of Ships (later Naval Ship Systems Command) an organization modeled after the old Bureau of Aeronautics. BuAer had been unique among the material bureaus before World War II because of its control over aviation personnel training and assignments. The first chief of BuAer had won and kept that power through nearly a decade of bureaucratic conflict with OPNAV and other bureaus, especially Navigation (later the Bureau of Naval Personnel). BuAer was able to get away with its sweeping authority because its first chief argued persuasively that the Navy's fledgling air arm needed special protection and support.[79]

By the mid-1960s, Rickover, as an official in both the Atomic Energy Commission and in BuShips, had used a similar approach and the same rationale to gain control over the design and construction of nuclear submarines for the U.S. Navy, and over the training and assignment of the personnel to man those submarines. He had, through his contacts in Congress and through his post at the Atomic Energy Commission, created a bureau-within-a-bureau, gradually insulating himself from effective control by the CNO. Instead of responding to his OPNAV sponsor, Rickover controlled the sponsor through his ties to Congress. As Rickover admitted, he was a "creature of Congress."[80] By the 1970s Rickover's influence was so great that it extended to submarine operations as well as design.

Rickover's story has been told in detail elsewhere.[81] What matters here is that his approach to weapons development and force planning was an alternative considered by the Benson Task Force. Although Rickover's tactics bypassed the chain of command, he had succeeded in creating, training, and supporting a large nuclear submarine force. Moreover, he was willing to work with other branches of the Navy. All he demanded was that, if they used nuclear power, the power plants be his designs manned by his crews. The task force avoided praising Rickover because the admiral had only reluctantly accepted OPNAV authority. Indeed, when Admiral Elmo R. Zumwalt Jr., served as CNO (1970–1974), he found that he had to negotiate with the nominally subordinate Rickover as an equal before drafting a ship construction program. What the task force did acknowledge, however, was that OPNAV could be restructured above and around "weapons systems directorates," or the reorganized systems commands. What the task force also understood, but did not say, was that such an organization might well head off future Rickovers in the bureaus.

After considering OPNAV's organizational possibilities for nine months, the Benson Task Force arrived at five basic structural alternatives:

1. The *"four forces"* structure with DCNOs for undersea warfare, surface warfare, air warfare, and mobile combat logistics support (or amphibious warfare); and two other DCNOs for strategic plans and policy, and programs and budget. The Chief of Naval Material would be subordinate to these deputy chiefs.

2. The *functional-processes* structure, with DCNOs for planning and programming, development, manpower, logistics, and fleet operations and readiness. Again, the Chief of Naval Material would be subordinate to the DCNOs.

3. The *weapons systems directorates,* with DCNOs for manpower, operations, logistics, plans, development, and programming/budgeting. Six special directorates—for ships, aviation, logistics, facilities, ordnance, and electronics—would replace the Naval Material Command. The head of each would report directly to the program sponsors in OPNAV.

4. The *sequential-processes* structure, with DCNOs for programming/budgeting, planning and policy analysis, execution and appraisal, and "futures." Assistant chiefs of naval operations for antisubmarine warfare (ASW), aviation, research and development, electronic warfare, amphibious warfare, communications, and intelligence would head other OPNAV offices. These program directors would work directly with project managers in the systems commands, and the identity of each special office headed by an ACNO would change as naval warfare changed.

5. The *existing* structure, organized around both functional (e.g., planning,) and force (e.g., air, surface, antisubmarine warfare (ASW)) concepts.[82]

The task force had been open to all the alternatives, but stressed that "one of the basic principles underlying our effort has been to assign functions at the lowest practicable level."[83]

In a memo to the CNO Advisory Board (CAB) in October 1966, Benson observed: "Implementation of the Four Forces concept . . . would not be difficult. We operate almost like that now." However, he also reminded the members of the advisory board that "a basic change in the structure of CNO's staff is not essential." Benson and his task force well knew of "the turmoil incident to change," and the changes in OPNAV forced by the Secretary of Defense had already taken enough time and energy to implement.[84] Although the task force was willing to accept OPNAV as it existed, it also reaffirmed the traditional commitment to delegation and decentralization.

The Benson study put some important issues on the table. OPNAV had been mostly functionally organized after World War II, but by 1966 it was a hybrid headquarters organization built around forces and functions, part platform-oriented, part OSD-oriented (especially Program Planning), and part JCS-oriented (Plans and Policy). The 1966 reorganization had not really dealt with the effects of this patchwork structure, and the Benson study clearly stated that certain problems in the Navy were a consequence of it. The study also showed that influence within OPNAV was focused around the three major operational communities—aviators, submariners, and surface ship officers. The idea of organizing around these communities, however, was not new. In 1950, for example, Vice Admiral Francis S. Low, the special advisor on undersea warfare to the CNO, argued in a then-classified but influential study that the "organization for Undersea Warfare should be . . . either under a specially appointed Deputy Chief of Naval Operations or as a fleet organization along the lines of the Tenth Fleet in World War II."[85] What was novel in 1966 was saying that such an organization could work.

The Dillon Board had stated this challenge to OPNAV in its 1962 report: "There is a compelling need for the establishment of a doctrine around which our executives and the organizations which they supervise can better coordinate their collective efforts." This doctrine was "essential to achievement of the discipline necessary for unity in their leadership."[86] But what doctrine? The "four forces" form of organization called for multiple doctrines. No one doctrine would meld all the pieces of OPNAV together. Rear Admiral

Figure 9-4. CNO Admiral Thomas H. Moorer had a distinguished career as a naval aviator, earning a Silver Star in World War II. He later commanded Carrier Division Six, Seventh Fleet, Pacific Fleet, and served as Commander-in-Chief, Atlantic Command/NATO Atlantic Command. He also participated in the Strategic Bombing Survey of Japan, served as an ACNO, and led OPNAV's Long Range Objectives Group.
(National Archives 428-KN 15045)

Benson tried to build a consensus among senior flag officers behind *some* doctrine in 1967, but CNO McDonald left office that year, handing over his position to Admiral Thomas H. Moorer. When Moorer came in, the search for a consensus had to begin all over again. This is not to say that there were no immediate consequences of the Benson study. The Office of Strategic Offensive and Defensive Systems (OP-97) and the Naval Communications and Intelligence commands were established. Several assistant chiefs were made Assistant Deputy Chiefs of Naval Operations in order to limit the number of people with access to the vice chief and the CNO.[87] But the major issue—the organizational doctrine for OPNAV—had been left unresolved.

Following the Benson Study

In 1968, the Director of the Long Range Objectives Group (OP-93) suggested to CNO Moorer that OPNAV be "organized in groups, each of which closely conforms to the organization of an outside organization which is a major communicant of the CNO."[88] OP-93's idea was to create three DCNOs—for program planning, fleet readiness, and strategic plans. The first would deal with the Secretary of the Navy, who was the link to the Office of the Secretary of Defense. The second would work with the Chief of Naval Material and with the naval component commanders at the unified commands. The third would deal with the Joint Staff. The DCNO for program planning would focus on the program categories of OSD and also on the congressional budget categories. The DCNO for fleet readiness would be organized by warfare area—ASW, amphibious assault, aviation, at-sea replenishment, and so forth. The DCNO for strategic plans would be supported by a functional directorate whose fields conformed to those of the JCS Joint Staff directorates. An OPNAV staff director and a director of naval analysis would assist the Chief and Vice Chief of Naval Operations. Each deputy chief would be assisted by a director of studies who would communicate directly with a director of studies and analysis reporting to the deputy for program planning.

OP-93's proposal recognized three major clients of OPNAV—the Secretary of the Navy (and the Secretary of Defense), the fleet commanders, and the JCS. The proposal also recognized the three primary functions of OPNAV—force planning, supporting the fleet by structuring, training and supplying naval forces, and providing the military capabilities needed to support national strategy. What was interesting about the proposal, however, was its admission that the primary duty of OPNAV was to respond, not to command. As OP-93 was preparing its proposal, Admiral Bernard A. Clarey, Vice Chief of Naval Operations, asked the Systems Analysis Division to study OPNAV's organization yet again. OP-96 found the same shortcomings with OPNAV:

- OPNAV is too large. There are about 1,100 officers alone.
- The rank structure is too top heavy.
- There is a great deal of duplication of effort.
- The span of control of the CNO/VCNO is too great.
- For many, if not most, complex issues there is no clear line of responsibility.

- The current OPNAV organization is not structured by either mission or weapons platform but rather by a mixture.
- The fact that Washington duty is a virtual prerequisite for selection to flag rank causes many billets to be designated as captain billets which could be filled by more junior officers.[89]

Under a mandate to recommend only those changes that would cause "minimum disruption of OPNAV," the OP-96 study group ran into a problem.[90] What if its study suggested major changes? Members of the study group thought the problem was solved when they found "Admiral Benson's notes of his briefing for SECNAV."[91] They were excited about the organizational alternatives studied by the Benson Task Force but they soon discovered that the alternatives were never presented in the final report. The OP-96 group concluded that the Benson study omitted the alternatives because any real change in OPNAV "would require time and legislation" and would therefore "be vulnerable to attack."[92] Nevertheless, the OP-96 officers recommended that the Chief of Naval Material be made a deputy chief for resources and that, consequently, the DCNO positions for Logistics (OP-04) and Development (OP-07) be eliminated.

What OP-96 proposed was a gradual change in OPNAV, with an OPNAV staff director under the Vice Chief of Naval Operations. Assistant directors would be appointed for manpower, JCS matters, communications and intelligence, general purpose forces, sealift, oceanography, and strategic offensive and defensive forces. An office of an assistant director for program appraisal would generate long-range objectives and systems analyses of ongoing programs. In making this proposal, the Systems Analysis Division was heavily influenced by the OP-93 (Long Range Objectives Group) study and by a staff reorganization of the Royal Navy, which had just become effective. What is so interesting about the OP-96 effort is that it reveals an incredible absence of institutional memory. The Benson Task Force put together a detailed, thoughtful study. By the time Admiral Moorer was considering reorganization, the ideas generated by the Benson study had lost their influence, despite the fact that Benson had explained them to a number of senior flag officers.

The McNamara Years: A Conclusion

The McNamara years (1961–1968) were a whirlwind time for OPNAV. As one commentator said, "From 1961 to 1964, McNamara proved himself an unrivaled master at establishing firm civilian control over the massive Pentagon program."[93] To attain that level of control he expanded the size and authority of the Office of the Secretary of Defense. Between 1962 and 1969, for example, the OSD staff increased by almost 50 percent, as did the staff of the office of the Joint Chiefs of Staff.[94] Using his legal authority, McNamara also established the Defense Intelligence Agency (DIA), the Defense Supply Agency, the Defense Communications Agency, and the Defense Contract Audit Agency. President Kennedy also approved McNamara's creation of the Logistics Management Institute, a nonprofit organization that could provide independent assessments of Defense Department management.[95] In contrast, during McNamara's first three years as Defense Secretary, the size of the Office of the Secretary of the Navy decreased by over a third, OPNAV stayed the same, and the headquarters of the Marine Corps grew by more than 25 percent.[96] McNamara deliberately used his authority to establish his office as the center of defense policymaking and overall military command. He yielded to no one except the President.

As Secretary of Defense, McNamara imposed uniform programming practices on the services through the use of the Planning, Programming, and Budgeting System (PPBS). He understood the difference between data collection as a means of tracking expenditures and data collection as a means of discovering what an organization is doing and of controlling that organization. Later secretaries altered McNamara's system, but they did not abandon programming as the major tool of implementing force planning decisions. Budgets, for example, are still expressed in terms of Total Obligational Authority, and in the PPBS (now Planning, Programming, Budgeting, and Execution [PPBE]) process the emphasis on the multiyear defense plan continues. Programming dramatically changed OPNAV's relationships with the rest of the Navy. OPNAV ceased to be the staff of the Navy's senior commander, becoming instead the staff of a deputy chief executive whose major responsibility was support of the operating forces.

As CNO McDonald noted, the Navy

> would present a budget which contained what we thought was needed. If such required a monetary outlay which OSD thought excessive then instead of coming back to us and simply saying the darn thing costs too much, please rearrange based on a specified reduction in cost, Mr. McNamara and his staff would do the same thing by simply saying that certain things weren't needed.[97]

This understated but serious criticism contrasted with what Nitze, said about CNO McDonald: "On many issues I came to consider his judgment superior to mine, particularly on the politics of the Washington bureaucratic scene." However, Nitze's compliment should not mask the fact that he was selected to make sure that McNamara's policies were implemented within the Navy Department. Nitze was all business. As he admitted in his memoir, "After I had fired one admiral who persisted in refusing to follow my guidance, I found I had earned a certain respect."[98]

Under McNamara everything changed—force planning, the programming process, the relative authority of the Chief of Naval Operations, and the means by which major systems were procured. In 1964, for example, Assistant Secretary of the Air Force Robert Charles introduced the concept of Total Package Procurement. McNamara adopted it and forced it on the other services. Total Package Procurement meant that "contractors competing for a weapon-system award were required to submit binding price bids for the entire program—production as well as development—before the award was made."[99] It looked like a great innovation. But the concept encouraged the services to enter into wholesale production deals that left no escape if there were problems with the firm that won the contract. By the end of McNamara's time as Secretary of Defense, data drawn from experience with Total Package Procurement strongly suggested that it had not been a success in lowering the acquisition costs of major systems.[100]

Before the World War II, for example, the Navy usually built the lead ship of a class in a government yard. The cost and schedule for this first ship was then used to gauge the performance of private shipyards. In the 1950s, when government shipyards focused on modernization of the fleet and new construction was left to private firms, the Navy often parceled out ships of the same class among different yards to encourage competition. Under Total Package Procurement, private firms were induced to bid on major systems by the promise that the low bidder would get the whole package, from initial design to final construction. The idea was a disaster for the Navy because it shifted responsibility for design work from the systems commands to private firms, leaving the Navy dependent on a few major construction yards. As Norman Friedman noted in his detailed study of destroyer designs, total procurement of the DD-963 type meant that "a company with no previous preliminary design experience had to create a new destroyer design from scratch."[101]

One of the better characterizations of Secretary McNamara was made by his Assistant Secretary of Defense for Installations and Logistics, Paul R. Ignatius, when Ignatius compared McNamara to his successor, Clark M. Clifford: "McNamara made quick decisions; Clifford pondered. [McNamara] talked; [Clifford] listened. McNamara had answers; Clifford asked questions. McNamara looked up at his clock on the wall to signal that time was running short; Clifford seemed to have plenty of time for business, and even some left over for small talk."[102] McNamara was a whirlwind, and his impact on the Department of Defense—for better or worse—was profound and lasting.

After McNamara: Melvin Laird

By the end of the McNamara regime, OPNAV looked like a patchwork organization, the morale of senior officers was extremely low, and the future of the office was in doubt. The policies of President Richard M. Nixon's Defense Secretary, Melvin R. Laird, however, both improved the management system left behind by McNamara and assuaged the battered morale of senior military leaders. Laird employed what former Assistant Secretary of Defense Lawrence J. Korb termed "participatory management." According to Korb, "Laird looked primarily to the military services and the Chiefs for the design of the force structure. The civilian systems analysts were limited to evaluating and reviewing the military's proposals."[103] The SecDef did "not attempt to exercise control of details in the defense budget. Once he established an annual budget, and 'set fences' around specific program categories within the budget, Laird allowed the services wide latitude in structuring the categories."[104]

Laird used other tactics to avoid antagonizing the services. He began the process of leavening cost effectiveness analyses with political, fiscal, and manpower factors. It was the difference between telling (as McNamara had done) and explaining; it was part of Laird's strategy of governing the services by listening to them and representing them in Congress. Laird allowed "the military to appeal his decisions whenever and wherever they wished," and he even permitted them to procure or develop systems with doubtful value in cost-effective terms—the B-1 bomber, for example.[105] Finally, Laird gave the services fiscal guidance at the beginning of the PPBS cycle instead of at the end. Under this system, the services bore "the burden of making the tough choices about which areas to cut during the 37.2 per cent reduction in the real level of defense spending which occurred in the 1969–75 period."[106]

Laird revealed his skill as an organizational politician when he simultaneously reduced military expenditures and tightened OSD's control over service acquisition. By creating the Defense Systems Acquisition Review Council (DSARC), he gained control over major systems development. As Laird's deputy, David Packard, the co-founder of the very successful electronics firm Hewlett-Packard, told the service secretaries, "The primary responsibility for the acquisition and management of our major systems must rest with the individual Services." Yet he also explained that, as Deputy Secretary of Defense, he was "most anxious of insuring, before we approve transitioning through the critical milestones of the acquisition of a major system, that all facets of the acquisition process are properly considered."[107] DSARC complemented the Five Year Defense Program that was part of the Planning, Programming, and Budgeting System by giving a council of assistant Defense secretaries the chance to review major programs before so many resources were committed that any decision to cut off those resources would have become organizationally or politically impossible. Creating the council was a way of getting OSD in on the "ground floor" of development programs and then subjecting them to continual OSD assessment.

Laird had to be a skilled Pentagon politician. The Nixon administration had pledged to reduce defense spending, end the draft, and leave the war in Vietnam to the Vietnamese. The services wanted to keep the draft, win the war, and rebuild inventories depleted by combat and age. That Laird accomplished the administration's goals without seriously antagonizing the service secretaries and chiefs is a testimony to his abilities. One of those abilities was an appreciation of the symbolic side to leadership. McNamara had outworked, outargued, and outmaneuvered the service chiefs. Laird's style was very different. Vice Admiral William P. Mack, Deputy Assistant Secretary of Defense for Manpower and Reserve Affairs, under Laird, commented:

> [I]t was thought by navy officials, officers, that you really weren't working right unless you worked at least ten hours a day, seven days a week. . . . And when you wrote a paper or a speech it had to be nitpicked to death . . . that's the way paper work and administration were done, particularly in the Navy Department. I'd been through this for years, and I didn't think it was the way it should be, so to me it was quite a clean breeze to come to the Defense Department and find . . . that it was staffed at the very highest level by businessmen who didn't believe this, who thought that if you couldn't do your work in eight hours a day on five days, perhaps occasionally six, you weren't doing it right. In other words, you weren't delegating responsibility properly.[108]

The key term is "delegating." It did not matter so much that Laird delegated the duty of finding ways to cut spending instead of increasing it. What really counted was that Laird and his associates in OSD recognized an area of service responsibility and respected it, making sure that the services knew why OSD was doing so.

As far as OPNAV was concerned, things were getting worse—organizationally. At least that was what a "Special Review" by the Naval Audit Service concluded at the beginning of 1969. Audit Service investigators reported that they had:

> been unable to identify, at any level below the immediate office of the Chief of Naval Operations, a unit, group, or board, where a truly objective decision is made for the best interest of the Navy, particularly with regard to allocations of available funds to the various programs.... The final recommendations to CNO for program priority rests [sic] with the Chief of Naval Operations Advisory Board (CAB).[109]

But the deputy chiefs and the assistant chiefs who sat on the board settled their major differences through back-stage bargaining *before* the meetings. Hence the board did not base its decisions after "an objective determination of priority need."[110] To do well in the bargaining sessions, "each DCNO/ACNO considers it his responsibility to be knowledgeable with respect to substantially all Navy actions."[111] Unfortunately, the need for intelligence on what other offices were planning and programming led to a wasteful duplication of staffs.

This requirement for intelligence on competing offices within the organization drove the deputy chiefs to demand reports from the fleet and from the Chief of Naval Material, burying OPNAV offices in paper. The Audit Service estimated that OPNAV received more than four times as much paper as was necessary.[112] But the paper was the essential fuel for the necessary studies. Because decisions about programs were reached through an essentially political process, the parties to the process (essentially a zero-sum game, especially under the cost-cutting imposed by OSD) needed not only information but also what is referred to in political lobbying literature as "partisan analysis"—studies showing the virtue of one position, or alternative, over another. Given the way OPNAV worked, studies were imperative. They were also wasteful:

> (1) Personnel are selected for Special Studies on the basis of rank and not on the basis of expertise in their individual specialty. (2) The basis of the need for Studies and the Study Objectives are vague. (3) Studies in progress are not adequately monitored. (4) There is little post evaluation of Study results and no evidence of concern for cost effectiveness.[113]

The auditors added another complaint: "A major portion of the total OPNAV effort is devoted to processing JCS papers."[114] In fiscal year 1968 alone, OP-06 (Plans and Policy) processed almost 18,000 JCS papers, many of which required an immediate reply. The presence of a larger Joint Staff, allowed by the 1958 DOD Reorganization Act, seemed to confirm former CNO Burke's fears that the Joint Chiefs would become a drain on both the CNO and OPNAV.

The Audit Service observed that "detail to OPNAV appears to have an adverse effect on morale and encourages separation from the Service."[115] High-ranking officers became involved in "clerical type detail and other routine functions not related to Navy policy, or not requiring any military expertise."[116] To compound matters, just as officers had mastered their office duties, they were rotated out of their positions. These new officers entering OPNAV often lacked sufficient training in administrative and fiscal matters.[117]

Navy auditors sharply criticized OPNAV for its lack of a "centralized management of Logistics within the Navy," noting that they "have been unable to arrive at a clear definition of what the logistics role of OP-04 is intended to be."[118] OP-04 was supporting the other deputy chiefs instead of formulating policy. Moreover, the Naval Material Command had "never developed any management capability related to Air programs," and the systems commands were "operating substantially according to the former Bureau organizational lines and this promotes bypassing in the reporting chain."[119] Finally, the Audit Service noted that the "relationship and relative responsibilities of the program sponsor and the appropriation sponsor" were "not entirely clear."[120] That is, the command links between OPNAV and the systems commands were not as clear as they needed to be.

The 1969 audit exposed all the cracks in OPNAV's structure, and showed that the Chief of Naval Operations was losing charge of his own staff. Authority in OPNAV was fragmented, and lines of authority crisscrossed and overlapped. The Naval Material Command was not really managing the systems commands, in part because it was not fully integrated into OPNAV. As the naval auditors argued, "the organization and the functions of OPNAV should be restricted to policy, coordination, and direction" and the "subordinate commands should be used for operational detail."[121]

The reactions of the deputy chiefs and the assistant chiefs to the audit report were "in the majority of instances . . . unfavorable."[122] The DCNO for Development, for example, argued that the competition among deputy chiefs for funds was "not harmful," while the DCNO for Logistics maintained that duty in the Pentagon was essential for a successful career. The DCNO for Air disagreed with the auditors' claim that OPNAV service was frustrating, and he also asserted that time spent on JCS papers kept the Chief of Naval Operations involved in JCS decisions. The prospect of consolidating the Naval Material Command and OP-04 was "appalling" to the DCNO for Logistics.[123] As the Assistant VCNO, Director of Naval Administration, had observed in a memo to his boss, the opposition to the suggestions and analysis of the Audit Service would keep the Vice Chief of Naval Operations from making any changes.[124] Put another way, no reorganization could be successful without the approval of officers who were the nominal subordinates to the Chief of Naval Operations. OPNAV was, indeed, a loose confederation of offices, which competed among themselves for the CNO's support. The CNOs who followed Admiral McDonald would find that leading OPNAV—let alone the Navy—was a great challenge made even greater by a strong Office of the Secretary of Defense.

Notes

[1] President Kennedy's Inaugural Address, 20 Jan. 1961, John F. Kennedy Presidential Library & Museum website https://www.jfklibrary.org/Research/Research-Aids/Ready-Reference/JFK-Quotations/Inaugural-Address.aspx.

[2] Charles J. Hitch, "Decision-Making in the Department of Defense," H. Rowan Gaither Lectures in Systems Sciences, University of California at Berkeley, 5–9 Apr. 1965, 17.

[3] Ibid., 18.

[4] As Paul H. Nitze, Assistant Secretary of Defense of International Security Affairs from 1961 to 1963, observed, McNamara "wanted to have a better understanding and more detailed control over logistics, base structure, pay scales, and a thousand and one different things." *From Hiroshima to Glasnost*, with Ann M. Smith and Steven L. Rearden (New York: Grove Weidenfeld, 1989), 274.

[5] Charles J. Hitch, "Decision-Making in the Department of Defense," 19.

[6] Ibid.

[7] Ibid., 17.

[8] Ibid.

[9] Ibid., 18.

[10] Ibid., Appendix G, "Statement of Asst. Secretary of Defense Charles J. Hitch Before the Military Operations Subcommittee of the House Committee on Government Operations," 25 July 1962, 184.

[11] Ibid., 191.

[12] As Paul Nitze recalled, "In the first few weeks of the administration, [McNamara] asked the Joint Chiefs of Staff to come up with answers to some ninety-six questions in the Pentagon review of our defense needs. The Joint Chiefs simply did not have the machinery in place to generate adequate responses by the time McNamara expected them on his desk. Consequently [McNamara] turned more and more to his handpicked civilian team in OSD for quick advice and action." *From Hiroshima to Glasnost*, 243.

[13] Draft Memorandum for the President, "Recommended FY 1964–FY 1968 Strategic Retaliatory Forces," from Secretary of Defense McNamara to President John F. Kennedy, 21 Nov. 1962. The number of warheads and the megatons of explosive power are on page 2. Secretary McNamara's justification for his decision is on page 3. The source of the declassified document was the records of the Office of Program Analysis and Evaluation, Office of the Secretary of Defense. On line version at https://history.state.gov/historicaldocuments/frus1961-63v08/d112.

[14] GEN Bernard A. Schriever, head of the USAF Systems Command from 1961 to 1966, noted after his retirement that "Mr. McNamara had no concept of management" and that he allowed his staff to "operate in . . . an undisciplined fashion." Interview No. 676 of GEN Bernard A. Schriever, USAF, by MAJ L. R. Officer and Dr. J. C. Hasdorff, 20 June 1973, USAF Oral History Program, Historical Research Center, Maxwell AFB, Alabama, 36–37.

[15] Rosenberg, "Arleigh Albert Burke," in Love's *The Chiefs of Naval Operations*, 308.

[16] Paul R. Schratz, "John B. Connally," in Coletta's *American Secretaries of the Navy*, vol. 2, 914.

[17] Lawrence Korb, "George Whalen Anderson Jr.," in Love's *The Chiefs of Naval Operations*, 321–32. Also see Nitze, *From Hiroshima to Glasnost*, and *TFX Contract Investigation*, Hearings before the Permanent Subcommittee on Investigations of the Committee on Government Operations, U.S. Senate, 88th Cong., 1st sess., Part 3, 2, 4, 5, and 10 Apr., and 1 May 1963. ADM Anderson's successor, ADM David L. McDonald, avoided the TFX issue because he saw no way of convincing McNamara to drop his support for the plane. What finally killed the TFX as the aircraft for both the Air Force and the Navy was the Navy's revival, under the leadership of VADM Thomas F. Connally, DCNO (Air), of a different fighter concept, represented by the combination of the F-14 and the Phoenix long-range, air-to-air missile. Floyd D. Kennedy Jr., "David Lamar McDonald," in Love's *The Chiefs of Naval Operations*, 333–50. See also Friedman, *U.S. Naval Weapons*, 177–78.

[18] Baer, *One Hundred Years of Sea Power*, 384.

[19] Paul R. Schratz, "Fred Korth," in Coletta's *American Secretaries of the Navy*, vol. 2: 931.

[20] Memo, The Need for a Look at DOD Organization," under cover ltr OP-06D, ser 109P06D, 15 May 1961, pt. 4, 5, folder 49, DOD Reorganization-1961, OP-602 File, NHHC Archives.

[21] Department of the Navy, *Navy Organization Study* (Roy S. Benson Task Force Report) (Washington, DC, 1966), A–i. (Hereafter, Benson Task Force Report).

[22] Department of the Navy, *Review of Management of the Department of the Navy*, study 1, vol. 2, *External Environmental Influences Study*, Study Director J. V. Smith (Washington, DC, 1962), 40.

[23] Ibid., 44.

[24] Ibid., 47.

[25] Department of the Navy, *Review of Management of the Department of the Navy*, study 2, vol. 1, *Planning, Programming, Budgeting, and Appraising Study*, Study Director H. A. Renken (Washington, DC, 1962), 22.

[26] Ibid., 23.

[27] RADM Draper L. Kauffman, USN (Ret.), *Reminiscences* (Annapolis, MD: U.S. Naval Institute, 1982), vol. I, 613.

[28] Ibid., 579–80.

[29] Ibid., 603.

[30] Ibid., 605.

[31] Ibid., 607.

[32] Ibid.

[33] Ibid., 611.

[34] Ibid., 622.

[35] Ibid., 581.

[36] Ibid., 603.

[37] Ibid., 589–90.

[38] Ibid., 592, 610.

[39] Ibid., 614, 621–22.

[40] Ibid., 584.

[41] Ibid., 599–600.

[42] ADM James L. Holloway III, USN (Ret.), *Aircraft Carriers at War* (Annapolis, MD: Naval Institute Press, 2007), 174–75. Holloway became "special assistant" to VADM Rivero. Rivero became Admiral and VCNO when ADM Ricketts died suddenly in 1964.

[43] Kauffman, *Reminiscences*, 618.

[44] Ibid.

[45] Ibid., 595.

[46] Ibid., 639–40. Paul Fay had served in the Navy with John Kennedy and was a close friend of the president. After Kennedy's assassination, Fay lost his standing with the White House, and Navy secretary Nitze could move Fay out of the office that connected to the Secretary's.

[47] Norman Friedman, "Elmo Russell Zumwalt Jr.," in Love's *The Chiefs of Naval Operations*, 366–67.

[48] CAPT E. T. Woolridge, USN (Ret.), ed., *Into the Jet Age: Conflict and Change in Naval Aviation, 1945–1975, an Oral History* (Annapolis, MD: Naval Institute Press, 1995), especially the chapter by ADM Thomas F. Connolly, "The TFX—One Fighter for All."

[49] Renken, *Planning, Programming, Budgeting, and Appraising Study*, vol. 1, 3, 5.

[50] Department of the Navy, *Review of Management of the Department of the Navy* (John H. Dillon Board Report) (Washington, DC, 1962), 85 (Hereafter, the Dillon Board Report).

[51] Ibid., 86.

[52] Ibid., 52.

[53] Ibid., 8, 102.

[54] Ibid. See final pages of the Dillon Board Report.

[55] Ibid., 12.

[56] Charles K. Duncan, interview by John T. Mason Jr., 1983, 3 vols., vol. 3, 1269, U.S. Naval Institute Oral History, Annapolis, MD (hereafter Duncan Oral History).

[57] Dillon Board Report, 28.

[58] Ibid., 110–11.

[59] Ibid., 9.

[60] Memo, "Erosion of the Military Profession," n.d., 1, JCS Organization-1960–68 folder, box 6, OP-602 File, NHHC Archives.

[61] Ibid., 5.

[62] Ibid., 6.

[63] U.S. Naval Institute, *Naval Leadership*, 3d ed. (Annapolis, MD, 1929), 163, 173.

[64] Benson Task Force Report, F-9. DOD Directive 5010.14 of 4 May 1965 and SECNAVINST 5000.21A of 8 Sept. 1965 directed the services to use the project manager concept.

[65] In his memoir, former SECNAV Paul H. Nitze noted that by the time he was appointed Secretary, "the service secretaries were excluded from participation in the mainstream of national security policy. Their tasks were to lead the effort to recruit, select, and train the personnel in their service; to develop, procure, and maintain the equipment their service needed; and to defend the interests of their service before the Congress and the public." Nitze, *From Hiroshima to Glasnost*, 253.

[66] Kennedy, "David Lamar McDonald," Love's *The Chiefs of Naval Operations*, 347.

[67] House of Representatives, *Communication from the President of the United States Transmitting a Plan for the Reorganization of the Department of the Navy*, 89th Cong., 2nd sess., 1966, H. Doc. 409, iv.

[68] Lawrence J. Korb, former Assistant Secretary of the Defense in the Reagan administration, noted in his 1979 study of defense policy making: "The first group of service secretaries appointed by McNamara all resigned within a year. To obtain stability, McNamara was eventually forced to place men from his own staff in those posts. McNamara's men really became vice-presidents of DOD rather than heads of the Army, Navy, or Air Force." Korb, *The Fall and Rise of the Pentagon* (Westport, CT, 1979), 86–87.

[69] Ltr, McNamara to L. Mendel Rivers, Chairman, House Armed Services Committee, 9 Mar. 1966, subj: Reorganization of the Navy, collection of Thomas C. Hone. Also in H. Doc. 409, 1966, iii–vi.

[70] Ibid., 23.

[71] Benson Task Force Report, F–9.

[72] Department of the Navy, *Review of Navy R&D Management, 1946–1973*, prepared by Booz, Allen & Hamilton Inc. (Washington, DC, 1976), 87.

[73] Benson Task Force Report, D–4.

[74] Ibid., E–3.

[75] Ibid., pt. 1, sec. 3, Summary, 3–5.

[76] Ibid., phase 2, pt. 2, tab G–2, 172.

[77] Secretary McNamara's deputies seem to have taken a very different view of his management style. See, for example, Paul R. Ignatius, *On Board: My Life in the Navy, Government,*

and Business (Annapolis, MD: Naval Institute Press, 2006), esp. ch. 5. Compare that with Paul H. Nitze's memoir, where he describes McNamara as performing "a tremendous amount of work, which resulted in his having a detailed and intimate knowledge of the complexities of the Department of Defense in a surprisingly short period of time." *From Hiroshima to Glasnost*, 274.

[78] Memo, Benson to DCNOs, 25 Nov. 1966, subj: Relationships between CNO's Staff and the "Bureaus," OPNAV Reorganization-1966, box 5, OP-602 File.

[79] Hone, "Navy Air Leadership: Rear Admiral William A. Moffett as Chief of the Bureau of Aeronautics," in Thompson's, *Air Leadership*, 83–118.

[80] Norman Polmar and Thomas B. Allen, *Rickover* (New York, 1982), 208.

[81] See Hewlett and Duncan, *Nuclear Navy*; and Polmar and Allen, *Rickover*.

[82] Benson Task Force Report, D–5–7.

[83] Ibid., F–4.

[84] Memo, Benson to CNO Advisory Board, 12 Oct. 1966, subj: Proposed Structure of CNO's Staff, OPNAV Reorganization-1966 folder, box 5, OP-602 File, NHHC Archives.

[85] F. S. Low, Study of Undersea Warfare, ser 001P003, 22 Apr. 1950, 11–12, CNO Studies, Command File, NHHC Archives.

[86] Dillon Board Report, 13.

[87] OPNAV Notice 5430, ser 130P09B3, 17 Apr. 1967, subj: Assistant Chiefs of Naval Operations (ACNO): change in billet titles, OP-09B2 Records.

[88] Memo, Director, Long Range Objectives Group to CNO, 2 Aug. 1968, subj: OPNAV Staff Organization, OPNAV Staff Organization Concept (1968) folder, box 5, OP-602 File, NHHC Archives.

[89] Briefing, OP-96 for VCNO, 1–2, OPNAV Reorganization (1968) folder, box 5, OP-602 File, NHHC Archives.

[90] Ibid., 2.

[91] Ibid., 3.

[92] Ibid., 4.

[93] Richard A. Stubbing, *The Defense Game* (New York, 1986), 285.

[94] McNamara formalized the growing authority of his staff by appointing Alain Enthoven, his chief analyst, assistant secretary of defense (Systems Analysis) in 1965. See "Acquisition in the Department of Defense, 1959–1968: The McNamara Legacy," by Walter S. Poole, in *Providing the Means of War: Historical Perspectives on Defense Acquisition, 1945–2000*, ed. by Shannon A. Brown (Washington, DC: U.S. Army Center for Military History and the Industrial College of the Armed Forces, 2005), 88.

[95] Ignatius, *On Board*, 83.

[96] Memo, OP-090 to CNO, 22 Sept. 1969, subj: Growth of Washington Headquarters, 5400, 00–1969 Subject file, OP-09B2 Records.

[97] Floyd D. Kennedy Jr., "David Lamar McDonald," in Love's *The Chiefs of Naval Operations*, 345.

[98] Nitze, *From Hiroshima to Glasnost*, 253.

[99] Stubbing, *The Defense Game*, 180. For an example of how defense contractors profited from Total Package Procurement, see the section on the Litton Ingalls Shipbuilding Division, 197–204.

[100] Walter S. Poole, "Acquisition in the Department of Defense, 1959–1968: The McNamara Legacy," in Brown's *Providing the Means of War: Historical Perspectives on Defense Acquisition, 1945–2000*, 82–84.

[101] Friedman, *U.S. Destroyers*, 371, 376–77.

[102] Ignatius, *On Board*, 170.

[103] Korb, *The Fall and Rise of the Pentagon*, 87.

[104] Ibid., 90.

[105] Ibid., 91.

[106] Lawrence J. Korb, "The Budget Process in the Department of Defense, 1947–77," *Public Administration Review*, 36 (July–Aug. 1977): 343.

[107] Memo, Deputy Secretary of Defense to Secretaries of the Military Departments, 30 May 1969, subj: Establishment of a Defense Systems Acquisition Review Council, 5420 File folder, "Boards and Committees," 00-1969 Subject File, OP-09B2 Records.

[108] William P. Mack Oral History, vol. 2: 546–47, (Annapolis, MD: U.S. Naval Institute, 1979).

[109] Naval Audit Service, "Special Review of the Organization and Mission of the Office of the Chief of Naval Operations and Subordinate Commands in the Washington Area," Report No. S00329, 31 May 1969, 8, Review of OPNAV Organization (1969) folder, box 5, OP-602 File, NHHC Archives.

[110] Ibid., 9.

[111] Ibid.

[112] Ibid., 13.

[113] Ibid., 15.

[114] Ibid., 14.

[115] Ibid., 11.

[116] Ibid.

[117] Ibid.

[118] Ibid., 17.

[119] Ibid., 18.

[120] Ibid., 22.

[121] Ibid., 11.

[122] Memo, ACNO, Director of Naval Administration to VCNO, subj: Auditor General's special review of OPNAV: 31 May 69, conducted by Naval Audit Service, OPNAV Audit 1969 folder, OP-09B92 Records.

[123] "OPNAV Responses," in ibid.

[124] Memo, ACNO, Director of Naval Administration to VCNO, subj: Auditor General's special review of OPNAV.

CHAPTER 10

Zumwalt: A Cultural Revolution

Introduction

At the beginning of the administration of President John F. Kennedy, then–Secretary of Defense Robert S. McNamara was faced with a very difficult problem, which was how to optimize the nuclear and conventional forces of the United States without increasing taxes. To increase employment, the Kennedy administration persuaded the Federal Reserve Board of Governors to reduce the cost of loans. It was feared that increased defense spending would lead the defense industry to take too great a percentage of that loan money—money that the Kennedy administration wanted invested in the civilian segment of the economy, and therefore Secretary McNamara reduced spending on strategic forces in order to make available money for investing in conventional forces without raising federal taxes.

However, after President Kennedy's assassination in the fall of 1963, then–Vice President Lyndon B. Johnson won the presidency in his own right with a landslide victory in the 1964 election. With what he considered a mandate from the electorate, and with majorities in both houses of Congress, Johnson set out to develop and implement a "Great Society" program. At the same time, the conflict in Vietnam grew more intense, more American forces were sent there, and defense spending increased. For example, one estimate has Vietnam War costs rising from $700 million in 1965 to over $15 billion in 1966.[1] This rapid rise in defense spending, coupled with an increase in spending on domestic programs, flooded the country with dollars. This increase, coupled with the Federal Reserve system's lower interest rates that facilitated borrowing, led to inflation—too many dollars chasing too few goods, in some cases dramatically, raising the cost of equipment, services, and fuel that the Defense Department had to purchase.[2]

The war in Vietnam also divided the country politically and socially. President Johnson was challenged from within his own political party in 1968 and chose not to campaign for re-election. Richard M. Nixon, the Republican Party candidate, won the bitterly contested presidential election and chose to reduce gradually the numbers of Americans fighting in the war. Within the political contests and controversies, many citizens—especially those subject to the Selective Service system—chose to participate in public demonstrations that at times turned violent. Adding to the sense of confrontation were the determined efforts of African Americans to challenge the *status quo* of race relations.

Admiral Elmo Zumwalt

Vice Admiral Elmo R. Zumwalt succeeded Admiral Thomas H. Moorer as CNO on 1 July 1970 and walked right into the political, economic, and racial controversies. Why had the young (49 years old) admiral been selected? Defense Secretary Melvin R. Laird had first met Zumwalt in Vietnam in February 1969 when the admiral was Commander, Naval Forces Vietnam, and he wanted Zumwalt as Chief of Naval Operations because he regarded Zumwalt as the right kind of young, ambitious, enthusiastic, intelligent, and aggressive officer who could shake up the Navy. Zumwalt was not outgoing CNO Moorer's choice as his successor because the youthful surface officer had already earned a reputation for being unorthodox.[3] However, both Defense secretary Laird and Navy secretary John L. H. Chafee—the latter a veteran Marine who had fought in World War II and Korea—were strong supporters of Zumwalt, and Moorer, who was moving up to serve as Chairman of the Joint Chiefs of Staff, could not block Zumwalt's appointment.

Zumwalt's most important mentor was Paul H. Nitze, a highly regarded strategist and negotiator. Zumwalt had worked as Nitze's executive assistant from 1963 to 1965 when Nitze had served as SECNAV. Zumwalt had also earned a reputation for being creative organizationally. While on the OPNAV staff in 1966, for example, he had set up OPNAV's first systems analysis division (OP-96). As the previous chapter of this study showed, OP-96 was part of the Navy's answer to then–Defense secretary McNamara's "whiz kids." Then-Commander Harry D. Train II, who in 1966 had succeeded Zumwalt as Nitze's assistant, considered "Zumwalt one of the most creative people I have ever known . . ."[4] and therefore an ideal candidate to set up and lead OP-96.

As expected (and in some quarters feared), Zumwalt took office as CNO "committed to changing Navy policy in a variety of areas" because he was convinced that the Navy "was confused about its justification for existence."[5] His policy initiatives in matters of discipline, naval dress, race relations, naval strategy, and cost overruns in warship construction are described in detail elsewhere, most notably in the admiral's memoirs. Many of those initiatives—and the methods used to implement them—were very controversial within the Navy and among some members of Congress. However, as historian Larry Berman revealed in his detailed 2012 biography of Zumwalt, the new CNO planned to work at two levels simultaneously.[6] The first level

Figure 10-1. CNO Admiral Elmo R. Zumwalt Jr. had never planned to make the Navy his career. However, his experiences as a young officer in China after the Japanese surrender led him to believe that he needed to remain in the Navy to defend the United States against the Soviet Union. Like his mentor, Secretary of the Navy Paul H. Nitze, Zumwalt was intelligent and articulate. (National Archives USN 1145559)

was that of the Navy as an institution; to make institutional changes, Zumwalt would change OPNAV. The second level was that of national strategic policy, and at that level what would matter was whether his views were compatible with the views of President Nixon and Henry Kissinger, the President's national security advisor. As it happened, the two levels were often not synchronized, forcing Zumwalt to compromise or abandon some of his goals.

Organizational Reform

Even before Zumwalt's tenure began, naval leaders had been concerned about calls for both Defense and Navy reorganization. In 1969, for example, the Nixon administration had commissioned a "Blue Ribbon Defense Panel" to study the organization and administration of the Defense Department. CNO Moorer had carefully tracked the panel's discussions through OP-06 (DCNO, Plans and Policy). The panel had made several recommendations to the President. One was to reduce the staffs in the service headquarters, the office of the service secretaries, the Joint Staff, the Office of the Secretary of Defense, and the unified commands. The reason? Because the existing situation encouraged "excessive paper work and coordination, delay, duplication and unnecessary expense." A second recommendation was that "management throughout the supply, maintenance and transportation systems of the Department [of Defense]" be better integrated. A third proposal was to reorganize the unified command staffs so that they were really under the control of the regional combatant commanders. A fourth called for removing the Navy's systems commands from OPNAV and giving them to a line command (or commands).[7] Indeed, like the Symington Committee of 1960, the Blue Ribbon Defense Panel suggested a wholesale reorganization of the Defense Department. Although the panel stopped short of recommending service unification, some of its proposed changes were just too politically controversial for Secretary of Defense (SecDef) Laird to accept as part of a larger package.

But that did not mean the services would escape the danger of serious organizational reform dictated from above. In October 1970, the Committee on Government Operations of the House of Representatives argued in its report that the U.S. military experience in Vietnam showed that the logistics organizations of the services needed reform. SecDef Laird noted, in a letter to the committee's chairman, that the Blue Ribbon Defense Panel had reached a similar conclusion, and that DOD had already acted to improve military logistics.[8]

"Project Sixty"

In April 1970, even before becoming CNO, Admiral Zumwalt had promised Secretary Laird that he could develop a plan for organizational change in OPNAV within 60 days of taking over from Admiral Moorer.[9] With the assistance of then–Rear Admiral Worth H. Bagley, Zumwalt developed what he called Project Sixty, a collection of more than 20 different initiatives.[10] The new CNO first had Rear Admiral (Select) Stansfield M. Turner brief a preliminary version of Project Sixty to flag officers in the Washington, D.C., area on 26 August 1970. Then, he and SECNAV John Chafee briefed Secretary Laird on 10 September. Laird accepted their approach.[11] In a letter to all flag officers in the Navy and Marines, Zumwalt noted that the Project Sixty paper would guide "actions we should take on the suitability of current programs" and serve as "a dynamic statement of the direction that the Navy is to move . . ."[12]

Jeffrey Sands of the Center for Naval Analyses summarized the contents of the Project Sixty paper and briefing as "emphasizing six basic principles: reprioritize naval missions; retire forces early to fund modernization; modernize following the 'high-low' mix; pursue 'new initiatives' in research and development; reduce support costs; and pursue people programs."[13] In his oral history, Admiral Bagley observed that "There wasn't one single policy paper I can remember in three-and-a-half years [in OPNAV with Zumwalt] in which it wasn't perfectly clear from the Project Sixty work the direction of decision that should be taken."[14]

Zumwalt's Changes to OPNAV

Zumwalt had already established his own "Organizational Review Panel" in OPNAV,[15] and in August 1970, while waiting for his panel's report, Zumwalt established the Naval Decision Center (NADEC). The NADEC was a "secure briefing room" where Zumwalt and his vice chief and their staffs could meet regularly in closed sessions to discuss policy decisions and internal organizational problems.[16] Zumwalt also created the CNO Executive Panel (CEP), a small group of experts from outside and inside the Navy to provide him with advice he was not likely to get from his own staff. As Jeffrey Sands discovered, however, the more important reason for creating the CEP was to "develop supporters in a wide variety of ever-changing government and non-government" posts who would be "conversant with naval issues" and who might hold "key positions long after [Zumwalt] had left the scene."[17]

To support the CEP, Zumwalt set up a special staff office, OP-00K. The Ad Hoc Priorities Analysis Group, formed that September, assisted OP-00K in developing "a clear statement of a Navy concept suitable for use in the next four years for reshaping the Navy, using it so that civilian members of the Office of the Secretary of Defense, White House, and Congress would more clearly understand the Navy's mission, purpose and vital importance to U.S. national objectives."[18] What Zumwalt and his supporters within the Navy wished to do was to shift the Navy's role from "power projection" to "sea control." As Zumwalt had argued to Chafee and Laird, the rise of the Soviet navy posed a direct challenge to the Navy's ability to dominate with relative impunity the seas near land targets. Though numbers of Navy aircraft had been lost to antiaircraft missile and gun attacks in Southeast Asia, no aircraft carriers had been lost or damaged through enemy action. The growth rate of the Soviet navy, however, promised to increase the challenge at sea to U.S. carriers and complicate the Navy's ability to operate across the world's oceans.[19]

One reason Admiral Zumwalt felt compelled to force his own colleagues to think about a shift in the Navy's role was because of OPNAV's preoccupation with the programming and budgetary process that had been established by OSD. This was evident in an OP-03G (Fleet Operations) memo in September 1970 to OP-090 (Program Planning), which noted: "Practically the entire OPNAV organization is tuned, like a tuning fork, to the vibrations of the budgetary process. . . . [T]here is a vast preoccupation with budgetary matters at the expense of considering planning, or readiness or requirements, or operational characteristics or any of the other elements contributing to the ability of the Fleets to fight."[20] The new CNO shared this view of OPNAV, and OP-00K's assignment revealed the essence of Zumwalt's organizational strategy: first defining the Navy's mission then directing OPNAV through the use of program planning and systems analysis.

To help him achieve these goals, Zumwalt created what became known as the "platform sponsors": OP-05 (DCNO for aviation), OP-02 (DCNO for submarines) and OP-03 (DCNO for surface forces). Each platform sponsor would be a vice admiral. The new CNO had wanted to place these platform sponsors—as rear admirals—under the DCNO for Fleet Operations and Readiness (OP-03). He was apparently argued out of that move by the members of his own Organizational Review Panel. They also convinced him to back away from a proposal to create two vice chiefs of naval operations—one for program development and review and the other for fleet construction and support.[21] As a former aide to the admiral commented later, Zumwalt "had an essential distrust of a bureaucracy."[22] This trait is precisely what could be expected of a talented, successful Navy "operator." As Zumwalt apparently suspected, however, his operator's credentials were not strong enough to secure his position as the Navy's chief officer. Zumwalt had never commanded one of the numbered fleets, and unlike predecessors such as Arleigh Burke, his operational command experience did not compensate for his relative youth.

Zumwalt Compared to Arleigh Burke

A point often forgotten is that Burke and Zumwalt, both relatively junior when appointed CNO, could not use the same techniques to first establish their legitimacy and then use that legitimacy to direct the Navy. For example, during Burke's first four years in office, the Navy began switching from analog to digital control technology, developed a submerged intermediate-range ballistic missile system, and fielded major missile air defense systems.[23] But Burke had moved cautiously and was careful to win allies in the service before making controversial decisions. Because of his work in OP-23 (Organizational Research and Policy) in the 1940s, Burke was identified as an independent Navy man, and drew on that image to win support from his fellow officers.

Zumwalt had no such image. Many of his peers regarded him as a decidedly "political" officer, dating from his time working for Paul H. Nitze, McNamara's Assistant Secretary of Defense for International Security Affairs (ISA) in 1962. When Nitze became Secretary of the Navy in 1963, there were Navy officers who thought that the new Navy secretary had rewarded then-Captain Zumwalt for his prior work in ISA by making him the secretary's executive assistant. Zumwalt's tie to Nitze could not compensate for his lack of experience at sea. Indeed, it worked the other way around, and there were officers in the Navy who felt that Zumwalt had made his career by writing papers instead of commanding ships. These critics conveniently ignored Zumwalt's successful command of American naval forces in Vietnam under General Creighton Abrams, Commander of Military Assistance Command Vietnam (MACV).

Figure 10-2. CNO Elmo R. Zumwalt Jr. (left), conferring with Vice Admiral Robert S. Salzer, Zumwalt's successor as Commander U.S. Naval Forces Vietnam, on board an aircraft flying over South Vietnam in May 1971. (National Archives USN 1148801)

Zumwalt's lack of experience did not keep him from arguing in 1970 that multiple crises were seriously threatening the Navy, and he moved quickly and directly to effect change. As a result, he sent a cluster of "Z-grams," messages directly from the CNO to the fleet, directing changes in policies that the CNO had real control over (e.g., dress codes and race relations).[24] Moorer, Zumwalt's predecessor, had begun reform in these fields, but he had worked gradually and quietly through the chain of command. Zumwalt bypassed the chain of command and spoke directly to the fleet, calling his action the "least-worst" choice.[25] Zumwalt's methods, however, were interpreted by some senior officers as a means of making the fleet dependent on the CNO and not on the various seagoing commanders. In this, they were expressing a traditional and deeply held view about the importance of delegating authority and responsibility within the Navy.

More Organizational Changes

In November 1970, members of the OPNAV Organizational Review Panel briefed Zumwalt on the results of their deliberations. Most of their suggestions resembled the proposals developed by earlier studies, particularly the Benson report of 1966. The panel proposed that OPNAV eliminate the DCNO positions of Logistics and Development and absorb the Naval Material Command to perform those duties. A second suggestion, which Zumwalt approved, elevated the authority and rank of the Director of Navy Program Planning to a principal assistant (OP-090) to the CNO. A third idea focused all nuclear warfare planning on the office of the DCNO for Plans and Policy (OP-06).[26] In implementing the proposals to alter the form of OPNAV, Zumwalt was constrained by Secretary Laird's decision that the service chiefs could not increase the sizes of their staffs. In fact, in September 1970 Laird had ordered the service secretaries to reduce headquarters (including OPNAV) civilian and military personnel by 15 percent.[27] However, it was also clear that Secretary Laird would not contravene Zumwalt's efforts to reorganize OPNAV so long as Zumwalt stayed within the personnel cap.

The battle over centralization of functions in the Defense Department continued, however. In January 1971, Deputy Secretary of Defense David Packard announced that he and Secretary Laird, contrary to the recommendation of the Blue Ribbon Defense Panel, did not "intend to establish a single Defense-wide Logistics Command at this time." However, they promulgated a "set of logistics systems policy objectives" that eventually formed the basis of a Department of Defense (DOD) Logistics Systems Plan.[28] In response to "an OSD drafted Blueprint for logistics change and to the numerous memoranda coming from OSD," Vice Admiral George E. Moore, the Vice Chief of Naval Material, had recommended the formation of a logistics policy committee.[29] Composed of logistics specialists from the services, this committee developed its own cross-service logistics plan. Upon its completion, the plan was viewed by Vice Admiral Moore and others as an effective means of blocking any OSD changes that the services regarded as threatening.[30] But Deputy Secretary Packard withheld from the Logistics Systems Policy Committee the authority to organize the plan's implementation. As an OP-06 (Plans and Policy) study noted, "a common Service view that the [committee] would provide Service control of the logistics systems changes has not emerged."[31]

OP-06 viewed Secretary Laird's concept of "participatory management" as "participation when you do what they [Office of the Secretary of Defense] want." Whether this was a fair assessment or not, the point is that Zumwalt attempted internal reforms while, from the Navy's standpoint, OSD was encroaching on service prerogatives and undermining service autonomy. The risk involved with Zumwalt's approach was that his changes, coupled with changes mandated from the Office of the Secretary of Defense, would make matters in OPNAV worse and not better. Like his predecessors, Zumwalt faced pressure from above and below. The pressure from below was not only a resistance to Zumwalt's policies in areas like race relations and military demeanor, but also opposition from high-ranking officers like Vice Admiral Hyman G. Rickover.

Corralling Admiral Rickover

Rickover ran a significant portion of the Navy directly, or indirectly, and he was virtually immune to CNO control. Zumwalt had tried to "bargain with Rickover . . . but Rickover—probably seeing that the deal was not a prerequisite to achieving his goals—refused."[32] In a sense, Rickover was acting logically because in his view OPNAV lacked the organizational discipline necessary to achieve his goals. Rickover felt that both his success and that of the Navy's nuclear power program depended on his demonstrated political skills and on the "culture" that he had created to guarantee the safe operation of nuclear attack and ballistic missile submarines.

Zumwalt did not see himself as a threat to Rickover, but Rickover regarded him (and openly accused him of being) a "political" admiral, attractive to the media and ready to charm the President and the SecDef. Zumwalt believed he had no choice but to act as he did, however. The CNO had to be political to be effective; the nature, or character, of the Navy's cultural problems required that he use what were essentially political means. Rear Admiral David R. Oliver, a nuclear submarine commander who closely observed the behavior of both Rickover and Zumwalt when he was "the communication path" between them, described both officers as "extraordinary" and "visionary leaders."[33]

Each was out to force a new culture on the Navy. Rickover realized that the Navy's nuclear submarine program would die if the nuclear reactors driving the submarines were not perceived to be safe, and making them safe and reliable meant creating a new type of engineering and operating culture within the Navy. Making them safe required Rickover to create a new class of officer and enlisted—men so skilled in nuclear reactor technology and so dedicated to the operating discipline that Rickover had created that they could operate a fleet of nuclear submarines safely as a matter of routine. "In contrast," to quote Rear Admiral Oliver, "Zumwalt inherited a Navy that badly needed immediate and dramatic transformation, and he had only four years to accomplish this change." Oliver believed that Zumwalt had "great substance," but he also felt that "Zumwalt was the king of style," and that the CNO needed to be such a "king" in order to make the changes in the Navy that he (and Secretary Laird) felt were essential.[34]

Still More Organization Changes

By the end of 1970, Zumwalt was like a baseball player caught in the act of stealing second base. To hesitate was to be thrown out, and so Zumwalt pressed ahead with further changes in OPNAV as his subordinates were engaged in making his initial changes work. In January 1971, he shut down the CNO Advisory Board and set up the CNO Executive Board (CEB). The permanent members of the CEB were the VCNO, the Assistant VCNO, the Director of Navy Program Planning (OP-090), the six DCNOs (OP-01 through OP-06), the Director of Tactical Electromagnetic Programs (OP-093), the Director of Antisubmarine Warfare (ASW) Programs (OP-095), the Director of Strategic Offensive and Defensive Systems (OP-097), and the Chief of NAVMAT. According to Sands, one purpose of the board was to give the CNO the chance to talk directly to his senior deputies and convince them to accept his decisions. But the board was also a place where Zumwalt could review how and how well his initiatives—especially program decisions—were being implemented.[35]

In March 1971, the CNO finally organized the deputies along the "four forces" concept as created by the Benson Task Force. The title of the Deputy Chief of Naval Operations for Fleet Operations and Readiness (OP-03) changed to DCNO for Surface, later Surface Warfare. The DCNO for Air (OP-05) inherited all the offices in the old OP-03 that programmed aviation activities. The Deputy Chief of Naval Operations for Submarines (OP-02), later Submarine Warfare, was established. Zumwalt also eliminated OP-07 (Development), re-designating its chief the Director of Research, Development, Test and Evaluation (RDT&E), so that the number of deputy

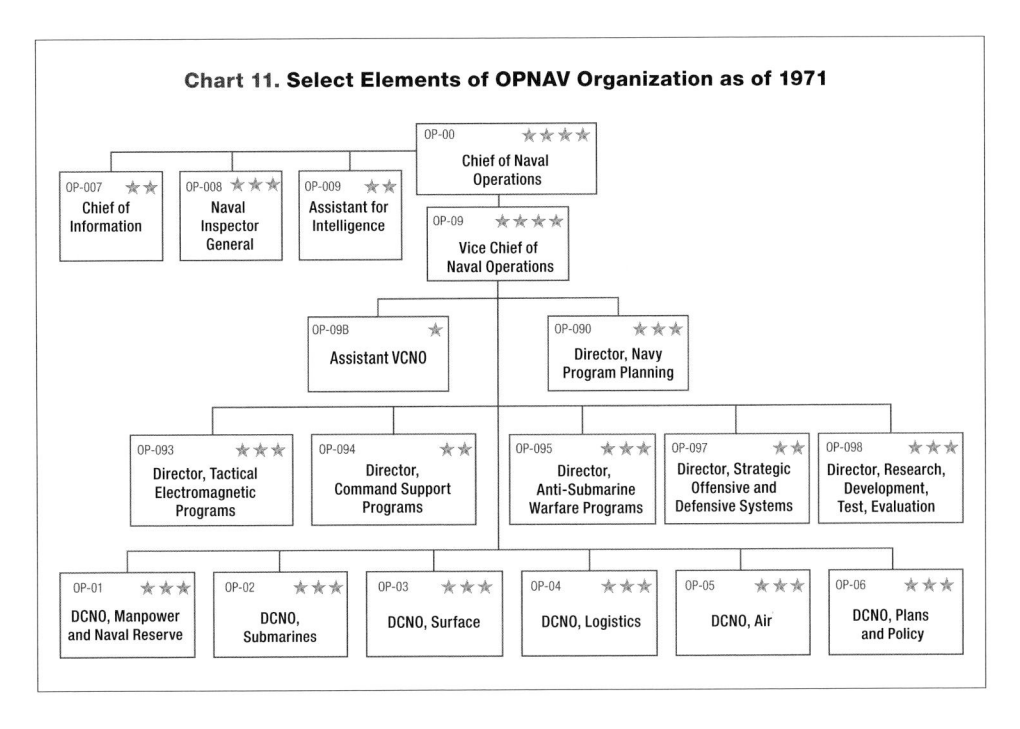

Chart 11. Select Elements of OPNAV Organization as of 1971

chiefs remained constant.[36] This move represented a major change in focus because it shifted the OPNAV organization further away from functional lines and more toward warfare, or platform, communities. OP-01 (Manpower and Naval Reserve), OP-04 (Logistics), and OP-06 (Plans and Policy) were the only DCNO offices whose interests stretched across the platform communities.

In effect, Zumwalt placated the three major warfare communities by vesting each with permanent and powerful representation in OPNAV. Programmatic integration of these communities was achieved in the directorates headed by deputies of the Vice Chief of Naval Operations: Director of Navy Program Planning (OP-090); Director of Tactical Electromagnetic Programs (OP-093); Director of ASW Programs (OP-095); the new Director of Research, Development, Test and Evaluation (OP-098); and Director of Naval Education and Training (OP-099).

These directorates under the vice chief became the CNO's immediate—and therefore more influential—staff. While Zumwalt reassured the deputy chiefs in January 1971 that they would retain the authority to manage programs over which they had cognizance, he also explained that the directorates were meant to "provide a systems overview . . . to ensure that . . . the Navy's resources are correctly allocated to those systems which provide the Navy with the best possible operational capability."[37] When it became clear to Zumwalt that OPNAV was too large to use effectively as the staff he felt he needed, he began creating his staff-within-a-staff.

As part of this process, Zumwalt disbanded OP-097, the directorate for Strategic Offensive and Defensive Systems, and shifted its functions and personnel to OP-06 in June 1971.[38] In August 1971, Zumwalt established the Fiscal Management Division (OP-92) under the Director of Navy Program Planning.[39] This was part of his plan to focus, in OP-090, enough staff support to enable him to review and evaluate all major Navy programs. Another part of his plan was to make the Systems Analysis Division (OP-96) both a source of ideas and a source of intelligence on what the deputy chiefs were planning. For example, Vice Admiral Worth H. Bagley, Director of Navy Program Planning, told the deputy chiefs and the Chief of Naval Material, "Ultimately, I expect OP-96 to provide Study Project Officers for all studies in the CNO program, insofar as this is agreeable."[40] These officers would be Bagley's "spies," but they would also work with officers in the surface, aviation, and submarine offices to tie together Navy programs.

Zumwalt continued to strengthen the directorates under the vice chief in 1972. In March he combined OP-92 with the Office of the Deputy Chief of Naval Material for Programs and Financial Management, thereby linking the fiscal control divisions of OPNAV and the Naval Material Command.[41] That August, the CNO shifted the Ship Acquisition and Improvement Division from OP-03 to OP-090 (Navy Program Planning).[42] When Rear Admiral Stansfield Turner returned from a destroyer-cruiser flotilla command in 1971, Zumwalt had appointed him head of OP-96. Under Turner, OP-96 replaced the Project Sixty paper with the "CNO Policy and Planning Guidance," or CPPG. The CPPG summarized the program guidance from the SecDef and any additions or modifications to that guidance from the CNO. The CPPG also described the national and international trends that were influencing Navy strategic thinking. In addition, it ranked the Navy's program areas in order of priority, and it gave programmers guidance as they prepared their inputs to the CNO's Program Analysis Memorandum (CPAM).[43]

Rear Admiral Turner and his staff had developed a version of what former SecDef McNamara had forced on the services—a planning and programming process—and with the same intent, which was to give a senior executive (the CNO in this case) the ability to direct force structure development. OP-96, OPNAV's systems analysis office, started the process off every year by issuing the CPPG at the beginning of October. Soon thereafter, OP-96 distributed CPAMs to the program sponsors in OPNAV (OP-01 through OP-06). The program sponsors assessed the tentative CPAMs against the guidance in the CPPG and the resource "requirements" from organizations such as the Naval Material Command and the Navy's systems commands. Then the sponsors would put together Sponsor Program Priorities, and send them to OP-090 for review. Once reviewed and approved, the Sponsor Program Priorities would be combined into a final CPAM. Then OP-96 and OP-92 would review them one last time before they were sent to OSD. Once approved by the Secretary of Defense, the program numbers would be transformed into the Navy's budget submission to the White House Office of Management and Budget (OMB).[44]

By May 1973, when this process of developing the Navy's program was no longer new, the new Director of OP-96, Rear Admiral Harry D. Train II, was told by CNO Zumwalt that his job

> had three equal parts. One of those ... was to preside over studies that started with a question and [worked] towards the answer. He charged me to be extremely sensitive to the progress of such studies, and if it appeared that the answer was going to be disastrous to the Navy in terms of its procurement program ..., then we'd have to try to short it to the ground before it damaged us too badly.[45]

The second part of Train's job

> was to preside over studies that supported decisions of the ... Defense System Acquisition Review Council ... Those studies were to start with the answer, which was 'buy the system,' and then work the study backwards.... It was a continual challenge to ensure that when you were proving that you needed one system you weren't disproving that you needed another.[46]

Train's third responsibility was to market the results of OP-96's studies and CNO Zumwalt's programs.[47]

These instructions from Zumwalt to Train might seem cynical, but they weren't. Zumwalt had already charted the course that he wanted the Navy to pursue. The function of analysis had changed from providing a stimulus to checking the validity of the changes that Zumwalt and his deputies had initiated. Admiral Train recalled that Zumwalt "didn't think you got answers from analysis. He thought from analysis you derived a way to communicate to other people who understood analysis..."[48] But the communication was essential to fostering and sustaining change. For example, the Navy conducted campaign analyses—usually warfare simulations at the tactical and operational levels of war—on a regular basis, and both Zumwalt and Train knew that such analyses were an important way of both bringing people from different parts of the Navy together *and* developing evidence to support the Navy's overall program.

During November 1972, Zumwalt shifted "mission and functions pertaining to aircraft carriers in the Fleet Modernization Program" from OP-05 to the new Ship Acquisition and Improvement Division in OP-090. At the same time he eliminated the office of the Program Coordinator for Nuclear-powered Carriers in OP-05, transferring its mission to OP-090.[49] The Secretary of the Navy approved the transfer of reserve programs from OP-01 to the Director of Naval Reserve (OP-09R), who formally received sponsorship authority in April 1973.[50] The directorate for Tactical Electromagnetic Programs was abolished, and its functions were shifted to OP-095, renamed the Office of Antisubmarine Warfare and Tactical Electromagnetic Programs.[51] The CEB recognized the shift of authority from the deputy chiefs to the directorates under the vice chief when it handed down a decision requiring the deputy chiefs to get permission from the CNO before issuing statements of force level requirements, ship and aircraft characteristics, characteristics of weapons systems whose development and procurement costs crossed certain thresholds, and modernization decisions for major weapons systems.[52]

Admiral Zumwalt shifted influence inside OPNAV from OP-06 (DCNO, Plans and Policy) to OP-090 (Program Planning). But he did so to achieve the goals he had set out in Project Sixty. One of those goals was to scrap a number of mothballed ships that the analysts tagged as no longer useful as a supplement to existing fleet strength. Another was to solve the growing problem of a Soviet nuclear submarine force that was spreading out into the Atlantic and Pacific and threatening the lines of communication between the United States and its overseas allies. The FFG-7, an antisubmarine escort designed from the first to deal with this challenge, was also a product of Project Sixty.

Were the Organizational Changes Working? Could They?

Zumwalt had already hired a consulting firm, Organization Resources Counselors, Inc., to study OPNAV, and he had also solicited suggestions, through OP-96, from Rear Admiral Tyler F. Dedman, Assistant VCNO and Director of Naval Administration.[53] The firm's study (later referred to as the Beaumont Study) was presented to Zumwalt in May 1973. Its conclusions were a warning to Zumwalt that all his organizational changes had not made OPNAV a more efficient organization:

- The lines of accountability and responsibility within OPNAV and CNO's major related areas of responsibility are unclear. . . . At any given point in time it is almost impossible to identify one single individual who is responsible for a project, program, or process.[54]
- [I]n the area of Program Coordinator/Project Manager, the massive duplication of channels of communications, lines of approval, access to financial resources, etc. make it extremely difficult to identify who is responsible, even though there are countless documents formally establishing authority.[55]

- The Navy's proclivity to create special units to get things done is detrimental to the integrity of any management system.[56]
- [A]llocation of resources across the many competing claimants is based on a highly complex system of personal priorities and negotiations.[57]
- Currently, OPNAV can be viewed as organized into a number of "little Navies." Each of these units attempts to remain an independent and autonomous whole, fighting to keep its boundaries (mission) intact, even to the point of departure from CNO's stated objectives. In the process, each unit attempts to acquire the organizational aspects, skills and capabilities of the others, thus remaining well-equipped for adversary proceedings even with OPNAV itself.[58]
- [B]ecause of the crisis nature of the management process, there is a tendency for OPNAV to reach into and run and direct many of the activities in subordinate commands.[59]

These conclusions were a strong critique; they repeated many of the observations found in earlier studies. After all the structural changes, what had really been achieved? A review committee, chaired by former VCNO Admiral James S. Russell, USN (Ret.), was not quite sure what to do with the study, and recommended only evolutionary changes in OPNAV's organization.

Part of OPNAV's problem—and Zumwalt's—was the growth of special project offices. This management technique, first established in 1955 for the Fleet Ballistic Missile Program (Polaris), was so successful that later CNOs and chiefs of Naval Material created other project offices to push through development and acquisition projects in emergency cases. By 1965, however, the Secretary of Defense had ordered the services to use these management organizations for *all* major acquisition projects. This directive struck at the authority of the CNO and the Secretary of the Navy to control the Navy's program budget. By the time Zumwalt became CNO, special project managers were concerned with meeting cost and schedule deadlines set by the Defense Systems Acquisition Review Council (DSARC)—not with whether their programs were tied systematically to the initiatives of the current CNO.

Moreover, because many projects continued through the terms of several CNOs, project managers with many years of experience could deal directly and expertly with both OSD and Congress. The scope of the resulting management problem is suggested by the numbers. Between 1955 and 1973, the chiefs of Naval Material designated 22 special projects. By 1976, the average life span of these projects was almost six years, or two years longer than the expected term of the Chief of Naval Operations. Thirty-one special projects in the Naval Ship Systems Command and 36 in the Naval Air Systems Command had been established, and 18 projects in each command still existed in 1973.[60]

Not all projects had the kind of visibility and status given to the Polaris project, the first special projects office (SPO). Nor did they operate under the same conditions. The SPO for Polaris reported to a special oversight and review committee headed by the CNO (then Arleigh Burke) and the Secretary of the Navy. Most of the project offices in 1973 reported only to their sponsors in OPNAV and up the chain of command in the systems commands. Coordination across projects and programs was the responsibility of the Naval Material Command and

OPNAV. However, as the Organization Resources Counselors' study showed, the Naval Material Command lacked authority and OPNAV was so splintered that project managers were often on their own. To protect their resources, they cultivated support in OPNAV and in Congress, constructing alliances directly with OPNAV and congressional staffs. This situation led Secretary of Defense James D. Schlesinger (Melvin Laird's successor) to note that "if service resistance is really entrenched, it cannot be overcome."[61]

Schlesinger's problem was that he dealt with program managers (PMs) only through the reviews of major acquisition programs done by the DSARC. Those reviews focused on the ability of PMs to meet schedule and performance milestones. Money for these special programs came from the services, which were supposed to review the programs to verify that they did in fact contribute to service goals by satisfying service requirements. This is why CNO Zumwalt was intent on adding to the authority of the Director of Navy Program Planning (OP-090). Though specific programs were sponsored by the warfare area DCNOs, Zumwalt could use the programming process to do what a Secretary of Defense could not do easily—that is, to force warfare community leaders to tie ongoing programs to larger goals.

Investing in Personnel

Zumwalt regarded the CNO's role as a leader of sailors as critical to the Navy and a major responsibility. In 1970, Zumwalt faced a rising personnel crisis in the Navy. Re-enlistment rates for enlisted personnel were down. Many wives of enlisted and officer personnel were extremely dissatisfied with housing, long deployment times, and what seemed to be a lack of concern for their welfare on the part of senior admirals.[62] Race was also a problem for the Navy—a time bomb that went off when African American sailors refused to obey orders on the carriers *Kitty Hawk* (CVA-63) and *Constellation* (CVA-64) in the fall of 1972.[63] After World War I and until the middle of World War II, African Americans who joined the Navy found that the officer ranks and enlisted skilled trades were closed to them. This history of discrimination had lingering negative effects on Navy personnel policy, and African American sailors found this situation intolerable. Zumwalt sided with them. While media coverage of the events on *Constellation* was still intense, Zumwalt had given a very pointed speech to Navy flag officers in the Washington, D.C., area. With reporters present, Zumwalt told his fellow admirals that "the Navy has made unacceptable progress in the equal opportunity area," and that the refusal of African American sailors to obey orders on *Constellation* was a sign that the Navy as a whole had not implemented the changes that he had already ordered.[64]

The incidents on the two carriers and the means used by Zumwalt and the on-scene commanders to defuse what could have been a violent situation nearly cost Zumwalt his job. Zumwalt's speech to his fellow admirals made matters even worse for the CNO. Navy secretary John Warner, Chafee's successor, did not stand by Zumwalt. Just as bad was the fact that, as Larry Berman documented, "A number of flag officers felt insulted and demeaned. They also resented that the CNO had allowed the press to attend the meeting."[65] Even worse was the reaction of President Nixon, who threatened to demand that Secretary of Defense Laird dismiss Zumwalt immediately.[66]

As historian Berman discovered, "a handful of retired admirals were working with key contacts in the media and [in Congress] to undermine [Zumwalt's] credibility. Their ringleader was Admiral George Anderson, who had succeeded the legendary Arleigh Burke..."[67] Representative F. Edward Hebert, (D-LA) Chairman of the Armed Services Committee of the House of Representatives, called for a special subcommittee investigation. Fortunately, Hebert and Zumwalt were well acquainted, but the clamor for Zumwalt's firing was strong, especially after news stories recounting his speech to his fellow admirals. Even Chairman Hebert was angry. To keep his post, Zumwalt had to mount a defense, and that included a special trip with Secretary Warner to speak with retired Representative Carl Vinson, then 89 years old and living in Milledgeville, Georgia.[68]

Zumwalt was under a great deal of pressure. The congressional subcommittee released its findings at the beginning of 1973. Berman called it "as harsh an indictment as could have been issued within the norms of congressional propriety."[69] Nevertheless, Zumwalt survived the public and private criticism. One reason was because William E. Timmons Sr., who was President Nixon's assistant for legislative affairs, criticized the investigating committee's report on the grounds that "The sweeping generalizations drawn from the two [aircraft carrier] cases are simply not supported by the evidence... To say as the report does that there is no racial discrimination in the Navy is obviously untrue."[70] Timmons was no stranger to politics. He had managed both the 1968 and 1972 Republican national conventions for Nixon. His view on the subcommittee investigation carried the day in the White House. Zumwalt was also saved by what Berman called "the dramatic reversal of reenlistment trends under Zumwalt (10 percent in 1970, 23 percent in 1972) and the great improvement of overall morale among both officers and enlisted."[71]

Yet the furor over race relations in the Navy revealed an Achilles heel in Zumwalt's approach to the service. To improve the lot of sailors, Zumwalt had to push his fellow flag officers hard. The incidents on *Kitty Hawk* and *Constellation* were seen by some very influential people as a sign that Zumwalt was failing. What he was trying to do in the Navy suddenly became front-page news, forcing him to wage what can only be called a political campaign to preserve his job. Put another way, as both the Navy's senior officer and a national figure, Zumwalt's image was controversial. To change the Navy as he had planned in Project Sixty, he needed to be able to look successful in both worlds. On the one hand, he had to be able to show the active and retired admirals who opposed him that his efforts to improve the service were in fact successful. On the other hand, he had to make sure that any negative publicity linked to a perception that he had failed did not rob him of support in the White House and Congress. Zumwalt could not build a wall between his effort to significantly change the Navy and his standing in Washington as the Navy's spokesman and uniformed leader. His "inside" moves affected his influence outside the Navy.

Fortunately for Zumwalt, his efforts to improve officer education in the Navy were both less visible publicly and more successful within the service. His most obvious effort was to send Rear

Admiral Stansfield Turner, a Naval War College alumnus, to Newport in 1972 to invigorate the college's curriculum. Turner set out to strengthen the teaching of strategy and also to educate officers in "defense economics" and in the sorts of management methodologies being used by their civilian counterparts and superiors in the Office of the Secretary of Defense.

Zumwalt and Turner were aware of the trend toward earlier career specialization within the Navy that had begun during the World War II. Before the war, the concept of a general line officer, broadly trained and by mid-career capable of taking on a variety of assignments, made sense. The growth of technology made the notion of the "general line" obsolescent, however, and the Navy gradually developed very different communities of line officers. In the 1930s, for example, Annapolis graduates could not begin aviation training or volunteer for submarine duty right after graduation. Regardless of their qualifications for flight training or submarines, they served for two years in the fleet. Moreover, once the aviators earned their wings, they were required to fly several types of aircraft under different conditions before specializing in one area. A carrier pilot had to spend a year or two flying floatplanes from battleships, or long-range seaplanes from tenders, before joining a carrier squadron. This policy gave younger officers a broad base of experience so that, when they reached higher command, they would understand the diversity of the Navy's forces. Former CNO Moorer was the last Navy chief to have this sort of background.

Necessarily abandoned during the war, the policy was not revived after the war largely because younger officers took longer to master the newer, more complex specialties. By the mid-1950s, the Navy found that allowing officers to specialize early in their careers was the most cost-effective approach to training. Aviation grew more specialized because of the unique training needed just to enable young fliers to maneuver the early jet aircraft on and off carrier decks safely. Nuclear propulsion (and the sorts of undersea operations it permitted) turned the submarine warfare community into a highly specialized, rather isolated branch of the service. Zumwalt could not arrest these trends, but he did search for something that would pull the warfare communities (submarine, surface, and air) back together. One of his solutions was to have Rear Admiral Turner make the Naval War College the premier war college—one that officers from any service would want to attend.

Zumwalt also wanted to give the Navy influence in offices outside those normally staffed by Navy officers, and he also wanted to begin creating a leadership cadre for the future. In August 1972, Zumwalt directed the Chief of Naval Personnel to establish a "small pool of exceptional young officers capable of filling key Washington slots (outside of Navy/JCS/ISA) that open up from time to time where no billets exist." Zumwalt wanted these six officers under the control and supervision of OP-96. He also directed Naval Personnel and OP-96 to "institute a system for tracking the subsequent assignment of these officers, to ensure strong consideration is given to future shore duty assignments in key Washington area billets."[72] In plain terms, he wanted to insert talented mid-career Navy officers in places in the government where Navy officers were not usually found.

There were two reasons for this. One was that the CNO wanted more Navy officers to gain familiarity with institutions like the Congress. The other was that Zumwalt wanted to know what was going on at the White House. President Nixon and his national security advisor, Henry Kissinger, undertook a number of diplomatic initiatives while Nixon was in office. One of the most important was the rapprochement with the government of the Peoples Republic of China. Another was the effort to negotiate an end to U.S. involvement in the war in Vietnam. Both Nixon and Kissinger feared that making their initial discussions with the Chinese and the North Vietnamese public would arouse intense political opposition, and so the discussions were highly secret. Defense secretary Laird, Chairman of the Joint Chiefs Moorer, and CNO Zumwalt were kept in the dark about these diplomatic initiatives.

To find out what was going on, Laird, Moorer and Zumwalt resorted to informal intelligence gathering. For example, Laird used the National Security Agency and the Defense Intelligence Agency (DIA) to monitor Kissinger's actions, and he planted senior military liaison officers on the White House staff to gain information about what President Nixon and Kissinger were planning. Zumwalt "persuaded Kissinger that he needed more navy personnel on the [National Security Council staff], and this started a regular yearly rotation" of officers through the Council's office. Kissinger appreciated the loan of these talented Navy officers, and they worked diligently for him, but they also kept Zumwalt up to date on what Kissinger was doing and planning. Moorer's staff went even farther, surreptitiously recruiting a Navy yeoman to actually

Figure 10-3. Then–Vice President Gerald R. Ford with outgoing CNO Admiral Elmo R. Zumwalt Jr. at Zumwalt's retirement ceremony at the Naval Academy on 29 June 1974. President Richard M. Nixon had told Vice President Ford not to attend the ceremony and speak in praise of Zumwalt, but Ford chose to attend, to speak, and to present Zumwalt with the Distinguished Service Medal.
(National Archives USN1159266)

rifle through Kissinger's papers and Xerox any that might be of interest to the Chairman.[73] It was an extraordinary—even bizarre—move.

Conclusion

By the end of 1973 Zumwalt had just about lost the influence necessary to implement further internal reform. That December he faced yet another demand by the Office of the Secretary of Defense to pare the Navy's headquarters staff. In a memo to Secretary of the Navy Warner, Zumwalt suggested that the Navy respond by abolishing the Naval Material Command, thereby avoiding a restructuring of OPNAV. Admiral Isaac C. Kidd Jr., Chief of Naval Material, concurred.[74] But Secretary of Defense Schlesinger did not appreciate the effort, and in April 1974 ordered personnel cuts in OPNAV and in the Marine Corps headquarters. He also ordered Secretary Warner to combine the Naval Ordnance Systems Command with the Naval Ship Systems Command to form the Naval Sea Systems Command. In June, when Zumwalt had lost favor with the White House, the directorate for Ship Acquisition and Improvement (OP-097) was abolished, and its personnel were returned to the offices of the DCNOs.[75]

As a CNO, Admiral Elmo Zumwalt was either admired or hated by his fellow senior Navy officers. His actions provoked strong, emotional responses within the Navy and within Congress. He approached OPNAV with a combination of compromise and aggressiveness. He gave the warfare communities their separate organizations within OPNAV, but he also increased significantly the power of the directorates that reported to the Vice Chief of Naval Operations. At the end of Zumwalt's term, OP-090 had divisions capable of systematic program analysis using a Navy-wide automated data processing and reporting system. By the summer of 1974, Zumwalt's staff-within-a-staff had taken permanent shape. The directorates—OPs 090, 094, 095 and 098—were Zumwalt's organizational legacy to his successors. All were staffed by competent senior officers who saw service in the directorates as a means of promotion.

Zumwalt's approach to being CNO reflected his creativity and his professional intensity. His manner of dealing with colleagues and subordinates was clear even before he became the Navy's chief officer. As one of his aides put it,

> The admiral's bias was to always go with the people that would get the job done, whom he could relate to and related to him, understood what he wanted to do, supported what he wanted in the sense of not just genuflecting to everything he said, but argued with him, gave him their thoughts, their objections, et cetera. He always accepted that. But [sic] who essentially moved out and got the job done. And those people who fought the program eventually were cut out . . .[76]

As far as many other Navy officers were concerned, Zumwalt had weakened the twin pillars of naval command authority—the chain of command and the emphasis on operations. At the time of his appointment, the admiral was quite concerned about retaining quality officers and enlisted personnel in the service and he moved aggressively to give talented younger officers responsibility and promotions. In the process, he undermined the tradition of seniority, thereby robbing himself (and his office) of some of the support he might otherwise have had from the officer corps.

Zumwalt also tried to stimulate thinking about naval operations, tactics, and strategy, and his efforts coined a vocabulary of new strategic terms, such as sea control, power projection, and peacetime presence. He created a Navy Net Assessment office in OP-96 to compare the U.S. and Soviet navies across the board, and circulated the reports of this office throughout OPNAV.[77] The short-range benefit of such innovations for Zumwalt was limited, but the long-term benefit for the Navy was substantial.[78]

When he took office, Zumwalt faced significant obstacles in his efforts to reform OPNAV and the Navy. Service morale and retention rates were extremely low. The Navy needed new modern ships, but the Secretary of Defense was under orders to reduce defense expenditures. Racial injustice and conflicts in the fleet led Zumwalt to address immediately the grievances of African American sailors, but many senior officers believed he moved too quickly to force solutions on the service, especially when he also extended significant opportunities to women.[79] Zumwalt had neither the command experience nor the network of allies in the Navy that might have helped his campaign for reform. In short, he lacked the resources necessary to sustain the kinds of changes that he proposed. Moreover, his policy initiatives often denied him the sympathy that he needed for successful reorganization. Lack of funds compounded the difficulties of reorganization because, to save money, the CNO retired ships whose commands might have been some compensation for those officers whom he forced into retirement.

Finally, Zumwalt ran up against the sheer size of OPNAV. In 1939, before the Navy really mobilized for World War II, about 125 officers worked in OPNAV. By 1970, their number had swelled to at least 1,000. A Chief of Naval Operations might run an organization of this size if he had the time and if he could rely on the special ethical and social relationships characteristic of operational command. But Zumwalt had neither. As a result, he could do no more than establish his staff-within-a-staff—the Navy directorates. Put another way, he developed innovative bureaucratic means to deal with what was in his mind a large and often unresponsive bureaucracy.

Notes

[1] Congressional Quarterly *Almanac*, "Vietnam Statistics—War Costs: Complete Picture Impossible," CQ Online Editions (article first published in the CQ Almanac in 1975, using figures from the Department of Defense).

[2] For a very critical assessment of the Johnson administration's management of the economy, see *Self-Inflicted Wounds*, by Hobart Rowen (New York: Random House, 1994), ch. 1.

[3] Zumwalt had served as aide to Paul H. Nitze when Nitze was Assistant Secretary of Defense for International Security Affairs in 1962. Later, when Nitze served as Navy secretary, he was regarded by some senior Navy officers as a "McNamara man." The "taint" of being

associated with McNamara rubbed off on Zumwalt. But what those suspicious of Zumwalt's ambition did not know was that he had been treated dismissively by Secretary McNamara during the Cuban Missile Crisis in October 1962. See Paul H. Nitze, *From Hiroshima to Glasnost*, 228.

[4] ADM Harry D. Train II, oral history interview with Paul Stillwell, 16 July 1986, U.S. Naval Institute, 145.

[5] Friedman, "Elmo Russell Zumwalt Jr.," in Love's *The Chiefs of Naval Operations*, 369.

[6] Larry Berman, *Zumwalt, The Life and Times of Admiral Elmo Russell "Bud" Zumwalt Jr.* (New York: HarperCollins, 2012).

[7] *Report to the President and the Secretary of Defense by the Blue Ribbon Defense Panel* (Gilbert W. Fitzhugh Report) (Washington, DC, 1970), Executive Summary, 1, 5, 6, 5400/1 Blue Ribbon Panel folder, Subject files, 00 File, in the Archives, NHHC.

[8] Ltr, Laird to Chet Holifield, Chairman, Military Operations Subcommittee, Committee on Government Operations, House of Representatives, 6 Nov. 1970, subj: Military Supply Systems, Creeping Centralization Presentation-1972 folder, box 4, OP-602 File, Archives, NHHC.

[9] Jeffrey L. Sands, *On His Watch: Admiral Zumwalt's Efforts to Institutionalize Strategic Change*, CRM 93-22 (Alexandria, VA: Center for Naval Analyses, 1993), 19. (Hereafter On His Watch.)

[10] Zumwalt and Bagley became close colleagues when Zumwalt was in command of Navy forces in Vietnam and Bagley was the commander of the Seventh Fleet's Cruiser-Destroyer Flotilla 7. See Sands, *On His Watch*, 23.

[11] Project Sixty is in *U.S. Naval Strategy in the 1970s: Selected Documents*, ed. by John Hattendorf, Newport Paper No. 30 (Newport, RI: Naval War College Press, 2007), 3–30.

[12] Ibid., The memo to all flag officers and Marine General Officers, dated 16 Sept. 1970, is the first page of the Project Sixty paper.

[13] Sands, *On His Watch*, 25.

[14] Ibid., 19.

[15] Memo, OP-09B to CNO via VCNO, 22 Nov. 1970, subj: OPNAV Organization, Report of the OPNAV Organizational Review Panel folder, OP-09B2 Records.

[16] Sands, *On His Watch: Admiral Zumwalt's Efforts to Institutionalize Strategic Change*, 52.

[17] Ibid., 43.

[18] Elmo R. Zumwalt Jr., *On Watch* (New York: Quadrangle Books, 1976), 285.

[19] Berman, *Zumwalt*, 236.

[20] Memo, OP-03G to OP-090, 23 Sept. 1970, subj: Concept of Reorganization, OPNAV Reorganization Concept (1970) folder, box 5, OP-602 File, NHHC Archives.

[21] Sands, *On His Watch*, 46–47.

[22] CAPT Howard J. Kerr Jr., USN (Ret.), Reminiscences, from interviews by Paul Stillwell,

22 Sept. and Nov. 1982, USNI Oral History, 92.

[23] See "The Rise of the Submarine Based Ballistic Missile: A Brief History," by RADM William J. Holland Jr., USN (Ret.), *The Submarine Review*, Apr. 2011, 69–72.

[24] The 70 "Z-grams," issued starting in July 1970 and continuing into Jan. 1971, are listed in the Wikipedia entry for ADM Zumwalt dated 31 Oct. 2015. The Z-grams are also reprinted in Zumwalt's memoir, *On Watch*.

[25] Ibid., 137.

[26] Memo, OP-09B2 to CNO via VCNO, 22 Nov. 1970, subj: OPNAV Organization, OP-09B2 Records.

[27] Memo, Deputy SECDEF to SECNAV, 14 Sept. 1970, subj: Reduction of Headquarters Personnel, OPNAV Organization folder, OP-09B2 Records.

[28] Memo, Deputy SECDEF to Secretaries of the Military Departments, 15 Jan. 1971, subj: Department of Defense Logistics Systems Policy objectives 1970–1975, Creeping Centralization Presentation-1972 folder, box 4, OP-602 File, Archives, NHHC.

[29] "An Overview: DOD logistics management in the 1950's," 15, box 4, OP-602 file, Archives, NHHC.

[30] Deputy Secretary Packard, for example, had argued that the Defense Supply Agency could best manage all the petroleum resources for the services. The Navy opposed this policy on the grounds that it weakened the ability of field commanders to plan operations. The purpose of the Logistics Systems Plan was to guard against such OSD intrusions. Ibid., 14.

[31] Ibid., 15.

[32] Friedman, "Elmo Russell Zumwalt Jr.," Love's *The Chiefs of Naval Operations*, 374.

[33] RADM Dave Oliver, USN (Ret.), *Against the Tide: Rickover's Leadership Principles and the Rise of the Nuclear Navy* (Annapolis, MD: Naval Institute Press, 2014), 88.

[34] Ibid., 89.

[35] Sands, *On His Watch*, 52–54.

[36] OPNAV Notice 5430, 5 Mar. 1971, subj: Changes to the organization of the Office of the Chief of Naval Operations, OP-09B2 Records.

[37] OPNAV Notice 5430, 23 Jan. 1971, subj: Office of Tactical Electromagnetic Programs; establishment of, OP-09B2 Records.

[38] OPNAV Note 5430, 18 June 1971, subj: Disestablishment of OP-97, OP-09B2 Records.

[39] OPNAV Notice 5430, 7 Aug. 1971, subj: Establishment of the Fiscal Management Division (OP-92) under the Director of Navy Program Planning (OP-090), OP-09B2 Records.

[40] Memo, OP-96 to DCNOs, DMSOs, and Chief, NAVMAT, subj: CNO FY-72 Study Program and OSG Officer Utilization, OP-09B2 Records.

⁴¹ OPNAV Notice 5430, 1 Mar. 1972, subj: Combining MAT-01 with OP-92, OP-09B2 Records.

⁴² OPNAV Notice 5430, 9 Aug. 1972, subj: Transferring the functions of the Ship Acquisition and Improvement Division from OP-03 to OP-090, OP-09B2 Records.

⁴³ Sands, *On His Watch*, 57.

⁴⁴ Robert R. Swistak, "Defense Resource Planning in the Navy: The CPAM Process," Defense Systems Management School, Ft. Belvoir, VA, Nov. 1974.

⁴⁵ ADM Train oral history, Part 4 (17 July 1996), 271.

⁴⁶ Ibid.

⁴⁷ Ibid.

⁴⁸ Ibid., 273.

⁴⁹ OPNAV Notice 5430, 2 Nov. 1972, subj: Transferring jurisdiction of the aircraft carrier modernization program from OP-05 to OP-97, the Ship Acquisition and Improvement Division, OP-09B2 Records.

⁵⁰ "Naval Reserve Command," OP-09E background paper for CNO, 24 Apr. 1978, RADM Synhorst's Orig. File folder, OP-09B2 Records.

⁵¹ OPNAV Notice 5430, 27 Nov. 1972, subj: Redesignating the Director, Antisubmarine Warfare Programs (OP-095) as the Director, Antisubmarine Warfare and Tactical Electromagnetic Programs, OP-09B2 Records.

⁵² "Establishing Requirements," relating to Secretary of the Navy Instruction 5400.13 of 24 Aug. 1971, OPNAV Organization folder, OP-09B2 Records.

⁵³ Memo, T. F. Dedman, Assistant VCNO, Director of Naval Administration to W. H. Bagley, Director, Navy Program Planning, 8 Mar. 1972, subj: OPNAV/NAVMAT Organization, Synhorst folder, OP-09B2 Records.

⁵⁴ Department of the Navy, *Major Organizational Considerations for the Chief of Naval Operations, vol. 1, Report,* Organization Resources Counselors, Inc. (Washington, DC, 1973), V–10.

⁵⁵ Ibid., V–12.

⁵⁶ Ibid., V–14.

⁵⁷ Ibid., V–15.

⁵⁸ Ibid., V–16.

⁵⁹ Ibid., VII–2.

⁶⁰ Booz, Allen & Hamilton Inc., *Review of Navy R&D Management, 1946–1973*.

⁶¹ Quoted in Stubbing, *The Defense Game*, 327.

⁶² Berman, *Zumwalt*, 252–55.

⁶³ Ibid., 256–66.

[64] Ibid., 285.

[65] Ibid., 287. Zumwalt's bitter remarks about Secretary Warner are given on page 284.

[66] Ibid., 288.

[67] Ibid., 292.

[68] Ibid., 300.

[69] Ibid., 308.

[70] Ibid., 310.

[71] Ibid.

[72] Memo, CNO to Chief of Naval Personnel, 14 Aug. 1972, subj: Officers for Key Washington Assignments, OPNAV/5430 OP-96 1971–79 folder, OP-09B2 Records.

[73] Berman, *Zumwalt*, 318–30.

[74] Memo, CNO to SECNAV, 18 Dec. 1973, subj: DOD Headquarters Review, OP-09B2 Records. According to Berman, CNO Zumwalt considered ADM Isaac C. Kidd Jr., head of the Naval Material Command, both devious and self-serving, and Zumwalt did not want Kidd to be his successor. See *Zumwalt*, 298, 359.

[75] OPNAV Notice 5430, 3 June 1974, subj: Disestablishment of the Office of the Director, Ship/Acquisition and Improvement (OP-97), OP-09B2 Records.

[76] CAPT Howard J. Kerr Jr., USN (Ret.), *Reminiscences*, 40, 46; Jeffrey I. Sands, *On His Watch*, 55n112.

[77] Friedman, "Elmo Russell Zumwalt Jr.," in Love's *The Chiefs of Naval Operations*, 370.

[78] Peter M. Swartz, "The Maritime Strategy Debates: A Guide to the Renaissance of U.S. Naval Strategic Thinking in the 1980s," OPNAV P–60–3–87 (Washington, DC, OP-06, 1987); and Stansfield Turner, "Missions of the U.S. Navy," *Naval War College Review* 26 (Mar./Apr. 1974): 2–17.

[79] This was Z-Gram 116, which opened the entire staff corps and the restricted line to women. This directive from the CNO also made women eligible for command at sea and ashore, opened all ratings to enlisted women, and combined the detailing of men and women.

CHAPTER 11

From Project Sixty to the Maritime Strategy

Introduction

Admiral James L. Holloway III, took over from Admiral Elmo R. Zumwalt on 29 June 1974, while a constitutional crisis threatened the presidency of Richard M. Nixon. The President had been implicated in the so-called "Watergate scandal," and members of Congress were seeking tape recordings of conversations in the President's office that were thought to be key pieces of evidence of the President's role. On 24 July 1974, the Supreme Court had ordered President Nixon to give up the recordings, and he had done so. After listening to the tapes, the Judiciary Committee of the House of Representatives on 30 July had passed articles of impeachment. In early August, it was revealed publicly that a 23 June 1972 tape recording showed President Nixon conspiring with his chief of staff to obstruct the investigation of the break-in at Democratic National Committee Headquarters in the Watergate Building in Washington. Fearing a vote against him in the upcoming Senate trial, President Nixon resigned on 9 August 1974. His successor was Vice President Gerald R. Ford Jr., who had served as the minority leader of House Republicans from 1965 to 1973 before replacing former Vice President Spiro T. Agnew. Agnew had been forced to resign in October 1973, when it was revealed that he had taken substantial bribes during his career as a public official.

If Admiral Zumwalt had turned OPNAV upside down, the presidential impeachment crisis had turned Washington inside out. Holloway, however, was not new to crises. As a very young officer, he had served on a fighting destroyer at the Battle of Surigao Strait, one of the engagements that taken together made up the Battle of Leyte Gulf. He was a decorated fighter squadron commander in the Korean War on carrier *Valley Forge* (CV-45) and the third captain of the first nuclear aircraft carrier, *Enterprise* (CVAN-65). He was also an experienced OPNAV hand, having formed and then led the nuclear carrier sponsor's office in OP-03 in the late 1960s.[1] From his memoir, *Aircraft Carriers at War*, a reader will not get a sense that Admiral Holloway lost his stride as the Navy's senior officer during the Watergate crisis and its aftermath.

Background

In July 1973, Vice Admiral Holloway was relieved as commander of the Seventh Fleet, promoted, and dispatched to Washington to serve as Zumwalt's Vice Chief of Naval Operations. To prepare him to serve as his "alter ego," Zumwalt reviewed with Holloway "the situation in the Pentagon and in Washington," candidly "discussing the personalities of the major players." The two officers knew one another well. They had been classmates at Annapolis and had been members of the same National War College class in 1962. In his memoir, Holloway observed that "there was very little disagreement between us," and "our professional careers complemented one another."[2] This was fortunate for the Navy. By the early 1970s, the Navy's carrier force consumed almost half the "investment and manpower" of the service, and Holloway was Zumwalt's authentic expert (and expert witness before Congress) on "nuclear carriers and air warfare."[3]

If there was any potential source of friction between the two officers, it was over their very different relationships with Admiral Rickover, head of the Navy's nuclear reactors office. Holloway had impressed Rickover when the nuclear-powered *Enterprise* was being built, and Rickover treated Holloway with a respect that he did not show CNO Zumwalt. Zumwalt could have taken out his frustration with Rickover on Holloway, but he didn't. As Holloway recalled, Zumwalt "did not want to put me on the spot. . . . Frankly, it was very helpful of him, and it kept me out of a difficult position." On his part, Holloway "steered completely clear of Admiral Rickover" while VCNO, and Rickover "was astute enough not to rock the boat."[4]

Admiral Holloway understood that Zumwalt had recommended him for VCNO to give Holloway the experience and exposure that would make him a contender for the CNO's job. As Holloway put it, "I believe [Zumwalt] favored as CNO Admiral Worth Bagley, who he felt would be better suited to continue . . . the Zumwalt reforms, but [Zumwalt] was scrupulously fair to me as a candidate." Holloway was also helped by the support of Admiral Thomas H. Moorer, Zumwalt's predecessor and the Chairman of the JCS.[5]

Holloway's Initial Actions

Once he became CNO, Holloway's immediate goal was to "heal and unify the Navy." As he said, "I'm going to wait a while before I consider changing the set of the sails."[6] But some things would not wait. Within two weeks of becoming CNO, Holloway was grilled in Congress about the poor material readiness of the fleet. As he said in his memoir, "I took a lot of heat, and it was well deserved."[7] But the CNO patiently explained what the sources of poor maintenance were: a shortage of spare parts, a lack of "experienced petty officers, who are our real maintenance and repair technicians," and neglect of the "entire professional area of naval engineering."[8] Members of Congress offered to write legislation that would mandate relieving any captain whose ship failed a readiness inspection, but Holloway persuaded them that legislation of that sort was not the solution.

Instead, he used his own authority to require Navy officers to serve in the "engineering department of a sea-going vessel" if they wished to command a commissioned ship. As the CNO knew, "When the younger officers realized the Navy meant business in this regard—no waivers—there [would be] a scramble from the best and brightest to get to sea promptly as a ship's engineer."[9] But what about the carriers? After consulting with Vice Admiral James D. Watkins, the chief of personnel (and a future CNO), Holloway decided to allow Watkins to move "top-performing commanders from the surface warfare community" to "the billet of chief engineer on a carrier for a normal head-of-department tour of two years." Watkins and Holloway knew that the officers so selected might be angry about this policy—they would want command of a missile cruiser, instead—but Watkins and Holloway were able to make the policy work.

To produce still more officers with a strong grasp of engineering, the two admirals fostered the development of a "cram course in the practical aspects of steam engineering in Navy ship propulsion plants"[10] and made it an essential part of prospective commanding officer training. Watkins and Holloway received some unanticipated but very welcome help from Secretary of the Navy J. William Middendorf II, who knew Holloway from the time when Holloway had been VCNO and Middendorf had been Under Secretary of the Navy. As Holloway recalled, "One day, in the spring of 1975, Bill Middendorf walked into the CNO's office, pulled up a chair, and began a conversation." The secretary told the CNO that he wanted to make a "real contribution" to the Navy, and he wondered how he might best do that. As Middendorf put it, "How can I be of more direct help to the people in the fleet?"[11]

Holloway immediately suggested that Middendorf visit operational ships, though not in the way that most Navy secretaries had done in the past. Holloway advised the secretary to head straight for the engineering spaces and talk with the officers and enlisted personnel on duty. At first, Middendorf might not know his way around the steam cycle, but he would learn because he was intelligent and observant. Then, he could engage the men he found in engineering in worthwhile conversations, and the word would spread through the fleet that the secretary had the knowledge required to gauge the extent of the engineers' problems. As Holloway noted, "The Secretary charged into this program with his customary vigor, and the results were almost immediately evident."[12] From this and from other positive interactions, there developed a sort of partnership between the CNO and the secretary. One consequence of this partnership was Middendorf's "strong and articulate support of the Navy's programs," including the Trident ballistic missile submarine system, the Aegis air defense system, and the F/A-18 carrier fighter/attack plane.[13]

The Issue of Fleet Modernization

When Admiral Holloway was appointed CNO at the end of June 1974, annual inflation in the shipbuilding industry was between 15 and 20 percent, or almost four times the amount that

Navy programmers estimated when they requested funds for new construction when Admiral Zumwalt was the CNO.[14] The level of inflation did not decline in 1975, which meant that the Navy was caught between cost increases it could not control and the need to modernize by constructing new ships and submarines. Making matters worse, the staff of the Secretary of Defense was not convinced that the Navy needed additional construction appropriations and criticized the quality of Navy ship and weapons designs. Vice Admiral Eli T. Reich, then working for the Deputy Secretary of Defense, observed in February 1975, "the Navy has done an inadequate job of specifying overall ship system integration design—systems engineering and total ship design integration have been seriously lacking in post-World War II surface ship acquisitions."[15]

There was evidence that the Soviet fleet was planning and training to engage the U.S. Navy with conventional weapons. There was also evidence that Soviet naval forces possessed tactical nuclear weapons and planned to use them. Consequently, the CNOs after Zumwalt were faced with the problem of how to compete with both the quantitative and qualitative arms challenges presented by Soviet naval forces.[16] For example, OPNAV's Director of Organizational Appraisal (OP-09E2), Rear Admiral Gerald E. Synhorst, told CNO Holloway in May 1976 that

> faced with real needs to support forces which have been employed in real wars or crises (and which can be expected to be called again), the OPNAV staff and the CINCs whittle away at support for [tactical nuclear weapons] (make-believe weapons which they don't really expect to be able to use), in favor of non-nuclear problems which are considered real, and solvable, problems.[17]

In this high-pressure environment, OPNAV needed all of its resources to fend off or satisfy critics in OSD and Congress. For Holloway, this meant that fleet modernization through new construction mattered much more than reorganizing OPNAV.

Achieving modernization, however, was not easy. By the early 1970s the Navy was developing a layered defense of its carrier battle groups against attacks by missiles launched by Soviet bombers. The outer layer of this air defense shield was composed of F-14 fighters, each capable of engaging simultaneously up to six enemy targets with advanced Phoenix missiles. Sophisticated carrier-based electronics surveillance aircraft orbiting above the battle group controlled the movements of the fighters. The Aegis missile-firing surface ship formed the next layer of defense. With electronically steered, phased-array radar beams, the ship could monitor the middle range around the battle groups and could strike at any enemy missiles that penetrated the outer screen of fighters. The final layer of defense consisted of the less expensive short-range missiles, guns, and electronic deception equipment carried by all the ships in a carrier task force.

This multilayered system was not complete in the mid-1970s; the Aegis missile ship was missing. Admiral Holloway wanted the sophisticated Aegis air defense system built into a nuclear-powered cruiser that would accompany the new *Nimitz*-class, nuclear-powered aircraft carriers then just beginning to join the fleet. The Office of the Secretary of Defense objected to

Figure 11-1. CNO James L. Holloway III salutes at the playing of the national anthem to start the commissioning ceremony for the nuclear-powered carrier *Dwight D. Eisenhower* (CVN-69) in October 1977. Standing behind Holloway is Admiral Isaac C. Kidd Jr., Atlantic Fleet commander. Kidd was one of the candidates to succeed Holloway, but President James E. Carter Jr. selected Thomas B. Hayward, a decorated naval aviator, instead. (National Archives 1171131)

these ships on the grounds of cost. However, largely at the insistence of Vice Admiral Rickover, Congress had already passed a law saying that all future "major combatant vessels" had to be nuclear powered. Aegis became caught in the dispute between OSD and Congress, and in January 1975, the Secretary of Defense decided against requesting funds for Aegis ship construction or conversion. As Rear Admiral Wayne E. Meyer, project manager for Aegis, told his superior, the chief of the Naval Sea Systems Command, "We are simply unable to accomplish sensible program planning, or useful contractual work."[18] Only when the President assured Congress that a conventionally powered Aegis ship was needed, and the CNO, reversing his position, stated that a conventionally powered ship would be effective, did funding for the Aegis ship survive.[19]

But the future of Aegis was not the only acquisition issue troubling CNO Holloway. Secretary of Defense James R. Schlesinger was a Nixon appointee retained by Nixon's successor, President Gerald R. Ford Jr. Schlesinger was just as concerned about the growing cost of combat aircraft as he was about the cost of the Aegis program. A group of analysts in OSD had convinced him that the Navy and the Air Force needed to move away from their focus on high-performance aircraft such as the F-14 and the F-15. Lighter, less expensive aircraft could save the services from a vicious cycle: As the costs of systems such as aircraft spiraled up, the numbers that the services could afford came down, and the services faced the prospect that they would not have enough systems to meet the nation's strategic and operational goals.[20]

Secretary Schlesinger became convinced that there was only one way out of the conflict between the need for numbers of aircraft and the growth of aircraft unit cost, and that was for him to force the Air Force and Navy to adopt a common lightweight fighter. The new aircraft would complement the sophisticated F-15s and F-14s in the Air Force and Navy inventories. It would be relatively low cost and much less expensive to maintain. It would break the cycle of higher unit costs and declining numbers of planes. This approach was championed within the defense secretary's staff, especially by Leonard Sullivan Jr., the assistant secretary in charge of the program analysis office in the Office of the Secretary of Defense.[21] The problem for CNO Holloway and his senior aviators was that the same "light fighter" would not work for both services. A lightweight fighter for the Air Force would not be adequate for carrier service in the Navy because carrier fighters had to be designed and built to withstand the stresses of being catapulted off the flight deck and then brought to a "controlled crash" when landing back aboard. The need to strengthen the aircraft necessarily meant making sacrifices in other areas, especially range and weight.

The issue came to a head in April 1975, when CNO Holloway, accompanied by Director of Navy Program Planning Vice Admiral Thomas B. Hayward and Naval Air Systems Command head Vice Admiral Kent L. Lee, met with members of Schlesinger's staff. In response to the staff argument that some variation of what became the F-16 would meet the Navy's requirement, Holloway pointed out that the projected lightweight fighter favored by Schlesinger's staff could not successfully attack enemy fighters and bombers in poor weather with long-range missiles. But that capability was central to the Navy's need, which meant that the Navy needed to pass on the F-16 and proceed with a separate design. Secretary Schlesinger recognized the validity of Holloway's argument and approved development of what became the F/A-18 the following month.[22]

But the F/A-18—the combination fighter and attack aircraft—remained a risk because its designers had to make sure that the plane could fulfill both the fighter and attack roles while still being relatively inexpensive. As Admiral Hayward noted,

> A number of people like myself, who had seen a number of claimed achievements by the technical people fail again and again in the 1950s and 1960s, were not very enamored of the thought we were going to have all kinds of new things none of us had seen before: Heads-up displays, computers that could be used for air-to-air as well as air-to-ground at a time our air-to-air radars were still having lots of trouble, and our air-to-air fire controls were still not all that good. Our air-to-ground computer system was certainly open to plenty of doubts. How, then, were we to believe the technical people could possibly be right in their claim that we were going to see one airplane do both roles very well?[23]

In April and May 1975, the F/A-18 program was like an iceberg. You could see 10 percent of the critical elements, and the 10 percent looked good on paper. But what about the bulk of the iceberg—the part that was underwater? Would it work? CNO Holloway had no way to be certain, but what he did know was that a modified F-16 was not adequate, and he had the confidence and presence to carry the day against the talented (but to Holloway's mind mistaken) members of Secretary Schlesinger's staff.

When it came to building new nuclear carriers, Holloway's nemesis was President Ford's successor, former Georgia Governor James E. ("Jimmy") Carter Jr. President Carter was an advocate of nuclear arms control and an opponent of expensive nuclear-powered aircraft carriers. On taking office in January 1977, he had cancelled the funding for a carrier that had been included in the fiscal year 1979 budget. In February 1977, he instructed the new Secretary of Defense, Harold Brown, to tell CNO Holloway that there would be no new nuclear carrier and that any future carrier would be smaller and not nuclear powered. Holloway was presented with a dilemma. On the one hand, he strongly supported building a new nuclear-powered carrier. On the other hand, he had received his "marching orders" from SecDef Brown. Knowing the risk he was taking, CNO Holloway testified to the military subcommittee of the Senate Appropriations Committee in mid-February that he did not support the administration's position. After the hearing, during which Brown had repeated the President's opposition to a new nuclear-powered carrier, the SecDef asked Holloway (according to Holloway's memory) why the CNO had not supported the President's policy. Holloway answered correctly that the law required him (and any chief of a service) to offer the Congress his personal view when asked for it at a hearing. Brown seemed surprised.[24]

Despite the President's opposition to a new nuclear-powered aircraft carrier, a majority of the members of Congress reaffirmed their support for one, and Congress added a carrier to the fiscal year 1979 budget. President Carter vetoed the entire budget for the Defense Department in order to close out the carrier. In response, Carter's opponents on this issue in Congress put a nuclear carrier in the FY 1980 budget. Carter vetoed it again, but Congress overrode the President's veto, and the ship was eventually built.

Managing Innovation

The struggle over Aegis illustrated not only the Navy's concern for modernization and the efforts by Congress to control major weapons systems development, but also the inevitable conflict between the CNOs and the program managers (PMs) who are supposedly responsible to them. Admiral Holloway hoped to field an effective, *integrated* air defense system for the Navy's carrier battle groups. At the same time, he was as concerned as Zumwalt had been about the enormous cost of modern weapons systems. The first Aegis missile-firing cruiser cost nearly $1 billion, and the projected cost of all Aegis ships was approximately $30 billion in 1976. Rear Admiral Meyer was convinced that the ships would perform as expected in the antiair warfare role and usher in a new era of battle management, with implications in all warfare areas. To him, developing this advanced capability was worth the cost. But the CNO had to worry about all Navy costs, for both present operations and future equipment.

In June 1979, Captain Victor Basiuk, USNR, in a paper that was part of a headquarters review analysis, termed this difference between the CNO and the project managers as a conflict between "requirements pull" and "technology push."[25] That is, the Chief of Naval Operations was concerned with meeting the needs of the fleet for cost-effective cruise missile defense, while the project manager saw Aegis as a chance to achieve a new breakthrough in battle management. The CNO necessarily stressed deploying an affordable system. His nominally subordinate PM, on the other hand, emphasized the system's potential as its software improved over time. As Basiuk understood, the problem was not limited to the Aegis project. It was, instead, a general characteristic of Navy development programs, many of which had their roots not in any overall analysis of the fleet's need, but in far more narrow concerns.

A major reason why "technology push" often overcame "requirements pull" was because the Naval Material Command (NAVMAT) had never fulfilled the intent of those who had created it as the Navy's major procurement and logistics office. In the summer of 1976, for example, the Office of Management and Budget (OMB) studied the Naval Material Command's organization. The study team discovered the following deficiencies:

- The staff of the Chief of Naval Material, because its duties were not clearly defined, was involved in "matters previously carried out by the systems commands or bureaus."
- The Chief of Naval Material could not do effective planning or policy analyses.
- The lines of authority between OPNAV and NAVMAT were unclear.
- The technical capability of systems commands had eroded, and much of the technical work was performed by contractors.
- The structure of the Naval Sea Systems Command was "complex and unwieldy."
- Most project managers lacked the authority to meet the goals set for them.
- Competent mid-career line officers regarded billets in NAVMAT and the system commands as harmful to their chance for promotion and avoided such posts.[26]

This diagnosis showed that the procurement side of the Navy lacked an effective chain of command. To succeed in such a confused command setting, project managers needed a secure source of support. In the case of Aegis, Rear Admiral Meyer cultivated support in Congress, in OPNAV, and in the fleet. He also asked for and got a special charter for the Aegis Shipbuilding Project, which gave him potentially sweeping powers as well as definite responsibilities. In effect, Meyer was "empire-building," but he believed that the situation left him with no alternative. This situation eventually helped nudge Congress toward a major reform of the acquisition process for major military systems.

Holloway and the Carter Administration's Defense Reform Effort

Although initially very pro-Navy, President Jimmy Carter's appointees in the Defense Department questioned the need for a large surface Navy. In May 1977, the President announced that he would ask Congress to authorize 160 new ships for the Navy over the next five years. Within a year, however, Carter had reduced that figure by half on the advice of Secretary of Defense Brown, a former Secretary of the Air Force. Carter also called for "a searching organizational review" of the Defense Department, beginning another series of defense management studies. OMB, which favored abolishing the positions of service secretaries and chiefs, was charged with coordinating all major studies of executive branch management.[27] The Navy perceived this renewed round of defense studies as a threat to its integrity because it was pushed by OMB.

The Carter administration ultimately sponsored three studies of Department of Defense (DOD) organization. The first, chaired by former Secretary of the Navy Paul R. Ignatius, focused on OSD and the service headquarters.[28] The second, headed by Dr. Donald Rice, president of the RAND Corporation, considered the acquisition and programming side to DOD. The third, chaired by business executive Richard C. Steadman, looked at the national military command organization. The Rice study suggested that Secretary Brown create a special board to "direct and supervise the OSD review of the Service POMs [Program Objective Memoranda] and Budget Submissions."[29] That board, created in 1979 and named the Defense Resources Board (DRB), would play an important role in the Navy's efforts to take advantage of the defense spending increases in the 1980s.

The Ignatius study concerned OPNAV the most because, as a consultant to the CNO observed, "over the past several years, there have been repeated cuts to the SECNAV and OPNAV staff.... What is badly needed is time to settle down."[30] And time was just what the Navy received. The Ignatius study recommended that the service secretaries and chiefs be retained, but did call for a smaller headquarters staff. As Ignatius began his study, OPNAV, to protect itself, followed a strategy that gave the office "the appearance of having one coordinated, integrated SECNAV/OPNAV staff. Otherwise outside agencies of higher authority such as OSD, OMB, and Congress will believe the Navy has too much redundancy in its *departmental* staff and will tend to take away some of our staff assets."[31]

Secretary of the Navy W. Graham Claytor Jr., a member of the Defense Department committee set up to advise Ignatius, opposed any effort to move functions out of the services and into the offices of the assistant secretaries of defense. Claytor took a very active approach to Navy programming and systems acquisition, and he eventually challenged Secretary Brown over the administration's policy of not funding naval expansion. An officer then in OPNAV recalled: "With the arrival of Secretary Claytor and Undersecretary [R. James] Woolsey, . . . OPA [Office of Program Appraisal, created in response to a Dillon Board recommendation] became very directly involved in the day-to-day program planning process. . . . The Secretariat was once again showing signs of being in charge."[32] With more influence in Claytor's hands, the Navy could indeed fend off charges that the secretariat simply duplicated functions performed in OPNAV.

But there was more to it than that. According to a 1976 study sponsored by the Comptroller General of the United States, because the services were organized to respond to the Office of the Secretary of Defense, the problem of large service headquarters staffs was directly linked to the growing influence and demands of OSD. "As requests in the name of the Secretary of Defense are made to the military departments, each organizes and staffs itself to respond to the level of detail imposed, responding almost always by creating new offices mirroring the organizational structure of the requesting authority."[33] The Carter administration, however, did not see the connection. As Captain Donald K. Forbes, head of the National Policy and Command Organization Branch of the Strategic, Plans and Policy Division in OP-06, put it in November 1977, "I don't think we should kid ourselves by thinking we can ride through the reorganization effort and come out intact."[34] Indeed, Forbes suggested that perhaps one motivation for the President's emphasis on reorganization was to give Carter "the leverage he is seeking or, as a minimum, may divert some of DOD attention from the President's give-away policy in SALT [the Strategic Arms Limitation Talks with the Soviet Union]."[35]

At the request of Ignatius, OP-06 developed papers on OPNAV and its history. One such paper argued that "no one individual knows enough about the intricacies of the work done in OPNAV to plan a proper reorganization. Thus, any attempt to reorganize will be planned by committee. All vested interests will be considered, and the new organization will look amazingly similar to the old."[36] The same paper also noted that the "CNO/VCNO tend to demand full coordination and agreement among the equal powers before making critical decisions. . . . Often, such coordination results in a watered-down position that may or may not be in the best interest of the Navy."[37] Further, "we see force and mission sponsors generating force requirements relating to their own parochial interests without regard for overall Navy need."[38] Former CNO Zumwalt had strengthened the directorates, but that move in itself had not broken the "unholy alliances" between successful programmers in OPNAV and some project managers in the systems commands who, together with industrial firms, forged their own "mini-navies."

Despite attempts by Carter to force restructuring, OPNAV's organization grew more cluttered. The directorates, such as OP-098 (Research, Development, Test and Evaluation), increased in number as officers working in areas such as training, reserve affairs, and intelligence argued that their fields cut across warfare area boundaries and so deserved representation "above" the DCNO level. One way to deal with this increase in offices was to consolidate some of them. In 1977, for example, CNO Holloway transferred the responsibility for conducting and analyzing joint and naval war games from OP-090 (Program Planning) to OP-06. He also moved the billets in OP-098 (Research, Development, Test and Evaluation) that were responsible for nontechnical nuclear weapons matters to OP-06.[39] OP-06 therefore became a place where the Navy's future was explored and planned.

Holloway and the Joint Chiefs of Staff

In mid-May 1975, Holloway, whom Admiral Harry D. Train II considered "enthusiastically a participant in JCS matters,"[40] won points with President Ford during the effort to release the crew of the merchant ship *Mayaguez* from Khmer Rouge captivity in the waters off Cambodia. Holloway had been in Boston touring a Soviet ship when the *Mayaguez* was captured. General George S. Brown, U.S. Air Force, the Chairman of the JCS, was in Europe. So General David Jones, Air Force Chief of Staff, was the acting chairman. Unfortunately for General Jones, his presentation to the President did not apparently help Ford determine what to do, and Ford had

Deputy Secretary of Defense William P. Clements Jr., summon Holloway back to Washington. On arriving at the White House, Holloway told the President that "Speed was essential." Ford "quickly agreed . . . and sent me back to the Pentagon to get things going."[41]

The next day, Ford convened a meeting of the National Security Council. Holloway was acting chairman of the JCS. The President believed that capturing the ship was "tantamount to piracy and could not be tolerated," and so the members of the JCS, joined by Defense Secretary Schlesinger, developed a plan to free the ship and its crew and then briefed members of Congress on it. The actual effort to free the ship and her crew began in the early morning of May 15th. Once they were free, the Navy and Marine forces that had forced their release were withdrawn, though not without casualties. Holloway believed that "The most important fallout from the *Mayaguez* incident was that, for the rest of the Ford administration, I was always acting chairman when George Brown was out of town." The President's decision meant that Holloway had to be ready to meet with Ford whenever Brown was not available. As Holloway admitted, "This amounted to about 20 percent of my time during the rest of the administration."[42]

While Holloway was CNO and often acting JCS chairman, General Louis H. Wilson, Marine Corps Commandant and Medal of Honor recipient in World War II, was pressing to have the Commandant given equal status with the other service chiefs on the JCS. Though the Commandant sat on the JCS and was recognized as having the lead in discussions of issues vital to the Marine Corps, no Commandant had been allowed to substitute for the JCS chairman when the chairman was unavoidably absent. So Wilson worked in the spring of 1978 with Senators John C. Stennis (D-MS) and Dewey F. Bartlett Sr. (R-OK) to change the language in Title 10, U.S. Code so that the Commandant was a "full" member of the JCS. But the change to the law was put in the FY 1979 defense authorization act, and (as previously noted) President Carter vetoed the act and the House of Representatives did not have the votes to override Carter's veto. To move the authorization process along, both the House and Senate authorizing committees agreed to resubmit the authorization act *without* the nuclear carrier. When that was done, and President Carter signed the law, Marine Corps Commandant Wilson achieved his goal.[43]

Restructuring the Fleet

CNO Holloway regarded his decision of 15 September 1977 to restructure the fleet as "probably [his] most significant contribution to the U.S. Navy in [his] tour as CNO."[44] As he noted in his memoir, "our fleet was organizationally structured in 1977 to reflect the administration of the Navy by types of ship . . . , rather than by groups of ships constituted to carry out a strategic or tactical mission."[45] Holloway reorganized the fleet into battle forces, and the battle forces were made up of battle groups. He wrote up the redesign over a weekend and sent the proposal to the commanders of the Atlantic and Pacific Fleets on Monday, 16 September. They accepted his proposal on Wednesday, 18 September. Holloway did not have to first consult with the Secretary of the Navy or the Secretary of Defense because at that time "it was the CNO's prerogative to establish the operating procedures of naval forces."[46]

> A battle group was a task group
>
> capable of conducting offensive operations at sea against the combined spectrum of hostile maritime threats . . . and be a task group consisting of one carrier, two cruisers, four surface combatants, and one or two submarines, operating together in mutual support with the task of destroying hostile submarine, surface, and air forces within the group's assigned area of responsibility."[47] The battle group's focus, however, was not exclusively on the sea. It would use its "air wing to establish air superiority over the objective area to project power ashore . . ."[48]

That was a key point; the Navy's purpose was to clear the sea and air so that the Marines, the Army, and the Air Force could get ashore and wage a campaign.

Holloway also argued in his memoir that the battle group concept led to a fleet organization "that accurately reflected the Navy's roles and mission as established by the laws enacted by the Congress of the United States." Significantly, it "provided that battle force and group commanders would be unrestricted line officers of any designation, selected on the basis of those flag officers best suited by virtue of their operational experience, warfare specialty qualification, and command maturity and judgment." This *was* a change. Since the 1920s, the rule had been that only aviators could command carriers and carrier task forces. In making the change, Holloway knew he was knocking down what he called "parochial boundaries" that were actually constraining the rise of talent within the Navy.[49]

But restructuring the fleet was just the first part of a two-part effort. Part two was documenting the "basic strategic concepts of the Navy." This would become *Naval Warfare Publication No. 1: Strategic Concepts of the U.S. Navy*, or NWP-1. Holloway found that "to preserve the lore and lessons learned in thirty-five years of a naval career" in his own style, he'd have to write NWP-1 himself, which he did, in the spring of 1978. The document "was written in longhand in pencil on ruled paper in the evenings at Quarters A in the. . . CNO's quarters." As the CNO revealed, writing NWP-1 was "pure relaxation," his thoughts spilling out of a mind that had been thinking for decades about what the Navy was for.[50] It was mostly finished by the time Holloway was relieved by Admiral Thomas B. Hayward on 1 July 1978.

Holloway was proud to learn over time that NWP-1 was used for several decades by many officers and by the staff of the Naval War College. But what made NWP-1 even more significant was that it rested on the assumption that fleet structure and fleet mission went together. You could not change one without at least thinking about the implications of that change for the other. After NWP-1, this awareness of the link between structure and function (or mission) was a given.

Holloway as CNO

Like Fleet Admiral William F. Halsey, CNO Holloway was a "fighting admiral." He was bright, very quick to size up any situation, aggressive, intelligent, clever, and—when necessary—calculating. In some respects, he was the ideal aviator admiral, and, almost always, well suited to the increasingly more responsible commands given him. However, whereas President Ford trusted Holloway and drew on the CNO's counsel, President Carter and Holloway had a difficult relationship. Proof of that is clear from Holloway's memoir, where he writes off as essentially inconsequential Carter's Navy experience.[51] Holloway then describes an awkward early encounter in 1977 between President Carter and his service chiefs over reducing the number of nuclear weapons.

The new President was committed to reducing the likelihood of a nuclear war by reducing—and eventually eliminating—nuclear weapons. He told the members of the JCS that he had been in touch with Soviet leader Leonid Brezhnev before his election, and that as President he was committed to nuclear disarmament. The new President said that, according to Holloway, "he expected the JCS to revise their war planning to be able to conduct the necessary operations to defend the United States and carry out our military war plans without the same reliance on nuclear weapons in the deployment of forces and resources."[52] Holloway realized immediately that the new President "was not aware of the degree to which the use of nuclear weapons, or more important, the threatened use of nuclear weapons was in our national security planning . . ."[53]

The CNO knew that he and the other service chiefs had a problem on their hands, and that it was imperative to teach President Carter what was really going on. Fortunately, the new President was eager to learn, and he readily participated in exercises designed to test nuclear command and control technology and explore the organizational issues related to the control and use of nuclear forces. The CNO also had confidence in Secretary of the Navy Claytor, with whom he enjoyed a "pleasant and straightforward relationship."[54] Holloway did not have the same relationship with Harold Brown, Carter's Defense secretary, whom Holloway described as "positive and somewhat didactic."[55] With Donald H. Rumsfeld, who had briefly succeeded James Schlesinger in November 1975, the CNO's relationship was less than professional. Holloway noted that Rumsfeld was absent from his office a good deal, and that, because he did not delegate authority, "the working relationship" was "quite uncomfortable" at times. Rumsfeld also acted as though he "felt that the people in uniform were assuming too much authority vis-à-vis the civilian leadership."[56] That Holloway and Secretary Rumsfeld did not "hit it off" is surprising because they had two experiences in common: both had been champion collegiate wrestlers and both were naval aviators.

In his diary, Chase Untermeyer, who served as Navy secretary John F. Lehman's assistant for manpower and reserve affairs starting in 1984, characterized Admiral Holloway as "an exuberant personality [with] the genial, crafty manner of a rural state senator."[57] Untermeyer's assessment should surprise no one. To succeed as CNO, Holloway had to be able to win over likely supporters of his initiatives and, when necessary, cleverly disguise his real thoughts. For example, he had been very adept at winning the approval and support of older officers as he moved through his career. In his memoir, Holloway mentions working diligently for Admiral Horacio Rivero Jr., when Rivero was in charge of Navy program planning in 1964. Rivero did not forget the younger officer, and he openly supported Holloway when the latter was CNO.[58] Holloway's positive relationship with Admiral Rickover has already been mentioned. Holloway knew the older man well enough to see that "Rickover had an excellent sense of humor, but not many people had an opportunity to experience his wit because he was usually too busy chewing someone out."[59] Despite their differences, Holloway made sure that Rickover had access to him. Finally, Holloway hired John F. Lehman Jr., a protégé of Henry Kissinger, in 1976 "mainly to advise in matters concerning [Strategic Arms Limitation] but also in a host of other operational and political subjects involving the Navy and, especially, carriers and Naval Aviation."[60] It was a prescient move.

CNO Hayward: The Roots of the Maritime Strategy

Like Admiral Holloway, Admiral Thomas B. Hayward was a decorated carrier pilot. He had flown combat missions in both the Korean and Vietnam conflicts. He took over as CNO on 1 July 1978, after a tour as Commander-in-Chief, Pacific Fleet. While in Hawaii, Hayward and his staff developed plans collectively called Sea Strike, for using Navy carrier battle groups against Russian bases in Siberia. The purpose of attacking Soviet targets in the Pacific in the event of a war with North Atlantic Treaty Organization (NATO) was to keep Soviet forces in the Pacific from reinforcing their comrades in Europe. Developing Sea Strike had convinced Hayward of the need to revitalize strategic and operational thinking in the Navy. He understood what former CNO Zumwalt had grasped in 1970: the Navy needed a new unifying *naval* concept around which to plan and program. Otherwise, Navy programs and budgets would be subordinated to the mission of protecting convoys as they steamed to Europe. Hayward rejected the idea that the Navy's primary role in a general conventional war should be defensive and not offensive.

Hayward had served as director of Navy program planning (OP-090) from 1973 to 1975. He understood the programming process. At the same time, however, he thought that too many senior Navy officers were preoccupied with the budget disputes between the Navy and the Office of the Secretary of Defense that had characterized the last year of Admiral Holloway's term as CNO. As Naval War College historian John Hattendorf correctly observed, "Hayward sought

Figure 11-2. CNO Thomas B. Hayward, after flying one of the Navy's new strike fighters, the F/A-18 Hornet, at the Patuxent River Naval Air Station. Hayward, while serving as Commander-in-Chief of the Pacific Fleet, developed Sea Strike, a plan for attacking Soviet bases in Siberia; this was one of the roots of what became the Maritime Strategy under Navy Secretary John Lehman. (National Archives USN 1178642)

to change . . . from a budget battle to an analysis of the strategic issues for a global maritime power."[61] Put another way, Hayward wanted to shift the focus of attention within OPNAV from the struggle for resources to a critique of U.S. military strategy.

Hayward's Primary Concerns

When Hayward became CNO, he had the following priorities:

- Instilling "a sense of ownership of the Navy and belonging—pride and professionalism. That was far and away my first priority. We had to address the fact that we were losing most of our best talent." As Hayward knew, fleet readiness declined drastically when talented enlisted and officer personnel left the service.
- Improving the "tactical competence of our commanders."
- Taking mine warfare seriously. As he said when interviewed years later, "Mine warfare just doesn't get appropriate support, and it never will if the CNO doesn't personally make it so."
- Creating a special study group of highly talented officers at the Naval War College who "would choose their own curriculum" and then study an important problem in depth. As far as Hayward was concerned, it didn't matter what they studied. What mattered was that they learned to think and learned how to intelligently direct their own thinking toward the Navy's major problems.
- Allowing and encouraging the OPNAV staff to "concentrate heavily on how to argue the global mission of the Navy and develop an updated maritime strategy."[62]

Making Changes to OPNAV

In the fall of 1978, Hayward began shaping OPNAV so that the staff would better help him achieve these goals. He first eliminated the "sponsorship" in OPNAV directorates of *concepts* such as sea control and power projection.[63] Hayward wanted to prevent specific platforms from appropriating certain concepts. To change the way that the existing concepts were understood and expressed, he authorized the Maritime Balance Study, which examined the way the Navy developed strategy and long-range plans.[64] The study concluded first, that the programming and budgeting "process has come to be seen as a strategy itself"; second, that research and development needed "specific mission-oriented and priority-ranked goals"; and third, that the Navy needed "a mechanism for institutionalizing its strategic planning beyond the time horizon of personnel rotation and replacement."[65] Hayward was trying to break ideas and concepts free from platforms so that he could pressure the platform communities, so strongly represented in OPNAV, to think together about missions.

Soon after the Maritime Balance Study was promulgated, Captain Victor Basiuk submitted his careful study of how OPNAV determined the priority of potential research and development and acquisition programs. The study accurately described the problem facing the new CNO. It described OPNAV as divided into two camps—one organized around the platform sponsors (DCNOs for submarine, surface, and air warfare); the other, around the OP-090 directorate

(Program Planning).[66] Basiuk noted that "platform sponsors have been, in effect, put in charge of the development of platforms and weapon systems that go with them from . . . the development stages of R&D to their retirement from the fleet."[67]

In 1979 the platform DCNOs exercised influence through their Sponsor Program Proposals, detailed program descriptions required before programs would obtain funding.[68] Basiuk recognized one positive aspect of this situation: "The Navy is a highly complex organization and platform orientation helps to reduce its fragmentation by focusing priorities and the human effort associated with them on something concrete."[69] He also saw drawbacks: "Platform orientation leads to incremental technological improvement"; worried more about their platform than what was in them, platform sponsors could "stall, and perhaps defeat," the development of new weapons that would compete with established ones; and mission sponsors, such as OP-095 (the director of antisubmarine warfare [ASW]), had to be especially persuasive and forceful to compete with the platform sponsors for resources.[70]

Although the CNO could override vetoes cast by the deputy chiefs, as Hayward did when he supported development of the land-attack version of the Tomahawk long-range cruise missile, such interventions were inevitably the exception given a CNO's many responsibilities. As Basiuk observed, "The Planning, Programming and Budgeting (PPB) process is perhaps the single most important vehicle through which the will of the CNO is projected into the shaping of priorities."[71] Unfortunately, "the budgetary process does not adequately counterbalance the power of platform sponsors," largely because OP-090 was a "microcosm of the Navy with individual loyalties finding their origins in platform constituencies."[72]

The day-to-day workings of OPNAV were no secret: "Programmers from OP-090 and platform sponsors reach informal understandings behind the scenes."[73] But the informal network of alliances that crisscrossed OPNAV and spread into the Naval Material Command and the systems commands did more than steer the acquisition process. As Basiuk discovered, "it is the PPB process and the studies directly or indirectly related to that process which, to a degree, marry strategic and tactical considerations with existing hardware."[74] In plain terms, OP-06 (Plans, Policy, and Operations), which considered strategic issues, was not the "focal point for the development and integration of strategic and tactical doctrines."[75]

Basiuk's analysis of how OPNAV actually worked went to the foundations of influence within the organization. Two activities mattered most in OPNAV—programming and setting the requirements for new systems—and the former was so decentralized that it was often insulated from direction by the CNO. The CNO started off and then reviewed the results of the programming process, but he lacked the time (and sometimes the knowledge) to direct it. Nor did he entirely control the requirements process because it was the buying commands that had to turn performance goals into actual hardware.[76] Even if he wished to, a CNO would find it almost impossible to dominate the programming and budget processes within the Navy. Ship construction, for example, could stretch across the tenures of three CNOs; once begun, such programs were legitimately the province of the deputy chiefs.

To overcome the problems described by Captain Basiuk, Hayward changed the title of OP-095 from Director of Antisubmarine Warfare Programs to Director of Naval Warfare, and he gave OP-095 two major divisions, one for force-level planning and a second for strike warfare. To give the restructured office influence in the programming process, Hayward assigned OP-095 the task of developing the CNO Program Analysis Memoranda, which guided the platform deputies as they drew up their annual contributions to the Navy's portion of the Five Year Defense Plan. Hayward also made OP-095 "responsible for implementing the CNO's policy for overall fleet readiness and modernization in regards to all phases of general purpose naval warfare."[77] His goal was to make the negotiations that characterized the programming process hinge on warfare issues that were developed before its start by an office subordinate to the CNO that could impose the CNO's priorities on the platform deputies. It was not enough to have a systems analysis office in OP-090 review proposals already prepared by the deputy chiefs. Hayward wanted to give the CNO the power of initiation in addition to the power of review.

The Genesis of the Maritime Strategy

Before becoming CNO, Hayward was bothered by the way that strategic planning placed the Navy in an essentially defensive role. In the event of a war in Europe—the one event that was "all the Defense Department staff ever thought about"—the Navy's role was to get reinforcements to NATO by keeping the Atlantic sea lanes open. As Hayward complained, "There wasn't any other strategic thinking. It was just the Fulda Gap [in Germany] and escalating into a nuclear war."[78] There really was no successor to the decades-old "containment" strategy for dealing with the Soviet Union. However, in the years since the Cuban Missile Crisis of 1962, the Soviet Union had strengthened and modernized both its conventional forces and its tactical nuclear forces in Europe. It appeared that Soviet leaders wanted to threaten America's European allies with overwhelming force and thereby undermine NATO. Hayward believed that the United States could confront the Soviet Union with a counter threat, and he further believed that the Navy and Marines would be an essential part of that.

To give substance to this idea of a counter threat, Hayward drew on the "Sea Strike" work performed under his leadership when he was Commander-in-Chief of the Pacific Fleet (CINCPACFLT) in 1977–1978. Starting in May 1979, he began meeting with senior admirals to explore the idea of countering Soviet threats and a conventional Soviet attack on NATO with a threatened American assault by the Navy and Marines on Soviet territory. Could the United States somehow endanger Soviet ballistic missile submarines hidden in far northern "bastions" without using nuclear weapons? The ballistic missiles on those submarines were the Soviet Union's nuclear reserve. What if they could be threatened by conventional U.S. naval and air forces? Would that threat deter a Soviet military offensive?

To discover the answer to that question, Hayward in the early fall of 1982 had the VCNO, Admiral William N. Small, direct the reorganized OP-095 to work with OP-603, the strategy concepts branch of OPNAV. OP-603 was then headed by Captain William B. Garrett, who acted under the general direction of OP-06, Vice Admiral Arthur S. Moreau Jr. Garrett passed the "buck slip" from Moreau to Commander W. Spencer Johnson IV, OP-605. Johnson was OP-06's liaison with OP-09, the CNO's programming directorate.[79] Johnson realized that he needed help with this task, and he was teamed with Lieutenant Commander Stanley B. Weeks from OP-603. The two officers built on a preliminary outline that Johnson had written on a yellow legal pad. That outline became the Maritime Strategy, so named by Johnson and Weeks because the strategic concept required concerted action among the Navy, the Marines, the Army, and the Air Force. As Johnson recalled, the Maritime Strategy was not cleared with the Army and Air Force before he and Weeks presented it to senior officers because there wasn't time. The process of building the Navy's POM was about to begin, and Johnson and Weeks had to respond to the tasking that they'd been given.[80]

Weeks and Johnson also consulted with Captain William H. J. Manthorpe, an intelligence officer charged with setting up OP-96N, the new "net assessment" office in OPNAV. In the meantime, Captain Garrett had been replaced by Captain Elizabeth G. Wylie, and Wylie, Johnson, and Weeks kicked off the POM process by briefing the rear admirals representing the DCNOs. Their presentation was a success. It showed how being able to deploy 15 carrier battle groups to the seas near Norway in a crisis could threaten a Soviet conventional invasion of Western Europe. The brief provided just the sort of guidance that the POM process needed.[81]

As Captain Johnson recalled years later, the Navy was going to receive an increase of approximately 15 percent in its budget for fiscal year 1983, and CNO Hayward didn't want the "plus-up wasted. He wanted an overarching framework that would allow him to discipline the programming process."[82] To help develop officers who could inherit and augment the thinking that Hayward had already initiated, the CNO created the Strategic Studies Group (SSG) at the Naval War College. He also set up the Center for Naval Warfare Studies at the Naval War College and the Long Range Planning Group (OP-00X) in OPNAV. His goal was to improve strategic and operational thinking in the Navy and then to tap that thinking for ideas that would turn out to be decisive over the long run.

At the same time, Hayward was at ease with his deputy CNOs. He later characterized the "Navy's system for making decisions" as one that produced "good, balanced, cooperative business decisions."[83] What about the platform sponsors? Hadn't the CNO already tried to reduce their influence inside of OPNAV? Hayward's position was that the task of the CNO was to create a process where the "barons" (platform sponsors for surface ships, aircraft, or submarines) were allowed to propose the strongest possible programs for their separate "kingdoms" while the CNO, aided by the VCNO and OP-090, struck a balance among them. As he said, "You want the best guy in that [DCNO] job fighting for the best he can get. He's not going to get it, or all of it, but that's what you want him striving for." If the CNO couldn't handle the arguments of his deputies and the competition among them at the CNO executive board (CEB) meetings, then he was "the wrong CNO."[84]

Strategic Arms Limitation

Hayward had been concerned that the Single Integrated Operations Plan—the SIOP—the tightly scripted plan for waging nuclear war with the Soviet Union, was inadequate. Hayward never regarded the SIOP as being based on "really good thinking," and he said so, starting when he was OP-090 from 1973 to 1975.[85] He carried that impression into OPNAV in July 1978. Unfortunately, it was in the field of strategic weapons that Hayward found himself unprepared and in need of a lot of hard work to catch up. As the former CNO recalled, "I was heavily involved with SALT I and SALT II, and participated pretty intensely in them." To get up to speed, Hayward relied on his executive assistant, Captain William J. Cockell Jr. Cockell "had done a lot of work in that area," and "He brought in not only our own staff to spend an hour or two on some issue, but he also helped me with the CNO Executive Panel; with Albert Wohlstetter, Henry Rowen, Sy Weiss and people like that, who had a lot of background in strategic nuclear balance and policies and theories." Hayward recalled spending "hours and hours and hours—one, to just understand the debate, and then two, to try to figure out what I thought the Navy's position should be in this."[86]

In 1979, as President Carter was preparing to travel to Vienna to sign the SALT II agreement, Hayward tried to get his fellow service chiefs to agree:

> to present a short paper to the President, suggesting that in the last minutes with [Leonid] Brezhnev . . . the President would say, 'Now, let's you and I rise above all of this detail and agree to 2,000 more cuts apiece. Take them any way you want. We're not going to argue about whether it's bombers or submarines. We're going to reduce by 2,000 [warheads], and we're going to tell our staffs we've agreed—we're sending a signal we want this escalation stopped.'

According to Hayward's memory, President Carter took the paper with him, "but Brezhnev got so sick that the President never had a chance to address it. So it never got in the record . . ."[87]

Readiness Challenges

In 1979, Hayward was cornered by a reporter in San Diego who accused the CNO of not wanting to recognize that the Navy had a drug problem. On returning to Washington, Hayward set in motion a comprehensive but anonymous survey of drug use in the Navy. The results, according to Hayward, "were stunning."[88] Almost half of the sailors (and significant numbers of Marines) were probably using illegal drugs of one sort or another, and drug use was blamed when an EA-6B electronic warfare aircraft crashed on the flight deck of carrier *Nimitz* (CVN-68) in May 1981, killing 14 sailors and injuring several dozen others. At first it wasn't clear to Hayward just what to do, but then urinalysis became reliable enough to serve as the test of drug use, and it "was a fabulous tool."[89] To help the anti-drug use program, the Navy's chief petty officers requested that they be held to the same high standards as commissioned officers.[90]

In 1980, Hayward spent time examining naval reserve units. Some were performing at very high levels—intelligence units, Seabees, and aircraft squadrons, for example. Others, particularly surface ship crews, often performed poorly because the ships they manned were obsolete and run down. Hayward decided to reduce the size of the Naval Reserve to eliminate those units that could not be brought up to a standard that would allow them to complement active fleet units in a crisis. The money saved would be used to improve the equipment and simulators for the remaining reserve units. As Hayward recalled, "Because the logic is so irrefutable, I got away with it. The Congress bought off on it."[91]

Hayward, like Holloway before him, was concerned about readiness, and in 1979 he created a new level-of-readiness measure, one that meant a ship was unsafe to steam or an airplane was unsafe to fly. He wanted the truth about readiness; he was certain that there were ships and aircraft that were essentially "broken." Hayward explained to members of Congress and members of the staff of the Defense secretary that he was not just grandstanding in order to squeeze more money from them. As he noted, "I had to personally deliver that . . . readiness message to all the operating commanders so that they would support anybody who blew that whistle. Otherwise, . . . [they] were not going to put themselves on report as being unable to handle the problem."[92] Sure enough, on 10 April 1980 the captain of the fleet oiler *Canisteo* (AO-99) said his ship could not get underway safely, and the captain's report was made public.

Hayward recalled that that particular case of "truth-telling" allowed him to "prove to the Secretary of Defense and to all the congressional committees that we had a major personnel problem in the military," starting with pay that was too low. Congressional staffers and others interviewed sailors and discovered that there was a pay problem. Then Congress came through with a raise. Hayward said that the "event with the oiler . . . got people in authority to start being realistic about what they'd been doing to the military for a decade."[93] According to Hayward, the all-volunteer force was in jeopardy. However, once Congress was shown how serious the problem was, the problem was solved—and soon helped along very much by the Reagan administration's commitment to bolstering defense.

The Stage Was Set for Navy Secretary John F. Lehman Jr.

As the successors to former CNO Zumwalt, Admirals Holloway and Hayward had wrapped up some of the issues that had engaged Zumwalt's time and energy, especially readiness, pay, race relations, drug abuse, and the Navy's mission in deterring military aggression by the Soviet Union in Europe. If the 1960s were a time of rapid social change—perhaps even a time of social revolution, then the 1970s were, for the Navy, a time of consolidation and not a counter-revolution led from the CNO's office.

CNO Hayward was "ecstatic" when President Ronald W. Reagan was elected in November 1980.[94] He welcomed a President who could champion the military services. As he would discover after Reagan was inaugurated in January 1981, the new President was also not satisfied with the concept of "mutually assured destruction," and that fit right into the Navy's Maritime Strategy. However, Hayward would also discover that Reagan's choice for Secretary of the Navy, John F. Lehman Jr., would turn out to be very different from his immediate predecessors.

Notes

[1] ADM James L. Holloway III, USN (Ret.), *Aircraft Carriers at War* (Annapolis, MD: Naval Institute Press, 2007), esp. 251–67.

[2] Ibid., 340, 342.

[3] Ibid., 271, 340.

[4] Ibid., 343.

[5] Ibid., 345. Critics of CNO Zumwalt favored ADM Isaac C. Kidd Jr. and opposed ADM Bagley. ADM Holloway was therefore a "compromise" candidate, acceptable to those opposed to Kidd or Bagley.

[6] Ibid., 345–46.

[7] Ibid., 349.

[8] Ibid., 349, 355.

[9] Ibid., 356.

[10] Ibid., 357. The course that CNO Holloway initiated was designed by ADM Rickover and conducted in Idaho, near where the nuclear submarine officers were trained. There were apparently some officers unhappy with the requirement to take a 17-week-long course.

[11] Ibid., 361.

[12] Ibid., 362.

[13] Ibid., 360–61.

[14] James K. Oliver, "Congress and the Future of American Seapower: An Analysis of US Navy Budget Requests in the 1970s," (Paper presented at the meetings of the American Political Science Association, 1976), 32.

[15] Memo, Assistant SECDEF, Program Analysis and Evaluation, to SECDEF, 4 Feb. 1975, subj: Navy shipbuilding, PMS-400 files, Naval Sea Systems Command, Washington, DC.

[16] See James J. Tritten, *Soviet Naval Forces and Nuclear Warfare* (Boulder, CO, 1986).

[17] Memo, OP-09E2 to OP-06, 14 May 1976, subj: OPNAV Strategic/Nuclear Organization, encl: Review of OPNAV Strategic/Nuclear Organization, 1, OP-098 1973–78 folder, OP-09B2 Records.

[18] Memo, W. E. Meyer to R. C. Gooding, Chief, Naval Sea Systems Command, 28 Apr. 1975, PMS-400 Records, Naval Sea Systems Command, Washington, DC.

[19] Thomas C. Hone, "The Program Manager as Entrepreneur: AEGIS and RADM Wayne Meyer," *Defense Analysis* 3 (Fall 1987): 197–212.

[20] See *Defense Facts of Life: the Plans/Reality Mismatch*, by Franklin C. Spinney (Boulder, CO: Westview Press, 1985).

[21] Franklin C. Spinney, an analyst in the Office of Program Analysis and Evaluation (PA&E) converted his initial briefing slides into a long and detailed staff paper and distributed it in 1980

as "Defense Facts of Life," 5 Dec. 1980. It was this staff paper that later became the 1985 book, *Defense Facts of Life: The Plans/Reality Mismatch.*

[22] Holloway, *Aircraft Carriers at War*, 367–69.

[23] Orr Kelly, *Hornet: The Inside Story of the F/A-18* (Shrewsbury, England: Airlife Publishing, 1990), 67.

[24] Holloway, *Aircraft Carriers at War*, 384.

[25] Victor Basiuk, "Organization and Procedures for Selection of Priorities in Navy R&D and Acquisition," June 1979, 10–15, OP-09B2 Records.

[26] National Security and International Affairs, OMB, "Review of Naval Material Command Organization," Aug. 1976 (revised Sept. 1976), Major Observations Section, Analysis of CNM folder, OP-09B2 Records.

[27] Memo, VCNO to CNO, 3 Mar. 1978, subj: Presidential Reorganization Project, 3 Mar. 1978, Mar.–May 78 folder, Synhorst's Original file, Mar.–May 78 folder, OP-09B2 Records.

[28] See Department of Defense, *Departmental Headquarters Study, A Report to the Secretary of Defense*, DOD Reorganization Study Project (Washington, DC, 1978).

[29] Memo, Synhorst to CNO, 25 Dec. 1977, subj: Departmental Headquarters Study Project, Synhorst's Original file, OP-09B2 Records.

[30] Memo, SECDEF to Secretaries of the Military Departments, 7 Apr. 1979, subj: Establishment of Defense Resources Board, DOD Reorganization folder, box 2, OP-602 File, NHHC Archives.

[31] Memo, OP-09E to VCNO, 6 Sept. 1977, subj: Secretariat/OPNAV Relationships, Mar.–May 78 folder, Synhorst's Original file, OP-09B2 Records.

[32] Donald Stoufer, interview with Thomas Hone, 20 July 1987. The Office of Program Appraisal (OPA) was created in 1962 in response to a Dillon Board recommendation.

[33] Comptroller General of the U.S., "Suggested Improvements in Staffing and Organization of Top Management Headquarters in the Dept. of Defense," FPCD-76-35, 20 Apr. 1976, OP-09B2 Records.

[34] Memo, Head, National Policy and Command Organization Branch, to Director, Strategy, Plans and Policy Division, 14 Nov. 1977, subj: Reorganization some random thoughts, p. 1, DOD Reorganization file, box 2, OP-602 File, NHHC Archives.

[35] Ibid.

[36] Point Paper, 2 Nov. 1977, subj: OPNAV Organization, OP-602, p. 1, OPNAV Organization folder, box 5, OP-602 File, NHHC Archives.

[37] Ibid., 2.

[38] Ibid.

[39] OPNAV Notice 5430, 21 Jan. 1977, subj: Transferring non RDT&E weapons functions from OP-985 to OP-06, OP-09B2 Records.

[40] ADM Harry D. Train II, Oral History, U.S. Naval Institute, 17 July 1996, Part 4, 323.

[41] Holloway, *Aircraft Carriers at War*, 399.

[42] Ibid., 402.

[43] Brewster, "The Commandant of the Marine Corps and the JCS," *Marine Corps Gazette*, 62–66.

[44] Holloway, *Aircraft Carriers at War*, 390.

[45] Ibid., 386.

[46] Ibid., 388.

[47] Ibid., 389.

[48] Ibid.

[49] Ibid., 390.

[50] Ibid., 392.

[51] Ibid., 415.

[52] Ibid., 416–17.

[53] Ibid., 417.

[54] Ibid., 383.

[55] Ibid., 384.

[56] Ibid., 365–66.

[57] Chase Untermeyer, *Inside Reagan's Navy: The Pentagon Journals* (College Station: Texas A&M Univ. Press, 2015), 94.

[58] Holloway, *Aircraft Carriers at War*, 174.

[59] Ibid., 375.

[60] Ibid., 307.

[61] John B. Hattendorf, "The Evolution of the Maritime Strategy: 1977–1987," *Naval War College Review* 51 (Summer 1988): 14.

[62] ADM Thomas B. Hayward, USN (Ret.), *Reminiscences*, interviewed by Paul Stillwell (Annapolis, MD: U.S. Naval Institute, 2009), 371–77.

[63] OPNAV Notice 5430, 19 Oct. 1978, subj: Eliminating the concept of sea control and power projection sponsorship, OP-09B2 Records.

[64] Office of the CNO, "The Maritime Balance Study, The Navy Strategic Planning Experiment," 15 Apr. 1979, Executive Summary, NHHC Archives.

[65] Ibid., 11–13.

[66] Basiuk, "Organization and Procedures for Selection of Priorities in Navy R&D and Acquisition," 8, OP-09B2 Records.

[67] Ibid.

[68] Ibid.

[69] Ibid., 10.

[70] Ibid., 9–10.

[71] Ibid., 11.

[72] Ibid., 12–13.

[73] Ibid., 13.

[74] Ibid., 16.

[75] Ibid., 18.

[76] The buying commands were the Naval Sea Systems Command (NAVSEA), the Naval Air Systems Command (NAVAIR), the Space and Naval Warfare Systems Command (SPAWAR), and the Naval Supply Systems Command (NAVSUP).

[77] OPNAV Notice 5340, 15 Jan. 1980, subj: Changing OP-095 from the Director, Antisubmarine Warfare Programs to the Director, Naval Warfare, OP-09B2 Records.

[78] Hayward, *Reminiscences*, 378–79.

[79] Interview, William Spencer Johnson IV, by Thomas C. Hone, 26 July 1916. Weeks was a 1970 graduate of the Naval Academy, and both he and Spencer Johnson were designated specialists in the field of strategy.

[80] Ibid. Johnson was confident that the Air Force and Army would be able to blend their own concepts with the one he and Weeks had developed.

[81] Ibid. According to Johnson, he and Weeks assessed three Navy battle forces in their initial brief. One was composed of the existing carrier battle groups. The second had 12 carrier battle groups, and the third had 15.

[82] Ibid.

[83] Hayward, *Reminiscences*, 282.

[84] Ibid.

[85] Ibid., 357.

[86] Ibid. Albert Wohlstetter was a well-known senior analyst at the RAND Corporation specializing in strategic nuclear issues. Henry S. Rowen had been president of RAND and was a former assistant director of the Bureau of the Budget. Seymour Weiss had headed the Office of Strategic Research and Intelligence in the State Department.

[87] Ibid., 359.

[88] Ibid., 393.

[89] Ibid., 393–94.

[90] Ibid., 394.

[91] Ibid., 471.
[92] Ibid., 416–17.
[93] Ibid., 418.
[94] Ibid., 428.

CHAPTER 12

Resurgence of the Navy Secretariat

Introduction

There is no way to be truly objective in discussing John Lehman's tenure as Secretary of the Navy. From his swearing in on 5 February 1981 to his departure on 10 April 1987, he was always at the center of Navy policy making and almost always controversial and larger than life. He took office committed, as he says in his memoir, to focus "on strategy and policy, not on engineering and facilities management, aircraft development, ship design, and contract law."[1] But he soon decided that the procurement problems that immediately confronted him were just symptomatic of fundamental flaws in the way that the Defense Department and the Navy Department were managed. It wasn't just the procurement process that was "a catastrophe."[2] No. The whole field of civil-military relations was littered with inefficient, "inbred" processes, and the armed services suffered accordingly.

Lehman's bitter enemy was bureaucracy—the offices that performed the routines of Defense Department and Navy management and, in Lehman's view, impeded sensible, swift action to deal with the nation's national security problems. Lehman could not fix the whole Pentagon, but he was determined to get control of the Navy secretariat and, using it and its legal authority, gain control of much of OPNAV and hence the Navy. In the process, he did not much care what most Navy officers thought of him, his methods, and his subordinates in the secretariat. As one officer who worked for him put it, Lehman was "very hands-on, and he wanted to make decisions on almost everything." Accordingly, he "was very upset if he wasn't consulted."[3] John Lehman, like his predecessors Josephus Daniels and James Forrestal, showed what a knowledgeable, determined Navy secretary could do if he had the support of the White House.

Background

President Ronald W. Reagan's Secretary of Defense, Caspar W. Weinberger, and his deputy, Frank C. Carlucci, informed the service secretaries early in 1981 that they would work "toward a system of centralized control of executive policy direction and more decentralized policy execution," where they would hold "each of the Service Secretaries responsible for the development and execution of the necessary programs and the day-to-day management of the resources under their control."[4] The service secretaries were encouraged to express their views and participate in the defense decision-making process. Weinberger and Carlucci promised to improve planning throughout the Planning, Programming, and Budgeting System (PPBS) cycle and pledged to avoid dictating to the services as they developed their own programs.[5] In addition, they changed the composition and responsibilities of the Defense Resources Board (DRB), which had been created by former Secretary of Defense Harold Brown to adjudicate disputes over program goals between OSD and the services. The service secretaries were made permanent members of the board and the service chiefs were permitted to attend board meetings as their advisors, and the board's responsibility was extended to assisting the Defense secretary in managing "the entire revised planning, programming and budgeting process."[6]

This was a major change to the programming process. As members of the DRB, service secretaries were given great *potential* initiative and influence. In his published memoir, *Command of the Seas*, Secretary Lehman noted that the board met almost daily once the Reagan appointees moved into the Pentagon in 1981, and he claimed that the "group was extremely effective as a decision-making body."[7] The Secretary of Defense held the service secretaries responsible for the management of their departments and encouraged them to take the initiative in making sure service programs met the guidelines outlined at the beginning of the PPBS cycle. Weinberger also changed the PPBS process itself. The Joint Chiefs of Staff continued to begin the process every fall by preparing a Joint Strategic Planning Document, a list of forces that the Joint Chiefs believed were needed to achieve the strategic goals of the United States. At the same time, however, the unified theater commanders, or CINCs, also prepared a list of programs and systems that were most important to them. At the beginning of the new year, the Office of the Secretary of Defense promulgated a draft Defense Guidance that was reviewed by the services and the Joint Chiefs. Once the reviews were complete, the DRB met for the first time in the PPBS cycle to recommend a final version of the Defense Guidance to the SecDef. After considering the DRB recommendations, the secretary issued the guidance to the services.

With the support of their headquarters staffs, the service secretaries and chiefs implemented the Defense Guidance through their service-specific POMs. Before the Reagan administration, the services were free to draft program documents without further review until they were forwarded to OSD in July. In 1985, however, Secretary Weinberger altered the process so that the

Joint Chiefs and the theater commanders could review preliminary service POMs in May.[8] In June, OSD analysts, working with comments from the Joint Chiefs and the theater commanders, negotiated with the service headquarters staffs when, and if, there were disagreements over the POM numbers. OSD could try, for example, to pressure a service to move funding for a program up or down if OSD analysts believed that the service POM did not conform to the Defense Guidance. Throughout June, negotiations between OSD and service headquarters staffs pared the number of POM issues to a minimum. The Defense Resources Board reviewed the POMs in August and the services were then allowed one final appeal before the Defense secretary made his judgment.

Office of the Secretary of Defense review of Program Objective Memoranda was not entirely analytical and never really had been. Organizational, doctrinal, and individual interests frequently came into play. This was inevitable. The programming process was characterized by negotiation and making trade-offs within each service headquarters and then between each headquarters and the OSD staff. Trade-offs were necessary because the cost of all the specific programs (research and development, training, acquisition, and personnel), that the service staffs wanted to support was greater than the funds available to support them. The relative scarcity of funds forced programmers to become advocates as well as analysts. The fact that Lehman had been schooled in advocacy while studying at Cambridge University in England helped the Navy's position vis-à-vis the other services.

The service secretaries became an integral part of defense programming through participation both in the development of the Defense Guidance and in the adjudication process of the Defense Resources Board. Concerned also with the separation of the programming process from the acquisition process, Weinberger and Carlucci ensured that membership on the DRB and on the Defense Systems Acquisition Review Council (DSARC) (the senior acquisition review board) overlapped. Although Weinberger tied the programming and acquisition committees together, he kept real control for himself and his chief deputy. However, his decision to rely on the DRB as a major initiation and review body in the PPBS process enhanced the influence of the Navy secretary both at the Department of Defense level and—more importantly—within the Navy.

Lehman's Influence over Navy Programs

Secretary Lehman eagerly grasped and used this new influence. Remember that he had been hired as an advisor by former CNO Holloway. Despite saying that he was a stranger to the Pentagon's bureaucracy, Lehman was no stranger to the Navy. Moreover, as a protégé of Henry Kissinger, Lehman knew how to use knowledge to advantage in bureaucratic contests. Lehman was also an A-6 (carrier attack plane) bombardier-navigator in the Navy reserves. The most personally aggressive and organizationally perceptive Navy secretary since James Forrestal, Lehman understood two things about OPNAV: first, its primary function was to produce the Navy's Program Objective Memorandum, or POM; second, OPNAV staff developed the Navy's

POM through a process of negotiation, review, and ratification that took place in several layers of committees.

The first committee level was the Program Development Review Committee, made up of rear admirals representing the CNO's major deputies and chaired by the Director of the General Planning and Programming Division (OP-90) within OP-090. The next level was the Program Review Committee, chaired by the Director of Navy Program Planning (OP-090). Capping the review process was the CNO Executive Board (CEB), chaired by the Vice Chief of Naval Operations and composed of the Chief of Naval Material, the Commandant of the Marine Corps, and the DCNOs.

To gain leverage in OPNAV's programming process, Secretary Lehman created the Navy Program Strategy Board, which he chaired, at a level above the CEB, and he used the new board as part of his effort to take control of the programming process. In his published memoir, Lehman asserted that he and his deputies "wanted to decentralize decision-making and delegate authority to the lowest appropriate level, but then to hold people accountable by name."[9] This is not quite accurate. What Lehman wanted to do was to get around the traditional separation of the secretary's acquisition authority and the CNO's programmatic duties. He wanted to know who made key decisions so that he could influence them. He could not stand the passive voice in memos, as in "it is the policy that . . ." or "a decision was made to . . ." because it disguised which officials had made or were making a decision. Similarly, he wanted to be able to see into the Navy's bureaucracy in order to locate the individuals who had authority; they were the ones he wanted to influence. He would give no "bureaucrat" *carte blanche*, and he recruited a civilian staff who shared his views and his assertiveness. Lehman went so far as to move senior civil servants from one systems command to another so that they could not obstruct his initiatives.[10]

At the same time, however, Lehman set his sights on getting the material that the Navy needed. In 1978, while working as a consultant for then–CNO James Holloway, Lehman had written *Aircraft Carriers: The Real Choices*, a strong and articulate defense of the modern carrier and its air wing.[11] He had also, while still a private citizen, lobbied contacts in the House and Senate in support of the *Nimitz*-class carrier that President Carter had chosen not to fund. In 1981, after being confirmed as Secretary of the Navy, Lehman had appointed George A. Sawyer, a former Navy submarine engineer officer, as the Assistant Secretary of the Navy (Shipbuilding and Logistics). Sawyer suggested that it might be possible to negotiate the purchase of two *Nimitz*-class carriers in the same fiscal year by renegotiating the contract for the ship that became CVN-71 (*Theodore Roosevelt*).[12]

However, Congress had not authorized two carriers in the same year since World War II, and Lehman was concerned that he would not gain the approval of Secretary of Defense Weinberger. Fortunately for the Navy, Deputy Secretary of Defense Carlucci "became excited about the idea and came up with an imaginative approach to fitting it to our annual budget cycle." Carlucci said the Navy could have additional funds in fiscal year 1983 for the two *Nimitz*-class ships. In return, the Navy would "pay back" the funds used to start procurement of the second carrier in the Navy's fiscal year 1984 budget.[13] As Lehman recalled, by the end of 1981, the Navy had gained funding to extend the useful lives of "all the older carriers, extend the *Coral Sea* [CV-43] to 1991, extend the *Midway* [CV-41] to the year 2000, and build three new Nimitz [sic] class carriers."[14] This was an impressive achievement. It was an essential part of the *quid pro quo* that Lehman established between himself and the Navy's senior officers.

But getting more ships, more sailors, and more funds for operations was just part of what Lehman intended to do. He also appropriated CNO Hayward's aggressive operational concept toward the Soviet Union and gave it widespread publicity as *the* "Maritime Strategy." He also monitored the work of the small but influential Strategic Studies Group (SSG), which Hayward had established at the Naval War College and considered one of the CNO's own sources of creativity. The new secretary also encouraged the faculty of the Navy's Postgraduate School in Monterey, California, to offer courses on strategic issues. Most importantly, Lehman used his public and political visibility to push for a 600-ship Navy, based on Hayward's concept of a force built around 15 aircraft carrier battle groups.

Secretary Lehman understood that success in Congress and in OSD would add to his credibility and his influence within the Navy. He would trade results—a larger and stronger Navy—for the loyalty of the Navy's officers. A careful student of the Congress, Lehman realized that the nature of the legislative process had changed in the 1970s, eroding the seniority system and creating many centers of influence. Accordingly, his strategy toward Congress had two parts. The first was a long-term approach to build, among members of the House and Senate, recognition of the Navy's importance and knowledge of its programs. Lehman assumed that he and his subordinates in the Office of Legislative Affairs (OLA) could build awareness, understanding, and ultimately support in Congress, but only if the secretary—and no competitors in uniform—spoke for the Navy. Accordingly, an essential part of his strategy was to have his staff work with OLA to review drafts of all Navy testimony being prepared for congressional committee hearings in order to make sure that all communications with Congress were in line with his annual posture statement. Any deviations from the statement were rejected.[15]

The second part of Lehman's congressional strategy included an annual ranking of programs. Each November, the secretary began a process of presenting congressional appropriation and authorization committees with briefings and papers in support of about eight programs most important to the secretary and the CNO. Between the fall of one year and committee mark-up time in the next, the Navy's presentations did not vary, even if Congress appeared unwilling to support all the programs suggested by the secretariat. The Office of Legislative Affairs became the focal point in this process. It tracked changes in congressional support for Navy programs and screened program managers (PMs) and senior Navy officers called to testify. Program managers in the systems commands who balked at the guidance of the secretariat were not permitted to speak for the Navy.[16]

Lehman also promoted the Maritime Strategy as a means of gaining visibility for the Navy in Congress and in the Office of the Secretary of Defense. To OSD, Lehman argued that

Navy programs were based on a military strategy that made optimal use of the resources that a nation like the United States could and would produce. After all, the North Atlantic Treaty Organization (NATO) could not field the ground strength of the Warsaw Pact, so why try? Why not use the maritime strength of the U.S. Navy to offset NATO's ground force weakness? To Congress, Lehman argued that Navy forces were effective across a wide range of conflicts and mobile enough to deploy to the scene of a conflict in time to deal with it. The Navy and Marines were effective for all sorts of missions, ranging from "peacetime presence" to major conventional war.

To gain support within the Navy, Lehman presented himself as the provider and defender of the 600-ship fleet and as the advocate of the only coherent military service strategy. He appealed to the fleet and its support units by visiting ships and bases, "campaigning" among the operating forces just as politicians work their constituents. Indeed, as Captain Donald A. Stoufer, a former member of Lehman's staff, observed, "Lehman's philosophy was . . . control belongs with the operators, not at the Pentagon."[17] And Lehman told everyone that he was *in* the Pentagon but not *of* the Pentagon.

Using this philosophy as a shield against criticism, Lehman deliberately undercut the influence of OPNAV and the CNO. According to Stoufer, "Secretary Lehman created an atmosphere of antagonism, fear, loathing, hate—almost any emotion. . . . Lehman was the consummate bureaucrat and yet he was antibureaucratic."[18] His goal was to break down the "Washington syndrome," or the view of OPNAV programmers that "the guy in the fleet doesn't know anything about the Navy or how the Navy operates, and therefore he—the programmer—is going to sit there and design a program that supports his view of the Navy."[19] Lehman's tactic in dealing with OPNAV was to threaten action, almost any action. "That was his tactic against OPNAV—not long hours. He didn't play their game."[20] The secretary used his formal powers to the utmost, guiding the deliberations of selection boards and the assignments of flag officers, controlling the public relations and congressional affairs aspects of the Navy Department, driving the programming process, and capturing the symbolic leadership role that was once the province of the Chief of Naval Operations.

Lehman and Hayward

Secretary Lehman's strategy while in office was to treat the Chief of Naval Operations as his deputy, but deputy in the sense that former CNO James Holloway described his time as the vice chief under CNO Elmo Zumwalt—as someone whose agenda was his superior's. Holloway said that his job under Zumwalt was to see to it that the CNO's policies were implemented; that "was the Navy way."[21] But that same relationship really wasn't meant to be translated into the relationship between the SECNAV and the CNO. The two officials had different legal responsibilities. That had been the foundation of the accepted distinction between the CNO deciding military requirements and the secretary finding ways to build a navy that could support those requirements. But Lehman didn't accept this distinction. As he testified to the Senate Armed

Services Committee in November 1983, service secretaries needed to "worry as much about the soundness of military strategy, military operations, military weapons and military leadership as they do about the soundness of contract procedures and spare parts procurement."[22]

Secretary Lehman's assertiveness and his expansive view of his authority led to a clash with CNO Hayward. As then-Commander Spencer Johnson recalled, "They couldn't stand each other. They really couldn't." As a result, they "didn't speak to each other for the better part of a year."[23] The "standoff" was not good for either of them, and so they gradually discovered that they could cooperate when they dealt with the Navy's program because they saw "eye-to-eye generally on programmatic issues," especially in 1981.[24] Years later, Hayward recalled that he "particularly enjoyed" testifying with Lehman before congressional committees "because he was quite forceful and strong, and we were really aligned on what we were trying to accomplish."[25]

Yet there was a negative side to Lehman's ability to think on his feet. He "didn't like people around him whom he couldn't manipulate."[26] Hayward believed that this was the reason Lehman and Admirals Carlisle A. H. Trost and M. Staser Holcomb did not get along. The two admirals "could out-think him, or at least think as fast as he could."[27] Before Secretary Lehman took office, Hayward relied on the CNO's Executive Panel (CEP) and the Center for Naval Analyses for advice and ideas. Captain William J. Cockell Jr., Hayward's executive assistant, kept the CNO in touch with the idea people.[28] But Cockell had to leave the Pentagon and take a seagoing command in 1981 in order to make flag rank.

When he became Navy secretary, Lehman already knew that one of his most difficult tasks would be to force Admiral Hyman G. Rickover, head of the Navy's nuclear propulsion program and an official in the Department of Energy, into retirement.[29] As it happened, CNO Hayward was also thinking about a way to retire Rickover. As Hayward recalled, "I had nothing but admiration for Admiral Rickover. . . . But he was 78 years old when I became CNO, and he'd had a couple of small heart attacks." Hayward decided the Navy needed a plan in case Admiral Rickover was suddenly incapacitated. He asked Admirals James D. Watkins and Robert L. J. Long (Commander-in-Chief, Pacific Command) for help. Both admirals had been trained by Rickover, and Hayward thought that they could help maneuver Rickover toward leaving active duty. But Rickover resisted, and so Lehman and Secretary of Defense Caspar Weinberger forced the issue. Lehman described the confrontation that ensued in the White House between him and Rickover in detail in his memoir. It was an awkward—and for Rickover very bitter—scene, but Lehman and Hayward had already isolated the old admiral politically, and Rickover had no choice but to retire. However, ever the consummate bureaucrat, Rickover struck a bargain with Lehman. He accepted retirement in exchange for Executive Order 12344 of 1 February 1982, which "insured" Rickover's successors eight-year terms and directed them to report directly to the CNO.[30] Though there would not be another Rickover, each of his successors would have eight years in office—time enough to make any needed changes to the "nuclear navy."

Lehman and CNO James D. Watkins (I)

Admiral James D. Watkins was brilliant, a disciplined and precise thinker, and socially a conservative. He had performed outstandingly as Chief of Naval Personnel from 1975 to the beginning of 1978, and his OPNAV experience (VCNO 1980–1981) was balanced by his command experience at sea in the Mediterranean (Sixth Fleet commander 1978–1979) and in the Pacific, where he had served as commander-in-chief of the Pacific Fleet (1981–1982). When he succeeded CNO Hayward on 30 June 1982, he immediately began examining the Navy as a whole, a demanding task given the Navy's operating tempo (OPTEMPO) and worldwide deployments.

He promised that he'd reveal the product of his thinking in 90 days, and he did. His message to senior admirals on 7 October 1982 spelled out where he wanted to put his energy as CNO.[31] His first concern was "warfighting readiness" against the forces of the Soviet Union. To help achieve this very high level of readiness, he wanted to "revitalize" the Naval War College "as the crucible for strategic and tactical thinking." He felt that a revitalized War College could provide an environment to "test and harmonize tactical thinking in a wide variety of strategic applications." He also intended to modify the "officer training pipeline" so that there would be enough trained officers for Secretary Lehman's 600-ship Navy. He planned to continue Admiral Hayward's effort to "integrate reserves" into the active Navy, and he pointed to a memorandum between himself and the Chief of Staff of the U.S. Air Force to improve Navy–Air Force cooperation in tactical air operations as an example of actions that would better prepare all the services for war.

Watkins also stressed the need to "find imaginative ways to reduce the ever-growing cost of doing business." These ways he lumped into two categories—"cost discipline" and "cost technology." As he said, "cost discipline requires weapon system configuration control, independent cost estimating, hard-nosed contracting and competition in a variety of forms . . ." Cost technology, by contrast, was "a mind set [sic] which emphasizes cost as a criteria [sic] in design, operation," and provides spare parts for weapons. As he argued, "Application of cost technology results not in missile components designed to perform at the leading edge of technology for an infinite life but rather with 100 percent reliability for the time of flight, be it 30 seconds or 30 minutes." He also stressed the need to "imbue our military and civilian

Figure 12-1. After his term as CNO, James D. Watkins retired and headed the Presidential Commission on the HIV epidemic. He also served as Secretary of the Department of Energy in the administration of President George H. W. Bush. (National Archives 428-KN 28899)

leaders with the quality of character that looks under the rug as a matter of professional conscience and routine."[32]

"Recall," he enjoined his fellow flag officers,

> how we took that approach in our war on drugs. Some said we had to accept drug usage as an American way of life. We said nonsense. We were right. Unwitting complacency to waste in the special sense outlined here is, like drug abuse, a societal problem which we cannot accept as a natural way of life in the Navy.[33]

These were the words of an educated and dedicated Catholic—a man who was not content to take people as they were but as they might be and could be. It explains Watkins's focus on the values and abilities of sailors and on the values of the larger society that produced them. Like so many of his predecessors, Watkins perceived a clear connection between personal excellence and national security.[34]

The Maturing of the "Maritime Strategy"

CNO Hayward's retirement in June 1982 did not bring work on what became the "Maritime Strategy" to an end. Quite the contrary. As CNO Watkins revealed his plans to senior Navy officers in October 1982, Lieutenant Commander Stanley B. Weeks and Commander W. Spencer Johnson were briefing the rear admirals who served on OPNAV's Program Development Review Committee. The chairman of the committee was then-Rear Admiral Joseph Metcalf III, the head of OPNAV's Planning and Programming Division, OP-90. According to Johnson, Metcalf picked up a phone, called the CNO's office and advised Watkins to see the presentation immediately. Soon thereafter, Weeks, Johnson, and Captain Elizabeth G. Wylie briefed Watkins, VCNO Admiral William N. Small, the deputy chiefs, and senior Marine officers.[35]

Watkins was apparently impressed with the presentation, part of which called for a "surge" of 11 carriers into the Atlantic and the Norwegian Sea in the event of an impending invasion of Western Europe by the armed forces of the Warsaw Pact. Johnson recalled Watkins turning to his deputy CNO for aviation and asking if that many carriers could be deployed in such an emergency. The answer was no—not 11, maybe as many as six. Watkins wondered why 11 could not be surged. The answer was that carriers returning from deployment had to transfer ordnance and even the tractors used to move aircraft on their flight decks to those carriers preparing to deploy. This response sobered the new CNO emotionally. As Johnson recalled, this response and others from the DCNOs was like a bucket of cold water thrown on Watkins. It showed him that his Navy was "hollow." It lacked the readiness and logistics to mobilize in the face of a threatened attack on NATO by the Soviet Union. He told his deputies that he would not purchase any new systems until the Navy's readiness problems were adequately addressed.[36]

From that time on, the program proposals of the CNO's deputies had to support the Maritime Strategy. In addition, CNO Watkins insisted that the strategy be part of the annual Global War Game at the Naval War College, that the elements of the strategy be tested in exercises at sea, and that it be reviewed annually to determine if there were major obstacles to its successful execution.[37] The Atlantic and Pacific fleet commanders were enthusiastic about the Maritime Strategy, and Secretary Lehman embraced it because it gave him a persuasive rationale for his efforts to field a "600-ship Navy."[38] He directed Vice Admiral Arthur S. Moreau Jr., head of OP-06, to have his staff show the brief to all the captains and rear admirals then holding posts in the Pentagon, and Lehman himself eventually presented a classified version of the brief to members of Congress.[39]

The Maritime Strategy continued to mature after Lieutenant Commander Weeks went to sea and Commander Johnson left OPNAV to serve as a special assistant to Secretary Lehman "for policy implementation." Vice Admiral Moreau was replaced by Vice Admiral James A. Lyons Jr., and Rear Admiral Ronald F. Marryott took over OP-60 (the Strategy, Plans and Policy Division of OP-06) from Rear Admiral Dudley L. Carlson. Captain Philip D. Smith relieved Captain Wylie as OP-603, and Captain Roger W. Barnett relieved Smith. Then he and Commander Peter M. Swartz picked up where Weeks and Johnson had left off. They altered the November 1982 brief intended to discipline Navy programming and budgeting into a full-blown strategic concept.[40] Rear Admiral Marryott presented their work to CNO Watkins and six former chiefs of naval operations on Coast Guard cutter *Chase* (WHEC-718) anchored off Newport, Rhode Island, in September 1983.[41] In October, the strategy was again the touchstone of the POM process, this time for fiscal year 1985.

In January 1984, Secretary Lehman and CNO Watkins briefed Secretary of Defense Weinberger on the Maritime Strategy, and Weinberger endorsed it. Lehman and Watkins presented it to the Subcommittee on Seapower of the Senate Armed Services Committee in March, and the "Maritime Strategy" was signed by CNO Watkins and formally promulgated in early May 1984.[42] Representatives of OP-06 and the Naval War College spread the strategy through the fleet, and the U.S. Naval Institute published both an unclassified version of it and Secretary Lehman's paper on the 600-ship Navy in a special supplement to the institute's January 1986 *Proceedings*.[43]

Their shared interest in the Maritime Strategy helped Lehman and Watkins cooperate at a time when many people feared that there might be a conventional or even nuclear conflict between NATO and the Warsaw Pact. The two men were also teamed under a President—Ronald Reagan—who wanted to end the Cold War and do it in a way that would break up the "evil empire" of the Soviet Union without war. To give Reagan the confidence and the sense of American power and resolve that he could use as the basis for his negotiations with the Soviet Union, both Lehman and Watkins had to show that American military power was growing, and that the armed forces of the United States were confident that they could more than stand up to anything that the Soviet Union could throw at them. Moreover, the exercises held to test the ideas in the Maritime Strategy not only improved it, they also served as a warning to the Soviet Union that the strategy could in fact be implemented.

Put another way, measures to reduce the cost of systems and eliminate waste dovetailed perfectly with the Maritime Strategy and the 600-ship Navy. To use a cliché of that time, the Navy and Marines would be "a lean and mean fighting machine." On that, Lehman and Watkins were agreed. They also agreed on the need for "cost discipline" and the need for a more cost-conscious approach to acquisition and logistics. But Lehman wanted to do more than cooperate with the CNO. He and his closest deputies understood that the key to dominating a bureaucracy was to gain and keep the initiative in ideas and in action. Lehman's strategy was "to integrate the uniformed staff of the chief of naval operations and the commandant of the marine corps with the staff of the secretary of the navy."[44] This was the area where Lehman and Watkins differed.[45]

Lehman and CNO Watkins (II)

The problem facing Watkins was that Secretary Lehman had taken the bureaucratic initiative in 1981.[46] By 1983, he was aggressively questioning the value of OPNAV offices that he suspected could or did provide the new CNO with ideas and programmatic insights that would conflict with his own. On 28 March 1983, Watkins disestablished OP-96, the pocket of systems analysts in the program planning office (OP-090), and replaced it with OP-91, the Program Resource Appraisal Division.[47] On 6 May 1983, Watkins transferred the functions of OP-00X, the Long-range Planning Group, to the Chief of Naval Operations' Executive Panel (OP-00K). Then, that same month, Lehman and Watkins eliminated the Naval Material Command (NAVMAT) and its headquarters staff. As Professor Frederick Hartmann of the Naval War College argued, "There was no issue, no question, in the Watkins years that divided opinion more in the navy than this one."[48]

Why abolish NAVMAT? It had been created in 1963 to serve as a focal point for the procurement and logistics concerns of the Secretary of the Navy. The idea was that the Secretary and a few members of his senior staff could work better with the Special Projects Office (SPO) (for ballistic missile submarine and missile development) and the major material bureaus if they didn't have to go to the different procurement offices separately. Secretary Lehman said this plan had not worked—that the platform DCNOs had gradually but steadily intruded into the relationship between the Secretary and the material bureaus (systems commands). But the reason that OPNAV offices had in fact gotten involved in development and acquisition was because they were responsible for military requirements. As Watkins pointed out, Secretary Lehman "put himself into a position where he thought he had to run the Navy all by himself. And he couldn't! One Secretary, no matter how talented, can't do it. You have to rely on the CNO and all the officers under him."[49] However, Watkins went along with abolishing NAVMAT because Admiral Isaac C. Kidd Jr., NAVMAT's chief, said that having another four-star admiral involved in procurement and development was costing more in time and energy than he was worth.

Was eliminating NAVMAT a "power play"? Yes and no. There was already dissatisfaction inside the Naval Sea Systems Command (NAVSEA) "with the lack of consistent and clear Navy guidance on the wide range of parameters that [drove] ship designs. Designs were started, modified and then cancelled after expending considerable time and money."[50] To remedy this problem, the vice commander of NAVSEA had sent a letter in February 1982 to the VCNO recommending "improvements to the process now in use within the Navy for determining the characteristics of our new ships." As the letter noted, "Creation of a ship design is by its nature, a series of compromises in which elements such as weapons system capability, survival in a wartime environment, speed, endurance, reliability, maintainability, and cost all must be properly evaluated and weighed against each other." That weighing was not happening effectively, and the letter recommended using a series of reviews "at the vice admiral level at set points in a program's development."

After months of discussions among representatives of NAVSEA, OPNAV, and NAVMAT, Vice Chief of Naval Operations Small established the Ship Characteristics and Improvement Board. The board took the place of the Ship Acquisition and Improvement Panel. The secretariat was given two non-voting members of the board, and a permanent staff supporting the board was set up inside OPNAV. Once it was up and running, the board served "as the advisory board to the [CNO Executive Board] on all matters related to ship acquisition and improvement" and also provided "staff liaison" to the Assistant Secretary of the Navy for Shipbuilding and Logistics.[51] Secretary Lehman was pleased with the board's work, and in a 4 August 1983 memo to CNO Watkins wrote that "The success of the Ship's [sic] Characteristics and Improvement Board has persuaded us to apply the same approach to aviation. Accordingly the [Assistant Secretary of the Navy (Shipbuilding & Logistics)] and CNO shall submit a plan for the establishment of an Air Characteristics and Improvement Board."[52]

This memo was not good news for the Naval Air Systems Command (NAVAIR), which was developing the F/A-18 fighter-attack aircraft to replace the older light and heavy attack bombers then on carriers. Secretary Lehman was a bombardier-navigator in the A-6 heavy attack plane, and continued to fly with a naval reserve squadron even while serving as Navy secretary. He did not regard the F/A-18 as an adequate substitute for the A-6 because the F/A-18 lacked range and the ability to carry a heavy bomb load. Creating an air board as an analog to the Ship Characteristics and Improvement Board could give the Secretary the opportunity to torpedo the F/A-18.[53] Lehman had already pressured the F/A-18's builder (McDonnell-Douglas) to reduce the cost of the airplane,[54] and aviation officers in NAVAIR and OPNAV believed he would find a way to cancel the program. But Lehman didn't.

What convinced him to accept it? Two things. First, he and his staff forced—with strong arguments and analysis—the builder to constrain the cost. Second, the new engine for the plane was reliable and responsive, and Lehman "became a big fan."[55] But if Lehman could force NAVAIR to create an Air Characteristics Improvement Board, he would be able to influence aircraft designs early in their development and avoid the sort of bureaucratic hair-pulling that he had been forced to engage in in his efforts to hold down the cost of the F/A-18. Put another way, he could institutionalize a role for the Secretary of the Navy that put the secretary in place of the CNO as a developer of military requirements.

In his published memoir, Lehman argued that the Navy's acquisition process was not responsive to civilian control—and for that reason ships and aircraft were costing too much and the number of ships and planes was coming down even though spending on them had been going up. The reason he had been hostile to NAVMAT was because he had seen it as a barrier to secretariat control of the acquisition process, even if it was presented as an aid to that control. As he said, "A single centralized procurement bureaucracy called the Navy [sic] Materiel Command reported to the chief of naval operations through his staff . . . [A]ll the procurement and business organizations were under the total domination of the headquarters staff of the chief of naval operations, the OPNAV staff."[56]

Lehman's assessment was not entirely correct. NAVMAT was not really under the control of the CNO. Indeed, that was one reason why senior Navy officers supported the decision to eliminate NAVMAT. But what Lehman was after was the ability to bypass the DCNOs for submarine, surface, and air warfare and reach the project managers. As he said,

> [T]he financial officer for every project worked for the project manager who wrote his fitness report, and not for the comptroller of the Systems Command, who reported to the assistant secretary for financial management. This violated the most fundamental management principles, and I directed it be changed immediately. There was tremendous resistance from the OPNAV staff, but Jim Watkins completely agreed.[57]

Lehman surmised that "Since . . . virtually all project managers were unrestricted line . . . officers who hoped to get good assignments back with the fleet, they danced to the tune of the [DCNOs]."[58]

To break the deputy chiefs' power over project managers in the Navy's major acquisition commands, such as NAVSEA and NAVAIR, Lehman and Watkins changed the way financial deputies in the project offices were evaluated. They gave authority to write the fitness reports for such officers to the systems command comptrollers, who reported to the Assistant Secretary of the Navy for Financial Management (the Navy comptroller), removing the PMs, in whose offices the financial deputy worked, from the chain of command.[59] Watkins also gave the Director of Naval Warfare the authority to sponsor acquisition programs, a power which the deputy chiefs had almost totally monopolized.[60]

Lehman described the change in *Command of the Seas*:

> [W]e changed the reporting authority to have the commander of each of the systems commands report directly to the secretary of the navy and, on a parallel line, to the chief of naval operations for informational purposes. I had direct through lines put on my telephone to each of the systems commanders, and we talked back and forth almost daily.[61]

The talk was mostly one way. Because "the blue suiters simply would not recognize any authority but the chief of naval operations," Lehman developed other means to increase or apply the influence of his office over acquisition and development.[62] He forced PMs in the Naval Sea Systems and Naval Air Systems Commands to submit all requests for engineering change proposals to special review boards in each systems command. Contractors often requested such proposals to cover the increased cost of modifying a design at the government's request, hence raising the systems' costs. Ideally, such change proposals were used only as a last resort, when an unforeseen and unplanned design change had to be made. In fact, engineering change proposals were an "out" for PMs—a loophole that allowed (and some said encouraged) sloppy design practices. Lehman made all Navy program managers run requests for engineering changes through special screening boards, and if they passed that hurdle, through the CNO, and then finally to Lehman himself.

Lehman also required the major Navy buying commands (NAVSEA and NAVAIR) to impose competition and fixed price contracts on the development and acquisition process. Using the legal authority vested in his office by Title 10 of the U.S. Code, he gave the Navy secretariat greater influence over Navy procurement, research and development, and the Navy's relationship with major civilian contractors. In exchange for this level of influence, Lehman persuasively and effectively advocated Navy programs within the Defense Department and with Congress. Much of the Reagan administration's military build-up was in fact a Navy build-up.

To better get his way within the Navy, Lehman supported officers he favored. A case in point was Vice Admiral James A. Lyons Jr., who commanded the Second Fleet from July 1981 to July 1983 and had been something of a professional mentor to Lehman before Lehman became Navy secretary.[63] Admiral Hayward described Lyons as "extremely close to the Secretary. Through this relationship [Lyons] made . . . very clear . . . his disloyalty in numerous respects to the CNO and to the Navy system. He was out for himself, and the Secretary was going to get him everything he could get him. . . . Unfortunately, I couldn't block it."[64] Admiral Harry D. Train II, then Supreme Allied Commander Atlantic, expressed his concern with Lehman's methods by saying "that in the wake of the personnel changes and the personnel policies and the philosophies that [Secretary Lehman] conveyed to the Navy, we ended up with an officer corps that was more politicized than I felt comfortable with. Even the younger officers, the lieutenants and lieutenant commanders, had their eyes on the political scene, as opposed to being consumed with their professional development."[65]

By contrast, Admiral William J. Crowe, who served as Chairman of the Joint Chiefs of Staff from 1 October 1985 to 30 September 1989, considered Secretary Lehman a good and "eminently successful" bureaucrat. According to Crowe, Lehman understood the political process "in his bones and [manipulated] it ruthlessly." As Crowe put it in his own memoir, Lehman exhibited the "spirit of a man who wanted later to be able to declare, I'm the one who built a real Navy." Crowe recognized the great sense of ambition that Lehman possessed and observed that Lehman "was not eager to be the Secretary who took the Navy from 60 percent spare parts to 95 percent spare parts . . ." Instead, Lehman wanted a 600-ship Navy. That was his theme in 1981; it remained his theme throughout his time as Navy secretary. But Lehman's focus on numbers of ships and submarines drove professional officers "to distraction" because they were always struggling to "get support for the mundane essentials"—fuel, weapons, and spare parts—that they needed.[66]

Lehman was determined to get *his* 600 ships. For example, after Hayward's departure at the end of June 1982, Lehman began holding a series of Navy Strategy Board "retreats," where the Secretary could confront the new CNO, Admiral James D. Watkins, in a setting where the admiral could not draw on the help of the OPNAV staff. As Lehman pointed out, the retreats in the American Security Council's conference space in Boston, Virginia, broke down "the institutional barrier between the uniformed navy and marine corps and between them and the civilian leadership."[67] What he did not say was that he purposefully wanted to break down those barriers because they were a source of influence for the Chief of Naval Operations, serving to shield the CNO from Lehman's efforts to influence him and set the CNO's agenda. It would be a mistake to make too much of these informal meetings, but they did give Secretary Lehman the opportunity to deal with Watkins and the Marine Corps commandant *outside the Pentagon*, and Lehman prided himself on his ability to be persuasive in such a setting.

The relationship between the secretary and his Navy chief was widely rumored at the time to be difficult, and Lehman did not openly contradict those rumors. Indeed, the rumors were part of the bureaucratic atmosphere that the secretary wished to create. Every strong Secretary of the Navy, from Josephus Daniels in World War I to Forrestal in the last year of World War II, had clashed with senior Navy officers, though not always with the CNO, and John Lehman knew it. By law, the secretary is responsible for the administration of the Navy Department. The CNO is his primary military assistant to whom the secretary usually delegates great authority. But John Lehman, like Forrestal, was anything but "normal" as a Navy secretary. Lehman's office—and sometimes the secretary personally—intervened in naval operations, planning, and acquisition to an unprecedented degree in peacetime. Lehman's audacity and brashness worked to keep the OPNAV bureaucracy off balance. His actions were unsettling and unusual, and his opponents claimed that they were detrimental to officer morale and bordered on the unethical.

In his oral history, Admiral Bruce DeMars, who served as DCNO for Submarine Warfare (OP-02) from 1985 to 1988, recounted an effort by Secretary Lehman in 1986 to improperly influence the captain selection board chaired by DeMars. The members of selection boards were sworn under oath to follow the guidance of the Secretary of the Navy as to the impartial evaluation of the service records of officers to be chosen for promotion. De Mars and his fellow board members followed that guidance. According to DeMars, Lehman did not. As DeMars recalled, Lehman "started telling me specific guys I should select: 'Okay, I want this guy'—by name," but DeMars reminded the secretary that "you're not allowed to do that." When Lehman continued to pressure DeMars, DeMars formally resigned as head of the selection board. DeMars's letter of resignation was leaked to *The Washington Post*, and that caught the attention of some senior senators. Their interest in the case led to an investigation by the Inspector General of the Department of Defense (DOD). The Inspector General's report on the matter, released before Lehman resigned in April 1987, sided with DeMars and against Lehman.[68] So long as John Lehman had the support of President Ronald Reagan and succeeded in pushing pro-Navy budgets and authorizations through Congress, his unorthodox (and even incorrect) methods were tolerated. By the time of Lehman's confrontation with then–Rear Admiral DeMars, however, things had changed.

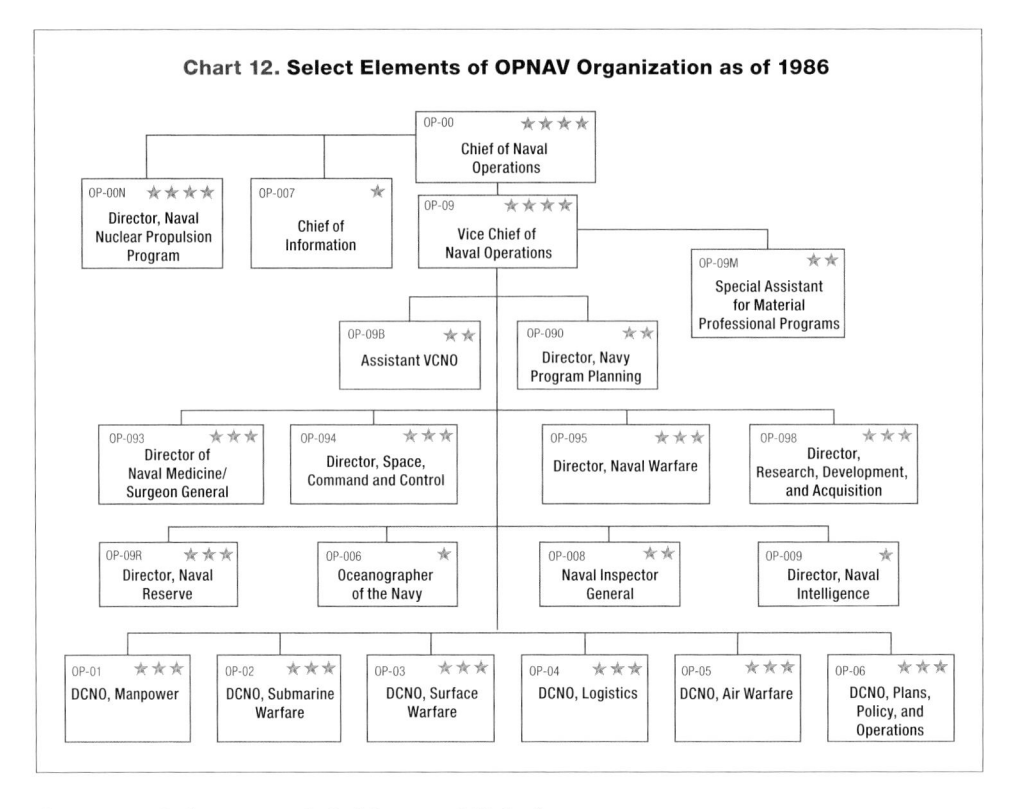

Chart 12. Select Elements of OPNAV Organization as of 1986

- OP-00 ★★★★ Chief of Naval Operations
  - OP-00N ★★★★ Director, Naval Nuclear Propulsion Program
  - OP-007 ★ Chief of Information
  - OP-09 ★★★★ Vice Chief of Naval Operations
    - OP-09M ★★ Special Assistant for Material Professional Programs
    - OP-09B ★★ Assistant VCNO
    - OP-090 ★★ Director, Navy Program Planning
      - OP-093 ★★★ Director of Naval Medicine/Surgeon General
      - OP-094 ★★★ Director, Space, Command and Control
      - OP-095 ★★★ Director, Naval Warfare
      - OP-098 ★★★ Director, Research, Development, and Acquisition
      - OP-09R ★★★ Director, Naval Reserve
      - OP-006 ★ Oceanographer of the Navy
      - OP-008 ★★ Naval Inspector General
      - OP-009 ★ Director, Naval Intelligence
      - OP-01 ★★★ DCNO, Manpower
      - OP-02 ★★★ DCNO, Submarine Warfare
      - OP-03 ★★★ DCNO, Surface Warfare
      - OP-04 ★★★ DCNO, Logistics
      - OP-05 ★★★ DCNO, Air Warfare
      - OP-06 ★★★ DCNO, Plans, Policy, and Operations

Secretary Lehman and Goldwater-Nichols

In the run-up to the 1 October 1986 signing of the Goldwater-Nichols Department of Defense Reorganization Act of 1986 (PL 99-433), Lehman consistently and openly opposed the legislation. In testimony before Congress, he often took the same position that Arleigh Burke, as a captain, had expressed in 1949: the nation was protected from poor military advice and inordinate military influence by separate, coequal services, linked only loosely at the level of the Joint Chiefs of Staff. Lehman's concern was that the new law gave too much authority to the Secretary of Defense and the Chairman of the JCS.

Although he was not able to block the legislation, he gained influence within the Navy by arguing forcefully against the weakening of the authorities of the service secretaries and the senior service officers, including the CNO.[69] Lehman did not disagree that the DOD was in need of reform. However, he asserted that the real sources of ineffectiveness and inefficiency were, first, a lack of disciplined legislative oversight from Congress; second, the growth of staffs at the service level and in the Office of the Secretary of Defense; and third, the desire of reformers to centralize control of the DOD, ignoring the evidence that such centralization was not effective and could even be harmful.[70]

A close look at the legislation will make clear Secretary Lehman's concerns. Section 511, paragraph 5013 listed the responsibilities of the Secretary of the Navy, "including the following functions:" recruiting, organizing, supplying, equipping (including research and development), training, servicing, mobilizing, demobilizing, administering (including the "morale and welfare of personnel"), maintaining, building and repairing military equipment, and military construction.[71] This was an impressive list. However, the powers of the Navy secretary were subject "to the authority, direction, and control of the Secretary of Defense," and what Secretary Lehman wanted was freedom for him and his successors from close scrutiny by the Secretary of Defense.

The law also listed the responsibilities of the Navy secretary to the Secretary of Defense to include:

> the functioning and efficiency of the Department of the Navy, the formulation of policies and programs . . . that are fully consistent with national security objectives and policies established by the President or the Secretary of Defense, effective and timely implementation of policy, program, and budget decisions and instructions of the President or the Secretary of Defense, and fulfilling (to the maximum extent practicable) the current and future operational requirements of the unified and specified combatant commands.[72]

Finally, the law allowed the Secretary of the Navy to "assign, detail, and prescribe the duties of members of the Navy and Marine Corps and civilian personnel of the Department of the Navy," and to "prescribe regulations" to carry out the Secretary's "functions, powers, and duties under this title."[73] This was definitely not enough for Secretary Lehman. He wanted the sort of authority and accessibility to the President that former Navy secretaries like Josephus Daniels and James Forrestal had had. Goldwater-Nichols did not give it to him. He was, instead, subject "to the authority, direction, and control of the Secretary of Defense," and enjoined legally to "implement the policy, program, and budget decisions and instructions of the President or the Secretary of Defense relating to the functions of the Department of the Navy." In plain terms, the law made the Navy secretary a bridge between the Navy and, above the Navy, to a hierarchy of command consisting of the Secretary of Defense and the President.

Unfortunately for Secretary Lehman, his campaign against the Goldwater-Nichols Department of Defense Reorganization Act of 1986 backfired. Unlike President Reagan, who had serious doubts about the wisdom of the legislation but refused to get into a bruising political battle over it, Lehman would not give up his campaign against the bill. Lehman's deputy undersecretary apparently described the proposed law as unconstitutional and an assault on civilian control of the armed services. When Senators Barry Goldwater (R-AZ) and Sam Nunn (D-GA), the senior members of the Armed Services Committee learned of this, they wrote a strong letter to Secretary of Defense Weinberger, urging him to curb Secretary Lehman's attacks on the law.[74] Lehman had gone too far. His intemperate private and public statements eventually cost him the support of Secretary Weinberger and, apparently, President Reagan.[75]

Admiral Watkins and the Strategic Defense Initiative

In his "Ninety-Day Message" on 7 October 1982, CNO Watkins had noted that, "From our sparse inventory of technological advantages over the Soviets, we should select those that can provide measurable force multiplication..."[76] Two of those technological advantages were computers and space, and Admiral Watkins wanted to combine them in order to develop a defense against ballistic missile attack. As it happened, his professional and personal interest in ballistic missile defense coincided with a similar interest on the part of President Reagan, and the two men—with the encouragement and cooperation of other officials—came together to support what the President termed the Strategic Defense Initiative.

CNO Watkins had had to work out his own position on the issue of strategic missile defenses after he became CNO and sat as a member of the JCS. By the beginning of 1983, Watkins had rejected the concept of "mutual assured destruction," which was the foundation of U.S. nuclear deterrence policy. As he explained to Naval War College Professor Frederick Hartmann,

> [T]he genius of this country is to take a new technological concept (which the Soviets may well have in their minds as we do) and build it—field it—which they can't do. So why don't we use our applied technical genius to achieve our deterrent instead of sticking with an offensive land-based rocket exchange which they will win every time?... We shouldn't continue to play in a game like that.[77]

Searching for a technological solution to the ballistic missile defense problem, Watkins considered several alternatives. On 20 January 1983, he listened as Dr. Edward Teller proposed a network of space-based X-ray lasers. Watkins, however, was less interested in any specific defense system than he was in the concept of a space-based system, especially one that did not rely (as the X-ray laser did) on nuclear technology.[78] After meeting—and arguing—with Teller, Watkins "directed Rear Admiral [W. J.] Holland [of OP-65] and his deputy, Captain Linton [F.] Brooks, to develop the concept further..." Brooks found the words that captured the CNO's thoughts—thoughts about the feasibility of some sort of strategic ballistic missile defense and also about the morality of defense vs. offense in nuclear war.[79]

Watkins first presented his ideas to the CNO Executive Panel, and then, after the panel had supported him, to his peers on the JCS on 5 February. Watkins did not just discuss strategic missile defense; he also covered the sea- and land-based offensive missile forces. But the Joint Chiefs of Staff were scheduled to provide their views on the composition of U.S. strategic nuclear forces to President Reagan, and Watkins wanted to make sure that the ballistic missile defense option was a subject for consideration. "Unexpectedly, the Joint Chiefs, with Air Force General Charles Gabriel in the lead, unanimously adopted his approach as their position." Captains Jake W. Stewart and Linton Brooks went to work on a version that JCS Chairman General John W. Vessey Jr., would present to the President.[80]

It was in the 11 February 1983 meeting with the President that Reagan picked up the words that a space-based ballistic missile defense system would "protect the American people, not just avenge them."[81] The President wanted that phrase to serve as the basis for the proposal that he would present to the public on 23 March. In April 1986, Robert C. McFarlane, who had served as President Reagan's National Security Advisor, told Professor Hartmann that the most important contribution CNO Watkins had made was to crystalize the thoughts of President Reagan regarding strategic missile defense. McFarlane, who had also been a strong supporter of ballistic missile defense, observed that "people haven't absorbed how historic a step this is, that it wasn't done frivolously at all, that it was born of intellectual and very rigorous concern on [Watkins'] part about the future of offensive deterrence that he believed strongly was becoming much less stable." As McFarlane stressed, the approach taken by the CNO "was both military and moral."[82]

Then–Vice President George H. W. Bush was also impressed with Admiral Watkins, selecting the Admiral as Secretary of Energy in 1989. Prior to that appointment, Watkins served in 1987 prominently and well as head of a Presidential commission on the HIV epidemic. Washington commentators speculated after his retirement from the Navy in 1986 that he might run for high public office, but he did not.[83]

Enduring Issues

The first chapter of this study of OPNAV raised some enduring issues, among them the "proper" balance between the powers and authority of the Secretary of the Navy and the Chief of Naval Operations. The history of John Lehman's tenure as secretary illustrates just how enduring those issues were. When Lehman became secretary, his potential authority was very large, as he knew, and he acted to increase the scope of his authority by using his staff to influence the workings of the Navy's systems commands. In 1915, when the office of the CNO was established, the incumbent did not have command authority or budget authority over the Navy's bureaus. In World War II, CNO Fleet Admiral Ernest King finally joined his statutory authority with actual influence (though not formal legal power) over the bureaus. In so doing, he inevitably clashed with Secretary of the Navy James Forrestal, who was fighting a bureaucratic and political campaign to resist the expansion of the CNO's authority. Their conflict was both bureaucratic and personal.

Something similar happened after John Lehman became secretary, and it was inevitable. Lehman had an expansive (and some would say expanding) view of his authority and Lehman's view had to clash with the views of CNOs Hayward and Watkins. Over time, CNOs and secretaries had worked out a relationship that allowed them to avoid bureaucratic confrontations. That's what senior officers expected to continue. When, under Lehman, just the reverse occurred, many senior officers were surprised and irritated, even angry. There were the legal rules, but there were also the unwritten rules, and one function of the unwritten rules was to reduce friction between the Secretary of the Navy and the Chief of Naval Operations.

What is interesting is that both Hayward and Watkins were able to achieve a number of their objectives despite having to deal with an aggressive, well connected, and knowledgeable

Figure 12-2. (Left to Right) Secretary of the Navy John F. Lehman Jr., Virginia Senator John W. Warner, and the new CNO Admiral Carlisle A. H. Trost at the Naval Academy on 30 June 1986. Admiral Trost was not Secretary's Lehman's choice as CNO. Lehman preferred Admiral Frank B. Kelso II. However, Trost had commanded nuclear submarines, served as a commander of the Seventh Fleet in the Pacific, and been Commander-in-Chief of the Atlantic Fleet. He had also headed the Navy's system analysis office and had served as the director of Navy programming. (U.S. Nay Photo DN-SN-86-10017)

Navy secretary who was not afraid to use what might be termed intemperate language in dealing with them and with others in OPNAV. However, on 1 July 1986, Admiral Carlisle A. H. Trost succeeded Admiral James D. Watkins as CNO, and it was clear to many in OPNAV and around Washington that Secretary Lehman had lost his close link to the President. Secretary Lehman had wanted Admiral Frank B. Kelso II, as the new CNO, but President Reagan selected Admiral Trost. As Lehman admitted, "It was a bitter blow. I had gone very far in lobbying for Kelso's appointment—too far in the opinion of some of my close friends."[84] He attributed his defeat to the fact that the President's National Security Advisor, Vice Admiral John M. Poindexter, was a close associate of Trost's.

The secretary argued in his memoir that "things went smoothly through the remainder of the year," but that was only a temporary armistice between bureaucratic opponents. Lehman and Trost could not work together. To use Lehman's own words, he left office on 10 April 1987 "like the retiring marshal of the Old West, backing out of the saloon with guns blazing because every punk wants to take a shot at him on the way out. Sad to say, Carl Trost was among them . . ."[85] As it happened, Lehman's sense that he had been betrayed was made worse after he left the Pentagon. In the summer of 1988, Lehman's former Assistant Secretary of the Navy for Research,

Engineering and Systems, Melvyn R. Paisley, was implicated in a widespread bribery scandal and admitted to accepting sizeable bribes. He was convicted and sentenced to four years in prison. John Lehman was not linked to Paisley's misdeeds, but his proximity to the scandal may have ended Lehman's prospects for a place in a future Republican administration.

Though his going was bitter, Lehman had had an extraordinary run as Secretary of the Navy. As Admiral Train noted in 1986, "John Lehman has shown what an enormous difference an individual can make in that job."[86] Years later, Captain W. Spencer Johnson agreed, but he turned that accolade around by noting that it was a good thing for the Navy that Lehman was not appointed Secretary of the Air Force.[87] According to Chase Untermeyer, one of Lehman's assistant secretaries, John Lehman developed over time "technical mastery of ships, aircraft, and weaponry," and possessed "unmatched skill at congressional relations," and the "ability to outfox bureaucratic foes." The result, according to Untermeyer, is that the 21st-century Navy "is at heart the one that John Lehman built in the 1980s."[88]

Notes

[1] John F. Lehman Jr., *Command of the Seas* (New York: Charles Scribner's Sons, 1988), 228.

[2] There is an official difference between "procurement" and "acquisition." In the Department of Defense, "procurement" refers to purchasing, as in purchasing reams of paper to be used in office computer printers. "Acquisition" refers to the whole process of developing a system, manufacturing it, testing it, fielding it, and then supporting it during operations. The text uses "procurement" as a synonym for "acquisition." That is technically incorrect, but readers are not assumed to be familiar with the official difference between the two words.

[3] Interview, CAPT W. Spencer Johnson IV, USN (Ret.), with Thomas C. Hone, 26 July 2016 (Hereafter, CAPT Spencer Johnson interview).

[4] Memo, Deputy SECDEF to the Secretaries of the Military Departments, 27 Mar. 1981, subj: Management of the DOD Planning, Programming and Budgeting System, 2, collection of Thomas C. Hone.

[5] Ibid., 3–4.

[6] Ibid., 6.

[7] Lehman, *Command of the Seas*, 151.

[8] Memo, Deputy SECDEF to members of Defense Resources Board, 14 Nov. 1984, subj: Enhancement of the CINCs' Role in the PPBS; see also OP-901R Memo, 8 Mar. 1985, subj: SPRAA Briefings to Service Chiefs-Potential DRB Issues.

[9] Lehman, *Command of the Seas*, 237.

[10] Untermeyer, *Inside Reagan's Navy*, 211. Untermeyer was Deputy Assistant Secretary of the Navy for Installations and Facilities (1983–1984) and then Assistant Secretary of the Navy for Manpower & Reserve Affairs (1984–1988).

[11] John F. Lehman Jr., *Aircraft Carriers: The Real Choices* (Beverly Hills, CA: Sage Publications, 1978).

[12] This was a major initiative of Lehman's administration. However, Assistant Secretary Sawyer was criticized openly in the press when he left the Navy secretariat in 1983 to take a senior position with General Dynamics, one of the firms he had overseen while serving as Assistant Secretary for Shipbuilding and Logistics.

[13] Lehman, *Command of the Seas*, 174.

[14] Ibid., 175.

[15] Secretary Lehman also went after contractors whom he believed were charging the Navy too much for their work or were producing systems that could not meet requirements. As Chase Untermeyer noted, "Getting tough on [General Dynamics, especially the Electric Boat Division] was one of Lehman's biggest and earliest achievements . . ." *Inside Reagan's Navy: The Pentagon Journals*, 124.

[16] CAPT John D. Fedor, Deputy Chief of Legislative Affairs, interview with Thomas C. Hone, 1985.

[17] CAPT Donald A. Stoufer, interview with Thomas C. Hone, 20 July 1987.

[18] Ibid.

[19] Ibid.

[20] Ibid.

[21] Holloway, *Aircraft Carriers at War*, 340.

[22] Frederick H. Hartmann, *Naval Renaissance, The U.S. Navy in the 1980s* (Annapolis, MD: Naval Institute Press, 1990), 44.

[23] CAPT Spencer Johnson, interview.

[24] Hayward, *Reminiscences*, 429.

[25] Ibid., 432.

[26] Ibid., 438.

[27] Ibid.

[28] RADM Cockell served on the staff of the National Security Council in 1986–87.

[29] See Patrick Tyler, *Running Critical: The Silent War, Rickover, and General Dynamics* (New York: HarperCollins, 1989).

[30] CAPT W. Spencer Johnson IV, USN (Ret.), phone conversation, 29 Aug. 2016.

[31] ADM James D. Watkins, "The Ninety-Day Message," 7 Oct. 1982, Appendix E in *Naval Renaissance*, by Frederick H. Hartmann, 283–86.

[32] Ibid.

[33] Ibid.

[34] Hartmann, *Naval Renaissance*, 82–86.

[35] CAPT Spencer Johnson interview. See also, *The Evolution of the U.S. Navy's Maritime Strategy, 1977–1986*, by John B. Hattendorf (Newport, RI: Center for Naval Warfare Studies, Naval War College, 1989), 120. Also at https://www.usnwc.edu/Publications/Naval-War-College-Press/-Newport-Papers/Documents/33-pdf.aspx.

[36] CAPT Spencer Johnson interview, and phone conversation with Thomas C. Hone, 29 Aug. 2016.

[37] Ibid.

[38] Ibid.

[39] The 4 November 1982 Maritime Strategy Presentation is in *U.S. Naval Strategy in the 1980s: Selected Documents*, ed. by John B. Hattendorf and CAPT Peter M. Swartz (Newport, RI: Naval War College Press, 2008), 19–43.

[40] Ibid., 45–47.

[41] John B. Hattendorf, *The Evolution of the U.S. Navy's Maritime Strategy, 1977–1986*, 132.

[42] Ibid., 134.

[43] "The Maritime Strategy," U.S. Naval Institute, Jan. 1986.

[44] Lehman, *Command of the Seas*, 265.

[45] Untermeyer, *Inside Reagan's Navy*, 50.

[46] See SecNav memo, "Realignment of Administrative Functions Within the Secretariat," 8 May 1981, File: DNS (OPNAV, SecNav, USMC), N09B1. See also SECNAV Notice 5430, "Reorganization of the Secretariat," 15 June 1981, File: DNS (OPNAV, SecNav, USMC), N09B1.

[47] ADM William N. Small, Oral History, U.S. Naval Historical Center, interview with David Winkler, 51–61, in *Navy/Chiefs of Naval Operations/Commandants of the Marine Corps, 1951–1985*, compiled by Senior Archivist Bernard F. Cavalcante, Naval Historical Center (now Naval History and Heritage Command), Library, 2000.

[48] Hartmann, *Naval Renaissance*, 119.

[49] Ibid., 120.

[50] Stuart Williams, "The Ship Characteristics and Improvement Board: A Status Report," *Naval Engineers Journal*, May 1984, 39.

[51] Ibid., 40, 44–45.

[52] Ibid., 46.

[53] See Kelly, *Hornet, The Inside Story of the F/A-18*.

[54] Lehman, *Command of the Seas*, 230–33.

[55] Kelly, *Hornet, The Inside Story of the F/A-18*, 111.

[56] Lehman, *Command of the Seas*, 240–41.

[57] Ibid., 438; ch. 7 n1.

[58] Ibid.

[59] Ibid.

[60] Memo, CNO to VCNO, 7 Sept. 1984, subj: Navy Headquarters Review, OP-09B2 Records.

[61] Lehman, *Command of the Seas*, 242.

[62] Ibid., 244.

[63] See Baer, *One Hundred Years of Sea Power*. In ch. 16, Baer describes the intellectual "disarray" among senior Navy officers in the mid-1970s. ADM Lyons, among many others, was far more optimistic and aggressive about the U.S. Navy's ability to influence the Soviet Union. As a consultant to CNO Holloway, Lehman listened to these aggressive-minded officers.

[64] Hayward, *Reminiscences*, 440.

[65] ADM Harry D. Train II, USN (Ret.), Oral History, Interview No. 7 with Paul Stillwell, 16 Oct. 1996 (Annapolis, MD: U.S. Naval Institute), 474. VADM Albert J. Herberger, USN (Ret.), was not impressed with Secretary Lehman and considered him "arrogant" and insensitive to the needs of senior officers on the OPNAV staff. VADM Herberger, interview, with Thomas C. Hone, 28 Oct. 2014.

[66] ADM William J. Crowe Jr., USN (Ret.), *The Line of Fire* (New York: Simon & Schuster, 1993), 240.

[67] See Lehman, *Command of the Seas*, 240.

[68] ADM Bruce DeMars, USN (Ret.), Oral History, Interview No. 4, 24 May 2012, conducted by Paul Stillwell for the U.S. Naval Institute, 213–17. See also George C. Wilson, "Navy Secretary Causes Fury Over Promotions: Admiral Calls Order 'Illegal,'" *The Washington Post*, 3 Mar. 1987, A1. DeMars was appointed Director, Naval Nuclear Propulsion, and promoted to admiral in 1988.

[69] House Committee on Armed Services, Subcommittee on Investigations, *Reorganization of the Department of Defense: Hearings* [H.A.S.C. No. 99-53], 99th Cong., 2d sess., 1987.

[70] See *Victory on the Potomac, The Goldwater-Nichols Act Unifies the Pentagon*, by James R. Locher III (College Station: Texas A&M University Press, 2002), 270–71. Also see, *Command of the Seas*, by John Lehman, ch. 15.

[71] Public Law 99-433 (1 Oct. 1986), "Goldwater-Nichols Department of Defense Reorganization Act of 1986," Title V, Part B, Sec. 511, para. 5013 (b).

[72] Ibid., para. 5013 (c).

[73] Ibid., para. 5013 (g).

[74] Locher, *Victory on the Potomac*, 419.

[75] See Caspar W. Weinberger's memoir, *Fighting for Peace: Seven Critical Years in the Pentagon* (New York: Warner Books, 1990), where Secretary Lehman is mentioned only very briefly

in passing, when in fact Lehman was one of the most influential sub-cabinet appointees in the Reagan administration.

[76] Hartmann, *Naval Renaissance*, Appendix E, 283.

[77] Hartmann, *Naval Renaissance*, 253.

[78] Ibid., 253–54.

[79] Ibid., 254. CAPT Linton F. Brooks later was appointed Chief Strategic Arms Reduction Negotiator in the State Department, and under his leadership both the START I (Strategic Arms Reduction Treaty) and START II agreements were negotiated.

[80] Ibid., 255.

[81] The story is told a just bit differently in Hartmann's Naval Renaissance, 255, and Caspar W. Weinberger, *Fighting for Peace, Seven Critical Years in the Pentagon* (New York: Warner Books, 1990), 304, but both accounts agree on the importance of ADM Watkins's words.

[82] Hartmann, *Naval Renaissance*, 256.

[83] ADM Watkins' mother had made an effort to gain the nomination of the Republican Party in California for a U.S. Senate seat in 1938, and the admiral had apparently always taken a sincere if strictly professional interest in political affairs.

[84] Lehman, *Command of the Seas*, 418.

[85] Ibid.

[86] ADM Train, Oral History, Interview No. 2, 16 July 1986, 176.

[87] CAPT Spencer Johnson interview.

[88] Untermeyer, *Inside Reagan's Navy*, xv.

CHAPTER 13

After Lehman's Regime

Introduction

When Admiral Carlisle A. H. Trost succeeded Admiral James D. Watkins as CNO on 1 July 1986, he faced—as he knew he would—some good news and some bad news. On the good side, the Navy was still growing; Navy secretary John Lehman and his allies in the White House and the Congress had been successful in increasing the size and power of the Navy. On the bad side was Lehman's way of acting arbitrarily. The new CNO had seen that up close when, in 1982, he had returned to OPNAV as Admiral Watkins's OP-090, where he had annually led the process of compiling the Navy's Program Objective Memorandum. Also on the good side was the recovery of the American economy from the recession of the early 1980s and some evidence that President Reagan's effort to work with Mikhail Gorbachev, the General Secretary of the Communist Party of the Soviet Union, to bring the Cold War to an end might bear fruit.

On the bad side was the Goldwater-Nichols Department of Defense Reorganization Act, signed into law by President Reagan on 1 October 1986. The law changed Title 10, USC, by eliminating the CNO as the principal naval advisor to the President and the Secretary of the Navy and as the secretary's principal executive. Chapter 505, paragraph 5033, of the Goldwater-Nichols Act preserved the status of the CNO as the Navy's highest ranking officer and also affirmed the CNO's position as a member of the Joint Chiefs of Staff. At the same time, it made the CNO "directly responsible" to the Navy secretary and defined the role of the CNO as advisor to the secretary and the secretary's "agent."

Publicly and privately, CNO Trost agreed with Secretary Lehman that there was no need "for massive reorganization," which was Admiral Trost's way of describing the Goldwater-Nichols legislation.[1] Like former CNOs such as Arleigh Burke, Trost was concerned with the new law's focus on increasing the authority on the Chairman of the Joint Chiefs of Staff. With Secretary Lehman, Trost feared that adding to the strength and prestige of the Joint Chiefs of Staff (JCS) would turn it into the Defense Department's primary decision-making body. The authors of the legislation argued back that its primary purpose was to make clear the powers of the Secretary of Defense and therefore improve civilian control of the military. With the bill's passage, however, the debates pro and con had to end, and Trost and other senior officers and civilians had to turn legislative direction into an accepted set of new authority relationships.

The commitment to the 600-ship Navy, coupled with an abiding suspicion of the Soviet Union, connected CNOs Hayward, Watkins, and Trost *and* gave continuity to work by the OPNAV staff as action officers came and went. This shared commitment also linked all three admirals—no matter their personal feelings—to Secretary Lehman. In *Naval Renaissance, The U.S. Navy in the 1980s*, Frederick Hartmann commented on this continuity by referring to a meeting Admirals Watkins and Trost had with the CNO's Executive Panel on 18 June 1986. At that meeting, Watkins explained why he believed that the early 1980s had ushered in a "naval renaissance," and he expressed his concern that the Navy would suffer in the ongoing struggles in Congress regarding federal spending. Admiral Trost said that his mission would be to protect the gains already made. As Hartmann observed, "Admiral Trost could count on a great deal of momentum coming from the navy's progress in the middle years of the 1980s. What was less certain was the support he would receive from Congress."[2]

Refashioning OPNAV: Lehman's Legacy

When Admiral Trost took on the duties of the Chief of Naval Operations on 1 July 1986, he and the OPNAV staff had to work within the Planning, Programming, and Budgeting System process adopted by Secretary Lehman. On 31 March 1986, for example, the secretary's office had issued its instructions for implementing PPBS for fiscal year 1988. The instruction listed the responsibilities of the secretary and the secretariat to include the following: first, the secretary would provide "planning and program guidance" to the CNO; second, the executive assistants to the secretary would advise him as he drew up that guidance; third, the assistant secretary for financial management would set "Overall [Navy Department] PPBS policy;" fourth, the head of the Office of Program Appraisal (OPA) would advise the secretary, represent the secretary on the Defense Guidance Steering Group, and "support" the secretary "during programming and budgeting;" fifth, the director of the Navy Program Information Center would be "responsible for the programming phase of PPBS."[3] By contrast, the CNO and the Commandant of the Marine Corps were responsible for following the guidance of the secretary, coordinating the planning phase of their work with one another and with the Joint Chiefs of Staff, preparing the detailed POM for the Navy Department, developing budget estimates for Congress based upon the POM numbers, and then implementing congressionally approved budgets.[4]

In one sense, the direction provided by this instruction was not unusual. After all, it was the secretary who was legally responsible for submitting and defending the Navy's budget. But the instruction made clear the secretary's authority within the Navy: *he* would provide the service-specific guidance, *his* assistants and his OPA would serve as his principal day-to-day advisors, and *his* assistant secretary for financial management and the Navy Program Information Center would lead and monitor the programming process. Before Lehman, PPBS had been dominated by the program sponsors in OPNAV because only they had the staffs large enough to review past programming proposals and prepare updated ones.[5] Lehman had used his own staff—the under and assistant secretaries, OPA, and the staff of the Navy Program Information Center—to gain and hold the initiative in the programming process—*not* by duplicating the work done in OPNAV but by guiding and monitoring that work and intervening in the process in areas of special interest to him. An example was his order in 1986 that OP-05 fund (and the Naval Air Systems Command develop) a digital mission planning system for the A-6E, an updated version of an attack airplane he had flown in and favored.[6]

On 12 January 1987, Lehman updated the instruction describing the Program Management Proposal (PMP) system. The revised instruction explained that the purpose of the system was to regulate research and development and control "configuration changes and modifications to ships, aircraft, missiles, weapons, systems, combat vehicles, and combat equipment both during and subsequent to production." The PMP system was intended to discipline the process by which new acquisition programs were managed and through which existing systems were modified. The primary goal was to make visible the cost consequences of changes to a system's "performance characteristics" as described in its "baseline" statement of cost, schedule, and performance. Related to that first goal was a second—making sure that the OPNAV sponsor of the responsible Navy systems command could actually fund any proposed change or upgrade.[7]

The formal instruction assigned the responsibility for administering the PMP system to OPA. It also directed the Assistant Secretary of the Navy for Shipbuilding and Logistics and the Assistant Secretary for Research, Engineering and Systems to review PMPs and "make recommendations for approval/disapproval." The head of OPA was directed to meet with the secretary every month to go over those PMPs that the assistant secretaries had evaluated.[8] The January 1987 instruction institutionalized the replacement—the PMP process—for the processes formerly used by the Naval Material Command. It complemented Secretary Lehman's 1985 instruction giving the assistant secretaries for shipbuilding and logistics and for research, engineering, and systems the authority to monitor and rate the performance of Navy material managers.[9] Lehman had already paid careful attention to Navy flag selection boards, so his instructions regarding acquisition programs, acquisition program managers (PMs) (the material managers), and the Navy's planning, programming, and budgeting process put in place a legal framework that any future Secretary of the Navy who was personally and professionally aggressive and politically astute could draw on. CNO Trost could not wipe that framework away. However, Trost knew what he wanted from the OPNAV staff, and he set about reorganizing the staff to get it once it was clear that Lehman would be resigning in the spring of 1987.[10]

Refashioning OPNAV Part 2: Trost's Changes

When Trost took over OPNAV, there were six deputy chiefs (for manpower, submarine warfare, surface warfare, logistics, air warfare, and plans, policy, and operations) and five key "directors" (program planning, space and command and control, naval warfare, research and development, and naval intelligence). Goldwater-Nichols reduced the number of deputy chiefs from six to five and limited the OPNAV staff to only three assistant chiefs. Taking advantage of the legislation, Trost reduced the standing of the so-called "barons" (the 3-star DCNOs for surface, undersea, and air warfare) to assistant chiefs. He created a new DCNO for naval warfare (OP-07) and another for Navy program planning (OP-08). The other three deputy chiefs were for plans, policy, and operations (OP-06), logistics (OP-04), and manpower and training (OP-01).

Trost later explained that his goal was to create tension between the "barons" and the DCNO for naval warfare.[11] Each "baron" would develop programs maximizing his arm of the Navy. The new DCNO for naval warfare (OP-07) would assess and analyze the whole mix of programs, looking across the Navy's platforms and warfare capabilities. OP-08 would be the referee in this conflict, balancing for the CNO the different perspectives and then turning that

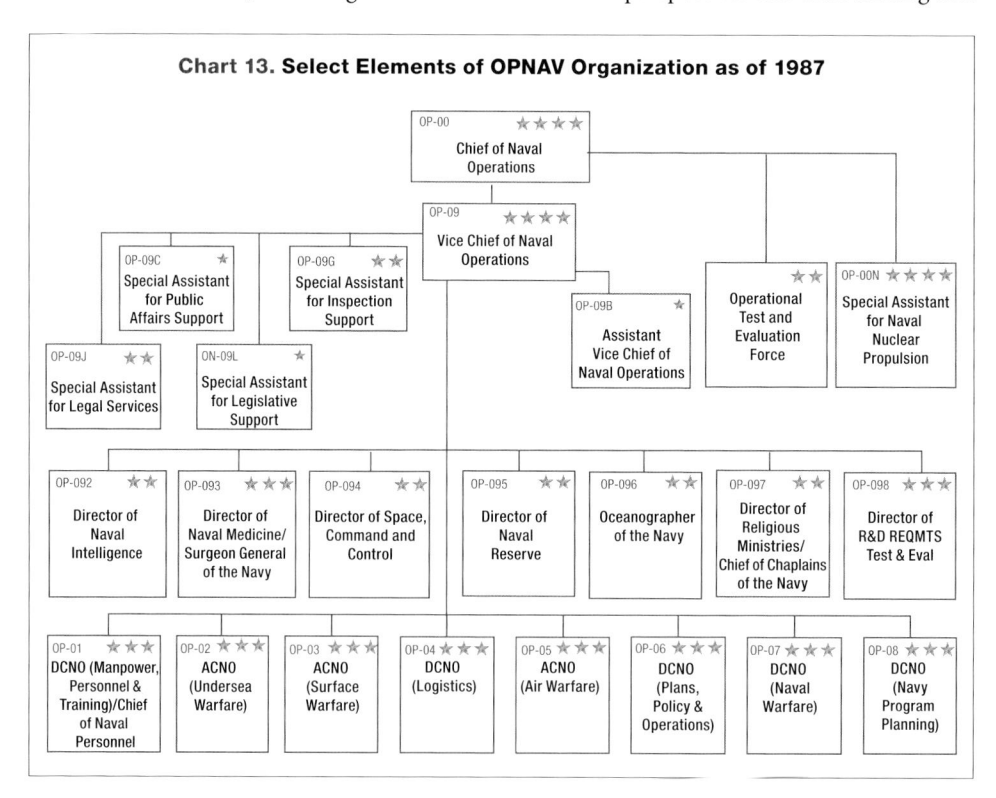

Chart 13. Select Elements of OPNAV Organization as of 1987

balance into a coherent set of programs. The surface, submarine, and aviation operators knew what they wanted. They were often innovative, but only within the boundaries set by the ways they fought. Trost wanted a deputy's office where there was space for "out of the box" thinking. To help get it, he wanted the executive assistant to OP-07 to be a graduate of the Strategic Studies Group at the Naval War College.

Trost modeled OP-07 on OP-96, the systems analysis division of OP-090, which he had headed in 1976–1977. Trost had watched as OP-96 and OP-00K responded to CNOs Holloway and Hayward. As he put it, these organizations within OPNAV were "quick acting, responsive to the CNO, and capable of tapping the rest of OPNAV."[12] This particularly mattered when the Navy needed an analysis or a point paper to present in a meeting of the Joint Chiefs, or to send to the State Department. The problem with OP-06 (Plans and Policy) was that it could be—and often was—consumed by details, especially in coordinating with the Joint Staff. Trost, like Hayward, wanted to be able to reach out and get some immediate help from bright and energetic staff officers—in effect his "inner staff."

However, Trost wanted more than information from this inner staff. For example, CNO Holloway had encouraged dissent among the officers in OP-96 if any of its members disagreed with him. Trost learned that Holloway could tolerate it—that Holloway could actually use it. For example, if members of Congress raised questions about carrier aviation, Holloway had almost always had someone in OP-96 already raise and explore the issue. That way, Holloway was ready with an answer or a rebuttal. As a side benefit, Holloway also had the benefit of some of that "out of the box" thinking that Trost also found useful.

The potential drawback to Trost's reorganization of OPNAV was clear enough: OP-07 didn't have the money; OP-08 did—and so did the "barons." Trost understood this problem. As he observed, it was critically important that the CNO talk frequently with his OP-08. The two officers needed to be close. Otherwise, the deputy and assistant chiefs, consumed as they were with building the Navy's POM, would give little weight to OP-07's assessments. Personalities mattered. It was essential that the CNO have a "POM builder" whom he trusted. Similarly, there was a need for a deputy like OP-07. OP-08 would be "eaten up" by the level of work associated with his responsibilities, and the right sort of OP-07 could actually help the OP-08 prepare a "balanced" and coherent POM.[13] No organization chart or organization charter could capture the critical but subtle relationship between an OP-07 and an OP-08.

By March 1988, the process of dialogue between OP-08 and OP-07 was focused on Navy master plans. As the then-VCNO, Admiral Huntington Hardisty, put it in an OPNAV instruction on long-range planning, "By design, the Navy does not maintain a formal, centralized Long-Range Plan." But the Navy did have plans—lots of them, including an electronic warfare master plan, an aviation plan, a space warfare plan, a command and control plan, a manpower and training strategy, and of course the Navy's POM. As Hardisty's instruction put it, ". . . individual master plans must be appropriately integrated and mutually supportive, and must reflect some level of fiscal reality, if their combination is to have the effect of a cohesive overall long-range plan." The key part of the instruction, however, was assigning OP-7 to "review all master plans to ensure compatibility with other platform master plans and applicable warfare area master plans."[14]

By contrast, OP-08 was to "review all master plans to ensure appropriate programmatic consistency and the compatibility of plans with pertinent fiscal projections." The difference between 07 and 08 was clear: In engaging the platform and program sponsors about how their plans fit with the many other plans, 07 would perform an "integrative function," putting the pieces together so that the Navy's program was coherent from an operational (or warfare) perspective. The director of research and development requirements in OPNAV would do something similar. Did the plans "fit" what the Office of Naval Research was investing in? Was there a future for these plans, or were they too dependent on existing technology? Once OP-07 did its work, OP-08 could find support for all the required programs. To facilitate the overall process, the Long-Range Planning Group (00K) held an annual conference where the CNO and senior officers could get a sense of where the Navy's program was going.[15] What did the future Navy look like? Is that what the many program sponsors intended? Had they followed the CNO's guidance?

It is clear that the 07/08 match depended on the personalities and skills of the admirals holding those positions. Both jobs, for example, required individuals who could master details, endure long hours of work, and understood the technical side to naval warfare.[16] In short, each needed to be a nice combination of operator and staff officer, and their personalities had to be compatible. The problem was that OP-07's influence was due more to controlling access to the CNO than it was to the appraisals done by the OP-07 analysts, and the major platform program sponsors (OP-02, OP-03, and OP-05) were able at times to bypass OP-07 and deal with the CNO or the vice chief.[17] Interviews with other senior officers suggest that Trost allowed this because he was very, very intelligent and organized in his own mind. Put another way, what the so-called "barons" (platform sponsors) wanted was access to the CNO, trusting that if their arguments were sound he would accept them.[18] Eventually, the platform (air, surface and submarine) sponsors reckoned that they and the staff in OP-08 could build an effective POM without OP-07.

That is not to say OP-07 did not matter. Under Vice Admiral James D. Williams, the last head of OP-07, selected members of the staff of OP-07 started doing assessments of "black" (highly classified) programs and combined those with less classified assessments to rank all the significant programs in the Navy. The staff also looked at alternative navies possible under different budget ceilings.[19] Yet even in its early days under CNO Trost, OP-07 was a counter to the incremental approach of the platform sponsors, which was "more of the same only bigger, faster, and farther."[20] As retired Rear Admiral David Oliver observed in 1997, developing a POM means enlisting in the process parties who have major stakes in the outcome. Once you do that, personalities matter; they can trump analysis. This produces a paradox: a system (PPBS) whose legitimacy rests on analysis must inevitably be "corrupted" (and not necessarily in a negative way) by the influence of personalities.[21]

Fiscal Stringency

The major problem facing Admiral Trost and John Lehman's successors was how to preserve the naval build-up of the first Reagan term. By late 1989, the irony of the build-up was that it had apparently succeeded. It had been set in motion to persuade the leaders of the Soviet Union that they could not be victorious in a war against the North Atlantic Treaty Organization (NATO) alliance. Once the Soviet leaders seemed to accept this notion—that is, once the policy appeared to be a success—Congress wanted to restrain the build-up, thereby threatening the existence of the 600-ship Navy. Moreover, Congress had been after savings ever since the passage of the Gramm-Rudman-Hollings Balanced Budget and Emergency Deficit Control Act of 1985. That legislation, designed to compel the Congress to stop running up federal deficits, put ceilings on discretionary spending. If Congress approved a budget that broke through the overall ceiling, then the executive branch agencies would have to deal with automatic across-the-board spending reductions ("sequestration") imposed by the Comptroller General.[22] This was a definite potential threat to the budget stability that was essential to the 600-ship Navy program, and the pressure to reduce defense spending grew through Admiral Trost's tenure.

This issue eventually convinced Secretary Lehman's successor, James H. Webb Jr., to resign. Webb, an accomplished author and decorated Marine Corps veteran, took over from Lehman in May 1987 after serving as Assistant Secretary of Defense for Reserve Affairs in OSD. In November 1987, Webb notified all Navy commands that ". . . the Department has to contend with the additional general, unspecified sequestration of appropriated funds across all programs for deficit reduction purposes. The impact of these FY 1988 reductions will carry forward into FY 1989, when even greater reductions may be mandated." Congress had tried to force itself to control deficit spending with the Gramm-Rudman-Hollings law, but it did not seem to be working. There was no consensus among members of the Congress on just how to dampen spending. But Webb believed "strongly that the force structure of the Navy must not be allowed to deteriorate."[23] Webb, who had been Secretary of Defense Weinberger's "personal choice to be Secretary of the Navy," remonstrated in the strongest terms with Weinberger's successor, Frank C. Carlucci III, but to no avail.[24] Webb therefore resigned on 23 February 1988. His place was taken first by William L. Ball III, and then, in May 1989, by H. Lawrence Garrett III.

Dealing with Fiscal Stringency Through Analysis

Admiral Trost provided managerial continuity in the Navy Department as Navy secretaries came and went. However, the budget news was frustrating. The "Maritime Strategy" was in place and generally accepted within the Navy and among the Navy's supporters in Congress. But the confrontation inside Congress between members of the two major political parties, coupled with a gradual reduction of tensions between the United States and the Soviet Union, threatened the survival of the 600-ship Navy. Was there any way that the Navy could draw on its analytical expertise to both save money and also show Congress that its decision making was effective and trustworthy?

For example, the Aegis anti-air warfare system, first deployed in 1983, was accepted as a technical and managerial success. In some very important ways, the systems engineering process by which the Aegis system had been developed was a model for other major acquisition programs. This process was F2D2, or "functional flow diagrams and descriptions." It was a rigorous functional analysis of any new shipboard system within a "system of systems." For example, Aegis began as an anti-air warfare system. It was developed to defeat attacking aircraft and missiles. Defeating those "threats" was its basic, or top-level, requirement. But what functions would have to be performed if the Aegis system were to successfully fulfill that requirement? One was finding the target. But how was this done? How was this function performed? It was done with a phased-array radar. But what functions would have to be performed if the phased-array radar were to work as needed?

Functional analysts began with a higher-level function (such as "finding the target") and then dug down into the supporting sub-functions that had to be fulfilled if that higher function were to be realized. As they did so, they branched out into ancillary but critical functions such as providing the necessary level of power and building fault-detection subsystems so that the higher-level weapon system function was protected.[25] As they were doing this, their colleagues would be specifying the sub-functions that had to be performed in order for the other top-level functions—such as hitting the target—to be met. The result of all their work was a collection of "functional flow diagrams and descriptions"—literally a very large and very detailed flow chart. The chart made clear where there were critical flows of information and energy, and where there were crucial interdependencies among subsystems.

If this process of functional analysis could work for a system as complex as Aegis, why not push it up to the next level—to the carrier battle group "system," composed of ships, aircraft, submarines, satellites, logistic support ships, and—here was the really innovative part—systems used by the other services? And why not apply a form of this functional analysis within OPNAV to reduce the longstanding tension between OPNAV and the Navy's systems commands? OPNAV was tailored to support programs that sustained the fleet and to decide which warfare "requirements" needed funding. Once that was done, the Navy's system commands (such as NAVSEA and NAVAIR) produced the needed hardware and software, plus the essential training and logistical support.

Ideally, the different programs being executed by the system commands would fit together more or less like the pieces of gigantic picture puzzle. Unfortunately, as Vice Admiral Eli T. Reich, then an assistant secretary of defense for logistics, noted in the mid-1970s, the Navy had "done an inadequate job of specifying overall ship system integration design" after World War II.[26] Rear Admiral Wayne Meyer, the Aegis system PM, had set out to remedy this problem, and he, his staff, and his prime contractor (initially RCA) had done so. Could F2D2 or *something like it* be used in OPNAV? Perhaps by Trost's OP-07?

The answer to that question was complicated. Experienced OPNAV program sponsors were already familiar with a process called "warfare system architecture and engineering." It was intended to force officers sponsoring ship, submarine, and aviation programs to step away from saying, "We need a new and better model of what we already have," and to ask instead, "What functions does a Navy battle group or battle force perform, and what's the optimal way to perform those functions?" Thinking like this existed in OP-095 (the Director of Naval Warfare) and in organizations like the Center for Naval Analyses before Admiral Trost took over as CNO, and he understood the potential value of this way of thinking. It was why he created OP-07. OP-07 would have what amounted to a dialogue with the "barons"—the assistant chiefs of naval operations for surface, subsurface, and air warfare—as the Navy's Program Objective Memorandum was being prepared. But what would be the basis of their negotiations? One answer was "warfare system architecture and engineering." It was an effort to root the negotiations within OPNAV over programs and budgets in a way of thinking that would tie together unrestricted line officers in the fleet and the specialist officers and civilian engineers who staffed the systems commands.

How did "warfare system architecture and engineering" work? The first step was to develop "top level warfare requirements," or systematic statements of what Navy systems were supposed to do if the fleet was to fulfill its missions. In 1986, for example, one primary mission of the Navy was to execute the operational-level maritime strategy. In May 1986, Vice Admiral Henry Mustin, commander of the Second Fleet, noted that NATO's "concept of operations" in the seas near Norway had four maritime objectives. The first was "to contain and destroy the Soviet Northern Fleet." The second was "to deny the Soviets the use of the Norwegian air fields." The third was to defend northern Norway against air and land attacks, and the fourth was to block any Soviet amphibious assault on northern Norway.[27] What requirements had to be met in order for Navy and Marine Corps forces to achieve these four objectives?

The first requirement was gaining air superiority. As Mustin observed, "Once you lose the air battle, then things unravel very quickly ashore in the land campaign."[28] To win that battle, Mustin proposed sending in three U. S. carriers and a Marine air wing. That would double the number of NATO fighters in the northern part of Norway, increase by three times "the all-weather capability for interceptors" and the "attack aviation capability," and add approximately "1,000 surface-to-air missiles, to a region that has none." As Mustin argued, "if you put that kind of reinforcement in there before the war starts, the striking fleet can make the difference between winning or losing the battle ashore."[29] The second requirement was for an anti-submarine campaign that would protect Mustin's aircraft carriers and amphibious ships and then threaten Soviet ballistic missile submarines. As Mustin recognized, by moving his forces into the Norwegian Sea before any military action commenced, Second Fleet and the Marines could "win rather than lose in North Norway, and we can win the ASW campaign in half the time than we can without, which is very important, because with the force structure that we have, we can't do everything at once . . ."[30]

Here was the second step in planning—the operational-level part. The strategy—the first step—was to deter or defeat a Soviet invasion of NATO territory. As far as OPNAV's officers were concerned, the subsequent steps had to support these two goals, especially the second one—the operational objective. Program sponsors had to examine their programs and decide whether they did or did not add to the functions that Second Fleet would have to perform in order to achieve Admiral Mustin's military objectives. Then they had to check to see how their individual programs "fit" with the programs of other sponsors.

But there had to exist a process that all the different sponsors could use. By 1988, this process—drawn from the sort of functional analysis used in the Aegis program—had five basic steps. The first was to ascertain the missions required of existing systems. The second was to consider how existing systems fit into the overall force. The third step was to consider possible opposition. Who was the likely enemy? The fourth step was to ask, "How will we know when we've achieved success? How will we know when we've performed the mission?' The final step was to search for important constraints and assumptions.[31] For example, Admiral Mustin had planned with the limits to his forces always in mind. As he had explained, "[W]e can't do everything at once . . ." There were only so many carriers and so many Marine air wings. Mustin also made certain assumptions, including one very critical one—that he would have advance warning of a Soviet attack. How would he get that? There were organizations responsible for seeing to it that he did, and their contributions to the overall campaign had to be sponsored and funded.

The Maritime Strategy has been described as a strategy that allowed operational commanders like Admiral Mustin to plan a campaign. But the Maritime Strategy also could serve as the basis for planning and programming inside OPNAV. Analysts in OP-07 could look across warfare areas (like ASW) and platform sponsors (surface ships, submarines, and aircraft) and use that "picture" as the basis for their rankings of programs.[32] To anticipate the analysts, the programmers could use the same "picture" to produce and defend their program requirements. Because not all programmers in OPNAV were technical specialists, they would need the support of a "systems architect." Eventually, senior officers hoped that the Space and Naval Warfare Systems Command (SPAWAR) would fill this role, but it apparently never quite did.[33] But the idea was a fascinating one. OPNAV programmers would not just use the last POM as their starting point. They would start with missions and see if their programs were likely to produce whole warfare *systems* (with trained sailors) that would achieve those missions.

There were two possible drawbacks to this approach. The first was that the "default position" among OPNAV programmers was to start with the last POM, check for changes that had taken place since that POM had been approved, and then negotiate with other programmers on that basis. That is what the staff would do unless the CNO and his deputies could show them a better way to proceed. The second drawback was that really sophisticated warfare analysis was expensive and time-consuming. For example, an important source of insights about warfare architectures was war games, but those games were costly and took people away from their regular jobs. That is not to say they were too expensive or time-consuming to be used. On the contrary, they were used again and again, but each had to be paid for by a sponsor, and that sponsor might not care about the "warfare architecture" approach. Moreover, just how did you structure a war game to get at the critical links between a system's architecture and its functions? Perhaps the best way was to run two games simultaneously. In game one, the system being examined would be set at one particular value (or set of values); in game two, that system would either not be there at all or would be set at some possible value that was different than the value (or set of values) used in game one. In this situation, the two games run simultaneously with a difference in one variable; this constitutes an experiment. How many experiments would be necessary to cover all the variables that mattered? And who would impose the results of the war games in the process by which the POM was built? This drawback would not go away.

There were only three other ways to deal with the fiscal stringency that squeezed the Navy during CNO Trost's tenure. One was to get more money from Congress. The second was to cut some major programs. That had been done by CNO Admiral Arleigh Burke in the 1950s in order to fund Polaris. The third was what the OPNAV staff ruefully referred to as "death by a thousand cuts," or taking small amounts of money from almost all programs. This last option was high-risk. If Congress saw that the Navy survived lots of little cuts in one year, then Congress was likely to expect more such cuts the following year. That is why so much energy was spent trying to justify the Navy's POM with techniques such as "warfare system architecture and engineering." If used properly and explained clearly, the technique could pay dividends within OPNAV and also outside, with congressional staff.

Figure 13-1. Admiral Carlisle A. H. Trost, who had opposed the Goldwater-Nichols legislation, had to contend with the results of that act, which diminished the power of the CNO and shifted greater authority to the Joint Staff and the Combatant Commanders. (NHHC Archives L38-90.04.01)

Implications of Goldwater-Nichols

What was it that Congress had intended by passing the Goldwater-Nichols Act? The controversy over the proposal to adjust and add to the Department of Defense Reorganization Act of 1958 had been intense.[34] When the dust settled with the signing of the new law on 1 October 1986, Navy leaders had to take stock. What had Congress directed? What had Congress intended?

The Senate's report on the bill listed 15 goals of the legislation. The following 11 applied to the Chief of Naval Operations and his staff: (a) improving the quality of "professional military advice," (b) strengthening "civilian control of the military," (c) improving "the performance of joint military duties," (d) making service in the Joint Staff a career advantage for professional officers, (e) "strengthening the authority of the unified and specified combatant commanders," (f) increasing "the decentralization of authority" within the Department of Defense, (g) reducing the size of the "defense bureaucracy," (h) reducing the "burdens of congressional oversight of the Department of Defense," (i) improving the formulation of military strategy, (j) providing "for the more efficient use of resources," and (k) clarifying "the roles, responsibilities, and authority of senior civilian officials and senior military officers of the Department of Defense."[35]

The body of the Senate's report provided the justifications for each of these goals. For example, the report noted that "the problem of undue Service influence arises not from Service malfeasance, but principally from the weaknesses of organizations that are responsible for joint military preparation, planning, and operations."[36] The report also described the unified commands as 'loose confederations of single-Service forces" that could not swiftly and effectively swing into "unified action."[37] The report called out strategic planning for special criticism: "DoD strategic planning resources are underutilized because they are not effectively applied to solving the major policy, strategy, and program issues that result from fiscal constraints."[38] The need to remedy flaws in the relationships between service secretaries and service military chiefs was also given much attention. The relationship between the Secretary of Defense and the service secretaries had to be made explicit in law, and then the "division of work between the Secretariats . . . and the military headquarters staffs" could be "adequately defined."[39]

But the Senate's report also noted that Congress itself was a major contributor to the problems that the bill aimed to deal with. "The Congress is becoming increasingly involved in the details of the national defense effort . . .," and there had been "a steady and dramatic increase in the extent of congressional involvement in the annual defense budget submission."[40] As a consequence, "Efforts to reorganize the Department of Defense will prove imperfect unless accompanied by fundamental changes on Capitol Hill."[41] Why had the Congress been remiss? First, Congress had spent "more time worrying about trivia than about fundamental defense issues and policies." Second, Congress actually cooperated with the Defense Department in "approaching the defense program with an accountant's mentality, viewing the budget as thousands of individual debit and credit entries."[42]

The solution? First, Congress had to shift to biennial budgeting. Second, congressional committees had to focus their inquiries on joint operations and missions. If the military services were to become more "joint," then it was up to congressional committees to adopt joint authorizing and budget perspectives. Third, members of Congress had to get rid of more than 250 "statutory reporting requirements" imposed on the Department of Defense. Finally, as the authors of the Senate's report recognized, "Committee jurisdictions must be reasserted and tightened to minimize overlap and duplication. Redundant legislative phases of budgeting, authorizing, and appropriating must be consolidated. The orderly process of deliberation within committees, rather than unending floor amendments, must again become customary in the Senate."[43] The House of Representatives, though, was another matter. If the Senate could be said to sometimes focus on the "big" issues, there was a tendency for the House to focus on the details of defense spending and management.

Much of what the Senate wanted concerned the Secretary of Defense. The secretary needed to be able to discuss and justify "major military missions" such as strategic deterrence with members of Congress. The secretary also needed the support of *qualified* political appointees instead of assistant secretaries and deputy assistant secretaries who were essentially "on-the-job trainees."[44] Without that support, the Secretary of Defense could not do what the report recommended, which was to "provide annually to the JCS Chairman written policy guidance for the preparation and review of contingency plans."[45] Yet what perhaps most concerned the Senate was the way that OSD emphasized—in its procedures and through its structure—"material inputs" and *not* "mission outputs."[46]

Critics of Goldwater-Nichols had complained that the legislation would reduce the roles of the service chiefs while strengthening the hand of the Chairman of the JCS. The danger, some argued, was that the President would not receive any dissenting views from the service chiefs once the chairman had decided what to advise the Secretary of Defense and the President. Supporters of strengthening the authority of the chairman had taken a very different view. "Logrolling," they insisted, had led the service chiefs to "harmonize their differences," leaving any given President with a set of compromises that often came to him too late for him and his Defense secretary to reject them.[47] Moreover, the delay built into the pre-Goldwater-Nichols deliberations among the service chiefs had led successive secretaries of defense to rely on civilian advisors and ignore the advice of the nation's senior military staff officers.[48] In the balance among the service staffs, the Joint Chiefs of Staff, and the staff of the Secretary of Defense, the Secretary of Defense's staff had the most influence. This troubled the senators who had listened to many days of testimony. They wanted a balance—and they assumed that several sources of well-developed advice would be of much more use to a president than advice from one source.

But were the service chiefs completely cut off from the Secretary of Defense and the President? Did the legislation aim at one problem—a weak Chairman of the Joint Chiefs of Staff (CJCS)—and then create another—a situation where the chairman monopolized the attention of the Secretary of Defense and the President? No. The bill drafted in the Senate contained several limits on the chairman's power. One was that a chairman could only have two 2-year terms beyond his first tour of two years; six years was the maximum amount of time he could hold the post of chairman, and extensions beyond the first two years required approval by the Senate. In addition, the chairman was required to hold "regular" meetings of the joint chiefs; he could not keep them in the dark about his actions and his professional views by simply refusing to see the service chiefs. The chairman was also directed to consult on an ongoing basis with the service chiefs and with the unified and specified combatant commanders.

The CJCS was not going to be an operational commander, but he was to have the responsibility and the authority "for preparing strategic plans that provide for the strategic direction of the armed forces."[49] However, the Senate wanted more than just plans. The Senate wanted the chairman to prepare "fiscally constrained plans," and not just the existing Joint Strategic Planning Document (JSPD), which was not fiscally constrained. As the report noted, the JSPD "does not help to establish priorities and to make difficult resource choices."[50] But the Joint Chiefs of Staff could not develop fiscally constrained plans unless and until the chairman was given clear and realistic fiscal guidance from the Secretary of Defense.[51] Using such guidance, the JCS could assess the risks "that would be incurred by the forces contained in the program recommendations of the Military Departments."[52] Those risks would be spelled out in the Joint Program Assessment Memorandum.

The chairman was also given the task of trying to link strategic (i.e., long-range) and contingency planning, developing joint doctrine, periodically evaluating the roles and missions of the armed forces, and selecting—after consulting the other service chiefs—a Director of the Joint Chiefs of Staff.[53] Creating new authority for the Chairman of the Joint Chiefs of Staff was one of the two major innovations of Goldwater-Nichols. The legislation's other hallmark was the enhanced authority it gave combatant commanders such as the leaders of the Pacific Command (PACOM) and Central Command (CENTCOM). The command authority of these officers was spelled out in law, and it included operational command and "coordination and approval of those aspects of administration and support, including planning for wartime logistics, necessary for the accomplishment of the missions assigned to the command."[54] They were also given the authority to select their subordinate commanders and to evaluate the performance of those subordinates.[55]

This grant of authority caused a problem for CNO Trost starting in December 1986, when Kuwait's government asked the U. S. government to "reflag" tankers transporting Kuwait's oil through the Persian Gulf. The so-called "tanker war" had started in 1984, and in the years after 1984 both Iranian and Iraqi forces had intermittently attacked tankers going to and from Kuwait. The story of the U. S. government's involvement has been told by historian Michael A. Palmer in his *On Course to Desert Storm, The United States Navy and the Persian Gulf*.[56] What matters here is that Trost was responsible both for supporting the Central Command commander through the Navy's Middle East Force and for developing policy as a member of the Joint Chiefs of Staff. But as the Navy's strength in the Gulf grew (from six ships to 13), the Secretary of Defense created a new command—Joint Task Force Middle East.[57]

This meant that Trost needed to support Marine General George B. Crist, the Central Command Commander, through both the Joint Task Force and the still operating Middle East Force. The command picture was cleared up when one rear admiral was made commander of both the Middle East Force and the Joint Task Force. But one difficulty remained. As CNO, Trost was responsible for supporting all Navy units spread among the combatant commanders. "Supporting" meant, among other things, developing and monitoring the rotation schedules of ships' crews. Historian Robert W. Love has argued that Trost erred in not seeing to it that the crews of frigates sent to the Gulf (especially *Stark* [FFG-31], hit by an Iraqi missile in May 1987) were properly trained.[58] Love also suggested that the Navy's minesweepers were not sent to the Persian Gulf in time.[59] As Michael Palmer pointed out, however, the relatively few Navy minesweepers were initially held back in U.S. ports because that's where they were needed in the event the Cold War became suddenly "hot."[60] The point here is that CNO Trost was inevitably caught between his obligation to support the combatant commander and his responsibility to keep the Navy trained, equipped, and organized to wage and win the "big" war. Goldwater-Nichols had not magically eliminated the conflicts of authority that senior officers could face. The military service chiefs were providers and—along with the Chairman of the JCS—participants in making key operational decisions.

Goldwater-Nichols also reached into the relationship between the Secretary of the Navy and the Chief of Naval Operations. The "specified powers and duties of the Secretary of the Navy would be substantially expanded," but "the Secretary of the Navy's direct responsibilities to the President" were removed. In addition, the Secretary of the Navy was directed to not duplicate "specific functions assigned to the Office of the Chief of Naval Operations and the Headquarters, Marine Corps."[61] The legislation also placed the office of the Navy inspector general and the Office of Naval Research in the secretariat. The CNO would remain the Navy's most senior admiral, but the CNO would not by law serve as "the principal naval advisor to the President and to the Secretary of the Navy on the conduct of war."[62]

The Senate's report makes one thing clear—that the senators on the Armed Services Committee wanted to consolidate the innovations in Department of Defense organization proposed but not realized in the 1958 Department of Defense Reorganization Act. Put another way, the 1986 legislation was not something brand new, or something devised to try to anticipate an uncertain future.[63] Instead, it was a "wrapping up" of issues that had been unresolved for almost 30 years. If the 1958 law was an effort to adapt the Defense Department to the Cold War, then the 1986 law had essentially the same goal—to enable DOD's civilian and military leaders to plan and conduct a long-haul "Cold War" with the Soviet Union. That conflict would require DOD to plan creatively, budget carefully, and invest efficiently. It was the policy approved in the early 1950s when Dwight Eisenhower was President—a policy to preserve the economic vitality of the United States while fielding forces that would "contain" the Soviet Union and also allow the government of the United States to influence events around the world.

But what happens to the "reforms" in the event that the Cold War ended? Would the new structure of authority be suited to a post–Cold War world? That would become an issue for the Chairman of the Joint Chiefs of Staff, Admiral William J. Crowe Jr. Admiral Trost and his successors would face that issue, too.

The Packard Commission, Goldwater-Nichols, and Defense Acquisition

In the summer of 1985, President Reagan had created the "Blue Ribbon Commission on Defense Management," which was usually referred to as "the Packard Commission" after the former Deputy Secretary of Defense, David Packard, who headed the group of experienced civilian and military leaders who served on the commission. The Packard Commission's studies proceeded in parallel with the investigations of the House and Senate Armed Services Committees as they considered what eventually became Goldwater-Nichols, and the commission provided both committees with its findings. The White House also knew what the Packard Commission was doing and what it would likely recommend in its final report.

President Reagan issued NSDD (National Security Decision Directive) 219 on 1 April 1986 in an effort to take advantage of the Packard Commission's deliberations. The directive covered the planning and budgeting process in the DOD, military command organization, Defense Department acquisition, government-industry accountability, and procedures for reporting how NSDD 219 was being implemented. The section on acquisition "organization and procedures" instructed the Secretary of Defense to prepare a directive "outlining the roles, functions, and responsibilities of the Under Secretary of Defense for Acquisition."[64] The occupant of this new, very senior position was expected to "have a solid industrial background" and would serve as the senior defense acquisition executive.

NSDD 219 also instructed the Secretary of Defense to "direct the Secretaries of the Military Departments to prepare Military Department Directives establishing Service Acquisition Executives," or—as they quickly became known as—SAEs. The Service Acquisition Executives, "acting for the Service Secretaries," were to "appoint Program Executive Officers (PEO) who will be responsible for a reasonable and defined number of acquisition programs." The program managers, or "PMs," would "be responsible directly to their respective PEO and report only to him on program matters." This was the innovation so strongly recommended by David Packard and his colleagues—to shorten the chain of command and reporting, so that PMs of major efforts had only one executive (a PEO) between themselves and a SAE.[65]

John Lehman objected to this three-level hierarchy (confirmed in Goldwater-Nichols) for the management of major acquisition programs. What he so strongly opposed was the provision of NSDD 219 and of the new law that each service's SAE would report directly to the Under Secretary of Defense for Acquisition (USD[A]). Lehman said publicly that he would appeal to Secretary of Defense Caspar Weinberger if a dispute arose between him and the first USD(A), Richard P. Godwin, formerly a senior executive at Bechtel Corporation.[66]

Lehman's opposition to granting the USD(A) authority over major acquisition programs was seconded by Edward C. Aldridge Jr., Secretary of the Air Force. Both service secretaries argued that Congress had not intended to rob their formal positions of authority over major acquisition programs. How could the service secretaries be accountable to Congress, for example, if the really important decisions about major acquisition programs were not in their hands? First Secretary Lehman, and then Secretary Aldridge, appealed to William H. Taft IV, the Deputy Secretary of Defense. After all, the service secretaries were members of the Defense Resources Board (DRB), the highest level of decision makers regarding defense expenditures.[67] How could they be shut out of the management of major programs?

"After consulting Pentagon lawyers, and receiving tacit approval from [Secretary of Defense] Weinberger,"[68] Deputy Secretary Taft ruled in favor first of Lehman and then of Aldridge by declaring that only the Deputy Secretary of Defense could overrule a service secretary in a dispute between a service secretary and the USD(A). But this move by Taft did not settle the matter. The squabbling over the new under secretary's authority went on for months. It only died down when Under Secretary Godwin resigned in frustration in September 1987, and it would flare up again later, during the investigation of the problems associated with the development of the A-12 carrier heavy-attack aircraft. Under Secretary Godwin captured the reason for his frustration when he resigned: "When we brought in a new system [of management] and superimposed it on top of the current one we came down on everyone's toes."[69] It would probably be more accurate to say that the change disrupted established procedures—procedures that dated back to World War II and that were therefore deeply ingrained.

But NSDD 219 also specified that "the Secretary of Defense shall establish procedures which call for the Joint Requirements Management Board to be co-chaired by the Under Secretary of Defense (Acquisition) and the Vice Chairman of the" JCS. This board was "to play an active and important role in all joint programs and in appropriate Service programs by defining weapons requirements, selecting programs for development, and providing thereby an early trade-off between cost and performance." The JRMB was instructed to coordinate its actions with those of the Defense Resources Board that sat at the top of the programming and budgeting management pyramid.

It's a cliché of defense management in the United States that the Pentagon's major management challenge is to integrate its three major decision processes: (a) programming and budgeting, (b) acquisition management, and (c) strategic and operational planning. In 1986, the DRB was the senior resource management committee. That took care of the top of the chain of authority for programming and budgeting. The JCS was supposed to review and coordinate operational plans developed by the staffs of the combatant commanders. That took care of the chain linking the operational planners in the field with the strategic planners in the Pentagon. NSDD 219 set up the JRMB to review major weapon system requirements and make trade-offs "between cost and performance." That innovation was supposed to allow senior officials to balance a major system's cost and performance in light of strategic requirements—to take care of the chain linking system developers with the Secretary of Defense. But would it work?

The Packard Commission had documented three major problems with systems development. First, the cost of the development of major weapons systems usually increased over time, leading to the procurement of fewer major systems and therefore smaller forces. Second, technology that met a military requirement at the start of an acquisition program was often only marginally effective when the new system was fielded years later. Third, "users" of major systems, aware that they would not get their new system for many years, "overstated" the threat from enemy systems in order to compensate for the slowness of the usual acquisition process.[70] The recommendations of the Packard Commission, initially implemented through NSDD 219, were supposed to "reform" the acquisition process and solve these problems.

For the Navy, a solution was overdue. In 1983, Navy Secretary Lehman had favored upgrading the existing A-6 carrier-capable bomber—a plane in which he had flown as a bomber-navigator—instead of replacing it with a brand new airplane. Deputy Secretary of Defense Taft had wanted a new aircraft—a "stealthy" all-weather, day/night bomber for the Navy's carriers. The two officials allegedly "struck a deal." Secretary Lehman would get OSD support for an upgraded A-6, and the Navy would begin work on developing a new stealth bomber (the A-12) for its carriers. By the summer of 1986, two industry teams had developed separate concepts of the stealth carrier bomber, and both teams were awarded contracts allowing them to move into the "demonstration and validation" phase of development. Unfortunately, the stage was set for a major acquisition failure—one that would still be argued over in a federal circuit court in 2014.[71]

The Strategic Environment Trumps the 600-Ship Navy

While the CNO, several Secretaries of the Navy, and Congress wrestled with fiscal constraints, the Cold War reached a peak and then with dramatic suddenness began coming to an end. The nuclear disaster at Chernobyl, in Ukraine, in April 1986 was emblematic of the economic and social problems affecting the Soviet Union, and the General Secretary of the Communist Party of the Soviet Union—Mikhail Gorbachev—made an unsuccessful effort to solve them. As the Cold War seemed to be ramping down, areas of U.S.-Soviet conflict, such as Nicaragua and the nuclear arms race, were either settled or began to slip as sources of U.S.-Soviet tension.

It was an uncertain time. In February 1988, for example, the Soviet frigate *Bezzavetnyy* deliberately collided with cruiser *Yorktown* (CG-48) during the latter's cruise in the Black Sea. Yet that same month, new regimes in Armenia and Azerbaijan began a bitter conflict over the disputed territory of Nagorno-Karabakh, acting as though rivalries that preceded the Russian Revolution of 1917 were important again. Was the Soviet Union more dangerous as the Soviet empire appeared to be coming apart, or was the Cold War coming to an end because leaders such as Mikhail Gorbachev refused to hold that empire together by force, as his predecessors had done? Adding to the uncertainty were the discussions between Gorbachev and President Reagan regarding limits on nuclear weapons. At their meeting in Reykjavik, Iceland, in October 1986, the two leaders had come close to working out a dramatic nuclear arms limitation agreement. Where would that lead?

1989 was an even more dramatic year—one not to be missed. In February, the Soviet Union withdrew its military forces from Afghanistan. Soon after, authoritarian regimes in Poland, Hungary, and Czechoslovakia lost support and were replaced. While the Warsaw Pact was unraveling, young Chinese openly demonstrated against the authoritarianism of the Chinese Communist Party in a place called Tiananmen Square. This was an extraordinary challenge to the successors of Mao Zedong. It seemed as though Bolshevik authoritarianism was on its way out all over the world. The Berlin Wall fell in November 1989, and there was talk about German reunification—where the regime of the former German Democratic Republic would be absorbed by the German Federal Republic, creating a united and democratic Germany.

Through this time of change, Admiral Trost stuck with the policies that he had affirmed when he was selected as CNO. He supported the 600-ship Navy, the policy of "strategic homeporting" (and the related need to support sailors' families), Admiral Watkins's "personal excellence" program, antisubmarine warfare (ASW) research and development, improved management of logistics and acquisition, and the need to deter the aggressive policies of the Soviet Union.[72] In an interview published in October 1986, Trost noted that, in his view, "Nothing has changed in the world to say that there is any less need for military forces."[73] Trost's view was also compatible with that of Admiral William J. Crowe, the Chairman of the Joints Chiefs of Staff. Crowe told the members of the Senate Budget Committee on 13 January 1987 that ". . . we cannot afford to relinquish naval superiority to the Soviets. To do so would jeopardize our coalitions, economic and trade dependencies (which are now necessary in war as well as peace), and capabilities to project our power overseas. Our ability to prevail at sea is a cornerstone of our overall strategy."[74] However, by the end of 1989, when the tenures of both four-star officers were ending or near to ending, the strategic situation was very different than it had been when both had taken office.

Notes

[1] ADM Carlisle A. H. Trost, USN, "The View from the Bridge," *Sea Power*, vol. 29, no. 1 (Oct. 1986), 22.

[2] Hartmann, *Naval Renaissance*, 265, 268.

[3] SECNAVINST 5000.16E, "Department of the Navy Planning, Programming and Budgeting System (PPBS)," 31 Mar. 1986, 4. Collection of Thomas C. Hone.

[4] Ibid., 4–5.

[5] ADM William D. Smith, USN (Ret.), interviewed by Thomas C. Hone, 11 Mar. 1998.

[6] Norman Friedman, *Network-Centric Warfare* (Annapolis, MD: Naval Institute Press, 2009), 321n14. As it happened, this system (referred to as TAMPS) could be—and was—upgraded and installed in the F/A-18.

[7] SECNAVINST 5000.33B, "Program Management Proposal Process," 12 Jan. 1987, 1–2. Collection of Thomas C. Hone.

[8] Ibid., 3.

[9] SECNAVINST 5000.32, SO, "Additional Reporting Responsibilities of the Assistant Secretary of the Navy (Shipbuilding and Logistics) and Assistant Secretary of the Navy (Research, Engineering and Systems)," 21 Feb. 1985. Collection of Thomas C. Hone.

[10] VADM Robert F. Dunn was appointed DCNO for Air Warfare (OP-05) in Jan. 1987. When John Lehman left the Pentagon, CNO Trost asked him, "What kind of things did John Lehman put in that you want to undo?" *Reminiscences*, VADM Robert F. Dunn, USN (Ret.), interviewed by Paul Stillwell, 26 Feb. 1996, U.S. Naval Institute Oral History, 2008, Interview No. 7, 556.

[11] ADM Carlisle A. H. Trost, USN (Ret.), interviewed by Thomas C. Hone, 10 Mar. 1998.

[12] Ibid.

[13] Ibid. Also ADM William D. Smith interview with Hone, 11 Mar. 1998.

[14] OPNAVINST 5000.51, "Long-Range Planning," 24 Mar. 1988. In the collection of Thomas C. Hone.

[15] Ibid.

[16] RADM Michael A. McDevitt, USN (Ret.), interviewed by Thomas C. Hone, 23 Jan. 1998. RADM McDevitt was the Director of the CNO Executive Panel in 1988–1990 and the Director of J-5 in 1993–1995.

[17] RADM J. J. Dantone Jr., USN (Ret.), interviewed by Thomas C. Hone, 17 Apr. 1998. RADM Dantone later was selected to be the first Director of the National Imagery and Mapping Agency.

[18] VADM Richard C. Allen, USN (Ret.), interviewed by Thomas C. Hone, 17 Feb. 1998.

[19] VADM James D. Williams, USN (Ret.), interviewed by Thomas C. Hone, 11 Feb. 1998.

[20] Email, from: Edwin M. Baldwin; to: Thomas C. Hone; subj: OP-07/95, 9 Feb. 1998. Baldwin was on the staff of OP-95 when it became OP-07.

[21] RADM David R. Oliver, USN (Ret.), interviewed by Thomas C. Hone, 19 Dec. 1997. RADM Oliver later served as the Principal Deputy Under Secretary of Defense for Acquisition, Technology, and Logistics and as a senior executive with EADS North America.

[22] The power of the Comptroller to calculate and then impose the reductions was challenged in federal court, and the Supreme Court of the United States ruled in 1986 that the Comptroller General lacked the constitutional authority to do so. See *Bowsher v. Synar* (478 U.S. 714). So Congress then passed the "Balanced Budget and Emergency Deficit Control Reaffirmation Act of 1987."

[23] James H. Webb Jr., Secretary of the Navy, ALNAV message 221500Z, Feb. 1988. 1, in the collection of Thomas C. Hone. See also, *The Nightingale's Song*, by Robert Timberg (New York: Simon & Schuster, 1995), 409–10.

[24] Weinberger, *Fighting for Peace*, 402.

[25] Thomas Hone, "The Program Manager as Entrepreneur: AEGIS and RADM Wayne Meyer," *Defense Analysis*, vol. 3, no. 3 (1987), 197–212.

[26] Ibid., 201.

[27] United States Naval Institute Professional Seminar Series, "The Maritime Strategy," 29 May 1986, Naval Air Station, Jacksonville, FL, 20–21.

[28] Ibid., 22.

[29] Ibid.

[30] Ibid., 23.

[31] Briefing, "Warfare System Architecture & Engineering," Status Report, 21 Apr. 1988. Collection of Thomas C. Hone.

[32] VADM James D. Williams, USN (Ret.), interviewed by Hone, 11 Feb. 1998.

[33] ADM Stanley R. Arthur, USN (Ret.), interviewed by Thomas C. Hone, 10 Feb. 1998.

[34] Locher, *Victory on the Potomac*.

[35] Senate Report No. 99–280, 1–2, also available at https://digitalndulibrary.ndu.edu/cdm/compoundobject/collection/goldwater/id/830/rec/11.

[36] Ibid., 7.

[37] Ibid., 8.

[38] Ibid., 9.

[39] Ibid.

[40] Ibid.

[41] Ibid., 10.

[42] Ibid., 11.

[43] Ibid., 12.

[44] Ibid., 15.

[45] Ibid.

[46] Ibid., 17.

[47] Ibid., 21.

[48] Ibid.

[49] Ibid., 25.

[50] Ibid.

[51] Ibid.

[52] Ibid., 26.

[53] Ibid., 27–33.

[54] Ibid., 40.

[55] Ibid., 41.

[56] Michael A. Palmer, *On Course to Desert Storm, The United States Navy and the Persian Gulf* (Washington, DC: Naval Historical Center, Department of the Navy, 1992).

[57] Ibid., 124.

[58] Love, *History of the U.S. Navy, Vol. Two, 1942–1991*, 776.

[59] Ibid., 783.

[60] Palmer, *On Course to Desert Storm*, 129.

[61] Senate Report No. 99-280, 63.

[62] Ibid., 66.

[63] Archie D. Barrett, "Empowering Eisenhower's Concept," *Joint Force Quarterly*, Autumn 1996, 13. Also www.dtic.mil/doctrine/jfq/jfq-13.pdf.

[64] "National Security Decision Directive Number 219, Implementation of the Recommendations of the President's Commission on Defense Management," 1 Apr. 1986, 4. Also www.reaganlibrary.archives.gov/arch.

[65] Ibid.

[66] J. Ronald Fox, *Defense Acquisition Reform, 1960–2009* (Washington, DC: Center for Military History, U.S. Army, 2011), 141. See also J. Ronald Fox, with James L. Field, *The Defense Management Challenge: Weapons Acquisition* (Boston: Harvard Business School Press, 1988).

[67] Weinberger, *Fighting for Peace*, 44.

[68] Fox, *Defense Acquisition Reform, 1960–2009*, 144.

[69] Ibid., 146.

[70] Ibid., 128.

[71] Office of the Inspector General, Dept. of Defense, "Review of the A-12 Aircraft Program," No. 91-059 (28 Feb. 1991) available at http://www.dodig.mil/Audit/Audit2/91-059.pdf. Also "A-12 Administrative Inquiry," Memorandum for the Secretary of the Navy, 28 Nov. 1990. Other accounts include Herbert L. Fenster, "The A-12 Legacy," U.S. Naval Institute *Proceedings*, Feb. 1999, and James P. Stevenson, *The $5 Billion Misunderstanding: The Collapse of the Navy's A-12 Stealth Bomber Program* (Annapolis, MD: Naval Institute Press, 2001). Also www.en.wikipedia.org/wiki/McDonnell_Douglas_A-12_Avenger_II.

[72] Cost control was addressed through instructions and messages. See, for example, the message from John Lehman in Dec. 1986, "FY 86 Results of Spare Parts Acquisition Initiatives," regarding Project BOSS (Buy Our Spares Smart), R012036Z, and the message of November 1988, "Action Plus Department of the Navy Follow-On to Action' 88," R101553Z. Both ALNAV messages in the Navy Department Library.

[73] Carlisle A. H. Trost, "A View from the Bridge," *Seapower*, vol. 29, no. 11 (Oct. 1986), 18.

[74] *Selected Works of Admiral William J. Crowe Jr., USN*, Joint History Office, Office of the Chairman of the Joint Chiefs of Staff (Washington, DC, 2013), 112.

CHAPTER 14

The Continuing Response to Goldwater-Nichols and the End of the Cold War

Introduction

When he became the Chief of Naval Operations on 29 June 1990, Admiral Frank B. Kelso II well and clearly understood the intent and implications of the Goldwater-Nichols Department of Defense Reorganization Act. For example, as Commander-in-Chief, Atlantic Fleet, from June 1986 to November 1988, Kelso had thought of himself and his command as a force provider to the joint theater commander. As he noted, "I saw that as what the law had changed for me to be, and that was what I was supposed to do . . . provide trained forces to the unified commanders."[1] Later, during Operations Desert Shield and Desert Storm, CNO Kelso stayed with this concept of his role: ". . . I felt our job was to provide whatever General [Norman] Schwarzkopf [the theater joint commander] wanted."[2]

Yet as CNO—the Navy's senior officer—Admiral Kelso could not confine his leadership only to what the law required. Goldwater-Nichols had shifted authority from the service staffs to the Joint Chiefs of Staff and from the service chiefs to the Chairman of the Joint Chiefs of Staff. But the senior service officers continued to represent and speak for their services. In very important ways, the service chiefs represented their organizations to the President, the Congress, the media, and the people. The CNO no longer had the authority to command operations, but he was still the "chief"—still the highest-ranking naval officer and the person looked to by sailors and citizens as the legitimate leader of the Navy. Admiral Kelso would find this side to his job very taxing, indeed.

The "Base Force"

As the Cold War moved in steps toward its end, Joint Chiefs of Staff Chairman General Colin L. Powell took the lead in planning an American military for the post–Cold War world. As a consequence of Goldwater-Nichols, he did not have to negotiate with the service chiefs before offering President George H. W. Bush an altered force structure, and in the fall of 1989 he set his J8 and J5 staffs to work on a new strategic vision.[3] General Powell foresaw a "drastically different strategic environment" by 1994, and he anticipated that there would be calls from members of Congress for a reduction in the size and strength of U.S. armed forces. He did not want to oversee a rushed demobilization or a spending reduction that would leave "hollow" forces in its wake.

Powell and his deputies on the JCS were one step ahead of the Bush administration. In June 1990—the month that Admiral Kelso succeeded Admiral Trost as CNO—Secretary of Defense Richard Cheney acknowledged in public that the Defense Department "might be willing to undertake major force reductions."[4] The service chiefs had already informed General Powell that they opposed the reductions he had put forward as possibilities. But in meetings with the chairman, they had not changed Powell's basic position—one that they thought would be reflected in Secretary Cheney's programming guidance scheduled to be issued that September. At the beginning of August, President Bush had formally announced that his administration would develop a new defense strategy and then propose the military forces needed to sustain it. Then Iraq's invasion of Kuwait and Operations Desert Shield and Desert Storm happened. For seven months, the focus was on preparing for and then fighting a campaign against the forces of Iraqi dictator Saddam Hussein.

Changing Minds and Changing Processes

With the end of Operation Desert Storm on 28 February 1991, Kelso and Navy secretary H. Lawrence Garrett III turned from supporting the theater commander back to dealing with General Powell's proposals—his plan for what was called "the Base Force." By that time, it was clear that the Warsaw Pact was breaking up and that the Communist Party of the Soviet Union was losing its power. Kelso, who "had found some aspects of the Base Force attractive," grasped what this meant for the Navy: "After Desert Storm, military spending took what I describe as a free fall."[5] By "free fall," Kelso meant his worst nightmare as CNO—a situation where initial spending reductions made by Congress would become a cascade of cuts that would go far beyond what he and General Powell thought sensible.

How could the Navy avoid such major reductions? One way was to develop a naval (or maritime) force structure better suited to the changed strategic environment. On 20 August 1990, General Powell informed the service chiefs and the unified and specified joint commanders (then referred to as "CINCs") that they needed to take the initiative in planning force reductions. Iraq's invasion of Kuwait would not let them off the hook; reductions would happen. Accordingly, on 23 August, CNO Kelso and Navy secretary Garrett promulgated a joint memorandum, "The Way Ahead." In that document, the two leaders of the Navy Department observed that the

Navy and Marine Corps were "first class" fighting forces. But they also cautioned their services that they faced three major challenges. The first was to preserve the necessary industrial base. The second was to decide which ships, submarines, and planes could be safely and effectively operated once Congress reduced defense funding. The third was to plan a future force that could meet the nation's needs and yet be affordable.[6] Kelso wanted to see "The Way Ahead" published quickly, but he said later that it was held up because of multiple reviews.[7]

However, months before Kelso and Garret sent out their joint memo, Navy and Marine officers met informally to develop a replacement to "The Maritime Strategy." According to then–Captain E. Richard Diamond Jr., who headed the strategic concepts branch of OP-06, this informal group—drawn from the CNO Executive Panel (CEP) (OP-00K), Marine Corps Headquarters, and OPNAV—developed a Navy-Marine Corps "strategy" and presented it— without official sanction—to other officers in the Pentagon on a Saturday toward the end of March 1990.[8] Diamond then orchestrated his "volunteers" in the creation of a brief that would argue that the Navy's future role would focus more on facilitating maneuver on land than on fighting a major engagement at sea. He presented the brief first to Vice Admiral Robert J. Kelly, OP-06, and then to Vice Admiral Paul David Miller, OP-07. Captain Peter Haynes, author of a detailed study of Navy and Marine Corps strategy-making from 1989 to 2007, has argued that Vice Admiral Miller, "a member of CNO Kelso's inner circle" from the days when both officers were part of Secretary John Lehman's staff, became the unofficial but influential sponsor of the draft of the new strategy.[9]

Captain Diamond briefed Marine Corps Commandant General Alfred M. Gray Jr., in September 1990. Gray endorsed the new approach.[10] Over the winter of 1990–1991, General Gray and Admiral Kelso collaborated on "The Way Ahead." Published in the April 1991 issues of the U.S. Naval Institute *Proceedings* and the *Marine Corps Gazette*, the paper was, according to Captain Haynes, "the first such document drafted, signed, and published with equality between the two services," and it had been allegedly finally approved in a meeting between Kelso and Gray over Kelso's kitchen table.[11] Kelso later said that he felt the paper was published about a year too late to seriously influence the thinking of General Powell and Secretary of Defense Cheney.[12] As he put it, "I felt we would be better off to put our foot forward to accept the reality [of reductions] than . . . to fall down the wall scratching with our fingernails reducing force structure all along the way down."[13]

Force structure and strategy were not the only issues that had to be addressed. In February 1989, President Bush directed the Secretary of Defense to verify that the services were implementing the recommendations made by the Packard Commission in 1986. The response to the President's requirement became known as the Defense Management Review, and the review process produced the Defense Management Report (DMR). Navy secretary Garrett's response to the DMR was to create the Department of the Navy Review Commission in November 1991.[14] The Review Commission was directed to "develop proposals to reduce the operating cost of the [Navy Department], while maintaining and sustaining required warfighting and deterrent capabilities."[15] This "ad hoc" commission was to work "in parallel to and in support of the POM/budget process" in order to "provide the mechanism through which cost savings proposals developed by other ad hoc [Navy Department] committees may be submitted for appropriate programming and budget consideration."[16] In plain terms, there was to be a scramble to find savings. The Review Commission was to go out of existence once the FY 1994 Program Objective Memorandum (POM) was produced.[17]

At the same time, however, Secretary Garrett sent a memo to Kelso and General Carl E. Mundy Jr., the Marine Corps Commandant, entitled "Post Cold War Navy/Marine Corps."[18] Garrett's direction emphasized developing "a new, zero-based plan for naval forces spanning the next fifteen to twenty years" that was "based on a fresh and realistic evaluation of our potential adversaries and a clear vision of the future role of naval forces as an instrument of national policy."[19] There were several obvious constraints on this Navy-USMC effort. The first was financial. As Garrett put it, "it must be apparent that our plan represents the least possible investment in naval forces which preserves a margin of maritime superiority and the economic well being of our country." The second constraint was keeping "faith with our people."[20]

But the end of the Cold War also meant that there could be "Some relaxation in the readiness of all of our operating forces," and a reevaluation of "those costly missions, capabilities and operating patterns—such as deep strike, continuous presence and over-the-horizon assault—which drive force level and resource requirements, with a view toward lower cost options."[21] Garrett also accepted the possibility that the Navy and Marine Corps might not be able to "fulfill certain traditional roles" if they were given less money. If so, they were to "consider relinquishing those roles."[22] In plain terms, Garrett was saying formally what Kelso had been saying privately—that the POM-building process that had become routine during the Cold War was no longer adequate. The times called for something different—innovative concepts and new processes.[23]

That was why Admiral Kelso wanted to change the programming process within OPNAV permanently. In early 1992, OPNAV programming continued to be based on back-and-forth negotiations and discussions among OP-07, OP-08, and the platform sponsors. Kelso believed that the programming process "had little rigor, little participation from the political leadership, and the officer leadership often was at odds over how the Navy's money was being divided. There was little buy-in for the plan,"[24] with two negative results. The first was a rush at the last minute to create a consensus among the senior members of the OPNAV and secretariat staffs. The second was weak support for the program sent to Congress. Indeed, members of Congress could often find senior Navy officers whose support for the Navy's overall program was lukewarm at best.[25]

How could the process be improved? Kelso rejected the idea of simply replacing incumbent officers with "fresh blood." He "wanted the Navy staff to develop a plan together that all the leadership put together and understood" in detail.[26] Programming tended to be done from the bottom-up, with spokesmen for the various warfare communities negotiating disagreements over the allocation of resources until a grand consensus was achieved. Kelso felt this model was inadequate. "I wanted the admirals of all warfare disciplines to have to work with and listen to the problems of the entire Navy." But he believed that "We needed a new culture to do that."[27] Yet an organization's culture was not easy to change. Was there some approach that could work in both OPNAV and down through all the Navy's organizations? Kelso thought there was—the approach of W. Edwards Deming, whose ideas on statistical process control had been credited with making Japanese industrial firms perhaps the most efficient in the world.[28] Taken together, these ideas were referred to as "total quality management," or TQM. Kelso suspected that Navy officers and senior enlisted personnel would not take to the word "management," so he changed the name of the approach to "Total Quality Leadership," or TQL.[29]

But what was TQL? The answer is that TQL (TQM in disguise) was (and remains) a focus on the processes of an organization *as the organization's primary outputs*. The usual model of production, for example, was that "inputs" such as raw materials, components, labor, and energy were combined to produce "outputs"—products or services. In the U.S. automobile industry, for example, the "outputs" had traditionally been numbers of cars and trucks. The "outcome" of the production of the "outputs" had been sales. Deming had turned this around. He argued that a satisfied customer—a returning customer—was the real outcome to be aimed for. The "output" had to be something that the customer would value and would therefore return to purchase again. The goal of management was therefore to work with labor to create a process that would routinely produce quality "outputs."

In the case of the automobile industry, that meant producing a car that was economical to operate, easy and safe to drive, and also affordable—and less expensive to manufacture than the cars produced by the competition. U.S. auto makers said it could not be done; quality, they said, cost real money, as any owner of a Cadillac could tell you. Honda and Toyota, however, proved that Deming was right—quality could be produced at a low monetary cost *so long as managers of production made the production process itself a quality human product*. This idea had been applied to assembly line production with success.[30] Kelso thought it could be applied to a number of processes in the Navy.

But first people had to know what TQL was. According to Kelso, there already was a "cell" of TQM (later TQL) advocates in the Navy secretariat, but spreading TQL beyond specialists in the Navy secretariat required a major training program. In OPNAV alone, officers convinced that there was something to TQL spent a "lot of hours . . . trying to make Deming's ideas improve" staff work and its outputs. Kelso wanted to make TQL courses mandatory throughout the Navy, but he had only partial success—though to his great pleasure most of the senior and master chiefs "were highly supportive of TQL."[31] They became supporters once they realized that adopting TQL principles would put more authority and responsibility—in equal amounts—in their hands.

Kelso wanted to merge the methods of TQL with a restructured OPNAV. In this effort, he was supported by his VCNO, Admiral Stanley R. Arthur. A decorated carrier aviator, Arthur had commanded U.S. naval forces during Operation Desert Storm. On arriving in Washington in early July 1992, he met with Kelso, and the CNO gave him "a single sheet of paper with a wiring diagram on it that he and Admiral Paul David Miller [OP-07] had discussed. He wanted to know what I thought of it." Arthur asked Kelso to wait while the new vice chief "retrieved a yellow legal sheet of paper" he had that "contained an outline for the OPNAV staff that reflected my views on how we could be better aligned to support the 'joint' world that we now lived in." On comparing the two sheets of paper, the two admirals discovered that "our two wiring diagrams were almost identical."[32] Their agreement meant two things to CNO Kelso. The first was that he was probably on the right track in his efforts to change OPNAV. The second was that he would have the strong support of his own vice chief. Kelso asked Arthur when OPNAV should be reorganized. Arthur's answer was "the sooner the better."

Kelso's choice as the officer who would implement his changes was Vice Admiral William Owens, then the Sixth Fleet commander. At the same time, Kelso also realized that his effort to change the POM process in OPNAV would not make sense to a lot of officers and civilians unless they understood why it was being done—why it *had* to be done. For that, Kelso and Navy secretary Garrett needed a new statement of the Navy's purpose—something that would have more impact than "The Way Ahead." Meanwhile, Vice Admiral Leighton W. Smith Jr., had replaced Vice Admiral Kelly in OP-06.[33] Smith (a carrier aviator known as "Snuffy, after the cartoon character") had worked as General John Galvin's operations deputy while serving on the European Command (EUCOM) staff. He recalled that, in EUCOM, "we had lots of discussions about where the next spats were coming, and so I began to formulate my own opinions about how the Navy ought to be shaping itself to meet future threats."[34]

So, by coincidence, Smith had been preparing himself for his new job as OP-06. In a sense, he was just what CNO Kelso needed. But developing a replacement for "The Maritime Strategy" was not easy. Smith's style was to aggressively push his staff to think broadly. He came up with the term "littoral," but his own staff had problems following his lead, and he was "so frustrated that Kelso was beating up on me."[35] Smith's problem was not process; it was finding staff officers and civilians with minds that could conceive of a new strategy and of the best way to express it. Smith knew that going "threat shopping" would not work. To create a forum that would produce the thinking that Vice Admiral Smith wanted, Secretary Garrett created the Naval Force Capabilities Planning Effort, a series of panels that met at the Center for Naval Analyses in Alexandria, Virginia, from October 1991 on and off through March 1992. Led by Vice Admiral Smith and Marine Lieutenant General Henry Stackpole, the participants—most of who initially came from Navy and Marine Corps programming and budget organizations—began by considering the likely future strategic setting. Then, they asked themselves what role the Navy could and should play in that setting. The meetings continued. Eventually, there were 40 participants, many from numbered fleet staffs.[36]

The work of these officers and civilians did not produce a coherent statement to rival the original Maritime Strategy, but they achieved several significant objectives. The first was to stress the role of the Navy as a facilitator for what became known as "littoral warfare." The second was to flesh out the concept of an "expeditionary task force" so that it would have standing in the minds of Navy officers similar to that of "carrier strike group." The third objective achieved was to give credibility to the concept of "capabilities planning." But it would be a mistake to see the work done by the participants in the Naval Force Capabilities Planning Effort as taking place in an isolated environment. The business of the Navy Department and OPNAV went on. Moreover, Smith had to oversee the many revisions of the initial draft of what would become ". . . From the Sea." As anyone who's served on a Pentagon staff can testify, this process of vetting a document can be exasperating. As Vice Admiral Smith put it, "I was literally . . . having chest pains, and my blood pressure was probably off the top of the scale . . ."[37]

"Well," recalled Smith, "we finally beat this damned thing to death, got it together, and we submitted it." Admiral Kelso and General Mundy approved the paper, but the new Navy secretary, Sean O'Keefe, insisted that seven pages be cut out of it.[38] Smith and one of his deputies did that, but then they had to choose one of several alternative titles for the paper. It turns out that the choice came almost by accident. Vice Admiral Smith's account is priceless:

> I had this document in my briefcase and I was sitting at my breakfast table at home . . . one morning about 5:00 o'clock [sic] eating my Cheerios or whatever the hell I was eating. The briefcase was open, and right on top of it was this piece of paper, and it had "Engagement From the Sea." . . . I looked at that thing and suddenly I said, 'You know, it could be anything from the sea. So why don't I just put three dots down here: '. . . From the Sea.' You can fill in what you want.[39]

That was it. ". . . From the Sea" was published in September 1992.

". . . From the Sea" was a revolutionary document. Under the Maritime Strategy of the 1980s, the Navy's mission was to deter war with the Soviet Union by showing that it could win a conventional fight on the USSR's doorstep and threaten the Soviet Union's ballistic missile submarine bastions in the far north. ". . . From the Sea" turned that earlier concept around. Now the Navy was to support joint forces fighting in areas close to the sea in regions distant from Europe. Under the Maritime Strategy, the Navy had to have more people than the Marines. Under the new concept, it was the Marines, along with expeditionary elements of the Army and Air Force that would do most of the fighting. The Navy would support them. Admiral Trost and his peers had not been convinced that it was time to make this change in thinking and planning. Admirals Kelso, Arthur, Smith, and Owens knew they had to begin shaping the Navy so that it could fulfill its new primary function.

While Vice Admiral Smith, his colleagues, and his subordinates wrestled with what became ". . . From the Sea," Vice Admiral Owens and Admiral Kelso reorganized the OPNAV staff. As Owens explained, "the staff organization built in the 1970s fit the times. The problem in 1992 was that times had changed."[40] Accordingly, OP-07 was disestablished in the fall of 1992 and its "warfare appraisal functions" were absorbed by a new office, "the Deputy Chief of Staff for

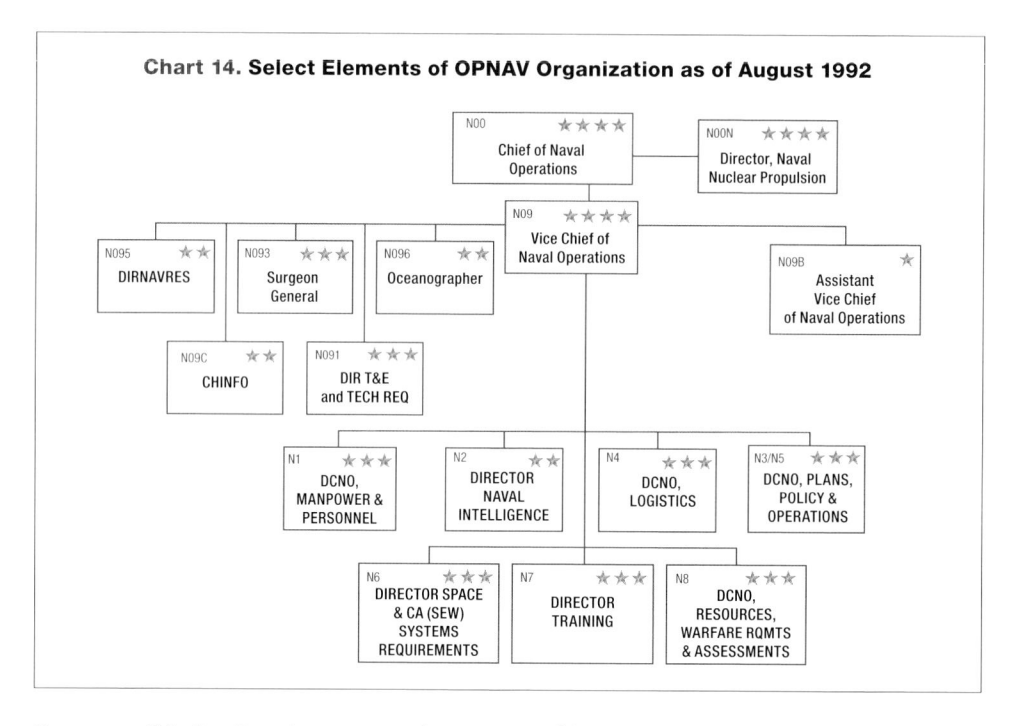

Chart 14. Select Elements of OPNAV Organization as of August 1992

- N00 ★★★★ Chief of Naval Operations
- N00N ★★★★ Director, Naval Nuclear Propulsion
- N09 ★★★★ Vice Chief of Naval Operations
- N095 ★★ DIRNAVRES
- N093 ★★★ Surgeon General
- N096 ★★ Oceanographer
- N09B ★ Assistant Vice Chief of Naval Operations
- N09C ★★ CHINFO
- N091 ★★★ DIR T&E and TECH REQ
- N1 ★★★ DCNO, MANPOWER & PERSONNEL
- N2 ★★ DIRECTOR NAVAL INTELLIGENCE
- N4 ★★★ DCNO, LOGISTICS
- N3/N5 ★★★ DCNO, PLANS, POLICY & OPERATIONS
- N6 ★★★ DIRECTOR SPACE & CA (SEW) SYSTEMS REQUIREMENTS
- N7 ★★★ DIRECTOR TRAINING
- N8 ★★★ DCNO, RESOURCES, WARFARE RQMTS & ASSESSMENTS

Resources, Warfare Requirements, and Assessment."[41] As was typical of him, Admiral Owens expressed the essence of the change succinctly:

> [T]he bureaucratic tension that earlier had been designed to balance a general warfare overview against program and budgeting realities was replaced by a more centralized structure in which the function of developing a vision of what the Navy should move toward—in terms of its size, shape, and character—and the function of converting that vision into program and budget reality were combined.[42]

Owens acknowledged that this change had given the new N8 the sort of "potential bureaucratic power" possessed by "few staff offices in any of the military services."[43]

Reorganizing OPNAV, however, was not enough. "It also was necessary," as Owens noted, "to incorporate new standards or criteria for deciding program priorities; a new vocabulary to the debates over the way the budget was to be allocated; and a new style of decision making. Both structure and process had to change..."[44] The success of the process hinged on the participation of "the most experienced members of the Navy staff." It depended on the willingness of flag and general officers to "play a much more direct and instrumental role than before."[45]

One way to tap the experience and knowledge of senior officers was through the Requirements and Resources Review Board, or R3B. On the surface, the R3B looked like other similar organizations in all three military departments—organizations that traditionally had reviewed staff program proposals and reconciled staff disputes. "In reality," asserted Owens, "the R3B was quite dissimilar. It did not meet so much to review staff positions as to try to develop a collective flag officer sense of what the size, structure, and character of the Navy ought to be in the future, independent of the ideas of the lower-ranking staff."[46] Note the deliberate phrase "independent of the ideas of the lower-ranking staff." Kelso and Owens wanted the rear admirals in OPNAV—especially those in N8—to take charge of mapping out the Navy's future so that there would be a shared consensus on it as those rear admirals became vice admirals and four-star officers.[47] So they encouraged and tolerated "open discussion" at R3B meetings. To facilitate candid discussion, no official minutes of R3B meetings were taken, and the board "spent a considerable effort critiquing and assessing its own interactions, sometimes with the help of outside observers."[48]

The second innovation put in place by Kelso and Owens was the use of joint mission area assessments during the programming process. As Owens acknowledged, "virtually all program advocates were required to justify their programs in terms of their contribution" to joint mission areas such as strike, littoral warfare, surveillance, and presence.[49] Owens had as his goal forcing "a horizontal flow of information" and then rewarding the members of the staff who had an intelligent appreciation of related Navy and joint programs.

> Advocates of a given program had to work with other advocates to arrive at priorities in each of the new mission areas. For example, for an advocate of submarine programs to ensure what he would define as adequate funding, he had to demonstrate to his competitors that his programs contributed more than theirs to joint littoral warfare, joint strike, and the rest of the mission areas. If he was successful in getting his programs ranked relatively high in each of the mission areas, the probability that they would be fully funded during the investment balance review increased.[50]

This process placed a premium on OPNAV program sponsors who looked across warfare areas and even across what the different services could do, but it also meant that the sponsors had to be good at explaining how their programs complemented systems or tactics in a range of joint areas. In short, OPNAV staff work was now intellectually challenging—as well as joint. This *was* new.

Owens was quite aware that, in implementing Kelso's guidance, he and his colleagues had developed something innovative, "not in response to direct tasking by the Secretary of Defense or any other external authority, at a time when the presidential campaign was entering the home stretch."[51] The proof that all the work had been worthwhile was the fact that the "Secretary of Defense accepted almost all the SecNav recommendations that flowed from the process" in the FY 1995 budget.[52]

Troubled Waters, Part I: Tailhook

Weaving in and out of the events marking the end of the Cold War were two major changes in American society. The first was the desire of women for more active roles in the military. The second was a similar desire on the part of homosexuals for the same opportunities. On 25 October 1990, Navy secretary Garrett and CNO Kelso co-signed a circular letter on the need

385

to eliminate sexual harassment in the Navy. At the same time, they put together a task force to consider how more positions that had been closed to female personnel could be opened to them.[53] In May 1991, the House Armed Services Committee voted to allow women pilots in the military to fly combat missions. In July of that year, the Senate followed the House. In September came the infamous "Tailhook" scandal, where female personnel were harassed and assaulted at a Tailhook Association convention in Las Vegas. The publicity surrounding this incident, and the appearance that the senior officers of the Navy had not taken it seriously enough, became a metaphorical millstone around Admiral Kelso's neck. As he noted, "[T]he social evolution/revolutions that burst upon us were not expected or understood by me and many of my peers."[54]

The Tailhook Association was "a non-profit corporation dedicated to foster, encourage, develop, study and support the aircraft carrier, sea-based aircraft, both fixed and rotary wing, and aircrew of the United States of America and to educate the public in the aircraft carrier's appropriate role in the Nation's defense system."[55] The association published a magazine called *The Hook*, encouraged studies of carrier aviation, and sponsored an annual convention. One major purpose of the convention was to bring together retired Navy aviators and those currently flying from carriers. It was routine for senior Navy aviation officers, including the Deputy Chief of Naval Operations (Air), the "type commanders" for aviation in the Atlantic and Pacific, and the Commander of the Naval Air Systems Command, to attend the convention.[56]

There was always a good deal of partying at the Tailhook conventions, but Vice Admiral Robert F. Dunn, who was the senior aviation officer in the Atlantic, thought that "things began to get a little bit out of hand" at the 1985 meetings.[57] As he recalled, "I was going up the elevator to my room when I encountered a couple of [junior officers] with Japanese headbands. I asked them what the headbands were for and they said, 'If you drink ten Kamikazes, you get a headband.'" Concerned, Dunn spoke with his counterpart in the Pacific, Vice Admiral James E. Service, and asked Service to go with him to speak to Vice Admiral Edward H. Martin, then DCNO (Air Warfare). The three admirals "then called together all the [commanding officers] whose squadrons had suites [in the hotel] and gave them instructions to take charge and cool it. They did, and nothing untoward happened that year."[58]

At the Tailhook convention in Las Vegas in September 1991, that sort of senior officer awareness and action was lacking. As a result, female aviators were harassed and some were actually assaulted by male aviators who'd had too much to drink. Kelso had attended the convention to defend his decision to develop the F/A-18E/F as a replacement for the canceled A-12. He didn't see any insulting behavior directed at female aviators, but others at the convention asserted that he must have. Initial investigations by Navy officers did not satisfy critics, especially some influential members of Congress and Assistant Secretary of the Navy for Manpower and Reserve Affairs Barbara Pope. The fact that the Navy broke off all relations with the Tailhook Association in October 1991 also did not lessen what became a storm of controversy over the events at the 1991 convention and what were eventually determined to be deliberately lax efforts by some senior officers in the Navy to investigate what had really taken place.

The media and political "fallout" from Tailhook, accompanied by the revelations regarding the A-12 program, almost sank carrier aviation. That is not an extreme assessment. Once it appeared that the report of the Naval Investigative Service (now the Naval Criminal Investigative Service) had glossed over the inappropriate behavior of a number of junior officers, the hunt was on for those responsible for the "cover up." With the release of the report by the Inspector General of the Department of Defense in September 1992, a number of officers not already implicated in the scandal were judged to have failed to intervene either to halt what happened in Las Vegas in September 1991 or to make sure the initial Navy investigation was thorough. One survey of the consequences of the events of September 1991 suggested that the careers of more than 300 senior and junior Navy officers suffered because of their involvement in the events of Tailhook or in what took place afterward.[59] Admiral Kelso suffered personally and professionally. As he recalled later, what undermined the Navy's credibility over Tailhook "were the expectations that you were going to have a lot of people fired, and not anybody was fired immediately. This caused all kinds of problems."[60] If the CNO had fired all the officers who had attended the convention and might have known of the assaults on female aviators, "this would have been almost the entire aviation leadership at the squadron commander level."[61] Accordingly, Kelso waited until all the facts were in—but that took a year, a year in which the Navy's reputation suffered.

Kelso was put through the legal and media wringer, too. In February 1994, Navy Captain William T. Vest Jr., the military judge in the Tailhook court-martials, argued in an opinion that Admiral Kelso had known what was happening at the Tailhook convention. The CNO was wounded deeply. "Everybody," he said, "wanted to kill somebody or shoot somebody over Tailhook."[62] But Kelso's role in the Tailhook convention and the subsequent investigation had been reviewed by President William J. Clinton, and the newly elected President had chosen to keep Kelso on as CNO and acting Secretary of the Navy (20 January 1993 to 21 July 1993). However, the new Navy secretary, John H. Dalton III, examined the evidence concerning Tailhook and on 1 October 1993 recommended publicly that Admiral Kelso be dismissed. The admiral stayed on until April 1994 because he had the support of the Secretary of Defense, but he and Dalton did not respect one another.[63]

The revolutions just roiled along: In April 1993, Secretary of Defense Les Aspin formally rescinded the ban on women flying combat missions, and Admiral Kelso, acting on his authority as CNO, opened six additional enlisted ratings for women. In November of that year, President Clinton directed the Navy to open billets on Navy combat ships to women. In response, Secretary Dalton announced that the first female sailors would be detailed to combat ships in June 1994. And, in December 1993, Secretary of Defense Aspin promulgated a policy of "don't ask, don't tell" regarding the presence of homosexuals in the armed forces. In taking the CNO's job, Admiral Kelso had not counted on dealing with all the complex social issues that he would face.

Figure 14-1. CNO Frank B. Kelso II speaks at the commissioning ceremony of the nuclear-powered carrier *George Washington* (CVN-73) at Norfolk, Virginia, on 4 July 1992. *George Washington* had been ordered in December 1982 as part of the Reagan administration's program to increase the size and power of the Navy. It was one of the Nimitz-class carriers that former Navy Secretary John F. Lehman Jr., had promised to build. (NHHC Archives Collection 2016-09 Vol. I)

As he admitted, they robbed him of a lot of sleep.[64]

Troubled Waters, Part II: The A-12

The A-12 program was supposed to produce a stealthy, long-range carrier bomber as a replacement for the veteran A-6. The program was already in trouble when Admiral Kelso became CNO in June 1990. Responsibility for the problems with the A-12 program could not be placed at his feet. The mistakes in that program—discussed later—had been committed before he walked into his office in the Pentagon for the first time, but CNO Kelso would have to deal with the serious consequences for the Navy of those mistakes.

With its "stealth" features, the A-12 was a dramatically different Navy carrier aircraft, and there was just as much drama in its eventual cancellation. The A-12 was intended to give Navy carriers a "heavy attack" capability against advanced Soviet air defenses (which were spreading or had spread to Soviet client states). In 1991, an air wing on a carrier usually consisted of 24 F-14 fighters, 24 A-7E bombers or F/A-18A/C fighter-bombers, ten A-6 bombers, 4 EA-6B electronic warfare aircraft, 10 S-3B antisubmarine warfare (ASW) planes, four E-2C airborne early warning and command aircraft, and six SH-3 ASW helicopters. But the F-14,

A-7E, and A-6 aircraft were growing old. The first F-14 had deployed operationally in 1974; the first A7Es in 1970; the first A-6Es in 1971; and the first S-3s in 1974. Under John Lehman's direction, the Navy had planned to upgrade the A-6E model to an A-6F version, arm the carrier heavy attack squadrons with a mix of A-6Fs and A-12s, upgrade the F-14, and replace the A-7Es with F/A-18A/C fighter-bombers. The goal in 1984 was to have one A-12 squadron ready for deployment in ten years.[65]

By June 1990, however, the A-12 program was in trouble. The developers of the plane, General Dynamics and McDonnell Douglas, had fallen behind schedule, and their projected costs for finishing work and initiating production were significantly higher than originally forecasted when they won the full-scale development contract in January 1988. As a detailed report submitted in November 1990 to the Assistant Secretary of the Navy (Research, Development and Acquisition) (ASN[RD&A]) put it, "the contractor team advised the Navy of a significant additional slip in the schedule for the first flight [of the aircraft], that the [full-scale development] effort would overrun the contract ceiling by an amount which the contractor team could not absorb, and that certain performance specifications of the contract could not be met."[66] This was a serious issue, but not necessarily one that should have caused Admiral Kelso and the Navy the problems that it did. After all, the decisions that had led to the problem had been made some years before Kelso had been appointed CNO.

As in the Tailhook scandal, however, embarrassing—even incriminating—matters took on lives of their own as the investigation unfolded and the controversy grew. In December 1990, John Betti, the Under Secretary of Defense for Acquisition, resigned because of the problems with the A-12 acquisition. In January 1991, Secretary of Defense Cheney decided not to ask the Congress for additional funds "to bail the contractors out."[67] The Navy Department then cancelled the A-12 contract. In late February 1991, the Inspector General of the Department of Defense issued the report that Secretary Cheney had used in his evaluation of the A-12 program.[68] The report noted that the initial issue was contractor performance. That is, General Dynamics (Fort Worth) and McDonnell Douglas suspected that the ceiling for full-scale development costs set in their contract with the Navy was probably unrealistic, and so they saw the ceiling as a target instead of an absolute limit.[69] To use a phrase widespread in the military acquisition community, the firms "bought in" and counted on being bailed out later.

However, in this case there was a fine line between actors in the A-12 drama making poor judgments and those same actors acting unethically. For example, the DOD Inspector General's audit report revealed that

> The contractor team experienced significant technical difficulties with the A-12 development program that were identified during phase II of the [critical design review] process, which occurred between August 15, and August 25, 1989. These problems were not resolved during the [critical design review] process, which was concluded in December 1989. The contractor team did not report the schedule and related cost impact of its technical difficulties to the Government. We consider the [critical design

review] Phase II to be the logical point at which the Government and the contractor team should have initiated corrective action to resolve program deficiencies.[70]

This was just one of a series of incidents that came to light in the initial Navy and Defense Department investigations.

For example, on 26 March 1990, Donald J. Yockey, the Principal Deputy to Under Secretary of Defense for Acquisition (USD[A]) asked Gaylord Christle, the Deputy Director for Cost Management under John Christie, Director of Acquisition Policy and Program Integration in the USD(A)'s office, to "perform an independent analysis of cost and schedule status on several 'special access' programs, including the A-12."[71] Christle's view, based on a comparison of the A-12 program with other aircraft programs, was that "the development contract, when completed, would be at least $1.0 billion over ceiling and at least one year behind schedule."[72] Why wasn't the acquisition chain of command for major programs (leading from the program manager [PM] to the program executive officer, and then to the service acquisition executive [SAE] and finally to the undersecretary of defense for acquisition) alerted? The answer is that Christle's assessment was shown to Donald Yockey on 27 March 1990 and to USD(A) Betti, on 5 April 1990. As the DOD Inspector General's report noted, "It would be unrealistic to expect that Mr. Christle's work could be evaluated and reconciled with existing projections of the A-12 status in the several days prior to the final [Major Aircraft Program Review] briefing to the Secretary of Defense on April 5, 1990."[73]

This argument ignored the previous warnings of problems with the A-12 program and how they had not been taken seriously within the Navy and in the Office of the Secretary of Defense.[74] Indeed, General Dynamics and McDonnell Douglas were convinced that the true fault with the A-12 program was the government's, and the firms filed suit against the government in the Court of Federal Claims in June 1991. That initial suit led to a whole string of court appearances, and the legal dispute between the government and the contractors wasn't settled until January 2014. There is not space here to review all the details of the affair, but as the story unfolded during CNO Kelso's tenure, the Navy's management of its aviation programs was subject to severe congressional scrutiny.

The criticisms began at a House Armed Services Committee hearing on 10 December 1990. Representative Andrew "Andy" P. Ireland (R-FL) had been instrumental in inaugurating the DOD Inspector General's investigation of the A-12 program. In questioning Navy secretary Lawrence Garrett, Ireland noted that Garrett had told the members of Congress that an effective oversight "system" existed but that individuals serving in it had not fulfilled their roles as competently as Garrett would have wished. Ireland responded to that claim by saying, "Actually, the ball went right through the shortstop's legs. It was not a small error. It was a big error."[75] Representative John R. Kasich (R-OH) used much stronger language:

> I can't really get outraged any more. . . . It is like a wake. . . . We come into the hearing room, we have our heads down and the body is laid out somewhere in the corner and

we hold each others' hands and we shake our heads. Wasn't it a tragedy. Then you guys get back in the car and you will think about this and say, how do you think it went? . . . I don't want to kick you when you are down . . . [but] The public is saying the system stinks.[76]

The criticisms continued. The Investigations Subcommittee of the House Armed Services Committee looked into the A-12 acquisition effort in April and July 1991.[77] A continuing issue for both the Investigations Subcommittee and the House Armed Services Committee was whether the A-12 cancellation was a consequence of poor judgment or a flawed acquisition "system." As Representative Ireland put it, "The system might be just fine. We have a lot of people who are stonewalling around here, and a lot of people who are absolutely passing the buck to other people." As members of the Investigations Subcommittee dug deeper into the events that led up to the Navy's decision to terminate the A-12 contract, the level of confusion did not necessarily go down, but the level of irritation among the legislators certainly went up. Representative Norman Sisisky (D-VA), for example, called the A-12 program "a national disaster with naval aviation . . . really a serious problem."[78] Representative Ireland seemed to grow more dissatisfied with each witness. As he fumed, "The lack of accountability in this case has sent a very strong signal, not just through the Department of Defense but through the entire Government, if we let a $3 billion plus mistake go by . . . our Navy, our Department of Defense, and indeed our whole government, is in bad trouble."[79]

There was that word—accountability. It would bring Tailhook together with the A-12, and both would be albatrosses around Admiral Kelso's neck. The Navy was in a peculiarly difficult spot with regard to the A-12 termination. If the Navy demanded that the General Dynamics (Fort Worth)/McDonnell Douglas team return the funds the government had paid them but they had not used to develop what their contract required, then McDonnell Douglas would face bankruptcy. However, as Terrence O'Donnell, the General Counsel of DOD, informed the House Armed Services Committee's Investigations Subcommittee, if McDonnell Douglas "were to go into chapter 11, they could reject key Department of Defense contracts, accept the profitable ones, and reject those under bankruptcy law that are not profitable." As O'Donnell put it, "The Department of Defense and the United States cannot sustain that type of risk." Punishing the contractors would mean collecting "some of the money up front by offsets, but we would not get it all by a long shot. We might jeopardize the collection of the entire amount."[80]

Moreover, if McDonnell Douglas went under, that would mean one less firm to compete for Navy aviation contracts—and that at a time when the Navy was trying to find a replacement for the A-12. It was like a line of falling dominoes. The decision to forego development of the A-6F meant that the only carrier-capable "heavy attack" plane was the A-12. When A-12 development was halted, it wasn't clear what would come next. Whatever the airplane was, it was DOD policy to sponsor a competition for its development and production, but serious competition might be impossible if there were only one realistic contender for the contract.

But there was one other factor to consider—the congressional pressure for joint development of systems. Both Navy aviation and the Air Force were caught off guard by the end of the Cold War. The Air Force, for example, had constructed four very modern "air logistics centers," which were some of the most sophisticated aviation depots in the world. What would become of them? The Air Force offered to do Navy aircraft maintenance at those installations—and even talked about doing maintenance there for the major commercial airlines. The Air Force was also officially interested in the Navy's plans to develop a replacement for the A-12. Dubbed A-X, the new design would carry about half the ordnance of the A-12 and have a range (fully loaded) of 700 nautical miles (nmi) instead of the 800 nmi of the A-12. In early May 1991, the House Armed Services Committee authorized the Navy to proceed with concept studies for the A-X. The Air Force and industry took a strong interest in the A-X, and the Navy agreed to include general Air Force requirements in the Navy's tentative operational requirement for the concept airplane. In the meantime, members of the Senate Armed Services Committee pressed Navy secretary Garrett to define A-X's operational requirements in terms broad enough to allow Lockheed Corporation to develop an attack version of the F-22 supersonic fighter.[81]

On 12 June 1991, CNO Kelso approved the tentative operational requirements for A-X, and on 19 June the Joint Requirements Oversight Council (JROC) approved the A-X's mission need statement, allowing the Defense Acquisition Board (DAB) to give the Navy permission to initiate studies of the A-X concept. Things were moving very fast. Just two years earlier, the Navy was considering a major upgrade to the A-6 (the A-6F), a possible upgrade of the remaining F-14 fighters as fighter-bombers, the new A-12, and upgrades to the existing F/A-18C/Ds. In the space of a few months, the range of Navy alternatives had narrowed dramatically, and now Navy and Air Force aviators were considering a joint attack aircraft program. But the Navy had a "hole card" of sorts—an upgraded version of the F/A-18C/D, the F/A-18E/F.

The Navy's argument in favor of the F/A-18E/F was that it was a modification of the already flying F/A-C/D—that it wasn't a new airplane but just an improved version of an already existing model, and therefore developing it would not entail the sort of technical, cost, and schedule risks that had so hampered the A-12 program. At the same time, the Navy and Air Force could proceed with the A-X. The two programs would overlap. The F/A-18E/F would come along in time to replace the ageing A-6Es, and the stealthy A-Xs would arrive a few years later—meeting both the Navy and Air Force requirements. But if this acquisition approach were to be successful, the Navy needed to get moving on the F/A-18E/F program. That meant bypassing the steady, measured "milestone" approach that was at the heart of the formal acquisition process.[82]

The milestone process was a series of sequential technical, cost, and schedule reviews conducted by the Defensive Acquisition Board (DAB), the highest review authority within the Defense Department. Milestone 2 was the review normally required before a major acquisition program could begin the engineering and manufacturing development phase—the phase where prototype aircraft were tested and a contractor made the tooling required for production. Milestone

3 was the review prior to beginning actual production. Milestone 4 was a review done before an existing system was modified in a significant way. In July 1991, the Navy proposed going to the DAB for a combined Milestone 2 and 4 review of the F/A-18E/F program in the spring of 1992.

But the failure (whether real or perceived) to the A-12 program had led to increased scrutiny of the F/A-18E/F "upgrade." In March 1992, the Inspector General's office in DOD issued a draft audit report critical of the Navy's estimated development and production costs for the F/A-18E/F. In May 1992, however, the DAB held a combined Milestone 2/4 review of the program and approved the Navy's program plans. In June, the DOD Inspector General's final audit warned that the Navy's effort to get the F/A-18E/F program moving entailed significant risks. The ball was back in Congress's court and on 30 June 1992 the Procurement and Military Nuclear Systems Subcommittee and the Research and Development Subcommittee of the House Armed Services Committee listened as Derek Vander Schaaf, the acting Inspector General, presented his office's case against the F/A-18E/F program. Vander Schaaf's basic argument was that the F/A-18E/F was not a modification or an upgrade to the existing F/A-C/D but an almost new airplane. As such, it should have gone through the steps required by the regulation covering the formal milestone process, including the step requiring a formal comparison of the F/A-18E/F with alternatives, including a modified F-14.

Representative Sisisky was concerned that the Navy might be hurrying along the F/A-18E/F, and that therefore Congress might see another failure like the A-12. As he put it to Vander Schaaf, "[I]s there a parallel, in your opinion, between the DoD oversight of the failed A-12 program and what you have seen in the F/A-18 program?" When Vander Schaaf replied that he wasn't sure, Sisisky observed that it was his belief that "we are not going to get both airplanes. You are not going to get the AX or the F/A-18." This lack of confidence was shared by other representatives at the hearing. Congressmen David O. Martin (R-NY) was obviously seriously irritated. As he said, "Aside from dairy price supports, I don't think anything has frustrated me more than naval aviation . . ." But he also felt that the Navy was neither stupid nor acting illegally, and he asked Vander Schaaf why there was a problem in the first place.

Vander Schaaf's answer was revealing: "Part of the difficulty is the Naval Air Systems Command. . . . They have a history of not being as straightforward about these matters as they should be. . . . They keep underpricing things, and don't come forth with all the documentation and then the thing gets in trouble." His point was that the Navy condoned "the underpricing of this stuff, getting your foot in the door thinking it is all going to go well and then finding out it doesn't go well."[83] The result, as DOD program analyst Franklin Spinney had noted years earlier, was that the higher unit cost of new systems meant that fewer were bought, and that therefore the overall size of U.S. forces declined.[84]

Representative Isaac N. "Ike" Skelton (D-MO) commented that there were really two questions confronting the members of Congress. One was whether the cost of the proposed F/A-18E/F would be reasonable; the second was whether the F/A-18E/F was a new airplane and therefore whether building it might entail major technical risks. Skelton also argued that the larger issue was whether there could be enough money to pay for both the F/A-18E/F and the A-X. He was right. The A-X was cancelled by the Clinton administration's "Bottom-Up Review" in the summer of 1993 and replaced by the Joint Advanced Strike Technology (JAST) program. JAST became the Joint Strike Fighter (JSF) in 1995. The F/A-18E/F first flew in November 1995.

The Cold War's End and Partial Demobilization

The buffeting that naval aviation took after the Secretary of Defense withheld funding for the A-12 program in January 1991 was extraordinary. Everything seemed to be happening at once. General Dynamics (Fort Worth) and McDonnell Douglas took the Navy to court, charging that the Navy's decision to cancel the A-12 was unwarranted. The staffs of OPNAV's aviation sponsor's office and the Naval Air Systems Command pitched in to gather, sort, and catalog all the documents pertinent to the court case. In addition, the Navy and Air Force were suddenly faced with the prospect of developing at least one new—and joint—strike aircraft. What was it to be? Which service would pay for it and be the lead developer? Would it be ready in time to fly from Navy aircraft carriers? And what about the Air Force's modern air logistics centers? Would they do the work that had been done by the Navy's aviation depots? With the end of the Cold War, did the Air Force and Navy need that many depots for aircraft repair and modernization? In the Naval Air Systems Command, for example, about 35 percent of the employees were no longer needed. Which skills had to be retained? Where was aviation technology going?

Over decades, the Cold War had become the normal state of affairs. Thousands of people, in uniform and out, had assumed that their Cold War roles would continue indefinitely. It was difficult for them to understand that 1992–1993 was like 1945–1946. The war—and the Cold War had been a real war—was over. It was time for thousands of people to do something else. It was also time for the defense industries to consolidate—to merge or to go out of business. They would do that with a vengeance in 1994, after Defense secretary William Perry informed their executives in the fall of 1993 that "restructuring" the industry was necessary and that the Defense Department expected the major defense firms to do the restructuring themselves. Grumman Aerospace aircraft, McDonnell Douglas, Rockwell, Martin Marietta, and Hughes Electronics were eaten up by larger or more solvent firms; IBM, GE, Goodyear, and Ford auctioned off their defense development divisions. Individuals and organizations scrambled to find or protect their jobs and functions. In the meantime, the work of the Defense Department went on—ships deployed, pilots trained on their aircraft, soldiers and Marines were recruited and taught their crafts, payrolls were met, equipment was bought and tested, and retirees were given their pensions and cared for in military hospitals and clinics.

Yet it was clear that bases and other installations had to be closed. Congress had developed an effective way to do that—the Base Realignment and Closure (BRAC) Commission would put together a list of places to be closed, the list would be sent to the Congress, and then Congress had only one choice to make: the whole list had to be approved or voted down. There could be no amendments—no nit-picking at the list. To draw up the Navy's list, Kelso, while serving as acting Navy secretary, selected Charles P. Nemfakos, the Associate Director of Budgets and Reports in the Navy Comptroller's office, to head a group of officers and civilians. As Kelso recalled, Nemfakos was not only "incredibly bright, tenacious, [and] persistent," he was also "smart enough to know that whatever we were going to do we had to have some rigor as to how we were going to do it, because we were going to get assailed from all sides."[85]

The standard developed by Kelso to determine what to keep and what to let go was "core capability." This term referred to (a) the skills and abilities that were at the heart of what the Navy did and (b) the supporting skills and abilities necessary to keep the Navy deployed and effective. Some core capabilities were obvious, such as the ability to land high-performance aircraft on a carrier's deck and the associated capability to develop the arresting gear and arresting gear cables that brought the planes safely to a stop. Other "core" capabilities were less obvious, and Kelso knew it, but some standard for deciding what to keep and what to let go was needed, and so debates and discussions about what was "core" and what was not echoed through the OPNAV and system command staffs.[86]

The BRAC process in 1993 was "very frustrating" for Kelso and the Navy, but that was not surprising to anyone. However, as the admiral later admitted, "Nothing I had to do as the CNO was probably more fraught with political peril than that base closure round."[87] Recommending the closing of the Philadelphia Naval Shipyard in the 1991 round of BRAC had been bad enough; Kelso acknowledged that the Navy "paid painfully" for that. But the 1993 round was both harder and even more necessary. Kelso "felt that if we did not effect substantial closures . . ., there would never likely be another opportunity to make the difficult decisions required to reduce the [Navy's] overhead."[88] Though subjected to vehement criticism and insulting remarks, Kelso persevered. As he said, "you have to do what you have to do sometimes regardless of the personal abuse."[89]

Paralleling (if not complementing the BRAC process) was acquisition reform initiated by Defense Secretary Aspin's successor, William J. Perry. Just six days after Aspin's departure from office for health reasons, Perry, who had served as Deputy Secretary of Defense in 1993–94, gave a special paper to the House Armed Services Committee. Entitled "Acquisition Reform: A Mandate for Change," it was a broad blueprint for reducing the costs of the military acquisition system while increasing its effectiveness.[90] Its proposals and succeeding instructions would alter the acquisition process, replacing the reforms put in place by then-Under Secretary of Defense for Acquisition Donald Atwood in 1992.[91]

The Effects of the Reorganization of OPNAV

CNO Kelso and his deputies had to embrace Goldwater-Nichols. Theirs was the task of organizing, training, and equipping naval forces. But to do that, they could not wall themselves off from operations. Like any organization that produced what its audience of consumers needed, OPNAV had to gauge future needs and requirements and make hard choices about what mattered and what didn't. The "good news" is that OPNAV and the CNO were at a crucial pivot point. On one side was the fleet, forward deployed. Determining what the fleet needed for operations could be done by examining all the information that flowed into the various OPNAV divisions. But what would it need in the future? That was the other side—the systems commands, and at their best, the technical specialists in the systems commands, were in touch with industry and with the Office of Naval Research. If there was "bad news," it was that what the fleet wanted in the short term and what the technical specialists wanted to invest in over the long run cost more than the Navy's budget.

Admiral Kelso was convinced when he became CNO that making the hard choices within OPNAV would be improved with the creation of Admiral Owen's R3B. The R3B was the place where the senior OPNAV staff confronted the conflicts between what the fleet and the systems commands wanted and what the Navy could afford. R3B agendas covered topics from base closings to ways to attract better educated recruits and from the Navy/Marine Corps relationship to ballistic missile defense at sea. Owens kept the members of the R3B busy. In just the month of October 1992, the group held lengthy meetings seven times, and the members discussed a wide range of issues, from how best to organize and utilize reserve personnel to unmanned vehicles.[92]

However, making OPNAV work more effectively was a work in progress in the fall of 1992. R3B meetings tended to be dominated by issues raised by the platform sponsors (N86, N87, and N88). Owens had to make sure that the R3B also considered and seriously discussed personnel, logistics, and training issues—to say nothing of the issues raised by the new N85 (Expeditionary Warfare). Accordingly, he set up subcommittees—ship and aircraft improvement panels, for example, and a panel to consider non-nuclear ordnance requirements, plus a "Program Review and Coordinating Committee." Owens was experimenting, trying to find the optimal way to use the staff resources (people and time) that were available. The new organizational structure and the authority of its components were not spelled out formally until the end of March 1993, in OPNAV Instruction 5430.48D.

But changing the way that OPNAV worked was not enough. Admiral Kelso understood the importance of ideas, which is why he sponsored and supported the writing and publication of ". . . From the Sea." He also understood the need to connect the ideas in that document with "what the Army and the Air Force were going to do." His plan was to create for the Navy something like the United States Army Training and Doctrine Command (TRADOC) and put it in Norfolk, where it would be physically close to both TRADOC and the Air Force's Air Combat Command.[93] The Marines apparently wanted any Navy/Marine Corps doctrine command to be located at their historic base in Quantico, Virginia, but Kelso insisted on Norfolk. His reasoning was clear: "I did not want to create a doctrine from the Navy. I wanted a joint doctrine for the Navy in a joint arena."[94] As it happened, the newly created Doctrine Command did not fulfill Kelso's hopes, and he took responsibility for that. ". . . I was not smart enough to get everybody to see" the potential of it, he later admitted.[95]

As CNO, Admiral Kelso was consistent in his approach to his responsibilities. He became CNO fully aware of the implications of Goldwater-Nichols. Though admittedly slow to grasp the dramatic implications of the end of the Cold War, he and Admiral Owens established a process that justified a forward-deployed naval force in a post–Cold War world. Pummeled by the Tailhook scandal and by the consequences of the decision to cancel the A-12, Kelso nonetheless gained the trust of a new President and a new Secretary of Defense early in 1993—trust that mattered a great deal during the "Bottom-Up Review" in the summer of 1993. As Admiral Leighton Smith told interviewer Paul Stillwell, "Frank Kelso doesn't know how to lie."[96]

Notes

[1] *The Reminiscences of ADM Frank B. Kelso II, USN (Ret.),* interviewed by Paul Stillwell (Annapolis, MD: U.S. Naval Institute, 2009), 511. (Hereafter cite as Kelso Oral History.)

[2] Ibid., 620.

[3] Lorna S. Jaffe, *The Development of the Base Force, 1989–1992* (Washington, DC: Joint History Office, Office of the Chairman of the Joint Chiefs of Staff, 1993), 14.

[4] Ibid., 35.

[5] Kelso Oral History, 651. See also Jaffe, *The Development of the Base Force, 1989–1992*, 40.

[6] Secretary of the Navy Lawrence Garrett III, and ADM Frank B. Kelso, Joint Memorandum, subj: "The Way Ahead," Navy Dept., OPNAV Ser. 00/0U500222, 23 Aug. 1990. Cited in "American Naval Thinking in the Post–Cold War Era: The U.S. Navy and the Emergence of a Maritime Strategy, 1989–2007," by CAPT Peter D. Haynes, USN, PhD Dissertation, Naval Postgraduate School, June 2013, 71–72.

[7] Kelso Oral History, 669.

[8] Haynes, "American Naval Thinking in the Post–Cold War Era: The U.S. Navy and the Emergence of a Maritime Strategy, 1989–2007," 76. See also John B. Hattendorf, ed., *U.S. Naval Strategy in the 1990s, Selected Documents*, Newport Paper No. 27, (Newport, RI: Naval War College Press, 2006), 7–11.

[9] Ibid., 77.

[10] Ibid., 80.

[11] Ibid., 81. "The Way Ahead" was published in the U.S. Naval Institute *Proceedings* of Apr. 1991, 36–47.

[12] Kelso Oral History, 669.

[13] Ibid., 668.

[14] SECNAV Notice 5200, from the Secretary of the Navy, subj: Navy Management Review, 20 Nov. 1991, in the collection of Thomas C. Hone.

[15] Ibid.

[16] Ibid., 2.

[17] Ibid.

[18] Memo from the Secretary of the Navy to the Chief of Naval Operations and Commandant of the Marine Corps, Subj: "Post Cold War Navy/Marine Corps," 20 Nov. 1991, in the personal papers of Thomas C. Hone.

[19] Ibid., 1.

[20] Ibid., 2.

[21] Ibid., 1.

[22] Ibid., 2.

[23] Kelso Oral History, 684.

[24] Ibid., 684.

[25] Ibid., 685.

[26] Ibid., 686.

[27] Ibid., 576.

[28] Ibid., 574.

[29] Ibid., 577.

[30] Here's an actual (and somewhat simplified) illustration. Honda had a factory in Ohio producing motorcycles. The fuel tanks for the motorcycles were painted by trained workers using spray guns. If the paint from the spray guns dripped and ran instead of adhering to the primed metal surface of a fuel tank, a worker could stop the moving line of fuel tanks. A supervisor would immediately duplicate the painting procedure to see if the problem also showed up when he did the work. If the paint still dripped and ran, the firm's paint shop would be called right away and a paint shop employee would appear to make sure that the painting was being done properly. If it was, the representative of the paint shop would accept the responsibility for remedying the error and a new batch of paint would be sent over. The result? Few defective paint jobs and a production line that was not stopped for very long. Employees were trained to identify problems, and both employees and managers were trained to solve them.

[31] Kelso Oral History, 579, 583.

[32] Ltr. from ADM Stanley R. Arthur, USN (Ret.), to Thomas C. Hone, subj: "OPNAV History—ADM Kelso," 20 May 2014.

[33] VADM Smith had been the Director of Operations in the European Command from 1989 to his appointment as OP-06 in 1991. As a young pilot, he had flown more than 280 combat missions from carriers off North Vietnam. ADM Arthur had flown even more combat missions and had been awarded the Distinguished Flying Cross 11 times.

[34] *The Reminiscences of ADM Leighton W. Smith Jr., USN (Ret.),* interviewed by Paul Stillwell (Annapolis, MD: U.S. Naval Institute, 2006), 639. Hereafter Smith Oral History. ADM Smith emphasized the role of GEN Galvin in his thinking in an email to Thomas C. Hone dated 22 May 2014: "Jack Galvin was a brilliant leader with whom I enjoyed a very special relationship."

[35] Smith Oral History, 640.

[36] Haynes, "American Naval Thinking in the Post–Cold War Era," 96–110.

[37] Smith Oral History, 643.

[38] Ibid.

[39] Ibid., 644.

[40] VADM William Owens, *High Seas, The Naval Passage to an Uncharted World* (Annapolis, MD: Naval Institute Press, 1995), 125.

[41] VADM William Owens, "The Quest for Consensus," U.S. Naval Institute *Proceedings*, vol. 120, no. 5 (May 1994), 70. The change was detailed in a "Personal For" message sent by ADM Kelso to "Commanders, Commanding Officers and Officers in Charge" on 22 July 1992. The message was augmented by a 22 July 1992 letter from ADM Kelso to Navy flag officers; the letter had attached to it charts showing the "wiring diagram" for the changed OPNAV organization. CNO Kelso and Secretary of the Navy Sean O'Keefe also held a press conference on 22 July to announce the Navy's reorganization plan.

[42] Ibid.

[43] Ibid.

[44] Ibid., 71.

[45] Ibid.

[46] Ibid.

[47] Interview, ADM Frank Kelso by Thomas C. Hone, 7 Apr. 1998.

[48] Owens, "The Quest for Consensus," 71. See also Owens, *High Seas,* 131.

[49] Owens, "The Quest for Consensus," 71. See also, Owens, *High Seas*, 128, where he illustrated the matrix built from the joint mission areas and the major POM-building divisions in OPNAV.

[50] Owens, "The Quest for Consensus," 71. The switch from "OP codes" to "N codes," which signified the importance of a joint perspective in the programming process, was directed in a message from ADM Kelso to Navy staff offices dated 6 Aug. 1992.

[51] Owens, *High Seas*, 130.

[52] Owens, "The Quest for Consensus," 71. Changing the organization OPNAV was not done overnight. Various subcommittees of a transition team had to arrange for the transfer of the files and people from the disestablished OP-07 to the new N8. Moving people and paper, creating new billets in N8, and altering office spaces took five months. See: memo, "Disposition of OP-7 Functions," from Chairman, Subcommittee A, to Chairman, Transition Management Team, N83, 30 Sept. 1992, 09B2 files.

[53] Jack Sweetman, ed., *American Naval History*, 2nd ed. (Annapolis, MD: Naval Institute Press, 1991), 305.

[54] Kelso Oral History, 724.

[55] From the table of contents page of *The Hook*, Aug. 1990.

[56] "Type commanders" were senior officers (usually vice admirals) who monitored aviation maintenance, training, doctrine, and operations in the fleet. They were not operational commanders. Instead, they made sure that aircraft carrier and land-based air squadrons met the standards of maintenance and support set by OP-05, the Deputy Chief of Naval Operations for Aviation.

[57] "The Reminiscences of Vice Admiral Robert F. Dunn, USN (Ret.)," interviewed by Paul Stillwell, U.S. Naval Institute, 2008, 543.

[58] Ibid.

[59] Neil Lewis, "Tailhook Affair Brings Censure of 3 Admirals," (*New York Times* 15 Oct. 1993).

[60] Kelso Oral History, 746.

[61] Ibid., 747.

[62] Ibid., 744.

[63] Ibid., 657.

[64] Ibid., 746.

[65] A discussion of the A-6 upgrade and development of the A-12 is in *Strike from the Sea, U.S. Navy Attack Aircraft from Skyraider to Super Hornet, 1948–Present*, by Tommy H. Thomason (North Branch, MN: Specialty Press, 2009). This book contains a number of excellent photographs of A-6 aircraft and drawings of the ill-fated A-12.

[66] Memo from Chester Paul Beach Jr., Inquiry Officer and Principal Deputy General Counsel, Navy Department, to the Secretary of the Navy via the Assistant Secretary of the Navy (Research, Development and Acquisition), subj: "A-12 Administrative Inquiry," 28 Nov. 1990, 1. Available at https://acc.dau.mil/adl/en-US/19583/file/1040/A-12_Administrative_Inquiry.pdf.

[67] Audit Report, "Review of the A-12 Aircraft Program," No. 91-059, 28 Feb. 1991, Office of the Inspector General, Dept. of Defense, Memorandum for the Record (20 Mar. 1991), subj: "Correction of Report Language," by Robert J. Lieberman, Assistant Inspector General for Auditing.

[68] Ibid., see Robert Lieberman's 28 Feb. 1991, memo to the Secretary of the Navy, the USD(A), the ASD(Production and Logistics), the DOD Comptroller, the ASN(Financial Management), and the Director, DLA. The memo is at the very beginning of the IG report.

[69] The best and final bids submitted by the two contractor teams for the fixed-price full-scale development contract were approximately 20 percent apart. See page 76 of *The Navy's A-12 Aircraft Program*, Joint Hearing before the Procurement and Military Nuclear Systems Subcommittee and the Research and Development Subcommittee and the Investigations Subcommittee of the Committee on Armed Services, House of Representatives, 101st Cong., 2nd sess., 10 Dec. 1990. The General Dynamics/McDonnell Douglas team was the low bidder and the

winner. But faced with such different bids, an experienced acquisition officer could reasonably infer that the team with the low bid was in fact "buying in" to get the business and would later return to the government for relief.

[70] Audit Report, "Review of the A-12 Aircraft Program," 28 Feb. 1991, 20. A critical design review, or CDR, is a multi-discipline technical review of an acquisition program's readiness to proceed to the next phase of development and production. It usually involves intense dialogue between contractor and government specialists.

[71] Ibid., 34. "Special access programs" were controlled above "top secret," and information about them was tightly restricted, even to officials within the Department of Defense.

[72] Ibid.

[73] Ibid., 35.

[74] Herbert L. Fenster, "The A-12 Legacy: It Wasn't an Airplane—It Was a Train Wreck," U.S. Naval Institute *Proceedings* (Feb. 1999). Also James P. Stevenson, *The $5 Billion Dollar Misunderstanding: The Collapse of the Navy's A-12 Stealth Bomber Program* (Annapolis, MD: Naval Institute Press, 2001). Congress also held hearings on the program. See *The Navy's A-12 Aircraft Program*, Joint Hearing before the Procurement and Military Nuclear Systems Subcommittee and the Investigations Subcommittee of the Committee on Armed Services, House of Representatives, 101st Cong., 2nd sess., 10 Dec. 1990, and *A-12 Acquisition*, Hearings before the Investigations Subcommittee of the Committee on Armed Services, House of Representatives, 102nd Cong., 1st sess., 9 and 18 Apr., 18, 23, and 24 July 1991.

[75] *The Navy's A-12 Aircraft Program*, Joint Hearing, 10 Dec. 1990, 77.

[76] Ibid., 80–81.

[77] *A-12 Acquisition*, Hearings before the Investigations Subcommittee of the Committee on Armed Services, House of Representatives, 102nd Cong., 1st sess., 9 and 18 Apr., 18, 23, and 24 July 1991 (Washington, DC: GPO, 1992).

[78] Ibid., 91.

[79] Ibid., 124.

[80] Ibid., 82.

[81] *Aerospace Daily*, 29 May 1991.

[82] Dennis R. Jenkins, *F/A-18 Hornet* (New York: McGraw-Hill, 2000), 108.

[83] *DOD Inspector General's Report on Defense Acquisition Board Review of F/A-18E/F Aircraft*, H201-12, 30 June 1992, Committee on Armed Services, House of Representatives, 102nd Cong., 2nd sess. (Washington, DC: GPO, 1993).

[84] Franklin Spinney, *Defense Facts of Life: The Plans/Reality Mismatch* (Boulder, CO: Westview Press, 1985).

[85] Kelso Oral History, 675.

[86] Ibid., 676.

[87] Ibid., 683.

[88] Ibid.

[89] Ibid.

[90] Fox, *Defense Acquisition Reform, 1960–2009*, 153–54.

[91] Charles B. Cochrane, "DOD's New Acquisition Approach, Myth or Reality?," *Program Manager* (Defense Systems Management College), July–August 1992, 38–46.

[92] "Resources & Requirements Review Board (R3B) Schedule, 1992–1993," 1 Oct. 1992, in the collection of Thomas C. Hone.

[93] Kelso Oral History, 696.

[94] Ibid., 697.

[95] Ibid.

[96] Smith Oral History, 638. In an email to Thomas C. Hone on 22 May 2014, ADM Smith recalled that "I played a lot of golf with [ADM Kelso] and [ADM Jerome L.] Johnson [Vice Chief of Naval Operations, 1990–1992] . . . He loved his golf and was able to escape the pressures of his position on the course."

CHAPTER 15

Following Kelso: Consolidating Changes

"They've been warned, they know better, they know all the bitter histories, but they just can't help themselves. They want to believe. Everybody, somewhere down the line, trusts a politician."

Donald E. Westlake, *Put a Lid on It*

Introduction

Under the leadership of CNO Frank Kelso, OPNAV had tailored its organization and its processes to the joint environment. At the same time, officers in OPNAV and in Marine Corps Headquarters had to ask themselves, "What's the role of the Navy in this new post–Cold War world, and what should be the relationship between the Navy and the Marine Corps?"[1] For the Navy and the Marines, joined as they are in one maritime service, these were critical questions. Though Goldwater-Nichols had confined the service chiefs to the role of organizing, training, and equipping their forces, all the chiefs and their staffs had to be heavily engaged in working out the post–Cold War roles of their respective services. They could not leave that task to the Joint Staff and the Office of the Secretary of Defense.

The Navy and Marine Corps had "... From the Sea," approved in September 1992, as a guiding maritime concept, but by the time Admiral Jeremy M. Boorda was confirmed as Admiral Kelso's successor at the end of April 1994, the roles of the Navy and Marines had been redefined by the Bottom-Up Review commissioned by Les Aspin, former Secretary of Defense.[2] Aspin, chairman of the House Armed Services Committee until nominated as Defense secretary by President William J. Clinton, initiated the Bottom-Up Review in March 1993. The report of the review was published in October 1993.[3]

The Consequences of the Bottom-Up Review

The Bottom-Up Review defined the nation's national strategy as one of "Engagement, Prevention, and Partnership."[4] "Engagement" meant not allowing the United States to withdraw politically, economically, and diplomatically from the post–Cold War world, especially from interactions with the nations of the former Warsaw Pact. "Prevention" meant using U.S. military force carefully but quickly to prevent political or ethnic conflicts from becoming military ones. "Partnership" meant working with other governments—especially established allies—to regulate what former President George H. W. Bush had called the "new world order." To make "prevention" a reality, the review argued that the United States had to "maintain sufficient military power to be able to win two major regional conflicts that occur nearly simultaneously."[5] If regimes wishing to attack a neighbor knew that the U.S. military possessed this capability, they would be less likely to start a conflict. Put another way, the review mandated the preservation of a significant conventional deterrent capability on the part of the United States.

The review expressed the Clinton administration's position as follows:

> Army and Air Force units are permanently stationed in regions where the United States has important and enduring interests and wants to make clear that aggression will be met by a U.S. military response. . . .
>
> Maritime overseas presence forces range widely across the world's oceans, demonstrating to both friends and potential adversaries that the United States has global interests and the ability to bring military power quickly to bear anywhere in the world. In addition, maritime forces have the operational mobility and political flexibility to reposition to potential trouble spots by unilateral U.S. decision. . .[6]

The Bottom-Up Review had laid out the major programmatic implications of the Clinton administration's strategy. For example, the Air Force's F-22 fighter would be fielded in order to guarantee U.S. forces' air superiority. The F/A-18E/F would replace A-6s, F-14s, and older versions of the F/A-18 in the Navy's carrier force. That would reduce the number of types of carrier aircraft, hopefully simplifying maintenance and training requirements. The A/F-X being developed by the Navy and the Air Force would be cancelled, as would the multirole fighter. They would be replaced by the Joint Advanced Strike Technology (JAST) program.[7] The Navy would get a new carrier (CVN-76), construction of which would begin in FY 1995, but advanced procurement for CVN-77 would be deferred "pending completion of a study evaluating alternative aircraft carrier concepts for the 21st century."[8]

Navy attack submarines were directed to "focus on regional conflicts and presence operations," and the Navy's leaders were enjoined to "develop and build a new attack submarine as a more cost-effective follow-on to the *Seawolf*-class, with construction beginning in FY 1998 or FY 1999 at the Groton, Connecticut, shipyard."[9] The previous administration had tried to shut down the V-22 "Osprey" program in 1989, but Congress had continued to fund the program. In spite of congressional action, the Bush Administration's Future Years Defense Program for

1994–1999 had not provided the resources necessary for the V-22 to enter production. The review went the other way, however, and supported the decision to move toward production.[10]

To facilitate the implementation of the Clinton administration's defense strategy, the review argued that "the majority of U.S.-based forces, including the Atlantic Fleet, Forces Command, Air Combat Command, and Marine Forces Atlantic," needed to be placed "under a single, unified combat command," the United States Atlantic Command. This altered joint command would "ensure joint training and readiness of forces stationed in the United States," enabling those forces to better support the regional combatant commanders if they were needed.[11] The Atlantic Command would also improve "joint tactics, techniques, and procedures" and develop and test joint doctrine.[12]

CNO Boorda and the Bottom-Up Review

Admiral Boorda was President Clinton's personal choice to be Admiral Kelso's successor. His experiences in the Navy marked him as a wise choice. Boorda was the first four-star admiral to rise from the enlisted ranks and perhaps the finest ship handler among the Navy's senior officers, fulfilling a dream of former Navy secretary Josephus Daniels that educating enlisted sailors would tap a latent source of talent, allowing some former enlisted sailors to hold major commands and thereby strengthen the Navy.[13] At a time when the Navy was shrinking, Boorda's experience with Congress as chief of the Navy's Bureau of Personnel was a plus for him. In addition, as Commander, United States Naval Forces Europe, and Commander, Allied Forces Southern Europe, Boorda had had first-hand experience with the social and ethnic tensions that surfaced in the Balkans after the end of the Cold War.

Admiral Boorda became Chief of Naval Operations on 23 April 1994. Secretary Aspin had resigned at the beginning of February 1994. His successor was Deputy Secretary of Defense William J. Perry. Dr. Perry had extensive experience as a scientist, business executive, and Defense Department official. Before being appointed Deputy Secretary of Defense in 1993, Perry had chaired the Carnegie Commission's Task Force on National Security, and he made it clear once he became Defense secretary that he would implement the Task Force's recommendations on defense management—recommendations that had been endorsed by

Figure 15-1. CNO Jeremy Michael Boorda speaks to the crew of fleet oiler *Kalamazoo* (AOR-6). Boorda, who began his Navy career as an enlisted sailor, qualified for Officer Candidate School and rose steadily through the ranks, serving as commander of NATO forces in southern Europe before becoming CNO. His suicide in May 1996 was a great tragedy. (NHHC Archives Collection 2016-05 Album I)

the Bottom-Up Review. Perry's argument was that the only way to preserve a strong military force was to create one that was "smaller, cheaper, and more flexible but still unmatched by any potential opponent."[14] How could that be done? Perry described his intentions in a paper, "Acquisition Reform: A Mandate for Change," that he gave to the Armed Services Committee of the House of Representatives on 9 February 1994. This paper had significant implications for the service secretaries and service chiefs.

However, Secretary Perry wasn't the only source of proposals for management change in the Defense Department. In November 1990, Congress had passed the Chief Financial Officer and Federal Financial Reform Act (Public Law 101-576), and President George H. W. Bush had signed it. The law created the position of "chief financial officer" in each executive branch department and established a new Deputy Director for Management in the Office of Management and Budget (OMB). The Deputy Director for Management was supported by the Comptroller, who headed the new Office of Federal Financial Management within OMB. In addition, the legislation had mandated the establishment of a Chief Financial Officers Council, whose members were the chief financial officers of the largest federal agencies, their immediate deputies, and senior officials from the Treasury Department and OMB.

The purpose of the new law was to compel the major federal agencies to "use a financial *accounting* and reporting system similar to the one used in the private sector" on the assumption that this would make federal "agency operations . . . more effective and efficient over time."[15] In 1994, Congress passed the Government Management Reform Act, which extended the 1990 law to all Defense Department activities and stressed the desire of Congress to see the Secretary of Defense produce a budget that could be audited by a major, credentialed, private audit agency. The pressure on the military departments to adopt budgeting and spending methods used in private industry was growing at a time when they were also being directed to reform their acquisition processes.

The advocates of acquisition and financial accounting reform seemed not to understand that a capital-intensive service like the Navy (or the Air Force) is like a huge freight train. You can't stop it quickly, and if you decide to change tracks you have to be careful you don't derail the train as it moves through the switch. CNO Kelso had started the process of changing tracks, but the process was by no means complete when Admiral Boorda became the Navy's senior officer.[16] Nor was there a consensus among civilian and military leaders about where the process should lead. The Navy and the Marines had to work out a new relationship in an environment where money was tight and likely to get tighter, and where the cost of new amphibious ships was increasing. The Navy also had to figure out how to stay forward deployed with fewer ships and personnel. And, as if these problems weren't enough, the new CNO had to fulfill his responsibilities as a member of the Joint Chiefs of Staff. For example, Operation Southern Watch, which maintained a no-fly zone in southern Iraq, was a significant military operation in 1994. So, too, were Operations Provide Promise and Deny Flight in the former Yugoslavia. CNO Boorda had to stay even with these operations.

Boorda's initial response to these challenges was to focus on the Navy, literally campaigning inside the Navy as he visited bases and ships in an effort to reassure Navy personnel that their interests and their futures were going to be protected.[17] He also drew on his charismatic personality, his intelligence, and his ability to act decisively to gain influence in the Pentagon and in Congress. As Admiral T. Joseph Lopez, Boorda's N8, noted later, Boorda's task was to consolidate the major changes initiated by Admirals Kelso and Owens.[18] Kelso, Owens, and the flag officers who supported them had "thrown the switch" that would set the Navy's "train" moving along a different track. Boorda was committed to keeping the train moving. In response to pressures from members of Congress for what had come to be called a "peace dividend," the admiral noted, "I don't ever plan on advocating a virtual Navy."[19]

Boorda's Leadership of OPNAV and the Navy

It was no surprise that the new CNO acted to re-establish the program that had given him his chance to move from the enlisted ranks to the officer corps. Given Boorda's experience and interest in personnel, it was also no surprise that he acted to improve the clarity and quality of officer fitness reports and enlisted evaluations.[20] Boorda also approved a change in Navy oceanographic policy, shifting the focus of the Navy's oceanographers from the open seas to the littorals, and he personally supported the concept of an "arsenal ship" that could provide fire support to Marines ashore. The "arsenal ship" concept was that of a large, tanker-like ship that would carry 500 Tomahawk land-attack missiles. It would provide fire support for Marines engaged in an amphibious assault or launch waves of Tomahawks against land targets. The concept was compatible with what a number of Navy officers thought was a primary need of the Marine Corps—persistent precision fire support. But it was also possible to see the arsenal ship as "the first important physical manifestation of a Navy in the early stages of transformation to a new battle fleet model—the distributed, networked battle fleet—in which the combined firepower of a widely dispersed naval battle network" could be concentrated against enemy sea or land forces.[21]

But was the arsenal ship what the Marines needed? Could it serve as an integral part of existing Navy carrier battle groups or was it like an amphibious ship, dedicated to supporting the Marines? The Navy was caught in a vise with multiple faces. One face was the requirement to be forward deployed in order to exert the "presence" called for in the Bottom-Up Review. Another was the need to integrate its concepts, systems, and operating doctrines with the Marines. A third was to shape its forces for joint operations. A fourth was to put to rest the controversy over Tailhook. A fifth was to implement the changes that Secretary of Defense Perry planned to impose on all the services. The many faces of this vise pressed on Boorda and OPNAV.

In responding to these challenges, Boorda drew on his own personality and on his personal energy, as well as on the authority given his office by OPNAV Instruction 5430.48D (29 March 1993). "A fine writer,"[22] he wrote a letter to senior Navy admirals every week; the greatly admired CNO Arleigh Burke had done the same in the 1950s. Boorda also consulted retired CNOs Thomas Moorer and Elmo Zumwalt. And, of course, Boorda had friends who were fellow flag officers, including Vice Admiral Michael P. Kalleres, who in 1989 was the rear admiral heading OP-80 in Navy Program Planning when Vice Admiral Boorda was OP-01, the DCNO for Manpower, Personnel and Training. The two officers had become close when they attended the Naval War College, and they stayed friends as they rose through the ranks.[23] Another close colleague of Boorda's was Rear Admiral Albert J. Herberger, who was head of the Military Personnel Policy Division in OPNAV when Boorda was an executive assistant to the chief of naval personnel and then executive assistant to the CNO.[24] In addition, in July 1995, Boorda recruited retired Admiral James R. Hogg to lead the Strategic Studies Group (SSG) at the Naval War College, and he directed Hogg to focus the SSG on likely future innovations that could revolutionize naval operations.[25]

CNO Boorda inherited from Admiral Kelso the November 1993 Navy Program Review and the 6 December 1993 Navy "Consolidated Planning and Programming Guidance." Both resulted from the work of Admirals Kelso and Owens. The Program Review followed the guidance of the Bottom-Up Review but especially stressed one very important element: An emphasis on "aggressively developing a mobile ballistic missile defense capability based on the proven technology of our Aegis cruisers (CG-47 class) and destroyers (DDG-51 class)."[26] The Consolidated Planning and Programming Guidance noted the need for program planning for the fiscal year 1996 to focus on the requirement for "heightened awareness of the sea-land interface and an improved *joint* capability to conduct operational maneuver from the sea (OMFTS). This will involve exploiting to the fullest extent possible the interaction between the Navy and the Marine Corps." The Guidance also asserted that the "Key to the success of our fighting forces is *technological superiority*."[27]

CNO Boorda also inherited the programming process created by Admirals Kelso and Owens. At the heart of this process was the work of "assessment" teams, small groups of knowledgeable officers who could evaluate Navy programs from a joint operational perspective. The Navy Department's forces were divided among the joint military (JMA) and support (SA) assessment teams within OPNAV. The teams were given the task of ferreting out major investment issues. The areas of responsibility of the teams were also designed to be roughly compatible with the Joint Staff's Joint Warfighting Assessments. N8's 1997 edition of its program guide described the process as follows:

> ... the assessment process relies upon analytical and assessment tools in considering the seven Joint Mission Areas [joint strike, joint littoral warfare, joint intelligence, surveillance & reconnaissance, joint command & control and information warfare, nuclear deterrence, maritime support of land forces, and engagement and conventional deterrence] and four Support Areas [readiness, infrastructure, manpower & personnel, and training]. The process thoroughly examines the Naval Services' contributions to joint war-fighting ... by examining Navy and Marine Corps programs in the context of all services' roles, missions, and functions.[28]

An example may help make clear what the assessment teams were supposed to do. Many Navy surface ships and some submarines carried Tomahawk long-range cruise missiles. Navy carrier strike aircraft also carried both missiles and bombs. Air Force attack aircraft also carried missiles and bombs. Which systems were more cost-effective? Was there a preference for one system over another in particular combat settings? How could you know? Under Kelso and Owens, program assessment teams were supposed to ask these sorts of questions. Money was tight. How could the Navy—and indeed the other services—get the most combat effectiveness for the least amount of money? Should the Navy purchase more Tomahawks, or fewer? If you added the Tomahawk inventory to what carrier strike aircraft could put on target, was that enough ordnance or not? And what about Air Force systems? Given the financial "squeeze," there was no need to duplicate what they could do.

Note the key terms: "analyze," "balance," and "options." It was a given among programmers in every service that there were more "requirements" than there were resources (financial and human) to satisfy them. Programmers therefore had to strike a balance, and they needed to do it based on analysis and not on horse-trading. Bruce Powers, who spent more than a decade on the OPNAV staff, described the analysis done by the Navy's programmers as the "examination of competing alternative solutions to a problem," where the cost and military effectiveness consequences were developed and "then portrayed to a decision-maker, tailored to enable selection."[29] The goal of Kelso and Owens had been to get the OPNAV staff to conduct serious analyses (including war games) at the beginning of the programming process. If lieutenant commanders and commanders did this, they would learn the ins and outs of OPNAV's programming process, bring their own operational experiences to bear on the analysis, learn something about relevant programs in the other services, and sift through all the possible issues to highlight the most difficult ones for the CNO and the Secretary of the Navy.

This was important work. The assessment teams presented the results of their efforts to the Integrated Resource and Requirements Review Board (IR3B) chaired by the Navy and Marine Corps chief programmers and composed of senior Navy and Marine Corps officers and members of the staff of the Navy secretariat. If the IR3B could not resolve an issue, then the matter was pushed one level of authority higher—to the Navy Department Program Strategy Board (DPSB). Ideally, the IR3B would produce an Investment Balance Review (IBR) that satisfied the CNO and the Secretary of the Navy, and that document—once approved by the DPSB—would be the basis for the Navy's POM. Because the Joint Mission Area teams paralleled the Joint Warfighting Capability Assessment teams, there was the opportunity for the Navy POM to dovetail with the Joint Strategic Planning System.[30]

Fitting together joint and service pre-POM analysis was a major innovation. In the past, OSD had been the "final" integrator of the service POMs. It was the Defense secretary and his staff that had reconciled severe service disagreements over programs and budgets. It was the OSD staff that had top-flight career program analysts—not the Joint Staff. As a result, this integrating and analysis function had been a source of significant influence for the Defense secretary and his deputies. By 1995, the integrating function was passing to the Joint Staff, a development that promised to reduce the influence of the SecDef over the Department of Defense. Prior to the passage of Goldwater-Nichols, the defense programming process had been dominated by the service and OSD staffs. After Goldwater-Nichols, the Joint Staff increased its influence by edging its way—through pre-POM analysis—into the process of POM preparation, though it was still the military service staffs that wrote the first drafts of their program memoranda.

But there was more to the Planning, Programming, and Budgeting System (PPBS) process than programming, despite what the programmers might say. There was also planning that was broader and more fundamental than program planning—strategic planning. In 1992, the Navy Department had published the product of this planning: ". . . From the Sea." In June 1994, Secretary Dalton "directed CNO Boorda, Commandant of the Marine Corps General Carl Mundy, and Undersecretary of the Navy Richard J. Danzig . . . to develop a new strategy" that took account of changes in national strategy made by the Clinton administration. The focus of the new statement of strategy, entitled "Forward . . . From the Sea," was not significantly different from its predecessor: ". . . the most important role of naval forces in situations short of war is to be *engaged* in forward areas, with the objectives of *preventing* conflicts and *controlling* crises."[31] However, as Dalton's speechwriter noted, the secretary was

> embarrassed trying to defend a strategy . . . that was signed by a Republican. . . . Critics would say that 'Forward . . . From the Sea' was really no different than '. . . From the Sea' (except emphasizing forward presence). They were right. It was not meant to be different, it was meant to be signed.[32]

For CNO Boorda, however, what mattered was showing that existing force structure was essential if the forward presence stressed by President Clinton in his June 1994 *A National Security Strategy of Engagement and Enlargement* was to be a reality.[33] "Forward . . . From the Sea" made a case for sustaining carrier battle groups *and* amphibious ready groups, and it had charts that showed, first, that it was the Navy that had taken the bulk of the budget hits in the 1990s and, second, that the Navy's financial support for "littoral warfare" had actually increased in the 1990s while its overall budget had dramatically declined.[34] By contrast, the Marine Corps had not suffered financially as much.

There was an important reason for this disparity. In World War II, the Navy built, trained, and equipped a huge force of amphibious ships and landing craft.[35] To many observers, this showed that an amphibious capability could be built relatively quickly. Moreover, the more durable ships of this force could be mothballed and rather promptly be brought back into service, as many were for the Korean War and the war in Vietnam.[36] But by the end of the Cold War, the far more modern ships (LHDs and LPDs, for example) and systems (V-22s and landing craft air cushion [LCACs] transporters) essential to the Marine Corps were neither cheap nor easy to design and build.[37] The amphibious capability of the Navy and the Marines had to be treated like the ships and aircraft that made up carrier battle groups—as ships and systems that would likely have long service lives and be very expensive to acquire.

It was therefore inevitable that acquiring them would take far more time than had been necessary to build and equip their ancestors of the 1940s. But if the world was changing rapidly, how could the Marines and Navy create an amphibious force that was affordable, long-lasting, and likely to be useful militarily for as much as 40 years? There was the danger that very expensive ships, aircraft and amphibious vehicles might become obsolete relatively quickly. At the same time, systems developed during the Cold War were becoming obsolete. For example, the USMC's CH-46 helicopter was wearing out. Marine Corps Commandant General Mundy called it "a decrepit flying machine," and he argued that its replacement should "be able to fly for the next 40 years," despite uncertainties about the future.[38] That replacement was the V-22, an extraordinary—and very expensive—tilt-rotor aircraft. Mundy strongly supported the V-22, despite the disastrous failure of the fourth pre-production aircraft before an audience of members of Congress at Quantico, Virginia, in July 1992.[39] The remaining V-22s were kept on the ground for 11 months until the problem that caused the crash had been solved.

Behind the V-22's teething problems was a more fundamental issue: In hard budgetary times, what mattered more—pressing on with the V-22 or making sure that the F/A-18E/F, the substitute for the failed A-12 and the aging A-6, was funded? After his retirement, General Mundy wrote a scathing critique of the Navy's leadership, insisting that "The determination of equipment and other warfighting requirements needed by Marines must be made by the Marines, and supported—not vetoed—by the Navy if the [Navy-Marine Corps] 'team' is to succeed and flourish."[40] Mundy's essay opened to the public a serious rift between the Navy and the Marines. The general had hinted at the conflict openly in his November 1994 interview with the editors of the U.S. Naval Institute's *Proceedings*, but his post-retirement writing revealed just how strong the tension was between the Navy and the Marines—and how the Marines had not wanted to accept the options for a "balanced" POM produced with the assistance of the joint warfighting capability assessment process. As Mundy noted, if the Navy and Marine Corps were equal partners on a "team," then "team" requirements and "team" budgeting would have to be developed "equitably."[41] Not analytically—equitably. It was no accident that the relationship between the Navy and the Marines was once described as "a difficult marriage that can't be terminated."[42]

CNO Boorda was caught in a bind. It wasn't just the Marines who wanted—and needed—new systems. What did the post–Cold War Navy need? One obvious answer was an attack aircraft to replace the existing attack aircraft, the A-6. But what about surface ships? The existing surface ships were optimized for antisubmarine warfare (ASW) and air defense, but in the post–Cold War world the need was obviously for more support of the Marines ashore. What was the future of the surface fighting ship? This issue had actually surfaced when Admiral Kelso was CNO. In 1992, Kelso directed that the Naval Sea Systems Command consider new surface ship concepts. Analysts focused on applying stealth technology and on building the conceptual ship's systems around modern computer hardware and software.[43] By June 1994, the Navy had gained the approval of the Joint Requirements Oversight Council (JROC) of a Mission Needs Statement for a new type of surface combatant, termed SC-21. SC-21 was not one system design but several. The Navy wanted to seriously evaluate each to determine which would be best in a post–Cold War world. The key step was to define and rank the missions that the new system or systems would have to perform. The mission that stood out was bombarding targets ashore—that is, supporting the Marines. In January 1995, the Defense Acquisition Board (DAB), responsible for approving major acquisition programs, granted the SC-21 effort major program status, and a program office (PMS 400R) was set up in October.

Then the really hard work began. The requirements officers in OPNAV had to sort through a variety of concepts. Each concept expressed a different balance of major characteristics, such as firepower, the ability of the ship to protect itself, its range, its speed, and its likely crew size. These officers were like the architects planning a building. Their goal was to develop an overall "plan," or concept, for the new ship. Then they could request that the "builders"—the engineers in the Naval Sea Systems Command—evaluate and compare the military suitability of each plan or concept. CNO Boorda favored a surface ship holding more than 500 missiles in vertical launch tubes; it was dubbed "the arsenal ship." It was put on a back burner when the admiral committed suicide in May 1996, and the requirements officers and engineers shifted their attention to a stealthy surface ship with long-range guns, various kinds of missiles in vertical launchers, an improved Aegis radar, and a not-then developed active sonar.[44] In effect, the analysts selected requirements for an updated, sophisticated multimission destroyer/cruiser. But could the Navy get enough such ships to meet the needs of the regional combatant commanders?

Problem-Solving and CNO Boorda's OPNAV

Admiral Boorda had a limited number of "tools" to use in his effort to direct the Navy and influence its future. One tool—already mentioned—was Boorda's own personality and his great energy. A second was the ability of the CNO to influence the programming process. A third tool was the ability of the CNO to become involved in major acquisition programs. A fourth was the way that a CNO could influence the Navy's interpretation of and support for national strategy. And of course every CNO can influence the standards used by selection boards to promote up-and-coming officers. In employing all these tools, no CNO works alone. All modern CNOs have a sizeable staff. This means that any CNO must know how to get the most out of the OPNAV staff.

This might not appear to be a major problem for a Chief of Naval Operations; the boss directs—the staff responds. But it isn't so simple. First, the time the CNO can devote to leading and shaping the OPNAV staff is limited. By law, the CNO has multiple, demanding responsibilities—to the Secretary of the Navy, to Congress, to the President, to the other members of the Joint Chiefs of Staff, and for sure to the enlisted and officer personnel of the Navy. There is no way a CNO can fulfill all those responsibilities except through a large staff, and there is no absolute guarantee that a particular CNO will have the experience necessary to orchestrate the work of the OPNAV staff. Second, the CNO's personality, as well as the personalities of the

CNO's principal deputies, matter a great deal. Can the CNO form from his deputies an effective team, and can that be done quickly? Third, the CNO does not get to hand pick his whole staff. Every CNO will find that there are officers and civilians on his staff whom he does not know well—whom he has to influence and rely on even though the CNO is often not certain how best to deal with them. Finally, the Navy, like all professional militaries, is a competitive organization. The rear admirals often want to be vice admirals, and the vice admirals want to be fleet commanders, regional combatant commanders, and even the CNO. All CNOs must therefore be aware of the competition for rank taking place around them all the time.

CNO Boorda inherited a programming process tailored for Admirals Owens and Kelso. That process made the Deputy CNO for Resources, Warfare Requirements and Assessments (N8) the key assistant to the CNO. It was N8 that was responsible for leading the process that produced the Navy's POM, and N8 under Boorda was Vice Admiral Lopez, who shared with Boorda the distinction of being promoted from the enlisted ranks. Lopez later noted that Admirals Kelso and Owens needed a "no nonsense process" that allowed them to make major changes in Navy programs and budgets. As Lopez saw it, "Owens had stirred the pot, and I had to keep that going."[45] At the same time, Admiral Lopez had to coordinate within N8 the joint warfare capability assessments—done by one group of officers and civilians—with the POM developers, who were *mostly* a different collection of officers and civilians. As Lopez told researchers working for the Center for Naval Analyses, the assessment process needed to present the CNO and the Secretary of the Navy with a "balanced" POM—one that was efficient in terms of both cost and warfighting.[46] At the same time, it was difficult to find space in the Navy's POM for "seed money" for new technologies and systems.

As already noted, with the cancellation of the stealthy A-12 bomber and the retirement of the A-6 attack aircraft, the Navy's carrier force was in danger of not having a carrier plane that could carry a heavy ordnance load. As Admiral Lopez recognized, "It's the carriers that make the Navy unique" as a conventional force. The Marines also wanted the Navy's carriers to have a replacement for the A-6 and the A-12. That plane—the F/A-18E/F—was actually being built, but until enough of the new planes were ready for deployment, the Navy lacked a long-range bomber. Rear Admiral Brent M. Bennitt, N88, proposed "filling the gap" with modified F-14Ds, or "Bombcats".

Taking a chance, Admiral Lopez worked with Vice Admiral Richard C. "Sweet Pea" Allen, commander of naval air forces in the Atlantic, to mount LANTIRN (Low Altitude Navigation and Targeting Infrared for Night) pods on a limited number of F-14s. According to Lopez, the pods "worked like a champ," allowing the modified F-14s to serve as heavy attack aircraft while their replacements (F/A-18E/Fs) were being built.[47] Indeed, there were reports in the trade press that the modified F-14Ds worked so well that there were some officers who believed that they should be preserved and used in place of the F/A-18E/F.[48] It was, again, "good news" and "bad news." The good news was that Lopez and Boorda had found a way to finance a solution to an urgent requirement. The bad news was that the F-14D—like any similar program—had taken on a life of its own, with its own constituency.

The case of the LANTIRN-equipped F-14Ds illustrates how programming—an essential element of Navy management—was far more than a bureaucratic exercise. Assume, for example, that you came from the Navy's surface ship community and were assigned to the "Maritime Support of Land Forces" Joint Military Assessment (JMA) team in the fall of 1995. Assume also that you knew about the work being done on a concept for SC-21 in the 400R program office. One of your tasks was to make sure that there was an adequate funding "wedge" in the POM for fiscal year 1998. John H. Dalton, the Secretary of the Navy, put out his guidance for the FY 1998 POM in September (1995). On the one hand, he stressed taking advantage of technology "through research, technological outreach and well-planned modernization programs." On the other hand, the SECNAV stressed "absorbing, controlling and constraining recapitalization costs . . . so that we are able to acquire systems and essential warfighting capabilities with the resources likely to be available for investment."[49] That was very general guidance.

What do you do if you're responsible for the SC-21 program? There is an approved requirement for SC-21, so you have to find resources for the program. The Secretary of the Navy did not mention the SC-21 program in his official guidance, so your task is to make sure that studies and war-games conducted or funded by your JMA include SC-21. Your task is to take the general guidance from the secretary and help turn it into an assessment that will include SC-21. Put another way, you become an advocate as well as an analyst, and you work among a number of others who are also both advocates and analysts. The JMA process, which was created to open up new possibilities for a new strategic setting, could instead tend toward becoming a bargaining process whose goal was primarily to find savings—to strike a fiscal and warfighting "balance." But was that what the Navy and Marines needed in a rapidly changing world? Was the OPNAV staff back to "the old days," when each warfare community worked to shield its own programs from "poaching" by its "competitors?"[50]

To forestall this sort of thinking, Admiral Lopez had created a new JMA, the Force Structure Assessment Team (or FSAT) in time for the POM-98 assessment process. The problem Lopez and the Navy faced was both simple and intractable: find some way to pay for a new aircraft carrier, a new submarine, and SC-21—all programs whose bills were estimated to come due with a vengeance in calendar years 2002 and 2003—without harming the rest of the Navy and the Marines.[51] There was no easy answer, and the FSAT did not produce one. As Major General Jeffrey W. Oster, acting for the Marine Corps commandant in the assessment process, told researchers from the Center for Naval Analyses, "The [POM-98] assessment is not really an assessment," and "We should narrow the issues and assign them to a study management group . . . an ad hoc group to study a particular issue." His point was that the senior officers knew that the Navy Department was going to be short of funds, and that they needed to make some difficult decisions that would satisfy Congress and the President. But the routine JMA process would not lead them to those decisions. They would have to step outside the process and rely on an ad hoc group.[52] In other words, the JMA process itself was not going to solve the Navy Department's near-term fiscal problem.

That is where matters stood when Admiral Boorda committed suicide on 16 May 1996. There was little warning that the CNO was considering taking his own life. On 15 May, he had participated in a long meeting with Secretary Dalton, Admiral Lopez, and Marine Corps Generals Oster and Charles C. Krulak (the Marine Corps Commandant) regarding Navy and Marine Corps budget priorities. Lopez talked with Boorda after the meeting about what had taken place, and Lopez recalled that the CNO "was in high spirits."[53] What apparently triggered Boorda's suicide was the criticism of his wearing decorations that he was not entitled to. As Vice Admiral Herberger put it, Boorda prized his integrity so much that he could not tolerate the perception that he had acted improperly.[54] Admiral Boorda also apparently regretted that he had not resisted the pressure by Senator David Durenberger (R-MN) to force President Clinton to deny the command of the Pacific Command (PACOM) to Admiral Stanley R. Arthur, the VCNO.

Admiral Johnson Takes Over

There was no good from Admiral Boorda's suicide. However, then-retired CNO Frank Kelso said later that he thought "Mike Boorda's death . . . really was the end of Tailhook."[55] Admiral Jay L. Johnson, the Vice Chief of Naval Operations and Boorda's successor, might have disagreed. After CNO Boorda's death, Admiral Johnson had served temporarily as the Chief of Naval Operations until approved by the Senate. In his confirmation hearing with the Senate Armed Services Committee at the end of July 1996, Johnson had to walk a fine line, praising Admiral Boorda for Boorda's work on behalf of Navy personnel while at the same time telling the senators that the "atmosphere" and shameful behavior that characterized the 1991 Tailhook meetings "will never again be tolerated."[56] Johnson had been officially "cautioned" by Secretary Dalton because he had attended the Tailhook meetings and had not stopped the scandalous actions of younger naval aviators, so he was at a disadvantage when dealing with the senators, and they knew it. The new CNO therefore had to be both contrite and firm, apologizing for mistakes and simultaneously putting forth his vision for the Navy.

Admiral Johnson presented his program to the senators and to the public. First on his list was maintaining "the care, the nurturing, and the betterment of the people of the Navy." This general goal included a stress on innovation, especially innovation that added to the ability of sailors to perform their missions. At the same time, modernization had to be balanced against readiness. As Johnson put it, "[T]he challenge, as we step into the next century, . . . will be balancing our readiness requirements against the need to recapitalize our force."[57] It is not as though the senators did not know what Johnson would say. He had already met with them one-on-one in private. But he and they had points they wanted on the record. For example, Senator Dirk Kempthorne (R-ID) wondered if Johnson, having been "cautioned" by Secretary Dalton, would have the personal stature necessary to lead the Navy. Kempthorne also led Admiral Johnson into saying that "I am very pleased with the integration of women aboard combat ships."[58]

Senator James Exon (D-NE) asked Johnson about "the bow wave cost of ship construction in the years ahead." Exon even asked if Congress needed to provide the Navy with "additional tools" to deal with the rising costs of acquisition. Johnson's response was that he was concerned about the "bow wave," that he was working with the Assistant Secretary of the Navy for Research, Development, and Acquisition, and that, "if I am confirmed, that will be my first order of business."[59] Later, in an exchange with Senator (and former naval aviator) John McCain (R-AZ) Johnson stressed the need to invest in carrier aircraft. Johnson also reassured Senator James Inhofe (R-OK) that the Navy would allocate funds to upgrade the Aegis system for its planned role in ballistic missile defense.[60]

Former Navy secretary Senator John Warner (R-VA) shifted the discussion before the committee to the costs of military operations in Bosnia. As Warner noted, "Prior to the current deployment of troops in this multi-national force, we were the principal logistician, principal one at sea, principal one in terms of air, and . . . it has drained the Department of Defense budget."[61] Had that harmed the Navy? Johnson agreed that it had, especially in the area of acquisition. Finally, Senator Dan Coats (R-IN) asked about the role of the JROC, of which Johnson was a member. Had the JROC developed an effective path for the modernization of the nation's tactical aviation? Was it acting to preserve the military's capability to conduct "deep" (i.e., long-range) attack? Johnson said that it was.[62]

Though the hearing on Admiral Johnson's nomination to be the next CNO was a staged and choreographed event, it was still revealing. Senators were able to make clear their concerns, and Johnson described the major elements of his program. It was clear what his (and the Navy's) problem was—a lack of funds to cover all the Navy's personnel and material expenses. What had begun under CNO Kelso as an effort to chart a very new path for the Navy had become a struggle to make ends meet. Innovation was becoming desperation. As CNO, Johnson did not want to cut Navy force structure. At the same time, he did not want to cut pay for sailors. The Navy had already reduced funding for acquisition. Could the Base Realignment and Closure Commission do another round? Not likely, given the opposition in Congress to the closures approved in 1995. What was left?

The answer was reorganization. Admirals Boorda, Arthur, and Lopez had considered reorganizing OPNAV in 1995. They then drafted an OPNAV reorganization plan, tentatively scheduled for implementation in June 1996.[63] At its heart was the creation of a deputy CNO's position "for generating warfare requirements and ensuring that they are satisfied during [Navy] POM development." The new deputy would be charged with focusing "research and development efforts" and with pressing for advances in information and electronic warfare. Under the new deputy chief of naval operations (N9/N6) would be seven divisions: Space, Command, Control and Communications (N60), Test and Evaluation and Technology (N90), Anti-Submarine Warfare and Maritime Superiority (N91), Air Defense (N92), Information Warfare (N94), Expeditionary Warfare (N95) and Strike Warfare (N98).

In a way, this was "back to the future." The concept had already been tested and found wanting in the eyes of many officers, but did that mean the concept was invalid? Or, instead, did it mean that it took a certain kind of officer to lead a POM process where requirements and assessments were divided between two directorates? Admiral Boorda had inherited an N8 organization tailored specifically for Admirals Owens and Kelso. By 1996, he and Admiral Lopez wanted something else. Admiral Johnson knew about this proposed reorganization, but he shelved it. Instead of reorganizing, he replaced Vice Admiral Lopez with Vice Admiral Donald Pilling when Lopez was given a fourth star on his promotion to Commander, Allied Forces, Southern Europe. Was Pilling, with his PhD in mathematics (from Cambridge) and his previous experience in N8, the individual who could reconcile all the demands on the Navy with the declining defense budget?

Pilling and Marine Lieutenant General Jeffery W. Oster issued their guidance for the FY 1999 program review Joint Mission Area and Support Area assessments on 17 September 1996. The guidance was essentially the same as that of the previous year, but the political environment had changed. Would President Clinton be reelected in November? Would the Republican Party, led by Speaker of the House Newt Gingrich (R-GA), retain its majority in that body? In 1995, Clinton had threatened to veto the fiscal year 1996 defense budget bill because—among other reasons—it provided funding for a national ballistic missile defense system, and a compromise between the President and his Republican opponents in Congress was reached only after a partisan political stand-off that lasted into 1996. In March 1996, Secretary of Defense Perry revealed a 5-year defense modernization plan that assumed the defense budget would stop declining in fiscal year 1997 and then grow in real terms in successive years. But would that really happen?

Congress responded to the defense budget debate by requiring the Secretary of Defense to conduct a review of the nation's defense program. The National Defense Authorization Act of 23 September 1996 contained a clause that provided for "an independent, non-partisan review of the force structure that is more comprehensive than prior assessments [and] . . . extends beyond the quadrennial defense review . . ." The review was to cover defense strategy and recommend "a revised defense program through the year 2005." The group conducting the review was called the National Defense Panel.[64] But the Quadrennial Defense Review (QDR) was already underway, and so two major reports would appear in 1997, both of them the results of legislation originally sponsored by Senator McCain.[65] It made sense for the new CNO and N8 to pause before they implemented any changes in the Navy's programming process, even though there is evidence that Vice Admiral Pilling had lost confidence in the ability of the Integrated Resource and Requirements Review Board (IR3B) to address the issues raised by the assessment committees.[66]

The new Secretary of Defense, replacing Perry in January 1997, was William S. Cohen of Maine, a former Republican senator and personal friend of President Clinton and a successful sponsor of defense-related legislation.[67] Cohen had decided to wait until the QDR and National Defense Panel reports were completed before making any changes to the general program that his predecessor had developed. As Cohen and others had anticipated, the QDR report of 19 May 1997 did not recommend major changes in the overall defense program. In his introduction to the report, Cohen argued that the Defense Department's plans were fiscally responsible; that is, they did not push against the budget "caps" agreed to by the President and the Congress. As Cohen put it, "There is a bipartisan consensus in America to balance the federal budget by the year 2002 . . . [This] fiscal reality did not drive the defense strategy we adopted, but it did affect our choices for its implementation and focused our attention on the need to reform our organization and methods of conducting business . . ."[68] There it was: funds for modernization and acquisition would have to be gleaned from savings achieved by slimming down existing organizations. The "freight train" that was the Navy would not necessarily be run down a new track; instead, it would just slow down.

This pause in the rate of change also showed up in the exchanges between the Navy and the Marines about naval doctrine. Admiral Boorda had been concerned in 1994 that the Marine Corps concept of "operational maneuver from the sea" (OMFTS) might so lessen the Navy's open ocean preparedness that the Navy would then be unable to perform the range of operations that the regional combatant commanders assumed the Navy could always do.[69] This concern was justified from the Navy's perspective. According to Navy Captain (and historian) Peter D. Haynes, *Naval Operations* (NDP-3), which was written to bring together Navy and Marine Corps doctrine, went "through almost forty iterations" between 1995 and 1997, "and each time they were rejected, mostly by the Marine Corps Combat Development Command's commanding general, Lieutenant General Paul K. Van Riper . . ."[70]

As Haynes has pointed out, there were very real differences between Navy and Marine Corps ideas; General Van Riper's refusal to accept drafts of NDP-3 was not based on any personality differences. Instead, the Marines differed with the Navy on two very important issues. The first was command of a "naval" expeditionary force. The Navy wanted such a force commanded at sea by a Navy officer; a Marine could take command once Marine units headed for shore. The Marines questioned this. If the point was to maneuver operationally from the ocean against the land, then the whole maneuver was one action—one effort, and a Marine needed to command that effort. The second issue was how Navy and Marine personnel should work together up and down the chain of command. The Marines wanted "integration"; the Navy favored "coordination."[71]

These were significant issues. If the future was one of operational (that is, very long-distance) maneuver from the sea against land objectives, then the old idea that the Navy carried the Marines to a hostile shore no longer applied. Instead, the Marines wanted to see all elements of the amphibious force as one unit, with one basic mission. It was as if the ocean were a huge plain, and the Navy and Marines operated on this plain against various objectives. The fact that the plain was water didn't matter. The Marines were out to abolish the traditional boundary between the sea and the land. That implied a thorough integration of Marine and Navy staffs, including—perhaps—headquarters staffs. The Navy could not accept this, and so *Naval Operations* (NDP-3) was never published. According to Haynes, this "undermined the other five NDPs, the Naval Doctrine Command's stature, and the expectation that the Navy could develop doctrine to explain its warfighting approach."[72] The inability to agree on a truly joint "warfighting" doctrine made it extremely difficult for the OPNAV and Marine Corps staffs to function in an integrated fashion. The vision of Admirals Kelso and Owen had not been achieved.

This apparently did not bother CNO Johnson. According to Haynes, the new CNO "was generally skeptical about the value of top-down statements of strategic vision," and he never signed the "2020 Vision" statement that Admiral Boorda had asked the CNO Executive Panel (CEP) to write.[73] Instead, Johnson accepted the National Military Strategy's emphasis on "engagement, deterrence, and conflict prevention."[74] As Johnson noted, "We will deploy carrier battle groups and amphibious ready groups with embarked Marines to provide naval expeditionary forces for the Combatant Commanders."[75] The same thing—with slightly different wording—could have been said by a senior Navy officer in 1947. As then, Johnson's 1997 concept of the Navy was that of a force that gained maritime superiority, "thus providing unimpeded use of strategic sea lanes and freedom of operation in littoral waters."[76] This concept of maritime superiority was like that of "air superiority." In both cases, one force was "the enabler," shielding and supporting the ground force while it fought its way to its objective. But was that all "operational maneuver from the sea" was about? If so, then it wasn't a revolutionary concept.

That was not CNO Johnson's problem. What he wanted, as historian Haynes learned, was "a *Navy* Operational Concept, as distinct from a *naval* one."[77] Johnson directed Commander Joseph Bouchard, who headed N513 (OPNAV's Strategy and Concepts branch), to work with Vice Admiral Arthur Cebrowski, the Director of Space, Information Warfare, and Command and Control (N6) to come up with this concept. Cebrowski, who had served as the Joint Staff J6 (Command, Control, Communications, and Computers), was one of a group of Navy officers working to usher the Navy into the so-called "digital age." He is credited with developing the ideas that linked together have the label "net-centric," or "network-centric" warfare.[78] As Haynes discovered, "Bouchard and Cebrowski agreed that network-centric warfare could take the theory of maneuver warfare to the next level of sophistication, thereby providing the Navy with an opportunity to drive joint doctrine instead of reacting to it."[79] The two produced what became "The Navy Operational Concept" in January 1997, and it was published in an unclassified form in May 1997.[80] From the Navy's point of view, it appeared just in time—though not necessarily as a guide to the preparation of the Navy's next program submission to the Office of the Secretary of Defense.

That same month, on the 20th and 21st, Secretary of Defense Cohen discussed the conclusions of the just-completed QDR with the Senate Armed Services Committee and the House National Security Committee. Few of the members were positive about the QDR's conclusions, but Secretary Cohen got the toughest treatment in the House. Committee Chair Representative Floyd Spence (R-SC) had this to say: "It would seem to me that the QDR's most glaring shortcoming is its demand on the one hand that America accept difficult trade-offs. Yet on the other hand the review fails to provide a clearly defined baseline from which to assess the risks and tradeoffs in an environment of fiscal restraint." Representative Ike Skelton, Missouri Democrat, was also critical. As he told Cohen, the Army had sent eight of its 18 divisions to fight Iraqi forces in Desert Storm in 1991. But in 1997, the Army had only ten divisions. The Air Force had 13 fighter air wings; there were 24 in 1991; the number of Navy warships had fallen from 546 to 346 between 1991 and 1997. How could the military services fight two serious conflicts at once?[81] These pointed criticisms were appropriate if the services fought future conflicts the way that they had fought Desert Storm in 1991, but "The Navy Operational Concept" argued that technology was in the process of changing how the services would fight. Technology could make a smaller force just as effective as the larger force had been.

Some of this thinking was reflected in the Program Objective Memorandum (POM) for FY 2000 assessment instructions to the Joint Mission and Support Areas, issued in August 1997. The goals for the assessment teams included identifying significant capability and programmatic issues and developing "Mission Area Concepts" that would dovetail with the "Naval Operational Concept." The teams also had to evaluate the proposals made by the National Defense Panel, the DOD Task Force on Defense, the Quadrennial Defense Review, and the authors of Joint Vision 2010. Finally, the teams had to establish a priority among the objectives in the first draft of the Navy's "Long-Range Planning Objectives."[82] The instructions also noted that the assessment teams could consider alternatives *beyond* the "usual" programming process—alternatives that included changes in doctrine, defense policy, and even what major business organizations were doing. This emphasis on not simply staying with the routine programming process was made by Vice Admiral Pilling, the N8, and his successor, Vice Admiral Conrad C. Lautenbacher Jr. Finally, the teams were told to assume that the Navy Department's budget would stay constant through FY 2005. In short, the members of the assessment teams could not count on any infusion of funds.

However, there were a number of ideas being discussed. For example, Bruce Powers, head of N812 (the Assessment and Affordability Branch), briefed the Navy Study Group in July 1997 to define and encourage some "out of the box" thinking. One of the ideas he proposed to the group was having the Navy buy satellite data from commercial firms. Another was copying corporate business practices in order to save money. Still another was moving most Navy training and education into the fleet via the internet.[83] How N81's analysts—expert programmers all—would approach such issues wasn't clear, but at least no one could say that they hadn't been considered. By November 1997, CNO Johnson was relying more on his special "brain trust," composed of the newly promoted Admiral Pilling (now the vice chief), Vice Admirals Cebrowski (N6), James Ellis (N3/N5), and Lautenbacher, Rear Admiral Kendall Pease (head of Navy public affairs), and Captain R. Robinson "Robby" Harris, who directed 00K, the CNO Executive Panel.

CNO Johnson also recognized the need for a vision statement printed in the Naval Institute's *Proceedings*, and he got it in time for the November 1997 issue. The paper, entitled "Anytime, Anywhere: A Navy for the 21st Century," defined the Navy's purpose as influencing, "directly and decisively, events ashore from the sea—anytime, anywhere." It also argued that the purpose of the Navy and Marine Corps was to give a smaller naval force "an impact so disproportionate to its numbers as to make it decisive in peace and in war." "Anytime, Anywhere" seemed to embrace the Marine Corps concepts of OMFTS and ship to objective maneuver, and it also argued that the right sort of naval (and not just Navy) presence could foreclose a potential opponent's options.[84] But could the Navy and Marines fill out this vision? Could the staffs consider truly different kinds of naval forces and compare them rigorously with existing forces? Was there any way to reduce the demand for forward presence so that the Navy and Marines could experiment with new formations, new operating concepts, and new prototype systems? It was one thing to have a vision, but could the staffs program to achieve it?[85]

Was there any reason to worry? Irving N. Blickstein, Vice Admiral Lautenbacher's principal assistant, did not think so when interviewed toward the end of December 1997. Blickstein instead insisted that both N8 and OPNAV had worked well and were still working well. For example, the Navy had recognized the importance of cybernetic conflict, fostered the use of Tomahawk cruise missiles against land targets, and embraced information technology (the replacing of analog electro-mechanical systems with digital ones). As he put it, "We [OPNAV] haven't had [long-range] planning for 30 years and [yet] we're the most powerful country in the world." N8 was attracting the best kind of younger officers and civilians, and any CNO could use the programming process to shape the Navy's future. The many efforts to reorganize OPNAV had not mattered as much as "having the right leaders."[86] Reorganizing OPNAV was therefore not a panacea for the Navy Department's problems.

Blickstein's thoughts—based on many years of successful experience—captured a dilemma facing any CNO. On the one hand, the nation's political leaders wanted a forward-deployed military with great potential fighting power. On the other hand, many of those same leaders expected a major "peace dividend." At the same time, events outside the Navy—especially conflicts between the President and the Republicans in Congress—and often quite outside the Navy's control constrained the range of potential solutions to the basic dilemma.

Blickstein was right in arguing that the Navy needed leaders who could manipulate the programming process to find the resources that would allow the Navy and Marines to become more effective while simultaneously shrinking in size, but the leaders coming to the summits of their careers had grown up in the Cold War, and the sort of ongoing fiscal crisis they faced under CNOs Boorda and Johnson was not something they had had significant experience with. At the same time, the structure of N8, where programming and budgeting were routinely integrated, gave the CNO and the Navy secretary opportunities to exercise their influence, but only they could identify the "correct" goals to pursue. It was a very frustrating situation.

Unfortunately, the post–Cold War budget reviews, done in the summer prior to the beginning of the next fiscal year at the start of October, had become more taxing to the Navy's comptroller staff and to the budget staffs in the Navy's systems commands. As the Naval Air Systems Command (NAVAIR) put it in a paper prepared for the Navy's Inspector General in the late winter of 1996, "the magnitude of budget reductions and the changes to the nature of military operations and changing threat have made adapting to these changes and reflecting them in the appropriate departmental documentation extremely difficult."[87] In plain language, budget officers in NAVAIR were finding it very difficult to roll with the punches. So were their colleagues in OPNAV.

The Devil Is Always in the Details

Secretary of the Navy Dalton, CNO Johnson and VCNO Pilling could not solve this problem because its roots lay outside the Navy—in the post–Cold War world and in the back-and-forth between the Congress and the President that led to unanticipated spending (and spending cuts). But Johnson and Pilling did understand that they needed—at the minimum—to do three things. One was to say openly and often what the Navy could do. That was the point to "Anytime, Anywhere." The second thing they had to do was to find savings in the operations accounts. That meant paying attention to details. Where did the money actually go? What was the Navy paying for? Pilling knew what it should be paying for, and that was readiness in the forward-deployed forces. Readiness in forces not deployed would have to be allowed to slip; it was a concept called "tiered readiness," as Pilling explained to newspaper correspondent George C. Wilson.[88] The third thing was to control the costs of modernizing the ships, aircraft, submarines, and related systems being developed by the Navy Department. In January 1998, for example, the DD-21 program office convinced the DAB that the program was ready to begin development; the required conceptual work was complete. In March, the program office issued a "Request for Proposals" to industry for planned development of a multi-mission ship "optimized for land attack."[89]

The program to acquire the F/A-18E/F had already moved ahead. The prototype F/A-18E had flown in November 1995, and the first "low-rate initial production" F/A-18E was scheduled to take to the air in December 1998. The Navy had opted for the F/A-18E/F over a strike version of the veteran F-14 and a joint attack aircraft program with the Air Force.[90] Congress, mindful of the failure of the A-12 program, had imposed a cost cap on the E/F: its "flyaway cost" could not exceed that of the F/A-18C/D by more than 25 percent.[91] Whereas the Joint Strike Fighter (JSF) program was focused on producing what could be termed "the airplane of the 21st century," the F/A-18E/F program aimed to produce a plane that would cover the transition from the Cold War carrier air wings to those of the years past 2005. The F/A-18E/F program was scheduled to complete the operational testing of the aircraft in early 2000, and full rate production was projected to begin at the start of 2002.[92]

The aircraft had not been without its critics.[93] They had pointed out that the new airplane would lack the range of the A-6 that it was replacing, and that it lacked the radar that made the F-14 a potent air defense fighter. The E/F also encountered an unanticipated "wing drop" problem during prototype testing. In a few mid-air maneuvers, the plane would suddenly and very briefly lose lift on one wing. Critics charged that the F/A-18E/F was potentially unstable and dangerous to fly in a dogfight. Defenders argued that the problems revealed in testing would be remedied, but they also argued that what really mattered was that the F/A-18E/F would reach the fleet in time. This was a version of the old argument about "a bird in the hand" being superior to "two in the bush." However, it masked another issue. The Cold War carriers and their Aegis escorts had fielded an extraordinary, multilayered air defense system. It was a sort of "buzz saw." The authors and defenders of the Maritime Strategy had realized that this buzz saw could be shoved against the Soviet Union's naval air force and deal with it. In effect, a system designed to defend the carriers could be employed offensively. By abandoning the F-14/Phoenix missile combination, the Navy was taking the first layer of "teeth" out of the buzz saw. Critics of the F/A-18E/F said that it was not a good fighter and not an attack airplane that could meet the Navy's requirement. But they also were reluctant to abandon the "buzz saw" even though Russia was no longer an enemy.

What really saved the F/A-18E/F was not just the way that the Naval Air Systems Command and the Boeing Company (which had purchased McDonnell-Douglas, the original developer of the F/A-18) worked together to stay on schedule and near the cost target, but also the way that the acquisition initiatives implemented by Secretary of Defense Perry fostered the birth of a new family of precision-guided munitions—the ordnance that the F/A-18E/F would carry. In 1994, Congress had passed the Federal Acquisition Streamlining Act. Section 5064 of the new law authorized the Defense Department to conduct acquisition pilot programs, programs exempt from the standard reviews mandated in the Federal Acquisition Regulation. One of these programs was a joint-service effort that produced the Joint Direct Attack Munition (JDAM). A JDAM was an unpowered bomb guided to its target by signals from Global Positioning System satellites. It was both accurate and very inexpensive compared to existing guided ordnance; as one wag put it, JDAM was a "smashing success." But JDAM was only one member of a family of precision-guided weapons. It was the short-range weapon; it had been developed both to provide the Navy and Air Force with a new accurate bomb and to show that acquisition reform would work. There were also a medium-range and a long-range weapon in the "family." The F/A-18E/F was designed to carry all three weapons and, if necessary, return with them to its home carrier. This new aircraft/weapon combination made possible a new era of aircraft strike operations for both the Navy and the Air Force.[94]

CNO Johnson and VCNO Pilling were not directly responsible for the F/A-18E/F, though their support for the program was crucial. The direct chain of authority ran from the Navy's assistant secretary for research, development, and acquisition to the Program Executive Office for Tactical Aircraft Systems and then to the F/A-18E/F program officer. But it was the CNO who led the programming and budgeting process and who defended the F/A-18E/F program to the Office of the Secretary of Defense and the Congress. And that defense was essential to the program's success.

That success was not guaranteed, certainly not at the program's beginning. In May 1991, for example, retired Navy Captain Floyd D. Kennedy Jr., USNR, who reviewed naval weapon and aircraft developments for the U.S. Naval Institute's *Proceedings*, noted that the "past eighteen months have been among the most trying in recent memory for naval programs in general and naval aviation in particular." Indeed, "the only new start proposed for the fiscal year 1992–93 budget . . . is one the Navy specifically did not request: upgrades to the F/A-18 Hornet."[95] A year later, Captain Kennedy did not have much better news. Cancellation of the A-12 carrier stealth bomber had thrown "the carefully planned naval aviation road map into disarray," and "development cost growth for the . . . F/A-18E/F" was "reminiscent" of the "A-12 cost overruns only a year ago."[96]

What had saved the program? One answer was that competing aircraft programs had not worked out. A second answer—already given—was that the F/A-18E/F could, like the cancelled A-12, carry the new "family" of precision-guided munitions. A third answer was that aviation officers in OPNAV and in NAVAIR had kept the program alive by making sure it worked and by answering the program's critics.[97] For example, Rear Admiral Bennitt, Director of Air Warfare (N88) in OPNAV, successfully steered the debate over the worth of the F/A-18E/F from the plane's performance in air combat maneuvering to its ability to strike enough targets with precision munitions. Vice Admiral John A. Lockard, commander of the Naval Air Systems Command in the mid-1990s, was adept at convincing members of Congress and officials in the Pentagon that the F/A-18E/F could form the heart of future carrier air groups. And Captain (later Vice Admiral) Joseph D. Dyer, the E/F's program manager (PM), imposed a disciplined risk reduction process on the plane's development that allowed his successors to stay within cost and schedule boundaries.[98]

CNO Johnson's Initiatives

The history of the F/A-18E/F program shows how any CNO is dependent on others in the Navy to do their jobs well. When Admiral Kelso succeeded Admiral Trost as CNO, the Navy's standing with Congress was low because Trost had resisted reducing spending on the Navy in light of the reduction in the tensions of the Cold War. Because Tailhook happened while Kelso was CNO (and also because he had attended), he could not improve the Navy's reputation in the minds of congressional critics. But Admirals Boorda and Johnson were able to do so. By CNO Johnson's second year in office, the sense that the Navy knew where it was going was decidedly enhanced. This could not help but give CNO Johnson added confidence, and that paid off as the fleet staged a series of battle experiments.

Starting in 1997, both the Third and Second Fleets conducted battle experiments developed by the Navy Warfare Development Command (NWDC). The experiments combined simulations with actual operations, and they carried over into 1998, when a battle experiment was made part of Joint Task Force Exercise 98-2, with the *Dwight D. Eisenhower* (CVN-69) battle

Figure 15-2. CNO Admiral Jay L. Johnson, Vice CNO when CNO Boorda committed suicide, was confirmed as Boorda's replacement in August 1996. Johnson, a carrier aviator, had flown combat missions during the war in Vietnam. He was commander of the Second Fleet when chosen to be the Vice Chief of Naval Operations. (NHHC Archives Bio File Copy)

group.[99] One of the problems looked at during this experiment was that of linking computer-assisted air and missile defense planning across a theater. In Desert Storm in 1991, Joint Force Air Component Command (JFACC) missile defense planning in the theater of operations was effectively jury-rigged by officers on the JFACC staff who worked on an ad hoc basis with personnel in the United States. That was clearly not satisfactory in the face of the proliferation of cruise missile systems across the world, and the Navy had developed an air defense command software module that it needed to test at sea. Other fleet battle experiments dealt with the coordination of missile and air attacks in support of a friendly land force and with the staging of amphibious assaults.[100]

To take advantage of the NWDC's concept development and experimentation capability, Johnson appointed Vice Admiral Arthur K. Cebrowski as President of the Naval War College and placed the Warfare Development Command under Cebrowski's control. As Vice Admiral Cebrowski said when he took command of the War College,

> I am here to link the long history of conceptual development at the Naval War College with information age technology, modern concepts [in economics and management], and rigorous operation experiments ... I am here to encourage and support a new type of officer, one who is naturally inclined to operational experimentation and innovation. I foresee officers who view doctrine as a dynamic adaptive process rather than a refuge for the uninformed.[101]

Cebrowski's view was that ideas mattered. His experience in OPNAV had convinced him that the PPBS process was not suited to the post–Cold War strategic environment. He aimed not at another reorganization or a new innovation in management, but at a change in the way that up-and-coming officers thought. Knowing he could not succeed with a frontal attack on the PPBS process, he intended to subvert it.

The Marines, however, kept using the process, bombarding the Navy with concept papers. "Operational Maneuver from the Sea" (OMFTS) in 1996 was followed by "Ship to Objective Maneuver" in 1997. The latter was followed in 1997 by "Maritime Prepositioning Force (MPF) 2010 and Beyond," and in 1998 the Marines issued "Seabased Logistics." These doctrinal statements followed logically from the earlier documents. The goal of "Operational Maneuver from the Sea" had been to smooth out the movement of troops and vehicles from assault ships to the shore. Under the OMFTS concept, the attacking force would not construct even a temporary base ashore. Instead, it would act as though there were no land-sea divide. Assault forces would move in one step from sea to objectives ashore, even to objectives located significant distances inland.

For ideas as to how this might be done, the Marines had drawn on the Defense Science Board Task Force on Strategic Mobility. The task force had considered the future of maritime prepositioning ships. These floating warehouses had not been thought of as an integral part of an amphibious assault force. Instead, they were to move inshore once the Marines had captured a port with enough deep water to take the prepositioned support ships. But that requirement tied the Marines to deep-water ports. OMFTS and "Sea Based Logistics" proposed to break that requirement. But that wasn't the only new idea. Traditionally, amphibious ships put organized and fully prepared forces ashore, even in the face of enemy resistance, and the maritime prepositioning ships came along later like buses. The Marines wanted the prepositioned ships to be more like assault ships, with Marines on board ready to fight once they landed. That would mean building something new or converting existing hulls. The Marines understood that such ships might be very expensive but argued that it was the only way for them to fight in the 21st century. Finally, the Marines wanted a fleet of prepositioned ships that could sustain a force ashore without having to rely on a deep-draft port.[102] They wanted sustained logistical support without a fixed presence. That *was* new.

It also put heavy pressure on the Navy's programs and budgets. The Navy was short of funds, but the Marines wanted some big-ticket items, including the V-22 tilt-rotor aircraft, new and rebuilt helicopters, the expeditionary fighting vehicle that could swim at high speed and provide fire support once ashore, an improved air cushion landing craft, and a new fleet of maritime preposition ships. It was "crunch time." In the 1990s, the Marines had worked on a new and exciting approach to what had been termed "amphibious operations." They had come up with what amounted to a new concept for a new fleet. At the same time, the Navy worked to fix the problems that Operation Desert Storm had revealed and changed the nature of the battle fleet so that it was better able to support just the sort of amphibious assault that the Marines were trying to move away from.[103] The lack of funds meant that the Marines and the Navy were in a zero-sum game. Gains by one side would come at the expense of the other—and this in what was supposed to be an effective *naval* force.

Richard Danzig: Another "Activist" Secretary

Richard Danzig, Secretary of the Navy starting on 16 November 1998, walked right into this conflict. But it was no surprise to him. Danzig, a PhD and brilliant Rhodes Scholar, had served as Under Secretary of the Navy from November 1993 until May 1997. He took office committed to action, and he lived up to that commitment. As historian Haynes observed, Danzig "was one of the few Clinton appointees in the Pentagon that had the support of both parties," and Danzig "quickly gained the reputation on Capitol Hill as an effective and innovative administrator, and as a figure brilliant enough to change what many saw as a hidebound and scandal-ridden" Navy.[104] Danzig was especially good at challenging Navy clichés. Just what was "presence," anyway? Could a nuclear submarine exercise it, even if the submarine wasn't seen? Did presence require a ship or submarine to be around all the time—or perhaps most of the time—or maybe only now and then? Was forward deployment more important for friends and allies than it was for neutrals or potential opponents? The new secretary knew there might not be answers to these sorts of questions, but he wasn't afraid to say so, and he definitely wasn't afraid to ask questions. But what could he do in the two years before the next presidential election? What did he *need* to do?

One thing he needed to do was see to it that the Navy went into the 2001 QDR with a new statement of its strategy. OPNAV's N51 had produced a tentative statement entitled "A Maritime

Strategy for the 21st Century." In his thesis, Captain Haynes argued that the early drafts of "A Maritime Strategy" did not win support from the Marine Corps or from other commentators familiar with the Navy.[105] He also argued that though CNO Johnson and Marine Corps Commandant General Krulak eventually signed "A Maritime Strategy," Secretary Danzig wanted to rewrite it. According to Haynes, "the two chiefs balked and rescinded it, and agreed not to send another [copy] to Danzig." As a result, "A Maritime Strategy for the 21st Century" was not published.[106]

Secretary Danzig was more successful in other areas. At the beginning of March 1999, he defended the Clinton administration's budget submission by arguing that it paid needed attention to sailors' pay and benefits, acquisition of needed systems (like the F/A-18E/F), and "much needed increases in our maintenance, spare parts, and training accounts."[107] The secretary had already sent two letters to Navy personnel describing his concerns and his goals, and he sent another, similar, letter several weeks before testifying to the Seapower Subcommittee of the Senate Armed Services Committee. In his third letter, he described the initiatives that he had been pursuing with the help of the CNO and the Commandant. One was setting aside money for the "Smart Work" program, an effort that was designed to reduce dramatically the hard and time-consuming maintenance and cleaning that sailors had done for decades. A second initiative was improving ship design to improve life on board and to facilitate the "Smart Ship" investments the Navy Department was making (and planned to continue to make). The secretary also told the Navy that he was just as committed to recruiting better qualified sailors as he was to making sure that the work they did was meaningful, rewarding, and effective. And he made it clear that he was reinstating the policy of paying retirees 50 percent of their basic pay after 20 years of service. He also wanted to reward the Navy's "best performers" with higher pay, and he informed Navy personnel that they could gain access to personally and professionally useful information via the internet.[108]

Danzig continued to "spread the word" about his initiatives. Speaking to the National Defense Industrial Association on 9 March 1999, he stressed acquisition successes (including information technology), his Smart Work and Smart Ship programs, the need to invest in research and development that would improve life aboard ships, fielding unmanned aerial vehicles (UAV) for reconnaissance, improving or replacing the Navy aircraft that were not fighter-bombers (like the E-2C airborne warning and control planes), sustaining the professionalism of the acquisition work force, and "integrating" the Navy and Marine Corps headquarters staffs.[109] He also raised the issue of what he called the "psychology of conscription." What he meant by that was that the Navy treated young sailors like they were a source of cheap labor. But they weren't cheap labor, and it was important to free them from tedious tasks like scraping old paint from ships' hulls so that they could do what mattered. What was the sense of having a 21st century Navy if the sailors running it were treated like it was still World War II? As Danzig put it in an article he wrote for the fall 1999 issue of the Navy League's *Seapower* magazine, "People are our most important asset."[110] The secretary carried the argument one step farther: Get the right people, and they will work *smarter*. That smarter work will actually get the job done faster and better—and therefore cheaper, and the money saved will buy modern ships and software.

If there was one area where Secretary Danzig was not so successful, it was in "integrating" the staffs of the Marine Corps and the Navy. For example, though Navy and Marine pilots "share the title 'naval aviator,' receive the same training, and fly many of the same aircraft, [why don't] our services . . . have well-coordinated plans for developing, maintaining, and using our aviation assets?"[111] He answered his own question by saying that the cause was a lack of coordination "and a lack of understanding of each other's culture and doctrine."[112] But was that so? Or was the reason that senior officers in both services had not done a good job of thinking through the implications of "operational maneuver from the sea," and "ship to objective maneuver," and "seabased logistics?"

In 1985, the Navy and Marines were committed to the Maritime Strategy. Once the Cold War ended, both services had searched for a new role. The Marines had it easier. The post–Cold War world wasn't necessarily peaceful or stable, and the Marines—who had historically been the shock troops of the republic—could see a critical role for themselves in this new environment. But Operational Maneuver from the Sea gave the Marines a new vision—they could maneuver from the sea in such a way as to play a *decisive* role in a conflict that was less than a major war. Their ability to be decisive was dependent on their own resources *and* on what the Navy could give them. It was possible to take a very big step and think of a new, maritime service, where the organizational integration that Secretary Danzig talked about was the "norm" and not the exception.

As his time as CNO wound down, Admiral Johnson took stock of his administration's accomplishments in an address he gave at the June 1999 Current Strategy Forum of the Naval War College. The future Navy, he argued, would be "network-centric," based on digital technology and a secure digital communications system. Speed would be a paramount necessity—"speed with which we understand our environment, speed with which we share that understanding, speed with which we make decisions, and most importantly, the speed with which our desired effects are achieved."[113] The ability to gain access "to information, people, ideas, and most importantly, to key domains of operations" (the sea, space, and cyberspace) would be essential to the future naval force. Would that future force be radically different than the one the CNO led? No. As Johnson put it, "The Navy After Next must blend the best capabilities of our current force with the capabilities of one specifically designed for assured access in the close littoral . . ."[114]

The CNO did not say, "Set the existing force aside, and we'll start over." The future would be reached through evolution and not revolution. Yet Admirals Johnson and Pilling, with Secretary Danzig and the senior officers of the Marine Corps, had set the foundation of a new type of naval force. It was not clear whether enough officers in both the Navy and the Marine Corps understood that and accepted it, but CNOs Kelso, Boorda, and Johnson had initiated and sustained a process and ways of thinking that were in fact changing the force that had, in the 1980s, planned to implement the Cold War Maritime Strategy. Moving the "train" from one "track" to another had taken ten years.

Notes

[1] An excellent statement of the Navy and Marine Corps task was "The Military After Next, Shaping U.S. Armed Forces for the Next Century," by ADM Paul David Miller, CINCLANT, U.S. Naval Institute *Proceedings*, vol. 120, no. 2 (Feb. 1994), 41–44.

[2] "Les" (Leslie Aspin Jr.) Aspin had served as a systems analyst in the Office of the Secretary of Defense when Robert S. McNamara was the Secretary of Defense.

[3] Les Aspin, *Report on the Bottom-Up Review* (Oct. 1993). https://www.dtic.mil/cgi-bin/GetTRDoc?AD=ADA359953 (24 Aug. 2016).

[4] Ibid., 3.

[5] Ibid., 7.

[6] Ibid., 8.

[7] Ibid., 36–38.

[8] Ibid., 53.

[9] Ibid., 57.

[10] Ibid., 69–70.

[11] Ibid., 85.

[12] Ibid.

[13] Tom Philpot, "As a Ship Handler," U.S. Naval Institute *Proceedings*, vol. 121, no. 4 (Apr. 1995), 33.

[14] Memo from David Z. Robinson, Executive Director of the Carnegie Commission on Science, Technology, and Government, to OPNAV staff, subj: "Carnegie Commission Statement on Defense Procurement," 10 Mar. 1993, in the collection of Thomas C. Hone. The memo is a comment on "A Radical Reform of the Defense Acquisition System," issued by the Carnegie Commission the previous Dec. (New York: Carnegie Commission, 1 Dec. 1992).

[15] Christopher H. Hanks, "Financial Accountability at the DOD: Reviewing the Bidding," *Defense Acquisition Review Journal*, vol. 16, no. 2 (July 2009), Defense Acquisition University, Ft. Belvoir, VA, 183.

[16] OPNAVINST 5430.48D ("Office of the Chief of Naval Operations [OPNAV] Organization Manual") of 29 Mar. 1993 specified that the CNO "takes precedence over all other officers on the naval service" and "also serves as a member of the Joint Chiefs of Staff," where he "serves as a military advisor to the President, the National Security Council, and the Secretary of Defense." 5430.48 also stated that the "CNO serves as the principal naval advisor and naval executive to the Secretary of the Navy on the conduct of the naval activities of the Department of the Navy." In the collection of Thomas C. Hone.

[17] Nick Kotz, "Breaking Point," *Washingtonian*, Dec. 1996, 93–121. Also see Malcolm Steinberg, *Admiral Boorda's Navy* (West Conshohocken, PA: Infinity Publishing, 2011). In his first ten months as CNO, ADM Boorda visited 66 ships, mixing with more than 60,000 sailors. See

"... We're Tinkering with Success Here," an interview with ADM Boorda, U.S. Naval Institute *Proceedings*, vol. 121, no. 4, (Apr. 1995), 30.

[18] Interview, ADM T. Joseph Lopez, USN, by Thomas C. Hone, 12 Nov. 2014.

[19] Tom Philpott, "Congressional Watch," U. S. Naval Institute *Proceedings*, vol. 121, no. 5 (May 1995), 165.

[20] "... We're Tinkering with Success Here," 34–35.

[21] Robert O. Work, "Naval Transformation and the Littoral Combat Ship," Center for Strategic and Budgetary Assessments, Washington, DC, Feb. 2004, 21. http://csbaonline.org/publications/2004/02/naval-transformation-and-the-littoral-combat-ship/ (24 Aug. 2016).

[22] According to VADM Albert J. Herberger, who had worked with ADM Boorda often, the CNO was "always able to get it right on the first draft—or at worst on the second draft," when he was writing letters, instructions, or memos. Interview with ADM Herberger by Thomas C. Hone, 28 Oct. 2014.

[23] VADM Michael P. Kalleres went from OPNAV to command (as a vice admiral) the Second Fleet. In 1992, Kalleres was appointed head of the Military Sealift Command, where he "re-engineered" the organization. It functioned so effectively that—for the first time—it actually earned $400 million. VADM Kalleres retired from the Navy in 1994. http://www.usspreble.org/kalleres.html (24 Aug. 2016).

[24] VADM Herberger was the first graduate of the U.S. Merchant Marine Academy to reach flag rank in the U.S. Navy. He was in no way an "outsider," but his background was different from that of most senior Navy officers who had graduated from the U.S. Naval Academy. http://www.liquisearch.com/albert_j_herberger (24 Aug. 2016).

[25] https://www.usnwc.edu/About/Chief-Naval-Operations-Strategic-Studies-Group.aspx (25 Aug. 2016).

[26] "Restructuring Naval Forces for New Challenges," The FY 1995–1999 Navy Program Review, Nov. 1993, 10. In the collection of Thomas C. Hone.

[27] "Department of the Navy Consolidated Planning and Programming Guidance (DNCPPG)," John H. Dalton, Secretary of the Navy, 6 Dec. 1993, 2–3. In the collection of Thomas C. Hone.

[28] DCNO, Resources, Warfare Requirements, and Assessments (N8), *Force 2001: Vision, Presence, Power* (1997), 29, in the collection of Thomas C. Hone. See also *Organizing OPNAV (1970–2009)*, by Peter M. Swartz, with Michael Markowitz, CAB D0020997. A5/2 Rev (Jan. 2010), Center for Naval Analyses, Alexandria, VA. https://www.cna.org/cna_files (25 Aug. 2016).

[29] Ltr. From Bruce Powers to Thomas C. Hone, Aug. 2015. In the collection of Thomas C. Hone.

[30] DCNO, Resources, Warfare Requirements, and Assessments (N8), *Force 2001: Vision, Presence, Power* (1997). Also, "Evolution of the Assessment Process," briefing by Mr. Matt Henry, N81, 2 May 1995, in the collection of Thomas C. Hone.

[31] John H. Dalton, ADM J. M. Boorda, and GEN Carl E. Mundy, USMC, "Forward . . . From the Sea," 1. http://www.dtic.mil/jv2010/navy/b014.pdf (25 Aug. 2016).

[32] CAPT Peter D. Haynes, USN, *American Naval Thinking in the Post–Cold War Era: The U.S. Navy and the Emergence of a Maritime Strategy, 1989–2007*, PhD Dissertation, Naval Postgraduate School, Monterey, CA (2013), 136.

[33] President William J. Clinton, *A National Security Strategy of Engagement and Enlargement* (Washington, DC: GPO, July 1994). http://nssarchive.us/NSSR/1994.pdf.

[34] John H. Dalton, ADM J. M. Boorda, and GEN Carl E. Mundy, USMC, "Forward . . . From the Sea," 9.

[35] FADM Ernest J. King, USN, "War Reports," in *The War Reports of General of the Army George C. Marshall, General of the Army H. H. Arnold, and Fleet Admiral Ernest J. King* (New York: J. B. Lippincott Company, 1947), Appendix B, 763. Including vessels supplied through Lend Lease, almost 110,000 mine craft, patrol craft, auxiliaries, district craft, landing craft, and small boats were completed for the Navy between 7 Dec. 1941 and 1 Oct. 1945.

[36] Friedman, *U.S. Amphibious Ships and Craft*.

[37] LHDs are large amphibious assault ships—as large as a World War II *Essex*-class aircraft carrier. They carry aircraft (fixed-wing and rotary-wing), Marines, vehicles, and landing craft. LPDs are very modern amphibious transport docks capable of carrying helicopters, landing craft, vehicles, Marines, and supplies. The V-22 is a large aircraft whose wings change direction to convert from vertical lift to level flight and then back again. LCACs are large air-cushion vehicles that can quickly move from ship to shore.

[38] "The Golden Age of Naval Forces Is Here," an interview with GEN Mundy, U.S. Naval Institute *Proceedings*, vol. 120, no. 11 (Nov. 1994), 78.

[39] The aircraft crashed into the Potomac River. All seven aboard were killed.

[40] GEN Carl E. Mundy, USMC (Ret.), "Navy-Marine Corps Team: Equalizing the Partnership," U.S. Naval Institute *Proceedings*, vol. 121, no. 12 (Dec. 1995), 29.

[41] Ibid., 28.

[42] Ltr from Bruce Powers to Thomas C. Hone, Aug. 2015.

[43] Friedman, *U.S. Destroyers*, rev. ed., 434.

[44] Ibid., 445.

[45] Interview of ADM T. Joseph Lopez, USN, by Thomas C. Hone, 12 Nov. 2014.

[46] Memo, from: Jeffrey Sands, "Interview with VADM Lopez on program planning process," 18 Apr. 1996, Center for Naval Analyses, Alexandria (now Arlington), VA. In the collection of Thomas C. Hone.

[47] Interview of ADM T. Joseph Lopez, USN, by Thomas C. Hone, 12 Nov. 2014.

[48] The process by which Grumman Aircraft's proposed "Quickstrike" variant of the F-14D became a reality is summarized in Thomason's *Strike from the Sea, U.S. Navy Attack Aircraft from Skyraider to Super Hornet, 1948–Present*, 192–94.

[49] John H. Dalton, Secretary of the Navy, "Fiscal Year 1998 Program Objectives Memorandum (POM98) Guidance," memo to the CNO, the Commandant of the Marine Corps, the Under Secretary of the Navy, the General Counsel, and the Assistant Secretaries of the Navy, 11 Sept. 1995, 2–3. In the collection of Thomas C. Hone.

[50] An example of how the joint military assessment process "helped" was the decision to retire the A-6 aircraft. N88, the OPNAV sponsor of aviation programs, agreed to accept the retirement of the A-6 even though it was not obvious that the F/A-18E/F would be a suitable replacement. This was a gamble on the part of N88.

[51] Thomas P. M. Barnett and Henry H. Gaffney Jr., "Force Structure Assessment Team (FSAT)," 5 Mar. 1996 Working Paper (05 96-0363), Center for Naval Analyses, Alexandria (now Arlington), VA. In the collection of Thomas C. Hone.

[52] J. Sands, "Interview with MGEN Oster, DC/S P&R, 27 Mar. 1996," 29 Mar. 1996, Center for Naval Analyses, Alexandria (now Arlington), VA. In the collection of Thomas C. Hone.

[53] Interview of ADM T. Joseph Lopez, USN, by Thomas C. Hone, 12 Nov. 2014.

[54] Interview of VADM Albert J. Herberger, USN, by Thomas C. Hone, 28 Oct. 2014. VADM Herberger also noted that ADM Boorda had not had any experience in dealing with media criticism. Boorda's career had been a string of successes, and therefore he did not know how to react to "perceived failure."

[55] "The Reminiscences of Admiral Frank B. Kelso II, USN (Ret.)," interviewed by Paul Stillwell, (Annapolis, MD: U.S. Naval Institute, 2009), 762.

[56] *Testimony of Adm. Jay L. Johnson, USN, before the Senate Armed Services Committee Hearing on His Reappointment to Admiral and to Serve as Chief of Naval Operations*, July 31, 1996, 2. Navy Public Affairs Library. http://www.navy.mil/navpalib/.www/welcome.html (25 Aug. 2016).

[57] Ibid., 3.

[58] Ibid., 6–7.

[59] Ibid., 9–10.

[60] Ibid., 11, 13, 15.

[61] Ibid., 17.

[62] Ibid., 21–22.

[63] Memorandum for the Chief of Naval Operations, subj: "OPNAV Reorganization," 20 June 1996. Bruce Powers had developed a reorganization plan and briefed it to ADMs Boorda, Lopez, and Arthur in 1995. Ltr, from Bruce Powers to Thomas C. Hone, Aug. 2015. Both documents in the collection of Thomas C. Hone.

[64] George C. Wilson, *This War Really Matters: Inside the Fight for Defense Dollars* (Washington, DC: CQ Press, 2000), 15.

[65] These reports were in addition to JCS Chairman GEN John M. Shalikashvili's *Joint Vision 2010*, released in July 1996. *Joint Vision 2010* offered a vision of future U.S. forces: they would be digitally connected, mobile, and lethal.

[66] Private conversations of Thomas C. Hone with N8 personnel in Oct. 1996.

[67] As a senator, Cohen had participated in the drafting of the Competition in Contracting Act (1984), the Federal Acquisition Reform Act (1996), and the Information Technology Management Reform Act (1996). The last was usually referred to as the "Clinger-Cohen Act."

[68] Wilson, *This War Really Matters*, 27.

[69] ADM J. M. Boorda, "Time for a '. . . Sea' Change," U. S. Naval Institute *Proceedings*, 120, No. 8 (Aug. 1994), 9–10.

[70] Haynes, *American Naval Thinking in the Post–Cold War Era*, 158.

[71] Ibid., 157.

[72] Ibid., 158.

[73] Ibid., 162–66.

[74] "Forward . . . From the Sea: The Navy Operational Concept," Mar. 1997, with a "Foreward" by ADM Jay L. Johnson, USN, Chief of Naval Operations, 1. http://www.navy.mil/navydata/policy/fromsea/ffseanoc.html (25 Aug. 2016).

[75] Ibid., 2.

[76] Ibid., 7.

[77] Haynes, *American Naval Thinking in the Post–Cold War Era*, 177.

[78] See Norman Friedman, *Network-Centric Warfare* (Annapolis, MD: Naval Institute Press, 2009), Part 3.

[79] Ibid., 178.

[80] ADM Jay L. Johnson, "The Navy Operational Concept: Forward . . . From the Sea," *Seapower*, vol. 40, no. 5 (May 1997).

[81] Wilson, *This War Really Matters*, 29–31.

[82] James R. East, et. al., *Assessing the Navy's Assessment Process for POM-00*, CRM 98-97/ Aug. 1998, Center for Naval Analyses, Alexandria, VA. See also briefing, "Navy Long Range Planning," CDR Sam Tangredi, Strategy and Concepts Branch (N513), Mar. 1998. Both documents in the collection of Thomas C. Hone.

[83] Bruce Powers, "Which Issues Belong in the Box?" a briefing to the Navy Study group, 10 July 1997, slide 9. In the collection of Thomas C. Hone.

[84] ADM Jay L. Johnson, "Anytime, Anywhere: A Navy for the 21st Century," U.S. Naval Institute *Proceedings*, Vol. 123, Nov. 1997.

[85] H. H. Gaffney, then a senior member of the staff of the Center for Naval Analyses, made these points in memos and papers produced while studying OPNAV on behalf of VCNO Pilling in the fall of 1997.

[86] Interview of Irving N. Blickstein, N8B, Center for Naval Analyses staff, 24 Dec. 1997, especially 3. In the collection of Thomas C. Hone.

[87] Enclosure (2) to "Command Inspection of Commander, Naval Air Systems Command (NAVAIRSYSCOM)," Naval Inspector General, Ser 02B/0786, 5 Mar. 1996 (in N09B1 files), 4.

[88] Wilson, *This War Really Matters*, 58–59.

[89] Robert O. Work, *Naval Transformation and the Littoral Combat Ship* (Washington, DC: Center for Strategic and Budgetary Assessments, 2004), 41.

[90] Thomason, *Strike from the Sea, U.S. Navy Attack Aircraft from Skyraider to Super Hornet, 1948–Present*, ch. 12. See also, *F/A-18 Hornet, A Navy Success Story*, by Dennis R. Jenkins (New York: McGraw-Hill, 2000).

[91] "Flyaway cost" was the cost of actually making one representative aircraft. It included the actual cost of production and the cost of the tools and machines required to produce that plane. By contrast, acquisition cost as measured covered the plane's life cycle and included costs of research and development and costs of maintaining the aircraft and the cost of training those who flew the plane and took care of it.

[92] Dates from "F/A-18E/F Acquisition Strategy," a briefing by Mr. Richard Gilpin, PMA-265, Naval Air Systems Command, to students at the Industrial College of the Armed Forces, 19 Oct. 1999. In the collection of Thomas C. Hone.

[93] See, for example, a strong critique by James P. Stevenson, author of a history of the failed A-12 program, in the Apr. 1998 U.S. Naval Institute *Proceedings*, 24.

[94] See "Spiral Development and the F/A-18," by RADM (Sel) Jeffrey A. Wieringa, USN, in *Program Manager*, May–June 2003, 50–52.

[95] Floyd D. Kennedy Jr., "U.S. Naval Aircraft and Weapon Developments in 1990," U.S. Naval Institute *Proceedings*, vol. 117, no. 5 (May 1991), 160. The systems canceled or dropped from the Navy's budget requests from the beginning of 1990 included the A-12 carrier bomber, the F-14D, the Advanced Tactical Support aircraft, the Navy's Advanced Tactical Fighter, the P-7 long-range antisubmarine patrol plane, and the V-22 Osprey. The V-22's funding was restored by Congress.

[96] Floyd D. Kennedy Jr., "U.S. Naval Aircraft and Weapon Developments in 1991," U.S. Naval Institute *Proceedings*, vol. 118, no. 5 (May 1992), 169.

[97] See the statement of Philip E. Coyle III, Director, Operational Test and Evaluation, Office of the Secretary of Defense, in *Hearings* before the Committee on Armed Services, United States Senate, Part 4, (3, 10, 17, and 24 Mar. 1998), 125–31.

[98] Interview of John J. Dicks, formerly of the Naval Air Systems Command and later Deputy Program Manager of the En Route Air Traffic Systems Development in the Federal Aviation Administration, by Thomas C. Hone, 3 Oct. 2000. In the collection of Thomas C. Hone.

[99] Floyd D. Kennedy Jr., "U.S. Naval Aircraft and Weapon Developments," U.S. Naval Institute *Proceedings*, May 1998, 120.

[100] Floyd D. Kennedy Jr., "U.S. Naval Aircraft and Weapon Developments," U.S. Naval Institute *Proceedings*, May 1999, 112, 114.

[101] ADM Jay L. Johnson, USN, Chief of Naval Operations, and VADM Arthur K. Cebrowski, USN, "Remarks at the Naval War College Change of Command and the Stand-up of the Navy Warfare Development Command," 24 July 1998, 5. http://www.navy.mil (25 Aug. 2016).

[102] Robert O. Work, "Thinking About Seabasing: All Ahead, Slow" (Washington, DC: Center for Strategic and Budgetary Assessments, 2006), 98–101.

[103] Ibid., 102–103.

[104] Haynes, *American Naval Thinking in the Post–Cold War Era*, 195.

[105] Ibid., 201.

[106] Ibid., 201–202.

[107] *Statement of the Honorable Richard Danzig, Secretary of the Navy*, before the Senate Armed Services Committee Seapower Subcommittee, 3 Mar. 1999. http://www.navy.mil (5 July 2014).

[108] Ltr, from the Secretary of the Navy to all Marines and Sailors, Feb. 1999. http://www.navy.mil (5 July 2014).

[109] Honorable Richard Danzig, Secretary of the Navy, remarks at the National Defense Industrial Association luncheon, 9 Mar. 1999. http://www.navy.mil (5 July 2014).

[110] Richard Danzig, Secretary of the Navy, "A Commitment to Principles," *Seapower* (Navy League of the United States), Fall 1999.

[111] Ibid.

[112] Ibid.

[113] ADM Jay L. Johnson, Chief of Naval Operations, address to the Current Strategy Forum, Naval War College, 15 June 1999. http://www.navy.mil (5 July 2014).

[114] Ibid.

CHAPTER 16

Admiral Vernon Clark: Readiness, Reorganization, and War

Introduction

Admiral Vernon E. Clark faced two major challenges as the Chief of Naval Operations. The first he understood well. Since the end of the Cold War in 1991, every CNO had had to justify the Navy's existence, lead efforts to determine the size and composition of the Navy, and support the unified and regional combatant commanders. Clark—the first CNO with a master's degree in business administration—had some very definite ideas about how OPNAV should be organized and how the OPNAV staff should support the fleet as the fleet supported the regional combatant commanders. As far as this challenge was concerned, the new CNO hit the ground running when he was sworn in as Chief of Naval Operations on 12 July 2000.

In one sense, Clark was just the right officer for the job. Donald Rumsfeld, appointed Defense secretary by President George W. Bush in January 2001, had in mind major changes in how the Department of Defense should be managed. As the military service chiefs discovered in 2001, Rumsfeld's leadership style was demanding. But President Bush had made Rumsfeld his Defense secretary in order to force change on the Pentagon. As the President and his Defense secretary saw things, it had been almost ten years since the Soviet Union had broken up, yet U.S. military forces—and U.S. military management practices—looked much like they had during the Cold War. The President and Rumsfeld wanted something else and were determined to get it.

But then, less than 14 months after he had taken over from former CNO Jay Johnson, Clark's Pentagon headquarters was attacked by suicidal Islamic terrorists—the young men who hijacked four large airliners and gone after targets in New York and Washington, D.C. on and after 11 September 2001, Clark and his newly organized staff had to work to support military operations against terrorists while at the same time fashioning a more modern fleet. Instead of driving events, Clark was suddenly faced with the prospect that events would drive him. His second challenge—applying the power of the Navy to the operations against terrorists around the world while simultaneously pursuing his management reforms—was not one he had planned for.

Clark Takes Command

On becoming Chief of Naval Operations, Admiral Clark quickly sent a message to all commands in which he said that, "Although there is more to the Navy than the Fleet, the Fleet must be the center of our thinking and action." He followed that statement with "OPNAV will be realigned to provide a strong advocate for war fighting and readiness."[1] In a "personal for" message to senior Navy leaders, the new CNO insisted that "We need to know what our readiness requirements really are and make strategic decisions that support those requirements, not just react to fiscal restraints . . ." As he would say again and again in the months to follow, "[W]e need to get this right!"[2]

By 17 August 2000, CNO Clark's "OPNAV Alignment Working Group" had a draft plan to reorganize the OPNAV staff, and he wanted it fully implemented by 30 September 2000.[3] The point to changing OPNAV's organization was to create "an OPNAV organization with a Navy-wide corporate perspective to provide independent analysis and advice to [the] CNO/VCNO." Clark's goal was to establish "a CNO/VCNO led formal, open decision-making process."[4] The major changes proposed by the Alignment Working Group were as follows:

> First, transfer sponsorship of fleet training programs to N4, the DCNO for Logistics, and eliminate an N7 dedicated only to Navy training.
>
> Second, focus the DCNO for Logistics (N4) on readiness and give N4 more authority in the acquisition process in order to make clear the manpower requirements of new systems.
>
> Third, create a DCNO for Warfare Requirements and Programs (initially N9; then N7).
>
> Fourth, reduce the size and scope of authority of N8. Focus N8 on programming and budgeting.
>
> Fifth, create the post of assistant CNO for theater missile defense.
>
> Sixth, reestablish the CNO Executive Board (CEB) and a Navy Requirements Oversight Council (NROC) chaired by the Vice Chief of Naval Operations.
>
> Seventh, change the IR3B to the IR2B/R2B (Integrated Resource Review Board/Resource Review Board).
>
> Eighth, focus N3/5 *away* from broad strategy and policy and toward assessing the "impact of current operations on readiness."[5] In October, as part of this change, Clark shifted the responsibility for preparing for quadrennial defense reviews (QDRs) from N3/5 to N8.
>
> Ninth, create "capability sponsors" to integrate "platform and system operational requirements and capabilities within a specific Mission Capability Package." These cross-platform sponsors would be proposed by N9 (later N7) and approved by the CEB.

The Alignment Working Group headed its summary slide with a quotation from Admiral J. Paul Reason, who had retired in 1999 after commanding the Atlantic Fleet: "Most corporations that have tried various solutions to their own problems have failed in *implementation*. . . . The real challenge is not to determine what the problems are and how to solve them, but to do what needs to be done."[6] Admiral Reason had captured CNO Clark's vision—to make sure that the Navy could stay forward deployed in adequate numbers by wringing the most efficiency out of its methods of training, acquisition, and operations.

On 28 August 2000, VCNO Admiral Donald L. Pilling sent a message to OPNAV and Navy secretariat staff describing the new alignment, scheduled to begin on 1 October. Pilling's message noted that the N84 (antisubmarine warfare), N85 (expeditionary warfare), N86 (surface warfare), N87 (submarine warfare), and N88 (air warfare) divisions would be moved from N8 to the new N7 (DCNO for Warfare Requirements and Programs). Pilling's brief message also noted the "refocusing" of N4 as the DCNO for Fleet Readiness and Logistics. The realignment, the message stressed, had to be "accomplished without growth in OPNAV military or civilian billets." Finally, the VCNO announced that "a flag-level study group will be established . . . to examine the appropriate alignment for Navy training responsibilities and resources." Hopefully, their work would lead to "a revolution in Navy training."[7]

In October 2000, the CNO and the new N7, Vice Admiral Dennis V. McGinn, announced that they had created N70, the Warfare Integration position, headed initially by Rear Admiral Daniel R. Bowler, who had served in the Joint Staff J8 (Force Structure, Resources and Assessments Directorate). Bowler was responsible for compelling the platform sponsors in N7 to

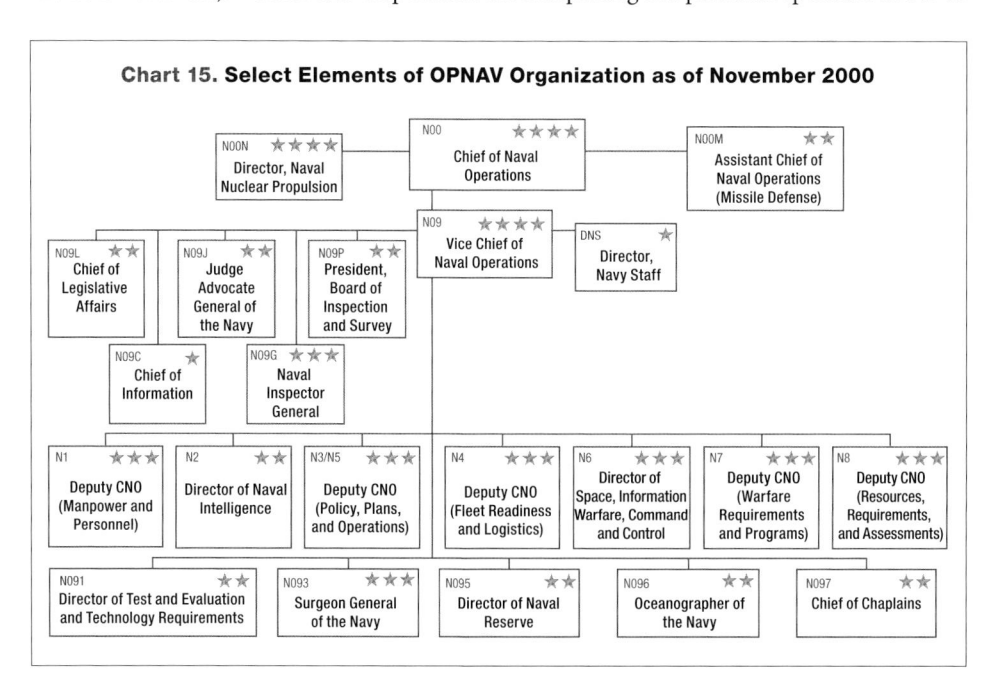

Chart 15. Select Elements of OPNAV Organization as of November 2000

justify their program proposals in terms of broad "warfighting requirements." Under the new organization, N8 focused on developing the current program and budget and on preparing for the QDR. N7 focused on requirements and the composition of the future Navy.[8]

CNO Clark justified the reorganization on several grounds. First, it was a means of moving his own staff and Navy officers in the fleet away from a focus on platforms (submarines, ships, and planes) and toward a focus on "capabilities." What capabilities did the Navy need in order to wage successful campaigns in support of the nation's goals? What combination of platforms and systems—what mix of capabilities—would work best? What would that mix cost? Second, Clark was after the "bow wave," the program costs that were put off to the future in anticipation of an increase in the Navy's budget. As he said in January 2001 to the members of the Surface Navy Association, "I don't want any more understated requirements. I've had enough of it . . . It's time to put that methodology behind us . . . it's wrong." What he meant was that there was a tendency for programmers to push unpleasant news about costs into the "out years"—the future, where it was often assumed that the Navy budget would be larger. As Clark argued, it was not going to be larger, and the OPNAV staff had to produce Program Objective Memoranda for the Office of the Secretary of Defense that adequately expressed what operating and maintaining the Navy cost in the next fiscal year and in the near-term future as well. If that meant making risky choices, then the choices had to be made and the risks made explicit.[9]

CNO Clark also had his eye on the Navy's shore-based systems commands, especially Naval Sea Systems Command (NAVSEA) and Naval Air Systems Command (NAVAIR). The number of people working in both had been cut after the end of the Cold War, but the demands on the systems commands stayed high because of naval operations in the Balkans and in Central Command's area of responsibility. The initial solution to this dilemma of reduced infrastructure and high demands for support from the fleet had been developed under former CNO Frank Kelso. It was based on a distinction between "core" support and readiness capabilities and those that were not "core." The latter could be contracted out, supposedly allowing the Navy to enlarge or shrink shore-based infrastructure relatively quickly in response to changes in national strategy or defense spending.

The Office of the Secretary of Defense (OSD) accepted this policy when the Deputy Under Secretary of Defense for Logistics said in November 1993 that the Defense Department's policy stressed retaining "core" capabilities under government control. A "core" capability was then defined as one needed to "meet readiness and sustainability requirements of the weapons systems" that supported the "contingency scenarios" of the Joint Chiefs of Staff. "Core" capabilities in the Navy's shore installations were those that minimized operational risks and guaranteed "required readiness." However, "core" depot capabilities were the minimum necessary; they were not those held in reserve in case of an extended national emergency.[10]

This policy was a compromise between the extremes of wholescale privatization and no privatization whatsoever. The compromise was written into law.[11] The decision to keep certain "core readiness capabilities" in the hands of the military services thus hinged on planning done by the regional combatant commanders and approved by the Joint Staff. This was a consequence of the Goldwater-Nichols legislation. In effect, the Navy's systems command became clients of the regional combatant commanders and their Navy component commanders. This was a dramatic change. It was also a development that former Navy secretary John Lehman had argued would harm the Navy because it would weaken the ability of the Navy secretariat to plan the future "naval" force.

An assumption shared by both CNO Clark and senior officials in the systems command in 2000 was that the adoption of automated information systems and digital communications within the Navy would facilitate fleet readiness while reducing its cost, thereby freeing up funds for other uses. NAVAIR in particular had begun adopting the notion of organizing internally by "core competencies" and creating "integrated product teams" to deal with major acquisition and support issues.[12] The maturing of digital data storage, digital quantitative analysis techniques, and digital communications aided these changes. At first, they had automated the personnel-intensive processes already in existence. Later, the more astute officers and civilians began what had come to be called "process reengineering," where support, maintenance, and logistics processes were first modified and then made digital. Even before Admiral Clark became CNO, the systems commands were finding that digital data systems could speed up parts delivery and reduce the overhead costs that were a consequence of keeping more spares on hand than were necessary. In effect, the "real time" (or "just in time") delivery of parts and services was becoming a reality, especially for Navy aviation, partially fulfilling the vision sketched out by former Secretary of Defense William Perry in 1994.[13]

At the same time, however, Clark had to deal with the claim by Marine Corps leaders that Navy requirements development and Navy budgets were often not responsive to their service's needs. On the one hand, the Marines argued that theirs was the more manpower-intensive service and therefore was less expensive man-for-man than the capital-intensive Navy. On the other hand, the Navy Department was still investing significant sums in Marine acquisitions such as the V-22 tilt-rotor aircraft, the expeditionary fighting vehicle, and the vertical take-off version of the Joint Strike Fighter (JSF). Balancing the "requirements" put forward by the Marine Corps against the "requirements" of the Navy had been a demanding responsibility of each CNO since Admiral Frank Kelso. It would remain a major task for Clark.

The Impact of Defense Secretary Rumsfeld

CNO Clark's initiatives in OPNAV were both complemented by and complicated by the way Donald Rumsfeld, the new Defense secretary, saw his job. In the presidential campaign of 2000, then-candidate George W. Bush had stressed creating a smaller, more mobile, and less expensive military, one that would cost the nation less but actually be more effective as a tool of U.S. policy.[14] After taking a series of briefings from various experts in the fields of defense policy and management in the late winter and early spring of 2001, Rumsfeld concluded that the major obstacle to the changes that President Bush had in mind was the Pentagon itself. In a speech to Defense Department employees on 10 September 2001, Rumsfeld said,

> The topic today is an adversary that poses a threat, a serious threat, to the security of the United States of America. This adversary is one of the world's last bastions of central planning. It governs by dictating five-year plans. From a single capital, it attempts to impose its demands across time zones, continents, oceans and beyond. With brutal consistency, it stifles free thought and crushes new ideas. It disrupts the defense of the United States and places the lives of men and women in uniform at risk.

That adversary? "It's the Pentagon bureaucracy. Not the people, but the processes. Not the civilians, but the systems. Not the men and women in uniform, but the uniformity of thought and action that we too often impose on them."[15]

Rumsfeld went on to say that "The modernization of the Department of Defense is a matter of some urgency." But he also noted that he had "no desire to attack the Pentagon; I want to liberate it. We need to save it from itself." The world had changed, "from a bipolar Cold War world where threats were visible and predictable, to one in which they arise from multiple sources, most of which are difficult to anticipate, and many of which are impossible even to know today." Changing the Pentagon, argued the new Defense secretary, would require a revolution in management. This

Figure 16-1. CNO Vernon E. Clark (left) arrives at Naval Air Facility Atsugi, Japan, on 2 September 2001. Clark was not a graduate of the Naval Academy; he was the first CNO to have an MBA. After the terrorist attacks on the United States on 11 September 2001, Clark began developing a Navy deployment concept that would allow a President to "surge" Navy forces in the event of an emergency.
(DIMOC Asset: 75M797599_x01 010902-N-QM876-005 [Released])

would entail taking risks, which in Rumsfeld's view ran counter to the Pentagon's management culture and processes, but as he said, "risk aversion is not America's ethic…"

Secretary Rumsfeld had already considered Admiral Clark as a possible successor to General Henry H. Shelton, the outgoing Chairman of the Joint Chiefs of Staff. According to journalist Bradley Graham, Shelton's "personal pick" as the next Chairman had been Admiral Clark, and Secretary Rumsfeld "had also looked hard at Clark."[16] But Clark and Rumsfeld had not—initially—gotten along. Clark felt that Rumsfeld "came in with certain prejudices and biases about the services being out of control," and according to Graham, Clark told Rumsfeld that he and the new Secretary of Defense "hadn't developed the kind of relationship [that] was important between a secretary and chairman."[17] At the same time, CNO Clark seemed to have an approach to his job that Rumsfeld liked, and Clark was to become one of Rumsfeld's favorite service chiefs, despite his feeling that "adjusting to Rumsfeld and the new administration team had been the most difficult challenge of his career."[18]

In his 10 September 2001 speech, Secretary Rumsfeld laid out a program of changes, including creating a Defense Business Board, changing the Planning, Programming, and Budgeting System (PPBS) by combining the programming and budgeting phases, consolidating health care in one program, reducing the size of headquarters staffs, modernizing the Defense Department's financial systems, outsourcing "non-core" activities, streamlining the acquisition process, altering the human resources rules in the department to keep skilled and experienced military personnel in their jobs longer, and creating a Senior Executive Council (which included the service secretaries) to advise him on changes and reforms in the Department. Rumsfeld emphasized that this reform program "begins with the personal endorsement, in fact the mandate, of the President of the United States."

An explanation of the new administration's thinking had been given earlier by Edward C. Aldridge Jr., the new Under Secretary of Defense for Acquisition, Technology and Logistics, who spoke at length about it with reporters in the Pentagon in late June.[19] Aldridge observed that Secretary Rumsfeld's position on pricing programs was essentially the same as CNO Clark's: "We're tired of going over to the Hill and telling what a program costs and knowing it's not truthful. So we have fully funded by several hundred million dollars programs that are currently in the budget…"[20] He also noted that the four-member Business Initiatives Council set up by Secretary Rumsfeld aimed to "take $15 to $30 billion a year out of the infrastructure and overhead of the Department of Defense" and use it to "start the process of doing transformation that we really need to do." In specific terms, the money saved could be plowed back into areas where there was real need—housing for military personnel, for example, and ballistic missile defense. Finally, Under Secretary Aldridge told the reporters that the results of the changes being implemented would be visible in the Fiscal Year 2003 budget—the one then being developed in the services. As he observed, "The [Quadrennial Defense Review] has been given out to [the Office of the Secretary of Defense] and the military departments. They're coming back in with their analysis. Once that analysis is done the defense planning guidance will be formulated."

With the promulgation of that guidance, the results of the QDR could be "fully integrated" with the defense budget.

Unfortunately, the process described by Aldridge was not working as he and others had anticipated, largely because Secretary Rumsfeld had not approved the draft QDR report. The delay in approving the QDR report held back the fiscal guidance necessary for the military services to finish building their programs. Rumsfeld and Deputy Secretary of Defense Paul Wolfowitz did not sign out the needed fiscal guidance for the services until August 2001—months behind schedule—and the service programmers had thrown up their hands and told the secretary's staff that they either had to get the guidance approved or the OSD staff could make up the service programs on its own.[21] This unfortunate bureaucratic stand-off was brought to an end by the attack on the Pentagon on 11 September. The suicidal attack destroyed the Navy's Command Center, which tracked the movement of Navy forces worldwide for the CNO and his staff.[22] Also decimated was OPNAV's Strategy and Concepts Branch (N513). Four of the ten members of the Branch, "including its chief, Captain Robert E. Dolan, were killed," and a fifth seriously injured.[23]

Operational Implications of the 11 September 2001 Attacks

The terrorist attacks of 11 September 2001 produced two consequences of immediate importance to the Department of Defense. The first was a dramatic increase in the defense budget. The confrontation over service programs between Rumsfeld and his staff and the staffs of the service secretaries vanished. Congress removed it. The second consequence, described by George J. Tenet, former Director of Central Intelligence and head of the Central Intelligence Agency (CIA), was a decision by President Bush to wage overt and covert campaigns, based on plans already drawn up by the CIA, against al Qaeda, the Islamist extremist group responsible for the 11 September 2001 killings in New York and Washington.[24] The President had decided to pressure—and then, when that failed—to remove the Taliban in Afghanistan because the Taliban leaders had refused to hand over Osama bin Laden, head of al Qaeda. The removing would be done by CIA operatives, U.S. special forces, and Afghans willing to side with the agents and soldiers of the United States—all supported by firepower from air forces stationed in the Persian Gulf area. This placed the military services in the position of supporting the CIA and the Joint Special Operations Command.

The CIA's "worldwide attack matrix," with objectives in places far afield from Afghanistan, became the campaign plan for the effort to fight organized Islamist extremists.[25] The President endorsed it and granted the CIA the authority necessary to implement it.[26] The President also signed National Security Presidential Directive 9, which instructed the Secretary of Defense to plan for attacks on Taliban and al Qaeda targets in Afghanistan. The directive also instructed the Secretary of Defense to support Joint Forces Command (JFCOM) and the regional combatant commanders in eliminating al Qaeda and its sanctuaries wherever they existed. That meant extending what later was called Operation Enduring Freedom (OEF) to the Philippines and the Horn of Africa.

Attacking the Afghan Taliban with a combination of local allies, trained CIA operatives, and U.S. special forces was just the sort of campaign that Secretary Rumsfeld had been advocating. For the campaign to succeed, it would have to have what the Taliban could not muster—accurate and reliable bombardment from the air, networked communications, advanced sensors, and effective logistics support. The hard combat on the ground in Afghanistan initially fell on the shoulders of CIA personnel, American special forces units, and anti-Taliban Afghan forces, but supporting them were the resources of the U.S. Air Force and the U.S. Navy, who supplied the U.S. Central Command and the CIA with the aircraft, supplies, and air-to-ground attacks essential to ousting the Taliban.

Managerial Implications of the 11 September 2001 Attacks

The suicide attacks on the United States, and the subsequent increase in defense spending that the Congress authorized in an emergency supplemental, did not remove the need of the services and OSD to follow the rules for the construction of the defense program and the budget that would sustain it. The procedure in place had the Secretary of Defense issuing defense planning guidance (DPG) to shape the programs of the military departments and fiscal guidance to discipline the military department budget officers. The departments would then develop their POMs and submit them to the staff of the Secretary of Defense for review. The secretary's staff would match the POMs against the planning guidance and inform the Deputy Secretary of Defense if any POM deviated from the guidance in a significant way. If so, the deputy secretary would consult with the other members of the Defense Resources Board (DRB) and then issue a Program Decision Memorandum that either accepted the deviation or rejected it.[27]

The 11 September attacks had cut into the timing of this process and further delayed it. The Secretary of Defense could have waived the programming process rules and arbitrarily selected certain spending increases from among all those put forward in the aftermath of the 9/11 attacks. However, that would have ignored the long-term implications of those initial increases. A key element of planning, programming, and budgeting is the way in which the process highlights the flow of resources into programs over time. Even in an emergency, that flow has to be projected and its implications made clear to the Defense secretary and the President. As Congress moved to add a substantial sum to the Pentagon's fiscal year 2001 and 2002 budgets, senior officials from OSD, the Joint Staff, and the service staffs met in marathon sessions to decide how to allocate the added funds. While the President and his advisors discussed how to combat al Qaeda, the Pentagon worked to make sure that the fiscal and human resources required to support their decisions were available.

However, the *routine* programming and budgeting process had not been entirely abandoned. It could not be. As a result, there was still tension after 9/11 between the Defense secretary's program review staff and the military department programmers. For example, the Defense Department's share of the $40 billion emergency supplemental funding authorized by Congress for fiscal year 2001 increased spending on some programs that had *not* been slated for increases by the 2002 DPG (issued before the 11 September attacks). These included aircraft upgrades (on existing F-16s, for example), improving protection of U.S. military bases, added support for the Joint Special Operations Command, and funds to pay for the increased operating tempo (OPTEMPO) of U.S. forces.[28] At the same time, the Department's share of the immediate supplemental allocation of $10 billion was not integrated with existing spending for fiscal year 2002. There had not been time for the Congress to rework the details of the fiscal year 2001 spending program in such a way as to fold the supplemental's dollars smoothly into the budgets of the military services and defense agencies. There had certainly not been time to sketch out for the Secretary of Defense all the long-term implications of the immediate emergency funding.[29] So within a few days of the 9/11 attacks, there grew up two program and budgeting processes—the "regular" one and one for the emergency supplementals. The consequence of this division would eventually become detrimental, but few of the officials in OSD who were engaged in the process of responding to the Congress in September and October 2001 thought that the campaign against terrorists would be a long and expensive one.

The managerial foundation of the campaign conducted against the Taliban in Afghanistan was important because one major challenge posed by the 11 September attacks was that of finding and then allocating the resources necessary to prosecute both the armed response to the attacks and the campaign of defense "transformation" that the President and the Secretary of Defense were committed to. That transformation effort was reaffirmed in the "Quadrennial Defense Review Report" published on 30 September 2001. In his "Forward" to the "Report," Secretary Rumsfeld informed his readers that "A central objective of the review was to shift the basis of defense planning from a 'threat-based' model that has dominated thinking in the past to a 'capabilities-based' model for the future."[30] In his statement written to accompany the QDR Report, General Henry H. Shelton, outgoing Chairman of the Joint Chiefs of Staff, noted that "the QDR calls for the capability to respond to overlapping major crises and defeat adversaries or their efforts in more than one region."[31] General Shelton also endorsed Rumfeld's desire for transformation; he said it was essential, and, like Rumsfeld, he defined it broadly, as something that would reform "key institutional planning, programming, budgeting, and acquisition processes."[32]

The Bush administration was committed both to fighting and to transforming. That was the policy. How could it be implemented? The first step was taken on 14 September—increasing the funds allocated to the military services and defense agencies. The next step was to put together a set of major requirements that the Deputy Secretary of Defense could issue as guidance for the services and defense agencies as they worked to modify their programs for fiscal year 2003 and beyond. On 19 October 2001, Barry D. Watts, then the director of OSD's Office of Program Analysis and Evaluation (OSD [PA&E])—the Secretary of Defense's program review office—produced a draft list of those requirements. The list included immediate costs of the campaign against al Qaeda and efforts to protect the United States and its armed forces from terrorist attack. The list also included "new or additional capabilities" that the services needed to support, plus "Hedges against demands we haven't yet anticipated," and "Programs and capabilities that should receive less emphasis or even be terminated."[33] It's important to recall that many senior officials feared that the attacks of 11 September were just the first phase of a string of dramatic terrorist acts, even including the possibility that al Qaeda might detonate a nuclear weapon on American soil.[34] Defense Department officials therefore had to balance the regular, or routine, work of allocating resources—work based upon anticipation of future requirements—against the possibility that the requirements might change dramatically and significantly disrupt the programming and budgeting procedures.

By the end of October, some things were clear to those charged with allocating and accounting for the funds to sustain the country's armed forces. As Dov S. Zakheim, the Comptroller of the Department of Defense, put it in a 31 October paper to the Deputy Secretary of Defense, "it is vital that we separate out the true costs of the War on Terrorism." Why? Because, as the Comptroller argued, paying for the conflict with year-end supplementals (last minute add-ons from the Congress), "a tried and true method for contingency funding," would make a hash of the assessment process that was essential to programming if the supplemental funding went on for very long. Moreover, "Setting aside funding within the POM for the war may also destroy budget discipline as Services and Agencies come to think of the funds as a new topline"—that is, as relatively permanent. In addition, "Near-term war investment costs have outyear tails that are not well understood and likely unfavorable to transformation efforts." Finally, "Beyond the budget tails associated with the current war effort, we must clarify the impact of the supplementals." To make matters even worse, "The Department has already allocated every penny of the increased topline, leaving no headroom for new transformation initiatives." As the comptroller concluded in his "bottom line" summary, "We need to agree on how we want to score war costs, defend them and pay for them."[35]

Very quickly after 11 September 2001, the Bush administration, along with the military staffs in the Pentagon, decided that the United States would likely have to fight with terrorists for a number of years. But that fight soon became an intelligence and special operations war, where the Navy and the Air Force played a supporting role and the Army and Marines began preparing for operations on the ground. At the same time, no one knew what the future held; the Bush administration therefore chose to pursue what became OEF and defense transformation *simultaneously* while quietly preparing for a possible major military campaign in the Middle East.[36] Before 9/11, the Navy's role for the near-term future had been to (a) proceed with the conversion of several older ballistic missile submarines to cruise missile–launching submarines that could also carry a small contingent of special operations personnel or Marines, (b) fully fund unmanned aerial vehicle (UAV) programs, (c) maintain adequate cargo ships in case they were needed to support a major operation overseas, and (d) fully fund major acquisition and critical research and development programs, especially ballistic missile defense. Starting in November, the members of the DRB affirmed those efforts and strengthened the Navy's programs aimed at operations in littoral areas.[37]

Secretary Rumsfeld's assumption was that a "transformed" military—more mobile, more linked through digital systems, and quick to respond to emergencies—would also be better able to combat terrorists. But was the struggle against terrorists the "operational concept" that was most important to the Defense secretary? Or was it the use of lighter, faster, and yet more lethal forces against the regimes that sponsored and shielded terrorists? After 11 September 2001, President Bush said the government of the United States would hunt down terrorists and go after those regimes that sheltered the likes of Osama bin Laden. Finding and attacking terrorists was not necessarily the same type of operation as attacking a regime that harbored terrorists, and it was important—eventually—to decide just what service transformation efforts should aim for.

In an essay in *Army* in June 2001, then-Colonel David A. Fastabend, who later would serve as a major general in Iraq, argued that an "operational concept is an image of combat: a concise visualization that portrays the strategic requirement, the adversary and his capabilities, and the scenario by which that adversary will be overcome to accomplish the strategic requirement."[38] In *At the Center of the Storm*, former CIA director George Tenet described the adversary and much of what the adversary was capable of, but he also noted that, as the CIA's knowledge of al Qaeda increased, it became more difficult to fulfill the "strategic requirement" of protecting the American citizenry from attack. Specifically, the CIA grew increasingly concerned about terrorists using chemical, biological, or nuclear "weapons of mass destruction" against the continental United States. What, then, was the proper "operational concept"? Could it be a pre-emptive attack against any regime that sheltered al Qaeda in particular or terrorists in general?[39] If so, then should transformation in the Department of Defense be achieved in such a way that it optimized U.S. forces for sudden attacks against other nations?

CNO Clark's Initial Response

Right after 11 September 2011, CNO Clark realized that the Navy needed to play a role in the military response to the attacks by the terrorists. He quickly told Rear Admiral James G. Stavridis, the new head of "Deep Blue," to begin drafting a briefing to Secretary of Defense Rumsfeld that would define the Navy's role in the war on al Qaeda.[40] According to Stavridis, "Admiral Clark knew how important that brief was going to be, blocked plenty of time on his schedule to create it, spent hours refining it," and then presented it to Rumsfeld personally.[41] Two elements to that briefing would shape the next decade of Navy operations. The first was an emphasis on keeping adequate naval forces deployed by changing the deployment cycle that had been developed during the Cold War. The second was an emphasis on sending individual sailors into war zones to augment personnel from the other services, especially the Marines and the Army.

Shifting the Navy and Marines to what Clark called "a wartime footing" for a "sustained conflict"[42] was made easier because of the Navy's participation in U.S. air combat patrols during Operations Northern Watch and Southern Watch in the skies over Iraq in the 1990s. Begun as Operation Provide Comfort in 1991, the air patrols over northern Iraq by planes from several countries was renamed Operation Northern Watch in January 1997. The Navy provided EA-6B electronic warfare aircraft to this campaign. Operation Southern Watch began in August 1992 to keep Iraqi aircraft out of the skies of southern Iraq. The Navy usually provided at least one carrier battle group and its air wing in the northern Persian Gulf to furnish aircraft for Southern Watch patrols and strikes. In mid-December 1998, a second carrier joined the first and boosted the attack aviation used to prosecute Operation Desert Fox, which was an effort by U.S. forces to wreck Iraq's capability to produce "weapons of mass destruction." By the late spring of 2001, planes of a coalition of forces were flying about 10,000 sorties over Iraq per year.[43] It was information regarding the human, financial, and material costs of these air campaigns that OPNAV staff could rely on to gain estimates of what any major campaign against al Qaeda in Afghanistan would cost.

But simply ramping up expenses for personnel, operations, and maintenance with the money Congress allotted the Defense Department after 11 September 2001 was not CNO Clark's goal. He wanted to answer once and for all the question, "What's the Navy for in this very different world?" As he said at the Naval War College in October, "We're going to have to think about some near-term and some long-term objectives." Thinking about objectives raised questions such as "[W]hat kind of concepts will our future operations entail?" and "How much capability should we keep forward?" But the more immediate question was, "How do we counter this transnational threat while meeting traditional concerns and conducting on-going operations that we have tasked around the world today, like the peacekeeping operations in Bosnia and Kosovo?" According to Clark, President Bush had said, "We're going to keep [the terrorists] on the run."[44] How could that be done?

Clark's first and primary focus was the fleet, and he deliberately created Fleet Forces Command on 1 October 2001 as a way to give the fleet a strong voice in the areas of requirements and logistics. According to the official message creating Fleet Forces Command, its commander was "responsible for coordinating, establishing, and implementing integrated requirements and policies for manning, equipping and training Atlantic and Pacific Fleet units during the inter-deployment training cycle." That made the Commander, Fleet Forces Command "the primary point of contact for all fleet and fleet type commander issues pertaining to policy and requirements related to manning, equipment and training."[45] The CNO wanted one four-star command to bring together what had been separate—the type commands in the Atlantic and Pacific fleets. The differences between the Atlantic and Pacific fleets stretched back to World War II, and Clark believed that those differences increased the cost of operating and maintaining the Navy as a whole. Clark felt that if there was just one very senior officer directing the process by which fleet units were prepared for deployment, the idea of "the fleet" would become a reality, simultaneously strengthening readiness and reducing its cost. The idea behind what became Fleet Forces Command had been around since Admiral Kelso had been CNO, but it was Clark who finally implemented it.[46]

When Clark became CNO, the Navy still had two chains of authority: one, the command chain, ran from the President and the Secretary of Defense to the senior operational commanders (in charge of the unified and specified commands); the other, the administrative chain, ran from the CNO to the "type commanders" in the Atlantic and Pacific fleets. The type commanders dated back to before World War II. By the end of the 1990s, there were three on each coast—one each for surface ships, naval aviation, and submarines. Their job was to provide for training and logistics broadly defined, to include maintenance and providing new equipment for ships scheduled for deployment.[47]

Clark came into office committed to changing the administrative chain of authority. He believed that having two separate sets of type commanders was inefficient. His goal was to create one support command—later named Fleet Forces Command—and have one senior type commander for each platform community (surface, aviation, and submarine). That way, the administrative chain would run from the CNO to the commander, Fleet Forces Command, and then to three type commanders. No longer would there be "two navies," one centered in Norfolk, Virginia, and the other based at Pearl Harbor, Hawaii. Clark's first step in implementing this change was to create "lead and follower" type commands, and he planned to follow that move with a second instruction to make the "follower" type commanders deputies to the senior type commander.[48]

At the same time, Clark wanted to make Fleet Forces Command the "lead voice for unified fleet requirements."[49] On the way to achieving that goal, he "double-hatted" the commander of the Atlantic Fleet as the head of the new Fleet Forces Command. The idea was that eventually the Atlantic Fleet would be disestablished and its place taken by Fleet Forces Command. Clark's goal was "aligning" the type commands with Fleet Forces Command and Fleet Forces Command with OPNAV. The desired alignment was from OPNAV (the CNO and his N4) to Fleet Forces Command and then to the type commanders. But of course it was a two-way street. The type commanders were very important advocates for readiness. They were the "canaries in the mine," ready to voice concerns that OPNAV might otherwise not respond to. But because the senior type commanders were only three-star admirals, they needed to have their concerns expressed to OPNAV by a four-star admiral—the commander of Fleet Forces Command.

As Clark moved toward the new "alignment" of OPNAV, Fleet Forces Command, and the type commands, he began promoting a "Total Force Integrated Readiness Model," or TFIRM. Clark's argument was that digital technology allowed the Navy's logisticians to construct models that would quantitatively link resources to readiness. If one unit—or one strike group—fell below readiness standards, the models would tell the logisticians in Fleet Forces Command just what resources they had to apply to the unit or group in order to bring it up to the required standard of performance. Clark's goal was to streamline the administrative chain so that the organizations in it could actually use the new digital systems that were either available or possible.[50]

What did all this activity produce? The answer is that it led to a new approach to naval operations, based initially on Clark's briefing to Rumsfeld in the immediate aftermath of the 11 September attacks.[51] This new approach was termed the Fleet Response Plan (and sometimes also the Fleet Readiness Program), and it was ready for testing under the supervision of Fleet Forces Command starting in the summer of 2003. Prior to the Fleet Response Plan, "the Navy's ship readiness objectives and maintenance needs for surface combatants were met through a two-year cycle" where ships were deployed forward for six months and then "spent the next 18 months primarily in maintenance and training." But both the QDR report and CNO Clark wanted the Navy—especially the carriers—to be able to deploy to a number of regions simultaneously.

For this to happen, the ships had to be able to come down off their high state of readiness after a deployment but also had to be able to stay at a high enough level of readiness so that six carrier strike groups (CSGs) could deploy within 30 days, with another two carrier strike groups ready within 90 days. Changing what the Navy called its "Inter-Deployment Readiness Cycle" almost doubled the numbers of carriers and escorts deployed or ready for deployment under the Cold War two-year cycle.[52] The proof of this new concept came in 2004, during a set of at-sea exercises ("Summer Pulse") conducted between 2 June and 27 July 2004. During this time, seven carrier strike groups operated simultaneously in five different operational theaters. They were complemented by 17 attack submarines. After 9/11, CNO Clark promised Secretary Rumsfeld that the Navy could deploy to meet multiple crises, and in the 2004 exercises the Navy delivered on the CNO's promise.

Admiral Clark revealed what this meant when he spoke at the Current Strategy Forum of the Naval War College in June 2002. Clark called this approach "a new operational vision," and he told his audience that he was presenting his vision for the first time in public. He illustrated this new vision with an example from Operation Enduring Freedom: "In Afghanistan, it is now widely reported that 80% of Navy strike sorties attacked targets that were unknown to the aircrews when they left the carrier. They relied upon networked sensors and joint communications to swiftly respond to targets of opportunity. This was a planned warfighting approach. As a result of this impressive capability, over 90% of the ordnance dropped has been precision guided, a dramatic change from [Operation] Desert Storm just a decade earlier."[53] CNO Clark also insisted that this combination of sensors, secure communications, and precision guided munitions was a joint capability—that it was not confined to Navy missions, and promised to "double the combat output [of naval forces] within ten years."[54]

Further Implications of 9/11 for CNO Clark and OPNAV

Admiral Clark had taken office committed to creating a new Navy—a 21st-century force—and he did not abandon that commitment after pledging that the Navy would be heavily involved in the "away game" against terrorism. Rear Admiral Phillip M. Balisle, head of the surface warfare office (N76) in OPNAV, described a very important part of this force to the Seapower Subcommittee of the Senate Armed Services Committee at the beginning of April 2002. The 21st century surface combatant force was to be built around the "DD(X) Family of Ships,"[55] which included a ship designed especially to provide fire support for Marines ashore, a "Littoral Combat Ship," an advanced cruiser, a joint command and control ship, a new version of the existing DDG-51 class of destroyers, and upgraded existing Aegis cruisers.[56]

As Rear Admiral Balisle informed the lawmakers, a "spiral technology development process of DD(X) and [littoral combat ships] will enable the most efficient insertion of high pay-off technologies into the Family of Ships with the least amount of risk." DD(X) and the littoral combat ship (LCS) would be "developed in parallel and on complementary time lines," allowing the "advanced automation technology, high density propulsion plants and increased modal and C4I connectivity" to "reduce crew size, increase Joint C4I connectivity, and reduce operating and support costs."[57] The Navy was going to use improved sensor and information technology to reduce crew size while also improving combat potential. As Balisle put it, "These combatants must be affordable to produce and less costly to operate. They must be designed from the keel up to enable dramatic, 50–70%, manpower reductions."[58] But even with fewer sailors to man them, the new and modified ships would operate together as "a netted, distributed force."[59]

This was the vision of the future: precision strike, directed by and from a fully networked Navy. The vision would be achieved through transformation—"The integration of multiple systems in a force with different levels of capability . . ."[60] CNO Clark was going to achieve this transformation *while still taking the fight to terrorists*. He would fulfill both missions simultaneously through what he called "alignment," which was a process of seeing to it that all major elements of the shoreside Navy—from OPNAV through the systems commands and the warfare centers—were focused on increasing the power and endurance of the forward-deployed fleets. Clark created N7 as the OPNAV directorate responsible for making sure that the warfare sponsors (N74 through N79) "and the requirements, programs, and training they produce [were] aligned across warfare areas."[61] As Clark explained, "This will help us ensure that in the future we are not involved in trying to cobble together systems that have been built independently."[62]

In partial pursuit of this goal, Navy secretary Gordon R. England promoted Rear Admiral Balisle to Vice Admiral and Commander of NAVSEA. Balisle "realigned" the headquarters of the Naval Sea Systems Command, establishing both a warfare systems engineering directorate and a "human systems integration" directorate in order to tap the discipline of systems engineering to improve the performance of sailors on the new ships—such as LCS—then being designed. Balisle also strengthened the role of key "warranted technical leaders" within the organization. His goal—one shared by both CNO Clark and Navy secretary England—was to make the Naval Sea Systems Command a systems integrator—an organization that could competently blend varieties of system engineering to produce ships that needed less maintenance and fewer sailors and were therefore more affordable.[63]

CNO Clark also accepted the concept of planning and programming in terms of "capabilities" instead of by specific ship, submarine, and aircraft programs. Chairman of the Joint Chiefs of Staff Instruction (CJCSI) 3170.01B, dated 15 April 2001, introduced the term "capabilities-based requirements," which essentially meant a requirement that was expressed in terms of a capability and not in terms of the performance of a specific military unit, platform or system. CJCSI 3170.01B directed the services to develop a "capability based requirement" as well as the routine "operational requirements document" for any new system.[64]

The introduction of this term—"capability"—provoked a good deal of debate inside the Pentagon, but initially Secretary Rumsfeld seemed to have a point. The staffs of the combatant commanders had grown accustomed to requesting specific forces—a carrier battle group, for example, or the 82nd Airborne Division, or a particular fighter wing. Rumsfeld's argument was that what they should have listed as force requirements as they drew up their actual or contingency plans were capabilities (such as "strike" or "counterinsurgency"), and then the service staffs could build joint "packages" of capabilities to meet the needs of the combatant commanders. Rumsfeld argued that a major element of Defense Department "transformation" had to be the creation and use of a new terminology—a new way of expressing military potential and power and therefore also a new way of planning forces and planning for the use of forces in operations.

To assist him in his efforts to sustain military operations against terrorists and the regimes that supported them while still developing a 21st-century fleet, Clark enlarged his "inner staff" by creating "new offices with overlapping responsibilities."[65] The Quadrennial Defense Review cell was kept together and was renamed the Navy Operations Group. In early 2002, the Group was given a new name—Deep Blue—and charged with coming up with innovative ways to wage the war against terrorists. Its first leader was Rear Admiral Joseph A. Sestak Jr. Rear Admiral Stavridis took over after Sestak left to lead N81, the Assessment Division of N8. Deep Blue, whose leader reported directly to the CNO, gradually became a "multi-mission think tank staffed by the Navy's best and brightest."[66] In 2002, Clark also created N00Z, the Strategic Actions Group, as a "mini-staff," and N00Z functioned much as N00K (the CNO Executive Panel [CEP]) had done under CNO Johnson.[67] N00Z was led by Captain (later Vice Admiral) Frank C. Pandolfe, who had headed N513 in 1997.

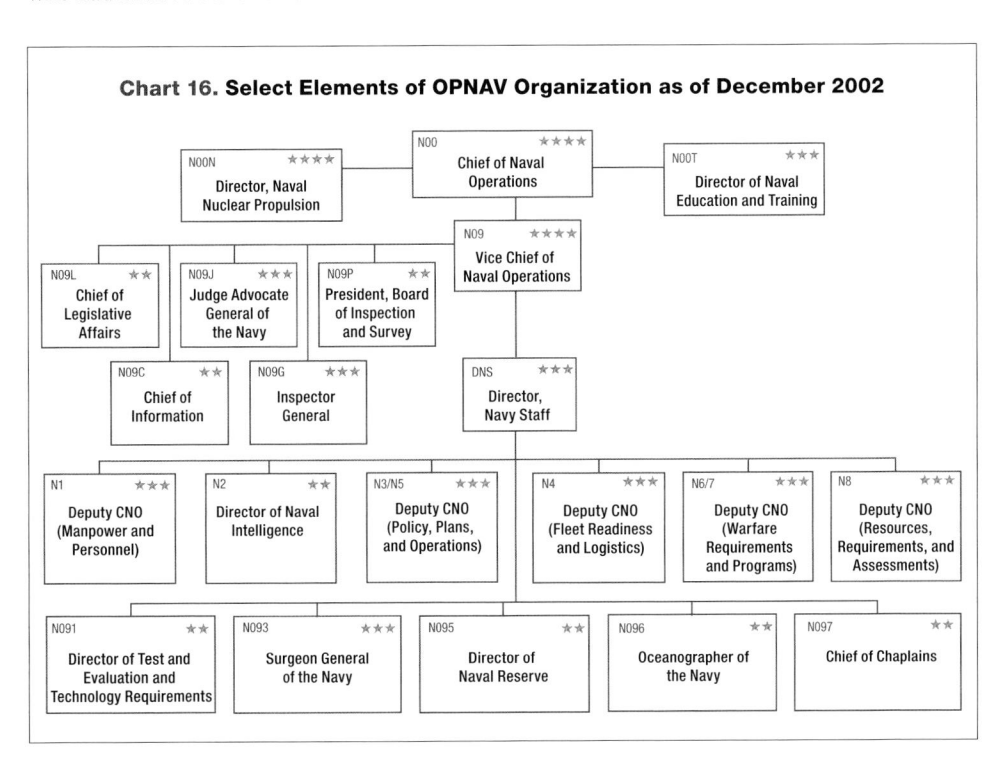

Chart 16. Select Elements of OPNAV Organization as of December 2002

- N00 ★★★★ Chief of Naval Operations
  - N00N ★★★★ Director, Naval Nuclear Propulsion
  - N00T ★★★ Director of Naval Education and Training
  - N09 ★★★★ Vice Chief of Naval Operations
    - N09L ★★ Chief of Legislative Affairs
    - N09J ★★★ Judge Advocate General of the Navy
    - N09P ★★ President, Board of Inspection and Survey
    - N09C ★★ Chief of Information
    - N09G ★★★ Inspector General
    - DNS ★★★ Director, Navy Staff
      - N1 ★★★ Deputy CNO (Manpower and Personnel)
      - N2 ★★ Director of Naval Intelligence
      - N3/N5 ★★★ Deputy CNO (Policy, Plans, and Operations)
      - N4 ★★★ Deputy CNO (Fleet Readiness and Logistics)
      - N6/7 ★★★ Deputy CNO (Warfare Requirements and Programs)
      - N8 ★★★ Deputy CNO (Resources, Requirements, and Assessments)
      - N091 ★★ Director of Test and Evaluation and Technology Requirements
      - N093 ★★★ Surgeon General of the Navy
      - N095 ★★ Director of Naval Reserve
      - N096 ★★ Oceanographer of the Navy
      - N097 ★★ Chief of Chaplains

As Captain Haynes noted in his history of strategic thinking in OPNAV, "Clark now had five offices—Deep Blue, N00Z, N00K, N81, and N513 [N3/5's strategy and concepts branch]—working on five overlapping strategy projects during 2002 and 2003, numbers unprecedented in the post–Cold War era."[68] CNO Clark also strengthened the position of Director of the Navy Staff by making the post one for a vice admiral. According to Navy regulations, the director did not appear to be a major actor inside OPNAV. In practice, however, the Director of the Navy Staff could serve as a senior deputy to the CNO, and the director's role grew in importance as the work load of the CNO and the VCNO increased after 9/11.

To make sure everyone in the Navy and the Marines understood what Clark's vision was, the Admiral gave it a name—*Sea Power 21*—and explained what it was in an article in the October 2002 *Proceedings* of the U. S. Naval Institute. As the article explained, there were three "fundamental concepts" critical to "the Navy's continued operational effectiveness: Sea Strike, Sea Shield, and Sea Basing. Sea Strike is the ability to project precise and persistent offensive power from the sea. Sea Shield extends defensive assurance throughout the world; and Sea Basing enhances operational independence and support for the joint force."[69] Clark argued that the "21st-century Navy will exert direct, decisive, and sustained influence in joint campaigns" through "the dynamic application of persistent intelligence, surveillance, and reconnaissance; time-sensitive strike; ship-to-objective maneuver; information operations; and covert strike to deliver devastating power and accuracy..."[70] The Marines were by no means forgotten. They would get "pre-positioned ships with at-sea-accessible cargo," plus the V-22 and a level of fire support that was unheard of in the 1990s.[71] The special warfare fighters would also be supported by precision-guided munitions. To drive these points home, Clark or his deputies published an additional eight articles in *Proceedings* from November 2002 through January 2004.[72]

In his study of Navy strategy-making from 1989 to 2007, Captain Haynes argued that "*Sea Power 21* did not resonate in the fleet," but CNO Clark seemed to believe that his Navy would catch on once it saw the difference his vision would make in operations. As Clark argued in his inaugural paper of October 2002, "the Sea Basing concept provides a valuable tool for prioritizing naval programs. Sea-based forces enjoy advantages of security, immediate employability, and operational independence. All naval programs should foster these attributes to the greatest extent feasible. This means transforming shore-based capabilities to sea-based systems whenever practical..."[73] Clark's decision to place both the Naval Network Warfare Command (NETWARCOM) and the Navy Warfare Development Command (NWDC) under Fleet Forces Command was consistent with this vision of sea-basing.

The last of the Sea Power 21 articles was published in the January 2004 *Proceedings*. In that paper, VCNO Michael G. Mullen struck a warning note: "Since 1990, the Navy has undergone a dramatic reduction in size—37% fewer ships, 26% decrease in number of aircraft, and 35% decrease in active-duty end strength. Despite this decline, our operational costs... continue to rise at about 7% per year... and consume critical recapitalization resources."[74] To solve this problem, the vice chief—speaking for CNO Clark—repeated the theme of "aligning" the whole

Navy to support the fleet. As he said, "It is not about the latest business fad, nor is it a 'do more with less' message." But it was clear that the Navy had to achieve cost savings within its shore establishment: "We must generate about $10 billion annually over the next five years" to recapitalize the fleet.[75] The Navy could not keep up the operational tempo that it had demonstrated in 2002 and 2003 and still develop its 21st century fleet. It had to sustain its forward-deployed forces by being smarter and more creative, both on shore and at sea. It also had to generate savings that the Navy could use to recapitalize its forces.

But what about the Marines? The Marines had not backed away from "Expeditionary Maneuver Warfare" and had continued their argument for more influence within the Navy Department in "Marine Corps Strategy 21." The Marines were the nation's overseas expeditionary force, and after 9/11 they could see a future filled with expeditionary operations. But CNO Clark asserted that advances in naval technology had given the Navy the ability to create a "controlled space" at sea and then extend this control across a beach and into the land. The Marines would operate within this umbrella of control. For that reason, it was the Navy that needed resources and authority over expeditionary operations. The visions of "Sea Power 21" and "Expeditionary Maneuver Warfare" seemed at odds, and Navy secretary Gordon England could not reconcile them.[76] As a result, the Navy did not release the new operational concept that the OPNAV staff had put together by the early spring of 2003.[77] This was a mistake, according to Haynes, because the Navy lost an opportunity to influence *joint* doctrine as it was developing after 9/11.[78]

Figure 16-2. CNO Vernon E. Clark appears before the Senate Armed Service Committee to discuss and answer questions concerning the 2004 fiscal year defense programs. (DIMOC asset: 75M636209_x01 030225-N-SW955-573 U.S. Navy photo by Chief Photographer's Mate Johnny Bivera. [Released])

However, by the beginning of Operation Iraqi Freedom (OIF) in March 2003, what really mattered was the conflict in Iraq. The need to support the conflict took first place on the agendas of the CNO, the Commandant, and the leaders of the other services. For example, the Navy's contribution to Operations Enduring Freedom and Iraqi Freedom in 2004 came to about 20,000 personnel. 12,000 of them were in one carrier strike group and two expeditionary strike groups, and 8,000 were serving in a variety of positions ashore for Central Command, including "2,500 medical personnel in direct support of ground combat missions."[79] In FY 2004, "Navy sea-based tactical aircraft flew more than 3,000 sorties and dropped more than 100,000 pounds of ordnance in close support missions." Other Navy aircraft flew nearly 5,000 hours of reconnaissance missions, and Navy small craft protected Iraqi oil terminals after Saddam Hussein's regime was toppled. Navy ships also supported counter-proliferation efforts and maritime domain awareness operations with the U.S. Coast Guard. Not all of this effort was funded by the "Global War on Terror" supplemental. As CNO Clark noted, "the Navy absorbed $1.5B in corporate bills . . ."[80]

Under the circumstances, this was a significant amount of money because it continued through the years of the long counter-insurgency campaign in Iraq. "Meanwhile," as Captain Haynes discovered, "many of the ships and aircraft that had entered the inventory in the 1970s and 1980s were being retired in advance because their maintenance was proving too expensive."[81] This led to a reduction in the size of the fleet—from 318 ships when Clark became CNO to 282 when he retired. Clark was willing to trade off ship and aircraft numbers because, as he put it, "I would rather muster two battle groups for three months and do something really significant internationally . . . than just go over and hang out for six months without purpose."[82]

A Renaissance of Strategy

The campaigns in both Afghanistan and Iraq did not end as originally planned. The outcome of the initial campaign against Hussein and his forces and supporters was never in doubt. But there was a catch. As Steven Metz of the Army War College pointed out, "[N]o senior policymaker anticipated that there would be extensive and protracted armed resistance after the dictator was gone."[83] The evidence from public sources suggests that U.S. military and civilian leaders were not prepared for the level and scale of that resistance. Even worse, it took some time for them to understand that what they faced was an insurgency. Why was this? Metz suggested it was because the President did not consult his military leaders regarding his strategy. Indeed, Metz went farther than that and argued that Bush "leaned toward detachment and delegation" until pressured by events in Iraq in 2006.[84] In *Fiasco*, correspondent Thomas Ricks took a somewhat similar view, arguing that the Joint Chiefs of Staff did not have a serious discussion of the President's direction of the war. As Ricks put it, "One of the unexplained oddities of this time was the absence of much of the nation's top military leadership . . ."[85] They appear not to have been seriously consulted. Determining whether the Joint Chiefs of Staff were or not will depend on the declassification of the Joint Staff's documents.

The lengthy counter-insurgency operations in Iraq led CNO Clark to revisit an issue that he thought he had put to rest: What was the role of the Navy in the post–9/11 world? To put the question another way, what was American global strategy and how did the Navy support it? To answer that question, CNO Clark—not a leader normally concerned with global strategy— selected Vice Admiral John G. Morgan Jr., to be the DCNO for Operations and Policy (N3/5) in 2004. Morgan's career could be thought of as almost ideal in terms of the Goldwater-Nichols legislation. He had served as a carrier battle group commander, as the deputy for acquisition strategy in the Ballistic Missile Defense Office, and as a senior military assistant to Secretary of the Navy England. Morgan understood that though the Navy was not active in the war against terrorists the way that the Army and Marines were, the Navy remained an important national asset and had to think clearly and creatively about its role.

Vice Admiral Morgan also knew that, as Captain Haynes put it, "The Pentagon was a place where being perceived as relevant was as important as actually being relevant."[86] Morgan therefore set out to show that the Navy was important to the long-term security of the nation. Haynes suggested that Morgan had some freedom to do so because he already had the confidence of Secretary of the Navy England.[87] Whatever the source of Morgan's influence—he was to hold his job for four years, across several CNOs—he had a kind of freedom that his predecessors had not enjoyed, and he set out to provoke a dialogue about strategy within OPNAV and then between the Navy and influential elements of the public.[88] His goal was to show the value of a forward-deployed Navy. Admiral Clark had overseen the creation of a "surge" Navy—one that could respond quickly to crises and regional conflicts. Morgan was after a Navy whose influence would be worldwide and lasting. Operations Enduring Freedom and Iraqi Freedom would not last forever, and the Navy had to be prepared for the long haul.[89]

To assist him, Morgan had Rear Admiral Charles W. Martoglio assigned as head of N51. Martoglio was an experienced seagoing commander and OPNAV staff officer, and he had worked in OSD and as an executive assistant to the VCNO. As Captain Haynes observed, Martoglio "knew how to peddle potentially controversial initiatives to the deputy CNOs and division directors, who were the caretakers of embedded billion-dollar programs, and therefore jealously guarded their turf."[90] By November 2004, Morgan and Martoglio had created a slide that captured the difference between the Navy's pre–9/11 capabilities and those it needed in 2004. The slide, dubbed "the bear paw," showed stability operations, the global campaign against terrorists, and "homeland defense/homeland security" as essential naval capabilities.

The central capability of the Navy would remain "major combat operations," but its combat capability needed to "feed" and support the other three capabilities. It was not a matter of saying that stability operations, counter-terrorism, and defense of the continental United States were lesser included capabilities under an umbrella of forces needed to wage a major theater war. Instead, it was a means of sorting out programs that needed support. The Navy's river patrol boats in Iraq, for example, were seen as components of two larger, strategic capabilities—the war on terrorists and the conduct of stability operations.[91] And of course the whole approach of Morgan and Martoglio recognized the importance of the Marines.

The experienced military correspondent Thomas E. Ricks had argued that "One of the roles of a president is to provide strategic context—to explain how the public, and especially how subordinate officials, should think about a situation."[92] A CNO had the same responsibility, and Morgan and Martoglio provided Clark and Navy secretary England with that context. In the last phase of the Cold War, the Navy's Maritime Strategy applied the capabilities of the Navy and the Marines to a major conventional war. Just as the Cold War ended, the United States fought alongside coalition partners to defeat a regional adversary; that was Operation Desert Storm in early 1991. After that conflict, the Navy began to shift from a focus on the open ocean to the littorals; that was the point of ". . . From the Sea" and "Forward . . . from the Sea." Both documents provided the "strategic context" for the Navy in a post–Cold War world. But as Morgan recognized, the Navy needed a new strategic context for the post-9/11 world, and he and Martoglio provided it.

Clark accepted this new strategic context, and Martoglio "began presenting the brief to audiences in OPNAV and (possibly unbeknownst to Clark) to local think tanks. In January 2005, Clark officially introduced the [new] Strategy at the annual Surface Navy Association [meeting] in Washington, DC."[93] In the meantime, Vice Admiral Morgan had sent the briefing and a paper to several senior Navy officers, including Admiral Michael Mullen, commander, United States Naval Forces, Europe, and Clark's successor. The paper was eventually entitled "Navy's 3/1 Strategy; The Maritime Contribution to the Joint Force in a Changing Strategic Landscape," and not every senior officer responded positively to it. After all, the proposed "strategic context" gave the Navy a role analogous to that performed by Britain's Royal Navy in the 19th century—as the enforcer of freedom of the seas. Moreover, this policing of the seas would have to be done—could only be done—with the assistance of other maritime nations.[94] This was a significant change. As Captain Haynes put it, "Never before in a Navy strategic statement had the Navy's constabulary role enjoyed such a prominent place alongside its other two roles of warfighting and diplomacy."[95]

The major opponent of the new strategy was Admiral John B. Nathman. A career naval aviator, Nathman had been the logistics chief for the commander of the North Atlantic Treaty Organization (NATO) Implementation Force in Bosnia (IFOR) and a carrier group commander. After a tour as N88 in OPNAV, he had served as the type commander for Navy air units in the Pacific. Then Nathman was selected as N6/7, and in August 2004 was appointed Vice Chief of Naval Operations. When Vice Admiral Morgan was sending out his "3/1 Strategy," Nathman was commander of Fleet Forces Command. In a discussion with Captain Haynes, Nathman said that "no one in OPNAV seemed to understand that the fleet and its high-end platforms had been adapting . . . well to the post–9/11 challenges, including the lesser included missions."[96] But of course Vice Admiral Morgan did not see them as "lesser included missions." That was Morgan's whole point—stability operations and the antiterrorist campaign were essential missions, requiring different systems and specially-trained personnel in adequate numbers. But "Nathman believed it was operationally and politically dangerous to downplay the Navy's blue-water capabilities." Indeed, the "3/1 Strategy" was "pandering to the Bush administration's new concepts while patently ignoring operational realities."[97] In Nathman's eyes, the danger of such a policy was that it would invite a challenge by China. CNO Clark did not sign out the paper, but the briefing was widely circulated.

Unresolved Issues

The war in Iraq did not snuff out the process of "transformation." Instead, it shifted the focus of the process to the battlefield and away from the Pentagon. The Office of Force Transformation in the Office of the Secretary of Defense defined "transformation" as "a process that shapes the changing nature of military competition and cooperation through new combinations of concepts, capabilities, people and organizations . . . to sustain our strategic position . . ."[98] The head of the new office was retired Vice Admiral Arthur K. Cebrowski, who had ended his time in uniform after leading the Naval War College and the Navy Warfare Development Command. Cebrowski was an audacious thinker. For example, he had used his position as President of the Naval War College to lease a civilian version of what became the high-speed vessel, or HSV. He had it brought up the Potomac River to Washington to show to other Navy officers and Navy civilians. His argument was that the Navy could lease such platforms in order to rapidly augment its capability to move personnel and equipment within a theater, thereby stymieing any enemy—whether conventional or terrorist—trying to get the jump on U. S. forces.

Cebrowski also promoted small naval combatants, both because they might be very useful in the littorals against enemy small craft and because building such a small but versatile boat *outside of* the normal acquisition community might lead to the creation of two acquisition processes, one for "regular" systems and a second available for use in emergencies.[99] Cebrowski's charter from Rumsfeld to encourage transformation extended to all the services, and the retired admiral's small office funded a number of "seed" projects, including an effort to create a capability to quickly loft small reconnaissance satellites in case an enemy tried to "blind" U.S. space systems.[100] However, innovation—whether termed "transformational" or not—was alive and well in the operating forces. For example, by the end of 2005, the Coalition forces in Iraq were using "overseas contingency operations" (OCO) funds to build a battlefield intelligence system that could provide real-time information about insurgent movements. It was just the sort of innovation that Cebrowski had advocated. But would it have a lasting effect within the Pentagon's routine processes of building, training, and sustaining forces?

The tension between winning the conflicts in Iraq and Afghanistan and developing U.S. military forces for the future was supposed to be overcome by the development of joint operating concepts that would guide the plans and programming of all the services. Responsible for this development was the Joint Forces Command (JFCOM), created in 1999 from the U.S. Atlantic

Command and charged with using experimentation and education to foster a transformation of the U.S. armed forces. In cooperation with the JCS and the military services, JFCOM developed joint concepts, conducted joint experimentation, and set joint standards for training and the interoperability of major digital systems. After 2004, until its disestablishment in 2011, JFCOM was also responsible for providing conventional forces to the combatant commanders.

Coinciding with the arrival of Donald Rumsfeld in the Pentagon, the JFCOM J9 staff produced both joint operating concepts and what were called joint integrating concepts. An example of a joint operating concept was "rapid decisive operations." An example of a joint integrating concept was "joint forcible entry." The integrating concept complemented and filled in the details of the operating concept. "Rapid decisive operations," for example, would not be possible without the capability for "joint forcible entry." The operating and integrating concepts were—obviously—supposed to be joint, which meant that they had to be general enough to cover all the services. At the same time, they were supposed to be produced or at least reviewed by the services and the Joint Special Operations Command and then tested in war games organized by the J9 staff. This need for joint reviews of concepts led to a lot of staff work, and it was eventually not clear just what that staff work had done to create a "transformed" and joint military force.

Fortunately, the discussions, war games and experiments orchestrated by JFCOM did lead to the development of the Standing Joint Task Force concept and what came to be called the Collaborative Information Environment. Ideally, standing joint task forces would train for deployment and therefore be ready to swing into action quickly, no matter what the conflict was. The Collaborative Information Environment would be the basis for the digital information systems that any such task force would use. It was a very bold idea—to create the concepts that would guide future spending and development across all the services, and it had a major implication for the services: They would have to try to make the programming process not only joint but also guided by joint concepts. Secretary Rumsfeld wanted to see JFCOM set the broad requirements that would guide service programming, and he hoped that those requirements would "fall out" logically from the joint concepts. But what if they did not? The Navy and the Air Force were "capital-intensive" services. Each developed weapons and platforms that were supposed to last for decades. In a sense, each service gambled on being able to anticipate the future. JFCOM's concepts were supposed to guide them to the future. But what if the concept-development process did not succeed? The Navy and the Air Force could not wait while the concept-development process was refined. Both services had industrial bases to nurture.

Conclusion: Two Reformers and War

Donald Rumsfeld strode into the Pentagon determined to yank the Defense Department into the 21st century. As national security correspondent Robert Kaplan suggested, Rumsfeld was not a failure, despite what some writers have argued was his deeply flawed understanding of the Iraq campaign.[101] His achievements included giving the Missile Defense Agency (the successor to the Ballistic Missile Defense Organization) the funds and the freedom from close supervision in order to promote the creation of a working national ballistic missile defense,[102] and an effort to support ongoing efforts to make U.S. forces, especially the Army, more expeditionary. Secretary Rumsfeld also created the Northern Command to defend North America (including Mexico) and Africa Command, and he used his authority to give Joint Special Operations Command the sort of authority that previously only a combatant command had possessed.

He also supported negotiations with South Korea that led to a reduction of U.S. forces there, and he worked successfully on a number of issues with Japan, including persuading the Japanese to accept a U.S. Navy nuclear-powered carrier in Japanese territory. As Kaplan noted,

> [J]ust as a new, more flexible, austere, and far-flung basing constellation was emerging worldwide, empowered by a more centrally controlled command structure, troubled relationships with crucial Asian allies were on the mend. Such developments, as Rumsfeld saw them, would help the United States react in expeditionary style to unforeseen emergencies, prosecute the war on terrorism, and hedge against a rising Chinese military without unnecessarily provoking it.[103]

Just as important to Rumsfeld was changing the defense planning process, which he claimed was too slow to deal with rapid changes in the world. As Rumsfeld put it after he became the Defense secretary, he could give guidance to the services, but then he had to wait months to see the results. He said it was like seeing a freight train load up on the West Coast, and then watching it leave—but not knowing for sure what would be unloaded when the train got to the East Coast. He wanted more control over program planning, and he proposed to get it by doing the following: (a) basing planning on the joint operating concepts developed in JFCOM; (b) continuing the use of defense planning scenarios, where different force structures were tested in likely conflict situations; (c) getting service and defense agency programmers to think in terms of capabilities; and (d) making capability trade-offs within realistic fiscal boundaries.[104] The process would be triggered by the issuing of the National Security Strategy and the National Defense Strategy, making it responsive to the guidance provided by the President.

CNO Clark had to thread his way and the Navy's way through Rumsfeld's initiatives. There was just enough similarity between the two clusters of reforms for the two leaders to avoid a confrontation. For example, Clark also thought that programming within OPNAV should consider capabilities and not just platforms, and Clark acted to free the Navy from Cold War deployment cycles that tied up ships and submarines in shipyards and rendered them unavailable to the regional combatant commanders. He eventually realized that he also needed to encourage his own service to think about and publicize its role in the post–9/11 world. In doing so, Clark accepted the argument that the Navy had to tailor itself for participation in *long-term* counter-insurgency and counter-terrorism operations.

Both Rumsfeld and Clark wanted changes that would better prepare U.S. armed forces for what they saw as a future where the quality of a force, its mobility, and its informational awareness counted for more than its quantity. Operation Iraqi Freedom seemed to vindicate Rumsfeld's vision for U.S. forces. As the insurgency in Iraq grew, however, Rumsfeld's view of conflict seemed inappropriate. Enemies of the United States would concede the high-technology realm of war to U.S. forces and strike back with simple, even primitive, methods, such as suicide bombers. Their goal was to drag out conflicts and to continuously inflict casualties on U.S. units with weapons such as improvised explosive devices. They realized that the smaller professional ground forces of the United States were a precious, limited asset, and they planned their campaigns to wear down that asset.

Clark and his colleagues had no solution to this problem, though the Marines argued and then demonstrated that the Iraq conflict was one they and the Army could handle. The Marines, planning in the 1990s to maneuver operationally from the sea, found themselves in two counterinsurgency campaigns where their amphibious expertise was not the key to success. Technology was of value in such campaigns, but in the end each conflict (in Iraq and in Afghanistan) would be settled by Marines interacting with the local populations, and there were people in those populations who hated the United States and who bent their energies and applied their resources to countering U.S. military technology.

The Clark years were tumultuous. Reorganization took place in parallel with wartime operations. Committed to "aligning" the whole Navy to support the fleet and thereby refinance recapitalization, Clark backed the military operations in Iraq (Iraqi Freedom) and Afghanistan (Enduring Freedom) "to the hilt."[105] But doing so meant wearing down the people and ships that Clark had promised to sustain—in spite of the overseas contingency funds that Congress approved. Initially dubious about the value of a strategy office in OPNAV, Clark felt compelled to invigorate Navy strategic thinking. Like Defense secretary Rumsfeld, a business-minded leader, Clark watched as his goal of "alignment" was overshadowed by war.

Notes

[1] Ronald E. Ratcliff, "CNO and OPNAV Reorganization," a Naval War College case study. The case quotes from two NAVOP messages—one (009/00) in July and a second (010/00) in early Aug. 2000, http://www.au.af.mil/au/awc/awcgate/navy/pmi/opnav_reorg.pdf (21 Aug. 2016).

[2] Ibid. The CNO's "personal Message to Senior Naval Leadership" was sent out in early Aug. 2000.

[3] The members of the Working Group were N1B (Mr. Matt Henry, chairman of the Working Group), N8B (Mr. Irving N. Blickstein), N80B (CAPT A. Worbey), N09B (RADM Gerald Talbot), N4A (CAPT Michael J. Plumkett), N7A (CAPT Marilyn J. Augstine), and a few others. See "OPNAV Alignment Plan," briefing, 17 Aug. 2000, slide 2. In the collection of Thomas C. Hone.

[4] "OPNAV Alignment Plan" briefing, 17 Aug. 2000, slide 2.

[5] CAPT Peter D. Haynes, "American Naval Thinking in the Post–Cold War Era: The U.S. Navy and the Emergence of a Maritime Strategy, 1989–2007," 211.

[6] Slide 24 of the 17 Aug. 2000 "OPNAV Alignment Plan" briefing.

[7] Message, from: Vice Chief of Naval Operations to Distribution, Subj: OPNAV Alignment, 28 Aug. 2000. In the collection of Thomas C. Hone.

[8] However, the N7 was very small at first, and according to rumor it did not grow at a pace commensurate with its responsibilities.

[9] *Inside the Navy*, 15 Jan. 2001, 3.

[10] James R. Klugh, Deputy Under Secretary of Defense (Logistics), "Policy for Maintaining Core Depot Maintenance Capability," 15 Nov. 1993, quoted on slide 5 in "NAVAIR Core Overview" brief to Commander, Naval Air Systems Command, 18 Dec. 2000. In the collection of Thomas C. Hone.

[11] U.S. Code, Title 10, ch. 146, Section 2464.

[12] John W. Mishler III, "Re-Organizing the Naval Air Systems Command," PhD Dissertation, George Washington University, 2000.

[13] The Defense Technical Information Center and the Defense Acquisition University have produced publications and guidebooks describing and analyzing "just in time" logistics support. The Navy's F/A-18E/F program was guided in the mid-1990s by an executive steering committee whose members represented the Navy component commanders, the aviation type commanders, the carrier strike wings, the Marine aviation groups, and OPNAV. The program office also worked closely with the Navy Aviation Warfare Center and the Navy's aviation depots to implement "full life cycle" management. See "Program Operating Guide," PEO(T) and PMA 265, 15 Nov. 1996. In the collection of Thomas C. Hone.

[14] As then-Governor Bush said in a speech ("A Period of Consequences") at the Citadel on 23 Sept. 1999, "Our forces in the next century must be agile, lethal, readily deployable, and require a minimum of logistical support. We must be able to project our power over long distances, in days or weeks rather than months."

[15] "Remarks as Delivered by Secretary of Defense Donald H. Rumsfeld," the Pentagon, Monday, 10 Sept. 2001, Office of the Assistant Secretary of Defense (Public Affairs), http://www.defense.gov/Speeches/Speech.aspx?SpeechID=430.

[16] Bradley Graham, *By His Own Rules, The Ambitions, Successes, and Ultimate Failures of Donald Rumsfeld* (New York: Public Affairs, 2009), 274.

[17] Ibid., 211, 274–75.

[18] Ibid., 358.

[19] Aldridge had served as Under Secretary of the U.S. Air Force from 1981 to 1986 and secretary of the Air Force from 1986 to 1988. He had agreed with John Lehman in 1986 that

the authority granted the first Under Secretary of Defense for Acquisition had encroached on the legitimate responsibilities of the service secretaries.

[20] DOD News briefing, Under Secretary of Defense Edward C. Aldridge, 27 June, 2001, www.defenselink.mil/news/Jun2001/t06272001_t627asda.html.

[21] Meetings of Thomas C. Hone, then–Deputy Assistant Secretary of Defense (PA&E), and the Director of OSD (PA&E), Barry Watts, with service deputy programmers in August 2001.

[22] The events at the Pentagon on 9/11 are described in *Pentagon 9/11*, by Alfred Goldberg, Sarandis Papadopoulos, Diane Putney, Nancy Berlage, and Rebecca Welch (Washington, DC: Historical Office of the Secretary of Defense, 2007).

[23] Haynes, "American Naval Thinking in the Post–Cold War Era," 229.

[24] George Tenet, with Bill Harlow, *At the Center of the Storm: My Years at the CIA* (New York: HarperCollins, 2007).

[25] Ibid., 121–22.

[26] See *The 9/11 Commission Report*, authorized edition (New York: W.W. Norton, 2004), 332–34.

[27] The members of the Defense Resources Board were the Deputy Secretary of Defense (chair), the Chairman of the Joint Chiefs of Staff (vice chair), the secretaries of the military departments, and the under secretaries of defense for (a) acquisition, technology and logistics, (b) policy, (c) comptroller, and (d) personnel and readiness. The Vice Chairman of the Joint Chiefs of Staff, the Assistant Secretary of Defense for Command, Control, Communications, and Intelligence, the General Counsel of the Defense Department, and the assistant secretary for legislative affairs could attend on a regular basis as observers.

[28] "FY01 Emergency Supplemental," information memo from the Under Secretary of Defense (Comptroller) to the Deputy Secretary of Defense, 25 Sept. 2001. In the collection of Thomas C. Hone.

[29] "Proposed First Release of funds from the $40 billion Emergency Supplemental," Office of the Director, Office of Management and Budget, Executive Office of the President, 20 Sept. 2001. This proposal followed an initial estimate of emergency spending made within the Defense Department on 13 Sept. 2001. The 20 Sept. Office of Management and Budget (OMB) memo is in the collection of Thomas C. Hone.

[30] *Quadrennial Defense Review Report*, Dept. of Defense, 30 Sept. 2001, iv., http://archive.defense.gov/pubs/qdr2001.pdf.

[31] Ibid., 67.

[32] Ibid., 68.

[33] "Topline Increases," from Barry Watts (Director, OSD [PA&E]) to the Deputy Secretary of Defense, 19 Oct. 2001. In the collection of Thomas C. Hone.

[34] CIA Director George Tenet certainly thought so, as he acknowledged in his memoir, *At the Center of the Storm*.

[35] Information memo, "Managing the Program/Budget Review," from Dov S. Zakheim, Under Secretary of Defense (Comptroller) to the Deputy Secretary of Defense, 31 Oct. 2014. In the collection of Thomas C. Hone.

[36] "FY 2003–07 Program/Budget Review," briefed to Deputy Secretary of Defense Paul Wolfowitz on 2 Nov. 2001, in the collection of Thomas C. Hone.

[37] Beginning the first week of Nov. 2001, the Defense Resources Board held a series of four major reviews, in which the service POMs submitted before 9/11 were reviewed in light of the increased funding from Congress. In the case of the Navy, the POM was added to. This was done to fight terrorism and, as the Bush administration had promised, to fund Navy transformation efforts. Thomas C. Hone's unclassified notes.

[38] David A. Fastabend, "That Elusive Operational Concept," *Army*, The Magazine of the Association of the U.S. Army, June 2001, 40.

[39] In his speech to the graduating cadets at the U.S. Military Academy on 1 June 2002, President George W. Bush said, "[O]ur security will require all Americans to be forward-looking and resolute, to be ready for preemptive action when necessary to defend our liberty and to defend our lives." He added that ". . . we must oppose [nuclear] proliferation and confront regimes that sponsor terror, as each case requires." Source: Ashbrook Center at Ashland University, http://teachingamericanhistory.org/library/document/president-bush-delivers-graduation-speech-at-west-point/.

[40] ADM James G. Stavridis, USN (Ret.), *The Accidental Admiral, A Sailor Takes Command at NATO* (Annapolis, MD: Naval Institute Press, 2014), 129.

[41] Ibid., 130.

[42] ADM Vernon E. Clark, "September 11, 2001: Attack on America," Remarks at a Naval War College Symposium, "Setting Our Course in the Terror War," 29 Oct. 2001, http://avalon.law.yale.edu/sept11/navy_002.asp (25 Aug. 2016).

[43] Tony Holmes, *US Navy Hornet Units of Operation Iraqi Freedom, Part One* (Botley, Oxford, England: Osprey Publishing, 2004), 9.

[44] Clark, "September 11, 2001: Attack on America," 3.

[45] Administrative message, from: CINCLANTFLT; to, GENADMIN/CINCLANTFLT; subj: US Fleet Forces Command, 1 Sept. 2001, RMKS/1, printed in *Inside the Navy*, vol. 14, no. 40 (8 Oct. 2001), 10.

[46] Interview, Thomas C. Hone with CAPT R. Robinson Harris, USN (Ret.), 23 Jan. 2015. As CAPT Harris recalled, "I saw Paul David Miller [CincLantFlt and then CINCLANT] work the idea of a forces command with Admiral Kelso, and [Miller] used the Air Force's Air Combat Command as an example." According to Harris, Miller told Kelso, "[CINCLANT] is Pentagon South. I ought to be the guy who's telling you, the CNO, what you need rather than the staff in OPNAV."

[47] Karen Domabyl Smith, Dean Cheng, Rebecca L. Kirk, Frederick Thompson, Alison Rimsky Vernon, with Kletus Lawler, "Aviation Type Command Alignment: The Promise and the Pitfalls," Center for Naval Analyses (CNR D0007438.A2/Final), Jan. 2003.

[48] ADM John C. Harvey Jr., with CAPT David E. Grogan, JAGC, and CDR (Ret.) Anthony J. Mazzeo, JAGC, "Course Corrections in Command and Control," U.S. Naval Institute *Proceedings*, vol. 138, no. 3 (Mar. 2012), 57.

[49] Smith, Cheng, Kirk, Thompson, Vernon, and Lawler, "Aviation Type Command Alignment: The Promise and the Pitfalls," 28.

[50] Dr. David A. Perin of the Center for Naval Analyses explained this innovation to his colleagues at the Center for Naval Analyses, and one of them explained it to Thomas C. Hone.

[51] Stavridis, *The Accidental Admiral*, 130.

[52] Roland J. Yardley, Raj Raman, Jessie Riposo, James Chiesa, and John F. Schank, "Impacts of the Fleet Response Plan on Surface Combatant Maintenance," RAND Corporation Technical Report (Arlington, VA: RAND, 2006), and *Naval Transformation Roadmap 2003*, Department of the Navy. On line at: http://www.au.af.mil/au/awc/awcgate/navy/naval_trans_roadmap2003.pdf.

[53] ADM Vernon E. Clark, "Sea Power 21: Operational Concepts for a New Era," a speech to the Current Strategy Forum, Naval War College, Newport, RI, 12 June 2002, 3, http://www.navy.mil (25 Aug. 2016).

[54] Ibid., 6.

[55] *Statement of RADM Phillip M. Balisle, Director, Surface Warfare Division*, before the Seapower Subcommittee of the Senate Armed Services Committee on Surface Warfare Systems, 9 Apr. 2002, 7.

[56] Ibid., 14.

[57] Ibid., 17.

[58] Ibid., 21.

[59] Ibid., 23.

[60] Ibid., 30.

[61] PERS FOR—221435Z Feb. 01, "Naval Warfare Requirements and Programs (OPNAV N7)." In the collection of Thomas C. Hone.

[62] Ibid., 5.

[63] George H. Labovitz and Victor Rosansky, "Rapid Realignment: Proven Strategies for Unbeatable Performance," briefly explain the methods used by VADM Balisle to alter the structure and processes of NAVSEA, http://www.lifehack.org/articles/work/rapid-realignment-proven-strategies-for-unbeatable-performance.html (26 Aug. 2016). CNO Clark had asked the Navy's flag officers to read Labovitz and Rosansky's *Rapid Realignment: How to Quickly*

Integrate People, Processes, and Strategy for Unbeatable Performance (http://rapidrealignment.com) and apply its methods to their organizations.

[64] "Requirements Generation System," CJCSI 3170.01B, 15 Apr. 2001, A-1. In the collection of Thomas C. Hone, https://info.aiaa.org/tac/SMG/SOSTC/Launch%20Management%20Documents/Appendix%20B%20Reference%20Documents/Charman_JCS_Instruction.pdf.

[65] Haynes, "American Naval Thinking in the Post–Cold War Era," 225.

[66] Ibid. Haynes based his conclusion on the research done by CAPT Peter M. Swartz, USN (Ret.), at the Center for Naval Analyses. See "Organizing OPNAV (1970–2009)," by Peter M. Swartz, with Michael C. Markowitz, Center for Naval Analyses (Jan. 2010). Also see *The Accidental Admiral*, by ADM James Stavridis, USN (Ret.), 129–30.

[67] This is the view of CAPT Swartz.

[68] Haynes, "American Naval Thinking in the Post–Cold War Era," 226.

[69] ADM Vernon E. Clark, "Sea Power 21: Projecting Decisive Joint Capabilities," U.S. Naval Institute *Proceedings*, vol. 128, no. 10 (Oct. 2002), 33–34.

[70] Ibid., 34.

[71] Ibid., 37.

[72] VADM Michael Bucchi (Commander, Third Fleet) and VADM Michael Mullen (N8), "Sea Shield: Projecting Global Defensive Assurance," U.S. Naval Institute *Proceedings*, vol. 128, no. 11 (Nov. 2002), 56–59. VADM Cutler Dawson (Commander, Second Fleet) and VADM John Nathman (N6/7), "Sea Strike: Projecting Persistent, Responsive, and Precise Power," *Proceedings*, vol. 128, no. 12 (Dec. 2002), 54–58. VADM C. W. Moore Jr. (N4) and LTGEN Edward Hanlon Jr., USMC (Commanding General, Marine Corps Combat Development Command), "Sea Basing: Operational Independence for a New Century," *Proceedings*, vol. 129, no. 1 (Jan. 2003), 80–85. VADM Richard W. Mayo (Commander, Naval Network Warfare Command) and VADM John Nathman (N6/7), "ForceNet: Turning Information into Power, *Proceedings*, vol. 129, no. 2 (Feb. 2003), 42–46. VADM Michael Mullen (N8), "Global Concept of Operations," *Proceedings*, vol. 129, no. 4 (April 2003), 66–69. ADM Vernon E. Clark, "Persistent Combat Power," *Proceedings*, vol. 129, no. 5 (May 2003), 46–48. VADM Alfred G. Harms Jr. (Commander, Naval Education and Training Command), VADM Gerald L. Hoewing (Chief of Naval Personnel), and VADM John B. Totushek (Commander, Naval Reserve Force), "Sea Warrior: Maximizing Human Capital," *Proceedings*, vol. 129, no. 6 (June 2003), 48–52. ADM Robert J. Natter, "Sea Trial: Enabler for a Transformed Fleet," *Proceedings*, vol. 129, no. 11 (Nov. 2003), 62–66. ADM Michael G. Mullen (VCNO), "Sea Enterprise: Resourcing Tomorrow's Fleet," *Proceedings*, vol. 130, no. 1 (Jan. 2004), 60–63.

[73] Clark, "Sea Power 21: Projecting Decisive Joint Capabilities," 37.

[74] ADM Michael G. Mullen, "Sea Enterprise: Resourcing Tomorrow's Fleet," U.S. Naval Institute *Proceedings*, vol. 130, no. 1 (Jan. 2004), 61.

[75] Ibid., 60.

[76] Haynes, "American Naval Thinking in the Post–Cold War Era," 243.

[77] Ibid., 245.

[78] Ibid., 246.

[79] *Statement of Admiral Vern Clark, U.S. Navy Chief of Naval Operations* before the Defense Subcommittee of the House Appropriations Committee, Posture Statement, 10 Mar. 2005, 3 under Fig. 1.

[80] Ibid., 22 accompanying Fig. 10.

[81] Haynes, "American Naval Thinking in the Post–Cold War Era," 263.

[82] "Surge Protectors [*sic*] Submarines Prove Vital to the Navy's Fleet Response Plan," Undersea Warfare (Fall 2004), 1.

[83] Steven Metz, "Decisionmaking in Operation Iraqi Freedom: The Strategic Shift of 2007," Operation Iraqi Freedom Key Decisions Monograph Series, U.S. Army War College, Strategic Studies Institute, May 2010, 1.

[84] Ibid., 15. See also 18.

[85] Thomas E. Ricks, Fiasco, *The American Military Adventure in Iraq* (New York: Penguin Press, 2006), 66.

[86] Haynes, "American Naval Thinking in the Post–Cold War Era," 273.

[87] Ibid., 271.

[88] Ibid., Haynes interviewed VADM Morgan.

[89] Ibid., 275.

[90] Ibid., 276.

[91] Ibid., 277.

[92] Ricks, *Fiasco*, 145.

[93] Haynes, "American Naval Thinking in the Post–Cold War Era," 277.

[94] Ibid., 283.

[95] Ibid., 286.

[96] Ibid., 288.

[97] Ibid., 289.

[98] "Transformation Planning Guidance," Office of Force Transformation, Office of the Secretary of Defense, April 2003, 3, http://www.acq.osd.mil/brac/Downloads/Prior%20BRAC%20Rounds/transformationplanningapr03.pdf.

[99] In that sense, the Littoral Combat Ship was not transformational. It was built essentially as an advanced concept demonstrator, and not as an example of a transformed acquisition process.

The argument for the Littoral Combat Ship was that its modularity and its digital links to other systems and platforms made it transformational. While there was some truth to that argument, what Cebrowski was after was a process that went from concept to operational system quickly enough to deter enemies from trying to match the U.S. effort.

[100] James R. Blaker, *Transforming Military Force: The Legacy of Arthur Cebrowski and Network Centric Warfare* (Westport, CT: Praeger Security International, 2007).

[101] For a strong critique of Rumsfeld, see Thomas E. Ricks, *The Gamble, General David Petraeus and the American Military Adventure in Iraq, 2006–2008* (New York: Penguin Press, 2009).

[102] Rumsfeld's decision to shield the Missile Defense Agency/Ballistic Missile Defense Organization from programmatic scrutiny (especially from the analysts in OSD/Program Analysis & Evaluation) was not necessarily a good move. It sent a message to other agencies: Get the support of the President or the Secretary of Defense, and you can avoid having some analysis group looking over your shoulder.

[103] Robert D. Kaplan, "What Rumsfeld Got Right, How Donald Rumsfeld Remade the U.S. Military for a More Uncertain World," *The Atlantic*, July/Aug. 2008, on-line version, 5, https://www.theatlantic.com/magazine/archive/2008/07/what-rumsfeld-got-right/306870/.

[104] "The Defense Planning Process, FY 2006–2011," briefing to the Deputy Secretary of Defense, 14 Nov. 2003, slide 5.

[105] Interview, Thomas C. Hone with CAPT Ronald R. Harris, USN (Ret.), 23 Jan. 2015.

CHAPTER 17

A Dramatic Two Years: Michael G. Mullen as CNO

Admiral Michael G. Mullen, Admiral Clark's successor as CNO, was also an aggressive leader. No one should have been surprised. Mullen had served as Clark's vice chief from August 2003 to October 2004. Before that, he had gained extensive Washington experience—in the Bureau of Naval Personnel (BUPERS), in the Office of the Secretary of Defense, and in OPNAV, where he was both N86 and, later, N8. Admiral Mullen also served as Commander, Allied Joint Force Command in Naples from October 2004 until his appointment as Chief of Naval Operations in July 2005. As Navy captain and historian Peter Haynes noted, Mullen possessed a very strong background in programming—as strong as that of any of the CNOs prior to his appointment. At the same time, Mullen's experience as an allied commander in Europe had "profoundly reshaped how he thought about the world."[1] Selected for his leadership abilities and for his programming experience, Mullen brought his own concept of naval strategy and a keen sense of public relations to his position. His two years as CNO (July 2005 to September 2007) would be filled with significant initiatives.

A Running Start

Mullen's appointment as CNO began on 22 July 2005. Three days later, the new CNO issued seven memos to the OPNAV staff and Fleet Forces Command. The memos dealt with Navy health care costs, a "human capital strategy" for the Navy, the readiness of Navy shore commands, the notion of recreating a coordinating organization for the Navy's systems commands,

Navy shipbuilding programs, OPNAV organization, and the proper relationship between Fleet Forces Command and OPNAV. But the action that garnered the most media attention was Mullen's decision to remove and reassign Vice Admiral Joseph A. Sestak Jr., DCNO for Warfare Requirements and Programs (N6/N7). Sestak, with both extensive operational experience and a PhD from the Kennedy School of Government at Harvard University, had a reputation within OPNAV for being both brilliant and for working his staff to exhaustion—a reputation that he took to the House of Representatives after retiring and winning a seat there in 2006. As media commentators noted when Sestak was removed, Mullen was sending a message about "command climate" to his deputies and the OPNAV staff.[2]

But Mullen's most important immediate tasks were to project future Navy readiness levels and to get shipbuilding costs under control. Readiness requirements directly affected Navy spending for operations and maintenance. If readiness costs went up, then there would be less money available for new ships. Yet if the cost of new ships increased, the size of the Navy's surface and carrier forces would still decline, even if readiness costs were held down. Mullen assigned the task of projecting future readiness needs to Fleet Forces Command. He gave the job of reviewing shipbuilding programs to his Vice Chief of Naval Operations, Admiral Robert F. Willard, an outstanding naval aviator and former head of the Joint Staff's Force Structure, Resources, and Assessment Directorate (J8). Willard was an experienced staff officer as well as a former carrier group and Seventh Fleet commander. While leading J8, for example, he had broken a logjam over the concept of "capability" that was at the heart of the Joint Capabilities Integration and Development System (JCIDS).

Admiral Willard would need all his skills to lead an effort to do what CNO Mullen directed: stabilize the Navy's relations with its shipbuilding industrial base, develop a future naval force structure, discipline the requirements process for ships, eliminate or highlight "statutory or regulatory barriers" that hampered efficient shipbuilding, and move the Navy toward "more modular and multipurpose ship designs."[3] In the 1990s, the Navy had monitored the Danish navy's apparently successful effort to use interchangeable modules as a way of making a basic hull design more versatile and at the same time more affordable. As historian Norman Friedman found, the reliance on interchangeable modules appeared to "be just what would be needed for the littoral combat ship. A littoral ship design might" be very valuable for forward deployment if it could swap in and out several different types of module, if the modules could be stored at a forward base near the deployment area, and if the ship could move quickly from a deployment to the forward base and then back again. This is the concept that had formed the basis of the original LCS solicitations—"unconventional hull forms offering substantial deck areas (for emplacing modules) and high sustained speed."[4]

The Navy was shrinking as old ships were retired and new ones did not replace them on a one-for-one basis, and CNO Mullen was determined to wring as much value as he could out of every shipbuilding dollar. Unfortunately, the actual or projected costs for ships were rising, and the money for ship construction was at best stable and at worst declining. On 31 March, 2005, then–CNO Clark had even advocated a sort of heresy: building smaller warships (including smaller aircraft carriers) as a means to maintain numbers of ships in the face of rising costs and diminishing resources.[5] To make matters worse for the new CNO, there was friction between the Navy and the Marine Corps over which types of ships should be built. Former CNO Clark, Marine Corps Commandant General Michael W. Hagee, and Secretary of the Navy Gordon R. England had signed an agreement that set the minimum number of new LPD-17 amphibious ships at nine, but the Marines wanted one more.[6] Unfortunately for the Marines, LPD-17 cost more than projected, and it was not clear that later ships of the same class would cost less.

This sort of problem was made even worse by the need to support the military operations in Iraq and Afghanistan. By the time Mullen took office as CNO, the United States had more than 143,000 troops in Iraq alone, at a total cost of about $140 billion per year. Army General George W. Casey Jr., the commander of Multi-National Force-Iraq, was struggling to develop and implement a successful counter-insurgency campaign in Iraq, and it was not clear in the summer of 2005 whether that campaign would succeed and when it would end.[7] The president asked for and received from Congress supplemental appropriations to cover war costs, but those "supplementals" were often not enough, and the Secretary of Defense would pull funds from existing programs to cover the difference between the supplementals and the actual war costs. Admiral Mullen therefore had two tasks. One was forced on him—to find the resources *from within the Navy* to build ships. The other task was to show that the Navy was actively and significantly involved in the global campaign against terrorists. The immediate "solution" to the second problem was to make sure that the Navy continued to rotate almost ten thousand individual augmentees through Central Command. Solving the first problem would prove frustrating, but VCNO Willard was told to go at it.

However, in his "American Naval Thinking in the Post–Cold War Era," Captain Haynes argues persuasively that Mullen brought more to his task than just a focus on finding funding for Navy ships and systems. Vice Admiral John G. Morgan Jr., N3/N5, had already put together the "Navy's 3/1 Strategy: The Maritime Contribution to the Joint Force in a Changed Strategic Landscape," and he had deliberately sent it to Admiral Mullen in Italy before Mullen's selection as CNO was made public. Morgan hoped that Mullen would find his new approach to the Navy's role in the world persuasive. It involved looking at the world in a different way. In a speech to a Navy League audience in New York, Morgan described his reaction when, as commander of *Enterprise* Battle Group, he learned of the attacks of 9/11. "What struck me was what a clear day it was," he recalled. "For some reason, I did not focus on the burning tower. I focused on what a bright, clear, pristine new day it was." Morgan told his Navy League audience that he then turned to his chief of staff and said, "The world has just changed." His next move was to call the captain of *Enterprise* and direct him to make "best speed for the coast of Pakistan."[8]

Morgan wanted Mullen to have a similar experience—a realization that indeed the world had changed and that the Navy could and would change to deal with it. Mullen did. In a 29 July 2005 memo to Vice Admiral Morgan, Mullen directed him and his subordinates to come up with a "Navy Strategic Plan" that could serve to influence the programming process in OPNAV and help the new CNO evaluate the quality of the Navy's program.[9] Fleet Forces Command was directed to describe what capabilities the Navy would need in the future and then develop a concept of operations (such as forward deployment) for the effective use of those capabilities, but N3/N5 was in charge of strategy development. If the fleet deployed forward, for example, what was it supposed to achieve? And why that and not something else? Morgan had set out to answer these questions, and in CNO Mullen he found someone of a similar mind.

The Genesis of the 1,000-Ship Navy

The link between then–CNO Admiral Frank Kelso in the summer of 1990 and CNO Mullen 15 years later is the way that both grasped how the world had changed. For Kelso, the Cold War was over, and the Navy needed to adapt to a world where there was no significant maritime challenge to U.S. dominance. For Mullen, the Navy's role was that of protecting world trade and encouraging world-wide maritime awareness. As Captain Haynes put it, "In a globalizing, more interdependent world where U.S. interests are increasingly linked to those of other nations, the United States needed a strategic approach that placed the system's security requirements at its core. In essence, for the United States, 'national' and 'systemic' security were so subtly intertwined as to be indistinguishable in practice."[10] But Morgan and Mullen agreed that "systemic" security could not be maintained by the United States alone. As the September 2005 *National Strategy for Maritime Security* put it, keeping the seas open and safe required "a common understanding and a joint effort for action on a global scale."[11] This meant that the Navy would be as much a "facilitator" of trade, safe passage, and maritime awareness as it would be a guardian of the sea lanes to and from the United States and an "enforcer" of security at sea.

Not every flag officer agreed with this approach. As noted in the previous chapter, Admiral John B. Nathman, head of Fleet Forces Command, "believed it was operationally and politically dangerous to downplay the Navy's blue-water capabilities."[12] Nathman was not one to be ignored. A veteran pilot and carrier commander, as a young flag officer he had been in charge of logistics for North Atlantic Treaty Organization (NATO) IFOR in Bosnia in the mid-1990s. He had also served as the first commander of U.S. Naval Air Forces, been N6/N7, had served as the VCNO, and had taken command of Fleet Forces Command in February 2005, before Admiral Mullen had been appointed CNO.

The U.S. Naval Institute's *Proceedings* published the different views of Nathman and Mullen in its January 2006 issue. Mullen argued that "the Navy cannot meet the threats of tomorrow by simply maintaining today's readiness and requirements." Nathman responded by arguing that, "if the past is prologue, America will again find itself confronting an aggressive state."[13] Based on his experience within N5, where he served as a branch chief from February to June 2006, Captain Haynes observed that "Over the next year and a half, the clashes between Nathman's U.S. Fleet Forces Command and Morgan's N3/N5 . . . grew fierce as the relationship between the two organizations descended into rancor."[14]

Mullen, though, was not moved; he would not retreat. As Haynes suggested, "Mullen and Morgan thought that relative to their costs, more specialized capabilities required for local stability and shaping operations and counter-terrorism would bring about disproportional political results in terms of their systemic effects."[15] The results of the Quadrennial Defense Review (QDR), published in February 2006, went Mullen's way. The 2006 review, "like the 3/1 Strategy, argued that the missions of Homeland Defense and War on Terror/Irregular Warfare were not subsets of traditional, conventional campaign-oriented challenges and thus required unique capabilities."[16] Indeed, what the writers of the QDR argued was that the policy of military pre-emption adopted by President George W. Bush for Iraq was not well suited to a world where cybernetic attacks, economic disruptions, and insurgencies in "failed states" were major threats to American national security. At the same time, the nation's military forces had to be prepared for "spikes of intense warfighting activity" like the combat in Iraq and Afghanistan—or worse.

What was the operations concept that went with the new naval strategy? CNO Mullen had directed Vice Admiral Morgan in January 2006 "to update" the "Naval Operational Concept for Joint Operations" that former CNO Clark and former Marine Corps Commandant Hagee had signed in 2003. Morgan was to work with Marine Lieutenant General James N. Mattis, the head of the United States Marine Corp's Combat Development Command (MCCDC). Mattis, intelligent and much more widely read than most officers in any service, also had a boatload of combat experience. He had led a battalion in Operation Desert Storm in 1991, was the first Marine ever to command a Navy task force in combat, and in 2003–2004 had commanded the 1st Marine Division in Iraq.[17] While heading the Combat Development Command, Mattis cooperated with the Army in crafting a new manual on counter-terrorism. Mattis also oversaw the drafting of the USMC's *Marine Corps Operating Concepts for a Changing Security Environment*, published in March 2006. The paper assumed that future conflicts would be irregular, but it also argued that the combined-arms approach of the Marines would be effective in such conflicts, as well as in more "traditional" operations like Operation Iraqi Freedom (OIF). As *Operating Concepts* put it, Marines "thrive in the chaotic and unpredictable environments in which our forces are employed." This was vintage Mattis. So, too, was his assertion in the Foreword to the document that "We are a nation at war and will remain so for the foreseeable future."[18] There was, in this, apparently enough similarity between the views of Morgan and Mattis to permit them to cooperate.

Working directly for Morgan and Mattis was Rear Admiral Philip H. Cullom, whom Mullen made director of strategy and policy (N51) in OPNAV in March 2006.[19] Cullom recruited a team of three OPNAV officers (one of whom was the deputy director of Deep Blue), two Marine officers from MCCDC, and one Marine staff officer from Marine Corps Headquarters to draft the "Naval Operations Concept," and they worked on it—with guidance from more senior officers—through the spring and summer. In the Preface to the document, the authors informed readers that the *Naval Operations Concept 2006* superseded "the 2002 *Naval Operating Concept for Joint Operations* . . . as well as earlier papers like *From the Sea* and *Forward . . . From the Sea*." Arguing that they had been guided by formal (that is, presidential) statements of national strategy, the authors went on to say that "this concept calls for *more widely distributed forces* to provide *increased forward presence*, security cooperation with an expanding set of international partners, preemption of non-traditional threats, and global response to crises in regions around the world where access might be difficult."[20] Later in the document, the concept was expressed as a challenge—"to remain capable of traditional naval missions while simultaneously enhancing our ability to conduct non-traditional missions in order to ensure that naval power and influence can be applied at and from the sea, across the littorals, and ashore, as required."[21]

According to Captain Haynes, the 2006 *Naval Operations Concept* was less important for what it said than for what the process of preparing it meant for OPNAV and the CNO. Haynes was very blunt about it: "Goldwater-Nichols had increased the power of the CINCs/combatant commanders and undermined the Services' stature, which bred a dismissive attitude . . . toward the service chiefs and their staffs. In this respect, Goldwater-Nichols made it more difficult for the ideas and initiatives of the strategy section of OPNAV to be taken seriously."[22] More generally, the continuing argument between the Fleet Forces Command staff and the OPNAV staff was a logical consequence of former CNO Clark's view that OPNAV's responsibility was primarily to support the combatant commanders.

In effect, Clark had created a counterweight to OPNAV *within the Navy*. Fleet Forces Command was supposed to make sure that the fleet was trained and ready—ready to accomplish the missions set by the Navy's component commanders who supported the regional combatant commanders. Therefore, Fleet Forces Command looked to the naval component commanders for guidance in developing the Navy's program. OPNAV was supposed to do the same thing, but with a focus on the future as well as the present. Intended or not, Fleet Forces Command challenged OPNAV and the CNO in an area—programming—where OPNAV had been dominant. As Captain Haynes realized, CNO Mullen had little choice but to fight back, and one tool he could use was strategic planning: "Mullen's Navy Strategic Plan was a new tool of governance. It allowed the CNO to broaden the analytical basis upon which programmatic decisions were made beyond operational-level capability gaps . . ."[23]

In effect, the two sides—OPNAV and Fleet Forces Command—to the debate over Navy (and Marine Corps) concepts competed in three arenas. The competition in the first arena was over what the Navy should do—and what it should be like—in order to support American national strategy. In this field of competition, there was room for honest argument, and the evidence suggests that the arguments between OPNAV and Fleet Forces Command were reasoned and sensible. The second arena was one of personalities. Both Mullen and Nathman were experienced, intelligent leaders; neither was used to giving way in an argument; both cared deeply about the Navy. We should not be surprised, therefore, that their professional disagreement over the proper shape of the Navy involved their loyal staffs. The third arena was institutional. What organization was at the heart of the Navy's commitment to train, equip, and organize naval forces? Who was the real boss—the head of Fleet Forces Command or the head of OPNAV? That this question might even be asked shows that honest disagreements among professionals could potentially escalate into a series of conflicts between OPNAV and Fleet Forces Command. If CNO Mullen allowed this to happen, it would set a precedent that would frustrate future Chiefs of Naval Operations.

In short, the debate prior to the adoption of the "1,000-ship" navy concept was more important than it seemed. What looked like a disagreement over naval or maritime strategy or an operating concept was more than that. It was also a disagreement about which organization—OPNAV or Fleet Forces Command—better understood the needs of the fleet and the fleet's role in national strategy. CNO Mullen was well suited to manage this disagreement. In the first place, he had allies. Marine Corps Commandant Michael Hagee was, to quote Mullen, "a friend," and had been since the time that both had entered the Naval Academy.[24] Mullen also had at least tacit support from former CNO Clark. As Mullen told reporters attending a 13 October 2005 "media roundtable," "from about '96 until very recently I had a lot of tours with Vernon Clark, so I was in many ways trained by him and appreciated greatly his leadership, and he left the Navy . . . in terrific shape . . ."[25] CNO Mullen also had support from his chief programmer, Vice Admiral Lewis W. Crenshaw Jr., who told a chapter of the Armed Forces Communications and Electronics Association on 13 October 2005 that the budget for national defense had "peaked out," and that the future was inevitably one of decreasing budgets. As Crenshaw told his audience of defense contractors at the beginning of his presentation, "For those of you who don't want to be sad, [it's] time for you to leave."[26] Finally, Mullen was not dogmatic. As he told the media roundtable participants, "I'm very supportive of 'Seapower 21'," and he wanted to continue promoting the concept on which it was based. But he also said, in almost the same breath, that he'd see how the idea worked out as it spread among the world's navies. "Then," he noted, "a year or two from now [I'll] see if or where I should adjust."[27]

Reorganizing OPNAV

Mullen was also deliberate and careful in the way that he implemented change within OPNAV. Details of the proposed changes "leaked out" in October, giving supporters and opponents a chance to argue their positions. In his 31 August 2005 speech at the Naval War College, Mullen compared policy-making in the Marine Corps and the Navy. The Marines would argue vigorously, but then "The commandant makes a decision, boom, everybody's singing from those first edition copies of the music. The Navy has a debate. It's a vigorous debate. The CNO makes a decision, and everybody goes, 'Holy Cow, he's serious, we'd better have a debate.'"[28] Though obviously meant to be humorous, Mullen's comment did suggest a real difference between the services, and it was a difference that he knew how to manage. For example, Mullen and General Hagee met for two whole days at the end of October 2005 to discuss what Hagee called "third rail" issues, including Navy-Marine Corps tactical aviation, future amphibious ships, the Navy's plan for a riverine force, and the issue of the command of expeditionary strike groups. Hagee emerged from the discussions, saying, "We talked about those issues that affect the Navy and the Marine Corps, and I think we came out better. And that is going to continue primarily because of the leadership of Mike Mullen."[29]

When Mullen and VCNO Willard were ready, they issued their "staff realignment" plan. The 8 November 2005 memo merged N6/N7 with N8 and placed Vice Admiral Crenshaw at the head of the combined organization. The memo also warned OPNAV staff to prepare for "a future breakout of a separate N6 directorate."[30] Why the merger of N7 and N8? One reason was to put the evaluation of near-term and long-term modernization programs under one OPNAV staff directorate. A second reason was to align the OPNAV staff with the Joint Staff. Responding to Secretary of Defense Donald Rumsfeld's direction, the Joint Staff—with much debate and discussion with the service staffs—had created a "capabilities-based" program and acquisition assessment process. This new process was designed to compel the combatant commanders' staffs and the service staffs to plan in terms of capabilities and not specific named forces (like the *Nimitz*-carrier battle group). Setting up this process was the job of the Joint Staff's J8 directorate.

Initially, there was a lot of confusion about the meaning of "capability." An example may help make the concept clear. Before Secretary Rumsfeld, combatant commanders' staffs had drawn up their tentative or actual operational plans according to the Joint Operation Planning Process (JOPP). An essential part of the JOPP was a review and assessment of available forces. Combatant command planners had to consult with military service liaison officers to see if the forces normally allotted to their region were capable of carrying out the planned operations that the staffs routinely devised to deal with likely contingencies. The planners used specific kinds of forces—carrier battle groups, Marine air-ground task forces, Army combat brigades, Air Force combat or transport wings, etc.—as they did their work. Rumsfeld wanted the process changed so that the combatant commander's staffs planned using notional capabilities such as long-range strike, airlift, or counterinsurgency. So if a combatant commander's operations planners wanted long-range strike, they would ask for just that, indicating the operating environment, the mission that had to be done, and the objective to be achieved. The Joint Staff might come back and say, "There's an aviation strike capability available, and a cruise missile strike capability. Which better fits your need?" For on-call strike, the planners would probably select land-based or sea-based tactical aviation. For something that could work at almost any time, they could select cruise missile or unmanned aerial vehicle (UAV) attacks.

This stress on capabilities put a burden on service staffs. They had to be able to think in terms of capabilities and not in terms of specific units or systems. Indeed, they had to *develop* capabilities and not simply acquire systems or maintain specific units. To enforce this new way of thinking, CNO Mullen created a new organization, the Naval Capabilities Board. The March 2006 charter for the Resources and Requirements Review Board (R3B) spelled out the relationship between the existing R3B and the new Naval Capabilities Board. The R3B remained the key flag-level decision board. As the charter explained,

> The R3B acts as the focal point for decision-making regarding Navy/[Joint Capabilities Integration Development System] [Acquisition Category] I-IV requirements, the validation of non-acquisition related, emergent, and Joint requirements, synchronization of Planning, Programming, Budgeting, and Execution (PPBE) milestones, and resolution

of cross-enterprise or cross-sponsor issues. The R3B shall conduct periodic reviews of the Navy's major program requirements and determine the affordability way ahead.[31]

The Naval Capabilities Board was a two-star panel; the R3B was a three-star panel.

For both acquisition and programming, there were two flag-level panels above the R3B—the Navy Corporate Board, chaired by the vice chief, and the CNO's Executive Board, chaired by the CNO. The CNO would issue general guidance to the OPNAV staff, and the staff offices would come back with their proposals. The proposals would be reviewed and filtered by the boards—from the Capabilities Board to the R3B, and from there to the Corporate Board and/or the CNO's Executive Board. This was a complex process; The Navy's "Acquisition and Capabilities Guidebook," published in December 2008, had more than 200 pages.[32] But the inability of the Joint Staff (and its contractors) to develop a rigorous definition of "capability" by 2005 left space for the Navy's own analysts. Mullen's reorganization of OPNAV moved those analysts from N7 to N8, in particular N81, the "Capability Analysis and Assessment Division."

The deputy chief of N81, retired Captain Arthur H. Barber III, believed that the concept of "capability" was inadequate as the basis for programming, and he set out to see to it that "capability assessments" did not influence the work of N81.[33] He was also opposed to the idea that N81's analysts should be the "honest brokers" in the programming process. As an officer who respected Barber put it after the latter's retirement, "[Barber] eradicated the term 'honest broker' from N81's vernacular, because he thought it implied that others on the Navy staff were somehow dishonest or unwilling to face the truth" about their programs.[34] Barber wanted to

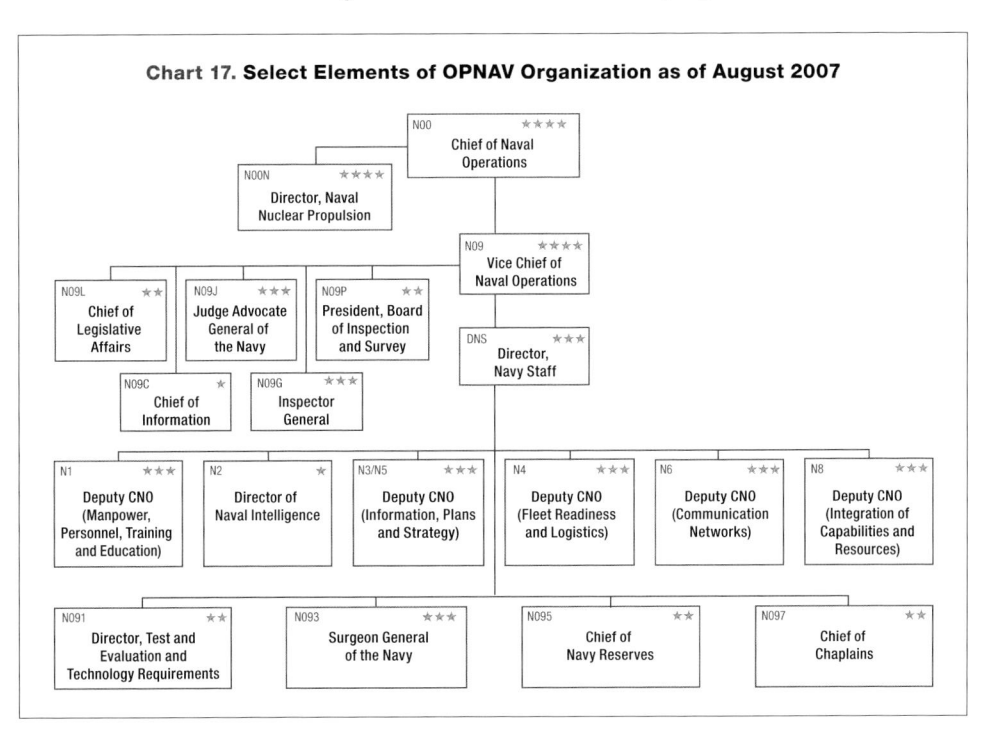

Chart 17. Select Elements of OPNAV Organization as of August 2007

root the programming process in rigorous, "dispassionate," campaign analysis—analysis so well done that it would gain support among diverse audiences in the Pentagon and in the Congress. The focus on N81's analysis was its work on the four "capability scenarios" developed by OSD.[35]

The rise in the importance of N81, and the concomitant reduction in the influence of J8 inside OPNAV, was one development that resulted from Secretary Rumsfeld's emphasis on "capabilities." Another was the invigoration of planning inside OPNAV. To produce the "right" capabilities called not only for a rigorous programming process, it also called for a rigorous *planning* process. It was the planners, after all, who reviewed the joint scenarios used by the analysts in N81. CNO Mullen, following the thinking of Vice Admiral John Morgan, understood this.

That is why the debate between Mullen and Nathman was so important. Both had visions of the Navy's future; those visions did not agree. Mullen had to keep up his back-and-forth with Admiral Nathman while at the same time drawing on Vice Admiral Morgan and Morgan's OPNAV staff for the strategic thinking that would be essential if the Navy were to plan an affordable and effective future. In his thesis, Captain Haynes noted that CNO Mullen did not turn to N8 for a Navy strategic plan—a look ahead to the Navy of the future. Instead, Mullen turned to Vice Admiral Morgan. It was from N3/N5 that Mullen drew the idea of the "1,000-ship Navy," while its complement, the Global Fleet Station, came originally from the work of Captain Wayne Porter, head of Mullen's Strategic Actions Group (N00Z).[36] A Global Fleet Station was "a self-sustaining, home base compromised of one or more large amphibious ships that would steam off the coast and play host and coordinate the activities of U.S. small-craft and riverine boats, helicopters, mobile training teams, Seabees, Army engineers, explosive ordnance personnel, salvage divers, medical and dental teams . . . using capabilities that would normally have been considered support functions."[37] Mullen was also an advocate of the "sea basing" concept, and he defined it broadly, to include the Navy's use of aircraft carriers to save and sustain survivors of the tsunami that swept Indonesia in 2004 and of those overwhelmed by Hurricane Katrina in 2005. As he told reporters in October 2005, "The sea base is made up of lots of different capabilities."[38]

Mullen's reliance on Morgan and N3/N5 made sense for several reasons. First, N8 was in the process of absorbing N6/N7 over the winter of 2005–2006 and into the spring of 2006. N8 personnel were also busy in the summer of 2006 with the Navy's Program Objective Memorandum. Second, Morgan and his staff were a "proven quantity." They did not have to be "broken in." Third, Morgan was adept at communicating with audiences within the Navy and those outside Washington. He began a program of "conversations with the country" in November 2006 after he had spent the summer of 2006 giving "a series of extraordinary presentations to Navy admirals" regarding the 1,000-ship Navy.[39] Fourth, Morgan could work with both the Marines and the Coast Guard. That was essential because they were critical players in both the 1,000-ship Navy idea and Mullen and Morgan's concept of "maritime domain awareness."

Working with Marine Lieutenant General James F. Amos and Assistant Coast Guard Commandant Rear Admiral Joseph L. Nimmich, Morgan put together a "tri-service core writing team" and began a series of "seminars, wargames, and workshops" at the Naval War College to produce "maritime strategy options" that could be reviewed by the flag officers and then used by the writing team.[40] To shield both the war gamers and the writing team from the programming process, Mullen kept Morgan's three-person executive committee and those working for it from considering force structure. As Haynes discovered, the commandants of the Coast Guard and the Marines supported this constraint.[41] They well knew that any consideration of programs and budgets would inhibit the ability of the analysts, war gamers, and staff officers to focus on a strategy.

In the meantime, on 1 September 2006 CNO Mullen and USMC Commandant Hagee signed "The Naval Operations Concept 2006." This document took strategy as a given, as something spelled out in *The National Strategy for Maritime Security* and in other, similar documents; it focused on *using* maritime forces. As the Introduction to the document stated, it was written for a "wide audience," including the public, other agencies of the federal government, "multinational partners," and "Sailors and Marines."[42] What made "The Naval Operations Concept 2006" interesting was its list of "Guiding Naval Principles," its use of one actual and two notional scenarios to illustrate its points, and a chart that showed how missions were related to principles and methods and therefore led to important outcomes.[43]

It's a given that staff officers are busy. Just because the CNO or the Commandant of the Marine Corps embraces an idea or a concept of operations doesn't mean that staff action officers see the idea or concept the same way as the flag officers do. Senior officers need to explain their ideas and approaches, and they need to do so in a way that busy staff subordinates will understand. "The Naval Operations Concept 2006" was a handy guide for those who received a copy. It was not too long, and it avoided the sort of conceptual language that might have left parts of its intended audience scratching their heads and wondering what the point was.

The "Concept" also provided guidance. The list of "naval principles," for example, contained some general points that were widely accepted, such as the need for "agility" and "interoperability." But the list also held some real guidance, such as "persistent presence," speed of response time, and "unpredictability for our adversaries and reliability for our friends." The same was true for the list of "foundation" practices. "Leadership and professionalism" were obvious enough, but there was "mission type orders," which drew on Navy and Marine Corps experiences reaching back to World War II, and "interdependence," which was something very different than "coordination" or "cooperation."[44] There was even a discussion of "desired outcomes and effects," which attempted to pull the discussions of principles, missions, and methods together in a coherent package. "The Naval Operations Concept 2006" was something that staff officers could quickly refer to, readily understand, and then use in the negotiations over programs and "capabilities."

They needed it. In December 2005, retired Marine Corps Lieutenant General Paul K. Van Riper, a decorated combat veteran and former commander of the Marine Corps Combat Development Command, sent an email very critical of the "capabilities-based planning" process to Commandant Hagee and other senior officers, including Chairman of the Joint Chiefs General Peter Pace, USMC. Van Riper, outspoken and brilliant, argued that the instructions

481

setting out capabilities-based planning were not clear and used terms that had "damaged the military lexicon to the point that it interferes with effective professional military discourse." Lieutenant General Mattis, then in command of MCCDC, agreed with Van Riper, saying "I think he is squarely on target."[45] "The Naval Operations Concept 2006," with its emphasis on clear language, was in line with what Generals Van Riper and Hagee were saying. It was part of an effort to use terms that would be clear, acceptable to the Joint Staff, and also helpful for younger staff officers. It also kept up the momentum of changes that CNO Mullen had initiated.

Donald C. Winter, who succeeded Gordon England as Secretary of the Navy, did not take office until 3 January 2006, and his first speech was to the Surface Navy Association on 12 January. Winter, a scientist and business executive, would find his hands full with acquisition issues, but Captain Haynes suggested the new secretary also intervened in Vice Admiral Morgan's strategy development process in the late spring of 2006. Winter was apparently concerned that the new strategy document draft placed too much stress on those capabilities that were not directly focused on winning a major fight at sea or against the land.[46] Winter was also obviously protecting the prerogatives of the secretary's office. He did not intend to simply stand by while Morgan put forward the views of the uniformed naval strategists.

CNO Mullen had enjoyed six months of relative—and extraordinary—freedom from interference by former Secretary England because England also served as acting Deputy Secretary of Defense after 13 May 2005. In the six months from July 2005 to and through December of that year, Mullen had led efforts to develop a multiservice maritime strategy, reinforced his personal authority and that of his office, used his position and his access to the media to reach beyond the boundaries of the Pentagon, and linked an altered OPNAV with a vision of the Navy's future. It was an impressive achievement. But acquisition problems would detract from it.

Navy and Marine Corps Acquisition Disappointments

Admiral Mullen inherited several major acquisition programs that were less than stellar. One was the new destroyer, DD(X); another was the littoral combat ship, or LCS; a third was the *Virginia*-class attack submarine; the fourth was the LPD-17 amphibious ship; the fifth was the Joint Strike Fighter (JSF). When Mullen became CNO, all these acquisition programs were in trouble—mostly cost trouble. Because major Marine Corps acquisitions are mostly paid for by the Navy, there were also some USMC programs in trouble that Mullen had to consider, especially the Expeditionary Fighting Vehicle (EFV), the H-1 helicopter program, and the vertical take-off and landing version of the JSF.

When it comes to major acquisitions, no CNO or Secretary of the Navy today enters office with the ability to work from a "clean slate." There are always ongoing acquisitions, and sometimes a secretary and CNO can do little to shape their progress. A classic example was the JSF, whose roots went back to the early 1990s. In November 1996, Lockheed Martin and Boeing were awarded contracts to produce competing prototypes, and the prototypes were tested in 2001, with Lockheed winning the competition. It looked as though the development effort was off to a good start, but by the time Admiral Mullen became CNO, there were signs that the Marine Corps and Navy variants would cost significantly more than originally projected, mainly due to the increased cost of the plane's complex software systems.

The classic dilemma of modern military acquisition is the inverse relationship between numbers and cost: the more expensive the system, the fewer of them that can be afforded and produced, especially if funds are limited. The performance of the individual systems—aircraft, ships, or submarines—may be much improved over those items they replace, but there is the danger of eventually not having enough ships, planes, and submarines. This is especially true when the defense budget is declining or when—as was the case after the invasion of Iraq in 2003—increases in defense spending must go to combat operations and their support. Two tendencies are usually the source of dramatic cost growth in acquisition programs. The first is to attempt to pack too much performance into a system—to require it to "push the envelope" of technology. The second is to conduct research and development concurrently with initial production. If not eliminated or constrained, these two tendencies will run up program costs dramatically, especially if both occur in the same program.

The tendency to "push the envelope" strongly affected the EFV, JSF, and LCS programs. The EFV was planned to replace the Marines' existing assault amphibious vehicle, or AAV, which dated back to the early 1970s. The requirements that drove the vehicle's design were high speed through the water and on paved roads, a range of operations great enough to be launched from amphibious ships that were out of sight of any beach, improved armor protection for the 20 Marines driving and riding in it, the ability to operate over rough terrain, and a powerful but relatively light gun. The EFV was to form one leg of a triad of new Marine systems; the other two legs were the V-22 Osprey and the landing craft air cushion (LCAC) vehicle. Initially christened the Advanced Amphibious Assault Vehicle (AAAV), work on its design began in 1988. In June 1996, General Dynamics began full-scale engineering development; in the summer of 2001, the firm won a contract to build the prototypes that would test the vehicle's performance. In September 2003, the name of the AAAV was changed to "Expeditionary Fighting Vehicle." Its projected cost was $20 million per copy.

However, studies by the USMC staff in 2005 and 2006 suggested that the EFV was not likely to be needed in large numbers in the future. Evaluations of operations in Iraq and Afghanistan were convincing Marines that the EFV was too expensive for the limited capability that it gave the Marine Corps in irregular and counter-insurgency operations. The QDR had emphasized the need for the services to plan for such operations, and Secretary Rumsfeld had directed the services to tailor their program plans and budgets to better support the global campaign against terrorists. In consequence, the Marine Corps reduced the number of EFVs it planned to purchase from over 1,000 to less than 600. It intended to use the funds saved to develop a "light tactical vehicle" and a vehicle that could be carried by the V-22 Osprey.[47]

But the EFV's troubles were not over. In operational tests, models of the EFV proved less reliable than expected and projected.[48] In November 2006, the Office of the Secretary of Defense directed the Navy to shift funds from the EFV program and other programs in order to fully finance the DD(X), by then renamed the DDG-1000.[49] By February 2007, the Marine Corps was officially searching for alternatives to the existing EFV design.[50] In June 2007, members of Congress wondered why the Marines were still pursuing the EFV when they were simultaneously procuring mine-resistant ambush-protected (MRAP) vehicles. MRAPs were designed to withstand explosions of improvised explosive devices (IEDs). If that was the sort of attack Marines could expect in the future, then why wasn't the EFV designed to survive it? As it happened, the EFV did shield its occupants from IEDs, as tests showed in 2010, but by then it was too late. The unit cost of the EFV had climbed as the Marines reduced the number they planned to purchase. Members of Congress had lost confidence in the vehicle and were concerned about its purchase price and likely maintenance cost. In addition, the Marine Corps was more concerned as the months passed with a new concept of amphibious operations—one that did not hinge on having a swarm of EFVs.

Ship acquisition programs also plagued CNO Mullen and Secretary of the Navy Winter. Mullen was a strong supporter of both the DD(X) program and LCS development. But the DD(X) program had problems, some of them not of the program office's making. For example, the Navy's original acquisition strategy was to build 12 DD(X)s and divide the production between Northrop Grumman's Ingalls shipyard and General Dynamics' Bath Iron Works. However, as fiscal constraints reduced the size of the Navy's planned purchase, the Navy switched to a different acquisition strategy: qualify competing contractors, have them build prototypes, evaluate the prototypes, and then "down select" to just one winner. A bipartisan group of members of Congress opposed this approach even before Admiral Mullen was appointed CNO.[51] To pressure the Navy, the House of Representatives reduced the funding for the program—slicing ship construction funds for the DD(X) out of the Navy's tentative budget.[52] On 17 March 2005, the full Senate weighed in and criticized the Navy's acquisition strategy as "ill-advised."[53]

After being sworn in, Mullen immediately directed VCNO Willard to chair a study group to see if there were ways to improve Navy shipbuilding. The idea was to bring together representatives of OPNAV, the Navy secretariat, the Marine Corps, Fleet Forces Command, and NAVSEA to rationalize the processes by which the Navy could obtain the necessary numbers of ships at a price that the Navy could afford. Mullen was concerned about the rising cost of ship construction, but he was also concerned about what Secretary Winter would call "industrial base elasticity" in the spring of 2007.[54] By "elasticity," Winter meant the ability of major defense firms to survive losing a major contract. As spending for ships declined, there was the possibility that ship construction firms and their suppliers would "drop out" of the market, leaving the Navy with just one major shipbuilder for each kind of product—surface combat ship, submarine, and aircraft carrier. That was already the case with carriers; there was only one builder (Newport News). Mullen and other senior officers did not want to see just one builder of surface ships. But what could they do? The option of nationalizing Newport News and having the Navy build its own carriers was not economically, organizationally, or politically feasible.

Several alternatives were on the table. One was to set aside a certain amount of funding each fiscal year for ship construction and alterations. The shipbuilders could see that and know that business was there for them to compete for. A second possibility was to sketch out the Navy's future force structure so that shipbuilders and their suppliers could understand what the Navy planned to build over time. A third proposal, strongly supported by Mullen, was to recreate the Ship Characteristics Improvement Board (SCIB) to force the Navy to discipline its requirements process and seriously consider cost as a major factor in deciding what ships to build. Mullen—like Clark before him—wanted to eliminate unnecessary rules and regulations that drove up the cost of ships. Mullen also wanted to see if the Navy could slim down the number of basic ship types. Was there such a thing as a multipurpose surface ship design?[55]

In the short run, it didn't matter, because in December 2005 Mullen and the Navy received a welcome holiday gift: the appropriations committees of the Senate and House of Representatives fully funded the DD(X) program for FY 2006 and added funds so that the Navy could procure two additional littoral combat ships.[56] At the same time, however, the appropriations committees' conference report noted that "The conferees are concerned over the unanticipated cost growth on existing Navy shipbuilding contracts, and agree that the plan directed by the House on this subject [a plan to cap ship costs] is to include details on the cost growth for all existing shipbuilding and conversion efforts."[57] But just what was the cause of spiraling costs, and could the CNO do anything about it?

In the case of DD(X), the cause was the technological sophistication of the ship. In 2001, the staff of the Secretary of Defense had criticized the Navy for planning a 12-ship buy of a design that was very experimental. DD(X) was stealthy, and stealth technology is expensive. DD(X) was supposed to carry a new dual-band radar; the new radar had not yet been developed by 2001. DD(X) was supposed to carry a new, long-range gun (the Vertical Gun for Advanced Ships) in order to provide fire support for U.S. forces ashore. But the gun was not developed in its original form, and the Extended Range Gun Munition (ERGM) program was already facing difficulties in 2005; it would be shut down in 2008. The DD(X) was supposed to be powered by a permanent magnet motor, but the motor was not ready in time to be installed in the ship's hull. Finally, the ship's missile battery was distributed around the external skin of the ship, supposedly giving DD(X)/DD-1000 a total of 80 Tomahawk missiles. But this new launcher design had not been fully tested by 2001. The staff of the Secretary of Defense therefore argued that DD(X) was in fact a research and design effort and not a mature acquisition program. The Government Accountability Office (GAO) agreed. The Navy's position was that the DD(X) was a coherent but revolutionary package, and that the only way to hold down the cost of the first 12 ships was to fund all of them. Procuring 12 would spread the total research and development cost among them so that the unit cost of DD(X) would not be too high.

Influential members of Congress did not agree. The House Armed Services Committee was concerned that the Navy was "attempting to insert too much capability into a single platform.... Originally, the Navy proposed building 32 next-generation destroyers, reduced that to 24, then finally to seven in order to make the program affordable. In such small numbers, the committee struggles to see how the original requirements for the next-generation destroyer, for example, providing naval surface fire support, can be met."[58] In June 2006, Representative Roscoe Bartlett (R-MD) and the chairman of the Projection Forces Subcommittee of the House Armed Services Committee, told *Inside the Navy* that "Six or seven DD(X) destroyers cannot cover the world's oceans any better than two . . . Building more than two would be stealing money from an affordable 'next generation' ship class for the Navy's future fleet."[59] As a result, the fiscal year 2007 defense appropriations bill, approved 21 September 2006, contained funding for just two ships, and the Navy eventually built them in separate yards.

DD(X) was not the only acquisition program in trouble while Admiral Mullen was CNO. In August 2006, the Navy proposed to delay procuring a number of Marine short takeoff and vertical landing versions of the Joint Strike Fighter for 14 months because of budget constraints. The Marines, however, reversed their decision to delay procurement that November, and, in December 2006, Deputy Secretary of Defense England directed the Navy to restore the funding. The Marines also had difficulty replacing aging helicopters, first proposing to purchase new rotary-wing aircraft and then opting to upgrade and repair existing models. The need for new systems kept bumping hard into cost increases.

The story of the Advanced SEAL Delivery System (ASDS), a midget submarine intended to carry Navy SEALs from offshore submarines into defended enemy coastal areas, illustrates some of the problems that beset Navy acquisition programs. Work on ASDS began in 1994, but the system was still not performing as required in 2005. Rear Admiral William H. Hilarides, the program executive officer for submarines and later head of NAVSEA, explained why: "We didn't know exactly what we wanted. The company didn't know exactly what we wanted. And at the end, we got there and we went, 'Oh, this isn't what we wanted.' So we really didn't build the community, both in the contractor [Northrop Grumman] and in the government, of people who knew how to design this new thing that's not really a submarine."[60] This was a very revealing comment. It showed how important the relationship needed to be between the Navy and its industrial base. It had to be a continuing relationship, with engineers on both sides who understood the technology involved. But in the post–9/11 world, much of the critical technology—especially the software—was new or very expensive to develop. That posed no problem for civilian firms like Microsoft and Apple, with their large networks of consumers willing or even eager for new software and hardware, but it presented a major problem for those elements of the Navy's industrial base whose engineering expertise had been shaped by the requirements of the Cold War.

Was there anything that either Secretary Winter or CNO Mullen could do about their shared acquisition problems? Historically, the Navy secretariat had been very active in the field of acquisition, and Secretary Winter, certainly possessed the background in technology and business to enable him to deal with the technical problems that were making new major acquisitions such as DD(X) so expensive. He also had the able assistance of Dr. Delores M. Etter, who had served as the Deputy Under Secretary of Defense for Science and Technology from 1998 to 2001 and who was appointed Assistant Secretary of the Navy (Research, Development and Acquisition) in November 2005. On his appointment, CNO Mullen had wanted a "ships configuration board" modeled after the defunct Ship Characteristics and Improvement Board of the 1980s, but he didn't get it. Moreover, it wasn't the ship's structure and layout that was the problem. Instead, it was the software in the ships and the integration of the various digital systems that were at the heart of all combat ship functions.

NAVSEA had worked to include computer software and firmware in its configuration management methodology, but of necessity NAVSEA had to "permit the maximum latitude during the early design and development phases [of a ship or system] and ensure the introduction of configuration control necessary during final design, production or construction, and operations."[61] This approach had worked for engines, hulls, masts, and the like, but it had not worked well for software and for the need to link all the software systems on a modern ship. For example, should all the software in all the systems be built using commercial specifications and "tools"? Or should the software be "Navy-only?" Was there even a need to link the different software systems? And what about changes in software over time? If a ship lasted a generation or more, how could its software be upgraded at a cost that the Navy could afford?

These sorts of issues were the ones that Dr. Etter had been hired to deal with, but hers was an uphill campaign, if only because so many senior industry and Navy executives were not experienced in hands-on software development. In the summer of 2006, for example, Vice Admiral Crenshaw, the N8, had told *Inside the Navy* that he was "really surprised" to learn how expensive software development and integration were.[62] That was why Etter had quickly decided to meet often with the program managers (PMs) for the littoral combat ship and DD(X). It was also why she and Vice Admiral Crenshaw promulgated a memo on 9 June 2006 creating a new requirements trade-off process within OPNAV. The Resources and Requirements Review Board was given the responsibility to determine "what requirements are driving acquisition cost." The R3B reviews were supposed to be "open and frank sessions during which the general status of system acquisition is discussed, risks understood and cost drivers defined."[63]

But the R3B reviews were not Assistant Secretary Etter's key software management initiative. What she was after was "software acquisition discipline"—an analog to the physical and military requirements discipline that had been practiced before World War II by the General Board and then after 1945 by the Ship Characteristics Board (SCB) and its 1980s successor, the Ship Characteristics Improvement Board. As she noted in a May 2006 memo, "Successful development and acquisition of software is paramount for acquiring Naval Warfighting and business systems." Moreover, there were "many parallel and related efforts underway [to] address improvement in the acquisition of software products . . ."[64] Her goal was to "consolidate these efforts into a focused initiative." To do that, she created a steering group of "senior engineering professionals" and five "focus teams," each of which took on one of the major software problem areas (such as software systems engineering). Her initiative also created two software education courses for senior program managers, one of which taught participants an introduction to Capability Maturity Model Integration (CMMI). Finally, she insisted that "software development efforts in software intensive system programs [be] conducted by contractors who have a software process improvement program" that would qualify for CMMI certification. Etter was stressing what was increasingly obvious—that one reason software development was so expensive was because not enough people in the Navy and inside contractor organizations knew how to manage it effectively.

Etter, Secretary Winter, and CNO Mullen inherited systems whose characteristics had been defined before they had any authority over the Navy's acquisition system. The dilemma facing developers of systems like DD(X) was that software in particular and technology in general continued to progress and change over time. On the one hand, system developers wanted or needed to take advantage of the changes. On the other hand, doing that often delayed the completion of the project and increased its overall cost. Project managers could therefore get into a very frustrating cycle where the length of development (especially software development) threatened to make their system somewhat obsolescent *unless* they continued to fund ongoing software modifications.

Compounding the severity of this problem was a change in projected naval operations. As Robert O. Work, who would later serve as Under Secretary of the Navy and Deputy Secretary of Defense, noted in his study of the littoral combat ship and fleet design, the Navy had spent the 1990s planning and developing a force of large surface fighting ships (Aegis cruisers, DDG-51 class destroyers, and the planned DD-21s). However, the 2001 QDR argued that this was the wrong path to go down. Over time, according to the authors of the QDR, the proliferation of netted sensors and precision-guided munitions was bound to give land-based defenses an advantage in a showdown with ships such as the DDG-51. What were needed were platforms and sensors that could oppose land-based area denial and anti-access defenses. As Work noted, "during the 2001 QDR, OSD planners quietly told the Navy that the Secretary of Defense would approve further development of the DD-21 [which became DD(X)] only if the Navy added a small combatant to its planned fleet design. The new Littoral Combat Ship was the direct result."[65] In short, firepower had been supplanted as the key requirement for surface ships. In its place were the factors of mission adaptability (hunting mines, for instance, and then switching quickly to hunting submarines), mobility (both tactical and strategic), and shallow draft. That meant the LCS was very dependent on sensors and software to survive. It could adapt to changes in its mission, but only if the software that it carried made such adaptability possible. Therefore the software had to work and it had to be relatively inexpensive. Otherwise, the Navy would never be able to afford the many small surface combatants that it needed.

By the time that Mullen, Winter, and Etter were in their positions, LCS was in trouble, both technically and financially. The Navy had issued its first LCS-related request for proposals in November 2001. But it took until February 2003 for OPNAV's surface warfare office (N76) to propose a concept of operations for the LCS, and the Navy proceeded to award design contracts to three design teams in July of that year. Ronald O'Rourke, a respected naval analyst at the

Congressional Research Service, warned early in 2003 that the LCS had been the product of an "analytical virgin birth," and that the Navy would regret the haste with which it launched the LCS program.[66] He was proved correct. The keel of LCS-1, christened *Freedom*, was laid down in early June 2005. The ship was launched at the end of September 2006. Construction of the second LCS design, the trimaran *Independence* (LCS-2), began in January 2006, and the ship was launched at the end of April 2008. On 12 January 2007, however, the Navy sent a 90-day "stop work" order to Lockheed Martin, halting work on the third ship of the class because of a dramatic increase in the estimated cost of *Freedom*.[67] After negotiations between the Navy and Lockheed Martin broke down, the Navy cancelled LCS-3 on 12 April 2007.

With LCS, the Navy had attempted to show that it and its contractors could respond relatively quickly to changes in national strategy. The result was a flawed acquisition plan. Indeed, the three modules for each LCS—for antisubmarine warfare (ASW), surface combat, and mine hunting—had not been developed when construction began on the two LCS designs. In addition, the Navy had planned to evaluate the two different LCS prototypes and then select just one for production; as in the case of DD(X), Congress intervened, and the Navy then planned to produce both variants. That decision was made without the whole LCS program passing an official review to ascertain whether the technology required for both LCS variants and their mission modules was mature.[68] In response, the Navy reorganized its ship acquisition organization, but Representative John Murtha (D-PA), chairman of the Defense Subcommittee of the House Appropriations Committee, said the problem was not one of organization but instead was due to the Navy's launching a production program before the final design of the ship was ready.[69]

The case of LCS was frustrating to Admiral Mullen. He had given that program—as well as DD(X)—his support, and both had been disappointments. As CNO, Mullen did not directly control Navy acquisition. He depended upon the acquisition command chain, which in the case of ships ran from the civilian service acquisition executive (SAE) to a program executive officer in NAVSEA and then to the LCS program manager. Mullen, like both Winter and Etter, also inherited both DD(X) and LCS. Despite their separate talents and their shared desire to make both programs successes, they were stymied by two flawed decisions that were taken before they took office. The first was to make DD(X) a revolutionary system. The second was to fail to recognize just how revolutionary LCS was. LCS was not a small combatant. Instead, it was a piece of a larger "system" designed to allow Navy and joint forces to overcome modern sensors and land-based precision munitions. Under Mullen's predecessor, the Navy had gambled that it could make the leap into the 21st century in one move. Under Mullen, the Navy learned that its DD(X) and LCS acquisition strategies were either too expensive or were subject to the sort of congressional interference that would push their already high costs even higher.

Conclusion

The goal of any CNO must be to leave the Navy stronger than he found it. Admiral Mullen believed that N7 needed to be merged with N8, and he did that. He wanted to better define the

Figure 17-1. CNO Michael G. Mullen meets with sailors following an all hands call in the hangar bay of *John C. Stennis* (CVN 74) in 2006. Mullen had served as VCNO under CNO Vernon E. Clark. He also held the post of Commander, Joint Force Command Naples/U.S. Naval Forces Europe before being selected as CNO Clark's replacement. (Official Navy photo by MC3 Philip V. Morrill [Released] DIMOC Asset 75M66N7_S0Y82UED4 060801-N-SO663-007)

relationship between OPNAV and Fleet Forces Command, and he did that, too. He wanted to improve the "command climate" within OPNAV, and the evidence suggests that he was successful. He was impressed with Vice Admiral Morgan's work, and so he allied himself with Morgan to express a notion of the Navy's role in national security that was a very new approach to maritime security. Mullen also worked very well with Marine Corps Commandant General Hagee and his successor, General James T. Conway. "Working well" didn't mean that there were no disagreements between the Navy and the Marine Corps. But the two services compromised on the very serious issues of tactical aviation and amphibious shipping, and the Marines finally accepted the fact that the expensive Expeditionary Fighting Vehicle program had lost the conceptual and political support that it needed to survive. What the Marines really wanted most was the V-22 Osprey.

When it came to the military campaigns in Iraq and Afghanistan, there was a gulf between the Navy and the Marine Corps. True, CNO Mullen provided individual augmentees to Central Command, and, yes, Navy tactical aviation supported ground operations and Navy surface ships kept the seas from being used by the nation's enemies. But the day-in, day-out patrolling and fighting was done by soldiers and Marines. Mullen supported the creation of a Navy riverine force and established the Navy Expeditionary Combat Command (NECC) in October 2005, but by no means was the NECC created to train and support a large force of "naval infantry."

The Marines would not accept that. So the Marines worked in two worlds simultaneously. One world was Iraq and Afghanistan and the Philippines. The other was the world of Washington, including the world of Congress. The operational theaters of conflict required support. But the Pentagon did not go on a war footing. Peacetime procedures continued.

In his memoir, for example, former Secretary of Defense Robert M. Gates described how difficult it was for him personally to see to it that the Army and Marines procured MRAP vehicles for use in Iraq and Afghanistan.[70] Army acquisition officials initially opposed procuring the different types of MRAPs. They argued correctly that having vehicles of different designs would create logistics problems in the field. They also argued correctly that the Army would be stuck with a bunch of the things once U.S. forces didn't need them. Then the MRAPs would have to be sold or scrapped. It was axiomatic that major acquisitions were developed on the assumption that they would last a long time and be useful in a variety of operations. The M-1 tank was a classic example; so were Navy aircraft carriers. But Gates worried that improvised explosive devices were taking too high a toll of U.S. soldiers and Marines, and he wanted something done to protect them. He eventually got his way, but his was not an easy task, even though he was the senior official in the Defense Department.

Peacetime procedures were also modified when it came to paying for the campaigns in Iraq and Afghanistan. As described in the previous chapter, after the attacks on the United States in September 2001, Congress provided the Defense Department and other agencies with "supplementals" to cover mostly operational, training, personnel, and medical expenses. In effect, the Defense Department began operating on two budgets. One was the "regular" budget, developed and reviewed as the defense budget had been in peacetime. The other was in fact (if not in name) a war budget. For example, the Marine Corps congressionally mandated strength was 175,000. But the USMC had an additional 5,000 personnel; they were paid for by a "supplemental." The idea was that the request for supplementals would not have to go through the armed services committees; they could be given directly to congressional appropriations committees and bypass the authorization process.

But this created two problems. One was that the military services might take advantage of the supplemental process to insert requests for acquisitions. This was an issue raised by Senators John McCain (R-AZ), the ranking Republican on the Senate Armed Services Committee, and Carl Levin (D-MI), the Committee's chairman, in 2006.[71] The second problem was that the supplementals did not really add to the long-term military strength of the nation, nor were they meant to. Senator McCain was especially concerned that year after year of supplementals corrupted the defense budget process, essentially exempting the Defense Department from careful legislative scrutiny. For example, it was the authorizing committees, especially the House Armed Services Committee that conducted investigations of Navy shipbuilding.[72] McCain did not want the Congress kept from performing its oversight function.

As it was, there was an intermittent siphoning effect, where shortages of funds for operations in Iraq and Afghanistan were "made good" by raiding military service accounts. This obviously disrupted efforts by military service programmers to manage spending according to the long-term plans of the service chiefs. For example, on 28 December 2005, the Defense Department comptroller pulled more than $2 billion from Navy accounts across fiscal years 2006 through 2011, including $187 million that had been set to fund joint experimentation, and $180 million intended for Marine Corps procurement.[73] In 2007, Congress forced the Defense Department to change its supplemental spending request to pay for the additional troops sent to Iraq as part of the "surge" intended to subdue the insurgency there. The change kept the Navy from purchasing six E/A-18G electronic warfare aircraft that had been part of the supplemental request.[74] If in fact the United States was engaged in a long and expensive war with terrorists— as Marine General Mattis claimed—then some way needed to be found to provide funds for waging that war and for simultaneously sustaining and improving U.S. forces over the long run. Otherwise, service programmers and budget officers would be forced to constantly improvise, which was contrary to the whole point of having the Planning, Programming, Budgeting, and Execution (PPBE) system.

Admiral Mullen acted quickly and aggressively on becoming CNO in order to take the organizational and psychological initiative. OPNAV had many external "stakeholders," including the combatant commanders (especially Central Command [CENTCOM]), the Congress, the President, the Secretary of Defense and his staff, and the Joint Staff. As CNO, Mullen had to work to make certain that he and his staff defined Navy responsibilities instead of having others do that for them. In early 2007, for example, the Air Force wanted to be the "executive agent" for unmanned aerial vehicles (UAVs), setting policy on UAV development and concepts of operations, especially for UAVs operating at higher altitudes. The Chief of Staff of the Air Force had argued that the proposal made sense because USAF planes routinely operated in that space and because it was often an Air Force officer who served as Joint Force Air Component Commander. The Air Force position was that having one service act as "executive agent" would streamline acquisition of UAVs and make sure that all UAV concepts of operations complemented one another. The Navy, Marine Corps, and Army opposed the USAF on this matter, both inside the Pentagon and before Congress. Despite their opposition, the Joint Requirements Oversight Council (JROC), chaired by the Vice Chairman of the JCS, backed the Air Force. However, in September 2007 Deputy Secretary of Defense England overturned the JROC.[75]

Far more important than any disagreements with the Air Force, however, was the relationship between the Navy and the Marine Corps. There, for 15 months, Mullen was fortunate to have as his Marine counterpart General Hagee, a longtime personal friend. But friendship could not overcome the problem that had dogged the Navy–Marine Corps relationship since the end of the Cold War: What was the future role of the Marines, and how did that affect the Navy? By 2005, that question had become very specific: How were the Marines to get to a fight? If the Marine Corps was an expeditionary force, then what ships did the Navy need to adequately move and support that force? The deployment of Marines to Iraq and Afghanistan had made answering that question less urgent, but the matter came up again and again in Navy-Marine conversations, especially once General Conway was appointed Commandant.[76] The Marines had traditionally planned to fight their way ashore if necessary, and to do that successfully they needed fire support from the air and the sea, amphibious assault vehicles, landing craft, and combat-loaded transports. But those systems were expensive, and it became clear while Mullen was the CNO that the Navy could not afford the ships that it wanted and still provide the Marines with the amphibious ships that the Marines demanded and expected. The result was a series of Navy-Marine negotiations that produced a series of compromises but not a clear solution. A solution satisfactory to both services might have been found if the Navy's shipbuilding programs had been less expensive or if Congress had been willing raise the defense budget for amphibious ships, but that did not happen while Admiral Mullen was CNO.

Mullen was successful in every area but acquisition, and there the problems the Navy and its major contractors encountered had their roots in decisions made before he or Secretary Winter took their posts. To their credit, Winter and Assistant Secretary Etter took on those problems, just as Navy secretaries and their deputies had done for over a century, but they faced a difficult challenge, which was the rising cost of materials and labor, especially the highly skilled and expensive labor involved in developing software. The "digital revolution" made Mullen and Vice Admiral Morgan's "1,000-ship" navy feasible, but it had a high price tag. Early in his time as CNO, Mullen said he intended to conduct reviews and make changes that would keep him busy for four years. As it happened, Mullen was promoted to Chairman of the Joint Chiefs of Staff in just two, after impressing both President George W. Bush and Rumsfeld's successor as Secretary of Defense, Robert M. Gates.[77]

Notes

[1] Haynes, "American Naval Thinking in the Post–Cold War Era," 278–79.

[2] *Inside the Navy*, vol. 18, no. 30 (1 Aug. 2005), 5.

[3] Ibid., 7.

[4] Friedman, *U.S. Destroyers, An Illustrated Design History*, rev. ed., 450.

[5] *Inside the Navy*, citing a speech by ADM Clark to the Heritage Foundation, vol. 18, no. 13 (4 Apr. 2005), 1.

[6] *Inside the Navy*, vol. 18, no. 14 (11 Apr. 2005), 15. The LPD-17 was a sophisticated "amphibious transport dock."

[7] For GEN Casey's account, see his *Strategic Reflections, Operation Iraqi Freedom, July 2004–Feb. 2007* (Washington, DC: National Defense University Press, 2012).

[8] VADM John G. Morgan Jr., "A Maritime Strategy for a Changed World," New York Council of the Navy League of the United States, *The Log* (Winter 2007).

[9] Haynes, "American Naval Thinking in the Post–Cold War Era," 295n4.

[10] Ibid., 283.

[11] *The National Strategy for Maritime Security*, the White House, Washington, DC, Sept. 2005, 2. http://www.state.gov/documents/organization/255380.pdf.

[12] Haynes, "American Naval Thinking in the Post–Cold War Era," 289.

[13] ADM Mullen's essay was "What I Believe: Eight Tenets That Guide My Vision for the 21st Century Navy," and ADM Nathman's paper was "Shaping the Future." Both were in *Proceedings*, vol. 132, no. 1 (Jan. 2006).

[14] Haynes, "American Naval Thinking in the Post–Cold War Era," 303.

[15] Ibid., 302.

[16] Ibid., 305.

[17] COL Nicholas E. Reynolds, USMCR (Ret.), *U.S. Marines in Iraq, 2003: Basrah, Baghdad and Beyond* (Washington, DC: History Division, USMC, 2007), 4–5.

[18] LTGEN James N. Mattis, *Marine Corps Operating Concepts for a Changing Security Environment*, 1st ed. (Quantico, VA: Marine Corps Combat Development Command, Mar. 2006), iii, viii.

[19] As CAPT Peter Haynes noted in his "American Naval Thinking in the Post–Cold War Era," the organizational analog of MCCDC was the Navy Warfare Development Command (NWDC), yet NWDC was not tapped for this project. Similarly, the organizational analog to N3/N5 was the USMC's office of Plans, Policies, and Operations, but MCCDC supplied the Marine staff officers to RADM Cullom. See Haynes, "American Naval Thinking in the Post–Cold War Era," 312n54.

[20] ADM Michael G. Mullen and GEN Michael W. Hagee, *Naval Operations Concept 2006*, (Washington, DC: Office of the Chief of Naval Operations, Sept. 2006), 1.

[21] Ibid., 11.

[22] Haynes, "American Naval Thinking in the Post–Cold War Era," 316.

[23] Ibid., 317.

[24] Speech by ADM Mullen at the Naval War College, 31 Aug. 2005. The speech was covered in detail by *Inside the Navy*, vol. 18, no. 36 (12 Sept. 2005), 1, 10–12.

[25] *Inside the Navy*, vol. 18, no. 42 (24 Oct. 2005), 6 of the media roundtable interview.

[26] *Inside the Navy*, vol. 18, no. 41 (17 Oct. 2005), 4. VADM Crenshaw was an outstanding naval aviator, and had served as an aide to the Secretary of the Navy, a member of the Joint Staff, and a carrier battle group commander. Perhaps more important were his three tours in N8—as deputy director of the assessment division (N81D), then N81, and N8 after Nov. 2004.

[27] *Inside the Navy*, vol. 18, no. 42 (24 Oct. 2005), 7.

[28] *Inside the Navy*, vol. 18, no. 36 (12 Sept. 2005), 12.

[29] *Inside the Navy*, vol. 18, no. 43 (31 Oct. 2005), 4.

[30] *Inside the Navy*, vol. 18, no. 46 (21 Nov. 2005), 12. The "breakout" of N6 was actually done in August 2006.

[31] Memo, "Resources and Requirements Review Board (R3B) Charter," N09 (5420), 23 Mar. 2006, 1. In the collection of Thomas C. Hone.

[32] Department of the Navy, Deputy Asst. Secretary of the Navy (Research, Development and Acquisition), "Acquisition and Capabilities Guidebook," SecNav M-5000.2 (Dec. 2008). http://www.public.navy.mil/cotf/OTD/SECNAV%20M-5000.2%20-%20DON.pdf.

[33] Interview of Arthur H. Barber III, by Thomas C. Hone, 21 Oct. 2014.

[34] VADM James G. Foggo III, "The 'Barber' Shop Is Now Closed," U.S. Naval Institute Blog Archive, July 2014. As a RADM, VADM Foggo had served as the Director of N81 and retired CAPT Barber had been his deputy.

[35] Interview of CAPT Arthur H. Barber III, USN (Ret.), 21 Oct. 2014. The scenarios were littoral conflict, ground conflict, maritime conflict, and preserving global maritime security in the face of a significant military challenge.

[36] When ADM Mullen was Commander, NATO Forces South, CAPT Porter was his director of operational net assessment. When Mullen became CNO, Porter headed N00Z. After leaving OPNAV, Porter was the Assistant Chief of Staff for Intelligence under the commander of naval forces in Central Command. In 2008, Porter became the Special Assistant for Strategy to the Chairman of the Joint Chiefs of Staff, ADM Mullen, and held that post until 2011.

[37] Haynes, "American Naval Thinking in the Post–Cold War Era," 297–98.

[38] *Inside the Navy*, vol. 18, no. 42 (24 Oct. 2005), 10.

[39] Haynes, "American Naval Thinking in the Post–Cold War Era," 321.

[40] Ibid., 324.

[41] Ibid., 327.

[42] ADM Michael G. Mullen and GEN Michael W. Hagee, "Naval Operations Concept 2006," given in full in *Inside the Navy*, vol. 19, no. 36 (11 Sept. 2006), 6.

[43] Ibid., 9, 11, 12, 13.

[44] Ibid., 11.

[45] *Inside the Navy*, vol. 19, no. 3 (23 Jan. 2006), 4. LTGEN Van Riper was a hard man to ignore. He had been awarded two Silver Stars and a Purple Heart, and he had performed brilliantly in a major ("Millennium Challenge") war game in 2002. Leading the "enemy" Red Team, Van Riper had defeated a much stronger "Blue Force," and the incident was publicized widely by the media.

[46] Haynes, "American Naval Thinking in the Post–Cold War Era," 340.

[47] *Inside the Navy*, vol. 19, no. 34 (28 Aug. 2006), 6.

[48] *Inside the Navy*, vol. 19, no. 39 (2 Oct. 2006), 1, 4.

[49] *Inside the Navy*, vol. 19, no. 46 (20 Nov. 2006), 1, 4.

[50] *Inside the Navy*, vol. 20, no. 7 (19 Feb. 2007), 1, 8.

[51] *Inside the Navy*, vol. 18, no. 9 (7 Mar. 2005), 1, 4.

[52] *Inside the Navy*, vol. 18, no. 29 (25 July 2005), 10.

[53] *Inside the Navy*, vol. 18, no. 11 (21 Mar. 2005), 1, 10.

[54] *Inside the Navy*, vol. 20, no. 13 (2 Apr. 2007), 7.

[55] *Inside the Navy*, vol. 18, no. 30 (1 Aug. 2005), 6–7.

[56] *Inside the Navy*, vol. 18, no. 51 (26 Dec. 2005), 1, 6–7.

[57] Ibid., 7.

[58] "Report of the Committee on Armed Services, House of Representatives, on H.R. 5122, Together With Additional and Dissenting Views," *National Defense Authorization Act for Fiscal Year 2007*.

[59] *Inside the Navy*, vol. 19, no. 26 (3 July 2006), 7.

[60] *Inside the Navy*, vol. 19, no. 21 (29 May 2006), 6.

[61] NAVSEA Instruction 4130.12B, "Configuration Management (CM) Policy and Guidance," from the Commander, Naval Sea Systems Command, 21 July 2004, 3. https://acc.dau.mil/adl/en-US/398362/file/53687/NAVSEAINST%204130.12B%20CM%20Policy%20Jul%2004.pdf.

[62] *Inside the Navy*, vol. 19, no. 26 (3 July 2006), 6.

[63] The memo signed by Crenshaw and Etter was printed in full in *Inside the Navy*, vol. 19, no. 26 (3 July 2006), 6–7.

[64] Etter's memo is printed in full in *Inside the Navy*, vol. 19, no. 28 (17 July 2006), 6–7.

[65] Robert O. Work, "Fleet Design and the Littoral Combat Ship," draft paper, n.d., 30. In the collection of Thomas C. Hone.

[66] Robert O. Work, "Naval Transformation and the Littoral Combat Ship," Center for Strategic and Budgetary Assessments, Feb. 2004, 5. See also "Navy Littoral Combat Ship (LCS) Program: Background and Issues for Congress," by Ronald O'Rourke, Congressional Research Service 7-5700 (RL 33741), 24 Dec. 2014, especially pages 3, 6. When the Navy announced that the LCS would have a helicopter, it was clear to observers outside the Navy that the ship would displace at least 3,000 tons.

[67] The Lockheed Martin contract for LCS-1 had originally been for approximately $198 million. But SECNAV Winter informed the House Armed Services Committee that he anticipated the actual cost would be between $350 and 375 million. Asst. Secretary Etter was rumored to have said she expected the cost to run to over $400 million. See *Inside the Navy*, vol. 20, no. 10 (12 Mar. 2007), 3.

[68] *Inside the Navy*, vol. 20, no. 30 (30 July 2007), 13.

[69] Ibid., 12.

[70] Robert M. Gates, *Duty* (New York: Knopf, 2014), 119–27.

[71] *Inside the Navy*, vol. 19, no. 6 (13 Feb. 2006), 2.

[72] *Inside the Navy*, vol. 20, no. 19 (14 May 2007), 8.

[73] *Inside the Navy*, vol. 19, no. 1 (9 Jan. 2006), 4.

[74] *Inside the Navy*, vol. 20, no. 10 (12 Mar. 2007), 5.

[75] See the following issues of *Inside the Navy*: vol. 20, no. 16 (Apr. 23, 2007), 3–4; vol. 20, no. 33 (20 Aug. 2007), 7–8; vol. 20, no. 37 (17 Sept. 2007), 1, 12–13.

[76] GEN Conway and ADM Mullen and senior members of their staffs met to discuss this issue and others three times between the beginning of February 2007 and the middle of June that same year.

[77] Gates, *Duty*, 100.

CHAPTER 18

Admiral Gary Roughead: Déjà Vu All Over Again?

Introduction

On 29 September 2007, Admiral Michael G. Mullen left his position as the Chief of Naval Operations and was sworn in as Chairman of the Joint Chiefs of Staff. His successor was Admiral Gary Roughead, who had been serving as Commander, Fleet Forces Command since the middle of May. Roughead inherited the OPNAV staff structure created by his predecessor and also several ongoing and very expensive acquisition programs, including the Joint Strike Fighter (JSF), the DDG-1000, and the expeditionary fighting vehicle for the Marine Corps. The new CNO also faced a relatively new Secretary of Defense—Robert M. Gates, a very experienced former head of the Central Intelligence Agency, who had replaced Donald Rumsfeld on 18 December 2006. One of Gates's major priorities as Secretary of Defense was, as he put it, "to tackle the military acquisition process and weed out long-overdue, over-budget programs . . ."[1] Finally, the major financial institutions of the United States and Europe were starting to go into a tailspin—that meant issues of importance inside the Pentagon would be overshadowed by issues outside. Was Roughead in a position similar to that of CNO Pratt in 1932? Was it a similar dilemma of having major responsibilities but not the funds to achieve them?

Admiral Roughead's background was oriented strongly toward operations. He had commanded the Pacific Fleet from July 2005 to May 2007. Though he had tours in the Navy secretariat's Office of Program Appraisal (OPA) and as the Navy's chief of legislative affairs, he had not had significant experience in OPNAV. Roughead needed time to understand how OPNAV worked, and especially to learn firsthand how changes in OPNAV could affect policies that he wanted to implement. He was also overshadowed to a degree by Admiral Mullen, who developed a strong working relationship with Secretary Gates. One reason Admiral Mullen had been selected as the Chairman of the JCS was because Mullen understood both politics and public relations. Moreover, Secretary Gates respected Mullen because the new chairman understood how important personal relationships among the nation's senior officers were yet he did not manipulate those relationships to achieve the parochial goals of the Navy.[2]

In addition, the timing of Roughead's appointment was awkward. Fiscal Year 2008 was supposed to begin at the beginning of October 2007, and the budget for FY 2009 would go to the Congress in early 2008. That timetable constrained the new CNO; he could only have a systematic impact on the Navy's Program Objective Memorandum (POM) for FY 2010. But the presidential election of 2008 promised to be a contentious one. Who knew what a new administration—whether Republican or Democrat—would do once a new President entered the White House in January 2009? A new administration might dramatically alter Navy programs worked out in the spring and summer of 2008 for implementation in 2010.

Roughead's Concerns

In July 2009, Roughead told *Defense Daily* that he was convinced that information was the key to success in combat on, under, above, or from the sea. He was concerned that the focus of the Navy on platforms—ships, aircraft, and submarines—instead of on information was hindering the optimal use of those platforms. Roughead wanted to shift the focus of the Navy to its capabilities as a network. As he noted, "We don't envision the whole . . . we still look at it in piece parts." His initial experience as CNO confirmed his inference that the programming process was not highlighting the importance of information: "Then when I got here and went through that [2007–08] budget cycle, it just continued to reinforce and reinforce and reinforce. And then at the end of the 2010 [budget] process, that's when I moved." But he had to pick his time—after the November 2008 elections and after the first months of the new administration when he and the OPNAV staff would know what the new President's policies were.[3]

By that time, unfortunately, what was beginning to matter most in Washington was the state of the American economy. In 2008, the financial system of the country almost collapsed. As then–Federal Reserve Chairman Ben S. Bernanke noted in a document filed in a 2014 lawsuit, "September and October of 2008 was the worst financial crisis in global history, including the Great Depression."[4] Roughead's desire to shift the Navy toward a systematic focus on "information warfare" was in danger of foundering as the result of a lack of resources.

The Management of Defense: From Rumsfeld to Gates

Every Chief of Naval Operations works within a set of informal and formal rules that govern what the CNO can and should do. After the passage of the Goldwater-Nichols legislation in 1986, the service chiefs were out of the chain of command that ran from the President to the regional combatant commanders. Like the other service chiefs, the CNO was given the role to supply the combatant commanders with trained and ready forces. Goldwater-Nichols had changed the chain of operational authority but not the "organize, train and equip" chain of authority. The regional combatant commanders were given increased operational authority but not commensurately increased authority over the planning, programming, and budgeting process. Under President George W. Bush, Secretary of Defense Rumsfeld had set out to change that aspect of defense.

Instead of going to Congress with a proposal to further increase the legal authority of the combatant commanders, Rumsfeld had set out to strengthen their hands in the Pentagon by using the authority inherent in his office. At the same time, Rumsfeld—along with some members of Congress—had argued that it was essential for the Defense Department to operate more like a private business. Two strands of thinking—on the authority of the combatant commanders and on how to improve defense management—merged under Secretary Rumsfeld. A consequence of this merging was Rumsfeld's attempt to modify the way that the Pentagon worked. For example, in 2001 he created the Senior Executive Council. He was the chairman, and the other members were senior civilian appointees—Rumsfeld's "executive vice presidents": the Deputy Secretary of Defense, the military service secretaries, and the Under Secretary of Defense for Acquisition, Technology and Logistics. The stated role for this group was to "implement modern business practices in the department and to guide transformation efforts in the services."[5]

However, over time Rumsfeld's primary "governing forum" became the Senior Leader Review Group, or SLRG. What Secretary Rumsfeld wanted was a panel of executives modeled after those often used in major private firms to develop strategic plans and policies. The service secretaries—the "executive vice presidents"—would be responsible for making sure that his guidance (which was guidance that they endorsed) was followed. They would also serve as his senior civilian advisors, complementing the roles of the appointed under secretaries of defense. Robert Gates, Rumsfeld's successor, accepted the SLRG, but the directive issued by his office in May 2008 that spelled out the SLRG's role in defense decision-making specified that the SLRG would convene "at the discretion of the Secretary of Defense to address DoD issues and priorities at the highest level." That was not quite the role for the service secretaries that Rumsfeld had created for them.

Over time, it became clear that the real senior day-to-day governing board under Rumsfeld and then Gates was the Deputy's Advisory Working Group (DAWG), and it met "at the discretion of the Deputy Secretary of Defense to provide advice and assistance to the Deputy . . . on matters pertaining to DoD enterprise management, business transformation, and operations; and strategic level coordination and integration of planning, programming, budgeting execution, and assessment activities of the Department."[6] In practice, because of the multiple responsibilities of the Secretary of Defense, the DAWG was the Department's senior day-to-day governing board—and it was chaired by Deputy Secretary of Defense Gordon England until he left the Defense Department in February 2009.

England, a former executive vice president at General Dynamics Corporation, had been selected in 2001 by then-President George W. Bush as Secretary of the Navy. In January 2003, however, President Bush had appointed England the first Deputy Secretary in the Department of Homeland Security to help get that new department organized. At the end of July 2003, the new Secretary of the Navy, Colin R. McMillan, committed suicide, and President Bush asked England to return to the Navy Department as its secretary. In October 2003, Secretary England told an interviewer that the United States was "a nation at war, and it is a totally different kind of war. I believe this war against terrorism will in one respect be similar to the war we fought against communism, which lasted 40 years."[7] The belief that the nation was in another lengthy struggle against a powerful adversary underlay many Bush administration policies and linked the senior members of the government. In May 2005 Bush nominated England as the Deputy Secretary of Defense to replace Paul Wolfowitz, who was leaving the Pentagon to become president of the World Bank.

Before Gordon England became the Deputy Secretary of Defense, service staffs had to contend with a growing number of policy and strategy guidance documents, including the National Security Strategy, the National Defense Strategy, the National Military Strategy, and the reports of the quadrennial defense reviews.[8] It was difficult for officers in the military service staffs to keep current with all these documents and to know just which elements of these official papers really mattered. England narrowed the number of guidance documents to four: The "Guidance for Employment of the Force" (GEF), which focused on the near term and was aimed at the combatant commanders; the "Guidance for Development of the Force" (GDF), which stated the Defense secretary's goals for long-term force development; the Joint Programming Guidance, which was intended to compel the programmers on the service staffs to look across service boundaries as they drew up service POMs; and the quadrennial defense review.[9]

Planning According to Desired Joint Capabilities

Rumsfeld and England also supported the creation of the Joint Capabilities Integration and Development System (JCIDS) managed by the chairman of the Joint Chiefs of Staff, and the use of "capabilities-based" planning. The latter was supposed to conform to the concepts produced by the Joint Operations Concepts Development Process.[10] Through this process, the Joint Forces Command (JFCOM) and the Joint Staff were supposed to develop a "capstone" concept and supporting operating and functional concepts that would tie the different staffs—those outside as well as inside the Pentagon—together. It was to be the first step in the creation of an "overarching capabilities-based framework within DOD."[11]

The keystone of the framework would be the capstone concept, such as "the protection of the people and territory of the United States and its allies." That would be the central concept. Other lesser and more detailed concepts would spring from it or enlarge on it. For example, protecting the people and territory of the United States and its allies would require a concept of defense against nuclear attack, and a concept for defense of the United States and its allies against conventional attack. Taking just one subordinate concept (defense against nuclear attack), there would have to be a concept of nuclear defense. Would that be nuclear deterrence or an effective anti-ballistic missile defense, or both? If nuclear deterrence, then there would have to be a concept for that—mutual assured destruction, perhaps, or a secure second strike capability, and certainly the adequate command and control of nuclear forces. Using this way of thinking, it is possible to move logically from a very general and obvious concept (or principle) to more detailed concepts (or principles), and eventually to an actual system, such as the Navy's sea-launched ballistic missiles and the nuclear submarines that carried them.

The concept development process, termed the JCIDS, was supervised by the Joint Requirements Oversight Council and managed by the Joint Chiefs of Staff. JCIDS was supposed to make the programming and acquisition processes more "joint" by highlighting "capability gaps" in the programs and acquisitions of the military services so that they could be dealt with *before* there were problems in the field. The concept development process, with its joint operating concepts, joint integrating concepts, and functional concepts, was supposed to build capability-based planning from the ground up by training staff officers in the Pentagon and at the combatant staffs to think in terms of capabilities. Each major joint concept had to be drafted and then reviewed by both military and civilian staff officers. Joint Forces Command also tested such concepts in war games. This process of developing, reviewing, and testing concepts entailed a great deal of staff work. Similarly, major joint programs and acquisitions were supposed to be developed and/or reviewed by groups of staff officers from different services using a "joint capabilities" approach. Was all that work worth it?

Civilian and military staff told the writers of the "Beyond Goldwater-Nichols" study in 2008 (after Secretary Rumsfeld had resigned) that the answer was no—the joint concepts were not guiding JCIDS effectively. Together, the concept development process and JCIDS were "among the most maligned efforts in the Department of Defense."[12] The directive governing JCIDS was revised three times between 2003 and 2008, and the arguments over "capabilities" and "concepts" had frustrated and disappointed many members of the service staffs and the Joint Staff.[13] As the writers of *Invigorating Defense Governance* put it, the whole capabilities-based planning process was "cumbersome" and "shallow," with the consequence that both concept development and JCIDS were "continually marginalized."[14] Moreover, most of the work on concepts was done by mid-career military officers and retired officers working as contractors, especially at Joint Forces Command in Suffolk, Virginia. The process of drafting concepts and reviewing them was corrupted by the fear within the service staffs that any major organization that did not "fit" into some concept would suffer when budgets were drawn up. Put another way, the whole concept development process was not routinely doing what it was supposed to do, which was ultimately to allow the Secretary of Defense and his subordinates to direct investment in such a way that it met the needs of the joint combatant commanders.

In an effort to salvage the goal of capabilities-based planning, Deputy Secretary England turned to "capability portfolio management." This was an effort to use a practice borrowed from the financial industry to "optimize capability investments across the defense enterprise (both materiel and non-materiel) and minimize risk in meeting the Department's capability needs in support of strategy."[15] If the service staffs were having trouble building their POMs on capabilities-based assessments, then England could at least create capability portfolio managers to advise the DAWG. Though the capability portfolio managers did not have any budget authority, they were able to present their findings to the DAWG, providing its members with "cross-Component alternatives and recommendations on current and future capability needs and investments."[16]

The Concept of the "Chief Management Officer"

But capabilities-based planning and a Deputy Secretary of Defense committed to it were not the only "outside-the-Navy" pressures on OPNAV. There was also the continuing pressure on the military services to adopt accrual-based accounting and the more recent pressure from Congress and the Bush Administration to compel the military services and the Office of the Secretary of Defense to adopt performance-based management through a chain of "chief management officers."[17] In private firms, chief management officers (CMOs) reported to chief executive officers; these private sector CMOs usually exercised "line authority" over a firm's financial, personnel, and information technology activities. One major reason for wanting a "chief management officer" inside the Pentagon was because of the need to coordinate defense department software acquisitions.

The Government Accountability Office (GAO) had for years tracked the growing cost to the federal government of information technology, and one of the biggest users of that technology had been the Department of Defense. In 1996, Congress passed the Information Technology Management Reform Act (known as "Clinger-Cohen" after its House and Senate sponsors). In implementing the law, the Office of Management and Budget (OMB) directed almost all federal agencies to develop compatible "information technology architectures" under the leadership of agency chief information officers. The major exception to the law were "national security systems," most of which were developed or maintained by the Defense Department. The CMOs were created in order to bring those systems under central control, with the long-term goal of dramatically reducing the costs of national defense.

However, instead of creating a new OSD-level position, Secretary Rumsfeld assigned the CMO role to the Deputy Secretary of Defense, and the deputy secretary was formally made the department's chief management officer in the Fiscal Year 2008 National Defense Authorization Act.[18] The law also created CMOs in the military departments and placed them under the authority of the military department under secretaries. In effect, Congress created a web, or network, of chief and deputy chief management officers inside the Pentagon, authorizing them to transform the business of the military departments subject to the direction of the Deputy Secretary of Defense, who acted as the Defense Department's chief management officer. In practice, because of the deputy secretary's extensive responsibilities inside the Pentagon, business "transformation" became the responsibility of the deputy chief management officer and the network of military department deputy chief management officers.

With the creation of a deputy CMO in the Office of the Secretary of Defense and the simultaneous creation of a deputy CMO in the office of the Secretary of the Navy, a majority of the members of Congress reached a goal that they shared with the leaders of the GAO: overhauling the "fundamental management structure" of the Department of Defense, a structure many members of Congress and critics of the Pentagon suspected was the primary cause of the high cost of defense acquisitions. What they were in fact after—though no senior official in the Bush administration could admit it—was a truly joint programming process. Had Rumsfeld and England said that was what they were trying to create, they would have had to admit that programming—and not a joint concept development process—was the means by which the leaders of the Defense Department could steer the military services and defense agencies.

One consequence of adopting programming was relying on the results of the systematic campaign analyses conducted by the skilled civilians and military officers in organizations like the Navy's N81. These specialists were the individuals who could discover the "maximum combat capability" that could be developed "against the identified threat."[19] As retired Captain Arthur H. Barber put it, "I managed to herd everybody into a business model that let the civilian deputy [of N81] be the chief analyst of the Navy."[20] Put another way, Rumsfeld and England could not escape the essential character of Defense Department programming, which was its dependence on a cadre of specialists in campaign analysis and operations research. Any Secretary of Defense could only do two things about this situation. The first was to create his own organization of program analysts, but in truth he already had that. The second was to promote the creation of quality program analysis *within* the service staff organizations. That had been done, too. The new "chief management officers" had to rely on these specialists.

Gates Takes Over

After Defense secretary Gates agreed to stay on as Defense secretary in the administration of President Barack H. Obama, he set to work fashioning a fiscal year 2010 defense budget that would reflect the new President's priorities. In his memoir, Gates described how he led this process: "During February and March 2009, I chaired some forty meetings as we considered which programs should have more money and which were candidates to be eliminated or stop production." The "we" were Gates, his deputy secretary, the Chairman and Vice Chairman of the Joint Chiefs of Staff, two members of Gates's personal staff, and the following members of the Office of the Secretary of Defense: the head of program evaluation and his deputy; the comptroller; the under secretary for acquisition, technology, and logistics; and the under secretary for policy. Gates wrote that "Every few days we would hold expanded meetings . . . that included the service secretaries and chiefs and other senior civilians. And twice we brought in the entire Defense leadership, including the combatant commanders." Gates's motive for these marathon meetings was clear: "I wanted the services intimately involved in the process," and therefore he was "prepared to give each service chief and secretary all the time he wanted to explain his views. . . . Everyone had a chance to weigh in . . . I wanted this to be a team effort, because when we were finished, I expected the chiefs, in particular, to support whatever decisions I made."[21] This was a change from the process employed by former Secretary Rumsfeld. The "overarching capabilities-based framework" had not worked as Rumsfeld had desired. In its place was a process that at the highest levels was dependent upon deliberations and negotiations among senior officials, a process that added to the workload of CNO Roughead and his staff at a time when, because of Goldwater-Nichols, some of the best military staff officers were avoiding tours in the service staffs in favor of tours in the Joint Staff.

The Great Recession

The recession officially began in December 2007, when the unemployment rate for the United States reached 5 percent and the real Gross Domestic Product (GDP) had declined for two consecutive three-month periods. The Federal Reserve created an auction process in mid-December so that banks could shed high-risk loans. The Federal Reserve also continued into 2008 to steadily reduce the interest rate charged to member banks. On 13 February, President George W. Bush signed the Economic Stimulus Act of 2008, which gave taxpayers a rebate and reduced taxes on business investment. Unfortunately, these measures to sustain the supply of fiduciary money did not stop the financial crisis.[22] On 16 March 2008, the brokerage firm of Bear Stearns folded; it was purchased by JPMorgan Chase. But investment banks and banks that had invested heavily in the housing market could not sustain their portfolios. At the end of April 2008, the Federal Reserve was charging only two percent interest on short-term loans, yet the supply of fiduciary money continued to decline as stock prices and home values fell.

On 7 September, the Treasury Department took control of the Federal National Mortgage Association ("Fannie Mae") and the Federal Home Loan Mortgage Corporation ("Freddie Mac"). On 15 September, the investment bank Lehman Brothers filed for bankruptcy; it was the largest such failure in the history of American banking. The next day, the Federal Reserve provided funds to keep the American International Group (AIG), a huge insurance firm, from declaring bankruptcy. On 3 October, President George W. Bush signed into law a bill creating the Troubled Asset Relief Program (TARP), an effort to sustain U.S. financial institutions. From 6 through 10 October 2008, the Dow Jones average of stock values suffered its worst weekly loss in its history.

On 28 October, the Treasury Department advanced $125 billion in TARP funds to nine banks in an effort to sustain confidence in the nation's banking system. Despite this move, the panic continued. The Treasury Department bailed out Citigroup at the end of November, and the Federal Reserve reduced its interest rate for short-term loans to zero in mid-December to make liquidity available to banks and businesses. On 19 December, the Treasury Department offered to loan General Motors and Chrysler Corporation $13.4 billion from the TARP fund. In January, the Treasury Department loaned $20 billion to Bank of America. On 17 February 2009, the new President, Barack H. Obama, signed a "stimulus package" bill that cut some taxes and provided money for public projects. On 9 March, the Dow Jones average hit bottom, almost 54 percent below its high point of 9 October 2007. On 1 June 2009, General Motors filed in court for bankruptcy, and by October 2009 the unemployment rate peaked at ten percent.

As Princeton Professor Alan S. Blinder noted, "During the quarter century from February 1984 through January 2009, Americans *never* witnessed an unemployment rate as high as 8 percent *for even a single month*. An entire generation entered the labor force and worked for decades without ever experiencing an unemployment rate as high as the *lowest* rate we had from February 2009 through August 2012."[23] Put another way, "the cumulative *jobs deficit* was around 12 million by February 2010—nearly the population of Pennsylvania."[24] Blinder argued that the recession of 2007–2009 was the worst of the recessions that the United States had suffered after World War II. But what made the recession even more devastating economically was that the recovery, measured in terms of jobs and GDP growth, was initially very weak. To add to the widespread sense of failure and frustration, what had begun in the United States as a collapse of a mortgage "bubble" had "touched off a worldwide financial crisis," making unemployment and lost income global problems.[25] The weakened economy meant fewer tax revenues, and fewer federal revenues meant serious reductions in defense spending. The Navy had not seen such reductions since the winter of 1932–1933.

Shipbuilding Programs

CNO Roughead inherited from CNOs Clark and Mullen acquisition programs that were over their planned budgets. He also inherited the split between OPNAV's management of programming and the acquisition management chain of authority that ran from the assistant secretary for research, development and acquisition down through "program executive officers" and then to "program managers (PMs)."

Even before Admiral Roughead took office as Chief of Naval Operations, it was clear that shipbuilding would be a major issue for him and the OPNAV staff. For example, on 24 July 2007, Vice Admiral Paul E. Sullivan, the commander of NAVSEA, outlined changes to the Navy's shipbuilding organization to the members of the Seapower and Expeditionary Forces Subcommittee of the House Armed Services Committee. These changes were initiated by then–Assistant Secretary of the Navy for Research, Development and Acquisition (ASN[RD&A]) Delores M. Etter in an effort to constrain the rising costs of surface combatants. The two littoral combat ships then building were not going to meet their Navy cost goals or the cost ceilings imposed by Congress in the FY 2006 Defense Authorization Act, and the Navy had already terminated the contract with Lockheed Martin for the third ship of the class because of a disagreement over the vessel's cost.[26] In its July 2007 mark-up of the FY 2008 defense spending bill, the House Appropriations Committee had allotted enough funds for only one additional littoral combat ship, and Representative John T. Murtha (D-PA), chair of the Defense Subcommittee of the House Appropriations Committee, had said publicly that he and his colleagues were not going to pay for further overruns.[27]

John J. Young Jr., the acting Under Secretary of Defense for Acquisition, Technology and Logistics (USD[AT&L]) was then aggressively pushing against changes in ship programs that led to cost increases. To give him the ability to block such changes, Young insisted in a 30 July 2007 letter to the services that the military departments would have to create "Configuration

Steering Boards" for every major acquisition program then under development. Each board would normally be chaired by a service acquisition executive (SAE) (such as the assistant secretary for research, development, and acquisition) and include among its members senior civilians from the office of the USD(AT&L). Young expected the Configuration Steering Boards to reject "significant technical configuration changes . . . deferring them to future blocks or increments."[28] Young knew what he was about. An engineer by training, he had served as Assistant Secretary of the Navy (Research, Development and Acquisition) (ASN[RD&A]) from July 2001 to November 2005. Then he had taken the post of Deputy Director of Research and Engineering in the Office of the Secretary of Defense (November 2005 to July 2007), where he helped to increase the production of mine-resistant, ambush-protected (MRAP) vehicles. As a new USD(AT&L), he was adamant about holding down acquisition costs. As he said in his 30 July letter, "The acquisition policy will be to adjust technical content and requirements to deliver as much as possible of the planned capability within the budgeted cost."[29]

In written testimony to the Senate Armed Services Committee in early October 2007, before he had been confirmed as the new USD(AT&L), Young noted that he had learned from his disappointing experience with the littoral combat ship (LCS) program, and it was why he would—if confirmed—insist that every service use two or more competing teams to produce prototypes of key elements of any new system. It was true that fostering and paying for this type of competition would be expensive, but Young was convinced that it would save time and improve the performance of new systems in the long run. In making this argument, Young was echoing the words of many of his predecessors. Only a few major Navy programs—one was Aegis in the 1970s and 1980s—had been successful without using the technique of competitive prototyping, and Young made it clear when he was confirmed that he would be an active and aggressive undersecretary, waging a serious campaign against rising ship construction costs.

The Navy had a problem. It was expected to produce both numbers of new ships and the most capable ships it could get. This policy placed the managers of ship programs in a bind. Because of the Goldwater-Nichols legislation, they had to respond to the "requirements" set by the users of the new ships, especially the regional combatant commanders. That meant

Figure 18-1. CNO Gary Roughead answers questions from the media following his tour of the littoral combat ship Pre-Commissioning Unit *Freedom* (LCS-1) at the Marinette Marine Shipyard, 14 January 2008. Before becoming CNO, Admiral Roughead had commanded the Pacific Fleet and headed Fleet Forces Command. (U.S. Navy photo by Mass Communication Specialist 1st Class Tiffini M. Jones [Released] DIMOC Asset: 75M313738_x01 080114-N-FI224-199)

that service secretaries and service chiefs had to provide the combatant commanders with the numbers of ships "required" by the combatant commanders' war and theater engagement plans. One obvious way to obtain numbers of ships and perhaps get them to sea in a shorter period of time was to reduce the capability (and hence the cost) of a given design. The problem there was that the officers who drew up specific performance requirements (firepower, endurance, range, etc.) for new ships often planned to take advantage of new and often "immature" technologies in order to deal with anticipated "threats" across the lifetimes of the ships. When those immature technologies turned out to be more expensive than planned, the cost of a class of ships increased. Faced with those increased costs, the Navy often reduced the numbers of ships being bought—which just made the cost of any individual ship even greater as it had to "absorb" a greater percentage of the research and development costs associated with the whole class of ships.

A classic example of this challenge was the fate of the DDG-1000, the *Zumwalt*-class destroyer. The planned buy for this class was 32. That number was steadily reduced—to 24, to 12, and then to seven. By the time Admiral Roughead became the CNO, the number of *Zumwalts* that the Congress was willing to support was three, and even that number was not firm. At the end of February 2008, for example, Representative Murtha proposed reducing funding for the third DDG-1000 and procuring instead two additional cargo ships and a tenth LPD-17 amphibious assault ship. Allison F. Stiller, the Deputy Assistant Secretary of the Navy for Ship Programs and a former ship acquisition manager in NAVSEA, responded that the shipbuilder, National Steel and Shipbuilding Company, was already assembling two cargo ships and lacked the capacity to shift quickly and efficiently to four.[30] As she said, "to go to four would be quite a leap for them."[31]

But Murtha persisted. He argued that the Navy had to purchase 10 ships a year in order to have enough ships to meet its own goal of a fleet of 313 modern ships. Secretary Winter told Murtha's subcommittee at a hearing in March 2008 that the Navy still planned to procure seven *Zumwalts* and that the "program is actually going along very nicely." As Winter pointed out in talking with reporters about the DDG-1000, "We've had six years worth of design effort before we went through and definitized the contracts. We've had a whole series of engineering development models that have been used to wring out all the technology."[32] But of course technology was not the real issue. The real issue for both Murtha and Representative Gary E. "Gene" Taylor (D-MS), who chaired the House Armed Services Subcommittee on Seapower and Expeditionary Forces, was numbers of ships. At a 12 March 2008 hearing, Taylor asked Pacific Command (PACOM) commander Admiral Timothy J. Keating if his command would be better off militarily with two DDG-1000s or five DDG-51s with new radars. Keating chose the DDG-51s.[33] So what would Congress support—a third DDG-1000, more DDG-51s, or a new cruiser?

As expected, two influential senators—Edward Kennedy (D-MA) and Susan Collins (R-ME)—supported the three-ship DDG-1000 program, but representatives Murtha and Taylor still favored holding the DDG-1000 buy to just two ships. John S. Thackrah, the new ASN(RD&A), told *Inside the Navy* on 20 March that "You can't get the reaction that we've gotten recently in testimony and not be looking at contingency plans. We're looking at the DDG-51—what could we do with it? Vice Admiral [Bernard J.] McCullough [the N8] likes to call it the gap-filler. We're looking at all the options." On 25 March 2008, CNO Roughead seemed to try to dampen that sort of thinking when he told reporters that he was opposed to using funds already allocated to the third *Zumwalt* to build other ships. The Admiral was concerned that disruptions to the DDG-1000 and LCS programs would "be very harmful to our future combatant programs and to our warfighting capability."[34] What was the Navy's true position?

As far as Representatives Murtha and Taylor were concerned, it didn't matter. They wanted the DDG-1000 program stopped at two ships.[35] In his subcommittee's recommendation for the fiscal year 2009 defense authorization bill, Taylor offered to give "the secretary of the Navy and the chief of naval operations the flexibility . . . for the continuation of the DDG-1000 class or for re-starting the procurement of DDG-51-class destroyers."[36] CNO Roughead, in a letter to Senator Kennedy on 7 May, said that it would cost "significantly less" to produce a DDG-51 than a DDG-1000. That opened the door to restarting the DDG-51 production line. But Under Secretary Young told the Senate Armed Services Committee on 3 June that the DDG-1000 program was sound and that restarting the DDG-51 production line would be more expensive than CNO Roughead had estimated. According to Young, the Navy didn't want more DDG-51s: "they would actually like to have a ship that has more radar and other features." Moreover, "If you don't want to produce the exact same ship, what will it cost to produce the new design and what do you do about stability" at Bath Iron Works and Ingalls? Young made it clear that he would not let the Navy cancel the third *Zumwalt* without a careful analysis of the costs associated with restarting DDG-51 production.[37]

On 12 June 2008, Deputy Secretary of Defense England met with Young, Winter, and Roughead to discuss the Navy's position on the DDG-1000. Both Winter and Roughead later informed reporters that the Navy was sticking to the seven-ship DDG-1000 program.[38] Within a month, however, the Navy did a complete about-face, agreeing to limit DDG-1000 production to two ships and to restart DDG-51 production.[39] What had led to the change? On 31 July 2008, in testimony to the House Armed Services Seapower and Expeditionary Forces Subcommittee, DCNO for Integration of Resources and Capabilities (N8) McCullough noted that "Our internal analysis says we have excess capacity in naval surface fires which DDG-1000 was predominantly designed for," but the "demand from combatant commanders is for ballistic missile defense, integrated air and missile defense, and anti-submarine warfare best provided by the DDG-51s and not the surface fire support optimized for DDG-1000."[40] As Arthur H. Barber, who led Navy campaign analysis in N8, recalled, "The nature of the ASW [antisubmarine] challenge fundamentally changed, and the anti-ballistic missile demand on the Navy" kept increasing.[41] The decision to close down DDG-1000 production was a done deal, according to McCullough; the Marines were on board. Representative Taylor was pleased: "All the factors—the threat, the amount of money that's available, the fact that the fleet's too small and we need to grow it—I think when you look at all those things, they made the right decision."[42] Taylor did not say anything about "capabilities." That perspective had not taken hold in Congress.

On 18 August, however, Taylor and his colleagues were surprised by yet another 180-degree turn by the Navy. That day, Secretary of the Navy Winter and Deputy Secretary of Defense England informed them that the Navy would in fact build a third DDG-1000, using fiscal year 2009 funds already programmed for its construction.[43] The builder would be Bath Iron Works, which understandably pleased Senator Collins, then facing a challenge in the upcoming congressional elections. Representative Taylor was disappointed, and he termed the Defense Department's decision "the wrong decision for the wrong reason." In a 21 August phone interview with *Inside the Navy*, Taylor said, "I think it's a situation where politics are outweighing the best interests of the Navy."[44] Representative Murtha later expressed his frustration this way: "They came to us right before the mark-up and said, 'No, no, we don't want the 1000, we want the [DDG-51 *Arleigh Burke*–class destroyer] back.' Then, before we mark up, they said, 'No, no, we want the third 1000.' Now that's what we're dealing with. That's what makes it so difficult for us to come up with a program and be able to stabilize."[45] In frustration, Secretary Gates said that the country "had a shipbuilding strategy that seemed to change whenever the Navy secretary or chief of naval operations changed."[46]

CNO Roughead told the Surface Navy Association in January 2009 that he had cut the DDG-1000 program because the ship lacked ballistic missile defense and antisubmarine warfare (ASW) capabilities. "DDG-1000 did not address these important challenges," according to Roughead, while the DDG-51 "has the right capabilities and provides greater capacity where we need it."[47] He did not say anything about the U.S. economy, yet the state of the economy mattered a great deal. One major problem with the acquisition process was that it sometimes took so long to produce a needed system that the reasons for deciding to produce it in the first place were no longer valid. Or, as in 2008 and 2009, the lack of resources caused by an unforeseen economic disruption could rob the Navy of the funds it wanted in order to produce and field the complex systems that it was developing.

The LCS program continued to be a problem for CNO Roughead and the Navy. In a careful study of the program, Robert O. Work, who would later serve as Under Secretary of the Navy in the Obama administration, showed that the primary reasons for the rapidly escalating costs of the first littoral combat ships were "changes made in the middle of the detailed design and early production phase" of the LCS program *by the Navy*. As Work noted, "the lead ships were placed into production well before their designs were stable. As a result, change orders became the program standard rather than the exception, further complicating and disrupting production and driving costs up."[48] In a situation where "change orders" become the "standard," it is impossible for a contractor to proceed without some guarantee that spiraling costs will be covered, and that requires a "cost" contract.

But the Navy was unwilling (and politically reluctant) to provide such an open-ended guarantee and wanted its LCS contractors (Lockheed Martin and General Dynamics) to accept fixed-price incentive contracts. When both firms balked, the Navy cancelled their contracts for the second ships of each hull type. The House of Representatives and the Senate reacted to the cancellations by agreeing on a defense appropriations bill that provided funds for just one additional LCS and dramatically reduced funds for the "mission modules" that were an essential part of the LCS concept. Representative Murtha said that he did not want to terminate the LCS program—"one of the highest priorities of the Navy"—but he also told *Inside the Navy* that the Congress expected the Navy to find a way to hold down the cost of individual ships.[49]

Robert Work traced the problem facing CNO Roughead back to decisions endorsed by former CNO Vernon E. Clark:

> Recall that in 2002–2003, the Navy planned to award each of two winning LCS design teams a contract for one Flight 0 prototype. The first was to be built in FY 2005 and the second in FY 2006. After a period of fleet testing, the Navy would down-select to a single Flight I variant, with the first two production ships being requested in FY 2008 and delivered in FY 2010.
>
> This plan proved unworkable for two reasons. First, the winning teams . . . indicated that stick-building a single Flight 0 prototype and then keeping their design teams and production lines idle until the Navy decided on the eventual Flight I winner would be prohibitively expensive. . . . [Second], the second builder would just be finishing its first Flight 0 seaframe as the down-select decision was being made. In other words, the Navy's plan allowed for little if any time for comparative testing between the two prototypes.[50]

Roughead, of course, had had no control over this process; he was, instead, left with the unfortunate consequences. In the Navy's favor, however, was the support for the LCS *concept* in Congress and on the part of the Defense Department's Acquisition Under Secretary, John Young. Young made clear his support for the program in a talk with reporters on 4 March 2008, when he expressed his confidence in the Navy's acquisition strategy to evaluate both competing bidders and their designs.[51]

In the first week of August, 2008, Secretary of the Navy Winter—fresh from a ride on the Lockheed Martin LCS-1—again voiced his support for the program. At the same time, however, he proposed to revise the major acquisition process.[52] CNO Roughead agreed with Winter that more effective oversight was necessary in the case of both the process by which requirements were prepared and the process by which ship designs were turned into the final product. In a speech to a conference of the American Society of Naval Engineers on 25 September, Roughead warned that "We have lost our credibility. We have got to get it back . . ." To restore its credibility, the Navy had to exert satisfactory control over the development of system requirements. "Requirements creep" could lead to almost impossible—and certainly unaffordable—systems and ships.

In addition, a lack of "technical" and "on-scene" oversight impeded effective supervision of the Navy's contractors. At the same time, Roughead admitted that "the career patterns that our officers have to follow really doesn't [sic] lend itself to someone becoming an expert in the area of requirements."[53] What the admiral was admitting was that there were few officers and civilians in the Navy who could master the technical complexities that were at the core of the littoral combat ship concept. As Robert Work noted,

> [T]he LCS would rely on the power of FORCEnet [netted sensors] for both situational awareness and survivability to a degree never seen before. This represented a big leap in battle force and ship design, as well as a major culture shift for a surface warfare community whose experiences were shaped predominantly by operating large, expensive, multimission combatants.[54]

Yet this revolution in what surface combatants would do, what they would be like, and how they would "fit" into the rest of the Navy's fighting formations was not seen for the engineering challenge that it was. It was as significant a change as the introduction of nuclear power had been, and as the development of Aegis had been. But where was the engineering expertise needed to manage and direct that change? It had largely migrated to industry. As retired Vice Admiral Wayne Meyer, the "father" of Aegis, observed in 1996, "Today virtually the entire acquisition process is oriented on business . . . Technical requirements don't reside any place in that process." But they needed to be there, according to Meyer. "The leadership must carry the burden of the technical discussion."[55] The evidence suggests that the Navy could do that with the DDG-1000, but the Navy had not been able to do it with the littoral combat ship because development and production of the LCS had been rushed. As a result, the arguments in Congress and in the media tended to focus on traditional acquisition concerns—how much did each ship cost? Were any behind schedule? Did they carry enough weapons to defend themselves? When would the modules be available? To the extent that those sorts of questions dominated the debate about LCS, the debate over the program missed the point—and could therefore not help solve the program's problems.

Nevertheless, something needed to be done about the LCS program, and especially about the information technology (hardware and software) in Navy ships. At the annual meeting of the Surface Navy Association in January 2008, Vice Admiral Mark J. Edwards, Deputy Chief of Naval Operations for Communications Networks (N6), warned that the Navy's digital technology was falling "further and further behind the capabilities of the civilian marketplace," and that the service would lose the next generation of sailors if it didn't catch up. "The *Arleigh Burke* destroyer is one of the most advanced fighting ships the world has ever seen," according to Edwards, but the "two-wave communication bandwidth of [a] single Blackberry is three times larger than the bandwidth of an entire *Arleigh Burke* destroyer." The Admiral knew what the problem was; it was proprietary software—software made exclusively for the Navy and tied intimately to proprietary hardware. As he noted, "In the past . . . the application and the hardware were linked together, so if you changed the application you had to change the hardware, and so it's very expensive to do that." Because it was so expensive, it was put off, with the result that most Navy software was obsolete. But this was something that the Navy could do something about—and was doing it. The solution was to switch to open software architecture.[56] Edwards had already begun this move, and he had the support of both CNO Roughead and Secretary Winter. But Roughead would take another step once the new presidential administration was in office.

The "Balisle Report"

CNO Roughead didn't just have problems with shipbuilding costs. He also faced a real problem with ship maintenance. The push to have the fleet deployed or ready for deployment *while still reducing Navy expenditures* had led to serious maintenance gaps among surface combat ships, especially within the DDG-51 class. The maintenance programs for the nuclear-powered submarines and aircraft carriers had been more rigorous, and therefore satisfactory. But for various reasons the "engineering underpinning" required to define the maintenance needed to guarantee 40-year life spans for the DDG-51s had not been done, and the number of surface combat ships ready for deployment had declined.[57] As Vice Admiral William R. Burke, then the Deputy Chief of Naval Operations for Readiness and Logistics (N4), told the members of the Subcommittee on Readiness of the House Armed Services Committee in July 2011, "an average of 50 ships a year since 2005" had "violated one or more of the . . . standards such as deployment length, . . . compared with an average of 5 in years prior to" 2005.[58]

This problem had not gone unnoticed. The Navy's chief engineer had tracked it, and Admirals Robert F. Willard and John C. Harvey Jr., had supported the chief engineer in bringing it to the attention of CNO Roughead when Willard was the Pacific combatant commander and Harvey was head of Fleet Forces Command. Accordingly, in September 2009, Roughead formed a panel, chaired by former NAVSEA chief Philip M. Balisle, to find the causes of the problem and recommend a solution to Admiral Harvey and the commander of the Pacific Fleet. On 26 February 2010, the panel ("Fleet Review Panel of Surface Forces Readiness") published its findings.[59] The Panel's findings were summarized in two sentences: ". . . Surface Force readiness has degraded over the last ten years. This degradation has not been due to a single decision or policy change, but the result of many independent actions."[60]

What were those actions? Ships had been manned for operations, and not also for essential shipboard maintenance requirements. Shore-based intermediate maintenance facilities were closed. "Readiness squadrons" had been eliminated and replaced by "regional support organizations" (termed Regional Maintenance Centers, or RMCs), but the RMCs had been replaced in 2007 by ship class squadrons that lacked "line authority over the ships they supported." The Fleet Review Board reduced the frequency of its inspections. Training in surface ship maintenance was cut for both officers and new enlisted personnel. The time allotted for shipyard maintenance was "shortened from 15 weeks to 9 weeks and the material maintenance management . . . program was scaled back."[61] As Vice Admiral McCoy, who as the Navy's chief engineer had recognized the problem, put it, every one of the changes in policy that led to the decline in material readiness "seemed to make sense at the time they were made. But when you looked at the impact across the surface-warfare community, the cumulative effect was highly negative."[62]

This explanation did not satisfy the members of the Readiness Subcommittee of the House Armed Services Committee, who grilled both Vice Admiral Burke and Vice Admiral McCoy in a public hearing on 12 July 2011. Burke explained the genesis of the maintenance problem as follows: ". . . the continuing demand for forces exceeds that which we have, which we can provide. So, we have the combatant commanders in a situation where they drive demand, and their demand is relatively unconstrained . . ."[63] Representative J. Randy Forbes (R-VA), chairman of the subcommittee, wanted a direct answer to a question: Was the Pentagon giving the Navy the resources its surface combatants needed to perform their missions? If not, then why not? As Forbes asked, "[D]o we have any objective bars, thresholds, or standards we use" to decide when to give the Navy more money for maintenance, "or is all this just kind of subjective, that we kind of know it when we see it? . . . In determining our readiness, do we rely on the QDR [Quadrennial Defense Review] at all?"[64] Burke's answer was "The QDR helps us decide what forces we procure. The COCOM [combatant commander] demand signal helps us determine how we prepare those forces to deploy."[65] Representative Forbes was not satisfied: "I don't know why we have the QDR if the QDR isn't going to help us make some assessments on our readiness." What alarm would sound to warn Congress when Navy readiness was beginning to significantly weaken? There was only one answer from the Navy. It was when Navy officers found evidence of it.

There were several major issues highlighted by the subcommittee's hearings and the written statement given the subcommittee by Vice Admirals Burke and McCoy. For example, the statement noted that the Fleet Response Plan had not worked as intended: ". . . readiness available for surge is being used for presence. This is unsustainable over the long term . . ." As a result, "to stabilize the surge readiness available under the [Fleet Response Plan], operational demand and force structure must be rebalanced."[66] This was a polite way of saying that the Navy needed both more surface combat ships like the DDG-51 and more funds for ship maintenance and training for sailors. Yet there was more to it than money, and the subcommittee included in its report a May 2011 memo from Fleet Forces Commander Admiral John Harvey discussing the "Balisle Report" in which Harvey explained why the material problems were quite serious. As Harvey noted, "Many years of doing whatever was necessary to meet operational commitments artificially suppressed the Surface Force's requirements for people, maintenance, training, equipment, and logistical support. Another unfortunate byproduct of this approach was the perception that broken and degraded equipment, inadequate proficiency, and poor risk management were tolerable."[67]

Roughead and OPNAV

By the end of 2008, CNO Roughead had laid the foundation for significantly changing OPNAV, starting with the creation of what became the Quadrennial Integration Group, or QIG, that May. Prior to that time, the Navy had not had a permanent office to plan for and develop the Navy's approach to the QDR. Instead, the Navy's leaders had been content with pulling together groups of officers and civilians to deal with the next QDR and then sending them back to their "home" offices when the QDR was completed. But the Air Force and Army had found that keeping a

QDR core staff together made preparing for the next review easier, and that mattered because, as described earlier in this chapter, the Quadrennial Defense Review report had become a major policy document. The services realized that preparing for the QDR and for the Quadrennial Roles and Missions study deserved to be done thoroughly.

To head the QIG, CNO Roughead selected then-Rear Admiral William R. Burke, a submariner and the same Admiral Burke questioned in Congress about readiness in July 2011; Burke reported to Roughead through the Director of the Navy Staff. To help Burke get his new organization off the ground, he was given the personnel of Deep Blue, an organization created after the attacks of 11 September 2001 to provide advice on anti-terrorist operations to CNO Clark and Navy component commanders. By 2007, Deep Blue's function was to help move new capabilities into the fleet, and Roughead decided to use it as the basis for a permanent organization that would be the Navy's lead office for the QDR. But Roughead also gave the new organization the task of assisting him in "aligning and integrating OPNAV staff activities." Burke and his staff were to "create an integrated description and view of how [the] Navy strategically addresses current and future operational environments via sustainable investment and execution plans."[68]

In June 2008, Roughead gave the Naval Network Warfare Command (NETWARCOM) type commander responsibilities for fleet intelligence "in addition to its information operations (IO), networks and space missions." As the CNO informed the fleet, "[T]he assignment of intelligence [type command] and fleet ISR advocacy functions to NETWARCOM is a key part of . . . intelligence transformation . . ." NETWARCOM would continue to report to the commander, Fleet Forces Command, and it would not assume the duties of the Office of Naval Intelligence, but it would have direct access to N2 "to ensure capabilities and processes are in place to deliver the best current/operational intelligence to the fleet."[69]

Significantly, Roughead's message mentioned maritime headquarters and maritime operations centers. The latter, referred to by the acronym "MOCs," were something new—naval planning staffs specializing in joint operational-level campaign planning based on a shared "picture" of the maritime environment. Numbered fleet staffs already existed, but the MOCs were intended to engage not only in joint planning across a potential theater of conflict, but also to meld the data from operational-level intelligence sources with data from other sensors to "keep pace with the increasingly complex and dynamic potential threat environments of the future."[70] This was a general way of explaining something that was potentially revolutionary—the creation of an operations planning process that could actually anticipate an enemy's moves across a wide swath of territory or ocean. The message from Roughead was also a sign of how he would reorganize OPNAV once a new presidential administration was in office.

In February 2009, Roughead, as part of a larger effort to change the role of intelligence in the Navy, selected Vice Admiral David J. Dorsett to be the first three-star Director of Naval Intelligence since the 1970s. Dorsett was charged with improving the education of intelligence personnel, with seeing to it that Navy intelligence personnel supported the conflicts in Iraq and Afghanistan, and with leading the Navy to what Roughead had termed "information dominance."[71] Roughead had also directed Dorsett to find out if software being used by naval intelligence personnel could fit into the Navy's Consolidated Afloat Networks and Enterprise Services, or CANES. Dorsett admitted that he faced a problem there—the same problem highlighted by the N6, Vice Admiral Edwards: Navy ships were "bandwidth-limited," and therefore, "until we get significant bandwidth, we will not be in an optimal operating environment."

To make progress toward getting that environment, Roughead directed the merger of N2 and N6 in a 26 June 2009 memorandum.[72] He wanted the reorganization to begin on 1 October and finish no later than 18 December 2009. Roughead's reorganization memo specified that the N6 "billet will be used to establish a Fleet Cyber Commander (FLTCYBERCOM) on 1 October 2009 to serve as the Navy Component Commander to U.S. Cyber Command."[73] The CNO also directed his reorganization team to "propose administrative and operational relationships between FLTCYBERCOM and other Navy and Joint Commands" while identifying "governance mechanisms across the Navy to optimally align and manage Navy's information capabilities."[74] In a 13 July 2009 memo for the staffs of N2 and N6, Vice Admiral Dorsett (N2) and Vice Admiral Harry B. Harris Jr., (N6), made it clear that the "CNO's expectations are very high," and the two of them agreed that the merger was "an historic opportunity to reshape the Navy for warfighting dominance in the Information Age."[75] At an OPNAV "all hands" meeting on 17 July 2009, Admiral Roughead explained why the staff was being restructured: "Biggest breakthrough of the current fight in OEF and OIF is the successful integration of intelligence and operations, and using the network to get information to the right person, at the right time, in the right way. That is where the power is."[76]

According to retired Vice Admiral Burke, Admiral Dorsett was selected as the head of the new N2/N6 "because he was the current N2 and had tremendous credibility in both Navy and joint intelligence circles." It would have been challenging for Admiral Roughead to "sell" the reorganization if he were to immediately choose an officer who was not an acknowledged intelligence specialist. "Because Admiral Dorsett was the current Director of Naval Intelligence, it was an easier transition. The new N2/N6 would become an incubator for future flag officers with a much broader perspective."[77] Vice Admiral Burke also noted that another reason for consolidating N2 and N6 was because N6 was often considered within the Navy as a communications office—as an office involved with what amounted to logistics, when in fact almost all communications were digital, and therefore communications were an essential element of any digital campaign and every logistical support plan. In fact, interfering with digital communications was essential to attacking an enemy's "kill chain" (the sequence of events from detecting a target to attacking it). "Conversely," according to Burke, "avoiding interference with our 'electromagnetic spectrum' was crucial to completing [the joint force's] kill chain." Protecting and attacking communications was just as important as "kinetic" attacks, hence the merger of N2 and N6.[78]

The memo establishing the "administrative and operational relationships between FLTCYBERCOM/Tenth Fleet and other Navy and Joint Commands" was signed by Admiral Roughead on 23 July 2009.[79] The memo made Fleet Cyber Command/Tenth Fleet the naval component to the United States Cyber Command (USCYBERCOM), which was in its turn under the command of the Strategic Command (STRATCOM) in Nebraska. However, Fleet Cyber Command/Tenth Fleet also had a formal administrative link to OPNAV. It was OPNAV that provided the training, equipment, and funds for Fleet Cyber Command, and it was to OPNAV and the CNO that the commander of Fleet Cyber Command/Tenth Fleet turned to for the personnel, supplies, and facilities that the Command needed. Finally, FLTCYBERCOM/Tenth Fleet was made "service cryptologic commander" for the National Security Agency. This arrangement of divided authority untangled a potentially thorny relationship—the need for Fleet Cyber Command/Tenth Fleet to be operationally subordinate to USCYBERCOM while coordinating with the National Security Agency and being sustained by OPNAV. The 23 July memo also made clear the relationship between Fleet Cyber Command/Tenth Fleet and the Naval Network Warfare Command: NETWARCOM was the subordinate command, charged with executing "network and space operations."[80]

In that same 26 June 2009 memorandum, Roughead altered the role of N00X from a focus on preparing for quadrennial defense reviews to one of "naval warfare assessment." N00X was directed to "[i]dentify gaps and shortcomings in warfighting capability," recommend ways that the Navy could better "allocate risk," and conduct program and other assessments for the CNO. Rear Admiral Burke, the first head of the altered organization, noted that his was a difficult role to play. On the one hand, he and his small staff had to respond quickly to the needs of CNO Roughead; they would serve as a sort of "inner staff." On the other hand, the deputy chiefs of naval operations and their senior aides and deputies would wonder what the N00X was telling the CNO. As Burke admitted, N00X could become a "boutique organization," doing things "that were more appropriately done by established OPNAV divisions."[81]

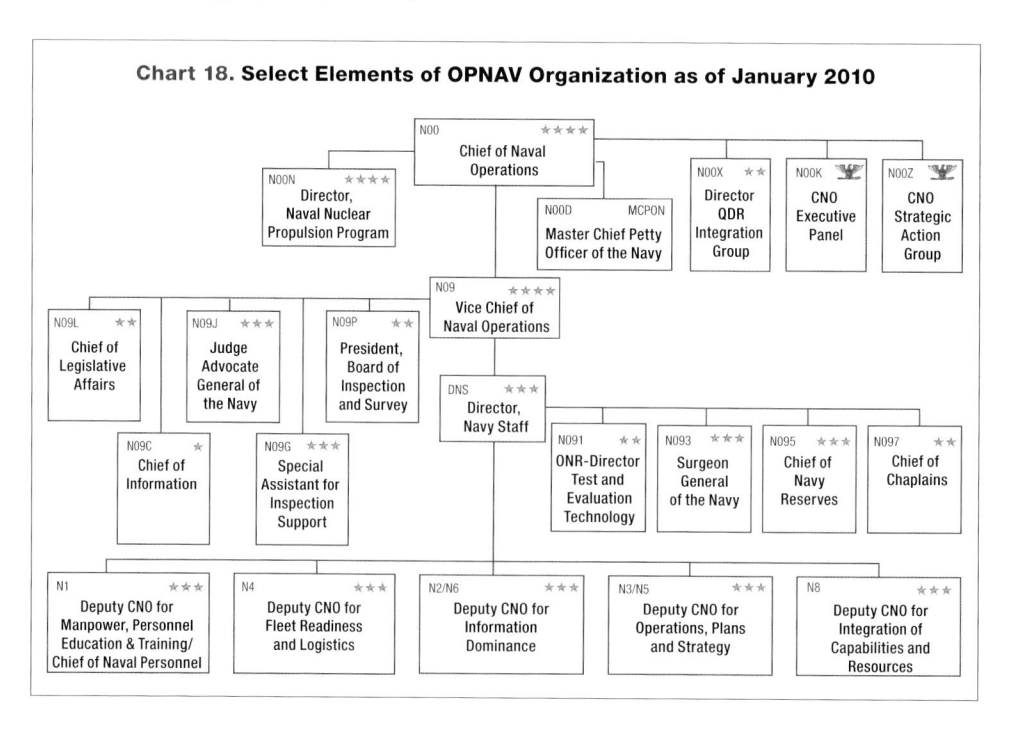

Chart 18. Select Elements of OPNAV Organization as of January 2010

The role of N00X was clarified by a January 2010 OPNAV Notice promulgated by Vice Admiral Samuel J. Locklear III, Director of the Navy Staff. The notice contained a new charter for N00X, and the charter stressed the responsibility of its Director to "identify strategic risks or gaps in the ability of the planned program to deliver the expected capability and capacity in key warfare areas across platforms and communities."[82] But the charter also noted that N00X would "facilitate senior leader discussion of areas where Navy's [sic] plans, program and strategy diverge from one another or national strategy or present opportunities for innovation or better integration."[83] In effect, N00X would look inside the Navy for things the CNO might otherwise miss, and look outside the Navy—through what was called the CNO's "Futures Forum"—for possible future issues that merited discussion by the CNO and his senior deputies. Vice Admiral Burke recalled that CNO Roughead "cared greatly about the 'futures' meetings. He credited those with keeping him up to date with new technological and social developments, and his improved understanding of them added to his performance as a member of the Joint Chiefs." In addition, Roughead "thought that the discussions during the futures meetings and then the write-ups afterward helped keep senior Navy officers on the same page, especially when they spoke with the media or to members of the public."[84]

Information and the Cooperative Strategy

In October 2007, CNO Roughead had co-signed "A Cooperative Strategy for 21st Century Seapower" along with Marine Corps Commandant James T. Conway and Coast Guard Commandant Thad W. Allen.[85] As the three officers noted, the strategy stressed "an approach that integrates seapower with other elements of national power," and described "how seapower will be applied around the world . . . as we join with other like-minded nations to protect and sustain the global, inter-connected system through which we prosper."[86] This was not a new concept. However, as Roughead knew, it was more than just a concept and more than just a goal. The specifics of a "cooperative strategy" had already been worked out during actual campaigns, especially those carried out by U.S. special forces.

The potential drawback of a "cooperative strategy" was that it could not be sustained in the face of the force and resource requirements of the conflicts in Iraq and Afghanistan. The Navy, Marines, and Coast Guard were executing multiple operations in different conflicts simultaneously. Their components, acting under one or more of the regional combatant commands, were also engaged in many other activities, usually in cooperation with the forces of other nations. What tied all these operations together? CNO Roughead answered that question in a talk he gave at the Center for Strategic and International Studies on 1 October 2009. In his presentation, he stressed that, in Iraq and Afghanistan, "in the area of special operations, . . . we have been able to fuse information and intelligence into operations in ways that we have never been able to do before. And in ways that have made our forces there extraordinarily more effective where we can use the power of the networks to get information, the right information, to the right person at the right time to be able to do the right thing."[87] Though the CNO stressed the actions of special

Figure 18-2. CNO Admiral Gary Roughead testifies and answers questions concerning the "Cooperative Maritime Strategy for 21st Century Seapower" strategy before the House Armed Services Committee at Washington, DC, 13 December 2007. (U.S. Navy photo by Mass Communication Specialist 1st Class Tiffini M. Jones [Released] DIMOC Asset 75M308028_x01 071213-N-FI224-043)

forces, the principle had much wider implications. It applied to both combat and engaging in exercises with the navies of other nations.

In the former, U.S. forces—even in relatively small numbers—could have the advantage of knowing where the enemy was and what he was likely to do next. In dealing with other navies, especially those of small or relatively poor nations, the U.S. Navy could provide a "picture" of what was happening at sea and thereby increase the effectiveness of those small navies. The navies of most nations were in fact coast guard forces. What those navies usually lacked was a clear picture, in near real-time, of what was happening in the waters that washed their shores. If they and their friendly neighbors could "see" what was happening, then they could use their small but often quite professional forces with success against smuggling and the illegal transportation of refugees and immigrants: "Overall, networking can make individual units more lethal, if they are equipped to take advantage of it."[88] Put another way, navies—particularly the U.S. Navy—with the technology to construct digital "pictures" of the movements of ships on the ocean could share those "pictures" with less wealthy navies and improve the military potential of such navies. This was an important inducement for routine naval cooperation.[89]

The Navy and the Marines

The leaders of the Navy and the Marine Corps continued to spar over the number of amphibious ships bought and built for the Marines, but that wasn't the most important development in the relationship between the two services. The most important development was the signing of Secretary of the Navy Instruction 4000.37, "Naval Logistics Integration," on 31 December 2007. The instruction aimed to *integrate* Navy and Marine Corps logistics. This wasn't an effort to improve coordination; it was, instead, what it said—a plan to integrate Navy and Marine Corps logistics, which was something new and daring.[90] By the spring of 2008, there was an executive board for naval logistics integration composed of flag and general officers from OPNAV, Marine Corps Headquarters, and the Defense Logistics Agency (DLA), to focus the efforts of the three organizations on taking advantage of their formal integration and informal "transformation" efforts.[91] Using approaches borrowed from private industry, subordinate organizations such as the Marine Corps Systems Command and the Naval Supply Systems Command sent experienced members to Integrated Product Teams (IPTs) that examined the "total life cycle management" of various items and services, ranging from clothing to medical supplies. The goal of these teams was to find ways to better manage the production and fielding of support needed by the operating forces. To the degree that they could be successful, they would improve the chances that the Navy's concept of "seabasing" would be a success.

As the logisticians went to work, senior Navy and Marine Corps officers tried to agree on what a future amphibious force would look like. At a conference on 23 October 2007, Marine Corps Commandant Conway argued again in public that the Marines needed 33 or 34 large amphibious ships in order to be able to count on having 30 available. As he noted, "You have multiple talks with the United States Navy and convince them that your cause is just and that we're in this together." But General Conway also revealed his bargaining strategy: "Our Navy admirals are reasonable people and it is now all in their court to tell us how they're going to do it, because again it's got to compete with other ships that they see as necessary."[92] In public, a Navy captain from the amphibious warfare office in OPNAV agreed with Conway, adding just a bit more to the pressure on the Navy's shipbuilding program.

This was at the same time that Congress was cutting funding for the LCS program back to two ships and funding for the DDG-1000 to three. Conway could make his case knowing that the Navy had lost standing in the eyes of some very influential members of Congress who wanted to improve the strengths of both the Navy and the Marine Corps. In response to Conway, the Navy suggested it might use the National Defense Sealift fund to purchase maritime prepositioning ships, thereby freeing up money for another large amphibious ship, but the Senate Armed Services Committee pointed out that the National Defense Sealift Fund was not intended by law to be used to procure amphibious assault ships like those that would be central to the Maritime Prepositioning Force (MPF) (Future).[93] CNO Roughead was in a corner. As he pointed out to reporters on 12 February 2008, it was not clear that the Navy would be able to afford the 313 ships that he had said were necessary in order for the Navy to fulfill the requirements of its own strategy.[94]

In the meantime, the Marines were reassessing their plans to implement a "distributed operations concept." The concept was developed as a means to take advantage of the "seabasing" capability and operational mobility of the Marines and Navy. For example, a naval force could remain over the horizon while it quickly moved small contingents of Marines ashore. These heavily armed squads, not tied to a landing beach, would be able to bypass static enemy defenses and attack key enemy objectives with the support of air and missile attacks launched from the distant ships. In the past, amphibious operations had been movements of two stages—from ship to shore and then, with the shore secured, from the landing point to an objective further inland. Under the new concept, there would be just one stage of movement—from the sea to relatively distant objectives ashore. The Marines on the ground would get most of their supplies and firepower from the seabase—using V-22s and helicopters flying from large amphibious ships and aircraft carriers. It was a very audacious concept, "seeding" an area dominated by an enemy with small Marine "fire teams" that could rely on "information superiority" to avoid the enemy until they could assemble to stage an attack. As Marine Corps Commandant Conway argued in May 2008, "Our value is not in the fact that we provide a second land army to this great country. Our value is that we provide an expeditionary force second-to-none that can get out of town quickly, be light on its feet, be adaptable wherever we go, and [be] very, very lethal."[95]

At the same time, however, the Marine Corps did not want to forego the option to wage a counterinsurgency campaign. The goal, noted General Conway, was to become a "two-fisted" force.[96] But it wasn't clear just how to become such a force. As Conway was describing a Marine Corps that was both extremely light and very lethal, the MCCDC was formally abandoning the distributed operations concept. In its place was "enhanced company operations." As Brigadier General Andrew W. O'Donnell, the "director of capabilities development" at MCCDC acknowledged, General Conway was "not comfortable" with "six-man teams going out on their own."[97] Simulations and exercises, along with combat experience in Iraq and Afghanistan, had suggested that the smallest effective unit for expeditionary operations was a reinforced platoon of approximately 100 Marines. But to move such units ashore from amphibious ships located over the horizon would require numbers of V-22 vertical lift transport aircraft, as well as the specialized amphibious ships to carry, service, and refuel them.

In short, the Navy and the Marines were trying to work out their disagreement about how many large amphibious ships to buy while the Marines were wrestling with how to specifically define and then build a "two-fisted" force. Given his legal responsibility for Navy Department acquisition, Secretary Winter was in the middle of the Navy–Marine Corps discussions. In an interview with *Inside the Navy* on 7 August 2008, the Navy secretary pointed out that, "If anything, one of the lessons learned over the last eight-to-10 years is the value of being able to operate from the sea and not being dependent on fixed bases."[98] Winter was convinced that "The whole future of the amphibious fleet is the next real challenge that the Navy and Marine Corps together have got to take on." Retired Captain Arthur H. Barber III, the head of OPNAV's N81, put it differently: "If you're serious, [seabasing] breaks the Navy."[99]

There were obviously many questions to answer in order to cope with this challenge. What about "selective offloading," where a Marine commander needed to pull just some "items from an amphibious ship without removing all the equipment aboard?" And what was the best way to move supplies from the over-the-horizon naval force to land? If Marines could be moved ashore quickly by V-22 aircraft, was there any way to move their heavier equipment just as quickly, or did the "heavy" equipment (artillery and ammunition, for example) have to be replaced by equipment that could be carried by helicopters and V-22s?[100] General Conway won a victory of sorts early in 2009 when he and CNO Roughead agreed that the Navy's amphibious force would have a minimum of 33 amphibious ships, but that was only the beginning of a Marine Corps effort to tailor its whole force to a future of both amphibious operations and counterinsurgency campaigns.

Conclusion

Admiral Roughead became CNO when the pressures on OPNAV were increasing. Over the four years of his tenure (September 2007–September 2011), the DDG-1000 and littoral combat ship programs were a source of frustration and often embarrassment. So was the "Balisle Report," which could be read as a case where the OPNAV staff did not fulfill its duty to monitor and reduce risks in the area of fleet support. But the merging of N2 and N6 was a daring stroke. The Navy needed to participate in a major way in the new world of cybernetic operations, and the merger was one way to pull whole classes of specialists out of their accepted career paths and throw them into a world that was changing at extraordinary speed. Defense secretary Gates was in the process of creating the United States Cyber Command and reorganizing the United States Strategic Command while the Navy was acting to support the change.[101] By December 2009, the Navy's "new main battery" was "information dominance," and dominating information meant interfering with an opponent's information systems while preventing your opponent from doing the same to yours.[102] By the summer of 2011, the deputy chief management officer of the Department of Defense was trying to convince Congress to create a single appropriations account for information technology.[103]

This shift took place despite the "great recession," and despite severe antagonism between the two major political parties. Two events from the same month illustrate how the Navy went ahead with efforts to achieve national security goals even in the face of the economic crisis. On 9 March 2009, the Dow Jones average of selected stocks was down almost 54 percent from its 9 October 2007 high. Huge amounts of fiduciary money had simply disappeared in about 16 months, despite efforts by the Federal Reserve banks to keep that from happening. On 23 March 2009, the CNO created N52, the directorate for "international engagement," in OPNAV. N52 was charged with fostering and sustaining cooperative relationships with more international partners, a key element of "A Cooperative Strategy for 21st Century Seapower."[104] As the first head of the new office put it, "This is the center of gravity for CNO for international engagement."[105] Though the economic downturn had affected the Navy Department's budget and therefore threatened the ability of the CNO and the Secretary of the Navy to manage the Department effectively, it had not halted naval forward deployments or totally disrupted acquisition programs.

What affected the Marines and the Navy were efforts to control the growth of federal deficits. If the recession was caused by a lack of demand on the part of consumers and businesses, then the customary solution was for the federal government to stimulate demand, usually by borrowing money. But the United States had developed a series of deficits, and it appeared to many members of Congress that drastic measures had to be taken to keep the overall federal debt from rising so high that it threatened the ability of the government to borrow money. After the Republican Party gained control of the House of Representatives in the 2010 congressional elections, its majority (and a majority of the Senate) approved what became the Budget Control Act of 2011, requiring the "sequestration" of federal funds if the President and the Congress could not agree among themselves on significant reductions in federal spending. The political confrontation that this law triggered between a Republican House of Representatives and a Democratic President was serious, and their ongoing dispute was not one that CNO Roughead could shape to the Navy Department's benefit. He was just as much a prisoner of events as his distant predecessor, CNO Admiral William V. Pratt (September 1930 to June 1933), had been during the Great Depression.

In a 16 December 2010 interview, Deputy Chief Management Officer of the Department of Defense Elizabeth A. McGrath said that the "overarching enterprise business priorities" in the Department's 2009 Strategic Management Plan were sustaining the all-volunteer force, reforming defense acquisition, strengthening the skills of the Defense Department's civilian workforce, improving the Department's financial management, and making sure that overseas contingency operations (OCO) were properly supported.[106] CNO Roughead had to keep his eye on these goals while he and the OPNAV staff found ways to improve the Navy's digital capabilities and implement the goals of 2007's "A Cooperative Strategy for 21st Century Seapower."

Under the circumstances, it was not an easy road to travel. The issue of what to do about the EFV program dragged on for almost all of Roughead's time as CNO. The JSF program was also a burden, as was the new amphibious ship, the LPD-17. And was the Navy going to be saddled with the development and production costs of the replacements for the *Ohio*-class ballistic missile submarines? Added to these issues for the CNO and the Navy secretary was the long-running dispute between the Navy and the Marines about the number and type of amphibious ships and the nature of amphibious operations. Since the end of the Cold War, the Marines had begun to sound less like an element of the Navy Department and more like a separate service. But why not? Who was doing the fighting in Iraq, Afghanistan, and in the other theaters of the "Global War on Terrorism?"

Finally, there was the relationship between the Navy Department and the regional combatant commanders. On 14 June 2011, CNO Roughead, Marine Corps Commandant General James F. Amos, and Secretary of the Navy Raymond E. Mabus Jr., sent Secretary of Defense Leon E. Panetta—Gates's replacement—a memo stating that the demand for naval forces by the combatant commanders "consistently exceeds available and even potential capacity, even without the anticipated fiscal constraints."[107] The Navy and Marines could be "stretched" only so far and for so long before people and machines wore out. Put another way, "swimming upstream" could not be done forever.

Notes

[1] Gates, *Duty*, 304.

[2] Ibid., 100–101.

[3] Geoff Fein, "N2/N6 Reorganization to Give Fleet Right Information at Right Time, CNO Says," *Defense Daily*, 24 July 2009.

[4] *Wall Street Journal*, 27 Aug. 2014, A2.

[5] Jeffrey M. Borns, "How Secretary of Defense Rumsfeld Sought to Assert Civilian Control Over the Military," written for Course 5603, "The Interagency Process," National War College, National Defense University, 8–9.

[6] "DOD Senior Governance Councils," Department of Defense Directive (DODD) 5105.79, 19 May 2008, Sections 3 and 4. http://www.dtic.mil/whs/directives/corres/pdf/510579p.pdf (29 Aug. 2016).

[7] Gordon R. England, "One War, One Team, One Fight," U.S. Naval Institute *Proceedings*, vol. 129, no. 10 (Oct. 2003), 70.

[8] Peter M. Swartz, with Karin Duggan, *U.S. Navy Capstone Strategies and Concepts: Introduction, Background and Analyses* (Alexandria, VA: Center for Naval Analyses, 2012).

[9] Conversations with COL Patrick C. Sweeney, U.S. Army (Ret.), a professor at the Naval War College, Newport, RI. COL Sweeney included in the list of important guidance documents the Unified Command Plan, which allocated responsibilities among the regional combatant commands.

[10] "Joint Capabilities Integration and Development System," Chairman of the Joint Chiefs of Staff Instruction 3170.01F, 1 May 2007. http://jitc.fhu.disa.mil/jitc_dri/pdfs/3170_01f.pdf (29 Aug. 2016).

[11] Kathleen Hicks, *Invigorating Defense Governance*, Center for Strategic and International Studies, Mar. 2008, 29.

[12] Ibid., 57.

[13] Ibid., 58, and the experience of Thomas C. Hone while he was a member of the Office of Force Transformation in the Office of the Secretary of Defense, 2003–2006.

[14] Hicks, et. al., *Invigorating Defense Governance*, 58–59.

[15] "Capability Portfolio Management," Department of Defense Directive 7045.20, 25 Sept. 2008, Section 4.a. http://www.dtic.mil/whs/directives/corres/pdf/704520p.pdf (29 Aug. 2016).

[16] Ibid., Section 4.e.

[17] Douglas A. Brook, *et. al.*, "Implementation of the Chief Management Officer in the Department of Defense, An Interim Report," Center for Defense Management and Research, Naval Postgraduate School, Monterey, CA, 2013.

[18] Ibid., 9.

[19] Interview with CDR James K. Kuhn, USN (Ret.), by Thomas C. Hone, 26 Jan. 2015. CDR Kuhn had served as an analyst in OPNAV N80 and N6/N7.

[20] Interview with CAPT Arthur H. Barber III, USN (Ret.) by Thomas C. Hone, 21 Oct. 2014.

[21] Gates, *Duty*, 315–16.

[22] Fiduciary money is money that is a number or set of numbers in an account and not cash. The assumption among economists has been that recessions can best be dealt with by making sure that the supply of fiduciary money is high enough so that there is adequate money to spend and invest.

[23] Alan S. Blinder, *After the Music Stopped, The Financial Crisis, the Response, and the Work Ahead* (New York: Penguin Press, 2013), 11.

[24] Ibid.

[25] Allan Sloan, "Taking Stock Five Years after the Meltdown," *The Washington Post*, 17 June 2012, G-6.

[26] *Inside the Navy*, vol. 20, no. 30 (30 July 2007), 10–13.

[27] Ibid., 12.

[28] *Inside the Navy*, vol. 20, no. 31 (6 Aug. 2007), 11.

[29] Ibid.

[30] Stiller had spent almost two decades—in government and in private industry—in the shipbuilding business, and she was especially knowledgeable regarding amphibious ships.

[31] *Inside the Navy*, vol. 21, no. 9 (3 Mar. 2008), 5.

[32] *Inside the Navy*, vol. 21, no. 11 (17 Mar. 2008), 1.

[33] Ibid., 6–7.

[34] *Inside the Navy*, vol. 21, no. 13 (31 Mar. 2008), 5.

[35] *Inside the Navy*, vol. 21, no. 16 (21 Apr. 2008), 1, 6.

[36] *Inside the Navy*, vol. 21, no. 19 (12 May 2008), 1.

[37] *Inside the Navy*, vol. 21, no. 23 (9 June 2008), 9.

[38] *Inside the Navy*, vol. 21, no. 25 (23 June 2008), 6.

[39] *Inside the Navy*, vol. 21, no. 28 (14 July 2008), 1.

[40] *Inside the Navy*, vol. 21, no. 31 (4 Aug. 2008), 1, 6. It is also no coincidence that a new ASN(RD&A), Sean G. J. Stackley, was sworn in on 28 July 2008.

[41] Interview of CAPT Arthur H. Barber III, USN (Ret.), by Thomas C. Hone, 21 Oct. 2014.

[42] Ibid., 7.

[43] As retired CAPT Arthur H. Barber III, noted, the Navy had to keep a major shipyard "from inadvertently going out of business." Interview by Thomas C. Hone, 21 Oct. 2014.

[44] *Inside the Navy*, vol. 21, no. 34 (25 Aug. 2008), 9.

[45] *Inside the Navy*, vol. 21, no. 50 (15 Dec. 2008), 3.

[46] Gates, *Duty*, 277.

[47] *Inside the Navy*, vol. 22, no. 2 (19 Jan. 2009), 5. According to retired CAPT Arthur H. Barber III, "We [the Navy] accepted the USMC requirement, did our best to meet it, but it was at the outer edge of the technically feasible envelope, and it turned out to be very hard, very expensive, and because it was so expensive, [it] . . .was too much." Interview of CAPT Barber by Thomas C. Hone, 21 Oct. 2014.

[48] Robert O. Work, "The Littoral Combat Ship: How We Got Here, and Why," no date, 26, 34–35. In the collection of Thomas C. Hone.

[49] *Inside the Navy*, vol. 20, no. 45 (12 Nov. 2007), 5–6.

[50] Robert O. Work, "The Littoral Combat Ship: How We Got Here, and Why," 33–34.

[51] *Inside the Navy*, vol. 21, no. 10 (10 Mar. 2008), 3.

[52] *Inside the Navy*, vol. 21, no. 32 (11 Aug. 2008), 8.

[53] *Inside the Navy*, vol. 21, no. 39 (29 Sept. 2008), 2.

[54] Work, "The Littoral Combat Ship," 22.

[55] "An Interview with Rear Admiral Wayne E. Meyer, USN (Ret.)," *National Security Studies Quarterly*, vol. II, issue 4 (Autumn 1996), 85–86.

[56] *Inside the Navy*, vol. 21, no. 3 (21 Jan. 2008), 2, 10. See also, "Ideas Become Reality as New Strategies Unfurl," by Rita Boland, *SIGNAL* (May 2008).

[57] Interview with VADM Kevin M. McCoy, "To Improve the Material Readiness of the Surface Fleet," U.S. Naval Institute *Proceedings*, vol. 139, no. 5 (May 2013), 19.

[58] VADM William R. Burke, testimony to the Readiness Subcommittee Hearing, House Armed Services Committee, 12 July 2011 (Washington, DC: GPO, 2012), 6.

[59] From VADM Philip M. Balisle, USN (Ret.) to Commander, Fleet Forces Command and Commander, U.S. Pacific Fleet, subj: "Fleet Review Panel of Surface Force Readiness," 26 Feb. 2010. In the collection of Thomas C. Hone.

[60] Ibid., 4.

[61] Ibid., 4–5.

[62] Interview with VADM Kevin M. McCoy, "To Improve the Material Readiness of the Surface Fleet," 21.

[63] VADM William R. Burke, *How Does the Navy Get Ready, and Where Are We Today?* Hearings before the Subcommittee on Readiness, House Armed Services Committee (Washington, DC: GPO, 2012), 12 July 2011, 6.

[64] Ibid., 13.

[65] Ibid., 14.

[66] *Statement of Vice Admiral William Burke, DCNO (Fleet Readiness and Logistics) and Vice Admiral Kevin McCoy, Commander, Naval Sea Systems Command*, before the House Armed Services Committee Subcommittee on Readiness on Navy Readiness, 12 July 2011, 46. https://www.gpo.gov/fdsys/pkg/CHRG-112hhrg68158/pdf/CHRG-112hhrg68158.pdf

[67] Memorandum for the Record, "Fleet Readiness Review Panel Report (One Year Later), ADM John C. Harvey Jr., Commander Fleet Forces Command, 11 May 2011 (3501 Ser N00/135), 2 (the House Armed Services Committee Subcommittee on Readiness Hearing on Navy Readiness, 12 July 2011, 58). https://www.gpo.gov/fdsys/pkg/CHRG-112hhrg68158/pdf/CHRG-112hhrg68158.pdf.

[68] Geoff Fein, "Deep Blue Gives Way to Bolstered Director Navy Staff Office," *Defense Daily*, 7 May 2008, no. 23.

[69] R 161250Z Jun 08, from CNO to NAVADMIN, "Stand-up of Intelligence TYCOM Functions within Naval Network Warfare Command (NETWARCOM)." In the collection of Thomas C. Hone.

[70] Ibid.

[71] Robert Ackerman, "Naval Intelligence Ramps Up Activities," *SIGNAL*, 1 Feb. 2009, no. 5. Also a phone interview of retired VADM William R. Burke by Thomas C. Hone, 23 July 2014.

[72] "Reorganization of the Office of the Chief of Naval Operations (OPNAV) Staff," from the Chief of Naval Operations, to the Director of Naval Intelligence (N2), Memorandum 5400 Ser N00/100052, 26 June 2009. In the collection of Thomas C. Hone.

[73] Ibid., Part 2.d.

[74] Ibid., Part 2.d.(1) and (2). RADM Burke was a member of the CNO's reorganization team, along with rear admirals from N3/5, N8F, and N39, and a senior civilian (N6FB). The group's leader was VADM Dorsett.

[75] "Re-organization of Chief of Naval Operations Staff," Memorandum for Deputy Chief of Naval Operations (Communications Networks) (N6) Staff and Director of Naval Intelligence (N2) Staff, 5400, N2/N6, 13 July 2009. In the collection of Thomas C. Hone.

[76] "CNO's Remarks, OPNAV Staff All Hand's—17 July 2009." The message formally announcing the creation of N2/N6 was promulgated on 9 Oct. 2009. See "Establishment of the Deputy Chief of Naval Operations for Information Dominance (N2/N6)," R 292237Z Oct 09, REF/A/RMG/CNO Washington DC/012135ZOct 09. In the collection of Thomas C. Hone.

[77] Phone interview of retired VADM William R. Burke by Thomas C. Hone, 23 July 2014.

[78] Ibid. See also, "The New Main Battery, The Navy Realigns Its Organization toward Information Dominance," by Richard R. Burgess, Managing Editor, *Seapower*, Dec. 2009, 16–18.

[79] "Fleet Cyber Command/Commander Tenth Fleet Implementation Plan," from CNO, 5440, Ser N00/100057, 23 July 2009. In the collection of Thomas C. Hone.

[80] "FLTCYBERCOM/COMTENTHFLT Organization Guidance," attached to "Fleet Cyber Command/Commander Tenth Fleet Implementation Plan." In the collection of Thomas C. Hone.

[81] Phone interview of retired VADM William R. Burke by Thomas C. Hone, 23 July 2014. CNO Roughead also had his very small personal staff—N00Z—to assist him, especially with congressional testimony and explanations of Navy policy to the public and other "outsiders" who might take an interest in naval affairs.

[82] "Establishment of the Naval Warfare Integration Group (N00X)," OPNAV NOTICE 5430, Ser N00X/9U106573, from the Chief of Naval Operations (through the Director of the Navy Staff), 20 Jan. 2010, 2. In the collection of Thomas C. Hone.

[83] Ibid.

[84] Phone interview of retired VADM William R. Burke by Thomas C. Hone, 23 July 2014.

[85] GEN James T. Conway, USMC, ADM Gary Roughead, and ADM Thad W. Allen, "A Cooperative Strategy for 21st Century Seapower," Oct. 2007. https://www.ise.gov/sites/default/files/Maritime_Strategy.pdf (29 Aug. 2016).

[86] Ibid., 1.

[87] "Information Dominance: The Navy's Initiative to Maintain the Competitive Advantage in the Information Age," ADM Gary Roughead, 1 Oct. 2009, 1. In the collection of Thomas C. Hone. Also see *You Cannot Surge Trust, Combined Naval Operations of the Royal Australian Navy, Canadian Navy, Royal Navy, and the United States Navy, 1991–2003*, ed. by Gary E. Weir (Washington, DC: Naval History and Heritage Command, 2013).

[88] Norman Friedman, *Network-Centric Warfare*, 241.

[89] The U.S. Navy and the U.S. Coast Guard formed a Global Maritime Situational Awareness office at Coast Guard headquarters before ADM Roughead became CNO. Its mission was "to create a collaborative global, maritime, information sharing environment through unity of effort across entities with maritime interests." See *Inside the Navy*, vol. 20, no. 33 (20 Aug. 2007), 1.

[90] LTCOL Randy Hodge, USMC (Ret.), CAPT Grisell Collazo, USN, and CDR Kerry Pearson, USN, "Naval Logistics Integration, Refocusing Efforts in 2009," *Marine Corps Gazette*, vol. 93, no. 5 (May 2009), 50–53.

[91] Ibid., 50.

[92] *Inside the Navy*, vol. 20, no. 44 (5 Nov. 2007), 9.

[93] *Inside the Navy*, vol. 21, no. 6 (11 Feb. 2008), 7.

[94] *Inside the Navy*, vol. 21, no. 7 (18 Feb. 2008), 11.

[95] *Inside the Navy*, vol. 21, no. 20 (19 May 2008), 4.

[96] Ibid.

[97] Ibid., 10.

[98] *Inside the Navy*, vol. 21, no. 32 (11 Aug. 2008), 2.

[99] Interview of CAPT Arthur H. Barber III, USN (Ret.), by Thomas C. Hone, 21 Oct. 2014.

[100] *Inside the Navy,* vol. 22, no. 3 (26 Jan. 2009), 3. GEN Conway admitted that "We must reconcile equipment size and weight limits to remain both operationally deployable by sea and tactically effective ashore, ensuring adequate protection for our Marines."

[101] "SECDEF Establishes Unified U.S. Cyber Command for Military Cyberspace Operations," *Information Domain* (Fall 2009).

[102] Richard R Burgess, "The New Main Battery, The Navy Realigns Its Organization toward Information Dominance," *Seapower* (Dec. 2009). In his history of the operations of carrier *Enterprise* (CV-6) in World War II, CDR Edward P. Stafford noted a message sent to the carrier's aircraft squadrons as they joined her in November 1943: "The Big E welcomes aboard her main battery." See *The Big E: The Story of the* USS *Enterprise*, by CDR Edward P. Stafford, USN (New York: Ballantine Books, 1962), 261.

[103] The effort by DCMO Elizabeth A. McGrath and her staff is described in *Inside the Navy*, vol. 24, no. 30 (1 Aug. 2011), 6–7.

[104] "A Cooperative Strategy for 21st Century Seapower," Oct. 2007, 9.

[105] *Inside the Navy*, vol. 22, no. 10 (23 Mar. 2009), 2.

[106] *Inside the Navy*, vol. 23, no. 51 (27 Dec. 2010), 16.

[107] Ibid., vol. 24, no. 28 (18 July 2011), 12.

CHAPTER 19

Admiral Jonathan W. Greenert as the 30th CNO

Introduction

Admiral Jonathan Greenert assumed his post as Chief of Naval Operations on 23 September 2011. According to one retired officer who had worked for several chiefs of naval operations, "There was no one better prepared to be CNO than Jon Greenert."[1] Greenert's credentials were certainly impressive. A nuclear submariner and former commander of the Seventh Fleet (2004–2006), he had served as Admiral Roughead's vice chief from 2009 to 2011, and he had been Commander, Fleet Forces Command from 2007 to 2009. He had served two tours in N8, the second as its director (2006–2007), and for two years (2000–2002), he had been the head of the operations division in the Navy comptroller office. However, this outstanding record of service did not guarantee that Greenert would be CNO.

In his memoir, Admiral James G. Stavridis, retired European Command commander, noted that then–Secretary of Defense Robert Gates had tentatively selected *him*—and not Admiral Greenert—to succeed Admiral Roughead. As it happened—and unfortunately for Admiral Stavridis—an anonymous complaint to the Defense Department's Inspector General led to an investigation that, though it exonerated Stavridis of any wrongdoing, prevented President Obama from nominating him to be the next CNO. That left the way open for Admiral Greenert.[2]

Greenert began his tenure as CNO by stating his vision for the Navy. It would be a navy that could fight ("warfighting first"). It would be a Navy that could operate forward—despite not having as many ships as the new CNO thought essential. It would be a Navy ready to conduct its missions. Those were the three elements of Greenert's "vision" for his Navy: warfighting, forward deployment, and readiness. But how would his "vision" play out? What policies would he and his deputies pursue?

Reorganizing OPNAV—Again

Even before assuming the CNO's position, Admiral Greenert had given serious thought to OPNAV's organization.[3] After he became the CNO he pulled together a "Realignment Team" headed by Vice Admiral William R. Burke, who had served as Admiral Roughead's N4, and gave the team the following guidance:

> Relieve N8 of responsibility for simultaneously integrating/balancing the POM and building the future Navy. N8 is the POM [Program Objective Memorandum] integrator (not CNO and VCNO).

> Introduce a new 3-star to focus on warfare systems wholeness and future capability.

> Improve CNO/VCNO oversight.

> Position OPNAV for the emerging fiscal environment. Realign the staff to make better informed trades while preserving critical capabilities.

> Unify accountability for vertically integrated platform wholeness. Restore platform-specific manpower and readiness programming authority and accountability to warfare, information and logistics systems sponsors.

> Consolidate trade-space decision authority at lowest practicable level. Empower 2 [and] 3-stars with the capability to make informed trades and investments which improve wholeness/simplify executive decision-making. Incentivize Total Ownership Cost behavior.

> Unify and strengthen analysis and assessment. Realign N00X back into N8. Clarify N1, N4 and N2N6 [sic] assessment responsibilities.

> Enable more effective engagement with OSD and ASN(RD&A) [Assistant Secretary of the Navy for Research, Development, and Acquisition]. Clarify who speaks for key topics and positions within the Navy program.[4]

What did CNO Greenert want from this "realignment"? He wanted a focus within OPNAV on "total ownership cost behavior." How did this differ from the "life cycle cost" concept already in use? The answer is that it reached beyond the existing concept by factoring in other costs that were often ignored, including the training of personnel to man and support the system being developed.

"Total ownership" can be compared with "life cycle cost" in terms of a private automobile. A consumer wanting a new car will obviously consider the car's initial cost (what you pay the dealer), and if a consumer wants to know the car's life-cycle cost he or she will add to the initial cost the cost of the interest charged for the loan that purchases the car, the cost of operating and repairing the car, and the cost of insuring the car for all the years that he or she drives the car. Total ownership adds to these costs several others. One is the cost across time of housing the car or protecting it from the weather. Another is the cost of training any adolescents to drive the car, as well as the added cost of insurance once any new drivers begin using the car. In short, total ownership cost is the sum of buying, owning, operating, training users, and finally disposing of an item across all the years of the item's service life.

Before Admiral Greenert became CNO, he had decided that the platform (ship, submarine, and aircraft) sponsors in N8 had not been programming adequately for this total ownership cost. To improve the accuracy of programming, CNO Greenert pulled the platform sponsors out of N8 and put them in a new organization—N9, headed by a new DCNO for Warfare Systems. So N85 (expeditionary warfare), N86 (surface warfare), N87 (undersea warfare), N88 (air warfare), and N89 (special programs) would become N95, N96, N97, N98, and N99; respectively. At the same time, Greenert took individuals from N1 (manpower, personnel, training and education) and N4 (fleet readiness and logistics) and "gave" them to the platform sponsors in the newly created N9. These reorganized program sponsor offices were supposed to develop their pieces of the overall Navy program in terms of "total ownership" costs. As Bryan Clark, the head of the CNO's Strategic Action Group (N00Z), put it, the platform sponsors had been "incentivized to buy more platforms and to do so without much regard for what it would cost to man them or maintain them."[5] Pulling people out of N1 and N4 and reassigning them to N9 was, according to Clark, "very painful," but it had to be done. The OPNAV model that stressed separate functional (personnel and logistics) deputies was "efficient, but the new model was optimized for the CNO's goals," the most important of which was controlling costs in order to maintain readiness in a forward-deployed fleet.[6]

Vice Admiral Burke reported to Greenert that

> The most significant theme of the realignment was the shift in the scope of responsibilities and span of control among resource sponsors. This required the re-integration of resource sponsorship . . . responsibilities and authorities for warfare systems manpower, training and afloat readiness resources from N1 [personnel] and N4 [readiness and logistics] back into [the platform sponsors and N2/N6].

At the same time, the new CNO wanted "wholeness," which worked against the possibility that the platform sponsors would promote their platforms at the expense of the rest of the Navy. To get "wholeness" into the routine of OPNAV staff work, Greenert and Burke created N9, the three-star deputy chief for warfare systems, and put the platform sponsors in N9.[7]

Greenert separated N9 from N8 because he felt that there was not a good balance among the OPNAV staff functions of "assessment, resource allocation and management." Though he wanted his N8 to be "first among equals," he did not want the programmatic analysis done in

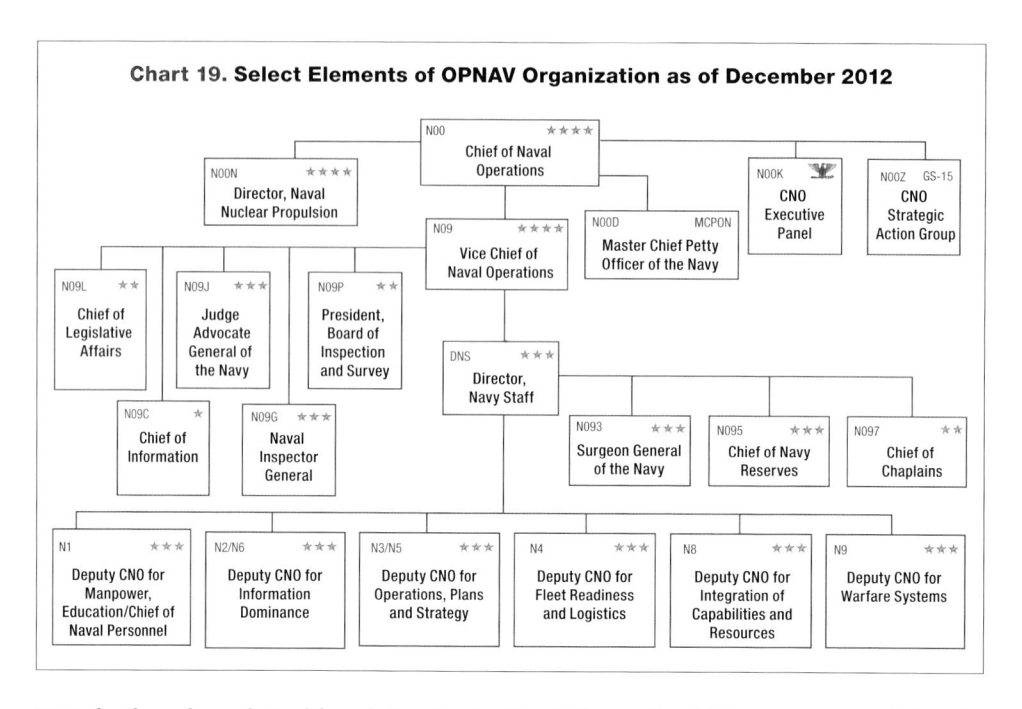

Chart 19. Select Elements of OPNAV Organization as of December 2012

- N00 ★★★★ Chief of Naval Operations
  - N00N ★★★★ Director, Naval Nuclear Propulsion
  - N00K CNO Executive Panel
  - N00Z GS-15 CNO Strategic Action Group
  - N09 ★★★★ Vice Chief of Naval Operations
  - N00D MCPON Master Chief Petty Officer of the Navy
    - N09L ★★ Chief of Legislative Affairs
    - N09J ★★★ Judge Advocate General of the Navy
    - N09P ★★ President, Board of Inspection and Survey
    - DNS ★★★ Director, Navy Staff
    - N09C ★ Chief of Information
    - N09G ★★★ Naval Inspector General
    - N093 ★★★ Surgeon General of the Navy
    - N095 ★★★ Chief of Navy Reserves
    - N097 ★★ Chief of Chaplains
    - N1 ★★★ Deputy CNO for Manpower, Education/Chief of Naval Personnel
    - N2/N6 ★★★ Deputy CNO for Information Dominance
    - N3/N5 ★★★ Deputy CNO for Operations, Plans and Strategy
    - N4 ★★★ Deputy CNO for Fleet Readiness and Logistics
    - N8 ★★★ Deputy CNO for Integration of Capabilities and Resources
    - N9 ★★★ Deputy CNO for Warfare Systems

N8 to be the only analytical foundation for the Navy's future. In addition, he suspected that the workload for the N8 staff was already too great and that the prominence of N8 within OPNAV weakened the prospects that all the deputy chiefs would work as a corporate body. He wanted N8 to focus on developing the Navy's POM. The new N9 was to look across platform boundaries, searching for the relationships among programs.

For example, the P-8 long range, antisubmarine warfare (ASW) aircraft was considered a replacement of the obsolete P-3. As Bryan Clark argued, however, P-8s did not necessarily have to replace P-3s on a one-for-one basis. How did the Navy intend to conduct antisubmarine operations? How would the new P-8 work with the Navy's other antisubmarine systems and platforms? CNO Greenert did not want to do one-for-one replacements of *any* platform unless and until these questions were asked and answered.[8] He believed that answering such questions through whole force-level analysis would improve both the requirements process and the relationship between the platform sponsors in OPNAV and the staff of the Navy's ASN (RD&A).[9]

The "End Game"

The "end game" is the most exciting and worrisome part of programming. To understand the importance of the "end game" and the risks involved for those who "play" it, imagine that you sit around a large table with a number of other "players." In the center of the table is a pile of "resources"—in this case, mostly money and people, but also authority. Each "player" is a claimant for resources. Each "player" comes to the table with a set of discrete programs, such as the *Virginia*-class submarine construction program, or the F/A-18E/F operations and maintenance program. Each "player" wants the resources required to sustain or begin the programs assigned to his or her office. The catch is that there are rarely enough resources to satisfy all the "players," and so some means must be found to determine which "players" get what they want and which don't.

As a "player," you know that you and your staff didn't get to the table without already having run a table of your own, with your own "players." In fact, the players at the final game approach the table after having had their preliminary program proposals examined by the analysts in N81. The analysts compare the preliminary proposals against the results of the conflict scenarios that have been approved by the Joint Chiefs of Staff. In effect, different versions of the Navy are matched against likely opposing forces in a series of war games to gain an understanding of the optimal mix of programs. Yet once that work has been done, there is still room for discussion and negotiation. Hence the "end game." As one of the "players," you have to be able to muster the best case that you can for your claim on the Navy's resources. You have to show that you have followed the guidance provided by the CNO and the Secretary of the Navy. Will you get the resources that you're convinced that your part of the Navy needs?

It's "high noon." Which claimants will get what they argue they need? CNO Greenert understood this process—this "end game." He knew it involved analysis, negotiation, and bargaining. It had to. The world was and is uncertain. No "player" had or can have a corner on what the future would or will be like. The level of risk attached to the outcome of the game was and is great. The nation's survival could depend on it. Though the whole programming process was designed to reduce risk through various forms of analysis, in the end it may come down to "making trades" around the table. Whose views of risk are accepted? Who's best able to inspire trust in the other "players" and the CNO? If you were to ask the CNO's senior deputies gathered around the table, "Are you 'playing' for the future of the world?" they would probably say "No"—that they were instead engaged in a difficult and often exhausting process of trying to meet essential needs with too few resources. The "end game" is dominated by very pragmatic individuals. They are there to make their cases to the chief programmer and to participate in a trade-off process.

CNO Greenert knew from experience that each claimant would be a strong and articulate advocate for his or her proposal. To make the bargaining and negotiation that were an unavoidable part of this process the best it could be for the Navy and Marine Corps, Greenert wanted each claimant to make his or her proposal based on "total ownership" costs. His assumption was that the agreements that led to a POM would be better to the degree that the "players" performed from the "same sheet of music." Inside OPNAV and Marine Corps headquarters, the terms used by those engaged in building a POM are often metaphorical. Claimants "game the system," or put on (or see through) "Kabuki dances," or "roll over the opposing team." Yet the process has to rest on analysis and the sort of negotiations among professionals that is the opposite of the negotiations between a consumer and a used car salesman. Forcing the claimants to use "total ownership" costs was one way CNO Greenert attempted to strengthen the annual process of building the Navy's POM.

"Wholeness"

Two concepts of "wholeness" came out of the work of Vice Admiral Burke's re-alignment team. The first concept had to do with "warfighting"—the ability to outfight and outlast an enemy. As the re-alignment team's report put it, "Warfighting wholeness is . . . about evaluating the capability and capacity of systems, units or forces required to achieve certain *performance outcomes* [emphasis in the original] in specific environments and scenarios." This was N81's territory, and the N81 staff was quite capable of doing this sort of analysis. But the realignment team also recognized that the new N9 "needed to [focus] on a view of wholeness that complements Warfighting Wholeness analysis." To do this, the staff of N9 needed to work with "an expanded definition of readiness," one that comprehended the factors required to keep fleet units deployed or ready to deploy. This "expanded definition of readiness" included modernization and procurement. As the team's final report put it, "it will be important for N9 to understand and articulate issues and trends in manpower, training, maintenance, etc. *across* [emphasis in original] programs in its portfolio to consider informed trades within and across accounts."[10]

This second notion of "wholeness" was intended to prevent a recurrence of the sorts of interrelated but unanticipated problems that had reduced the readiness of the Navy's surface ships. According to Bryan Clark, previous N1 and N4 chiefs had saved scarce funds by allowing the surface fleet's readiness to decline because "The surface fleet was the one place you could go to take people and reduce maintenance and planes wouldn't fall out of the sky and nuclear reactors wouldn't be at risk of having an accident."[11] In addition, Greenert and his deputies had inherited some innovative platforms such as the DDG-1000 and the littoral combat ship (LCS), and it wasn't clear just how much it would cost to operate and maintain these ships. If the operating, maintenance, and manning costs were too high, the Navy's component commanders would not be able to use them the way that they had planned.[12] Greenert wanted to make sure that the process of developing requirements in OPNAV did not lead to systems that were too expensive to man and to operate in a constrained fiscal environment.

"Logistics" needed to be thought of in very broad terms, especially given the high cost of recruiting, training, and compensating personnel. At the same time, the team did not suggest creating a "super DCNO" charged with overseeing the team's broad definition of readiness "wholeness." Neither did the team want to bring back some version of the Naval Material Command. As the team's final report observed, "wholeness" was an "overloaded" term.[13] It meant different things to different people because it was an effort to put into one word what CNO Greenert thought was a very important conceptual approach to developing the Navy's short-term, mid-term, and long-term programs. As the final report noted, it would "require more than one PPBE [Planning, Programming, Budgeting, and Execution] cycle to stabilize/mature" the "connections between . . . platform/system wholeness and warfighting wholeness, and its adoption as a 'standard' POM framework."[14]

Implementing the OPNAV Reorganization

CNO Greenert outlined some of his reorganization proposals in an OPNAV "all hands" meeting in December 2011. The admiral wanted the "realignment" of OPNAV "to be completed by 1 August 2012, ready to begin POM [20]15."[15] On 5 March 2012, Director of the Navy Staff Vice Admiral John M. Bird sent a message to all OPNAV staff explaining the changes about to be made public.[16] On 9 March, Vice Admiral Burke sent an "action memo" to Vice Admiral Bird and the N8 describing how fiscal resources would be realigned—how, for example, dollars would be shifted from N8, N1, and N4 to the new N9.[17] On 12 March, Admiral Greenert sent a message throughout the Navy describing the realignment.[18] And on 4 May 2012, Vice Admiral Burke sent a second memo to the Director of the Navy Staff and the new N8, Vice Admiral Allen G. Myers, wrapping up the resource and workforce changes required by the realignment.[19]

The Purpose of the Reorganization

In 2012, CNO Greenert issued a "Navigation Plan" that revealed the programmatic implications of his tenets of "warfighting first," "operate forward," and "be ready."[20] What were his priorities? The first was to field 11 aircraft carriers and ten air wings, with one of each in Japan, and ten amphibious ready groups, one of which would also be based in Japan. Something of a surprise was the second item on his list of "warfighting first" priorities: "Increase near-term mine warfare capability . . .," which meant both the offensive use of sea mines and the ability to defeat mines put in the water by an enemy. Mining and mine sweeping were the "forgotten stepchildren" of the Navy. Several past CNOs, reaching back to Admiral Thomas B. Hayward in 1978, had put mine warfare on their priority lists only to see other priorities elbow ahead of mining and mine sweeping.[21] Other items on the CNO's list were not surprises, including efforts to counter fast-attack craft, procuring more ships and aircraft, developing new missiles and a new air and missile defense radar, constructing additional *Virginia*-class submarines and a special "payload module" for them, exploiting cyberspace while shielding the Navy's own computer networks, and developing a new ballistic missile submarine.

For CNO Greenert, "operate forward" meant sustaining bases such as Guam and preserving the right to use facilities in places such as Spain, Bahrain, and Singapore. It also meant stationing littoral combat ships in Singapore and deploying Aegis ballistic missile defense ships to Rota, Spain. It meant finding the resources to deploy an "afloat forward staging base" and providing "amphibious lift for U.S. Marines operating out of Australia." "Be ready" was very much a matter of "establishing a sustainable deployment schedule that affords sufficient time for maintenance and training," but it also meant providing "a place for each single Sailor to live ashore by 2017." Readiness was acknowledged to be a function of providing opportunities for sailors and support for their families. The problems that affected civilians, including alcohol and drug abuse, were present in the Navy, too, and they needed to be addressed. Maintenance funding would be increased by—and here was a sensitive issue with Congress—inactivating but not discarding seven older Aegis cruisers and two LSD-41 class amphibious ships. There was also a need for more "decoys, sonobuoys, and torpedoes for Fleet [antisubmarine warfare] training." Finally, the Navy needed to invest "in new technologies such as hybrid-electric drive."

Partisan Politics Intervenes

What CNO Greenert, Vice Admiral Burke, and the re-alignment team had put together was an OPNAV that could avoid repeating the existing readiness problems of the surface fleet. OPNAV could also provide forces to support military campaigns against terrorist movements, and reassure other nations by providing what those nations needed, which included "freedom of the seas" and mobile ballistic missile defense. But the reorganized and hopefully smooth-running OPNAV that Greenert wanted depended on a reasonably smooth-running Congress—one that could conduct the public's business through routine negotiations with the White House. Relations between the Congress and the presidency were the key. They could be contentious; that was a given. But if they continually disrupted the budget process, then OPNAV would be constantly "fighting political fires" instead of implementing Greenert's notions of "wholeness." Put another way, serious and irreconcilable day-to-day partisan turmoil could thwart the new CNO, even if he had strong support for his ideas and initiatives inside the Navy.

The warning signs were there. On 26 January 2010, the Senate defeated a resolution to adopt a procedure that would have produced a "sweeping plan to solve the U.S.'s debt problem . . ."[22] What was important about this event was the fact that seven Republican cosponsors of the resolution voted against it, something that was extraordinary in the modern history of the Congress. Cosponsors were supposed to back their bills, not repudiate them. What did this mean for the Navy? It meant that the normal and expected partisan disagreements about elements of the federal budget had become so bitter that compromise with President Obama over critical pieces of legislation might become impossible. Republicans in Congress demanded a reduction in federal deficits and the federal debt.[23] The President and his supporters in Congress wanted to couple debt reduction with tax increases. The two sides could not find a compromise they could accept.

In the 2010 congressional elections, the Republican Party won a majority of seats in the House of Representatives. In January 2011, the Republicans in the House met to discuss their legislative agenda, and their majority leader, Representative Eric I. Cantor (R-VA), proposed using the budget process and the need for Congress to approve an increase in the national debt as sources of influence over the President.[24] Cantor's fellow House Republicans accepted his proposal, setting the stage for a series of political confrontations with President Obama. The first came at the beginning of April 2011, when the continuing resolution under which the federal government was operating was set to expire.[25] Only a last minute compromise to extend the continuing resolution put off a severe curtailment of federal government activity.

The second confrontation was over extending the federal government's debt limit. The Treasury Department estimated that the federal government had to be able to borrow more money by the beginning of August to avoid defaulting on the federal debt. The President, the leaders of the Senate, and the House leadership could not agree on a law that would extend the federal debt limit and at the same time meet the debt and deficit reduction goals set by the Republican majority in the House. After a lengthy and increasingly tense series of negotiations among members of the House and Senate and members of the Obama administration, with the prospect of the federal government defaulting on its debts hanging over them, all sides agreed to a compromise. The new bill was signed into law on 2 August 2011.

It provided for an immediate increase in the federal debt ceiling to keep the federal government solvent. It also cut federal discretionary spending by an amount greater than the increase in the debt ceiling, and it authorized Congress to create a joint select committee to write legislation that would significantly reduce the federal debt. The law also contained a threat: if Congress did not find a way to slice $1.2 trillion from the deficit over ten years, then the Congress could increase the debt ceiling by that amount—but that action would trigger automatic across-the-board reductions in discretionary *and* mandatory spending starting on 2 January 2013. The law also required the Congress to vote on a constitutional amendment to balance the federal budget by the end of 2011.[26] As it happened, the joint select committee was unable to reach a compromise between its Democratic and Republican members, and Congress did not pass a constitutional amendment to force the federal government to balance its budget each year. That left the automatic reductions—"sequestration"—as a possibility starting in January 2013.

Through 2012, OPNAV and the Navy secretariat went ahead with "normal" business, responding, for example, to the Defense Department's strategic guidance that "rebalanced" the focus of U.S. forces from Europe to the "Asia-Pacific" area. In April 2012, CNO Greenert signed and promulgated an OPNAV instruction clarifying the "missions, functions, and tasks" of Fleet Forces Command. This was an effort to clear up confusion about the roles of Fleet Forces Command and the type commands. When former CNO Vernon E. Clark created Fleet Forces Command in 2001, his goal was to have one "unified Fleet Commander responsible for manning, training, and equipping Atlantic and Pacific Fleet units." Admiral Clark wanted the Commander, Fleet Forces Command to have administrative control of the type commanders in the Atlantic and Pacific fleets. To avoid having to create another four-star command, Admiral Robert J. Natter, then–Atlantic Fleet commander, assumed "concurrent duties as commander, United States Fleet Forces Command" on 1 October 2001.[27] As Admiral John C. Harvey Jr., Fleet Forces Command commander from July 2009 to September 2012, wrote, "the next logical step would have been to align the operating forces on both coasts under" the administrative control of Commander, Fleet Forces Command.[28]

But Congress balked, using a provision of the FY 2004 Department of Defense appropriations act to prohibit "the expenditure of funds to transfer [administrative control] or operational control of Navy forces from" commander, Pacific Fleet, to commander, Fleet Forces Command.[29] In effect, Congress had blocked the creation of a unified fleet readiness commander with administrative authority over all the Navy's type commanders. Admiral Clark had made his intent clear. It was to unify the type commanders under Fleet Forces Command and thereby streamline and simplify the administrative structure that standardized manning, training, and equipping throughout the whole fleet. Congress had rejected his ultimate goal but not his interim reorganization. As a result, it wasn't clear which commands were in fact responsible for maintaining readiness and for developing readiness requirements.[30]

CNO Mullen tried to make the readiness chain of command clear by revising the instruction spelling out the "missions, functions, and tasks" of Fleet Forces Command in 2007, but the confusion continued. To clear it up, Admiral Harvey and Pacific Fleet commander Admiral Patrick M. Walsh worked together in 2009 and 2010 "to eliminate ambiguity and reestablish clear lines of authority, responsibility, and accountability" and "clarify the [administrative control] chain of command within [their] respective Fleets."[31] The result was a new OPNAV instruction, but there were still some issues remaining, and CNO Greenert had to revise the 2010 instruction in 2012.[32]

This administrative restructuring proceeded despite the possibility that the President and the Congress would again be at odds over financing the federal government. After the presidential and congressional elections of 2012, which returned President Obama to the White House and a Republican majority to the House of Representatives, the two sides quickly squared off over raising the federal debt ceiling and over "sequestration," the across-the-board cuts in federal spending required by the Budget Control Act of 2011.[33] In January 2013, the Congress put off sequestration until 1 March and postponed another confrontation over the federal debt limit until 18 May. On 6 March, Congress extended the fiscal year 2013 continuing resolution until September 2013, with sequestration adding to the spending reductions already embedded in the resolution.[34] In November, CNO Greenert testified to the Senate Armed Services Committee that "the continuing resolution and sequestration reductions in FY 2013 compelled [the Navy] to reduce both afloat and ashore operations, which created ship and aircraft maintenance and training backlogs."[35] This included furloughing Navy civilian employees for six days.

As Greenert told the senators, the actions taken by the Navy "in 2013 to mitigate sequestration only served to transfer bills amounting to over $2 billion to future years for many procurement programs," and therefore what the Navy was forced to do in 2013 was "not a sustainable course for future budgets."[36] As if in response, Congress passed the Bipartisan Budget Act of 2013 in December, changing the sequestration "caps" for fiscal years 2014 and 2015. With the resulting fiscal flexibility, Greenert was able to sustain the Navy's aircraft carrier and amphibious group deployments in fiscal year 2014. As he said publicly, "Ten years ago we had 300 ships. We provided 100 forward. Today, we have about 285 ships. We provide 100 forward. It is this presence that is as important today as it was 20 years ago, and will be in the future."[37]

Unfortunately, there was inadequate back-up for the forces deployed. As the CNO testified, "maintenance and training backlogs [have] meant delayed preparation for deployments, forcing us, in turn, to extend the deployments of those units already on deployment." The negative effects of the backlogs also cascaded into the "Navy's ability to maintain required forces for contingency response . . . Although the requirement calls, on average, for three additional [carrier strike groups] and three additional [amphibious ready groups] to deploy within 30 days for a major crisis, [the] Navy has only been able to maintain an average of one group each in this readiness posture."[38] Greenert was candid: "Continuing along this budget trajectory means by 2020 (the [Defense Strategic Guidance] benchmark year), [the] Navy will have insufficient contingency response capacity to execute large-scale operations in one region, while simultaneously deterring another adversary's aggression elsewhere."[39]

Greenert's testimony in Congress echoed the concerns of Secretary of Defense Charles T. Hagel. When sequestration went into effect in March 2013, Hagel commissioned the Defense Department Strategic Choices Management Review, requiring its members to report by the end of July 2013 on ways to "ensure the Department of Defense is prepared in the face of unprecedented budget uncertainty."[40] The members of the review panel provided the following options for the Secretary: first, continue reducing management overhead by cutting the sizes and costs of various headquarters; second, reduce compensation for active duty personnel and pensions for retirees; third, alter the composition of U.S. forces by pursuing options such as reducing the size of the Army.[41] As Secretary Hagel pointed out, however, "cuts to overhead, compensation, and forces generate savings slowly," and he noted that if the Defense Department combined "all the reductions I've described, including significant cuts to the military's size and capability—the savings fall well short of meeting sequester-level cuts, particularly during the first five years of these steep, decade-long reductions."[42]

Hagel's words were criticized as partisan—as reflecting the views of the President and not necessarily of the military services. But Hagel had made sure to say in his remarks about the process that produced the review that the military service chiefs and secretaries had fully participated in the discussions. Moreover, he deflected criticism of the review's work by asserting that a "modest reduction in force structure, when combined with management efficiencies and compensation reforms, would enable us to meet the $150 billion in savings required by the President's budget proposal while still defending the country and fulfilling our global responsibilities."[43] In short, embracing the President's budget would achieve the goal of reducing the federal deficit while preserving an effective force. Rejecting the President's position and continuing a ten percent across-the board sequestration would force "senseless, non-strategic cuts that damage military readiness, disrupt operations, and erode our technological edge."[44] As had become the case in Washington, serious analysis of a problem was wrapped up with bitter partisan political strife. The Vice Chairman of the JCS, Admiral James A. Winnefeld Jr., expressed his frustration by saying, "We don't know how much money we're going to have. We don't know when we will know how much money we're going to have. And we don't know what the rules are going to be when we know."[45]

Shipbuilding Problems Persist

CNO Greenert could have been forgiven if, like Samuel Taylor Coleridge's ancient mariner, he had felt that Navy shipbuilding was like a dead albatross hanging around his neck. When Greenert assumed the post of Chief of Naval Operations, the Navy was in the process of implementing a dual-award acquisition strategy for the LCS. Both Lockheed-Martin and Austal USA would build ten "sea frames." But the modules for surface combat, mine hunting, and ASW were still not fully developed. Moreover, the results of war games and reviews of the LCS program conducted between February and August 2012 led the CNO to create an LCS Council that could guide the preparation of the LCS "sea frames" already constructed for their initial deployment to Singapore in 2013.[46] Admiral Greenert directed the council's members (four vice admirals) to prepare a detailed plan for preparing the existing littoral combat ships for routine overseas deployment.

Unfortunately, development of the LCS modules stayed behind schedule. The surface warfare module would not be ready for initial operational test and evaluation (IOT&E) until March 2014.[47] The mine countermeasure module would not be ready for IOT&E until 2015. The antisubmarine module was farther behind schedule, with IOT&E scheduled for 2016.[48] These schedule delays, coupled with the increased costs of the modules, drew ongoing criticism from members of Congress and led Secretary of Defense Hagel in February 2014 to limit the total LCS buy to 32 ships.[49]

The Navy was embarrassed. Congressional critics of the LCS program had pointed out that the program was in trouble in 2012 and 2013, even while Assistant Secretary of the Navy (Research, Development and Acquisition) (ASN[RD&A]) Sean J. Stackley had claimed as late as mid-January 2014 that "We have a valid requirement for 52 ships, and the program is performing strongly."[50] In May 2013, for example, Senator John S. McCain III, (R-AZ) in a hearing on Navy shipbuilding programs, told Assistant Secretary Stackley that "the Navy plans for the littoral combat ship to comprise over one-third of the Nation's total surface combatant fleet by 2028 and yet the littoral combat ship has not yet demonstrated adequate performance of assigned missions. We need to fix it or find something else rather rapidly."[51] McCain's later words were prophetic:

> I asked whether these problems [with the modules] were envisioned, particularly in a new platform . . . No problem. There is no problem. We have got that all planned out. And obviously, . . . quote, the Navy's own analysts have only about 10 percent confidence in the current estimate of the cost to operate and support.[52]

It was frustration with unmet promises that led Secretary of Defense Hagel to direct the Navy in February 2014 to "submit alternative proposals to procure a capable and lethal small surface combatant, generally consistent with the capabilities of a frigate."[53] The Navy did so later in the year, and in December 2014 Secretary Hagel announced that the last 20 littoral combat ships would be modified versions of the two designs already built.[54] LCS seemed to have a charmed life. On 11 January 2015, *Defense News* reported that the littoral combat ship program had received effective support from Secretary of the Navy Raymond E. Mabus Jr., and former Under Secretary of the Navy Robert O. Work. The two officials had sustained the littoral combat ship program despite both bad publicity and opposition from within the Office of the Secretary of Defense. But *Defense News* also noted that the "changes being made for the modified ships are not unusual or illogical. Rather, they are logical mid-course changes that could be expected in a 52-ship production run."[55] If there were any basic flaws in the littoral ship concept, they would likely carry on in its successor.

LCS was not the only source of frustration in the Navy's shipbuilding program. The Navy had estimated in its fiscal year 2008 budget that the new nuclear carrier *Gerald R. Ford* (CVN-78), the first in a series of three newly designed attack carriers, would cost $10.5 billion. By May 2013, the estimated cost was $12.8 billion. Senator McCain, who had verbally sparred with Assistant Secretary Stackley over the littoral combat ship program, asked Stackley, "How do I explain . . . to my constituents in Arizona that we have a $2.5 billion cost overrun on an aircraft carrier?"[56] McCain was well aware that the Newport News shipyard was the only one in the United States that could build *Ford* and her sisters, and the Navy was not about to cancel so critical a program. But he pressed Stackley to explain how such cost overruns could be avoided in the future. Stackley acknowledged that "Far too much risk was carried into the design of the first of the *Ford* class . . . the design was moving at the time production started."[57] Senator McCain cut him off: "I understand all that. What are we going to do to Newport News to make sure that they get a ship built according to the cost since there is no competition?" Indeed. The Navy faced a classic problem in military acquisition—there was only one qualified producer. Of course the shipbuilder faced the other side of the coin—that there was only one buyer, and the buyer might simply walk away from the very high cost of the item it wanted produced, leaving the shipbuilder facing bankruptcy.

Assistant Secretary Stackley and Senator McCain also covered another sensitive part of the Navy's long-range shipbuilding program: Who was going to pay for the replacements for the *Ohio*-class ballistic missile submarines? As Stackley testified, "the *Ohio* replacement dominates our shipbuilding plan . . . outside of the" Future Years Defense Program (FYDP).[58] He also noted that the Navy had made a strong effort to reduce the initial estimate of $7 billion for each new ballistic missile submarine. "The current estimate," he said, was approximately $5.6 billion, and "we are working through the design process to get it down with an objective of about $5 billion, $4.9 billion." However, "That by itself does not bring the shipbuilding plan within the reach of affordability." After listening to this, McCain got right to the point that he wanted to make: "If the Navy builds the *Ohio* replacement submarine within existing funds, will it be able to afford 300 ships?" Stackley made it clear that the answer was no.[59]

The back-and-forth between the assistant secretary and the senator illustrated the constraints placed on the Chief of Naval Operations. The CNO, in responding to strategic guidance from the President and demands for forces from the combatant commanders, was only responsible for the general requirement—for the "force structure assessment" that projected requirements and likely ship acquisitions over the next 30 years. Once that projection was complete, it was up to the acquisition wing of the Navy to commission the studies and the research required to move from a requirement (such as an all-weather, day/night heavy attack aircraft using precision weapons) to an actual system. True, the OPNAV sponsors for platforms and "capabilities" were responsible for reviewing and defending acquisition budgets, but the actual design and fabrication of expensive systems and "capabilities" was done through a chain of command that ran from the Secretary of the Navy, through the Assistant Secretary for Research, Development, and Acquisition, to the program executive officers and then to the program managers and their staffs. That is why the often contentious back-and-forth in hearings was between a civilian assistant secretary and a member of Congress.

The formal requirement for what became aircraft carrier *Gerald R. Ford* was approved in 1996. *Gerald R. Ford*, like the LCS, the *Virginia*-class submarine, and the DDG-1000 destroyer, was a critical part of the 21st century Navy, a Navy built on the assumption that combat capability and long life were the characteristics that mattered most in fighting ships. But these ships—even the littoral combat type—and the *Virginia*-class attack submarine were very expensive and took years to develop and construct. One CNO might lead the effort to develop the requirement, but the ship or system might not be at sea or mature for another ten years, or even more. Critics of the littoral combat ship, for example, were not happy when the Secretary of Defense decided in 2014 that the successor to the LCS would be modified versions of the existing ships, but they had to admit that the Navy had brought down the costs of the existing "sea frames" and that therefore Secretary Hagel's decision had a logic to it. At the same time, it was clear that the rising cost of new ships was making it unlikely if not impossible for the Navy to have the 300 combatants that it said were required. CNO Greenert was right in the middle of this dilemma, having inherited both expensive ships and a budget process in crisis.

One possible way to deal with this dilemma was to separate the acquisition of "platforms" (ships, submarines and aircraft) from "payloads" (sensors, computers, and weapons). This approach was not new. Indeed, it was the basis of the LCS program, and the idea of modularity in shipboard systems went back to 1967.[60] The idea was to produce a basic "platform" (usually a ship) in numbers, thereby reducing its cost. The platform would have adequate volume, load-carrying capacity, range, survivability, and electric power. Separately, various programs would produce "payloads" for this "platform," just as the LCS could carry different "modules" for mine countermeasures or antisubmarine warfare. The challenge facing developers would then be more manageable. The platform and payload (or payloads) would not be tied together in such a way that modules could not be swapped out when the need for a change arose.

The Navy and the Marines

Shipbuilding was not the only problem CNO Greenert inherited. Just as important—perhaps even more so—was the relationship between the Navy and Marine Corps. The desire of the Marines for more amphibious ships had remained constant over a number of years. In the Navy's 2005 force structure assessment, the goal was 31 amphibious ships. After five years of back-and-forth talks between the chiefs of naval operations and the Marine Corps commandants, the goal had increased to 33 ships, and there it stayed in the Navy's 2012 force structure assessment.[61] The goal was to field—by fiscal year 2018—11 amphibious assault ships, 11 amphibious transport docks, and 11 ships to replace the aging dock landing ships. These 33 ships could carry two Marine expeditionary brigades. The Marines actually had wanted 38 amphibious ships, but the number had stayed at 33; that was all that then-CNO Roughead would agree to.

But there was more involved here than numbers of amphibious ships. The basic issue was the mission of the Marine Corps. What was it? In 2010, at the end of his time as Secretary of Defense, Robert Gates challenged the Marines to "redefine" their role. That same summer, Marine Corps

Commandant General James T. Conway set up a Force Structure Review Group to do just that. The Secretary of the Navy told the members of this panel that the Marines needed to be able to "rapidly disaggregate and aggregate to increase forward engagement, rapidly respond to crisis, and rapidly project power in austere locations."[62] The Marines themselves argued that they were the nation's "Middleweight Force," with mobility that the Army lacked and firepower and mass that special forces did not have.[63]

As Navy senior program analyst Robert P. Kozloski argued in the Summer 2013 issue of the *Naval War College Review*, the Navy was becoming "unable to support fully the Marine Corps's [sic] amphibious-lift requirements" because of the size of the Corps. After the end of the Cold War, Navy personnel numbers had dropped more than 40 percent over a 20-year period. Over that same interval of time, the number of Marines had increased by 4.5 percent.[64] General Conway and his successor, General James F. Amos, did not want the Marines to be a smaller version of the Army. They wanted the Marines to shift back to being a seaborne expeditionary force. They were also concerned about the cost of training and sustaining their new and veteran Marines. The size and composition of the Marine Corps was set by legislation: no less than three combat divisions and three air wings.[65] Was that also an effective upper limit to the size of the Corps, given the budget constraints?

To work all this out, Marine Corps Commandant General James F. Amos created the Ellis Group (named after famed USMC Lieutenant Colonel Earl H. Ellis) at Quantico, Virginia, in December 2011. The military and civilian members of the group were directed to study how combat was changing, to find ways to better cooperate with the Navy, and to suggest ways that Marine Corps leaders could develop a firm partnership with their counterparts at the U.S. Special Operations Command. They reported directly to General Amos, just as the members of the CNO's Strategic Studies Group (SSG) reported directly to CNO Greenert. General Amos had already signed a memorandum of agreement with CNO Roughead in May 2011 that brought together senior Navy and Marine officers to "identify naval war fighting, operational employments and force development issues that should be considered in order to optimize the contributions of the naval services across the range of military operations in the naval domain."[66] This memorandum led to the creation of a new organization: the Naval Board. If Marine Corps combat expertise lay at the company and battalion levels and in the ability of Marine units to operate from the sea, then what were the implications for the Navy? And how would changes in technology—through the further development of unmanned systems and cybernetic "weapons"—affect future amphibious operations? The new board was designed to be a place where these questions could be asked and answered.

OPNAV and the Navy Secretariat

The Navy secretariat was a strong organization during the Obama presidency. The Secretary, Raymond E. Mabus Jr., was an experienced and effective politician from Mississippi, a Navy veteran, and a former Ambassador to Saudi Arabia. The Under Secretary, Robert O. Work, was a retired Marine Corps colonel who had served as military assistant for former Secretary of the Navy Richard J. Danzig. Work also wrote extensively and well about Navy issues. The ASN (RD&A) was Sean J. Stackley, an Annapolis graduate and former engineering duty officer in the Navy, a manager (from 2001 to 2005) of the *San Antonio* (LPD-17) acquisition program, and a former professional staff member of the Senate Armed Services Committee.

Bryan Clark recalled that the relationship between OPNAV and the Secretariat was a strong one. For example, the CNO wanted requirements for new systems to be both technically feasible and fiscally realistic. Under Secretary Work and Assistant Secretary Stackley agreed. They supported Greenert's argument that making major investments in existing ships would pay dividends over time. But Secretary Mabus was concerned that the Navy was becoming too small, and that taking some ships out of service in order to better maintain others was a mistake. Clark's view was that the Navy secretary was for a time too focused on numbers of platforms and not enough on the "health of those platforms across time," though eventually Mabus perceived the soundness of CNO Greenert's policy.[67]

Under Secretary Work was also the Navy's Chief Management Officer (CMO), "responsible for the performance of the department's business operations."[68] It was his responsibility to respond to the pressures from the Congress to manage the Navy in a businesslike way. His mission was to "Build an Effective Business Enterprise Architecture" and to promote "Strategic Business Management" inside the Navy Department. That meant reducing overhead costs,

Figure 19-1. CNO Jonathan W. Greenert (left) testifies during a posture hearing before the Senate Armed Services Committee in support of the proposed budget for the Department of the Navy for Fiscal Year 2016 and the Future Years Defense Program. Secretary Ray Mabus, (right) and Commandant of the Marine Corps General Joseph Dunford also testified. (U.S. Navy photo by Mass Communication Specialist 1st Class Nathan Laird [Released] DIMOC Asset: 77975PT_CP13VAOKM 150310-N-AT895-144)

developing a "lean" (small but very productive) Navy organization ashore, and producing a comprehensive financial audit for the department.[69] The under secretary, acting as the CMO, was in charge of the Navy's "business mission area," which was composed of "Policies, processes, information and systems relating to the end-to-end financial, logistical, facility management, human capital, acquisition, administrative and other functions that support the warfighter."[70] Assisting the under secretary in this endeavor were two new offices: OPNAV's N41, the Navy's Business Operations Office, and the Marine Corps Business Enterprise Office.[71]

Congress had started down a path to pressure the executive branch agencies to become more businesslike once the impetus for federal deregulation in the late 1970s and 1980s had appeared to be a success. The notion that the executive agencies could become more productive had gained increasing numbers of supporters in Congress, and they pressured successive administrations to adopt more business practices. One of these was to adopt accrual accounting in order to be able to prepare annual agency balance sheets and income statements. A balance sheet in a private firm listed the firm's current and long-term assets, its current and long-term liabilities, and stockholder's equity. The sum of the liabilities and owners' equity comprised the firm's assets. Private firms also produced annual income statements, which were often referred to as earnings statements or statements of operations. These reports matched income against expenses to yield "net income" in a given year.

The last time that the Navy Department had published a "balance sheet of the general ledger" was probably in 1930.[72] The following table contains essential elements of that balance sheet.

FINANCIAL ACCOUNTS	DEBIT BALANCE	CREDIT BALANCE
Appropriation—Treasury balances	------------------	$123,510,861.48
Available funds	$91,893,625.99	------------------
Cash in hands of disbursing officers	$28,069,003.94	------------------
COST AND APPROPRIATION ACCOUNTS	DEBIT BALANCE	CREDIT BALANCE
Appropriations—Unexpended balances	$118,342,625.07	------------------
Appropriations, 1789–1930	------------------	$12,934,673,839.91
Cost of the Navy, 1789 to 1930	$11,440,835,700.61	
PROPERTY ACCOUNTS	DEBIT BALANCE	CREDIT BALANCE
First cost of ships on Navy list, 6-30-1930	$1,275,200,947.61	------------------
Stores, purchases	------------------	$2,771,626.68
Property investment	------------------	$2,727,777,030.34
Total	$15,820,622,528.82	$15,820,622,528.82

When this balance sheet was published, the American Institute of Certified Public Accountants had not yet developed a comprehensive list of "generally accepted accounting principles." But even in 1930, several of those principles applied. For example, in this chart, ship costs are what they were at the time the ships were acquired—not the "fair market value" that the ships would have had in 1930. The concept of "constant dollars," so familiar today, was not used in 1930. This chart reflected the practice of professional accountants in 1930 of simply applying the same basic accounting methods across time, even though in the case of the Navy that time span reached from the end of the 18th century to one-third of the way through the 20th.

But to what purpose? What's missing from this chart is the purpose or the consequences of these expenditures. The income (appropriations) side of the ledger is clear enough, and so is the debit (cost) side. But what did these expenditures achieve? A balance sheet today tells actual and potential stock owners what a firm's assets are and separates current assets (such as accounts receivable) from long-term assets (such as buildings). An income statement prepared for a firm today balances sales against operating expenses to calculate net income and earnings per share. The Navy, however, "sells" nothing except obsolete equipment and ships that it throws away or auctions off. It is not in the business of making items or providing services for sale in a competitive market.

In 1930, as the Great Depression was getting under way, the Congress wanted to know what it was getting for its appropriations to the Navy Department. The 1930 "balance sheet of the general ledger" was one answer. The Navy's Bureau of Supplies and Accounts in 1930 also provided members of Congress with detailed reports of what it cost to purchase, operate, repair, and alter ships, and what it cost to operate and maintain shipyards and other installations.[73] The fiscal "inputs" to the Navy were well documented. The "outputs"—ships, planes, trained sailors, and bases—were also well documented. But no one could show precisely what the consequences were of that spending and the force the spending had produced.

From the mid-to-late 1990s to Admiral Greenert's time as CNO, more and more members of Congress wanted the Defense Department to be more businesslike. The number of members who supported imposing business procedures on the components of the Department seems to have increased as the conflicts in Iraq and Afghanistan continued. However, both the Center for Strategic and International Studies and the Center for Strategic and Budgetary Assessments—two very accomplished Washington think tanks—argued that the growth of defense spending was due to something deeper than the military campaigns in Iraq and Afghanistan. As Todd Harrison of the Center for Strategic and Budgetary Assessments claimed in an analysis in 2011, "The base budget now supports a force with essentially the same size, force structure, and capabilities as in FY 2001 but at a 35 percent higher cost. The [Defense] Department is spending more but not getting more."[74] What was causing these increased costs, and how could the increase be constrained?

The congressional answer was to make the Navy more like a business. The secretariat was given that task. Was the deputy chief management office, along with N41 and the USMC's

Business Enterprise Office successful? In the FY 2013 transformation plan and FY 2012 annual report, Under Secretary Work noted that $300 million had been saved through the restructuring of a human resources management "modernization effort," that the number of redundant software applications in the "Logistics and Readiness portfolio" had been or would soon be cut by more than 40 percent, and that the Marine Corps was well on the way to fielding its digital Global Combat Support System.[75] The business "train" was moving. Was that enough?

Perhaps, but only if business modernization were coupled with "transformation." In July 2014, Secretary Mabus approved the "Department of the Navy Transformation Plan, FY 2014–2016." The process of developing and updating the Plan was supposed to aid the secretariat by using "business challenges and opportunities to meet the DoD directed 20 percent Headquarters reduction."[76] As the plan stated, "The past decade of expanded defense budgets permitted an environment that resulted in organizational growth and increased support for mission demands. Now, as defense budgets contract, the approach of the business enterprise must shift to create a cost-management culture. . . . Difficult tradeoffs are inevitable . . ."[77] How could the secretariat promote a "cost-management culture?" One way was by using "analytics," including "business process reengineering, continuous process improvement, and Lean Six Sigma . . ."[78] Another way was to use the Business Transformation Council, "the senior level governing body which assesses, approves and governs transformation efforts that cross organizational or functional boundaries." The Council, composed of the Assistant Commandant of the Marine Corps, the VCNO, the Assistant Secretaries of the Navy, "Deputy Under Secretaries of the Navy and Special Staff Advisors" was created to "improve collaboration and [optimize] the involvement of senior leadership to directly support the Chief Management Officer's decision making needs."[79]

How could Secretary Mabus know that a "cost-management culture" was being created? By checking to see if the following goals were being achieved: "financial auditability," increased energy efficiency in operations and in shore-based support organizations, more efficient acquisition spending, a reduction in headquarters staffs, and improved business operations.[80] It was ironic that the secretariat was telling the rest of the Navy that reductions in headquarters personnel were imperative when in fact, as the Government Accountability Office (GAO) found, "Within the Navy Secretariat and Office of the Chief of Naval Operations, the number of authorized military and civilian positions has increased from 2,061 in fiscal year 2005 to 2,402 in fiscal year 2013, with increases in authorized civilian positions, primarily at the Navy Secretariat, driving the overall increase."[81] Where were these individuals? In the secretariat, 298 of the total of 1,260 were in the offices of the ASN (RD&A) and the Assistant Secretary for Financial Management and Comptroller.[82] Of course. If the goal of the Secretary of the Navy was to improve cost-management, then there were two obvious places where the secretary needed people to do that—in acquisition and financial management. But the GAO found another 523 people in the "Department of the Navy Assistant for Administration, headquarters elements of the Naval Criminal Investigative Service, the Office of Civilian Human Resources, and the Naval Center for Cost Analysis."[83]

What about OPNAV? How large was it, and what OPNAV codes had the most people? N2/N6 (DCNO for Information Dominance) had 147 positions, 88 military and 59 civilian. N3/N5 (DCNO for Operations, Plans and Strategy) had 144 positions, 120 military and 24 civilian. N4 (DCNO for Fleet Readiness and Logistics) had 163 positions, 68 military and 95 civilian. N8 had 181 positions, 118 of them military, though 28 of the total of 86 positions in N81 were civilian. N9 had 235 positions, 157 of them military. The immediate Office of the Secretary of the Navy had 44 positions; the CNO's had 52. The VCNO had 16; the Under Secretary of the Navy had five. The Director of the Navy Staff had 78—about as many as all of OPNAV had in 1916. Total staff positions (military and civilian) for the Secretary of the Navy in FY 2013: 1,260; for the CNO, it was 1,116.[84]

Whatever the reasons behind these numbers, they make one thing clear: OPNAV and the secretariat are large *staff* organizations. But just what is it that staff offices do—or are supposed to do? They are supposed to gather information for the men and women holding the most senior positions so that those senior officials can make well-informed decisions and lead the crafting of Navy policy. Once decisions are made, the staffs ideally communicate those decisions and their implications throughout the Navy and then track what is happening in the Navy to learn if decisions made in Washington are being implemented and policies properly followed. But what you see today in OPNAV and the secretariat are large complex organizations that require very careful management if they are to be what Secretary Mabus said he wanted them to be: engines of innovation and creators of a "cost-management" culture. The danger is that elements of the secretariat and perhaps even of OPNAV will become like *line* organizations, charged with actually making things or executing policies—as against monitoring what others charged with operational responsibilities are doing. The congressional pressure to make the services more businesslike may actually be making the Secretariat and OPNAV more directive and therefore—perhaps—more difficult for the Secretary and the CNO to lead.

The Hidden But Always-Present Danger: Cybernetic Warfare

The sorts of cultural changes that members of Congress and senior Navy officials have advocated may be taking place in the office of the Deputy Chief of Naval Operations (N2/N6). In July 2014, Vice Admiral Ted N. Branch, the DCNO(Information Dominance, N2/N6) argued in an issue of the U.S. Naval Institute's *Proceedings* that information dominance would give the Navy three advantages over an enemy: strong and resilient command and control, "Superior knowledge of . . . the physical environment as well as threat capability, disposition, and intent," and "integrated fires."[85] To gain those advantages, the "restricted-line communities of Naval Oceanography, Information Warfare, Information Professional, Intelligence, and the Space Cadre" were being integrated "into the Information Dominance Corps."[86] One function of the corps that was often overlooked was protecting the Navy Department's transportation links. A number of Navy officers, especially those exposed to major Red/Blue war games, had recognized that the United States could not take its air and sea links to the far Pacific for granted. The ships and aircraft using those links needed to be able to hide from an enemy. To do that, they would have to make their way while "electromagnetically silent," and U.S. forces would have to deny an enemy the ability to integrate many different pieces of evidence that would reveal the positions of friendly ships and aircraft.[87]

This mission had to be accomplished despite two challenges. One was training restricted line officers to think and act like combat commanders. As one Navy officer put it, line officers made "life and death decisions" as they increased in rank, while intelligence officers traditionally made *recommendations* regarding "life and death decisions" as *they* increased in rank. Former CNO Roughead understood that difference, and therefore he knew that it would be difficult to change the way that restricted line officers thought of their roles and the way that line officers thought of the restricted line.[88] There was nothing to it, however, but to merge N6 and N2 and trust to the leadership of the senior officers who led the merger. The second challenge was to compensate for the sale by the U.S. government of many of the radio frequencies it once owned. In effect, the military forces of the United States were trying to shove many more messages through a narrower band of frequencies.

As Alan Shaffer, the Principal Deputy to the Assistant Secretary of Defense for Research and Engineering, told an audience at the National Press Club in September 2014, the United States had "lost the electromagnetic spectrum." The proliferation of cheap but effective digital communication devices meant that "The kind of electronic eavesdropping and jamming that used to require a nation-state's resources" was now open to "small countries and even guerillas." As Shaffer warned his audience, "People are able to create very agile, capable systems for very little money, and those agile, capable systems—if we don't develop counters—can impact the performance of some of our high-end platforms."[89]

Vice Admiral Branch was aware of this danger. He argued that the Navy had developed a "concept of [electromagnetic] Maneuver Warfare . . . which anticipates future conflicts in the battlespace created where cyber and the [electromagnetic] spectrum converge." To implement this concept of warfare, naval forces would need "a complete awareness of our [electromagnetic] signature and others' in real time; the ability to manipulate our [electromagnetic] signature to control what others can detect, maximize our ability to defeat jamming and deception, and guarantee our use of the spectrum when needed; and use of [electromagnetic] and cyber capabilities as non-kinetic fires to inhibit" any adversary's sensing and combat capability.[90] He also pointed to the creation in 2014 of the Navy Information Dominance Forces, "an integrated type command" dedicated to information dominance that would report to the Commander, Fleet Forces Command.[91] It was just in time. In January 2014, retired Admiral James G. Stavridis had advocated strengthening the U.S. Cyber Command because "the cyber domain requires precisely the core competencies that none of the other [services] possess."[92] Stavridis's point was that it was time for the Congress to create what amounted to a new service, though this new service would be unlike any other.

Sex and "Officer Detachment for Cause"

The manual for the Naval Personnel Command defines "Officer Detachment for Cause" as "the administrative removal of an officer, whether on active duty or in the Selected Reserve, from the officer's current duty assignment before their [sic] normal transfer or planned rotation date."[93] The manual goes on to say that "The need for [Detachment for Cause, or DFC] arises when an officer's performance or conduct detracts from accomplishing the command mission . . ." A DFC "has a serious effect on the officer's future naval career, particularly with regard to promotion, duty assignment, selection for schools, and special assignment. The initiation of a DFC, therefore, should be undertaken with full appreciation of its gravity."[94] In 2004, the Navy's inspector general had commissioned a study of the rate at which DFCs were approved.[95] In 2010, the inspector general again organized a panel of officers to ask whether the rate at which DFCs were being approved had increased since 2004, and, if so, why.[96]

The 2004 study examined the records of 78 commanding officers in pay grades from lieutenant to captain "who were relieved from command from January 1999 through June 2004." Not surprisingly, the study panel found that officers were relieved for the following reasons: some serious event (grounding a ship, for example), the inability of the officer's command to perform its mission or achieve the required level of readiness, an "abusive or unhealthy climate attributable" to the commanding officer, or misconduct by the commanding officer.[97] The study panel noted in its report that "No significant career commonalities were found that could be attributed to the COs being relieved for cause."[98] Indeed, "in every case, there was no indication or documentation of prior problems in the fitness report file. On the contrary, fitness reports were uniformly outstanding in every case."[99] What was going on? Did the officers who were removed lack training? No.[100] Did the officers in question not know the rules? No. "*In nearly every case, the officers relieved for personal behavior clearly knew the rules. In some cases, they had been specifically counseled, but ultimately chose to violate the regulation.*" [emphasis in the original]

The study panel observed that events such as grounding a ship or running a ship into a pier were inherent in the naval profession. Commanding a ship or submarine, as well as leading an aviation squadron or an air wing, were high-risk endeavors. A certain level of error was probably unavoidable. But the panel focused on personal behavior that could easily have been avoided, including inappropriate relations with members of the opposite sex who were under the CO's command, sexual assault and harassment, drinking and driving, falsifying documents, and using a government computer to view pornographic images.[101] As the panel's report pointed out, the "most significant factor in the increase in reliefs has been CO misconduct or inappropriate personal behavior."[102] At the same time, the members of the panel

> could not conclusively determine whether the significant rise in reliefs from adultery and alcohol related incidents was due to a recent increase in such behavior, or rather, from a growing intolerance for such behavior in COs. Subordinates today have a greater level of awareness of the CO's behavior and are much less reticent to report misconduct.

Greatly improved connectivity with the Internet, email, and hotlines have made it nearly impossible for a CO's personal indiscretions to remain private.[103]

Whatever the cause or causes, the 2004 study panel "found no systemic factors relating to the increase in CO reliefs." The 2010 study came to a similar conclusion: "There was no correlation between CO [detachments for cause] and career paths, personality traits, accession sources, time in command, or year groups."[104] But the 2010 study panel also found that "The recommendations implemented from the 2004 CO DFC study had no discernable impact on the CO DFC rate."[105] Yet "the preponderance of Navy-wide CO reliefs were for Personal Misconduct. Within the category of Personal Misconduct, the preponderance of reliefs were for adultery, inappropriate relationships, harassment, or sexual assault."[106] In response to this report, various senior officers, including Admiral Greenert, went to schools for prospective commanding officers to hammer away at the need to obey the rules.[107]

In 2012, however, the number of commanding officers relieved for cause increased again, almost to the 2003 level that had triggered the 2004 study. CNO Greenert was quoted as saying that he was "concerned" and also unable to explain why the efforts to deal with personal misconduct had not seemed to work.[108] Navy Captain Mark F. Light took on this issue while a student at the Army War College in 2011. As Captain Light discovered, "the most prevalent cause of CO DFCs in every community [surface, aviation, and subsurface] has been sexual misconduct, including inappropriate relationships, fraternization, and sexual harassment."[109] Based on his analysis, Light argued that the fundamental cause of this sexual misconduct was "*not* mixed gender crews," but instead "a lack of integrity on the part of the offending officers."[110] However, that lack of integrity was not due to a lack of awareness of the rules or a lack of sensible training. What, then? As Light found, "every flag officer interviewed for" his study saw "CO misconduct as an issue requiring attention," but there was no consensus among those flag officers that the issue of sexual misconduct "urgently demands transformational change."[111] It was ironic that the technologically sophisticated Navy had discovered that "social problems are very much harder than scientific ones, and . . . we usually don't get anywhere when we do think about them."[112]

According to Bryan Clark, the issue of sexual assault took a great deal of the CNO's time, but it was not the issue that concerned him the most. What mattered more was that no flag officer in OPNAV said, "I'll take this issue on. I own it. I'll work with the Secretariat to deal with it." It was that willingness to aggressively take on issues that the CNO wanted to see in the younger flag officers. Indeed, Admiral Greenert's reorganization of OPNAV could not be successful unless the "junior flags" (the new rear admirals) took the initiative.[113] As Greenert knew, how best to tailor what might be called the Navy's "culture" for the post–Cold War world was a serious challenge. The perceived failure to do so had stained the reputation of CNO Frank Kelso. The military services were committed to mixing young men and women and to opening fields to women that had been closed to them for generations. The "blending" of genders would be done, but it needed to be done by leaders who knew how to make the required changes without disrupting the lives and careers of service members any more than was necessary.

"Managers" vs. "Executives"

In his "terms of reference" that he had written for Vice Admiral Burke and Burke's OPNAV realignment team, CNO Greenert had directed Burke and his team to carefully consider organizational challenges and opportunities. The assumption behind the terms of reference had been that the officers and civilians in OPNAV would work to make the new organizational structure effective. As Burke had warned, however, the organizational realignment in itself would not necessarily "achieve the CNO's intents and objectives." As Burke's report to Greenert put it, "Almost the entire OPNAV staff was affected by this realignment, either by changes in reporting, functions, seams, or relationships, and it will take commitment from every code to realize [your] intents and objectives . . ."[114]

To improve matters, CNO Greenert assigned the Strategic Studies Group at the Naval War College the task of exploring the organizational function of "talent management." Every bureaucratic organization like the Navy had to manage the talents of its members to maximize their contributions to the organization's missions. But an organization like the Navy valued operational experience more than investing in the procedures to make sure that people with the necessary talent rose through the ranks. In wartime, the leaders stood out. They were—to use Greenert's terms—clearly "bold, confident and accountable." In peacetime, such officers might offend higher-ranking opponents who could block their rise to the top.

Greenert discussed this problem with successful business executives.[115] How could a bureaucratic organization promote its most qualified operational leaders *and* those officers best able to cultivate the executives of the future? The Navy needed both outstanding operational leaders and effective executives, but selection boards understandably favored the aggressive and successful operators. Those so selected might not be very effective in OPNAV, especially in the role of nurturing future executives. This difference between "operators" and "executives" reaches back to the years before World War I. Admiral King, for example, modeled his career and his behavior on that of his World War I superior, Admiral Mayo. But which admiral "seeded" the future Navy with younger protégés? Not Mayo, but Admiral Sims. It was the protégés of Sims (Joseph Reeves, William Pratt, and Harris Laning) who went on to command the fleet or serve as CNO in the 1930s. Similarly, after World War II it was not the protégés of Admiral King who led the Navy but those of Admiral Nimitz (Forrest Sherman and Robert Carney).

As CNO Greenert recognized, this was a difference between "managers" and "executives." The analogy used by Bryan Clark was the difference between a firm's plant managers and its front office executives. The former had to be focused; the immediate success of a manufacturing firm hinged on the effectiveness of its plant managers and its supply chain managers. Over the long run, however, a manufacturing firm's prosperity depended on its having executives who could see a much broader picture and position the firm to take advantage of changes in technology, finance, and consumer expectations. Similarly, the Navy, led by the naval component commanders, had to be able to plan and conduct operations in the present. The CNO and the

OPNAV staff had to be able to tackle current problems (like the budget and sexual assault) while at the same time laying the foundation for the future through research and development and through programs to bring intelligent and energetic young people into the Navy. This could not happen—as Greenert well knew—if the rising flag officers were not willing to act as "executives" in the best sense of that word.

Conclusion: The Hurricane Years

Cameron Hawley, a retired business executive turned writer, published the novel *The Hurricane Years* (Little, Brown) in 1968.[116] The story is about a business executive in a very competitive market who has to weather a series of business and personal challenges while surviving and recovering from a heart attack. The title of Hawley's book, though not its plot, is relevant to Admiral Jonathan Greenert's tenure as Chief of Naval Operations. If CNO Gary Roughead, Greenert's predecessor, was concerned about the Navy's future, Greenert was more concerned about the present—about the Navy's role as a forward-deployed force ready to fight. His argument was simple: an obviously ready force operating across the globe was suited to deterring conflicts, as well as to winning them. That sort of deterrence—stemming from presence and from cooperation with other navies—fit the Obama administration's national security policy. But it was overshadowed by the tumultuous relations between Democrats and Republicans in Washington.

The Republicans in Congress demanded that the components of the Defense Department act more like businesses, even though the Congress acted anything but businesslike, especially after the Republican Party gained a majority in the House of Representatives in the 2010 congressional elections. The PPBE process is difficult in "normal" times. It wears down those doing it when money is very, very tight or when, as happened, the legislative process becomes chaotic. CNO Greenert was placed in a difficult position. His role was to faithfully execute the policy of the government's leaders, but how could that be done when the partisan debates over the federal budget and over the federal debt limit came close again and again to paralyzing effective decision-making and management within OPNAV?

CNO Greenert's ability to lead the Navy was hampered by a political process that he could not control. It was also hampered by honest debates over the proper role of the Navy and the Marines. What could the Navy do about what came to be called "hybrid war," where opponents of the United States combined insurgency tactics, terrorism, media manipulation, and money laundering to gain their ends, while never, in their campaigns, directly challenging American naval forces? The changing nature of conflict was also a problem for the Marine Corps. The Marines did not want to be a "second Army," and they had initially resisted being teamed with special operations forces, but the conflict in Iraq was a "big army" fight in 2003, changed into a counter-insurgency campaign in 2004–2005, and then pulled Marines back in for heavy close combat during the "surge" in 2006.

Enough of the Global War on Terrorism (GWOT) became targeted operations that blended agents of the Central Intelligence Agency, intelligence specialists, special operations units, and unmanned aircraft to suggest to some influential political leaders that the nature of war had fundamentally changed.[117] At the same time, the Navy had to be able to operate in the Western Pacific. Navy operations there, especially by the Seventh Fleet, had been a touchstone of U.S. policy for several generations, and it was clear by the time Admiral Greenert became CNO that the regime in China was hostile to that long-standing policy. How could the Navy do what was expected of it in a demanding international environment with an uncertain domestic political environment and with inadequate funds?

As far as CNO Greenert was concerned, the primary problem for OPNAV was "to develop new programs that leverage innovative operating concepts and harvest proven technologies in an affordable way." OPNAV needed to develop operating concepts and then plan and program in terms of them. Bryan Clark argued that the next step in reorganizing OPNAV was to create an organization in N8 that could develop and test these concepts.[118] N81 already did campaign analysis. What if there was a group in N8 that developed "whole Navy" operating concepts? That sort of analysis had been done in OP-96 when Admiral Hayward was CNO, but it had been "threat-driven." Alternate force structures and operating concepts were matched against what the Soviet Union had and what its armed forces could do. But what would drive concept development now? Was the "Air-Sea Battle" concept the answer? No one quite knew.

Despite all the uncertainty of politics in Washington and events around the world, there was continuity in OPNAV during "the hurricane years." Evidence of that was the 12 February 2015 OPNAV instruction on "force structure assessments."[119] The instruction affirmed that the Director, Assessment Division (OPNAV N81) served as "the executive agent and lead for force structure assessment." That is testimony to the quality of N81's work across time, and to the ability of a CNO to hold in his hands the key to the Navy's programmatic success, even during "the hurricane years."

Notes

[1] Interview with CAPT R. Robinson Harris, USN (Ret.), by Thomas C. Hone, 23 Jan. 2015.

[2] Stavridis, *The Accidental Admiral*, 119–24.

[3] Interview, Mr. Bryan Clark with Thomas C. Hone, 9 April 2015. Clark enlisted in the Navy in 1982, earned a college degree and a commission, and served as a submarine officer. He served in OPNAV from 2004 to 2011 and participated in the quadrennial defense reviews of 2006 and 2010. In 2013, he was head of N00Z, the CNO's strategic action group. He was on the staff of the Center for Strategic and Budgetary assessments when he was interviewed.

[4] Information Memo for Chief of Naval Operations from VADM Bill Burke, OPNAV Realignment 2011–2012 Team Leader, subj: OPNAV Realignment Final Report, 11 Sept. 2012, "Introduction," 1–2. In the collection of Thomas C. Hone.

[5] Interview, Bryan Clark with Thomas C. Hone, 9 Apr. 2015.

[6] Ibid.

[7] Information Memo for Chief of Naval Operations from VADM Bill Burke, subj: OPNAV Realignment Final Report, 11 Sept. 2012, 7. In the collection of Thomas C. Hone.

[8] Interview, Bryan Clark with Thomas C. Hone, 9 Apr. 2015.

[9] Information Memo for Chief of Naval Operations from VADM Bill Burke, subj: OPNAV Realignment Final Report, 11 Sept. 2012, 2.

[10] Ibid., 40–41.

[11] Interview, Bryan Clark with Thomas C. Hone, 9 Apr. 2015.

[12] Ibid.

[13] Information Memo for Chief of Naval Operations from VADM Bill Burke, subj: OPNAV Realignment Final Report, 11 Sept. 2012, 57. See endnote 7.

[14] Ibid., 5.

[15] Ibid., 8.

[16] Memo from VADM John M. Bird, DNS, to All OPNAV Distribution List; subj: OPNAV Realignment Update, 05 Mar. 2012. In the collection of Thomas C. Hone.

[17] Action Memo from VADM Bill Burke to Director, Navy Staff and Deputy Chief of Naval Operations for Integration of Resources and Capabilities (N8), subj: Chief of Naval Operations Staff Realignment of Resources, 09 Mar. 2012. In the collection of Thomas C. Hone.

[18] Message from CNO to NAVADMIN, subj: OPNAV Realignment, R 121702Z, 12 Mar. 2012. In the collection of Thomas C. Hone.

[19] Action Memo from VADM Bill Burke to Director, Navy Staff and Deputy Chief of Naval Operations for Integration of Resources and Capabilities (N8), subj: Chief of Naval Operations Staff Realignment of Resources, 4 May 2012. In the collection of Thomas C. Hone.

[20] "CNO's Navigation Plan, 2013-2017," Office of the Chief of Naval Operations. http://www.navy.mil/cno/Navplan2012-2017-V-Final.pdf (29 Aug. 2016).

[21] See, for example, *Damn the Torpedoes, A Short History of U.S. Naval Mine Countermeasures, 1777–1991*, by Tamara Moser Melia (Washington, DC: Naval Historical Center, Department of the Navy, and GPO, 1991).

[22] Thomas E. Mann and Norman J. Ornstein, *It's Even Worse than It Looks* (New York: Basic Books, 2013), xix. Mann and Ornstein are respected students of the political process in Washington. Mann is based at the Brookings Institution and Ornstein is a resident scholar at the American Enterprise Institute.

[23] The federal deficit is the difference in any given year between what the Treasury takes in and what it spends. The federal debt is the total of deficits across all fiscal years. Republicans regarded the debt as far too great. The way they proposed to reduce it was to immediately begin to eliminate yearly deficits.

[24] Mann and Ornstein, *It's Even Worse than It Looks*, 11.

[25] A continuing resolution, passed by the Congress, authorizes federal agencies to continue operating with the fiscal obligation authority that they had in the preceding fiscal year. Note that Article I, Section 7 of the Constitution specifies that "All bills for raising revenue shall originate in the House of Representatives . . ." This rule gave the Republican Party majority in the House significant political influence.

[26] See *The Price of Politics*, by Bob Woodward (New York: Simon & Schuster, 2012), and Lawrence P. Farrell Jr., "Budget Control Act of 2011 Forces Real Cuts to Defense, and Difficult Choices," *National Defense* (Sept. 2011). www.nationaldefensemagazine.org/archive/2011/September/Pages/Budget (29 Aug. 2016).

[27] ADM Robert J. Natter, "New Command Unifies the Fleet," U.S. Naval Institute *Proceedings*, vol. 128, no. 1 (Jan. 2002). Also administrative message R 281053Z SEP 01 ZYB PSN 317065F22 from CINCLANTFLT, subj: US Fleet Forces Command. Printed in *Inside the Navy*, 8 Oct. 2001, 10.

[28] ADM John C. Harvey Jr., CAPT David E. Grogan, and CDR Anthony J. Mazzeo, "Course Corrections in Command and Control, U.S. Naval Institute *Proceedings*, vol. 138, no. 3 (Mar. 2012), 56–57.

[29] Ibid., 58.

[30] Ibid.

[31] Ibid., 59. See also OPNAV Notice 3111, "Disestablishment of Commander, Fleet Forces Command (CFFC) and Change in Name for Commander, U.S. Atlantic Fleet (COMLANTFLT), 23 May 2006, Ser DNS-33/6U827232. See http://www.public.navy.mil/usff/Pages/history.aspx (29 Aug. 2016). Also OPNAV Instruction 5440.77, from: Chief of Naval Operations, subj: Missions, Functions and Tasks for U.S. Fleet Forces Command (USFLTFORCOM), 16 July 2007, in the collection of Thomas C. Hone.

[32] OPNAV Instruction 5440.77B, from Chief of Naval Operations, subj: Missions, Functions, and Tasks of United States Fleet Forces Command, 25 Apr. 2012. In the collection of Thomas C. Hone.

[33] Entitlement spending on programs such as Social Security was protected. Discretionary spending included funds for the federal departments and for a majority of Department of Defense programs.

[34] Undersecretary of Defense (Comptroller) Robert F. Hale and LTGEN Mark F. Ramsay (USAF), Director, Force Structure, Resources and Assessment, Joint Staff (J8), "DOD News Briefing on the Fiscal 2014 Defense Budget Proposal," 10 Apr. 2013. As Hale pointed out, under sequestration "2,500 line items in the department budget have to be cut by the same percentage." He also noted that "Sequestration cuts $11 billion out of [the] base O&M budget for active forces. We've decided to protect our wartime operations . . . That means we've got to take that [Overseas Contingency Operations] money out of the base. That's another $4 billion." http://archive.defense.gov/transcripts/transcript.aspx?transcriptid=5215 (29 Aug. 2016).

[35] *Statement of Admiral Jonathan Greenert, USN, Chief of Naval Operations*, before the Senate Armed Services Committee on "The Impact of Sequestration on National Defense," 28 Jan. 2015, 1.

[36] Ibid., 2.

[37] Interview with ADM Jonathan W. Greenert, USN, in Jane's *Navy International*, 17 Dec. 2013.

[38] *Statement of Admiral Jonathan Greenert, USN, Chief of Naval Operations*, 28 Jan. 2015, 2.

[39] Ibid., 4. What Greenert did not say was that sequestration was a hardship for the military department budget officers because it was a 10 percent cut across programs, projects and activities. It was not, for example, a 10 percent cut across the broad budget categories of Operations and Maintenance, Personnel, and Acquisition. If it were, the military departments could shift funds within those broad budget categories. But the Budget Control Act of 2011 specified across-the-board reductions down into the military department program line items, making no allowance for the comparative importance of programs. This is what was causing such serious problems for the CNO and his counterparts in the other services.

[40] Secretary of Defense Charles T. Hagel, "Statement on Strategic Choices and Management Review," 31 July 2013, Dept. of Defense Press Operations, Washington, DC, 1.

[41] Ibid., 2–3.

[42] Ibid., 3.

[43] Ibid.

[44] Ibid., 4.

[45] Ibid., 7.

[46] Ronald O'Rourke, "Navy Littoral Combat Ship (LCS) Program: Background and Issues for Congress," Congressional Research Service Report (7-5700), RL33741, 24 Dec. 2014, 11.

[47] Initial Operational Test and Evaluation (IOT&E) describes that part of the acquisition process where one or more of the initial production items of a new system or platform are subjected to testing under operational conditions. Unlike full operational testing, IOT&E is not an "up or down" review. Instead, it is the first step in deciding if a new system or platform (such as an airplane) will function as intended while being employed by regular service personnel under operational conditions.

[48] *Statement of the Honorable Sean J. Stackley (ASN[RD&A]), VADM Joseph P. Mulloy (DCNO, Integration of Capabilities & Resources [N8]), and VADM William H. Hilarides, Commander, Naval Sea Systems Command, on Department of the Navy Shipbuilding Programs*, before the Subcommittee on Seapower of the Senate Armed Services Committee, 10 Apr. 2014, 11.

[49] Ronald O'Rourke, "Navy Littoral Combat Ship (LCS) Program: Background and Issues for Congress," 24 Dec. 2014, 13.

[50] Ibid., 15.

[51] *Statement of the Honorable Sean J. Stackley (ASN[RD&A]), VADM Joseph P. Mulloy (DCNO, Integration of Capabilities & Resources [N8]), and VADM William H. Hilarides, Commander, Naval Sea Systems Command, on Department of the Navy Shipbuilding Programs*, 10 April 2014, 8.

[52] *Hearing to Receive Testimony on Navy Shipbuilding Programs in Review of the Defense Authorization Request for Fiscal Year 2014 and the Future Years Defense Program*, U.S. Senate, Subcommittee on Seapower, Committee on Armed Services, 8 May 2013, 14.

[53] Secretary of Defense Hagel quoted in Ronald O'Rourke, "Navy Littoral Combat Ship (LCS) Program: Background and Issues for Congress," 24 Dec. 2014, 13. See also "An Analysis of the Navy's Fiscal Year 2015 Shipbuilding Plan," Congressional Budget Office, Dec. 2014, 28–29.

[54] Congressional Budget Office, "An Analysis of the Navy's Fiscal Year 2015 Shipbuilding Plan," Dec. 2014, 29.

[55] Christopher P. Cavas, "In the End, LCS Dodges the Critics," *Defense News,* 11 Jan. 2015. www.defensenews.com/story/defense/naval/ships/2015/01/11/littoral-lcs-ssc-small-surface-combatant-ship-navy-work-mabus-mccain/21513247/ (29 Aug. 2016).

[56] *Hearing to Receive Testimony on Navy Shipbuilding Programs in Review of the Defense Authorization Request for Fiscal Year 2014 and the Future Years Defense Program*, 13.

[57] Assistant Secretary Stackley explained in some detail the problems that had bedeviled the *Gerald R. Ford* acquisition in testimony to the Senate Armed Services Committee in October 2015. He pointed to a change in the acquisition strategy documented in a December 2002 program decision memorandum as the source of most of the program's problems. See his comments in the hearing on *Procurement, Acquisition, Testing and Oversight of the Navy's Gerald R. Ford Class Aircraft Carrier Program*, 1 Oct. 2015, Senate Armed Services Comm.

[58] *Hearing to Receive Testimony on Navy Shipbuilding Programs in Review of the Defense Authorization Request for Fiscal Year 2014 and the Future Years Defense Program*, 12.

[59] Ibid.

[60] See Friedman, *U.S. Destroyers, An Illustrated Design History, rev. ed.*, 374, 422.

[61] Congressional Budget Office, "An Analysis of the Navy's Fiscal Year 2015 Shipbuilding Plan," Dec. 2014, Table 2, 4.

[62] Briefing, "USMC Force Structure Review," COL Russell E. Smith, Director, MAGTF Integration Division, Strategic Vision Group (CDD, CD&I) Headquarters, USMC, 30 Apr. 2011, slide 4. https://www.scribd.com/presentation/54644121/Marine-Corps-Force-Structure-Review-April-30-2011 (29 Aug. 2016).

[63] Ibid., slide 5. See also, "Reshaping America's Expeditionary Force In Readiness: Report of the 2010 Marine Corps Force Structure Review Group," 14 Mar. 2011. http://www.nationaldefensemagazine.org/blog/Documents/FSR_Final_14Mar11_ExecSum.PDF (29 Aug. 2016). Also *Crisis Response: Institutional Innovation in the United States Marine Corps*, LTCOL Brian

Bruggeman and Ben Fitzgerald (Washington, DC: Center for a New American Security, Nov. 2015). http://www.cnas.org/institutional-innovation-usmc#.V8S62GD6vcs (29 Aug. 2016).

[64] Robert P. Kozloski, "Marching Toward the Sweet Spot, Options for the U.S. Marine Corps in a Time of Austerity," *Naval War College Review*, vol. 66, no. 3 (Summer 2013), 14 and Fig. 2.

[65] Title 10, USC, ch. 507, sec. 5063.

[66] Robert P. Kozloski, "Marching Toward the Sweet Spot," 21.

[67] Interview, Bryan Clark with Thomas C. Hone, 9 Apr. 2015.

[68] Deputy Under Secretary of the Navy and Deputy Chief Management Officer, "Department of the Navy Business Transformation Plan, Fiscal Year 2013 & Fiscal Year 2012 Annual Report," approved by the Under Secretary of the Navy, 28 Dec. 2012, 3. http://www.doncio.navy.mil/uploads/0222UYF27728.pdf (29 Aug. 2016).

[69] Ibid.

[70] Ibid., 4.

[71] Ibid., 6.

[72] *Annual Reports of the Navy Department For the Fiscal Year 1930*, (Washington, DC: GPO, 1930), 1238.

[73] See "Spending Patterns of the U.S. Navy, 1921–1941," by Thomas C. Hone, *Armed Forces and Society*, vol. 8, no. 3 (Spring 1982), 443–62.

[74] Todd Harrison, *Analysis of the FY 2012 Defense Budget* (Washington, DC: Center for Strategic and Budgetary Assessments, 2011). See also *Planning for a Deep Defense Drawdown*, part 1, "A Proposed Methodological Approach," by Clark Murdock (Washington, DC: Center for Strategic and International Studies, 2012), 8–12. Both reports are cited in Robert P. Kozloski, "Marching Toward the Sweet Spot," 17.

[75] Deputy Under Secretary of the Navy and Deputy Chief Management Officer, "Department of the Navy Business Transformation Plan, Fiscal Year 2013 & Fiscal Year 2012 Annual Report," 10–11. http://www.doncio.navy.mil/uploads/0222UYF27728.pdf (29 Aug. 2016).

[76] Secretary of the Navy, "Department of the Navy Transformation Plan, FY 2014–2016," July 2014. www.navy.mil/secnav/secnav-dtp/opportunities.html (29 Aug. 2016).

[77] Ibid., 13.

[78] Ibid., 14.

[79] Ibid., 15.

[80] Ibid., 4.

[81] "Defense Headquarters: DOD Needs to Reassess Personnel Requirements for the Office of the Secretary of Defense, Joint Staff, and Military Service Secretariats," Government Accountability Office, Report to the Committee on Armed Services, House of Representatives, GAO-15-10 (Jan. 2015), 16.

[82] Ibid., Appendix VI, 64–65

[83] Ibid., 65, footnote a.

[84] Ibid., Appendix VI, 64–65.

[85] VADM Ted N. Branch, USN, "A New Era in Naval Warfare," U.S. Naval Institute *Proceedings*, vol. 140, no. 7 (July 2014), 19.

[86] Ibid., 20.

[87] Ibid., 21.

[88] Interview of CDR James K. Kuhn, USN (Ret.), by Thomas C. Hone, 26 Jan. 2015. VADM Branch was aware of the need to change the thinking of both types of officer, as his article in the July 2014 *Proceedings* made clear.

[89] Sydney J. Freedberg Jr., "US Has Lost 'Dominance In Electromagnetic Spectrum': Shaffer," *Breaking Defense*, 3 Sept. 2014. Besides his work in the office of the Asst. Secretary of Defense (Research and Engineering), Principal Deputy Shaffer had been the Executive Director of the very successful Mine Resistant Ambush Protection (MRAP) Task Force.

[90] VADM Ted N. Branch, "A New Era in Naval Warfare," 23.

[91] Ibid.

[92] ADM James Stavridis, USN (Ret.) and David Weinstein, "Time for a Cyber Force," U.S. Naval Institute *Proceedings*, vol. 140, no. 1 (Jan. 2014), 40–44. Note that the Department of Homeland Security is the agency responsible for leading any effort to protecting American digital systems that are not national security assets. See "Cyber Operations in DOD Policy and Plans: Issues for Congress," Catherine A. Theohary and Anne Harrington, Congressional Research Service, R43848, 5 Jan. 2015.

[93] MILPERSMAN 1611-020, CH-18, 30 Mar. 2007, 1. http://www.public.navy.mil/bupers-npc/reference/milpersman/1000/1600Performance/Documents/1611-020.pdf (29 Aug. 2016).

[94] Ibid.

[95] "Commanding Officer Detach for Cause Study," Naval Inspector General, 2004. http://www.secnav.navy.mil/ig/FOIA%20Reading%20Room/NAVINSGEN%20Commanding%20Officer%20Dismissed%20For%20Cause%20(DFC)%20Study%202004.pdf (29 Aug. 2016).

[96] "Commanding Officer Detach for Cause Study 2010," Naval Inspector General, 2010. http://www.secnav.navy.mil/ig/FOIA%20Reading%20Room/NAVINSGEN%20Commanding%20Officer%20Dismissed%20For%20Cause%20(DFC)%20Study%202010.pdf (29 Aug. 2016).

[97] "Commanding Office Detach for Cause Study, 2004, 4.

[98] Ibid.

[99] Ibid., 5.

[100] Ibid., 8.

[101] Ibid., 11.

[102] Ibid., 18.

[103] Ibid., 14.

[104] "Commanding Officer Detach for Cause Study 2010," i (Executive Summary).

[105] Ibid.

[106] Ibid., ii (Executive Summary).

[107] Sam Fellman, "High-Profile Firings in the Navy on the Rise," *Navy Times*, 3 Jan. 2011.

[108] Alex Jackson, "Annapolis Grads, Like Mids, Face Conduct Scrutiny," *The Capital* (Annapolis, MD), 31 Dec. 2012.

[109] CAPT Mark F. Light, USN, "The Navy's Moral Compass: Commanding Officers and Personal Misconduct," (Carlisle Barracks, PA: U.S. Army War College, 2011), 16.

[110] Ibid., 17.

[111] Ibid., 23.

[112] Richard P. Feynman, *The Pleasure of Finding Things Out* (Cambridge, MA: Perseus Books, 1999), 142.

[113] Interview, Bryan Clark with Thomas C. Hone, 9 Apr. 2015.

[114] Information Memo for Chief of Naval Operations from VADM Bill Burke, subj: OPNAV Realignment Final Report, 11 Sept. 2012, 57. In the collection of Thomas C. Hone.

[115] Interview, Bryan Clark with Thomas C. Hone, 9 Apr. 2015.

[116] Cameron Hawley published four acclaimed novels about business executives: *Executive Suite* in 1952, *Cash McCall* in 1955, *The Lincoln Lords* in 1960, and *The Hurricane Years* in 1968. *Executive Suite* and *Cash McCall* were made into movies.

[117] See Mark Mazetti, *The Way of the Knife: The CIA, a Secret Army, and a War at the Ends of the Earth* (New York: Penguin Press, 2013).

[118] Interview, Bryan Clark with Thomas C. Hone, 9 April 2015.

[119] OPNAVINST 3050.27, from: Chief of Naval Operations (N81), subj: Force Structure Assessments, 12 Feb. 2015. https://cryptome.org/dodi/2015/opnav-3050.27.pdf (29 Aug. 2016).

CHAPTER 20

Conclusion

*"... it is power, i.e., the ability to make something happen, that,
in the final analysis and however broadly defined, is the core of leadership."*
Robert Merton, in *The Contradictions of Leadership*

Introduction

So what has the Chief of Naval Operations become after a century? "Logistician in chief," using "logistics" in its broadest sense to include all the "costs" that CNO Greenert meant when he used the term "total ownership cost"? No. The CNO and OPNAV do not manage the acquisition process—one of the key elements of total fleet logistics—but do shape it in two very important ways: by developing the "requirements" for new systems and by providing funding as new systems are developed. Even in "the requirements process," however, other officials and other organizations matter. Major system requirements, for example, have to be vetted by the Joint Requirements Oversight Council. Of course. The whole point to the Goldwater-Nichols law was to shift initiative and influence from the separate military service staffs to the Joint Staff. The path to promotion ceased to run through OPNAV and instead ran through joint billets. In one sense, the advocates of a unified service won—not by merging the military services, but by luring the most talented and energetic officers to joint career paths.

This change in career paths undercut the influence of the service staffs. John Lehman saw this clearly. Why be a Secretary of the Navy when in fact the best officers—the raw material of influence in the Pentagon—would go to the joint commands and joint offices? Talent, like money, is a scarce commodity. Adding talent to money is a sure path to influence in Washington. Members of Congress who supported what became Goldwater-Nichols understood that, which is why the law preserved the military secretariats and the military service staffs as a "balance" against the strengthened Joint Staff. James Madison's lesson about dividing power was not lost on the supporters of Goldwater-Nichols. They left the programming process in the hands of the service staffs while placing the responsibility for planning in the hands of the joint organizations.[1]

One result has been the dominant influence of the Navy's programming office. The Joint Staff, under the guidance of the Secretary of Defense and the Chairman of the Joint Chiefs of Staff, produces a variety of scenarios—likely conflicts, given the state of the world. The programmers in the Navy build models of these possible conflicts in order to test the ability of the planned naval force to defeat its likely enemies. In a sense, it's like the plans in the 1920s and 1930s for the Orange war in the Pacific, which were checked against the war games at Newport and the annual fleet problems. It's as close to major war as the Navy can get in peacetime. One consequence of this process of "checking" the draft Program Objective Memorandum (POM) against today's conflict models is that it gives influence within OPNAV to the military officers and civilians who build the models. To balance that influence with another, recent CNOs have created DCNOs for requirements or for "wholeness." The fear of too much centralized authority has kept OPNAV's organization—its structure—in turmoil for almost a generation.

Historical Background

Military organizational reforms have tended to target the ills of the last conflict. After the Spanish–American War, energetic, reform-minded Army and Navy officers wanted more coordination of planning and operations. To get that coordination, they wanted to centralize authority and responsibility in senior officers serving under civilian cabinet secretaries. The Navy reformers and their allies in Congress also wanted to impose selection on the process of officer evaluation and promotion. After World War I, the naval reformers wanted greater control over industrial mobilization. After World War II, they wanted to revert to a peacetime organization but with a "catch." The "catch" was that the CNO would have greater authority.

Unfortunately, the post–World War II Navy reformers faced a formidable opponent in President Dwight D. Eisenhower, the former general who had participated in the sometimes bitter debates between the Army and the Navy during the war, and who did not want that to continue. Eisenhower supported the passage of the Department of Defense Reorganization Act of 1958, which rendered the service chiefs and their staffs subordinate to the secretaries of defense and their staffs. Under Secretary of Defense McNamara, it was civilian control with a vengeance. The service chiefs had no operational authority, though they kept their membership on the Joint Chiefs of Staff and therefore their access to the President. By 1986, however, with the passage of the Goldwater-Nichols Act, the service chiefs didn't even have the authority to do operational planning. The regional combatant commanders would do that. As this was being written, congressional committees, having watched the Defense Department wage war in the Middle East and Afghanistan, were considering changes to the relationship between the Secretary of Defense and the service secretaries and service chiefs, especially in the field of acquisition. Reform is again in the air. Maybe the authority of the CNO has been weakened too much.

Does the CNO Matter?

The answer is "yes," and the reason it is "yes" is because the Navy is the nation's constantly deployed force, whether you refer to the fleets steaming in international waters thousands of miles from the coast of the United States or to the ballistic missile submarines that cruise—also in international waters—quietly hundreds of feet beneath the sea. The Chief of Naval Operations does not command those forces, but the CNO must see to it that those forces are trained, manned, equipped, and so organized that they can carry out the directions of the President acting as commander-in-chief of the military forces of the United States.

As retired Navy Captain Peter Swartz has shown in a brilliantly conceived series of briefings, the shape and deployment of the Navy and the Marines has always changed to deal with the nation's interests and its strategies.[2] Today's Navy is not the same as the Navy of 1915, or the Navy of 1935, or the Navy of 1955. The Navy's structure and its patterns of deployment have been changed by its leaders *in response to* a number of factors, but especially to changes in national strategy. Across a century, from 1915 to 2015, the primary responsibility of the Chiefs of Naval Operations and their staffs has been to shape and field naval forces capable of supporting national strategy. As part of that effort, successive chiefs have worked to persuade the political leaders of the nation to support them as they have built and maintained those forces. CNOs have also altered the structure of OPNAV to suit the changes in the Navy's role in national defense and diplomacy.

In the pages to follow, we will first talk about the development of OPNAV as an organization. We will identify some patterns across OPNAV's 100-year history. Then we will focus on the Chiefs of Naval Operations. What skills does a CNO need? What experiences help make an officer a successful CNO? Indeed, what is "success" to a CNO? Have the answers to those questions changed over time? We will also look at the ways that a CNO can successfully direct an organization as large and complex as OPNAV has become while still fulfilling the responsibilities the CNO has outside of OPNAV—to the Secretary of Defense, the President, and the Congress. Finally, we will consider what "lessons" can be learned by examining the history of the office and the experiences of those who have held it.

OPNAV: Responding to Change

When OPNAV was created in 1915, the Chief of Naval Operations could not fulfill his responsibilities to the Secretary of the Navy without a staff of subordinates. Secretary of the Navy Josephus Daniels did not believe that the CNO needed a large staff. The technical specialists were in the Navy's bureaus. What value did the CNO's staff add to the task of directing the Navy and planning its future? Part of that answer is apparent from the January 1916 OPNAV organization chart. Three of the subordinate offices in OPNAV were concerned directly with improving the professionalism of the Navy. Target Practice and Engineering tested the ability of ships and their crews to perform their military functions; it developed and refined measures of performance. The Board of Inspection and Survey provided quantitative measures of ship capability.

Were new ships adequate? Were existing ships in need of repair? The Naval War College had two purposes. One was to prepare officers for high command. The other was to assist OPNAV planners by testing plans in war games and through the use of systematic analysis. For example, in 1916 the fleet was short of cruisers for scouting. Could destroyers fill that role? Could aircraft?

OPNAV was also "home" to new technologies, especially radio communications and aviation. Aviation would later move to its own bureau, but communications stayed in OPNAV. Radio messages quickly became the "web" (or network) that tied the Navy together. Breaking into the networks of other navies while protecting the Navy's own network also soon became an OPNAV responsibility. The Office of Naval Intelligence (ONI) gathered information on other navies but also became a sort of counterintelligence organization, with a very diverse portfolio. In addition, the CNO supervised the work of the naval district commanders because the naval districts existed to support the fleet. It was up to the naval district commanders to provide a variety of services, ranging from communications to drydocking. Only the officer who supervised the fleet's movements—the CNO—had the capacity to shift resources among the naval districts in a way that would adequately support the fleet.

OPNAV's structure remained stable through most of the 1920s and 1930s. In 1932, there were ten major divisions in OPNAV: War Plans, Intelligence, Material (dealing with Navy yards, ship repairs, and ship modernization), Ships' Movements, Fleet Training, Naval Districts, Inspections, Communications, Central (handling communications with the State Department), and the Naval War College.[3] The Naval War College was moved under the Bureau of Navigation in 1933, but as late as April 1941, the structure of OPNAV was basically the same as in 1932, with just two additions. One was a division for Naval Reserve Policy; the second was a division for "Interdepartmental Communication Liaison."[4] The peacetime size of OPNAV stayed relatively constant across the interwar years, ranging from 109 officers in June 1920 to 136 at the beginning of 1939. There were six admirals in OPNAV in 1929 and six ten years later.

However, the continuity of OPNAV's basic structure does not mean OPNAV did not mature as an organization between 1919 and 1939. Recall that the problem facing CNO Coontz, the second CNO, was to find a way to shape the Navy. He chose to do so through the development of war plans that then shaped the budget proposal sent to Congress. By the end of CNO Eberle's term, the planning function had become more sophisticated.[5] War plans were tested in the war-gaming process at the Naval War College, and operational-level maneuvers were tested in the annual fleet problems. OPNAV was at the center of a "feedback loop" that allowed the fleet to "learn" even in a time when expenditures on the Navy were dangerously small. Under the fifth CNO, Admiral Pratt, OPNAV was developing long-range shipbuilding plans as part of Pratt's response to the naval arms limitation policy of President Hoover.

After Admiral King became both Commander-in-Chief and CNO in March, 1942, however, OPNAV's structure was altered significantly. The Vice CNO, assisted by various aides and OPNAV's Central Division, handled liaison with the Army, the British staff in Washington, and the Navy's bureau chiefs. Under the vice chief was a sub-chief. Planners

(OP-12) and communicators (OP-20), along with the Naval Districts Inspection Board and the Board of Inspection and Survey, reported to that individual, along with the assistant CNOs for operations, information & security, and maintenance.

The other major change in OPNAV's structure during World War II was the creation of the Deputy Chief of Naval Operations (Air), or OP-03, in August 1943. Under the DCNO (Air) were offices for aviation planning, personnel, and training, plus Marine Corps aviation and the Naval Air Transport Service. The creation of OP-03 gave OPNAV a split personality. On one side were functional offices, such as those for intelligence, communications, fleet maintenance, inventory control, and base maintenance. Side-by-side with these functional offices were what might be termed "equipment" offices, including the DCNO (Air), an electronics office (OP-25, under the assistant CNO for Material), the Board of Inspection and Survey, the hydrographic office, the Naval Observatory, and the Naval Transportation Service.

This division was carried over into the postwar era. Executive Order 9635 of 29 September 1945 blended what had been the Commander-in-Chief's staff with that of OPNAV, creating six deputy CNOs—for personnel, administration, operations, logistics, air, and special (i.e., nuclear) weapons. The CNO was "the principal adviser [sic] to the President and to the Secretary of the Navy on the conduct of war, and principal naval adviser [sic] and military executive to the Secretary of the Navy on the conduct of the activities of the naval establishment." At Fleet Admiral King's insistence, the CNO was given "command of the operating forces comprising the several fleets, seagoing forces, sea frontier forces, district and other forces, and the related shore establishments of the Navy," though the CNO was also "responsible to the Secretary of the Navy" for the use of these forces in wartime. The CNO was also "charged, under the direction of the Secretary of the Navy, with the preparation, readiness and logistic support of the operating forces . . . and with the coordination and direction of effort to this end of the bureaus and offices of the Navy Department."[6]

The structure of OPNAV in January 1947 reflected the merging of the Navy's commander-in-chief with the CNO. There were the functional offices—deputy CNOs for personnel, administration, and operations—and the one platform deputy CNO (for air). The DCNO for Special Weapons had been eliminated and in its place was an assistant CNO's office for guided missiles. This was the post–World War II pattern—a mix of functional and platform deputy CNOs (vice admirals), plus various rear admirals and captains for special offices such as research and development and the Naval Reserve. This mix continued. In 1962, there were six deputy chiefs of naval operations—for personnel, fleet operations and readiness, logistics, aviation, plans and policy, and development. There were assistant chiefs for planning and programming, intelligence, and communications. In 1971, the six DCNOs were manpower, submarines, surface ships, aviation, logistics, and plans and policy. Because Congress deliberately limited the number of deputy chiefs, there were also six "directors" in OPNAV: electromagnetic programs, program planning, command support programs, antisubmarine warfare (ASW), strategic offensive and defensive systems, and research, development, test and evaluation (RDT&E).

By 1992, this basic mix of platform and functional offices had taken on a new form. The functional DCNOs survived: logistics, personnel, plans and policy, intelligence, and training. However, the platform "sponsors" (for aviation, surface ships, and submarines) were subordinate to the DCNO for "resources, warfare requirements, and assessments." There was also a new director—for space and for command, control, communications and computers. OPNAV's organization chart for November 2000 showed the split between N7 (DCNO for Warfare Requirements and Programs) and N8 (DCNO for Resources, Requirements and Assessments). The chart also showed a new N6, the Director of Space, Information Warfare, Command and Control. The former OP-06 (Plans, Policy, and Operations) was still a part of OPNAV, but its designation had changed to N3/N5. CNO Clark also created the post of Director of the Navy Staff, a vice admiral's billet directly subordinate to the Vice Chief of Naval Operations. By 2012, the six deputy CNOs were personnel, education and training, information dominance, plans and strategy, readiness and logistics, "integration of capabilities and resources," and "warfare systems."

There's a pattern here. Successive CNOs have changed the size and the structure of OPNAV in response to events and to the demands of war at and from the sea. In wartime, OPNAV grew—from 51 officers in January 1916 to 360 officers at the signing of the Armistice on 11 November 1918, and from 294 in April 1941 to 702 at the beginning of March 1942. Though OPNAV shrank after World War II—down to 276 billets in January 1947—it grew again for the Cold War. There were almost 1,400 officers and senior civilians serving in it in the early 1980s; they were led by two dozen admirals. If you divide the number of officers in OPNAV by the total number of officers in the Navy, you find the following ratios: .023 in 1929; .0195 in 1939; .117 in 1942; and .038 in 1986. The increased ratio for 1942 is no surprise. The ratio for 1986 is no surprise, either. For the Navy, the latter half of the Cold War was intensely technological as the navy of the Soviet Union challenged the U.S. Navy's dominance of the oceans. In response, successive Navy secretaries and CNOs (to say nothing of Admiral Rickover) tried very hard to recruit young people with educations in technology. They also tried to move the best of this group to positions of responsibility, both in the fleet and in OPNAV.

The Chiefs of Naval Operations

For some of the many below [the leader] in the hierarchy, he is secure, knowing, decisive, powerful, dynamic, threatening, driving, and altogether remote . . . At eye level, he is more often seen as filled with troubled doubts . . .

Robert Merton, in *The Contradictions of Leadership*

The CNO is the Navy's most senior officer, despite the fact that as of this writing he has no direct operational authority. The CNO's counterparts in the Air Force and Army are called chiefs of staff. That title would more accurately reflect the CNO's current power and responsibilities. But "chief of staff" would not reflect the full potential of the office. That potential—to shape the Navy and to influence national policy as well as Navy policies—is inherent in the CNO's position, and it is an attribute of the office that links CNOs across the century of OPNAV's existence.

If the potential in the office has survived a century of change, what personal characteristics have CNOs drawn on to exploit that potential? One is an understanding of how to lead a complex bureaucracy. This is not a skill easily learned because the learning is best done "on the job," and senior leadership jobs are scarce. For that reason, CNOs often learn how (or how not) to lead a bureaucracy by serving as a responsible subordinate on a senior officer's staff, as future CNO Ernest J. King learned by watching fleet commander Admiral Henry T. Mayo in World War I. Younger officers can also learn by taking on significant staff responsibilities, as future CNO William V. Pratt did while serving on the OPNAV staff as deputy to CNO William S. Benson in that same conflict.[7] Several more recent CNOs had experience as aides to more senior officers or served as executive assistants to a secretary of the Navy. Admiral Elmo R. Zumwalt had a great deal of experience of this sort, as did Admiral Carlisle A. H. Trost. It is also no accident that several Vice Chiefs of Naval Operations moved up to be CNO, including Admirals James L. Holloway III and Michael G. Mullen.

However, even the most experienced leaders—those with experience leading a bureaucracy—may find themselves frustrated by developments over which they have little or no control. CNO Frank B. Kelso II was caught off guard by the Tailhook scandal, and CNO George W. Anderson Jr. could not have anticipated the confrontations he would have with Secretary of Defense Robert S. McNamara over the multiservice fighter plane (TFX) aircraft and during the Cuban Missile Crisis. Yet it's essential for a CNO to be able to weather such incidents, as CNO Arleigh Burke was able to carry through several major initiatives—especially the Polaris missile system project—even after the Soviet Union's Sputnik space satellite launches had publicly humiliated the Navy's Vanguard satellite effort in the fall of 1957.[8] Any CNO walks a tightrope. Any number of events can upset the "balance" that every CNO strives to achieve between directing events and responding to them. With luck, a CNO will have been through enough to know how to react to surprises. It is also essential for a CNO to have the support of a President if and when crises occur.

CNOs have often been skilled at what might be called "public relations," but in fact this skill is the more sophisticated ability to shape perceptions of a situation in their favor. CNO Arleigh Burke was very good at this, as were CNOs Forrest P. Sherman and Elmo R. Zumwalt Jr. Sometimes a CNO comes up against a Navy secretary who's even better at it, as were Josephus Daniels and John Lehman. This "shaping of perceptions" skill is essentially political. It is a way of influencing how people see some aspect of the world in an effort to shape their thinking or their feelings. It requires a fine "touch"—the ability to know how and when to send a message to several audiences at once that will influence them all. Presidents often have this ability. If they do, then the incumbent CNO wants it used to the Navy's advantage.

CNOs also have to be able to recognize what really matters to them and to their programs and at the same time possess the ability to avoid being distracted. The need to focus on what really matters to the Navy is one reason CNOs form "inner" staffs. For example, CNO Elmo Zumwalt had an "inner staff" to assist him in developing the Navy's program and to communicate his

Figure 20-1. CNO Frank B. Kelso, with former CNOs at the Pentagon 19 October 1990. Those present are (from left to right): Admiral Carlisle A. H. Trost, CNO in 1986–1990; Admiral Thomas Hayward, CNO in 1978–1982; Admiral Elmo Zumwalt, CNO in 1970–1974; Admiral Arleigh A. Burke, CNO in 1955–1961; Admiral Kelso CNO in June 1990–April 1994; Admiral Thomas Moorer, CNO in 1967–1970; Admiral James Holloway, CNO in 1974–1978; and Admiral James Watkins, CNO in 1982–1986. (Photograph by Dave Wilson. Image NH 9667-KN)

concerns throughout OPNAV and the rest of the Navy. The "inner staff" could serve as a conduit to the staffs of the DCNOs, explaining the CNO's guidance and intent. The inner staff, the first of which may have worked for CNO William Pratt in 1930, could also alert the CNO to developments that he might otherwise not perceive—developments that were taking place outside the Navy or that were not captured in the routine process of developing the Navy's programs. In addition, the "inner staff" could act quickly; it was a creature of a specific CNO; it existed only for his use. The need for such a staff continues. It can be an important tool for a CNO. Indeed, small "inner" staffs called "commander's action groups" have proliferated. In 2015, all the military service chiefs and combatant commanders had them.

Bryan Clark, who served as head of Admiral Greenert's "Strategic Actions Group" (00Z) in 2012–2013, described what are likely to be the functions performed by such groups, no matter which CNOs the groups supported. The first function was "to help the CNO think through problems . . . by looking at things being presented to him—tying together different, disparate issues that are on his desk . . . and integrating [them] for him. It's all in his head, but he wants somebody else to be doing the same thing at the same time to back him up."[9] The second function was to identify things that required the personal attention of the CNO. As Clark phrased it, the small inner staff could identify issues "that he's not running into because nobody's bringing them up to him." Does this mean circumventing the routine chain of command? Yes, and so this "intelligence gathering" has to be done carefully, and with discretion. According to former DCNO Vice Admiral Robert F. Dunn, there is always the danger that the CNO may become isolated by a "palace guard" that "inhibits free communications" with the rest of OPNAV.[10] The third basic function was to serve as "translator": "You need people who have internalized what the CNO wants to do and can translate that [to others] on demand." At the same time, these "translators" must be accountable. If they substitute their message for that of the Chief of Naval Operations, they will do him a disservice and find themselves searching for another job. The fourth function was to study a problem on behalf of the CNO in a way that the CNO wanted it studied.

Any CNO must also be aware of and pay attention to the competition for position and prominence that takes place within the Navy. Officers dedicate themselves to a life of service. They also engage in serious contests to see which of them will get to the top. They will not get to the top if they ignore the need to make names for themselves within the fleet or impress the most capable senior leaders in the Navy and in the political world of Washington. To win the competition for the CNO's job, the aspirants must be outstanding operationally and also must be recognized as such. They must also gain the attention and the favor of mentors. The best of them will learn what creative leadership means through commanding at sea, working in a position of real executive responsibility within OPNAV, and often by serving as an aide to a Secretary of the Navy. They must. We must not forget that admirals—and especially CNOs—are constantly evaluated by their near-peers and by their subordinates. The competitive, ambitious admirals are well aware of this and act accordingly.

At the same time, however, CNOs must recognize that many capable officers deliberately escape competition for the rank of admiral by avoiding service in the Pentagon. They stay in the Navy and perform their duties well, even superbly, because they enjoy the service. They relish command responsibility and the chance to lead capable young men and women at, under, or above the sea. But the bureaucratic life of the Pentagon does not appeal to them. Staff work in "the five-sided building that talks" is something they do because they have to and not because they see it as a useful rung on the ladder to very high rank. Such officers are also often not attracted to the political life of Washington. Though this history does in fact focus on the officers holding the highest posts, these other officers should not be ignored. In some ways, they—along with the senior enlisted personnel—are the heart of the Navy.

Obstacles to a CNO's Leadership

The obstacles to any CNO's leadership are many. One is the presence of a strong willed and clever Navy secretary. John Lehman was just such a secretary. Another is a clever and bureaucratically skilled President. Franklin Roosevelt was just such a President. A third is an influential congressional leader such as Representative Carl Vinson. A fourth is a determined Secretary of Defense. Robert McNamara left his mark on the Defense Department, and, though he antagonized several CNOs, the Navy, in responding to his initiatives, eventually developed an effective programming office and skilled officers to man it. Civilian office-holders constrain what a CNO can do. They can also be allies. Much depends on what their agendas are, and whether a given CNO can perceive those agendas and react to them in a constructive way.

When Admiral Thomas Hayward was appointed CNO in July 1978, one of his priorities was mine warfare. In 1985, while serving as the Navy representative to a Defense Science Board study, Captain W. Spencer Johnson IV discovered that the Navy still lacked the sort of mine hunting and minesweeping systems that former CNO Hayward had advocated. Johnson, who then worked as a special assistant to Navy secretary John Lehman, documented the problem in a paper cleared by the DCNO for Surface Warfare. When Lehman read the paper, he—to use Johnson's words—"went ballistic," and demanded to know the truth. The capability to find and sweep mines was indeed lacking, and so Lehman called all the senior surface officers in the Pentagon into his office, "read them the riot act," and demanded that the DCNO for surface warfare complete a class of modern mine hunter/sweepers.[11] The first of the new ships (MCM-1, *Avenger*) was sent to the Persian Gulf in 1990 as part of Operation Desert Shield even before her trials were complete.[12] This case illustrates the two-sided nature of a service secretary's authority: it can be used to oppose or support a service chief's initiatives.

The basic obstacle to any CNO's leadership, however, has not been the authority of secretaries of the Navy. Instead, it's been the successive and gradual reduction in the CNO's command authority. At the end of World War II, Fleet Admiral King acted to eliminate the post of Commander-in-Chief, U.S. Fleet, and plant its powers in the CNO and his staff. Almost immediately, however, those powers were weakened. Eventually, once the Department of Defense Reorganization Act of 1958 (PL 85-899) was signed, the CNO's actual authority over the fleet was based on his personality, his standing with the President and other senior officials, and the ability of his staff (OPNAV) to produce plans for use by operational commanders.

As a consequence of the 1986 Goldwater-Nichols legislation (PL 99-433), the CNO lost even the authority to produce operational plans. The law defined the "function of the Office of the Chief of Naval Operations" as assisting "the Secretary of the Navy in carrying out his responsibilities."[13] The secretary's authority was broad, ranging from recruiting and training sailors to supplying the fleet, from military construction to maintaining the fleet's ships, planes, and submarines. Moreover, the secretary was immediately responsible to the Secretary of Defense for "the functioning and efficiency of the Department of the Navy," and the law even provided for the formal structure and authority of the secretariat, giving the office of the Secretary of the Navy "sole responsibility" for acquisition, auditing, financial management, legislative and public affairs, and information management.[14] In effect, through legislation and directives, the CNO has been moved farther and farther away from operations while not losing the responsibility to prepare the Navy for precisely those operations. At the same time, the regional combatant commanders have been moved closer to the programming process. As this study has pointed out, however, the planning horizon of the CNO is inevitably very different from that of any regional combatant commander.

Moreover, as a member of the Joint Chiefs of Staff, the CNO and his fellow military service chiefs must look across time, across geographic boundaries, and across strategic issues to provide a president with the best possible military advice. This gives a CNO the chance to become known outside the Pentagon in peacetime and in areas of endeavor where a CNO might not be expected to be competent. You see this in the case of CNO James Watkins, who after retiring from the Navy chaired a presidential commission studying the impact of AIDS on the American population. Watkins was also a successful Secretary of Energy. Former CNO Admiral James Holloway served in 1986 on a commission headed by the Under Secretary of Defense for Policy to develop "grand strategy" for the period from 1990 to 2010, and this was not the first time he had been called upon to serve in this way. In 1985, Holloway had served on President Reagan's Task Force on Combating Terrorism. In the spring of 1980, Holloway had chaired the Special Operations Review Group that investigated the failure of the Iranian hostage rescue mission. There is a pattern here, and it is not one unique to Admiral Holloway—and it shows how a CNO's access to senior officials may lead to further responsibilities.

Of course the classic case of a former CNO wielding great influence is that of Fleet Admiral William D. Leahy. Chief of the Bureau of Ordnance from 1927 to 1931, and Chief of the Bureau of Navigation from 1933 to 1935, Leahy, who also held major fleet commands, was CNO from January 1937 to August 1939, when he retired. In retirement, he first served as Governor of Puerto Rico (September 1939 to December 1940) and then as United States Ambassador to France, where, under the instructions of President Franklin D. Roosevelt, he worked to keep the French fleet out of the hands of Germany. Recalled to active duty in Washington in the spring of 1942, Leahy was, in July of that year, appointed by Roosevelt to serve as the President's chief military advisor and a member of the Joint Chiefs of Staff. He held that position through the remainder of the war, and he remained in the White House as President Harry Truman's chief military advisor until 1949.

It is ironic that, as CNOs have gradually lost the authority to act as naval commanders and planners, they have gained the opportunity to become national military leaders. Ironically, as their power of command has been deliberately reduced, they have become more visible as representatives of the Navy and the nation's military forces. This has been a mixed blessing, as CNOs Frank Kelso and Mike Boorda discovered. Any CNO, on assuming the office, must be prepared for surprises like the Tailhook convention scandal, for personal attacks in the media, and for unfair criticism. CNOs inhabit the spotlight, and they can be lightning rods for congressional and media criticism. They must beware of being too much or too little in the public's eye because so much of their leadership depends on their public reputations and their standings among their Navy peers.

In a March 1981 speech, former Secretary of Defense Harold Brown argued that there was a "basic limitation of any attempt to manage the Defense Department in an idealized textbook fashion." Brown conceded that

> To manage defense efficiently and at the lowest possible cost along presumed business lines of management and organization is a useful standard. But there are prices we cannot afford to pay for meeting it exactly. One is the abandonment of democratic

control. Another is the loss of a war. Defense cannot be 'managed' like a business. But it can be led so as to preserve most effectively our national security interests.[15]

These thoughts can be usefully applied to successive Chiefs of Naval Operations. At the same time, the pressure from Congress to manage the Defense Department and the Navy more like a business has added to the strain placed upon both CNOs and Secretaries of the Navy. This is because many members of Congress do not understand what former Secretary Brown understood well—that there is a significant difference between the armed services, where the highest authority is deliberately divided, and private enterprises, where that authority must be formally united if the chief executive officer of the enterprise is to be accountable to the stockholders.

The CNO Compared with a President

The CNO can be compared to the President. Both must govern within the American constitutional tradition, which means that they share power with other office holders. Because power is divided and shared among political leaders working within different institutions, most of those leaders—including both Presidents and CNOs—must argue from evidence, persuade, bargain, and communicate. Both always have competitors, allies, subordinates, and audiences. They must therefore support allies without being their tools, lead subordinates without appearing arrogant or thoughtless, and turn just the right face to the appropriate audience at the appropriate time. In an e-mail to the authors, Professor Donald Chisholm of the Naval War College, a long-time student of organizations in general and of Navy administration in particular, argued that any CNO, on taking office, would have to do the following:

- Negotiate the "boundaries" between the secretariat's authority and OPNAV's authority.
- Negotiate the "boundaries" with other senior naval officers in the fleets and the systems commands.
- Assess the "fit" between the existing organization and what outside organizations expect. A new CNO must consider whether and how OPNAV can deal effectively with demands and expectations from the White House, the Secretary of Defense, the Chairman of the Joint Chiefs of Staff, and the Congress.
- "Appoint the right senior naval officers to the right billets."
- Build and maintain "mutual trust" among other senior officers, the Secretary of Defense, the President, and the Secretary of the Navy.
- Construct a "dominant governing coalition" within the Navy.[16]

Note the key terms: "negotiate," "assess," "appoint," "trust," and construct "a dominant governing coalition." This is what the best political leaders do. It is leadership in a free society's government. There is of course a negative side to these actions. A leader can refuse to negotiate, or negotiate only from a position of strength. A leader can appoint or decline to appoint. A leader can build trust or act warily where that option is foreclosed. And leaders must always put together coalitions if they are to govern intelligently in a setting where power is deliberately divided and constrained.

Conclusion

In 1988, Penguin Books published military historian John Keegan's *The Mask of Command*, an analysis of senior military commanders from the time of Alexander the Great to World War II. In that book, Keegan argued that the "face" worn by military commanders had changed as war itself had changed. He also argued that a commander's "face"—his presentation of himself as battle or war leader—was something that every successful commander had to deliberately fashion. This point also applies to commanders in peacetime. They too have to fashion "faces" that are appropriate for the audiences they deal with.

In his memoir, *The Line of Fire*, Admiral William J. Crowe Jr., former Chairman of the Joint Chiefs of Staff, emphasized this point by recounting a suggestion he made at a party that what the Navy needed as a CNO was not a Navy officer but "a good lawyer." Crowe remembered telling the others at the party that "The biggest things that happen in the Navy are winning the battles in [the Joint Chiefs of Staff], the Secretary of Defense's office, the White House, and Congress. We have to convince all these people; otherwise we lose. What we need is a lawyer, preferably a New York lawyer. . . . He doesn't have to know a lot about the Navy, he has to know how to win arguments."

In response to objections from his listeners, Crowe asserted that "we ought to hire a professional advocate. If you want a Navy man, we can put a hat and a coat with some stripes on him." As Crowe recalled, "You could hear a pin drop." His basic point was that naval officers needed to be trained "to be advocates, because the large peacetime decisions are made in dialogue, debate, and argument."[17] It's therefore no accident that some of the more effective recent CNOs—Admirals Zumwalt, Trost, Mullen, and Greenert come quickly to mind—were articulate heads of the programming process in OPNAV before they became CNOs.

Yet this creates, as we have tried to show, a dilemma for the Navy. It sets up a conflict between how a CNO gains legitimacy within OPNAV and how a CNO gains and holds legitimacy outside OPNAV. To use the terminology of John Keegan, these are two different "faces" of command. One is acquired through operational command. The other is fashioned from what Admiral Crowe had seen as a younger officer working in OPNAV. It is the "face" of an advocate, a diplomat, a negotiator, and a conciliator. An effective CNO must wear at least these two faces, though the operator's "face" is one that must be based on a record compiled before wearing the CNO's four stars. The fact that Navy secretary John Lehman acted as though he had an "operator's" legitimacy, even though in the eyes of many officers he did not, was a major reason why he was often resented within the Navy. And the need of Navy secretaries for at least a piece of that operator's legitimacy is why so many of the recent secretaries have served in the Navy as young men.

Any CNO will find it easier to govern if he (or someday she) can build a dominant coalition of senior officers and civilians within the Navy.[18] If that's not done, then any major changes made by a CNO will probably not outlast his or her term of office. Today, a CNO's term is limited by law to one notional four-year term, with the possibility of a two-year extension.[19] Before 1986, it was limited to two years with the possibility of two additional two-year terms. Only CNOs

Burke and Clark have served longer than four years since World War II. This limited time in office poses a challenge to Chiefs of Naval Operations determined to make changes. They have to act fast, and to see to it that their changes "stick" they usually make those changes right at the beginning of their terms. It takes time to communicate a new vision, and it may take even longer to build a "dominant coalition" to support and sustain that vision. A CNO may enter office with a cluster of supporters, but almost every CNO has had to try to enlarge that cluster in order to make it a real governing coalition.

As we think this history has shown, this need to build a coalition makes the CNO like other political executives—governors and presidents. Like them, the CNO needs to persuade, argue, bargain, use the media, and negotiate. Like them, a CNO has to know who's already in his coalition, why they are there, and what it will take to keep them there. A CNO also has to know who his opponents are, why they are opponents, and what might shift them from opposition to support. But at no time should a CNO forget that every senior Navy officer's legitimacy is tied to his or her performance—or at least perceived performance—in operations.

There once was a deep seated hostility in the Navy toward "political" admirals, and some of that hostility lingers today. There are two understandable reasons for it. The first reason is that the Navy is deployed around the world at all times. To keep that up—to keep the Navy at sea armed and ready—officers and enlisted personnel must perform to a very, very high standard. This is an old requirement—the requirement that Navy officers be intensely professional. Admiral Benson, CNO during World War I, would have understood it even though the Navy he headed was not routinely "forward" deployed. In the not-too-distant past, this requirement was seen as being incompatible with being a "political" admiral. The second reason is that the Navy's ballistic missile submarine force holds a major portion of the nation's nuclear deterrent. That deterrent must be safe from destruction and at the same time be under the President's immediate control. Every CNO since Arleigh Burke has been responsible for seeing to it that this force is ready and capable. The Goldwater-Nichols Act of 1986 may have removed the CNO from the chain of command, but the CNO and his subordinates are responsible for making sure that the forces available to the combatant commanders function as required. The intent to fulfill this responsibility at an economical cost is what led to the creation of Fleet Forces Command.

Any CNO must also have an appreciation of the American constitutional tradition. If the Navy's tradition is a combination of peacetime professionalism and wartime aggressiveness, a CNO must understand that the nation's constitutional tradition emphasizes the division of powers, the subordination of the military to civilian authority, and respect for the notion that political life must be governed by written rules and unwritten but important customs. Recall how this was the case even in World War II, when the authority granted to CNO-COMINCH King was great but not so great that he could ignore civilian authority. Despite his fierce reputation and very real temper, King was no dictator. President Roosevelt was his patron and his boss, and King knew it—and also knew why it was so.

In World War II, a war when the nation's future was thought to be endangered, the political and military leaders of the country nevertheless generally respected the nation's constitutional tradition. In the Cold War, when the very existence of the nation was put at risk by nuclear weapons, the successors of the military and political leaders of World War II did the same. Now the nation faces some very real but different challenges to its interests and its values, and current and future CNOs must find ways to respond to those challenges within the larger American constitutional tradition. Put simply, the Navy must be effective, but it must also be legitimate, and it can only be legitimate if it stays within the bounds set for it by law and regulation. Any CNO must work within those bounds. Past CNOs have certainly done so. Clearly, to be effective a CNO must have a nice sense of the politically feasible and an understanding of the larger political world.

The CNO as Chief Programmer

The Planning, Programming, and Budgeting System (PPBS) was imposed on the Navy by Secretary of Defense Robert McNamara. At first the Navy resisted McNamara's reform. The Navy had its own systematic means of developing its budget. However, Secretary Fred H. Korth established the Office of Program Appraisal (OPA) in 1963 to complement the systems analysts working for Secretary of Defense McNamara, and then a similar office was created in OPNAV.[20] From that time forward, programming in the McNamara sense became an essential function—some would say *the* primary function—of OPNAV. CNO Elmo Zumwalt understood the importance of McNamara's programming concept, instituted programs to train Navy officers in this way of building a budget, and then used McNamara's concept within the Navy to achieve his own goals. In the years since, as we have shown, some of the brightest and most professional senior officers have had experience in Navy programming and programmatic analysis, and that commitment to the programming function has paid dividends to the Navy by allowing the service to deal with the reductions in the Navy's budget in the post–Cold War period.

One of the major criticisms of military service programming during the Cold War was that program costs were too often pushed into the "out years"—the years beyond the Future Years Defense Program. These costs were termed the "bow wave" because they looked like a wave of spending out ahead of the programmed years. For example, projected spending on Navy programs in 1984 was a bit less than $200 billion, while actual spending was closer to $140 billion. The projection for 1986 was close to $210 billion, while actual spending was closer to $165 billion. This "gap" between projected costs and actual spending did not seem to be a problem during the height of the Cold War because service programmers assumed that rising defense expenditures would continue to increase. But they did not continue to increase. In fact, they went in the other direction. The "gap" between projected and actual spending could not be justified by the assertion that the gap would be closed in the "out years." As CNO Vernon Clark pointed out, projections had to conform to political and strategic realities.

As the Cold War came to an end, programming had to be realistic. The future was one of declining or flat defense budgets. The curve of spending on the Navy rose through FY 1986 and then began to drop, slowly at first and then rapidly after 1989, reaching a low point in FY 2000. Navy program projections across these years steadily became more realistic; the gap between projected and actual spending narrowed dramatically. Put another way, the downsizing of the Navy (in terms of personnel and funding) was *managed*, and it was managed because Navy programming had become more sophisticated. Moreover, the downsizing was managed through negotiations with the Office of the Secretary of Defense (OSD), a task facilitated by the fact that programmers in both the Navy and OSD shared the same concepts, methodologies, and data.

Once the programming function became a CNO's major tool for directing the Navy and a major tool of the Secretary of Defense to direct the CNO, it attracted some of the most capable officers in the Navy. Programming had to be coordinated across the subordinate OPNAV offices, and that meant creating a "chief programmer"—an officer to reconcile disputes over elements of the program and work closely with the CNO to determine the trade-offs among the many different programs. But what happened when the CNO met with his chief programmer to work out the Navy's submission to the Office of the Secretary of Defense? Each DCNO would wonder whether his piece of the overall program was being given fair treatment. Put another way, the deputies and their assistants would be tempted to "game the system" in order to obtain the resources that they were convinced were necessary for their particular parts of the Navy.

To constrain that sort of "gaming," each CNO needed an "inner staff." In a small staff organization, the commander can impress his or her vision and direction on the organization personally. Once the staff gets to a certain size, doing that becomes impossible because the people several layers below the senior leader almost inevitably adopt the ideas and loyalties that matter within their pieces of the overall organization. To overcome the fragmentation of effort that results from this adoption of different loyalties, CNOs tend to rely on their "inner staffs," or even several inner staffs with different functions. Admiral Roughead, for example, had N00X to alert him to the technological, economic, and social changes that would affect the Navy in the future, but his successor, Admiral Greenert, eliminated N00X because he felt that he had no need for it. "OPNAV watchers" have learned to keep an eye on how any given CNO sets up his "inner staff" because its structure and composition can serve as a policy "weather vane."

The Influence of Strategic Issues

The history of OPNAV and the CNOs reveal three other sources of influence on CNOs and on OPNAV that need to be discussed. One is strategy; another is technology; the third is personality. We will deal with changes in strategy first. Even before OPNAV was created, President Theodore Roosevelt was intent on making what had been a minor navy into a major one. We have discussed what Roosevelt and his contemporaries in the U.S. Navy had to do in order for that to happen. They had to make the Navy modern in order for it to be effective. To make it modern, they had to create a truly professional officer corps, which meant that the line officers had to be merged with the engineering officers and all officers had to be subject to regular evaluation and periodic *selection*.

At the same time, Navy officers had to create those standards of evaluation necessary to make selection effective. This was not easy. It was not easy because the Congress directed the Navy to consider both effectiveness and fairness in evaluating and selecting officers. Members of Congress did not want *arbitrary* evaluation and selection. Officers needed to know how they would be evaluated and why, and they needed to know both how and why at stages in their careers that allowed them time to learn required skills and demonstrate their mastery of them. This story has been told in detail by Donald Chisholm in his *Waiting for Dead Men's Shoes*.[21] Inevitably, making the Navy modern in personnel terms required a bureaucracy dedicated to detailing officers to commands, developing training for them, evaluating their performances, and tracking their career moves. In turn, specific officers had to make sure that this bureaucracy was both effective—producing top-notch officers—and legitimate—untainted by corruption or favoritism.

Creating a truly modern navy also required engineers and scientists to make modern technologies such as electricity and radio compatible with ships at sea. The Navy also needed to develop new technology, such as model tests of a ship's hull resistance in specially built towing tanks and electrical circuits that could link the output of fire control optical devices with fuze setters used by gunners. The Navy also needed to produce what private industry would not make or could not afford to produce, including naval ordnance, advanced steam power plants for use at sea, and aircraft engine test equipment. A century ago, most of these technologies were monitored, encouraged, or applied by the Navy's bureaus, and so one of the most persistent issues in the history of the modern Navy became—and remains—the relationship of the Navy secretariat and the CNO with the bureaus (now "systems commands").

A modern navy also needed officers who could think creatively at the operational and strategic levels of national competition and conflict. Rear Admiral Stephen B. Luce understood this as early as 1884, when he became the first President of the Naval War College. There was a need for a place to learn how to think strategically and operationally, and that meant there would also have to be a place where that thinking could be applied to war plans, as indeed it was in OPNAV. There would also have to be a way or ways to test strategic and operational ideas. Hence the intensive use of war games and simulations at the Naval War College and eventually the use of major "fleet problems" before World War II to test tactical and operational ideas and give officers at all levels the opportunity to command in simulated conflicts.

A major navy had to have all of this—an educated and professionally competent officer corps, a sophisticated engineering and technology base, and officers capable of thinking at the operational and strategic levels of war. It became clear over time to many officers and some influential political leaders that the civilian Navy secretary and his assistants could not personally coordinate and direct all these activities. The Navy would need a professional military staff.[22] To avoid following the German model (or what was perceived as the German model) of a naval general staff, Congress created the Office of the Chief of Naval Operations. At the time of its creation, OPNAV was an experiment. Older officers knew what the bureaus were for and the sources of their authority and resources. They also knew what squadron commanders did.

By 1915, however, the Navy needed a senior officer heading a competent staff to orchestrate the Navy's development and operations. There would have been no need for that staff if there had been no need for a fleet, and there would have been no need for a fleet if political leaders of the United States had not become intent on making the United States a "world power."

After World War II, with the development and deployment of nuclear weapons, individual leaders in the Navy responded by creating a secure nuclear deterrent, the ballistic missile submarine. Again, a strategic change—in this case the deployment of intercontinental ballistic missiles coupled with the Soviet menace—led to a change in the Navy. The bureau system was altered in favor of the "project office," and even before that was done CNO Arleigh Burke made sure that Navy officers participated in the nuclear weapons targeting process. In the 1980s, CNO James Watkins became an influential advocate of ballistic missile defense as a means to offset large numbers of Soviet nuclear warheads. At the same time, Secretary Lehman promoted "the Maritime Strategy" as a conventional counter to the threat of a Soviet assault on Western Europe. In the 1920s and 1930s, the strategic opponent of the United States was Japan, and the Navy planned and built forces to deter or, if necessary, defeat Japan. After World War II, the opponent was the Soviet Union, and senior Navy officers—along with Navy secretaries such as Thomas S. Gates and John Lehman—planned and acted accordingly, altering the Navy's policies and its organization to deal with the new situation.

The Influence of Technology

Technology continues to have a strong effect on OPNAV and on CNOs. Indeed, the challenge of digital conflict—fought via the internet—may be more than current organizations can handle. But the challenge from technological change is not new. From its beginnings, OPNAV has had to deal with new and revolutionary technologies—submarines, aircraft, nuclear weapons, satellites, and computers, to name just a few. A century ago, the management of technology was a bureau responsibility. That's how aircraft were dealt with; creating the Bureau of Aeronautics, for example, gave aviation a "home" and a budget. But by the time nuclear weapons and long-range missiles were developed, what was needed was a way to coordinate across bureau boundaries, and the need for that coordination led to organizational "experiments" such as the creation of the Bureau of Naval Weapons (BuWeps). Later, the Space and Naval Warfare Command was established to tie digital technology to the Navy. OPNAV changed in parallel with changes to the bureaus and systems commands. Today the challenge is to coordinate across *service* boundaries—which raises the question, "Are the services the best form of organization to take advantage of modern technology?"

Creating an organization—an element perhaps of a larger bureaucracy—is a widespread way to deal with a new problem or the consequences of a new technology. But as problems or technologies proliferate, there needs to be some organizational restructuring or the primary leaders of the organization will be overwhelmed as those subordinates who are developing new technologies demand the attention of the CNO and his deputies and the resources that they control. The Navy's leaders traditionally dealt with this problem by decentralization—by turning problems over to the bureaus or to the commanders of forces at sea. But officers such as Bradley Fiske realized at least a century ago that there was a need for a senior admiral with proper staff support to monitor and direct this decentralized organization.

Several generations later, Elmo Zumwalt resorted to decentralization as a means of organizing OPNAV itself. His goal was to turn the so-called "Barons"—the DCNOs for Aviation, Submarines, and Surface Warfare—loose and coordinate among them. The problem with this structure was that it challenged the ability of a CNO to control the programming process. At best, the three warfare area staffs would build their pieces of the Navy's overall program and then debate among themselves how the funding "pie" would be divided, making the CNO as much an adjudicator as an instigator of policy and planning. At worst, the "Barons" would negotiate without the CNO's knowledge. As retired Admiral Bruce DeMars, a former DCNO for Submarine Warfare, admitted, "We [Barons] supported each other at meetings. Even if we didn't know anything about the other programs being discussed, we always supported each other." Was there "horse-trading" behind the scene? Yes. As DeMars recalled, "we weren't *totally* altruistic."[23] This role was not really what Admiral Zumwalt had in mind when he became CNO.

The need to produce a POM led to the creation of, first, OP-090 (with OP-96 as its systems analysis office) and then N8. But dissatisfaction with N8 led to the creation of N7 and later N9. There has been an almost constant back-and-forth between the desire to have an overarching program office (like N8) and the desire to divide that part of the OPNAV staff into an N8 programming office and an N7 "requirements" office. This back-and-forth (or point-counterpoint) is not a sign of confusion as much as it is a sign of frustration on the part of some CNOs. The repeated reorganizations within OPNAV suggest that programming inevitably becomes the stronger of the two "P's" in the Planning, Programming, Budgeting, and Execution (PPBE) (formerly PPBS) process, and that recent CNOs have sensed this and acted to balance programming with some sort of "requirements" office.

Indeed, the 2012 edition of the Naval Postgraduate School's *Practical Financial Management* handbook for Navy comptrollers acknowledged that the programming process within OPNAV was relatively straightforward when compared with the planning process that was supposed to "feed" it.[24] The complexity of the planning process in 2012, and the fact that the planning process leading up to the Defense Planning Guidance (DPG) was not done under fiscal constraints, prevented the planning process from blending smoothly into the programming process. As a result, most programmers did what they had already been doing, which was to focus on marginal changes to their programs.[25]

This did not mean that programmers in OPNV had relaxed schedules. Quite the reverse. As *Practical Financial Management* pointed out, OPNAV resource sponsors (N4, N2/N6, N86, etc.) had to spread available funds across "multiple programs" which required "multiple appropriations" in order to "meet capability requirements all [sic] within a fiscal constraint."[26]

In effect, as the staff of a resource sponsor adjusted the resources allocated to a given program, the resources given to other, related programs might have to change. As the authors of *Practical Financial Management* noted, "No one acts without affecting the plans [actually the programs] of others." The amount of work it took to balance resources across numbers of specific programs was intended to "maximize the likelihood that the most efficient, effective, economical, and worthwhile mix of money, manpower, hardware and capabilities results in the end."[27] Note that the phrase "strategically meaningful" was not used.

Balancing the need to develop force requirements against the need to put together workable programs is difficult. If there were an optimal solution that applied regardless of who was CNO, it would already have been found. No conscientious officer wants the POM-building process to be chaotic or confused or so punishing that competent officers run from it. The need is there and it won't go away. What the Navy needs has to be balanced against what the Navy has in the way of funds, people, and equipment; that balancing can't be done using some hands-off process. Instead, officers have to apply their professional judgments to programs with results that often entail significant risks. Then they have to defend those judgments. Should these programs be funded or not? Are the risks acceptable or not? If there is some risk that a given program will fail, how can that risk be estimated and the likelihood of failure reduced? These are not easy questions to answer, and so some of the most talented Navy officers have worked hard to develop ways to strike a "least-risk" balance among programs.

For example, in the 1990s the question facing CNO Frank Kelso and his N8, William Owens, was whether to scrap existing ships, thereby freeing up funds for research and development and new ship construction. If they went ahead with plans to reduce the size of the fleet, would Congress agree to allow them to invest in the ships and technologies that they believed the future fleet needed? Or would Congress balk at investing in new and more costly ships and systems? CNOs and Navy secretaries are like gamblers in a casino. They usually like to "play" to reduce risk. But how can they do that when the technology is changing rapidly, as it is today? Can "long-range planning" have any serious meaning in a digital world?

The story of Admiral Hyman G. Rickover makes this issue of how to adopt and control new technology particularly significant. Rickover was clever enough to plant one bureaucratic foot in a quasi-independent office (nuclear reactors) that reported to the CNO and his other bureaucratic foot in the Atomic Energy Commission, whose overseers were members of Congress. Over time, three factors gave him influence within the Navy rivaling that of the CNO. The first was Rickover's careful and thorough cultivation of congressional support. The second was his ability to attract many of the best and brightest younger officers in the Navy. The third was the performance of his organization: no Navy nuclear reactors installed in operational ships or submarines failed catastrophically. The success of his organization added to its influence. So, too, did Rickover's ability to influence Navy programs, an influence he exercised through Congress. But it was obvious what the weakness of Rickover's strategy was. It depended very much on him. What would happen when he was too old to serve?

Admiral Rickover had thought that issue through. He realized that he had to stay in his post long enough to make what retired Rear Admiral David R. Oliver has termed "cultural change." It would take a generation for Admiral Rickover to make that change, and he did so, knowing that his long-term goal was to instill a culture of "engineering competency" in the submarine force and perhaps in the Navy generally.[28] But there were other competencies that the Navy needed, including tactical prowess and creative strategic and operational thinking. Several successive CNOs and Secretary Lehman knew that and were determined to counter Rickover's influence. There was such a thing as being too *narrowly* successful.

Personalities

Working in the Pentagon can be boring, exhausting, and exasperating. Civilians in OPNAV, working at the same basic routines year after year, often envy the naval officers and enlisted personnel who cycle through Navy spaces in the building. The civilians are also subject to the pressures, frustrations, and challenges that sometimes vex and always tire officers detailed to the OPNAV staff. The danger for civilians is that they will become jaded and even cynical. The humorist Dave Barry once said that it wasn't true that men were "from Mars and women were from Venus." No, he said, men were from Mars and women were like huge comets crashing into Mars. In some sense, Navy officers detailed to OPNAV often "crash into" the civilians in OPNAV.

Officers usually roll into OPNAV fresh from the fleet, fresh from some of the most exhilarating and satisfying (and even incredibly dangerous) experiences of a lifetime, only to find their days taken up by the tasks required to produce the Navy's POM, or by the need to support and serve superior officers preoccupied by budget issues, or by the need to prepare for the next roles and missions review, or for the next iteration of the Navy's proposed 30-year shipbuilding plan. How these officers react to this dramatic change in professional work often shapes how they deal with the career civilians who exist to train, assist, and guide them. There was, for example, a problem in the mid-1990s when commanders began moving into positions in N8 that had been previously occupied by captains. The younger officers lacked experience, and apparently some found it difficult to take guidance from more experienced civilians.[29]

Work in a bureaucratic hierarchy is often very different from work under a command hierarchy. In operations, delegation is essential. Officers and senior enlisted personnel must be always prepared for emergencies and for unanticipated crises. No written guide can prepare them for all contingencies. On 12 October 2000, for example, *Cole* (DDG-67) was attacked by suicidal terrorists while refueling in Yemen. The terrorists detonated a large bomb against the port side of the ship, blowing in the ship's hull. Though 17 members of the crew were killed and 39 injured, the crew, under the leadership of *Cole*'s captain, Commander Kirk Lippold, kept the ship afloat. One minute *Cole* was at peace; the next minute, she was at war. Only prompt action by officers and enlisted personnel kept the ship from sinking after the surprise attack. This ability to respond is precisely what the operating Navy trains for—action. Inside the Pentagon, by contrast, what usually matters is a briefing, and briefings have to be carefully crafted. In the

OPNAV of the 1930s and even the 1950s, what often mattered was a paper. Who could make a succinct argument or raise a critical issue in a few paragraphs? By the mid-to-late 1960s, the issue paper was being replaced by the issue briefing, and soon after that information papers were also replaced by briefings, many of which were not "brief" at all.

In operations, subordinates show what they can do through action, deliberate and careful operations planning, and leadership of those they are responsible for. Junior officers either learn to lead and demonstrate their professional skills or they leave the service. In the Pentagon, junior officers are often not allowed any discretion. They usually make their marks (if at all) by working long hours, fashioning, refashioning, and refashioning yet again programmatic details or briefings for superiors. If they are fortunate, they get to work for an outstanding superior and "learn the ropes."

It's no accident that the recent CNOs—from Trost to Greenert—spent time as responsible and hard-working leaders of the process of building the Navy's program submission to the Office of the Secretary of Defense. That's an essential task. If they are fortunate, younger officers in OPNAV also get time to work with officers in the other services. If they are really fortunate, the younger officers, including rising young rear admirals, learn what OPNAV does from senior civilians. Our history has necessarily focused on the CNOs and Navy secretaries. But what makes OPNAV progress from day-to-day is a small army of younger officers, experienced civilians, and contractors who do the actual detail work.

But is it all a grind? Not necessarily. CNOs and their subordinates must retain their senses of humor. Recall then-Captain Pratt's account of dashing into a female typist during World War I. She did not realize who he was and told him off. He could only smile and hurry on. Or the unnamed admiral, in uniform, who was standing alone one evening at the entrance to New York's Algonquin Hotel in the late 1920s. The slightly inebriated humorist Robert Benchley emerged from the hotel, mistook the admiral for the hotel doorman, and asked the admiral to call him a taxi. The officer replied that he was an admiral, not the doorman. Benchley came back with, "Very well, then get me a battleship."

Retired Navy Captain John Byron, an accomplished diesel submarine commander, was the executive assistant to then-Rear Admiral Frank Kelso when Kelso was head of the Office of Program Appraisal in the Navy secretary's office. Byron had to schedule the first Boston, Virginia, conference with Secretary Lehman that the new CNO, Admiral James Watkins, attended. Watkins planned to fly by helicopter with the Commandant of the Marine Corps to a small airstrip in Culpepper, Virginia. From there the two were supposed to be driven to Boston. But the driver and car did not appear. The two senior officers were left standing in their full uniforms at the airstrip. Then, according to Byron,

> A Culpepper volunteer fireman who'd been standing by at the field . . . saw them and asked if he could give them a ride . . . They jumped on it and got driven to the Boston conference . . . both sitting in back in the bed of an old pickup truck, Watkins ready to kill someone and the Commandant laughing . . . No wonder Watkins may have been a bit rattled.[30]

Personalities matter. A "hard charger" from the fleet may be dismayed by OPNAV's routines and procedures and may even go so far as to swear that he or she will never take a position there again. Or an officer may have to work with a Navy secretary whose outlook on the Navy is very different from his or her own. But these different personalities have to work within (to use Professor Chisholm's term) "boundaries." They have to establish "working relationships." They have no other choice. OPNAV must work. The staff must manage the organizing, training, and equipping of the fleet under the direction of the Secretary of the Navy and the Navy secretariat. It must produce the program that the Secretary of Defense's staff needs, the budget that Congress needs, and the "vision" that the Navy needs. The CNO must develop the policies that guide the planning and programming that OPNAV does, and the OPNAV staff must support those policies.

Bureaucracy

At the end of the Cold War in December 1991, the government of the United States had to decide what to do with its huge military establishment. The focus of that effort was on safely downsizing—on avoiding the sort of massive and rapid demobilization that had been done deliberately after World War II. However, those involved in the downsizing seemed to forget that the demobilization after World War II was accompanied by an effort to revamp the organization of national defense. Indeed, you can see the congressional investigation of the Pearl Harbor attack (November 1945–June 1946) as part of a larger effort to learn how to restructure that organization. The products of that effort included the National Security Act of 1947 and the National Selective Service Act of 1948. Both were attempts to codify the lessons of World War II.

Similarly, the Department of Defense reorganization acts of 1958 and 1986 were efforts to better structure the nation's defense organization for the Cold War. The changes to the law were based upon lessons learned in using the existing structure. However, at the end of the Cold War, the national security structure finally put in place to wage the Cold War was largely left in place.

The nation's forces were reduced, but its defense bureaucracy was not revamped. The Goldwater-Nichols legislation had left the structure and authority of the Office of the Secretary of Defense essentially unchanged. However, the law had added to the authority of the Chairman of the Joint Chiefs and to the authority of the Joint Staff. The importance of the law became clear when it was the Chairman, Army General Colin Powell, who presented the "Joint Chiefs and regional commanders" with the concept of the "Base Force" in February 1990. Neither CNO Admiral Carlisle Trost nor the OPNAV staff had participated in the development of the "Base Force" concept, and Trost believed that Powell's recommendation of a reduced Navy force structure was inadequate. As retired Navy officer Steven Wills observed, the Chairman "rather than the CNO or even the Secretary of the Navy made the recommendation to Congress and the president about what naval forces would be retained."[31]

Thus was the prediction of John Lehman fulfilled? Goldwater-Nichols had removed control of the Navy's force structure from both the CNO and the Secretary of the Navy. However, as retired Captain Robert C. Rubel, a former head of the Center for Naval Warfare Studies at the Naval War College, put it, the collapse of the Soviet Union made a dramatic reduction in the Navy's strength seem reasonable. The great "threat" of the Cold War went away with the official end of the Soviet Union in December 1991. In such a situation, strategy gives way to "competition among the services for a share of the shrinking defense budget," a change that can only add (and did add, as we have shown) to the influence of OPNAV's skilled programmers.[32]

Because of the stronger role given them by Goldwater-Nichols, the unified and specified commanders increased the sizes of their staffs. The work to implement Goldwater-Nichols was carried on, as though a structure designed for the Cold War was suited well for the post–Cold War world. But was it? Is it? From the point of view of a Chief of Naval Operations, the answer has to be "no." From the CNO's perspective, there are too many layers—too many organizations and individuals with authority. That made sense during the Cold War when it was essential to avoid conflicts that could escalate into a major or nuclear war between the United States and the Soviet Union. But it may well be a mistake now, when the need is not to restrain action but to initiate it quickly and then rapidly assess its effects.

Go back to the beginning of OPNAV. In *United States Navy Regulations, 1920* (1941 edition), the CNO was

> charged, under the direction of the Secretary of the Navy, with the operations of the fleet, with the preparation and readiness of plans for its use in war, and with the coordination of the functions of the Naval Establishment afloat . . . All orders issued by the Chief of Naval Operations in performing the duties assigned him are performed under the authority of the Secretary of the Navy, and his orders are considered as emanating from the Secretary and have full force and effect as such.[33]

The chain of command was very short—from the President to the Secretary of the Navy and then to the CNO. That made sense in peacetime, especially before World War II changed the strategic role of the United States.

However, thoughtful critics inside the government and out argued that both the President and the Secretary of the Navy lacked adequate staff support given their great responsibilities, *even in peacetime*. That is, the short chain of command was a burden, even a hazard, without adequate staff support. When World War II came, all bets were off. The Navy's command structure changed dramatically, though the basic concept at its foundation—civilian control—did not, which led to a series of disputes between CNO-COMINCH King and Navy secretary James Forrestal during and immediately after the war. After the war, those disputes were resolved mainly in favor of the Secretary of the Navy.

Then, after 1958, it was clear where the real authority lay—in the Secretary of Defense and in the Secretary's staff. The 1958 law altered the respective authorities of the Secretary of Defense and the service secretaries but it didn't eliminate the latter. The secretariat stayed; its authority was given firm legal basis in 1986. As we have noted, pulling the CNO out of the command chain and eventually replacing the CNO with unified and specified commanders in 1986 led to a further weakening of the CNO's authority (even over acquisition) and yet did not make the CNO's job any easier because what might be best referred to as "the chain of decision-making" never shrank. It just grew in bulk. There were more offices and individuals at each link of the chain. Bureaucracies exist to get things done. From the CNO's perspective, however, the current national security bureaucracy may seem to be designed to do the opposite.

The CNO as Actual and Symbolic Leader

Like the President, the Chief of Naval Operations is an actual and symbolic leader. Like the President, the CNO has definite responsibilities. The CNO is also responsible for the image of the Navy in the minds of citizens. Weakening the operational authority of the office of the CNO and the standing of the service chiefs in the Joint Chiefs of Staff has forced individual CNOs to rely on what are essentially political skills. In 1959, veteran Washington journalist Allen Drury's *Advise and Consent* appeared to rave reviews and became a best seller, winning the Pulitzer Prize for fiction in 1960.[34] In one scene from the book, an influential politician watching a president deal with a controversial issue decides that the president's tactic is "both politically perceptive and quite symbolic of the government in which it occurred." It was "a perfect democratic solution, not wholly satisfying anybody, not wholly antagonizing anybody . . . not good, not bad; pragmatic, realistic, sensible . . ."[35] If that is a description of presidential decision making in a democracy, then can it apply also to the Chief of Naval Operations?

If the CNO were not a symbolic leader, the answer would be "yes." However, the CNO, like any President, is also the representative of the Navy as a powerful symbol. A CNO may draw on the positive effects of that symbol, just as a President draws support from the symbols of the nation. At the same time, though, the CNO's symbolic role can be a trap. If enough citizens perceive that there is something wrong with the Navy, as so many did after the Tailhook incident, then the CNO may find influence fading like a sand castle left to the mercy of the incoming tide at the seashore. Or, as may have been the case with CNO Michael Boorda, the harsh spotlight of adverse publicity can rob an individual of the self-respect so necessary in a leader who's built a reputation for competence and integrity.

How can a CNO combine pragmatism and bureaucratic skills with a reputation as an operator and the ability to inspire the whole naval service, or even a sizeable segment of the nation? Consider World War II: What U.S. Navy leader comes to mind? Commander-in-Chief and CNO King? Not often. Instead, the admiral who comes to mind is William Halsey, a hard-working and talented professional who had also developed the ability to create an aggressive, even pugnacious, "mask" of command. Who can forget his message to the South Pacific Force before the Battle of the Santa Cruz Islands in late October 1942: "Attack—Repeat—Attack"?[36] Yet there would not have been much of anything to attack *with* if it hadn't been for the efforts of bureau chiefs like Rear Admiral John Towers or the Deputy CNO Vice Admiral Frederick Horne.

To a great degree, the CNO has been deprived of both actual and symbolic authority. At the same time, the CNO is still the highest ranking officer in the Navy. If the CNO weren't, then what Secretary of the Navy, what Secretary of Defense, or what President would listen? Any successful CNO will draw on what authority is left in the office to improve the Navy and to shape the public's image of the Navy. But what authority is left? For starters, CNOs can change the structure of OPNAV and the patterns of work within the organization. This history has shown that OPNAV has been deliberately shaped—and reshaped—by CNOs trying to improve its ability to support them. In addition, the CNO can influence promotions as well as the Navy's POM and budget. Like a President, the CNO can also "go to the people," visiting the fleet and shore installations, using his or her personality to influence the sailors and the civilians who are the Navy. The CNO can also build personal relationships with a President and members of Congress, and, in so doing, influence more than just the Navy. Finally, a CNO can "set the tone" of Navy service.

In short, the position of Chief of Naval Operations offers opportunities for any intelligent, persuasive, and articulate leader. The story of OPNAV and the CNOs is full of drama, even if that drama was not or is not apparent to outsiders. How is the fleet to be organized? Where are sailors to come from? How are they to be trained? What equipment does the Navy require, and in what quantities? Who will design and build the ships, submarines and aircraft, and how will all this sophisticated equipment be maintained? The issues go on and on, and it has been the responsibility of a succession of CNOs and members of the OPNAV staff to deal with them. The CNO's authority may have declined. The CNO's accountability has not, and therefore any successful CNO must find a way to involve many others in the work of leading the Navy.

If the CNO doesn't do that, then others—a Secretary of the Navy, or a Secretary of Defense, or a President—will lead and shape the Navy. As recent CNOs have recognized, however, the Navy draws on American society. As American society changes, the Navy must change with it *without losing its effectiveness*, and that is a great challenge. Ultimately, the Navy fights, and the sailors and civilians who *are* the Navy must be prepared for that, and they must not allow other goals to impede the will or the ability of the Navy to fight the nation's enemies and defeat them.

Notes

[1] It took several years after the passage of the Goldwater-Nichols bill for the combatant commanders' staffs to fully assert their legal responsibility to plan major regional operations. An illustration of this point is the Air Staff's Checkmate organization's role in planning the air campaign for Operations Desert Shield and Desert Storm. See Alexander Cochran, et. al., *Gulf War Air Power Survey, Vol. I, Planning* (Washington, DC: Dept. of the Air Force, 1993).

[2] CAPT Peter M. Swartz, USN (Ret.), with artwork by Karin Duggan, S*ea Changes: Transforming U.S. Navy Deployment Strategy, 1775–2002* (Alexandria, VA: Center for Naval Analyses, 31 July 2002). See also Peter Swartz (with Karin Duggan), *The U.S. Navy in the World (1970–2010): Context for the U.S. Navy Capstone Strategies and Concepts* (2 volumes, Center for Naval Anal-

yses, 2011), and Swartz (with Duggan), *U.S. Navy Capstone Strategies and Concepts (1970–2010): Comparisons, Contrasts, and Changes* (also 2 volumes, Center for Naval Analyses 2011).

[3] *Navy Directory*, 1 Oct. 1932, Bureau of Navigation (Washington, DC: GPO, 1932), 193.

[4] *Navy Directory*, 1 Apr. 1941, Bureau of Navigation (Washington, DC: GPO, 1941), 356.

[5] In the second volume of his history of the Office of Naval Intelligence (*Conflict of Duty, The U.S. Navy's Intelligence Dilemma, 1919–1945* [Annapolis, MD: Naval Institute Press, 1983], 17), Jeffery M. Dorwart noted that Coontz's director of naval intelligence had "mastered the naval intelligence dilemma by balancing nicely between secret operations and traditional strategy and information."

[6] *Manual for the Office of the Chief of Naval Operations*, ch. 1, "General Statement of Duties," OPNAV-P21, 1-100 (Nov. 1945), Historic OPNAV Org Manuals File, OPNAV Organization, Feb. 42–May 48, Folder, N09B1.

[7] For King's experience and its implications, see "A King's Navy: The First World War Education of Fleet Admiral Ernest J. King," by David Kohnen, U.S. Naval War College, a paper presented at the 2015 McMullen Naval History Symposium, U.S. Naval Academy, Annapolis, MD, 18 Sept. 2015. In the collection of Thomas C. Hone.

[8] Thomas, *Ike's Bluff: President Eisenhower's Secret Battle to Save the World*.

[9] Bryan Clark, interview, with Thomas C. Hone, 9 Apr. 2015.

[10] Dunn, *Reminiscences*, Interview No. 7, 26 Feb. 1996, by Paul Stillwell, 581.

[11] CAPT W. Spencer Johnson IV, interview, with Thomas C. Hone, 26 July 2016.

[12] Despite the minesweeper's presence, two combatant ships were seriously damaged: *Tripoli* (LPH-10) and *Princeton* (CG-59). One modern minesweeper was simply not enough to shield the many Navy ships operating in the Persian Gulf.

[13] 10 USC 5031, part (a), 1986. However, 10 USC 5033 established the term of the CNO as four years, thereby breaking the pattern of two-year appointments (with the option of a second two-year term) to the post of Chief of Naval Operations.

[14] 10 USC 5013 and 5014, 1986.

[15] Entry for Harold Brown in *Wikipedia*, 19 Oct. 2014.

[16] Email from Prof. Donald Chisholm, Naval War College, to Thomas C. Hone and Curtis Utz, 28 Feb. 2015.

[17] ADM William J. Crowe Jr., with David Chanoff, *The Line of Fire* (New York: Simon & Schuster, 1993), 44–45.

[18] See "The Business Firm as a Political Coalition," by James G. March, *The Journal of Politics*, vol. 24, no. 4 (Nov. 1962), 662–78.

[19] 10 USC 5033.

[20] Kauffman, *Reminiscences*, vol. I, 578–95.

[21] Chisholm, *Waiting for Dead Men's Shoes*.

[22] See "Memorandum on General Staff for the U.S. Navy," by CAPT H. C. Taylor, USN, U.S. Naval Institute *Proceedings*, vol. XXVI, no. 3 (Sept. 1900), 441–48.

[23] DeMars, *Oral History*, Interview no. 4, 24 May 2012, by Paul Stillwell, 203.

[24] Lisa Potvin, ed., *Practical Financial Management: A Handbook for the Defense Department Financial Manager*, 11th ed., revision 1 (Monterey, CA: Naval Postgraduate School, Graduate School of Business & Public Policy, 2012), 49.

[25] Ibid., 53–54.

[26] Ibid., 58.

[27] Ibid.

[28] RADM David R. Oliver, *Against the Tide, Rickover's Leadership Principles and the Rise of the Nuclear Navy* (Annapolis, MD: Naval Institute Press, 2014), 123.

[29] Off-the-record conversations of Thomas C. Hone with OPNAV and NAVAIR personnel.

[30] Email, from CAPT John Byron, USN (Ret.), to Thomas C. Hone, 4 Mar. 2010.

[31] Steven Wills, "The Effect of the Goldwater-Nichols Act of 1986 on Naval Strategy, 1987–1994," *Naval War College Review*, vol. 69, no. 2 (Spring 2016), 29.

[32] Robert C. Rubel, "Response to Steven Wills's 'The Effect of the Goldwater-Nichols Act of 1986 on Naval Strategy, 1987–1994': Some Missing Pieces," *Naval War College Review*, vol. 69, no. 3 (Summer 2016), 166.

[33] *United States Navy Regulations, 1920* (1941 edition), Article 392.

[34] Allen Drury, *Advise and Consent* (Garden City, NY: Doubleday, 1959).

[35] Ibid., 612–13.

[36] Samuel Eliot Morison, *History of United States Naval Operations in World War II, Vol. V: The Struggle for Guadalcanal* (Boston: Little, Brown, 1950), 204.

EPILOGUE

Toward the end of Admiral Jonathan W. Greenert's time as the Chief of Naval Operations, there was growing criticism of the strategic planning process within OPNAV. In October 2014, for example, Representative J. Randy Forbes (R-VA), Chairman of the Seapower and Projection Forces Subcommittee of the House Armed Services Committee, said publicly that the Navy needed a long-term strategy. His argument echoed that of Arthur H. Barber III, the recently retired deputy director of N81, OPNAV's Assessment Division, in a May 2014 article in the U.S. Naval Institute's *Proceedings*.[1] In June 2015, members of the Naval Postgraduate School issued "Navy Strategy Development: Strategy in the 21st Century," a study written "in support of" OPNAV's strategy and policy division (N3/N5).[2] In the spring 2016 issue of the *Naval War College Review*, retired Navy officer and Naval War College graduate Steven Wills argued that the Goldwater-Nichols Act had taken the responsibility for naval strategy away from OPNAV and "effectively dispersed the naval service's informal but highly effective cohort of strategic experts . . ., removed them from naval control, and scattered them in assignments on the Joint Staff and the regional and functional commanders' (CINC) staffs."[3]

These statements and arguments were both a sign of concern and a call to action. Admiral Greenert's successor, Admiral John M. Richardson, alluded to likely action in his "commander's intent," issued in January 2016 as "A Design for Maintaining Maritime Superiority," when he noted that there was a need for a comprehensive "assessment of the security environment."[4] On 18 October 2016, CNO Richardson announced that as of 1 October 2016 the "Navy headquarters staff (OPNAV) realigned to develop a Program Objective Memorandum (POM) process" that would be "transparent, collaborative and [an] efficient culture of decision making."[5] The process would have "three overlapping phases," the first of which was "A Strategy Phase, . . ., in which the Deputy Chief of Naval Operations (DCNO) for Operations, Plans and Strategy (N3/N5) is the supported DCNO and all other DCNOs, the Fleets, and Budget Submission Offices (BSOs) are supporting."[6]

Would this change solve the problem that the Navy's own strategists and Representative Forbes had pointed to? Following the Strategy Phase already described was a "Requirements-Program Integration Phase" led by N9 and then a "Resources Integration Phase" led by N8. Would this revised process actually produce "a strategy-based, fiscally balanced and defendable Navy Program . . ., which appropriately implements [Office of the Secretary of Defense] fiscal and programming guidance, addresses [Secretary of the Navy] and CNO priorities, and achieves the best balance of strategic guidance as provided" by the CNO?[7] Richardson's directive certainly emphasized the role of N3/N5 in working with the Under Secretary of Defense for Policy (USD[P]). The latter's office was responsible for writing and updating the formal guidance issued by the Secretary of Defense to the military services. USD(P)'s planning was supposed to draw on military service level evaluations of "the operational utility and cost effectiveness of major decision options."[8] Formally, then, CNO Richardson's reorganization was in line with the directive from the Office of the Secretary of Defense. Whether Richardson's change will work, however, and whether it will persist into his successor's time as CNO, are obviously questions that can only be answered with the passage of time.

Notes

[1] Sam LaGrone, "Randy Forbes to CNO Greenert: 'The Navy desperately needs a strategy,'" *USNI News*, 1 Oct. 2014, http://news.usni.org/2014/10/01/randy-forbes-cno-greenert-navy-desperately-needs-strategy. Arthur H. Barber III, "Rethinking the Future Fleet," U.S. Naval Institute's *Proceedings*, vol. 140, no. 5 (2014).

[2] James A. Russell, James J. Wirtz, Donald Abenheim, Thomas-Durrell Young, and Diana Wueger, "Navy Strategy Development: Strategy in the 21st Century," Naval Research Program, Naval Postgraduate School, Project No. FY14-N3/N5-0001, Dudley Knox Library, Monterey, CA, http://www.nps.edu/library.

[3] Wills, "The Effect of the Goldwater-Nichols Act of 1986 on Naval Strategy, 1987–1994," 22.

[4] CNO John M. Richardson, "A Design for Maintaining Maritime Security," *Naval War College Review*, vol. 69, no. 2 (Spring 2016), 11–18.

[5] R 182128Z Oct 16, from CNO, to NAVADMIN (231/16), subject "POM Process Reorganization and OPNAV Staff Realignment."

[6] Ibid., Paragraph 3.a.

[7] Ibid., Paragraph 5.

[8] See Enclosure 4 to Dept. of Defense Directive 7045.14, "The Planning, Programming, Budgeting, and Execution (PPBE) Process," (25 Jan. 2013). www.dtic.mil/whs/directives/corres/pdf/704514p.pdf.

BIBLIOGRAPHY

Primary Sources

Archival and Special Collections

The major collections used in the preparation of this study are located in Washington, D.C., and in the collection of Archives II in College Park, Maryland: the records held by the Organization and OPNAV Resources Management Division (OP-09B2, renamed N09B1); the files of the Plans, Policy, and Command Organization Branch (OP-602) of the Office of the DCNO for Plans, Policy, and Operations (OP-06) held by the Archives in the Naval History and Heritage Command (NHHC): the U.S. Naval Institute Oral History Collection; interviews conducted by Thomas Hone, copies of which are in the NHHC Archives; the Naval War College library, and the Navy Department Library, which holds the major organizational studies and the World War II draft histories cited in the work.

Congressional and Executive Documents

U.S. Congress. House. *Communication from the President of the United States Transmitting a Plan for the Reorganization of the Department of the Navy.* 83rd Cong., 1st sess., 1966. H. Doc. 409.

———. *Reorganization Plan No. 6 of 1953, Relating to the Department of Defense.* 83rd Cong., 1st sess., 1953. H. Doc. 136.

———. Subcommittee of the Committee on Armed Services. *Reorganization of the Department of Defense: Hearings* [H.A.S.C. No. 99–53]. 99th Cong., 2nd sess., 1987.

———. Committee on Appropriations. *Navy Department Appropriations Bill for 1934, Hearings before a Subcommittee of the Committee on Appropriations.* 72nd Cong., 2nd. sess., 23 Jan. 1933.

———. Committee on Appropriations. *Navy Department Appropriations Bill for 1936, Hearings before a Subcommittee of the Committee on Appropriations.* 74th Cong., 1st. sess., 25 Feb. 1935.

———. Committee on Armed Services, Subcommittee on Investigations, *Reorganization of the Department of Defense: Hearings* [H.A.S.C. No. 99–53], 99th Cong., 2nd. sess., 1987.

———. Committee on Armed Services, Subcommittee on Readiness, *How Does the Navy Get Ready and Where Are We Today: Hearing* [H.A.S.C. No. 112–50], 112th Cong., 1st. sess., 2011.

Bibliography

U.S. Congress. Senate. Committee on Department of Defense Organization. *Report of the Rockefeller Committee on Department of Defense Organization.* 83rd Cong., 1st sess., 1953.

———. Armed Services Committee. *Department of Defense Reorganization Act 1986: Report to accompany S. 2295.* 99th Cong., 2nd sess., 1986.

———. Committee on Naval Affairs. *Unification of the War and Navy Departments and Postwar Organization for National Security: Report to the Hon. James Forrestal Secretary of the Navy* (Ferdinand Eberstadt Report). 79th Cong., 1st sess., 1945.

———. Committee on Government Operations, Permanent Subcommittee on Investigations *TFX Contract Investigation, Hearings*, 88th Cong., 1st sess., Part 3, 1963.

———. Committee on Naval Affairs. *Hearings before the Subcommittee of the Committee on Naval Affairs.* 66th Cong., 2nd. sess., 1921.

U.S. Congress. Joint Committee on the Investigation of the Pearl Harbor Attack. *Investigation of the Pearl Harbor Attack: Hearings.* 39 vols. 79th Cong., 2nd sess., 1946.

———. *Investigation of the Pearl Harbor Attack: Report.* 79th Cong., 2nd sess., 1946. S. Doc. 244.

U.S. Congress. Joint House–Senate Conference Committee. *Goldwater-Nichols Department of Defense Reorganization Act of 1986: Conference Report.* 99th Cong., 2nd sess., 1986. H. Rept. 99–824.

U.S. Congress. Seapower and Strategic and Critical Materials Subcommittee, House Armed Services Committee. "Hearings" on the Maritime Strategy. 99th Cong., 1st sess., 24 June and 5, 6, and 10 Sept. 1985.

U.S. Congress. Congressional Budget Office. "An Analysis of the Navy's Fiscal year 2015 Shipbuilding Plan." Dec. 2014.

U.S. Navy. *NWP 2, Organization of the U.S. Navy.* Washington, DC: Government Printing Office (GPO hereafter, also Government Publishing Office 2014), 1987.

———. U.S. Navy. *Ships' Data, U.S. Naval Vessels.* Washington, DC: GPO, various years.

U.S. Statutes. *An Act to establish the composition of the United States Navy with respect to the categories of vessels limited by the treaties signed at Washington, February 6, 1922, and at London, April 22, 1930, at the limits prescribed by those treaties; to authorize the construction of certain naval vessels; and for other purposes*, [Vinson-Trammell Act/First Vinson Act] Public Law 135. Vol. 48, part 1, 1934.

———. U.S. Statutes. *An Act to Establish the Composition of the United States Navy, to Authorize the Construction of Certain Naval Vessels, and for Other Purposes*, [Naval Expansion Act/Second Vinson Act] Public Law 528. Vol. 52, 1938.

———. U.S. Statutes. *An Act to Establish the Composition of the United States Navy, to Authorize the Construction of Certain Naval Vessels, and for Other Purposes*, [Third Vinson Act] Public Law 629. Vol. 54, part 1, 1940.

———. U.S. Statutes. *An Act to Establish the Composition of the United States Navy, to Authorize the Construction of Certain Naval Vessels, and for Other Purposes*, [Two-Ocean Navy Act] Public Law 757. Vol. 54, part 1, 1940.

———. U.S. Statutes. *An Act Making Certain Changes in the Organization of the Navy Depatment, and for Other Purposes*, Public Law 432. Vol. 62, part 2, 1948.

———. U.S. Statutes. *National Security Act Amendments of 1949.* Public Law 216. Vol. 63, part 1, 1949.

Report of the President's Committee, The President's Committee on Administrative Management. Washington, DC: GPO, 1937.

Report to the President and the Secretary of Defense by the Blue Ribbon Defense Panel (Gilbert W. Fitzhugh Report). Washington, DC: July 1970.

U.S. Department of the Navy, *Annual Reports of the Navy Department.* Washington, DC: Government Printing Office, various years.

———. U.S. Department of the Navy, General Order 94 [1921 Series] "Organization of Naval Forces." Washington, DC: 6 Dec. 1922.

———. U.S. Department of the Navy, General Order 143 [1935 Series] "Organization of Naval Forces of the United States." Washington, DC: 3 Feb. 1944.

———. U.S. Department of the Navy, *United States Navy Regulations, 1920.* Reprint. Washington, DC: Department of the Navy, 1979.

———. U.S. Department of the Navy, Bureau of Navigation, Navy *Directory: Officers of the United States and Marine Corps.* Washington, DC: Government Printing Office, various issues 1915–1942.

———. U.S. Department of the Navy, Bureau of Supplies and Accounts, "Historical Record of the Activities of the Bureau of Supplies and Accounts during the War with Germany," no date.

———. U.S. Department of the Navy, Bureau of Supplies and Accounts, "Naval Expenditures 1940." Washington, DC: Government Printing Office, 1941.

———. U.S. Department of the Navy, Office of Naval Intelligence, *Information Concerning the U.S. Navy and Other Navies.* Washington, DC: Government Printing Office, 1919.

———. U.S. Department of the Navy, "Revised Organization Orders of the Office of Naval Operations," 1 Aug. 1919. Washington, DC: Government Printing Office, 1919.

Published and Unpublished Studies

Aspin, Les, Secretary of Defense, *Report on the Bottom-Up Review*, Washington, DC: Department of Defense, October 1993.

Byron, John L. *Reorganization of U.S. Armed Forces.* National War College Strategic Study. Washington, DC: National Defense University, 1983.

Russell, James A., James J. Wirtz, Donald Abenheim, Thomas-Durrell Young, and Diana Wueger, "Navy Strategy Development: Strategy in the 21st Century," Naval Research Program, Naval Postgraduate School, Project No. FY14-N3/N5-0001, Dudley Knox Library, Monterey, CA, 2015.

Walsh, Rep. David I, Chairman of the Committee on Naval Affairs, U. S. Senate. "The Decline and Renaissance of the Navy, 1922–1944," 7 June 1944. Washington, DC: GPO, 1944.

U.S. Department of Defense. *Departmental Headquarters Study, A Report to the Secretary of Defense.* Washington, DC: 1978.

U.S. Department of the Navy. *Major Organizational Considerations for the Chief of Naval Operations. Vol. 1, Report.* Prepared by Organization Research Counselors, Inc. Washington, DC: 1973.

Bibliography

———. "The Naval Establishment: Its Growth and Necessity for Expansion, 1930–1950." Office of the Comptroller of the Navy (NavExos-P-1038). Washington, DC: 1951.

———. *Navy Organization Study* (Roy S. Benson Task Force Report). Washington, DC: 1966.

———. "Report of the Board Convened by the Chief of Naval Operations to Study and Report Upon the Adequacy of the Bureau System of Organization" (R. V. Libby Board Report). Serial 05754, 14 Mar. 1956.

———. *Report of the Committee on Organization of the Department of the Navy* (Thomas S. Gates Committee Report). Washington, DC: 1954.

———. *Report of the Committee on Organization of the Department of the Navy* (William B. Franke Board Report). Washington, DC: 1959.

———. *Report of the Committee on Organization of the Department of the Navy.* Washington, DC: 1954.

———. *Review of Management of the Department of the Navy* (Robert S. Dillon Board Report). Washington, DC: 1962.

Review of Management of the Department of the Navy. Study 1, vol. 2, External Environmental Influences Study. Prepared under Study Director John V. Smith. Washington, DC: 1962.

———. *Review of Management of the Department of the Navy.* Study 2, vol. 2, Planning, Programming, Budgeting, and Appraising Study. Prepared under Study Director H. A. Renken. Washington, DC: 1962.

Review of Navy R&D Management. Prepared by Booz, Allen & Hamilton Inc. Washington, DC: 1947.

Statement of Rear Admiral Ernest J. King, Chief, Bureau of Aeronautics, Hearing before the Subcommittee of the House Committee on Appropriations, Navy Department Appropriation Bill for 1935, 6 Dec. 1933. Washington, DC: 1934

Office of the Chief of Naval Operations. *The Maritime Balance Study: The Navy Strategic Planning Experiment.* Washington, DC: 16 April 1979.

The United States at War, Development and Administration of the War Program by the Federal Government. Prepared by the War Records Section of the Bureau of the Budget. Washington, DC: 1946.

Diaries
Millis, Walter, ed. with the collaboration of E. S. Duffield. *The Forrestal Diaries.* New York: Viking Press, 1951.

Interviews and Oral Histories
Interviews with Thomas Hone.
  Allen, Richard C. February 1998.
  Arthur, Stanley R. February 1998.
  Barber, Arthur H., III. October 2014.
  Blickstein, Irving N. December 1997.
  Burke, William R. July 2014.

Clark, Bryan. April 2015.
Dantone, Joseph J. April 1998.
Dicks, John J. October 2000.
Fedor, John D. 1985.
Harris, R. Robinson. January 2015.
Herberger, Albert J. October 2014.
Johnson, W. Spencer. July 2016.
Kelso, Frank B., II. April 1998.
Kuhn, James K. January 2015.
Lopez, T. Joseph. November 2014.
McDevitt, Michael A. January 1998.
Oliver, David R. December 1997.
Smith, William D. March 1998.
Stewart, Jake W., Jr. 22 December 1987.
Stoufer, Donald A. 20 July 1987.
Trost, Carlisle A. H. March 1998.
Williams, James D. February 1998.

U.S. Naval Institute Oral History Collection. Annapolis, MD.
    DeMars, Bruce. Interviewed by Paul Stillwell, 2012.
    Duncan, Charles K. Interviewed by John T. Mason Jr. 3 vols. 1983.
    Dunn, Robert F. Interviewed by Paul Stillwell, 2008.
    Hayward, Thomas B. Interviewed by Paul Stillwell, 2009.
    Kauffman, Draper L. Interviewed by John T. Mason Jr., 1982.
    Kelso, Frank B., II. Interviewed by Paul Stillwell, 2009.
    Kerr, Howard J., Jr. Interviewed by Paul Stillwell. 1982.
    MacDonald, David L. Interviewed by John T. Mason Jr. 1976.
    Mack, William P. Interviewed by John T. Mason Jr. 2 vols. 1979.
    Smith, Leighton W. Interviewed by Paul Stillwell, 2006.
    Train, Harry D., II. Interviewed by Paul Stillwell, 1986.

USAF Oral History Program, Historical Research Center, Maxwell AFB, AL
    Schriever, Bernard A., interviewed by MAJ L. R. Officer and Dr. J. C. Hasdorff, 1973.

Secondary Sources
Books
The 9/11 Commission Report (authorized ed.). New York: W.W. Norton, 2004.
Acker, David D. *Acquiring Defense Systems: A Quest for the Best*. Ft. Belvoir, VA: Defense Systems Management College (now Defense Acquisition University), Technical Report TR 1-93, 1993.

Bibliography

Albion, Robert Greenhalgh, and Robert Howe Connery. *Forrestal and the Navy.* New York: Columbia University Press, 1962.

Albion, Robert Greenhalgh, ed. by Rowena Reed. *Makers of Naval Policy, 1798–1947.* Annapolis, MD: Naval Institute Press, 1980.

Albion, Robert Greenhalgh, and Samuel H. P. Read Jr. *The Navy at Sea and Ashore.* Washington, DC: Department of the Navy, 1947.

Allston, Frank J., RADM, SC, USNR (Ret.). *Ready for Sea, The Bicentennial History of the U.S. Navy Supply Corps.* Annapolis, MD: Naval Institute Press, 1995.

Ambrose, Stephen E. *Eisenhower. Vol. 2, The President.* New York: Simon & Schuster, 1984.

Baer, George W. *One Hundred Years of Sea Power, The U.S. Navy, 1890–1990.* Stanford, CA: Stanford University Press, 1994.

Ballantine, Duncan S. *U.S. Naval Logistics in the Second World War.* Princeton, NJ: Princeton University Press, 1949.

Barlow, Jeffrey G. *From Hot War to Cold, The U.S. Navy and National Security Affairs, 1945–1955.* Stanford, CA: Stanford University Press, 2009.

———. *Revolt of the Admirals, The Fight for Naval Aviation, 1945–1950.* Washington, DC: Naval Historical Center, Dept. of the Navy, 1994.

Baruch, Bernard M., and Richard H. Hippelheuser, ed. *American Industry in the War, A Report of the War Industries Board.* New York: Prentice-Hall, 1941.

Berman, Larry. *Zumwalt, The Life and Times of Admiral Elmo Russell "Bud" Zumwalt Jr.* New York: HarperCollins, 2012.

Blaker, James R. *Transforming Military Force: The Legacy of Arthur Cebrowski and Network Centric Warfare.* Westport, CT: Praeger Security International, 2007.

Blinder, Alan S. *After the Music Stopped, The Financial Crisis, the Response, and the Work Ahead.* New York: Penguin Press, 2013.

Boghardt, Thomas. *The Zimmermann Telegram: Intelligence, Diplomacy, and America's Entry into World War I.* Annapolis, MD: Naval Institute Press, 2012.

Bradford, James C., ed. *Admirals of the New Steel Navy.* Annapolis, MD: Naval Institute Press, 1990.

Braisted, William R. *The United States Navy in the Pacific, 1909–1922.* Austin: University of Texas Press, 1971.

Broadwell, Paula, with Vernon Loeb. *All In: The Education of General David Petraeus.* New York: Penguin Books, 2012.

Buell, Thomas B. *Master of Seapower, A Biography of Fleet Admiral Ernest J. King.* Annapolis, MD: Naval Institute Press, 2012.

Burns, James M. *Roosevelt: The Soldier of Freedom.* New York: Harcourt, Brace, Jovanovich, 1970.

Bush, George W. *Decision Points.* New York: Crown Publishers, 2010.

Casey, George W., Jr., GEN, USA (Ret.). *Strategic Reflections, Operation Iraqi Freedom, July 2004–Feb. 2007.* Washington, DC: National Defense Univ. Press, 2012.

Chisholm, Donald. *Waiting for Dead Men's Shoes, Origins and Development of the U.S. Navy's Officer Personnel System, 1793–1941.* Stanford, CA: Stanford University Press, 2001.

Coakley, Robert W., and Richard M. Leighton. *Global Logistics and Strategy, 1943–1945*. Washington, DC: Office of the Chief of Military History, U.S. Army, 1968.

Cohen, Eliot A. *Supreme Command: Soldiers, Statesmen, and Leadership in Wartime*. New York: The Free Press, 2002.

Coletta, Paolo E., ed. *American Secretaries of the Navy. Vol. 1 and Vol. 2*. Annapolis, MD: Naval Institute Press, 1980.

Connery, Robert H. *The Navy and the Industrial Mobilization in World War II*. Princeton, NJ: Princeton University Press, 1951.

Cooling, Benjamin F. *U.S.S. Olympia, Herald of Empire*. Annapolis, MD: Naval Institute Press, 2000.

Coontz, Robert E., RADM, USN (Ret.). *From the Mississippi to the Sea*. Philadelphia, PA: Dorrance and Co., 1930.

Cote, Owen R. Jr. *The Third Battle, Innovation in the U.S. Navy's Silent Cold War Struggle with Soviet Submarines*. Newport, RI: Naval War College, 2003.

Crowe, William J. Jr., ADM. *The Line of Fire*. New York: Simon & Schuster, 1993.

Daniels, Josephus. *Our Navy at War*. New York: George H. Doran, 1922.

Davidson, Joel R. *The Unsinkable Fleet, The Politics of U.S. Navy Expansion in World War II*. Annapolis, MD: Naval Institute Press, 1996.

Davis, M. Thomas. *Managing Defense After the Cold War*. Washington, DC: Center for Strategic and Budgetary Assessments, 1997.

Davis, Vincent. *The Admirals Lobby*. Chapel Hill: University of North Carolina Press, 1967.

———. *Postwar Defense Policy and the U.S. Navy, 1943–1946*. Chapel Hill: University of North Carolina Press, 1962.

DeWolfe Howe, Mark A. *George von Lengerke Meyer, His Life and Public Services*. New York: Dodd, Mead & Co., 1920.

Dibner, Martin. *The Deep Six*. New York: Doubleday & Co., 1953.

Drucker, Peter. *Concept of the Corporation*. New York: John Day, 1946.

Duncan, Robert C. *America's Use of Sea Mines*. Silver Spring, MD: U.S. Naval Ordnance Laboratory, 1962.

Feynman, Richard P. *The Pleasure of Finding Things Out*. Cambridge, MA: Perseus Books, 1999.

Fiske, Bradley A., RADM, USN (Ret.). *From Midshipman to Rear Admiral*. New York: The Century Co., 1919.

———. *The Navy as a Fighting Machine*. New York: Charles Scribner's Sons, 1916.

Forester, C. S. *Mr. Midshipman Hornblower*. New York: Grosett and Dunlap, 1950.

Fox, J. Ronald. *Defense Acquisition Reform, 1960–2009*. Washington, DC: Center for Military History, U.S. Army, 2011.

Fox, J. Ronald, with James L. Field. *The Defense Management Challenge: Weapons Acquisition*. Boston, MA: Harvard Business School Press, 1988.

Friedman, Norman. *Fighting the Great War at Sea: Strategy, Tactics and Technology*. S. Yorkshire, UK: Seaforth Publishing, 2014.

Bibliography

———. *Network-Centric Warfare*. Annapolis, MD: Naval Institute Press, 2009.

———. *The Postwar Naval Revolution*. Annapolis, MD: Naval Institute Press, 1986.

———. *U.S. Aircraft Carriers: An Illustrated Design History*. Annapolis, MD: Naval Institute Press, 1983.

———. *U.S. Amphibious Ships and Craft*. Annapolis, MD: Naval Institute Press, 2002.

———. *U.S. Battleships: An Illustrated Design History*. Annapolis, MD: Naval Institute Press, 1985.

———. *U.S. Cruisers: An Illustrated Design History*. Annapolis, MD: Naval Institute Press, 1984.

———. *U.S. Destroyers: An Illustrated Design History*. Annapolis, MD: Naval Institute Press, 1982.

———. *U.S. Destroyers: An Illustrated Design History, Revised Edition*. Annapolis, MD: Naval Institute Press, 2004.

———. *U.S. Naval Weapons*. Annapolis, MD: Naval Institute Press, 1984.

———. *U.S. Submarines Through 1945: An Illustrated Design History*. Annapolis, MD: Naval Institute Press, 1995.

Furer, Julius Augustus, RADM, USN (Ret.). *Administration of the Navy Department in World War II*. Washington, DC: Division of Naval History, Dept. of the Navy, and GPO, 1959.

Futrell, Robert Frank. *Ideas, Concepts, Doctrine: A History of Basic Thinking in the United States Air Force, 1907–1964*. Maxwell AFB, AL: Aerospace Studies Institute, Air University, 1971.

Gannon, Michael. *Operation Drumbeat: Germany's U-Boat Attacks Along the American Coast in World War II*. New York: HarperCollins, 1990.

Gates, Robert M. *Duty*. New York: Knopf, 2014.

Gough, Terrence J. *Establishment and Evolution of the Office of the Deputy Chief of Staff for Operations and Plans, 1903–1983*. Washington, DC: Dept. of the Army, 1983.

Graham, Bradley. *By His Own Rules, The Ambitions, Successes, and Ultimate Failures of Donald Rumsfeld*. New York: Public Affairs, 2009.

Grossnick, Roy A., with contributions from William J. Armstrong, W. Todd Baker, John M. Elliott, Gwendolyn J. Rich, and Judith A. Walters. *United States Naval Aviation, 1910–1995*. Washington, DC: Department of the Navy and GPO, 1997.

Harrison, Todd. *Analysis of the FY 2012 Defense Budget*. Washington, DC: Center for Strategic and Budgetary Assessments, 2011.

Hartmann, Frederick H. *Naval Renaissance, The U.S. Navy in the 1980s*. Annapolis, MD: Naval Institute Press, 1990.

Hattendorf, John B. *The Evolution of the U.S. Navy's Maritime Strategy, 1977–1986*. Newport, RI: Center for Naval Warfare Studies, Naval War College, 1989.

Hattendorf, John B., ed. *U.S. Naval Strategy in the 1990s: Selected Documents*. Newport, RI: Naval War College Press, 2006.

———. ed. *U.S. Naval Strategy in the 1970s: Selected Documents*. Newport, RI: Naval War College Press, 2007.

Hattendorf, John B., and Peter M. Swartz, eds. *U.S. Naval Strategy in the 1980s: Selected Documents*. Newport, RI: Naval War College Press, 2008.

Hattendorf, John B., and Bruce A. Elleman, eds. *Nineteen-Gun Salute, Case Studies of Operational, Strategic, and Diplomatic Naval Leadership during the 20th and Early 21st Centuries*. Washington, DC, and Newport, RI: GPO and Naval War College Press, 2010.

Hawley, Cameron. *The Hurricane Years*. Boston, MA: Little, Brown, 1968.

Hayes, John D., and John B. Hattendorf, eds. *The Writings of Stephen B. Luce*. Newport, RI: Naval War College, 1975.

Haynes, Peter D. *Toward a New Maritime Strategy, American Naval Thinking in the Post–Cold War Era*. Annapolis, MD: Naval Institute Press, 2015.

Hendrix, Henry J. *Theodore Roosevelt's Naval Diplomacy: The U.S. Navy and the Birth of the American Century*. Annapolis, MD: Naval Institute Press, 2009.

Hewlett, Richard G., and Francis Duncan. *Nuclear Navy*. Chicago: University of Chicago Press, 1974.

Hicks, Kathleen. *Invigorating Defense Governance, A Beyond Goldwater-Nichols Phase 4 Report*. Washington, DC: Center for Strategic and International Studies, Mar. 2008.

Hicks, Kathleen, and David Berteau, Samuel J. Brannen, Eleanore Douglas, Nathan Freier, Clark A. Murdock, and Christine E. Wormuth. *Transitioning Defense Organizational Initiatives, An Assessment of Key 2001–2008 Defense Reforms*. Washington, DC: Center for Strategic and International Studies, Dec. 2008.

Historical Division, Joint Secretariat, Joint Chiefs of Staff. *Chronology, Functions and Composition of the Joint Chiefs of Staff*. Washington, DC: Joint Chiefs of Staff, 1979.

———. *A Concise History of the Organization of the Joint Chiefs of Staff,* 1942–1978. Washington, DC: Joint Chiefs of Staff, 1980.

Holley, I. B., Jr. *Ideas and Weapons*. New Haven, CT: Yale University Press, 1953.

Holloway, James L., III, ADM. *Aircraft Carriers at War*. Annapolis, MD: Naval Institute Press, 2007.

Holmes, Tony. *U.S. Navy Hornet Units of Operation Iraqi Freedom, Part One*. Botley, Oxford, England: Osprey Publishing, 2004.

Holwitt, Joel Ira. *Execute Against Japan: The U.S. Decision to Conduct Unrestricted Submarine Warfare*. College Station: Texas A&M University Press, 2009.

Hone, Thomas C. *Power and Change: The Administrative History of the Office of the Chief of Naval Operations, 1946–1986*. Washington, DC: Naval Historical Center, 1989.

Hone, Thomas C., and Trent Hone. *Battle Line, The United States Navy, 1919–1939*. Annapolis, MD: Naval Institute Press, 2006.

Hone, Thomas C., and Norman Friedman and Mark D. Mandeles. *American & British Aircraft Carrier Development, 1919–1941*. Annapolis, MD: Naval Institute Press, 1999.

———. *Innovation in Carrier Aviation*. Newport, RI: Naval War College Press and GPO, 2011.

Howeth, L. S., CAPT *History of Communications-Electronics in the United States Navy*. Washington, DC: Bureau of Ships and the Office of Naval History, 1963.

Hughes, Wayne P. CAPT, USN (Ret.). *Fleet Tactics: Theory and Practice*. Annapolis, MD: Naval Institute Press, 1986.

Hurley, Alfred F. *Billy Mitchell: Crusader for Air Power*. Bloomington: Indiana University Press, 2006.

Bibliography

Hurley, Alfred F., and Robert C. Ehrhart, eds. *Air Power and Warfare.* Proceedings of the 8th Military History Symposium. U.S. Air Force Academy. Washington, DC: Office of Air Force History and U.S. Air Force Academy, 1979.

Ignatius, Paul R. *On Board: My Life in the Navy, Government, and Business.* Annapolis, MD: Naval Institute Press, 2006.

Jaffe, Lorna S. *The Development of the Base Force, 1989–1992.* Washington, DC: Joint History Office, Office of the Chairman of the Joint Chiefs of Staff, 1993.

Janeway, Eliot. *The Struggle for Survival, A Chronicle of Economic Mobilization in World War II.* New Haven, CT: Yale University Press, 1951.

Jenkins, Dennis R. *F/A-18 Hornet.* New York: McGraw-Hill, 2000.

Johnson, Alfred W., VADM, USN (Ret.), *The Naval Bombing Experiments Off the Virginia Capes, June and July 1921: Their Technological and Psychological Aspects* Washington, DC: Naval Historical Foundation, 1959.

Joint History Office, Office of the Chairman of the Joint Chiefs of Staff. *Selected Works of Admiral William J. Crowe Jr., USN.* Washington, DC, 2013.

Kaplan, Fred. *The Insurgents: David Petraeus and the Plot to Change the American Way of War.* New York: Simon & Schuster, 2013.

Karsten, Peter. *The Naval Aristocracy: The Golden Age of Annapolis and the Emergence of Modern American Navalism.* New York: Free Press, 1972.

Kaufman, Herbert. *The Administrative Behavior of Federal Bureau Chiefs.* Washington, DC: Brookings Institution, 1981.

Kelly, Orr. *Hornet, The Inside Story of the F/A-18.* Shrewsbury, England: Airlife Publishing, 1990.

King, Ernest J., FADM, USN. The *War Reports of General of the Army George C. Marshall, General of the Army H. H. Arnold, and Fleet Admiral Ernest J. King.* New York: J. B. Lippincott Co., 1947.

Kittredge, Tracy Barrett. *Naval Lessons of the Great War.* Garden City, NY: Doubleday, Page & Co., 1921.

Klachko, Mary, with David F. Trask. *Admiral William Shepherd Benson, First Chief of Naval Operations.* Annapolis, MD: Naval Institute Press, 1987.

Klein, Maury. *A Call to Arms, Mobilizing America for World War II.* New York: Bloomsbury Press, 2013.

Knight, Austin M. RADM, USN. *Modern Seamanship.* New York. Van Norstrand, 1918.

Knott, Richard C. CAPT, USN. *The American Flying Boat: An Illustrated History.* Annapolis, MD: Naval Institute Press, 1979.

Koistinen, Paul A. C. *Arsenal of World War II, The Political Economy of American Warfare, 1940–1945.* Lawrence: University Press of Kansas, 2004.

———. *State of War, The Political Economy of American Warfare, 1945–2011.* Lawrence: University Press of Kansas, 2012.

Korb, Lawrence. *The Fall and Rise of the Pentagon.* Westport, CT: Greenwood Press, 1979.

Kuehn, John T. *Agents of Innovation: The General Board and the Design of the Fleet that Defeated the Japanese Navy.* Annapolis, MD: Naval Institute Press, 2008.

Land, Emory S., VADM, USN (Ret.). *Winning the War with Ships*. New York: Robert M. McBride, 1958.

Lambert, Nicholas. *Planning Armageddon: British Economic Warfare and the First World War*. Cambridge, MA: Harvard Univ. Press, 2012.

Laning, Harris, ADM, USN (Ret.). *An Admiral's Yarn*, ed. by Mark Russell Shulman. Newport, RI: Naval War College Press, 1999.

Lassman, Thomas C. *Sources of Weapons Systems Innovation in the Department of Defense, The Role of In-House Research and Development, 1945–2000* Washington, DC: Center for Military History, 2008.

Lehman, John F., Jr. *Aircraft Carriers: The Real Choices*. Beverly Hills, CA: Sage Publications, 1978.

———. *Command of the Seas*. New York: Charles Scribner's Sons, 1988.

Leighton, Richard M., and Robert W. Coakley. *Global Logistics and Strategy, 1940–1943*. Washington, DC: Office of the Chief of Military History, U.S. Army, and GPO, 1995.

Locher, James R. III. *Victory on the Potomac, The Goldwater-Nichols Act Unifies the Pentagon*. College Station: Texas A&M University Press, 2002.

Love, Robert William Jr., ed. *The Chiefs of Naval Operations*. Annapolis, MD: Naval Institute Press, 1980.

———. *History of the U.S. Navy, Volume 1 1775–1941*. Harrisburg, PA: Stackpole Books, 1992.

———. *History of the U.S. Navy, Volume 2 1942–1991*. Harrisburg, PA: Stackpole Books, 1992.

Edward Marolda, ed. *FDR and the U.S. Navy*. New York: St. Martin's Press, 1998.

Mann, Thomas E., and Norman Ornstein. *It's Even Worse than It Looks*. New York: Basic Books, 2013.

Mazetti, Mark. *The Way of the Knife: The CIA, a Secret Army, and a War at the Ends of the Earth*. New York: Penguin Press, 2013.

Melhorn, Charles M. *Two-Block Fox: The Rise of the Aircraft Carrier, 1911–1929*. Annapolis, MD: Naval Institute Press, 1974.

Melia, Tamara Moser. *Damn the Torpedoes, A Short History of U.S. Naval Mine Countermeasures, 1777–1991*. Washington, DC: GPO, 1991.

Metz, Steven. *Decisionmaking in Operation Iraqi Freedom: The Strategic Shift of 2007*. U.S. Army War College, Strategic Studies Institute (May 2010).

Miller, Edward S. *Bankrupting the Enemy, The U.S. Financial Siege of Japan before Pearl Harbor*. Annapolis, MD: Naval Institute Press, 2007.

———. *War Plan Orange, The U.S. Strategy to Defeat Japan, 1897–1945*. Annapolis, MD: Naval Institute Press, 1991.

Miller, Jerry (Gerald E.) VADM, USN (Ret.). *Nuclear Weapons and Aircraft Carriers: How the Bomb Saved Naval Aviation*. Washington, DC, 2001.

Morison, Elting E. *Admiral Sims and the Modern American Navy*. Boston: Houghton Mifflin, 1942.

———. *Naval Administration, Selected Documents on the Navy Department Organization, 1915–1940*. Washington, DC: Navy Department, 1945.

Morison, Samuel Eliot. *History of United States Naval Operations in World War II*. Multiple volumes. Edison, NJ: Castle Books, 2001.

Bibliography

Muir, Malcolm Jr. *Black Shoes and Blue Water, Surface Warfare in the United States Navy, 1945–1975*. Washington, DC: GPO, 1996.

Murdock, Clark. *Planning for a Deep Defense Drawdown, Part 1*. Washington, DC: Center for Strategic and International Studies, 2012.

Nitze, Paul H., with Ann M. Smith and Steven L. Rearden. *From Hiroshima to Glasnost: At the Center of Decision—A Memoir*. New York: Grove Weidenfeld, 1989.

Nofi, Albert A. *To Train the Fleet for War, The U.S. Navy Fleet Problems, 1923–1940*. Naval War College Historical Monograph Series No. 18. Washington, DC: GPO, 2010.

O'Hara, Vincent P., W. David Dickson, and Richard Worth, eds. *To Crown the Waves: The Great Navies of the First World War*. Annapolis, MD: Naval Institute Press, 2013.

Oliver, Dave, RADM, USN (Ret.). *Against the Tide: Rickover's Leadership Principles and the Rise of the Nuclear Navy*. Annapolis, MD: Naval Institute Press, 2014.

Ordnance, Bureau of. *Navy Ordnance Activities, World War, 1917–1918*. Washington, DC: GPO, 1920.

Owens, William, ADM. *High Seas, The Naval Passage to an Uncharted World*. Annapolis, MD: Naval Institute Press, 1995.

Palmer, Michael A. *On Course to Desert Storm, The United States Navy and the Persian Gulf*. Washington, DC: Naval Historical Center, Dept. of the Navy, 1992.

———. *Origins of the Maritime Strategy: American Naval Strategy in the First Postwar Decade*. Washington, DC: Naval Historical Center, 1988.

Panetta, Leon, with Jim Newton. *Worthy Fights, A Memoir of Leadership in War and Peace*. New York: Penguin Books, 2015.

Paullin, Charles Oscar. *Paullin's History of Naval Administration, 1775–1911*. Annapolis, MD: U.S. Naval Institute, 1968.

Perry, Glen C. H. *"Dear Bart," Washington Views of World War II*. Westport, CT: Greenwood Press, 1982.

Polmar, Norman, and Thomas B. Allen. *Rickover*. New York: Simon & Shuster, 1982.

Prange, Gordon, with the collaboration of Donald M. Goldstein and Katherine V. Dillon. *At Dawn We Slept: The Untold Story of Pearl Harbor*. New York: McGraw-Hill, 1981.

Rearden, Steven L. *History of the Office of the Secretary of Defense*. Vol. 1, *The Formative Years, 1947–1950*. Washington, DC: Historical Office, Office of the Secretary of Defense, 1984.

Rauchway, Eric. *Blessed Among Nations: How the World Made America*. New York: Hill and Wang, 2007.

Reynolds, Clark G. *Admiral John H. Towers, The Struggle for Naval Air Supremacy*. Annapolis, MD: Naval Institute Press, 1991.

Reynolds, Terry S., ed. *The Engineer in America: A Historical Anthology from Technology and Culture*. Chicago: Univ. of Chicago Press, 1991.

Ricks, Thomas E. *Fiasco, The American Military Adventure in Iraq*. New York: Penguin Press, 2006.

———. *The Gamble. General David Petraeus and the American Military Adventure in Iraq, 2006–2008*. New York: Penguin Press, 2009.

Roskill, Stephen. *Naval Policy Between the Wars, II, The Period of Reluctant Rearmament, 1930–1939.* Annapolis, MD: U.S. Naval Institute, 1976.

Rowen, Hobart. *Self-Inflicted Wounds.* New York: Random House, 1994.

Rowland, Buford, and William Boyd. *U.S. Navy Bureau of Ordnance in World War II.* Washington, DC: GPO, 1954.

Sands, Jeffrey L. *On His Watch: Admiral Zumwalt's Efforts to Institutionalize Strategic Change,* CRM 93-22. Alexandria, VA: Center for Naval Analyses, 1993.

Shapack, Arnold R., ed. *Proceedings, Naval History Symposium.* U.S. Naval Academy, 27–28 April 1973. Annapolis, MD: U.S. Naval Academy, 1973.

Sherwood, Robert. *Roosevelt and Hopkins.* New York: Harper & Brothers, 1948.

Shlaes, Amity. *Coolidge.* New York: HarperCollins, 2013.

Simpson, B. Mitchell, III. *Admiral Harold R. Stark, Architect of Victory, 1939–1945.* Columbia: University of South Carolina Press, 1989.

Spector, Ronald H. *In the Ruins of Empire: The Japanese Surrender and the Battle for Postwar Asia.* New York: Random House, 2008.

Spinney, Franklin C. *Defense Facts of Life: The Plans/Reality Mismatch.* Boulder, CO: Westview Press, 1985.

Spout, Harold and Margaret. *Toward a New Order of Sea Power.* Princeton, NJ: Princeton University Press, 1940.

Starr, Paul. *The Social Transformation of American Medicine.* New York: Basic Books, 1984.

Stavridis, James G., ADM, USN (Ret.). *The Accidental Admiral, A Sailor Takes Command at NATO.* Annapolis, MD: Naval Institute Press, 2014.

Steinberg, Malcom. *Admiral Boorda's Navy.* West Conshohocken, PA: Infinity Publishing, 2011.

Stevenson, James P. *The $5 Billion Misunderstanding: The Collapse of the Navy's A-12 Stealth Bomber Program.* Annapolis, MD: Naval Institute Press, 2001.

Stillwell, Paul, ed. *Air Raid: Pearl Harbor! Recollections of a Day of Infamy.* Annapolis, MD: Naval Institute Press, 1981.

Stirling, Yates, RADM, USN (Ret.). *Sea Duty: The Memoirs of a Fighting Admiral.* New York: G. P. Putnam's Sons, 1939.

Stubbing, Richard A. *The Defense Game.* New York: Harper & Row, 1986.

Swartz, Peter M., with Karin Duggan. *U.S. Navy Capstone Strategies and Concepts: Introduction, Background and Analyses.* Alexandria, VA: Center for Naval Analyses, 2012.

———, et. al. *"Old Links, Young CINCs and Component Commanders": How the US Navy Has Organized for Joint Operations.* Alexandria, VA: Center for Naval Analyses, 1997 (CNA 97-1262).

———, with Michael C. Markowitz. *Organizing OPNAV (1970–2009).* Center for Naval Analyses, 2010 (CAB D0020997. A5/2 Rev).

———, with Karin Duggan. *U.S. Navy Capstone Strategies and Concepts (1970–2010): A Brief Summary.* Center for Naval Analyses, 2011 (D0026437 .A1/Final).

Bibliography

———, with Karin Duggan. *U.S. Navy Capstone Strategies and Concepts: Introduction, Background and Analyses.* Center for Naval Analyses, 2011 (D0026421 .A1/Final).

———, with Karin Duggan. *U.S. Navy Capstone Strategies and Concepts (1970–1980): Strategy, Policy, Concept, and Vision Documents.* Center for Naval Analyses, 2011 (D0026414 .A1/Final).

———, with Karin Duggan. *U.S. Navy Capstone Strategies and Concepts (1981–1990): Strategy, Policy, Concept, and Vision Documents.* Center for Naval Analyses, 2011 (D0026419 .A1).

———, with Karin Duggan. *U.S. Navy Capstone Strategies and Concepts (1991–2000): Strategy, Policy, Concept, and Vision Documents.* Center for Naval Analyses, 2012 (D0026416 .A2/Final).

———, with Karin Duggan. *U.S. Navy Capstone Strategies and Concepts (1970–2010): Comparisons, Contrasts, and Changes, Vol. I.* Center for Naval Analyses, 2011 (D0026422 .A1/Final).

———, with Karin Duggan. *U.S. Navy Capstone Strategies and Concepts (1970–2010): Comparisons, Contrasts, and Changes, Vol. II.* Center for Naval Analyses, 2011 (D0026423 .A1/Final).

Jack Sweetman, ed. *American Naval History*, 2nd ed. Annapolis, MD: Naval Institute Press, 1991.

Tenet, George, with Bill Harlow. *At the Center of the Storm: My Years at the CIA.* New York: HarperCollins, 2007.

Thomas, Evan. *Ike's Bluff: President Eisenhower's Secret Battle to Save the World.* Boston: Little Brown 2012.

Thomason, Tommy H. *Strike from the Sea, U.S. Navy Attack Aircraft from Skyraider to Super Hornet, 1948–Present.* North Branch, MN: Specialty Press, 2009.

Thompson, Wayne, ed. *Air Leadership.* Washington, DC: Office of Air Force History, 1986.

Timberg, Robert. *The Nightingale's Song.* New York: Simon & Schuster, 1995.

Tooze, Adam. *The Deluge: The Great War, America and the Remaking of the Global Order, 1916–1931.* New York: Viking Press, 2014.

Trimble, William F. *Admiral William A. Moffett: Architect of Naval Aviation.* Washington, DC: Smithsonian Institution Press, 1994.

———. *Wings for the Navy: A History of the Naval Aircraft Factory, 1917–1956.* Annapolis, MD: Naval Institute Press, 1990.

Tritten, James J. *Soviet Naval Forces and Nuclear Warfare.* Boulder, CO: Westview Press, 1986.

Tyler, Patrick. *Running Critical: The Silent War, Rickover, and General Dynamics.* New York: HarperCollins, 1989.

Ulbrich, David J. *Preparing for Victory, Thomas Holcomb and the Making of the Modern Marine Corps, 1936–1943.* Annapolis, MD: Naval Institute Press, 2011.

Untermeyer, Chase. *Inside Reagan's Navy: The Pentagon Journals.* College Station: Texas A&M University Press, 2015.

U.S. Naval Institute. *Naval Leadership.* 3d ed. Annapolis, MD: 1929.

Weinberger, Caspar W. *Fighting for Peace, Seven Critical Years in the Pentagon.* New York: Warner Books, 1990.

Weir, Gary E. *Building American Submarines, 1914–1940.* Washington, DC: Naval Historical Center, 1991.

———, Sandra J. Doyle, ed. *You Cannot Surge Trust: Combined Naval Operations of the Royal Australian Navy, Canadian Navy, Royal Navy and the United States Navy, 1991–2003.* Washington, DC: Naval History and Heritage Command, 2013.

Wheeler, Gerald E. *Admiral William Veazie Pratt, U.S. Navy.* Washington, DC: Naval History Division and GPO, 1974.

Wilson, George C. *This War Really Matters: Inside the Fight for Defense Dollars.* Washington, DC: CQ Press, 2000.

Wood, Dakota L. *The U.S. Marine Corps: Fleet Marine Forces for the 21st Century.* Center for Strategic and Budgetary Assessments. Washington, DC, 2008.

Woodward, Bob. *Obama's Wars.* New York: Simon & Schuster, 2010.

———. *The Price of Politics.* New York: Simon & Schuster, 2012.

Woolridge, E. T. CAPT, USN (Ret.), ed. *Into the Jet Age: Conflict and Change in Naval Aviation, 1945–1975, an Oral History.* Annapolis, MD: Naval Institute Press, 1995.

Work, Robert O. *Naval Transformation and the Littoral Combat Ship.* Washington, DC: Center for Strategic and Budgetary Assessments, 2004.

———. *Thinking About Seabasing: All Ahead, Slow.* Washington, DC: Center for Strategic and Budgetary Assessments, 2006.

Yards and Docks, Bureau of. *Activities of the Bureau of Yards and Docks, World War, 1917–1918.* Washington, DC: GPO, 1921.

Zogbaum, Rufus F. *From Sail to Saratoga.* Rome: S. Nib, n.d.

Zumwalt, Elmo R., Jr. *On Watch.* New York: Quadrangle, 1976.

Articles

Ackerman, Robert. "Naval Intelligence Ramps Up Activities. A Global Reach Now Embraces Maritime Domain Awareness Across Agencies." *Signal* 5 (Feb. 2009).

"Admiral Pratt Forming Planning Section" *Army Navy Journal* 4 October 1930: 101.

Barber, Arthur H., III, "Rethinking the Future Fleet," U.S. Naval Institute *Proceedings*, vol. 140, no. 5 (2014).

Barnett, Thomas P. M., and Henry H. Gaffney Jr. "Force Structure Assessment Team (FSAT)." Center for Naval Analyses Working Paper 05 96-0363 (Mar. 1996).

Barrett, Archie D. "Empowering Eisenhower's Concept." *Joint Force Quarterly* (Autumn 1996): 13.

Beers, Henry P. "The Development of the Office of the Chief of Naval Operations, Part I." *Military Affairs* 10 (Spring 1946): 40–68.

———. "The Development of the Office of the Chief of Naval Operations, Part II." *Military Affairs* 10 (Fall 1946): 10–38.

———. "The Development of the Office of the Chief of Naval Operations, Part III." *Military Affairs* 11 (Summer 1947): 88–99.

Bibliography

———. "The Development of the Office of the Chief of Naval Operations, Part IV." *Military Affairs* 11 (Winter 1947): 229–37.

Boorda, J. M., ADM. "Time for a '. . . Sea' Change." U.S. Naval Institute *Proceedings* 120 (Aug. 1994): 9–10.

———. "What Are the Bedrock Requirements?" U.S. Naval Institute *Proceedings* 120 (Oct. 1994): 27–28, 53–55.

———. ". . .We're Tinkering with Success Here." U.S. Naval Institute *Proceedings* 121 (Apr. 1995): 30–36.

Brewster, Albert E., BGEN, USMC (Ret.). "The Commandant of the Marine Corps and the JCS." *Marine Corps Gazette* 92 (Mar. 2008): 58–66.

Branch, Ted N., VADM (USN). "A New Era in Naval Warfare." U.S. Naval Institute *Proceedings* 140 (July 2014): 18–23.

Brook, Douglas A., with Christina Hajj, Sally Baho, and LT Anthony Macaluso. "Implementation of the Chief Management Officer in the Department of Defense: An Interim Report." Center for Defense Management and Research, Naval Postgraduate School (Mar. 2013): 1–40.

Burgess, Richard R. "The New Main Battery, The Navy Realigns Its Organization toward Information Dominance." *Seapower* (Dec. 2009): 16–18.

Cancian, Mark. "Acquisition Reform: It's Not as Easy as It Seems." *Acquisition Review Quarterly* (Summer 1995): 189–98.

Cavas, Christopher P. "In the End, LCS Dodges the Critics." *Defense News* (11 Jan. 2015).

Clark, Vernon E., ADM, USN. "Sea Power 21: Projecting Decisive Joint Capabilities." U.S. Naval Institute *Proceedings* 128 (Oct. 2002): 32–41.

Cochrane, Charles B. "DOD's New Acquisition Approach, Myth or Reality?" *Program Manager* (July–Aug. 1992): 38–46.

"Daniels Names Naval Advisors. Announces Makeup of Board of Inventors Headed by Thomas A. Edison." *New York Times*, 13 Sept. 1915.

Danzig, Richard. "Today's Navy and Marine Corps: 'Always There When the Nation Calls'." *Seapower* 42 (Oct. 1999): 11–17.

Eaton, George B., MAJ, USA. "General Walter Krueger and Joint War Planning, 1922–1938." *Naval War College Review*, vol 48, no.2, (Spring, 1995): 91–113.

Farrell, Lawrence P., Jr. "Budget Control Act of 2011 Forces Real Cuts to Defense, and Difficult Choices." *National Defense* (Sept. 2011) at www.nationaldefensemagazine.org/archive/2011/September/Pages/Budget.

Fastabend, David A. "That Elusive Operational Concept." *Army* (June 2001): 37–44.

Fein, Geoff. "Deep Blue Gives Way to Bolstered Director Navy Staff Office." *Defense Daily* 23 (May 2008).

———. "N2/N6 Reorganization to Give Fleet Right Information at Right Time, CNO Says." *Defense Daily* 24 (July 2009).

Fellman, Sam. "High-Profile Firings in the Navy on the Rise." *Navy Times*. 3 Jan. 2011.

Fenster, Herbert L. "The A-12 Legacy: It Wasn't an Airplane—It Was a Train Wreck." U.S. Naval Institute *Proceedings* 125 (Feb. 1999): 33–39.

Foggo, James G., III, VADM. "The 'Barber Shop' Is Now Closed." U.S. Naval Institute Blog Archive (July 2014).

Freedberg, Sydney J. "U.S. Has Lost 'Dominance In Electromagnetic Spectrum': Shaffer." *Breaking Defense* (3 Sept. 2014): 1–3.

Gackle, Jonathan O., LTCOL, USMC. "Redefining MAGTF Logistics." *Marine Corps Gazette* 89 (Aug. 2005): 31–33.

Gortney, William, ADM, USN, and ADM Harry Harris, USN. "Applied Readiness." U.S. Naval Institute *Proceedings* 140 (Oct. 2014): 40–45.

Greenwood, John T. "The Emergence of the Postwar Strategic Air Force, 1945–1953." In *Air Power and Warfare,* Proceedings of the 8th Military History Symposium, U.S. Air Force Academy, 18–20 October 1978, 215–44. Edited by Alfred F. Hurley and Robert C. Ehrhart. Washington, DC: Office of Air Force History and U.S. Air Force Academy, 1979.

Hancock, William, VADM, USN. "The Officer in Charge of Risk." U.S. Naval Institute *Proceedings* 123 (Aug. 1997): 46–49.

Hanks, Christopher H. "Financial Accountability at the DoD: Reviewing the Bidding." *Defense Acquisition Review Journal*. Defense Acquisition University (July 2009): 181–96.

Harvey, John C. Jr., ADM, USN, with CAPT David E. Grogan, USN, and CDR Anthony J. Mazzeo, USN (Ret.). "Course Corrections in Command and Control." U.S. Naval Institute *Proceedings* 138 (Mar. 2012): 56–61.

Hattendorf, John B. "The Evolution of the Maritime Strategy: 1977–1987." *Naval War College Review* 51 (Summer 1988): 7–28.

Hitch, Charles J. "Decision-Making in the Department of Defense." H. Rowan Gaither Lectures in Systems Sciences, Univ. of California at Berkeley, (Apr. 1965): 2–52.

Hodge, Randy, LTCOL, USMC (Ret.), and CAPT Grisell Collazo, USN, and CDR Kerry Pearson, USN. "Naval Logistics Integration, Refocusing Efforts in 2009." *Marine Corps Gazette* 93 (May 2009): 50–53.

Hone, Thomas C. "The Effectiveness of the Washington Treaty Navy." *Naval War College Review* 32 (Nov.–Dec. 1979): 35–59.

———. "Spending Patterns of the U.S. Navy, 1921–1941." *Armed Forces and Society* 8 (Spring 1982): 443–62.

———. "Navy Air Leadership: Rear Admiral William A. Moffett as Chief of the Bureau of Aeronautics." In *Air Leadership,* 83–118. Edited by Wayne Thompson. Washington, DC: Office of Air Force History, 1986.

———. "The Program Manager as Entrepreneur: AEGIS and RADM Wayne Meyer." *Defense Analysis* 3 (Fall 1987): 197–212.

———. "Fighting on Our Own Ground: The War of Production, 1920–1942." *Naval War College Review* vol. 45, no. 2 (Spring 1992): 93–107.

———. "Force Planning Cycles: The Modern Navy as an Illustrative Case of a Frustrating Trend." *Defense Analysis* 9 (No. 1, 1993): 31–42.

———. "Naval Reconstitution, Surge, and Mobilization: Once and Future." *Naval War College Review* vol. 47, no. 3 (Summer 1994): 67–85.

———. "The Disestablishment of OP-07." Center for Naval Analyses, CQR 98-3/July 1998.

———. "Replacing Battleships with Aircraft Carriers in the Pacific in World War II." *Naval War College Review* 66 (Winter 2013): 56–6.

Hone, Thomas C., and Norman Friedman. "Innovation and Administration in the Navy Department: The Case of the *Nevada* Design." *Military Affairs* (Apr. 1981): 57–62.

Hone, Thomas C. and Mark Mandeles. "Interwar Innovation in Three Navies: USN, RN, IJN." *Naval War College Review* 40 (Spring 1987): 63–83.

———. "Managerial Style in the Interwar Navy: A Reappraisal." *Naval War College Review* 32 (Sept.–Oct. 1980): 88–101.

Hone, Trent. "The Evolution of Fleet Tactical Doctrine in the U.S. Navy, 1922–1941." *Journal of Military History* 67, no. 4 (Oct. 2003): 1107–1148.

———. "U.S. Navy Surface Battle Doctrine and Victory in the Pacific." *Naval War College Review*, 62, no. 1 (Winter 2009): 67–105.

———. "The U.S. Navy." In *To Crown the Waves: The Great Navies of the First World War*, 257-307. Ed. by Vincent P. O'Hara, W. David Dickson, and Richard Worth. Annapolis, MD: Naval Institute Press, 2013.

Jackson, Alex. "Annapolis Grads, Like Mids, Face Conduct Scrutiny." *The Capital*. Annapolis, MD (31 Dec. 2012).

Johnson, Jay, ADM, USN. "Included in Our Sticker Price." U.S. Naval Institute *Proceedings* 123 (Mar. 1997): 6–10.

———. "The Navy Operational Concept: Forward . . . From the Sea." *Seapower* 40 (May 1997): 15–22.

———. "Anytime, Anywhere: A Navy for the 21st Century." U.S. Naval Institute *Proceedings* 123 (Nov. 1997): 48–50.

Kaplan, Robert D. "The Atlantic: What Rumsfeld Got Right, How Donald Rumsfeld Remade the U.S. Military for a More Uncertain World." *CFR.org*. Council on Foreign Relations, 1 Aug. 2008. Web. 21 July 2014.

Kelly, Richard L., LTGEN, USMC. "Logistics Modernization: Lethality and Effectiveness." *Marine Corps Gazette* 89 (Aug. 2005): 16–19.

Kennedy, Floyd D. Jr. "U.S. Naval Aircraft and Weapon Developments in 1990." U.S. Naval Institute *Proceedings* 117 (May 1991): 160–66.

———. "U.S. Naval Aircraft and Weapon Developments in 1991." U.S. Naval Institute *Proceedings* 118 (May 1992): 169–77.

———. "U.S. Naval Aircraft and Weapon Developments." U.S. Naval Institute *Proceedings* 119 (May 1993): 150–54.

———. "U.S. Naval Aircraft and Weapon Developments." U.S. Naval Institute *Proceedings* 120 (May 1994): 152–64.

———. "U.S. Naval Aircraft and Weapon Development in Review." U.S. Naval Institute *Proceedings* 121 (May 1995): 150–60.

———. "U.S. Naval Aircraft and Weapon Developments." *U.S. Naval Institute Proceedings* 122 (May 1996): 122–30.

———. "U.S. Naval Aircraft and Weapon Developments: The Budget." *U.S. Naval Institute Proceedings* 122 (June 1996): 50–53.

———. "U.S. Naval Aircraft and Weapon Developments." *U.S. Naval Institute Proceedings* 124 (May 1998): 120–30.

———. "U.S. Naval Aircraft and Weapon Developments." *U.S. Naval Institute Proceedings* 125 (May 1999): 112–20.

Kester, Randall B. "The War Industries Board, 1917–1918: A Study in Industrial Mobilization." *American Political Science Review* 34 (Aug. 1940): 655–84.

Korb, Lawrence J. "The Budget Process in the Department of Defense, 1947–77: The Strength and Weaknesses of Three Systems." *Public Administration Review* 36 (July–Aug. 1977): 334–46.

Kotz, Nick. "Breaking Point." *Washingtonian* (Dec. 1996): 93–121.

Kozloski, Robert P. "Marching Toward the Sweet Spot, Options for the U.S. Marine Corps in a Time of Austerity." *Naval War College Review* 66 (Summer 2013): 13–36.

LaGrone, Sam. "Randy Forbes to CNO Greenert: 'The Navy desperately needs a strategy,'" *USNI News*, 1 Oct. 2014, http://news.usni.org/2014/10/01/randy-forbes-cno-greenert-navy-desperately-needs-strategy.

Landau, Martin, and Donald Chisholm. "The Arrogance of Optimism." *Journal of Contingencies and Crisis Management* 3 (June 1995): 67–80.

Linkowitz, Nicholas. "Future MAGTF Logistics and Support From the Sea (2010+)." *Marine Corps Gazette* 87 (Aug. 2003): 23–29.

Locher, James R., III. "Taking Stock of Goldwater-Nichols." *Joint Force Quarterly* (Autumn 1996): 10–16.

———. "Has It Worked? The Goldwater-Nichols Reorganization Act." *Naval War College Review* 54 (Autumn 2001): 95–115.

Manthorpe, William H. J., CAPT, USN (Ret.). "The Secretary and CNO on 23–24 October 1962, Setting the Historical Record Straight." *Naval War College Review* 66 (Winter 2013): 21–40.

March, James G. "The Business Firm as a Political Coalition." *The Journal of Politics* 24, no. 4 (Nov. 1962): 662–78.

McBride, William M. "Powering the U.S. Fleet, Propulsion Machinery Design and American Naval Engineering Culture, 1890–1945." In *New Interpretations in Naval History*, 51–68. Edited by Marcus O. Jones. Newport, RI: Naval War College Press, 2016.

McCoy, Kevin M., VADM USN. "To Improve the Material Readiness of the Surface Fleet." *U.S. Naval Institute Proceedings* 139 (May 2013): 18–23.

Merton, Robert K. "The Ambivalence of Organizational Leaders." In *The Contradictions of Leadership*, 1–26. Edited by James F. Oates Jr. New York: Appleton-Century-Crofts, 1970.

Messina, Barry P. "Development of U.S. Joint and Amphibious Doctrine, 1898–1945." Arlington, VA: Center for Naval Analyses, 1994.

Bibliography

Miles, Paul L. "Roosevelt and Leahy: The Orchestration of Global Strategy." In *FDR and the U.S. Navy*, 147–62. Edited by Edward J. Marolda. New York: St. Martin's Press, 1998.

Miller, Paul David, ADM, USN. "The Military After Next." U.S. Naval Institute *Proceedings* 120 (Feb. 1994): 41–44.

Morgan, John G., VADM, USN. "A Maritime Strategy for a Changed World." *The Log*. New York: New York Council of the Navy League of the United States (Winter 2007).

Mullen, Michael G., VADM, USN. "Global Concept of Operations." U.S. Naval Institute *Proceedings* 129 (Apr. 2003): 66–69.

Mullen, Michael G., ADM, USN. "Sea Enterprise: Resourcing Tomorrow's Fleet." U.S. Naval Institute *Proceedings* 130 (Jan. 2004): 60–63.

———. "What I Believe: Eight Tenets That Guide My Vision for the 21st Century Navy." U.S. Naval Institute *Proceedings* 132 (Jan. 2006): 12–16.

Mundy, Carl E., GEN, USMC. "The Golden Age of Naval Forces Is Here." U.S. Naval Institute *Proceedings* 120 (Nov. 1994): 27–28, 78–80.

Mundy, Carl E. GEN, USMC, (Ret.). "Navy-Marine Corps Team: Equalizing the Partnership." U.S. Naval Institute *Proceedings* 121 (Dec. 1995): 27– 30.

Nathman, John B., ADM, USN. "Shaping the Future." U.S. Naval Institute *Proceedings* 132 (Jan. 2006): 18–21.

Natter, Robert J., ADM, USN. "New Command Unifies the Fleet." U.S. Naval Institute *Proceedings* 128 (Jan. 2002): 72–74.

Naval Studies Group, Center for Naval Analyses. "The Defense Planning, Programming, and Budgeting System (PPBS): Past, Present, and Future." Conference Report. Coordinators: Dr. Bernard Rostker and Dr. Lewis Cabe (Mar. 1983).

O'Rourke, Ronald. "Navy Littoral Combat Ship (LCS) Program: Background and Issues for Congress." Congressional Research Service Report RL33741 (24 Dec. 2014).

Paullin, Charles Oscar. "A Half Century of Naval Administration." U.S. Naval Institute *Proceedings* 40 (Jan.–Feb. 1914): 111–28.

Peniston, Bradley. "Congressional Watch." U.S. Naval Institute *Proceedings* 124 (May 1998): 131–34.

———. "Congressional Watch." U.S. Naval Institute *Proceedings* 125 (May 1999): 121–24.

Petersen, Peter B. "Fighting for a Better Navy: An Attempt at Scientific Management (1905–1912)." *Journal of Management*, vol. 16, no. 1 (1990): 151–66.

Potter, David, CAPT, USN (SC). "The Annual Naval Appropriation Bill: How It Becomes a Law." U.S. Naval Institute *Proceedings*, vol. 58, no. 358 (Dec. 1932): 1723–28.

Pratt, William V., ADM. "Naval Policy and the Naval Treaty." *North American Review*, vol. 215, no. 798 (May 1922): 590–99.

———. "Disarmament and the National Defense," U.S. Naval Institute *Proceedings*, vol. 55, no. 9 (Sept. 1929): 751–64.

———. "Our Naval Policy." U.S. Naval Institute *Proceedings*, vol. 58, no. 353 (July 1932): 953–70.

Puleston, William D., CAPT, USN. "Modernizing the U.S.S. *Mississippi* [(BB-41)]," *Scientific American*, vol. 150, no. 6 (June 1934): 298–300.

Richardson, John M., ADM. "A Design for Maintaining Maritime Security," *Naval War College Review*, vol. 69, no. 2 (Spring 2016): 11–18.

Rochlin, Gene I., Todd R. La Porte, and Karlene H. Roberts. "The Self-Designing High-Reliability Organization: Aircraft Carrier Flight Operations at Sea," *Naval War College Review* 40 (Autumn 1987): 76–90.

Rosenberg, David A. "American Postwar Air Doctrine and Organization: The Navy Experience." In *Air Power and Warfare,* Proceedings of the 8th Military History Symposium, U.S. Air Force Academy, 18–20 October 1978: 245–78. Edited by Alfred F. Hurley and Robert C. Ehrhart. Washington, DC: Office of Air Force History and U.S. Air Force Academy, 1979.

Roughead, Gary. "Information Dominance: The Navy's Initiative to Maintain the Competitive Advantage in the Information Age." Remarks delivered at the Center for Strategic and International Studies (CSIS), Washington, DC, 1 Oct. 2009.

Rubel, Robert C. "Slicing the Onion Differently: Sea Power and the Levels of War." *Joint Force Quarterly* 64 (Jan. 2012): 107–14.

———. "Response to Steven Wills's 'The Effect of the Goldwater-Nichols Act of 1986 on Naval Strategy, 1987–1994': Some Missing Pieces." *Naval War College Review* 69 (Summer 2016): 165–69.

Sloan, Allan. "Taking Stock Five Years after the Meltdown." *The Washington Post* (17 June 2012): G-6.

Smith, Karen Domabyl, with Dean Cheng, Rebecca L. Kirk, Frederick Thompson, Alison Rimsky Vernon, and Kletus Lawler. "Aviation Type Command Alignment: The Promise and the Pitfalls." Center for Naval Analyses D0007438.A2/Final (January 2003).

Stavridis, James G., ADM, USN (Ret.), and David Weinstein. "Time for a U.S. Cyber Force." U.S. Naval Institute *Proceedings* 140 (Jan. 2014): 40–44.

Stirling, Yates, CDR, USN. "Organization for Navy Department Administration," U.S. Naval Institute *Proceedings*, vol. 39, no. 2 (June 1913): 435–99, and "Discussion," 501–502.

Swartz, Peter M. "The Maritime Strategy Debates: A Guide to the Renaissance of U.S. Naval Strategic Thinking in the 1980s." OPNAV P-60-3-87 (Washington, DC: OP-06, 1987).

Swartz, Peter M., CAPT, USN (Ret.) and Michael C. Markowitz. "Organizing OPNAV, 1970–2009." Center for Naval Analyses (Jan. 2010).

Sweetman, Jack. "Take Veracruz at Once," *Naval History* (April 2014): 34–41.

Theohary, Catherine A., and Anne Harrington. "Cyber Operations in DOD Policy and Plans: Issues for Congress." Congressional Research Service Report R43848 (5 Jan. 2015).

Trost, Carlisle A. H., ADM, USN. "The View from the Bridge." *Sea Power* 29 (Oct. 1986): 11–30.

———. "Looking Beyond the Maritime Strategy." *U.S. Naval Institute Proceedings* 113 (Jan. 1987): 13–16.

Turner, Stansfield, VADM, USN. "Missions of the U.S. Navy," *Naval War College Review* 26 (Mar.–Apr. 1974): 2–17.

U.S. Naval Institute. "The Maritime Strategy." *Proceedings* 112 (Jan. 1986 Supplement).

Washington, James W., LTCOL, USMC (Ret.). "Sea Viking Joint Deployment Operations." *Marine Corps Gazette* 89 (Mar. 2005): 14–16.

———. "Joint Deployment Process Transformation." *Marine Corps Gazette* 91 (May 2007): 43–46.

Bibliography

Wieringa, Jeffrey A., RADM, USN. "Spiral Development and the F/A-18." *Program Manager* (May–June 2003): 50–52.

Williams, Stuart. "The Ship Characteristics and Improvement Board: A Status Report." *Naval Engineers Journal* 96 (May 1984): 39–46.

Williams, William J. "Josephus Daniels and the U.S. Navy's Shipbuilding Program during World War I," *The Journal of Military History* 60 (Jan. 1996): 7–38.

Wills, Steven. "The Effect of the Goldwater-Nichols Act of 1986 on Naval Strategy, 1987–1994," *Naval War College Review* 69 (Spring 2016): 21–40.

Work, Robert O. "Fleet Design and the Littoral Combat Ship." Draft paper. Collection of Thomas C. Hone.

———. "The Littoral Combat Ship: How We Got Here, and Why." Draft paper. Collection of Thomas C. Hone.

Yardley, Roland J., and Raj Raman, Jessie Riposo, James Chiesa, and John F. Schank. "Impacts of the Fleet Response Plan on Surface Combatant Maintenance." RAND Corporation Technical Report (2006).

PhD Dissertations

Haynes, Peter D., CAPT, USN. "American Naval Thinking in the Post–Cold War Era: The U.S. Navy and the Emergence of a Maritime Strategy, 1989–2007." Naval Postgraduate School (2013).

Mishler, John W., III. "Re-Organizing the Naval Air Systems Command." George Washington University (2000).

Woodall, Stephen R. "Strategic Forecasting in Long-Range Military Force Planning: With an Application to the Naval Case." The Catholic University of America (1985).

Papers

Borns, Jeffrey M. "How Secretary of Defense Rumsfeld Sought to Assert Civilian Control Over the Military." National War College, National Defense University Course 5603, 2002.

Light, Mark F., CAPT, USN. "The Navy's Moral Compass: Commanding Officers and Personal Misconduct." U.S. Army War College, Carlisle Barracks, PA, 2011.

Oliver, James K. "Congress and the Future of American Seapower: An Analysis of US Navy Budget Requests in the 1970s." Paper presented at the meetings of the American Political Science Association, Washington, 1976.

Swistak, Robert R. "Defense Resource Planning in the Navy: The CPAM Process." Defense Systems Management School (now the Defense Acquisition University). Ft. Belvoir, VA, 1974.

APPENDIX 1

Secretaries of the Navy and Chiefs of Naval Operations, 1915–2015

SECRETARIES	DATES	CHIEFS OF NAVAL OPERATIONS	DATES
Josephus Daniels	Mar. 1913–Mar. 1921	ADM William S. Benson	May 1915–Sept. 1919
Edwin C. Denby	Mar. 1921–Mar. 1924	ADM Robert E. Coontz	Nov. 1919–July 1923
Theodore Roosevelt Jr. (Acting)	10 Mar. 1924–19 Mar. 1924	ADM Edward W. Eberle	July 1923–Nov. 1927
Curtis D. Wilbur	19 Mar. 1924–Mar. 1929	ADM Charles F. Hughes	Nov. 1927–Sept. 1930
Charles F. Adams III	Mar. 1929–Mar. 1933	ADM William V. Pratt	Sept. 1930–June 1933
Claude A. Swanson	Mar. 1933–July 1939	ADM William H. Standley	July 1933–Jan. 1937
		ADM William D. Leahy	Jan. 1937–Aug. 1939
Charles Edison	7 July 1939–24 June 1940	ADM Harold R. Stark	Aug. 1939–2 Mar. 1942
Lewis Compton (Acting)	24 June 1940–11 July 1940		

619

Appendix 1

Secretaries of the Navy and Chiefs of Naval Operations, 1915–2015

SECRETARIES	DATES	CHIEFS OF NAVAL OPERATIONS	DATES
Frank Knox	11 July 1940–Apr. 1944	ADM Ernest J. King	2 Mar. 1942–15 Dec. 1945
Ralph A. Bard (Acting)	28 Apr. 1944–19 May 1944		
James V. Forrestal	19 May 1944–17 Sept. 1947		
		FADM Chester W. Nimitz	Dec. 1945–Dec. 1947
John L. Sullivan	Sept. 1947–May 1949	ADM Louis E. Denfeld	Dec. 1947–Nov. 1949
Francis P. Matthews	May 1949–July 1951	ADM Forrest P. Sherman	Nov. 1949–July 1951
Dan A. Kimball	July 1951–Jan. 1953	ADM William M. Fechteler	Aug. 1951–Aug. 1953
Robert B. Anderson	Feb. 1953–Mar. 1954	ADM Robert B. Carney	Aug. 1953–Aug. 1955
Charles S. Thomas	May 1954–Apr. 1957		
		ADM Arleigh A. Burke	Aug. 1955–Aug. 1961
Thomas S. Gates Jr.	Apr. 1957–June 1959		
William B. Franke	June 1959–Jan. 1961		
John B. Connally	Jan. 1961–Dec. 1961	ADM George W. Anderson Jr.	Aug. 1961–Aug. 1963
Frederick H. Korth	Jan. 1962–Nov. 1963	ADM David L. McDonald	Aug. 1963–Aug. 1967
Paul B. Fay (Acting)	2 Nov. 1963–28 Nov. 1963		
Paul H. Nitze	29 Nov. 63–30 June 67		
Charles F. Baird (Acting)	1 July 1967–31 Aug. 1967		
Paul R. Ignatius	Sept. 1967–Jan. 1969	ADM Thomas H. Moorer	Aug. 1967–July 1970

Secretaries of the Navy and Chiefs of Naval Operations, 1915–2015

SECRETARIES	DATES	CHIEFS OF NAVAL OPERATIONS	DATES
John H. Chafee	Jan. 1969–May 1972	ADM Elmo R. Zumwalt	July 1970–June 1974
John W. Warner	May 1972–Apr. 1974		
J. William Middendorf	Apr. 1974–Jan. 1977	ADM James L. Holloway III	June 1974–July 1978
W. Graham Claytor Jr.	Feb. 1977–Aug. 1979	ADM Thomas B. Hayward	July 1978–June 1982
Edward Hidalgo	Oct. 1979–Jan. 1981		
John F. Lehman Jr.	Feb. 1981–Apr. 1987	ADM James D. Watkins	June 1982–June 1986
		ADM Carlisle A. H. Trost	July 1986–June 1990
James H. Webb Jr.	May 1987–Feb. 1988		
William L. Ball	Mar. 1988–May 1989		
Henry L. Garrett III	May 1989–June 1992	ADM Frank B. Kelso II	June 1990–Apr. 1994
Daniel Howard (Acting)	7 July 1992–2 Oct. 1992		
Sean C. O'Keefe	2 Oct. 1992–20 Jan. 1993		
ADM Frank B. Kelso II (Acting)	20 Jan.–July 1993		
John H. Dalton	July 1993–Nov. 1998	ADM Jeremy M. Boorda	Apr. 1994–May 1996
		ADM Jay L. Johnson	May 1996–July 2000

Appendix 1

Secretaries of the Navy and Chiefs of Naval Operations, 1915–2015			
SECRETARIES	DATES	CHIEFS OF NAVAL OPERATIONS	DATES
Richard J. Danzig	Nov. 1998–Jan. 2001	ADM Vernon E. Clark	July 2000–July 2005
Robert B. Pirie Jr. (Acting)	Jan. 2001–May 2001		
Gordon R. England	May 2001–30 Jan. 2003		
Susan Livingstone (Acting)	30 Jan. 2003–7 Feb. 2003		
Hansford T. Johnson (Acting)	7 Feb. 2003–30 Sept. 2003		
Gordon R. England	1 Oct. 2003–29 Dec. 2005		
Dionel M. Aviles (Acting)	29 Dec. 2005–3 Jan. 2006	ADM Michael G. Mullen	July 2005–Sept. 2007
Donald C. Winter	3 Jan. 2006–Mar. 2009	ADM Gary Roughead	Sept. 2007–Sept. 2011
B. J. Penn (Acting)	13 Mar. 09–19 May 2009		
Raymond E. Mabus Jr.	19 May 2009–20 Jan. 2017	ADM Jonathan W. Greenert	Sept. 2011–Sept. 2015

APPENDIX 2

Abbreviations

AAAV	Advanced Amphibious Assault Vehicle
AAF	Army Air Forces
ACNO	Assistant Chief of Naval Operations
ASDS	advanced SEAL delivery system
ASN(RD&A)	Assistant Secretary of the Navy (Research, Development and Acquisition)
ASW	antisubmarine warfare
BRAC	base realignment and closure commission
BSO	budget submission offices
BuAer	Bureau of Aeronautics
BuC&R	Bureau of Construction and Repair
BuDocks	Bureau of Yards and Docks
BuNav	Bureau of Navigation, later became BuPers
BuOrd	Bureau of Ordnance
BuPers	Bureau of Naval Personnel
BuSandA	Bureau of Supplies and Accounts
BuShips	Bureau of Ships
BuWeps	Bureau of Naval Weapons
C4I	Command, Control, Communications, Computers and Intelligence
CAB	CNO Advisory Board
CANES	Consolidated Afloat Networks and Enterprise Services
CCS	Combined Chiefs of Staff
CDR	Critical Design Review
CEB	CNO Executive Board
CENTCOM	Central Command
CEP	CNO Executive Panel
CIA	Central Intelligence Agency
CINCLANT	Commander-in-Chief, Atlantic Command
CINCLANTFLT	Commander-in-Chief, Atlantic Fleet

Appendix 2

CINCPAC	Commander-in-Chief, Pacific Command
CINCUS	Commander-in Chief, U.S. Fleet, 1922–1942
CJCS	Chairman of the Joint Chiefs of Staff
CJCSI	Chairman of the Joint Chiefs of Staff Instruction
CMMI	Capability Maturity Model Integration
CMO	chief management officer
CNO	Chief of Naval Operations
CO	commanding officer
COMINCH	Commander-in Chief, U.S. Fleet, 1942–1945
CPAM	CNO's Program Analysis Memorandum
CSG	carrier strike group
DAB	Defense Acquisition Board
DAWG	Deputy's Advisory Working Group
DCNO	Deputy Chief of Naval Operations
DE	destroyer escort
DFC	Detachment for Cause
DIA	Defense Intelligence Agency
DLA	Defense Logistics Agency
DMR	Defense Management Report
DOD	Department of Defense
DPG	Defense Planning Guidance
DPSB	Navy Department Program Strategy Board
DRB	Defense Resources Board
DSARC	Defense Systems Acquisition Review Council
EFV	expeditionary fighting vehicle
EO	executive order
ERGM	Extended Range Gun Munition
EUCOM	European Command
F2D2	Functional Flow Diagrams and Descriptions
FLTCYBERCOM	Fleet Cyber Command
FSAT	Force Structure Assessment Team
FY	fiscal year
FYDP	Five Year, and later Future Years Defense Program
GAO	Government Accountability Office
GDF	Guidance for Development of the Force
GDP	gross domestic product
GEF	Guidance for Employment of the Force
GWOT	global war on terrorism
HSV	high speed vessel

IBR	Investment Balance Review
IED	improvised explosive device
IFOR	Implementation Force in Bosnia
ihp	indicated horsepower
IO	information operations
IOT&E	Initial Operational Test and Evaluation
IPT	Integrated Product Team
IR2B/R2B	Integrated Resource Review Board/Resource Review Board
IR3B	Integrated Resource and Requirements Review Board
ISA	International Security Affairs
ISR	intelligence, surveillance, and reconnaissance
JAG	judge advocate general
JAST	Joint Advanced Strike Technology
JCIDS	Joint Capabilities Integration and Development System
JCS	Joint Chiefs of Staff
JDAM	Joint Direct Attack Munition
JFACC	joint force air component command
JFCOM	Joint Forces Command
JMA	Joint Military Assessment later Joint Mission Assessment
JOPP	joint operation planning process
JROC	Joint Requirements Oversight Council
JSF	Joint Strike Fighter
JSPD	Joint Strategic Planning Document
JSTPS	Joint Strategic Target Planning Staff
LANTIRN	Low Altitude Navigation and Targeting Infrared for Night
LCAC	landing craft air cushion
LCS	littoral combat ship
MACV	Military Assistance Command Vietnam
MCCDC	Marine Corps Combat Development Command
MOC	maritime operations center
MPF	maritime prepositioning force
MRAP	mine-resistant, ambush-protected
NADEC	Naval Decision Center
NATO	North Atlantic Treaty Organization
NAVMAT	Naval Material Command
NAVWAG	Naval Warfare Analyses Group
NECC	Navy Expeditionary Combat Command
NETWARCOM	Naval Network Warfare Command
NROC	Navy Requirements Oversight Council

Appendix 2

NROTC	Naval Reserve Officer Training Corps
NSC	National Security Council
NSDD	national security decision directive
NWDC	Naval Warfare Development Command
NWP	Naval Warfare Publication, later became Navy warfare publication
OCO	overseas contingency operations
OEF	Operation Enduring Freedom
OIF	Operation Iraqi Freedom
OLA	Office of Legislative Affairs
OMB	Office of Management and Budget
OMFTS	operational maneuver from the sea
ONI	Office of Naval Intelligence
OP&M	Office of Procurement and Material
OPA	Office of Program Appraisal
OPNAV	Office of the Chief of Naval Operations
OPTEMPO	operating tempo
OSD	Office of the Secretary of Defense
OSD (PA&E)	Office of the Secretary of Defense Office of Program Analysis and Evaluation
OWM	Office of War Mobilization
PACOM	Pacific Command
PEO	program executive office
PM	program managers
PMP	Program Management Proposal
POM	program objective memorandum
PPB	Planning, Programming, and Budgeting
PPBE	Planning, Programming, Budgeting, and Execution, previously known as PPBS
PPBS	Planning, Programming, and Budgeting System, later known as PPBE
QDR	quadrennial defense review
QIG	Quadrennial Integration Group
R3B	Requirements and Resources Review Board
R&D	research and development
RDT&E	research, development, test and evaluation
RMC	regional maintenance center
SA	support assessment
SAC	Strategic Air Command
SAE	Service Acquisition Executive
SALT	Strategic Arms Limitation Treaty/talks
SCB	Ship Characteristics Board
SCIB	Ship Characteristics Improvement Board

SCOROR	Secretary's Committee on Research and Reorganization
SecDef	Secretary of Defense
SECNAV	Secretary of the Navy
SIOP	Single Integrated Operations Plan
SLRG	Senior Leader Review Group
SPAWAR	Space and Naval Warfare Systems Command
SPO	Special Projects Office
SSG	Strategic Studies Group
START	Strategic Arms Reduction Treaty
STRATCOM	Strategic Command
TARP	Troubled Asset Relief Program
TFIRM	Total Force Integrated Readiness Model
TFX	Multiservice fighter plane
TQL	Total Quality Leadership
TQM	Total Quality Management
TRADOC	United States Army Training and Doctrine Command
UAV	Unmanned Aerial Vehicle
USCYBERCOM	United States Cyber Command
USD(A)	Under Secretary of Defense for Acquisition
USD(AT&L)	Under Secretary of Defense for Acquisition, Technology and Logistics
USD(P)	Under Secretary of Defense for Policy
VCNO	Vice Chief of Naval Operations
WPD	War Plans Division
WPL	Navy War Plan

INDEX

Key: n indicates mention in endnotes, **bold** denotes an image

A-6, 331, 340, 357, 372, 388–89, 391–92, 404, 411, 413, 422
A-12, 372, 386–90, 392–94, 397, 411, 413, 422–24; investigation of, 371, 389–92
Adams, Charles F., 94, 96–98, 100, 103, 105, 110, 119
advanced SEAL delivery system (ASDS), 486
Aegis: air defense system, 305–6, 362, 364, 412, 416, 422, 451, 488; shipbuilding project, 307, 309–10, 508, 513; ships, 306, 408, 537
Aeronautical Board, 118
aids (later aides), Navy (1909), 10–12, 21n, 22n
Air Characteristics and Improvement Board, 340
Air Force, U.S., 195, 199, 267, 314, 320, 383, 404, 406, 409, 419, 422–23, 445, 447, 478, 515, 570; and Air Combat Command, 396, 465n; and "Black Book," 236; and DoD reorganization (1958), 231; and Navy, 196–97, 199–204, 206, 207n, 220, 224–25, 231–32, 236, 248, 254, 273n, 307–8, 336, 349, 391–92, 394, 460; and nuclear technology/weapons, 191, 196–97, 199–201, 248; and roles and missions debate, 199–200
Albion, Robert G., 94, 109, 149–50, 166, 193–94
Aldridge, Edward C., Jr., 370, 443–44
Allen, Ezra G., 149, 194
Allen, Richard C. "Sweet Pea," 413
Allen, Thad W., 519
Amos, James F., 480; creates Ellis Group, 545; as USMC Commandant, 524, 545
amphibious ships, 145, 147–48, 150–51, 188, 363, 406–7, 410–11, 426, 473, 477, 480–83, 490, 493, 521–24, 537, 544; LST, LSD, LSI, and LCT in World War II, 150–51
Anderson, George W., Jr., **249**, 252–53, 260, 571
Anderson, Robert B., 216, 219
Andrews, Adolphus, 90n, 116
antiaircraft trials (1939) and Antiaircraft Defense Board (1940), 139
Arcadia Conference (22 Dec. 1941–14 Jan. 1942), 150
Armed Forces Communications and Electronics Association, 477
Army Air Service/Forces, U.S., 74–75, 82, 147–48, 189–91, 196–97
Army–Navy Petroleum Board, 172
Army, U.S., 1, 29, 33, 43, 118, 123, 383, 396, 404, 419, 447–48, 461; and DoD reorganization (1958), 231; and Navy, 1, 5, 34–35, 37, 56, 63–64, 75–76, 90n, 101–2, 115, 118–21, 124, 126, 143, 147–48, 151, 153–57, 159–60, 164, 167, 172, 457; and unification, 190, 202
Army War College, 90n, 102–3, 456, 553
Arnold, Henry H., 153, 175
arsenal ship, 407, 412
Arthur, Stanley R., 381–83, 415–16
Aspin, Leslie, 387, 395, 403, 405
Assistant Chiefs of Naval Operations: Assistant to/Assistant Chief of Naval Operations (OP-11), 40–43, 56–57, 94, 98, 117–18, 125, 163, 172, 192, 197; for Air (1942), 143; for Air Warfare (OP-05), 360; for Communications (OP-94), 260; for General Planning, later for General Planning and Programming (OP-90), 238–39, 251, 259, 583; for Guided Missiles, 198; for Intelligence (OP-92), 231, 260; for

629

Personnel and Material (1942), 143; for Surface Warfare (OP-03), 358, 360; for Undersea Warfare (OP-02), 358, 360. *See also* Deputy Chiefs of Naval Operations and Chief of Naval Operations, Office of (OPNAV), organizations within
Assistant Commandant of the Marine Corps, 238, 549
Assistant Vice Chief of Naval Operations, Director of Naval Administration (OP-09B), 238, 271, 290. *See also* Chief of Naval Operations, Office of (OPNAV), organizations within
Atlantic Charter (1941), 124
Atlantic Command and Commander-in-Chief, Atlantic (CINCLANT), 214, 241n
Atomic Energy Commission, 262, 584
Atwood, Donald, 395
Aviation Supply Office (World War II), 167
A-X, 392–94

B-1, 268
B-29, 191, 196
B-36, 197, 204, 206
Baer, George, 120, 122, 352n
Bagley, Worth, 282, 288, 298n, 304, 323n
Balisle, Phillip M., 451–52; as commander, NAVSEA, 452, 466n; and Fleet Review Panel of Surface Forces Readiness (Balisle Report), 514–15, 523
Ball, William L., III, 361
Ballantine, Duncan, 152, 154, 157–58, 163–65
Barber, Arthur H., III, 479, 495n, 505, 510, 522, 527n, 593
Barlow, Jeffrey G., 188–89, 192, 197, 201–2, 218
Base Realignment and Closure Commission (BRAC), 394–95, 416
Basic Logistical Plan for Command Areas Involving Joint Army and Navy Operations (Mar. 1943), 155–56
Basiuk, Victor, 309–10, 317–19
Bath Iron Works, 484, 510–11
Beaumont Study, 290–91
Belknap, Reginald R., 5, 22n
Bennitt, Brent M., 413, 424
Benson, Roy S., and Benson Task Force study, 260, 262–66, 285, 287
Benson, William S., 94, **156**, 571; accompanies President Wilson to Europe after the Armistice, 45; as CNO, 17, 25–27, 29, 31–33, 35, **36–41**, 46–48, 52n, 58, 61, 578; issues "Action Doctrine," 48; promulgates Organization Orders of the Office of Naval Operations (1919), 46–47
Berman, Larry, 280, 292–93
Bethlehem Steel Company, 114–15
Betti, John, 389–90
Bipartisan Budget Act of 2013, 540
Bird, John M., 537
Blandy, William H. P., 198
Blickstein, Irving N., 421, 462n
Blinder, Alan S., 507
Bloch, Claude C., 89n, 109, 194
Blue Ribbon Commission on Defense Management (Packard Commission), 369–71, 379
Blue Ribbon Defense Panel, 281–82
Board on Construction, 2–3
Bonaparte, Charles, J., 6–8
Boorda, Jeremy M.: as Chief of BuPers/OP-01, 405, 408; as CNO, 403, **405**–8, 410–13, 415–19, 421, 424, 428, 429n, 430n, 432n, 575, 589
Booz, Fry, Allen & Hamilton (in World War II), 152
Bottom-Up Review, 393–94, 396–97, 403, 406–8
Bowen, Harold G., 107
Bowler, Daniel R., 439–40
Braisted, William, 48, 80
Branch, Ted N., 550–51, 562n
Brooks, Linton F., 346, 353n
Brown, George, 313
Brown, Harold, 309–11, 315, 330, 575–76
Budget and Accounting Act (1921), 55, 63, 65, 87n, 193
Budget Control Act of 2011, 524, 540, 559n
Buell, Thomas B., 140–41, 148, 150, 160, 163, 170–71
Bureau of Aeronautics (BuAer), 66–67, 71, 75, 79, 82–83, 97, 99–100, 107, 109, 124, 138, 152–53, 157, 161, 166–67, 192, 223, 233, 262, 568, 582
Bureau of Construction and Repair (BuC&R), 4, 7, 9, 17, 28, 32, 36, 40, 60, 64, 66, 97, 99–100, 107, 121. *See also* Bureau of Ships
Bureau of Engineering, 107, 114, 121. *See also* Bureau of Ships
Bureau of Equipment, 11
Bureau of Medicine and Surgery (BuMed), 10, 16–17, 36, 157, 259
Bureau of Naval Weapons (BuWeps), 233, 582. *See also* Bureau of Aeronautics and Bureau of Ordnance

Bureau of Navigation (BuNav), 1, 3, 7–8, 10–11, 15, 17, 28, 37, 66, 104, 114, 116, 262, 568. *See also* Bureau of Personnel

Bureau of Ordnance (BuOrd), 6–8, 15, 17, 26–27, 34, 36–37, 42, 44, 60, 98, 100, 107, 114, 119, 139, 144, 157, 166–167, 194, 223, 239; and immune zone concept, 98

Bureau of Personnel (BuPers), Navy, 166, 262; Mullen as chief of, 471. *See also* Bureau of Navigation

Bureau of Ships (BuShips), 121, 124, 144, 149, 150–51, 153, 157, 159, 166, 223–24, 254, 262

Bureau of Steam Engineering, 8, 15, 17, 27, 36, 40, 60, 100

Bureau of Supplies and Accounts (BuSandA), 16–17, 27, 36–38, 46, 157, 167, 255, 548

Bureau of the Budget (Department of the Treasury, later Executive Office of the President), 65, 95, 109–10, 115, 118, 149, 193, 195. *See also* Office of Management and Budget

Bureau of Yards and Docks (BuDocks), 17, 36, 157

bureaus, Navy, 2, 6–8, 10, 12, 16–18, 31, 41, 59, 60, 63, 65, 71, 94, 109, 112, 117–18, 150–53, 163, 177n; abolishment of, 259; and CNO's authority, 16–17, 26–28, 34, 36, 42, 44, 46–47, 57, 100, 107–8, 124–25, 138, 144, 168–69, 174–75, 347, 567, 569, 581; and COMINCH authority, 140, 158; lead bureau system, 224, 255; officer strength in July 1942, 144; organization of, 3, 582; and planning, 61–62, 71–72, 77, 83, 98, 109–10, 164, 567; producer/consumer distinction in, 170, 184n, 237; role of, 4, 8–9, 26, 266, 581–82; weapons development in, 582. *See also* individual bureaus

Burke, Arleigh A., 240–41, 254, 257, 284, 293, 344, 356, 407, **572**, 578, 582, 620; and Ad Hoc Committee to Review Navy Department Organization, 230, 233; appointment as CNO, 221; and BuWeps, 233; command experience of, 175; and command tradition, 203, 239; and Congress, 229, 231, 235–36; and defense reorganization, 229–**31**, 233–34, **235**–36, 270; as head of OP-23, 201–3, 221; and JCS, 231, 270; and Libby Board, 222–24; management style of, 225, 234–35; on McNamara, 248; and NAVWAG, 223; and New Look, 222; and planning, 237–39, 247; and Polaris, 222, 224, 241n, 291, 365, 571; and "public relations," 571; on quality of officers, 256; and Reed study, 231–32; on unification, 203–5, 235–36

Burke, William R., 514–19, 528n, 532–33, 536–38, 554

Bush, George H. W., **336**, 347, 378–79, 404, 406

Bush, George W., 437, 441–42, 444, 448–49, 456, 463n, 465n, 475, 493, 501–2, 506

Business Initiatives Council, 443

Business Transformation Council, 549

Byron, John, 586

Calhoun, William L., 156–57

Carlucci, Frank C., 330–32, 361

Carney, Robert B., 175, 202–3, **220**, 241; as CNO, 218–21, 225; as DCNO for Logistics (OP-04), 197–98; and long-range planning, 220–21, 223, 238

Carter, Jimmy (James E.), 307, 309–10, 312–13, 315, 321

Casey, George W., Jr., 473

Cebrowski, Arthur K., 419–20, 425, 459, 469n

Center for Naval Analyses, 262, 335, 363, 382

Center for Naval Warfare Studies (Newport), 320, 588

Center for Strategic and Budgetary Assessments, 548, 556n

Center for Strategic and International Studies, 519, 548

Central Command, U.S. (CENTCOM), 368, 492

Central Intelligence Agency (CIA), 199, 241, 444–45, 448, 499, 555

Cheney, Richard, 378–79, 389

Chief Financial Officer and Federal Financial Reform Act (PL 101-576), 406; and Chief Financial Officers Council, 406

Chief Management Officer, 504–5, 546, 549; and deputy chief management officers, 523–24

Chief of Naval Operations (CNO): and acquisition, 412, 415–16, 486, 488, 512, 565; authority of, xx, xxii, 15–17, 25–26, 32, 34, 37, 42, 44–45, 48, 57–58, 61, 65, 71, 108, 111, 125, 131n, 137–38, 161, 168–69, 187, 192–93, 215, 233–34, 267, 313, 355, 377, 429n, 566–67, 574, 590; and Base Force, 378, 587; and Basic War Plan, 61–62; and bureaus, 16–17, 26–28, 31, 34, 36, 42, 44, 46–48, 57, 100, 107–8, 124–25, 138, 144, 168–69, 174–75, 233, 259, 347, 567–69, 581; and Chief of Naval Material, 192, 259–60;

631

Index

and COMINCH, 137, 140–42, 144–45, 161, 167–70, 175, 578, 588; and Congress, xxi, 2, 15, 33, 65–66, 71, 74, 81, 83, 95–96, 105, 109, 114–16, 126, 140, 150, 201, 215, 221, 231, 304, 356, 364–67, 424, 538–39; and DoD reorganization (1958), 234, 270, 566; and DoD reorganization (1986), 355, 365–67, 369, 377, 476, 565; establishment of, 1, 14–16, 18; and Fleet Forces Command, 449–50, 471, 474–77, 490, 578; and fleet modernization, 107, 290, 305–6; and fleet problems, 73, 76–77, 83–84, 111–12, 566, 568, 581; and "inner staff," 571–73, 580; as JCS member, xx–xxi, 138, 201, 221, 231, 315, 346, 406, 566, 575–77, 589; as Navy budget officer, 65, 72; planning process, 25, 34, 40–41, 55, 61–63, 71–72, 77, 103; planning process and operational versus logistic planning, 152–55, 158, 161–64; political influence of, 83, 204; and programing, 318, 332, 364, 412; and programming and link to long range planning, 237–39, 420, 584; and readiness, 304–9, 322, 337, 415, 440–41, 451, 471–72, 514–15, 533, 540–41; relation to General Board, 62, 71; and Reorganization Plan 7, 215–18; and requirements, 318, 407, 441, 524–25, 543, 583; role of, xix, xx–xxi, 15, 28, 33, 44, 47, 55–56, 58–59, 61, 73, 117–20, 126, 334, 403, 412, 437, 443, 501, 565, 570–71; and the SECNAV, xxi, 16–17, 25, 31, 55, 110, 160–61, 168, 173, 203, 218, 233, 252–53, 280, 315, 335, 340–41, 343, 347, 355, 369, 426–27; and shipbuilding programs, 451–52, 472, 484–86, 488–89, 493, 507–14, 521, 541–45; and systems commands, 516, 581; workload of, 42, 45, 65, 234, 261, 412, 454

Chief of Naval Operations, Office of (OPNAV): 1995 draft reorganization, 416–17; Action Doctrine, 48; audit of, 270–71; and Balisle Report, 514–15; Beaumont study of, 290–91; and Benson Study, 260–64, 266; and capabilities planning, 383, 411, 452–53, 474, 478–79; and decision making, 239–40; and Dillon Board, 250–51, 254–56; duties and roles of, xxi–xxii, 1, 28, 32–33, 43, 46, 61–62, 93, 143, 152, 163–64, 203, 331, 334, 478–80, 565; establishment of, 14–15, 33–34; and "Estimate of the Situation," 77–78, 81, 84, 102, 110, 118, 130n; "Estimate of the Situation" and Base Development Program, 109, 127n; and forward presence, 410, 421; and Franke Board, 232–34; and Libby Board, 222–24; logistic support of fleets in World War II, 154–57, 161–65; management of, 234, 269, 437, 442, 554–55; and Marine Corps, post–Cold War, 415, 418, 425–26, 428, 441, 477, 481–84, 486, 490–91, 521–23, 544–45; and OP-96 study, 265–66; organization charts for, 32, 63, 72, 100, 117, 144, 162, 198, 234, 261, 287, 344, 358, 384, 439, 453, 479, 518, 534; personnel numbers from different years, 36, 45, 85n, 144, 177n, 265, 297, 550, 568, 570; and planning process, 55, 61–63, 67–69, 71–72, 77–78, 82–83, 97, 167, 205, 364; and platform sponsors, 283, 317–18, 320, 360, 364, 380, 396, 438–39, 533–34; post–World War II organization of, 188–89, 569; and PPBE, 478, 492, 536, 555, 583; and PPBS, 261–62, 268–69, 356, 360, 410, 425, 579, 583; pre–World War II organization of, 126, 568; producer/consumer distinction in, 170, 184n, 217, 237, 255, 259; programming in, 262, 332, 364, 384, 408–10, 444, 474, 479–80, 534–35, 566, 583, 586; and project managers, 258, 260, 262–63, 310, 312, 341, 488; and Reed study, 231–32; reorganization of, 229–30, 255–56, 264, 285–86, 288, 290–91, 297, 312, 358–59, 384, 395–96, 421, 437–40, 477–79, 532–34, 537–38, 554, 569–70; and shipbuilding in World War II, 158–60; special projects office in, 223–24, 291; systems analysis in, 362–63; under Lehman, 340–42; warfare communities in, 232; wartime organization of, 142–44

Chief of Naval Operations, Office of (OPNAV), organizations within: Ad Hoc Priorities Analysis Group, 283; Air Warfare, Director of (N88, later N78, later N88, later N98), 396, 413, 432n, 439, 458, 533; Air Warfare Division (OP-55), 205–6; Antisubmarine Warfare Programs, Director of (OP-095), 287–88, 290, 318–19 (later redesignated Antisubmarine Warfare and Tactical Electromagnetic Programs, (OP-095), 290; redesignated Naval Warfare, Director of, (OP-095) (*see* below)); Antisubmarine Warfare Division (N84), 439; Assessment and Affordability Branch (N812), 420; Assessment Division (later Capability Analysis and Assessment) (N81), 420,

632

453–54, 479–80, 505, 522, 535–36, 550, 556; Central Division (OP-13), 98, 143, 568; CNO Executive Panel (CEP) support staff (OP-00K, later N00K), 283, 339, 359, 379, 453–54; Code and Signal Section (OP-20G), 126; Communications Division (OP-20), 33, 143, 568; Convoy and Routing Section, 172; Electronics Office (OP-25), 569; Expeditionary Warfare, Director of (N85, later N95), 396, 416, 439, 533; Fiscal Management Division (OP-92), 288–89; Fleet Maintenance Division (OP-23), 130n, 131n; Fleet Maintenance Division (OP-23), planning fleet support in World War II, 152, 154; Fleet Training Division (OP-22), 76, 80, 99, 125, 141–42, 152, 568; General Planning and Programming Division (OP-90) (in OP-090), 332, 337; General Planning Group (OP-001), 201; Hydrographic Office in OPNAV (OP-28), 143, 569; Inspection and Survey, Board of, in OPNAV (OP-21), 26, 143, 567, 569; Inspection and Survey, Board of, in OPNAV (OP-21), as Inspection Division (OP-21), 568; Inspector General, Navy (OP-08, later OP-008, later N09G), 198, 369, 421, 552; Interdepartmental Communications Division, 568; Logistic Organization Planning Unit (World War II), 161–62; Long Range Objectives Group (OP-93), 220, 223, 238, 265–66; Long Range Planning Group (OP-00X), 320; Long Range Planning Group (OP-00X), functions transferred to as OP-00K, 359; Material Division, 33, 62, 568; Mine Warfare Section, 172; National Policy and Command Organization Branch, 312; Naval Administration, Director of (OP-09B), 238, 271, 290 (*see also* Assistant VCNO); Naval Districts Division (OP-30), 33, 568; Naval Districts Inspection Board (OP-31), 143; Naval Education and Training, Director of (OP-099), 288; Naval Intelligence, in OPNAV, as Director of Naval Intelligence (OP-009, later OP-092), 288, 358; Naval Intelligence, in OPNAV as N2, 516–17; Naval Intelligence, in OPNAV, as Intelligence Division (OP-16), 143, 148, 568; Naval Intelligence, in OPNAV, as Office of Naval Intelligence, 32, 45, 59, 85 (*see also* ACNO for Intelligence, DCNO for Information Dominance, and Office of Naval Intelligence); Navy Net Assessment (OP-96N), 297, 320; Naval Observatory, in OPNAV (OP-29), 144, 569; Naval Reserve, in OPNAV, as Director of Naval Reserve (OP-09R), 290; Naval Reserve, in OPNAV, as Naval Reserve Policy Division (OP-15), 568; Navy Staff, Director (DNS), 454, 516, 519, 537, 550, 570 (*see also* Assistant VCNO, Director of Naval Administration (OP-09B)); Naval Transportation Service (OP-39), 84, 144, 172, 569; Naval War College, in OPNAV, 16, 26–27, 33, 42, 65, 568 (moved to BuNav in 1933, 568) (*see also* Naval War College); Naval Warfare Analyses Group (NAVWAG), 223; Naval Warfare, Director of (OP-095), 319, 358, 363; Naval Warfare, Director of (OP-095), as OP-07 (*see* DCNO for Naval Warfare); Operations Division, 33; OPNAV Alignment Working Group, 438–39; Organizational Appraisal, Director of (OP-09E2), 306; Organizational Research and Policy Division (OP-23), 201, 204; Pan American Division (OP-17), 143; Planning Section (1930 "inner staff"), 98–99; Plans Division, 33, 60, 64–65; Plans Division, changed to War Plans Division (WPD) (OP-12), 62, 68, 71, 77–79, 81, 83, 97–99, 120, 125, 141, 152, 568; Plans Division, changed to Logistic Plans Division (OP-12), 143, 164, 171, 568–69; Program Evaluation Center (in OP-90), 239; Program Planning, Director of (OP-090), 252–54, 260, 283, 285, 287–88, 290, 292, 296, 312, 316–20, 332, 339, 355, 358–59, 569; Program Planning, Director of (OP-090), and program sponsors, 318; Program Planning, Director of (OP-090), system analysts in, 296 (*see also* DCNO for Naval Program Planning); Program Resource Appraisal Division (OP-91) (in OP-090), 339; Publicity Division, 33; Quadrennial Integration Group (QIG) (N00X), 515–16; Quadrennial Integration Group (QIG) (N00X), changed to Naval Warfare Integration Group (N00X), 518–19, 529n, 532, 580; Regulations, Division, 33; Research, Development, Test and Evaluation, Director of (OP-098), 288, 312, 358, 569; Ship Acquisition and Improvement Division (OP-097), 290,

Index

296; Ship Acquisition and Improvement Division (OP-097), transferred from OP-03 to OP-090, 288; Ships' Movement Division, 33, 56, 62–63, 71–72, 100, 117, 172; Space and Command and Control (OP-094), 358; Strategic Action Group (N00Z), 453–54, 480, 495n, 529n, 533; Strategic Offensive and Defensive Systems, Director of (OP-97), 288; Strategic Plans and Policy Division (OP-60), (in OP-06), 312; Strategic Plans and Policy Division (OP-60), (in OP-06), as Strategy, Plans and Policy Division (OP-60), 338; Strategic Plans Division (in OP-03), 200; Strategy and Concepts Branch (N513), 419, 444, 453–54; Strategy and Policy, Director of (N51), 426–27, 457, 475; Strategy Concepts Branch (OP-603), 319–20, 338; Surface Warfare, Director of (N86, later N76, later N86, later N96), 396, 439, 451, 488, 533, 583; Systems Analysis Division (OP-96), 243n, 254, 262, 280, 294, 297, 339, 359, 556, 583; Systems Analysis Division (OP-96), study of OPNAV organization, 265–66; Tactical Electromagnetic Programs, Director of (OP-093), 288, 569; Target Practice and Engineering Competitions, 26; Technical Studies Group (OP-06D), 235–36; Training, Director of (N7), 438; Undersea Warfare, Director of (N87, later N77, later N87, later N97), 396, 439, 533, 583; Warfare Integration Office (N70), 439
China, 65, 67, 88, 113–14, 116, 188, 206, 295, 372, 459, 556
Chisholm, Donald, 18n, 34, 87n, 576, 581, 587
Christie, John, 390
Christle, Gaylord, 390
Churchill, Winston S., 123–24, 150, 177
Clarey, Bernard A., 265
Clark Bryan, 533–34, 536, 546, 553–54, 556, 556n, 572
Clark, Vernon E.: and alignment, 438–39, 450, 462, 471, 539; as CNO, 437–41, **442–43**, 448–**55**, 456–59, 461–62, 467n, 473, 475–77, 485, 493n, 507, 512, 516, 570, 578–79, 622; as VCNO, 454; and Sea Strike, Sea Shield, and Sea Basing, 454, 467n
Claytor, W. Graham, Jr., 311, 315
Clinger-Cohen Act (Information Technology Management Reform Act, 1996), 433n, 504
Clinton, William J., 387, 403, 405, 410, 415, 417

CNO Advisory Board (CAB), 238, 264, 270, 287
CNO Executive Board (CEB), 287, 290, 320, 332, 438, 479
CNO Executive Panel (CEP), 282–83, 335, 379, 419, 453, 546. *See also* Chief of Naval Operations, Office of (OPNAV), organizations within
Coast Guard, U.S., 142–43, 169, 456, 480–81, 519, 529n
Cochrane, Edward L., 150–51
Cockell, William J., Jr., 335, 350n
Cohen, William S., 417, 419, 433n, 504
Cold War, 175, 213, 240, 355, 369, 372, 378, 380, 385, 392, 394, 397, 405, 410–11, 421–22, 424, 428, 440, 442, 448, 451, 458, 461, 474, 486, 492, 524, 545, 570, 579, 587–88; and arms control, 245, 309, 312, 321, 372; and the breakup of the Soviet empire, 338, 372, 378, 588; and the Warsaw Pact, 206, 334, 337–38, 372, 378
Cole (DDG-67), 585
Cole, William C., 111
combatant commands, 345, 501, 519, 525n. *See also* various commands
Combined Chiefs of Staff (CCS), 138, 147
Commandant of the Marine Corps, xxi, 16, 99, 143, 169, 199, 216, 239, 313, 332, 339, 343, 356, 379–80, 410–11, 414–15, 427, 456, 473, 475, 477, 481, 490, 493, 519, 521–22, 524, 544–45, 586
Commander in Chief, U.S. Fleet (CINCUS), 74, 111, 135n, 139–40
Commander in Chief, U.S. Fleet (COMINCH), 137, 140; headquarters organization, 140–41, 144, 171–72; headquarters organization elements transferred from OPNAV to COMINCH, 141; Tenth Fleet in, 171–72, 264
Comptroller General of the United States, 311, 361, 374n
Congress, 8, 30, 71; and the bureaus, xxi, 15, 27, 43, 60, 64; and CNO's authority, 215; and Committee on Legislative Reorganization and Act, 193, 195; and defense appropriations, 309, 361, 378, 417, 444, 493, 541; and defense reorganization, 187, 214–15, 250, 365–67; and DoD management, 504–5; and National Security Act, 201, 216, 235; and naval appropriations, 4, 6, 11, 33–34, 42, 56, 63, 65–66, 73–74, 87n, 88n, 97, 115–16, 193, 199; and OPNAV, 28, 255, 521; and procurement, 38, 121; and project managers, 291;

and Symington Committee report, 237; and systems commands, 424; and unification, 190–91
Connally, John B., 249
Connally, Thomas F., 273n
Conolly, Richard L., 198, 214, 225n
Consolidated Planning and Programming Guidance (CPPG), 408
Constellation (CVA-64), 292–93
Converse, George A., 7
Conway, James T., 490, 493, 497n, 519, 521–23, 530n, 545
Cooke, Charles M., Jr., 141, 163, 171
Coolidge, Calvin, 75, 78–81, 83, 95
Coontz, Robert E., 56–57, **69;** as assistant to CNO Benson, 56–57; as CNO, 56–59, 61–72, 75, 83–84, 193–94
Council of National Defense (1916), 34, 38; creates Munitions Standard Board and then General Munitions Board, 37
Crenshaw, Lewis W., Jr., 477–78, 487, 494n, 496n
Crist, George B., 368
Crowe, William J., Jr., 342, 369, 373, 577
Cruiser Bill (1929), 81
Cuban Missile Crisis, 297n, 319, 571
Cullom, Philip H., 475, 494n

Dalton, John H., III, 387, 410, 414–15, 422
Daniels, Josephus, 2, 18, 25–34, **36**–42, 44–46, 60, 63–64, 104, 168, 330, 343, 345, 405, 567, 571; Adm. Benson's assessment of, 47; and Adm. Coontz, 57, 59, 72; agenda, 12–13; versus Adm. Sims, 43, 48, 53n, 57–59, 63, 85n, 93, 103; and Rear Adm. Fiske, 13–18
Danzig, Richard J., 410, 426–28, 546
Darling, Charles H., 3–4, 19n
DD-963 (*Spruance*) class, 268
DDG-51 (*Arleigh Burke*) class, 408, 451, 488, 509–11, 514–15
DD(X)/DD-1000, 451, 482, 484–89; as DD-21, 422, 488; and Extended Range Gun Munition (ERGM), 485. *See also* SC-21, *Zumwalt*-class destroyer
Defense Acquisition Board (DAB), 392, 412
Defense, Assistant Secretaries of: for Administration, 249; for Command, Control, Communications, and Intelligence, 464n; Comptroller, 239–40; for Installations and Logistics, 268; for International Security Affairs, 259, 272n, 284, 297n; for Logistics, 362; for Systems Analysis, 276n
Defense Business Board, 443
Defense Cataloging and Standardization Act (1953), 216
Defense Communications Agency, 266
Defense Contract Audit Agency, 266
Defense, Department of (DoD): acquisitions of, 369, 459; appropriations of, 540–41; Inspector General of, 343, 389–90; management in, 229, 248–49, 329, 371, 437, 442–43, 504–5; and National Security Act, 202; reorganization of, 214–15, 229; reorganization (1958) of, 246; reorganization (1986) of, 344–45, 366–67
Defense, Deputy Under Secretaries: for Acquisition (USD[A]), 370–71, 389–90, 464n; for Acquisition (USD[A]) as Acquisition, Technology and Logistics (USD[AT&L]), 443, 507–8; for Logistics, 440; for Science and Technology, 487
Defense Guidance, 330–31, 356
Defense Intelligence Agency (DIA), 266, 295
Defense Management Review and Defense Management Report (DMR), 379
Defense, Office of the Secretary (OSD), 214–15; and acquisition process, 269, 370; authority under McNamara, 256–57; and capabilities based planning, 446, 461, 478, 502–4; comptroller in, 193 (*see also* ASD Comptroller); criticism by Dillon Board, 250–51; Deputy's Advisory Working Group (DAWG), 501, 504; and the Navy, 283, 286; and PPBE, 583; and PPBS, 246–48, 330–31, 357, 410, 443, 579; and project managers, 291; and OPNAV, 257; and reform, 281–82; and service POMs, 331–32; Systems Analysis, Directorate of, 248, 254
Defense Resources Board (DRB), 311, 330–31, 370–71, 445, 447
Defense, Secretary of, 195; authority of, 210n, 215, 345; and DoD reorganization, 215, 367; and programming process, 330–31, 459, 461, 505–6; and special projects offices, 291; and unification, 201
Defense Supply Agency, 266, 299n
Defense Supply Management Agency, 216
Defense Systems Acquisition Review Council (DSARC), 269, 291–92, 331
DeLany, Walter S., 165

635

Index

Denby, Edwin, 59, 64, 67, 70, 72, 75, 94
Denfeld, Louis E., 198, 201–**2**, 203–6
Department of Defense Reorganization Act of 1958, 214, 230, 232, 246, 365, 369, 566, 574, 587
Department of Defense Reorganization Act of 1986 (Goldwater-Nichols Act), 344–45, 355–58, 365, 367–70, 377–78, 395–96, 403, 410, 441, 457, 476, 500–501, 503, 506, 508, 565–66, 574, 578, 587–88, 590n, 593
Department of the Navy Review Commission (1991), 379–80
Deputy Chiefs of Naval Operations (DCNO): for Administration (OP-02), 197–98; [for] (Air) (OP-03), 157, 166, 183n, 569; for Air, later for Air Warfare (OP-05), 197–98, 223, 232–33, 238, 283, 287, 290, 357, 373n, 400n; for Communications Networks (N6), 513; for Development (OP-07), 238, 266, 287; for Information Dominance (N2/N6), 517, 528n, 532–33, 550, 583; for Logistics (OP-04), 197, 238, 266, 271, 358; for Logistics (OP-04), later for Readiness and Logistics (N4), 438–39, 450, 532–33, 536–37, 550, 583; for Naval Warfare (OP-07), 358–60, 362–64, 374n, 379–80, 382–83, 399n; for Navy Program Planning (OP-08), 358–60, 380; for Navy Program Planning (OP-08), as Resources, Warfare Requirements, and Assessments (N8), 383–85, 399n, 408, 413, 478–80, 570, 583, 585; for Navy Program Planning (OP-08), as for Integration of Resources and Capabilities (N8), 510, 533–34, 537, 550, 556, 583–84, 594; for Operations, later Fleet Operations and Readiness (OP-03), 197, 200, 220, 255, 263, 283, 304, 569; for Operations, later Fleet Operations and Readiness (OP-03), changes to DCNO for Surface (OP-03), 287; for Personnel (OP-01), 197, 238; for Personnel (OP-01), as for Manpower (OP-01), 569; for Personnel (OP-01), as for Manpower and Naval Reserve/Chief of Personnel (OP-01), 255, 287, 289–90; for Personnel (OP-01), as for Manpower and Training (OP-01), 358; for Personnel (OP-01), as for Manpower, Personnel and Training/Chief of Personnel (OP-01), 408; for Personnel (OP-01), as for Manpower, Personnel, Education and Training/Chief of Naval Personnel (N1), 532–33, 536; for Personnel (OP-01), as for Manpower, Personnel, Education/Chief of Naval Personnel (N1), 537; for Plans and Policy, later Plans, Policy and Operations (OP-06), 220–21, 230, 232–33, 235, 257, 262, 270, 281, 285–90, 312, 318, 320; for Plans and Policy, later Plans, Policy and Operations (OP-06), as N3/N5, later DCNO for Information, Plans and Strategy, later DCNO for Operations, Plans and Strategy, 473–74, 480, 494n, 550, 570, 593–94; for Special Weapons (OP-06), 197; for Submarines, later for Submarine Warfare (OP-02), 287, 343; for Surface, later Surface Warfare (OP-03), 283, 287, 320; for Warfare Requirements and Programs (N7, initially N9), 438–40, 452, 463n, 479, 570; for Warfare Requirements and Programs (N7, initially N9), as N6/N7, 472, 478, 480; for Warfare Systems (N9), 533–34, 536–37 (*see also* Assistant Chiefs of Naval Operations and Chief of Naval Operations, Office of (OPNAV), organizations within)
Dewey, George, 3–5, 8, 19n, 34, 71; Diamond, E. Richard, Jr., 379
digital technology, 224, **235**, 428, 450, 513, 582
Dillon, John, 250; Dillon Board, 250–51, 254–56, 258–59, 264, 311, 324n;
Director of the Navy Staff (DNS). *See* Chief of Naval Operations, Office of (OPNAV), organizations within
DoD Directive 5158.1, 216, 220
Dorsett, David J., 516–17, 528n; and Navy Consolidated Afloat Networks and Enterprise Services (CANES), 517
Duncan, Charles K., 255
Duncan, Donald B., 146, 160, 178n, 215, 219
Dunn, Robert F., 373n, 386, 573
Dwight D. Eisenhower (CVN-69), 424
Dyer, Joseph W., 424

Eagle Boats, 44
Eberle, Edward W., **76**, 79, 83; background, 73; as CNO, 61–63, 73, 76–80, 84; as head of Eberle Board, 75
Eberstadt, Ferdinand, 190, 199, 215
Edison, Charles, 115, 120, 134n, 139
Edwards, Mark J., 513–14, 517

636

Edwards, Richard S., 140–41, 168, 178n; as deputy COMINCH-CNO, 159, 163, 166, 172, 189
Eisenhower, Dwight D., 207, 213–14, 218–21, 225, 229, 369; and Burke, 221, 230–31, 240, 243n; and defense reorganization, 214–16, 220, 230, 241n, 566; and the New Look, 213, 222
Ellis, James, 420
Emergency Deficit Control Act of 1985 (Gramm-Rudman-Hollings), 361
Emergency Fleet Corporation (World War I), 40
end game (in the Navy POM development process), 534–35
engineering change proposals, 341–42
Engineering Duty Only (EDO) officers, 223, 546
England, Gordon R., 482; as Deputy Secretary of Defense, 482, 486, 492, 501–2, 505, 510–11; as Deputy Secretary of Homeland Security, 502; as SECNAV, 452, 455, 457–58, 473, 501; sponsor of capability portfolio management, 503–4
Enterprise (CVAN/CVN-65), **249**, 304, 473
Espionage Act (1917), 114
Etter, Delores M.: as Assistant Secretary of the Navy (Research, Development and Acquisition), 486–89, 493, 496n, 507; and Capability Maturity Model Integration (CMMI), 487–88
Executive Council for Development and Production, 224
Executive Orders 8244 and 8245 (8 Sept. 1939), 118
Executive Order 8248 (8 Sept. 1939), 118
Executive Order 8984 (18 Dec. 1941), 140, 169
Executive Order 9096 (12 Mar. 1942), 137–38, 141, 165, 168–69, 176n
Executive Order 9635 (Sept. 1945), 168–69, 184n, 187, 569
Executive Order 12344 (1 Feb. 1982), 335
Expeditionary Combat Command, Navy (NECC), 490
expeditionary fighting vehicle (EFV), originally advanced amphibious assault vehicle (AAAV), 426, 441, 482–84, 490, 499, 524

F-14, 404; as attack aircraft, 388, 392–93, 413–14, 422, 432n, 434n; as carrier fighter, 273n, 306–8, 388, 422–23
F-16, 308, 446
F-22, 392, 404
F/A-18, 305, 308, 340, 373n, 388, 392–93, 422–23
F/A-18E/F, 386, 392–93, 404, 411, 413, 422–24, 427, 432n, 463n, 534–35
Farber, William S., 154, 172–73
Fastabend, David A., 448
Federal Acquisition Streamlining Act (1994), 423
Federalist Paper No. 10, 205
FFG-7 (*Oliver Hazard Perry*) class, 290
Fiske, Bradley, 5, 12–**13**, 14–18, 26, 34, **36**, 47–48, 138, 583
Five Year Defense Program (formerly Five Year Force Structure and Financial Program later Future Years Defense Program) (FYDP), 247, 543
Fleet Ballistic Missile Program, 291
Fleet Cyber Command, 517–18
Fleet Forces Command (U.S. Navy), 450, 458, 471–72, 474, 476–77, 484, 490, 514, 516, 539–40, 551, 578; creation of, 449; and Naval Network Warfare Command, 454, 516; and Naval Warfare Development Command, 454
Fleet Modernization Program, 290
fleet problems, 73, 76–77, 79, 83–84, 90n, 93, 97, 111–12, 126; Fleet Problem IX (1929), 82, 91n
Fleet Response Plan (aka Fleet Readiness Program), 450; and Inter-Deployment Readiness Cycle, 451
Fleet Review Board, 514
Fletcher, Frank F., 29
Forbes, Donald K., 312
Forbes, J. Randy, 515, 593–94
Force Structure Assessment Team as an element of Joint Military Assessment process, 414
Ford, Gerald R., Jr., **295**, 303, 307, 309, 312–13, 315
Forrestal, James V.: and Eberstadt, 190, 199, 215; and King, 143, 160–61, 163, 166–69, 173, 183n, 233, 347, 588; and naval aviation, 167; and Nimitz, 192; and Organization Top Policy Group (1944–1945), 165–66; and postwar Navy organization, 168, 190–91, 194–95; as Secretary of Defense (SecDef), 195, 200–202, 210n; as Secretary of the Navy, 160, 165–66, 187, 192–93, 205, 254, 330–31, 343, 345, 620; created Special Committee on Cutbacks (1944), 160; as Under Secretary of the Navy, 142, 149, 159, 194; and unification, 190–91
Foster, Edwin D., 166
"four forces" structure for OPNAV, 263–64, 287
Franke, William B., 233; Franke Board report, 232–34

637

Index

Friedman, Norman, 7, 97, 107, 150, 196, 206, 268, 472
Fullam, William, 43
functional flow diagrams and descriptions (F2D2), 362
functional-processes structure for OPNAV, 263

Gabriel, Charles, 346
Galantin, Ignatius J., 259
Galvin, John, 382, 398n
Garrett, H. Lawrence, III, 361, 378–80, 382, 385, 390, 392, 621
Gates, Artemus L., 166, 168
Gates, Robert M., 491, 493, 499–501, 505, 511, 523–24, 531, 544
Gates, Thomas S., Jr., 216, 582
Gates Board (1945), 168–70
Gates Committee (1954), 216
Geddes, Eric, 43
General Board, 2–3, 5, 11–12, 16, 19n, 26–27, 32, 35, 38–39, 57, 59, 66–69, 73, 79, 80–83, 94, 98, 111–12, 128n, 129n, 138, 172, 176n, 195, 201, 203, 224, 226n, 240, 487; and Adm. Pratt, 93, 95, 99–100; created, 2–4, 16–18; hearings in 1919, 59–60; and Navy strategy, 11, 18, 26, 33, 56, 61–62, 64, 71–72, 77, 189; role in ship design, 5, 8, 21n, 22n, 26, 32, 62, 64, 71, 81, 83, 97–98, 107, 153, 166; in World War I, 38–43; in World War II, 153, 157, 159–60, 165–66
General Dynamics, 350n, 389–91, 394, 400n, 483–84, 501, 511
General Motors, 165, 182n, 506
General Orders. *See* Navy General Order
Geneva Conference (1927), 78–81, 83, 95, 98
Gerald R. Ford (CVN-78), 542–44, 560n
Global Combat Support System (USMC), 549
Global Fleet Station, 480
Global War on Terrorism (GWOT), 475, 524, 555
Godwin, Richard, 370–71
Goldwater Nichols Act. *See* Department of Defense Reorganization Act of 1986
Gorbachev, Mikhail, 355, 372
Government Accountability Office (GAO), 485, 504–5, 549
Government Management Reform Act (1994), 406
Graham, Bradley, 443
Gray, Alfred M., 379
Greenert, Jonathan W., 540–41, 544–45, **546**, 548, 553–55, 559n, 577, 580, 586, 593, 622; career, 531; creates LCS Council, 542; creates N9, 533; and Fleet Forces Command, 539–40; "Navigation Plan," 537; total ownership cost, 532–33, 535, 565; vision for the Navy, 531–32; "wholeness" concept, 532–33, 536–38, 556, 566
Guam, 64, 69, 116, 537
Guderian, Heinz, 204
Guidance for Development of the Force (GDF), 502
Guidance for Employment of the Force (GEF), 502
"Gun Club," 223

Hagee, Michael W., 473, 475, 477, 481–82, 490, 492
Hagel, Charles T., 541–42, 544
Hale, Eugene, 3, 9
Hale, Frederick, 96
Halligan, John, Jr., 98–99, 128n
Halsey, William F., 146, 156, 314
Harding, Warren G., 56, 64–65, 67, 70
Hardisty, Huntington, 359
Harriman, W. Averell, 142
Harris, Harry B., Jr., 517
Harris, R. Robinson, 420, 465n
Hartmann, Frederick, 339, 346–47, 356
Harvey, John C., Jr., 514–15, 539–40
Hawley, Cameron, 555, 563n
Haynes, Peter D., 379, 418–19, 426–27, 454–58, 467n, 471, 473–76, 480–82, 494n
Hayward, Thomas B., 314, **316**, 335–36, 342, 356, 359, 537, 556, **572**, 574, 621; as CINCPACFLEET, 316; and directorates, 317–18; and drug abuse, 321; established Strategic Studies Group, Center for Naval Warfare Studies, and OP-00X, 320; and Lehman, 335, 347; and maritime strategy, 316–17, 319–20, 322, 333, 337; as (OP-090), 308, 316, 321; and readiness, 322
Hebert, F. Edward, 293
Hepburn, Arthur J., 126
Herberger, Albert J., 352n, 408, 415, 430n, 432n
high-low concept, 282
Hilarides, William H., 486
Hitch, Charles J., 246–47
Hobson, Richmond P., 14
Hogg, James R., 408
Holcomb, M. Staser, 335
Holland, W. J., 298n, 346
Holloway, James L., III, 274n, 303–4, **307**, 311–16, 323n, 331–32, 334, 352n, 359, 571–**72**, 575, 621; and fleet reorganization for missions, 313–14; and readiness and modernization, 305–9, 322

638

Hoover, Herbert C., 79–81, 97–98, 103–5, 110–11, 127n, 195, 568; conflict with CNO Hughes, 79–81, 83–84; conflict with CNO Pratt, 94–97, 103; relationship with Ramsay MacDonald, 80, 95
Hopkins, Harry, 153, 177n; letter to King on 13 Mar. 1942, 141
Horne, Frederick J.: relationship with King, 148; responsibilities in July 1942, 143–44; as VCNO, 143, 150, 152–55, 157–59, 589
Horwitz, Sol, 249
House, Edward, 31, 33, 44–45, 48
House Appropriations Committee, 105, 130n, 489, 507
House Armed Services Committee, 193, 203, 246, 250, 259, 293, 386, 390–93, 395, 403, 485–86, 491, 496n, 507, 514–15, 593
House Committee on Government Operations Committee, 282
House Naval Affairs Committee, 3, 11, 14, 26, 33, 42, 70, 81, 100, 109, 116, 190, 193–94
Hughes, Charles Evans, 56, 65, 67–69
Hughes, Charles F., 79–81, **82**–84, 95, 104, 619
Hughes, Wayne P., Jr., 196
Hull, Cordell, 125
Hussein, Saddam, 378, 456

Ignatius, Paul R., 268, 311; and Ignatius study, 311–12
Imperial Japanese Navy, 47, 62, 69, 84, 123, 125, 138, 151, 156
Ingalls Shipbuilding, 277n, 484, 510
Ingersoll, Royal E., 125, 162–63, 172
Integrated Resource and Requirements Review Board (IR3B), 409, 417, 438
Integrated Resource Board/Resource Review Board (IR2B/R2B), 438
intermediate range ballistic missile, 222, 229, 284
Investment Balance Review (IBR), 385, 409
Iraq, 368, 378, 406, 448–49, 456–62, 473, 475, 483, 490–92, 516, 519, 522, 524, 548, 555
Ireland, Andrew P., 390–91
Irish, James M., 149
Irwin, Noble E., 59, 61

Johnson, Jay L., 415–17, 419–23, **424**–25, 427–28, 437, 453, 621
Johnson, Louis A., 202, 205
Johnson, Lyndon, 249, 279–80
Johnson, William S., IV, 320, 326n, 335, 337–38, 349, 574

Joint Advanced Strike Technology (JAST) Program, 393–94. *See also* Joint Strike Fighter
Joint Aircraft Committee (Sept. 1940), 124
Joint Army and Navy Board, 5, 31, 35, 64, 101, 118; and Joint Planning Committee and the Orange war plan, 101
Joint Army and Navy Munitions Board, 118
Joint Army-Navy-War Shipping Administration Ship Operations Committee (1943), 155
Joint assessments: joint military assessment, 408, 414, 432n; joint warfighting capabilities assessments, 408–9, 411; support assessment, 408
Joint Capabilities Integration and Development System (JCIDS), 472; criticisms of, 503; origin of, 502–3
Joint Chiefs of Staff (JCS), viii, 142, 151, 157, 167, 171–72, 180n, 189–90, 197–98, 200–201, 205, 214, 217, 229, 231, 237, 265–66, 271, 272n, 294, 312, 315, 346, 367, 371, 378, 440, 456–57, 460, 503, 535, 566, 577; authority of, 175, 189, 199, 215, 230, 356, 377, 587; and capabilities-based programs, 452, 478, 502; Chairman of, 198, 216, 220, 230, 280, 312–13, 344, 346, 356, 367–69, 377–78, 443, 446, 464n, 481, 493, 500, 505, 566; determining force requirements in World War II, 138, 148; and Eisenhower, 213–14, 216; Joint Staff of, 199, 216, 231, 368, 478, 587; and logistics program in World War II, 152, 158–60; Marine Corps Commandant as member of, 216, 313; and National Security Act (1947), 199; and OP-06, 220–21, 235, 262, 264, 270, 359; and PPBS, 330–31; size of, 199, 230, 266, 270; Vice Chairman of, 371, 464n, 492, 505, 541
Joint Direct Attack Munition (JDAM), 423
Joint Forces Command (JFCOM), 444, 460, 502–3
Joint Merchant Vessel Board, 173
Joint Munitions Board, 215
Joint Operation Planning Process (JOPP), 478
Joint Operations Concepts Development Process, 502
Joint Production Survey Committee, King's opposition to, 159–60
Joint Program Assessment Memorandum, 368
Joint Programming Guidance, 502
Joint Requirements Management Board (JRMB), 371

Index

Joint Requirements Oversight Council (JROC), 392, 412, 416, 492
Joint Special Operations Command, 444, 446, 460–61
Joint Strategic Planning Document, 330, 368
Joint Strategic Target Planning Staff (JSTPS), 231, 236
Joint Strike Fighter (JSF), 394, 483, 499; Marine Corps version, 441, 482; Navy acquisition program, 422, 482, 524
Joint Task Force Exercise 98-2, 424
Jones, David, 312
Jones, Hillary P., 73, 79
Judge Advocate General (JAG), Navy, 11, 16, 109, 120, 135n, 169, 179n, 194, 236–37

Kalleres, Michael P., 408, 430n
Kaplan, Robert, 460–61
Kauffman, Draper, 251–54
Keating, Timothy J., 509
Kellogg, Frank B., 79, 81
Kelly, Robert J., 379, 382
Kelso, Frank B., II, 348, 377–87, **388**–92, 394–96, 402n, 403, 406–9, 411, 413, 415–18, 424, 428, 440–41, 449, 465n, 474, 553, 571–**72**, 575, 584, 586, 621
Kempff, Clarence S., 112
Kennedy, Floyd D., Jr., 423
Kennedy, John F., 236, 245–46, 248–49, 266, 274n, 279; and Kennedy administration, 245–46, 249, 279
Key, Albert L., 5, 8
Key West agreements, 200
Kidd, Isaac C., Jr., 252, 254, 296, 301n, **307**, 323n, 339
Kilday, Paul, 230
Kimmel, Husband E., 89n, 125–26, 135n, 171
King, Ernest J., 138, 187, 191–92; and BuAer, 109; changes CINCUS to COMINCH, 140; COMINCH staff structure, 140–41, 144, 163, 177n; as COMINCH/CNO, 125–26, 137–38, 140–41, 146, 149–52, 154–**56**, 162, **170**–75, 179–80n, 185n, 189, 240, 554, 568–69, 574, 578, 589, 620; as commander Atlantic Fleet, 124–25, 139; early career, 138–39, 176n; and Forrestal, 142–43, 160–61, 163, 165–67, 169, 183n, 233, 588; on General Board, 138–39, 176n; and James Byrnes, 158–59, 163; and Navy reorganization plan (1942), 142–43; and Navy reorganization plan (1943), 157–58; and relations with the press, 173; and reorganization, 163, 168, 182–83; shortage of escort ships in 1942, 145; subordinate to VADM Mayo in World War I, 142, 554, 571, 591n
Kitty Hawk (CVA-63), 292–93
Knight, Austin M., 12, 22n, 35
Knoll, Denys W., 235–36
Knox, Dudley W., 14, 68
Knox, Frank, 121, 125–26, 140, 142–43, 146, 151–52, 157–61, 173, 182n, 183n, 188, 194; created OP&M, 149; "destroyers for bases" exchange, 122; supporter of King, 139
Korb, Lawrence J., 268, 275n
Korean War, 207, 213, 225, 280, 304, 316, 410
Korth, Fred H., 249, 251–52, 254, 259, 579
Kozloski, Robert P., 545
Krulak, Charles C., 415, 427
Kuwait, 368, 378

Laird, Melvin, 268–69, 280, 282–83, 285–86, 292, 295
Land, Emory S., 66, 98–99, 128n, 132n, 145
landing craft air cushion (LCAC) vehicle, 410, 431n, 483
Langley (CV-1), 76, 99
Lautenbacher, Conrad, 420–21
Leahy, William D.: as chief, BuNav, 105, 114, 575; as chief, BuOrd, 114, 575; as chief of staff to Pres. Roosevelt, 151, 175, 179n, 180n, 575; as CNO, xx, 94, 113–18, 133n, 619; on OPNAV staff, 61
Lee, Kent L., 308
Legislative Affairs, Office of, 333
Lehman, John F., Jr., 316, 322, 329, 341–42, **348**–49, 350n, 352n, 353n, 361, 372, 376n, **388**, 463n, 464n, 565, 571, 573–74, 577, 586, 621; and Congress, 332–35, 342–43, 349; member, Defense Resources Board, 330–31; and DOD Reorganization Act of 1986 (Goldwater-Nichols), 344–45, 356, 369–70, 441, 587–88; management style of, 329–30, 335, 355; and Maritime Strategy, 333–34, 337–38, 582; and NAVMAT, 339–41; and Navy Program Strategy Board, 332; as Navy reserve officer, 331, 340; use of Office of Legislative Affairs (OLA), 333; and OPNAV, 331–32, 334–35, 338–40, 347–48, 357–58, 373n; and Rickover, 335, 585; and systems commands, 332, 341–43

Lend-Lease Act (Mar. 1941), 124, 150
Leverton, Joseph, 233–35, 242n
Levin, Carl, 491
Lexington (CV-2), 74–**76**, 82, 139
Libby, Ruthven, and the Libby Board, 222–24, 255
Light, Mark F., 553
Line Personnel Act of 1916, 34
littoral combat ship (LCS), 451–52, 468n, 469n, 472, 482–85, 487–89, 496n, 507–8, 510–13, 521, 523, 536–37, 541–44
Lockard, John A., 424
Locklear, Samuel J., 519
Lodge, Henry Cabot, 68
Logistics, "consumer" and "producer," 170, 184n, 217–18, 238, 255, 259
Logistics Systems Plan, 285, 299n; and Logistics Systems Policy Committee, 285
London Conference (1930), 81, 83, 95, 97–98; subsequent treaty (Apr. 1930), 82, 94–99, 102–3, 105–6, 110–11, 116
London Conference (1936), 106, 110–11, 113; subsequent agreement, 111, 115
Long, John D., 1–4, 16–17
Long, Robert L. J., 335
Long Range Objectives, 238–39, 266
Long Range Requirements, 238–39
Lopez, T. Joseph, 407, 413–17, 432n
Lord, Herbert M., 95
Love, Robert, 171, 175, 368
LPD-17 (*San Antonio*) class, 473, 482, 493n, 509, 524, 546
Luce, Stephen B., 3, 581
Lusitania, 31, 35
Lyons, James A., Jr., 338, 342, 352n

Mabus, Raymond E., Jr., 524, 542, 545–**46**, 549–50, 622
MacArthur, Douglas, 96, 101–2, 147, 151, 167
MacDonald, Ramsay, 80, 95
Mack, William P., 269
Madison, James, 205, 566
Mahan, Alfred Thayer, 4, 9, 18
Management and Budget, Office of (OMB), 289, 310–11, 406, 504
Management Engineer, 202
Manthorpe, William H. J., Jr., 320
Marine Corps, U.S., xx, 10, 12, 29, 34, 60, 62, 104–5, 118, 124, 138, 143, 148, 151, 155, 163–64, 168, 174, 187, 189, 199–200, 202, 208n, 216, 251, 257, 267, 282, 296, 313, 319, 321, 334, 337–38, 343, 345, 363–64, 369, 379–80, 382–83, 396, 403, 406–8, 410–14, 418–21, 425–28, 441, 447–48, 451, 454–58, 462, 473, 475, 477, 480–84, 486, 490–93, 499, 510, 521–25, 535, 537, 545–49, 555, 567, 569
Maritime Balance Study, 317
maritime operations centers (MOCs), 516
Maritime Strategy, 322, 337–38, 361, 363–64, 379, 382–83, 422, 428, 458, 481–82; and Adm. Hayward, 316–17, 319–20; and Secretary Lehman, 333, 338, 582; and Secretary Danzig, 427
Marshall, George C., 120, 122, 124–25, 147–48, 155, 158–59, 171, 173, 175, 179n, 187, 189; proposes single head of Army and Navy, 147
Martin, David O., 393
Martin, Edward H., 386
Martoglio, Charles W., 457–58
Massachusetts Institute of Technology (MIT), 4
Matthews, Francis P., 203
Mattis, James N., 475, 482, 492
Mayo, Henry T., 29, 39, 142, 554, 571
McCain, John S., III, 416–17, 491, 542–43
McCoy, Kevin M., 514–15
McCrea, John L., 141
McCullough, Bernard J., 510
McDonald, David L., 252–**53**, 254, **258**–60, 265, 267, 271, 273n, 620
McDonnell Douglas, 340, 389–90, 394, 400n, 423
McFarlane, Robert C., 347
McGinn, Dennis V., 439
McGowan, Samuel, 27–28, 38, 46
McGrath, Elizabeth A., 524, 530n
McKean, Josiah S., 17, 31, 43
McMillan, Colin R., 502
McNamara, Robert S., 279–80, 289, 297n, 429n, 566, 571, 573; and Five Year Defense Program, 247; management style of, 246, 248–49, 258, 266–69, 272n, 275n, 276n; and PPBS, 246–50, 252, 261–62, 267, 579; Navy response to, 248–65, 273n
Merchant Marine Act (1928), 107; (1936), 113
Metz, Steven, 456
Mexico: intervention in by the United States, (1914), 29
Meyer, George von Lengerke, 2, 9–12, 16, 18, 21n, 45
Meyer, Wayne E., 307, 309–10, 362, 513
Meyers, Allen G., 537
Miles, Paul, 151

641

Index

Military Order 2786 (1 July 1939), 118
Miller, Paul David, 379, 382, 465n
mine resistant ambush protected vehicle (MRAP), 484, 491, 508, 562n
Mitchell, William, 60, 63–64, 75
Mitscher, Marc A., 99
Moffett, William A., 66–67, 71–72, 75, 79, 83, 99, 128n, 138
Monthly Progress Report of the Navy Logistic Program (World War II), 165, 183n, 208n
Moody, William H., 3–6, 19n
Moore, Charles J., 189, 207n
Moore, George E., 285
Moorer, Thomas H., 243n, **264**–66, 280–81, 285, 294–95, 304, 407, **572**, 620
Moreau, Arthur S., Jr., 320
Morgan, John G., Jr., 457–58, 473–75, 480–82, 490, 493; and the Navy's 3/1 strategy 458–59, 473, 475
Morrow Board (1925), 75–76, 97; and Dwight Morrow, head of, 75
Morton, Paul, 6
Mullen, Michael G.: career, 471; as CJCS, 500; as CNO, 458, 471–77, 480–**90**, 492–93, 494n, 495n, 497n, 499, 507, 540, 577, 622; as Commander Naval Forces Europe, 458; and staff realignment plan, 478–80; as VCNO, 454, 571
Mundy, Carl E., Jr., 380, 383, 410–11
Murtha, John P., 489, 507, 509–12
Mustin, Henry, 363–64
Mustin, Henry C., 66

N codes: creation of, 381–82, 399n; under CNO Boorda, 413, 416; under CNO Clark, 438–40, 452–53; under CNO Johnson, 420; under CNO Kelso, 395–96; under Greenert, 532–34; under Mullen, 478, 480; under Roughead, 516–17. *See also* Deputy Chiefs of Naval Operations and Chief of Naval Operations, Office of (OPNAV), organizations within
Nathman, John B., 458–59, 467n; as commander Fleet Forces Command, 474, 476, 480, 494n
National Defense Act (1916), 33
National Defense Advisory Commission (May 1940), 121, 124
National Defense Industrial Association, 427
National Defense Panel, 417, 420
National Defense Strategy, 461, 502

National Industrial Recovery Act (1933), 105
National Military Establishment, 199, 202. *See also* Defense, Department of
National Military Strategy, 419, 502
National Security Act (1947), 199–202, 204–5, 210n, 215–16, 235, 587
National Security Agency (NSA), 295, 518
National Security Council (NSC), 199, 207, 241, 295, 313, 350n, 429n
National Security Decision Directive (NSDD) 219 (1 April 1986), 370–71; and program executive officers (PEOs), 370; and Service Acquisition Executives (SAEs), 370, 390, 489, 508
National Security Presidential Directive 9, 444
National Security Strategy, 461, 502
Naval Aircraft Factory, 106, 130n
Naval Appropriation Act of 1916, 32, 34–35, 56–57, 70
Naval Audit Service, 270–71
Naval Board, 545
Naval Capabilities Board, 478–79
Naval Communications Command, 260, 265
Naval Consulting Board (1915), 28, 32
Naval Consulting Board (1940), 120
Naval Electronic Systems Command, 259
Naval Establishment, 96, 137, 167, 168–69, 192, 208n, 217–18, 569, 588
Naval Facilities Engineering Command, 259
Naval Force Capabilities Planning Effort, 382–83
Naval Intelligence Command, 260, 265
Naval Material Command, 259, 296, 310; abolishment of, 339; and the acquisition process, 192, 260, 339, 340; and bureaus, 255, 259; chief of, 192, 332; and Logistics (OP-04), 265, 271; and OMB study of, 310; and OP-96 study, 265; and OPNAV, 270, 339; in the programming process, 238, 278, 332; and project offices, 291; and systems commands, 271
Naval Material Support Establishment, 259
Naval Network Warfare Command, 454, 516, 518
Naval Nuclear Propulsion Program, Director of, 233; becomes a direct report to the CNO, 332
Naval Ordnance Systems Command, 259, 296. *See also* Naval Sea Systems Command
Naval Overseas Transportation Service, 43, 45
Naval Research Laboratory, 71
Naval Reserve Force, 10–11, 35
Naval Reserve Officer Training Course (NROTC), 70, 74

Index

Naval Sea Systems Command (NAVSEA), 326n, 339–42, 362, 411–12, 440, 452, 466n, 467n, 484, 487, 489, 507; chief of, 307, 507, 514; and OMB study, 310; as systems integrator, 452

Naval Ship Systems Command, 29, 259, 262, 291. See also Naval Sea Systems Command

Naval Supply Systems Command, 259, 326n, 521

Naval War Board, 3

Naval War College, 1–3, 5, 7–8, 19n, 35; "Estimate of the Situation," 77, 102; and maritime strategy concepts, 293–94, 337, 480–81; pre–World War II gaming, 65, 67, 77, 81–83, 87–88, 90n, 568, 581

Navy, Assistant Secretaries of the, 3, 15, 28, 39, 67–68, 85n, 100, 104, 110, 115, 120, 126, 151n, 157, 165–66, 168, 217–18; for Air, 157, 218, 233; for Financial Management (Comptroller) (later Financial Management and Comptroller), 218, 333, 341, 356–57, 394–95, 549; for Material, 218; for Personnel and Reserve Forces (later Reserve Affairs), 218, 386; for Research and Development, 233; for Research, Development and Acquisition, 389, 416, 423, 487, 507–8, 532, 542–43, 546; for Research, Engineering and Systems, 348–49, 357; for Shipbuilding and Logistics, 332, 340, 350n, 357

Navy, Department of: authority in, 63, 335, 345; and civilian control, 2–3, 15–16, 26, 45, 47, 57–58, 85n, 93, 174, 193, 225; and congressional affairs, 10–12, 17, 77, 109, 115, 194–95; and defense reorganization (1958), 232–34; management of, 6–7, 9, 17, 44, 57, 99, 269, 379–80, 437; organization of, 7, 9, 41, 100, 117

Navy, Secretary of the, 1–2, 5, 35, 45, 115–16, 121–22, 137–38, 169, 192, 249; and bureaus, 63; and Dillon Report, 251, 255; and DoD reorganization, 215; and DRB, 331; and Franke Board 232–33; and Secretary's Committee on Research on Reorganization (SCOROR), 190

Navy, Secretary of the, Office of (Secretariat): Analysis and Review, Office of, 218, 239; Comptroller, 195, 202–3 (see also ASN for Financial Management (Comptroller)); Fiscal Director, 195; and OPNAV, 252–55, 327, 338–39, 545–46, 548–49; Organizational Policy Group, 165; Procurement and Material, Office of (OP&M), 149, 152–54, 165, 182n, 183n, 189; procurement authority of, 142–43, 149, 160–61, 168, 183n, 267–68, 341; Program Assessment (or Appraisal), Office of (OPA), 251–54, 311, 324n, 499, 579; in program planning, 311, 380; and Reorganization Plan 6, 215–17, 221; and requirements, 340; and reserve programs, 290; and special projects offices, 223–24, 339

Navy, Under Secretary of, 126, 135n, 166, 223, 237, 426, 432n, 511, 542, 545–47, 549

Navy, U.S.: bilinear organization of, 217, 233, 255, 258, 262; command traditions of, 71, 102, 155, 203–4, 230, 232, 257–58, 296, 577–78; and deployment cycles, 448, 451; expansion in World War I, 31–36, 40, 55; expansion in World War II, 120–21, 138, 146, 161; as a "Fighting Machine," 14; and fleet modernization, 290, 305–6; under Lehman, 342–43; and line officers, 116–17, 223, 233, 256–57, 310, 363, 551, 580; and littoral warfare, 382–83; and manning of, 40, 55–56, 70–71, 103–6, 118; and National Security Act (1947), 199; and naval aviation, 32, 56, 59–60, 66–67, 72, 74–76, 79, 84, 93, 97, 99, 102, 117, 128n, 190–91, 197, 203, 206, 232, 331, 393–94, 423; and nuclear weapons, 188, 196–97, 201, 225, 579, 582; pre–World War II organization of, 123, 138; professionalism in, 2, 6, 18, 34, 83, 171, 305, 317, 342, 413, 427, 481, 567, 578–81, 585; shore establishment, 4, 26, 109, 118, 146, 154, 161, 169, 173, 455, 569; technology in, 7, 37, 73, 83, 93, 188, 196–97, 221–22, 225, 371; and unification, 189–91, 197, 199, 201, 203–4, 207, 235–37, 282

Navy Corporate Board, 479

Navy (or Naval) Decision Center, 282

Navy General Order 5 (Nov. 1954), 217, 233, 259

Navy General Order 9 (Nov. 1955), 217, 233

Navy General Order 19 (May 1949), 217

Navy General Order 65 (Aug. 1921), 66

Navy General Order 94 (Dec. 1922), 69

Navy General Order 143 (Feb. 1941), 123, 135n

Navy General Order 166 (Jan. 1942), 149

Navy General Order 230 (Jan. 1946), 169–70

Navy Management Council, 217

Naval Postgraduate School, 86, 333, 583, 593

Navy Program Strategy Board, 332

Navy Warfare Development Command (NWDC), 424–25, 454, 494n

643

Nemfakos, Charles P., 395
Neutrality Act (1935, and as amended in 1936, 1937, and 1939), 113–15, 118–19, 133n, 135n
New Look, 213, 221–22
Newberry, Truman H., 21n, 57, 85n
Nimitz, Chester W., 61, **119**, 554; appointed commander of Pacific Fleet, 140; as commander Pacific Fleet, 147, 151, 153–54, **156**–57, 161, 163, 165, 168, 171, 174; as CNO, **191**–92, 197–98, 201, 620
Nimitz (CVN-68) class carriers, 306, 321, 332–33, **388**, 478
Nimmich, Joseph L., 480
Nitze, Paul H., 252, 254, 259, 267, 272n, 274n, 275n, 276n, 280, 284, 297n
Nixon, Richard M., 268, 280–81, 292–95, 303, 307; and Nixon administration, 269, 281
North Atlantic Treaty Organization (NATO), 206, 207n, 214, 225, 316, 319, 334, 337–38, 361, 363, 458, 474
NSDD 219 (1986), 370–71

Obama, Barack H., 505–6, 531, 538, 540
O'Donnell, Andrew W., 522
O'Donnell, Terrence, 391
Office of Naval Intelligence, 3, 6. *See also* Chief of Naval Operations, Office of (OPNAV), organizations within
Office of Naval Research, 360, 369, 395–96
Office of War Mobilization (OWM), 158–59
Ohio-class (SSBN-726) ballistic missile submarines, 447, 524, 543
O'Keefe, Sean, 383, 399n
Oliver, David R., 286, 360, 374n, 585
Omaha-class (CL-4) cruisers, 74
operational maneuver from the sea (OMFTS), 408, 418, 420, 425–26, 428
Operations: Deny Flight, 406; Desert Fox, 449; Desert Shield, 377–78, 574, 590n; Desert Storm, 377–78, 381, 419–20, 425–26, 451, 458, 475, 590n; Enduring Freedom, 444, 447, 451, 456–57, 462, 517; Iraqi Freedom, 456–57, 462, 475, 517; Northern Watch, 448; Provide Promise, 406; Sledgehammer, 147; Southern Watch, 406, 448–49; Torch 147–48
ORANGE war plan, 61, 65, 73, 77, 81, 84, 87n, 93–94, 98, 101, 109–10, 115–16, 123, 133n, 173, 566
Organization Resources Counselors, Inc., 290
O'Rourke, Ronald, 488–89

Oster, Jeffrey W., 414–15, 417
Overman Act (1918), 44
Owens, William, 382–84, 407–9, 413, 417, 584; creating the R3B, 384–85, 396

Pace, Peter, 481
Pacific Command (PACOM) and Commander in Chief, Pacific Command (CINCPAC), 230, 234, 368, 509
Packard, David, 269, 285, 299n, 369, 370
Panay (PR-5), 113, 133n
Pandolfe, Frank C., 453
Panetta, Leon E., 524
Paullin, Charles Oscar, 16
Pearl Harbor, 64–65, 67, 125–26, 140–41, 146, 191, 450, 587
Pease, Kendall, 420
Perry, William J., 394–95, 405–7, 417, 423, 441
Philippines, 3, 64–65, 69, **94**, 126, 444, 491
Pihl, Paul E., 161–62
Pilling, Donald, 417, 420, 422–23, 428, 434n, 439
Poindexter, John M., 348
Pope, Barbara, 386
Porter, Wayne, 480, 495n
Pound, Dudley, 142
Powell, Colin L., 378–79, 587
Powers, Bruce, 409, 420, 432n
Pratt, William V., 56–58, **101**, 499, 524, 554; as assistant CNO, 28, 40–44, 52n, 571, 586; as CINCUS, 81; as CNO, 93–94, 97–100, 103, 105, 110–11, 123, 125–26, 128n, 129n, 130n, 568, 572, 619; command background, 94; command philosophy, 102–3; differences with President Hoover, 94–97, 103; letter to Adm. King when King was made COMINCH-CNO, 175; at London conference, 95–96; Pratt-MacArthur agreement, 101–2; and "rotating reserve," 103–4; and Washington conference/treaty, 67–68, 94–95
Procurement Review Board (World War II), 158–59
Program Coordinator for Nuclear-powered Carriers, 290
Program Development Review Committee, 332, 337
Program Management Proposal (PMP) system, 357
programming and budgeting, 338, 364, 445, 447, 464n, 491; emergency supplements after 11 Sept. 2001, 445–47, 464n; gap between

projected and actual spending, 472–73, 579–80
Program Objective Memorandum (POM), 311, 320, 330–32, 338, 355–57, 359–60, 363–65, 380, 382, 399n, 409–11, 413–14, 416, 420, 440, 445, 447, 465n, 480, 500, 502, 504, 532, 534–37, 566, 583–85, 590, 594
Program Review Committee, 332
Program Strategy Board, 332, 409
project (program) managers, 260, 262–63, 291–92, 309–10, 312, 333, 341–42, 357, 370, 390, 487–89, 507, 543
Public Law 432, 192, 208n, 220
Pye, William S., 61, 78, 171

Quadrant Conference (Aug. 1943), 161
Quadrennial Defense Review (QDR), 417, 419, 420, 426, 438, 440, 443–44, 446, 450, 453, 475, 483, 488–89, 502, 515–16, 518, 556n

Radford, Arthur W., 168, 183n, 190, 198, 219, 220–21; as head of a board reviewing aviation logistics (1944), 167–68
Rainbow Plans, 120, 124
Ramsey, Dewitt C., 192
Reagan, Ronald, 322, 338, 343, 345, 348, 355, 361, 369–70; and meeting with Mikhail Gorbachev in Reykjavik, 372; Reagan administration, 322, 330, 342, 353n, **388**, 575; and Strategic Defense Initiative, ix, 346–47
Reason, J. Paul, 439
recession, great, 506–7, 523
Reconstruction Finance Corporation, 121
Reed, Allan L. and Reed study, 231–32
Reeves, Joseph M., 61, 76, 83, **101**, 111–12
Regional Maintenance Centers (Navy), 514
Reich, Eli T., 306
Reorganization Act (1939), created Executive Office of the President, 118
Reorganization of the Department of Defense (JAG study), 236
Requirements and Resources Review Board (R3B) (1992), 384–85, 396
Requirements Review Board (World War II), 165–66, 173, 183n
Research and Development Board, 215
Resources and Requirements Review Board (R3B) (2006), 478–79
Reuben James (DD-245), 125
Rice, Donald, 311

Richardson, James O., 89n, 117, 120, 123, 190, 194
Richardson, John M., 593–94
Ricketts, Claude V., 252–55, 274n
Rickover, Hyman G., 570; and Congress, 307; and Lehman, 335; and the nuclear power program, 224, 584–85; relations with CNO and OPNAV, 233, 262–63, 304, 323n; and Zumwalt, 263, 286, 304, 315–16
Ricks, Thomas E., 456, 458
Robinson, Samuel M, 124, 134n, 149, 165–66, 168
Rockefeller, Nelson A. and Rockefeller Committee, 214–15, 225n, 229–30
Rockefeller Foundation, 229
Rodgers, Eustace B., 57, 85n
Roosevelt, Franklin D.: as advocate of joint logistics planning in World War II, 158–59; "Arsenal of Democracy" speech (1940), 123; as Assistant Secretary of the Navy, 28, 39; criticizing *Midway*-class carriers, 146; as President, xx, 98, 100, 103–4, 106–7, 110–11, **113**, 115–26, 131n, 133n, 138–41, 143, 145–48, 150–51, 153, 157–58, 160–61, 166, 168, 171, 174–75, 177n, 179n, 180n, 184n, 241, 573, 575, 578; "Quarantine" speech (1937), 114
Roosevelt, Henry L., 100, 104
Roosevelt, Theodore, 10, 18; as President, 5–9, 580; "Roosevelt Corollary," 8
Roosevelt, Theodore, Jr., 67–68
Rosenberg, David, 201, 205, 224, 231, 239, 248
Roughead, Gary, 499–500, 506–**8**, 509–12, 514–19, **520**–21, 523–24, 529n, 531, 544–45, 551, 555, 622
Rowen, Henry, 321, 326n
Royal Navy, 5–6, 8, 29–31, 59–60, 69, 74, 79, 81, 90n, 98, 266, 458; issue of gun elevation, 73–74; and the U.S. Navy in World War I, 37–41, 43, 52n; and the U.S. Navy in World War II, 123–24, 142–43, 150
Rumsfeld, Donald H., 315, 437, 441–48, 450–53, 459, 460–62, 469n, 478, 480, 483, 499–506
Russell, James S., 291
Russo-Japanese War, 8, 18

SALT I (Strategic Arms Limitation Treaty), 321; SALT II, 312, 321
Sands, Jeffrey L., 282–83, 287
Saratoga (CV-3), 74–75, 82, 99
Sawyer, George A., 332, 350n
SC-21, 412, 414. *See also* DD(X)/DD-1000 and *Zumwalt*-class destroyer

645

Schindler, Walter G., 235
Schlesinger, James R., 292, 296, 307–9, 313, 315
Schofield, Frank, 73, 79, 81
Schratz, Paul, 220, 248
Schwarzkopf, Norman, 377
Seabees, 321, 480
Sea Power 21 concept, 454
Sea Strike (Hayward), 316, 319
Seawolf-class (SSN-21) submarine, 404
Second Fleet, 342, 363–64, **424**, 430n, 467n
Second World War: Anglo-American cooperation in, 104, 111, 123–26, 139–40, 142–43, 147–48; CNO in, 122, 140, 170–75; Navy organization before, 121; and new technology, 187–88; and OPNAV, xx, 152–58; shipbuilding program for, 150, 153, 163, 174–75; and unification, 189
Selective Service Act (1940), 123
Selective Service Act (1948), 201, 587
Senate, 15, 25, 47, 65, 68, 81–82, 121, 160, 191, 208n, 221, 303, 332, 365–68, 386, 415, 484, 511, 524, 538, 539
Senate Appropriations Committee, 65, 158, 309, 485
Senate Armed Services Committee, 193, 199, 230, 313, 334–35, 338, 369–70, 392, 415, 419, 427, 451, 491, 508, 510, 521, 540, 546, 560n
Senate Budget Committee, 373
Senate Military Affairs Committee, 190
Senate Naval Affairs Committee, 3, 8–9, 26, 42, 48, 57, 117, 199
Senior Executive Council, 443, 501
Senior Leader Review Group (SLRG), 501
sequential-process structure for OPNAV, 263
Service, James E., 386
Service Forces Pacific and establishment South Pacific Service Squadron (April 1942), 153
Sestak, Joseph A., Jr., 453, 472
Seventh Fleet, 556
Shaffer, Alan, 551, 562n
Shelton, Henry H., 443, 446
Shenandoah (ZR-1), 75
Sherman, Forrest P., 198–99, **205**–6, 214, 554, 571, 620
Sherwood, Robert, 114
Ship Characteristics Board (SCB), 166, 487
Ship Characteristics Improvement Board (SCIB), 340, 485, 487
Shoemaker, William R., 77–78
Sims, William S., 5–6, 8–9, 11, 13, 17–18, 29, 34, 40–42, 57, 68, 73, 93–94, 103, 123, 142, 149, 554; and congressional investigation of his criticisms of the Navy Department in World War I, 43, 48, 57–58, 63, 72; in London in World War I, 38–41, 43, 51n, 53n; as President of the Naval War College, 38, 57, 67, 85n
Sisisky, Norman, 391, 393
Sixth Fleet, 188
Skelton, Isaac N., 393, 419
Small, William N., 337, 340
Smedberg, William R., III, 126, 251
Smith, Leighton W., Jr., 382–83, 396–97, 398n, 402n
Smith, Philip D., 338
Snyder, Charles P., 165
Somervell, Brehon B., 153, 155, 157–58, 172
South Korea, 461
Soviet Union (USSR), 104, 114, 142, 147, 188, 202, 240, 245, 297, 312, 316, 319, 336, 338, 346, 372, 378, 437, 571; air defenses, 200, 388; collapse of, 588; efforts to build ships in the United States, 114–15; future war with, 196–97, 200–201, 206, 225, 320–21, 333, 338, 361, 363–64, 369, 383; and Lend-Lease, 124; navy, 363, 422–23, 570; threat of, 191, 198, 205–6, 214, **281**, 283, 290, 306, 322, 337, 352n, 356, 373, 556, 582, 588
Space and Naval Warfare Systems Command (SPAWAR), 364
Spaatz, Carl, 191
Special Projects Offices (SPOs), 223–24, 291, 339
specified commands, 215, 345. *See also* combatant and unified commands
Spence, Floyd, 419
Spinney, Franklin, 323n, 393
Sponsor Program Proposals, 318
Stackley, Sean J., 542–43, 546, 560n
Stackpole, Henry, 382
Standard Stock Catalogue, Navy, 38
Standley, William H., 78, **108;** as CNO, 94, 100, 104–8, 110–12, 123
Stark, Harold K., **119;** author of "Plan Dog" memo, 122–23; as chief of BuOrd, 119; as CNO, 94, 118–20, 122–26, 137, 141, 147, 152; in London in World War I, 123, 142; and in London in World War II, 126, 142; relationship with Adm. King, 125, 139–41
Stark (FFG-31), 368
State Department, 30, 50n, 65, 114–15, 120, 126, 143, 159, 190, 359, 568

Stavridis, James G., 448; as EUCOM commander, 531; as head of Deep Blue, 448, 453
Steadman, Richard C., 311
Stewart, Jake W., 346
Stiller, Allison F., 526n; responding to Congress about National Steel and Shipbuilding Co. (NASSCO), 509
Stimson, Henry L., 81
Stirling, Yates, Jr., 12, 22n
Stoufer, Donald A., 334
Strategic Air Command (SAC), 188, 191, 202, 230, 241n
Strategic Command (STRATCOM), 518
Strategic Defense Initiative, 346
Strategic Materials Act (1939), 119
Strategic Studies Group (Naval War College), 320, 333, 359, 408, 545, 554
Strauss, Joseph, 72, 194
Sub-Chief of Naval Operations (OP-11, later OP-02), 143, 166
Sullivan, John L., 195, **202**
Sullivan, Leonard, 308
Sullivan, Paul E., 507
Surface Navy Association, 440, 458, 482, 511, 513
Swanson, Claude A., xx, 100, 104, 106–7, 109, **113**–14, 119–20, 129n, 131n, 194
Swartz, Peter, 338, 467n, 567
Swift, William and the Swift Board, 10, 21n
Symington, Stuart, and Symington Committee, 236–37, 282
Synhorst, Gerald E., 306
systems commands, xxi, 289, 296, 310, 312, 318, 333, 421, 440–41; and combatant commanders, 441; establishment of, 259–60; management of, 271, 332, 452; officers in, 310, 341; and OPNAV organization, 260, 262–63, 282, 339, 362, 395–96, 471–72, 582; and Total Package Procurement and shift of design work, 267

Taft, William H., 9–10, 12
Taft, William H., IV, 370–72
Tailhook Association, convention of (1991), 385–87, 389, 391, 397, 407, 415, 424, 571, 575, 589
tanker war (reflagging Kuwaiti oil tankers), 368
Taylor, David W., 28, 32, 40, 42, 64, 66
Taylor, Gary E., 509–11
Taylor, Henry C., 1, 3–7, 17, 19n
Taylor, Montgomery M., 76, 98–99
Tenet, George J., 444, 448, 464n

Tenth Fleet: reestablished in 2009 for cyber, 517–18; in World War II, 171–72, 264
TFX, 249, 254, 273n, 571
Thackrah, John S., 509
Theodore Roosevelt (CVN-71), 332
Thomas, Charles S., 219
three "Ts" program (Terrier, Tartar, and Talos missiles), 222
Tomahawk missile, 318, 407, 409, 421, 485
Top Policy Group, 165–66
torpedo boats and torpedo boat destroyers (before World War I), 7
Total Force Integrated Readiness Model (TFIRM), 450
Total Obligational Authority, 247, 267
Total Package Procurement, 267–68, 277n
Total Quality Leadership (TQL) and Total Quality Management (TQM), 381
Towers, John H., 60, 66, 161; as BuAer chief, 124, 152–53, 589
Train, Harry D., II, 280, 289, 312, 342, 349
Training and Doctrine Command (TRADOC), U.S. Army, 396
Transformation Plan, Navy Department, FY2014–2016, 549
"Trends in Unification" memo, 203
Tripartite Pact (Sept. 1940), 122, 124
Trost, Carlisle A. H., 335, **348**, 355, **365**, 373, 373n, 378, 383, 424, 571–**72**, 577, 586–87, 621; and DOD Reorganization Act of 1986, 355–56, 365–69; as OP-090, 355; and relations with OP-07 and OP-08, 358–60, 362–63
Truman, Harry S., 159, 174, 196, 202, 207, 575; and conscription, 200; executive orders of, 168–69, 187; and Forrestal, 168, 187, 190, 202; and the Navy, 191, 193; and unification, 190–91, 198
Turner, Richmond K., 125, 154
Turner, Stansfield, 252, 282, 288–89, 293–94
Two Ocean Navy Act (19 July 1940), 121, 134n
type commands (TYCOMS), 112, 386, 400n, 449–50, 463, 539; Adm. Pratt's explanation of, 102; lead and follower, 450; in World War II, 145–46

U-Boats: World War I, 31, 35–36, 38–40, 52n, 173; World War II, 119, 141–42, 147, 154
unification, 189–91, 197, 199, 201, 203–4, 206–7, 229, 236–37, 239, 256, 282

unified commands, 215, 220, 234, 265, 281, 330, 345, 386; authority of, 215, 366; staff sizes of, 281–82. *See also* combatant and specified commands
United States (CVA-58), cancellation of, 202
United States Steel, 165, 182n
unmanned aerial vehicles (UAVs), 427, 447, 478, 555–56; Navy opposition to U.S. Air Force as executive agent, 492
Untermeyer, Chase, 315, 349, 350n
Urgent Deficiencies Act (1917), 42
U.S. Naval Academy, 4, 32, 47, 70, 140, 223
Utley, Johnathan, 104

V-22 (Osprey), 404–5, 410–11, 426, 431n, 434n, 441, 454, 483, 490, 522–23
Van Riper, Paul K., 418, 495n; as critic of capabilities-based planning, 481–82
Versailles Treaty (1919), 45, 48, 63, 65
Vessey, John W., Jr., 346
Vest, William T., Jr., 387
Vice Chief of Naval Operations (VCNO) (OP-10, later OP-01, later OP-09, later N09), 143, 148, 154, 163, 168, 192, 215, 219, 232, 239, 243n, 255, 261, 265–66, 274n, 282–83, 291, 304–5, 312, 319–20, 415, 438, 473, 484, 568; on Business Transformation Council, 549; on CNO Advisory Board 238; on CNO Executive Board, 287, 332, 438; on CNO Executive Panel, 282, 321; and Director of the Navy Staff (DNS), 454, 570; and directorates, 288, 290, 296; and naval audit, 271; on Naval Requirements Oversight Council, 438; office of, 201, 260, 550; OPNAV realignment, 478; position of, 143–44, 152; and program planning, 188–89, 252–53, 260, 359, 422–23, 472, 532; and Ship Characteristics and Improvement Board, 339–40; and training, 439; workload of, 261–62, 454
Vietnam, 269, 279–80, 282, 284, 295, 410
Vinson, Carl, 99, 113, 117, 121, 179n, 293, 573; as chairman, House Armed Services Committee, 230; as chairman, House Naval Affairs Committee, 96, 100, 105, 115–16, 120, 150, 171; co-author of "second Vinson bill" (1938), 116; co-author of Vinson-Trammell Act (1934), 106–7, 110, 121, 130n
Virginia-class (SSN-774) attack submarines, 482, 534, 537, 544

Wainwright, Richard, 12
Walsh, David I., 133n, 179n
Walsh, Patrick M., 540
War Industries Board (World War I), 34, 42, 44–45
War Powers Act (18 Dec. 1941), 149, 184n
War Production Board, 149, 158, 181n, 190; Navy members of, 149
War Resources Board (1939), 118, 133n
War Shipping Administration, 128n, 145, 155
War Shipping Board, 118
warfare (platform) communities, 198, 256, 288, 292, 294, 296, 305, 317, 380, 414, 450, 513–14
Warner, John W., 292–93, 296, 300n, **348**, 416
Warsaw Pact, 206, 334, 337–38, 372, 378, 404
Washington Naval Conference (1921), 67–69; Five Power Naval Treaty, 68; Four Power Treaty, 68; subsequent treaty (Treaty for the Limitation of Armament), 71, 94; "treaty system," 56, 73–74, 80, 82–83, 93–96, 98, 103, 109–13, 115, 126
Watkins, James D., 305, 335–**36**, 343, 347–48, 353n, 355–56, 373–**72**, 575, 586, 621; and cost of the Navy, 336–37; and the Maritime Strategy, 337–39; and Naval War College, 336; and NAVMAT, 339–41; and readiness, 337; and Strategic Defense Initiative, xxi, 346–47, 582; as VCNO, 336; and the "war on drugs," 337
Watts, Barry D., 446
Webb, James H., Jr., 361
Weeks, Stanley B., 320, 326n, 337–38
Weinberger, Caspar W., 330–32, 335, 338, 345, 361, 370–71
Weiss, Sy, 321, 326n
Wheeler, Gerald, 42, 67–68, 95–96, 103, 128n
Wheelock, Charles D., 224
Whitehill, Walter M., 152
Wilbur, Curtis D., 75, 79–81
Willard, Robert F., 472–73, 478, 484, 514
Williams, Clarence S., 62, 68
Williams, Henry, 149
Williams, James D., 360
Willson, Russell, 140
Wilson, Charles, 218–19, 221
Wilson, George C., 422
Wilson, Henry B., 58
Wilson, Louis H., 313
Wilson, Woodrow, 13, 16, 26, 29, 33–34, 37–41, 44–46, 48; and neutrality policy, 25, 29–31, 35, 43
Winnefeld, James A., Jr., 541

648

Winter, Donald C., 482, 484, 486, 488–89, 493, 509–12, 514, 522, 622
Wohlstetter, Albert, 321
Wolfowitz, Paul D., 444, 502
Woodson, Walter B., 61
Work, Robert O., 488, 511; as Navy chief management officer, 546; Under Secretary of the Navy, 542, 545–46, 549
WPL-46 (Pacific Fleet War Plan, 1941), 124–25
Wylie, Elizabeth G., 337–38

Yarnell, Harry E., 61, 65, 133n, 189
Yockey, Donald J., 390
Yorktown (CG-48) collision with Soviet frigate, 372
Young, John J., Jr., 507–8, 510, 512

Z-grams, 285, 299n, 301n
Zumwalt, Elmo R., Jr., 243n, 252, 280, 334, 407–8, 571–**72**, 577, 579, 583, 621; and directorates, 288, 290, 296; and OPNAV reorganization, 281–83, 285–90; and Rickover, 263, 286; and Systems Analysis Division (OP-96), 254
Zumwalt-class destroyer (DDG-1000), 509–10. *See also* DD(X)/DD-1000, SC-21